CLARK'S REGIMENTS

AN EXTENDED INDEX

to the

Histories of the Several Regiments and Battalions from North Carolina in the Great War 1861-65

★★★

Written by Members of the Respective Commands

Edited by Walter Clark
Lieutenant Colonel Seventieth Regiment N. C. T.

By Charles C. Davis

PELICAN PUBLISHING COMPANY
Gretna 2001

Copyright © 2001
By Charles C. Davis
All rights reserved

The word "Pelican" and the depiction of a pelican are trademarks of Pelican Publishing Company, Inc., and are registered in the U.S. Patent and Trademark Office.

Library of Congress Cataloging-in-Publication Data

Davis, Charles C. 1951-
Histories of the several regiments and battalions from North Carolina in the Great War, 1861-65 : an extended index / by Charles C. Davis.
p. cm.
Original work was edited by Walter Clark.
ISBN 1-56554-938-4
1. Histories of the several regiments and battalions from North Carolina in the Great War, 1861-65—Indexes. 2. North Carolina—History—Civil War, 1861-1865—Regimental histories—Indexes. 3. United States—History—Civil War, 1861-1865—Regimental histories—Indexes. 4. North Carolina—Militia—History—19th century—Indexes. 5. United States—History—Civil War, 1861-1865—Campaigns—Indexes. I. Histories of the several regiments and battalions from North Carolina in the Great War, 1861-65. II. Title.

E573.4 .D38 2001
973.7'456—dc21

2001036804

Printed in the United States of America

Published by Pelican Publishing Company, Inc.
1000 Burmaster Street, Gretna, Louisiana 70053

CONTENTS

Preface 5
Abbreviations and Conventions 9
A 13
B 33
C 89
D 140
E 161
F 170
G 187
H 207
I 246
J 248
K 262
L 271
M 291
N 330
O 339
P 343
Q 367
R 368
S 398
T 436
U 452
V 454
W 466
Y 500
Z 503
Bibliography 505

PREFACE

Some thirty years after the conclusion of the great War Between the States the State Confederate Veterans Association appointed Judge Walter Clark to be the editor of what was to become the Histories of the Several Regiments and Battalions from North Carolina in the Great War 1861-'65, Written by members of the respective commands. This collection of five volumes has been the finest set of first person accounts of North Carolina's contributions to the Confederate States of America ever published. Assuredly, written as it was by some seventy odd different writers—none of whom were trained historians—the quality of the entries for the many commands are varied. There are of course in a work of its type known factual errors which must, with the greatest kindness, be attributed to the lack of resource materials at hand rather than any conscious attempt at deception. The reader of "Clark's Regiments," as this set of books has come to be known, must keep in mind that the majority of troop rosters and official military records had been forcibly confiscated by Lincoln's hordes or wantonly destroyed. Writing from memory and what few personal accounts were available the minor errors of history are easily overlooked in favor of the huge value of these volumes as a whole.

Yet there has always existed a deficiency in the works of Clark and his fellows that in no small way has caused the many researchers who have delved into their pages considerable anguish and frustration. A lacking that has seen these outstanding collections of memories and experiences put back on the shelf and omitted from bibliographies and research works. That hateful deficiency has always been its poor and wholly inadequate index.

The professional historian is accustomed to long frustrating and diligent research. He knows that in the great quest for knowledge, the answers to his questions and the ever illusive facts that he seeks will mean, many pages, if not entire volumes read, before gleaning some of the most sought after information.

The student or amateur historian on the other hand does not always understand the difficulty of research. They do not fully understand that over the generations writing styles and conventions have changed. Nor do they appreciate the fact that the index of any given work can be its weakest and most misleading feature. Unfortunately, when the information they seek does not leap forward from the collection of entries presented in a nearly century old index they too often relegate that work to the reshelve pile, move on to works easier to use and deny themselves the benefit of thorough research. Even the professional historian sometimes tires faced with the prospect of reading several works cover-to-cover to find that one missing bit of information.

In the case of "Clark's Regiments," having been questioned thousands of times for assistance in locating information in these great works, by the bewildered student and the frustrated professional alike, it has been my goal to in some small way reduce such problems for others whose love of history is nearly as great as my own. An attempt to be of assistance has been made by compiling an Extended Index for The Histories of the Several Regiments and Battalions from North Carolina in the Great War 1861-'65, Written by members of the respective commands.

The goal in compiling this index has been to include every person, place and thing no matter how insignificant it's mention. Where possible an attempt has been made to positively identify every individual including his rank, company and unit. In some cases additional information and editorial comment has been made. Places and things have also been identified by their state, relative location to other more familiar entities or type. By doing these things it has been the hope of this researcher not only to make "Clark's Regiments" a more useful collection of research materials in their own right but also to allow the information found within the pages of "Clark's" and this "Extended Index" to point the researcher to further cross references in other reference material.

As with any effort in writing and the presentation of historical data there are bound to be errors no matter how careful and diligent the researcher has attempted to be. For any unintended mistakes in the pages of this work this historian takes full responsibility and humbly apologizes to you the reader in advance.

No book is written and published wholly on the efforts of its author or compiler. There are always others who contribute in endless ways whose assistance is invaluable to the completion of every book. At the least it would be horribly bad manners not to mention these unsung individuals. In light of their real contributions it would be the height of arrogance not to do so. Of the unsung firstly it must be noted that without the patience and understanding of Amy G. Greene, of whom the words friend, even partizan, seem wholly inadequate, this nor any other of this life's works would be possible. She has lived and learned and worried over these Confederate ancestors every page of the way from beginning to end. To Mrs. Susan Zolkowski, Chief Librarian and Archivist and her staff of the Olivia Raney Local History Library, Raleigh, Wake County, North Carolina thanks must be extended for the privilege of being granted free run of their stacks and their facility. Also, to Mr. Douglas Jarrett, Commander of the Colonel Robert F. Webb Chapter Military Order of the Stars and Bars, compatriot and fellow lover of books, whose loans of reference materials from his personal collection saved me countless hours of exhausting research away from home thanks must be given. To my editor at Pelican Publishing, Nina Kooij, your skill and experience has certainly saved this novice writer great embarrassment and ultimately quickened the publication of my humble efforts. Last and certainly not least there is Professor William S. Powell. Former keeper of the treasures of the Southern Collection, Wilson Library, University of North Carolina, Chapel Hill; eminent professor of history; currently Professor Emeritus, University of North Carolina, Chapel Hill; Chairman of The North Carolina Historical Commission; author and editor of eighty some odd articles, pamphlets and books, it is he who has encouraged this amateur historian to write. Always he has reminded any who have listened that some of the best works of history have been written by those of us whose love and passion for historical truth far surpasses that of many of those in the ivy towers who write strictly for others of their ilk.

Through my own efforts and with the help of dedicated friends this work is presented to generations of yet uneducated historians with the hope that truth will always and ultimately overcome the myths and propaganda of revisionism.

ABBREVIATIONS AND CONVENTIONS

RANK

Pvt	Private
Cpl	Corporal
Sgt	Sergeant (6th to 1st)
Sgt Maj	Sergeant-Major
Ensign	Ensign (Navy, Lowest ranking officer)
3rd Lt	Third Lieutenant
Jr 2nd Lt	Junior Second Lieutenant
2nd Lt	Second Lieutenant
1st Lt	First Lieutenant (Army & Navy)
Capt	Army
Lt Cmdr	Lieutenant Commander (Navy)
Maj	Major
Cmdr	Commander (Navy)
Lt Col	Lieutenant Colonel
Capt	Captain (Navy)
Col	Colonel
R Adm or R Admr	Rear Admiral
Brig Gen	Brigadier-General
Adm or Admr	Admiral
Maj Gen	Major-General
Lt Gen	Lieutenant-General
Gen	General (Full) (No full generals in USA)

POSITIONS

ACS	Assistant Commissary Sergeant
ADC	Aide-de-Campe
Adjt	Adjutant
AAG	Assistant Adjutant-General
AG	Adjutant-General
AIG	Assistant Inspector-General
A & IG	Adjutant and Inspector General
AQM	Assistant Quartermaster
AQS	Assistant Quartermaster Sergeant

ASG	Assistant Surgeon-Genaral
Ass't Comm	Assistant Commissary
Ass't Surg	Assistant Surgeon
Comm	Commissary
IG	Inspector-General
QM	Quartermaster
SG	Surgeon-General
Surg	Surgeon

MILITARY UNIT OR BRANCH

Art	Artillery
Light Art	Light Artillery
Horse Art	Horse Artillery
Hvy Art	Heavy Artillery
Cav	Cavalry
Co	Company
CSN	Confederate States Navy
USN	United States Navy
NCST	North Carolina State Troops (Regiment)
AoG	Army of the Gulf
ANV	Army of Northern Virginia
AoT	Army of Tennessee
AoW	Army of the West
CSA	Confederate States Army
USA	United States Army

CONVENTIONS

General Robert E. Lee does not appear as an item in this index. His name is used so often within the text as to be more akin to an adjective than as a reference to himself. No notable quotes are attributed to him within the language of the several authors. For these reasons his name has been omitted.

Lt Gen U.S. Grant does not appear as an item in this index. His name is used most often as an adjective or term of discriptive possessiveness. No notable quotes are attributed to him within the language of the several authors. For these reasons his name has been omitted. Army of Northern Virginia has been omitted as an item in this index because it was the unit to which most of North Carolina's soldiers were attached. Reference to it is virtually as common as a comma. Where possible an attempt has been made to identify every individual mentioned in the original text by Walter Clark, et al.

Unfortunately the several authors, due to the variance of reference material at hand or the accuracy of their memories, made numerous errors in identification. Where errors occurred in any part of an individual's name or his rank and unit an alternate is given within square brackets, [ ]. When the available records do not support the identification of an individual or the original text has provided insufficient information for certain identification the mark ** will be found following that particular name. Such a notation should not be taken by researchers to mean that that person did not exist, only that this historian was unable to properly identify him.

The symbol, **, follows the name of an individual whose identity could not be verified in troop records or who may have been a civilian not fully identified in the text of Clark's. Further research will be required to positively identify these persons.

(A)

Abaco Lighthouse, Nassau, V: 355, 356, 391, 449.
Abbott, ______, (Lt, Mi., USA), V: 655.
Abbott, Joseph, Carter, (Brig Gen, USA), II: 10, 647; V: 163, 238.
Aberdeen, N.C., IV: 608.
Abernathy, Columbus, (Pvt, Co G, 34th NCST), V: 556.
Abernathy, F.S., [See: Sidney S.], IV: 705.
Abernathy, G.S., (2nd Lt, Co D, 30th NCST), II: 496.
Abernathy, H.W., (Lt Col, 34th NCST), I: 118, 581, II: 581.
Abernathy, J., (Pvt, Co C, 10th NCST, 1st Art & Engs, Brem-Graham-Williams' Battery, Light Art), V: 567.
Abernathy, J.W., (Pvt, Co K, 35th NCST), V: 193.
Abernathy, J.W.C., (Ordnance Sgt, 37th NCST), V: 545.
Abernathy, Dr. James M., (Ass't to N.C. Surgeon-General Warren), I: 133; IV: 630.
Abernathy, John A., (Hospital Steward, 28th NCST), II: 466, 475.
Abernathy, L.D., (Pvt, Co K, 35th NCST), V: 563.
Abernathy, M.A., (Pvt, Co F, 32nd NCST), V: 496.
Abernathy, R.D., (Sgt, Co E, 32rd NCST), V: 496.
Abernathy, S.O., (Pvt, Co F, 13th Vols/23rd NCST), V: 510.
Abernathy, Sidney, S., (1st Lt, Co D, 30th NCST), II: 496; IV: 722.
Abingdon, Va., III: 523, 740, 741; IV: 386, 606.
Acquia Creek, Va., I: 137, 138, 179, 216, 227, 500; II: 598.
Acworth, Ga., II: 742.
Adairsville, Ga., II: 741.
Adams, ______, (Capt, AG, Trimble's Brigade), IV: 237.
Adams, ______, (Capt, 1st S.C. Art), III: 207; V: 162.
Adams, Charles Francis, (U.S. Minister to the Court of St.James), V: 349.
Adams, Benjamin, (Pvt, Co D, 30th NCST), V: 492.
Adams, D.T., (Pvt, Co D, 26th NCST), V: 531.
Adams, E., (2nd Lt, Co E, 78th NCST, 8th Senior Reserves), IV: 107.
Adams, E.W., (AQM, 50th NCST), III: 202.
Adams, G.H.A., (Pvt, Co E, 1st Vols, "Bethel"), I: 128.
Adams, G.W., (Pvt, Co C, 48th NCST), V: 526.
Adams, J.L. (Sgt, Co I, 63rd NCST, 5th Cav), V: 674.
Adams, J.F., (Pvt, Co G, 8th Vols/18th NCST), II: 64; V: 540.
Adams, James, (Capt, Adjt Gen., Hoke-Godwin-Lewis Brigade), IV: 526.

Adams, James T., (Lt Col, 26th NCST), II: 300, 330, 358, 371, 380, 390, 393, 395, 396, 397, 403,411-412, 415, 420; V: 529.
Adams, James T., (Capt, Co K, 49th NCST), III: 147, 148, 153.
Adams, Jesse, (Pvt, Co E, 55th NCST), V: 528.
Adams, Jesse A., (Sgt Maj, 55th NCST), III: 289; V: 527.
Adams, John, (2nd Lt, Anderson's Battalion, Co I, 71st NCST, 2nd Junior Reserves), IV: 29.
Adams, John, (Brig Gen), III: 495.
Adams, Meredith, (3rd Cpl, Co G, 27th NCST), II: 462.
Adams, "Old Hike," IV: 727.
Adams, Miss R.S., (Clerk, University Publishing Company), V: xv.
Adams, Samuel, F., Jr., (Capt, Co E, 45th NCST), V: 494.
Adams, Samuel H., (2nd Lt, Co B, 12th Vols/22nd NCST), II: 164, 165, 167.
Adams, Samuel T., Jr., (Capt, Co E, 45th NCST), IV: 705; V: 494.
Adams, T.J., (Capt, Co K, 49th NCST), V: 15.
Adams, W., (Sgt, Co E, 37th NCST), V: 545.
Adams, W.H., (Pvt, Co C, 6th NCST), V: 512.
Adams, Warren, (Lt, Butler's 1st S.C.), V: 641.
Adams William M., (2nd Lt, Co D, 50th NCST), III: 203.
Adams, Z.T., (Capt, Co D, Adam's Battery, Starr's 13th Battalion NCST, Light Art), II: 642, 645, 774; IV: 341, 353; V: 229, 232, 240.
Adams Street, (Plymouth), V: 189.
Adcock, Henry C., (Musician, 55th NCST), V: 527.
Addington, W.M., (Capt, AQM, Co K, 9th NCST, 1st Cav), I: 451, 485, 486.
Aderhold, Dr. W.V., (Surg, 16th Battalion/75th NCST, 7th Cav), IV: 643.
Aderholt, J.F., (4th Cpl, Co I, 1st Vols/11th NCST), V: 531.
Aderholt, M., (Sgt, Co G, 57th NCST), V: 517.
Aderholt, Thomas, (Pvt, Co F, 32nd NCST), V: 496.
Aderholt, William, (Pvt, Co F, 32nd NCST), V: 496.
Adjutant-General, ANV, II: 370.
Adjutant-General's Department, N.C. (and Adjutant-General. North Carolina had four Adjutant-Generals during the war. They were: J.G. Martin, J.F. Hoke, R.C. Gatlin, D.G. Fowle), I: 3, 5, 8, 9, 10, 11, 13, 15, 16, 17, 18, 19, 21, 22, 44, 50, 52, 53, 74, 77, 124, 125, 126, 705; II: 161, 162, 202, 662; III: 319, 719; IV: 66, 402, 403, 483, 531, 555, 556; V: xi, 1, 466, 471, 630.
Adjutant & Inspector General, CSA, II: 334.
Adkins, J.F. (2nd Lt, Co F, 1st NCST), I: 137.
Adkins, J.M., (Pilot, Ella and Annie), V: 357.
Adkins, James, (Pvt, Co G, 3rd Vols/13th NCST), V: 551.
Adkins, L., (Pvt, Co G, 3rd Vols/13th NCST), V: 551.
Adkins, W.H., (Pvt, Co G, 3rd Vols/13th NCST), V: 551.
Adkinson, E.C., (Capt, Co B, 50th NCST), III: 161.
Adkinson, Joseph H., (Capt, Co H, 50th NCST), III: 161.
Admiralty, British, V: 414, 415.
Agricultural and Mechanical College, (now NCSU), I: 57.
Ahearn, James, A., (Jr 2nd Lt, Co E, 6th Battalion NCST, Fayetteville Armory Guard), IV: 297.

Aiken, Robert, A., (Capt, Co H, Walker's Battalion, Thomas' Legion; 80th NCST), III: 738; IV: 117, 118, 119 120 127, 128; V: 653.
Ainsworth, F.C., (Gen, Chief of Records and Pensions, USA), I: xi; III: 549, 592; IV: 66.
Alabama, I: 70 II: 119, 367, 701, 737, 801; III: 494, 496, 500, 501, 738; VI: 121; V: 386.
Alamance, Battle of, (Revolution), II: 359; IV: 22, 32, 60.
Alamance County, N.C., II: 303, 725; III: 108, 264, 406, 427; IV: 101, 105, 483.
Alamance River, N.C., I: 413; III: 200; IV: 32, 60.
Albany, N.Y., II: 360.
Albea, J.M., (1st Sgt, Co H, 4th NCST), I: 233.
Albemarle, N.C., (section of), II: 88; IV: 22, 357, 431.
Albemarle River, N.C., III: 178.
Albemarle Sound, N.C., III: 134, 719; IV: 392, 646; V: 17, 57,192, 311, 315, 321.
Albemarle & Chesapeake Canal, III: 177; V: 17.
Albert, Robert, J., (Sgt, Co F, 6th NCST), V: 512.
Albertin, Daniel, [Albertini], (Pvt, Co A, 5th NCST), I: 291; V: 504.
Albertson, Elbert J., (2nd Lt, Co G, 40th NCST, 3rd Cav), II: 747.
Alberty, J.J., (Pvt, Co K, 11th Vols/21st NCST), V: 515.
Albright, A.G., (Capt, Co F, 53rd NCST), III: 262, 265.
Albright, G.N., (2nd Lt, Co F, 6th NCST), IV: 722.
Albright, G.W., (2nd Lt, 6th NCST), IV: 705.
Albright, George, N., IV: 722.
Albright, H.A., (Lt, Co C, 10th NCST, 1st Art & Engs, Brem-Graham-Williams' Battery, Ligth Art), I: 547.
Albright, Henry A., (2nd Lt, Co C, 10th NCST, 1st Art & Engs, Brem-Graham-Williams' Battery, Light Art), V: 567.
Albright, Henry C., (Capt, Co G, 26th NCST), II: 304, 336, 358, 359, 372, 373, 389, 390, 396, 397, 403, 417.
Albright, John G., (1st Lt, Co A, 77th NCST, 7th Senior Reserves), IV: 65, 99, 101, 105.
Albright, R.H., (Pvt, Co E, 49th NCST), V: 564.
Albright, S.A., (Musician, 6th NCST), V: 511.
Albright, S.J., (2nd Lt, Co F, 53rd NCST), III: 263.
Albright, William A., (Capt, Co I, 57th NCST), III: 405.
Alden, Alonzo, (Col, 169th N.Y.), II: 649; V: 235, 238.
Alden, James, (Capt, USN), V: 242.
Aldie, Va., (and Battle of, 1863), I: 424; II: 438; III: 1, 472, 561, 563, 567.
Aldred, R., (Pvt, Co B, 52nd NCST), V: 535.
Aldridge, John W., (Lt, Co B, 67th NCST), III: 711.
Aldridge, W.J., (Pvt, Co H, 6th NCST), V: 513.
Aleutian Islands, V: 348.
Alexander, ______, (Capt, Signal Corps), V: 406.
Alexander, A.M., (AQM, Henry's 14th Battalion, 79th NCST, 8th Cav), IV: 113.
Alexander, Abdon, (Lt, Co C, 10th NCST, 1st Art & Engs, Brem-Graham-William's Battery, Light Art), I: 547, 549.
Alexander, Abner, (Lt, Co H, 61st NCST), III: 504.
Alexander, B.J., (QMS, 6th Battalion/60th NCST), III: 484.
Alexander, C., (Lt, Co C, 64th NCST), III: 660.

Alexander, Charles W., (1st Lt, Co A, 1st Vols/11th NCST), I: 77, 120, 583.
Alexander, Claudius S., (Capt, Co C, 4th NCST), I: 232, 269.
Alexander, Eben (Professor, UNC), IV: 120.
Alexander, Edward Porter, (Brig Gen, Chief of Artillery, A.N.V.), I: 622; V: 123, 138, 139, 140, 142.
Alexander, Elias C., (Capt, Co I, 48th NCST), III: 114.
Alexander, F., (Sgt, Co F, 57th NCST), V: 517.
Alexander, Frank R., (Capt, Co K, 56th NCST), III: 317, 323, 358, 360; V: 191, 663.
Alexander, George, (ACS, 6th Battalion/60th NCST), III: 497.
Alexander, George W., (Teamster, Co H, 35th NCST, Detailed, QM Corps), V: 571.
Alexander, Ham S., (Pvt, Co F, 63rd NCST, 5th Cav), III: 577.
Alexander, J.A., (Pvt, Co I, 37th NCST), V: 546.
Alexander, Dr. J.B. (Ass't Surg, 37th NCST), IV: 474, 637.
Alexander, J.J., (2nd Lt, Co B, 43rd NCST), V: 663.
Alexander, J.L., (Pvt, Co A, 6th Battalion/60th NCST), III: 481.
Alexander, J.M., (Pvt, Co K, 56th NCST), V: 566.
Alexander, J.M., (1st Cpl, Co A, 1st Vols/11th NCST), V: 530.
Alexander, J.M., (Pvt, Co F, 6th Battalion/60th NCST), III: 496.
Alexander, J.M.W. (Lt, Co H, 7th NCST), I: 378.
Alexander, J.P., (Lt, Co C, 9th NCST, 1st Cav), I: 485, 782.
Alexander, J.W., (Lt Cmdr, CSN, Captain, Raleigh), IV: 733, 743; V: 300, 304, 307, 312; V: 680.
Alexander, James F., (2nd Lt, Co E, 1st Vols/11th NCST), I: 585.
Alexander, Jasper, (Musician, 3rd Vols/13th NCST), V: 549.
Alexander, John M., (Capt, Co H, 35th NCST), II: 591.
Alexander, John Marion, (Capt, Co A, 52nd NCST), III: 223; V: 529.
Alexander, John Milton, (Lt, Co H, 7th NCST), I: 369.
Alexander, John O., (AQMS, 37th NCST), II: 653; V: 545.
Alexander, Julius, (2nd Lt, Co B, 43rd NCST), III: 3; V: 680.
Alexander, Marshall E., (2nd Lt, Co B, 53rd NCST), I: 120; III: 261; IV: 700, 705.
Alexander, McGrader W.R., (Capt, Co I, 6th Battalion/60th NCST), I: 120; III: 482, 484, 491, 497.
Alexander, O., (Musician, 3rd Vols/13th NCST), V: 549.
Alexander, R.B., (2nd Lt, Co A, 1st Vols/11th NCST), I: 584.
Alexander, R.W., (Pvt, Co K, 6th Battalion/60th NCST), III: 482.
Alexander, S.B., (Capt, Co K, 42nd NCST, brother of Ham S. Alexander, Hoke's Staff), I: 119; II: 791, 792, 807; III: 577; IV: 537.
Alexander, T.L., (Pvt, Co C, 37th NCST), V: 545.
Alexander, W.E., (Pvt, Co A, 35th NCST), V: 495.
Alexander, W.J.,(Capt, Co A & H, 37th NCST), IV: 721.
Alexander, W.W., (Musician, 3rd Vols/13th NCST), V: 549.
Alexander, William S., (Pvt, Co I, 6th Battalion/60th NCST), III: 482.
Alexander, Wilson W., (Pvt, Co B, 5th Vols/15th NCST), V: 521.
Alexander College, (Burkesville, Ky.), IV: 618.
Alexander County, N.C., II: 654; IV: 387, 398; V: 287, 292, 293, 295.
Alexander's Bridge, (Chickamauga River, Tenn.), III: 450, 487, 678.

Alexander's Hotel, N.C., III: 474.
Alexandria, Va., I: 86, 223, 224, 419, 753; II: 193, 683; III: 582; IV: 412, 552.
Alexandria & Leesburg Pike, I: 223.
Alexandria & Manassas Gap Railroad, II: 30.
Alford, A.J., (1st Lt, Co C, 1st Battalion Junior Reserves; Co D, 70th NCST, 1st Junior Reserves), IV: 13.
Alford, H.M., (1st Lt, Co I, 42nd NCST), II: 791, 807.
Alford, Rev. J.B., (Chaplain, 51st NCST), III: 205, 206; IV: 617.
Alford, J.H., (Pvt, Co C, 4th Vols/14th NCST), I: 731.
Alger, Russell A., (Col, 5th Mi.), III: 598, 599.
Allatoona, Ga., [Altonna], (and Battle of, 1864), I: 768; II: 492, 720.
Alle, John M., (1st Cpl, Co D, 52nd NCST), III: 224.
Alleghany County, N.C., II: 162, 163; III: 504; IV: 484, 609.
Alleghany Mountains, I: 318; II: 701; IV: 169.
Allen, ______, (Engineering Officer, Fort Hatteras), V: 45, 54.
Allen, ______, (Col, 1st N.Y.,) I: 88, 89, 97.
Allen, Austin, (Pvt, Co F, 2nd Vols/12th NCST), I: 639; V: 265, 268, 507.
Allen, Champion, (Musician, 34th NCST), V: 554.
Allen, Charles N., (Capt, Co D, 30th NCST; Battalion Junior Reserves, 72nd NCST, 3rd Junior Reserves), II: 485, 496; IV: 50, 51, 444.
Allen, D.J., (2nd Lt, Co G, 69th NCST, Thomas' Legion), III: 731.
Allen, Daniel, (Pvt, Co F, 2nd Vols/12th NCST), I: 639.
Allen, David C., (Capt, Co C, 30th NCST), II: 495, 496, 503, 504, 505; V: 484.
Allen, Davis, (Pvt, Co H, 34th NCST), V: 556.
Allen, Davis A., (Pvt, Co C, 25th NCST), V: 561.
Allen, Denarcus S., (Sgt, Co E, 5th Vols/15th NCST), V: 521.
Allen, Dr. G.D.S., (Ass't Surg, 62nd NCST), III: 515; IV: 641.
Allen, G.W., (Cpl, Co K, 26th NCST), V: 532.
Allen, H., (Pvt. Co G, 56th NCST), III: 348.
Allen, H., (Pvt, Co K, 6th NCST), V: 513.
Allen, H.P., (Capt, Co B, Freeman's 20th Battalion NCST; Capt, Allen's Unattached Company), IV: 401, 753; V: 626.
Allen, Hugh J., (Cpl, Co F, 2nd Vols/12th NCST), I: 639.
Allen, J., (Pvt, Co A, 5th Vols/15th NCST; Invalid Battalion), V: 571.
Allen, J.A.,[Junius A.], (Lt, Co B, Wynn's 15th Battalion NCST, Cav), IV: 365.
Allen, James, (Pvt, Co C, 6th Vols/16th NCST), V: 552.
Allen, Jerry, (Pvt, Co D, 32nd NCST), V: 496.
Allen, John L., (Pvt, Co H, 14th Vols/24th NCST), V: 560.
Allen, John W., (2nd Lt, Co D, 3rd Vols/13th NCST), V: 547.
Allen, Lawrence M., (Col, 64th NCST), III: 659, 661, 671.
Allen, M.A., (Pvt, Co D, 59th NCST, 4th Cav), III: 471.
Allen, Peter H., (Cpl, Co F, 2nd Vols/12th NCST), I: 639.
Allen, R.B., (Pvt, Co K, 26th NCST), V: 533.
Allen, R.F., (1st Lt, Co C, 38th NCST), II: 675, 678.

Allen, R.P., (Lt, Co C, 9th Battalion NCST, 1st Hvy Art), IV: 303, 312.
Allen, Robert, (Pvt, Co D, 14th Vols/24th NCST), V: 560.
Allen, S.F., (Capt, Co A, 2nd Battalion NCST), IV: 245.
Allen, S.J., (1st Lt, Co D, 30th NCST), II: 496.
Allen, Dr. T.A., (Civilian), III: 670.
Allen, T.M., (Capt, Co E, 4th NCST) I: 232, 270; IV: 722.
Allen, T.W., (Lt, Co D, 64th NCST), III: 660.
Allen, Thomas H., (Lt, Adjt, 10th NCST, 1st Art & Engs), I: 500, 501, 502, 536.
Allen, Thomas W., (2nd Lt, Co D, 64th NCST), I: 489; IV: 705; V: 54.
Allen, Turner, (Pvt, Co F, 2nd Vols/12th NCST), I: 639.
Allen, W.G., (Sgt Maj, 1st NCST), I: 136.
Allen, W.N., (Lt Cmdr, USN, Pioneer, Tuscarora), V: 244.
Allen, William, (Capt, Co D, 39th NCST), II: 705, 733, 734.
Allen, William A., (Col, 51st NCST), III: 205, 206, 218; IV: 483.
Allen, William A., (Maj, 7th Battalion Home Guard), III: 205, 218; IV: 483, 650.
Allen, William A., (2nd Lt, Co A, 43rd NCST), III: 19.
Allen, William B., (5th Sgt, Co A, 10th NCST, 1st Art & Engs, Ramseur-Manly's Battery, Light Art), I: 551.
Allen, William J., (Pvt, Co B, 6th NCST), V: 512.
Allen, Wyatt B., (1st Lt, Co I, 6th NCST), IV: 705, 722.
Allen, Ky., IV: 674.
Alligood, Stephen H., (Pvt, Co G, 2nd NCST), I: 176; V: 486.
Allison, J.H., (2nd Lt, Co I, 41st NCST, 3rd Cav), II: 772.
Allison, James, (Pvt, Co K, 56th NCST), V: 566.
Allison, Jonathan, (Pvt, Co K, 6th Battalion/60th NCST), III: 482.
Allison, John B., (Pvt, Co B, 25th NCST), V: 561.
Allison, John G., (Pvt, Co B, 25th NCST), V: 561.
Allison, Joseph F., (Capt, Co E, 31st NCST), II: 512.
Allison, Joseph W., (2nd Lt, Co E, 31st NCST), II: 507, 512.
Allison, M.B., (3rd Lt, Co H, 62nd NCST), IV: 723.
Allison, M.B., (Lt, 6th NCST), IV: 705, 723.
Allison, M.L., (2nd Lt, Co E, 62nd NCST), III: 516.
Allison, Norris, [Morris], (Pvt, Co H, 25th NCST), V: 561.
Allison, Richard, (Pvt, Co H, 25th NCST), V: 561.
Allison, Richard M., (1st Lt, Co B, 9th Vols/19th NCST, 2nd Cav), II: 89; V: 666.
Allison, Richard W., (Capt, Co B, 9th Vols/19th NCST, 2nd Cav), II: 80, 89; V: 666.
Allison, W.T., (Pvt, Co B, 28th NCST), V: 541.
Allison, William P., (Pvt, Co B, 25th NCST), V: 561.
Allman, Robert, (Pvt, Co D, 10th NCST, 1st Art & Engs, Reilly-Ramsay's Battery, Light Art), I: 574.
Allred, Clement M., (Pvt, Co B, 4th Vols/14th NCST), V: 490.
Allred, Henry C., (2nd Lt, Co M, 12th Vols/22nd NCST), II: 165, 166.
Allred, W.B., (Pvt, Co G, 26th NCST), V: 532.
Alman, Robert, (Pvt, Co D, 10th NCST, 1st Art & Engs, Reilly-Ramsay's Battery, Light Art), V: 568.

Allridge, W., (Pvt, Co M, 12th Vols/22nd NCST), V: 554.
Almond, Dr. A.J., (Ass't Surg, 8th NCST), IV: 633.
Almond, D., (Pvt, Co K, 28th NCST), V: 543.
Almore, Issac Taylor, (Sgt, Co I, 2nd NCST), I: 163.
Alred, W.R., (2nd Sgt, Co I, 12th Vols/22nd NCST), V: 554.
Alrich's, Va., III: 595.
Alston, B., (Pvt, Co K, 2nd Vols/12th NCST), V: 508.
Alston, Edward, (Lt, Co I, 2nd Vols/12th NCST), I: 620.
Alston, J.D., (Sgt, Co K, 2nd Vols/12th NCST), V: 508.
Alston, P.G., (Lt, Co K, 2nd Vols/12th NCST), I: 642.
Alston, Robert W., (Maj, 2nd Vols/12th NCST), I: 608, 627, 631, 644, 648, 650; II: 121.
Alston, Samuel T., (Lt, Co K, 2nd Vols/12th NCST), I: 642.
Alston, Dr. Solomon Williams, (Ass't Surg, 2nd Vols/12th NCST), I: 606; IV: 633.
Alston, W.T., (AQM, 2nd Vols/12th NCST), I: 606.
Alton, Pa., IV: 665.
Amelia Court House, Va., I: 210, 330, 480, 549, 651, 685, 781, 782; II: 62, 266, 300, 458, 482, 577, 589, 696, 783, 784; III: 17, 32, 58, 100, 252, 283, 399, 470; IV: 95, 210, 452, 453; V: 250.
Amelia Springs, Va., II: 285; IV: 454.
American Bible Society, III: 736.
Ames, Adelbert, (Brig Gen, USA), II: 91, 647; V: 233.
Amhurst, Mass., IV: 618.
Amhurst Court House, Va., III: 748.
Amis, Rufus, (Capt, Co I, 13th Vols/23rd NCST), II: 187.
Amisville, Va., I: 223, 422; III: 572.
Ammon, D.V., [Ammen], (Cmdr, USN), V: 242.
Ammons, Allen, (Chaplain, 39th NCST), II: 707; IV: 613-614.
Amory, Thomas Jonathan, (Brig Gen, USA), III: 508.
Amos, Richard, (Pvt, Co A, 10th NCST, 1st Art & Engs, Ramseur-Manly's Battery), I: 554.
Amosville, Va., IV: 184.
Ancient and Honorable Artillery Company of Boston, I: 131.
Anderson, A.A., (Pvt, Co A, 1st Battalion NCST), V: 503.
Anderson, A.J., (Sgt, Co C, 4th NCST), I: 232.
Anderson, D.D., (Capt, McLin's Cav), III: 739.
Anderson, D.W., (Capt, Co F, 64th NCST), III: 660, 665.
Anderson, Davis, T., (Pvt, Co H, 52nd NCST), V: 536.
Anderson, George Burgwyn, (Brig Gen) I: xi, 167, 224, 225, 230, 234, 235, 237, 241, 244, 245, 246, 248, 249, 266, 269, 271, 280, 558, 563; II: 5, 114, 377, 498, 499, 500; IV: 149, 445, 446, 447, 448, 463, 506; V: 9, 65, 78, 467, 639, 649.
Anderson, George Thomas "Tige," (Brig Gen), I: 633; II: 456; IV: 522.
Anderson, H.L., (Lt Col, 2nd Battalion NCST), V: 11, 65.
Anderson, Henry, (Virginian who fed North Carolina soldiers on their way home after the war), IV: 217.
Anderson, J.W., (Pilot, Mary Celesta), V: 357, 358.
Anderson, James Patton, (Maj Gen), II: 711; III: 436; IV: 142.
Anderson, John, (Pvt, Co G, 3rd Vols/13th NCST), V: 551.
Anderson John H., (Lt, Adjt, 48th NCST), III: 115, 124.

Anderson, John H., (Maj, 2nd Battalion Junior Reserves; Lt Col, Anderson's Battalion Junior Reserves; Col, 71st NCST, 2nd Junior Reserves), I: 118, 120; IV: 3, 5, 25, 27, 53, 358, 392, 499, 587, 594.
Anderson, John N. (1st Lt, Co H, 33rd NCST), II: 540, 579.
Anderson, Joseph Reid, (Brig Gen), I: 581; II: 467, 497, 677; IV: 244, 246, 421, 422.
Anderson, J. Sanhope, (Capt, Co A, 29th NCST), II: 485, 486, 493.
Anderson, L.R., (Capt, Co D, 44th NCST), III: 23.
Anderson, M.O., (Pvt, Co K, 30th NCST), V: 493.
Anderson, R.B., (2nd Lt, Co C, 5th Battalion Junior Reserves; Co H, 71st NCST, 2nd Junior Reserves), IV: 29.
Anderson, Richard Heron, (Lt Gen), I: 558; II: 205, 383; III: 45, 371; IV: 300, 537.
Anderson, Rev. Robert B., (Chaplain, 4th NCST), I: 230, 270; IV: 29, 605.
Anderson, R. Walker, (Lt, ADC to G.B. Anderson; Ordnance Officer, Cooke's Brigade), IV: 506, 507, 508.
Anderson, Samuel, (Antebellum-Maj and commander at Fayetteville Arsenal; Chief of Artillery Huger's Staff; Chief of Staff to R.H. Anderson), IV: 300.
Anderson, W.N., (Pvt, Co K, 8th Vols/18th NCST), II: 64; V: 540.
Anderson, W.S.G., (Capt, Co F, 10th NCST, 1st Art & Engs, Cogdell's Hvy Art), I: 525.
Anderson, W.W., (Cpl, Co I, 33rd NCST), II: 540.
Anderson, Walker, (Ordnance Officer, 4th NCST), I: 276.
Anderson, William, (Pvt, Co C, 34th NCST), V: 555.
Anderson, William, S., (AQM, 61st NCST), III: 503.
Anderson, William T., (1st Lt, Co B, 39th NCST), II: 705, 728.
Anderson, William T., (1st Lt, Co A, 5th NCST), I: 289; IV: 722.
Anderson, S.C., IV: 126.
Anderson's Turnout, (aka Anderson Station, Virginia Central Railroad), I: 384; IV: 195, 196, 197.
Andersonville Prison, (Camp Sumter at Andersonville, Ga.), IV: 730, 753.
Anderton, W., (Pvt, Co G, 2nd Vols/12th NCST), V: 507.
Andrews, ______, V: 213.
Andrews, A.B., (Capt, Co B, 9th NCST, 1st Cav), I: 445, 453, 485, 446, 450, 486; III: 553.
Andrews, B., (Cpl, Co I, 6th NCST), V: 513.
Andrews, Benjamin, [J.B.], (Pvt, Co C, 7th Vols/17th NCST), II: 5.
Andrews, Clinton M., (Col, 9th Vols/19th NCST, 2nd Cav), I: 433; II: 80, 82, 87, 88, 99, 102, 103; III: 537, 539, 603; IV: 255, 256, 258; V: 10, 649.
Andrews, E.M., (Pvt, Co H, 1st Vols/11th NCST), V: 530.
Andrews, Edward, (4th Sgt, Co G, 3rd Vols/13th NCST), V: 550.
Andrews, G.A., (Capt, Co C, 4th NCST), I: 232, 270.
Andrews, G.W., (Capt, Co G, 50th NCST), III: 161, 202.
Andrews, George, (Pvt, Co F, 63rd NCST, 5th Cav), III: 581.
Andrews, H.L., (Lt Col, 2nd Battalion NCST), IV: 252, 255, 256, 258, 259; V: 11.
Andrews, Henry C., (2nd Lt, Co G, 28th NCST), IV: 723.
Andrews, J.L, (Sgt, Co I, 6th NCST), V: 513.

Andrews, J.L., (Ordnance Sgt, 38th NCST), II: 678.
Andrews, J.W., (Pvt, Co E, 12th Vols/22nd NCST), V: 553.
Andrews, John, (Cpl, Co B, 33rd NCST), II: 538.
Andrews, John B., (Capt, Co C, 4th NCST), I: 231, 243, 268.
Andrews, L.D., (Maj, 38th NCST), II: 676, 678, 682.
Andrews, R.H., (2nd Lt, Co B, 70th NCST, 1st Junior Reserves), IV: 12.
Andrews, S.A., (Pvt, Co A, 10th NCST, 1st Art & Engs, Ramseur-Manly's Battery, Light Art), V: 567.
Andrews, Sandy, (Pvt, Co E, 3rd Vols/13th NCST), I: 670.
Andrews, S. Jay, (Capt, Co B, 9th Vols/19th NCST, 2nd Cav), II: 80, 89, 91.
Andrews, T., (Pvt, Co B, 2nd Vols/12th NCST), V: 506.
Andrews, T.W., (Capt, Co F, 2nd Battalion NCST), IV: 245.
Andrews, W.M., (2nd Lt, Co E, 3rd Vols/13th NCST), V: 547.
Andrews, W.S.G., (Capt, Co F, 10th NCST, 1st Art & Engs, Cogdell's Hvy Art), I: 489, 501, 525; IV: 418, 419; V: 39, 40, 41, 43, 45, 46, 48, 51, 52, 301, 302, 502, 536.
Andrews, William W., (1st Sgt, Co H, 38th NCST), V: 558.
Andrews, N.C., (was Valley River, See: Valley River).
Angel, Thomas M., (Capt, Co H, 6th Vols/16th NCST), I: 751; IV: 137.
Angle, The, (aka Copse of Trees, nr Gettysburg, Pa.), V: 103, 104, 106, 107, 108, 110, 111, 148, 157.
Angola Bay, N.C., IV: 424.
Angerman, W.H., (Sgt Maj, 33rd NCST), II: 537.
Angerman, W.H., (2nd Lt, Co D, 28th NCST), V: 538.
Anna River, North, Va., (and Battle of, 1864), I: 205, 588, 597, 640; II: 120, 173, 240, 387; III: 11, 246; IV: 195, 196, 197, 411, 426; V: 114.
Anna River, South, Va., I: 259, 588, 640; II: 54, 120, 240, 440, 679; III: 24, 25, 235, 419, 596; IV: 197.
Annapolis, Md., III: 287, 733; IV: 421.
Annapolis Naval College, V: 327.
Annas, Hezekiah, (Pvt, Co F, 26th NCST), V: 602.
Anson, Dr. I., (Ass't Surg, 9th Vols/19th NCST, 1st Cav), II: 88; IV: 635.
Anson County, N.C., II: 182, 303, 419, 421; III: 457; IV: 483, 516, 611, 760; V: 67.
Antarctic Ocean, V: 349.
Antohny, H.G., (Sgt, Co A, 28th NCST), V: 540.
Anthony, Peyton T., (2nd Lt, Co B, 33rd NCST), II: 583.
Anthony, W.H., (Capt, Co B, 9th NCST, 1st Cav), I: 441, 485, 782.
Antietam, (The battle and town of Sharpsburg were incorrectly called Antietam after the name of the creek that flowed near that town. See also: Sharpsburg, Md.), I: 166, 246, 265, 307, 663; II: 32, 41, 222; IV: 165; V: 82, 627.
Antietam Creek, (nr Sharpsburg, Md.), I: 141, 184, 185, 225, 307, 308, 372, 573, 576; II: 32, 71, 222, 656; III: 109, 116, 129, 235, 588, 589; IV: 165; V: 71, 72, 74, 79, 80, 589.
Antietam and Fredericksburg, II: 603; V: 77.
Antone, Andrew, (Resident of Richmond, Va.), IV: 188.
Apperson, Thomas V., (Capt, Co F, 28th NCST), II: 482, 483.
Apple, E.R., (3rd Cpl, Co I, 3rd Vols/13th NCST), V: 557.
Apple, Mat., (Pvt, Co I, 3rd Vols/13th NCST), I: 660.

Apple, Peter, (Pvt, Co F, 54th NCST), V: 516.
Apple, Pinkney, (Pvt, Co F, 54th NCST), V: 516.
Applewhite, _____, (ADC to Mat. Ransom), II: 283; V: 179.
Applewhite, Issac C., (Lt, Co D, 2nd NCST), I: 159.
Applewhite, W.H., (Lt, Co D, 2nd NCST), I: 159, 160.
Appomattox Bridge, (nr Petersburg, Va.), IV: 450.
Appomattox Campaign, I: 156, 580; II: 391, 484; III: 96.
Appomattox Court House, Va., I: v, 122, 161, 175, 177, 211, 265, 266, 279, 290, 291, 330, 332, 334, 534, 550, 560, 582, 588, 685, 686, 729, 748; II: 40, 62, 76, 77, 102, 173, 238, 266, 392, 460, 461, 482, 536, 589, 696; III: 18, 32, 33, 58, 59, 76, 122, 147, 159, 252, 256, 284, 344, 393, 400, 401, 403, 409, 425, 426, 467, 470, 471, 472; IV: 90, 94, 95, 96, 210, 211, 212, 215, 362, 453, 457, 471, 510, 516, 554, 568, 577, 579, 582, 612; V: viii, 253, 256, 468, 628.
Appomattox River, Va., I: 330, 406, 407, 678; II: 4, 6, 60, 61, 87, 264, 266, 288, 298, 402, 455, 456, 460, 482, 577, 589, 695, 696, 797; III: 10, 58, 96, 99, 100, 112, 121, 122, 140, 144, 247, 252, 276, 283, 354, 355, 359, 364, 379, 386, 391, 398, 399; IV: 93, 95, 138, 203, 204, 208, 209, 210, 357, 362, 450, 455, 471, 478, 529, 534, 576; V: 250, 251, 326.
Appomattox, Last Guns Captured, II: 108, IV: 580; V: xi.
Appomattox, Last Shot, II: 108, 505-506; IV: 96, 458, 580; V: xi, xiii, 225, 260.
Appomattox, Parole List, I: xii; V: 483, 573, 657.
Appomattox, Surrender at, (aka Lee's Surrender), I: 117, 212, 228, 413, 443, 497, 499, 549, 597, 602, 651, 686, 703, 709, 765; II: 62, 107, 108, 111, 124, 144, 177, 178, 267, 290, 301, 341, 393, 394, 402, 409, 412, 415, 421, 460, 461, 471, 482, 504, 523, 530, 536, 577, 600, 620, 626, 654, 670, 696, 701, 804; III: 18, 20, 29, 37, 38, 79, 100, 112, 200, 259, 260, 281, 284, 312, 332, 542, 653, 654, 671, 700, 710, 722, 760; IV: 31, 32, 60, 63, 128, 210, 213-215, 242, 258, 260, 354, 359, 369, 431, 438, 441, 460, 461, 472, 476, 479, 500, 510, 516, 524, 526, 562, 577, 593, 694; V: ix, xii, 81, 131, 247-256, 257-268, 277, 573-574, 641.
Archer, James Jay, (Brig Gen), I: 350, 374, 375; II: 29, 35, 117, 341, 344, 345, 553, 554, 556, 557, 657, 658, 684, 686; III: 236, 310; IV: 467; V: 104, 117, 248, 613.
Archibald, C.C., (Sgt, Co I, 4th NCST), I: 234.
Ardrey, James P., (Capt, Co F, 49th NCST), III: 137, 138, 148, 152.
Ardrey, W.E., (Capt, Co K, 30th NCST), I: 119; II: 496; III: 138; V: 484.
Arendell, Bridges, (1st Lt, Co G, 40th NCST, 3rd Art, Hvy), II: 746.
Arendell, Thomas, (Lt, Co F, 10th NCST, 1st Art & Engs, Cogdell's Hvy Art), I: 496, 529.
Arents, William R., (Jr 2nd Lt, Co H, 52nd NCST), III: 225.
Aretic Ocean, V: 347, 349.
Arey, Charles R., (AQM, Starr's 13th Battalion NCST, Light Art), IV: 348.
Argo, T.M., (Lt, Co D, 9th Battalion NCST, 1st Hvy Art), IV: 305.
Arizona, IV: 511.
Arkansas, I: 216; III: 427; IV: 9, 35; V: 4.
Armfield, B.F., [David F.] (2nd Lt, Co A, 9th NCST, 1st Cav), IV: 705.

Armfield, D.T., (Lt, Co A, 9th NCST, 1st Cav), I: 441, 485, 782.
Armfield, M.B., (Capt, Co B, 1st Vols/11th NCST), I: 584, 591.
Armfield, M.D., (Capt, Co B, 1st Vols/11th NCST), I: 113, 119; V: 88.
Armfield, R.F., (Lt Col, 38th NCST), II: 675, 678, 681, 682, 686, 687.
Armistead, Frank S., (Col, 70th NCST, 1st Junior Reserves; IG N.C. Reserves; Cmdr Junior Reserve Brigade), I: xiii; IV: 4, 11, 12, 18, 30, 37, 39, 53, 56, 591.
Armistead, Lewis Addison, (Brig Gen), I: 619; IV: 12; V: 107, 108, 110, 148, 157.
Armistead, Thomas, S., (Sgt Maj, 41st NCST, 3rd Cav), II: 769, 785.
Armistice, The, I: 61.
Arms, Need of, I: 41.
Armstrong, Rev. Dr. ______, (Resident of Norfolk, Va.), IV: 210.
Armstrong, A., (Pvt, Co G, 57th NCST), V: 517.
Armstrong, B.C., (Pvt, Co K, 5th Vols/15th NCST), V: 522.
Armstrong, Edward H., (Capt, Co G, 3rd NCST), I: 196. 204, 213.
Armstrong, G.W., (Lt, 63rd NCST, 5th Cav), IV: 705.
Armstrong, Dr. James Y., (Ass't Surg, 7th Vols/17th NCST), IV: 634.
Armstrong, N.C., (Lt, Co I, 9th NCST, 1st Cav), I: 486.
Armstrong, Nicholas E., (Capt, Co A, 38th NCST), II: 678, 686; V: 548.
Armstrong, T.J., (Capt, Co K, 37th NCST), V: 538.
Armstrong, Thomas E., (Capt, Co K, 3rd NCST), I: 212.
Armstrong's Mill, Va., (and Battle of 1864), III: 30, 248, 251, 628, 629; IV: 93; V: 207.
Army of Tennessee, (aka Bragg's Army), II: 491, 706, 708, 729, 730, 731; III: 434, 448, 449, 453, 481, 499, 500; IV: 120.
Army of Tennessee, (aka Hood's Army), II: 11; III: 190, 439, 493, 500; IV: 320.
Army of Tennessee, (aka Johnston's Army, Western Army), I: 12, 13, 55, 59, 60, 64, 133, 386, 412, 560, 768; II: 491, 492, 720, 741, 786; III: 437, 440, 442, 444, 500; IV: 57, 114, 120, 371, 750.
Army of Northern Virginia, (aka Lee's Army): Most of North Carolina's men and resources went to this most famous of all Confederate armies. This being the case the Army of Northern Virginia is mentioned or referred to on nearly every page of these several volumes. For that reason page listings are not given for this particular item.
Army of Virginia, (Pope's, USA), I: 306, 623, 759; II: 29, 30, 31, 134, 149, 150, 151, 153, 655, 656, 683; IV: 551.
Army of Wilmington, (The grandiose title given by the incompetent Bragg to the forces he so dramatically mislead in southeastern North Carolina), V: 217.
Army of the James, (USA, See also: B.F.Butler), III: 354, 383, 385; IV: 492, 538.
Army of the Potomac, (USA, See also: listings for the various generals who commanded this army; ie., Burnside, Hooker, McClellan, Meade), I: 146, 167, 200, 206, 309, 310, 318, 322, 373, 425, 428, 462, 465, 482,

546, 548, 592, 601, 602, 612, 617, 618, 625, 626, 628, 631, 632, 640, 666, 697, 701, 715, 720, 721, 738, 743, 762, 777; II: 41, 46, 66, 136, 228, 233, 344, 381, 386, 624; III: 13, 43, 91, 93, 159, 239, 258, 382, 401, 567, 597, 611, 615, 617, 625, 626, 630; IV: 494, 534, 562, 581; V: 72, 79, 113, 114, 115, 118, 119, 122, 125, 130, 257, 270.

Army of the Shenandoah, (aka Johnston's Army), I: 347.

Army of the West, (See also: J.E. Johnston), I: 36; III: 454; IV: 137, 746; V: vii, xii, 4, 633, 640, 643.

Army Navy Yard, (Wilmington), IV: 426.

Arnett, Alexander, (2nd Cpl, Co K, 38th NCST), V: 558.

Arney, B.F., (Pvt, Co K, 35th NCST), V: 563.

Arney, George, (Pvt, Co F, 26th NCST), V: 602.

Arney, J.E., (Pvt, Co K, 46th NCST), V: 525.

Arney, J.P., (Pvt, Co K, 35th NCST), V: 563.

Arney, P.E., (Pvt, Co K, 46th NCST), V: 525.

Arnold, F.A., (Pvt, Co H, 63rd NCST, 5th Cav), III: 587.

Arnold, J.L., (1st Lt, Co I, 9th Vols/19th NCST, 2nd Cav), II: 80.

Arnold, Neill T., (2nd Sgt, Co H, 46th NCST), V: 525.

Arnold, Richard, (1st Cpl, Co C, 52nd NCST), III: 223.

Arnold, Soloman, (Pvt, Co F, 5th Vols/15th NCST), V: 521.

Arnold, Thomas H., (Pvt, Co F, 5th Vols/15th NCST), V: 521.

Arrington, ______, V: 461.

Arrington, A.S., (Sgt, Co H, 30th NCST), V: 492.

Arrington, I.D., [John D.], (Lt, Co H, 32nd NCST), IV: 705.

Arrington, J.V., [J.D.], (2nd Lt, Co H, 32nd NCST), IV: 705.

Arrington, John W., (Ensign, Co I, 2nd Vols/12th NCST), I: 630, 642.

Arrington, K.W., (1st Lt, Co I, 30th NCST), II: 486, 498.

Arrington, L.P., (AQM, 2nd Vols/12th NCST), I: 651.

Arrington, P.W., (Adjt, 30th NCST), II: 502.

Arrington, S.P., (AQMS, 2nd Vols/12th NCST), I: 606; V: 506.

Arrington, William T. (Capt, Co I, 30th NCST), II: 496; V: 667.

Arrowood, _____(Pvt, Mi.; An allegation has been made that he was the last man killed east of the Mississippi. Supposition at best, the undocumented allegation should be given little credence), V: 653.

Arsenal Military Academy, (Charleston, S.C.), V: 637.

Arthur, David G., (2nd Lt, Co B, 12th Battalion NCST, Cav), IV: 339.

Artillery, Confederate:

- Adam's, (1st S.C., Light Art), V: 18, 162, 167.
- Adams', (Co D, Starr's 13th Battalion NCST, Light Art), II: 774, 775; IV: 341, 353, 775.
- Anderson's, (Co D, 36th NCST, 2nd Art & Engs), II: 630, 634.
- Andrew's, (See: Cogdell's).
- Atkins', (Co B, Starr's 13th Battalion, Light Art), V: 679.
- Badham's, (Co B, 3rd Battalion NCST, Light Art; See also: Moore's), II: 513; IV: 261, 263, 264, 265, 268, 269; V: 88, 89, 90.
- Beckham's, (Horse Art./ Beckman's Battalion), I: 454; III: 582.

Bienvenu's, (La., Light Art), IV: 26.
Blake's, (Batter of Howitzers at Ft. Wagner), V: 162, 167.
Blocker's, (Co C, 36th NCST, 2nd Art & Engs), II: 630, 634.
Blount's, (Battalion NCST, Light Art), IV: 362; V: 573.
Blount's, (Co K, 10th NCST, 1st Art & Engs, Hvy Art), I: 489, 497, 501, 508, 514, 525, 528, 529, 531, 536; II: 642; IV: 573; V: 183, 184.
Bondurant's, (Ala., "Jeff Davis," Light Art), IV: 444.
Borrough's, (Light Art), III: 739.
Bradford's, (Miss., Light Art), V: 175, 179, 195.
Branch's, (Va., "Petersburg Battery," Light Art), III: 134, 141, 330; IV: 573; V: 175, 178, 182.
Brander's, (Va., "Richmond Letcher," Light Art), IV: 470, 478.
Braxton's, (Va., "Fredericksburg Battery," Light Art) Battalion), I: 374; II: 472, 551.
Breathed's, (Horse Art./Battalion), II: 90, 96, 98; III: 562.
Brem's, (See: Graham's and Williams').
Buckner's, (Company/Battery 63rd Ga., Hvy Art), III: 207; V: 161, 162, 167.
Bunting's, (Light Art), I: 365, 493, 515; IV: 325, 326.
Cabdell's, (Light Art), I: 82.
Cabell's, (Battalion, Light Art), I: 553, 555, 556, 557, 558, 559.
Capehart's, (Co D, 3rd Battalion NCST, Light Art), IV: 264.
Carlton's, (Ga., "Troup Battery," Light Art), I: 556.
"Charleston Battalion," (S.C.), III: 207; V: 162, 165, 167.
Cogdell's, (Co F, 10th NCST, 1st Art & Engs, Hvy Art, See also: Andrew's), I: 489, 496, 497, 498, 500, 501, 502, 508, 509, 514, 515, 518, 519, 527, 529, 531, 535, 536.
Cooper's, (Va., "Stafford Battery," Light Art), III: 66.
Crenshaw's, (Va., "Richmond Battery," Light Art), I: 371; IV: 161, 168, 356.
Culpepper's, (Army of Tenn., Light Art), II: 716, 718.
Cumming's, (Co C, Starr's 13th Battalion NCST, Light Art), III: 400; IV: 341, 361-362, 437, 442; V: 16, 569, 573, 631, 679.
Cutt's, (Ga., "Sumter Battery,"/ Battalion, Light Art), I: 664, 665.
Dabney's, (Va., "Richmond Battery," Light Art), III: 169.
Davidson's, (Va., "Letcher Battery," Light Art), II: 472, 551.
Dearing's, (See: Washington Artillery).
DePass', (aka DeSaussure's, Light Art), III: 207; V: 162, 167. Deshler's, (Battalion, Light Art), III: 163.
Dickson's, (Co E, Starr's 13th Battalion NCST, Light Art), IV: 17, 589; V: 679.
Dixon's, (63rd Ga., Hvy Art), III: 207; V: 162, 167.
Dixon's, (N.C., Light Art), III: 349.
"Donaldsonville Artillery," (La., Light Art), V: 115.
Earl's, (Light Art), II: 661.
"Ellis Light Artillery," (See: Ramseur-Manly's Battery).

Ellis', (Co A, 3rd Battalion NCST, Light Art, See also: Flanner's and Pott's), IV: 261, 265, 266, 267, 268, 269.

Flanner's, (Co F, Starr's 13th Battalion NCST, Light Art, See also: Ellis' and Potts'), IV: 354, 442; V: 569, 573, 617-618.

Fraser's, (Ga., "Pulaski Battery," Light Art), I: 556.

French's, (Va., "Stafford Battery," Light Art), II: 429; V: 668.

Graham's, (See: Brem's, William's).

Graham's, (Va., "Petersburg Battery," Light Art), III: 337, 360; V: 83, 668.

Grandy's, (Va., "Norfolk Light Artillery Blues," Light Art), II: 5; IV: 532.

Greenough's, (Light Art), II: 434.

Griffin's, ("Salem Battery," Horse Art), III: 575.

Guion's, (Co B, 10th NCST, 1st Art & Engs, Hvy Art), I: 489, 491, 493, 497, 498, 500, 501, 502, 508, 509, 514, 515, 518, 519, 527, 529, 531, 535, 536.

Hampton's, (Light Art, units attached to Hampton's Division) IV: 429.

Hardy's, ("Middlesex Battery," Light Art), III: 473.

Hart's, (S.C., "Washington Battery," Horse Art), III: 565, 566, 596, 633.

Haskell's, (Battalion, Light Art), I: 580; IV: 354.

Hebert's (Brigade: 9th Battalion NCST, 1st Hvy Art; 36th NCST, 2nd Art & Engs; 40th NCST, 3rd Art, Hvy), IV: 306, 439.

Henry's, (Battalion, Light Art), I: 16, 51, 579, 580; IV: 363, 380.

Howell's, (Light Art), III: 678.

Hunter's, (Co F, 36th NCST, 2nd Art & Engs, "Pamlico Artillery"), II: 630, 635.

Imboden's, (Va., Light Art), I: 341.

Johnston's, (1st Stuart's Horse Art), III: 596.

Kain's, (Light Art), III: 522, 523.

King's, (Co A, 36th NCST, 2nd Art & Engs), II: 630, 634.

Kolb's, (Ala., Light Art), III: 434.

Lamb's, (aka Potter's, Co G, 36th NCST, 2nd Art & Engs), II: 630, 634.

Latham's, (Co F, "Branch Battery," Starr's 13th Battalion NCST, Light Art), I: 364, 366, 579, 609; II: 21, 308, 310, 311, 320, 326, 427, 469, 542, 545, 594; III: 374; IV: 341, 354, 437; V: 618.

Latta's, (Light Art), IV: 229, 230.

Lattimore's, (Light Art),

Lee's, (Ala., "Montgomery Blues," Light Art), III: 680, 721; IV: 15, 16, 573; V: 75, 175, 184.

Levy's, (Tenn., Thomas' Legion, Light Art), III: 735.

Lloyd's, (Light Art), I: 554, 577; V: 589.

"Louisiana Tigers," (Co K, Walker's Battalion, Thomas' Legion, 80th NCST, Battery, Light Art), IV: 119.

"Macon Light Artillery," (Light Art), II: 615.

Manly's, (Co A, 10th NCST, 1st Art & Engs; See also: Ramseur's), I: 4, 489, 551-560, 562; III: 131; IV: 266, 356, 437, 442; V: 567, 573, 589.

Mann's, (Co B, 36th NCST, 2nd Art & Engs, "Balden Stars"), II: 630, 635, 636.
Manny's (Co G, 10th NCST, 1st Art & Engs, Hvy Art), I: 363, 489, 493, 496, 497, 498, 500, 501, 502, 508, 514, 515, 518, 519, 525, 526, 529, 531, 535, 536; II: 642.
Marshall's, (Light Art), V: 184.
Marye's (Va., "Fredericksburg Battery," Light Art), III: 297.
McCarthy's, (Va., 1st Co, Richmond Howitzers, Light Art), I: 556, 559, 723.
McClees', (See also: Moore's), V: 88.
McGregor's, (2nd Stuart's Horse Art, Barringer's Brigade), I: 431, 439, 460, 468, 469; III: 573, 574, 610, 612, 613, 614, 629, 631, 633, 649, 651, 653.
McIntosh's (S.C., "Pee Dee Battery"/Battalion, Light Art), II: 691.
Miller's, (Co E, 10th NCST, 1st Art & Engs, Moore-Miller's), I: 4, 489, 581; II: 3, 287, 497, 582-582, 642; III: 337; IV: 437, 442; V: 175, 179, 569, 573.
Moore's, (See: 3rd Battalion Light Art).
Moore's, (See: Miller's).
Moore's, (Co C, 3rd Battalion NCST, Light Art; See also: Badham's), IV: 262, 264, 265, 268, 269.
Moseley's, (Battalion, Light Art), I: 581; III: 337; IV: 361.
North Carolina, 3rd Battalion, (Moore's Battalion: Ellis', McCleese's and Moore's Batteries), I: 119; III: 725; IV: 261-269, 439, 643; V: 88, 240.
North Carolina, 9th Battalion, (1st Hvy Art), IV: 5, 224, 303-313, 439; V: 2, 6, 240.
North Carolina, 10th Battalion, (2nd Hvy Art), III: 191, 197; IV: 105, 315-323, 325-327, 439, 440, 643.
North Carolina, 10th NCST, (1st Art & Engs), I: xii, 4, 12, 14, 118, 489-582, 490, 499, 537, 551; II: 79, 163, 513, 635, 640; III: 382; IV: 116, 221-222, 290, 294, 325, 356, 439, 540; V: 9, 113, 175, 183, 240, 680.
North Carolina, 11th Battalion, (Whitford's Hvy Art; See also: 32nd NCST and 67th NCST), III: 174; IV: 81, 224, 270, 338.
North Carolina, 13th Battalion, (See also: Starr's Artillery), I: 133; IV: 17, 56, 341, 342, 355, 361, 362, 379, 403, 439, 644; V: 16, 240, 269, 282, 618, 679.
North Carolina, 36th NCST, (2nd Art), I: xii, 7, 12, 528; II: 629-651, 709, 754, 756, 759, 761; III: 709; IV: 116, 304, 306, 311, 334, 423, 439, 637; V: 14, 222, 239.
North Carolina, 40th NCST, (3rd Art, Hvy), I: xii, 7, 12, 489, 502, 503, 518; II: 640, 745-765; IV: 115, 116, 304, 306, 327, 334, 421, 439, 638; V: 240, 664, 679.
Owens', (Va., 1st Co, Washington Art/Battalion, Light Art), IV: 489.
Otey's, ("Davidson Battery," Light Art), V: 247.
Paris', (Light Art), II: 3; IV: 43, 528.
Patterson's, (Co H, 36th NCST, 2nd Art & Engs, "Clarendon Artillery"), II: 630, 635.

Pegram's, (Va., "Purcell Battery," Light Art), II: 388, 450, 501, 623; III: 30, 141, 159, 248, 249, 337, 362, 370, 372, 374; IV: 159; V: 16, 179, 184.
Pegram's (Battalion, Light Art; aka Pegram's Artillery), II: 691; III: 30, 248; V: 208.
Pender's, (See: Manney's).
Pendleton's, (Artillery Corps/Reserve Artillery Corps, ANV), III: 166.
Pogue's, [Poague's], (1st Rockbridge Battery, Battalion, Va.), I: 541; IV: 176, 186; V: 567, 573.
Pool's, (Co. H, 10th NCST, 1st Art & Engs, Pool's Battery, Hvy Art.), I: 489, 491, 493, 497, 498, 499, 500, 501, 502, 505, 508, 514, 515, 518, 519, 525, 526, 529, 531, 535, 536; III: 290.
Pool's, (Battalion NCST: Co B, G, H, 10th NCST, 1st Art & Engs and Bunting's Battery), I: 493, 494, 495, 496, 515, 517, 518, 519, 521, 522, 523, 524, 525, 526, 527, 532, 533, 534, 535; IV: 325.
Pott's, (Co F, "Branch Battery," Starr's 13th Battalion NCST, Light Art, See also: Ellis' and Flanner's), II: 470; IV: 354.
Powell's, (Co E, 36th NCST, 2nd Art & Engs, "Columbus Artillery"), II: 630, 635.
Ramsay's, (Co D, 10th NCST, 1st Art & Engs, Reilly-Ramsay's Battery, Light Art; See also: Reilly's), I: 561-580; III: 374; V: 573.
Ramseur's, (See: Manly's).
Randolph's, ("Randolph's Howitzers," Va., Light Art), I: 85, 91, 94, 95, 105, 106, 127; III: 48.
Reade's, [Read], (Ga., Battery/Battalion, Light Art) III: 337.
Reid's, (Va., Battalion, Light Art), IV: 531; V: 175, 177.
Reilly's, (Reilly's Battalion NCST, Hvy Art: Co F, G, K and I, 10th NCST, 1st Art & Engs and Sutherland's Battery), I: 496; V: 528.
Reilly's, (Co D, 10th NCST, 1st Art & Engs, aka, "Rowan Artillery," Reilly-Ramsay's Battery, Light Art; See also: Ramsay's), I: 4, 489, 525, 561-580; II: 640; IV: 437; V: 24, 589.
Richardson's, (Co I, 36th NCST, 2nd Art & Engs, "Bladen Artillery"), II: 630, 634.
Robertson's (AoT, Light Art), (Rockbridge County, Va., McLaughlin's), IV: 616.
Rowan Artillery, (See: Reilly's, Ramsay's, Reilly-Ramsay's Battery).
Southerland's, (Co I, 10th NCST, 1st Art & Engs), I: 4, 489, 496, 528; IV: 540.
Sparrow's, (See: Blount's).
Standard's, (Va., Light Art), I: 341.
Starr's, (Battery: Co B, 13th Battallion NCST, Light Art; Starr's 13th Battalion NCST), I: 133, 231, 325, 345, 346, 493, 494, 515, 517, 518, 519, 520; II: 513; III: 231; IV: 17, 56, 325, 341-362, 484, 644.
Stevenson's, (Battalion, Light Art: Co A, C, D, G, I, 36th NCST, 2nd Art & Engs), II: 634.
Stribling's, (Va., "Fauquier Battery," Light Art), II: 88; III: 337.
Stuart's (Horse Artillery, See: Pelham's).

Sturdivant's, ("Albemarle Battery," Light Art), II: 515; IV: 86, 489, 499.
Tansil's, (3rd Va., Light Art), II: 679.
Tatum's, (1st S.C., Light Art), V: 162, 167.
Taylor's, (Co K, 36th NCST, 2nd Art & Engs, "Brunswick Artillery"), II: 630, 635.
Virginia, 12th, (Bogg's Hvy Art), IV: 355, 356, 403.
"Washington Artillery," (New Orleans, La., Battery/Battalion, Light Art), I: 187, 572, 741; II: 362, 609, 610; III: 353, 377; IV: 82, 572; V: 140.
Webb's, (Co A, Starr's 13th Battalion NCST, Light Art), IV: 341, 355-360, 437, 438; V: 271, 273, 274, 279.
William's, (Co C, "Charlotte Battery," 10th NCST, 1st Art & Engs, Light Art; See also: Brem-Graham's) I: 4, 123, 364, 489, 537-550; II: 308, 310, 313, 321, 324, 429, 446, 542, 594; III: 162, 165; IV: 437, 442; V: 273, 274, 567-568, 573, 668.
Wright's, (Va., "Halifax Battery," Light Art), III: 142, 363, 373, 374.

Artillery, Federal:
Ames', (Light Art), III: 580.
Arnold's, (Light Art), III: 580.
Battery D, (New York, Light Art), I: 150, 200.
Belger's, (Rhode Island), II: 337.
Bennett's, (Light Art), II: 311.
Calif's, (Horse Art), II: 344.
Connecticut, 1st, (Hvy Art), V: 238.
Cooper's, (Light Art), II: 346, 347, 350, 351, 361.
Cushing's, (Battery A, 4th U.S., Light Art), II: 364; V: 107, 147.
Dayton's, (Light Art), II: 311.
Fuller's, (Light Art), III: 565, 566.
Hall's, (Light Art), III: 298.
Howard's, V: 143, 152.
Maine, 2nd, (Light Art), II: 345.
Massachusetts, 1st, (Hvy Art), III: 60.
Massachusetts, 2nd, (Hvy Art), III: 345; V: 77, 175.
McGilvery's, (Light Art), II: 363, 364.
New York, 3rd, (Light Art), II: 337.
New York, 12th, (McKnight's, Light Art), III: 30.
New York, 16th, (Hvy Art),V: 238.
New York, 24th, (Independent Battery, Light Art), III: 345; V: 175.
Rhode Island, Battery D, (Light Art) III: 30.
Rhode Island, 3rd, (Light Art), I: 183, 219.
Ricketts', (1st U.S. Regulars, Light Art), I: 298, 332, 343, 345; III: 580; V: 29, 30, 31, 583.
Robertson's, (U.S. Regulars, Light Art), III: 596.
Sherman's, (Light Art), I: 343; V: 583.
Stewart's, (Battery B, 4th U.S. Regulars, Light Art), II: 350.
United States, 1st, (Light Art), I: 330.
United States, 2nd, (Light Art), I: 82, 87, 88, 93, 98, 106.
United States, 3rd, (Light Art), V: 238.
United States, 4th, (Light Art), II: 350.
Wade's, (New York, Light Art), I: 556.
Weidrick's, (Light Art), I: 332.
Woerner's, (New Jersey, Light Art), III: 30.
Woodruff's, (Light Art), II: 364; V: 108.

Asbell, James, (Pvt, Co K, 9th Vols/19th NCST, 2nd Cav), II: 92.
Asbury, Daniel M., (Jr 2nd Lt, Co G, 52nd NCST), III: 224.
Ash Landing, Va., V: 213.
Ashby, Turner, (Brig Gen), IV: 230, 231.
Ashby, N.C., (Roanoke Island), II: 509, 510.
Ashby's Gap, Va., I: 298, 578; III: 69, 464, 534, 535, 559, 561, 563, 564, 567, 569, 571; IV: 168; V: 676.
Ashby's Landing, (Roanoke Island), II: 509, 510; V: 59, 60, 63.
Ashcraft, John B., (Lt Col, 37th NCST), II: 653; IV: 474.
Ashcraft, Thomas, E., (Capt, Co I, 53rd NCST), III: 263, 264.
Ashe, Dr. A.S., (Ass't Surg, N.C.), IV: 630.
Ashe, Richard J., (Capt, Co D, 1st Vols, "Bethel"), I: 77, 90, 124, 125, 127, 129; II: 410.
Ashe, Samuel A'court, (1st Lt, Engineering Officer; Capt, AAG, to Pender), II: 685; IV: 296, 299, 413, 416, 421, 422, 551, 552; V: ix, 137, 158.
Ashe, Thomas S., (Congress, CSA), IV: 356.
Ashe, William S., (Maj, N.C. Quartermaster Department), I: 23.
Ashe County, N.C., II: 303, 359; III: 445, 447, 504; IV: 271, 371, 379, 387.
Asheboro, N.C., [Ashboro], IV: 102, 103.
Asheville, N.C., I: 130, 417; II: 80, 81, 293, 489, 493, 704, 705, 722, 727, 731; III: 34, 302, 307, 436, 473, 496, 516, 524, 527, 644, 663, 664, 669, 670, 679, 683, 738, 755, 756, 757, 759, 760; IV: 3, 6, 110, 111, 114, 115, 116, 123, 127, 128, 202, 218, 371, 373, 379, 380, 386, 397, 425, 431, 535, 594; V: 5, 110, 653, 654.
Ashford, John, (Col, 38th NCST), II: 47, 675, 678, 679, 682, 684, 685, 686, 687, 689, 692, 694, 695; IV: 209, 420; V: 548.
Ashland, Va., I: 300, 303, 366, 430, 567, 570, 612, 613; II: 23, 66, 470, 654; III: 608, 609; IV: 37, 150, 197, 233.
Ashley, A.J., (Capt, Co E, 51st NCST), III: 219.
Ashley, James P., (2nd Sgt, Co A, 26th NCST), V: 531.
Ashley, William, (1st Lt, Co C, Walker's Battalion, Thomas' Legion; 80th NCST), IV: 118.
Ashley River, S.C., II: 758; V: 450.
Ashworth, W.T., [W.R.], (2nd Lt, Co C, 6th Battalion Junior Reserves; Co F, 70th NCST, 1st Junior Reserves), IV: 13.
Askew, ______, (Resident of Madison County), III: 662.
Askew, Frank, (Pvt, Co G, 47th NCST), V: 535.
Askew, George H., (Pvt, Co K, 38th NCST), V: 558.
Askew, Joe, (Pvt, Co B, Wynn's 15th Battalion NCST, Cav), IV: 367.
Askew, Levi, (Capt, Co D, 68th NCST), III: 714.
Askew, R.J., (Pvt, Co F, 1st NCST), V: 485.
Askew, W.A.W., (2nd Lt, Co D, 66th NCST), III: 686.
Association of the Maryland Line, I: 34; V: 353.
Astooga Stoga, John, [Astoogatogch], (2nd Lt, Co A, Indian Co, 69th NCST, Thomas' Legion), II: 487; III: 730, 736.
Atgo, T.M., (Lt, Co C, 9th Battalion NCST), IV: 305.
Atkins, Rev. D., (Civilian), IV: 120.

Atkins, George B., (Capt, Co B, Starr's Battery, Starr's 13th Battalion NCST, Light Art), I: 119; IV: 56, 57, 347, 350, 351.
Atkins, J.B., (Pvt, Co F, 1st NCST; Pvt, Co C, 7th Vols/17th NCST), IV: 350.
Atkins, James, (Pvt, Co F, 5th Vols/15th NCST), V: 521.
Atkins, N.T., (Pvt, Co H, 45th NCST), V: 500.
Atkinson, Atlas, (1st Lt, Co B, 50th NCST), III: 203.
Atkinson, E.C., (Capt, Co B, 50th NCST), III: 202.
Atkinson, J.S., (Pvt, Co A, 10th NCST, 1st Art & Engs, Ramseur-Manly's Battery, Light Art), I: 559.
Atkinson, James W., (Ensign & Color-bearer, 33rd NCST), I: 548; II: 57, 62, 537, 576, 577, 579; IV: 470; V: 544.
Atkinson, Joseph H., (Capt, Co H, 50th NCST), III: 202.
Atkinson, Octavius A., (Sgt, Co E, 43rd NCST; Detailed, 2nd Corps Provost Guard), V: 498, 569.
Atkinson, Roger P., (Capt, AQM, 3rd NCST), I: 213.
Atkinson, Robert W., (Capt, AQM, Co E, 9th Vols/19th NCST, 2nd Cav), II: 80, 89; IV: 723.
Atkinson, Miss Virginia, (Resident of Pitt County), IV: 77.
Atkinson, W., (Pvt, Co K, 43rd NCST), V: 499.
Atlanta, Ga., (and Battle of, 1865), I: 730; II: 492, 702, 756; III: 438, 484, 493, 500; IV: 58, 327, 415, 498.
Atlanta Campaign, II: 704; III: 437, 443, 492, 493, 500.
Atlantic & North Carolina Railroad, N.C., I: 363, 537; II: 541, 543, 594; III: 7, 173, 226, 705, 727; IV: 528.
Atlee's Station, Va., I: 367, 428, 453, 459-464; II: 25; IV: 198; V: 197.
Atwater, M. (Pvt, Co G, 28th NCST), V: 542.
Atwell, George, (Sgt Maj, 34th NCST), II: 582.
Atwell, J.B., (Capt, Co F, 10th Vols/20th NCST), II: 112, 115.
Atwell, W.L., (2nd Lt, Co G, 42nd NCST), II: 791.
Atwood, Jesse W., (Capt, Co K, 48th NCST), III: 114, 115.
Auburn, Ala., III: 683.
Auburn, Va., I: 427; III: 578, 579, 580, 582, 589, 629.
Auburn Mills, Va., (Skirmish, 1863, aka "Buckland Races"), I: 426, 453, 454, 455, 456, 457, 458, 459, 481, 484.
August, T.P., (Col, N.C. Conscription Bureau) IV: 407.
Augusta, Ga., II: 756, 757; III: 179; IV: 320, 327, 333.
Auldred, John, (Pvt, Co F, 6th Vols/16th NCST), V: 552.
Aumack, Samuel M., (Pvt, Co D, 68th NCST), III: 715.
Aurora, Ind., III: 525.
Ausbon, William James, (Pvt, Co H, 7th Vols/17th NCST), V: 15.
Ausburn, Zach, (Pvt, Co A, 26th NCST), V: 531.
Austin, Benjamin P., (2nd Cpl, Co I, 52nd NCST), III: 225.
Austin, D.P., (Pvt, Co K, 28th NCST), V: 543.
Austin, Daniel B., (Pvt, Detached Co, 68th NCST), III: 723.
Austin, E., (Pvt, Co B, 8th Vols/18th NCST), II: 63; V: 539.
Austin, G.D., (Pvt, Co A, 26th NCST), V: 531.
Austin, Green B., (Musician, 4th NCST), I: 234; V: 488.
Austin, J.H., (Sgt Maj, 37th NCST), V: 545.
Austin, James E., (1st Lt, Co I & E, 48th NCST), III: 122.

Austin, John C., (Pvt, Co I, 48th NCST), V: 527.
Austin, John W., (Pvt, Co I, 2nd NCST), I: 176; V: 486.
Austin, Milton S., (1st Lt, Co E, 52nd NCST), III: 224.
Austin, Rufus, (Pvt, Co C, 53rd NCST), V: 501.
Austin, Thomas A., (Pvt, Co I, 48th NCST), V: 527.
Austin, W., (Pvt, Co F, 12th Vols/22nd NCST), V: 553.
Austin, W.A., (1st Lt, Co I, 48th NCST), V: 520.
Austin, W.M., (Lt, Co C, 58th NCST), III: 433, 435.
Auten, W., (Pvt, Co K, 56th NCST), III: 348.
Autrey, ______, (Capt, Co C, 2nd Home Guard), IV: 653.
Autrey, Phillip, (Pvt, Co I, 46th NCST), V: 525.
Autry, David, (Sgt, Co C, 3rd NCST), V: 487.
Avent, G.W., (Capt, Co D, 35th NCST), IV: 722.
Averasboro, N.C., (and Battle of, 1865), II: 12, 803; III: 193-195, 197, 454; IV: 20, 58, 104, 322, 336, 440, 592.
Averill, Willaim Woods, (Maj Gen, USA), I: 645.
Averitt, R.H., (Pvt, Co B, 56th NCST), III: 347.
Avery, Alphonso C., (ADC to Hood; Adjt District of Western N.C.; Maj, Avery's 17th Battalion; Col, 6th NCST), I: vi, vii, 22, 78, 90, 95, 116, 118, 122, 125, 127, 129, 133, 337, 339, 340, 345, 347, 348, 349, 351, 355, 365, 376; IV: 191, 371, 378, 373, 375; V: 581, 650.
Avery, Clark Moulton, (Col, 33rd NCST), I: 78, 90, 95, 114, 118, 125, 129, 130, 145, 365, 376, 380; II: 37, 47, 48, 311, 315, 317, 318, 319, 320, 321, 537, 542, 543, 544, 556, 557, 561, 564, 565, 566, 567, 578, 654; IV: 191, 473; V: 10, 94, 95, 97, 98.
Avery, H., (Master, USN), V: 243.
Avery, Isaac Erwin, (Col, 6th NCST), I: 296, 303, 313, 316, 344, 345, 349, 354, 357, 358; II: 137; III: 411, 413, 415, 416; IV: 237, 525; V: 9, 31, 32, 583, 606, 649.
Avery, L.A., (Sgt, Co G, 3rd NCST), V: 487.
Avery, Waighstill W., I: 22; III: 718; IV: 372, 382; V: 583.
Avery, Willoughby F., (Capt, Co I, 33rd NCST), II: 539, 540, 558.
Avery, Willoughby F., (2nd Lt, Co F, 41st NCST, 3rd Cav), II: 771.
Avery House, (nr Petersburg, Va.), II: 298.
Axley, Felix P., (1st Lt, Co G, 39th NCST), II: 706.
Aycock, E.S., (Pvt, Co B, 30th NCST), V: 491.
Aycock, J.R., (Pvt, Co I, 16th Battalion/75th NCST, 7th Cav), V: 660.
Aycock, Larry, (Pvt, Co A, 27th NCST), II: 461; V: 522.
Ayres, David, (Pvt, Co A, 5th NCST), I: 291.
Ayres, John, (Pvt, Co D, 43rd NCST), V: 498.
Ayres, S.P., (Pvt, Co B, 1st NCST), V: 485.

(B)

Babb, Lewis H., (1st Lt, Co E, 33rd NCST), II: 539.
Babb, William K., (2nd Lt, Co E, 33rd NCST), II: 539, 562, 578; IV: 467.
Babcock, ______, (Col, USA), III: 184.
Bache, Professor ______, (U.S. Coast Survey), V: 386.
Bache, George M., (Lt, USN, Pioneer, Powhatan) V: 244.
Bachelder, ______, (Brig Gen, USA), V: 143, 150.
Bachelor, J.A., (Pvt, Co K, 10th Vols/20th NCST), V: 509.
Bachelor's Creek, N.C., (and Battle of, 1864; aka Bachelder's Creek and Batchelor's Bridge), I: 321, 334, 396, 397, 526; III: 6, 7, 132, 210, 273, 333, 334; IV: 241, 486, 487; V: 327.
Bachman, ______, (Capt, Co D, 10th NCST, 1st Art & Engs, Ramseur-Manly's Battery, Light Art.), I: 565.
Back River, Va., I: 84, 85.
Bacon Race Church, Va., IV: 149, 150.
Badger, ______, (Resident of Raleigh), I: 116,
Badger, Edward S., (Lt, Co C, 56th NCST), III: 314, 398.
Badger, Hon. George E., (Grandfather of Sgt G.B. Badger), IV: 51.
Badger, Richard C., (Maj, ACS, Daniel's Brigade), I: 540; IV: 513, 517, 540; V: 651.
Badger, S.P., (Pvt, Co F, 26th NCST), V: 602.
Badger, Sherwood, (Pvt, Co D, 43rd NCST; Courier, Daniel-Grimes' Brigade), IV: 519; V: 498.
Badget, John R., (Pvt, Co B, 2nd Battalion NCST), V: 495.
Badgett, A.H., (Sgt, Co G, 30th NCST), V: 492.
Badgett, C.L., (2nd Lt, Co A, 6th Battalion Junior Reserves; Co C, 70th NCST, 1st Junior Reserves), IV: 13.
Badgett, J.D., (Pvt, Co G, 30th NCST), V: 492.
Badgett, J.W., (Capt, Co G, 30th NCST), V: 484.
Badgett, Joseph W., (Sgt, Co G, 30th NCST), V: 492.
Badham, John C., (Lt Col, 5th NCST), I: 281, 282, 284, 285; V: 11.
Badham, William, (Capt, Co B, Badham's 3rd Battalion NCST, Light Art), IV: 261, 264, 265, 268.
Baggerly, John A., [J.F. Baggerly, Bagley], (Pvt, Courier, Co G, 4th NCST), I: 271; II: 499; V: 489.
Bagley, ______, (Clerk, NCN), V: 311.
Bagley, Alvin, (1st Lt, Co K, 66th NCST), III: 686.
Bagley, William H., (Maj, 68th NCST), III: 713, 714.
Bagley, Worth, (Son of Maj W.H. Bagley), III: 714.

Bagwell, Stanhope H., (Pvt, Co C, 34th NCST), V: 555.
Bahamas, (aka Bahama Islands), V: 355, 356, 358, 430.
Bailey, _____, (Sgt, Color-bearer, 6th Battalion/60th NCST), III: 491.
Bailey, A.G., (Lt, Co K, 64th NCST), III: 660.
Bailey, Amos, (Pvt, Co D, 6th Vols/16th NCST), V: 552.
Bailey, Benjamin, (Pvt, Co F, 30th NCST), V: 492.
Bailey, Dempsey, (2nd Lt, Co E, 77th NCST, 7th Senior Reserves), IV: 100.
Bailey, Dr. G. Pink, [Baily], (Capt, Co K, 3rd Vols/13th NCST), I: 653, 654, 656, 692.
Bailey, Isaac H., (Capt, Co B, 58th NCST), III: 432, 435, 447, 448, 449, 450, 452, 453; V: 169.
Bailey, J.E., (Lt, Co K, 12th Vols/22nd NCST), II: 166.
Bailey, James C., (Capt, Co H, 14th Vols/24th NCST), II: 272.
Bailey, Lemuel Johnston, (Pvt, Co H, 63rd NCST, 5th Cav), III: 590.
Bailey, Thomas B., (Brother of L.J. Bailey), III: 590, 655.
Bailey, W.H., (Pvt, Co K, 12th Vols/22nd NCST), V: 554.
Bailey, W.H., (2nd Lt, Co F, 42nd NCST), II: 791, 806.
Baily, Wilson, (Lt, Co A, 47th NCST), III: 84.
Baines, James P., (Pvt, Co G, 33rd NCST), V: 544.
Baines, William, (Pvt, Co A, 47th NCST), V: 534.
Baird, Alfred H., (Maj, 5th Battalion; Lt Col, 65th NCST, 6th Cav), I: 118; III: 673, 674, 683; IV: 271, 273, 274, 275, 291, 301.
Baird, B.F., (Capt, Co D, 58th NCST), III: 433, 447.
Baird, D.F., (Lt, Co D, 58th NCST), III: 433; V: 169.
Baird, Dr. J.S.T., (2nd Lt, Co E, 6th Battalion/60th NCST), III: 474.
Baird, J.V., (Capt, Co I, 64th NCST), III: 660.
Baird, William W., (Sgt Maj, 14th Vols/24th NCST), II: 269.
Baker, A., (Pvt, Co D, 26th NCST), V: 531.
Baker, A.J., (Pvt, Co A, Webb's Battery, Starr's 13th Battalion NCST, Light Art), V: 282.
Baker, Alexander, (Pvt, Co G, 11th Vols/22nd NCST), V: 515.
Baker, B.T., (Pvt, Co C, 44th NCST), V: 533.
Baker, Benjamin, (Pvt, Co H, 11th Vols/22nd NCST), V: 515.
Baker, D.D., (Pvt, Co I, 53rd NCST), V: 502.
Baker, F.J., (Pvt, Co G, 11th Vols/22nd NCST), V: 515.
Baker, George B., (Lt, AQM, Conscript Camp), I: 118, 213.
Baker, H.F., (Pvt, Co C, 57th NCST), V: 517.
Baker, Henry H., (Capt, Co A, 33rd NCST), II: 538, 567.
Baker, J., (Pvt, Co D, 26th NCST), V: 531.
Baker, J.F., (Pvt, Co K, 14th Vols/24th NCST), V: 193.
Baker, J.C., (Pvt, Co G, 11th Vols/22nd NCST), V: 515.
Baker, J.R., (2nd Lt, Co H, 35th NCST), II: 598.
Baker, Jackson, (Pvt, Co A, 10th NCST, 1st Art & Engs, Ramseur-Manly's Battery, Light Art), V: 567.
Baker, Jackson, (Pvt, Co D, 26th NCST), II: 375.
Baker, Jasper, (Pvt, Co D, 6th NCST), V: 512.
Baker, John A., (Col, 41st NCST, 3rd Cav), I: 429, 430, 431, 432;

II: 769, 776, 778, 779, 780; III: 608, 610, 644; IV: 490, 582, 721.
Baker, John C., (2nd Lt, Co I, 9th Vols/19th NCST, 2nd Cav), II: 89.
Baker, John, Sr., (Pvt, Co D, 68th NCST), III: 715.
Baker, John W., Jr., (Resident of Fayetteville), I: 112.
Baker, Joseph, (Pvt, Co D, 68th NCST), III: 715.
Baker, Joseph, (Sgt, Co D, 42nd NCST), II: 799.
Baker, Dr. Joseph H., (Ass't Surg, 1st Vols. "Bethel"), I: 77; IV: 631.
Baker, Joseph S., (1st Lt, Co D, 9th Vols/19th NCST, 2nd Cav), II: 80, 89, 98, 101.
Baker, Lawrence S., (Brig Gen) I: xi, xii, xiii, 77, 417, 420, 422, 423, 425, 426, 481, 484, 485, 498, 527, 533, 534; II: 99; III: 186, 464, 465, 558, 572, 644, 727; IV: 4, 11, 15, 18, 19, 30, 39, 42, 359, 360, 381, 440, 581, 591; V: 269, 271, 273, 275, 276, 278, 279, 280, 281, 282, 589, 674.
Baker, Richard, (Pvt, Co D, 68th NCST), III: 715.
Baker, Dr. Richard B., (Surg, 33rd NCST), II: 537, 579, 580; III: 715; IV: 474, 636.
Baker, Rufus, (Pvt, Co B, 4th Vols/14th NCST), I: 731.
Baker, Theodore G., (Maj, AAG, Hampton's Division), III: 593.
Baker, Thomas W., (1st Lt, Co D, 43rd NCST), I: 120; III: 3.
Baker, W.H., (Pvt, Co A, 10th NCST, 1st Art & Engs, Ramseur-Manly's Battery, Light Art), V: 567.
Baker, W.J., (Pvt, Co C, 8th NCST), V: 193.
Baker, W.T., (Pvt, Co B, 26th NCST), V: 531.
Baker, William J., (Pvt, Co B, 4th Vols/14th NCST; Maj, Commissary, Pettigrew's Brigade), I: 731; IV: 556, 568; V: 193.
Baker Wrecking Company, V: 329.
Baker's Command, Surrender of, V: 269.
Bakersville, N.C., III: 719.
Balch, A., (Cpl, Co C, 28th NCST), V: 541.
Balch, F.H., (Pvt, Co C, 28th NCST), V: 541.
Balch, J., (Pvt, Co C, 28th NCST), V: 541.
Balch, J.W., (Lt, USN), V: 243.
Balch, M., (Pvt, Co C, 28th NCST), V: 541.
Bald Mountain, N.C., IV: 381
Bald Head Island, N.C., (aka Smith's Island, and Bald Head Lighthouse, See also: Smith's Island), II: 745, 748, 749, 750, 753, 754, 756, 761; IV: 47, 50, 265, 268, 307, 311, 421; V: 336, 358, 396, 409.
Baldwin, A.J., (Pvt, Co B, 28th NCST), V: 541.
Baldwin, Alfred, (Pvt, Co C, 10th NCST, 1st Art & Engs, Brem-Graham-William's Battery, Light Art), V: 568.
Baldwin, Charles M., (Sgt, Co H, 8th Vols/18th NCST), II: 64; V: 540.
Baldwin, Hiram, (Pvt, Co C, 4th Vols/14th NCST), I: 731; V: 490.
Baldwin, John R., (Pvt, Co H, 8th Vols/18th NCST), II: 64; V: 540.
Baldwin, Joseph, (Pvt, Co F, 26th NCST), V: 602.
Baldwin, Thomas R., (Jr 2nd Lt, Co E, 52nd NCST), III: 224.
Baldwin, W.G., (Lt, 10th Vols/20th NCST), IV: 705.
Bales, E.M., (Sgt, Co K, 30th NCST), V: 493
Bales, J.P., (Pvt, Co K, 30th NCST), V: 493.

Balfour, _____, (Capt, IG Cooke's Brigade), IV: 510.
Ball, C.N., (Pvt, Co B, 1st Battalion NCST), V: 504.
Ball, Franklin, (Pvt, Co H, 48th NCST), V: 527.
Ball, T., (Pvt, Co K, 54th NCST), V: 516.
Ball, T.M., (Sgt, Co H, 4th NCST), I: 233.
Ball, W., (Pvt, Co K, 54th NCST), V: 516.
Ball's Bluff, Va., III: 750.
Ballance, _____, (Seaman, Sea Bird), V: 309.
Ballard, J.C., (Pvt, Co I, 43rd NCST), V: 499.
Ballard, John, (Capt, Co I, 43rd NCST), III: 2, 3.
Ballard, John, (Pvt, Co I, 43rd NCST), V: 499.
Ballard, Junnius, (ACS, 1st Regt, 3rd Class, Home Guard), IV: 654.
Ballard, Kedar J., (Cpl, Co C, 5th NCST; Detailed, 2nd Corps Provost Guard), I: 291; V: 505, 569.
Ballard, M.T., (2nd Lt, Co B, 31st NCST), II: 512.
Ballard, Robert E., (2nd Lt, Co I, 32nd NCST; ADC to Daniel), I: 736; IV: 513, 518.
Ballard, W.H., (Capt, Co E, 5th Vols/15th NCST), I: 735.
Ballard, W.M., (Sgt, Co E, 28th NCST), V: 542.
Ballard, W.W., (Pvt, Co F, 8th Vols/18th NCST), V: 539.
Ballentine, John W., (Lt, Co E, 7th NCST), I: 383, 385.
Ballew, Joseph R., (Capt, Co F, 26th NCST), II: 304, 328, 330, 331, 336, 396, 416, 417.
Ballinger, Joseph D., (Jr 2nd Lt, Co K, 31st NCST), II: 508.
Ballinger, Tx., IV: 619.
Balsam Gap, N.C., III: 760; V: 654, 655.
Balsam Mountains, N.C., III: 518, 758, 759; IV: 127, 381.
Baltimore, Md., I: 36, 325, 632; II: 246, 671; III: 91, 610, 749, 750; IV: 662, 663, 665, 725, 735, 741, 742; V: 82, 353, 358, 361, 401, 422, 623.
Baltimore Crossroads, Va., I: 566.
Baltimore Pike, (nr Gettysburg, Pa.), I: 148, 196; III: 235.
Baltimore & Ohio Pike, (to Fredericksburg, Va.), I: 306.
Baltimore & Ohio Railroad, I: 189, 373, 573; II: 34, 233, 246, 479, 556, 657; IV: 164, 167.
Baltimore & Susquehannah Railroad, IV: 665.
Bamberger, Jacob, (Lt, Co H, 51st NCST), III: 219.
Bamburg, S.C., III: 190.
Band, 11th Regimental, II: 399.
Bandy, J.M., (2nd Lt, Co B, 8th Battalion Junior Reserves; Co E, 72nd NCST, 3rd Junior Reserves), IV: 41, 595.
Bank of England, V: 455.
Bank of Havana, V: 386.
Banks, _____, (Lt, Adjt, 1st Regt Home Guard in the Field), V: 631.
Banks, Charles R., (1st Lt, Co C, 6th Battalion/60th NCST), IV: 296.
Banks, Joseph, (Pvt, Co E, 56th NCST), III: 347.
Banks, Nathaniel Prentis, (Maj Gen, USA), I: 623, 659; II: 66, 131, 149, 150, 153, 154, 564, 682; IV: 230, 551.
Banks, R.B., (Pvt, Co I, 8th Vols/18th NCST), II: 64; V: 540.
Banner, H.C., (Lt, Co K, 48th NCST), III: 117.
Banner, John E., (Sgt, Co A, 2nd NCST), I: 175; V: 485.

Banner, W.O.T., (Lt, Co A, 2nd NCST), I: 158.
Bannerman's Bridge, (nr Wilmington), IV: 358.
Baply, Peter, (Pvt, Co A, 6th NCST), V: 512.
Baptist Gap, Tenn., II: 487, 708, 728; III: 736.
Baptist Valley, Tenn., III: 736.
Barbee, A., (Pvt, Co D, 28th NCST), V: 542.
Barbee, D.C., (Cpl, Co I, 6th NCST), V: 513.
Barbee, H., (Pvt, Co D, 28th NCST), V: 542.
Barbee, George, (Color-Sgt, 44th NCST), III: 33.
Barbee, William F.G., (Pvt, Co D, 56th NCST), III: 347.
Barbee's Cross Roads, Va., I: 422.
Barber, A.P., (Pvt, Co C, 53rd NCST), V: 501.
Barber, Charles, (Pvt, Co A, Webb's Battery, Starr's 13th Battalion NCST, Light Art), V: 282.
Barber, E.F., (Sgt, Co B, 4th NCST), I: 232.
Barber, H.A., (Pvt, Co C, 53rd NCST), V: 501.
Barber, J.W., (Pvt, Co C, 5th NCST), I: 291; V: 505.
Barber, Jackson, (Pvt, Co I, 14th Vols/24th NCST), V: 560.
Barber, John Y., (Musician, 4th NCST), I: 234.
Barber, Joseph, (2nd Lt, Co B, 4th NCST), I: 232, 269.
Barber, Kimmon, (Pvt, Co I, 14th Vols/24th NCST), V: 560.
Barber, S., (Pvt, Co K, 26th NCST), V: 533.
Barber, William M., [Barbour], (Col, 37th NCST), I: 385; II: 56, 57, 559, 574, 575, 653, 655, 657, 659, 662, 663, 668, 669; III: 332; IV: 474; V: 10.
Barberry, Elic, (Pvt, Co G, 56th NCST), V: 566.
Barbot, ______, (Ass't Engineer, Sirene), V: 404, 448, 449.
Barbour, J.Y., (Musician, 4th NCST), V: 488.
Barboursville, Ky., II: 708; IV: 271, 273, 289.
Barden, Allen, (1st Cpl, Co I, 46th NCST), V: 525.
Barden, Isaac V., (2nd Lt, Co C, 68th NCST), III: 727.
Barden, R.T., (Capt, Co K, 27th NCST) II: 425, 426.
Barden, Reddin C., (1st Lt, Co C, 68th NCST), III: 725, 727.
Bardin, William, (Pvt, Co K, 27th NCST), II: 463; V: 524.
Bardon, Miss., II: 735.
Bare, Jacob, (Pvt, Co A, 34th NCST), V: 554.
Bare, R., (Pvt, Co A, 26th NCST), V: 531.
Barefoot, Joel, (Pvt, Co B, 56th NCST), III: 366.
Barfield, S.A., (2nd Lt, Co C, 7th Battalion Junior Reserves; Co I, 72nd NCST, 3rd Junior Reserves), IV: 40.
Barger, Henry, (Pvt, Co I, 25th Ark.), II: 719.
Barger, Hosea, (Pvt, Co A, 13th Vols/23rd NCST), V: 509.
Barham, A., (Pvt, Co G, 45th NCST), V: 500.
Barham, Dr. R.G., (Ass't Surg, 28th NCST), II: 466; IV: 473, 636.
Barhamsville, Va., (aka Eltham's Landing), I: 301, 334; IV: 151, 152.
Barill, J.H., (Pvt, Co A, 1st NCST), V: 485.
Barker, Cicero R., (8th Vols/18th NCST), V: 665.
Barker, D.D., (Pvt, Co D, 2nd Vols/12th NCST), V: 507.

Barker, E.R., (Lt, Co A, 9th NCST, 1st Cav), I: 485.
Barker, L.J., (Hospital Steward, 28th NCST), II: 465; V: 540.
Barker, Theodore G., (AAG, Hampton's Division, Cav), III: 593.
Barkley, James M., (2nd Lt, Co B, 8th Battalion Junior Reserves; Co E, 72nd NCST, 3rd Junior Reserves), IV: 41, 42.
Barksdale, William, (Brig Gen), I: 556.
Barlow, D.H., (2nd Lt, Co I, 5th Vols/15th NCST), I: 735.
Barlow, Francis Channing, (Maj Gen, USA), I: 431; II: 47, 780.
Barlow, P., (2nd Sgt, Co A, 12th Vols/22nd NCST), V: 553.
Barnard, Hezekiah E., (1st Lt, Co 7, 79th NCST, 8th Cav), IV: 115.
Barnard, Joe, (Capt, Co 7, 79th NCST, 8th Cav), IV: 115.
Barnard, John C., (Pvt, Co H, 4th NCST), V: 489.
Banard House, (nr Hamilton's Crossing, Va.), I: 309.
Barnard's Mills, Va., IV: 573.
Barncastle, H.L., (Pvt, Co B, 1st Battalion NCST), V: 504.
Barnes, A.L., (Pvt, Co H, 2nd Vols/12th NCST), I: 630.
Barnes, Arthur, (Capt, Co H, 59th NCST, 4th Cav), III: 457.
Barnes, B., (Pvt, Co H, 2nd Vols/12th NCST), V: 507.
Barnes, B.J., (Capt, Co A, 2nd NCST), I: 158, 159.
Barnes, Bennett, (2nd Lt, Co C, 43rd NCST), III: 3.
Barnes, Calvin, (Capt, Co B, 2nd NCST), I: 158, 159; II: 746.
Barnes, Calvin, (Capt, Co H, 40th NCST, 3rd Art, Hvy), II: 746.
Barnes, Daniel, (Pvt, Co D, 68th NCST), III: 715.
Barnes, E., (Pvt, Co E, 9th Vols/19th NCST, 2nd Cav), V: 658.
Barnes, Dr. E., (Ass't Surg, 59th NCST, 4th Cav), III: 457; IV: 641.
Barnes, Elias, (Pvt, Co I, 43rd NCST),V: 499.
Barnes, G.L., (Pvt, Co G, 2nd Vols/12th NCST), V: 507.
Barnes, George B., (Capt, AQM, 56th NCST; AQM, M.W. Ransom's Brigade), III: 315, 318, 322; V: 559, 669.
Barnes, H.L., (Pvt, Co A, 54th NCST), V: 516.
Barnes, H.M., (Capt, Co B, 10th Battalion NCST, Hvy Art), IV: 329, 336.
Barnes, J.B., (Pvt, Co G, 63rd NCST, 5th Cav), V: 658.
Barnes, James, (Sgt, Co I, 26th NCST), V: 532.
Barnes, Jesse D., (Lt, Co F, 61st NCST), III: 504.
Barnes, Jesse S., (Capt, Co F, 4th NCST), I: 231, 267; II: 425.
Barnes, John, (Pvt, Co C, 14th Vols/24th NCST), V: 560.
Barnes, John C., (2nd Lt, Co A, 31st NCST), II: 512.
Barnes, R., (Pvt, Co H, 2nd Vols/12th NCST), V: 507.
Barnes, Rory, (2nd Lt, Co F, 5th Vols/15th NCST), I: 735.
Barnes, Ruffin, (Capt, Co C, 43rd NCST), III: 2, 3.
Barnes, S., (Pvt, Co A, 33rd NCST), V: 543.
Barnes, Spencer, (Pvt, Co F, 30th NCST), V: 492.
Barnes, S. Mose, (Pvt, Co A, 4th NCST), V: 488.
Barnes, William S., (Capt, Adjt, 4th NCST; ADC to Grimes), I: 230, 269; IV: 516, 518.
Barnett, E.S., (Pvt, Co B, 53rd NCST), V: 501.

Barnett, G.P., (Pvt, Co G, 30th NCST), V: 492.
Barnett, George W., (Musician, 6th Vols/16th NCST), V: 552.
Barnett, J.A., (Capt, Co G, 30th NCST), II: 495, 496.
Barnett, John, (Sgt, Co H, 4th NCST), I: 233, 274.
Barnett, R.S., (Ordnance Sgt, 53rd NCST), III: 261.
Barnett, W.P., (Lt, Co F, 49th NCST), III: 138, 148.
Barnett, William, (Pvt, Co K, 6th NCST), V: 513.
Barnett's Ford, (Rapidan River, Va.), II: 693; III: 572; IV: 184, 187, 189, 190, 609.
Barney, Albert M., (Lt Col, 142nd N.Y.), V: 237.
Barneycastle, J.R., (Pvt, Co B, 1st Battalion NCST), V: 504.
Barnhardt, George E., (Pvt, Co H, 63rd NCST, 5th Cav), III: 618.
Barnhardt, Jacob R., (Color-bearer, Co H, 8th NCST), I: 401, 408.
Barnhart, Robert, (Pvt, Co D, 10th NCST, 1st Art & Engs, Reilly-Ramsay's Battery, Light Art), V: 568.
Barnhart, C.M., (Pvt, Co H, 28th NCST), V: 542.
Barnhart, R.W., (Pvt, Co C, 33rd NCST), V: 544.
Barnhart, W., (Pvt, Co C, 33rd NCST), V: 544.
Barnhart, W.E., (Pvt, Co C, 33rd NCST), V: 544.
Barnhill, C., (Pvt, Co E, 8th Vols/18th NCST), II: 64.
Barnhill, J.W., (Pvt, Co I, 37th NCST), V: 546.
Barnwell, T.J., (Pvt, Co H, 56th NCST), III: 348.
Barr, John W., (1st Lt, Co L, Art, Louisiana Tigers, Walker's Battalion, Thomas' Legion), IV: 119.
Barr, William H., (2nd Lt, Co D, 3rd NCST), I: 213.
Barrett, ______, (Cpl, Color-bearer, Co E, 27th NCST), II: 442.
Barrett, David S., (Capt, Co D, 49th NCST), III: 152.
Barrett, Isaac A., (Sgt, Co A, 33rd NCST), II: 538.
Barrett, J.A., (Lt Col, 77th NCST, 7th Senior Reserves), IV: 99.
Barrett, J.W., (Pvt, Co A, 33rd NCST), V: 543.
Barrett, James, (Cpl, Co H, 32nd NCST), V: 497.
Barrett, L.J., (Capt, Claiborne-Dearing's 7th C.S. Cav; 16th Battalion/75th NCST, 7th Cav), IV: 91, 93.
Barrett, T.S., (Superintendent Fayetteville Arsenal), IV: 294.
Barrett, W.A., (2nd Lt, Co D, 49th NCST), III: 133, 148; V: 559.
Barrett's Ferry, Va., II: 201.
Barrier, D.M., (Sgt, Co H, 57th NCST), V: 517.
Barrier, Jacob, (Lt, Co F, 9th NCST, 1st Cav), I: 486, 782.
Barrier, John D., (Pvt, Color-bearer, Co F, 57th NCST), III: 427.
Barrier, Rufus A., (Lt Col, 8th NCST), I: 388, 405.
Barrier, Wiley A., (Capt, Co I, 9th NCST, 1st Cav), I: 422, 481, 486.
Barringer, David, (Pvt, Co K, 8th NCST), I: 397.
Barringer, J.A., (1st Sgt, Co G, 8th NCST), V: 194.
Barringer, J.E., (Pvt, Co G, 8th NCST), V: 194.
Barringer, J.L., (Pvt, Co C, 57th NCST), V: 517.
Barringer, John, (Pvt, Co E, 5th NCST), I: 292.
Barringer, Nelson, (Pvt, Co G, 8th NCST), V: 194.

Barringer, Dr. Paul B., (Son of Brig Gen Rufus Barringer), III: 636.
Barringer, Rufus, (Brig Gen, aka "Aunt Nancy"), I: xi, 417, 418, 422, 424, 427, 428, 429, 430, 432, 435, 438, 439, 440, 441, 442, 443, 445, 454, 456, 457, 458, 464, 470, 471, 472, 473, 476, 477, 478, 483, 485, 486, 775; II: 780, 781, 784; III: 538, 539, 547, 609, 610, 618, 619, 620, 635, 636, 640, 641, 642, 643, 647, 648, 650, 651, 652, 653; IV: 88, 582; V: 210, 212, 649.
Barringer, Victor C., (Maj, 9th NCST, 1st Cav; AAG & IG Robert Ransom's Brigade), I: 417, 485; IV: 569.
Barringer, W.J., (Pvt, Co G, 5th NCST), I: 292; V: 505.
Barringer, William D., (Lt Col, 28th NCST), II: 465, 466; IV: 473.
Barrington, Adam, (1st Lt, Co D, 40th NCST, 3rd Art, Hvy), II: 746.
Barrington, Stephen C., (Capt, Co B, 67th NCST; Capt, Barrington's Co, Whitford's 11th Battalion NCST), III: 704, 727; V: 17.
Barrington's Farm, (Neuse River nr New Bern), II: 339.
Barron, Samuel, (Commodore, CSN), V: 39, 40, 44, 45, 47, 48, 49, 51, 52, 301, 302.
Barrow, Charles, (Sgt, Co D, 11th Vols/21st NCST), V: 514.
Barrow, R.A., (Capt, Co D, 11th Vols/21st NCST), II: 145.
Barrow, Thaddeus P., (2nd Lt, Co I, 3rd NCST), IV: 722.
Barry, John D., (Temp. Brig Gen), I: xii; II: 21, 34, 39, 41, 47, 56, 63, 73, 74, 75, 96, 574; IV: 435, 467, 469, 472, 473; V: 95, 96, 649.
Barry, William Farquher, (Maj Gen, Chief of Artillery, USA), II: 96; V: 31.
Bartlett, ______, (Col, 3rd N.C., USA, Horse thief), V: 655.
Bartlett, ______, (Col, N.Y.), III: 759, 761.
Barlett, J.S., (1st Sgt, Co K, 1st Vols/11th NCST), V: 531.
Bartlett, James, (Pvt, Co B, 3rd Vols/13th NCST), I: 684; II: 541, 579.
Bartlett, James, (Cpl, Co K, 33rd NCST), II: 541.
Bartlett, W.R., (Pvt, Co K, 6th Battalion/60th NCST), III: 482.
Barton, Benjamin B., (Pvt, Co E, 25th NCST), V: 561.
Barton, Seth Maxwell, (Brig Gen), I: 526; III: 333, 334, 335, 349; IV: 82, 573.
Barton, William Brainerd, (Brig Gen, USA), V: 163.
Barton Creek Township, (Wake County), III: 112.
Bartonsville, Va., II: 250.
Bartow, Francis S., (Col, 8th Ga.), I: 299, 349; V: 582.
Basinger, John C., (Pvt, Co E, 5th NCST; Detailed, 2nd Corps Provost Guard), V: 505, 570.
Basket, ______, (Sgt, Co A, 2nd Engineers, CSA), IV: 431.
Baskerville, George Thomas, (Capt, Co I, 13th Vols/23rd NCST), II: 187, 221, 236, 239, 240.
Baskerville, Mrs. G.T., II: 239.
Basler, John, (Pvt, Co M, 3rd Vols/13th NCST), V: 551.
Bason, ______, [George F., Sgt Maj], (Color Sgt, 6th NCST), I: 351.
Bason, G.F., (Capt, Ordnance Officer, Scales' Brigade), IV: 553.
Bason, J.D., (Capt, Co E, 3rd Vols/13th NCST), V: 547.
Bason, W.H., (Pvt, Co E, 3rd Vols/13th NCST), V: 550.

Bass, Bryant, (Pvt, Co A, 55th NCST), V: 527.
Bass, T.R., (Lt, Co A, 55th NCST), III: 295.
Bass, W.R., (Capt, Co C, 68th NCST), III: 725, 727.
Bass, Hodge, (Pvt, Co B, 2nd NCST), I: 175; V: 486.
Bassett, G.W., (1st Lt, Ordnance Officer, Barringer's Brigade), V: 657.
Basinger, Joseph, (Pvt, Co B, 46th NCST), V: 524.
Bassinger, G.H., (Pvt, Co K, 4th NCST), V: 489.
Bassinger, James, (Lt, Co D, 34th NCST), II: 585.
Batchelder, ______, (Col, U.S. Gettysburg Commission), III: 300.
Batcheler, Wright, (Pvt, Co A, 47th NCST), V: 534.
Bate, William Brimage, (Maj Gen), II: 491, 712, 731.
Bateman, J.A., (Pvt, Co E, 45th NCST), V: 500.
Bateman's, James, (A Federal redoubt was erected at his residence near Plymouth), III: 339, 341; V: 176.
Bates, ______, (Maj, Cav), IV: 88.
Bates, ______, (Color-bearer, 21st Mass.), II: 312.
Bates, Benjamin, (Lt, Cmdr N.C. Invalid Battalion), V: 571.
Bath Alum, Va., IV: 149.
Bath Court House, Va., (was Warm Springs), IV: 149.
Baston, D.F., (Musician, Co G, 35th NCST), V: 563.
Batson, W.A., (Lt, Co B, 64th NCST), III: 660; IV: 705.
Battalion, Organization, IV: 224.
Battalions, Infantry, Confederate:
  Alabama, 5th, III: 300.
  Anderson's, John H., (2nd & 5th Battalions Junior Reserves; 71st NCST, 2nd Junior Reserves), IV: 15, 25, 27, 28.
  Avery's, (See: 17th Battalion NCST).
  Bates', (Invalid Battalion), V: 571.
  Beasley's, (See: 5th Junior Reserves).
  Beckett's, (N.C.), IV: 710.
  Bingham's, (See: 25th Battalion NCST).
  Brittian's, (Home Guard), IV: 652.
  Broadfoot's, (See: 1st Junior Reserves).
  Cadet Battalion, (Hillsboro Military Academy), V: 643-644.
  Caper's, (Ga.), III: 434.
  Charleston, III: 207.
  Clark's, H.J.B., (N.C. Militia), I: 364; II: 308, 310, 316, 317, 326, 327, 542, 543, 594.
  Clark's, (See: 6th Junior Reserves).
  Coleman's, (Became 39th NCST), I: 767; II: 704, 706, 723, 727.
  Coleman's, (Consolidated 58th & 60th NCST), III: 444, 454.
  Confederate, 1st, III: 290.
  Ellington's, (See: 8th Junior Reserves).
  Erwin's (See: 21st Battalion, 1st Senior Reserves).
  Evan's, (See also: 63rd NCST), IV: 224.
  Florida, 2nd, II: 197.
  Freeman's, (Three companies at Salisbury Prison; See also: 26th Battalion), IV: 753, 757, 769; V: 626.
  French's, (See: 7th Junior Reserves).
  Georgia, 2nd, (Ross'), II: 429, 430, 438, 677; III: 66; IV: 501, 502, 504.

Georgia, 10th, II: 634.
Georgia, 12th, III: 737.
Georgia, 40th, II: 634.
Georgia, 50th, II: 634.
Haskell's, IV: 354.
Hill's, (See: 22nd Battalion, 2nd Senior Reserves).
Hook's, (See: 3rd Senior Reserves).
Huger's, (Va.), I: 557.
Kennedy's, (Ga. & N.C.), I: 16.
Littlejohn's, (See: 23rd Battalion, 3rd Senior Reserves).
Louisiana, 3rd, II: 677.
Louisiana Zouaves, IV: 389, 390.
MacRea's, (See: 18th Battalion NCST, Cav).
Mallett-Hahr's, (See: 19th Battalion NCST).
McDowell's, (See: 6th Battalion NCST).
McKamy's, (See: Walker's), IV: 121.
Millard's, (See: 9th Junior Reserves and 20th Junior Reserves).
Mississippi, 2nd, IV: 509.
Mississippi, 26th, II: 453.
Montaque's, (Va.), I: 91, 93.
Moore's, (Became the 68th NCST), III: 725.
Mumford's "Irish," I: 673; IV: 142, 143.
Nethercutt's, (See: 8th Battalion NCST).
North Carolina, 1st, (Six com panies. Became 32nd NCST), I: 16; II: 521, 640; III: 7, 290; IV: 225, 436, 441, 523, 525, 643; V: 240, 503-504, 588.
North Carolina, 1st Junior Reserves, IV: 3,4, 9, 10, 11, 15, 587.
North Carolina, 1st Sharpshooters, II: 267; IV: 225-242.
North Carolina, 2nd, II: 523, 533; III: 5, 41, 42, 162, 256; IV: 243-260, 436, 513, 515, 519, 643; V: 11, 62, 494-495.
North Carolina, 2nd Home Guard, IV: 650.
North Carolina, 2nd Junior Reserves, IV: 3, 4, 5, 12, 25, 587.
North Carolina, 3rd, (See Artillery).
North Carolina, 3rd Home Guard, IV: 650.
North Carolina, 3rd Senior Reserves, (Became a part of the 78th NCST), II: 640; IV: 3, 6, 108, 587.
North Carolina, 4th, (See also: Nethercutt's 8th Battalion), I: 13; III: 685; IV: 224, 270, 302.
North Carolina, 4th Home Guard, IV: 650.
North Carolina, 4th Junior Reserves, IV: 3, 4, 6, 38, 41, 43, 46, 47, 49, 108, 270, 587, 588, 589, 590.
North Carolina, 5th, (See: Cavalry).
North Carolina, 5th Junior Reserves, II: 640; IV: 3, 4, 6, 25, 587.
North Carolina, 6th, (Fayetteville Arsenal "Armory Guard"), I: 119; IV: 224, 293-300.
North Carolina, 6th Junior Reserves, IV: 3, 4, 6, 9, 10, 11, 587.
North Carolina, 6th, (Became 60th NCST), III: 473.
North Carolina, 7th, (See: Cavalry).
North Carolina, 7th Home Guard, IV: 650.
North Carolina, 7th Junior Reserves, IV: 3, 4, 6, 29, 38, 40, 43, 47, 108, 301, 587, 588, 589, 590.

North Carolina, 8th, (aka Nethercutt's Rangers or Nethercutt's Partisan Rangers, 8th Battalion; Became 68th NCST), I: 13; II: 513, 774; III: 173, 685, 687, 725; IV: 270, 224, 302, 442; V: 19.
North Carolina, 8th Junior Reserves, IV: 3, 4, 6, 29, 38, 40, 41, 43, 47, 108, 302, 587, 588, 589.
North Carolina, 9th, (1st Hvy Art, See: Artillery).
North Carolina, 9th Junior Reserves, (See also:20th Battalion), IV: 3, 4, 18, 29, 43, 53, 358, 587, 588, 589, 590, 591.
North Carolina, 10th, (See: Artillery).
North Carolina, 10th, (aka Young's Sharpshooters), I: 680; II: 757; III: 188, 191, 197, 198, 199; IV: 6, 100, 101, 105, 302.
North Carolina, 10th Home Guard, IV: 650.
North Carolina, 11th, (See: Artillery).
North Carolina, 12th, (See: Cavalry).
North Carolina, 13th, (See: Artillery).
North Carolina, 14th Home Guard, IV: 650.
North Carolina, 15th, (See: Cavalry).
North Carolina, 16th, (See: Cavalry). North Carolina, 17th, (Two companies of infantry and one company of cavalry), IV: 224, 371-377.
North Carolina, 18th, I: 118; II: 651; IV: 224, 354, 379-382.
North Carolina, 18th Home Guard, IV: 650.
North Carolina, 19th, (Light Duty Men), I: 119, 493, 516; IV: 3, 14, 224, 301, 303, 325, 383, 399.
North Carolina, 20th, 1st Junior Reserves, (See also: 9th Junior Reserves. The 9th Battalion Junior Reserves became the 20th Battalion and then 1st Junior Reserves after all the other battalions were combined into regiments.), III: 385, 496; IV: 3, 4, 18, 29, 53, 225, 358-396, 397, 439, 496, 587, 588.
North Carolina, 21st Home Guard, IV: 650.
North Carolina, 21st, 1st Senior Reserves, II: 774; IV: 6, 100, 224, 397.
North Carolina, 22nd Home Guard, IV: 650.
North Carolina, 22nd, 2nd Senior Reserves, IV: 6, 224, 398.
North Carolina, 23rd Home Guard, IV: 650.
North Carolina, 23rd, 3rd Senior Reserves, IV: 6, 100, 224, 399; V: 678.
North Carolina, 24th, (Detailed Men; See also: 81st NCST), IV: 129, 224, 400.
North Carolina, 24th Home Guard, IV: 650.
North Carolina, 25th, IV: 224, 365, 401; V: 2, 6.
North Carolina, 26th, Salisbury Prison Guard, (See also: Freeman's), V: 626, 678.
North Carolina, 26th Home Guard, IV: 650.
North Carolina, 27th Home Guard, IV: 650.
North Carolina, 29th Home Guard, IV: 650.

North Carolina, 37th Home Guard, IV: 650.
North Carolina, 48th Home Guard, IV: 650.
North Carolina, 59th Home Guard, IV: 650.
North Carolina, 63rd Home Guard, IV: 650.
North Carolina, 64th Home Guard, IV: 650.
North Carolina, 68th Home Guard, IV: 650.
North Carolina, 69th Home Guard, IV: 650.
North Carolina, 72nd Home Guard, IV: 650.
North Carolina, 80th Home Guard, IV: 650.
Petersburg Junior Reserve, III: 58.
Reece's, (See: 4th Junior Reserves).
Rencher's, (See: 24th Battalion NCST).
Rogers', (See also: 47th NCST), IV: 224.
Ross', (See: 2nd Ga. Battalion).
Singletary's, (See also: 27th NCST), II: 426; IV: 224.
Smith's, "Extra Billy", Va., I: 342, 347, 348.
South Carolina, 7th, V: 24.
Trenholm's, (S.C.), II: 18.
Tucker's, (Naval Battalion), II: 400; IV: 403.
Virginia, 22nd, III: 300.
Walker's, (Walker's Battalion; Walker's Regiment of Thomas' Legion; Became the 80th NCST), III: 737; IV: 117-128, 177, 439.
Webb's, (On the way to Appomattox when the remaining men of the 27th NCST finally gathered it was found that only seventy some odd men and officers remained. Agreeing that if necessary some of the officers and some of the non-commis sioned personnel would serve in the ranks this group of sol diers formed themselves into a two company battalion. Thus they fought the last days of the war.) II: 457.
Wright's, (See: 4th Battalion NCST).
Young's, (See: 10th Battalion NCST).
Battalions, Infantry, Federal:
McIntosh's, I: 545.
Rhode Island, 5th, II: 317, 318, 326.
Washburn's, (1st Vt., 4th Mass.), I: 87, 93, 96.
Battalions, Reserve, IV: 224.
Batten, Wesley, (Pvt, Co C, 53rd NCST), V: 501.
Battery, Confederate, Artillery unit, (See: Artillery).
Battery, Confederate (Fixed gun emplacement):
Anderson, (nr Wilmington; See Fort Anderson).
Bolles, [Bowles], (nr Fort Fisher, at Confederate Point), II: 17, 631; IV: 307, 308, 353; V: 28.
Buchanan, (nr Fort Fisher), II: 635, 639, 640, 644, 647, 648, 761; IV: 46, 47, 307, 308, 423, 590; V: 219, 220, 221, 223, 225, 226, 230, 232, 234, 235, 237, 241.
Campbell, (Cape Fear River), IV: 419, 427.
Cobb's Point, (nr Elizabeth City), V: 308.
Confederate Point, (aka Federal Point, See: Battery Bolles).
Croatan, (Floating Battery), V: 307.
Flag Pond, (nr Fort Fisher), IV: 46.
Gatling, [Gatlin], (nr Fort Fisher), IV: 357, 539.

Gregg, (Cumming's Point, Morris Island, S.C.), I: 394; IV: 470; V: 161, 163, 166, 620.
Gregg, (nr Petersburg, Va.), II: 576.
Half Moon, (nr Fort Fisher), IV: 46, 49.
Huger, (Roanoke Island, aka Fort Huger), I: 389.
Lamb, (Cape Fear River), II: 649; V: 235.
Midgett's Hammock, (Roanoke Island), V: 58.
Mound, (nr Fort Fisher), II: 634, 635, 636; IV: 307, 423; V: xvi, 219, 221, 226, 228, 234, 397, 423, 424, 425.
Pork Point, (Roanoke Island), V: 305, 306, 308.
Pulpit Battery, (Fort Fisher), V: 227.
Purdie, (nr Fort Fisher), IV: 353.
Radcliffe, (Oak Island), IV: 419.
Reeve's Point, (South side of Cape Fear), IV: 305.
Rollins', (Fort Fisher), IV: 307.
Sewell's Point, (Va.), I: 607, 608.
Shaw's, (Oak Island), IV: 487.
Shepherd's (Fort Fisher), IV: 307.
Wagner, (Morris Island, S.C Both CSA & USA, See also: Fort Wagner), I: 392, 393, 394, 395; III: 206-211, 218, 219, 505, 511-512, 590; IV: 485, 716; V: 161-167, 435, 620, 621, 622.
Water Battery, (Cape Fear), IV: 427.
White Point, (nr Charleston, S.C.), II: 758.
Worth, (nr Plymouth, both CSA & USA, aka Fort Worth, See also: Fort Worth), III: 339, 340, 342, 343, 354; IV: 573; V: 320.
Zeke's Island, (New Inlet), II: 631, 633; IV: 416.
No. 2, (Potomac River, Va.), II: 164, 167.
No. 4, (nr Columbia, S.C.), IV: 327.
No. 4, (nr Petersburg, Va.), IV: 327.
No. 5, (nr Petersburg, Va.), II: 621.
No. 6, (nr Petersburg, Va.), II: 621.
No. 7, (nr Mechanicsville, Va.), IV: 90, 262, 355.
No. 8, (nr Petersburg, Va.), II: 621.
No. 9, (nr Petersburg, Va.), II: 621.
No. 14, (nr Petersburg, Va.), II: 622.
No. 45 (nr Petersburg, Va., aka Battery 45), II: 57, 58, 59, 60, 61, 62, 76, 174, 175, 534, 588; III: 112, 158, 396; IV: 203, 204, 207, 208, 470; V: 247.
Battery, Federal, Artillery unit, (See: Artillery).
Battery, Federal (Fixed gun emplacement):
No. 10, (nr Petersburg, Va., both CSA & USA), II: 143.
Battery Hill, (nr Gettysburg, Pa.), I: 311.
Battery Park Hotel, (Asheville), III: 670.
Battle, T.W., (Capt, Co I, 5th Vols/15th NCST), I: 735.
Battle, Cullen Andrew, (Brig Gen), I: 171, 173, 255.
Battle, Dorsey, (1st Lt, ADC, Lewis' Brigade), V: 511.
Battle, James S., (ADC to W.R. Cox), IV: 458, 463; V: 483.
Battle, Lewis, [Weslwy Lewis], (Lt, Co D, 37th NCST), II: 661, 674.
Battle, Dr. Kemp P., (of UNC), I: 76, 133; V: 647.

Battle, Richard, (Master, CSN), IV: 404.
Battle, Richard H., Jr., (1st Lt, Co I, 43rd NCST), III: 3.
Battle, Dr. William H., (Surg, 31st NCST; Surg, Wilmington Hospital), II: 511; IV: 636.
Battle After the War, V: 285.
Battle Cotton Factory, (nr Rocky Mount), III: 173.
Battlefield Commission, Report of, (Chicamauga), V: 179. (Sharpsburg), V: 587.
Battles and Leaders of the Civil War, I: 614, 622, 625.
Battley, W.T., (2nd Lt, Co E, 6th Battalion, "Fayetteville Armory Guard"), I: 120; IV: 297.
Batts, W., (Pvt, Co I, 30th NCST), V: 493.
Batts, William C., (Cpl, Co B, 2nd NCST; Detailed, 2nd Corps Provost Guard), I: 175; V: 486, 569.
Baucom, G.W., (Sgt, Co D, 37th NCST), V: 545.
Baugh, W.A., (Pvt, Co A, 10th NCST, 1st Art & Engs, Ramseur-Manly's Battery, Light Art), I: 554.
Baugh, William F., (2nd Lt, 12th Va.), IV: 403.
Baughn, R.K, (Pvt, Co H, 31st NCST), V: 551.
Baugle, W.H.H., (Pvt, Co B, 10th Vols/20th NCST), V: 508.
Baum, Joseph, (Sgt, Detached Co, 68th NCST), III: 723.
Baxter, DeWitt Clinton, (Brig Gen, USA), I: 634, 635.
Baxter, Dr. J.J., (Ass't Surg, 8th NCST), IV: 633.
Baxter, Peter Z., (Capt, Co K, 49th NCST), III: 128, 153.
Baxter, Sidney S., (Judge), IV: 754.
Baxter Road, (nr Petersburg, Va.), III: 359, 360, 362, 390; V: 16.
Bay of Biscay, Florida, V: 383.
Bay of Fundy, New Brunswick, V: 375.
Beacon Island, N.C., V: 36, 43.
Beal, Dallas M., (2nd Lt, Co K, 59th NCST, 4th Cav), III: 458.
Beal, Peter S., (2nd Sgt, Co H, 52nd NCST), III: 225.
Beal, W., (Pvt, Co H, 48th NCST), V: 526.
Beale, C.B., (Sgt Maj, 31st NCST), II: 511.
Beale, J.A., (1st Lt, Co B, 2nd Battalion Junior Reserves; Co C, 71st NCST, 2nd Junior Reserves), IV: 28.
Beale, Richard Lee Turberville, (Brig Gen), I: 438, 441; II: 94.
Beall, James F., (Maj, 11th Vols/21st NCST), II: 131-146 personal account; IV: 525, 526; V: 666.
Bealle, Thomas B., [Beall], (Capt, Co I, 4th Vols/14th NCST), I: 248, 708; II: 142.
Bealton, Va., III: 558.
Beam, David H., (Pvt, Co F, 34th NCST), V: 555.
Beam, John, (Pvt, Co B, 34th NCST), V: 555.
Beam, M.R., (Musician, 55th NCST), V: 527.
Beam, O.P., (2nd Lt, Co I, 38th NCST), II: 676, 678.
Beam, W.C., (Cpl, Co I, 56th NCST), III: 356.
Beam, W.P., (Capt, Co B, 34th NCST), V: 548.
Beaman, Benjamin C., (Sgt, Co K, 33rd NCST), II: 541, 544, 579.
Beaman, G.W., (1st Lt, Co D, 41st NCST, 3rd Cav), II: 770.
Beaman, Henry C., (2nd Lt, Co H, 43rd NCST), III: 3.
Beaman, J.T., (Capt, Co A, Wynn's 15th Battalion NCST, Cav), IV: 365.

Bean, J.W., (Pvt, Co K, 4th NCST), V: 489.
Bean, Moses L., (Capt, Co K, 4th NCST), I: 234, 272, 279; V: 484.
Bean, R.T., (Pvt, Co F, 46th NCST), V: 524.
Bean, W.W., (Pvt, Co F, 26th NCST), V: 602.
Bean's Station, Tenn., III: 448.
Bear's Ford, N.C., III: 757.
Beard, J.F.M., (Cpl, Co C, 37th NCST), V: 545.
Beard, John, (Capt, Co C, 57th NCST), III: 405, 418, 420, 421, 422, 425, 426, 428; IV: 441, 526; V: 511.
Beard, John, Jr., (Pvt, Co C, 57th NCST), V: 517.
Beard, John W., (Capt, Co F, 11th Vols/21st NCST), II: 132, 145.
Beard, M.P., (Pvt, Co C, 4th NCST), V: 488.
Beard, R.C., (Pvt, Co C, 4th NCST), V: 488.
Beard, W.W., (Capt, Co B, 6th Battalion Junior Reserves; Co E, 70th NCST, 1st Junior Reserves), IV: 13.
Bearden, William M., (Jr 2nd Lt, Co D, 39th NCST), II: 705.
Beardon, M.J., (Capt, AQM, 58th NCST; AQM, 6th Battalion/60th NCST), III: 432, 496; IV: 705.
Beardon, M.P., (Maj, AQM, J.F. Hoke's 2nd Brigade Junior Reserves), IV: 6.
Beasley, Mrs. ______, (Resident of Plymouth; Head Nurse, 1st N.C. General Hospital, Petersburg, Va.), IV: 624.
Beasley, S.H., (Pvt, Co I, 3th Vols/23rd NCST), V: 510.
Beasley, W.F., (Maj, 5th Battalion Junior Reserves; Maj. Anderson's Battalion NCST; Lt Col, 71st NCST, 2nd Junior Reserves), IV: 3, 5, 25, 28, 587, 594; V: 640.
Beasley, William R., (2nd Lt, AQM, 44th NCST), III: 22.
Beattie's Ford, N.C., IV: 375.
Beatty, J.D., (Pvt, Co C, 10th NCST, 1st Art & Engs, Brem-Graham-Williams' Battery, Light Art), V: 567.
Beatty, J.F., (Pvt, Co B, 28th NCST), V: 541.
Beatty, W., (Pvt, Co C, 10th NCST, 1st Art & Engs, Brem-Graham-Williams' Battery, Light Art), V: 567.
Beaty, F.A., (Pvt, Co H, 63rd NCST, 5th Cav), III: 587.
Baety, Alexander S., (Pvt, Co G, 34th NCST), V: 556.
Beau, R.T., (Pvt, Co F, 46th NCST), V: 524.
Beaufort, N.C., (and Beaufort Harbor), I: 500, 503; II: 3, 18, 541; III: 431, 705; IV: 413, 620; V: 23, 222, 299, 312, 374.
Beaufort County, N.C., II: 337, 748, 772; III: 503, 504, 723, 724; IV: 353, 354, 484.
Beaufort Road, (nr New Bern), I: 363, 364; II: 309.
Beaumont, J.C., (Cmdr, USN), V: 242.
Beauregard, P.G.T., (Gen and Beauregard's Army), I: 55, 298, 340, 342, 343, 347, 348, 359, 403, 404, 481; II: 4, 6, 7, 8, 130, 285, 286, 514, 619, 621, 622, 755, 778, 800; III: 9, 10, 130, 135, 136, 137, 139, 140, 179, 209, 211, 306, 350, 352, 353, 355, 359, 360, 370, 380, 381; IV: 93, 141, 362, 490, 491, 529, 530, 531, 534, 535, 537, 575, 626, 731, 656, 678; V: 7, 15, 16, 29, 270, 437, 618, 632, 633, 639.
Beavans, John, (Sgt, Co D, 43rd NCST), I: 122; V: 498.

Beavans, William, (2nd Lt, Co D, 43 NCST), I: 120; III: 3.
Beaverdam, N.C., (aka Beaver Dam Church), II: 493; III: 319.
Beaver, Joseph, (Pvt, Co K, 5th NCST), V: 506.
Beaver, M., (Pvt, Co K, 4th NCST), V: 489.
Beaver Dam Creek, Va., (and Battle of, 1862), I: 609, 613, 613, 614, 615, 622; II: 209, 210.
Beaver Dam Station, Va., I: 580; III: 596; IV: 198.
Beavers, Joseph, (Pvt, Co I, 5th NCST), I: 292.
Bebee, Judge ______, (U.S.), V: 445.
Beck, ______, (Deserter, Outlaw, Yankee), V: 294.
Beck, John M., (Pvt, Co E, 4th Vols/14th NCST), V: 490.
Beck, John W., (1st Sgt, Co K, 52nd NCST), III: 225.
Beck, S.C., (1st Lt, Co K, 62nd NCST), III: 516.
Beckham, N.L., (Pvt, Co G, 6th NCST), V: 513.
Bechnell, John L., (Pvt, Co A, 25th NCST), V: 561.
Bedford County, Va., IV: 218.
Bedingfield, B.K., (Musician, Co G, 35th NCST), V: 563.
Bedsole, C., (Pvt, Co H, 46th NCST), V: 525.
Bedsole, W., (Pvt, Co H, 46th NCST), V: 525.
Bee, Barnard Elliott, (Brig Gen), I: 297, 298, 299, 339, 340, 341, 347; IV: 162.
Beef Raid (Hampton's), I: 436; II: 105; III: 622.
Beek, J.F., (Cpl, Co D, 11th Vols/21st NCST), V: 194.
Beggarly, J.B., (Courier, Anderson-Ramseur-Cox's Brigade), IV: 464.
Behan, Edwin A., (Lt, 3rd N.Y.), V: 237.
Behring Sea, V: 348.
Belch, R.D., (Pvt, Co D, 32nd NCST), V: 496.
Belcher, John R., (Lt, Co F, 61st NCST), III: 504.
Belcher's Mill, Va., I: 437, 482; II: 105.
Belfield, Va., [Bellfield], (aka Belfield Station, and Warren's Raid on), I: xiii, 321, 437, 471, 747; II: 105, 390, 450, 588, 782; III: 78, 122, 311, 633-637, 680; IV: 16, 17, 29, 40, 41, 43-45, 88, 89, 94, 205, 388-390, 391, 589.
Belk, Samuel E., (1st Lt, Co B, 53rd NCST), III: 261.
Belknap, George E., (Lt Cmdr, USN), V: 242.
Bell, A.W., (Capt, Co B, 39th NCST), II: 705, 711, 728.
Bell, B.F., (Pvt, Co K, 28th NCST), V: 543.
Bell, Benjamin H., (Scout, Co H, 10th NCST, 1st Art & Engs, Pool's Hvy Art), I: 490, 508, 535.
Bell, C.E., (1st Lt, Co K, 30th NCST), II: 496.
Bell, D.A., (Capt, Co I, 1st Vols, "Bethel"), I: 125.
Bell, D.B., (Capt, Co, I, 1st Vols, "Bethel"), I: 78, 113, 124.
Bell, Demosthenes, (Capt, Co G, 59th NCST, 4th Cav), III: 457,468; IV: 705.
Bell, Frank, (Pvt, Detached Co, 68th NCST), III: 723.
Bell, J.C., (Pvt, Co B, 28th NCST), V: 541.
Bell, James, (Post war Pilot at Fernandine, Florida), V: 370, 374.
Bell, John, (Pvt, Detached Co, 68th NCST), III: 723.
Bell, Joseph A., (Scout, Co H, 10th NCST, 1st Art & Engs, Pool's Hvy Art), I: 535.
Bell, Louis, (Col, Bell's Brigade, USA), V: 238.

Bell, R.R., (1st Lt, Co D, 38th NCST), II: 675, 678.
Bell, Shade, (Pvt, Co I, 8th Vols/18th NCST), II: 64; V: 540.
Bell, W.A., (Pvt, Co I, 14th Vols/24th NCST), V: 560.
Bell, W.R., (Capt, Co B, 51st NCST), III: 218.
Bell, William, (Architect of the Fayetteville Arsenal), IV: 293, 294.
Bell, William, (Hospital Steward, Co F, 14th Vols/24th NCST), V: 560.
Bell, William B., (Lt, Co K, 2nd NCST), I: 175; V: 486.
Bell's Bridge, Tenn., III: 448, 676.
Belle Grove, Va., (See also: Cedar Creek), I: 644, 647, 649, 650.
Belle Island, (James River nr Richmond, Va.).
Belle Island Prison, (Prison, CSA), I: 460.
Belle Plaine Landing, Va., V: 619.
Belo, Alfred H., (Col, 55th NCST), III: 288, 292, 293, 294, 295, 297, 298, 302, 303, 304, 306, 318, 676; V: 110, 633.
Belo, Robert W., (2nd Lt, Co H, 56th NCST), III: 316, 356.
Beltch, Robert D., (Pvt, Co D, 32nd NCST; Detailed, 2nd Corps Provost Guard), V: 570.
Belton, J.H., (Pvt, Co H, 3rd Vols/13th NCST), V: 551.
Belton, William B., (Pvt, Co L, 11th Vols/21st NCST), V: 515.
Belvin, _____, (Maj, USA, at Johnson's Island Prison), IV: 678, 683.
Belvin, P., (Lt, Co L, 58th NCST), III: 434.
Belvins, W., (Pvt, Co A, 26th NCST), V: 531.
Bemer, Logan, (2nd Lt, Co E, 53rd NCST), III: 262, 316, 356.
Ben Hur, (Novel written by Maj Gen, Lewis Wallace, USA), I: 172; II: 246.
Ben's Church, (nr Smithfield, Va.), I: 552, 654, 689.
Benbow, _____, (Col, S.C.), III: 146.
Benbury, John, [John A. Benberry], (Capt, Co A, 1st NCST), I: 136, 140.
Benbury, L.C., (Lt, Co A, 1st NCST), I: 136.
Bender, W.G., (Lt, Engineering Officer), IV: 415.
Bendix, John E., (Brig Gen, USA), I: 87, 88, 89, 93, 107.
Benely, W., (Sgt, Co B, 33rd NCST), II: 538.
Benfield, J.R., (Pvt, Co H, 35th NCST), V: 563.
Benjamin, Hon. Judah P., (Sec of War, CSA) I: 25, 41, 42; V: xiv, 417.
Benner Barn, "Farthest at Gettysburg," III: 299, 300, 301.
Benner's House, (nr Gettysburg, Pa.), III: 6.
Bennett, Rev. Mr. _____, (One of the several Chaplains that served at Salisbury Prison), IV: 765.
Bennett, C.G., (Pvt, Co B, 59th NCST, 4th Cav), V: 659.
Bennett, Charles W., (Orderly Sgt, Co E, 13th Vols/23rd NCST), II: 221, 256.
Bennett, David N., (Pvt, Co C, 4th Vols/14th NCST), I: 728, 731; II: 125, 127.
Bennett, Frank, (Capt, Co A, 13th Vols/23rd NCST), II: 182, 204, 256, 262.
Bennett, Hugh C., (1st Lt, Co F, 41st NCST, 3rd Cav), II: 771.
Bennett, I.H., (Lt, AAG N.C.), I: 51.
Bennett, J.E., (Pvt, Co B, 2nd Vols/12th NCST), V: 506.

Bennett, J.S., (1st Lt, Co D, 5th Vols/15th NCST), I: 735.
Bennett, J.W., (Ensign, USN), V: 244.
Bennett, John G., (Pvt, Co K, 59th NCST, 4th Cav), V: 660.
Bennett, Dr. John W., (Co F, 11th Vols/21st NCST; Ass't Surg, 11th Vols/21st NCST), II: 138; IV: 631.
Bennett, Riley, (Pvt, Co G, 53rd NCST), V: 502.
Bennett, Risden Tyler, (Col, 4th Vols/14th NCST), I: 246, 248, 249, 253, 705-732 personal account; II: 50; IV: 461; V: xi, xii, 78.
Bennett, S.W., (1st Lt, Co C, 30th NCST), II: 496; IV: 701.
Bennett House, (at Bentonville), III: 200.
Bennett Place, (nr Durham), III: 514; IV: 22, 32.
Bennick, A.R., (Chaplain, 34th NCST), II: 581; IV: 613.
Benning, Henry Lewis, (Brig Gen), II: 174; IV: 192.
Bensel, Joseph, (Pilot, City of Petersburg), V: 357.
Benson, Harrison, (Musician, 6th Vols/16th NCST), V: 552.
Benson, James C., (Musician, 10th Vols/20th NCST), II: 113; V: 508.
Benson, James R., (Cpl, Co D, 5th NCST), I: 291; V: 505.
Benson, R.L., (Pvt, Co C, 49th NCST), V: 564.
Bentley, Allen, (2nd Lt, Co D, 30th NCST), II: 496.
Bentley, Richard, (Englishman, publisher), V: 414.
Bently, J.J., (Pvt, Co G, 37th NCST), V: 546.
Benton, ______, [William A.], (2nd Lt, Co A, 59th NCST, 4th Cav), III: 465.
Benton, A.M., (Courier, Garland-Iverson-Johnston's Brigade), IV: 523.
Benton, B.H., (1st Lt, Co D, 2nd Battalion Junior Reserves; Co F, 71st NCST, 2nd Junior Reserves), IV: 28.
Benton, H.E., (Pvt, Co F, 1st Vols, "Bethel"), I: 128.
Benton, J.L., (Pvt, Co F, 10th Vols/20th NCST), V: 509.
Benton, James H., (AQMS, Co H, 10th Vols/20th NCST), II: 113.
Benton, M.M., (Lt, CSN, Tallahassee), V: 438.
Benton, S.M., (Lt, 2nd NCST), IV: 705.
Benton, W.H., (Pvt, Co H, 10th Vols/20th NCST), V: 509.
Benton County, Tenn., V: 615.
Bentonville, N.C., (and Battle of, 1865,) I: xiii, 56, 412, 499, 531, 582; II: 8, 12, 518, 650, 701, 702, 763, 764, 803, 804; III: 194, 195-196, 197, 198, 216, 217, 355, 359, 412, 431, 440-444, 454, 496, 502, 505, 513-514, 681, 698-699, 709, 727; IV: 4, 20-22, 31, 38, 56-59, 104, 105, 108, 222, 269, 302, 311, 312, 322, 328, 335, 336, 350-352, 353, 359, 362, 383, 386, 393-394, 398, 436, 438, 440, 483, 498, 499, 547-549, 591, 592, 593; V: 29, 641, 670.
Berdan, Hiram, (Maj Gen, Berdan's Sharpshooters, USA), I: 609.
Berdan's Sharpshooters, III: 598.
Bergin, J.M., (Lt, 12th Vols/22nd NCST), IV: 705.
Berlin, Pa., I: 311.
Bermuda, I: 53; II: 412; IV: 326, 625; V: 335, 340, 341, 355, 361, 362, 369, 371, 377, 379, 380, 397, 405, 407, 409, 416, 418, 419, 420, 422, 427, 429, 430, 440, 457, 458, 459, 460, 461, 471.

Bermuda Hundred, Va., (and Battle of, 1864, aka Bermuda Hundred Neck), I: 117, 403, 404, 581; II: 4, 87, 286, 298, 516, 519, 620, 621, 779, 797, 798; III: 10, 137, 139, 276, 350, 359, 512, 688; IV: 85, 93, 361, 489, 491, 492, 529-531, 575; V: 16, 100, 197.
Bernard House, (nr Fredericksburg, Va.), II: 691.
Bernard's Mill, (Black Water River nr Suffolk, Va.), I: 398; III: 337.
Berrier, H.R., (Orderly Sgt, Co B, 10th Va. Cav-an N.C. company), V: 627-628.
Berrier, Henry J., (Pvt, Co B, 4th Vols/14th NCST), I: 731.
Berry, Rev. ______, [L.M.], (Chaplain, 13th Vols/23rd NCST), II: 189; IV: 610.
Berry, Andrew C., (Jr 2nd Lt, Walker's Battalion, Thomas' Legion; 80th NCST), IV: 118.
Berry, C.C., (Capt, Co A, Walker's Battalion, Thomas' Legion, 80th NCST), IV: 117.
Berry, Dr. David, (Ass't Surg, 78th NCST, 8th Senior Reserves), IV: 108, 643.
Berry, Dr. J., (Ass't Surg, 26th NCST), IV: 636; V: 529.
Berry, James, (Pvt, Co D, 56th NCST), III: 361.
Berry, James D., (Sgt, Co D, 6th NCST), V: 512.
Berry, John H., (2nd Lt, Co E, 31st NCST), II: 507, 512.
Berry, William, (Pvt, Co D, 6th NCST), V: 512.
Berry's Mill Pond, (nr Wilmington), IV: 372.
Berryville, Va., (and Battles of), I: 160, 253, 261, 325, 373, 381, 541, 696; II: 233, 248; III: 5, 41, 235, 270, 750, 751, 753; VI: 168, 254; V: 213, 629.
Berryville Pike, Va., I: 645; II: 251, 252, 255; V: 213, 214, 215.
Bertie County, N.C., II: 769, 796; III: 134, 321, 457, 458, 715, 716, 717; VI: 262, 339, 646; V: 271.
Bess, Thomas, (Pvt, Co K, 49th NCST), V: 565.
Bessent, R.P., (AQM, 42nd NCST), II: 789, 805.
Best, Benjamin S., (Cpl, Co K, 27th NCST), II: 263, 462; V: 524.
Best, D.R., (Pvt, Co C, 8th Vols/18th NCST), II: 63.
Best, J.R., (Pvt, Co A, 3rd NCST), V: 487.
Best, Robert A., (Sgt, Co D, 4th NCST), I: 232.
Best, Samuel, (Pvt, Co C, 25th NCST), V: 561.
Best, W.B., (Capt, Co D, 50th NCST), III: 202, 203.
Bethel, George J., (Lt, Co B & C, 55th NCST), III: 296.
Bethel, George T., [George J.], (Lt, Co B, 55th NCST), IV: 702, 705.
Bethel, N.C., VI: 612.
Bethel, Va., (and Battle of, 1861, aka Bethel Church), I: v, 40, 70, 83, 85, 88, 102, 103, 108, 109, 110, 111, 112, 114, 122, 123, 128, 448, 736; II: 58, 410; III: 113, 159, 217, 281, 313, 496, 502; VI: 62; V: viii, xiii, 646.
Bethel, Big, Va., I: 86, 87, 89, 130.
Bethel, Little, Va., I: 86, 87, 98.
Bethel Flag, I: 130.
Bether, W.J., (2nd Lt, Co I, 31st NCST), II: 512.
Bethesda Church, Va., [Bethsaida], I: 139, 183, 205, 614, 706, 726, 727; II: 210; III: 12, 95, 258, 261, 578.
Bethleham Baptist Church, III: 715, 716.
Bethune, ______, (Congressman), III: 574.

Bethune, Alexander, (Pvt, Co A, 63rd NCST, 5th Cav), III: 574.
Betts, Rev. A.D., (Chaplain, 30th NCST), II: 495; IV: 597, 599, 601, 602, 603, 604, 612, 616.
Betts, Andrew N., (Jr 2nd Lt, Co C, 31st NCST), II: 507.
Betts, Andrew W., (Capt, Co C, 31st NCST), II: 507.
Beverly, Hampton, (Capt, Co H, 43rd NCST), III: 2, 3.
Beverly, J.L., (Pvt, Co H, 43rd NCST), V: 499.
Beverly Ford, (Rappahannock River, Va.), I: 423; II: 90, 95; III: 557.
Bevil, A., [Bevill], (Pvt, Co H, 27th NCST), II: 462; V: 524.
Bevil's House, (at Battle of Boydon Plank Road, Va.), III: 630.
Bickers, Dr. William A., (Ass't Surg, 6th NCST), IV: 632; V: 511.
Bickerstaff, Harvey W., (Pvt, Co C, 5th Vols/15th NCST), V: 521.
Bicket, James S., (Pvt, Co B, 5th Vols/15th NCST; Courier, Cooke's Brigade), V: 521.
Bickett, Dr. T.W., (Lt, Adjt, 10th Battalion NCST, Hvy Art; Ass't Surg, N.C.), IV: 329, 330.
Biddle, James, (Brig Gen, Biddle's 1st Brigade, Cav, USA), II: 346, 347; III: 90.
Bickle, L.A., (Chaplain, 10th Vols/20th NCST), II: 112.
Biddle, J.W., (Lt, Co H, 9th NCST, 1st Cav), I: 486.
Biddle, S.S., (Capt, Co C, 61st NCST), III: 504.
Biddle's Ferry, N.C., III: 710.
Bienvenu, ______, (Lt., Louisiana Art), IV: 26.
Big Black River, Miss., III: 485.
Big Creek, Tenn, III: 474, 518.
Big Creek Gap, (Cumberland Mountains, Tenn.), III: 434, 448, 662, 676, 678; IV: 273, 274, 275, 289, 290.
Big Laurel Mountain, N.C., III: 666; VI: 381.
Big Northeast Bridge, (nr Jacksonville), II: 775.
Big Pond, Canton, Miss., II: 734.
Big Sewell Mountain, Va., II: 270.
Big Spring, Va., II: 685; III: 279; VI: 141, 147, 164.
Biggers, J.B., (AQM, Robert's Brigade, Cav), IV: 580.
Biggs, John D., (Capt, Co H, 61st NCST), III: 504.
Biggs, W.L., (Pvt, Co A, 35th NCST), V: 495.
Biggs, William, (Capt, Co A, 7th Vols/17th NCST), II: 2, 3, 13; IV: 548.
Bikle, Rev. Dr. L.A., (Chaplain, 10th Vols/20th NCST), IV: 609; V:503.
Biles, Huston T., (Pvt, Co H, 4th Vols/14th NCST), V: 491.
Billeter, Amos, (Pvt, Co K, 11th Vols/21st NCST), V: 515.
Billeter, P.L., (Pvt, Co D, 11th Vols/21st NCST), V: 514.
Billings, Daniel, (Pvt, Co B, 55th NCST), V: 527.
Billings, J., (Pvt, Co K, 3rd Vols/13th NCST), V: 551.
Billingsley, Edward F., (Pvt, Co C, 4th Vols/14th NCST), I: 725.
Billingsley, James I., (Pvt, Co C, 4th Vols/14th NCST), I: 732; V: 490.
Billups, J., (Pvt, Co K, 1st NCST), V: 485.
Billups, Lawrence, (Cpl, Co I, 5th Vols/15th NCST), V: 522.
Bingham, ______, (Maj, Hancock's Staff, USA), III: 631.
Bingham, J.W., (2nd Cpl, Co A, 1st Vols/11th NCST), V: 530.
Bingham, Alvin, (4th Sgt, Co B, 52nd NCST), III: 223.

Bingham, Mrs. Della Worth, (Wife of Capt. Robert Bingham), III: 34.
Bingham, G.A., (2nd Lt, Co B, 10th Va. Cav-a N.C. company), V: 627.
Bingham, G.M., (Sgt, Co E, 16th Battalion/75th NCST, 7th Cav), V: 660.
Bingham, Green L., (Pvt, Co F, 63rd NCST, 5th Cav), III: 588, 606.
Bingham, Harvey H., (Maj, Bingham's 25th Battalion NCST), IV: 371, 373, 374, 401; V: 287, 295.
Bingham, Henry, (Pvt, Co F, 57th NCST), V: 517.
Bingham, Robert, (Capt, Co G, 44th NCST), III: 21, 23; IV: 705; V: 210, 529.
Binion, A.H., (Ass't Surg, 57th NCST), II: 405, 427; III: 405; IV: 641; V: 511.
Binkley, J.W., (Pvt, Co D, 11th Vols/21st NCST), V: 514.
Bird, A.L., (Pvt, Co K, 6th Battalion/60th NCST), III: 482.
Bird, Francis W., (Lt Col, 1st Vols/11th NCST), I: 110, 118, 584, 590, 591, 599; V: 11, 88, 131.
Bird, James T., (Pvt, Co F, 4th Vols/14th NCST), V: 490.
Bird, Joshua C., (2nd Lt, Co B, 39th NCST), II: 705.
Birdford, ______, (Lt Col, 3rd La. Battalion), II: 677.
Birdsong, L.N., (Pvt, Co C, 32nd NCST), V: 496.
Birdsong Farm, (nr Vicksburg, Miss.), II: 734.
Birkhead, Burwell W., (1st Lt, Co I, 22nd NCST), IV: 722.
Birkhead, Solon G., [Solon E.], (2nd Lt, Co H, 56th NCST), III: 316, 356.
Birmingham, Ala., VI: 594.
Birney, David Bell, (Maj Gen, USA), II: 623.
Birney, William, (Maj Gen, USA), II: 47.
Birtchet, J.F., (Pvt, Co E, 13th Vols/23rd NCST). V: 510.
Bisaner, C.F., (2nd Lt, Co B, 2nd Battalion Junior Reserves; Co C, 71st NCST, 2nd Junior Reserves; ACS, 71st NCST, 2nd Junior Reserves), IV: 28.
Biscoe, H.L., (Maj, Commissary, Pender-Scales' Brigade), IV: 551; V: 547.
Bishop, George, (2nd Lt, Co H, 9th Vols/19th NCST, 2nd Cav), II: 80.
Bishop, Henry H., (Pvt, Co F, 3rd NCST), V: 487.
Bishop, T.H., (2nd Lt, Co G, 1st NCST), I: 137; V: 484.
Bissett, J.J., (Pvt, Co B, 47th NCST), V: 534.
Bivens, J.W., (Pvt, Co I, 53rd NCST), V: 502.
Bivins, R.M., (Pvt, Co D, 37th NCST), V: 545.
Bizzell, Hardy R., (Pvt, Co B, 38th NCST), V: 557.
Bizzell, Dr. James A., (Surg, 10th Vols/20th NCST), II: 112; IV: 635.
Bizzelle, A.T., [A.F.], (Lt, Co B, 7th NCST), I: 385.
Black, Calvin M., (1st Lt, Co D, 10th NCST, 1st Art & Engs, Reilly-Ramsay's Battery, Light Art), I: 561.
Black, D.A., (Pvt, Co K, Color-bearer, 38th NCST), II: 676.
Black, Duncan, (Lt, Co G, 38th NCST), II: 685.
Black, G.W., (Pvt, Co K, 25th NCST), V: 193.
Black, J.M., (Sgt, Co A, 37th NCST), V: 545.

Black, James A., (2nd Lt, Co A, 52nd NCST), III: 223, 229.
Black, John F., (Pvt, Co H, 48th NCST), V: 527.
Black, Dr. Kenneth, (Surg, 3rd NCST), I: 213; IV: 632.
Black, M., (Pvt, Co H, 37th NCST), V: 546.
Black, Noah, (Pvt, Co F, 49th NCST), V: 564.
Black, Pinkney, (Pvt, Co B, 13th Vols/23rd NCST), V: 509.
Black, S.A., (Pvt, Co G, 49th NCST), V: 564.
Black, T., (Pvt, Co H, 37th NCST), V: 546.
Black, W.H., (Pvt, Co D, 10th NCST, 1st Art & Engs, Ramseur-Manly's Battery, Ligth Art), I: 563.
Black, William, (Pvt, Co F, 49th NCST), V: 564.
Black, William M., (Capt, Co D, 49th NCST), II: 593; III: 152.
Black, Zero, (Pvt, Co F, 26th NCST), V: 602.
"Black Fox," (Capt, Co K, Indian Company, Walker's Battalion, Thomas' Legion; 80th NCST), IV: 119.
Black Jack, N.C., III: 507.
Black River, N.C., III: 194.
Black's & White's, Va., (now Blackstone), I: 433, 468; II: 102; III: 538-539, 611-618; IV: 87, 90, 93; V: 673.
Blackburn, A.W., (1st Lt, Co B, 38th NCST), II: 675, 678.
Blackburn, James O., (Capt, Co G, 11th Vols/21st NCST), II: 139; V: 194.
Blackburn, Julius C., (Capt, Co K, 52nd NCST), III: 225, 237, 239.
Blackburn, W., (3rd Sgt, Co K, 12th Vols/22nd NCST), V: 554.
Blackford, B.L., (Capt, Engineering Officer), IV: 425, 426.
Blackley, E.J., (Capt, Co B, Littlejohn's 23rd Battalion Senior Reserves), IV: 399.
Blackley, William A., (Sgt, Co E, 5th Vols/15th NCST), V: 521.
Blackman, A.M., (Col, 27th U.S., Colored), V: 238.
Blackmer, E.B., (Capt, Co G, 66th NCST), III: 686.
Blackmer, E.G., (Lt, Co F, 7th NCST), I: 369.
Blacknell, Charles C., (Col, 13th Vols/23rd NCST) I: 644; II: 185, 188, 189, 197, 199, 205, 206, 229, 231, 236, 238, 244, 245, 248, 249, 250, 251, 253, 254, 255, 256; IV: 705; V: 10.
Blacknell, Rev. John, (Great grand-father of C.C. Blacknell), II: 254.
Blacknell, Thomas, (Grandfather of C.C. Blacknell), II: 254.
Blackney, Dr. Julius C., (Ass't Surg, 61st NCST), IV: 641.
Blackstocks, S.C., III: 439.
Blackstone, R., (Pvt, Co C, 1st Vols/11th NCST), V: 530.
Blackwater Church, Va., II: 793; III: 228.
Blackwater River, Va., [Black Water], I: 398, 494, 522, 587, 737; II: 277, 278, 515, 772, 775, 776, 785, 793, 796; III: 87, 228, 229, 232, 321, 322, 335, 616, 617, 622, 623; VI: 15, 72, 74, 87, 176, 357, 358, 366, 368, 487; V: 17, 83, 84, 269, 271, 282.
Blackwater River, Fort on, V: 83.
Blackwater River, Service on, III: 321, 458.
Blackwelder, Benjamin F., (Pvt, Co A, 10th Vols/20th NCST), II: 119.
Blackwelder, D.M., (Pvt, Co B, 43rd NCST), V: 497.
Blackwelder, Daniel, (Pvt, Co E, 59th NCST, 4th Cav), V: 659.
Blackwelder, J.A., (Capt, Co G, 42nd NCST), II: 791, 806.

Blackwelder, John N., (2nd Lt, Co G, 12th Vols/22nd NCST), II: 165, 166.
Blackwelder, Joseph, "Joe," (Pvt, Co F, 63rd NCST, 5th Cav), III: 618.
Blackwelder, Thomas J., (Capt, Co B, 35th NCST), II: 622.
Blacknell, John, (Pvt, Co C, 57th NCST), V: 517.
Blackweld, William M., (Pvt, Co K, 55th NCST), V: 528.
Blackwell, John N., (2nd Lt, Co G, 12th Vols/22nd NCST), II: 165, 166.
Blackwell, Moses M., (Pvt, Co F, 6th Vols/16th NCST), V: 552.
Blackwood, J.M., (Pvt, Co F, 33rd NCST), V: 544.
Blackwood, S.D., (Cpl, Co F, 33rd NCST), V: 544.
Blackwood, Washington, (Pvt, Co D, 56th NCST), III: 355.
Bladen County, N.C., II: 16, 66, 68, 73, 754; VI: 303, 312.
Blain, J.A., [John A.], (Pvt, Co H, 6th Vols/16th NCST), IV: 723.
Blain's Cross Raods, Tenn., III: 743.
Blair, Francis Preston, (Postmaster, U.S.), I: 325; III: 279, 388, 749.
Blair, Francis Preston, Jr., (Maj Gen, USA), I: 56; II: 247.
Blair, Jesse, (Pvt, Co E, 6th NCST), V: 512.
Blair, John A., (Maj, 2nd Miss.), II: 345.
Blair, John C., (Capt, Co D, 9th NCST, 1st Cav), I: 441, 460, 463, 484, 485, 782; IV: 721.
Blair, J. Caldwell, (Drum Major, 58th NCST), III: 432.
Blair, M.B., (1st Lt, Co I, 26th NCST), II: 353, 358, 371, 372, 397.
Blair, Milton P., (Jr 2nd Lt, Co I, 26th NCST), II: 304, 353.
Blair, Hon. Montgomery, (Federal Postmaster), III: 55; V: 627.
Blair, S.W., (Pvt, Co H, 1st Vol/11th NCST), V: 530.
Blair, W.M., (Lt, Co D., 9th NCST, 1st Cav), I: 485, 782.
Blake, F.B., (Lt. Cmdr, USN; Pioneer, Susquehanna), V: 244.
Blake, Frederick R., (Capt, Co H, 25th NCST; AIG, Clingman's Brigade), II: 292; IV: 482, 493; V: 201, 205.
Blakemore, ______, (Capt, AAG, Coleman's Brigade), II: 719.
Blakemore, J.H., (Lt, Ordnance Officer, M.W. Ransom's Brigade), V: 559.
Blalock, Alfred, (2nd Lt, Co D, 77th NCST, 7th Senior Reserves), IV: 100, 104.
Blalock, J.C., (Pvt, Co E, 26th NCST), V: 532.
Blalock, James A., (Capt, Co F, 25th NCST), II: 292.
Blalock, John C., (Capt, Co I, 29th NCST), II: 485, 493.
Blalock, L.M., "Keith," (Pvt, Co F, 26th NCST), II: 330, 331.
Blalock, Samuel, (Pvt, Co F, 26th NCST), Samuel was actually Malinda Blalock who presented herself as a man to stay with her husband, Keith. Both left the service, became traitors and outlaws. II: 330, 331.
Blalock, W.D., (Pvt, Co C, 6th NCST), V: 512.
Blalock, W.M., (Pvt, Co E, 35th NCST), V: 562.
Blalock, W.T., (1st Lt, Co A, 50th NCST), III: 203.
Blalock, William B., (Pvt, Co A, 43rd NCST), III: 20; V: 497.
Bland, Christopher C., (Pvt, Co K, 36th NCST, 2nd Art & Engs, Brunswick Artillery), II: 636.
Bland, J.J., (1st Lt, Co I, 44th NCST), III: 23.

Blandford's Cemetery, (nr Petersburg, Va.), III: 140, 362, 372, 373; VI: 450.
Blandon, E.J., (Pvt, Co C, 5th Vols/15th NCST), V: 521.
Blanks, William, (ACS, 61st NCST), III: 503.
Blanton, Elijah, (Pvt, Co B, 34th NCST), V: 555.
Blanton, G., (1st Lt, Co I, 38th NCST), II: 676.
Blanton, James, (Pvt, Co B, 34th NCST), V: 555.
Blanton, S.T., (2nd Lt, Co B, Millard's 9th/20th Battalion NCST, Junior Reserves), IV: 386.
Blanton, William, (Pvt, Co I, 34th NCST), V: 556.
Blanton, William H., (2nd Lt, Co I, 38th NCST), V: 549.
Blasengame, John, (Jr 2nd Lt, Co G, 9th NCST, 1st Cav, Woodfin's Battalion), IV: 109.
Blasingame, John G., (1st Lt, Co F, 9th Vols/19th NCST, 2nd Cav), II: 89, 91.
Blasingame, J.L., (Lt, Co G, 9th NCST, 1st Cav), I: 486.
Blaylock, James, A., (Capt, Co F, 25th NCST), II: 292.
Blaylock, John, (2nd Lt, Co C, 77th NCST, 7th Senior Reserves), IV: 99.
Blaylock, John C., (Capt, Co I, 29th NCST), II: 485, 493.
Bledsoe, G., (Pvt, Co D, 30th NCST), V: 492.
Bledsoe, H., (Pvt, Co H, 56th NCST), III: 356.
Bledsoe, Moese A., (Capt, N.C. Quartermaster Department), I: 23, 24.
Bledsoe, Dr. Powhatan, (Ass't Surg, 36th NCST, 2nd Art & Engs), II: 630; IV: 637; V: 240.
Blevens, A.C., (Pvt, Co K, 37th NCST), V: 546.
Blevin, P., (Lt, Co L, 58th NCST), III: 434.
Blizzard, A.B., (Pvt, Co D, 27th NCST), II: 462; V: 523.
Blizzard, D.P., (Pvt, Co B, 56th NCST), III: 352, 356.
Blizzard, J.D., (Pvt, Co B, 56th NCST), III: 366.
Block Island, N.Y., V: 441.
Blockade Runners, (See: Vessels).
Blockade Runners, Pilots of, V: 357.
Blockade Running, II: 631-633; IV: 319, 332, 625; V: ix, xvi, 217, 341, 353-451.
Blockade Running, Termination of, V: 355.
Blockade and the Cruisers, V: 414.
Blockaders, Fight with, V: 351-352.
Blocker, Charles H., (Capt, Co F, 14th Vols/24th NCST, Capt, ACS, 36th NCST, 2nd Art & Engs, ADC to Lamb), II: 269, 630, 641, 643; V: 228, 230, 233, 239.
Blocker, O.H., (Capt, Co C, 36th NCST, 2nd Art & Engs, Blocker's Battery Hvy Art), II: 630.
Bloodworth, J.H., (1st Lt, Co C, 59th NCST, 4th Cav), III: 457; IV: 705, 723.
Bloodworth, Jesse F., (Pvt, Co K, 8th Vols/18th NCST), II: 64, 72.
"Bloody Angle," (nr Gettysburg), V: 605.
"Bloody Angle," (nr Spotsylvania, Va., aka "Horse Shoe," "Mule Shoe," "Lee's Salient"), I: 166, 257, 315; II: 216, 243, 244; III: 47; VI: 523; V: 78.
"Bloody Lane," (nr Sharpsburg, Md., aka the "Sunken Road"), I: 166, 187, 246, 248, 711; II: 116, 223, 499, 500; V: xii, 78, 590.
Bloomington, Ind., V: 408.
Blount, Gen. ______, (and Blount's Plantation nr Ruff's Mill), VI: 76.

Blount, ______, (Maj, ADC to Branch), II: 23.
Blount, Benjamin H., (Lt, Co H, 55th NCST), III: 296.
Blount, David, (Negro, valet to Capt Robert D. Graham), III: 403.
Blount, George W., (AQM, 55th NCST), III: 288.
Blount, John, (Pvt, Co G, 7th Vols/17th NCST), V: 46.
Blount, John G., (1st Lt, AQM, 40th NCST, 3rd Art, Hvy), II: 745, 746.
Blount, John M., (2nd Lt, Co K, 10th NCST, 1st Art & Engs, Hvy), I: 491, 501; V: 278, 279.
Blount, Richard H., (Capt, Co F, 40th NCST, 3rd Art, Hvy; Maj, Moseley-Blount's Art Battalion), I: 489, 502, 503, 582; II: 746, 747; V: 183.
Blount, Thomas H., (Capt, AQM, 4th NCST), I: 230, 244, 268.
Blount, Dr. William A., (Surg, 9th NCST, 1st Cav; ADC, Branch-Lane's Brigade), I: 485; II: 23; IV: 472, 633; V: 658.
Blount, William A., (Brig Gen), V: 622.
Blount, William H., (Capt, Co H, 2nd Vols/12th NCST), I: 652.
Blount, William H., (Lt, Co D, 47th NCST), III: 84.
Blount County, Tenn., III: 738; VI: 126.
Blount's Creek, N.C., (and Affair at, 1864, aka Blount's Mill, Blount's Creek Bridge), I: 588; II: 340; III: 172, 234; IV: 74, 76, 90, 361, 557.
Blountsville, Tenn., III: 664, 742-743.
Blowing Rock, N.C., VI: 374, 375; V: 285.
Blue, J.A.B., (1st Lt, Co H, 46th NCST), III: 76, 82.
Blue, Evander McN., (Capt, Co C, 35th NCST), II: 600, 627; IV: 721.
Blue Ridge Mountains, I: 13, 147, 194, 206, 244, 259, 303, 308, 310, 318, 327, 366, 424, 578, 628; II: 21, 30, 71, 116, 148, 150, 170, 258, 438, 469, 493, 545, 556, 700, 703; III: 14, 69, 72, 88, 279, 462, 559, 567, 571, 719, 746, 758; VI: 114, 122, 138, 168, 169, 177, 233, 376, 381, 452, 465, 552; V: 285, 291.
Blue Springs, Tenn., III: 740.
Blue Sulphur Springs, Va., II: 270.
Bluff City, Tenn., (aka Zollicoffer or Union Depot), III: 518, 519, 524, 737, 740, 744; VI: 119.
Blume, George C., (1st Cpl, Co A, 52nd NCST), III: 223.
Blythe, C.N., (Pvt, Co K, 13th Vols/23rd NCST), V: 510.
Board of Auditors, I: 20.
Board of Claims, I: 45.
Bobbitt, A., (Lt, Littlejohn's 23rd Battalion NCST, Senior Reserves), IV: 399.
Bobbitt, B.B., (Pvt, Co F, 43rd NCST), V: 498.
Bobbitt, J.M., (Pvt, Co F, 2nd Vols/12th NCST), V: 265, 507.
Bobbitt, P.A., (Sgt, Co F, 2nd Vols/12th NCST), V: 265, 507.
Bobbitt, Samuel H., (2nd Lt, Co H, 4th NCST), I: 233.
Bobbitt, T.H., [Joseph H.], (Sgt, Co G, 43rd NCST), V: 194.
Bobbitt, W.H., (Pvt, Co F, 2nd Vols/12th NCST), V: 507.
Bobcock, Thomas S., (Speaker of the House, CSA), III: 471.
Body, John W., (Pvt, Co G, 38th NCST), V: 557.
Boernstein, A.S., (Maj, 6th U.S., Colored), V: 238.
Bogan, James, (Capt, Co E, 39th NCST), II: 705.
Boger, Joseph A., (Sgt, Co A, 57th NCST). V: 516.
Boggan, James, (Capt, Co K, 43rd NCST), III: 2.

Boggan, John, (Pvt, Co H, 43rd NCST), V: 499.
Boggan, John A., (Lt, Co K, 43rd NCST), III: 3; V: 494.
Boggan, W.W., (2nd Lt, Co H, 43rd NCST), III: 3.
Boggan, William C., (Jr 2nd Lt, Co K, 26th NCST), II: 304, 397.
Boggan, Walter J., (Maj, 43rd NCST), III: 1, 2.
Boggs, Francis J., (Maj, Bogg's 12th Va. Battalion, Hvy Art), VI: 355, 356.
Boggs, J., (Pvt, Co G, 27th NCST), II: 462.
Boggs, Jeha, (Pvt, Co G, 27th NCST), V: 573.
Bogle, G.W., (Pvt, Co H, 56th NCST), III: 356.
Bogue, Richard, (Pvt, Co A, Webb's 13th Battalion NCST, Light Art), V: 282.
Bohannon, S.S., (Capt, Co I, 28th NCST), IV: 721.
Boisseau's Farm, (and Battle of 1864; aka Boisseau's House), I: 436; II: 104; III: 469, 472; IV: 88, 89, 90.
Bolch, F., (Pvt, Co H, 28th NCST), V: 542.
Boles, Geta, (Pvt, Co I, 11th Vols/21st NCST), V: 515.
Bolick, B.T., (Pvt, Co D, 6th NCST), V: 512.
Bolick, H.I., (Pvt, Co B, 32nd NCST), V: 495.
Bolick, Robert A., (Lt, Co A, 7th NCST), I: 377, 467; VI: 467.
Bolin, Alexander, (1st Lt, Co F, 50th NCST), III: 203.
Bolin, J., (Pvt, Co H, 56th NCST), III: 356.
Bolin, John, (Pvt, Co E, 35th NCST), V: 563.
Bolin, Lee, (Pvt, Co E, 35th NCST), V: 563.
Boling, P., (Pvt, Co E, 13th Vols/23rd NCST), V: 510.
Bolivar Heights, Va., I: 206, 372; II: 32, 432, 473, 553, 585, 685; III: 13; VI: 466, 570; V: 77, 685.
Bolles, Charles P., (Capt, Co A, 6th Battalion NCST; Cmdr Fayetteville Arsenal), IV: 296, 298, 299.
Bolton, W.M., (Pvt, Co K, 32nd NCST), V: 497.
Bomer, J.P., (Pvt, Co G, 33rd NCST), V: 544.
Bonarva, N.C. (Pettigrew's home), II: 377.
Bond, ______, (Maj, AG, Leventhorpe's Home Guard), V: 631.
Bond, F.W., (Capt, Co A, 1st NCST), I: 136.
Bond, M., (2nd Lt, Co I, 59th NCST, 4th Cav), III: 458.
Bond, R.H.L., (Capt, Co I, 68th NCST), III: 714.
Bond, W.J., (Sgt, Co E, 5th NCST), I: 291; V: 505.
Bond, W.M., (Co M, 1st Vols, "Bethel"), I: 133.
Bond, William R., (2nd Lt, Co F, 43rd NCST; ADC Daniel's Brigade), III: 3; IV: 257, 513, 518, 705.
Bond House, (at Battle of Boydton Plank Road, Va.), III: 632.
Bondurant, ______, (Capt, Bondurant's Miss. Battery), VI: 444.
Bone, David, (Sgt, Co G, 33rd NCST), II: 540.
Bone, J.W., (Pvt, Co I, 30th NCST), V: 493.
Boney, Christopher C., (Pvt, Co A, 38th NCST), V: 557.
Boney, W.F., (2nd Lt, Co E, 30th NCST), II: 496.
Bonham, Milledge Luke, (Brig Gen), I: 342; VI: 226.
Bonneau, Frank, (Capt, CSN, Ella and Annie), V: 194, 443, 445.

Bonner, B.T., (1st Lt, Co I, 4th NCST), I: 233, 270.
Bonner, Bryan S., (2nd Lt, Co I, 4th NCST), I: 231, 270.
Bonner, Bryan T., (Lt, Co I, 4th NCST), I: 270; V: 664.
Bonner, J.M., (2nd Lt, Co G, 5th Vols/15th NCST), I: 735.
Bonner, James, (Color-bearer, Co K, 4th NCST), I: 239; V: 664.
Bonner, Macon, (1st Lt, Co B, 40th NCST, 3rd Art, Hvy), II: 746, 762.
Bonner, W.C., (Pvt, Co C, 11th Vols/21st NCST), V: 514.
Bonner, W.O.L., IV: 701.
Bonner, Dr. William V., (Pvt, Co I, 5th Vols/15th NCST; Ass't Surg, I: 734; IV: 634.
Booe, A.M., (Col, 3rd Regt 3rd Class Home Guard), IV: 653, 654.
Booe, William E., (Capt, Co H, 63rd NCST, 5th Cav), III: 530, 550, 587.
Booker, Abraham, (Capt, Co H, 39th NCST), II: 706.
Booker, G., (Pvt, Co D, 26th NCST), V: 531.
Booker, G.W., (Pvt, Co F, 45th NCST), V: 500.
Booker, P.P., (2nd Lt, Co H, 5th Vols/15th NCST), I: 735.
Booker, W.E., (Pvt, Co D, 26th NCST), V: 531.
Booker's Chapel, VI: 602.
Booles, J.C., (Pvt, 21st Ga.), V: 194.
Boomer, Benjamin, III: 723.
Boomer, Caleb S., (Sgt, Co H, 33rd NCST), II: 540, 578.
Boon, D.H., (Pvt, Co M, 11th Vols/21st NCST), V: 515.
Boon, H.Z., (Pvt, Co M, 11th Vols/21st NCST), V: 515.
Boon, J.D., (Pvt, Co M, 11th Vols/21st NCST), V: 515.
Boon, Jacob, (Lt, Co K, 47th NCST; Capt, Co B, 77th NCST, 7th Senior Reserves), III: 85; IV: 99.
Boon, Patterson, (Pvt, Co K, 47th NCST), V: 535.
Boon, W.R., (2nd Lt, Co B, 51st NCST), I: 120.
Boon, William H., (Pvt, Co A, 38th NCST), V: 557.
Boone, ______, (Lt, Co 6, Henry's 14th Battalion NCST; 79th NCST, 8th Cav), IV: 113.
Boone, A., (Pvt, Co H, 1st NCST), V: 485.
Boone, Daniel, (Famed Frontiersman, politician, etc.), V: 286.
Boone, H.A., (Capt, Co B, 25th NCST), II: 301.
Boone, J.B.F., (AQM, 1st Vols, "Bethel"), I: 113.
Boone, J.D., (AQM, 1st Vols, "Bethel"; AQMS, 1st NCST), I: 136; V: 485.
Boone, Jesse B., (1st Lt, Co C, Wheeler's 2nd Battalion; Co H, 16th Battalion/75th NCST, 7th Cav), IV: 91, 339, 705.
Boone, Thomas D., (Capt, Co F, 1st NCST), I: 137, 150, 154; V: 484.
Boone, W.F., (Pvt, Co F, 1st NCST), V: 485.
Boone, W.R., (Lt, Co D, 51st NCST), I: 120; III: 219.
Boone, N.C., III: 684; V: 285.
Boone's Mill, N.C., [Boon's], (and Battle of, 1863), II: 277, 614, 616; III: 330; IV: 339, 572.
Booney, S.B., (Pvt, Co K, 46th NCST), V: 525.
Boonsboro, Md., (and Battle of, 1862; aka South Mountain), I: 142, 184, 225, 244, 246, 334, 610, 624, 625, 626, 627, 628, 643, 695; II: 115, 219-222; III: 278; IV: 164, 447; V: 71.

Boonsboro Gap, (See: Turner's Gap).
Boonsboro Pike, I: 184; II: 222; III: 271.
Booth, J.H., (Cpl, Co H, 47th NCST), V: 535.
Booth, John C., (Maj, Cmdr Fayetteville Arsenal), IV: 295, 296, 299.
Booth, John Wilkes, (Alleged assassin of Abraham Lincoln), VI: 150.
Boothe, John G., [Booth], (Capt, Co C, 9th Vols/19th NCST, 2nd Cav), II: 80, 82, 87, 88, 775.
Bordeaux, Richard L., (2nd Lt, Co C, 78th NCST, 8th Senior Reserves), IV: 107.
Borden, E.B., (AQM, 50th NCST), III: 161, 202.
Borden, James C., (Capt, Co H, 9th NCST, 1st Cav), I: 486.
Borden, W.H., (1st Lt, Adjt, 50th NCST; Staff of Hardy), III: 161, 202, 203, 334; IV: 334.
Borders, Albert J., (Cpl, Co F, 34th NCST), V: 555.
Borders, Henry J., (Pvt, Co F, 34th NCST), V: 555.
Borough, William C., (3rd Lt, Co I, 3rd Vols/13th NCST), I: 655.
Boseman, J.D., (Pvt, Co K, 5th Vols/15th NCST), V: 522.
Bost, A.T., (Capt, Co K, 46th NCST), III: 65, 76, 78, 82.
Bost, E.G., (Sgt, Co A, 2nd Vols/12th NCST), V: 506.
Bost, J.M., (Pvt, Co B, 10th Vols/20th NCST), V: 508.
Bost, Jackson L., (Maj, 37th NCST), II: 670; IV: 474; V: 538.
Bost, Morris, (Pvt, Co E, 32nd NCST), V: 496.
Bost, R.A., (Capt, Co K, 46th NCST), III: 82; V: 519.
Bost, W.W., (Pvt, Co K, 32nd NCST), V: 497.
Bostian, T.C., (Sgt, Co E, 32nd NCST), V: 496.
Bostic, Thomas J., (2nd Lt, Co A, 43rd NCST), III: 3, 11, 20; V: 494.
Bostic, W., (Pvt, Co I, 6th NCST), V: 513.
Bostic, W.H., (Pvt, Co E, 2nd Vols/12th NCST), V: 507.
Bostick, S.E., (2nd Lt, Co I, 50th NCST), III: 203.
Boston, Mass., I: 103; II: 405, 747; III: 209; IV: 734, 735; V: 375, 393, 422, 621.
Boswell, Mrs. ______, (Resident of Shepherdstown), I: 249.
Boswell, Alexander, (Pvt, Co I, 43rd NCST), V: 499.
Boswell, J.A., (Pvt, Co D, 1st NCST), V: 485.
Boswell, Joe, (Fayetteville and Harper's Ferry Arsenals), IV: 298.
Boswell, M., (Pvt, Co M, 33rd NCST), V: 544.
Boswell, Thomas, (Fayetteville and Harper's Ferry Arsenals), IV: 298.
Boswell, William S., (Lt, Co A, 5th NCST), I: 285.
Botler, Mrs. ______, (Resident of Shepherdsville, Md.), I: 249.
Boteler's Mill, Va., (and Fight at 1862), II: 34; VI: 177.
"Bottling Up of Butler," I: 321; II: 4; III: 276, 354-355, 512; VI: 85, 93, 361, 492, 529-531; V: 16.
Bottom's Bridge, (Chickahominy River, Va.), I: 616; II: 278, 287, 613; III: 131, 247, 358, 609; VI: 152.
Botts, John Minor, (and Botts' House nr Culpepper, Va.), II: 90; III: 460, 575, 585; IV: 657.
Bouchell, T.S., (Capt, Co B, 1st NCST; Col, 83rd NCST, Detailed Men), I: 136, 142; IV: 129, 133, 400.

Bouchelle, _____, (Lt, Lane's Brigade), VI: 467.
Bouge, J., (Pvt, Co F, 1st Vols/11th NCST), V: 530.
Bouge, Richard, (Pvt, Co A, Webb's Battery, Starr's 13th Battalion NCST, Light Art), V: 282.
Bouge Banks, N.C., I: 503.
Bouge Island, N.C., I: 362; II: 307.
Bough, W.F., (1st Lt, Co G, 61st Va.), V: 569.
Boudlin, _____, (Col, 30th Va.), VI: 501.
Bouldin, Ephraim, (1st Lt, Co H, 12th Vols/22nd NCST), II: 165, 166, 168.
Bourden, B.C., (Lt, Co B, 9th Battalion NCST, 1st Hvy Art), IV: 303.
Bourgin, F., (Drum Maj, 34th NCST), II: 582.
Boushall, Joseph D., (1st Lt, Co E, 33rd NCST), II: 539, 562, 578; IV: 467.
Bowden, J.W., (Pvt, Co G, 26th NCST), V: 532.
Bowden, L.H., (1st Lt, Co I, 10th NCST, 1st Art & Engs, Sutherland's Battery, Light Art), IV: 221.
Bowden, W.H., (Pvt, Co C, 2nd Vols/12th NCST), V: 507.
Bowden, William, (Pvt, Co B, 56th NCST), III: 366.
Bowden, William, (Pvt, Co D, 56th NCST), III: 378.
Bowen, Daniel A., (Pvt, Co B, 34th NCST), V: 555.
Bowen, E.J., (1st Lt, Co K, 31st NCST), II: 508, 512.
Bowen, G.W., (Pvt, Co D, 55th NCST), V: 528.
Bowen, George F., (Pilot, Keystone State, captured and illegally forced into service by the USN), V: 374.
Bowen, Henry E., (Pvt, Co B, 7th Va.), V: 194.
Bowen, William, (Pvt, Co D, 56th NCST), III: 378.
Bowers, Frank, (Pvt, Co A, 13th Vols/23rd NCST), II: 224-225.
Bowers, George, (Capt, Co D, 56th NCST), III: 322, 354.
Bowers, Giles, (1st Lt, Co C, 49th NCST), III: 146.
Bowers, Green, (Pvt, Co D, 56th NCST), III: 354.
Bowers, James, (Cpl, Co K, 4th NCST), I: 234, 278.
Bowling, Joseph M., (1st Lt, Co I, 41st NCST, 3rd Cav), II: 771.
Bowling Green, Ky., I: 41.
Bowling Green, Va., I: 460, 721; VI: 150.
Bowlinng Green Road, (nr Fredericksburg, Va.), III: 407, 408.
Bowman, _____, (Pvt, Co I, 6th Vols/16th NCST), VI: 182.
Bowman, G., (Pvt, Co K, 54th NCST), V: 516.
Bowman, Jacob W., (Capt, Co B, 58th NCST), III: 432.
Bowman, John, (Pvt, Co F, 26th NCST), I: 732; V: 602.
Bowman, Joseph, (Pvt, Co I, 11th Vols/21st NCST), V: 515.
Bowman, P.C., (Pvt, Co A, 2nd Vols/12th NCST), V: 506.
Bowman's Ford, (Shenandoah River, Va.), I: 154.
Boyce, C.B., (2nd Lt, Co H, 1st Vols/11th NCST), I: 585.
Boyd, _____, [W.W., 19th Ga.], (Col, 14th Ga.), VI: 150.
Boyd, Mr. _____, (Owner of residence where Pettigrew died), II: 377.
Boyd, A.J., (Lt Col, 22nd Battallion Home Guard), IV: 650.
Boyd, Andrew J., (Maj, 45th NCST), III: 35, 38.

Boyd, B.F., (2nd Lt, Co H, Vols/11th NCST), I: 586.
Boyd, Miss Belle, (Alleged Confederate spy), II: 232; IV: 662, 663.
Boyd, D., (Pvt, Co B, 33rd NCST), V: 544.
Boyd, George, (Pvt, Detached Co, 68th NCST), III: 723.
Boyd, J.R., (Pvt, Co I, 4th NCST), V: 489.
Boyd, John H., (Lt, Co G, 57th NCST), III: 411.
Boyd, McD., (Capt, Co C, 5th Battalion Junior Reserves; Co H, 71st NCST, 2nd Junior Reserves), IV: 25, 28.
Boyd, Samuel H., (Col, 45th NCST), III: 36, 37, 38, 54; IV: 705; V: 10.
Boydton, Va., I: 433.
Boydton Plank Road, Va., (and Battle of, 1864), I: 436, 702; II: 105, 411, 782; III: 36, 37, 54, 249, 251, 281, 627-633, 644; IV: 203, 705; V: 10.
Boyette, Larry B., (2nd Lt, Co B, 2nd NCST), I: 158, 159, 175; V: 484.
Boukin, D.W.,(Musician, Battalion/75th NCST, 7th Cav), V: 660.
Boykin, Edward A., (Capt, Co K, 25th NCST), III: 348.
Boykin, Irvin, (Pvt, Co B, 2nd NCST), I: 175; V: 486.
Boykin L.W., (2nd Lt, Co A, 5th Vols/15th NCST), I: 734.
Boykin, M.V., (ACS, 9th NCST, 1st Cav), I: 485.
Boykin, Solomom, (Lt, Co K, 51st NCST), III: 206, 220.
Boykin, Dr. Thomas J., (Surg, 26th NCST; Medical Purveyor at Wilmington), II: 306, 395, 412; IV: 630, 636.
Boykin's Depot, (Seaaboard & Roanoke Railroad), VI: 16; V: 271.
Boykins, N.C., VI: 26.
Boylan, D.L., (Cpl, Co B, 1st NCST), V: 485.
Boyle, Francis A., (Sgt, Adjt, Co A, 32nd NCST), II: 523.
Boyle, M.F., (Mail carrier, Co B, 26th NCST), II: 408.
Boyle's Mill, (nr Plymouth, redoubt at), III: 339, 345; V: 183, 320.
Boyle's Mill Road, (nr Plymouth), V: 176.
Boyles, Alexander, (1st Lt, Co H, 53rd NCST), III: 263.
Boynton, Henry VanNess, (Brig Gen, USA), III: 449; V: 170.
Boynton, H.V., V: 170.
Brabble, Edward C., (Col, 32nd NCST), II: 521, 522, 527-529, 530; III: 49; IV: 255, 515; V: 10.
Brabble, John J., (2nd Lt, Co D, 40th NCST, 3rd Art, Hvy), II: 747.
Bracken, T.H., (Pvt, Co H, 5th NCST; Detailed, Invalid Battalion), V: 571.
Bracken, Thomas, (Pvt, Co H, 63rd NCST, 5th Cav), III: 587.
Bracket, W.D., (Pvt, Co B, 12th Vols/22nd NCST), V: 553.
Brackett, W., (Pvt, Co C, 10th NCST, 1st Art & Engs, Brem-Graham-Williams' Battery, Light Art), V: 567.
Braddock Road, (Crampton Gap, Battle of South Mountain, Md.), I: 141.
Braddock Road, (nr Centerville, Va.), I: 563.
Braddy, K.J., [Bradley], (Capt, Co C, 36th NCST, 2nd Art & Engs, Blocker-Bradley's Battery Hvy Art), I: 120; II: 634; V: 239.
Bradford, ______, [Joseph H., Capt, Co B, 12th Ala.], (Capt, Ala., Art), III: 399.

Bradford, J.A., (Pvt, Co B, 10th Vols/20th NCST), II: 119.
Bradford, James A.J., (Col, 10th NCST, 1st Art & Engs), I: 500, 501, 518, 525, 536; IV: 294, 299, 300, 347; V: 9, 44, 680.
Bradford, John R., (Pvt, Co B, 10th Vols/20th NCST), II: 119.
Bradford, N.G. (Capt, Co I, 26th NCST), II: 336, 358, 372, 397; IV: 701, 705, 721.
Bradford, W.W., (Pvt, Co F, 26th NCST), V: 602.
Bradford, William B., (2nd Lt, Co B, 10th Vols/20th NCST), IV: 705.
Bradley, Isaac T., (Pvt, Co H, 6th Vols/16th NCST), V: 552.
Bradley, J.G., (1st Lt, Co B, 31st NCST), II: 507.
Bradley, J.J., (2nd Lt, Co D, 4th NCST), I: 231.
Bradley, J.T, (Pvt, Co D, 54th NCST), V: 516.
Bradley, James Y., (Capt, Co B, 31st NCST), II: 512.
Bradley, John N., (Pvt, Co G, 6th Vols/16th NCST), IV: 178, 179.
Bradley, Lemuel, (Pvt, Co D, 43rd NCST), V: 498.
Bradley, Lorenzo, (Pvt, Co C, 39th NCST), II: 736.
Bradley, Marcus, (Musician, 10th Vols/20th NCST), II: 113.
Bradley, R.H., (Pvt, Co A, 1st Vols, "Bethel"), I: 100, 101; V: 577, 579.
Bradley, S.B., (1st Lt, Co E, 34th NCST), V: 548.
Bradshaw, ______, (Maj, 11th Tenn.), II: 489.
Bradshaw, B., (Pvt, Co E, 30th NCST), V: 492.
Bradshaw, Charles W., (Lt Col, 42nd NCST), II: 789, 797, 805; IV: 538.
Bradshaw, J.A., (Maj, 37th Battalion Home Guard), IV: 650.
Bradshaw, J.I., (Pvt, Co I, 26th NCST), V: 532.
Bradshaw, John, (Cpl, Co G, 33rd NCST), II: 540, 579.
Bradshaw, John S., (Pvt, Co G, 38th NCST), V: 557.
Bradshaw, Nathan, (Pvt, Co F, 26th NCST), V: 602.
Bradshaw, W.S., (Capt, Co A, 77th NCST, 7th Senior Reserves), IV: 99, 101, 104.
Bradshaw, William F., (Pvt, Co B, 58th NCST), III: 453.
Brady, Samuel, (Pvt, Co E, 14th Vols/24th NCST), V: 560.
Bragg, ______, (Seaman, Sea Bird), V: 309.
Bragg, Braxton, (Gen), I: xii, 103, 532, 720; II: 9, 10, 12, 421, 518, 621, 634, 638, 639, 640, 641, 643, 645, 646, 647, 648, 649, 650, 708, 709, 710, 711, 712, 720, 735, 736, 778, 779, 802; III: 196, 381, 435, 448, 475, 480, 481, 486, 493, 678, 681, 693, 708, 733, 736, 737, 738, 742; IV: 50, 55, 58, 100, 120, 121, 123, 129, 268, 397, 428, 430, 431, 498, 539, 541, 542, 543, 544, 547, 652, 754; V: 170, 197, 217, 222, 223, 225, 226, 227, 230, 232, 234, 235, 239, 240, 241, 270.
Bragg, Thomas, (Governor of North Carolina), I: 9.
Bragg, W.C., (Pvt, Co B, 8th Vols/18th NCST), V: 539.
Bragg, W.P., (Pvt, Co C, 47th NCST), V: 534.
Braine, D.L., (Lt Cmdr, USN, Pequot), V: 242.
Brame, J.M., (1st Lt, Co B, NCST), II: 496.

Branch, ______, (Lt Col, Va., Art), V: 175, 178, 184.
Branch, C., (1st Lt, Co K, 1st NCST), I: 137.
Branch, J.G., (Lt, Co C, 51st NCST), III: 219.
Branch, Bolin, (Pvt, Co D, 43rd NCST), V: 498.
Branch, George N., (Pvt, Co D, 43rd NCST), V: 498.
Branch, H.K., (Lt, 10th NCST, 1st Art & Engs), IV: 705.
Branch, J., (Pvt, Co F, 26th NCST), V: 532.
Branch, J.F., (Lt, Wynn's 15th Battalion NCST, Cav), IV: 365, 368.
Branch, John H., (1st Lt, Claiborne-Dearing's 7th C.S. Cav; Co F, 16th Battalion/75th NCST, 7th Cav), IV: 91
Branch, Lawrence O'Brien, (Brig Gen), I: xi, 9, 23, 24, 48, 112, 115, 350, 363, 364, 365, 366, 371, 372, 390, 503, 538, 608, 737; II: 20, 21, 22, 23, 24, 25, 26, 28, 29, 31, 32, 33, 65, 68, 71, 308, 309, 310, 317, 320, 327, 328, 377, 427, 461, 468, 469, 471, 473, 474, 537, 541, 542, 543, 544, 545, 546, 547, 548, 550, 552, 553, 554, 555, 556, 593, 595, 653, 654, 656, 682; IV: 155, 165, 414, 465, 466, 472, 473, 647; V: 9, 10, 57, 79, 649.
Branch, Mrs. L.O'B., II: 579.
Branch, W.A.B., (Lt, ADC to Hoke, son of L.O.B. Branch), IV: 537.
Branch, W.R., (Pvt, Co K, 1st NCST), V: 485.
Branch's Command at New Bern, (7th, 26th, 27th, 33rd, 35th, 37th NCST, Berm's Battery, Spruill's 9th Vols/19th NCST 2nd Cav, H.J.B. Clark's Militia Battalion), II: 308.
Branchville, S.C., III: 191, 439, 501; IV: 103.
Brandon, Joseph, (Pvt, Co H, 63rd NCST, 5th Cav), III: 587.
Brandon, W.C., (2nd Lt, Co G, 66th NCST), III: 686.
Brandon, W.J., (4th Cpl, Co C, 3rd Vols/13th NCST), V: 550.
Brandon, Miss., III: 486.
Brandy Station, Va., (and Battles of), I: 253, 310, 382, 423, 426, 453, 462, 484, 609, 717; II: 89, 90; III: 5, 40, 41, 272, 417, 461, 472, 531, 532, 555, 557-558, 559, 575, 576, 577, 645; IV: 110, 160, 183, 186, 253, 254, 657, V: 628.
Branner, John A., (Sgt Maj, 45th NCST), V: 499.
Brannock, J., (Pvt, Co A, 28th NCST), V: 540.
Brannon, John Milton, (Maj Gen, USA), III: 436.
Branson, Isaac N., (1st Sgt, Co F, 46th NCST), V: 524.
Branson, L., (Capt, Co F, 46th NCST), III: 77, 454; IV: 442.
Branson, Thomas A., (Capt, Co F, 46th NCST), III: 81.
Brantley, ______, [William F.] (Maj, 15th Miss.), V: 633.
Brantley, John, (2nd Lt, Co H, 50th NCST), III: 203.
Brantly, B.F., (2nd Lt, Co H, 50th NCST), III: 203.
Brantly, David H., (Pvt, Co G, 38th NCST), V: 557.
Brantly, Wiley H., (Pvt, Co K, 38th NCST), V: 558.
Brantly, William F., [Brantley], (Brig Gen), III: 497.
Braswell, A.O., (Pvt, Co H, 32nd NCST), V: 497.
Braswell, James, (Pvt, Co F, 30th NCST), V: 492.
Braswell, R.H.,(Pvt, Co K, 5th Vols/15th NCST; Courier, Cooke's Brigade), V: 522.
Braswell, R.W., (Pvt, Co F, 26th NCST), V: 602.

Braswell, Robert M., (Pvt, Co F, 26th NCST), V: 601.
Braswell, W.D., (2nd Lt, Co K, 5th Vols/15th NCST), I: 736.
Braswell, W.D., (Lt, Co A, 1st NCST), I: 736.
Bratten, J.L., (1st Lt, Co A, 1st NCST), I: 136.
Brawley, W.R.J., (Musician, 4th NCST), I: 234; V: 488.
Brawley, John M., (Capt, Co A, 76th NCST, 6th Senior Reserves), IV: 97.
Braxton, Carter Moore, (Maj, Carter's Battalion, Art), I: 374.
Braxton, E.M., (Maj, QM Walker-Cooke's Brigade), IV: 503, 512; V: 519.
Bray, Benjamin, F., (Lt, Co A, 2nd NCST), I: 158.
Bray, S.C., (Pvt, Co B, 8th Vols/18th NCST), II: 63.
Bray, William P., (2nd Lt, Co C, 56th NCST), III: 314; V: 559.
Braysville, Ga., III: 678.
Brazie, William R., (Maj, 5th U.S., Colored), V: 238.
Brazil, IV: 490.
Breast Plates, III: 170.
Breckinridge, John Cabell, (Maj Gen, Sec of War, CSA), I: 61, 63, 205, 384, 645; II: 391, 408, 490; III: 437, 480, 481, 486, 488, 491, 524, 748, 750, 752; IV: 124, 198, 199, 209, 687; V: 171.
Breedlove, James A., (Capt, Co G, 13th Vols/23rd NCST), II: 186.
Breedon, William, (Ensign, Color-bearer, 39th NCST), I: 767; II: 732, 737.
Breese, K.R., (Lt Cmdr, USN), V: 241, 244.
Breitz, Edward A., (Jr 2nd Lt, Co B, 26th NCST), II: 371, 372, 396, 397; IV: 702.
Brem, Charlie, (Pvt, Co F, 63rd NCST, 5th Cav), III: 619.
Brem, M.S., (Lt, Co C, 48th NCST), III: 117.
Brem, Thomas H., (Lt Col, 63rd Battalion Home Guard), I: 537, 538; IV: 650; V: 668.
Brendle, H.F., (Pvt, Co D, 53rd NCST), V: 501.
Brenizer, A.G., (Col, 82nd NCST, Detailed Men), IV: 129, 131, 400.
Brent, Oscar J., (Chaplain, 28th NCST), II: 466; IV: 473, 611.
Brevard, J.A., (Capt, Co H, 29th NCST), II: 493.
Brevard, N.C., IV: 381.
Brewer, A.H., (Cpl, Co A, 30th NCST), V: 491.
Brewer, E., (Pvt, Co E, 26th NCST), V: 532.
Brewer, H., (Pvt, Co H, 46th NCST), V: 525.
Brewer, James, (Sgt, Co D, 4th NCST), I: 232.
Brewer, John, (Pvt, Co E, 26th NCST), V: 532.
Brewer, R., (Pvt, Co A, 67th NCST), III: 710.
Brewer, Samuel W., (Sgt, Co D, 5th Vols/15th NCST), V: 521.
Brewer, Stephen W., (Capt, Co E, 26th NCST), II: 304, 330, 365, 366, 371, 372, 374, 396, 397, 416, 419; IV: 705.
Brewer, W., (2nd Lt, Co G, 5th Vols/15th NCST), I: 735.
Brewer, William C., (Lt, Co F, 2nd NCST), I: 161, 162.
Brewer, Dr. William T., (2nd Lt, Co C; Surg, 43rd NCST), III: 1, 3; IV: 638.
Brewster, _____, (Col), II: 685.
Brice, Bailey, (Hospital Steward, 56th NCST), III: 319.
Brice, John D., (Pvt, Co H, 5th NCST), I: 292; V: 505.
Brice, O.D., (Pvt, Co I, 56th NCST), V: 566.

Brice's Creek, N.C., (nr New Bern), III: 335, 349; IV: 573.
Brick Church, (nr Orange County Court House, Va.), IV: 160.
Brickell, Sterling, (Capt, Co G, 2nd Vols/12th NCST), I: 642.
Bridgers, Alfred W., (Capt, Co G, 43rd NCST), III: 2, 3.
Bridgers, B.H., (1st Sgt, Co D, 45th NCST), V: 528.
Bridgers, George V., (Pvt, Co A, 10th NCST, 1st Art & Engs, Ramseur-Manly's Battery, Light Art), I: 357.
Bridgers, H.N., (Pvt, Co A, 6th Battalion/60th NCST), III: 481.
Bridgers, John L., (Lt Col, 10th NCST, 1st Art & Engs, Cmdr of Fort Macon), I: 77, 90, 94, 100, 101, 113, 118, 125, 127, 489, 500, 502, 515, 536; IV: 551, 650.
Bridgers, Hon. R.R., (Congress, CSA), I: 16.
Bridgers, S.G.H, (Pvt, Co H, 28th NCST), V: 542.
Bridgers, Sidney H., (Lt, Co A, 47th NCST), III: 84.
Bridgers, Thomas B., (Lt, Co A, 10th NCST, 1st Art & Engs, Ramseur-Manly's Battery, Light Art), I: 551.
Bridgeman, Laban, (AQM, Detached Co, 68th NCST), III: 723.
Bridgford, D.E., (Maj, Provost Marshal, ANV), V: 572.
Bridgman, Seth, (2nd Lt, Co I, 40th NCST, 3rd Art, Hvy), II: 747.
Bridges, Francis M., (2nd Sgt, Co I, 38th NCST), V: 558.
Bridges, K.A., (Pvt, Co E, 47th NCST), V: 535.
Bridges, Samuel, (Pvt, Co B, 34th NCST), V: 555.
Bridges, T.S., (Pvt, Co, H, 28th NCST), V: 542.
Bridges, Washington W., (2nd Sgt, Co B, 34th NCST), V: 555.
Brietz, Edward A., (2nd Lt, Co D, 11th Vols/21st NCST), IV: 705.
Brigade Histories, IV: 433-596.
Brigades, Confederate:
Anderson's, G.B., (4th NCST, 49th Va., 27th & 28th Ga.; 2nd, 4th, 14th & 30th NCST; See also: Ramseur's and Cox's), I: 167, 224, 235, 242, 244, 245, 246, 248, 249, 250, 633; II: 57, 204, 210, 221, 223, 238, 498, 499, 588, 783, 784; III: 451, 481; IV: 142, 435, 437, 443-464; V: 78, 208, 589, 590.
Anderson's, J.R., (3rd Brigade ANV: 1st S.C., 34th NCST, 3rd La. Battalion, 2nd Ga. Battalion, 45th Ga., 49th Ga.), II: 456, 677.
Anderson's, J.P., (AoT), III: 436, 451, 481; IV: 142.
Anderson's, R.H., (Ga.), II: 205, 696.
Archer's, (Tenn./Va.), I: 374, 352, 375; II: 29, 31, 35, 44, 171, 341, 343, 344, 345, 346, 347, 361, 363, 367, 553, 555, 565, 566, 657, 683, 684, 685, 686; III: 72, 236, 237, 297, 298, 300; IV: 159, 467, 508, 552, 559; V: 101, 102, 104, 107, 111, 117, 118, 119, 124, 125, 129, 139, 142, 144, 147, 150, 151, 153, 156, 157, 158, 613.
Archer's, (Va. Junior Reserves), V: 247, 248, 250, 252.
Archer-McComb's, (Ala.), II: 453.
Archer-Thomas-McConnel's, (See Also: Individual Listings), II: 394.
Armistead's, (9th, 14th, 38th, 53rd, 57th, Va.), I: 619; II: 44, 363, 367; III: 300; V: 101, 102,

103, 107, 139, 140, 144, 149, 157, 588.
Armistead's, F.S., (See: Junior Reserves).
Avery's, (See: Hoke's).
Baker's, (aka Hardy's; 67th, 68th NCST, 65th NCST 6th Cav), III: 186, 188, 191, 198, 199, 727.
Baker's, (See: Junior Reserves).
Barksdale's, (Miss.), I: 556, 629, 738.
Barry's, (7th, 18th, 28th, 33rd, 37th NCST), IV: 435.
Barton's, (Va.), I: 526; III: 132, 333; IV: 486, 573.
Bate's, (See: Raines'), II: 731.
Battle's, (Ala.), I: 201, 255, 277, 635, 637; II: 235, 259, 524, 535; III: 46, 48; V: 247, 248, 250, 252.
Bee's, (7th, 8th Ga., 4th Ala., 2nd Miss.; 2nd, 11th Miss, 4th Ala., 6th NCST), I: 297, 339, 341, 347, 350; III: 291.
Benning's, (Ga.), II: 174; IV: 192.
Blacknell's, (Temp Cmdr of a brigade at Petersburg, 1863), II: 244.
Bonham's, (S.C.), I: 342, 343; IV: 226.
Branch's, (7th, 18th, 28th, 33rd, 37th NCST; See also: Lane's), I: 12, 365, 366, 367, 369, 370, 371, 372, 373, 538; II: 20, 21, 24, 25, 27, 28, 29, 30, 32, 33, 65, 66, 68, 69, 77, 313, 398, 400, 468, 469, 470, 471, 473, 474, 544, 545, 546, 547, 549, 550, 551, 553, 556, 654, 655, 656; III: 134; IV: 166, 435, 437, 465-475; V: 588, 589.
Branch-Lane's, (See: Individual Listings).
Branch-Lane-Barry's, (See also: Individual Listings), IV: 435, 465
Brantley's, (AoT), III: 454, 497; IV: 442.
Brockenborough's, (Va., See also: Heth's), II: 44, 341, 343, 346, 347, 354, 361, 363, 364, 478, 561, 565, 661, 685; III: 300; V: 101, 102, 106, 108, 119, 124, 125, 130, 139, 144, 146, 154.
Brown's, (AoT), III: 438.
Clingman's, (8th, 31st, 51st, 61st NCST), I: 390, 397, 403, 404, 406, 407, 408, 519, 742; II: 5, 6, 423, 513, 515, 516, 517, 518, 519, 616, 764, 798; III: 132, 205, 206, 213, 214, 273, 274, 333, 337, 357, 505, 511, 512, 513, 691; IV: 22, 346, 435, 437, 438, 442, 465, 481-500, 531; V: 175, 197, 199, 202, 241, 244.
Cobb's, (S.C.), I: 738, 739, 740, 741; II: 297, 436, 438, 610; IV: 441, 504, 571; V: 588.
Coleman's, (See: Johnson's), II: 714, 718.
Colquitt's, (1st, 3rd NCST, 10th, 23rd, 37th Va.; 6th, 19th, 27th, 28th Ga.), I: 143, 145, 186, 188, 377, 408, 625; II: 5, 6, 11, 205, 219, 223, 232, 434, 517, 763, 798, 801; III: 357, 691; IV: 312, 444, 490, 493, 495, 531, 535, 536, 541, 546, 547; V: 199, 203, 205, 241.
Colston's, (Va.), I: 192, 655, 657, 709; II: 39; IV: 441.
Colston-Steuart's, (See also: Individual Listings), I: 147, 193, 199, 200.
Connally's, John K., (Temp. Cmdr of F.S. Armistead's Brigade: 4th 7th, 8th Battalion Junior Reserves, 78th NCST 8th Senior Reserves), II: 168, 170, 388,

679, 781; III: 333, 469, 565; IV: 6, 18, 108, 155, 440, 557; V: 212.
Cook's, (Ga.), IV: 508, 512; V: 247, 248, 250, 252.
Cooke's, (15th, 27th, 46th, 48th, 55th NCST), I: 207, 262, 385, 471, 545, 593, 595, 599, 741, 742, 743, 744, 745, 746, 747; II: 45, 57, 58, 76, 178, 379, 385, 388, 394, 395, 420, 438, 439, 440, 441, 442, 443, 446, 447, 448, 449, 450, 451, 455, 458, 459, 460, 480, 575, 588, 610, 613, 609, 695, 696, 781; III: 26, 30, 68, 71, 72, 73, 74, 75, 76, 77, 78, 79, 92, 94, 95, 97, 111, 117, 118, 120, 122, 242, 244, 247, 249, 290, 303, 308, 311, 322, 324, 328, 329, 330; IV: 184, 185, 435, 437, 438, 441, 442, 458, 50-512, 565, 566; V: xiii, 208, 209, 211, 212, 519-528, 573.
Corse's, (Va.), II: 438; III: 132, 235, 273, 274, 333, 351, 396, 741; IV: 486, 504.
Cowand's, (See also: Daniel's and Grimes'), IV: 516; V: 247, 248, 249, 250, 252.
Cox's, (2nd, 4th 14th & 30th NCST and later the consoil dated 1st & 3rd NCST; See also: Anderson's and Ramseur's), I: v, 152, 162, 173, 205, 207, 210, 212, 261, 262, 263, 265, 266, 279, 748; II: 503, 504, 505; III: 400, 401; IV: 206, 435, 437, 441, 443-464, 580; V: vii, xi, 247, 250, 251, 252, 254, 255, 260, 483-493, 573.
Crittenden's, (See also: Trimble's), IV: 441.
Cumming's, (Ga.), III: 197, 443.
Curtis', (Va.), IV: 49.
Daniel's, (32nd, 43rd, 45th, 53rd, 2nd Battalion NCST; See also: Grimes'), I: 12, 289, 539, 637; II: 50, 51, 334, 522, 523, 524, 527, 529, 530, 531, 535; III: 1, 4, 5, 6, 16, 17, 36, 39, 40, 41, 42, 43, 44, 45, 46, 47, 49, 50, 56, 61, 162, 163, 166, 167, 170, 172, 173, 255, 256, 258, 260, 322, 324, 329; IV: 247, 252, 253, 255, 256, 258, 259, 436, 437, 513-519, 601; V: xiii, 611.
Daniel-Grimes', (See also: Individual Listings), II: 523; IV: 436, 513; IV: 260.
Davidson's, (AoT), III: 678; V: 170, 173.
Davis', (2nd, 11th, 26th, 42nd Miss., 55th NCST, 57th NCST, 1st Battalion CSA), I: 353, 543, 743; II: 341, 343, 345, 346, 347, 348, 361, 363, 364, 367, 394, 439, 451, 454, 478, 527, 563, 565, 566, 573; III: 72, 98, 290, 291, 293, 294, 295, 297, 298, 299, 300, 303, 304, 306, 308, 309, 310, 406; IV: 435, 441, 508, 563; V: xii, 101, 102, 106, 108, 110, 111, 117, 119, 124, 125, 126, 127, 129, 139, 144, 146, 154.
Dibbrell's, (AoT), III: 679.
Doles', (Ga.), I: 202, 719; II: 227, 242, 524, 530; III: 46, 47; IV: 253, 259.
Donaldson's, [Donelson], IV: 142.
Early's, (5th, 23rd NCST, 20th GA., 24th, 38th Va.; 5th, 23rd NCST, 24th Va., 2nd Fla. Battalion), I: 282, 283, 342, 347, 611; II: 192, 197, 198, 602, 655; IV: 45, 160, 441.
Echol's, (Va.), IV: 532.
Ector's, (Tx., Army of the West), II: 491, 492, 720, 742; IV: 438, 442; V: 4, 170, 173.

Elliott's, (S.C., See Also: Evan's and Walker's), II: 298, 624; III: 141, 193, 361, 363, 367, 371, 372, 374.
Elzey's, (4th CSA; See also: Smith's), I: 343.
Evans', (S.C.), I: 207, 262, 347; III: 86, 349, 357, 508; IV: 325, 454; V: 86, 588.
Evans-Walker's, (S.C.; See also: Individual Listings), III: 349, 351, 356.
Field's, (See also: Brockenborough's), I: 613; II: 35, 686; V: 139.
Finnegan's, (Fla.), IV: 532.
Floyd's (Va.), II: 270.
Frazer's, (AoT), III: 434, 448.
French's, II: 167, 596.
Frye's, [Fry's], (See: Archer's).
Gardner's, III: 680.
Garland's, (5th, 12th, 13th, 20th, 23rd NCST; See also: Iverson's and Johnston's), I: 139, 186, 224, 245, 286, 610, 615, 618, 620, 621, 625, 626, 657, 658, 659, 660, 661, 662, 663, 694, 695; II: 114, 115, 204, 207, 208, 210, 212, 217, 219, 221; IV: 436, 437, 441, 521-524, 552; V: 589.
Garland-Iverson-Johnston, (See also: Individual Listings), IV: 436, 521-524; V: 679.
Garnett's, (8th, 18th, 19th, 28th, 56th, Va.), II: 363, 364, 367; III: 172, 300; V: 101, 102, 103, 106, 107, 140, 142, 144, 148, 157, 588.
Gilham's, William, (6th Vols/16th NCST, 14th Ga.), IV: 142. }
Girarady's, [Girardey], (Ga.), V: 617.
Godwin's, (See also: Hoke's and Lewis'), I: 326; III: 279, 406, 418, 420, 421; IV: 436, 437, 525-526.
Gordon's, J.B., (Ga.), II: 241; III: 413; IV: 522, 602.
Gracie's, (Ala.), II: 7; III: 139, 357, 359, 373, 449, 520; IV: 439.
Gregg's, (S.C., Tx.), I: 744; II: 31, 35, 552, 553, 555, 557, 679, 683, 716, 717, 736; III: 619.
Grimes', (32nd, 43rd, 45th, 53rd, 2nd Battalion NCST; See also: Daniel's), I: 261; II: 62, 523, 531, 532, 533, 534, 536; III: 11; IV: 247, 258, 437, 441, 513-519; V: 247, 256, 260, 264, 494-502, 573.
Hagood's, [Haygood's], (S.C.), II: 5, 6, 11, 640, 650, 763, 764, 798; III: 135, 350, 357, 691; IV: 105, 312, 353, 489, 531, 541, 547; V: 199-200, 226, 240, 241.
Hampton's, (Hampton's Legion; 14th, 19th Ga.; 6th Vols./16th NCST; 4th Ark. Battalion), IV: 149, 155.
Hardy's, [Hardie's], (10th Battalion, 36th, 40th, 50th, 77th 7th Senior Reserves), III: 198; IV: 6, 101, 103, 104, 334, 440.
Harris's, (Miss.), II: 50, 51, 62.
Harrison's, (AoT, Cav), III: 678, 679; IV: 101.
Hatton's, (Tx.), I: 350, 352.
Hays', [Hayes], (La.), I: 313, 314, 316, 317, 319, 354, 355, 356, 357, 358, 382; II: 31, 139, 569; III: 73, 270, 272, 300, 413, 414, 415, 417, 584 IV: 658, 659; V: 606, 608.
Hebert's, (9th Battalion, 1st Hvy Art, 36th, 40th, and attached companies NCST), IV: 306, 439.

Henderson's, (AoT), III: 443.
Hill's, D.H., (N.C.), I: 121.
Hoke's, J.F., (73rd, 74th, 76th Senior Reserves), IV: 67, 98, 440; V: 5.
Hoke's, R.F., (6th, 21st, 54th, 57th, 1st Battalion NCST; See also: Godwin's, Lewis' and Trimble's), I: 121, 309, 310, 314, 316, 317, 318, 319, 320, 325, 335, 354, 355, 356, 357, 358, 382, 644; II: 36, 136, 138, 139, 140, 146, 248, 249, 284, 569, 616; III: 6, 7, 8, 11, 73, 132, 269, 272, 273, 274, 275, 291, 333, 337, 338, 341, 342, 400, 407, 410, 411, 413, 414, 415, 416, 417, 418, 419, 428, 584; IV: 237, 241, 436, 441, 486, 489, 525-526, 573, 602, 609, 658, 659, 680; V: 175, 177, 178, 180, 182, 183, 190, 191, 194, 197, 606, 608.
Hoke's, W.J., (81st, 82nd, 83rd Detailed Men), IV: 129, 133, 440.
Holmes', (N.C.), I: 137. 342.
Hood's, (Tx.), I: 304, 548, 567, 621; II: 26, 27, 48, 446, 602; IV: 152, 504.
Howard's (S.C.), I: 678.
Humphrey's (Miss.), I: 722.
Hunton's, (Va.), V: 204.
Iverson's, (5th, 12th, 20th 23rd NCST; See also: Garland's and Johnston's), I: 287, 628, 634, 635, 636, 637, 640, 644, 697; II: 94, 118, 119, 225, 227, 228, 229, 230, 231, 233, 235, 236, 237, 239, 240, 524; III: 41; IV: 253, 436, 52-524, 601, 703.
Iverson-Johnston, Robert D., (5th, 12th, 20th 23rd NCST), I: 640, 641, 642, 644, 646, 647, 648, 649, 650; II: 50, 119, 120, 122, 123, 124, 125, 231, 234, 239, 240, 241, 242, 243, 244, 245, 246, 247, 248, 249, 251, 252, 260, 261, 262, 263, 264, 267, 480, 571, 666, 716, 777; III: 48, 417, 421, 727; IV: 242, 436, 437, 438, 441, 521-524; V: 249, 259, 260, 264, 276.
Jackson's, Alfred E., (AoT), III: 520, 736, 742, 751; IV: 119, 121, 383, 399.
Jackson's, George, (7th, 8th, 9th Battalions Junior Reserves), IV: 29, 41, 108, 383, 398, 440, 589.
Jackson's, T.J., (aka Stonewall Brigade; See also: Baylor's, Garnett's, Grigsby's, Paxton's, J.A. Walker's and Winder's; 2nd, 4th, 5th, 27th, 33rd Va.), I: 341; II: 28, 68, 550, 551.
Johnson's, Bushrod, (Tenn.), I: 403; II: 287, 716; III: 138, 139, 311, 353, 360; IV: 489, 492.
Johnston's, R.D., (1st Battalion, 5th, 12th, 20th, 23rd NCST; See also: Garland's and Iverson's), III: 48, 422; VI: 242, 437, 521-524, 525, 602; V: 213, 215, 249, 259, 260, 261, 264, 503-510, 573.
Jones', John Marshall, (Va.), III: 43.
Junior Reserves, (Cmdrs.: F.S. Anderson, L.S. Baker, J.H. Nethercutt; 71st, 72nd, 73rd, Millard's Battalion Junior Reserves), IV: 4, 18, 19, 12, 20, 21, 22, 30, 31, 37, 53, 55, 56, 57, 58, 59, 302, 351, 393, 438, 439, 442, 547, 549, 583-596; V: 4, 269-284.
Kelly's, (AoT, 65th Ga., 5th Ky., 58th NCST, 63rd Va.), III: 439, 449, 451.
Kemper's, (1st, 3rd, 7th, 11th, 24th Va.), II: 363, 367; III: 132, 237, 300, 337, 351;

IV: 573; V: 101, 102, 103, 106, 107, 140, 142, 144, 147, 149, 151, 175, 177, 182, 184, 191.
Kemper-Corse-Terry's, (See: Individual Listings).
Kershaw's, (S.C.), I: 555; II: 434; III: 116; IV: 571; V: 199, 200.
Kirkland's, (See also: MacRae's, Martin's and Pettigrew's), I: 592, 593, 594, 597, 743, 744, 745, 746; II: 8, 10, 11, 12, 13, 45, 379, 382, 385, 440, 443, 445, 446, 802, 803; III: 26, 27, 28, 29, 30, 72, 73, 74, 77, 78, 92, 95, 118, 139, 199, 241, 242, 244, 246, 247, 687, 691, 698, 699; IV: 45, 49, 105, 270, 302, 436, 438, 440, 442, 506, 527-549, 555-568; V: 221, 241, 573.
Lane's, (7th, 18th, 28th, 33rd, 37th NCST; See also: Branch's), I: 121, 372, 373, 374, 375, 376, 378, 379, 380, 381, 382, 384, 385, 471, 543, 599, 664, 665, 668, 675, 676, 745, 747; II: 33, 34, 35, 36, 37, 38, 40, 41, 42, 43, 45, 48, 49, 50, 51, 52, 54, 55, 57, 58, 59, 61, 65, 71, 73, 74, 75, 76, 77, 173, 174, 178, 363, 364, 367, 388, 447, 448, 465, 476, 477, 478, 479, 480, 482, 483, 545, 555, 556, 559, 560, 561, 562, 563, 564, 566, 567, 568, 569, 571, 572, 573, 574, 575, 576, 588, 657, 659, 660, 661, 662, 663, 665, 666, 667, 668, 669, 670, 674, 686, 692, 693, 781; III: 30, 31, 97, 111, 249, 300, 331, 332, 333, 358, 367; IV: 175, 188, 194, 198, 199, 207, 208, 435, 438, 442, 465-475, 565, 566; V: xii, xiii, 93, 94, 95, 96, 97, 98, 101, 102, 107, 111, 124, 138, 139, 140, 144, 146, 147, 153, 154, 155, 156, 157, 158, 208, 209, 211, 212, 537-546, 573.
Laws', (6th, 21st, 54th, 57th NCST), I: 305, 309; III: 268, 291, 406; IV: 441; V: 122, 588.
Lawton's, (Ga.), II: 36; V: 588.
Ledbetter's, (AoT), II: 706.
Leventhorpe's, (N.C. Home Guard), IV: 650.
Lewis', (See also: Hoke's and Godwin's), I: 121, 550; II: 535; III: 11, 277, 279, 281, 282, 284, 349, 351, 400, 422, 424, 426; IV: 436, 438, 441, 455, 525-526; V: 260, 511-518, 573.
Liddell's, (AoT), II: 421.
Longstreet's, (Va.), I: 282.
Lowrance's, (See: Scales').
McElroy's, (N.C. Home Guard), IV: 650.
MacRae's, (11th, 26th, 44th, 47th, 52nd NCST; See also: Pettigrew's, and Kirkland's), I: 385, 471, 593, 594, 598, 599, 600, 601, 602, 747; II: 57, 174, 178, 220, 385, 387, 388, 390, 394, 411, 412, 414, 447, 448, 455, 480, 575, 588, 695, 781; III: 27, 29, 30, 31, 32, 33, 95, 97, 98, 111, 247, 249, 250, 252; IV: 184, 185, 436, 438, 442, 469, 555-568; V: xiii, 208, 209, 210, 211, 212, 529-536, 573.
Mahone's, (Va.), I: 384, 555, 603, 607, 608, 609, 739; II: 51, 56, 75, 299, 383, 572, 574, 666; III: 143, 144, 157; IV: 441; V: 211, 617.
Manigault's, (AoT), II: 711, 718, 719.
Manning's, (See also: Cooke's and Walker's), III: 166; IV: 502.
Marshall's, (See: Pettigrew's).
Martin's, (11th, 17th, 44th, 47th, 52nd NCST; 17th, 26th,

42nd, 50th, 66th NCST; 17th, 42nd, 50th, 66th NCST; 17th, 26th, 42nd, 56th, 61st NCST, See also: Pettigrew's, Kirkland's and MacRea's), I: 12; II: 3, 4, 5, 6, 8, 334, 601, 796, 797, 798; III: 132, 173, 226, 320, 349, 357, 690; IV: 270, 302, 436, 527-549, 555; V: 5.
McGowan's, (S.C.), I: 380, 666, 675, 744; II: 41, 51, 54, 60, 76, 455, 456, 561, 695; III: 30; IV: 198, 199, 466; V: 93, 96, 208, 211.
McNair's, (AoT), II: 712, 714, 716, 718, 719, 720, 730, 734, 736; IV: 438; V: 170.
Nethercutt's, (See: Junior Reserves).
Nicholls', (La.), I: 196.
O'Neal's, (Ala.), III: 41.
Palmer's, Joseph B., (AoT), III: 440, 441, 442, 443, 444, 454, 496, 527, 662; IV: 442.
Palmer's, John B., (AoT), III: 434, 448.
Paxton's, (aka Stonewall Brigade; 5th, 24th, 27th, 33rd Va.), I: 140, 147, 193, 194, 251; II: 232.
Pegram's, (Va.), II: 248, 249; III: 311; IV: 509; V: 260.
Pemberton's, (Miss.), I: 552, 709; IV: 441.
Pender's, (13th, 16th, 22nd, 34th, 38th NCST; See also: Scales'), I: 373, 613, 614, 633, 659, 663, 664, 665, 666, 667, 668, 670, 755, 759, 760, 765, 762; II: 29, 35, 42, 43, 168, 170, 230, 231, 555, 556, 582, 583, 584, 585, 586, 679, 680, 682, 683, 684, 685, 686, 687, 688, 689, 690, 691; III: 237; IV: 155, 161, 165, 167, 436, 437, 156, 159, 163, 164, 166, 169, 172, 174, 176, 422, 436, 467, 522, 551-554; V: 589, 590.
Perry's, (Fla.), II: 363, 364; V: 108, 109, 140.
Pettigrew's, (11th, 26th, 44th, 47th, 52nd NCST; See also: Kirkland's and MacRae's), I: 352, 543, 544, 588, 589, 590, 591, 592; II: 42, 43, 44, 167, 171, 344, 335, 336, 339, 340, 341, 343, 344, 346, 347, 348, 349, 352, 354, 357, 358, 361, 362, 363, 364, 365, 366, 367, 378, 399, 562, 563, 565, 566, 567, 601; III: 24, 26, 87, 88, 103, 105, 106, 109, 228, 232, 233, 235, 236, 237, 240, 241, 300, 321, 322, 416, 441; IV: 180, 252, 436, 555-568, 569; V: xiii, 101, 102, 104, 107, 111, 113-159, 601.
Pettus', (AoT), III: 441.
Pickett's, (Va.), I: 621.
Preston's, (AoT), III: 476, 478, 484, 486.
Pryor's, (Va.), III: 232.
Raines', [Rain's], (Ala., AoT), II: 204, 490, 708, 709, 728, 731; IV: 438.
Ramseur's, (aka Ironsides of the Army of Northern Virginia; 2nd, 4th, 14th, 30th NCST; See also: Anderson's and Cox's), I: 172, 250, 251, 253, 255, 256, 259, 260, 278, 325, 711, 714, 716, 719, 721, 722, 723, 724, 727; II: 50, 117, 232, 501, 500, 502, 503, 504, 524, 530, 531; III: 45, 48, 51, 53, 116; IV: 253, 435, 443-464, 603; V: 96, 247.
Ransom's, M.W., (24th, 25th, 35th, 49th, 56th NCST; See also: Robert Ransom's), I: 398, 399, 400, 402; II: 277, 282, 284, 285, 286, 287, 288,

289, 290, 299, 333, 334, 612, 613, 616, 617, 619, 620, 621, 622, 624, 625, 626, 799; III: 67, 138, 139, 140, 141, 142, 143, 144, 145, 156, 212, 276, 329, 330, 335, 336, 337, 338, 339, 340, 349, 351, 352, 353, 373, 375, 377, 378, 389, 390, 394, 396, 397, 400, 401; IV: 365, 435, 436, 438, 442, 448, 482, 486, 488, 490, 495, 569-579; V: 175, 177, 178, 179, 180, 184, 186, 187, 276, 321, 559-566, 573, 588, 589, 590.

Ransom's, Robert, (24th, 25th, 26th, 27th, 35th, 48th, 49th NCST; 24th, 25th, 35th, 49th, 56th NCST; See also: M.W. Ransom's), I: 12, 598, 742; II: 20, 273, 275, 276, 294, 295, 328, 331, 332, 412, 428, 431, 439, 440, 535, 544, 596, 598, 599, 600, 601, 602, 605, 608, 610, 612; III: 114, 115, 116, 127, 129, 130, 131, 132, 134, 135, 136, 322, 324, 328, 329; IV: 346, 436, 437, 502, 503, 505, 556, 569-579; V: 76, 77, 79.

Reynold's, A.W., (AoT; 5th Ky., 58th, 60th NCST, 55th, 63rd Va.), III: 436, 437, 438, 453, 476, 492.

Reynolds', (Ark.; Army of the Gulf), II: 710, 720, 727, 739, 742; III: 454, 476, 492; IV: 439.

Rhett's, (S.C.), III: 193, 194.

Ripley's, (1st, 3rd NCST, 4th, 44th Ga.), I: 138, 139, 141, 181, 184, 217, 218, 222, 223, 224, 225, 613, 614; IV: 441, 571; V: 589.

Rodes', (Va.), I: 283; II: 39, 204; IV: 447, 522.

Robertson's, (Tx.), I: 587; II: 438, 718, 776; III: 459, 461, 463, 551, 552, 562, 564, 569.

Sander's, (Ala.), III: 143; V: 617.

Scales', (13th, 16th, 22nd, 34th, 38th NCST; See also: Pender's), I: 380, 680, 685; II: 41, 42, 43, 44, 50, 60, 171, 173, 174, 176, 177, 225, 363, 364, 367, 455, 459, 562, 563, 565, 566, 567, 575, 586, 587, 588, 589, 661, 691, 692, 693, 695, 696, 697, 701; III: 30, 300, 367; IV: 175, 177, 180, 184, 185, 187, 189, 196, 199, 203, 206, 208, 210, 436, 438, 442, 551-554; V: 101, 102, 104, 107, 111, 124, 139, 140, 144, 146, 147, 150, 151, 156, 157, 158, 208, 547-558, 573.

Scott's, (Ga.), IV: 291, 301.

Semmes', (Ga.), I: 552, 553, 554.

Smith's, E. Kirby, (4th CSA), I: 341.

Smith's, T.A., (36th, 45th, 51st, 60th Va., 69th NCST), III: 746, 751, 752, 753; IV: 437, 439.

Smith's, Extra Billy, (Va.), I: 148, 347, 356; IV: 437, 439.

Steuart's, George H., [Stewart], [Stuart], I: 147, 194, 196, 200, 201, 202, 204; II: 49, 50; III: 396; IV: 435, 441.

Stovall's, [Stoval's], (AoT), III: 488, 489, 499; IV: 439; V: 172, 173.

Taliaferro's, (Va.), II: 472, 550, 551, 655.

Taylor's, (La.), IV: 228.

Terry's, (Va., See also: Kemper's), II: 616, III: 396.

Thomas', (Ga.), I: 380, 670, 671, 675, 676; II: 35, 41, 60, 61, 62, 75, 578, 683, 684, 685, 686, 691; III: 305; IV: 191, 196.

Toomb's, (Ga.), V: 79, 589.

Toon's, (5th, 12th, 20th, 23rd, 1st Battalion NCST; See also: Garland's, Iverson's and Johnston's), IV: 436, 523.
Trigg's, (AoT), III: 436.
Trimble's, (12th, 21st Ga.; 21st NCST, 1st Battalion NCST; 15th Ala.; 16th Miss.), I: 116; II: 39, 130, 133, 135, 151, 167; IV: 228, 230, 232, 233, 234, 235, 236, 441, 525; V: 128, 588.
Vance's, R.B., (AoT), II: 711.
Walker's, J.A., (Va.), I: 650; III: 72.
Walker's, J.G., (1st Ark., 1st, 3rd NCST, 13th Va.; 3rd Ark., 2nd Ga. Battalion, 27th, 46th, 48th NCST, 30th Va., Cooper's Battery; See also: Cooke's, Evans' and Walker's), I: 188, 217; II: 167, 428, 429, 438, 601; III: 66, 115, 116, 163; IV: 119, 437, 501, 502, 564, 570, 571; V: 588, 589.
Wallace's, (S.C.),II: 625; III: 145, 146, 147, 390, 396; IV: 576.
Walthall's, (AoT), II: 711; IV: 438.
Weisiger's, (Va.), II: 51; III: 374; V: 569.
Wharton's, (Va.), I: 384; II: 574; III: 741.
Whitford's, (67th & 68th NCST), III: 708, 709; IV: 312.
Whiting's, (6th NCST, 2nd, 11th Miss., 4th Ala.), I: 299, 303, 304, 350; II: 212; III: 291; IV: 441, 750.
Wickham's (Va.), I: 429, 607.
Wilcox's, (Ala.), II: 42, 363, 364, 562; V: 108, 109, 124, 128, 140.
Williams', John S., III: 740.
Wise's, (Va.), II: 6, 287, 621, 622; III: 212, 357, 360; IV: 86, 403, 457, 494, 529 530, 531, 534.
Wright's (Ga.), II: 57, 274, 363, 438; III: 143, 373; IV: 195, 504.
Brigades, (Federal):
[Note: In general one finds that in the Confederate armies a general officer remained with the same brigade unless wounded or transferred to a different army or department. In the Federal armies the colonels and brigadier-generals who commanded brigades seemingly switched commands nearly as often as did the commanders of the armies. For that reason the information attached to a commander's name may have been true for only one battle or one season.]
Abbott's, (6th & 7th Conn., 3rd & 7th N.H., 16th N.Y. Hvy Art.), II: 647; IV: 542; V: 238.
Ames' (4th, 6th, 30th, 39th U.S., Colored), II: 91; V: 238.
Amory's, III: 508.
Baxter's, (Robinson's Division, 1st Corps), I: 634, 638.
Beale's, I: 436.
Bell's, (4th N.H., 13th Ind., 115th & 169 N.Y.), V: 238.
Biddle's, (121st, 142nd, 151st Pa.; 80th N.Y.), II: 346, 347, 350, 354, 361.
Boynton's, III: 449.
Caldwell's (Douch's Division), II: 213.
Curtis', (3rd, 112th, 117th, 142nd N.Y.), II: 643; IV: 49; V: 237.
Cutler's, (56th Pa., 76th, 84th, 95th, 147th N.Y.), II: 345; III: 279.
First, (U.S. Regulars), III: 208.
Foster's, (23rd, 24th, 27th Mass.), II: 309, 318.
French's, (3rd Brigade, 1st Division, 2nd Corps), I: 616.

Gordon's, (3rd Brigade, 1st Division, 7th Corps), V: 77.
Gorman's, (1st Brigade, 2nd division, 2nd Corps), V: 76.
Griffin's, (2nd Brigade, 1st Division, 5th Corps), III: 373.
Hall's, V: 106, 142, 147, 151, 157.
Harrow's, V: 106, 142, 147, 150, 151, 157.
Kirby's, III: 527.
Martindale's (N.Y.), II: 470.
Meaghar's, (aka Iron Brigade: 19th Ind., 24th Mich., 2nd, 6th, 17th Wis.), I: 166, 167, 554, 616; II: 213, 344, 345, 346, 347, 348-349, 350, 351, 354, 361; III: 298; V: 118, 119, 613.
Meredith's, (Commanded the Iron Brigade; See: Meaghar's), V: 613.
Paine's, (Colored Brigade and Division), II: 10.
Parke's, (Part of Burnside's and Foster's command at New Bern), II: 308, 309, 311.
Paul's, (1st Brigade, 2nd Division, 1st Corps), I: 638.
Pennypacker's, (47th & 47th N.Y., 76th, 97th, 203rd Pa.), V: ?
Philadelphia, (and monument to), I: 166.
Putnam's, (7th N.H., 62nd & 67 Oh., 100th N.Y.), III: 208; V: 163.
Reno's, (21st Mass., 9th N.J., 51st Penn.), II: 308, 312, 317, 318.
Russell's, (of 5th Corps), III: 273.
Schimmelfennig's, I: 145, 192.
Seymour's, II: 120.
Sherman's, I: 346.
Sherrill's, V: 142.
Sickles', II: 213.
Smyth's, V: 107, 142.
Spear's, IV: 572.
Stannard's, (Vt.), II: 364; V: 106, 149.
Stevenson's, (Mass.), III: 208, 508.
Stone's, (143rd, 149th, 150th Pa.), II: 346, 347, 350, 361; III: 42.
Strong's, (3rd H.H., 6th & 7th Conn., 9th Ma., 48th N.Y., 54th Mass. Colored, 76th Pa.), V: 163.
Taylor's (N.J.), I: 370; II: 473, 551, 655; IV: 466.
Tyler's, (N.Y.), II: 5.
Upton's, (of 5th Corps), III: 273.
Van Derveer's, [Vandeveer], V: xi.
Vincent's, III: 565.
Webb's, V: 106, 107, 142, 143, 147, 148, 156, 157.
Wessell's, (Garrison at Plymouth), III: 508.
Willard's, (N.Y.), V: 105, 107, 111. Wright's, (1st, 5th, 10th, 27th, 37th U.S., Colored), II: 10; V: 238.
Brigades, Cavalry, IV: 436, 580-582.
Briggs, B.F., (Maj, 6th Vols/16th NCST), I: 751; III: 433, 447; IV: 137, 462, 463, 636, 644.
Briggs, B.F., (Lt, Co A, 55th NCST), III: 295, 307, 310.
Briggs, Dr. G.W., (Surg, 30th NCST; Surg, Anderson-Ramseur-Cox's Brigade), IV: 462, 463, 636, 644.
Briggs, P.M., (2nd Lt, Co A, 55th NCST), V: 520.
Briggs, Peter M., (2nd Lt, Co D, 40th NCST, 3rd Art., Hvy), II: 747.
Briggs, S.B., (Capt, Co C, 58th NCST), III: 433, 447.
Bright, John J., (Lt, Co C, 9th Battalion, 1st Hvy Art), IV: 303.
Briley, Elihu, (3rd Cpl, Co E, 55th NCST), V: 528.

Briley, W., (Pvt, Co B, 33rd NCST), V: 544.
Brincefield, G.H, (Pvt, Co K, 3rd Vols/13th NCST), V: 551.
Brinchfield, Stanlin, (Capt, Co G, 12th Vols/22nd NCST), II: 166.
Brindle, Daniel, (Pvt, Co I, 8th Vols/18th NCST), II: 64; V: 540.
Brindletown, N.C., IV: 218.
Bringle, John, (Pvt, Co D, 10th NCST, 1st Art & Engs, Reilly-Ramsay's Battery, Light Art), I: 574.
Brinkle, Thomas, (Sgt, Co D, 7th NCST), I: 378.
Brinkley, Henry, (Cpl, Co A, 11th Vols/21st NCST), V: 514.
Brinkley, James, (Pvt, Co F, 2nd NCST), I: 176; V: 486.
Brinkley, James, (Pvt, Co D, 68th NCST), III: 715.
Brinkley, William, (Cpl, Co E, 33rd NCST), II: 539
Brinkman, Thomas, (Pilot, Condor), V: 357.
Brinson, William N., (Pvt, Co A, 43rd NCST), III: 20; V: 497.
Brison, J.H., (Pvt, Co H, 13th Vols/23rd NCST), V: 510.
Bristoe Campaign, (1863), I: 149, 426, 544, 545, 546; II: 99; III: 416, 465, 536, 574-578.
Bristoe Station, Va., [Bristow], (and Battle of, 1863), I: 288, 299, 318, 334, 370, 382, 454, 592, 593, 720, 742; II: 30, 45, 87, 177, 178, 360, 372, 378-379, 381, 385, 401, 436, 478, 569, 587, 663, 773; III: 26, 42, 72, 79, 84, 92-94, 117, 118, 241-243, 244, 302, 417, 581;IV: 161, 184-186, 505, 536, 553, 562, 611, 662, 663; V: xiv, 672.
Bristol, George E., (Capt, Co E, 39th NCST), II: 705.
Bristol, Lambert A., (Capt, Co C, 8th Battalion Junior Reserves; Co G, 72nd NCST, 3rd Junior Reserves), IV: 42, 47, 53, 56, 595.
Bristol, Lambert A., Jr., IV: 595.
Bristol, Tenn., II: 486, 707; III: 524, 733, 738, 739, 744; IV: 117, 123, 273, 275, 374; V: 654.
Bristol, Va., III: 578; IV: 123, 401.
Bristol & Chattanooga Railroad, IV: 119.
British Road, (nr Wise's Fork), IV: 54, 55.
Britt, Frank J., (Sgt, Co B, 4th Vols/14th NCST), I: 731.
Britt, George, W., (Lt, Co C, 2nd NCST), I: 159.
Britt, J.P., (Pvt, Co C, 16th Battalion/75th NCST, 7th Cav), V: 660.
Britt, John, (2nd Lt, Co E, 68th NCST), III: 714.
Britt, Thomas A., (AQMS, 5th Vols/15th NCST), V: 520.
Brittain, Benjamin, (1st Lt, Co 2, Woodfin's Battalion; Co 8, 79th NCST, 8th Cav), IV: 111, 115.
Brittain, James, (Jr 2nd Lt, Co G, 6th Battalion/60th NCST), III: 474.
Brittain, M.L., (Maj., Cherokee Battalion Home Guard), IV: 652.
Brittle, J.T., (Pvt, Co D, 32nd NCST), V: 496.
Britton, S., (Pvt, Co D, 1st Vols/11th NCST), V: 530.
Britton, Henry T., (Pvt, Co A, 5th Vols/15th NCST), V: 520.
Britton, J., (Pvt, Co K, 35th NCST), V: 563.
Britton, Jesse T., (2nd Lt, Co C, Wheeler's 12th Battalion; Co H, 16th Battalion/75th NCST, 7th Cav), IV: 91, 339.
Britton, O.J., [Brittain], (2nd Lt, Co D, 1st Vols/11th NCST), I: 120, 584.
Broad River, S.C., III: 439.

Broad Run, Va., (aka Broad Run Station, Broad Run River), I: 427, 428, 458, 593; II: 130; III: 242, 582, 583.
Broadfoot, Charles W., (1st Lt, ADC to Holmes; Maj, 1st Battalion Junior Reserves; Lt Col, 70th NCST, 1st Junior Reserves), I: 117, 118; III: 681, 721; IV: 3, 5, 9, 11, 12, 16, 17, 23, 37, 53, 499, 587, 594; V: 650, 663.
Broadhurst, D.J., (Sgt Maj, 10th Vols/20th NCST), II: 112.
Broadhurst, Thomas W., (Sgt Maj, Co E, 10th Vols/20th NCST), II: 113.
Broadnax, Dr. J.G., (Surg, Wake Forest Wayside Hospital), IV: 627, 629.
Broadnax, John W., (Maj, Commissary, Robert Ransom's Brigade), IV: 569, 572.
Broadnax, Thomas W., (Maj, QM, Ransom's Brigade), 577.
Broadnax, W.E., (Lt, ADC to Robert Ransom), I: 486; IV: 569, 577.
Broadway Church, (nr Petersburg, Va.), IV: 86, 90.
Brock, ______, [James, Pvt, Co G], (33rd NCST), II: 579.
Brock, J.W., (2nd Lt, Co G, 46th NCST), III: 78, 81.
Brock, James V., (2nd Lt, Co E, 42nd NCST), II: 790, 806.
Brock Road, (Wilderness, Va.), II: 48, 446; III: 244; IV: 191, 193, 507; V: 97.
Brockenbrough, James Mercer, (Col, 40th Va., 2nd Reserves), II: 44, 341, 354, 561.
Brodie, E.G., (Sgt, Co K; Ordnance Sgt, 54th NCST), III: 268.
Bromley, C.R., [Ozni R.], (Capt, Co B, 10th Vols/20th NCST), IV: 721.
Bronze Book, (nr Gettysburg, Pa.), III: 300.
Brook, Thomas, (Cpl, Co D, 33rd NCST), II: 539.
Brook, Church, Va., (aka Meadow Bridge), I: 484; II: 25; III: 602, 603, 644; IV: 581.
Brook Turnpike, [Brooke], (nr Ashland, Va.), I: 366; II: 546; III: 596, 601.
Brook's Station, (nr Acquia Creek, Va.), I: 137, 179, 216; II: 164.
Brookfield, Jacob, I: 281.
Brookfield, Rayner, (Capt, Co C, 5th NCST), I: 288.
Brooklyn, N.Y., V: 439.
Brooks, George, (Pvt, Co D, 26th NCST), V: 531.
Brooks, Rev. H.E., (Chaplain, 2nd Battalion NCST), IV: 245, 601.
Brooks, James M., (1st Sgt, Color-bearer, Co E, 26th NCST), II: 366, 374.
Brooks, John, (Pvt, Co A, 1st Battalion NCST), V: 504.
Brooks, John S., (Lt Col, 10th Vols/20th NCST), II: 111, 112, 114, 117, 118, 121, 126, 242; V: 12.
Brooks, R.D., (Cpl, Co G, 30th NCST), V: 492.
Brooks, R.H., (Sgt, Co A, 10th NCST, 1st Art & Engs, Ramseur-Manly's Battery, Light Art), I: 553, 554, 558.
Brooks, Royal, (Jr 2nd Lt, Co H, 6th Battalion/60th NCST), III: 474.
Brooks, S.J., (Pvt, Co A, 1st Battalion NCST), V: 504.
Brooks, T.H., (1st Lt, Co D, 77th NCST, 7th Senior Reserves), IV: 100.
Brooks, T.J., (Capt, Co D, 41st NCST, 3rd Cav), I: 119; II: 770.
Brooks, Thomas J., (Capt, Co D, 41st NCST, 3rd Art, Hvy), II: 770.
Brooks, Terrell, (Maj, 76th NCST, 6th Senior Reserves), IV: 97.

Brooks, W.A., (2nd Lt, Co G, 30th NCST), II: 496.
Brooks, W.N., (Pvt, Co I, 56th NCST), III: 317.
Brooks, William, (Pvt, Co B, 34th NCST), V: 555.
Brooks, William F., (Capt, Co K, 36th NCST, 2nd Art & Engs, Hvy Art), V: 239.
Brooks, William N., (Pvt, Co I, 56th NCST), I: 772.
Brooks, William T., (Capt, Co K, 36th NCST, 2nd Art & Engs, Brunswick's Battery Hvy Art), II: 630, 635, 651.
Brookshire, Thomas, (Pvt, Co E, 6th Battalion/60th NCST), III: 482.
Brookshire, W.F., (ACS, 52nd NCST), III: 226.
Brookville, (Va.), I: 425.
Broom, H.A., (Pvt, Co B, 43rd NCST), V: 497.
Broom, J.P., (Pvt, Co F, 33rd NCST), V: 563.
Broom, S., (Pvt, Co B, 43rd NCST), V: 497.
Broughton, Gaston H., (Capt, Co D, 26th NCST), II: 371, 372, 380, 396, 397, 403, 419, 420; IV: 705; V: 152.
Brothers, J.W., (1st Lt, Co C & D, 67th NCST), IV: 722.
Brotherton, Hiram, (Pvt, Co H, 52nd NCST), V: 536.
Brotherton, William, (Pvt, Co G, 34th NCST), V: 556.
Brower, W.L., (Pvt, Co G, 46th NCST), V: 525.
Brower, Dr. William, (Ass't Surg, 8th Vols/18th NCST), IV: 473.
Brower, William H., (Pvt, Co C, 4th Vols/14th NCST), V: 490.
Brown, ______, (Col), III: 745.
Brown, A.D., (2nd Lt, Co C, Cumming's Battery, Starr's 13th Battalion NCST, Light Art), IV: 361; V: 569.
Brown, A.H., (2nd Lt, Co H, 31st NCST), II: 497; IV: 705, 723.
Brown, A.I., [A.J.], (2nd Lt, Co F, 64th NCST), IV: 705.
Brown, A.J., (Lt, Co F, 64th NCST), III: 660; IV: 705.
Brown, Adam, (Fayetteville and Harper's Ferry Arsenals), IV: 298.
Brown, Alexander H., (2nd Lt, Co H, 30th NCST), IV: 723.
Brown, Alfred J., (Sgt, Co F, 40th NCST, 3rd Art, Hvy), II: 765.
Brown, Alsa J., [Alsa E.], (Capt, Co C, 38th NCST), II: 675, 678, 686, 689, 690, 691, 692; IV: 705; V: 548.
Brown, B.A., (Sgt, Co I, 10th Vols/20th NCST), II: 120.
Brown, B.R., (Capt, Co A, 65th NCST, 6th Cav), III: 673, 675, 677, 678, 679, 680, 683; IV: 15, 16.
Brown, Barton F., [Barton R.], (Capt, Co F & A, 65th NCST, 6th Cav), III: 681.
Brown, Hon. Bedford, (Resident of Caswell County), I: 65.
Brown, Dr. Bedford, (2nd Lt, Surg, 14th Vols/24th NCST; Surg, 43rd NCST; Medical Director Smith's Division), II: 269; III: 1, 24; IV: 635, 638.
Brown, Calvin S., (Capt, Co D, 1st Vols/11th NCST), I: 78, 90, 91, 94, 95, 119, 584.
Brown, Campbell, (Capt, ADC to Rodes), IV: 449.
Brown, D., (Pvt, Co B, 44th NCST), V: 533.
Brown, D.F., (Lt, Co G, 62nd NCST), III: 516; IV: 705.
Brown, D.M., (Pvt, Co B, 30th NCST), V: 491.
Brown, Dave, (Negro servant to Col J.E. Brown), II: 797.

Brown, Dempsey S., (Lt, Co G, 2nd Battalion NCST), IV: 259; V: 494.
Brown, E.W., (Pvt, Co F, 54th NCST), V: 516.
Brown, Elbert, (Sgt, Co B, 25th NCST), V: 561.
Brown, Eli, (Pvt, Co G, 38th NCST), V: 557.
Brown, Frank, (Pvt, Courier, Co H, 63rd NCST, 5th Cav), III: 600, 601, 639, 640, 642, 647, 651. 652, 653.
Brown, G.L., (Capt, Co G, 3rd Vols/13th NCST), V: 547.
Brown, G.W., (Pvt, Co G, 3rd Vols/13th NCST), V: 550.
Brown, George H., (2nd Cpl, Co A, 52nd NCST), III: 2, 223.
Brown, H., (Pvt, Co D, 33rd NCST), V: 544.
Brown, H., (Pvt, Co E, 30th NCST), V: 492.
Brown, Hamton A., (Col, 1st NCST and 1st & 3rd Consolidated), I: 134, 136, 140, 146, 149, 155, 156, 182, 193, 203, 209, 219, 372, 450, 459; IV: 372, 450, 459; V: 595.
Brown, Henry, (Pvt, Co D, 6th NCST), V: 512.
Brown, Hezekiah, (2nd Lt, Co C,, 43rd NCST), III: 2, 3; V: 194.
Brown, I.W., (Capt, Co I, 47th NCST), III: 85.
Brown, J., (Pvt, Co A, 28th NCST), V: 540.
Brown, J.A., (Pvt, Co B, Starr's Battery; Starr's 13th Battalion NCST, Light Art), IV: 349.
Brown, J.A.C., (Capt, Co L, 12th Vols/22nd NCST), II: 165, 166.
Brown, J.D., (Lt, Co C, 37th NCST), II: 668, 670.
Brown, J.F., (Pvt, Co D, 56th NCST), III: 380.
Brown, J.H, (Pvt, Co A, 1st Battalion NCST), V: 504.
Brown, J.H., (Sgt, Co I, 8th Vols/18th NCST), II: 64.
Brown, J.J., (Pvt, Co B, 16th Battalion/75th NCST, 7th Cav), V: 660.
Brown, J.M., (Lt, Co E, 2nd Vols/12th NCST), I: 621.
Brown, J.S.W., (Pvt, Co E, 55th NCST), V: 528.
Brown, J.W., (Capt, Co I, 47th NCST), III: 108.
Brown, J.W., (Musician, 3rd Vols/13th NCST), V: 549.
Brown, J.W., (Pvt, Co F, 37th NCST; Detailed, Invalid Battalion), V: 571.
Brown, Jack, (Col, 59th Ga.), II: 88.
Brown, James, (Ensign, USN), V: 243.
Brown, James D., (Pvt, Co A, 43rd NCST), III: 20; V: 497.
Brown, Jesse, (Pvt, Co E, 43rd NCST), V: 498.
Brown, Jesse, (Pvt, Co D, 56th NCST), III: 355.
Brown, John, (Abolitionist, Terrorist, Murderer), II: 342; IV: 177.
Brown, John B., (Capt, AIG, Cox's Brigade), IV: 463; V: 483.
Brown, John Calvin, (Maj Gen), I: 63; III: 438.
Brown, John Edmunds, (Col, 42nd NCST), I: 361, 365; II: 3, 789, 792, 739, 794, 795, 796, 797, 801, 804-805; IV: 472, 527, 538, 539; V: 15.
Brown, John Kent, (Lt, Engineering Officer), IV: 418.
Brown, John S., (Pvt, Co. B, 55th NCST), V: 527.
Brown, Jones, (at Battle of Fort Hamby), V: 290, 291, 292, 294, 295.
Brown, Joseph Emerson, (Governor of Georgia), III: 179, 180.

Brown, Julian S., (Pvt, Co A, 6th NCST), V: 511.
Brown, LaFayette W., [N.], (Pvt, Co A, 43rd NCST; Detailed, 2nd Corps Provost Guard), III: 20; V: 570.
Brown, Lawson, (Lt, Co K, 57th NCST), III: 409.
Brown, Merrill W., (2nd Sgt, Co A, 38th NCST), V: 556.
Brown, Murray S., (Pvt, Co A, 65th NCST, 6th Cav), III: 680.
Brown, Nathaniel L., (Lt, Co C, 47th NCST), III: 84; IV: 702, 705.
Brown, Owen N., (Maj, 37th NCST), I: 379; II: 661, 674; IV: 468, 474; V: 12.
Brown, P.P., (Col, 157th N.Y.), IV: 717.
Brown, Peter M., (Pvt, Co B, 27th NCST), II: 461; V: 523.
Brown, R.B., (Lt, Co D, 9th NCST, 1st Cav), I: 485.
Brown, R.D., (1st Lt, Co G, 4th NCST), I: 233.
Brown, R.G, (Sgt, Co E, 2nd Vols/12th NCST), V: 507.
Brown, R.H., (Lt, Co A, 6th Vols/16th NCST, 39th NCST), I: 768.
Brown, Robert C., (Capt, Co B, 44th NCST), III: 22.
Brown, Robert W., (Pvt, Co A, 35th NCST), V: 193.
Brown, S.J., (1st Lt, Co F & A, 65th NCST, 6th Cav), III: 673.
Brown, T.L., (Cpl, Co B, 33rd NCST), V: 543.
Brown, Thomas E., (Lt, Adjt, Millard's 9th/20th Battalion Junior Reserves), IV: 386, 392.
Brown, Thomas J., (Maj, 42nd NCST), I: 231, 269, 271; II: 789, 790, 791, 794, 800, 805, 807; III: 538.
Brown, Thomas W., (Capt, Co A, 8th Vols/18th NCST), II: 20.
Brown, Van, (Capt, Co A, 2nd Battalion NCST), IV: 245, 256.
Brown, Dr. W.C., (Surg, 42nd NCST), II: 789, 805; IV: 638.
Brown, W.D., (Cpl, Co D, 57th NCST), V: 517.
Brown, W.H., (Lt, Co C, 9th Battalion NCST, 1st Hvy Art), IV: 303, 306.
Brown, W.H., (Pvt, Co B, 2nd Vols/12th NCST), V: 506.
Brown, W.H., (Pvt, Co H, 41st NCST, 3rd Cav), V: 658.
Brown, W.L., (2nd Sgt, Co C, 55th NCST), V: 527.
Brown, W.L., (Pvt, Co B, 56th NCST), III: 366.
Brown, Dr. W.M., (Surg, N.C.), IV: 629.
Brown, W.P., (Capt, Co B, 82nd NCST), IV: 131.
Brown, William, (2nd Lt, Co K, 4th NCST), I: 231, 234.
Brown, William C., (2nd Lt, Co E, 69th NCST, Thomas' Legion), III: 730.
Brown, William E., (Pvt, Co E, 30th NCST; Detailed, 2nd Corps Provost Guard), V: 491, 570.
Brown, William H., (2nd Lt, Co D, 29th NCST), II: 485.
Brown, William S., (Capt, Co B, 57th NCST), III: 405.
Brown, Wilson, (Pvt, Co G, 27th NCST), II: 462; V: 523.
Brown, Dr. Wyatt M., (Surg, 7th Vols/17th NCST), II: 1; IV: 634.
Brown's Gap, Va., II: 116; III: 421.
Brown Mountain, N.C., IV: 372.
Browne, London, (Lt, Co E, 14th Vols/24th NCST), II: 276.
Browning, W., (Pvt, Co C, 6th NCST), V: 512.
Brownlow, William G., "Parson," (Editor of the "Knoxville Whig," perpetual political wannabe and

radical scalawag in the truest meanings of the term. His so-called narrative, Parson Brownlow's Book, stands as a prime examples of Radical propaganda. Its inaccuracies and intentional lies have been foisted upon the general public as history in a near criminal manner by alleged historians and purveyors of the false Lincoln myth. The lies of his book, just as the lies of his radical rag, have done immeasurable harm throughtout the ages.) III: 733, 734.
Bruce, James, (Pvt, Co E, 3rd NCST), V: 487.
Bruel, J.J., (Pvt, Co I, 53rd NCST; Detailed, Invalid Battalion), V: 571.
Brumley, O.K., [O.R.], (Capt, Co B, 10th Vols/20th NCST), IV: 705.
Bruner, ______, (Resident of N.C.), I: 278.
Brushy Mountains, N.C., V: 286, 288, 289.
Brunswick, N.C., II: 631.
Brunswick County, N.C., II: 111, 127; IV: 303.
Brunswick River, N.C., IV: 428.
Bryan, A.S., (Pvt, Co H, 48th NCST), V: 527.
Bryan, A.T., (Pvt, Co H, 5th Vols/15th NCST), V: 522.
Bryan, Billie, (Pvt, Co I, 2nd NCST), I: 163.
Bryan, Charles L., (1st Lt, Co K, 40th NCST, 3rd Art, Hvy), II: 746.
Bryan, Cornelius, (Pvt, Co I, 4th Vols/14th NCST), V: 491.
Bryan, D.O., (Capt, Co I, 9th Vols/19th NCST, 2nd Cav), II: 80, 89.
Bryan, Edward K., (Lt, Adjt, 31st NCST), I: 163; II: 511, 518, 519, 520; V: 167.
Bryan, Frederick D., (Sharpshooters, 10th Vols/20th NCST), II: 125.
Bryan, George Pettigrew, (Capt, Co G, 9th Vols/19th NCST, 2nd Cav), I: 435; II: 80, 89, 96, 104; IV: 705.
Bryan, George W., (2nd Lt, Co D, Adam's Battery; 1st Lt, Co F, Latham-Potts-Flanner's Battery, Starr's 13th Battalion NCST, Light Art), IV: 353, 354.
Bryan, James, (2nd Lt, Co H, 41st NCST, 3rd Cav), II: 771.
Bryan, Hon. James, I: 15.
Bryan, James A., (Capt, Ordnance Officer, Lane's Brigade), I: 59; II: 594; IV: 472.
Bryan, Jesse L., (Capt, Co I, 9th Vols/19th NCST, 2nd Cav), II: 80.
Bryan, John G., (Capt, Co G.; Maj, 37th NCST), II: 653; IV: 474.
Bryan, John H.P., (Pvt, Co B, 33rd NCST), II: 544.
Bryan, John W., (Capt, Co A, 47th NCST), III: 84.
Bryan, Johnson H., (Lt, Co H, 9th NCST, 1st Cav), I: 486.
Bryan, Joseph B., (2nd Lt, Co D, Adam's Battery, Starr's 13th Battalion NCST, Light Art), IV: 353.
Bryan, Joseph O., (Pvt, Co G, 32nd NCST), V: 496.
Bryan, S.H., (2nd Lt, Co D, 31st NCST), II: 512.
Bryan's Barn, (nr Gettysburg, Pa.), V: 103, 106, 108, 110, 111.
Bryant, J.H, (Sgt, Co I, 30th NCST), V: 493.
Bryant, John G., II: 653.
Bryant, L., (Pvt, Co K, 4th NCST), V: 489.
Bryant, Ruffin L., (Capt, Co D, 31st NCST), II: 507, 512.
Bryant, S.A., (Pvt, Co C, 55th NCST), V: 527.

Bryce, John Y., (Capt, Co K, 42nd NCST), II: 791, 807.
Bryce, John Y., (Capt, Co E, 59th NCST, 4th Cav), III: 457; V: 88.
Bryce, William, (2nd Lt, Co E, 59th NCST, 4th Cav), III: 457; V: 663. 664.
Bryce's Creek, [Brice's], (nr New Bern), II: 311, 322, 325, 329, 594.
Bryson, ______, (Ensign, Co K, 39th NCST), II: 739.
Bryson, A.W., (Lt, Co A, 6th Vols/16th NCST), I: 758.
Bryson, J.N., (1st Lt, Co A, Walker's Battalion, Thomas' Legion; 80th NCST), IV: 117.
Bryson, John G., (Maj, 37th NCST), II: 653.
Bryson, Samuel, C., (Lt Col, 25th NCST), II: 292, 294, 297.
Bryson, Thaddeus D., (Capt, Co B, 25th NCST), II: 292, 301.
Bryson, W.H., (1st Lt, Co E, 62nd NCST), III: 516; IV: 705.
Bryson, W.H., (Lt, AQM, 25th NCST), II: 291.
Bryson, Walter M., (Capt, Co G, 35th NCST), II: 605; III: 516; V: 76.
Bryson City, N.C., (aka Deep Creek), III: 750, 757, 758.
Buchan, George C., (Capt, Co G, 40th NCST, 3rd Art, Hvy), II: 746, 756, 760; V: 240.
Buchanan, George W., (Pvt, Co E, 12th Vols/22nd NCST), V: 553.
Buck Tails, (3rd Reg, 3rd Div, 1st Corps, Army of the Potomac, USA), IV: 236.
Buckittsville, Va., I: 421.
Buckland, Va., I: 427, 457, 458.
"Buckland Races," (Battle of, 1863), I: 428, 454, 457, 459; III: 582, 584, 617.
Buckner, ______, [James T., Co B, 63rd Ga.], (Capt, Ga., Art), V: 162.
Buckner, E., (Pvt, Co G, 26th NCST), V: 532.
Buckner, Simon Bulivar, (Lt Gen), III: 435.
Buckner, Taylor, (2nd Lt, Co 7, 79th NCST, 8th Cav), IV: 115.
Buckstarf, A., (Pvt, 7th Vols/17th NCST), V: 39.
Bucktown, Md., (aka Bucket Town, Buckeytown), I: 573; II: 431; III: 67.
Buell, Don Carlos, (Maj Gen, USA), II: 709, 710.
Budd, Dr. A.V., (Ass't Surg, 32nd NCST), IV: 637.
Buena Vista, (Battle in Mexican War), I: 103.
Buenos Ayres, Brazil, V: 346.
Buff, H., (Pvt, Co C, 10th NCST, 1st Art & Engs, Brem-Graham-Williams' Battery, Light Art), V: 567.
Buffalo Gap, Va., IV: 139.
Buffalo Springs, Va., IV: 618.
"Buffaloes," (Deserters and draft doggers from Confederate and Federal forces, outlaws, and other assorted dregs of society who formed into bands to murder, rob and terrorize mainly civilians in eastern and western sections of North Carolina.) II: 793, 794; III: 176, 705, 721; IV: 16, 348; V: 374, 630.
Buford, John, (Maj Gen, USA), I: 423, 451, 481, 633; II: 91, 93, 344; III: 236, 572, 573, 574, 576; V: 117.
Bufford's Bridge, (Salkehatchie River, S.C.), III: 189; IV: 103.
Bufford's Gap, Va., [Buford's], I: 205, 324; III: 12.
Buford's Still, Va., III: 277.
Buhmaun, Beaman G.W., (Lt, Co D, 41st NCST, 3rd Cav), I: 120, 128.
Buie, Bailey, (Hospital Steward, 56th NCST), V: 565.

Buie, James D., (Capt, Co G, 6th Battalion Fayetteville Armory Guard), IV: 297, 620.
Buie, Neil M., (Hospital Steward, 41st NCST, 3rd Cav), II: 769.
Bule, S.T., (Pvt, Co K, 8th Vols/18th NCST), II: 64.
Bule, Neil M., (Hospital Steward, 41st NCST, 3rd Cav), II: 769.
Bull's Gap, Tenn., III: 664, 665, 740, 756.
Bull Run, (aka Manassas, Va., Battle of, 1862; See also: Manassas), I: 306; II: 30, 31, 154, 682; III: 582; IV: 226, 227.
Bull Run Creek, Va., (and Bull Run Swamps), I: 223, 299, 341, 348, 370, 739; II: 30, 31, 130, 192, 193, 473, 551, 584, 655, 683, 684; III: 581, 582; IV: 161, 163, 466.
Bull Run Gap, Va., IV: 227.
Bull Run Mountains, Va., IV: 227; V: 676.
Bulla, Calvin, (Capt, Cmdr, Fayetteville Arsenal, USA), IV: 295.
Bullaboa, Lorenzo, (Pvt, Co D, 10th NCST, 1st Art & Engs, Reilly-Ramsay's Battery, Light Art), I: 577.
Bullard, A., (Pvt, Co D, 35th NCST), V: 562.
Bullard, Davis S., (2nd Lt, Co A, 8th Vols/18th NCST), IV: 723.
Bullard, Elisha, [Elisa], (Pvt, Co. C, 10th Vols/20th NCST), II: 114.
Bullard, J.D., (Cpl, Co H, 43rd NCST), V: 499.
Bullard, J.W., (Pvt, Co C, 10th Vols/20th NCST), V: 508.
Bullard, W.W., (Pvt, Co F, 8th Vols/18th NCST), II: 64.
Bullen, B.H., (Pvt, Co G, 53rd NCST), V: 502.
Bullen's Creek, (nr New Bern), II: 309, 310, 314, 321.
Bullerson, ______, (Lt, Co D, 56th NCST), III: 348.
Bullock, ______, (Capt, CSN, Agent to Europe), V: 386.
Bullock, B.F., (Capt, Co D, 13th Vols/23rd NCST), II: 184, 185.
Bullock, George B., (Lt, 10th Vols/20th NCST; Capt, Co I, 13th Vols/23rd NCST; AAG, Johnston's Brigade), II: 121, 187; V: 503.
Bullock, George Burns, (Lt, Co I, 13th Vols/23rd NCST), II: 187, 231, 238, 244.
Bullock, J.B., (Pvt, Co D, 3rd NCST), V: 487.
Bullock, J.E., (Pvt, Co E, 55th NCST), V: 528.
Bullock, James D., (Capt, CSN, Agent to Europe), V: 414, 415, 416.
Bullock, John T., (1st Lt, Co. E, 13th Vols/23rd NCST), II: 185; IV: 722.
Bullock, R.H., [R.A.], (ACS, 2nd Vols/12th NCST), I: 606, 651.
Bullock, Riley, (Pvt, Co, B, 33rd NCST), II: 544.
Bullock, W.A., (Lt, Co E, 51st NCST), III: 219.
Bullock, Walter, (Lt, Drill Master, Camp Vance), IV: 42.
Bullock, William J., (Capt, Co A, 55th NCST), III: 287.
Bumgarner, A., (Pvt, Co C, 28th NCST), V: 541.
Bumgarner, W.P., (Pvt, Co H, 58th NCST), III: 453.
Bunch, J.J., (Pvt, Co C, 47th NCST), V: 534.
Bunch, Nehemiah, (2nd Lt, Co F, 68th NCST), III: 714.
Buncombe County, N.C., II: 493, 704, 722, 723, 741; III: 432, 473,

499, 516, 665, 683; IV: 109, 110, 113, 115, 386, 481; V: 655.
Bundront, Joel, (Pvt, Co A, 2nd Battalion NCST), V: 494.
Bunford, W.B., (Lt, 10th Vols/20th NCST) IV: 705.
Bunker Hill, Va., (and Battles of), I: 154, 189, 207, 261, 373, 579, 591, 645, 663, 672, 761, 762, 766; II: 34, 116, 224, 377, 399, 437; III: 14, 92, 110, 241, 751, 753; IV: 167, 183, 229.
Bunn, B.H., (Lt, Co A, 47th NCST), III: 84; V: 667.
Bunn, Elias, (Adjt, 2nd Vols/12th NCST), I: 609; V: 667.
Bunn, J.H., (Pvt, Co I, 30th NCST), V: 493.
Bunn, J.H., (Pvt, Co I, 30th NCST), V: 493.
Bunn, William F., (Pvt, Co D, 10th NCST, 1st Art & Engs, Reilly-Ramsay's Battery, Light Art), V: 568.
Bunting, D.E., (2nd Lt, Co I, 10th NCST, 1st Art & Engs, Sutherland's Battery, Light Art), IV: 221.
Bunting, Gray, (Pvt, Co B, 44th NCST), V: 533.
Bunting, J.B., (Jr 2nd Lt, Co B, 66th NCST), III: 686.
Bunting, Samuel R., (Capt, Co I, 10th NCST, 1st Art & Engs, Sutherland's Battery, Light Art), IV: 221.
Bunting, William, (Pvt, Co E, 43rd NCST), V: 498.
Burch, ______, (Lt, 25th NCST), II: 299.
Burch, A.J., (1st Cpl, Co C, 3rd Vols/13th NCST), V: 550.
Burch, J.J., (Pvt, Co K, 33rd NCST), V: 545.
Burch, James A., (Capt, Co A, 50th NCST), III: 202, 203.
Burch, W.R., (Pvt, Co K, 46th NCST), V: 525.
Burchett, J., (Pvt, Co D, 33rd NCST), V: 544.
Burchett, Jackson, (Pvt, Co H, 11th Vols/21st NCST), V: 515.
Burdett, W., (Master, USN, Pioneer, Mohican), V: 244.
Bureau of Pensions and Records, IV: 65-66.
Burgaw, N.C., I: 742; II: 439.
Burgess, Edward, (Pvt, Detached Co, 68th NCST), III: 724.
Burgess, Edward W., (ACS, 33rd NCST), II: 537.
Burgess, Hardy, (Pvt, Co F, 30th NCST), V: 492.
Burgess, James P., (3rd Sgt, Co D, 6th Vols/16th NCST), V: 552.
Burgess, Joseph J., [Joseph I.], (Sutler, 27th NCST), II: 463; V: 522.
Burgess, Terrill, (Pvt, Co K, 7th NCST), V: 539.
Burgess Mills, Va., (and Battle of, 1864, aka Hatcher's Run, Burgess Mill pond, Burgess house), I: 328, 334, 601, 682; II: 389, 390, 411, 420, 421, 449, 450, 533; III: 31, 32, 78, 98, 112, 145, 249-251, 310, 396, 466, 472, 627, 628, 629, 632, 678, 683, 724; IV: 88, 90, 93, 566, 576, 621.
Burgin, Alney, (Capt, Co K, 12th Vols/22nd NCST), II: 162, 163, 165, 166.
Burgin, Charles H., (Capt, Co K, 12th Vols/22nd NCST), II: 165, 166.
Burgin, Elisha, (2nd Lt, Co A, Walker's Battalion, Thomas' Legion; 80th NCST), IV: 118.
Burgin, J.B., (Lt, Co K, 12th Vols/22nd NCST), II: 166.
Burgin, John A., (2nd Lt, Co K, 1st Vols/11th NCST), I: 120, 585.

Burgin, John M., (2nd Lt, Co K, 12th Vols/22nd NCST), II: 166; IV: 723.
Burgin, John W., (2nd Lt, Co K, 1st Vols/11th NCST), I: 120, 585.
Burgin, Samuel D., (ACS, Millard's 9th/20th Battalion Junior Reserves), IV: 386.
Burgoyne, ______, (Englishman, Capt, Royal Navy, Blockade Runner), V: 413.
Burgwyn, Henry King, Sr., (Father of Col Burgwyn), II: 405, 406, 407, 408.
Burgwyn, Mrs. Henry King, Sr., (Anna Greenough, Mother of Col Burgwyn), II: 405, 406.
Burgwyn, Henry K., Jr., (Col, 26th NCST), I: 126, 589; II: 304, 305, 306, 307, 310, 321, 322, 324, 325, 328, 329, 330, 335, 336, 338, 339, 342, 343, 350, 351, 352, 353, 358, 368, 371, 372, 374, 380, 395, 397, 399, 403, 404, 405-408, 410, 411, 418, 593, 607; III: 319; IV: 138, 555; V: 10, 111, 120, 133, 601, 650.
Burgwyn, William H.S., (Capt, AAG, Clingman's Brigade), II: 423, 605, 606, 608, 610, 613, 614, 628; IV: 481, 482, 486, 493, 497, 569, 579; V: 205.
Burke, ______, (Historian), V: 475.
Burke, James E., (Color-bearer, Pvt, Co I, 32nd NCST), II: 535; V: 497.
Burke, James P., (2nd Lt, Co B, 4th NCST), I: 232, 269.
Burke, Joseph K., (Maj, 74th NCST, 5th Senior Reserves), IV: 69.
Burke's Station, Va., I: 422; II: 193.
Burke County, N.C., II: 573, 771; III: 480; IV: 218, 271, 372, 374, 376, 382, 595, 604; V: 474.
Burkeville, Va., (aka Burkeville Junction, Burkeville Station), I: 330, 432; II: 62, 784; III: 396, 400, 401, 611, 653; IV: 90, 206, 454.
Burkesville, Ky., IV: 618.
Burkhart, George, (Fayetteville and Harper's Ferry Arsenals), IV: 298.
Burkhart, Joseph, (Fayetteville and Harper's Ferry Arsenals), IV: 298.
Burkhart, Phillip, (Master Armorer, Fayetteville and Harper's Ferry Arsenals), IV: 297, 298.
Burkhart, Phillip, Jr., (Fayetteville and Harper's Ferry Arsenals), IV: 298.
Burkhead, Burwell W., (1st Lt, Co I, 12th Vols/22nd NCST), II: 166, 172.
Burkhead, J.A., (Pvt, Co B, 57th NCST), V: 517.
Burkhead, William A., (Sgt, Co B, 4th NCST), I: 232.
Burleyson, A., (Pvt, Co D, 28th NCST), V: 542.
Burleyson, Jesse M., (Capt, Co K, 25th NCST), II: 293; III: 348.
Burlington, N.C., (aka Company Shops), I: 294, 338.
Burlington, N.J., II: 405.
Burnet, J.A., (2nd Lt, Co I, 62nd NCST), III: 516.
Burnett, James H., (Pvt, Co G, 5th Vols/15th NCST), V: 522.
Burnett, Orlander, (Pvt, Co A, 10th NCST, 1st Art & Engs, Ramseur-Manly's Battery, Light Art), I: 557.
Burnett, Thomas S., (1st Lt, Co H, 53rd NCST), III: 263, 514.
Burney, William C., (Cpl, Co H, 27th NCST), II: 402; V: 524.
Burney Place, N.C., III: 174, 175.
Burns, J.A., (Capt, Co G, 12th Vols/22nd NCST), II: 163, 166.

Burns, J.H., (Lt, Co E, 6th NCST), I: 345, 354.
Burns, James, (Pvt, Co C, 10th NCST, 1st Art & Engs, Brem-Graham-Williams' Battery, Light Art), V: 568.
Burns, M., (Pvt, Co I, 12th Vols/22nd NCST), V: 554.
Burnside, Ambrose E., (Maj Gen and Burnside's Army, USA), I: 9, 11, 12, 164, 168, 179, 216, 309, 310, 371, 372, 373, 384, 420, 422, 490, 491, 503, 508, 509, 510, 623, 628, 664, 665, 696, 760, 762, 763; II: 33, 34, 36, 81, 83, 84, 85, 86, 117, 169, 226, 228, 308, 309, 318, 327, 329, 497, 504, 541, 542, 553, 558, 564, 572, 593, 594, 609, 610, 656, 657, 686; III: 69, 83, 373, 374, 521, 522, 523, 736, 737, 738, 739, 740, 743; IV: 87, 93, 119, 123, 125, 126, 169, 171, 203, 236, 237, 245, 251, 262, 263, 325, 414, 448, 482, 552, 572; V: viii, 68, 79.
Burnside's Bridge, (aka Stone bridge nr Sharpsburg, Md.), II: 169, 220; V: 74, 79, 80.
Burnside's Mud March, I: 310.
Burnside's Negro Soldiers, II: 288.
Burnsville, N.C., IV: 123, 271, 651; V: 7.
Burr, James G., (Col, 7th Home Guard), I: 56, 59; IV: 650, 652; V: 359.
Burress, Wiley, (Pvt, Co E, 43rd NCST), V: 498.
Burris, James, (Owner of property nr Carolina Beach that was the site of Camp Wyatt), II: 17.
Burrougs, ______, (Maj, Cav), III: 163.
Burroughs, ______, [William A.], (Cpl, Co G, 30th NCST), IV: 602.
Burroughs, ______, (Capt, Cornubia), V: 406, 407.
Burroughs, W.H.H., (Musician, Co G, 27th NCST), II: 462; V: 523.
Burrows, E., (2nd Lt, Co H, 1st NCST), I: 137.
Burrows, John A., (Pvt, Co G, 13th Vols/23rd NCST), V: 510.
Burruss, E.T., (Pilot, Let Her Be), V: 357.
Burruss, J.N., (Pilot, Hansa), V: 357.
Burruss, George, (Pilot, Hebe), V: 357.
Burruss, T.J., (Pilot, Let Her Be), V: 357.
Burruss, Thomas, (Pilot, Banshee), V: 357.
Burt, James G., (Pvt, Co A, 2nd NCST), I: 175; V: 486.
Burt, W.P, (1st Sgt, Co D, 26th NCST), V: 531.
Burton, ______, (Passenger, Advance), V: 341, 343.
Burton, Andrew J., (Lt, Adjt, 72nd NCST, 3rd Junior Reserves), IV: 51.
Burton, Augustus W., (Maj, 2nd Vols/12th NCST), I: 606, 607; III: 19.
Burton, D.P., (Pvt, Co F, 3rd Vols/13th NCST), V: 550.
Burton, J.A, (4th Sgt, Co C, 3rd Vols/13th NCST), V: 550.
Burton, J.B., (Pvt, Co G, 12th Vols/22nd NCST), V: 554.
Burton, J.C., (Pvt, Co K, 30th NCST),V: 493.
Burton, J.H., (2nd Sgt, Co D, 3rd Vols/13th NCST), V: 550.
Burton, J.F., (2nd Lt, Co H, 45th NCST), IV: 705.
Burton, J.W., (Pvt, Co B, 1st NCST), V: 485.
Burton, James T., (3rd Lt, Co K, 6th NCST), IV: 701, 702.
Burton, John, (Pvt, Co B, 59th NCST, 4th Cav), V: 659.

Burton, John L., (Cpl, Co F, 4th NCST), I: 233.
Burton, N.E., (Pvt, Co F, 3rd Vols/13th NCST), V: 550.
Burton's Theater, (N.Y., N.Y.), V: 444.
Burwell, John B., (Capt, AQM, 53rd NCST), III: 261.
Burwell, P.L., (Capt, Co E, 50th NCST), III: 202.
Burwell, R.B., (QM Sgt, 53rd NCST), III: 261.
Burwell, Robert T., (2nd Lt, Co B, 43rd NCST), III: 2, 3; V: 664.
Burwell, W.R., (Pvt, Co B, 43rd NCST), III: 18; V: 497.
Burwell's Bay, Va., I: 709.
Busbee, Charles M., (Sgt Maj, 5th NCST), I: 289, 291; IV: 723; V: 504, 619, 625 personal account.
Busbee, Fabius H., (2nd Lt, Co B, 8th Battalion Junior Reserves; Co E, 72nd NCST, 3rd Junior Reserves), I: vi; IV: 42, 583.
Busbee, William J., (Ass't Surg, 31st NCST), II: 507, 511; IV: 636.
Bush, J.A., (2nd Lt, Co I, 26th NCST), V: 529.
Bush Hill, N.C., (now Archdale), I: 413; II: 519, 520; III: 217, 218, 219, 700; IV: 22, 32, 62, 328, 394.
Bushall, William J., (2nd Lt, Co H, 10th NCST, 1st Art & Engs, Pool's Hvy Art), I: 525.
Bushwackers, (and Bushwacking; See also: G.W. Kirk and Kirk's Command), II: 708; III: 664-669, 677, 718; IV: 113, 272, 276, 288, 380, 381, 382.
Busick, Andrew J., (1st Lt, Co E, 12th Vols/22nd NCST), II: 166, 172, 178; V: 548.
Butler, ______, [William], (Col, 1st S.C.), III: 193.
Butler, Benjamin Franklin, (Maj Gen and Butlers: Army, Command and Fleet, USA), I: 52, 81, 82, 83, 86, 87, 88, 89, 92, 96, 98, 102, 103, 106, 107, 108, 109, 117, 496, 528, 691; II: 1, 4, 9, 285, 286, 440, 516, 519, 520, 619, 620, 637, 778, 797; III: 9, 135, 137, 139, 211, 212, 215, 275, 336, 350, 354, 355, 357, 359, 390, 419, 512, 603, 694; IV: 45, 46, 47, 49, 50, 85, 210, 254, 297, 307, 361, 367, 391, 424, 491, 495, 529, 530, 531, 538, 540, 572, 573, 575, 590, 591; V: 16, 51, 52, 53, 54, 220, 221, 222, 236, 237, 301, 302, 396.
Butler, Benjamin L., (Sgt, Co C, 30th NCST; Detailed, 2nd Corps Provost Guard), V: 491, 569.
Butler, C., (Pvt, Co D, 1st Vols/11th NCST), V: 530.
Butler, E., (Pvt, Co D, 1st Vols/11th NCST; Detailed, Invalid Battalion), V: 571.
Butler, H.A., (Adjt, 3rd Ark.; Adjt, Manning's Brigade), IV: 503.
Butler, H.A., (AAG, Cooke's Brigade), V: 519.
Butler, Haywood, (Pvt, Co C, 38th NCST), V: 557.
Butler, J.M., (Pvt, Co D, 1st Vols/11th NCST), V: 530.
Butler, Matthew Calbraith (Maj Gen), I: 421, 424, 775; III: 621, 630; IV: 150.
Butler, R.R., (Scalawag, Congressman, Tenn.), III: 734.
Butler, Ransom, (4th Cpl, Co A, 10th NCST, 1st Art & Engs, Ramseur-Manly's Battery, Light Art), I: 551.
Butler, Rees H., (Fayetteville and Harper's Ferry Arsenals), IV: 298.

Butler, T.A., (Capt, Co K, 69th NCST, Thomas' Legion), III: 731, 744.
Butler, Thomas, (Capt, 69th NCST), III: 760.
Butler, W.F., (Pvt, Co D, 1st NCST), V: 485.
Butler, W.H., (4th Sgt, Co D, 1st Vols/11th NCST), V: 530.
Butler's Bridge, (nr Sharpsburg, Md.), III: 235, 720; IV: 16.
Butler's Bridge, (nr Hamilton), III: 681, 720, 721; IV: 16-17.
Butler's Powder Ship, IV: 539; V: 220.
Butler's Tower, (nr Bermuda Hundred, Va.), I: 559.
Butner, A.B., (Pvt, Co B, 1st Battalion NCST), V: 504.
Butner, E.J., (Capt, Co. D, 57th NCST), III: 409.
Butner, Francis A., [F.M.], (AQMS, 33rd NCST), II: 537; V: 543.
Butner, Will N., (Musician, 33rd NCST), II: 537; V: 543.
Butt, Dr. H.F., (Surg, 32nd NCST), IV: 637.
Butterfield, Daniel, (Maj Gen, Hooker's Chief of Staff, USA), I: 695; III: 560, 561.
Button, P.C., (Pvt, Co K, 54th NCST; Detailed, Invalid Battalion), V: 571.
Buxton, S.N., (Capt, Co H, 9th Vols/19th NCST, 2nd Cav), II: 89, 98.
Buzzard Bay, N.C., II: 756.
Byars, J.S., (2nd Lt, Co C, 5th Vols/15th NCST), I: 734.
Byerly, G., (Pvt, Co B, 49th NCST), V: 564.
Byers, Augustus, (Pvt, Co A, 4th NCST), I: 258, 271.
Byers, John H., (Pvt, Co A, 25th NCST), V: 561.
Byers, Joseph R., (1st Lt, Co H, 25th NCST), V: 559.
Bynum, James, (Pvt, Co H, 52nd NCST), V: 536.
Bynum, Dr. Joseph A., (Surg, 44th NCST), III: 22; IV: 638.
Bynum, Joseph F., (Pvt, Co G, 32nd NCST; Detailed, 2nd Corps Provost Guard), V: 570.
Bynum, Lewis, (2nd Lt, Co D, 66th NCST), III: 686.
Bynum, William Preston, (Lt Col, 2nd NCST), I: 157; II: 117.
Byrd, C.R., (Lt, Co G, 58th NCST), III: 433, 435.
Byrd, David S., (2nd Lt, Co H, 50th NCST; Capt, Co A, 7th Battalion Junior Reserves; Co H, 72nd NCST, 3rd Junior Reserves), III: 203; IV: 40, 52.
Byrd, P., (Pvt, Co H, 37th NCST), V: 546.
Byrd, S.D., (Lt Col, 72nd Battalion Home Guard), IV: 650.
Byrd, Rev. S.M., (Chaplain, 41st NCST, 3rd Cav), II: 769; IV: 614.
Byrd, W.J., (2nd Lt, Co C, 6th Vols/16th NCST), IV: 705.
Byrd, William S., (Capt, Co E, 61st NCST), III: 504.
Byrne, M.A., (Capt, Co H, 8th Vols/18th NCST), II: 20.

(C)

Cabarrus County, N.C., I: 498, 533; II: 111, 113, 126; III: 406, 408, 411, 427, 457, 545, 626; IV: 132, 483, 595, 609.
Cabell, Henry Coalter, (Col, Cabell's Battalion, Art; Chief of Art McLaw's Division), I: 553, 554, 556.
Cabiness, H.D., (1st Lt, AQM, 5th Vols/15th NCST), I: 734.
Cabiness, Joseph B., [Cabaness], (Lt, Co D, 55th NCST), III: 296; IV: 706.
Cabiness, T.P., (Pvt, Co F, 56th NCST), III: 348.
Cable, David F., (Resident of Ohio), III: 387.
Caddell, Edward B., (Pvt, Co D, 49th NCST), V: 564.
Caffey, W.F., (Lt, Co I, 8th NCST), I: 402.
Cagle, George, (Pvt, Co F, 2nd Battalion NCST), V: 495.
Cagle, M., (Sgt, Co B, 56th NCST), III: 366.
Cahill, John C., (Pvt, Co F, 63rd NCST, 5th Cav), III: 588, 589, 651, 654.
Cahill, T.J., (Capt, Co D, 7th NCST), I: 380; IV: 706.
Caho, Joseph M., (Hospital Steward, 2nd NCST), I: 160.
Caho, W.T., (4th Sgt, Co C, 68th NCST), III: 725, 726, 727.
Cahoon, ______, (Capt, Co E, 7th Vols/17th NCST), V: 40, 41, 42, 48, 680.
Cahoon, Thomas, (Capt, Co E, 7th NCST), III: 314.
Cain, D.J., (1st Lt, Co G, 4th NCST), I: 233, 272.
Cain, James F., (1st Lt, Co E, Cameron's Battery, Starr's Battalion NCST, Light Art), IV: 353.
Cain, L.D., (2nd Lt, Co C, 30th NCST), II: 496.
Cain, S.H., (Pvt, Co D, 53rd NCST), V: 501.
Cain, S.S., (Pvt, Co E, 44th NCST), V: 533.
Cain, William, (Cadet Capt, Co A, Hilliboro Military Academy Battalion), V: 637, 641, 643.
Calder, E.S., (Lt, 1st Battalion NCST, Hvy Art; AAG, Nethercutt's Brigade), IV: 5.
Calder, J.A., (Pvt, Co F, 8th Vols/18th NCST), II: 64; V: 539.
Calder, Robert E., (Adjt, 30th N.C. Militia; Lt, Co B, 2nd NCST), I: 158, 159; V: 25, 26.
Calder, William, (AQM, 30th N.C. Militia; Lt, Adjt, 1st Battalion NCST, Hvy Art; AAG, Nethercutt's Brigade), I: 164; IV: 5, 306, 313, 591; V: 25.
Caldwell, ______, [Samuel P.], (Lt, Co D, 9th NCST, 1st Cav), I: 485.
Caldwell, C.H.B., (Cmdr, USN), V: 243.
Caldwell, Denson A., (Pvt, Co F, 63rd NCST, 5th Cav), III: 555, 654.

Caldwell, J.A., (2nd Lt, Co K, 13th Vols/23rd NCST), II: 188; IV: 706.
Caldwell, J.E., (2nd Lt, Co B, 82nd NCST), IV: 131.
Caldwell, J.F., (Sgt, Co G, 52nd NCST), V: 536.
Caldwell, J.L., (Pvt, Co E, 32nd NCST), V: 496.
Caldwell, John, (2nd Lt, Co E, 33rd NCST), II: 539, 578; V: 640.
Caldwell, John Curtis, (Maj Gen, USA), II: 213; III: 580.
Caldwell, Dr. Julius A., (Ass't Surg, 6th NCST), IV: 632; V: 30.
Caldwell, Moses F., (1st Cpl, Co G, 52nd NCST), III: 224.
Caldwell, R. Baxter, (Pvt, Co F, 63rd NCST, 5th Cav), III: 555, 570, 654.
Caldwell, Robert M., (Sgt, Co H, 7th NCST), I: 378.
Caldwell, Dr. T.C., (Ass't Surg, Vols/23rd NCST), II: 190; IV: 635.
Caldwell, T.R., (Governor, N.C.), V: 640.
Caldwell County, N.C., II: 163, 303, 330, 358, 359, 410, 411, 417, 628; III: 432, 447, 683; IV: 54, 218, 372, 373, 375, 619; V: 285, 286, 287, 292.
Calf Pasture River, (nr Cheat Mountain, Va.), IV: 139.
Calhoun, John C., (Col, 4th S.C., Cav), II: 18.
Calhoun, W.J., (Sgt, Co B, 33rd NCST), V: 543.
Calhoun, Ga., II: 741.
Calicut, A., (Pvt, Co D, 5th Vols/15th NCST), V: 521.
California, I: 113; II: 416; III: 405; IV: 608.
Call, P.C., (Sgt, Co B, 1st NCST), V: 485.
Call, W.H., (Sgt, Co D, 16th Battalion/75th NCST, 7th Cav), V: 660.
Call, W.H., (Sgt, Co G; Ordnance Sgt, 16th Battalion/75th NCST, 7th Cav), IV: 72, 93.
Callahan, David, (Capt, Co D, 78th NCST, 8th Senior Reserves), IV: 107.
Callahan, John D., (Capt, Co G, 33rd NCST), II: 540, 562, 578; IV: 467.
Callahan, Robert S., (Pvt, Co G, 6th Vols/16th NCST), IV: 216; V: 552.
Callais, William J., (Capt, Co G, 33rd NCST), II: 540, 578, 678; V: 538.
Callis, John B., (Brig Gen, USA), V: 611-616.
Calloway, Abner S., (Lt Col, 55th NCST), III: 287, 288.
Callum, Archibald, (Pvt, Co H, 3rd NCST), V: 487.
Calton, Benjamin, (26th NCST), V: 474.
Calton, Thomas, (Resident of Burke County), V: 474, 475.
Calvert, S.J., (Capt, 56th NCST), IV: 706.
Calvin, Thomas R., (Musician, 8th Vols/18th NCST), V: 539.
Camden County, N.C., III: 318, 335, 366, 456, 713, 717.
Cameron, John W., (Maj, N.C. Quatermaster Department), I: 23.
Cameron, T.H., (1st Lt, CSMC), V: 572.
Cameron, Willian, (Capt, Co E, Camerson's Battery, Starr's 13th Battalion NCST, Light Art), IV: 341, 353.
Camm, ______, (Midshipman, NCN, Executive Officer, Ellis), V: 306, 310.
Camp, A., (Pvt, Co D, 2nd Vols/12th NCST), V: 507.

Camp, C., (Sgt, Co K, 2nd Vols/12th NCST), V: 508.
Camp, David C., (Lt, Co G, 41st NCST, 3rd Cav), II: 785.
Camp, J.C., (Capt, Co K, 6th Vols/16th NCST), IV: 137, 141, 216.
Camp, John C., (Pvt, Co G, 6th Vols/16th NCST), V: 552.
Camp, Jospeh A., (1st Lt, Co H, 34th NCST), IV: 701, 706.
Camp, L.A., (Pvt, Co G, 49th NCST), V: 564.
Campaign of 1864, III: 591.
Campaign of 1865, III: 637.
Campaigns of Stuart's Cavlery, The, II: 94.
Campaigns with Grant, II: 49.
Campbell, ______, (Southern, traitor at Fort Delaware, Md. who became a Federal Lieutenant), IV: 729.
Campbell, A., (Pvt, Co D, 48th NCST), V: 526.
Campbell, A.N., (Sgt, Co H, 63rd NCST, 5th Cav), III: 601.
Campbell, Amos A., (Musician, 10th Vols/20th NCST), II: 113.
Campbell, D., (Pvt, Co I, 32nd NCST), V: 497.
Campbell, D.A., (Lt, USN), V: 243.
Campbell, Ezekiel, (Pvt, Co F, 4th Vols/14th NCST), V: 490.
Campbell, E. Mansfield, (Lt, Co A, 7th NCST), I: 377; IV: 467.
Campbell, Frank, (Pvt, Co F, Drum Corps, 42nd NCST), V: 15.
Campbell, Freisan, (Pvt, Co H, 4th NCST), V: 489.
Campbell, G.W., (Pvt, Co H, 30th NCST), V: 493.
Campbell, H.H., (Capt, Co G, 53rd NCST), III: 263.
Campbell, J.A., (Ass't Sec of War, CSA), III: 386.
Campbell, J.B., (Pvt, Co K, 2nd Vols/12th NCST), V: 508.
Campbell, John C., (Pvt, Co H, 38th NCST), V: 558.
Campbell, M., (Pvt, Co I, 72nd NCST, 3rd Junior Reserves), IV: 590.
Campbell, Reuben P., (Col, 7th NCST), I: 361, 362, 363, 365, 367, 368, 472, 538; II: 23, 310, 313, 317, 327, 471, 542, 547, 654; IV: 472; V: 9.
Campbell, T.R., (Pvt, Co I, 56th NCST), III: 348.
Campbell, W.F., (1st Lt, Co G, 53rd NCST), III: 263, 265.
Campbell, Dr. Wesley M., (Surg, 7th NCST; Surg, Branch-Lane's Brigade), I: 361, 362; IV: 405, 472, 632, 644.
Campbell, William H., (Pvt, Co G, Color-bearer, 27th NCST), II: 436.
Campbell, William H., (Orderly Sgt, 35th NCST), II: 608, 621.
Campbell County, Va., IV: 218.
Campbell Court House, Va., IV: 215; V: 265.
Campe, J.W., (Pvt, Co I, 56th NCST), III: 357.
Camps, Confederate:
  Camp Advance, (nr Weldon), I: 500, 502; II: 753.
  Camp Alamance, (nr Company Shops-now Burlington),
  Camp Arrington, (nr Sewell's Point Battery, Va.), I: 607, 608.
  Camp Ashe, (nr Old Topsail Sound), I: 392; IV: 484.
  Camp Baker, (nr Hamilton), IV: 15, 16, 17.
  Camp Beauregard, (nr Ridgeway), I: 417.
  Camp Bee, (nr Burwell's Bay, Va.), I: 709.
  Camp Black Jack, (nr Moseley Hall-now LaGrange), III: 226.

Camp Bragg, (nr Suffolk, Va.), I: 709.
Camp Branch, (nr Fredericksburg, Va.), II: 687.
Camp Burgwyn, (Roanoke Island), I: 388, 389.
Camp Campbell, (nr Drewry's Bluff, Va.), III: 227.
Camp Campbell, (nr Kinston), I: 391.
Camp Canal, (nr Carolina City - now Morehead City), II: 751.
Camp Caroline, (Ward's Farm nr Norfolk, Va.), I: 607.
Camp Clingman, (nr Asheville), IV: 376, 386.
Camp Collier, (nr Goldsboro), III: 605. Camp Crab Tree, (Camp of Instruction nr Raleigh), II: 303, 304.
Camp Daniel, (nr Weldon on the property of John M. Moody), IV: 10, 14.
Camp Davis, (nr Masonboro Sound), I: 586; IV: 39, 42, 99, 103.
Camp Devil's Misery Hole, (nr Pocataligo, S.C.), III: 70.
Camp Ellis, (nr Manassas, Va.), II: 192.
Camp Ellis, (nr Suffolk, Va.), I: 709.
Camp Fayetteville, (nr Cocklestown, Va.), I: 112, 114, 129.
Camp Fisher, (High Point), II: 466, 581.
Camp Fisher, (nr Dumfries, Va.), I: 349, 552.
Camp Floyd, (nr Weldon), II: 677.
Camp French, (nr Petersburg, Va.), III: 227, 228.
Camp Goldsboro, (Base Camp of 10th NCST, 1st Art. & Engs.), I: 511.
Camp Gregg, (nr Guinea Station, Va.), I: 666, 696; II: 72, 73, 74, 687; IV: 171, 174, 175.
Camp Gregg, (nr Moss Neck, Va.), II: 477.
Camp Hill, (nr Weldon), I: 164, 230, 234, 563.
Camp Hill, (nr Asheville), II: 705, 727.
Camp Hill, (nr Petersburg, Va.), III: 210.
Camp Holmes, (nr Raleigh), IV: 9, 10, 25, 38, 42, 102.
Camp Holmes, (Va.), II: 289.
Camp Hopkins, (nr Wilmington),
Camp Hurricane, (nr Brandon, Miss.), III: 486.
Camp Johnston, (nr Kinston), III: 226, 227.
Camp Lamb, (New Hanover County), II: 759; III: 215, 322, 505; IV: 40, 388, 391, 392.
Camp Lee, (nr Richmond, at Fair Grounds), III: 329; IV: 264.
Camp Leventhorpe, (nr Garysburg), II: 677.
Camp Macon, (nr Warrenton), I: 387, 388; IV: 482.
Camp Mangum, (nr Raleigh), I: 9, 11, 13, 23, 41, 79, 125, 390, 391, 583, 586, 772; II: 2, 495, 511, 513, 541, 591, 592, 593, 596, 598, 675; III: 1, 19, 21, 35, 64, 66, 85, 113, 114, 161, 199, 223, 226, 260, 267, 287, 313, 317, 318; IV: 3, 138, 243, 483; V: 643.
Camp Marshall, (nr Orange Court House, Va.), III: 244.
Camp Mason, (Alamance County), I: 361.
Camp Mason, (nr Goldsboro), II: 677.
Camp McLean, (nr Goldsboro), IV: 50, 51, 52.

Camp Patton, (nr Asheville), II: 291, 485, 486. 704, 705; IV: 110, 386.
Camp Pickens, (nr Manassas, Va.), I: 563.
Camp Radcliff, (nr Smithville), III: 505.
Camp Rains, (nr Cocklestown, Va.), I: 114.
Camp Ransom, (nr Weldon), IV: 10.
Camp Rattlesnake, (Pensacola Bay, Fla.), II: 737, 738.
Camp Robinson, Dick, (Ky.), II: 730.
Camp Stephens, (Hufuenin's Farm, S.C.), II: 18.
Camp Vance, (nr Sulphur Springs), II: 485; IV: 42.
Camp Vance, (nr Goldsboro), II: 677.
Camp Vance, (nr Morganton), II: 677; IV: 41, 42, 387.
Camp Whiting, (nr Wilmington), I: 391, 409; IV: 103, 484, 497.
Camp Wigfall, (nr Manassas Junction, Va.), II: 191.
Camp Woodfin, (nr Asheville, III: 669; IV: 110.
Camp Wyatt, (nr Fort Fisher), I: 165; II: 17, 497, 754; IV: 48, 416.
Camp at New Bern Fair Grounds, I: 362, 363.
Camp of Instruction, (nr Asheville, See: Camp Patton).
Camp of Instruction, (at Company Shops), I: 294.
Camp of Instruction, (nr Garysburg), I: 164, 215, 216, 605, 653; IV: 73, 629.
Camp of Instruction, (nr Halifax), I: 281.
Camp of Instruction, (nr Kitrell's Springs), II: 79; III: 433.
Camp of Instruction, (nr Manassas, Va.), I: 563.
Camp of Instruction, (nr Morganton), IV: 3, 588.
Camp of Instruction, (nr Murfreesboro), IV: 365.
Camp of Instruction, (nr Raleigh, See: Camp Mangum).
Camp of Instruction, (nr Warm Springs), III: 474.
Camp of Instruction, (nr Warrenton), I: 388.
Camp of Instruction, (nr Weldon), I: 500; II: 188, 269.
Camp of Instruction, (nr Wilmington), IV: 3.
Camps, Federal:
Camp Chase, (Federal Prison, Ohio), II: 724; III: 664; IV: 132, 400, 440.
Camp Douglass, (Federal Prison Camp), III: 525, 663.
Camp Live Oak, (Chicamacomico), V: 56.
Canada, III: 37; IV: 691, 741.
Canady, Joshua, (Pvt, Co I, 24th NCST), V: 193.
Canady, William P., (Lt, Co G, 10th NCST, 1st Art & Engs, Pool's Hvy Art), I: 525.
Candler, C.N., (Capt, Co C, 64th NCST), III: 662, 665.
Candler, Thomas J., (Capt, Co D, 6th Battalion/60th NCST), III: 473, 475, 488.
Candler, William G., (1st Lt, Co D, 6th Battalion/60th NCST), III: 474.
Candler, Zachariah M., (2nd Lt, Co C, 64th NCST), IV: 702.
Cane Creek Factory, N.C., IV: 102.
Cane Creek Mountain, N.C., IV: 102.
Canipe, F., (Pvt, Co C, 10th NCST, 1st Art & Engs, Brem-Graham-Williams' Battery, Light Art), V: 568.

Canipe, John A., (Pvt, Co F, 55th NCST), V: 528.
Canipe, John C., (Pvt, Co F, 34th NCST), V: 555.
Cannady, A.L., (Pvt, Co D, 1st NCST), V: 485.
Cannady, Evans A., (Cpl, Co G, 33rd NCST), II: 540.
Cannady, Dr. Isaac G., (Ass't Surg, 55th NCST), III: 288; IV: 604; V: 520.
Cannady, John P., (2nd Sgt, Co K, 55th NCST), V: 528.
Cannady, W.E., [Cannaday], (AAG, Branch-Lane's Brigade), IV: 472.
Cannon, James C., (Capt, Co F, 57th NCST), III: 405, 409.
Cansler, James, (Capt, Co C, 65th NCST, 6th Cav), III: 675, 684.
Cansler, M.S., (3rd Cpl, Co C, 10th NCST, 1st Art & Engs, Brem-Graham-Williams' Battery, Light Art), V: 567.
Canton, Miss., II: 734; III: 485.
Canton, N.C., (aka Locust Old Field), III: 757.
Cantrell, F.P., (Pvt, Co E, 25th NCST), V: 561.
Cantwell, Edward, (Lt Col, 2nd Vols/12th NCST), I: 606; III: 19.
Cantwell, Edward, (Lt Col, 59th NCST, 4th Cav), III: 467; IV: 706.
Cantwell, John L., (Col, 13th N.C. Militia; Col, 30th N.C. Militia; Col, 51st NCST), III: 205, 218, 456, 467; IV: 361, 483, 645, 718, 719, 721; V: 23, 25, 26, 27, 28, 664.
Cape Charles, V: 440.
Cape Canavoral, Fla., V: 382, 383, 411.
Cape Fear, N.C., (Bar, Lighthouse, Region, River, etc.), I: 428; II: 9, 18, 518, 631, 635, 639, 640, 643, 745, 749, 750, 751, 752, 753, 754, 755, 756, 759, 761, 768, 772, 802; III: 4, 193, 215, 681, 726; IV: 39, 43, 45, 47, 49, 104, 267, 303, 304, 305, 307, 308, 309, 310, 311, 312, 317, 318, 319, 326, 327, 330, 331, 343, 344, 361, 413, 418, 421, 423, 426, 427, 428, 429, 430, 484; V: 6, 23, 28, 217, 218, 220, 225, 226, 235, 356, 362, 363, 364, 367, 368, 369, 374, 382, 392, 396, 397, 399, 402, 405, 406, 407, 413, 422, 424, 425, 426, 433, 434, 437, 438, 439, 440, 442.
Cape Fear & Yadkin Valley Railroad, III: 536.
Cape Henry, Va., II: 752; V: 339.
Cape Lookout, N.C., V: 343, 407.
Cape Lookout Lighthouse, N.C., III: 705; V: 336, 362, 365.
Cape Romain, (S.C.), IV: 714.
Cape of Good Hope, V: 416.
Capehart, B.A., (Capt, AQM, Wynn's 15th Battalion NCST, Cav), IV: 365, 366-369.
Capehart, Cadmus, (2nd Lt, Co K, 68th NCST), III: 714.
Capehart, Henry, (Maj Gen, USA), III: 644.
Capehart, Thomas, (Capt, Co D, 3rd Battalion NCST, Moore's, Light Art), I: 110, 119, 133; IV: 264.
Capehart, Dr. W.R., (Surg, Poague's Battalion, Light Art), V: 567.
Capel, Thomas R., (3rd Sgt, Co E, 52nd NCST), III: 224.
Capell, R.W., (Capt, Co E, 38th NCST), II: 676, 677.
Capetown, South Africa, V: 347.
Capps, Henry, (Pvt, Co K, 6th NCST), V: 194.
Captain Bell's School, (Rutherfordtown), IV: 212.
Capture Before the War, V: 23-28, 438, 439, 440, 441, 445.
Carawan, William R., (2nd Lt, Co H, 33rd NCST), II: 540, 578.

Caraway, Zack B., (Sgt, Co I, 4th NCST), I: 234.
Carden, S.L., (Pvt, Co H, 56th NCST), III: 357, 730, 744.
Cardenas, Cuba, III: 714.
Cardon, J., (Pvt, Co A, 33rd NCST), V: 543.
Carland, E., (Pvt, Co G, 56th NCST), V: 566.
Carland, Felix C., (Pvt, Co H, 25th NCST), V: 561.
Carlile, P.A., (Pvt, Co G, 6th NCST), V: 513.
Carlin, E., (Pvt, Co G, 56th NCST), III: 348.
Carlisle, Pa., (aka Carlisle Barracks), I: 148, 195, 425, 632, 633, 636, 718; II: 97, 233, 234, 502, 525, 526, 527; III: 5, 41, 256, 463; IV: 238, 255, 514, 601; V: 115.
Carlton, _____, (Capt, 10th NCST, 1st Art & Engs), I: 556.
Carlton, A., (Pvt, Co I, 6th NCST), V: 513.
Carlton, Charles, (5th Sgt, Co F, 52nd NCST), III: 224.
Carlton, F.D., [F.A.], (Sgt Maj, 4th NCST; 1st Lt, Co A, 4th NCST), I: 230, 231, 269; V: 665.
Carlton, P.C., (Lt, Co A, 7th NCST), I: 378, 382, 385; V: 665, 666.
Carmack, Alexander R., (Sgt Maj, 69th NCST, Thomas' Legion), III: 730, 733, 744.
Carmady, James M., (Barrington's Co, Whitford's 11th Battalion, Hvy Art; Co B, 67th NCST), V: 18.
Carmer, John R., (Capt, Co I, 3rd NCST), I: 179, 228.
Carmichael, Abner R., (Maj, 26th NCST), II: 303, 305, 306, 311, 314, 315, 316, 317, 322, 323, 329, 395, 396, 397, 595; V: 12.
Carmichael, William W., (2nd Lt, Co F, 52nd NCST), III: 224.
Carnes, James, (1st Lt, Co D, Walker's Battalion, Thomas' Legion; 80th NCST), IV: 118.
Carney, A.S., (Pvt, Co G, 10th Vols/20th NCST), II: 120.
Carolina Beach, N.C., I: 410; III: 215, 693; V: 358.
Carolina Central Railroad, V: 401.
Carolina City, N.C., (now Morehead City), I: 362, 363, 489, 490, 503; II: 306, 307, 308.
Caroline County, Va., I: 460, 554.
Carpenter, _____, [Pinkney D., Pvt., Co G], (Color-bearer, 6th Vols/16th NCST), IV: 191.
Carpenter, A., (Pvt, Co D, 28th NCST), V: 541.
Carpenter, Benjamin F., (Sgt, Co E, 34th NCST), V: 555.
Carpenter, C., (Pvt, Co B, 28th NCST), V: 541.
Carpenter, Elbert, (Pvt, Co D, 61st NCST), III: 508.
Carpenter, Hezekiah B., (Pvt, Co C, 4th Vols/14th NCST), V: 490.
Carpenter, J., (Pvt, Co D, 61st NCST), III: 507.
Carpenter, J.P., (Sgt, Co G, 57th NCST), V: 517.
Carpenter, K.J., (Sgt, Co I, 50th NCST), III: 189, 203.
Carpenter, M., (Pvt, Co B, 28th NCST), V: 541.
Carpenter, Philip W., (Capt, Co G, 57th NCST), III: 424.
Carpenter, R., (Sgt, Co K, 1st NCST), V: 485.
Carpenter, W.R., (Pvt, Co E, 4th NCST), V: 488.
Carpenter, Wyatt, (Pvt, Co D, 61st NCST), III: 507.
Carr, _____, (Col, 2nd N.Y., Cav), I: 88, 89, 97.
Carr, Albert S., (Sgt, Co E, 27th NCST), II: 462; V: 523.
Carr, D.C., (Pvt, Co E, 43rd NCST), V: 498.

Carr, Elias, (Governor of North Carolina), II: 714; V: 169.
Carr, J.C., (2nd Lt, Co E, 30th NCST), II: 496.
Carr, Julian S., (Pvt, Co K, 41st NCST, 3rd Cav; Cmdr. N.C. U.C.V.), II: 786; III: 635; IV: 581, 582.
Carr, O.W., (Capt, Co G, 46th NCST), III: 81.
Carr, Robert B., (1st Lt., Co A, 43rd NCST), III: 3, 19; IV: 706, 722.
Carr, Titus, (Sgt, Co E, 41st NCST, 3rd Cav), III: 709.
Carraway, Daniel T., (Commissary, Branch-Lane's Brigade; Maj, Commissary, Wilcox's Division), IV: 472; V: 537.
Carraway, James C., (Capt, Co K, 26th NCST), II: 304, 397.
Carraway, James G., (Lt, Ordnance Officer, 7th Vols/17th NCST), V: 46, 47, 50.
Carraway, W.W., (Capt, Co E, 41st NCST, 3rd Cav), II: 771, 774.
Carraway, Zack B., (Co I, 4th NCST), I: 234.
Carrier, Calvin C., (Lt, Co F, 12th Vols/22nd NCST), II: 166.
Carrier, Joseph B., (AQM, 34th NCST), II: 582.
Carrigan, W.A., (Pvt, Co D, Millard's 9th/20th Battalion Junior Reserves), IV: 392.
Carrington, ______, (Maj, N.C. Subsistence Department), I: 38.
Carrington, Dr., George W., (Surg, 2nd NCST), IV: 631; V: 484.
Carrington, T.R., (2nd Lt, Co I, 13th Vols/23rd NCST), II: 187.
Carroll, ______, (Ass't Engineer, CSN), V: 382, 384, 410.
Carroll, Benehan, (Lt, Co I, 9th NCST, 1st Cav), I: 486.
Carroll, Calvin, (Cpl, Co G, 11th Vols/21st NCST), V: 515.
Carroll, Francis M., (Lt, Co A, 61st NCST), III: 503.
Carroll, J.L., (AQMS, 46th NCST), V: 524.
Carroll, Levi, (Capt, Co B, 76th NCST, 6th Senior Reserves), IV: 97.
Carroll, Thomas D., (Pvt, Co K, 45th NCST), III: 53; V: 501.
Carroll, W.R., (Pvt, Co A, 10th NCST, 1st Art & Engs, Ramseur-Manly's Battery, Light Art), I: 556.
Carrsville, N.C., III: 321, 337.
Carson, ______, [James M.], (Capt, 25th S.C.), V: 240.
Carson, Rev. ______, (Chaplain), IV: 603.
Carson, Adolphus B., (Pvt, Color-bearer, 6th Vols/16th NCST), IV: 202.
Carson, Bill, (Negro servant to Capt Joseph Mills), IV: 218.
Carson, E.W., (Cpl, Co H, 49th NCST), V: 565.
Carson, John, (2st Lt, Co I, 26th NCST), II: 304, 397.
Carson, John, (1st Lt, Co D, 6th NCST; Capt, Co A, Avery's 17th Battalion NCST), IV: 373, 374, 376.
Carson, R.W., (Cpl, Co B, 28th NCST), V: 541.
Carson, Thomas L., (Sgt, Co I, 34th NCST), V: 556.
Carswell, Robert H., (Pvt, Co F, 26th NCST), V: 601.
Carter, ______, (Col), I: 634.
Carter, ______, (Purser, Advance), V: 338.
Carter, ______, (Pvt, Co E, Millard's 9th/20th Battalion Junior Reserves), IV: 394.
Carter, A.C., (2nd Sgt, Co K, 4th NCST), I: 272; V: 489.
Carter, Albert T., (Musician, Co E, 4th Vols/14th NCST), I: 711, V: 490.

Carter, Charles R., (Pvt, Co E, 33rd NCST), II: 544.
Carter, David, (Pvt, Co B, 34th NCST), V: 555.
Carter, David M., (Capt, Co E, 4th NCST; Col, Associate Judge Military Court, Jackson's Corps), I: 231, 244, 267; IV: 238, 239, 574; V: 8, 650.
Carter, E.A., (Lt, Co A, 37th NCST), II: 668.
Carter, H.B., (Pvt, Co I, 3rd Vols/13th NCST), V: 551.
Carter, J.C., (Pvt, Co C, 28th NCST), V: 541.
Carter, J.H., (Capt, Co E, 4th NCST), I: 232, 272.
Carter, J.R., (Pvt, Co G, 33rd NCST), V: 544.
Carter, James E., (Col, 1st Tenn., Cav), III: 745.
Carter, Jim, (Negro servant to Capt D.M. Carter), I: 273.
Carter, John, (Pvt, Co D, 10th NCST, 1st Art & Engs, Reilly-Ramsay's Battery, Light Art), I: 569.
Carter, John, (Pvt, Co F, 47th NCST), V: 535.
Carter, John Carpenter, (Brig Gen), III: 495.
Carter, Julius F., (Pvt, Co H, 4th Vols/14th NCST), V: 491.
Carter, L.H., (Pvt, Co D, 33rd NCST; Detailed, Invalid Battalion), V: 571.
Carter, Melvin E., (Capt, Co A, 64th NCST), III: 660, 662.
Carter, Nathan, (Pvt, Co F, 6th NCST), V: 513.
Carter, R.J., (Musician, 33rd NCST), V: 543.
Carter, R.M., (Adjt, 30th NCST), II: 495, 499.
Carter, Robert A., (1st Lt, Co F, 6th NCST), V: 582.
Carter, Robert A., (Capt, Co C, 42nd NCST), II: 790, 806.
Carter, S.W., (1st Cpl, Co H, 3rd Vols/13th NCST), V: 551.
Carter, Samuel Powhatan, (Maj Gen, USA), III: 519.
Carter, S. Sidney, (2nd Lt, Co F, 66th NCST), II: 305; III: 686.
Carter, Thomas M., (1st Lt, Co B, 44th NCST), III: 22.
Carter, W.B., (Pvt, Co H, 3rd Vols/13th NCST), V: 551.
Carter, W.G., (Pvt, Co G, 26th NCST), II: 305.
Carter, W.H., (1st Lt, Co H, 44th NCST; Capt, Co D, 6th Battalion Junior Reserves; Capt, Co H, 70th NCST, 1st Junior Reserves), III: 23; IV: 10, 13, 121.
Carter, Wilson, (Pvt, Co A, 1st Battalion NCST), V: 504.
Carter's, Tenn., (aka Carter's Depot), III: 518, 739, 740, 743.
Carter County, Tenn., III: 676; IV: 301.
Carter House, (nr Stephenson's Depot, Va.), I: 147.
Carteret County, N.C., I: 534; III: 686.
Cartersville, Ga., II: 742.
Carthage, N.C., IV: 431.
Cartland, J.M., (Pvt, Co H, 25th NCST), V: 193.
Caruth, Alexander R., (Capt, Co B, 56th NCST), I: 119; III: 313, 344, 352, 356.
Caruth, William, (Pvt, Co G, 6th Battalion/60th NCST), III: 482.
Carver, E.A., (2nd Lt, Co I, 1st NCST), I: 137; IV: 722.
Carver, John, (Pvt, Co G, 9th NCST, 1st Cav), I: 427.
Carver, W., (Pvt, Co B, 56th NCST), III: 347.
Carvin, John Y., (Pvt, Co A, 4th NCST), V: 488.

Case, John, (Pvt, Co I, 8th Vols/18th NCST), II: 64; V: 540.
Case, John J., (Capt, Co G, 35th NCST), II: 605.
Casey, George W., (Sgt, Co D, 4th NCST), I: 232.
Casey, Silas, (Maj Gen, USA), II: 203, 205.
Cash, A.G., (Pvt, Co I, 5th NCST), I: 292; V: 506.
Cash, J.W., (Capt, Co D, 65th NCST, 6th Cav), III: 675, 684.
Cash, Norfleet C., (Pvt, Co E, 3rd Vols/13th NCST; Detailed, 2nd Corps Provost Guard), V: 570.
Cash's Mountain, Pa., IV: 177.
Cashtown, Pa., I: 316, 541, 589, 632, 633; II: 42, 234, 342, 344, 527, 562; III: 88, 235, 296, 569; V: 114, 117, 118, 177, 239.
Cashtown Road, (nr Gettysburg, Pa.), I: 698; V: 597.
Caskiel, W., (Pvt, Co K, 28th NCST), V: 543.
Cason, Samuel R., (Pvt, Co E, 27th NCST), II: 462; V: 523.
Casote, J.L., (Pvt, Co H, 56th NCST), III: 357.
Cassell, D., (Ensign, USN; Pioneer, Brooklyn), V: 244.
Cassidy, J., (Boatswain, CSN, Tallahassee), V: 438.
Cassville, Ga., (and Battle of, 1864), II: 741, 742; III: 454, 493.
Castle, Y.B., (Ordnance Sgt, Co K, 11th Vols/21st NCST), V: 515.
Castleman's Ford, (aka Castleman's Ferry, Shenandoah River, Va.), I: 160, 172, 645; II: 248, 474.
Caswell Bar, N.C., IV: 305.
Caswell Beach, N.C., V: 358.
Caswell County, N.C., II: 769, 770, 804; III: 35, 38, 457; IV: 615.
Cataloochee, N.C., [Cattaloochee], III: 518, 758.
Catawba County, N.C., II: 182, 234, 591, 792; III: 126, 406, 545; IV: 6, 372, 398, 483, 523.
Catawba River, N.C., III: 439, 440; IV: 431; V: 635.
Cates, S.P., (Pvt, Co G, 44th NCST), V: 534.
Catharine Furnace Road, (Wilderness, Va.), I: 714; V: 97.
Catharine Iron Furnace, (Wilderness, Va.), I: 376; II: 36.
Catharpin Road, Va., (Skirmish on), II: 118; III: 594.
Cathey, Alfred, (Pvt, Co G, 34th NCST), V: 556.
Cathey, Benjamin H., (1st Lt, Co A, 39th NCST), II: 704.
Cathey, Benjamin H., (1st Lt, Co A, 6th Vols/16th NCST), I: 751, 752, 755, 761, 764, 766, 767, 768, 769, 771; II: 702; V: 666.
Cathey, H., (Pvt, Co B, 3rd Vols/13th NCST), V: 549.
Cathey, J.L., (Sgt, Co I, 6th Battalion/60th NCST), III: 488.
Cathey, James M., (Capt, Co F, 25th NCST), II: 292, 299.
Cathy, A.A., [Cathey, Alexander A.], (1st Lt, Co G, 34th NCST), IV: 723.
Catlett's Station, Va., III: 578, 579, 580; IV: 185.
Catoctin Creek, Va., I: 421.
Catoosa Station, Ga., II: 717.
Caudle, A.B., (Pvt, Co D, 37th NCST), V: 545.
Caudle, Jacob, (Pvt, Co B, 57th NCST), V: 517.
Caudle, Shadrach G., (Capt, Co F, 12th Vols/22nd NCST), II: 166, 172.
Causbey, W.N., (Pvt, Co D, 1st Vols/11th NCST), V: 530.
Causby Creek, Tenn., III: 518.
Causey, H.C., (1st Lt, Co C, 6th Battalion Junior Reserves; Capt, Co F, 70th NCST, 1st Junior Reserves), IV: 13.

Causey, J.C., (Pvt, Co H, 46th NCST), V: 525.
Causler, _____, [Cansler, James], (Capt, Co G, 65th NCST, 6th Cav), III: 684.
Causley, Thomas, (Pvt, Co E, 6th Vols/16th NCST), V: 552.
Causley, William, (Pvt, Co E, 6th Vols/16th NCST), V: 552.
Cavanaugh, _____, (Resident of Onslow County), II: 283.
Cavaniss, J.F., (1st Cpl, Co G, 46th NCST), V: 525.
Cavaniss, W.J., (Pvt, Co G, 46th NCST), V: 525.
Cavalry, Confederate:
Alabama, 55th, III: 727.
Ashby's, (Va.), IV: 229, 230.
Baker's, J.A., (Brigade: 1st, 2nd, 5th N.C. Cav; See also: L.S. Baker's, Barringer's, Gordon's, Johnston's, Robertson's, Young's Cav), III: 608.
Baker's, L.S., (Brigade: 1st, 2nd, 4th, 5th N.C. Cav; See also: J.A. Baker's, Barringer's, Gordon's, Robertson's, Young's Cav), I: 449, 450, 451, 453; II: 775, 776, 778, 779; III: 199, 464, 532, 558, 572, 645; IV: 490, 590; V: 590.
Ball's Legion, IV: 708.
Barringer's, (Brigade: 1st, 2nd, 3rd, 5th, N.C. Cav; See also: J.A. Baker's, L.S. Baker's, Gordon's, Robertson's, Young's Cav), I: 430, 433, 435, 437, 438, 440, 442, 470, 472, 475, 775, 776; II: 107, 780, 781, 782, 783, 784, 785; III: 538, 540, 541, 545, 546, 547, 609, 612, 614, 615, 617, 619, 620, 621, 626, 627, 629, 636, 637, 648, 650, 653; IV: 89, 96, 436, 438, 442, 581-582; V: 210, 212, 567, 573, 657-658, 675, 680.
Beale's, (10th Va.; Company E was raised in Davidson, Davie and Rowan counties), I: 438, 439, 441, 474, 475, 477, 778; III: 629, 650; V: 569.
Butler's, (Brigade & Division), I: 775; III: 30, 192, 574, 628, 629, 630, 633, 681; V: 208.
Calhoun's, (S.C.), II: 18, 19.
Chambliss,' (Va.), I: 432, 434; II: 95; III: 540, 562, 563, 570, 592, 595, 596, 616, 621.
Choctaw, 2nd, (Choctaw Indian), IV: 696.
Claiborne's, (See: Dearing's & Robert's 7th Confederate and 7th N.C. Cav).
Cobb's Legion, I: 420, 451.
Company Q, (Cavalry troopers without mounts. While await ing new horses these troopers functioned as infantry.), I: 61, 425; II: 91; III: 534.
Confederate, 1st, ANV, (1st 2nd, 4th, 6th Va., 9th NCST, Jeff Davis Legion), I: 419.
Confederate, 7th, ANV, (aka Claiborne's, Dearing's & Robert's Brigades and Divisions), I: 268, 432, 433; II: 106, 283, 778; III: 134, 335, 337, 349, 465, 595, 612, 613, 615, 622, 623, 645, 681; IV: 73, 74, 76, 82, 83, 85, 86, 87, 92, 93, 370, 437, 463, 438, 439, 580; V: 177, 192, 332.
Confederate, 10th, Goode's Ala., III: 677, 678; IV: 275, 278, 282, 290.
Davidson's, (Brigade), IV: 439; V: 170, 173.
English's, (Co C, 5th Battalion NCST), III: 447; IV: 271.
Evans', (See: 63rd NCST, 5th Cav).
Everett's, (aka Walker's Regiment of Thomas' Legion;

80thNCST; See also: Gromley's & Walker's), III: 758.
Ferebee's, (See: 59th NCST, 4th Cav).
Folk's, (See: 5th Battalion NCST).
Forrest's, (Brigade, Division, Coprs), III: 678; IV: 439; V: 170.
Funston's, (See also: Jones'), I: 454; III: 578.
Georgia, 1st, III: 679.
Georgia, 8th, II: 108.
Georgia, 16th, III: 739, 740.
Georgia, 62nd, (See also: Kennedy's, 16th Battalion NCST & 75th NCST, 7th Cav), IV: 71, 72, 73, 74, 82, 83, 92, 93, 370.
Gordon's, (Brigade: 1st, 2nd, 4th N.C. Cav; See also: J.A. Baker's. L.S. Baker's, Barringer's, Johnston's, Robertson's, Young's), I: 311, 356, 357, 426, 429, 450, 454, 457, 640; II: 100, 241, 788; III: 464, 536, 572, 575, 578, 583, 585, 586, 589, 591, 592, 593, 595, 596, 597, 598, 600, 602, 604; IV: 436, 581-582.
Gormley's, [Ghormley's], (aka Walker's Regiment of Thomas' Legion; 80th NCST; See also: Everett's & Walker's), III: 758.
Graham's, (Battalion: Companies C & K, 2nd N.C. Cav; Co C, 3rd N.C. Cav), II: 88; IV: 534.
Gray's, (S.C.), II: 173; III: 619.
Hampton's, (Brigade, Division, Corps; 9th NCST, 10th Va., Cobb's, Hampton's, Jeff Davis & Phillips' Legions), I: 324, 352, 420, 421, 422, 424, 425, 429, 434, 449, 450, 451, 453, 460, 470; II: 91, 103, 174, 780; III: 30, 192, 195, 199, 443, 460, 531, 558, 564, 568, 572, 578, 582, 584, 592, 596, 616, 620, 621; IV: 104, 352, 390, 425, 438; V: 210, 589, 627.
Hampton's Legion, I: 421, 753, 754.
Harrison's, (AoT), III: 678. 679; IV: 439.
Hart's, (Ga.), III: 678.
Henry's, (See: 14th Battalion NCST).
Humes,' (Division, AoT), III: 679; IV: 439.
Imboden's, (Va.), II: 257, 258; III: 746; IV: 181.
Jackson's, (Va.), II: 248, 252.
Jeff Davis Legion, I: 421, 423.
Jenkins,' (S.C.), I: 718; II: 613, 775; III: 330, 570.
Jones,' (Va.), I: 147, 152, 153, 193, 201, 202, 203, 204, 449; II: 91, 96; III: 460, 462, 463, 565, 574, 578, 742.
Johnson's, Bradley, (Va.), I: 646; II: 251; V: 213, 214.
Johnston's, (See: J.A. Baker's, L.S. Baker's, Barringer's, Robertson's, Young's).
Kelly's, (AoT), III: 449; IV: 439; V: 173.
Kennedy's, (16th Battalion NCST; 75th NCST, 7th Cav; See also: 7th Confederate Cav), II: 280; III: 174, 175; IV: 71-93, 370.
Kentucky, 4th, III: 739, 740.
Lee's, Fitzhugh, (Brigade, Division, Corps), I: 424; II: 391; III: 100, 397, 401, 460, 561, 575, 576, 592, 596, 638; IV: 454, 457; V: 197, 254.
Lee's, W.H.F., "Rooney," (Brigade and Division, 9th, 10, 13th 15th Va., 2nd N.C. Cav), I: 424, 429, 435, 440, 470;

II: 87, 91, 94, 95, 96, 97, 99, 100, 391, 781, 784; III: 30, 397, 460, 562, 563, 564, 565, 592, 595, 608, 609, 612, 615, 622, 627, 628, 629, 630, 633, 638, 644, 649; IV: 142, 438, 442; V: 208, 210, 573.

Lipscomb's, (See: 2nd S.C.).

Lomax's, (11th Va.,), I: 429, 454, 648; II: 252, 253, 257, 258, 259; III: 578, 579, 596, 598, 638.

Louisiana, 1st, (aka Scott's), IV: 274, 275, 285, 286.

Lusk's, (Co A, 5th Battalion NCST; See also: 5th Battalion NCST), III: 675; IV: 271, 272, 273, 274, 290.

Martin's, (Corps, AoT), III: 678.

McLin's, (Battalion), III: 739.

Miller's, (See also: Avery's 17th Battalion NCST), III: 622, 623; IV: 375.

Munford's, (2nd Va.), II: 873.

Newkirk's, II: 497.

North Carolina, 5th Battalion, (aka, Baird's; See also: Lusk's & Scott's 65th NCST, 6th Cav), I: 118, 119; III: 434, 673, 674, 676; IV: 224, 271-292, 301, 341.

North Carolina, 7th Battalion, (aka Folk's; See also: 65th NCST, 6th Cav), III: 673, 676; IV: 291, 301.

North Carolina, 9th, (1st N.C. Cav), I: xiii, 3, 4, 111, 417, 418-487, 775-783; II: 79, 99, 100, 102, 103, 104, 106, 107, 163, 597, 599, 700; III: 399, 464, 534, 535, 536, 537, 538, 545, 546, 547, 548, 549, 553, 556, 558, 569, 572-573, 575, 576, 581, 584, 592, 593, 595, 597, 602, 605, 608, 610, 612, 613, 620, 629, 630, 635, 636, 638, 639, 644, 647, 648, 650, 651, 652, 673, 674, 760; IV: 109, 110, 113, 116, 390, 437, 581, 582, 606, 633; V: xii, 9, 11, 13, 589, 657, 666.

North Carolina, 12th Battalion, (aka Wheeler's; See also: 59th NCST, 4th Cav & 16th Battalion/75th NCST, 7th Cav), II: 398; III: 458; IV: 72, 93, 224, 270, 339-340, 370.

North Carolina, 14th Battalion, (aka Woodfin's & Henry's; See also: Woodfin's), III: 664; IV: 109, 112, 114, 363, 380, 439, 643; V: 2, 6.

North Carolina, 15th Battalion, (aka Wynn's), IV: 365-369, 644; V: 2, 6, 677.

North Carolina, 16th Battalion, (aka Kennedy's; See also: Kenndey's & 75th NCST, 7th Cav), II: 208; IV: 89, 90, 93, 224, 340, 437, 643.

North Carolina, 19th, (2nd N.C. Cav; aka Spruill's & Robert's), I: xiii, 4, 5, 12, 50, 418-487, 609; II: 79-109, 308, 324, 539, 541, 700; III: 464, 466, 532, 536, 538, 539, 545, 556, 572, 586, 592, 593, 594, 595, 602, 608, 609, 610, 612, 613, 614, 620, 627, 634, 646, 647, 650, 651, 652; IV: 88, 110, 111, 116, 297, 358, 367, 437, 580, 581, 635, 641; V: 10, 13, 210, 273, 629, 657, 666, 676.

North Carolina, 41st, (3rd N.C. Cav), I: xiii, 7, 50, 429, 430, 431, 432, 435, 437, 439, 440, 442, 480, 482, 778; II: 88, 767-787; III: 545, 553, 608, 610, 620, 635, 636, 645, 650, 688; IV: 116, 437, 490, 581, 582, 614, 638; V: 18, 658, 666, 676.

North Carolina, 59th, (4th N.C. Cav), I: xiii, 13, 118, 429, 449,

451; II: 108, 337, 338, 777; III: 453, 455, 531, 550, 553, 556, 562, 570, 572, 574, 575, 576, 595; IV: 94, 116, 263, 340, 437, 534, 581, 634, 641; V: 83, 85, 86, 659-660.
North Carolina, 63rd, (5th N.C. Cav), I: xiii, 13, 118, 119, 424, 431, 432, 435, 436, 437, 439, 440, 441, 442, 443, 450, 451, 465, 472, 473, 474, 776; II: 3, 88; III: 459, 462, 464, 465, 525, 529-657; IV: 116, 224, 263, 270, 437, 534, 581, 619, 641; V: 10, 11, 12, 83, 85, 86, 88, 658, 666, 671, 672, 673, 676.
North Carolina, 65th, (6th N.C. Cav; See also: Lusk's Co 5th Battalion NCST, Scott's), I: xiii, 13, 118; II: 700, 701; III: 673-684, 706, 721, 726; IV: 15, 16, 116, 291, 292, 437, 439, 642; V: 169, 170, 171, 173.
North Carolina, 75th, (aka Claiborne's 7th C.S. Cav; Dearing's 7th C.S. Cav; 16th Battalion N.C. Cav; 7th N.C. Cav; See also: Spruill-Robert's 19th NCST, 2nd Cav), I: xiii, 15, 16; IV: 71-96, 340, 370, 437, 580; V: 631, 660.
North Carolina, 79th, (8th N.C. Cav; The regimental history of this unit does not desig nate the companies by letters as is traditionally done. For the purposes of this index they have been identified with the numbers 1-10. This con venience has also been used to identifying the men of the 79th.), IV: 109-116, 363, 439, 442, 643; V: 2, 6, 12, 654, 677.
Payne's, (Va.), I: 208.
Pegram's, (Brigade & Division), III: 678; IV: 301, 439.
Phillips' Legion, (Ga.), I: 421, 451.
Roberts', (Brigade: 59th NCST, 4th Cav; 16th Battalion/ 75th NCST, 7th Cav; 8th Ga. Cav), I: 268, 438; II: 106, 108, 780; III: 466, 467, 470, 645; IV: 88, 89, 90, 95, 96, 437, 438, 442, 463, 580; V: xi, 251, 567, 573, 659-660, 680.
Robertson's, Beverly H., (See also: J.A. Baker's, L.S. Baker's, Barringer's, Johnston's, Young's), II: 21, 93; III: 459, 460, 461, 462, 463, 531, 534, 550, 551, 555, 558, 562, 564, 566, 569, 570, 571.
Rosser's, (See also: Claiborne's & Dearing's 7th C.S. Cav), I: 436, 457; II: 258, 259, 783; III: 280, 397, 466, 583, 585, 586, 608, 622, 623, 746; IV: 88.
Scott's, J.S., (See: 1st La.).
Scott's, J.S., (AoT, Brigade: 1st La., 5th Battalion NCST, 10th C.S., 5th Tenn.; See also: 5th Battalion NCST), III: 676; : 275, 276, 288, 289, 290, 291, 301.
South Carolina, 1st, III: 578.
South Carolina, 2nd, (aka Lipscomb's), I: 451; IV: 431, 540, 541; V: 241.
South Carolina, 5th, II: 779; IV: 266, 528.
South Carolina, 7th, II: 779.
Spruill's, (See: 19th NCST, 2nd Cav; 16th Battalion NCST; 75th NCST, 7th; Claiborne's 7th C.S. Cav; Dearing's 7th C.S. Cav).
Stuart's, J.E.B., (Division & Corps), II: 232, 516, 568; III: 531, 556, 557, 559, 572, 581, 595; IV: 168, 328; V: 72, 78, 113.
Stuart-Hampton's, (Division & Corps), II: 106.

Tennessee, 1st, III: 732, 745.
Tennessee, 3rd, III: 732, 745.
Tennessee, 5th, IV: 275, 280, 282.
Tennessee, 14th, III: 745.
Texas, 8th, III: 197, 198.
Vaughn's, J.C., (AoT), III: 745, 753; IV: 123.
Virginia, 1st, I: 419.
Virginia, 2nd, I: 419.
Virginia, 3rd, I: 420.
Virginia, 4th, I: 419; II: 87, 93.
Virginia, 6th, I: 419.
Virginia, 7th, III: 575, 577.
Virginia, 9th, I: 474, 480, 778, 779; II: 87, 91, 92, 94, 104, 107; III: 556.
Virginia, 10th Battalion, IV: 403.
Virginia, 10th, (See also: Beale's), I: 420; II: 87, 90, 91, 92, 96, 103; V: 569, 627-628.
Virginia, 11th, II: 45.
Virginia, 12th, III: 575, 576, 578, 582.
Virginia, 13th, I: 475; II: 87, 91, 92, 94; IV: 678.
Virginia, 15th, II: 87; IV: 678.
Virginia, 16th, IV: 71, 89, 90, 93, 370, 437, 580.
Walker's, (Regiment of Thomas' Legion; 80th NCST), III: 320, 758.
West's, (See: Woodfin's 14th Battalion NCST).
Wharton's, (Division, AoT), II: 489; III: 678.
Wheeler's, (Disivion & Corps), I: 60, 92; II: 710, 757; III: 181, 189, 190, 192, 199, 321, 443, 679, 727; IV: 219.
Wheeler's, (See: 12th Battalion NCST).
White's, (Va.), I: 719.
Wickham's, III: 596, 598.
Woodfin's, (14th Battalion NCST: Fortune's, Harris' & West's companies, 9th Vols./19th NCST, 2nd Cav; See also: Henry's 14th Battalion), II: 81; IV: 109-112, 113, 363.
Wynn's, (See: 15th Battalion NCST).
Young's, (See also: J.A. Bakr's, L.S. Baker's, Barringer's, Gordon's, Johnston's, Robertson's), I: 457, 775; III: 197, 558, 575, 581, 583, 585, 586, 608, 621, 628, 629.

Cavalry, Federal:
Averill's, (Division), I: 645; II: 123, 248, 249; III: 751, 754.
Bragg's, (Division), IV: 43.
Buford's, (Brigade & Division), I: 633; II: 119, 343, 344, 369; III: 236, 565, 572, 575; V: 114, 115, 116, 118, 615.
Capehart's, III: 644.
Carter's, III: 519.
Chapman's, III: 616.
Cole's, 2nd U.S., (Colored), III: 336.
Custer's, (Brigade), III: 576, 644, 646, 647, 651, 652, 753, 754; V: 214.
Davies', III: 576, 644.
Dennington's, III: 644.
Devin's, (Brigade), III: 596, 644; V: 214.
Dodge's, (N.Y. Mounted Rifles), III: 330; IV: 366.
Gamble's, II: 361.
Gregg's, (Division), I: 729; II: 390; III: 30, 563, 564, 566, 580, 628, 629, 630; V: 207.
Illinois, 8th, II: 344.
Illinois, 12th, II: 344.
Indiana, 3rd, III: 743.
Indiana, 12th, II: 344.
Kautz's, (Division), I: 467; III: 350, 465, 612; V: 207.
Kilpatrick's, (Division), II: 238; III: 463, 465, 565, 572, 574, 575, 579, 582, 589; IV: 104, 257, 725; V: 270, 597.

Maine, 1st, (aka Weber's), I: 465, 466; II: 376; III: 567, 597, 598, 600, 601, 630, 631.
MacKenzie's, III: 644.
Michigan, 5th, III: 598.
Michigan, 6th, I: 591.
Michigan, 9th, III: 743, 744.
New York, 2nd Cav., I: 88, 97, 106.
New York, 3rd, II: 82; III: 173; V: 272.
New York, 5th, III: 585.
New York, 8th, II: 344.
New York, 10th, III: 597, 598, 748.
New York, 12th, III: 345; IV: 80; V: 175.
Ohio, 7th, III: 742.
Pennsylvania, 4th, III: 567.
Pennsylvania, 8th, I: 145, 192; II: 360.
Pennsylvania, 18th, III: 576, 577, 583, 584-585.
Pleasanton's, (Division), III: 461, 557, 562; V: 72, 588.
Rhode Island, 1st, III: 461, 562, 563.
Schocknett's, II: 785.
Sheridan's, (Division & Corps, See: Philip Sheridan).
Spear's, (Brigade), II: 277; III: 30, 330; V: 207.
Stoneman's, (Division), IV: 374, 375, 376, 387; V: 633, 635-636, 654.
Tennessee, 2nd, III: 742.
Torbert's, [Torbet's], (Brigade), II: 258; V: 214.
Weber's, (See: 1st Maine).
Well's, II: 784; III: 651.
Wilder's, III: 679.
Wilson's, (Division), II: 173; III: 612; IV: 93.
Wolford's, III: 677; IV: 292.
Cavalry Review, Stuart's, II: 89; III: 460, 531, 555, 557; IV: 186.
Cave, Reuben, (Pvt, Co B, 2nd Battalion NCST), V: 495.
Cave Spring, Ga., III: 500.
Cavetown Road, (nr Hagerstown, Md.), III: 570.
Cawsey, James F., (1st Lt, Co G, Walker's Battalion, Thomas' Legion, Cav; 80th NCST), IV: 118.
Cazaux, Anthony D., (Capt, AQM, 8th Vols/18th NCST; QM, Branch-Lane's Brigade), II: 17, 20; IV: 472, 473.
Cedar Creek, N.C., V: 279.
Cedar Creek, Va., (and Battle of, 1864; aka Battle of Belle Grove), I: 164, 172, 174, 208, 263, 325, 326, 327, 334, 647, 648, 728; II: 259, 260, 261, 533; III: 14, 37, 55, 256, 280, 281, 422, 733, 755-756.
Cedar Mountain, Va., (and Battle of, 1862; aka Cedar Run), I: 140, 184, 318, 370, 623, 698, 758; II: 28, 29, 68, 124, 133, 150, 151, 168, 438, 472, 549, 551, 584, 655, 680; III: 66, 579, 580; IV: 159-161, 235, 465, 551, 555; V: 71, 116.
Cemetery, English, (at Scutari), V: 426.
Cemetery Hill, (nr Gettysburg, Pa.), I: 171, 312, 313, 314, 315, 316, 317, 332, 354, 355, 356, 358, 380, 590, 672; II: 136, 171, 362, 363, 364, 661; III: 6, 237, 414, 415, 416, 463; IV: 179, 405, 525; V: ix, 102, 137, 139, 143, 150, 152, 605-609.
Cemetery Heights, (nr Gettysburg, Pa.), II: 42, 136, 138, 353, 415.
Cemetery Ridge, (nr Gettysburg, Pa.), I: 315, 380, 698; III: 416; IV: 595; V: ix, xi, 102, 104, 110, 120, 121, 122, 125, 126, 129, 131, 132, 137, 139, 609.
Centerville, Va., (and Battle of, 1863), I: 346, 419, 563, 564, 720;

II: 30, 31, 69, 87, 663; III: 242, 563, 582; IV: 162, 226, 227; V: 30.
Central's Bridge, (South Anna River, Va.), III: 24, 25.
Centre Church, N.C., [Center], (aka Old Centre Meeting House), II: 13, 804; III: 700; IV: 62, 352, 549.
Centre Cross, Va., II: 87.
Century Magazine, I: 342, 626; IV: 547.
Chadwich, N.N., (Capt, Co F, 2nd NCST), I: 161, 162.
Chaffin's Bluff, Va., II: 287, 621; III: 163, 247; IV: 536.
Chaffin's Farm, Va., (and Battle of, 1864), III: 275, 358, 512; IV: 495.
Chamberlin, Madison, (Pvt, Co G, 53rd NCST; Detailed, 2nd Corps Provost Guard), V: 570.
Chamberlain, Matthew, (Pvt, Co L, 11th Vols/21st NCST), II: 145.
Chamberlain's Hill, Va., II: 66.
Chamberlain's Run, Va., (and Battle of, 1865), I: 439, 440, 441, 442, 453, 471-477, 480, 483, 485, 777; II: 23, 25, 107; III: 638-645, 654; V: 671.
Chambers, Alexander, (Pvt, Co A, 43rd NCST), III: 20; V: 497.
Chambers, Henry A., (Capt, Co C, 49th NCST), III: 128, 132, 138, 144, 145, 146, 152, 401; V: 559.
Chambers, Jack, (Chief Engineer, Susan Beirne), V: 380, 381.
Chambers, John Gregg, (2nd Lt, Co C, 6th Battalion/60th NCST), III: 473, 484.
Chambers, Pickney B., (Maj, 49th NCST), III: 127, 147, 148, 152.
Chambers, Riley, (2nd Lt, Co B, 6th Battalion/60th NCST), III: 474.
Chamber's Street, N.Y., N.Y., V: 444.
Chambersburg, Pa., I: 148, 194, 311, 421, 541, 555, 579, 632; II: 233; III: 5, 235, 462, 569; IV: 177; V: 115.
Chambersburg Pike, (nr Gettysburg, Pa.), I: 316, 379; II: 342, 343, 344, 586, 691; III: 42, 236, 296, 297; IV: 553.
Chamblee, William B., (Lt, Co B, 47th NCST), III: 553.
Chambliss, John Randolph, (Brig Gen), I: 434; II: 94, 104; III: 540, 563, 565, 619.
Chambray, John, (Pvt, Co D, 68th NCST), III: 715.
Champion, C.W., (2nd Lt, Co G, 13th Vols/23rd NCST), II: 186, 236.
Champion, D.O.P., (Pvt, Co H, 28th NCST), V: 542.
Champion, John C., (Pvt, Co C, 5th Vols/15th NCST), V: 521.
Champion Compress, (Wilmington), V: 451.
Chancellor, G.B., (Pvt, Co E, 32nd NCST), V: 496.
Chancellor House, (Chancellorsville, Va.), I: 145, 146, 192, 193, 377, 554; II: 228, 231, 477, 560, 659, 688; IV: 173, 176.
Chancellorsville, Va., (and Battle of, 1863), I: 144, 146, 147, 154, 158, 160, 161, 163, 164, 169, 170, 172, 174, 191, 193, 212, 250, 251, 287, 375-379, 422, 546, 554, 555, 620, 623, 628, 630, 631, 643, 647, 666, 667, 668, 669, 670, 675, 696, 697, 707, 714, 715, 716, 763, 764; II: 36, 39, 40, 41, 42, 51, 72, 112, 117, 121, 135, 170, 171, 176, 177, 182, 183, 184, 185, 186, 187, 188, 227-232, 240, 254, 262, 476, 477, 500, 502, 559-562, 586, 658-660, 672, 688-690, 700, 713; III: 40, 159, 255, 269, 410, 556; IV: 11, 33, 172-175, 176, 177,

237, 241, 313, 411, 459, 464, 467, 471, 522, 525, 552, 558, 703, 718; V: xiv, xvi, 93-100, 114, 646, 665.
Chancellorsville Campaign, I: 144; II: 341.
Chancellorsville Road, Va., (aka Chancellorsville Pike), I: 667, 668; V: 97, 98.
Chancey, E.B., (Sgt, Co B, 26th NCST), V: 531.
Chancey, J.J., (Pvt, Co H, 8th Vols/18th NCST), II: 64; V: 540.
Chandler, George, (Pvt, Co C, 59th NCST, 4th Cav), V: 659.
Chandler, J.J., (2nd Lt, Co F, 77th NCST, 7th Senior Reserves), IV: 100.
Chandler, M., (Capt, Co G, 29th NCST), II: 485, 493.
Chandler, W.B., (2nd Lt, Co C, 3rd Vols/13th NCST), IV: 723.
Chanler, R., (Lt Cmdr, USN), V: 242.
Chantilly, Va., (aka Ox Hill and Battles of), I: 184, 224, 623; II: 169, 216, 217; IV: 164; V: 71.
Chapel Hill, N.C., I: 412, 413; II: 13, 403, 598, 804; III: 200, 217, 375; IV: 22, 32, 60, 606.
Chapan, ______, [Chapin], (Capt, 85th N.Y.), III: 338; V: 180.
Chapman, ______, (Col, USA), III: 608, 612, 613, 614, 615.
Chapman, D.P., (Pvt, Co A, Millard's 9th/20th Battalion Junior Reserves), IV: 392.
Chapman, George, (Pvt, Co A, 45th NCST), V: 499.
Chapman, James, (Sgt, Co G, 37th NCST), V: 546.
Chapman, M., (3rd Sgt, Co C, 10th NCST, 1st Art & Engs, Brem-Graham-Williams' Battery, Light Art), V: 567.
Chapman, R.F., (Capt, CSN), II: 640; V: 234, 241.
Chapman, R.L., (2nd Sgt, Co C, 10th NCST, 1st Art & Engs, Brem-Graham-Williams' Battery, Light Art), V: 567.
Chapman, W.F., (Pvt, Co C, 10th NCST, 1st Art & Engs, Brem-Graham-Williams' Battery, Light Art), V: 567.
Chapman, Willie, (Cpl, Co H, 6th Battalion/60th NCST), III: 482.
Chappel, James H., (1st Lt, Co D, 13th Vols./23rd NCST), II: 184; IV: 701, 706.
Chappel, M.C., (Pvt, Co F, 52nd NCST), V: 536.
Chappewamsic Creek, Va., II: 164.
Charles II, (King of England), II: 593.
Charles, H.E., (1st Lt, Co E, 12th Vols/22nd NCST), II: 164.
Charles, J.G., (Pvt, Co A, 10th NCST, 1st Art & Engs, Ramseur-Manly's Battery, Light Art), I: 556.
Charles, P.E., (Lt, Adjt, 12th Vols/22nd NCST), II: 168, 169.
Charles City County, Va., IV: 158.
Charles City Court House, Va., II: 28, 786.
Charles City Road, (nr Richmond), I: 617, 657; II: 8; III: 77, 618, 691; IV: 356, 536.
Charleston, S.C., I: 71, 293, 391, 392, 393, 395, 396, 742; II: 18, 161, 184, 185, 244, 416, 439, 513, 514, 757, 758, 759; III: 70, 179, 180, 190, 191, 206, 210, 324, 354, 440, 509, 510, 511, 512; IV: 58, 101, 243, 319, 322, 327, 333, 415, 419, 421, 424, 437, 484-486, 505, 556, 562, 713; V: 24, 161, 166, 343, 354, 355, 356, 384, 386, 397, 399, 400, 401, 412, 434, 435, 436, 441, 446, 450, 453, 454, 620, 621, 624, 639.
Charleston Railroad, II: 758.
Charleston & Savannah Railroad, III: 179, 180.

Charlestown, Va., [Charleston], (and Battles of), I: 154, 189, 207, 707, 727; III: 14, 235, 279, 752; IV: 168, 177, 502, 525; V: 213.
Charlotte, N.C., I: 61, 293, 338, 537, 537, 538; II: 58, 416, 605, 628, 694, 804, 805, 807; III: 128, 192, 368, 439, 443, 502, 589, 654; IV: 129, 132, 133, 189, 400, 405, 406, 615, 694; V: 270, 340, 645.
Charlotte Court House, Va., V: 266.
Charlottesville, Va., I: 303, 451, 567; II: 245; III: 636, 745; IV: 138, 233.
Chase, Samuel P., (Chief Justice, U.S. Supreme Court), I: 57.
Chase City, Va., (was Christianburg), V: 266.
Chastian, ______, [Abner], (Chaplain, 29th NCST), IV: 612.
Chatfield, J.L., (Col, 6th Conn.), V: 163, 164, 165.
Chatham Coal, V: 338.
Chatham County, N.C., I: 282, 386; II: 303, 359, 390, 408, 416, 535, 596, 771; III: 78, 262, 504, 507, 512, 545; IV: 216, 379, 484, 606, 611, 613.
Chatahoochee River, IV: 372.
Chattanooga, Tenn., (and Battle of, 1863), I: 37; II: 486, 491, 707, 708, 716, 737; III: 435, 436, 448, 489, 490, 491, 492, 500, 663, 678, 733; IV: 117, 120, 124, 273, 275, 276, 357; V: 173.
Chattanooga River, Tenn., III: 494.
Chattanooga Road, II: 716, 717; III: 451.
Cheares, Benjamin, (Ass't Surg, 48th NCST), IV: 639.
Cheat Mountain, Va., IV: 639.
Cheatham, Benjamin Franklin, (Maj Gen), III: 200, 513; IV: 60.
Cheatham, Edwin G., (AQM, 13th Vols/23ed NCST), II: 189.
Cheatham, Isham G., (AQMS, 44th NCST), III: 22.
Cheek, Dr. A., (Ass't Surg, 2nd Vols/12th NCST), IV: 633.
Cheek, A.W., (2nd Lt, Co D, 1st NCST), I: 137.
Cheek, Alexander, (Pvt, Co B, 59th NCST), V: 659.
Cheek, Dr. Benjamin A., (Ass't Surg, 12th Vols/22nd NCST), II: 162, 171; IV: 635.
Cheek, Charles C., (Cpl, Co G, 5th Vols/15th NCST), V: 522.
Cheek, G.W., (Pvt, Co K, 6th NCST), V: 513.
Cheek, J.D., (Sgt, Co G, 4th NCST), V: 489.
Cheek, W.R., (Pvt, Co F, 2nd Vols/12th NCST), V: 507.
Cheek, J.W., (Pvt, Co G, 28th NCST), V: 542.
Cheek, William, (Pvt, Co H, 14th Vols/24th NCST), V: 560.
Cheek William H., (Col, 9th NCST, 1st Cav), I: 418, 426, 428, 429, 430, 435, 441, 442, 443, 445, 446, 447, 449, 451, 452, 453, 454, 464, 466, 468, 469, 470, 472, 473, 474, 475, 476, 477, 478, 479, 480, 481, 482, 483, 484, 485, 775-783 personal account; II: 100, 104, 781; III: 399, 547, 548, 621, 622, 636, 638, 639, 651; IV: 706; V: xii, 219, 666.
Cheek, Mrs. William H., I: 781, 782.
Cheek's Famine, I: 454.
Cheek's Ford, (Potomac River, Va.), II: 601.
Cheevis, John H., (Sgt, Co B, 47th NCST), V: 534.
Chenault, W.W., (Capt, Co I, 49th NCST), III: 128, 153.
Cheraw, S.C., II: 725; III: 191, 192; IV: 104.
Cherokee, N.C., III: 757; IV: 612.
Cherokee County, N.C., I: 767; II: 700, 705, 706, 724, 725; III: 730,

731, 758; IV: 122, 125, 126, 127, 128, 481, 613.
Cherokee Indians, III: 128, 153, 518, 727, 736, 757, 759; IV: 124, 126, 127, 380.
Cherry, Dr. _____, (S.C.), IV: 104.
Cherry, George O., (1st Lt, Co F, 59th NCST, 4th Cav), III: 457; IV: 701, 706.
Cherry, James J., (Capt, Co A, 4th Vols/14th NCST), I: 706.
Cherry, Joseph B., (Capt, Adjt, 8th NCST), I: 387.
Cherry, Joseph B., (Capt, Co F, 59th NCST, 4th Cav), III: 457, 462, 468.
Cherry, Joseph O., (Capt, Co I, 59th NCST, 4th Cav; Capt, Co B, 12th Battalion NCST, Cav), III: 458; IV: 339.
Cherry, Macon G., (Capt, Co C, 44th NCST), III: 23; V: 529.
Cherry, W.D., (Pvt, Co C, 10th Vols/20th NCST), II: 114.
Cherry, William L., (Capt, AQM, 44th NCST), III: 22, 23.
Cherry, Willis W., (1st Lt, Co H, 66th NCST), III: 686.
Cherry Grove, Va., III: 321.
Cherryville, N.C., III: 152; IV: 202.
Chesapeake Bay, Va., I: 111; IV: 411.
Chesapeake & Ohio Railroad, IV: 149.
Chesson, J.A., (Sgt, Co D, 26th NCST), V: 531.
Chester, L.R., (Ensign, USN; Pioneer, Pontoosuc), V: 245.
Chester, Sidney, (Pvt, Co D, 6th NCST), V: 512.
Chester, S.C., IV: 431.
Chester, Va., III: 350.
Chester Gap, Va., I: 147, 194; III: 559, 571; IV: 177, 183.
Chester Hill, Va., III: 583.
Chesterfield, Va., (aka Chesterfield Court House), I: 330; III: 135, 425.
Chesterfield County, Va., IV: 209, 529.
Chestnut, C.L., (Capt, Co I, 10th Vols/20th NCST), II: 112.
Chestnut, Julius M., (Lt, Co A, 61st NCST), III: 503, 505.
Chestnut Street Sharf, (Wilmington), V: 368.
Chestnutt, Columbus L., (Capt, AQM, Starr's 13th Battalion NCST, Light Art), IV: 341.
Chestnutt, J.E., (Pvt, Co G, 3rd NCST), V: 487.
Chestnutt, Owen L., [Chesnutt], (Capt, Co C, 38th NCST), IV: 420; V: 548.
Chew, _____, [Robert Stanard], (Col, Va.), III: 334.
Chicago Convention, Democrat, (The only national political convention in American history to have been broken up by the military forces of the United States at the behest of the sitting president to protect his reelection bid.), IV: 685.
Chicamacomico, N.C., I: 388; V: 55-56.
Chickahominy, Va., (Bridge, Creek, River, Swamp), I: 138, 139, 161, 180, 182, 183, 217, 218, 222, 236, 242, 283, 285, 302, 303, 305, 323, 351, 366, 367, 369, 404, 431, 553, 567, 580, 597, 612, 613, 614, 616, 617, 657, 661, 693, 737, 746, 754, 755, 772; II: 21, 23, 24, 25, 66, 200, 201, 203, 207, 208, 209, 254, 471, 546, 547, 548, 549, 583, 679, 700, 799; III: 96, 115, 131, 139, 247, 358, 601, 602, 603, 609; IV: 152, 155, 157, 158, 198, 200, 235, 357, 465; V: 467.
Chickamagua, Tenn., (and Battle of, 1863), I: v, 35, 36, 720, 767, 768; II: 421, 491, 702, 712-720, 725, 735, 736, 739; III: 432, 433,

435, 448, 449-453, 476, 487-491, 497, 500, 674, 679, 740; IV: 291, 394, 438, 498; V: xi, 3, 104, 169-173, 354, 471, 670.
Chickamagua River, Tenn., II: 716, 735, 736; III: 678; V: 172.
Chijinsk Bay, V: 348.
Childers, H.H., (Pvt, Co K, 35th NCST), V: 563.
Childers, J., (Pvt, Co A, 37th NCST), V: 545.
Childers, J., (Pvt, Co D, 33rd NCST), V: 544.
Childers, John, (Cpl, Co E, 33rd NCST), II: 539, 578; V: 544.
Childers, William, (Pvt, Co C, 56th NCST), III: 356.
Childers, William, (Pvt, Co E, 32nd NCST), V: 496.
Childress, Hiram, (Pvt, Co A, 1st Battalion NCST), V: 504.
Childs, Mrs. ______, (Resident of Fayetteville), I: 730.
Childs, Ebbin, (Orderly to Col Palmer, 58th NCST), III: 453.
Childs, Francis L., (Lt Col, Cmdr Fayetteville Arsenal; Engineering Officer), IV: 296, 297, 298, 299, 413, 421.
Childsburg, Va., III: 596.
Chilton, Robert Hall, (Col, Lee's Staff; Brig Gen; A & IG CSA), II: 449; IV: 571.
China Sea, V: 416.
Chinnis, S.R., (Lt, Co G, 51st NCST), III: 219.
Chisenhall, John, (Pvt, Co H, 56th NCST), III: 348; V: 566.
Chisholm, M., (Pvt, Co E, 28th NCST), V: 542.
Chitwood, William, (Pvt, Co F, 56th NCST), III: 348; V: 566.
Choate, William T., (Capt, Co I, 61st NCST), III: 504, 505.
Choctaw Indians, IV: 696.
Chocwinity, N.C., II: 748.
Chopin, Dr. ______, (Surg, Medical Director to Beauregard), IV: 626-627.
Chowan, N.C., II: 793.
Chowan County, N.C., III: 716, 717; IV: 261, 262, 594.
Chowan River, N.C., II: 508, 790, 793, 794; III: 134, 335, 458, 553, 716, 717; IV: 11, 27, 29, 72, 339, 358, 368, 369, 392, 415, 573; V: 17, 57, 84, 175, 269, 270, 271, 283.
Christian, E.J., (Maj, 13th Vols/23rd NCST), I: 183, 189, 201, 206; V: 12.
Christian, Samuel H., (Confederate Congress), II: 206.
Christian, William Jasper, (1st Lt, Co C, 6th NCST), IV: 702, 706.
Christianburg, Va., (now Chase City), V: 266.
Christie, Daniel Harvey, (Col, 13th Vols/23rd NCST), I: 644; II: 117, 181, 189, 191, 201, 205, 211, 215, 220, 236, 238-239, 256; V: 10.
Christie, Mrs. Daniel Harvey, II: 238.
Christie, J.H., (Pvt, Co C, 4th NCST), V: 488.
Christman, D.P., (Sgt, Co F, 4th NCST), V: 488.
Christmas, Guilford, (Negro servant to Lt Col W.J. Green), IV: 251, 257.
Christmas Dinner, 1864, IV: 204.
Chuckatuck, Va., II: 88.
Chunky Gal Mountains, N.C., IV: 381.
Church, ______, (Deserter, Outlaw, Yankee), V: 294.
Church, ______, (Capt, Potter's Command, USA), IV: 79, 80.
Church, Redman, (Pvt, Co F, 26th NCST), V: 602.
Church Street, (Asheville), IV: 381.
Churchill, ______, (Sgt, Color-bearer, Barringers Brigade), I: 778, 779, 780; III: 641, 643, 647, 651, 652.

Cilley, Clinton A., (Capt, AAG VanDerveer's Brigade, USA), II: 714; V: xi, 169, 173.
Cincinnati, Ohio, IV: 275.
City Hall Park, N.Y., N.Y., V: 444.
City Point, Va., I: 436, 539, 737; II: 274, 400, 515, 612, 671, 793; III: 114, 140, 211, 359, 395, 604, 624; IV: 73, 88, 93, 534, 575, 742, 743.
City Point Railroad, III: 378, 379, 386, 390, 391; IV: 86.
City Point Road, (between Petersburg and City Point), IV: 489, 534.
Civil War in East Tennessee, IV: 124.
Civils, V., (Pvt, Co I, 27th NCST), V: 524.
Civils, Virgil, (2nd Lt, Co G, 30th NCST), II: 462.
Claiborn, R.F., (2nd Lt, Co G, 30th NCST), II: 496.
Claiborne, Thomas, (Col, Claiborne-Dearing's 7th C.S. Cav), IV: 73, 74, 75, 76, 80.
Clanton, John B., (1st Lt, Co E, 1st Vols/11th NCST), I: 584.
Clarendon Iron Works, (Wilmington), V: 368.
Clark, ______, (Col, 21st Mass.), II: 543.
Clark, ______, (Pvt, 25th Battalion NCST; Killed after the war by a Yankee outlaw), V: 287, 294.
Clark, A.S., (Pvt, Co I, 13th Vols/23rd NCST), V: 510.
Clark, Albertus W., (Pvt, Co B, 53rd NCST; Detailed, 2nd Corps Provost Guard), V: 570.
Clark, Dr. Benjamin A., (Ass't Surg, 12th Vols/22nd NCST), II: 176.
Clark, C.C., (ACS, 31st NCST), II: 511.
Clark, Charles D., (AQMS, 14th Vols/24th NCST), II: 269.
Clark, Clate, (Capt, Md.), IV: 142.
Clark, Daniel J., (Capt, Co K, 40th NCST, 3rd Cav), II: 746, 765.
Clark, David C., (Capt, Co D, 14th Vols/24th NCST; Adjt, 2nd Home Guard), II: 269, 271; IV: 653.
Clark, David C., (Col, 15th N.C. Militia; N.C. Brig Gen, Clark's Militia Brigade), I: xiii; IV; 645, 646, 647; V: 6-7, 287.
Clark, Davis C., (Lt Col, 1st Regt 3rd Class Home Guard), IV: 653.
Clark, Exum B., (Sgt Maj, 3rd Battlaion NCST, Light Art), IV: 261.
Clark, G.C., (Pvt, Co C, 2nd Vols/12th NCST), V: 507.
Clark, George M., (Maj, 34th NCST), II: 581, 586, 692; V: 12.
Clark, Henry J.B., (Col, N.C. Militia), I: 364; II: 308, 310.
Clark, Henry J.B., Jr., (Lt, Co F, 2nd NCST), I: 161, 162.
Clark, Henry T., (2nd War Governor of North Carolina), I: 9, 16, 17, 18, 22, 28, 41, 42, 43, 44, 48, 80, 339, 346, 349, 511, 581; II: 81; IV: 80, 624, 646; V: xiv, 581, 638.
Clark, J., (Pvt, Co E, 44th NCST), V: 533.
Clark, J.A., (Pvt, Co K, 6th Battalion/60th NCST), III: 482.
Clark, J.B., (Pvt, Co E, 44th NCST), V: 533.
Clark, J.C., (Pvt, Co E, 12th Vols/22nd NCST), V: 553.
Clark, J.E., (Pvt, Co B, 33rd NCST), V: 544.
Clark, J.F., (Pvt, Co I, 37th NCST), V: 546.
Clark, J.L., (Pvt, Co I, 13th Vols/23rd NCST), V: 510.
Clark, J.N., (Sgt, Co E, 56th NCST), III: 356.

Clark, J.W., (Pvt, Co K, 6th Battalion/60th NCST), III: 482.
Clark, James, (Pvt, Co I, 13th Vols/23rd NCST), V: 510.
Clark, James M., (Color-Sgt/Ensign, 56th NCST), III: 318, 355, 392; V: 191.
Clark, Jesse, (Pvt, Co D, 56th NCST), III: 355, 380.
Clark, Jim, [Clarke, James Foreman], (2nd Lt, Co G, 3rd NCST), I: 185.
Clark, John, (Col, Chief Engineer to Johnston), IV: 425.
Clark, John, (Pvt, Co D, 56th NCST), III: 355, 366.
Clark, John T., (Lt, Co G, 5th NCST), I: 285.
Clark, John W., (AQM, 34th NCST), II: 582.
Clark, Joseph B., [Clarke], (1st Lt, Co A, 12th Vols/22nd NCST), II: 164, 165, 170, 171.
Clark, M., (Pvt, Co D, 1st Vols/11th NCST), V: 530.
Clark, R.B., (Pvt, Co A, 12th Vols/22nd NCST), V: 553.
Clark, R.F., (Pvt, Co A, 3rd Vols/13th NCST), V: 549.
Clark, Sidney P., (Capt, Co H, 59th NCST, 4th Cav), III: 457; IV: 702, 706.
Clark, W.A., (Pvt, Co B, 28th NCST), V: 541.
Clark, W.H., (Pvt, Co C, 33rd NCST), V: 544.
Clark, W.S., (Lt Col, 21st Mass.), II: 312, 313, 314, 317.
Clark, Walter, (2nd Lt, Drill Master, 12th Vols/22nd NCST; Lt, Adjt, 35th NCST; Maj, 6th Battalion Junior Reserves; Lt Col, 70th NCST, 1st Junior Reserves), I: vii, x, 37; II: 166, 465, 598, 603, 605, 606, 611; III: 129, 549, 656, 680; IV: 5, 10, 11, 12, 13, 15, 16, 19, 21, 26, 35, 57, 65, 69, 315-316, 408, 435, 499, 587, 594, 646; V: 71 -82 personal account, 353, 593, 640, 651.
Clark, William B., (Capt, Co A, 12th Vols/22nd NCST), II: 165, 171.
Clark's Mountain, Va., I: 235; IV: 506.
Clarke, D.J., (Capt, Co K, 40th NCST, 3rd Cav), V: 240.
Clarke, Durell, (Pvt, Co H, 14th Vols/24th NCST), V: 560.
Clarke, G.W., (Capt, Co G, 53rd NCST), III: 263.
Clarke, J.C., (Pvt, Co F, 26th NCST), V: 602.
Clarke, J. Edward, (2nd Lt, Co B, 5th Battalion Junior Reserves; Co G, 71st NCST, 2nd Junior Reserves), IV: 28, 428.
Clarke, M.Y., (Pvt, Co B, 49th NCST), V: 564.
Clarke, William, (Pvt, Co F, 26th NCST), V: 602.
Clarke, William J, (Col, 14th Vols/24th NCST), II: 202, 269, 271, 272, 273, 279, 280, 285, 323, 332; III: 136, 138, 146, 212, 339, 353; IV: 569; V: 183, 184, 627, 650.
Clarke, Mrs. William J., II: 275.
Clarke, County, Va., II: 100, 474; V: 213.
Clarkson, ______, (Maj, 12th N.Y., Cav), IV: 79.
Clarksville, N.C., II: 263.
Clarksville, Va., I: 131.
Clary, William, (Pvt, Co G, 4th NCST), V: 489.
Clasby, George, (Fayetteville and Harper's Ferry Arsenals), IV: 298.
Clasby, James, (Fayetteville and Harper's Ferry Arsenals), IV: 298.
Clasby, John, (Fayetteville and Harper's Ferry Arsenals), IV: 298.

Clay, _____, (Lt, Breckenridge's Staff), III: 491.
Clay, G.P., (2nd Lt, Co F, 13th Vols/23rd NCST), II: 185.
Clay, J.H, (Pvt, Co D, 1st Vols/11th NCST), V: 530.
Clay, Miles M., (Pvt, Co G, 38th NCST), V: 557.
Clay County, N.C., II: 493, 700, 723, 724; IV: 122, 380, 381.
Clay's Brickyard, (nr New Bern), III: 7.
Clay's Farm, Va., (See also: Ware Bottom Church), III: 355, 356; IV: 362.
Clayton, A.J., (Pvt, Co E, 35th NCST), V: 563.
Clayton, Edward M., (Capt, Adjt, 6th Battalion/60th NCST), I: 118, 119, 131; III: 473, 484, 493, 497.
Clayton, Gideon E., (3rd Sgt, Co K, 52nd NCST), III: 225.
Clayton, G. Westly, (Col, 62nd NCST), III: 515, 516, 517, 518, 521, 524, 527, 759; IV: 381.
Clayton, Henry L., (Sgt, Co I, 4th NCST), I: 234.
Clayton, M.C., (Cpl, Co D, 11th Vols/21st NCST), V: 514.
Clayton, Robert M., (Jr 2nd Lt, Co B, 6th Battalion/60th NCST), I: 120; III: 474, 497.
Clayton, S.D., (Pvt, Co E, 35th NCST), V: 563.
Claywell, S.A., (2nd Lt, Co C, 4th NCST), I: 232, 271.
Clear Creek Township, (Mecklenburg County), II: 608.
Cleburne, Patrick R., [Cleburn], (Maj Gen), II: 742; III: 495.
Clegg, C.B., (2nd Lt, Co G, 48th NCST), V: 520.
Clegg, H.C., (2nd Sgt, Co G, 48th NCST), V: 526.
Clegg, M.D., (Lt, Co D, 48th NCST), III: 121.
Clegg, Thomas J., (Capt, Co D, 48th NCST), III: 115.
Clement, B.C., (Capt, Claiborne-Dearing's 7th C.S. Cav; Co E, 16th Battalion/75th NCST, 7th Cav), IV: 72, 91, 93, 94.
Clement, J.H., (1st Lt, Co F, 42nd NCST), II: 791, 806.
Clement, Jesse A., (Capt, Co F, 3rd Vols/13th NCST; Capt, Claiborne-Dearing's 7th C.S. Cav; Co G, 16th Battalion/75th NCST, 7th Cav), I: 654; IV: 72, 92, 93.
Clement, Wiley A., (Capt, Co F, 42nd NCST), II: 791, 792, 806.
Clement, William B., (Maj, 10th Battalion Va. Cav.), II: 96; IV: 403; V: 626, 678.
Clements, Lycurgus L., (Capt, Co G, 7th Vols/17th NCST), V: 35, 39, 40, 42, 43, 680.
Clements, W.B., (Capt, Co B, 10th Va., Cav), V: 627.
Clements, W.W., (2nd Lt, Co I, 41st NCST, 3rd Cav), II: 772.
Clemer, L.R., (Pvt, Co B, 28th NCST), V: 541.
Clemmer, G.P., (Pvt, Co H, 49th NCST), V: 565.
Clemmons, W.C., (Pvt, Co G, 10th Vols/20th NCST), V: 509.
Clemmons, W.J.P., (Pvt, Co H, 2nd Battalion NCST), V: 495.
Clendenin, G.A., (2nd Lt, Co H, 5th Vols/15th NCST), I: 735.
Clendenin, J.N.H., (2nd Lt, Co H, 5th Vols/15th NCST), I: 735.
Clenny, L.M., (Pvt, Co K, 43rd NCST), V: 499.
Cleveland, Tenn., III: 733.
Cleveland County, N.C., III: 125, 128, 299, 318, 458; IV: 61, 594, 595; V: 110.
Clewis, Zach, (Pvt, Co D, 8th Vols/18th NCST), II: 64; V: 539.

Clifton, F.A., (Pvt, Co C, Color-bearer, 38th NCST), II: 676.
Clifton, Francis A., (5th Sgt, Co D, 38th NCST), V: 557.
Clinard, F.C., (Sgt, Co A, 11th Vols/21st NCST), V: 194.
Clinard, Francis, (Pvt, Co A, 11th Vols/21st NCST), II: 139.
Clinard, William, (Capt, Co H, 77th NCST, 7th Senior Reserves), IV: 100.
Clinard's Store, N.C., I: 62.
Clinch Mountain, Tenn., IV: 274.
Clinch River, Tenn., II: 706; IV: 273, 274, 290.
Cline, A.K., (Pvt, Co E, 32nd NCST), V: 496.
Cline, J.M., (Chaplain, 52nd NCST), IV: 617.
Cline, L.W., (Pvt, Co E, 2nd Vols/12th NCST), V: 507.
Cline, M.C., (Pvt, Co B, 10th Vols/20th NCST), II: 119.
Cline, W.H., (Pvt, Co I, 1st Vols/11th NCST), V: 531.
Clingman, Thomas L., (Brig Gen), I: xi, xii, 390, 397, 407; II: 6, 291, 293, 294, 513, 516, 517, 518, 519, 723; III: 205, 213, 229, 231, 512; IV: 345, 346, 481, 482, 484, 486, 487, 488, 489, 493, 494, 495, 499; V: xii, 29-33 personal account, 167, 175-205 personal account, 584, 649.
Clingman's Dome, N.C., IV: 123.
Clinton, W.S., (Lt, Co K, 6th NCST), V: 194.
Clinton, N.C., II: 412; IV: 607, 613.
Clinton, Tenn., II: 706, 727; III: 434, 448, 661, 662, 663; IV: 271, 273, 290.
Clitz, J.M.B., (Cmdr, USN), V: 243.
Clodfelter, ______, [John A., Sgt], (Cpl, Co B, 10th Va., Cav), V: 628.
Clodfelter, A.W., (3rd Sgt, Co H, 48th NCST), V: 526.
Cloninger, W.W., (1st Lt, Co B, 28th NCST), II: 475.
Close, Y.D., (Pvt, Co B, 1st Battalion NCST), V: 504.
Closs, William A., (Lt, Co E, 7th NCST), I: 369.
Clothing, Furnished, I: 27; V: xiv.
Cloud, A.S., (Lt Col, 6th Vols/16th NCST), IV: 174, 180, 184, 192, 706; V: 547.
Clouts, J.M., (Pvt, Co F, 26th NCST), V: 601.
Clover, W.F., (Pvt, Co E, 49th NCST), V: 564.
Clover Depot, Va., (aka Clover Station), III: 542, 653.
Clover Lick, Va., IV: 141.
Clouts, J.M., V: 601.
Clowe, W.H., (Fayetteville and Harper's Ferry Arsenals), IV: 298.
Clowe, Hamson, (Fayetteville and Harper's Ferry Arsenals), IV: 298.
Clowe, John H., (Fayetteville and Harper's Ferry Arsenals), IV: 298.
Clowe, Richard, (Fayetteville and Harper's Ferry Arsenals), IV: 298.
Clyde, England, V: 405.
Coala, U.M., (Lt, 64th NCST), IV: 706.
Coan, William B., (Lt Col, 48th N.Y.), V: 238.
Coast Guard, IV: 410; V: 678.
Cobb, ______, (Capt, 10th NCST, 1st Art & Engs, Pool's Hvy Art), I: 492, 511.
Cobb, Andrew J., (2nd Lt, Co A, Wynn's 15th Battalion NCST, Cav), IV: 365.
Cobb, B., (Pvt, Co E, 12th Vols/22nd NCST), V: 553.
Cobb, Bryan W., (Capt, Co H, 2nd NCST), I: 162.

Cobb, Gaston D., (Capt, Co I, 8th NCST), I: 388.
Cobb, George S., (2nd Lt, Co G, 44th NCST), III: 23; IV: 706, 723.
Cobb, H.M., (Pvt, Co F, 53rd NCST), V: 502.
Cobb, J.B., (Pvt, Co F, 30th NCST), V: 492.
Cobb, J.L., (Capt, Co G, 76th NCST, 6th Senior Reserves), IV: 97.
Cobb, Jeff, (Sgt, Co I, 30th NCST), V: 493.
Cobb, John P., (Col, 2nd NCST), I: 162, 162, 173; IV: 460; V: 649.
Cobb, K., (Pvt, Co G, 61st Va.), V: 569.
Cobb, Martin H., (2nd Lt, Co G, 12th Vols/22nd NCST), II: 166, 172.
Cobb, Rev. Dr. N.B., (Chaplain, 4th Vols/14th NCST), IV: 601, 604, 607.
Cobb, R.A., (2nd Lt, Co F, 13th Vols/23rd NCST), II: 185.
Cobb, R.H., (Pvt, Co G, 61st Va.), V: 569.
Cobb, S.A., (Pvt, Co G, 44th NCST), V: 534.
Cobb, Stephen J., (Pvt, Co D, 51st NCST), III: 217, 220.
Cobb, Thomas Reade Rootes, (Brig Gen), I: 738; II: 297, 439; IV: 504.
Cobb, W.H.H., (Ass't Surg, 2nd NCST), I: 159, 160; IV: 631.
Cobb, W.H.H., (Lt, Co K, 55th NCST), III: 296.
Cobb, Wiley J., (Capt, Co E, 43rd NCST), III: 2, 3, 16; V: 494.
Cobb's Mill, N.C., (aka Wise's Fork), II: 650; III: 696, 722.
Cobham's Depot, Va., I: 580.
Coble, A.M., (Pvt, Co E, 3rd Vols/13th NCST), V: 550.
Coble, Alfred, (Pvt, Co F, 6th NCST), V: 513.
Coble, D.O., (Pvt, Co E, 3rd Vols/13th NCST), V: 550.
Coble, David, (Pvt, Co G, 44th NCST), V: 534.
Cochran, A.D., (Pvt, Co C, 10th NCST, 1st Art & Engs, Brem-Graham-Williams' Battery, Light Art), V: 567.
Cochran, A.J., (Pvt, Co C, 10th NCST, 1st Art & Engs, Brem-Graham-Williams' Battery, Light Art), V: 568.
Cochran, David R., (Capt, Co K, 34th NCST), II: 581.
Cochran, James G., (Musician, 6th Vols/16th NCST), V: 552.
Cochran, R.B., (Pvt, Co H, 35th NCST), V: 563.
Cochrane, C.J., (Capt, Co C, 13th Vols/23rd NCST), II: 183.
Cochrane, John M, (Capt, Co D, 37th NCST), V: 538.
Cochrane, R.E., (Capt, AQM, 63rd NCST), V: 672.
Cochrane, W.R., (Pvt, Co B, 53rd NCST), V: 501.
Cocke County, Tenn., III: 474, 496, 499, 518, 738.
Cockerham, David S., (Capt, Co H, 54th NCST), III: 267; IV: 706, 721.
Cocklestown, (nr Yorktown, Va.), I: 112.
Coddle, John, (Pvt, Co E, 8th NCST), V: 193.
Codori's House, [Cordori], (nr Gettysburg, Pa.), V: 102, 138, 142.
Cody, Andrew J., (Capt, Co F, 39th NCST), II: 706.
Cody, James, (Pvt, Co I, 1st Vols/11th NCST), V: 531.
Cody, John, (Pvt, Co I, 1st Vols/11th NCST), V: 531.
Coe, A., (Pvt, Co A, 28th NCST), V: 540.
Coffee, J., (Pvt, Co E, 37th NCST), V: 545.

Coffey, A.J., (Pvt, Co F, 26th NCST), V: 602.
Coffey, Cleveland, (Pvt, Co F, 26th NCST), V: 601.
Coffey, D.D., (Sgt Maj, 58th NCST), III: 432.
Coffey, H.C., (Pvt, Co F, 26th NCST), V: 602.
Coffey, Henry, (Sgt, Co F, 26th NCST), V: 600, 601.
Coffey, I.H., (Pvt, Co F, 26th NCST), V: 601.
Coffey, J.G., (Pvt, Co F, 26th NCST), V: 601.
Coffey, J.P., (Pvt, Co F, 26th NCST), V: 602.
Coffey, Thomas J., (Capt, Co E, 58th NCST), III: 433.
Coffey, Thomas M., (Pvt, Co F, 26th NCST), V: 601.
Coffey, W., (Pvt, Co F, 1st NCST; Detailed, Invalid Battalion), V: 571.
Coffey, W.E., (Lt, Co E, 58th NCST), III: 433.
Coffey, W.S., (Pvt, Co F, 26th NCST), V: 602.
Coffie, C.B., (Pvt, Co A, 16th Battalion/75th NCST, 7th Cav), V: 660.
Coffield, Cornelius H., (1st Lt, Co I, 31st NCST), II: 508.
Coffield, J.B., (AQMS, 5th Vols/15th NCST), I: 734.
Coffield, Joseph B., (2nd Lt, Co H, 1st NCST), IV: 722.
Coffin, G.W., (Ensign, USN, Pioneer, Ticonderoga), V: 244.
Coffin Detail, (Fort Delaware Prison, Md.), IV: 729.
Cogdale, Adney, (Pvt, Co F, 56th NCST), III: 348.
Cogdale, Allen, (Pvt, Co F, 56th NCST), III: 348.
Cogdell, Daniel A., [Cogdale], (Capt, Co F, 10th NCST, 1st Art & Engs, Cogdell's Hvy Art; Capt, Co D, 67th NCST), I: 489, 491, 496, 498, 501, 502, 522, 527, 535, 536; III: 704, 706.
Cogdill, Z.T., (Pvt, Co H, 2nd Battalion NCST), V: 495.
Coggin, I., [Jeremiah], (3rd Lt, Co C, 13th Vols/23rd NCST), IV: 706.
Coggin, Jeremiah, (2nd Lt, Co C, 13th Vols/23rd NCST), II: 184, 244; IV: 706, 723.
Coggin, Joseph B., (1st Lt, Co D, 56th NCST), III: 314, 331, 360.
Coggin's Point, (James River, Va.), I: 539; III: 622, 624, 625.
Coggins, Thomas, (Pvt, Co A, 64th NCST), III: 668.
Cogwell, Daivd, (Lt, Co C, 2nd NCST), I: 159.
Cohen, ______, (Engineering Officer), III: 379.
Cohen, A.D., (Chaplain, 46th NCST), IV: 615.
Cohen, E.B., (1st Lt, Co C, 1st Vols, "Bethel"), I: 77, 127.
Coinjack, N.C., III: 177.
Coir, J.C., (Pvt, Co C, 4th Vols/14th NCST), I: 732.
Coke, George H., (ASC, 52nd NCST), III: 225.
Coke, Dr. Lucius C., (2nd Lt, Co G; Surg, 1st NCST), I: 136; IV: 631; V: 484.
Cold Harbor, Va., (and First Battle of, 1862, aka Gaines' Mill), I: 139, 172, 181, 182, 205, 218, 242, 243, 304, 323, 384, 558, 609, 614, 620, 621, 623, 628, 629, 640, 643, 659, 694, 757; II: 25, 42, 112, 114, 148, 149, 173, 186, 189, 210, 211, 213, 238, 471, 547, 682, 798; III: 12, 84, 120, 358, 512, 688; IV: 157, 234, 444, 532, 551, 563; V: 16, 104, 258, 627.
Cold Harbor, Va., (Second Battle of, 1864), I: 160, 163, 164, 172, 205, 323, 334, 384, 404, 405, 430,

432, 549, 597, 640, 643, 677, 726, 746; II: 5, 6, 56, 75, 122, 140, 141, 146, 173, 245, 386, 387, 447, 480, 502, 516, 531, 573, 588, 621, 651, 790, 798, 806; III: 12, 37, 54, 79, 91, 95, 96, 111, 120, 211-212, 219, 220, 306-307, 332, 357, 358, 373, 419, 505, 512, 688, 689; IV: 198-200, 427, 469, 488, 492-493, 507, 525, 531, 532-534, 554, 563, 583; V: 16, 104, 197-205, 208, 258.
Cole, _____, (Col, Chief Commissary, ANV), II: 390; III: 638.
Cole, A.D., (Capt, Co A, 3th Vols/23rd NCST), II: 244.
Cole, Alexander T., (Capt, Co D, 13th Vols/23rd NCST), II: 184, 205, 206, 214, 215, 224, 231, 242, 244; IV: 721.
Cole, Barzillai F., (Capt, Co F, 9th Vols/19th NCST, 2nd Cav), II: 80.
Cole, Columbus C., (Lt Col, 12th Vols/22nd NCST), II: 162, 171; IV: 159, 169; V: 11.
Cole, Elijah, (Cpl, Co D, 5th Vols/15th NCST), V: 521.
Cole, Elisha, (Pvt, Co G, 6th Vols/16th NCST), IV: 216; V: 552.
Cole, G.B., (Sgt, Co H, 30th NCST), V: 492.
Cole, George O., (Cpl, Co D, 5th Vols/15th NCST), V: 521.
Cole, Hugh L., (Maj, 2nd NCST), I: 161, 162; IV: 27, 379, 381.
Cole, Isaiah S., (Cpl, Co D, 5th Vols/15th NCST), V: 521.
Cole, J.M., (Jr 2nd Lt, Co D, 6th Battalion/60th NCST), III: 476; IV: 705.
Cole, James A., (2nd Lt, Co I, 9th Vols/19th NCST, 2nd Cav.), II: 89, 96.
Cole, James H., (Lt, Co G, 6th Battalion/60th NCST), III: 500.
Cole, James R., (Col, 4th Regt Home Guard; Col, 1st Regt Home Guard in the Field; Chief QM, N.C.), IV: 650, 653; V: 629-636 personal account.
Cole, James R., (Lt, Adjt, 12th Vols/22nd NCST), II: 169, 179.
Cole, John W., (2nd Lt, Co D, 13th Vols/23rd NCST), II: 184.
Cole, Joseph, (Pvt, Co G, 6th Vols/16th NCST), IV: 216.
Cole, R.T., (Pvt, Co H, 30th NCST), V: 493.
Cole, Robert W., (Capt, Co E, 12th Vols/22nd NCST), II: 166, 169, 172, 178; V: 548.
Cole, W.B., (Cpl, Co D, 5th Vols/15th NCST), V: 521.
Cole, W.F., (Pvt, Co B, 3rd NCST), V: 487.
Cole, W.T., (Pvt, Co B, 7th NCST), V: 572.
Cole, William, (Pvt, Co D, 56th NCST), III: 370.
Cole, William C., (Pvt, Co D, 13th Vols/23rd NCST), II: 206.
Cole, William W., (2nd Lt, Co C, 54th NCST), IV: 701, 706.
Coleman, _____, [Thaddeus], (1st Lt, Co C, 10th NCST, 1st Art & Engs, Brem-Graham-Williams' Battery, Light Art), V: 668.
Coleman, _____, [William J.], (1st Lt, Co F, 30th Va.), II: 431.
Coleman, A.W., (Capt, Co A, 6th Vols/16th NCST), I: 751, 758; II: 707; IV: 137, 158.
Coleman, Cynthia Swain, (Mother of Col D.C. Coleman), II: 722.
Coleman, D.R., (Chief Musician, 10th Vols/20th NCST), II: 113; V: 508.
Coleman, Daniel, (Pvt, Co F, 10th Vols/20th NCST), II: 118.
Coleman, David C., (Maj, Coleman's Battalion; Col, 39th NCST),

I: 767; II: 487, 492, 704, 707, 711, 712, 713, 714, 715, 716, 718, 719, 720, 722-723, 727, 731, 732, 733, 734, 736, 737, 738, 740, 741; III: 517; IV: 442; V: xii, 4, 171, 650.
Coleman, E., (Pvt, Co C, 30th NCST), V: 491.
Coleman, Henry, (Capt, Co G, 9th NCST, 1st Cav), I: 441, 475, 486, 488, 782; IV: 110-111.
Coleman, Henry, (1st Lt, Co C, 10th Vols/20th NCST), V: 503.
Coleman, Henry E., (Col, 2nd Vols/12th NCST), I: 607, 639, 642, 643, 644; II: 119.
Coleman, J.A., (Pvt, Co E, 45th NCST), V: 500.
Coleman, J.L., (Cpl, Co A, 45th NCST), V: 499.
Coleman, Levi P., (Capt, Co G, 43rd NCST), III: 2, 3.
Coleman, McQueen, (Lt, Co K, 10thVols/20th NCST), II: 118, 125; IV: 706.
Coleman, Milton, (Pvt, Co I, 3rd Vols/13th NCST), I: 660.
Coleman, Robert L., (Capt, ACS, 6th Battalion/60th NCST; Chief Commissary, Department of Western N.C.; Col, 79th NCST, 8th Cav), I: 118, 585; III: 473, 497; IV: 115.
Coleman, S.H., (1st Lt, Ordnance Officer, Ramseur-Cox's Brigade), IV: 462, 463; V: 483.
Coleman, Thaddeus, (Capt, Engineering Officer; Lt Col, 58th NCST), I: 501, 504, 507; III: 432, 444, 454, 497; IV: 418.
Coleman, William, (Father of Col D.C., Coleman), II: 722.
Coleman, Yancey, (Pvt, Co I, 3rd Vols/13th NCST), I: 660.
Coleraine, N.C., II: 793; IV: 26, 358, 368, 392.
Coleraine's Mill, N.C., IV: 62.
Coletrane, D.B., [Coltrane], (Pvt, Co I, 63rd NCST, 5th Cav), III: 589, 625, 633, 641, 655.
Coletrane Expedition, IV: 29-30, 392.
Coley, Charles N., (Pvt, Co K, 52nd NCST), V: 536.
Coley, J.N., (Cpl, Musician, Co K, 11th Vols/21st NCST), V: 515.
Colhoun, E.R., (Cmdr, USN), V: 242.
Collett, E., (Pvt, Co F, 42nd NCST), II: 795.
Collett, Dr. W.A., (Ass't Surg, 6th NCST; Surg, 58th NCST), III: 432; IV: 630, 632, 641.
Collett, William J., (Pvt, Co B, 4th Vols/14th NCST), I: 731.
Colley, L.R., (Sgt, Co E, 2nd NCST), I: 176; V: 486.
Collie, Alexander, & Co., (Financial House, Manchester, England), V: 454, 455, 456, 457, 458, 459.
Collier, Samuel P., (Sgt Maj, 2nd NCST; Lt, Co H, 2nd NCST), I: 175; V: 486.
Collierstown, Va., II: 358; V: 599.
Collins, ______, (Maj, 4th NCST), I: 249.
Collins, B.M., (1st Lt, Co C, 2nd Vols/12th NCST; ADC, Johnston's Brigade), I: 627, 639, 642, 650, 651; II: 265, 267; V: 503.
Collins, C.R., (Capt, Engineering Officer, Fort Caswell), IV: 418.
Collins, David D., (Pvt, Co B, 38th NCST), V: 557.
Collins, E.W., (Lt, Co D, 10th Vols/20th NCST), II: 118.
Collins, George P., (Maj, QM, Prttigrew's Brigade), II: 407, 408, 414; IV: 555, 556.
Collins, H.H., (Lt, Co E, 64th NCST), III: 660.
Collins, H.W., (Pvt, Co A, 28th NCST), V: 540.

Collins James A., (2nd Lt, Co F, Latham-Potts-Flanner's Battery, Starr's 13th Battalion NCST, Light Art) IV: 354, 379; V: 569.
Collins, John, (ACS, 30th NCST), II: 495.
Collins, John A., (2nd Lt, Claiborne-Dearings's 7th C.S. Cav; Co F, 16th Battalion/75thNCST, 7th Cav), IV: 91.
Collins, Joseph, (Lt, Ordnance Officer), I: 51.
Collins, Kimsey, [Kimzey], (Pvt, Co F, 69th NCST, Thomas' Legion), III: 750.
Collins, R.P., (2nd Lt, Co B, 50th NCST), III: 203.
Collins, S.A., (Pvt, Co G, 30th NCST), V: 492.
Collins, Samuel P., (Capt, Co A, 31st NCST), II: 512.
Collins W.B., (Cpl, Co D, 10th Vols/20th NCST), II: 114.
Collis, S.M., (Chaplain, 29th NCST), IV: 612.
Colquitt, Alfred Holt, (Brig Gen), I: 377, 403; II: 477, 646; IV: 535, 537; V: 167, 234, 235, 241.
Colquitt's Salient, (nr Petersburg, Va.; aka Hare's House, Hare's Hill, Fort Stedman), II: 8; III: 370, 371, 379, 380, 381; IV: 535.
Colston, Raleigh Edward, (Brig Gen), I: 143, 190, 654, 709; II: 232, 561, 658; V: 93, 97.
Colton, James H., (Chaplain, 53rd NCST), III: 261; IV: 618; V: 494.
Colton, Rev. Dr. Simeon, (Father of James H. Colton), IV: 618.
Columbia, Pa., I: 311.
Columbia, S.C., III: 388, 439, 502; IV: 103, 126, 202, 327, 335, 613, 614.
Columbia, Tenn., III: 438, 494, 501.
Columbia Road, (nr Plymouth), III: 339, 341; V: 176, 178, 182, 184, 186.
Columbus County, N.C., II: 66, 74, 111, 123, 125, 127; III: 205; IV: 49, 303, 590; V: 16.
Colvin, James A., (Lt Col, 169th N.Y.), V: 238.
Colvin, T.R., (Pvt, Co E, 8th Vols/18th NCST), II: 64.
Comal, S., (Pvt, Co C, 28th NCST), V: 541.
Combs, N.P., (Pvt, Co H, 56th NCST), III: 357.
Comic Battle, III: 74.
Commissary Department, CSA, I: 37, 38, 613; II: 390; III: 411, 638.
Commissary Department, N.C., I: 5, 23, 37, 48.
Committee of Safety, V: 24.
Company A, 2nd N.C. Volunteers, Mexican War, I: 131.
Company Shops, N.C., (now Burlington), I: 59, 294, 295, 297, 338; II: 304.
Companies, Confederate (Named): The military unit know as a company consisted of, at its maximum strength, 100 men plus officers and was usually assigned a letter or number designation (A-K excepting the letter "I" not used or numbers 1-10). In the rare cases where more than ten companies were organized into one unit (regiment) successive letters or numbers were employed. Especially in the South where ante-bellum Militia and Home Guard units were as much social organizations as reserve military organizations there was a tradition of entitling companies with somewhat quaint although to their mem-

bers inspirational names. Many of these names survived the transformation from Militia to Confederate service and many companies that did not exist prior to the war chose to give their units a title other than a mere letter designator.

Alleghany True Blues, (Co. F, 12th Vols./22nd NCST), II: 162, 163.
Allen's, (Co B, Freeman's 26th Battalion NCST), V: 626.
Anson Ellis Rifles, (Co A, 13th Vols/23rd NCST), II: 182, 188, 224, 237, 256, 263.
Anson Guard, (Co C, 4th Vols/14th NCST), I: 706, 731-732 Roll of Honor.
Armory Guard, (aka Fayetteville Armory/Fayetteville Arsenal Guard; Co A, 6th Battalion NCST), IV: 293-300.
Athens Guards, (A company in H.J.B. Clark's N.C. Militia), IV: 647.
Barden's Company, (Co K, 27th NCST), II: 426, 434.
Beattie's Ford Riflemen, (Co K, 13th Vols/23rd NCST), II: 187, 205, 215, 229, 236.
Beauregard Rifles, (Co I, 2nd NCST), I: 163.
Bladen Guards, (Co K, 8th Vols/18th NCST), II: 66.
Bladen Light Infantry, (Co B, 8th Vols/18th NCST), II: 65.
Bold Mountain Tigers, (Co 29th NCST), II: 493.
Brunswick Guards, (Co A, 10th Vols/20th NCST), II: 111.
Buncombe Life Guards, (Co H, 29th NCST), II: 490.
Buncombe Riflemen, (Co E, 1st Vols, "Bethel," Color Guard Company), I: 77, 85, 90, 125, 127, 128, 130, 131; III: 497.
Burke Rifles, (Co G, 1st Vols, "Bethel"), I: 78, 90, 93, 95,96, 99, 109, 113, 125, 127, 128, 133.
Burke Tigers, (Co E, 6th Vols/16th NCST), IV: 148.
Cabarrus Black Boys, (Co F, 10th Vols/20th NCST), II: 112.
Cabarrus Guards, (Co E, 10th Vols/20th NCST), II: 112.
Caldwell Guards, (Co I, 26th NCST), II: 304, 305, 330, 335, 353, 359, 401, 410, 413.
Caldwell Rough & Ready Boys, (Co A, 12th Vols/22nd NCST), II: 162, 163, 170, 176, 177.
Cape Fear Light Artillery, (As a Militia unit it was connected with the early war capture of Fort Caswell), V: 27.
Cape Fear Minute Men, (Co F, 36th NCST; Upon giving up their Militia status and organizing for the war as a Confederate unit this compa ny also changed its name. Formerly known as Cape Fear Light Artillery.), V: 24, 27.
Carolina Boys, (Co K, 38th NCST), II: 676, 678, 686, 690.
Caswell Rangers, (Co C, 41st NCST, 3rd Cav), II: 770, 774.
Caswell Rifles, (Co G, 12th Vols/22nd NCST), II: 162, 163.
Catawba Blues, (Co D, 4th Vols/14th NCST), I: 707.
Catawba Guards, (Co F, 13th Vols/23rd NCST), II: 185, 246.
Catawba Rifles, (Co K, 2nd Vols/12th NCST), I: 607, 608.
Catawba Wildcats, (Co F, 38th NCST), II: 675, 678, 681, 690.
Charlotte Grays, (Co C, 1st Vols, "Bethel"), I: 77, 90, 94, 99, 109, 124, 127, 128, 133.

Chatham Boys, (Co G, 26th NCST), II: 304, 305, 314, 332, 333, 335, 350, 359, 389, 390, 401, 408, 417.
Chatham Rifles, (Co M, 5th Vols/15th NCST; Co. K, 32nd NCST), IV: 517.
Clarendon Guards, (Co H, 36th NCST, 2nd Art), I: 132; IV: 402.
Clark Skirmishers, (Co K, 41st NCST, 3rd Cav), II: 772, 774, 775, 777, 785, 786.
Cleveland Guards, (Co H, 2nd Vols/12th NCST), I: 607.
Cleveland Marksmen, (Co I, 38th NCST), II: 676, 678, 688, 690.
Columbus Guards, (Co C, 8th Vols/18th NCST), I: 124; II: 65.
Columbus Guards No. 1, (Co B, 10th Vols/20th NCST), II: 111.
Columbus Guards No. 2, (Co C, 10th Vols/20th NCST), II: 112, 125.
Columbus Guards No. 3, (Co D, 10th Vols/20th NCST), II: 112.
Columbus Vigilants, (Co H, 8th Vols/18th NCST), II: 66.
Confederate Grays, (Co E, 10th Vols/20th NCST), IV: 245, 420.
Cow Creek Volunteers, (A com pany in H.J.B. Clark's N.C. Militia), IV: 647.
Davidson Wild Cats, (Co I, 4th Vols/14th NCST), I: 708.
Davis Dragoons, (Co F, 41st NCST, 3rd Cav), II: 771, 775.
Davis Guards, (Co I, 12th Vols/22nd NCST), II: 162, 163, 164, 167, 176.
Dee's Company, IV: 71, 89.
Dixie Rifles, (Co H, 27th NCST), II: 425.
Duplin Greys, (Co G, 10th Vols/20th NCST), II: 112.
Duplin Rifles, (Co C, 2nd Vols/12th NCST; Co A, 43rd NCST), I: 124, 607, 608; III: 19.
Edgecombe Guards, (Co A, 1st Vols, "Bethel"; Co G, 3rd Vols/13th NCST), I: 77, 90, 100, 105, 108, 113, 118, 121, 125, 127, 128, 133, 692; V: 577.
Enfield Blues, (Co I, 1st Vols, "Bethel"), I: 78, 91, 113, 124, 125, 127, 133.
Faucett's Company, (Co K, 47th NSCT), III: 108.
Fayetteville Independent Light Artillery, (Co H, 1st Vols, "Bethel"), I: 40, 75, 78, 91, 96, 99, 109, 114, 126, 127, 128, 131, 133; IV: 294.
Freeman's, (Co A, Freeman's 26th Battalion NCST), V: 626.
Galloway's Coast Guard, IV: 401.
Gaston Guards, (Co H, 13th Vols/23rd NCST), II: 186, 190, 226, 236.
Gatling Dragoons, (Co B, 41st NCST, 3rd Cav), II: 770, 774.
German Volunteers, (30th N.C. Militia; Co A, 8th Vols/18th NCST), II: 16, 65; V: 27.
Goldsboro Rifles, (Co A, 27th NCST), II: 425.
Goldsboro Volunteers, (Co D, 4th NCST), II: 425.
Granville Grays, (Co B, 2nd Vols/12th NCST), I: 124, 607, 608; III: 295.
Granville Plough Boys, (Co E, 13th Vols/23rd NCST), II: 184, 221, 224, 236.
Granville Rifles, (Co G, 13th Vols/23rd NCST), II: 185, 197, 199, 205, 206, 209, 215, 231, 236, 247, 254.
Guilford Grays, (Co B, 27th NCST), II: 425, 426, 427, 443, 452, 453, 457; III: 260, 314.

Guilford Men, (Co E, 12th Vols/23rd NCST), II: 162, 163.
Guion's Company, (See: Artillery).
Halifax Light Infantry, (Co E, 2nd Vols/12th NCST), I: 607, 608.
Hamilton Guard, (Co F, 7th Vols/17th NCST), V: 42.
Hardy's Light Artillery, (1st Co, 6th Battalion; Co A, 60th NCST), III: 473.
Hatteras Avengers, (Co F, 31st NCST), V: 63, 65, 66, 67.
Hertford Light Infantry, (Co C, 7th Vols/17th NCST), V: 36, 40, 42, 44.
Hibriten Guards, (Co F, 26th NCST), II: 304, 306, 328, 330, 336, 338, 350, 358, 359, 368, 413, 416, 417.
Highland Rangers, (Co D, 41st NCST, 3rd Cav), II: 770.
Hog Hill Guards, (Co B, 13th Vols/23rd NCST), II: 183, 231.
Hornet's Nest Rifles, (Co B, 1st Vols, "Bethel"), I: 77, 90, 93, 96, 99, 109, 113, 124, 125, 127, 128, 133; V: 377, 577, 578.
Humphrey Troops, (Co H, 41st NCST, 3rd Cav), II: 771, 776.
Independent Guards, (Co E, 26th NCST), II: 303, 306, 321, 330, 350, 359, 365, 366, 387, 416, 419, 422.
Independent Grays, (Co E, 7th NCST; Co C, 56th NCST), III: 314; V: 42.
Jefferson Davis Mountain Rifles, (Co D, 12th Vols/22nd NCST), II: 162.
Jeff Davis Mountaineers, (Co A, 26th NCST), II: 303, 305, 314, 323, 350, 359, 415, 421.
John Harvey Guards, (7th Vols./17th NCST), II: 2.
LaFayette Light Infantry, (Co F, 1st Vols, "Bethel"; After the term of enlistment for the "Bethel" Regiment expired this company split itself with a portion becoming a part of Co. B, 56th NCST and anoth er portion becoming a part of Co. B, Starr's Battery, Starr's 13th Battalion NCST, Light Art.), I: 75, 78, 85, 90, 113, 125, 126, 127; III: 313; IV: 294, 341.
Lenoir Braves, (Co A, 10th NCST, 1st Art & Engs), V: 42.
Lumberton Guards, (Co D, 2nd Vols/12th NCST), I: 124, 607, 608; II: 403; III: 19.
Lusk's Company, (Co A, 5th Battalion NCST, Cav; See: 5th Battalion NCST and 65th NCST, 6th Cav), IV: 272.
Macon Mounted Guards, (Co E, 41st NCST, 3rd Cav), II: 771, 774.
Marlboro Guards, (Co E, 27tth NCST), II: 425, 426, 427, 437, 442, 444.
McCarthy's Company, (Richmond Howitzers, Va., Art), I: 552.
McCullough's Rangers, (A com pany in Wise's Legion), V: 65.
McDowell Boys, (Co K, 12th Vols/22nd NCST), II: 162, 163.
McDowell Rifles, (Co B, 12th Vols/22nd NCST), II: 162, 163.
Men of Yadkin, (Co B, 38th NCST), II: 675, 678, 690, 691.
Montgomery Volunteers No. 1, (Co C, 13th Vols/23rd NCST), II: 183, 190, 203, 206.
Moore Independents, (Co H, 26th NCST), II: 304, 305, 323, 328, 332, 352, 359, 418, 420, 421.

Moore's Creek Riflemen, (Co E, 8th Vols/18th NCST), II: 65.
Morris Guards, (7th Vols/17th NCST), V: 36, 37, 40, 42, 43.
Nash Boys, (Co I, 2nd Vols/12th NCST), I: 607, 620.
North Carolina Defenders, (Co D, 7th Vols/17th NCST; Co A, 56th NCST), V: 42.
North Carolina Guards, (Co C, 27th NCST), II: 425, 426, 427, 438, 448.
North Carolina Rangers, (Co B, 10th Va., Cav), V: 627.
Oak City Guards, (Co E, 4th Vols/14th NCST), I: 707, 711.
O.K. Boys, (Co B, 31st NCST), V: 67.
Old Dominion Dragoons, (Co , Va.), I: 82.
Orange Guards, (Co G, 27th NCST), II: 425, 426, 427, 434, 436, 437, 438, 443, 448, 452, 453, 455; III: 314.
Orange Light Infantry, (Co D, 1st Vols, "Bethel"), I: 77, 90, 106, 124, 125, 127, 128, 133; II: 410.
Pee Dee Guards, (Co D, 13th Vols/23rd NCST), II: 184, 190, 200, 205, 214, 215, 216, 224.
Pee Dee Wildcats, (Co K, 26th NCST), II: 304, 306, 321, 330, 332, 337, 353, 360, 380, 393, 418, 419, 422.
Perquimans Beauregards, (Co F, 27th NCST), II: 426, 427, 434, 442.
Pitt Volumteers, (Co H, 27th NCST), II: 425, 426, 427, 444, 452, 453.
Preston Guards, (7th Vols/17th NCST), V: 42.
Raleigh Rifles, (4th Vols/14th NCST), IV: 517.
Randlesburg Rifles, (Co B, 3rd Vols/13th NCST), I: 125.
Randolph Hornets, (Co M, 12th Vols/22nd NCST), II: 162, 163, 170, 174, 176.
Rebel Rangers, (Co A, 41st NCST, 3rd Cav), II: 770, 774.
Richmond Blues, (A company in Wise's Legion), V: 65.
Richmond Boys, (Co E, 38th NCST), II: 675, 678, 681, 690.
Roanoke Guards, (Co A, 7th Vols/17th NCST), V: 42.
Roanoke Minute Men, (Co A, 4th Vols/14th NCST), I: 706.
Robeson Light Infantry, (Co D, 8th Vols/18th NCST), II: 65.
Rocky Face Rangers, (Co G, 38th NCST), II: 676, 678, 681, 685, 690.
Rough and Ready Guards, (Co F, 4th Vols/14th NCST; Co G, 66th NCST), I: 708, 718, 723; II: 306.
Sampson No. 1, (Co H, 10th Vols/20th NCST), II: 112.
Sampson No. 2, (Co I, 10th Vols/20th NCST), II: 112.
Sampson No. 3, (Co K, 10th Vols/20th NCST), II: 112.
Sampson Farmers, (Co C, 38th NCST), II: 675, 6678, 690, 691.
Sampson Ploughboys, (Co D, 38th NCST), II: 675, 678, 681, 690.
Savannah Guards, II: 186.
Scotch Boys, (Co F, 8th Vols/18th NCST), II: 16, 65.
Scotland Neck Mounted Ridles, (Co G, 41st NCST, 3rd Cav), II: 497, 771, 785.
Smithville Guards, (Co B, 3rd N.C. Militia), V: 24, 25.
Sneed's, (Co C, Freeman's 26th Battalion NCST), IV: 401; V: 626.
Southern Stars, (Co K, 1st Vols, "Bethel"), I: 75, 78, 91, 98,

106, 114, 116, 123, 125, 126, 127.
Spartan Band, (Co A, 38th NCST), II: 675, 678, 686, 690, 693.
Stanly Marksmen, (Co H, 4th Vols/14th NCST), I: 707.
Steel's, (Co B, 26th NCST), II: 306.
Stokes Boys, (Co H, 12th Vols/22nd NCST), II: 162, 163.
Surry Regulators, (Co C, 12th Vols/22nd NCST), II: 162.
Tar River Boys, (Co C, 7th Vols/17th NCST), V: 36, 37, 42, 43.
Thomasville Rifles, (Co B, 2nd Vols/12th NCST), I: 124, 607, 608.
Topsail Rifles, (Co C, 2nd NCST; Co H, 10th NCST, 1st Art & Engs, Pool's Hvy Art), I: 500.
Townsville Guards, (Co F, 2nd Vols/12th NCST), I: 638, 607.
Trinity Guards, (Salisbury Prison Gaurds), IV: 746.
Tuckahoe Braves, (Co D, 27th NCST), II: 425, 426, 427.
Uwarrie Boys, (Co H, 38th NCST), II: 676, 678, 681, 690.
Uwharrie Rifles, (Co L, 12th Vols/22nd NCST), II: 162, 163, 174, 176.
Wake Guards, (Co D, 26th NCST), II: 303, 306, 314, 319, 330, 338, 380, 403, 411, 414, 415, 419, 420, 421.
Wake Rangers, (Co I, 41st NCST), 3rd Cav), II: 771, 773, 775, 777, 786.
Ward's Company, (Co I, 27th NCST), II: 426.
Warren Guards, (Co F, 2nd Vols/12th NCST), I: 124, 605, 607, 639; IV: 243.
Warren Rifles, (Co G, 2nd Vols/12th NCST), I: 605, 607, 608.
Warrenton Guards, (1st Vols, "Bethel"), I: 124.
Washington Grays, (Co G, 7th Vols/17th NCST), V: 36, 39, 41.
Waxhaw Jackson Guards, (Co B, 26th NCST), II: 303, 305, 321.
Whitaker's Company, (Co E, 80th NCST), III: 738.
Wilkes Volunteers, (Co C, 26th NCST), II: 303, 306, 389, 398, 408, 421.
Wilmington Light Infantry, (30th N.C. Militia; Co G, 8th Vols/18th NCST), I: 216, 221; II: 16, 66; V: 27, 28.
Wilmington Rifle Guard, (30th N.C. Militia; Co I, 8th Vols/18th NCST), II: 16, 66; V: 27, 379.
Wilson Light Infantry, (Co E, 27th NCST; Co F, 4th NCST), II: 425.
Companies, Unattached, IV: 401.
Bass', IV: 402.
Croom's, IV: 402.
Dawson's, IV: 402.
Foy's, IV: 402.
Griswold's, IV: 402.
McDougal's, II: 651.
Pitt's, IV: 401.
Spencer's, IV: 401.
Swindell's, (see also: 68th NCST), IV: 402.
Whitehurst's, II: 310.
Compton, James W., (2nd Lt, Co G, 44th NCST), III: 23.
Comte de Paris, (French Officer on McClellan's Staff), II: 213.
Conaby Creek, [Coneby], (nr Plymouth), I: 398; II: 617; III: 339, 341; IV: 83, 573; V: 176, 182, 183, 186.
Conally, Leander R., (1st Sgt, Co G, 30th NCST), V: 557.

Concord, Mass., II: 603; V: 77.
Concord, N.C., I: 498, 533; II: 806; III: 589. 654, 655; IV: 609, 613.
Concord, Tenn., IV: 290.
Concord National Bank, III: 589.
Condell, _____, (Lt, Co A, 2nd Battalion NCST), IV: 245.
Condrey, A.G., (Pvt, Co B, 35th NCST), V: 562.
Condrey, J.V., (Pvt, Co B, 35th NCST), V: 562.
Confederate Badges, (and Medals), II: 690.
Confederate Flag, 2nd National, II: 525, 526.
Confederate Military History, I: 100, 622; II: 573, 601; III: 327.
Confederate Monument, (at Raleigh), I: 332.
Confederate Pike, III: 162.
Confederate Point, (Formerly known as Federal Point at the mouth of the Cape Fear River), II: 631, 760; IV: 307; V: 217, 218.
Confederate Treasury, III: 388.
Confederate Veterans Association, (aka United Confederate Veterans or U.C.V.), I: vi, ix.
Congaree River, S.C., III: 439.
Congleton, Ashley, (1st Lt, Co C, 40th NCST, 3rd Art, Hvy), II: 746.
Conigland, Edward, (Maj, AQM, H.J.B. Clark's N.C. Militia), IV: 646.
Conine, Creek, N.C., IV: 645.
Conley, C.O., (Capt, Co F, 58th NCST), III: 433, 447; V: 670.
Conley, H.C., (Pvt, Co A, 49th NCST), III: 138.
Conley, J.A., (2nd Lt, Co F, 41st NCST, 3rd Cav), II: 771.
Conley, J.C., (Lt, Co B, 58th NCST), III: 432.
Conley, J.T., (Capt, Co B, 12th Vols/22nd NCST), II: 165.
Conley, James, (2nd Lt, Co F, 29th NCST), II: 485.
Conley, James, (2nd Lt, Co F, 69th NCST, Thomas' Legion), III: 731, 747.
Conley, John H., (Lt, Co B, 35th NCST), II: 610.
Conley, Robert T., (1st Lt, Co F, 69th NCST, Thomas' Legion), III: 731, 743, 750, 759, 761.
Conley, W., (Capt, Co F, 58th NCST), III: 433.
Conly, H. Clay, (2nd Lt, Co A, 49th NCST), I: 734; III: 138.
Conly, T.W., (Sgt, Co K, 35th NCST), V: 193.
Conn, D.G., (1st Sgt, Co F, Naval Battalion, CSA), IV: 404; V: 666.
Connally, John K., (Capt, Co A, 1st Battalion NCST; Col, 55th NCST; Cmdr, Junior Reserves Brigade), III: 287, 288, 289, 291, 292, 293, 294, 295, 297, 302; IV: 6, 108, 182, 225, 440, 508; V: 110.
Connecticut, II: 367; V: 385.
Connell, J.H, (Pvt, Co C, 19th NCST, 1st Art & Engs, Brem-Graham-Williams' Battery, Light Art), V: 568.
Connell, J.W., (Sgt, Co F, 22nd S.C.), II: 624.
Connell, Ira J., (2nd Lt, Co G, 30th NCST), II: 497.
Connelly, Horace W., (2nd Lt, Co C, 8th Battalion Junior Reserves; Co G, 72nd NCST, 3rd Junior Reserves), IV: 42, 595.
Connelly, W.A., (Lt, Co A, Avery's Battalion NCST), I: 120.
Connelly Springs, N.C., II: 628.
Conner, E.C., (Pvt, Co F, 69th NCST, Thomas' Legion), III: 753.
Conner, George J., (Pvt, Co E, 34th NCST), V: 555.
Conner, Humphrey, (Pvt, Co A, 25th NCST), V: 561.

Conner, James, [Connor], (Brig Gen), I: xii, 471; II: 57, 58, 168, 170, 388, 575, 679, 781; III: 333, 469, 565; IV: 155, 469, 551, 565; V: xii, 208, 212.
Conoly, J.A.P., (2nd Lt, Co D, 9th Vols/19th NCST, 2nd Cav), II: 189.
Conolly, Burrel, V: 290.
Connolly, James Harvey, V: 293.
"Conquered Banner," (Poem), IV: 62-63.
Connor, Charles F., (Capt, Co I, 49th NCST), III: 128, 148, 153.
Conrad, J.C., (Pvt, Co F, 32nd NCST), V: 496.
Conrad, James H., (Sgt, Co I, 33rd NCST), II: 540, 578, 579.
Conrad, Joseph, (1st Lt, Co A, 42nd NCST), II: 789, 805.
Conrad, S.F., (Capt, Co E, Millard's 9th/20th Battalion Junior Reserves), IV: 387, 395, 396.
Conscript Act, Confederate, II: 177, 181, 201, 582, 677; III: 79, 676, 733-736; IV: 2, 125, 407, 652; V: 630.
Conscript Bureau, I: 16, 18; IV: 407-408; V: 6.
Conscription, Enforcement of, II: 733.
Consolva, Charles, (Musician, Co B, 32nd NCST), V: 495.
Conspiracy, IV: 321.
Constitution of the United States, V: 476.
Constitutional Convention, 1887, I: 132.
Contentnea Creek, N.C., I: 524; III: 135, 349, 704.
Cook, Aaron, (Pvt, Co F, 55th NCST), V: 528.
Cook, B.B., (2nd Lt, Co H, 77th NCST, 7th Senior Reserves), IV: 100.
Cook, Benjamin, (Pvt, Co K, 2nd NCST), I: 164.
Cook, Charles Betts, (2nd Lt, Co A, 63rd NCST, 5th Cav), I: 78, 91, 120, 127.
Cook, Isam, (Pvt, Co A, 1st Battalion NCST), V: 504.
Cook, J.F., (Pvt, Co K, 21st Ga.), V: 194.
Cook, J.H., (Pvt, Co B, 2nd Vols/12th NCST), V: 506.
Cook, J.T., [Cooke], (Sgt Maj, 2nd Vols/12th NCST), I: 609, 620, 629.
Cook, J.W., (Pvt, Co I, 48th NCST), V: 527.
Cook, James M., (Lt, Co A, 52nd NCST), III: 223, 229.
Cook, John, (Maj Gen, USA), III: 750.
Cook, Jonas, (Capt, Co H, 8th NCST), I: 401, 404.
Cook, Joseph, (Pvt, Co D, 59th NCST), V: 659.
Cook, Josiah, (Pvt, Co G, 2nd Battalion NCST), V: 495.
Cook, L. (Pvt, Co C, 28th NCST), V: 541.
Cook, Philip, (Brig Gen), IV: 508, 512.
Cook, R.B., (Pvt, Co C, 4th NCST), V: 488.
Cook, Richard F., (1st Cpl, Co A, 52nd NCST), III: 223; V: 535.
Cook, T.D., (Pvt, Co A, 10th NCST, 1st Art & Engs, Ramseur-Manly's Battery, Light Art), I: 555.
Cook, Thomas, (Pvt, Co I, 57th NCST), V: 518.
Cook, W.L, (Pvt, Co A, 3rd Vols/13th NCST), V: 549.
Cook, W.P., (Jr. 2nd Lt, Co B, 6th Battalion/60th NCST), III: 473, 482.
Cook, W.R., (Pvt, Co B, 6th Battalion/60th NCST), III: 482.
Cooke, C.L., [Cook], (Capt, Co B, 38th NCST), II: 675, 678.

Cooke, Charles M., (Lt, Adjt, 55th NCST), III: 287, 288, 296, 304, 305; V: xi, 669.
Cooke, E.M, (2nd Lt, Co C, 38th NCST), V: 548.
Cooke, Henry, (CSN), V: 327.
Cooke, James W., (Lt. Cmdr, NCN, Capt, Ellis; Capt, CSN, Albemarle), I: xiv; II: 616, 618; III: 8, 9, 177, 338; IV: 404, 416, 573; V: 181, 188, 192, 298, 303, 304, 305, 307, 309-311, 312, 318, 319, 320, 321, 322, 396.
Cooke, John R., (Brig Gen), I: xi, xii, 187, 471, 593, 741, 743, 747; II: 388, 427, 429, 434, 435, 436, 438, 439, 441, 442, 443, 447, 448, 449, 452, 453, 454, 461; III: 68, 69, 72, 74, 75, 117, 118, 247; IV: 442, 501, 502, 503, 504, 505, 506, 507, 509, 510, 511, 512, 565, 566, 568; V: 519.
Cooke, Oliver D., (Adjt, 14th Vols/24th NCST), II: 271.
Cooke County, Tenn., IV: 371.
Cooke's Bridge, (Blackwater River, Va.), III: 622.
Cooley, Thomas L., (1st Lt, Co B, 6th NCST), IV: 702, 706.
Coon, A., (Pvt, Co I, 1st Vols/11th NCST), V: 531.
Coon, David A., (1st Lt, Co I, 1st Vols/11th NCST), I: 120, 133, 585; IV: 722.
Coonce, Henry, (Pvt, Co E, 32nd NCST), V: 496.
Cooper, C.A., (Pvt, Co G, 54th NCST), V: 516.
Cooper, Columbus, (Pvt, Co F, 4th Vols/14th NCST), V: 490.
Cooper, D.M., (Capt, Co H, AQM, 2nd Battalion NCST), IV: 245, 252.
Cooper, David Y., (Hospital Steward, 38th NCST), V: 556.
Cooper, George W., (4th Cpl, Co B, 52nd NCST), III: 223.
Cooper, Henry S.S., (AQMS, Co C, 10th NCST, 1st Art & Engs, Reillly-Ramsay's Battery, Light Art), V: 568.
Cooper, James W., (Capt, Co H, 69th NCST, Thomas' Legion), III: 731, 743.
Cooper, John A., (Capt, 1st Battalion NCST; ADC, Hoke's Brigade), IV: 241, 242.
Cooper, John C.E., (2nd Lt, Co E, 33rd NCST), II: 539, 578; IV: 723.
Cooper, L.R., (Capt, 9th Vols/19th NCST, 2nd Cav), I: 435.
Cooper, Dr. Robert, (Lt, Ass't Surg, 6th Battalion/60th NCST), III: 484, 493; IV: 641.
Cooper, S.T., (Sgt, Co H, 32nd NCST), V: 497.
Cooper, Samuel, (A & IG, CSA), II: 483, 776, 778; III: 335, 381, 550, 556; IV: 245, 246, 248, 419; V: 14, 467.
Cooper, Thomas J., (Capt, Co H, 69th NCST, Thomas' Legion), III: 731.
Cooper, Thomas W., (Capt, Co C, 1st Vols/11th NCST), I: 119, 584, 590.
Cooper, W.J., (Pvt, Co B, 1st Battalion NCST), V: 504.
Cooper, W.R., (Musician, 6th NCST), V: 511.
Cooper River, S.C., II: 758.
Cooper's Iron Works, Ga., II: 742.
Coosawhatchie, S.C., I: 581, 742; III: 186, 187; IV: 101, 333, 505.
Cope, E.B., (Col, Engineer, Gettysburg Park Commission), V: 110.
Cope, E.W., (Col, Corps of Engineers, USA), III: 300.
Copeland, ______, [Virginius], (Lt, Co H, 9th Vols/19th NCST, 2nd Cav), II: 89.
Copeland, J.H., (Pvt, Co E, 12th Vols/22nd NCST), V: 553.

Copeland, William, (Fayetteville and Harper's Ferry Arsenals), IV: 298.
Copeland, Dr. Winfield S., (Surg, Camp of Instruction, Garysburg), IV: 629.
Coppedge, John H., (Capt, Co G, 43rd NCST), III: 2, 3.
Coppedge, W.B., (2nd Lt, Co A, 70th NCST, 1st Junior Reserves), IV: 12.
Coppens, ______, [Gaston], (Lt Col, 1st Battalion, La.), I: 82.
Coppens, Alfred, (Col), II: 766.
Corbett, ______, (English, Capt, Shenandoah), V: 346.
Corbett, Carr B., (Jr 2nd Lt, Co I, 1st Vols, "Bethel"), I: 113.
Corbett, George W., (1st Lt, Sharpshooters, 8th Vols/18th NCST), II: 46; IV: 722.
Corbett, Warren, (Pvt, Co H, 2nd NCST), I: 176.
Corbett, William (Pvt, Co E, 27th NCST), II: 462; V: 523.
Corbett, William S., (Capt, Co B, 49th NCST), I: 734; III: 152.
Corbin, ______, (Col, Owner of the residence at Moss Neck, Va. where Jackson once had his headquarters), IV: 172.
Corbin, ______, (Sgt, Co I, 39th NCST), II: 739.
Corbin's Farm, (nr Port Royal, Va.), II: 116, 117; IV: 172.
Corbin's Neck, Va., II: 36.
Corbit, Augustus, (Pvt, Co C, 5th NCST), I: 291; V: 505.
Corbitt, W.M., (1st Lt, Co I, 50th NCST), III: 189, 203.
Corbitt, Warren, (Pvt, Co G, 2nd NCST), V: 486.
Corcoran, Michael, (Brig Gen, USA), IV: 532, 747.
Corcoran's Irish Legion, (USA), IV: 532.
Cord, John, (Fayetteville and Harper's Ferry Arsenals), IV: 298.
Cordle, Thomas, (Pvt, Co C, 13th Vols/23rd NCST), V: 509.
Cordon, W.W., (7th Vols/17th NCST), V: 43.
Core, Arthur, (Pvt, Co F, 14th Vols/24th NCST), V: 560.
Core Creek, N.C., (nr Kinston), I: 391, 742; II: 612; III: 173, 205, 273, 324.
Core Sound, N.C., I: 502; IV: 620.
Corinth, Miss., III: 439.
Corl, G.F.C., (Capt, Co D, 5th Battalion Junior Reserves; Co E, 71st NCST, 2nd Junior Reserves), IV: 25, 28.
Corn, F.M., (Jr 2nd Lt, Co 1, Woodfin's Battalion, Cav; Lt, Co 8, 79th NCST, 8th Cav), IV: 111, 115.
Corn, John P., (Pvt, Co K, 6th Vols/16th NCST), IV: 218; V: 552.
Corn, Mathew W., (Pvt, Co K, 6th Vols/16th NCST), V: 552.
Corn Cake Inlet, N.C., II: 756.
Corn Field, The, (nr Sharpsburg, Md.), I: 225; II: 32, 33, 223, 434, 435.
Cornehlson, C., (Capt, 30th N.C. Militia; Co A, 8th Vols/18th NCST), II: 16; V: 27.
Cornell, ______, (Engineering Officer, Fort Hatteras), V: 43.
Cornish, Wilie A., (Hospital Steward, Co H, 8th Vols/18th NCST), II: 64; V: 539.
Cornwallis, Lord General, I: 655, 754; II: 196; III: 599.
Cornwell, O.M., (2nd Lt, Co I, 54th NCST), V: 511.
Corpening, David J., (Col, 74th Senior Reserves), IV: 69.
Corpening, Julius A., (2nd Lt, Co G, 56th NCST), III: 316.

Corps, Confederate (Infantry):
Anderson's, (4th Corps ANV; See also: Gordon's), II: 446, 461, 784, 798; III: 374, 398, 399, 400; IV: 438, 454, 524; V: 573.
Beauregard's, (1st Corps prior to the reorganization of the army under Lee) II: 192.
Breckenridge's, (AoT), III: 749, 751, 752.
Buckner's, (AoT), III: 435, 449; IV: 438, 439.
Early's, (2nd Corps, ANV, aka Early's Army, Early's Army of the Valley), I: 153, 154, 155, 205, 209, 287, 290, 323, 324, 325, 326, 327, 328, 644, 727; II: 124, 241, 245, 247, 250, 253, 255, 256, 260, 441, 503, 532, 694; III: 12, 13, 15, 55, 277, 278, 279; IV: 194, 515, 629.
Ewell's, (2nd Corps, ANV), I: 200, 254, 257, 316, 378, 279, 555, 589, 594, 631, 632, 726; II: 41, 48, 49, 50, 135, 138, 233, 234, 240, 351, 381, 525, 531, 660, 693, 784; III: 5, 6, 40, 41, 44, 45, 47, 54, 269, 270, 277, 399, 400, 559, 561, 570, 578; IV: 176, 181, 184, 190, 191, 193, 237, 238, 253, 437, 449, 454, 514, 515, 563; V: 118, 121, 138, 606, 611, 613.
Gordon's, (See also: Anderson's), I: 175, 209, 212, 265, 330, 651, 686; II: 266, 451, 452; III: 15, 144, 389, 390, 400, 426 IV: 454, 524, 547; V: 253, 254, 261, 263, 573.
Hardee's, (AoT/AoW), II: 702, 756, 757; III: 440, 484, 513; IV: 9, 31, 32, 56, 58, 59, 350, 351, 591.
Hill's, A.P., (3rd Corps, ANV), I: 202, 204, 378, 379, 382, 385, 541, 575, 582, 588, 589, 594, 595, 598, 599, 601, 631, 632, 638, 641, 672, 675, 742, 764; II: 18, 41, 42, 47, 59, 174, 176, 178, 233, 241, 344, 350, 357, 379, 381, 383, 388, 441, 443, 445, 448, 455, 461, 479, 562, 569, 660, 661, 690, 691, 693; III: 5, 44, 47, 52, 72, 88, 92, 98, 117, 235, 236, 241, 242, 243, 245, 246, 248, 304, 305, 559, 578; IV: 176, 183, 184, 212, 390, 438, 467, 476, 506, 507, 532, 558, 559, 563, 573, 613.
Hill's, Daniel Harvey, (Aot/AoW), II: 491; III: 488; IV: 438, 439, 563; V: 173.
Hood's, (AoT), III: 437, 492; IV: 439.
Huger's, IV: 437.
Jackson's, T.J. "Stonewall," (2nd Corps, ANV, aka Jackson's Valley Army, Jackson's Foot Cavalry), I: 142, 144, 169, 186, 191, 251, 373, 376, 567, 628, 629, 658, 659, 663, 665, 666, 672, 707, 714, 715, 764; II: 30, 36, 41, 66, 68, 71, 73, 132, 133, 151, 153, 154, 158, 170, 218, 222, 431, 432, 461, 474, 477, 501, 525, 545, 546, 556, 562, 585, 620, 655, 656, 657, 658, 682, 683, 688, 690; III: 117, 269; IV: 169, 171, 173, 234, 235, 328, 551; V: 8, 72, 96, 588.
Lee's, S.D., (AoT), I: 386; III: 438, 454, 497; IV: 592, 665.
Longstreet's, (1st Corps, ANV), I: 35, 36, 373, 378, 379, 522, 523, 547, 548, 553, 555, 557, 558, 580, 590, 592, 594, 595, 601, 622, 623, 625, 628, 631, 632, 633, 675, 676, 720, 744, 762; II: 41, 42, 233, 288, 382, 383, 431, 461, 588, 655, 657, 660, 665, 702, 703, 713, 800, 801; III: 30, 44, 45, 76, 94, 119, 139, 140, 299, 300, 304, 305, 399, 400, 401, 414, 436, 470,

559, 561, 571, 743; IV: 161, 169, 176, 191, 208, 212, 239, 371, 437, 457, 507, 536, 538, 541, 571; V: 72, 123, 124, 138, 208, 354, 471, 573, 588.
Polk's, (AoT), II: 492, 731, 732, 737, 739, 742.
Smith's, E. Kirby, (AoT), II: 706, 708, 709; V: 8.
Smith's, G.W., (2nd Corps prior th the reorganization of the army under Lee), I: 349, 350; V: 8.
Stewart's, (AoT/AoW), III: 495, 698; IV: 58.
Corps, Federal (Infantry):
Birney's, (II), III: 630.
Birney's, (X), II: 623.
Blair's, (XVII), III: 194, 197, 198; IV: 57, 352.
Burnside's, (IX), I: 288, 640, 721; II: 6, 33, 49, 241, 480, 621, 622, 623, 667, 799; III: 141, 373; IV: 165, 469, 475; V: 72, 79, 80, 588, 589.
Couch's, (IV), I: 618; V: 588.
Crittenden's, (IX), III: 678.
Crook's, (VIII), I: 173, 209; II: 257.
Davis', (XIV), II: 803; III: 194, 196.
Franklin's, (VI), I: 301, 601; II: 47, 120; III: 258, 753; V: 72, 89, 588.
French's, (III), I: 198, 592; III: 575, 579, 580; IV: 562.
Gibbon's, (XXIV), II: 62.
Hancock's, (II), I: 289, 385, 596, 598, 747; II: 47, 48, 49, 50, 363, 383, 443, 450, 454, 621, 665; III: 31, 628; IV: 191, 534, 564; V: 121, 126, 149, 150, 158, 208, 210.
Heintzelman's, (III), II: 203.
Hooker's, (XX), II: 739; III: 194, 196; V: 588.
Hooker's, (I), V: 72, 80.
Howard's, (XI), I: 629, 638; II: 501; V: 114, 118, 121.
Humphrey's, (II), I: 592, 593, 600, 601; III: 400; IV: 43.
Keye's, (IV), II: 203.
Lockwood's, (VIII), III: 753.
Logan's, (XIV), III: 194, 195, 197.
Mansfield's, (VII), I: 185, 186; V: 72, 80, 588.
Martindale's, (XVIII), II: 723.
Meade's, (V), III: 560, 565, 567.
Paine's, (XXV, Colored), V: 238.
Parke's, (IX), I: 600, 601, 602.
Porter's, (V), I: 612, 613, 615, 618; II: 654; V: 72, 79, 80, 82, 588, 589.
Reno's, (IX), II: 220, 221.
Reynold's, (I), I: 634, 638; II: 344, 345, 368; V: 114, 121, 613.
Schofield's, (XXIII), I: 532; IV: 312.
Sedgwick's, (VI), I: 595, 629, 640, 745; II: 48; III: 269, 273, 582; IV: 678, 683; V: 122.
Sickle's, (III), II: 40, 43; V: 114, 121.
Siegle's, (XI), I: 169, 170, 376, 697, 715; II: 36, 40, 66, 229, 232.
Slocum's, (XIX), I: 647; II: 12, 532, 803; III: 258, 753.
Smith's, W.F., (XVIII), II: 621.
Sumner's, (II), I: 186, 188, 351, 352; II: 213, V: 72, 77, 80, 588.
Sykes', (V), III: 575; V: 122.
Terry's, (Provisional), II: 647; IV: 429, 541, 542, 543, 547, 591, 592.
Warren's, G.K., (II), II: 379; III: 580, 581; IV: 184, 185, 562.
Warren's, G.K., (V), I: 599, 600, 601, 602, 743; II: 5, 6, 48, 105, 173, 378, 390, 391, 443, 622, 623, 798, 800; III: 26, 29, 92, 97, 146, 242, 397, 401, 469,

595, 628, 631, 644; IV: 29, 43; V: 207. Weitzel's, (XVIII), I: 647; II: 637; IV: 590.
Wright's, H.G., (VI), I: 200, 602, 647; II: 61, 62, 259, 532.
Corps of Engineers, CSA, IV: 409; V: 4.
Correll, E.M., (Color Sgt, 7th NCST), I: 378.
Correll, J.W., (Pvt, Co G, 6th Vols/16th NCST), IV: 198.
Correll, Phillip A., Jr., (2nd Lt, Co A, 52nd NCST), III: 223, 229.
Correll, W.B., (Musician, 10th Vols/20th NCST), V: 508.
Corse, Montgomery, (Brig Gen), III: 235, 333, 334, 400.
Corzine, J.C., (Pvt, Co C, 33rd NCST), V: 544.
Cosand, William, (Pvt, Co H, 34th NCST), V: 556.
Cosart, E.H., (Musician, 6th NCST), V: 511.
Cosart, J.H., (Musician, 6th NCST), V: 511.
Costin, S.B., (Pvt, Co E, 8th Vols/18th NCST), II: 64.
Costin House, (Wilmington), IV: 221.
Costner, E.S., (Pvt, Co H, 49th NCST), V: 565.
Costner, Thomas, (Pvt, Co I, 38th NCST), V: 558.
Coston, E.M., (Pvt, Co A, 35th NCST), V: 562.
Cotten, M.A., (Lt, Adjt, 7th Vols/17th NCST), II: 2, 3, 5.
Cotten, Richard C., (Lt, Co D, 61st NCST), III: 504, 505; IV: 706.
Cotten, Richard C., (Lt Col, 44th NCST), III: 21, 22, 23.
Cotten, Thomas, (Pvt, Co D, 61st NCST), III: 507.
Cotten, W.J., (Pvt, Co F, 10th Vols/20th NCST), II: 120.
Cotter, John A., (Jr 2nd Lt, Co H, 39th NCST), II: 706.
Cotton, _____, (Col, 6th Ky., USA), II: 491.
Cotton, Mrs. _____, (Wife of Col), II: 491.
Cotton, Augustus, (2nd Lt, Co E, 7th Vols/17th NCST), I: 120.
Cotton, G.A., (2nd Lt, Co E, 7th Vols/17th NCST), I: 120.
Cotton, James C., (Lt, Co D, 4th NCST), I: 232.
Cotton, John, (Pvt, Co I, 35th NCST), V: 563.
Cotton, R., (Pvt, Co D, 35th NCST), V: 562.
Cotton Bonds, V: 453-461.
Cottrill, W.S., (Pvt, Co K, 14th Vols/24th NCST), V: 560.
Couch, Darius Nash, (Maj Gen, USA), I: 351; II: 203, 205, 214.
Coughenour, William C., (Capt, AIG Robert's Cav Brigade; AIG Ramseur-Cox's Brigade), I: 231, 234, 267, 279; II: 108, 109; IV: 462, 463, 580.
Council, A., (Pvt, Co D, 33rd NCST), V: 562.
Council, E.D., (Pvt, Co E, 5th NCST), I: 292; V: 505.
Council, J.W., (Lt, Co D, 9th NCST, 1st Cav), I: 485.
Council, T.T., (Pvt, Co B, 33rd NCST), V: 544.
Council, Thomas C., (Cpl, Co D, 5th Vols/15th NCST), V: 521.
Council, W.B., (Capt, Co B, 65th NCST, 6th Cav), III: 674, 675, 683.
Council, W.H., (Cpl, Co D, 35th NCST), V: 193.
Council of Ahitopel, IV: 715.
Courtney, A.H., (Cpl, Co F, 26th NCST), V: 602.
Courtney, C.C., (Pvt, Co A, 13th Vols/23rd NCST), II: 215.
Courtney, H.C., (Pvt, Co F, 26th NCST), V: 602.
Courts, Dr. W.H., (Surg, 2nd NCST), I: 157; IV: 631.

Cousins, ______, (Capt, AAG Law's Brigade), III: 291, 292.
Cousins Road, (nr Namozine Church), III: 650.
Cove Gap, N.C., V: 289, 292.
Covert, N.L., (Pvt, Co D, 61st NCST), III: 507.
Covey, Dr. ______, (Surg, Medical Director of N.C. Hospitals), IV: 625.
Covington, B.H., (2nd Lt, Co D, 13th Vols/23rd NCST), II: 184.
Covington, E.A., (Hospital Steward, Co C, 4th Vols/14th NCST), I: 731.
Covington, E.D., (Sgt Maj, 44th NCST), III: 22; V: 533.
Covington, H.R., [William R.], (2nd Lt, Co E, 38th NCST), IV: 706.
Covington, H.T., (Pvt, Co K, 26th NCST), V: 533.
Covington, M.T., (Jr 2nd Lt, Co E, 38th NCST), II: 675, 678, 681.
Covington, Nathaniel, (Pvt, Co B, 59th NCST), V: 659.
Covington, R., (Pvt, Co H, 3rd Vols/13th NCST), V: 551.
Covington, S.T., (Pvt, Co C, 3rd Vols/13th NCST), V: 550.
Covington, W.T., (2nd Lt, Co H, 6th NCST), V: 511.
Cowan, ______, (Capt), V: 292, 295.
Cowan, A.B., (Capt, Co F, 62nd NCST), III: 516, 524.
Cowan, Benjamin A., (Lt, Co G, 51st NCST), III: 219.
Cowan, Isaac A., (Capt, Co B, 4th NCST), I: 232, 269.
Cowan, J.A., [Isaac A.], (Lt, Co B, 4th NCST), I: 270.
Cowan, John, (Capt, Co D, 3rd NCST), I: ix, 177, 196, 215; IV: 719, 721; V: 624.
Cowan, J. Pink, (2nd Lt, Co A, 4th NCST), I: 232, 370.
Cowan, Robert H., (Col, 8th Vols/18th NCST), I: 178, 179, 215, 216; II: 15, 20, 21, 23, 25, 26, 27, 34, 37; IV: 473; V: 649.
Cowan, Robert V., (Col, 33rd NCST), II: 537, 538, 547, 572, 578, 664; IV: 473, 474; V: 538, 667.
Cowan, Thomas, (Lt, Co B, 3rd NCST), I: 213.
Cowan, Thomas A., (2nd Lt, Co A, 33rd NCST), II: 538, 567, 571, 572, 575, 576, 577, 578.
Cowan, N.V., (Pvt, Co B, 4th NCST), V: 488.
Cowan, W.W., (Cpl, Co I, 3rd NCST), V: 487.
Cowan, W.W., (Jr 2nd Lt, Co G, Walker's Battalion, Thomas' Legion, 80th NCST), IV: 118.
Cowan House, (nr Murfreesboro), III: 477.
Cownad, David G., (Col, 32nd NCST), II: 522; III: 17, 264; IV: 441, 516; V: 247, 248, 494.
Coward's Bridge, N.C., III: 174, 704; IV: 338.
Cowdy, ______, (Capt, Prisoner, USA), III: 334.
Cowee Mountains, N.C., III: 757, 758.
Cowles, C.L., (Lt, Co B, 51st NCST), III: 218; V: 673.
Cowles, Miles M., (Adjt, 38th NCST), II: 676, 678, 680, 681.
Cowles, W.H.H., (Lt Col, 9th NCST, 1st Cav), I: 422, 428, 429, 433, 441, 449, 454, 455, 456, 457, 458, 460, 461, 4662, 467, 470, 474, 475, 481, 485, 775, 782; II: 102; III: 538, 604;
Cowley, Stephen, (Capt, IG Bate's Division), IV: 420.
Cowpens Landing, N.C., (Neuse River), III: 710.
Cowpens, S.C., (Site of Revolutionary War battle), III: 735.
Cowper, J.C.E., [J.C.C.], (2nd Lt, Co E, 33rd NCST), IV: 723.

Cowper, L.R., (Capt, Co C, 9th Vols/19th NCST, 2nd Cav), II: 89, 104.
Cowper, Pulaski, (1st Lt, N.C. Conscription Bureau), I: 22, 39, 279; IV: 407, 408.
Cox, _____, (Capt, Co D, 12th Vols/22nd NCST), II: 162.
Cox, Rev. A.B., (Chaplain, 12th Vols/22nd NCST), II: 162; IV: 609.
Cox, Abram, (Capt, AQM, 44th NCST), III: 21, 22, 23.
Cox, Aras B., (Capt, Co I, 61st NCST), III: 504.
Cox, Braxton, (Pvt, Co D, 58th NCST), III: 453.
Cox, C.H., (Pvt, Co C, 4th Vols/14th NCST), I: 732.
Cox, Dr. Cader G., (2nd Lt, Ass't Surg, 35th NCST; Ass't Surg, 56th NCST), II: 593; III: 318, 322; IV: 637, 641; V: 559.
Cox, Charley, (Pvt, Co C, 4th Vols/14th NCST), I: 724, 728.
Cox, F.C., (Capt, AAG, ANV), V: 572.
Cox, Dr. F, (Ass't Surg, 28th NCST), IV: 636.
Cox, G.H., (Ass't Surg, 76th NCST, 6th Senior Reserves), IV: 97, 743.
Cox, G.W., (Pvt, Co F, 2nd Battalion NCST), V: 495.
Cox, H., (Pvt, Co I, 3rd Vols/13th NCST), V: 551.
Cox, H.B., (Sgt, Co D, 48th NCST), III: 122.
Cox, H.V., (Pvt, Co I, 1st Vols/11th NCST), V: 531.
Cox, J., (Pvt, Co F, 45th NCST), V: 500.
Cox, Jacob Dolson, [Coxe], (Maj Gen, USA), II: 11, 650, 803; III: 708; IV: 543, 544.
Cox, John J., [Joseph], (AQM, 31st NCST), II: 511; V: 667.
Cox, Joshua, (Lt, Co I, 61st NCST), III: 504.
Cox, M.H., (1st Lt, Co A, 6th NCST), IV: 701.
Cox, Romulus M., (2nd Lt, Co K, 52nd NCST), III: 225.
Cox, Uz, (Capt, Co H., 10th Vols/20th NCST), II: 112.
Cox, William Ruffin, (Brig Gen), I: xi, xii, 139, 156, 157, 160, 169, 170, 172, 173, 174, 175, 207, 208, 210, 212, 251, 252, 253, 261, 262, 268, 175, 275; II: 503, 505; IV: 206, 207, 441, 443, 464 personal account, 516, 554; V: xi, xii, 247, 250, 255, 260, 483.
Cox Road, (nr Appomattox River and Petersburg, Va.), II: 61, 482; III: 111, 612.
Cox's Bridge, N.C., (Neuse River nr Goldsboro), III: 727.
Cozart, Thomas J., (Pvt, Co F, 26th NCST), II: 374; V: 601, 603.
Cozine, David M., (Capt, Co C, 33rd NCST), II: 538, 359, 578.
Carb Apple Section, (of East Tennessee), III: 719.
Crab Creek, N.C., III: 668.
Crab Orchard, Ky., II: 708; IV: 288.
Crabtree, Abraham, (Pvt, Co G, 4th Vols/14th NCST), V: 490.
Crabtree, Henry, (Pvt, Co A, 14th Vols/24th NCST), V: 560.
Crabtree, R., (Pvt, Co D, 1st NCST), V: 485.
Crabtree, W.H., (2nd Lt, Co C, 1st Battalion Junior Reserves; Co D, 70th NCST, 1st Junior Reserves), IV: 13.
Craddock, Charles Egbert, (Journalist), IV: 120.
Craddock's Cross Roads, N.C., III: 507.
Craft, V.B., (1st Cpl, Co D, 3rd Vols/13th NCST), V: 550.
Crafts, E.P., (Master, USN), V: 243.
Craig, A.M., (1st Lt, Co B, 4th Battalion Junior Reserves; Co

D, 72nd NCST, 3rd Junior Reserves), IV: 38.
Craig, Archiblad, (Lt, Co D, 3rd NCST), I: 194.
Craig, Charles, (Pilot, Sirene), V: 445.
Craig, Charles W., (Pilot, Margaret and Jesse), V: 357.
Craig, J.S., (Pvt, Co H, 37th NCST), V: 546.
Craig, James A., (Pvt, Co B, 5th Vols/15th NCST), V: 521.
Craig, James W., (Pilot, Lynx), V: 357, 369, 374.
Craig, John T., (Pvt, Co B, 5th Vols/15th NCST), V: 521.
Craig, T.N., (2nd Lt, Co H, 13th Vols/23rd NCST), II: 187.
Craig, T.W., (Pilot, Pet), V: 357.
Craig, William, (Pilot), V: 369.
Craig's Landing, (nr Fort Fisher), II: 639; IV: 306; V: 225.
Craige, Cicero H., [Craig], (2nd Lt, Co I, 3rd NCST), I: 203, 213, 220, 221, 222.
Craige, Francis B., (1st Lt, Co C, 33rd NCST), II: 539, 578.
Craige, James, (Capt, Co G, 6th NCST), V: 584.
Craige, James A., (Maj, 57th NCST), I: 296, 345; III: 405, 406, 418, 420; V: 584.
Craige, Kerr, (Capt, Co I, 9th NCST, 1st Cav; ADC to Gordon), I: 477, 486; III: 537, 601, 602; IV: 582.
Craige, S.W., (Pvt, Co F, 35th NCST), V: 563.
Crampton's Gap, Md., I: 140, 184, 206, 553, 625, 739, 740; II: 218, 222; III: 13; V: 72.
Cranberry Iron Works, N.C., I: 22.
Cranford, H.G., (Cpl, Co A, 57th NCST), V: 517.
Cranor, W.E., (Pvt, Co B, 1st NCST), V: 485.
Crapon, George M., (2nd Lt, Co F, 3rd NCST), IV: 722.
Crater, Ruben J., (Musician, 33rd NCST), II: 537.
Crater, The, (nr Petersburg, Va., and Battle of 1864), During the siege of Petersburg Grant ordered a tunnel dug under the Confederate lines and at its end a chamber filled with explosives. When the work was completed this huge store of explosives was detonated rending men, animals and earth in one of the largest explosions of the war. The slaughter that ensued as the Federals attempted to breach the Confederate line after the explosion was horrific. Supposedly the Federals troops charged giving a yell of "no quarter" and the Confederate defenders who rushed to the scene of devastation happily consented to a battle with no mercy. Federals who found themselves trapped at the bottom of that Crater of their own making were shot down as easily as fish in a barrel. The amazing thing about this scheme was that from the opening days of the war the Federal army had complained bitterly when they happened to encounter that new innovation of war, the torpedo (land mine). They branded it barbaric and sought through negotiation to ban their use. And in the main, for their part, the Confederates discontinued the use of the land mine-the naval variety remained in use by both sides. But, Sherman and Grant adopted the use of land mines, other types of hidden explosives and this powder charged tunnel whenever the notion struck

them. Obviously barbarity was in the eye of the beholder. I: 407, 559, 598, 678, 747; II: 60, 288, 292, 298, 386, 534, 624, 801; III: 56, 97, 121, 126, 141, 152, 156, 157, 307-308, 371-375, 378, 380, 394, 690; IV: 87, 203, 362, 495, 564, 575, 576; V: 16, 247, 617-618.
Craton, Marshall D., (Col, 50th NCST), II: 425, 426, 592, 593, 595; III: 161, 163, 202.
Craven, Rev. Dr. B., (Capt, "Trinity Guards," Salisbury Prison Guards), IV: 746.
Craven, F., (2nd Sgt, Co F, 46th NCST), V: 524.
Craven, Newton, (Pvt, Co B, 57th NCST), V: 517.
Craven County, N.C., I: 534; II: 162, 771; III: 131, 504, 704, 710; IV: 354, 424, 483, 489, 604; V: 17, 18.
Crawford, A.W., (2nd Lt, Co K, 12th Vols/22nd NCST), II: 165, 166.
Crawford, B.F., (Pvt, Co D, 44th NCST), V: 533.
Crawford, C.M., (1st Lt, Co B, 72nd NCST), III: 515.
Crawford, Eli, (Pvt, Co K, 34th NCST), V: 556.
Crawford, J.A, (Sgt, Co E, 28th NCST), V: 542.
Crawford, J.M., (1st Lt, Co B & E, 62nd NCST), IV: 701.
Crawford, J.R., (Capt, Co B, 42nd NCST), II: 790, 791, 805; III: 320.
Crawford, James, (Cpl, Co K, 4th NCST), I: 234.
Crawford, James G., (Capt, Co I, 39th NCST), II: 706, 739.
Crawford, John T., (Lt, Co E, 49th NCST), III: 143, 148.
Crawford, L.W., (1st Lt, Co D, 42nd NCST), II: 790, 799, 806.
Crawford, Leonard, (Pvt, Co K, 34th NCST), V: 556.
Crawford, Marley, [Cranford], (2nd Lt, Co H, 38th NCST), II: 678.
Crawford, R.R., (Capt, Co D, 42nd NCST), II: 790, 792, 799, 806, V: 663.
Crawford, S.N., (Pvt, Co G, 28th NCST), V: 542.
Crawford, Samuel J., (1st Lt, Co K, 6th NCST), IV: 700, 706.
Crawford, Samuel Wylie, (Maj Gen, USA), III: 628, 631.
Crawford, T.D., (2nd Lt, CSN), IV: 723.
Crawford, W.H., (Capt, Co B, 42nd NCST), II: 790, 792, 805.
Crawford Farm, (nr Salisbury), II: 792.
Crawley, ______, (Col, QM, ANV), V: 197.
Crawley, A.B., (Pvt, Co B, 53rd NCST), V: 501.
Crayton, W., (Cpl, Co D, 28th NCST), V: 541.
Creasman, A., (Pvt, Co K, 1st Vols/11th NCST), V: 531.
Creasman, J., (Pvt, Co L, 12th Vols/22nd NCST), V: 554.
Creasman, William B., (Col, 29th NCST), II: 485, 491, 493.
Credle, C.N., (Pvt, Co F, 6th NCST), V: 513.
Credle, Dave, (Jr 2nd Lt, Detached Co, 68th NCST), III: 723.
Credle, Elisha, (Sgt, Detached Co, 68th NCST), III: 723.
Credle, Frank, (Pvt, Detached Co, 68th NCST), III: 724.
Creech, ______, (Pvt, Co E, 14th Vols/24th NCST), II: 286.
Creech, John, (Pvt, Co H, 8th Vols/18th NCST), II: 64; V: 540.
Creech, Nasrow, [Nasoow], (Pvt, Co C, 5th NCST), I: 291; V: 540.
Creed, Anderson, (Pvt, Co B, 2nd Battalion NCST), V: 495.
Creed, J.D., (Pvt, Co C, 11th Vols/21st NCST), V: 514.

Creed, J.W., (Pvt, Co C, 11th Vols/21st NCST),V: 514.
Creek, Indians, III: 759.
Creekman, L.R., (1st Lt, Co I, 4th NCST), I: 231, 270; V: 664.
Crenshaw, ______, (Lt, CSMC, Tallahassee), V: 438.
Crenshaw, H.A., (Capt, Co A, 10th NCST, 1st Art & Engs, Ramseur-Manly's Battery, Light Art), I: 558; IV: 161.
Crenshaw, John, (Pvt, Co F, 49th NCST), V: 564.
Crenshaw's Bridge, II: 547.
Cress, Absalom, (Pvt, Co I, 5th NCST), I: 292; V: 506.
Cress, H.W., (Pvt, Co F, 57th NCST), V: 517.
Crews, Alexander, (2nd Lt, Co G, 30th NCST), II: 497; V: 572.
Crews, D.G., (Sgt, Co E, 13th Vols/23rd NCST), V: 510.
Crews, E.W., (Pvt, Co A, 1st Battalion NCST), V: 504.
Crews, J.H., (Cpl, Co C, 32nd NCST), V: 496.
Crews. John, (Pvt, Co D, 45th NCST), V: 500.
Crews, John M., (2nd Sgt, Co K, 52nd NCST), III: 225.
Crews, R.L., (Capt, Co B, 70th NCST, 1st Junior Reserves), IV: 12.
Crews, S.B., (Pvt, Co F, 37th NCST), V: 546.
Crews, T.J., (Capt, Co D, Littlejohn's 23rd Battalion Senior Reserves), IV: 399.
Crews, W.F., (Pvt, Co G, 30th NCST), V: 492.
Crichton, H.R., (Lt, Co F, 47th NCST), III: 84.
Craiglersville, Va., II: 545; IV: 465.
Crisp, Robert, (Pvt, Co I, 34th NCST), V: 556.
Crisp, S.E., (Pvt, Co F, 30th NCST), V: 492.
Crisp, S.W., (Pvt, Co F, 26th NCST), V: 602.
Critcher, A.S., [Andrew J.], (Capt, C. B, 37th NCST), IV: 723.
Critchton, H.R., (Lt, Co F, 47th NCST), III: 84.
Crittenden, Thomas Leonidas, (Maj Gen, USA), III: 678.
Croatan Sound, N.C., V: 61.
Croatan Station, N.C., I: 537.
Crocker, T.J., (Capt, Co G, 13th Vols/23rd NCST), II: 185, 186.
Crocker, Luther R., (2nd Lt, Co G, 43rd NCST), III: 3.
Crockett, George W., (Capt, Co C, 14th Vols/24th NCST), II: 269.
Cromartie, James A., (Cpl, Co K, 8th Vols/18th NCST), II: 64; V: 540.
Cromwell, Elisha, (Lt Col, 44th NCST), III: 21, 22.
Croner, H.H., (Cpl, Co K, 11th Vols/21st NCST), V: 515.
Cronstadt, Russia, V: 425.
Crook, ______, (Col, Wilson's Cav, USA), III: 618.
Crook, George, (Maj Gen, USA), I: 173; II: 123, 250, 257.
Croom, Allen G., [Croome], (Capt, Co E, 61st NCST), II: 541.
Croom, Charles T., (Lt, Co E, 61st NCST), III: 504.
Croom, N.R., (Pvt, Co E, 37th NCST), V: 545.
Crosby, Pierce, (Capt, USN, Keystone State), V: 373.
Cross, Elbert, (Pvt, Co H, 5th NCST), I: 292; V: 505.
Cross, J., (Pvt, Co E, 47th NCST), V: 535.
Cross, J.F., (1st Lt, Co B, 5th Battalion NCST), IV: 701, 703.
Cross, J.P., (Capt, Co K, 5th Vols/15th NCST), I: 736.
Cross, M.H., (2nd Lt, Co B, 4th Vols/14th NCST), V: 484.
Cross, W., (Pvt, Co E, 47th NCST), V: 535.

Cross Creek, (District of Cumberland County), IV: 294.
Cross Keys, Va., (and Battle of, 1862), I: 623; II: 132; IV: 231-323.
Cross Roads Church, N.C., III: 319, 320.
Crossan, Thomas M., (N.C. Col sent to England to purchase and command the Advance), I: 17, 30; V: 299, 302, 312, 336, 341, 343, 344, 359, 361, 453, 458, 460, 461, 471.
Crotts, William, (Pvt, Co F, 34th NCST), V: 555.
Crouch, J.N., (1st Lt, Co A, 4th Battalion Junior Reserves; Co A, 72nd NCST, 3rd Junior Reserves), IV: 38.
Crouch, S.C., (1st Cpl, Co E, 52nd NCST), III: 224.
Crouse, D.T., (Musician, Mickey's Band, 26th NCST), II: 398.
Crouse, L.I., (Pvt, Co E, 32nd NCST), V: 496.]
Crow, John S., (Pvt, Co F, 55th NCST), V: 528.
Crow, Thomas W., (Lt, Co C, 2nd NCST), I: 159.
Crow House, (nr Hatcher's Run, Va.), II: 262.
Crowder, James, (2nd Lt, Co A, 13th Vols/23rd NCST), II: 183, 237, 245.
Crowder, M., (Pvt, Co F, 56th NCST), III: 357.
Crowder, N., (Pvt, Co B, 1st Battalion NCST), V: 504.
Crowder, William P., (Pvt, Co I, 38th NCST), V: 558.
Crowell, B.K., (1st Sgt, Co I, 52nd NCST), III: 225.
Crowell, J.W., (Sgt, Co I, 30th NCST), V: 493.
Crowell, James M., (Capt, Co K, 28th NCST), II: 478; IV: 468.
Crowell, Richard, (Pvt, Co D, 10th NCST, 1st Art & Engs, Reilly-Ramsay's Battery, Light Art), I: 572.
Crowell, S.W., (Pvt, Co B, 3rd Vols/13th NCST), V: 549.
Crowell's, N.C., V: 405.
Crowninshield, W.W., (Ensign, USN, Niphon), V: 351.
Crudup, Archibald D., (Lt Col, 47th NCST), III: 83.
Crump, H.C., (Pvt, Co F, 26th NCST), V: 602.
Crump, John J., (Capt, Co E, 44th NCST), II: 23, 28; V: 529.
Crump, Stephen, (Jr 2nd Lt, Co B, 31st NCST), II: 507.
Crump, Thomas, (Pvt, Co F, 26th NCST), V: 601.
Crump, W.F., (Pvt, Co I, 48th NCST), V: 527.
Crump's Farm, Va., (and Battle of, 1863), III: 330, 350.
Crumpler, J.A., (Cpl, Co G, 11th Vols/21st NCST), V: 515.
Crumpler, R.M., (Sgt, Co A, 30th NCST), V: 491.
Crumpler, Thomas N., (Maj, 9th NCST, 1st Cav), I: 418, 420, 483, 485; V: 11, 651.
Cruse, Adam, (Pvt, Co D, 10th NCST, 1st Art & Engs, Reilly-Ramsay's Battery, Light Art), I: 569.
Cruse, J., (Pvt, Co G, 33rd NCST), V: 544.
Cruse, Joseph, (Cpl, Co D, 57th NCST), V: 517.
Crutchfield, ______, [Stapleton], (Col, Chief of Artillery, 2nd Corps), IV: 65.
Crutchfield, E.F., (Pvt, Co F, 6th NCST), V: 513.
Crutchfield, F., (Pvt, Co E, 44th NCST), V: 533.
Crutchfield, G.P., (Cpl, Co F, 6th NCST), V: 512.
Crutchfield, H., (Pvt, Co E, 44th NCST), V: 533.

Crutchfield, James, (Pvt, Co F, 6th NCST), V: 513.
Crutchfield, W., (Pvt, Co E, 44th NCST), V: 533.
Crutchfield's, Va., III: 277.
Cub's Run, Va., I: 318.
Culberson, J.J., (1st Lt, Co A, Millard's 9th/20th Battalion Junior Reserves), IV: 386.
Culbreth, Calvin, (Pvt, Co B, 56th NCST), III: 366; V: 565.
Culbreth, Nathaniel, (Pvt, Co F, 26th NCST), V: 602.
Cullen, Thomas, (Cpl, Co I, 82nd N.Y.), II: 177, 178.
Cullowee Mountains, N.C., IV: 381.
Cullum, Benjamin F., (Pvt, Co F, 43rd NCST), V: 498.
Culp's Hill, (nr Gettysburg, Pa.), I: 148, 149, 312, 313, 315, 316, 317; II: 528; III: 6, 415; IV: 689; V: 121, 122, 138, 595, 606, 612.
Culp's House, (nr Gettysburg, Pa.), I: 355.
Culpepper, J., (Pvt, Co I, 30th NCST), V: 493.
Culpepper County, Va., II: 87, 88; III: 464.
Culpepper Court House, Va., (and Battle of, 1863), I: 223, 310, 318, 373, 381, 382, 423, 426, 544, 554, 555, 577, 578, 592, 594, 639, 742, 762; II: 29, 45, 87, 233, 240, 275, 378, 438, 444, 478, 479, 568, 569, 587, 609, 657, 693, 716, 718; III: 26, 40, 41, 66, 69, 73, 88, 235, 241, 242, 269, 272, 417, 460, 465, 472, 555, 557, 558, 559, 574, 575, 637; IV: 110, 149, 159, 177, 183, 184, 187, 262, 503, 570, 657; V: 627.
Culpepper Road, Va., I: 674; IV: 159, 184.
Cumberland Coal, V: 421.
Cumberland County, N.C., III: 205, 210, 262, 318, 319, 545; IV: 303, 342, 353, 355, 379, 483, 620.
Cumberland Ford, Tenn., II: 492.
Cumberland Gap, Tenn., II: 486, 487, 488, 493, 706, 708, 727, 728, 731; III: 434, 448, 516, 517, 519, 520-524, 525, 526, 659, 663, 736, 737, 739, 740, 756; IV: 271, 275, 439.
Cumberland Militia, (Ante-bellum military unit), IV: 356.
Cumberland Mountain, Tenn., II: 492; III: 678, 736.
Cumberland Mountains, Tenn., II: 706, 710; III: 434, 734; IV: 271, 273, 274, 275, 288, 289, 290.
Cumberland River, Tenn., II: 706, 710; III: 677, 678; IV: 271, 273, 289, 290; V: viii.
Cumberland Road, (nr Farmville, Va.), V: 252.
Cumberland, Valley, N.C., I: 80, 632; II: 234.
Cumming, Alfred, (Brig Gen), III: 197.
Cumming, James D., (Capt, Co C, Cumming's Battery, Starr's 13th Battalion NCST, Light Art), IV: 341, 361; V: 16.
Cumming, William A., (Capt, ACS, Co D, 3rd NCST), I: 213.
Cumming's Point, (Morris Island, S.C.), V: 161.
Cummings, Dr. J.T.F., (Ass't Surg, 68th NCST), III: 713.
Cummings, J.W., (Pvt, Co C, 11th Vols/21st NCST), V: 514.
Cummings, W.F., (Cpl, Co A, 10th NCST, 1st Art & Engs, Ramseur-Manly's Battery, Light Art), I: 556, 559.
Cummings, Yancey, (Pvt, Co I, 3rd Vols/13th NCST), I: 678.
Cummins, M.F., (Cpl, Co A, 10th NCST, 1st Art & Engs, Ramseur-Manly's Battery, Light Art), III: 54.
Cummins, P.A., (Sgt Maj, 79th NCST, 8th Cav), V: 677.

Cunningham, Alexander, (Cadet Adjt, Hillsboro Military Academy Battalion), V: 644.
Cunningham, Alexander T., (Capt, Ordnance Officre, MacRae's Brigade), IV: 564.
Cunningham, H., (Sgt, Co B, 27th NCST; Detailed, Invalid Battalion), V: 571.
Cunningham, J.P., (Adjt, 7th NCST), IV: 472.
Cunningham, R.M., (Pvt, Co G, 4th NCST), V: 489.
Cunningham, Solomon, (Capt, Co H, 25th NCST), II: 292.
Cunningham Farm, (nr Rappahannock River, Va.), II: 90.
Cureton, Taylor G., (Ordnance Sgt, 10th Battalion NCST, 2nd Hvy Art; 2nd Lt, Co B, 26th NCST), II: 303, 396; IV: 329.
Cureton, Thoams J., (Capt, Co B, 26th NCST), II: 328, 329, 336, 358, 366, 372, 372, 378, 394, 396, 397, 403, 415-416; V: 529.
Curiosities of Literature, I: 729.
Currie, D.W., (Hospital Steward, 6th NCST), V: 511.
Currie, Edward, (Pvt, Co F, 14th Vols/24th NCST), V: 560.
Currie, F.S., (Lt, Co D, 51st NCST), III: 214, 219.
Currie, H.A., (Cpl, Co C, 35th NCST), V: 562.
Currie, J.B., (Pvt, Co A, 30th NCST), V: 491.
Currie, Lauchlin W., (1st Lt, Co G, 6th Battalion Fayetteville Armory Guard), IV: 297.
Currie, Dr. Richard O., (Chief Surg, Salisbury Prsion), IV: 763, 765.
Currie, Stephen A., (1st Sgt, Co I, 10th NCST, 1st Art & Engs, Sutherland's Battery, Light Art), IV: 222.
Currituck County, N.C., I: 405; III: 457, 717; IV: 482, 483.
Curtin, Andrew Gregg, (Governor of Pennsylvania), III: 750; V: 81, 82.
Curtis, A.J., (Pvt, Co B, 1st NCST), V: 485.
Curtis, Alexander, (Master, CSN, Tallahassee), V: 438.
Curtis, John Henry, (Pvt, Cadet Battalion, Hillsboro Military Academy), V: 640.
Curtis, L.J., (1st Lt, Adjt, 1st NCST), I: 136.
Curtis, Larkin, (Lt, Co B, 1st NCST), I: 152.
Curtis, Newton Martin, (Maj Gen, USA), II: 643; V: 237.
Curtis, Thomas, (Pvt, Co F, 26th NCST), V: 602.
Curtis, W.A., (Sgt, Co A, 9th Vols/19th NCST, 2nd Cav), II: 98.
Curtis, William, (Pvt, Co C, 26th NCST), V: 602.
Cushing, Alonzo Hersford, (Lt, Battery A, 4th U.S. Art), V: 147.
Cushing, William B., (Cmdr, USN; Capt, Monticello), II: 756; III: 178, 707; IV: 27, 40, 317, 318; V: 242, 243, 245, 323, 374.
Cushman, C.H., (Lt Cmdr, USN; Pioneer, Wabash), V: 244.
Custer, George Armstrong, (Maj Gen, USA), I: 291, 428, 481, 686; III: 583, 584, 646; IV: 212; V: 261, 264.
Custis, Dr. Peter, (Surg, 31st NCST; Surg, Wilmington General Hospital), II: 507; IV: 636.
Cuthberston, D.G., (2nd Lt, Co B, 5th Vols/15th NCST), I: 734.
Cuthberston, G.B., (2nd Lt, Co B, 5th Vols/15th NCST), I: 734.
Cuthberston, John D., (1st Lt, Co I, 53rd NCST), III: 263; V: 494.
Cuthberston, T.L., (Musician, 53rd NCST), V: 501.

Cuthberston, W.F, (Pvt, Co I, 48th NCST), V: 527.
Cutlar, R., (2nd Lt, Co E, 10th NCST, 1st Art & Engs, Moore-Miller's Battery, Light Art), I: 581.
Cutler, Dr. ______, (Surg, 21st Mass.), V: 67.
Cutler, Joseph, (Cpl, Co E, 4th NCST), I: 233..
Cutler, Lysander, (Maj Gen, USA), II: 345; III: 41.
Cutrell, S., (Pvt, Co F, 33rd NCST), V: 544.
Cutts, ______, (Col, Art), I: 665.
Cutts, A.D., (Capt, Co F, 5th Vols/15th NCST), I: 735.
Cyrus, G.W., (Pvt, Co H, 2nd Vols/12th NCST), V: 507.

(D)

Dabbs, John J., (Sgt, Co I, 43rd NCST), III: 18.

Dabney, Chiswell W., (Capt, IG, Barringer's Brigade), IV: 582.

Dabney, R.L., (Maj, Jackson's Staff), II: 437.

Dabney, William J., (Capt, Co E, 20th Battalion, Va., Hvy Art), III: 169.

Daganheart, Levi, (Pvt, Co F, 32nd NCST), V: 496.

Dahlgren, Ulric, (Col, ADC to Sigel, Burnside, Hooker & Meade. Co-leader of the Dahlgren-Kilpatrick Raid on Richmond which embodied as some of its goals; the freeing of the Federal prisoners in Richmond, the burning of the city, the instigation of riots and disturbances subsequent to the firing of the city, and the assassination of President Jefferson Davis and his cabinet.) I: 428, 459, 461, 640; II: 100, 240.

Dailey, A.C., (Pvt, Co K, 6th NCST), V: 514.

Dailey, G.G., (Pvt, Co K, 6th NCST), V: 514.

Dailey, J., (Sg., Co F, 33rd NCST), V: 544.

Daily, Joel J., (Pvt, Co B, 34th NCST), V: 555.

Daingerfield, J.E.P., (Capt, 6th Battalion, Fayetteville Armory Guard), IV: 298, 299.

Dalby, A.C., (Pvt., Co K, 6th NCST), V: 513.

Dale, Bartlett, (Lt, 33rd NCST), II: 579.

Dale, Thomas Q., (Sgt, Co K, 33rd NCST), II: 541.

Dallas, Daniel Boone, (Pvt, Co G, 6th Vols/16th NCST), IV: 216; V: 552.

Dallas, Ga., II: 742.

Dallas, N.C., II: 672.

Dallas, Tx., I: 227.

Dalrymple, J., (Pvt, Co I, 19th NCST, 2nd Cav), V: 658.

Dalrymple, James, (2nd Lt, Co F, 50th NCST), III: 203.

Dalton, John Z., (1st Lt, Co H, 4th NCST), I: 231, 270.

Dalton, R.F., (Capt, Co C, 4th Battalion Junior Reserves; Co C, 72nd NCST, 3rd Junior Reserves), IV: 38, 51.

Dalton, Ga., (and Battle of, 1864), I: 768; II: 702, 720, 738, 740; III: 432, 433, 437, 438, 492, 498, 500, 733; IV: 498.

Dam No. 10, [Dam No. 1], (nr Yorktown, Va.), I: 552, 690.

Dameron, F.L., (2nd Lt, Co E, Cameror-Dickson's Battery, Starr's 13th Battalion NCST, Light Art), IV: 354.

Dameron, J.S.R., (Pvt, Co H, 13th Vols/23rd NCST), V: 510.

Dancey, James R., (Sgt, Co G, 8th Vols/18th NCST), II: 64; V: 540.

Dancey, John S., (AQM, 7th Vols/17th NCST; QM,

Martin-Kirkland's Brigade), II: 1, 2; IV: 527.
Dandridge, Dr. _____, (Surg, 49th NCST), III: 139.
Dandridge, Tenn., III: 664; IV: 380.
Dandy, George Brown, (Col, 100 N.Y.), V: 163.
Danford, A., (Pvt, Co C, 30th NCST), V: 491.
Daniel, B.T., (Pvt, Detached Co, 68th NCST), III: 723.
Daniel, G.F., (Lt, Co H, 45th NCST), V: 494.
Daniel, G.T., (Pvt, Co B, 44th NCST), V: 533.
Daniel, George B., (Capt, Co F, 7th Vols/17th NCST), II: 2; IV: 535, 545.
Daniel, H., (Pvt, Co G, 43rd NCST), V: 498.
Daniel, H.O., (Pvt, Co G, 44th NCST), V: 534.
Daniel, J.D., (Lt, USN; Pioneer, Vanderbilt), V: 245.
Daniel, John W., (AAG, Early's Division), III: 413.
Daniel, Junius, (Brig Gen), I: xi, 539, 710, 711; II: 87, 334, 523, 525, 526, 529, 530, 533, 536; III: 1, 6, 11, 35, 36, 39, 40, 42, 43, 45, 49, 52, 61, 162, 165, 170, 171, 172, 256, 258; IV: 10, 247, 252, 253, 255, 256, 259, 418, 449, 513, 514, 515, 516, 517, 518, 519; V: 9, 668.
Daniel, W.W., (Lt, Co I, 2nd Vols/12th NCST), I: 630.
Daniel, William, (Lt, Co C; Adjt, Littlejohn's 23rd Battalion Senior Reserves), IV: 399.
Daniels, C., (Sgt, Co F, 33rd NCST), V: 544.
Daniels, E.T., (Pilot, Coquett), V: 357.
Daniels, F.S., (2nd Lt, Co B, 70th NCST, 1st Junior Reserves), IV: 12.
Daniels, J.D., (Acting Vice-Lt, USN), V: 245.
Daniels, John, (Resident of Tarboro area), IV: 80.
Daniels, Jesse W., (Pvt, Detached Co, 68th NCST), III: 723.
Daniels, Kenneth, (Pvt, Co K, 41st NCST, 3rd Cav), II: 786.
Daniels, Richard, (Pvt, Detached Co, 68th NCST), III: 723.
Daniels' School House, (nr Tarboro), IV: 78-81, 90.
Danner, J.W., (Pvt, Co H, 9th NCST, 1st Cav), V: 657.
Danville, Ky., II: 487, 708, 728.
Danville, Va., I: 64, 386, 409, 446, 687, 781; III: 368, 542, 654, 692; IV: 90, 93, 225, 454, 539, 768; V: 265, 270, 654.
Danville Railroad, Va., I: 467, 617, 738.
Darbytown Road, Va., I: 385, 408, 409; II: 574, 575, 796, 801; III: 77, 215, 332, 618, 690, 691; IV: 536.
Darden, Alfred M., (1st Lt, Co C, Moore's 3rd Battalion, Light Art), IV: 262, 268.
Darden, Andrew J., (Lt, Co F, 61st NCST), III: 504.
Darden, George F., (Capt, Co K, 31st NCST), II: 512, 518.
Darden, H.C., (2nd Lt, Co D, 38th NCST), II: 675, 678, 681.
Darden, J.P., (Pvt, Co F, 1st NCST), V: 485.
Darden, J.H., (Ass't Surg, 38th NCST), V: 548.
Darden, Joseph H., (1st Lt, Co A, 3rd NCST), IV: 722.
Darden, J.W., (2nd Lt, Co D, 38th NCST), II: 678; V: 548.
Darden, W.A., (Capt, Co F, 61st NCST), III: 504.
Dare County, N.C., III: 715, 724.
Darnell, Mr. _____, (Hospital Steward), I: 249.

Darr, A.W., (Pvt., Co B, 48th NCST), V: 526.
Darnell, Jonathan, (Cpl, Co D, 33rd NCST), II: 539.
Daughtry, Allen, (Pvt, Co D, 10th NCST, 1st Art & Engs, Reilly-Ramsay's Battery, Light Art), V: 568.
Daughtry, Harrison R., (Pvt, Co A, 5th Vols/15th NCST), V: 520.
Daughtry, W.M., (Capt, Co I, 68th NCST), III: 714.
Daughtry, William, (Pvt, Co K, 49th NCST), V: 565.
Davenport, J.R., (Sgt, Co B, 33rd NCST), V: 543.
Davenport, William C., (Cpl, Co B, 33rd NCST), II: 538.
Daves, Graham, (Private Secretary to Governor Ellis; Acting Adjt Gen N.C. Militia; 1st Lt, ADC to Holmes; Capt, AAG Pender's Brigade; Maj, 12th Vols/22nd NCST). I: 18; II: 162, 168, 177, 180; IV: 11, 37, 551, 609; V: 17, 25.
Daves, Stephen, (Pvt, Co E, 5th NCST), I: 292.
Daves, W.C., (Pvt, Co F, 8th Vols/18th NCST), II: 64.
Daves, William, (Cpl, Color-bearer, Co I, 56th NCST), III: 346, 347, 348.
David, H., (2nd Lt, Co E, 10th NCST, 1st Art & Engs, Moore-Miller's Battery, Light Art), I: 581.
Davidson, A. Brevard, (Father of Sgt Robert A Davidson), III: 589.
Davidson, Elizabeth Vance, (Mother of H.H. Davidson), II: 723.
Davidson, G.W., (Cpl, Co I, 6th NCST), V: 513.
Davidson, Harvey H., (Lt Col, 39th NCST), II: 705, 707, 723-726 personal account; V: xi.
Davidson, Henry B., (Brig Gen), III: 678.
Davidson, John M., (1st Lt, Co C, 39th NCST), II: 704. 727-744 personal account; IV: 613.
Davidson, Joseph, (Pvt, Co D, 68th NCST), III: 715.
Davidson, Robert A., (Sgt, Co I, 63rd NCST, 5th Cav), III: 589.
Davidson, Samuel W., (2nd Lt, Co C, 6th Battalion/60th NCST), I: 120; III: 483, 491, 497.
Davidson, T.M.C., (2nd Lt, Co A, 4th NCST), I: 232, 271.
Davidson, Hon. Theodore, F., (Lt, ADC to R.B. Vance), I: 117, 133; II: 699, 703, 704, 707, 711, 718, 723, 725, 731; V: xi.
Davidson, Theodore H., (Pvt, Co A, 4th NCST), V: 488.
Davidson, Thomas F., (2nd Lt, Co F., 6th Battalion/60th NCST), I: 120; III: 492.
Davidson, W.L., (Capt, Co A, 4th NCST), I: 231.
Davidson, William Lee, (Col, 7th NCST), I: 361, 377, 383, 386; II: 570; IV: 472.
Davidson, William M., (Father of H.H. Davidson), II: 723.
Davidson College, Davidson, N.C., I: 78; II: 417, 418; III: 368; IV: 613, 745; V: 651.
Davidson County, N.C., II: 792; III: 317, 594; IV: 132, 241, 608; V: 627.
Davie County, N.C., II: 792, 799, 806; III: 428, 545, 550; IV: 387, 403, 760; V: 15, 627.
Davies, Henry Eugene, (Maj Gen, USA), III: 576, 584.
Davis, ______, (Acting Master, CSN, James Funk), V: 439.
Davis, ______, [Joseph],(Pvt, Co A, Wynn's 15th Battalion, Cav), IV: 367.

Davis, A., (Pvt, Co C, 1st Vols/11th NCST), V: 530.
Davis, A.B., [Joseph B.], (2nd Lt, Co F, 16th Battalion/75th NCST, 7th C.S. Cav), IV: 723.
Davis, A.E., (Lt, Co G, 64th NCST), III: 660.
Davis, A.F., (Lt, Co D, 58th NCST), III: 433.
Davis, A.T., (Pvt, Co G, 5th NCST), I: 292; V: 505.
Davis, Alfred, (ADC to J.A. Walker), I: 650.
Davis, Bartlett, (2nd Lt, Co I, 32nd NCST), I: 736.
Davis, Benjamin Franklin, (Maj Gen, USA), IV: 254.
Davis, Champ T.N., (Col, 6th Vols/16th NCST), I: 751, 753, 755; IV: 137, 139, 146, 151, 153, 154; V: 10.
Davis, Charles F., (Pvt, Co G, 56th NCST), V: 566.
Davis, David S., (Lt Col, 66th NCST), III: 686, 689, 696, 697, 699; IV: 538.
Davis, Elias, (Pvt, Co I, 7th Battalion Junior Reserves; 72nd NCST, 3rd Junior Reserves; First man killed at Fort Fisher), IV: 47.
Davis, Elkanah, (Pvt, Co I, 38th NCST), V: 558.
Davis, E. Hayne, (AIG, Garland-Iverson-Johnston's Brigade), IV: 523.
Davis, G.B., IV: 700.
Davis, G.W., (Pvt, Co K, 28th NCST), V: 543.
Davis, G.W., (Pvt, Co I, 1st NCST), V: 485.
Davis, George, (Pvt, Co B, 54th NCST), V: 659.
Davis, George W., (2nd Lt, Co G, 40th NCST, 3rd Art, Hvy), II: 747.
Davis, H.H., (Pvt, Co F, 49th NCST), V: 564.
Davis, J.C., (1st Sgt, Co H, 46th NCST), V: 525.
Davis, J.E., (Pvt, Co E, 2nd Vols/12th NCST), V: 507.
Davis, J.H, (Pvt, Co K, 43rd NCST), V: 499.
Davis, J.J., (Pvt, Co K, 49th NCST), V: 565.
Davis, J.L., (Lt Cmdr, USN), V: 243.
Davis, J.L., (Pvt, Co H, 6th NCST), V: 513.
Davis, J.T., (Lt Col, 49th NCST), V: 663.
Davis, J.T., (Pvt, Co G, 1st Vols/11th NCST), V: 530.
Davis, Jake, (Pvt, Co 1, Woodfin's Battalion; Co , 79th NCST, 8th Cav) IV: 112.
Davis, James, (Pvt, Co I, 49th NCST), V: 565.
Davis, James, (Pvt, Co D, 27th NCST), II: 462; V: 523.
Davis, James G., (Capt, Co H, 66th NCST), III: 686.
Davis, James H., (Lt, Co H, 64th NCST), III: 660.
Davis, James M., (Pvt, Co F, 34th NCST), V: 555.
Davis, J. Lucius, (Col, 10th Va., Cav), V: 627.
Davis, James M., (Orderly Sgt, Co H, 35th NCST), II: 628.
Davis, James M., (2nd Lt, Co G, 56th NCST), III: 315.
Davis, James Taylor, (Lt Col, 49th NCST), III: 138, 143, 144, 147, 148, 152; V: 11.
Davis, Jefferson, (President, CSA), I: 15, 38, 56, 57, 59, 61, 81, 103, 109, 138, 165, 181, 277, 297, 303, 304, 339, 340, 346, 350, 352, 378, 419, 463, 614, 624, 719, 781;II: 58, 200, 209, 240, 350, 353, 354, 378, 383, 385, 386, 387, 391, 392, 395, 398, 484, 500, 505, 515, 556, 618,

619, 729, 736, 754, 774; III: 10; IV: 2, 12, 36, 37, 316, 319, 367, 412, 425, 445, 453, 537, 581, 584, 588, 623, 665, 718, 728, 731, 748, 754; V: xvii, 193, 263, 354, 407, 417, 437, 438, 475, 478, 584, 588.

Davis, Jefferson Columbus, (Maj Gen, USA), II: 12.

Davis, John C., (Sgt, Co G, 33rd NCST), II: 540.

Davis, John Z., (2nd Lt, Co A, 40th NCST, 3rd Art, Hvy), II: 746, 747, 762.

Davis, Johnson, (Pvt, Co A, 14th Vols/24th NCST), V: 560.

Davis, Jospeh B., (2nd Lt, Claiborne-Dearing's 7th C.S. Cav; 16th Battalion/75th NCST, 7th Cav), IV: 91.

Davis, Joseph J., (Capt, Co G, 47th NCST), III: 84, 85, 91, 109; IV: 691, 700, 706; V: 107, 153.

Davis, Joseph R., (Brig Gen), III: 290, 291, 311.

Davis, Joseph R., (Brig Gen, nephew of Jefferson Davis), I: 353; II: 341.

Davis, L.D., (2nd Sgt, Co A, 44th NCST), V: 533.

Davis, Lawson B., (1st Lt, Co I, 6th Battalion/60th NCST), III: 475.

Davis, Lewis B., (Sgt, Co D, 21st Ga.), V: 194.

Davis, Luther M., (Capt, Co K, 5th NCST), I: 288.

Davis, M.J., (1st Lt, Co E, 42nd NCST), II: 790.

Davis, Martin, (Pvt, Co A, 1st Battalion NCST), V: 504.

Davis, Matthew L., Jr., (Col, 9th Vols/19th NCST, 2nd Cav), II: 83, 781; IV: 110; V: 10.

Davis, R.E., (1st Lt, Co C, 66th NCST), III: 686, 688.

Davis, R.S., (Capt, Co D, 77th NCST, 7th Senior Reserves), IV: 100.

Davis, Raleigh, (Pvt, Co B, 2nd Battalion NCST), V: 495.

Davis, Rufus, (Pvt, Co I, 56th NCST), III: 378.

Davis, S.B., (Pvt, Co C, 3rd Vols/13th NCST), V: 550.

Davis, S.D., (Lt, 6th Battalion/60th NCST), IV: 706.

Davis, S.J., (2nd Lt, Co H, 48th NCST), V: 520.

Davis, S.M., (Pvt, Co G, 11th Vols/21st NCST), V: 515.

Davis, Samuel A., (2nd Lt, Co G, 4th NCST), I: 231.

Davis, Samuel C., (Musician, 4th NCST), V: 488.

Davis, Simpson, (Pvt, Co E, 30th NCST), V: 492.

Davis, Stephen, (Pvt, Co E, 5th NCST), V: 505.

Davis, Dr. Sylvester D., (Hospital Steward, 33rd NCST), II: 537; V: 543.

Davis, T.C., (Sgt, Co G, 40th NCST, 3rd Art, Hvy), II: 745, 765; IV: 421.

Davis, T.H, (2nd Lt, Co D, 34th NCST), V: 548.

Davis, Thomas E., (Pvt, Co A, 43rd NCST), III: 20; V: 497.

Davis, Thomas R., (3rd Cpl, Co K, 52nd NCST), III: 225.

Davis, W.E., (Pvt, Co C, 2nd Vols/12th NCST), V: 507.

Davis, W.E., (Cpl, Co C, 3rd NCST), V: 487.

Davis, W.L., (Resident of Rutherford County), IV: 202.

Davis, W.L., (Pvt, Co C, 47th NCST), V: 534.

Davis, W.S., (Lt, Co I, 58th NCST), III: 434.

Davis, Weldon E.,(Capt, Co B., 30th NCST), II: 495, 496; IV: 600.

Davis, William, (Pvt, Co A, 59th NCST, 4th Cav), V: 659.
Davis, William, (Pvt, Detached Co, 68th NCST), III: 723.
Davis, William S., (Lt, Co H, 64th NCST), III: 660; V: 169.
Davis, William S., (Lt Col, 2nd Vols/12th NCST, part time commander of the 11th Vols/21st NCST, Col, 13th Vols/23rd NCST), I: 631, 637, 639, 642, 643, 644; II: 121, 188, 236, 240, 241, 246, 249, 781.
Davis, William T., (Pvt, Co G, 14th Vols/24th NCST), V: 560.
Davis' Farm, Va., (nr Petersburg, aka Davis House), I: 431; II: 58, 102, 387, 625, 694; III: 80, 81, 112, 309-310, 314, 317, 376, 377, 610; IV: 88, 90, 93, 470, 477.
Davoust, R.R., (Pvt, Co C, 10th NCST, 1st Art & Engs, Brem-Graham-Williams' Battery, Light Art), V: 568.
Dawes, Rufus R., (Lt Col, 6th Wisconsin), II: 345.
Daws, S.O., (Pvt, Co K, 5th Vols/15th NCST), V: 522.
Daws, William, (Pvt, Co K, 5th Vols/15th NCST), V: 522.
Dawson, F.H, (Musician, 6th NCST), V: 511.
Dawson, J., (Capt, Dawson's Unattached Co, Senior Reserves), IV: 402.
Dawson, L.L., (Capt, USMC), V: 244.
Dawson, William P., (4th Sgt, Co K, 52nd NCST), III: 225.
Day, R.J., (2nd Lt, Co K, 1st NCST), I: 137; V: 484.
Day, Robert J., (Pvt, Co G, 2nd Vols/12th NCST), I: 639.
Day, W.H., (Capt, Co K, 1st NCST), I: vi, 137, 150, 721.
Dayton, E.G., (Ensign, USN; Pioneer, Nereus), V: 245.
Dayton, G.H, (Pvt, Co A, 10th Vols/20th NCST), V: 508.
Dayvaukt, A., Jr., (Pvt, Co F, 3rd Vols/13th NCST), V: 550.
Deal, A.J., (Cpl, Co A, 12th Vols/22nd NCST), V: 553.
Deal, Alonzo, (Jr 2nd Lt, Co F, 38th NCST), II: 678.
Deal, Calvin J., (2nd Sgt, Co G, 38th NCST), V: 577.
Deal, J.A., (Ordnance Sgt, 2nd Vols/12th NCST), I: 606, 651; V: 506.
Deal, James, (Pvt, Co F, 26th NCST), V: 601.
Deal, Josiah, (Pvt, Co C, 5th NCST), I: 291; V: 505.
Deal, M.M., (1st Sgt, Co A, 12th Vols/22nd NCST), V: 553.
Deal, Marcus, (Lt, Co A, 12th Vols/22nd NCST), II: 165.
Deal, Rufus, (Lt, Co I, 26th NCST), II: 397.
Deal, W.E., (Pvt, Co A, 57th NCST), V: 517.
Dean, George W., (Pvt, Co A, 34th NCST), V: 554.
Dean, Josiah, (Pvt, Co C, 5th NCST), I: 291.
Dean, Moore, (Pvt, Co I, 43rd NCST), V: 499.
Deans, Robert D., (Pvt, Co H, 59th NCST, 4th Cav), V: 659.
Dearing, James, (Brig Gen), I: 433; II: 106, 618, 621, 778; III: 134, 335, 337, 343, 344, 346, 465, 466, 613, 623, 634; IV: 73, 82, 83, 85, 86, 87, 88, 90, 93; V: 175, 177, 178, 182, 189, 192, 331.
Dearing, St. Clair, II: 283, 291, 293, 294.
DeArmond, J.A., (Pvt, Co K, 56th NCST), V: 566.
Deaton, Andrew, (Pvt, Co B, 45th NCST), V: 500.
Deaton, Burton, (Pvt, Co B, 43rd NCST), V: 497.

Deaton, J.A., (Pvt, Co K, 35th NCST), V: 563.
Deaton, J.B., (Pvt, Co C, 37th NCST), V: 545.
Deartheridge, W.A., (Pvt, Co A, 33rd NCST), V: 543.
Deatonsville, Va., I: 330; III: 252, 283; IV: 362.
Deaver, James P., (Lt, Co 2, Woodfin's 14th Battalion; Lt, Co 2, Henry's 14th Battalion; Capt, Co A, 79th NCST, 8th Cav), IV: 114.
Deaver, R.M., (Capt, Co G, 64th NCST), III: 660, 668.
Deaver, W. Henry "Harry", (Lt Col, 6th Battalion/60th NCST), III: 473, 475, 479, 499.
Debass, E.G., (Lt, 64th NCST), IV: 706.
DeBerry, David D., (Capt, Co F, 44th NCST), III: 23.
Deberry, E.A., (1st Lt, Co A, 5th Vols/15th NCST), I: 734.
DeBerry, E.J., (Hospital Steward, 52nd NCST), III: 226.
DeBerry, James R., (Capt, Co H, 4th Vols/14th NCST), I: 707.
Deberry, Junius B., (Capt, Co D, 54th NCST), IV: 706.
Debnam, C.F., (Pvt, Co H, 47th NCST), V: 535.
Debnam, Charles, (Cpl, Co H, 47th NCST), V: 535.
Debnam, Robert W., (2nd Lt, Co H, 31st NCST), II: 512.
Debnam, Walter, (2nd Lt, Co H, 31st NCST), II: 508.
DeBose, Anthony, (Pvt, Co I, 3rd NCST), V: 487.
DeBruhl, E.F., (Cpl, Co A, 16th Battalion/75th NCST, 7th Cav), V: 660.
Debush, J., (Lt, Co I, 64th NCST), III: 660.
DeCamp, Charles, (Musician, 52nd NCST), III: 226.
Decker, George W., (Capt, Co C, 6th Battalion/60th NCST), IV: 296.
Decker, George W., (Fayetteville and Harper's Ferry Arsenals), IV: 298.
Decker, Levi, (Fayetteville and Harper's Ferry Arsenals), IV: 298.
Declaration of Independence, V: 465.
DeCourey, ______, [John F.], (Brig Gen, USA), II: 487; III: 521.
Deeds of Daring, Other, V: 17-18.
Deeds of Daring-Six Heroes, V: 15-16.
Deems, Rev. Dr. Charles F., (Chaplain), IV: 598.
Deep Bottom, Va., (and Deep Bottom Bridge), II: 56, 76, 669; III: 29, 121, 330; V: 207.
Deep Creek, N.C., (now Bryson City), III: 578.
Deep Creek, (Dismal Swamp Canal, N.C.), IV: 365.
Deep Creek, Va., II: 456, 695; III: 252; IV: 509.
Deep Gap, N.C., V: 285.
Deep Gully, (nr New Bern), I: 742; II: 83, 277, 513, 751; III: 5, 171, 349, 680, 705; IV: 221.
Deep River, N.C., I: 386; V: 629.
Deep Run, (nr Fredericksburg, Va., aka Hazel Run), I: 309, 310; II: 35, 657.
deErlanger & Co., Messrs., (Financial House, England), V: 455.
Dees, George T., (Capt, Co E, 62nd Ga. Cav; Capt, Co K, 16th Battalion/75th NCST, 7th Cav), IV: 71, 72, 73, 89, 91, 370.
Dees, John, (Pvt, Co I, 27th NCST), II: 462.
Dees, John, (Pvt, Co I, 43rd NCST;

Detailed, 2nd Corps Provost Guard), V: 499, 570
DeFontanges, ______, (Frenchman, Cmdr; Capt, Proney), V: 303, 304.
Dehart, John H., (3rd Lt, Co G, 65th NCST, 6th Cav), III: 680.
Deita, W.P., (Pvt, Co K, 33rd NCST), V: 563.
DeLagnel, J.A., (1st Lt, U.S. Art, Ass't Chief of Ordnance, Fayetteville Arsenal; Lt Col, Cmdr, Fayetteville Arsenal), IV: 294, 295, 296, 298, 300, 347.
Delancey, Thomas, (Pvt, Co H, 3rd Vols/13th NCST), V: 551.
Delaware, II: 367; IV: 321.
Delaware, Cape of, V: 440.
Delaware River, Pa., V: 619.
Dellinger, Daniel C., (Pvt, Co D, 5th Vols/15th NCST), V: 521.
Dellingrer, J.F., (Pvt, Co E, 13th Vols/23rd NCST), V: 510.
Dellinger, Jacob, (Pvt, Co E, 34th NCST), V: 555.
Dellinger, James, (Pvt, Co F, 32nd NCST), V: 496.
Dellinger, John C., (3rd Cpl, Co H, 52nd NCST), III: 225.
Dellinger, Lawson A., (Capt, Co A, 52nd NCST), I: 119; III: 225.
Deloatch, A.R., (Pvt, Co G, 16th Battalion/75th NCST, 7th Cav), V: 660.
Demarcus, W.A., (Pvt, Co A, 52nd NCST), V: 535.
Dement, W., (Pvt, Co G, 13th Vols/23rd NCST), V: 510.
DeMills, James, (Maj, ACS, Martin-Kirkland's Brigade), IV: 527.
Democratic Convention, 1860, III: 354.
Dempsey, John, (Pvt, Co H, 21st Ga.), V: 194.
Dempsey, William, (Pvt, Co H, 25th NCST), V: 561.
Denison, C.W., (Chaplain, Fortress Monroe, USA), V: 51.
Denison, W.E., (Lt, USN), V: 243.
Dennis, Reuben, (Pvt, Co I, 48th NCST), V: 527.
Dennis, W.M., (2nd Lt, Co E, 66th NCST), III: 686.
Denny, A.H, (Pvt, Co E, 35th NCST), V: 563.
Denny, B.J., (Pvt, Co E, 35th NCST), V: 563.
Denny, J.G., (2nd Lt, Co E, 6th Battalion Junior Reserves; Co G, 70th NCST, 1st Junior Reserves), IV: 13.
Denny, Washington, (Pvt, Co B, 1st Battalion NCST), V: 504.
Denson, C.B., (2nd Lt, Co A, 2nd Engineers, CSA; Capt, Co E, 10th Vols/20th NCST; AAG, Martin's Brigade), II: 112; IV: 403, 409, 411, 417, 420, 424, 425, 427, 428, 429, 430, 431, 432; V: xvi.
Denson, W.T., (Pvt, Co H, 3rd Vols/13th NCST), V: 551.
Denson's School, V: 637.
Denton, D., (Pvt, Co K, 35th NCST), V: 193.
Denton, Edward C., (Pvt, Co H, 14th Vols/24th NCST), V: 560.
Denton, Laban T., (Pvt, Co K, 14th Vols/24th NCST), V: 560.
Denton, W.F., (Pvt, Co G, Vols/13th NCST), V: 550.
Department, Ordnance, I: 39; IV: 356, 415.
Department, Pay, I: 45.
Department, Quartermaster-General's, I: 23.
Department, Subsistence, I: 37.
Department of Annapolis, I: 81, 86.
Department of East Tennessee, IV: 273, 290.
Department of East Tennessee and Western North Carolina, III: 661, 676, 729, 739, 760; IV: 117.

Department of Eastern North Carolina, III: 314, 679; V: 7.
Department of Norfolk, II: 508; V: 57.
Department of North Carolina, II: 308, 328, 334, 339, 593, 597, 612, 616, 769, 778; III: 5, 8, 299; IV: 244, 372, 410, 418, 541, 557; V: 57, 240.
Department of Northern Virginia, IV: 415.
Department of Richmond, II: 613.
Department of Virginia, I: 81.
Department of Western North Carolina, III: 436; V: 5, 653.
Department of the Cape Fear, IV: 305, 487; V: 217, 239.
Department of the Gulf, II: 720, 721, 734, 737.
Department of the Mississippi, II: 714.
Department of the Pamlico, III: 289.
Department of the Peninsula, I: 82.
Department of the Trans-Mississippi, II: 438, 492; IV: 36, 37, 431, 503, 682, 694.
DePass, ______, [W.L.], (Capt, DeSaussure's Art, S.C.), III: 208; V: 162, 167.
DePriest, J.R., (Pvt, Co G, 6th Vols/16th NCST), IV: 168.
DeRosset, Armand L., IV: 296.
DeRosset, Dr. Moses John, (Surg, 56th NCST), III: 318, 322; IV: 640; V: 559.
DeRosset, Thomas C., (See: Fayetteville Arsenal), IV: 299.
DeRosset, William Lord, (Capt, 30th N.C. Militia; Col, 3rd NCST), I: 138, 178, 179, 180, 184, 185, 189, 190, 215, 216, 217, 220, 221, 222, 224, 225, 226; V: 27, 74, 649.
DeRosset & Brown, (Wilmington), V: 368.
Desertion, in the 26th NCST, II: 400-402.
Deshler, James, (Brig Gen), III: 163, 164, 165, 490; IV: 254.
Deshler, James, (Col, Chief of Artillery to Gen. Holmes), V: 668.
Deshong, N.P., (Pvt, Co K, 6th NCST), V: 513.
Destruction and Reconstruction, II: 551.
Detailed Men, (See: 81st, 82nd, 83rd NCST).
Detailed Men, Quartermaster, Ordnance, Medical Departments, V: 571-572.
Detroit, Mi., II: 355.
Devalt, Frederick, (Lt, Co I, 64th NCST), III: 660.
DeVane, R.M., (Maj, 8th Vols/18th NCST), II: 21; IV: 473.
DeVane, Duncan J., (Maj, 10th Vols/20th NCST), I: 530; II: 112, 122, 124; V: 503.
DeVane, Dr. J. Stuart, (Ass't Surg, 2nd NCST; Ass't Surg, 38th NCST), I: 157; II: 676; IV: 631, 638.
DeVane, William S., (Col, 61st NCST), III: 503, 505, 507; IV: 483; V: 203.
DeVault's Ford, (Watauga River, Tenn.), III: 740.
Devereux, John, (Maj, Chief N.C. Quartermaster), I: 24, 25, 28, 30, 31, 32, 37, 48, 51, 56.
Devereux, Thomas P., (Pvt, Co D, 43rd NCST; Courier, Daniel-Grimes' Brigade), III: 18; IV: 519; V: 498.
"Devil's Den," (nr Gettysburg, Pa.), V: 137, 605.
"Devil's Half Acre," (The yard at Fort Delaware Prison, Md.), IV: 727.
Devin, Thomas Casimer, [Deven], (Maj Gen, USA), III: 573.

Dew, James, (Pvt, Co E, 47th NCST), V: 535.
Dew, Moses D., (Sgt, Co C, 43rd NCST), V: 498.
Dew, W.L., (Sgt, Co C, 43rd NCST), V: 498.
Dewar, W.A., (Capt, Co I, 31st NCST), IV: 721.
Dewese, Arthur A., (1st Lt, Co D, 29th NCST), II: 485, 487.
Dewy Celebration, New York, I: 132.
Dewey, George S., (Capt, Adjt, 9th NCST, 1st Cav), I: 441, 452, 453, 475, 486, 782; III: 635.
Dewey, Thomas W., (Resident of Charlotte), I: 61; IV: 694.
Dial, R.A., (Pvt, Co A, 10th NCST, 1st Art.& Engs, Ramseur-Manly's Battery, Light Art), I: 553.
Dibbrell, George Gibbs, (Brig Gen), III: 679.
Dick, Frederick N., (2nd Lt, Co G, 44th NCST), III: 23; IV: 700, 706.
Dick, S.W., (Pvt, Co I, 11th Vols/21st NCST), V: 194.
Dickens, Jesse, (Pvt, Co D, 59th NCST, 4th Cav), V: 659.
Dickerson, J.R., (Pvt, Co K, 1st Vols/11th NCST), V: 531.
Dickerson, M.O., (Capt, Co C, 34th NCST), II: 581; IV: 700.
Dickerson, S.W., (2nd Lt, Co K, 1st Vols/11th NCST), I: 120.
Dickerson, W., (Pvt, Co F, 47th NCST), V: 535.
Dickerson, W.J., (Lt, Co G, 2nd NCST), I: 162; IV: 706.
Dickerson, William T., (1st Lt, Co H, 1st Vol/11th NCST), I: 120, 586.
Dickey, E.M., (Pvt, Co B, 6th NCST), V: 512.
Dickey, J.H., (Capt, Co I, 57th NCST), V: 511, 514.
Dickey, W.N., (Lt, Co I, 7th NCST), I: 369.
Dickey, Z., (Pvt, Co D, 30th NCST), V: 492.
Dickinson, Calvin, (Lt, Co B, 26th NCST; Lt, Co D, 10th Battalion, 2nd Hvy Art), II: 396; IV: 330, 332.
Dickinson, S.L., (Pvt, Co K, 30th NCST; Detailed, Invalid Battalion), V: 571.
Dickson, Edward D., (Capt, Co C, 55th NCST), IV: 701.
Dickson, H.C., (Lt, Co F, 6th NCST), IV: 706.
Dickson, Henry, (Capt, Co E, Cameron's Battery, Starr's 13th Battalion, Light Art), IV: 353, 354.
Dickson, John A., (2nd Lt, Co G, 1st Battalion NCST), I: 78, 113.
Dickson, John R., (1st Sgt, Co E, 27th NCST), V: 523.
Dickson, P., (Pvt, Co G, 8th Vols/18th NCST), II: 64; V: 540.
Dickson, S.A., (Musician, Co G, 27th NCST), II: 462; V: 523.
Dickson, W.H., (Pvt, Co F, 28th NCST), V: 542.
Dickson, W.W., (2nd Lt, Co A, 12th Vols/22nd NCST), II: 164, 165; IV: 701, 706.
Diggs, W., Riley, (Pvt, Co B, 31st NCST), V: 63.
Dillard, Edward, (Pvt, Co K, 5th Vols/15th NCST), V: 522.
Dillard, James H., (Sgt, Co K, 5th Vols/15th NCST), V: 522.
Dillard, John H., (Capt, Co G, 45th NCST), III: 36, 39.
Dillard, Levi, (Pvt, Co K, 5th Vols/15th NCST), V: 522.
Dillard Farm, N.C., II: 793.
Dillard's Wharf, (James River, Va.), II: 776.
Dillehay, John G., (Capt, Co A, 14th Vols/24th NCST), II: 269.

Dillinger, S.A., [Dellinger, Lawson A.], (1st Lt, Co H, 52nd NCST), IV: 706.
Dillingham, J.W., (Pvt, Co C, 6th Battalion/60th NCST), III: 482.
Dillingham, John F., (Pvt, Co K, 25th NCST), V: 562.
Dillingham, John P., (Lt, Adjt, 2nd NCST), I: 163.
Dillingham, W.G., (Pvt, Co C, 6th Battalion/60th NCST) III: 482.
Dills, J.R., (Capt, Co E, 62nd NCST), III: 516; IV: 706.
Dilworth, N.C., IV: 406.
Dimmick, ______, (Col, Mass., Cmdr, Fort Warren Prison), IV: 735, 742.
Dingler, John, (Cpl, Co E, 1st Battalion NCST), I: 128.
Dinkins, Thomas, (Pvt, Co B, 38th NCST), II: 690.
Dinkins, William H., (Sgt Maj/Adjt, 49th NCST), III: 128.
Dinwiddie Court House, Va., I: 432, 438, 439, 441, 472, 777; II: 391, 783; III: 145, 158, 396, 397, 467, 642, 644; IV: 94, 576.
Dinwiddie Plank Road, Va., II: 61.
Dismal Swamp, N.C., IV: 84.
Dismal Swamp Canal, N.C., I: 390; II: 280; III: 133, 335; IV: 365; V: 307, 308.
Dismukes, W.W., (Pvt, Co E, 44th NCST), V: 533.
D'Israel, ______, I: 729.
Distance Between Lines, V: 665.
District of Eastern North Carolina, III: 703.
District of North Carolina, III: 685; IV: 18, 527.
District of North Carolina, 2nd Military, V: 269, 280, 281, 282.
District of Pamlico, II: 308, 328.
District of Southeastern North Carolina, IV: 424.
District of Southern Virginia and Eastern North Carolina, IV: 39.
District of Western North Carolina. IV: 115, 371, 372, 373, 379, 380, 535.
District of Wilmington, II: 774.
District of the Cape Fear, I: 10; II: 467, 497, 629, 634; IV: 416, 418; V: 223, 239.
Divisions, Confederate:
Anderson's, R.H., I: 404, 592, 594, 641, 744; II: 241, 375, 383, 621, 629, 677; III: 28, 72, 105, 236, 304; V: 118, 121, 124, 140,.
Bate's, (AoT), IV: 420.
Battle's, I: 173.
Breckinridge's, (AoT), I: 384; II: 734, 735; III: 476, 480, 481, 482, 484, 486, 488, 499, 749; IV: 198, 439, 532.
Cleburne's, (AoT), II: 421.
Colston's, (See also: Trimble's), II: 658, 688; V: 93, 97.
Dole's (Ga.), I: 638.
Early's, I: 316, 382, 629, 638, 641, 644; II: 50, 54, 120, 139, 241; III: 37, 94, 269, 270, 272, 277, 410, 411, 412; IV: 166, 237, 242, 437, 438, 441, 449, 522; V: 120, 573, 606.
Evans', V: 254.
Ewell's, I: 614; II: 30, 147, 683; IV: 163, 212, 227.
Field's, III: 364, 365; IV: 538, 541; V: 252.
French's, (AoT, AoG), II: 492, 734.
Gordon's, I: 205, 601, 645, 647, 648; II: 141, 241, 245, 248, 252; III: 281; IV: 450, 452.
Grimes', (and Rodes-Grimes'), I: v, 174, 209, 210, 211, 212, 261, 263, 265, 650; II: 264, 505, 523, 533, 534, 535, 536; III: 17, 57, 59, 399; IV: 438, 441, 453, 454, 456, 458, 459,

516, 576; V: xi, 247, 252, 254, 255, 260, 573.
Heth's, (Archer's, Cooke's, Davis', Kirkland's, MacRae's, Pettigrew's Brigades), I: 379, 380, 381, 382, 547, 588, 589, 590, 592, 594, 596, 600, 601, 602, 633, 742, 745, 746; II: 42, 43, 44, 45, 47, 171, 172, 174, 176, 178, 341, 343, 345, 346, 357, 358, 361, 363, 365, 366, 375, 378, 382, 388, 390, 394, 395, 420, 439, 440, 562, 564, 565, 589, 660, 662, 665, 691, 693; III: 28, 30, 72, 88, 90, 96, 97, 117, 118, 235, 236, 237, 243, 246, 249, 295, 299, 300, 301, 302, 303, 305; IV: 178, 184, 438, 442, 505, 536, 558, 563, 564; V: 96, 101, 103, 104, 115, 116, 117, 118, 120, 123, 124, 125, 126, 127, 128, 129, 130, 133, 139, 140, 143, 144, 146, 147, 151, 157, 197, 208, 573.
Hidman's, (AoT), II: 717; III: 436.
Hill's, A.P., (See: Light Division).
Hill's, Daniel Harvey, (Anderson's, Garland's, Raines', and Rodes' Brigades), I: 140, 143, 166, 168, 180, 185, 187, 190, 246, 286, 356, 386, 539, 613, 618, 621, 623, 625, 627, 628, 657, 658; II: 114, 115, 203, 204, 205, 210, 211, 212, 213, 214, 216, 217, 219, 498, 499, 501, 504, 602; III: 79, 87, 166, 454, 459, 497; IV: 54, 158, 163, 234, 346, 437, 442, 444, 446, 447, 544, 572; V: 467, 591.
Hoke's, (Clingman's, Colquett's, Hagood's and Martin-Kirkland's Brigades), I: xiii, 121, 403, 404, 405, 407, 409, 560, 597; II: 5, 6, 9, 10, 11, 12, 515, 516, 517, 647, 650, 764, 778, 798, 802, 803; III: 10, 135, 196, 199, 200, 215, 357, 359, 440, 513, 687, 688, 689, 690, 691, 692, 693, 694, 695, 696, 699, 700, 705, 708, 722; IV: 4, 9, 18, 20, 21, 22, 30, 31, 32, 53, 54, 55, 56, 57, 58, 60, 87, 198, 350, 351, 352, 393, 394, 428, 438, 439, 442, 489, 490, 492, 493, 494, 495, 497, 499, 531, 534, 536, 538, 540, 541, 543, 544, 545, 547, 598, 591; V: 241, 318, 468, 573.
Holmes', II: 753; III: 4, 39, 40; IV: 437, 501.
Hood's, I: 305, 306, 556; III: 268, 406; IV: 192, 571.
Hood-Field's, II: 7.
Huger's, I: 618, 619; II: 203, 294, 599; IV: 437, 570.
Jackson's, H.R., IV: 400.
Jackson's, I: 143, 144, 147, 190, 197, 614; II: 29, 147, 683, 684; V: 467.
Jenkin's, I: 548.
Johnson's, Bushrod, (Evans', Gracie's, Ransom's, Wise's), I: 582; II: 285, 713, 716; III: 15, 139, 357, 389, 396, 416, 436; IV: 90, 438, 442, 457, 459, 490, 534; V: 252, 254.
Johnson's, Edward, (Jones', Paxton's, Stewart's), I: 116, 147, 193, 255, 356, 383, 548, 596, 641, 742; II: 49, 50, 57, 243, 383, 384, 530, 621, 666, 694; III: 6, 47, 50, 51, 270, 271; IV: 193, 449, 469, 523; V: 121, 173, 573, 596.
Kershaw's, I: 647, 648; II: 5, 7, 258, 784, 798; III: 279, 305, 365; IV: 538, 541.
Light Division, (An affectionate title given the division by Major General A.P. Hill to recognize its supposed speed

of march. Division Cmdrs.: A.P. Hill, Pender, Heth, Wilcox), I: 116, 370, 376, 613, 663, 755, 757, 758, 759, 760, 761, 762, 765; II: 25, 28, 32, 33, 34, 35, 36, 38, 39, 40, 41, 118, 168, 169, 170, 471, 546, 549, 561, 562, 568, 577, 583, 656, 658, 680, 682, 683, 684, 685, 686, 687, 688, 689; III: 407; IV: 155, 158, 162, 163, 165, 166, 176, 196, 197, 215, 234, 437, 465, 466, 476, 477, 551, 552; V: 71, 72, 79, 80, 93, 96, 97, 467, 588, 589, 591.

Longstreet's, I: 612; II: 203; V: 467.

Loring's, IV: 695.

Magruder's, I: 618, 619; II: 599, 600; IV: 446, 570.

Mahone's, I: 407; II: 624, 694; III: 30, 281; IV: 524, 564; V: 208.

McLaw's, I: 186, 188, 553, 555, 556, 623, 624, 628, 629; II: 216, 431, 432, 553, 685; III: 184, 186, 191, 196, 197, 559; IV: 101, 447, 570; V: 71, 72, 80, 128, 588, 591.

Pegram's, (See also: Walker's), I: 186, 187, 188, 650; II: 262, 264, 265; III: 281, 282; IV: 524, 570, 571; V: 259, 260, 590.

Pender's, (Lane's, Scales'), I: 378, 379, 380, 381, 589, 632; II: 41, 42, 171, 346, 348, 363, 375, 660, 661, 662, 691, 692, 693; III: 5, 300; IV: 177, 553; V: 101, 118, 119, 121, 124, 151.

Pender-Wilcox's, I: 381, 547, 594, 675, 681, 682, 683, 685, 686, 744; II: 665; III: 78, 118, 208, 281; IV: 215, 438.

Pettigrew's, (While called Pettigrew's Division during the Battle of Gettysburg it should be remembered that this was actually Heth's Division. Heth having been wounded Pettigrew was placed in temporary com mand), II: 363, 366, 367, 368, 562, 563, 564, 565, 566, 567; IV: 45; V: 106, 107, 110, 111, 112, 127, 130.

Pickett's, I: 353, 526, 543, 590, 602; II: 42, 43, 44, 124, 363, 365, 366, 367, 529, 535, 562, 563, 565, 566, 567; III: 90, 132, 145, 235, 237, 258, 299, 300, 301, 359, 393, 396, 397, 400, 645, 646; IV: 180, 258, 528, 576; V: xiii, 101, 103, 104, 106, 108, 112, 124, 125, 126, 128, 129, 133, 134, 139, 140, 144, 147, 1148, 151, 152, 155, 156, 157, 158, 159, 326.

Polk's, (AoT), II: 731, 734.

Preston's, (AoT), III: 435, 449; IV: 439; V: 173.

Ramseur's, (See also: Rode's), I: 174, 205, 207, 208, 209, 263, 290, 325, 327, 328, 644, 645, 648; II: 123, 141, 142, 143, 248, 249, 250, 251, 252, 253, 260; III: 280, 281, 420; IV: 438, 516, 523.

Ramseur-Pegram's, I: 290, 328, 648, 650; II: 256, 257, 258, 259, 260, 262.

Ransom's, Robert, (Cooke's, Jenkins' and Ransomm's Brigades), I: 403; II: 609, 610, 613, 620, 776; III: 10, 741; IV: 121, 503, 572, 575.

Robertson's, III: 41.

Rodes', (Battle's, Doles', Iverson's and Ramseur's Brigades), I: 171, 202, 205, 206, 207, 252, 255, 259, 261, 262, 278, 287, 326, 328, 356, 376, 380, 628, 629, 633, 641, 645, 648, 682, 718; II: 118, 227, 228, 230, 241,

248, 252, 501, 502, 523, 524, 525, 527, 529, 530, 658, 688; III: 5, 12, 13, 14, 15, 16, 17, 40, 41, 49, 55, 260, 269, 270; IV: 253, 254, 437, 449, 514, 515, 522, 600; V: 93, 97, 118, 120, 611.

Rodes-Ramseur's, II: 256.

Smith's, G.W., II: 203; III: 406; IV: 152, 638, 701.

Stevenson's, (AoT), II: 708; III: 434, 437, 443, 492; IV: 439.

Stewart's, (AoT), II: 717, 731, 732; III: 196.

Taliaferro's, (AoT), III: 332, 443.

Trimble's, (See also: Colston's), II: 171, 366, 367, 368, 562, 563, 566, 567, 661; V: 97, 101, 108, 109, 110, 111, 112, 124.

Van Dorn's, (AoT), II: 193.

Walker's, J.A., (See also: Pegram's), III: 259, 260, 282.

Walker's, J.G., (Ransom's and Walker's Brigades), II: 296, 431, 432, 433, 434, 437, 553, 601, 685; III: 116, 423; IV: 447, 502, 570, 571; V: 71, 72, 74, 75, 79, 80, 253, 254, 591.

Walker's, W.H.T., (AoT), II: 491, 712; IV: 438.

Wharton's, I: 648; III: 678, 751, 752, 754; IV: 439.

Whiting's, I: 614, 618; II: 26, 27; IV: 418.

Wilcox's, (Lane's, McGowan's, Scales'), II: 45, 46, 47, 59, 60, 172, 173, 176, 178, 382, 483, 589, 693, 694; III: 30, 72, 77, 118, 119, 243, 281, 305; IV: 211, 438, 442, 453, 554, 537, 573.

Divisions, Federal:

Ames', II: 647; V: 233, 237.

Barlow's, I: 431, 596; III: 610.

Barney's, II: 47. Barry's, II: 96.

Brannan's. III: 436.

Butterfield's, I: 695.

Caldwell's, III: 580.

Casey's, II: 203, 205.

Couch's, II: 203, 205, 212, 213.

Cox's, II: 11, 115, 220, 650.

Crawford's, III: 628.

Crook's, II: 250.

Doubleday's, V: 118, 142.

Ferrero's, (Colored Division), II: 387; III: 373.

Franklin's, IV: 374, 375, 401.

Getty's, II: 47.

Gibbon's, II: 47, 363; V: 126, 142, 151, 207.

Hay's, II: 364; III: 580, 581; V: 126, 142, 152, 153, 154, 157.

Henry's, V: 130.

Hooker's, II: 203.

Kearney's, II: 203, 205, 212, 213, 599.

Ledlie's, III: 373.

Leslie's, II: 622.

McCall's, I: 615.

Miles', III: 29; V: 207.

Morell's, I: 609, 615; II: 213.

Mott's, II: 47.

Ord's, III: 401; IV: 454, 458.

Paine's, (Colored), IV: 542.

Palmer's, II: 11.

Porter's, (Fritz-John), II: 66, 546.

Potter's, III: 373.

Prince's, III: 575.

Reno's, IV: 521.

Richardson's, V: 78.

Robinson's, I: 634; V: 118.

Russell's, I: 722.

Schurz's, V: 118.

Sedgwick's, II: 48, 546; III: 417; V: 77.

Sheridan's, (Cav), I: 472.

Slocum's, I: 615.

Stannard's, V: 142.

Sykes', I: 615.

Turner's, III: 373.

Wadsworth's, II: 344; V: 117, 118.

Wallace's, I: 206; III: 13.

Warren's, I: 471.

Wilcox's, III: 30, 373; V: 207.

Wilson's, I: 467.

Dix, Mrs. Dorthea, I: 539.
Dix, John Adams, (Maj Gen, USA), III: 330, 750.
Dixon, ______, [W.J.], (Capt, 63rd Ga., Hvy Art), V: 162.
Dixon, B.F., (Capt, Co G, 49th NCST), III: 138, 151-160 personal account, 549.
Dixon, Columbus H., (Capt, Co G, 49th NCST), III: 128, 143, 148, 153.
Dixon, Edward, (Maj, 4th Vols/14th NCST), V: 11.
Dixon, Edward D., (Capt, Co C, 55th NCST), III: 296; IV: 706; V: 669.
Dixon, Henry C., (1st Lt, Co F, 6th NCST), IV: 700.
Dixon, Hugh M., (Capt, Co H, 35th NCST), II: 591, 598, 627; IV: 721.
Dixon, James, (Pvt, Co F, 6th NCST), V: 512.
Dixon, James W., (1st Lt, Co K, 40th NCST, 3rd Art, Hvy), II: 746.
Dixon, John F., (Pvt, Co D, 4th Vols/14th NCST), V: 490.
Dixon, S.A., (Musician, Co G, 27th NCST), II: 462.
Dixon, S.L., (Pvt, Co K, 30th NCST), V: 493.
Dixon, William J., (Sgt, Co D, 4th Vols/14th NCST), I: 724.
Dixon, William W., II: 164, 165.
Dobbin, D.P., (Pvt, Co C, 4th NCST), I: 232.
Dobbin, J.C., (Maj, 77th NCST, 7th Senior Reserves), IV: 99.
Dobbin, John H., (Pvt, Co B, Starr's Battery, Starr's 13th Battalion NCST, Light Art), IV: 349.
Dobbins, M.H., (Pvt, Co C, 10th NCST, 1st Art & Engs, Brem-Graham-Williams' Battery, Light Art), V: 568.
Dobbs, John L., (Sgt, Co I, 43rd NCST), V: 499.
Dobson, E.J., (Capt, Co K, 12th Vols/22nd NCST), II: 166, 172, 178, 391, 396, 548.
Dobson, J.E., (Pvt, Co A, Millard's 9th/20th Battalion Junior Reserves), IV: 391, 396.
Dobson, Joseph, (Capt, Co C, 65th NCST, 6th Cav), III: 675, 684.
Dobson, Silas C., (Pvt, Co B, 27th NCST), II: 461.
Dock, David, (Musician, Co A, 11th Vols/21st NCST), V: 514.
Dockery, Alfred, (2nd Lt, Co E, 38th NCST), II: 678.
Dockery, Oliver H., (Maj, 26th Battalion Home Guard; Lt Col, 38th NCST), II: 675, 676, 677; IV: 650; V: 68, 650.
Dodd, G.H., (Pvt, Co K, 14th Vols/24th NCST), IV: 650; V: 68, 650. 560.
Dodd, Isaac, (Pvt, Co B, Starr's Battery, Starr's 13th Battalion, Light Art), IV: 349.
Dodd, James, (Pvt, Co B, Starr's Battery, Starr's 13th Battalion NCST, Light Art), IV: 349.
Dodd, W.H., (Druggist & Ass't to Dr, E. Burke Haywood, Pettigrew Hospital, Raleigh), V: 577, 578.
Dodson, C.C., (Chaplain, 46th NCST), IV: 615.
Dodson, E.J., (Capt, Co K, 12th Vols/22nd NCST), II: 178.
Dodson, J.F., (2nd Lt, Co B, 42nd NCST), II: 790, 806.
Dodson, Silas C., (Pvt, Co B, 27th NCST), II: 461; V: 523.
Dog River Factory, Ala., II: 737.
Doggett, ______, (Lt, CSN, Signal Corps), V: 406.
Doherty, D.A., (Sgt, Co A, 4th NCST), I: 232.

Dolchite, P.A., [Dollarhite], (Pvt, Co A, 33rd NCST), II: 544.
Doles, George Pierce, (Col, 4th Ga.; Brig Gen), I: 141, 152, 224, 226, 277, 638, 641; II: 120; III: 49.
Doles, W.F., (2nd Lt, Co H, 32nd NCST), IV: 723.
Donald, J., (Pvt, Co E, 12th Vols/22nd NCST), V: 553.
Donaldson, Daniel S., [Donelson], (Brig Gen), III: 737; IV: 142, 149.
Donkey Island, S.C., II: 19.
Donoho, C., (Pvt, Co H, 56th NCST), III: 348.
Dorothy, W.W., [Doherty], (Lt, 37th NCST), II: 661.
Dorsey, A. (Pvt, Co F, 2nd Vols/12th NCST), V: 507.
Dorsey, E.W., (1st Lt, Co B, 1st Vols/11th NCST), I: 584; IV: 723.
Dortch, W.T., (Lt Col, 6th NCST; Speaker of N.C. House of Commons; Senator CSA), I: 295, 338, 339; V: 638.
Dosher, J.H., (2nd Lt, Co C, 30th NCST), II: 496.
Dosier, J.H., (Lt, Co G, 10th Vols/20th NCST), II: 127.
Dosher, Julius, (Pilot, North Heath), V: 357.
Dosher, Richard, (Pilot, Old Dominion), V: 357.
Doubleday, Abner, (Maj Gen, USA), II: 344, 347, 349; V: 147.
Douge, S.B., (Capt, Co H, 5th NCST), I: 281.
Douglas, J.A., (Pvt, Co D, 5th NCST), I: 291.
Douglas, James H., (Pvt, Co D, 5th NCST), V: 505.
Douglass, Joseph A., (Pvt, Co D, 34th NCST), V: 555.
Douglass, W.G., (Pvt, Co H, 43rd NCST), V: 499.
Douthatt, Robert, (Capt, Co D, 3rd Va. Cav), I: 89, 98.
Douthit, Dr. J.E., (Ass't Surg, 11th Vols/21st NCST), IV: 635.
Douthit, James B., (1st Lt, Co F, Millard's 9th/20th Battalion Junior Reserves), IV: 387, 393, 396.
Douthit, T.B., (Pvt, Co B, 11th Vols/21st NCST; Co B, 1st Battalion NCST), IV: 242; V: 504.
Dove, Jacob, (Wagon master, Co F, 9th NCST, 1st Cav), I: 419, 420.
Dover, N.C., III: 322.
Dover Swamp, N.C., (and Road), II: 81, 82, 83; III: 132, 273, 323, 324, 325, 333; IV: 54.
Dowd, C.D., (Capt, Co B, 6th Battalion Junior Reserves; Co E, 70th NCST, 1st Junior Reserves), IV: 10, 13.
Dowd, Clement, (Lt Col, 2nd Regt, 3rd Class Home Guard), IV: 650, 654; V: 651.
Dowd, Clement, (Capt, Co H, 26th NCST), II: 304, 328, 397, 418.
Dowd, C. Firmin, (Lt Col, 2nd Regt 3rd Class Home Guard), IV: 654.
Dowd, Henry A., (Col, 5th Vols/15th NCST), I: 24, 51, 733, 735.
Dowd, J.D., (Capt, Co D, 48th NCST), III: 117.
Dowd, John W., (Pvt, Co E, 26th NCST), V: 532.
Dowdle, John, (Pvt, Co G, 6th Vols/16th NCST), IV: 146.
Downing, John, (Pvt, Co D, 68th NCST), III: 715.
Downing, Joseph, (Pvt, Co B, 44th NCST), V: 533.
Downing, Rufus, (1st Lt, Co G, 6th Battalion/60th NCST), III: 474.
Downing, Thaddeus, (Pvt, Co D, 10th NCST, 1st Art & Engs, Reilly-Ramsay's Battery, Light Art), V: 568.

Downing, William, (1st Cpl, Co D, 68th NCST), III: 715.
Downs, Franklin C., (Pvt, Co G, 34th NCST), V: 556.
Downs, J.T., (ACS, 63rd NCST), I: 118.
Downs, J.T., (2nd Lt, Co K, 30th NCST), II: 497.
Downs, T.J., (Pvt, Co G, 32nd NCST), V: 496.
Dowtin, William A., (Capt, Co G, 43rd NCST), III: 2.
Dowton, William A., III: 2.
Doyle, ______, (Capt, 2nd Ga. Battalion), II: 677.
Draft Riot, III: 383.
Drainesville, Va., [Dranesville] I: 419, 573, 663; II: 96.
Drake, Benjamin F., (Lt, Co D, 47th NCST), III: 84.
Drake, J.C., (Sgt, Co C, 2nd Vols/12th NCST), V: 506.
Drake, John A., (Capt, Co H, 2nd Vols/12th NCST), I: 620, 645.
Drake, John J., (Capt, Co H, 32nd NCST), I: 620.
Drake, Richard F., (Capt, Co D, 47th NCST), III: 84; IV: 700, 706.
Drake, T.S., (Pvt, Co E, 35th NCST), V: 193.
Drake, W.C., (Capt, Co B, 30th NCST), II: 495.
Drake, W.F., (Pvt, Co H, 2nd Vols/12th NCST), V: 507.
Drake, W.R., (Pvt, Co D, 35th NCST), V: 562.
Drake's Branch, (aka Drake's Creek, nr Gettysburg, Pa.), V: 582, 584.
Drakesville, Va., II: 526, 527; III: 7, 751.
Draper, Jerry, (Pvt, Co F, 2nd Vols/12th NCST), I: 630.
Draughan, H.H., (Lt, 10th Vols/20th NCST), IV: 700, 706.
Draughan, James Walter, (1st Lt, Co A, 5th Battalion Junior Reserves; Co A, 71st NCST, 2nd Junior Reserves), IV: 26, 28.
Draughan, Walter F., (Col, 3rd Regt Home Guard; Brig Gen N.C. Militia), II: 495, 497; IV: 294, 295, 650.
Draughn, Isaac, (Pvt, Co A, 28th NCST), V: 540.
Draughorn, ______, [G.B.], (Pvt, Co D, 10th NCST, 1st Art & Engs, Reilly-Ramsay's Battery, Light Art), I: 577.
Drayford, Alexander, (Sgt, Co B; A.C. Sgt., 14th Vols/24th NCST), V: 560.
Drew, B.W., (Pvt, Co B, 3rd NCST), V: 487.
Drew, Benjamin, (Pvt, Co A, 10th NCST, 1st Art & Engs, Ramseur-Manly's Battery, Light Art), I: 555.
Drew, Solomon, (Pvt, Co F, 43rd NCST), V: 498.
Drew, W.H., (Pvt, Co G, 32nd NCST), V: 496.
Drewet, W.H., (Pvt, Co C, 32nd NCST), V: 496.
Drewry, Clay C., (Maj, QM, M.W. Ransom's Brigade), IV: 572, 577.
Drewry's Bluff, Va., (and Battles of), I: 12, 13, 402, 403, 404, 539, 540, 581, 702; II: 4, 6, 75, 76, 88, 140, 274, 278, 285, 296, 298, 428, 429, 515, 516, 519, 522, 523, 619, 620, 678, 778, 779, 793, 799; III: 4, 10, 11, 39, 40, 66, 77, 86, 135, 136, 139, 152, 153, 162, 163, 166, 169, 170, 211, 212, 227, 275, 276, 308, 315, 329, 353,359, 390, 419, 512; IV: 252, 403, 489-491, 501, 502, 514, 525, 531, 534, 556, 575; V: 326.
Drum, Cyrus, (Pvt, Co G, 38th NCST), V: 557.
Drum, Philip, (Pvt, Co I, 49th NCST), V: 565.

Drum, Rufus, (Pvt, Co I, 49th NCST), V: 565.
Drum, Thomas, (Pvt, Co I, 49th NCST), V: 565.
Dry, Moses, (Pvt, Co G, 8th NCST), V: 194.
Drysdale, Robert H., (Capt, Co A, 3rd NCST), I: 178, 227; II: 425, 426.
Dublin, Ireland, V: 335, 359, 470.
Dubose, _____, [D.G.], (Capt, Co H, 21st S.C.), V: 240.
DuBose, _____, [Wilds S.], (Capt, Co E, 2nd Battalion), IV: 245.
Dubose, Dudley M., (Brig Gen), III: 400.
Dubose, Dr. W.L., (Ass't Surg, 16th Battalion/75th NCST, 7th Cav), IV: 642.
Duck River, Tenn., III: 494, 501.
Ducker, William, (Lt, Co 10, 79th NCST, 8th Cav), IV: 115.
Duckett, Belton, [Ducket], (Capt, Co B, 6th Battalion/60th NCST), III: 473, 474, 481, 483.
Ducktown, Tenn., III: 735, 739.
Duckworth, John W., (Pvt, Co E, 6th Vols/16th NCST), V: 552.
Dudley, Eli, (Lt, Co K, 51st NCST), III: 220.
Dudley, Edward B., (Capt, Co D, 36th NCST, 2nd Art & Engs, Anderson-Dudley's Hvy Art), II: 630, 634; V: 239.
Dudley, G.L., (Capt, AQM, 1st NCST), I: 122, 136, 137.
Duees, A.A., (Capt, Co D, 64th NCST), III: 660.
Duels Between Officers, III: 291.
Duff, J.T., (Pvt, Co E, 30th NCST), V: 492.
Duffie, _____, (Col, 1st Rhode Island Cav), III: 562, 563.
Duffy, Dr. Charles, Jr., [Duffie], (Ass't Surg, 14th Vols/24th NCST; Surg, 49th NCST), II: 271; IV: 579, 635, 640; V: 559.
Duffy, George T., (Capt, Co B, 14th Vols/24th NCST), II: 269, 271, 274.
Duffy, Lawrence E., (Orderly Sgt, 14th Vols/24th NCST), II: 269.
Duffy, Dr. Walter, (Surg, 50th NCST), III: 161, 202; IV: 640.
Duggan, Dr. W.A., (Ass't Surg, N.C.), IV: 630.
Dugger, John E., (Lt, Co F, 8th NCST), I: 394, 408; II: 237; IV: 485.
Dugger's Ferry, (Watauga River, Tenn.), III: 676.
Duguid, Edward M., (Capt, Co D, 5th NCST), I: 290.
DuHeaume, _____, (Lt, Ordnance Officer, Clingman's Brigade), IV: 482.
Duke, G.M., (Cpl, Co F, 2nd Vols/12th NCST), V: 507.
Duke, H, (Pvt, Co E, 13th Vols/23rd NCST), V: 510.
Duke, J., (Pvt, Co F, 2nd Vols/12th NCST), V: 507.
Duke, J., (Pvt, Co G, 43rd NCST), V: 498.
Duke, Joseph H., (Pvt, Co F, 2nd Vols/12th NCST), V: 265.
Duke, Lewis, (Pvt, Co G, 43rd NCST), V: 194.
Duke, S.G., (Pvt, Co C, 2nd Vols/12th NCST), V: 507.
Duke, Tollect, (Fayetteville and Harper's Ferry Arsenals), IV: 298.
Dula, Aurelius J., (Pvt, Co A, 12th Vols/22nd NCST), II: 177.
Dula, Felix G., (2nd Lt, Co A, 12th Vols/22nd NCST), II: 164, 165.
Dula, George T., (2nd Lt, Co C, 9th Battalion Junior Reserves; 72nd NCST, 3rd Junior Reserves), IV: 42.
Dula, S.P., [S.T.], (Lt, Co I, 26th NCST), II: 397, 401.

Dula, Thomas J., (Lt Col, 58th NCST), III: 432, 433, 435, 452.
Dulin, John, (Sgt, Co H, 35th NCST), V: 193.
Dulin, William, (Pvt, Co I, 55th NCST), V: 528.
Dull, Edwin C., (Chief Musician, Sgt, Co I, 33rd NCST), II: 537, 540; V: 540.
Dumas, H.C., (Sgt, Co K, 26th NCST), V: 532.
Dumas, John C., (2nd Cpl, Co C, 4th Vols/14th NCST), V: 490.
Dumfries, Va., I: 300, 349, 422, 564.
Duncan, Rev. Mr. ______, (Va.), I: 101.
Duncan, B.M., (Pvt, Co K, 10th Vols/20th NCST), V: 509.
Duncan, Benjamin M., (Orderly Sgt, 10th Vols/20th NCST), II: 113.
Duncan, David, (Pvt, Co I, 13th Vols/23rd NCST), V: 510.
Duncan, J.W., (Lt, Co K, 58th NCST), III: 434.
Duncan, P.H., (Sgt, Co K, 58th NCST), III: 453.
Duncan, W.W., (Pvt, Co I, 53rd NCST), V: 502.
Duncan, Wesley, (Sgt, Co D, 33rd NCST), II: 539.
Dunevant, J.H., (Pvt, Co H, 6th NCST), V: 513.
Dunevanat, W.W., (Pvt, Co H, 6th NCST), V: 513.
Dungan, T.H., (Sgt, Co F, 2nd Battalion NCST), V: 495.
Dunham, John W., (Maj, 8th Battalion Home Guard), I: 230, 231, 233, 267; IV: 650.
Dunham, Jonathan, (Pvt, Co K, 8th Vols/18th NCST), II: 64; V: 540.
Dunkard Church, (nr Sharpsville, Md., aka St. Mumma's), I: 142, 148, 185, 188, 189, 194, 225, 307, 308; II: 435, 602; IV: 503, 571; V: 75, 76, 78, 79, 589, 590.
Dunlap, Bryant C., (2nd Lt, Co E, 26th NCST), II: 304, 396.
Dunlap, John L., (Pvt, Co C, 4th Vols/14th NCST), V: 490.
Dunlap, Seth, (Pvt, Co C, 10th NCST, 1st Art & Engs, Brem-Graham-Williams' Battery, Light Art), V: 568.
Dunlap's Farm, Va., [Dunlop's], (nr Richmond, Va.), II: 274; III: 211.
Dunlap's Station, (nr Burgess' Mill, Va.), I: 678.
Dunn, A.H., (AQM Sgt, 55th NCST), III: 288.
Dunn, Elias, (1st Lt, Co I, 30th NCST), II: 496; V: 667.
Dunn, J.E., (Sgt, Co K, 54th NCST), V: 516.
Dunn, J.R., (Pvt, Co I, 43rd NCST), V: 499.
Dunn, J.R., (Cpl, Co F, 49th NCST), V: 564.
Dunn, John, (Pvt, Co K, 55th NCST), V: 528.
Dunn, John, (Pvt, Co B, 21st Mass.), II: 313.
Dunn, Joseph, (Pvt, Co F, 46th NCST), V: 524.
Dunn, Junius H., (Sgt, Co A, 10th NCST, 1st Art & Engs, Ramseur-Manly's Battery, Light Art), I: 557, 559.
Dunn, Mitchell, (Pvt, Co H, 44th NCST), V: 534.
Dunn, Sidney M., (Lt, Co A, 10th NCST, 1st Art & Engs, Ramseur-Manly's Battery, Light Art), I: 551, 556, 558, 559.
Dunn, T.C., (Lt, USN), V: 243.
Dunn, Walter, (2nd Lt, Co F, 40th NCST, 3rd Art, Hvy), II: 747.
Dunn, Wiley, (Musician, 16th Battalion/75th NCST, 7th Cav), V: 660.

Dunn, William A., (Lt, Co E, 47th NCST), III: 84.
Dunn's Farm, Va., (nr Petersburg, Va.), III: 330; IV: 85.
Dunn's Hill, Va., (nr Petersburg, Va.), III: 114, 162.
Dunnavant, Andrew, (Pvt, Co I, 45th NCST), V: 500.
Dunnavant, L.H., (Pvt, Co H, 56th NCST), V: 566.
Duplin County, N.C., II: 111; III: 19, 20, 205, 215, 686, 704; IV: 267, 303, 331, 483, 523, 595, 608, 609, 613, 694; V: 384.
Duplin Cross Roads, (nr Wilmington), II: 762; III: 696.
Dupont, ______, (Chief Justice, Fla.), IV: 754.
Dupree, R.W., (2nd Lt, Adjt, 44th NCST), III: 22, 23.
Dupree, Willis R., (2nd Lt, Co E, 43rd NCST), III: 3.
Durell, William M., (Pvt, Co E, 4th NCST), I: 270.
Durham, C., (Pvt, Co E, 2nd Vols/12th NCST), V: 507.
Durham, Cicero, (Capt, Mat Ransom's Staff, aka "Fighting QM of the 49th NCST), II: 281, 284, 285, 619; III: 128, 133, 134, 136, 148, 153, 336, 351, 490; IV: 490, 575, 578; V: 183, 249.
Durham, F.R., (Cpl, Co G, 28th NCST), V: 542.
Durham, J.S., (Sgt, Co G, 28th NCST), V: 542.
Durham, Plato, (Capt, Co E, 2nd Vols/12th NCST), I: 642, 650, 651; II: 125, 619; V: 264, 503, 508.
Durham, R., (Pvt, Co D, 33rd NCST), V: 544.
Durham, R.J., (2nd Lt, Co C, 2nd Battalion Junior Reserves; Co D, 71st NCST, 2nd Junior Reserves), IV: 28.
Durham, Robert A., (Pvt, Co B, 34th NCST), V: 555.
Durham, W.P, (Pvt, Co G, 28th NCST), V: 542.
Durham, N.C., I: 413, 764; III: 200; IV: 32, 394, 539.
Duryea, Hiram, (Brig Gen, USA), I: 87, 88, 89, 93, 96, 97, 98, 109.
Dutch Gap, Va., I: 384, 549; III: 357.
Duvall, J.M., (Lt, Co A, 26th NCST), II: 396, 397.
Duvall, T.R., (Capt, Co I, 62nd Ga. Cav; Co. C, 16th Battalion, 75th NCST, 7th Cav), IV: 72, 73, 91, 92.
Duvall, W.C., (Lt, NCN; Capt, Beaufort), V: 300, 500.
Duvan, William A., (Capt, Co I, 31st NCST), II: 512.
Duych, John J., (Lt, Co F, 64th NCST), III: 660.
Dwiggens, James P., (Pvt, Co H, 63rd NCST, 5th Cav), V: 572.
Dwire, Daniel, (4th Cpl, Co F, 3rd Vols/13th NCST), V: 550.
Dyal, D., (Pvt, 21st Ga.), V: 194.
Dyche, Arthur M., (Capt, Co A, 39th NCST), II: 704, 728.
Dyche, John R., (1st Lt, Co A, 39th NCST), II: 704.
Duycus, Anselm N., (Pvt, Co B, 34th NCST), V: 555.
Dye, D.J., (2nd Lt, Co B, 6th Battalion Junior Reserves; Co E, 70th NCST, 1st Junior Reserves), IV: 13.
Dye, E.J., (2nd Lt, Co B, 6th Battalion Junior Reserves; Co E, 70th NCST, 1st Junior Reserves), IV: 13.
Dye, J.P, (Pvt, Co H, 37th NCST), V: 546.
Dye, M.E., (Pvt, Co F, 1st Vols, "Bethel), I: 128.

Dyer, A.B., (Capt, Cmdr, Fayetteville Arsenal; Maj Gen, Chief of Ordnance, USA), IV: 300.

Dyer, Thomas, (Pilot, Agnus Fry), V: 357.

Dyer's Field, Tenn., (nr Chickamauga), II: 703, 713, 714, 716; V: 171, 173.

Dyvall, A.B., (Capt, Co A, 26th NCST), II: 371, 373, 396, 397, 403.

(E)

Eades, Joel, (Pvt, Co A, 13th Vols/23rd NCST), V: 509.
Eagle, ______, (Maj, Ark.), II: 742.
Eagle, J.E., (Pvt, Co B, 53rd NCST), V: 501.
Eagle Island, N.C., IV: 428.
Eagles, L.D., (2nd Lt, Co F, 30th NCST), II: 496.
Eagles, T.R., (Sgt, Co F, 30th NCST), V: 492.
Eaker, Peter, (Pvt, Co M, 6th Vols/16th NCST), V: 553.
Eakes, J.S., (Pvt, Co B, 2nd Vols/12th NCST), V: 506.
Earles, Jubal, (Col, 38th Va.), II: 192.
Earls, J.H., (Pvt, Co G, 49th NCST), V: 564.
Earls, Jacob T., (Pvt, Co F, 34th NCST), V: 555.
Early, Jubal A., (Maj Gen and Early's Army), I: 117, 153, 154, 172, 209, 257, 324, 325, 326, 327, 342, 346, 355, 356, 596, 611, 629, 638, 641, 644, 645, 646, 647, 648, 649, 650, 727; II: 122, 123, 124, 125, 129, 139, 192, 193, 198, 199, 223, 225, 245, 249, 250, 251, 253, 257, 258, 259, 260, 261, 479, 532, 560, 571, 572, 694, 780; III: 12, 28, 37, 55, 94, 246, 257, 258, 259, 272, 280, 281, 298, 412, 413, 420, 421, 748, 749, 750, 752, 754, 755, 756; IV: 160, 166, 194, 449, 476, 477, 515, 522, 523, 659, 687; V: 115, 138, 213, 216, 468, 679.
Early, Robert, (Lt, ADC to Garland), IV: 521.
Earnhardt, J.A., (Capt, Co I, 42nd NCST), II: 791.
Earnhardt, James, (1st Lt, Co B, 82nd NCST), IV: 131.
Earnhart, Abram, (Pvt, Co D, 10th NCST, 1st Art & Engs, Reilly-Ramsay's Battery, Light Art), I: 569.
Earnhart, Wiley, (Pvt, Co D, 10th NCST, 1st Art & Engs, Reilly-Ramsay's Battery, Light Art), I: 574.
Earnheart, P.C., (Pvt, Co A, 10th Vols/20th NCST), V: 508.
Earp, H., (1st Lt, Co C, 14th Vols/24th NCST), IV: 722.
Earpsboro, N.C., V: 280.
Eason, T.L., (Pvt, Co D, 37th NCST), V: 545.
East Mountain, Tenn., III: 522.
East River, N.Y., V: 410.
East Tennessee & Georgia Railroad, IV: 273, 290.
East Tennessee & Virginia Railroad, I: 462; III: 519.
East Tennessee, Virginia & Georgia Railroad, II: 720, 727, 731.
East Woods, The, (at Sharpsburg, Md.) I: 225, 307; V: 78.
Easter, H., (Pvt, Co H, 48th NCST), V: 526.
Eastman, Edwin, (Pvt, Co A, 55th NCST), V: 527.
Easton, John S., (1st Lt, Co D, 44th NCST), III: 23.

Easton, Langdon, (Brig Gen, USA), III: 184.
Eastport, Maine, IV: 739; V: 375.
Eastwood, Benjamin W., (Cpl, Co F, 33rd NCST), II: 540, 578.
Eatman, T.J., [Eatmon], (Chaplain, 33rd NCST), II: 537, 538, 539, 578, 579; IV: 474, 612; V: 538.
Eaton, ______, (Col, Uncle of M.F. Taylor), V: 267.
Eaton, Riley, (Pvt, Co D, 53rd NCST), V: 501.
Eaves, Dr. A.E., (Ass't Surg, 59th NCST, 4th Cav), III: 457; IV: 641, 643.
Eaves, J.L., (Capt, Co B, Millard's 9th/20th Battalion Junior Reserves), IV: 386, 396.
Eaves, John B., (Capt, Co I, 50th NCST), III: 161, 188, 189; IV: 216.
Eaves, John P., (Pvt, Co G, 6th Vols/16th NCST), IV: 216; V: 552.
Ebbitt House, D.C., I: 466.
Ebenezer Church, Va., III: 623.
Eberstein, William H., (Drum Major, 61st NCST), III: 503.
Eccles, F.M., (1st Sgt, Co A, 11th Vols/21st NCST). V: 514.
Echenwalder, A., (Pvt, Co K, 45th NCST), V: 501.
Eckard, Simon, (2nd Sgt, Co K, 46th NCST), V: 525.
Ector, Matthew Duncan, (Brig Gen), II: 491, 492.
Eddings, J.R., (Pvt, Co K, 26th NCST), V: 533.
Edelin, John B., (Lt Col, 1 6th Battalion/75th NCST, 7th Cav), IV: 71, 89, 93, 94, 370.
Edens, James T., (Pvt, Co E, 3rd NCST), V: 487.
Edenton, N.C., II: 80, 81, 793; III: 337; IV: 13, 77, 556, 594.
Edgecombe County, N.C., I: v, 533; II: 499; III: 456; IV: 15, 462, 483.
Edgerton, J.B., (Capt, Claiborne-Dearing's 7th C.S. Cav; 16th Battalion/75th NCST, 7th Cav), IV: 72, 77, 78, 79, 85, 91, 94.
Edisto River, North, S.C., III: 439.
Edisto River, South, S.C., III: 439; IV: 103.
Edmonds, John H., (Pvt, Co B, 1st Battalion NCST), V: 495.
Edmondson, W.J., (2nd Lt, Co H, 57th NCST), V: 511.
Edmonson, J.W., (Lt, 50th NCST; ADC to Hardy), IV: 334.
Edmundson, James, (Maj, AQM, Daniel's Brigade), IV: 513, 517-518.
Edmundson, Jesse, (Sgt, Maj, 50th NCST), III: 161.
Edmunston, B.B., (Adjt, 25th NCST), II: 295, 301.
Edmunston, J.T., (Pvt, Co D, 2nd NCST), I: 176.
Edmonston, Jesse W., (Adjt, 50th NCST), III: 161., 202.
Edmonston, P.M., (Lt Col of Militia, Chief of Staff to Brig Gen David Clark), IV: 646.
Edmonston, R.A., (Capt, Co E, 62nd NCST), III: 516.
Edney, ______, (Col, N.C. Militia), III: 662.
Edney, Baylis M., (Capt, Co A, 25th NCST), II: 292.
Edney, John B., (2nd Lt, Co A, 25th NCST), V: 559.
Edney, Joseph L., (Pvt, Co A, 25th NCST), V: 193.
Edney, Leven, (Orderly Sgt, Woodfin's Battalion; Co G, 9th NCST, 1st Cav), IV: 110.
Edney, Thomas B., (Pvt, Co A, 25th NCST), V: 561.
Edray, Va., IV: 141, 147, 148.
Edward's Ferry, N.C., I: 495, 525; III: 331; IV: 528; V: 175, 312, 315.
Edward's Station, Miss., II: 734.

Edwards, Alexander, (Pvt, Co G, 6th Battalion/60th NCST), III: 482.
Edwards, Benjamin F., (Pvt, Barrington's Co, Whitford's 11th Battalion NCST, Hvy Art; Co B, 67th NCST), V: 18.
Edwards, Cal, (Pvt, Co F, 11th Vols/21st NCST), V: 194.
Edwards, D.W., (Capt, Co C, 67th NCST), III: 704.
Edwards, David, (1st Lt, Co F, 12th Vols/22nd NCST), II: 166, 172.
Edwards, Davidson, (Pvt, Co G, 6th Battalion/60th NCST), III: 482.
Edwards, E.B., (Pvt, Co F, 30th NCST), V: 492.
Edwards, E.S., (1st Lt, Co G, 28th NCST), II: 480.
Edwards, F.M., (Pvt, Co K, 26th NCST), V: 532.
Edwards, G.W., (Pvt, Co K, 56th NCST), III: 357.
Edwards, Gilmore, (1st Lt, Co B, 8th Vols/18th NCST), II: 40.
Edwards, Guilford, (Pvt, Co C, 10th Vols/20th NCST), II: 122.
Edwards, H.A., (Sgt, Co G, 28th NCST), V: 542.
Edwards, J.C., (Pvt, Co H, 43rd NCST), V: 499.
Edwards, J.F., (Pvt, Co E, 43rd NCST), V: 498.
Edwards, J.H., (Pvt, Co G, 45th NCST), V: 500.
Edwards, J.T., (Pvt, Co F, 37th NCST), V: 546.
Edwards, John G., (Capt, Co B, 34th NCST; ACS, Wilcox's Division), II: 581; V: 537.
Edwards, Jonas W., (Pvt, Co E, 43rd NCST), V: 498.
Edwards, Joseph J., (Maj, 68th NCST), III: 713, 716.
Edwards, M.M., (Pvt, Co G, 6th Battalion/60th NCST), III: 482.
Edwards, Q., (Pvt, Co D, 26th NCST), V: 531.
Edwards, R.J., (Pvt, Co C, 32nd NCST), V: 496.
Edwards, R.P., (1st Lt, Claiborne-Dearing's 7th C.S. Cav; Co D, 16th Battalion/75th NCST, 7th Cav), IV: 91.
Edwards, S.P., (Pvt, Co H, 5th NCST), V: 489.
Edwards, S.W., (Pvt, Co E, 43rd NCST), V: 498.
Edwards, T.W., (Pvt, Co H, 4th NCST), V: 489.
Edwards, Thomas H., (Capt, Co B, 28th NCST), II: 466.
Edwards, W.D., (Cpl, Co G, 16th Battalion/75th NCST, 7th Cav), V: 660.
Edwards, W.L., (2nd Lt, Co E, 50th NCST), III: 203.
Edwards, W.W., (Pvt, Co E, 26th NCST), II: 422.
Edwards, William Bryant, (Pvt, Co E, 27th NCST), II: 462; V: 523.
Edwards, William F., (2nd Lt, Co F, 40th NCST, 3rd Art, Hvy), II: 747.
Edwards, Weldon N., (President N.C. State Convention), IV: 646.
Edwards, William R., (2nd Lt, AQM, 1st Vols, "Bethel"; AQM 38th NCST), I: 114, 118; II: 678.
Efird, Martin S., (1st Lt, Co C, 42nd NCST), II: 790.
Efland, Madison L., (1st Lt, Co D, 53rd NCST), III: 262; IV: 702, 706.
Egan, Solomon E., (1st Lt, Co I, 69th NCST, 8th Cav), III: 731.
Egerton, James, (Pvt, Co G, 13th Vols/23rd NCST), V: 510.
Egerton, Joseph J., (Ordnance Sgt, 43rd NCST), V: 497.
Egg Harbor, New Jersey, V: 438.
Egg Island Reef, Nassau, V: 447.
Eggers, John, (Sgt, Co I, 58th NCST), III: 453.
Egypt Coal, V: 338.

Elam, Philip R., (Lt, Co C, 55th NCST), III: 296; IV: 701, 706.
Elberson, J.H., (Pvt, Co F, 2nd Battalion NCST), V: 495.
Eleno, John J., (Ordnance Sgt, 56th NCST), III: 319.
Elevation Church, N.C., (Johnston County), III: 194, 195.
Eleventh Street Pike, (to Washington, D.C.), I: 259.
Eley, William H., (Pvt, Co D, 68th NCST), III: 715.
Elias, Louis, (1st Lt, Co D, 1st Vols/11th NCST), I: 584.
Eliason, William A., (Lt Col, 49th NCST), I: 583.
Eliason, William A., (AQM, 7th NCST), IV: 472.
Eliason, William K., (1st Lt, Co A, 4th NCST), I: 231, 269; IV: 472; V: 665.
Eliason, William K., (Lt Col, 49th NCST), III: 125, 127, 153.
Elbow Key, V: 450.
Election, State, (1 August, 1862), III: 167. 375.
Elizabeth City, N.C., I: 390; IV: 77, 251, 556, 605, 606, 616; V: 68, 304, 306, 307, 308, 309, 310, 311, 312.
Elizabeth Creek, (nr Smithville), II: 752.
Elizabethtown, N.C., IV: 312, 429.
Elk Ford, Va., IV: 147.
Elk Mountain, Va., I: 753; IV: 148.
Elk River, Va., IV: 148.
Elkins, John Q., (2nd Lt, Co H, 8th Vols/18th NCST), IV: 723.
Eller, Calvin, (Capt, Co L, 58th NCST), III: 434.
Eller, D.W., (Lt, Co A, 9th NCST, 1st Cav), I: 485.
Eller, J., (Pvt, Co H, 13th Vols/23rd NCST), V: 510.
Eller, Jesse F., (Capt, Co K, 53rd NCST), III: 264; V: 494.
Eller, William, (2nd Lt, Co 4, Henry's 14th Battalion, Cav; 79th NCST, 8th Cav), IV: 113.
Ellerbee, Stephen W., (2nd Lt, Co I, 43rd NCST), III: 3.
Ellington, G., (Pvt, Co E, 26th NCST), V: 532.
Ellington, J.C., (2nd Lt, Co C, 50th NCST), III: 161, 165, 166, 167, 168, 169, 170, 175, 176, 185, 187, 201, 203; V: 668.
Ellington, J.P., (1st Lt, Co D, 4th Battalion Junior Reserves; Co K, 72nd NCST, 3rd Junior Reserves), IV: 38, 39.
Ellington, James B., (Lt, Co D, 61st NCST; Capt, Co D, 4th Battalion Junior Reserves; Maj, 8th Battalion Junior Reserves; Maj, 72nd NCST, 3rd Junior Reserves), III: 504, 505; IV: 3, 38, 39, 41, 42, 43, 51, 302, 587, 588.
Ellington, Jesse T., (1st Lt, Co C, 50th NCST), III: 181, 182, 203.
Ellington's Expedition, III: 187.
Elliott, ______, (Col, Evans' S.C. Brigade), III: 194, 356.
Elliott, ______, (Commodore, USN), V: 385.
Elliott, Alexander, (Lt, Co K, 51st NCST), III: 205, 212, 220.
Elliott, Charles Gilbert, (Capt, Adjt, 7th Vols/17th NCST; AAG to Martin & Kirkland, Builder of the Ironclad Albemarle), II: 1, 2, 8, 11, 12; IV: 525-549 personal account; V: 312, 315-323.
Elliott, H.E., (Pvt, Co B, 1st Vols/11th NCST), V: 530.
Elliott, J.E., (Lt, Co B, 9th NCST, 1st Cav), I: 485.
Elliott, James S., (Cpl, Co I, 38th NCST), V: 558.
Elliott, John T., (Capt, Co A, 68th NCST), III: 713; V: 17, 18.
Elliott, Lauriston F., [Elliot], (2nd Cpl, Co K, 52nd NCST), III: 225.

Elliott, S.H., (1st Lt, Co F, 49th NCST), I: 120; III: 137; V: 559.
Elliott, Sameul T., (Pvt, Co H, 47th NCST), V: 535.
Elliott, Stephen, (Brig Gen), III: 357.
Elliott, W.A., (Cpl, Co N, 11th Vols/21st NCST), V: 515.
Elliott, W.G., (Pvt, Co E, 48th NCST), V: 526.
Elliott, William, (Cpl, Co E, 48th NCST), V: 526.
Elliott, William H., (Pvt, Co C, 34th NCST), V: 555.
Ellis, ______, [William L.A.], (Capt, Co C, 62nd Ga., Cav), IV: 77, 78.
Ellis, ______, (Capt.), V: 290.
Ellis, Anderson, (Sister of Governor Ellis), III: 655.
Ellis, Anderson, (Lt Col, 54th NCST), III: 267, 269, 271, 278, 281; IV: 662, 677, 702, 706.
Ellis, Andrew J., (1st Lt, Co A, 44th NCST; Capt, Co A, Ellis' Battery, 3rd Battalion, Light Art), III: 22, 281; IV: 261, 264, 265, 266, 267; V: 529.
Ellis, B., (Pvt, Co I, 16th Battalion/75th NCST, 7th Cav), V: 660.
Ellis, B.P., (Lt, Co K, 9th NCST, 1st Cav), I: 486.
Ellis, Charles D., (Capt, Co B, 9th Battalion, 1st Hvy Art), IV: 303, 304.
Ellis, D.R., (Pvt, Co B, 10th Vols/20th NCST), II: 118.
Ellis, J.R., (Pvt, Co H, 48th NCST), V: 527.
Ellis, J.W., (Capt, Co C, 8th Vols/18th NCST), I: 124.
Ellis, J.W., (2nd Lt, Co E, 30th NCST), II: 496.
Ellis, James, (Cpl, Co F, 30th NCST), V: 492.
Ellis, Dr. James R., (Capt, Co A; Surg, 35th NCST), II: 593; IV: 637.
Ellis, Jesse J., (Cpl, Co D, 4th NCST), I: 232.
Ellis, John W. (The first of three war Governors of North Carolina.), I: 3, 18, 39, 48, 71, 104, 109, 134, 215, 220, 295, 296, 337, 339, 417, 483, 500, 550, 561, 562, 653; II: 15, 305, 521, 599; III: 386, 655; IV: 244, 294, 295, 319, 356, 361, 421, 513, 515, 578, 597, 623, 646; V: 25, 26, 27, 577, 645, 646.
Ellis, Laban, (Pvt, Co E, 26th NCST), II: 387.
Ellis, Thomas G., (Pvt, Co F, 5th Vols/15th NCST), V: 521.
Ellis, W.H., (4th Sgt, Co A, 44th NCST), V: 533.
Ellis, W.J., (1st Lt, Co E, 42nd NCST), II: 790, 794, 799, 806.
Ellis, William A., (Capt, Co I, 35th NCST), II: 620.
Ellis, Z., (Lt, Co B, 9th Battalion, 1st Hvy Art), IV: 303.
Ellison, D.P., (Pvt, Co L, 12th Vols/22nd NCST), II: 174.
Ellison, George, (Pvt, Co G, 6th Battalion/60th NCST), III: 482.
Ellison, J.W., (Pvt, Co H, 14th Vols/24th NCST), V: 560.
Ellison, John, (2nd Sgt, Co K, 6th Vols/16th NCST), V: 552.
Ellison, Nicholas, (Pvt, Co H, 6th Battalion/60th NCST), III: 482.
Ellyson's Mill, Va., [Ellison's], I: 168, 181, 367, 613, 738; II: 168; IV: 157.
Elmo, William, (Sgt, Co C, 1st Vols, "Bethel"), I: 128
Elmore, C.E., (3rd Lt, Co G, 57th NCST), IV: 706.
Elmore, John, (Pvt, Co C, 16th Battalion/75th NCST, 7th Cav), V: 660.

Elms, J.P., (2nd Lt, Co I, 37th NCST), I: 120; II: 661.
Elms, W.D., (Capt, Co I, 37th NCST), I: 119, 128.
Elmyra Prison, (Prison at Elmyra N.Y., USA), I: 531; II: 761.
Eltham's Landing, Va., (aka Barhamsville), I: 301, 334.
Elwing, Nere A., (Maj, 48th N.Y.), V: 238.
Elwood, William H., (4th Sgt, Co D, 4th Vols/14th NCST), V: 490.
Ely, ______, (Col, Mi.), III: 391.
Ely, ______, (Seaman, NCN, Curlew), V: 306.
Ely's Ford, (Rapidan River, Va.), I: 594, 640; II: 37, 38, 381, 693; III: 584, 585; V: 677.
Elyson's Mills, Va., [Ellyson's], I: 139, 738.
Elzey, Arnold H., (Maj Gen), I: 343; II: 88, 439, 461; III: 329; IV: 26, 505.
Emack, James W., (Lt, Co F, 7th NCST), I: 377; IV: 467; V: 95.
Emanuel Church, Va., (aka Brook Church), III: 601.
Embler, D, (Cpl, Co H, 48th NCST), V: 526.
Emerson, John R., (1st Lt, Co E, 26th NCST), II: 358, 371, 372, 396, 397, 419.
Emery, ______, (Col, 9th Maine), V: 163.
Emery, J., (Pvt, Co K, 33rd NCST), V: 545.
Emmettsburg, Pa., IV: 181.
Emmettsburg Road, [Emmitsburg], (nr Gettysburg, Pa.), I: 315, 317, 379, 556; II: 43, 344, 363, 364, 366, 661; III: 236; V: 102, 103, 105, 106, 107, 109, 124, 137, 142, 147.
Emory, Aaron, (Pvt, Co A, 44th NCST), V: 533.
Emory, William, (Sgt, Co H, 33rd NCST), II: 540.
Emory River, Tenn., IV: 273.
Emory and Henry College, III: 732.
Emry, Thomas L., (Pvt, Color-bearer, Co G, 2nd Vols/12th NCST), I: 621; IV: 490.
Emuckfau, ______, III: 735.
Encyclopaedia Britanica, I: 39.
End of the Confederacy, I: 59-65.
Endy, W.H., (Pvt, Co F, 5th NCST), I: 292.
Enfield, N.C., I: 535.
Engelhard, Joseph A., (Capt, AQM, 33rd NCST; QM, Branch-Lane's Brigade; Maj, AAG Wilcox's Division), I: 353; II: 537,554, 557; IV: 472, 474, 477; V: 148, 151, 537, 651.
Engineer Corps, CSA, (aka Engineer Bureau), II: 103; IV: 326, 409-432, 453; V: 4, 663.
Engineer Corps, Federal, V: 338.
  New York, 15th, V: 238.
Engineer Corps, N.C., (See: Artillery Regiments).
Engineer Corps, Collins', IV: 415.
Engineer Corps, Topographical, I: 689.
Engineer Troops, IV: 403, 409, 412.
Engineers, 1st CSA, IV: 403, 412, 413, 427.
Engineers, 2nd CSA, IV: 403, 412, 413, 425-432.
England, T.P., (Pvt, Co B, 35th NCST), V: 562.
England, William, (Cpl, Co B, 54th NCST), V: 516.
England, I: 11, 17, 28, 34, 42, 46; V: ix, xiv, xvii, 345, 359, 395, 396, 409, 415, 419, 425, 436, 441, 455, 457, 458, 459.
England, North Carolina's Financial Operations In, V: 453-461.
Englehard, Joseph A., (Maj, QM, Branch's Brigade; Adjt Pender's

Brigade), I: 353; II: 554, 557; IV: 477.
English, J. Milton, (Capt, Co C, 5th Battalion Cav; Capt, Co K, 65th NCST, 6th Cav), III: 447, 674, 675; IV: 271.
Enloe, L.H., (2nd Lt, Co D, 62nd NCST), III: 515; IV: 700.
Enloe, Thomas J., (Pvt, Co A, 25th NCST), V: 561.
Enloe, William A., (Capt, Co F, 29th NCST), II: 485, 493.
Ennett, Dr. William T., (Maj, 3rd NCST), I: 191, 212, 213; IV: 460; V: 484.
Ennis, W.C., (Pvt, Co K, 57th NCST), V: 518.
Enzor, W.H., (Pvt, Co C, 19th NCST, 2nd Cav), II: 117.
Eppes, J.A., (Pvt, Co A, 2nd Vols/12th NCST), V: 506.
Eppes, Richard F., (2nd Lt, Co G, 33rd NCST), II: 540.
Epps, Robert F., (1st Lt, Co E, 6th Battalion/60th NCST), IV: 297.
Epps, T.P., (Lt, Co F, 58th NCST), III: 433.
Ernhart, W.B., (Lt, 50th NCST), IV: 706.
Ernet, Augustus, (Color-bearer, Co K, 24th Mi.), II: 356.
Ernul, McG., (1st Lt, Co E, 27th NCST), II: 457, 462; V: 519.
Erson, Eric, (Lt Col, 52nd NCST), I: 118, 395; II: 395; III: 224, 239; V: 529.
Ervin, J.C., (Pvt, Co B, 35th NCST), V: 562.
Ervin, Rufus, (Pvt, Co F, 26th NCST), V: 602.
Erwin, A.R., (Pvt, Co B, 3rd Vols/13th NCST), V: 549.
Erwin, A.A., (Capt, Co B, 3rd Vols/13th NCST), I: 125, 126, 653.
Erwin, Alfred M., (Maj, QM, Clingman's Brigade), IV: 482.
Erwin, C.A., (Pvt, Co A, 10th Vols/20th NCST), V: 508.
Erwin, Frank, (Lt, Co K, 45th NCST), III: 53.
Erwin, J.B., (Lt, Co K, 64th NCST), III: 660.
Erwin, J.F., (Lt, Co K, 45th NCST), V: 494.
Erwin, John R., (Capt, Co E, 63rd NCST, 5th Cav), I: 441, 442; III: 529, 541. 594, 603, 642, 646, 647, 652, 653, 654.
Erwin, L.P., (Capt, Co G, 6th Vols / 16th NCST; Maj, 21st Battalion Senior Reserves), IV: 6, 153, 397.
Erwin, Marcus, (Maj, 2nd Battalion NCST), IV: 245, 246, 635.
Erwin, Mark, (Lt, 8th Regt Home Guard), V: 635.
Erwin, Phifer, (AQM, 6th Battalion/60th NCST), III: 484, 496.
Erwin, Rufus, (Pvt, Co F, 26th NCST), V: 602.
Erwin, S.E., (Capt, Co K, 64th NCST), III: 660.
Erwin, Stanhope, (Sgt Maj, 6th Battalion/60th NCST), III: 480, 481, 484.
Escape from Fort Warren, IV: 733.
Eskridge, G.M., (Pvt, Co E, 2nd Vols/12th NCST), V: 507.
Essex County, Va., II: 87.
Essic, Theof., (Pvt, Co B, 1st Battalion NCST), V: 504.
Essington, Heber B., (Capt, 203rd Pa.), V: 238.
Estes, H., (Drum Maj, 58th NCST), III: 432.
Estes, W.W., (Pvt, Co A, 44th NCST), V: 533.
Etheridge, Edwin, (Pvt, Co A, 55th NCST), V: 527.
Etheridge, J.D., (Pvt, Co D, 43rd NCST), V: 498.
Estridge, William M., (Lt, Co B, 26th NCST), II: 396, 397.

Etheredge, Amos R., (Pvt, Detached Co, 68th NCST), III: 723.
Etheredge, H., (Pvt, Co B, 47th NCST), V: 534.
Etowah River, Ga., II: 742.
Eubank, A., (Pvt, Co I, 32nd NCST), V: 497.
Eubank, J.T., (2nd Lt, Co K, 32nd NCST), I: 736.
Eubanks, T.C., (2nd Lt, Co E, 48th NCST), V: 526.
Eubanks, William G., (Cpl, Co I, 32nd NCST; Detailed, 2nd Corps Provost Guard), V: 497, 569.
Eudy, J. (Pvt, Co K, 28th NCST), V: 543.
Eudy, L., (2nd Lt, Co E, 6th Battalion Junior Reserves; Co G, 70th NCST, 1st Junior Reserves), IV: 13.
Eudy, W.H., (Pvt, Co F, 5th NCST), I: 292; V: 505.
Eudy, W.M., (Sgt, Co H, 57th NCST), V: 517.
Euker, H.A., (Lt, Co D, 28th NCST), II: 483.
Euliss, E.S., (Capt, Co H, 5th Vols/15th NCST), I: 735; V: 519.
Euliss, William H., (Pvt, Co H, 5th Vols/15th NCST), V: 522.
Euten, N.H., (Lt, 62nd NCST), IV: 706.
Eure, Elisha H., (Pvt, Co E, 7th NCST), I: 378.
Eure, J.E., (Pvt, Co E, 33rd NCST), V: 544.
Eure, Mills, L., (Capt, Co G, 19th NCST, 2nd Cav), II: 80, 89; IV: 701, 704, 706.
Eutaw Band, (S.C.), II: 801.
Evans, ______, (Capt, Wynn's 15th Battalion NCST, Cav), IV: 365.
Evans, A., (Pvt, Co E, 35th NCST), V: 193.
Evans, Abram C., (2nd Lt, Co A, 19th NCST, 2nd Cav), II: 89.
Evans, Clement A., (Brig Gen), I: 354.
Evans, Francis L., (Pvt, Co D, 68th NCST), III: 715.
Evans, Freeman, (Pvt, Co D, 68th NCST), III: 715.
Evans, Gustavus H., (Pvt, Courier, Co H, 27th NCST), II: 462; V: 524.
Evans, Henry C., (Lt, Co B, 9th Battalion, 1st Hvy Art), IV: 303, 305.
Evans, Jacob A., (Lt, Co G, 51st NCST), III: 211, 219.
Evans, James W., (Pvt, Co G, 38th NCST), V: 557.
Evans, James S., (Capt, Co F, 14th Vols/24th NCST), II: 271.
Evans, John, (Pvt, Co D, 44th NCST), V: 533.
Evans, John, (Pvt, Co I, 1st Vols/11th NCST), V: 531.
Evans, John B., (Capt, Co I, 50th NCST), III: 202.
Evans, John W., (4th Cpl, Co D, 68th NCST), III: 713, 714, 715, 717, 719, 720, 722.
Evans, Jonathan, (Maj, 14th Vols/24th NCST), II: 269; III: 269; V: 651.
Evans, Judson L., (Pvt, Co D, 68th NCST), III: 715.
Evans, L.H., (Pvt, Co K, 2nd NCST; Detailed, Invalid Battalion), V: 571.
Evans, Nathan George "Shanks," (Brig Gen), I: 341, 347, 493, 515, 516, 517, 518, 520; III: 86, 231, 507, 508, 509; IV: 325, 345, 383; V: 84, 85, 86, 90.
Evans, Peter G., (Col, 63rd NCST, 5th Cav), I: 424; II: 3; III: 462, 529, 530, 533, 534, 535, 536, 550, 551, 554, 566, 567, 569, 587; V: 10, 650.
Evans, Richard W., (Jr 2nd Lt, Co F, 10th NCST, 1st Art & Engs, Cogdell's Hvy Art), I: 501.

Evans, Robert C., (Jr 2nd Lt, Co D, 6th Battalion/60th NCST), III: 484.
Evans, Stephen B., (Lt Col, 63rd NCST, 5th Cav), III: 529, 530, 537, 538, 540, 551, 552, 572, 595.
Evans, Sherrod J., (Lt, Co B, 47th NCST), III: 84; IV: 700, 707.
Evans, T.C., (Capt, Co C, 3rd Vols/13th NCST), I: 677; V: 547.
Evans, Thomas H., (Pvt, Co B, 59th NCST, 4th Cav), V: 659.
Evans, Thomas H., (Pvt, Co D, 68th NCST), III: 715.
Evans, W.J., (Pvt, Co I, 45th NCST), V: 500.
Evans, William, (Pvt, Co E, 35th NCST), V: 563.
Evans, William, (Cpl, Co I, 30th NCST), V: 493.
Evans, William H., (Pvt, Co G, 38th NCST), V: 557.
Evans' Mill, N.C., IV: 82-84, 90.
Evansport, Va., (now Quantico Station), I: 300; II: 164, 167, 598.
Eve, A.E., (Ass't Surg, 16th Battalion/75th NCST, 7th Cav), V: 659.
Everett, ______, (Capt, 69th NCST), III: 760.
Everett, J.D., (Pvt, Co E, 43rd NCST), V: 498.
Everett, John, (Pvt, Co D, 10th NCST, 1st Art & Engs, Reilly-Ramsay's Battery, Light Art), V: 568.
Everett, John L., (2nd Lt, Co G, 31st NCST), II: 512.
Everett, Lawrence, (Adjt, 13th Vols/23rd NCST), II: 189.
Everett, R.M., (Pvt, Co B, 56th NCST), V: 565.
Everett, S.H., (2nd Lt, Co C, Cumming's Battery, Starr's 13th Battalion, Light Art), IV: 361.
Everett, W.I., (AQM, 13th Vols/23rd NCST), II: 189.
Everhart, M., (Pvt, Co B, 49th NCST), V: 564.
Everitt's, N.C., III: 299.
Eves, Dr. A.E., (Ass't Surg, 59th NCST, 4th Cav; Ass't Surg, 16th Battalion/75th NCST, 7th Cav), III: 457; IV: 72, 641, 643.
Eves, Dr. S., (Ass't Surg, 66th NCST), IV: 642.
Ewell, Richard S., (Lt Gen) I: 150, 152, 260, 274, 275, 356, 378, 379, 383, 545, 608, 616, 632, 633, 637, 644, 726; II: 41, 48, 75, 95, 96, 119, 125, 135, 147, 381, 382, 383, 384, 392, 525, 560, 563, 572; III: 11, 41, 47, 48, 242, 270, 277, 400, 559, 571; IV: 160, 184, 212, 228, 229, 230, 237, 238, 239, 449, 468, 514; V: 121, 122, 123, 138, 468.
Ewer, ______, (Capt, USA, at Plymouth), III: 552.
Ewing, John W., (1st Sgt, Co E, 52nd NCST), III: 224.
Ewing, Orville, (Adjt, 58th NCST), III: 432.
Ewing, Orville, Jr., (Adjt, 6th Battalion/60th NCST), III: 484.
Examining Board, (aka Officer Examining Board; Members: Majs Broadfoot, Anderson and Clark; This body was to judge the qualification of men elected or appointed to be officers of the Junior Reserves.), IV: 5, 13.
Exemptions, (Type and Number), V: 2.
Exum, J.H., (Lt, Co F, 61st NCST), III: 504.
Ezzell, A.W., (Capt, Co A, 40th NCST, 3rd Art, Hvy), II: 745, 746, 747, 748, 756.
Ezzell, J.A., (Sgt, Co F, 49th NCST), V: 564.

(F)

Fagan, Levi J., (Color Sgt, 41st NCST, 3rd Cav), II: 769, 774.
Fagan, N.B., (1st Lt, Co H, 1st NCST), I: 137.
Fagan's House, Frank, (nr Plymouth), III: 338.
Faggart, Paul, (Pvt, Co B, 10th Vols/20th NCST), II: 119.
Fain, John D., (Capt, Co C, 33rd NCST), II: 538, 577, 578.
Fair Bluff, N.C., II: 125, 127.
Fair Grounds, Old, (at Richmond, Va.), I: 297.
Fair Oaks, Va., (aka Seven Pines), I: 237, 302, 303, 334, 350, 352, 627, 738; II: 203; V: 627.
Fair Oaks Station, Va., I: 351.
Fair View, [Fairview], (aka Chancellors Hill, Va.), II: 36, 39, 40, 477, 659.
Faircloth, J.W., (Pvt, Co G, 33rd NCST), II: 544.
Faircolth, W., (Pvt, Co F, 10th Vols/20th NCST), V: 509.
Faircloth, William T., (Capt, AQM, 2nd NCST; QM Cox's Brigade), I: 157, 159, 175; IV: 463.
Faires, E.M., (Capt, Co H, 13th Vols/23rd NCST), II: 186.
Fairfield, Pa., III: 463, 569.
Fairfield, Tenn., III: 484.
Fairfield Road, (nr Gettysburg, Pa.), II: 660.
Fairfax County, Va., II: 149.
Fairfax Court House, Va., I: 421, 422, 424, 564, 573; II: 31, 96, 473, 552.
Fairly, David, (Chaplain, 27th NCST), IV: 611.
Faison, Alexander, (Capt, Co K, 10th Vols/20th NCST), II: 112.
Faison, Franklin J., (Lt Col, 10th Vols/20th NCST), II: 112, 114; V: 11.
Faison, Frank S., (Capt, 6th Battalion Junior Reserves; Co K, 70th NCST, 1st Junior Reserves), IV: 13.
Faison, J.A., (Capt, Co D, 6th Battalion Junior Reserves; Co H, 70th NCST, 1st Junior Reserves), IV: 13.
Faison, John W., (Adjt, 56th NCST), III: 318, 333, 347, 398.
Faison, Rev. Julian P., (Chaplain, 38th NCST), II: 676; IV: 613.
Faison, Paul F., (Col, 56th NCST), II: 287, 601; III: 136, 174, 318, 319, 320, 321, 322, 323, 325, 327, 328, 337, 338, 341, 343, 344, 345, 358, 359, 365, 367; IV: 357, 569, 575; V: 178, 183, 189, 559.
Faison. T.M., (Pvt, Co E, 10th Vols/20th NCST), V: 509.
Faison, W.L., (Adjt, 61st NCST), V: 16.
Faison, William E., (1st Lt, Co D, 38th NCST), V: 548.
Faison, N.C., II: 125.
Fallant, D., (Pvt, Co C, 10th NCST, 1st Art & Engs, Brem-Graham-Williams' Battery, Light Art), V: 568.

Falling Creek, N.C., I: 365; II: 654, 748, 749; III: 86, 727.
Falling Waters, Va., (and Battle of, 1864), I: 381, 425, 591, 699; II: 45, 74, 240, 335, 357, 373, 375-378, 378, 568, 579, 587, 662, 693, 720; III: 92, 109, 110, 239, 240-241, 301, 302, 416; IV: 164, 183-184, 468, 559.
Fallon, Thomas, (Pvt, Co A, 1st Vols, "Bethel"), I: 100, 101, 127.
Falls, J.G., Jr., (2nd Lt, Co C, 2nd Battalion Junior Reserves; Co D, 71st NCST, 2nd Junior Reserves), IV: 28.
Falls, Dixon, (Capt, Co C, 55th NCST), III: 287; V: 668.
Falls, George L., (Musician, 55th NCST), V: 527.
Falls, Thomas D., [T.J.], (Lt, Co C, 55th NCST), III: 296, 299; IV: 701, 707; V: 110, 669.
Falls, W.G., (Capt, Co A, 4th NCST), I: 231, 269.
Fallstown, N.C., III: 299.
Falmouth, Va., I: 300; IV: 150, 171.
Fanner, W.H., (Musician, 16th Battalion/75th NCST, 7th Cav), V: 660.
Fanning, P.W., (Chairman of the Board of Commissioners of Navigation) V: 360-361.
"Fanny," (English Terrier owned by J.W. Alexander), IV: 743.
Faribault, George H., (Col, 47th NCST), III: 83, 94, 103, 104, 107, 246; IV: 555, 556, 563.
Farley, Augustus, (Pvt, Co C, 10th NCST, 1st Art & Engs, Brem-Graham-Williams' Battery, Light Art), V: 568.
Farley, W.C., (Orderly Sgt, Co K, 4th NCST), V: 489.
Farley, W.T., (2nd Sgt, Co C, 3rd Vols/13th NCST), V: 550.
Farmer, J.B., (Cpl, Co F, 4th NCST), I: 233.
Farmer, James, (Pvt, Co A, 45th NCST; Detailed, Headquarters QM Corps), V: 572.
Farmer, Sylvester B.M., (Jr 2nd Lt, Co C, 39th NCST), II: 705.
Farmer Hotel, Flat Rock, N.C., III: 667.
Farmington, N.C., IV: 259.
Farmville, Va., I: 117, 210, 211, 213, 290, 330, 550, 685, 729, 780; II: 402, 459, 482, 577, 589, 696; III: 17, 58, 100, 252, 283, 400, 470, 542; IV: 209, 210, 211-212, 454, 509, 526, 615.
Farmville Road, Va., V: 251.
Farnsworth, Robert, (ACS, Henry's 14th Battalion, Cav; 79th NCST, 8th Cav), IV: 113.
Farquhar, N.H., (Lt, USN, Pioneer, Santiago de Cuba), V: 245.
Farr, J., (Pvt, Co H, 4th NCST), V: 489.
Farrar, J.B., (Musician, Co D, 55th NCST), V: 562.
Farrell, G.W., (Pvt, Co I, 32nd NCST), V: 497.
Farrell, John, (Capt, AQM, M.W. Ransom's Brigade), V: 559.
Farrior, Stephen D., (2nd Lt, Co A, 43rd NCST), III: 3, 11.
Farris, Archibald, (Pvt, Co A, 1st Battalion NCST), V: 504.
Farris, J.T., (Pvt, Co E, 49th NCST), V: 564.
Farris, Joseph, (Pvt, Co L, 11th Vols/21st NCST), V: 515.
Farrow, Isaac L., (1st Lt, Co H, 33rd NCST), II: 540, 561, 570, 578.
Farrow, William T., (Sgt, Co F, 33rd NCST), II: 539.
Farrow, Wilson, (1st Lt, Co H, 33rd NCST), II: 540.
Farthing, J.S., [James S.], (Capt, 1st Battalion Junior Reserves; Co I, 70th NCST, 1st Junior Reserves), IV: 13.

Farthing, William Y., (Capt, Co E, 37th NCST II: 653.
Fatherly, Matthew W., (1st Lt, Co C, 56th NCST), III: 314, 321, 378.
Faucet, A.F., (2nd Lt, Co K, 9th Vols/19th NCST, 2nd Cav), II: 89.
Faucet, W.H., II: 164, 166; IV: 650.
Faucett, _____, (Capt, Faucett's Partisan Rangers; Capt, 63rd NCST, 5th Cav), III: 550.
Faucett, Albert C., (1st Lt, Co A, 66th NCST), III: 685.
Faucett, J., (Cpl, Co D, 56th NCST), V: 566.
Faucett, James A., (Pvt, Co F, 38th NCST), V: 557.
Faucett, James N., (Pvt, Co G, 27th NCST), II: 462; V: 523.
Faucett, John W., (Pvt, Co F, 6th NCST), V: 194.
Faucett, R.G., (1st Sgt, Co E, 3rd Vols/13th NCST), V: 550.
Faucett, Robert T., (1st Lt, Co D, 56th NCST), III: 315, 316, 391, 398.
Faucett, W.H., (Lt Col, 4th Regt Home Guard), IV: 650; V: 630.
Faucett, W.H., (2nd Lt, Co E, 12th Vols/22nd NCST), II: 164, 166.
Faucett, William, (Pvt, Co I, 13th Vols/23rd NCST), V: 510.
Faucett, William A., (Pvt, Co G, 27th NCST), II: 462; V: 523.
Faucett, William E., (Pvt, Co D, 56th NCST), III: 355.
Faucette, Robert H., [Faucett], (Capt, Co K, 47th NCST), III: 85, 100; V: 529.
Faulk, Jonas, (Pvt, Co C, 5th NCST), I: 291; V: 505.
Faulk, Richard, (Cpl, Co C, 10th Vols/20th NCST), II: 118.
Faulkner, _____, (Col, 2nd Miss.), I: 347.
Faulkner, John, (Pvt, Co G, 43rd NCST), V: 498.
Fauquier County, Va., II: 95; III: 559.
Faust, John, (Pvt, Co F, 6th NCST), V: 512.
Faw, Alexander, (Pvt, Co B, 1st NCST), I: 145.
Fayetteville, N.C., I: 92, 112, 113, 131, 525; II: 446, 518; III: 193, 197, 216, 217, 223, 323, 347, 393, 577, 655, 656, 696, 726; IV: 30, 41, 51, 55, 56, 104, 132, 293, 296, 297, 299, 342, 350, 353, 400, 421, 429, 547, 592, 593, 607, 608; V: 385, 612, 615, 643.
Fayetteville, Pa., I: 379; II: 342, 398, 660.
Fayetteville, Va., III: 578.
Fayetteville Arsenal, I: 18, 39, 40, 47, 109, 500, 551; III: 193; IV: 293-300, 347, 356, 400.
Fayetteville Street, (Raleigh), IV: 59.
Fayetteville and Greenwich Road, Va., III: 578, 581.
Fearing, _____, (Capt, Co L, 7th Vols/17th NCST), II: 1.
Featherston, M.M., (Pvt, Co K, 32nd NCST), V: 497.
Featherston, Winfield Scott, (Brig Gen), V: 664.
Featherstone, T.W., (4th Sgt, Co D, 3rd Vols/13th NCST), V: 550.
Federal Point, N.C., (Renamed Confederate Point after secession), IV: 361, 422; V: 28.
Federal Point Lighthouse, II: 17.
Feimster, John A.S., (2nd Lt, Co C, 4th NCST), I: 232, 271.
Feimster, John W., III: 223.
Fellows, John R., (Capt, Ark., Prisoner at Johnson's Island), IV: 671.
Felter, John W., (4th Sgt, Co A, 52nd NCST), III: 223.
Felton, Eli, (Pvt, Co F, 30th NCST), V: 492.
Fender, John, (Pvt, Co F, 12th Vols/22nd NCST), V: 553.

Fennell, G.L., [George L.], (Pvt, Co D, 21st Ga.), V: 194.
Fennell, H.L., (1st Lt, Co C, 1st NCST), I: 136.
Fennell, N.H., (2nd Lt, Co G, 61st NCST), III: 504; IV: 723.
Fennell, Owen, (2nd Lt, ACS, 1st NCST), I: 136.
Fennymore, E.R., IV: 701.
Fenoni, William, (Drum Maj, 56th NCST), III: 319.
Fenton, Edmund, [Edmund F.], (Pvt, Co C, 4th Vols/14th NCST), I: 716.
Fentress, George W., (Pvt, Co A, Webb's Battery, Starr's 13th Battalion NCST, Light Art), V: 282.
Fentress Cooper Mine, (Guilford County), IV: 326.
Ferebee, ______, (Col, 4th NCST), II: 779.
Ferguson, E.R., [Ebed R.], (2nd Lt, Co A, 62nd NCST), IV: 707.
Ferguson, Ebed J., (Lt, Co F, 25th NCST), II: 298.
Ferguson, Franklin C., (Musician, 6th Vols/16th NCST), V: 551.
Ferguson, Garland S., (2nd Lt, Co F, 25th NCST), II: 291, 296, 299, 300, 301.
Ferguson, J.T., (Sgt, Co C, 26th NCST), V: 531.
Ferguson, J.T., (Pvt, Co A, 3rd Vols/13th NCST), V: 549.
Ferguson, Jesse T., [Jesse F.], (AQMS, 26th NCST), II: 307, 371, 396, 408.
Ferguson, John D., (Lt, Co D, 9th NCST, 1st Cav), I: 485.
Ferguson, L., (Pvt, Co H, 46th NCST), V: 525.
Ferguson, Thomas J., (Capt, Co E, 69th NCST, Thomas' Legion), III: 730, 742.
Ferguson, Thomas L., (Capt, Co C, 26th NCST), II: 396.
Ferguson, William B., (1st Lt, Co E, 29th NCST), II: 485.
Fernandina, Fla., V: 370, 384.
Ferrall, ______, [Francis B.], (Pvt, Co G, 41st NCST, 3rd Cav), II: 785.
Ferrebee, Dennis D., [Ferebee], (Col, 63rd NCST, 5th Cav; Col, N.C. Militia), I: 59, 449, 450; II: 338, 779; III: 456, 465, 467, 531, 550, 574, 646; V: 650.
Ferrel, John, (AQM, 14th Vols/24th NCST), II: 269, 271.
Ferrell, J.B., (Pvt, Co C, 43rd NCST), V: 498.
Ferrell, J.E., (2nd Lt, Co D, 30th NCST), II: 496; IV: 701, 707.
Ferrell, S.B., (Pvt, Co D, 30th NCST), V: 492.
Ferrell, T.G., (Cpl, Co A, 56th NCST), III: 347.
Ferrell, W.G., (Lt, Co B, 2nd NCST), I: 158, 159.
Ferrell, W.H., (Pvt, Co E, 54th NCST), V: 516.
Ferrell, William C., (2nd Lt, Co H, 59th NCST, 4th Cav), III: 458; IV: 700.
Ferrero, Edward, (Maj Gen, USA), II: 387.
Fesmire, Reuben C., (1st Cpl, Co B, 52nd NCST), III: 223.
Fesperman, H.D., (Pvt, Co B, 26th NCST), V: 531.
Fessenden, Dr. B.F., (Surg, Wilmington General Hospital), IV: 626, 627, 629.
Fetter, Hal, (Lt, MacRae's 18th Battalion NCST, Cav), IV: 379.
Fetter, William M., (2nd Lt, Co E, 8th Vols/18th NCST), II: 64; V: 537, 663.
Fetzer, John W., (1st Sgt, Co A, 52nd NCST), V: 535.
Fetzer, Nevin D., (1st Lt, Co A, 2nd Battalion Junior Reserves; Co B, 71st NCST, 2nd Junior Reserves), IV: 28, 595.

Fewell, William, (2nd Lt, Co D, 4th Battalion Junior Reserves; Co K, 72nd NCST, 2nd Junior Reserves), IV: 38.
Ficer, ______, (Col, Ga.), III: 188, 189.
Field, Charles William, (Maj Gen), I: 613; II: 7, 686; III: 364.
Field, W.B., (Lt, Co C, 9th NCST, 1st Cav), I: 485.
Fields, Alexander, (Lt, Co E, 61st NCST), III: 504.
Fields, Elias, (Pvt, Co D, 61st NCST), III: 507.
Fields, L.H., (Pvt, Co C, 27th NCST), II: 462; V: 523.
"Fifteen Negro Law," IV: 649, 652.
Fight, Henry T., (Color-bearer, Co F, 7th NCST), I: 368.
File, Jefferson, (Cpl, Co C, 33rd NCST), II: 539; V: 544.
Financial Operations in Europe, V: 453.
Fincannon, Isaac, (Pvt, Co G, 25th NCST), V: 561.
Fincannon, J.D., (Pvt, Co G, 25th NCST), V: 561.
Finch, J.C., (Pvt, Co F, 56th NCST), V: 566.
Fincher, H.H., (Pvt, Co D, 37th NCST), V: 545.
Fine's Creek, N.C., II: 493.
Finegan, Joseph, [Finnegan], (Brig Gen), IV: 532.
Fingan, Monroe, (Pvt, Co G, 32nd NCST), V: 496.
Finger, Sydney M., (Maj, QM Department), I: 585.
Finger, William L., (Pvt, Co B, 13th Vols/23rd NCST), V: 509.
Fink, H.H., (Pvt, Co A, 10th Vols/20th NCST), V: 508.
Fink, J., (Pvt, Co C, 33rd NCST), V: 544.
Finley, A.L., (1st Sgt, Co B, 12th Vols/22nd NCST), V:553.
Finley, G.A., (Pvt, Co B, 12th Vols/22nd NCST), V: 553.
Finley, G.P., (Pvt, Co B, 12th Vols/22nd NCST), V: 553.
Finley, N., (Pvt, Co B, 35th NCST), V: 562.
Fipp, James W., (Pvt, Co G, 25th NCST), V: 561.
First National Bank of Gastonia, N.C., V: 600.
First North Carolina Soldier Who Died, (See also: Henry L. Wyatt), V: 579.
Fisher, Alfred, (Pvt, Co I, 6th Battalion/60th NCST), III: 482.
Fisher, Cephas, (Pvt, Co K, 10th Vols/20th NCST), V: 508.
Fisher, Charles F., (Col, 6th NCST; Fort Fisher named in honor and memory of the 1st Colonel of the 6th NCST), I: 294, 295, 298, 299, 331, 332, 337, 338, 339, 341, 343, 346, 349, 542; V: 9, 29, 30, 31, 32, 33, 581, 582, 583, 585.
Fisher, Daniel G., (Capt, Co G, 69th NCST, Thomas' Legion), III: 731.
Fisher, Elwood, (Pvt, Co B, 1st Battalion NCST), V: 504.
Fisher, J.A., (Capt, Co F, 9th NCST, 1st Cav), I: 486.
Fisher, J.H., (Pvt, Co F, 13th Vols/23rd NCST), V: 510.
Fisher, J.R., (1st Lt, Co D, 82nd NCST), IV: 131.
Fisher, John V., (Color-bearer, Co H, 8th NCST), I: 408.
Fisher, R.H., (Pvt, Co F, 13th Vols/23rd NCST), V: 510.
Fisher, W.L., (4th Sgt, Co I, 48th NCST), V: 527.
Fisher, Willis C., (Sgt, Co K, 5th Vols/15th NCST), V: 522.
Fisher's Farm, Va., (nr Richmond), I: 434; III: 619.
Fisher's Hill, Va., (and Battle of, 1864), I: 154, 164, 173, 206, 207,

208, 262, 275, 290, 326, 327, 334; II: 142, 146, 253, 257, 259, 261, 533; III: 14, 37, 55, 256, 262, 264, 279, 421, 428, 533; IV: 463.
Fisher's Landing, (nr New Bern), II: 310, 327.
Fishing Creek, Ky., (and Battle of, 1862), III: 736; IV: 125, 284.
Fitch, G.S., (Sgt, Co H, 6th NCST), V: 513.
Fitch, John, (Pvt, Co H, 6th NCST), V: 513.
Fitchet, M.L., (Pvt, Co D, 35th NCST), V: 562.
Fitts, F.M., (Sgt Maj, 30th NCST), V: 491.
Fitts, F.M., (Capt, Co D, 30th NCST), II: 503.
Fitts, G.H., (Sgt, Co E, 26th NCST), V: 532.
Fitzgerald, A.L., (Ordnance Sgt, 41st NCST, 3rd Cav), II: 769.
Fitzgerald, Frederic, (Chaplain, 2nd NCST), V: 679.
Fitzgerald, H.H., (Lt, Co F, 9th NCST, 1st Cav), I: 486.
Fitzgerald, I.A., [J.A.], (2nd Lt, Co A, 54th NCST), III: 273.
Fitzgerald, O.W., (Lt, Co G, 12th Vols/22nd NCST), II: 166.
Fitzgerald, R.T., (1st Cpl, Co A, 3rd Vols/13th NCST), V: 549.
Fitzgerald, W.P., (Sgt, Co F, 4th NCST), I: 233.
Five Forks, Va., (aka Five Cross Roads, and Battle of, 1865), I: 330, 439, 440, 441, 442, 477-481, 602; II: 61, 107, 290, 300, 391, 393, 611, 626, 670, 783, 784; III: 126, 135, 145-147, 158, 251, 393, 396-399, 401, 425, 469, 472, 531, 541-542, 644, 645-648; IV: 88, 89, 110, 206, 452, 576, 579; V: 266, 671.
Flack, S., (Pvt, Co F, 54th NCST), V: 516.
Flagler, _____, (Lt, USA; Violated a cease fire and flag of truce), I: 510.
Flake, E.W., (Pvt, Co K, 26th NCST), V: 532.
Flake, F.E., (Pvt, Co K, 43rd NCST), V: 499.
Flake, Francis E., (2nd Lt, Co K, 43rd NCST), III: 3.
Flake, Robert J., (Pvt, Co F, 2nd NCST; Detailed, 2nd Corps Provost Guard), I: 176; V: 486, 570.
Flanigan, Robert, (Pvt, Co F, 63rd NCST, 5th Cav), III: 563.
Flanner, _____, (Purser, Advance), V: 341.
Flanner, Bennett, Jr., (2nd Lt, Co F, Latham-Potts-Flanner's Battery, Starr's 13th Battalion NCST, Light Art), IV: 354; V: 569.
Flanner, Charles, (Ordnance Sgt, 8th Vols/18th NCST), II: 63; V: 539.
Flanner, Henry G., (Capt, Co F, Latham-Potts-Flanner's Battery, Starr's 13th Battalion NCST, Light Art), IV: 354; V: 569, 617-618.
Flat Creek, N.C., III: 474.
Flat Rock, N.C., III: 667.
Flat Woods, (Yadkin Valley, N.C.), V: 286.
Flea Hill, (District of Cumberland County), IV: 294.
Fleetwood Heights, Va., (aka Fleetwood or Brandy Station), I: 609; II: 91; III: 531, 576.
Fleetwood Hill, Va., III: 558.
Fleetwood House, Va., I: 423; III: 532.
Fleming, _____, [Robert R., Cpl], (Sgt, Co H, 27th NCST), II: 494.
Fleming, C. Fletcher, (Pvt, Co I, 2nd Vols/12th NCST; Detailed, 2nd Corps Provost Guard), V: 570.

Fleming, E.L., (Sgt, Co E, 13th Vols/23rd NCST), V: 510.
Fleming, J.W., (Pvt, Co E, 13th Vols/23rd NCST), V: 510.
Fleming, John A., [Flemming], (Lt Col, 49th NCST), III: 127, 129, 138, 142, 143, 147, 148, 152, 372, 374; V: 11.
Fleming, N.N., (Capt, Co B, 46th NCST), III: 76, 80.
Fleming, Robert, (Cpl, Co H, 27th NCST), V: 524.
Fleming, Robert A., (Sgt Maj, 53rd NCST), III: 261.
Fleming, W.B., (Lt, Co C, 2nd Vols/12th NCST), I: 651.
Fleming, W.B., (2nd Lt, Co C, 2nd Vols/12th NCST), V: 503.
Fleming, W.L., (Sgt Maj, 53rd NCST), III: 261.
Fleming, W.W., (2nd Lt, Co D, 6th NCST), V: 511.
Fleming, William, (Pvt, Co F, 26th NCST), V: 601.
Fleming's Ford, N.C., [Flemming's Ford], (Catawba River above Morganton), IV: 376; V: 635, 636.
Flemming, E.P., (1st Cpl, Co B, 44th NCST), V: 533.
Flemming, Greenlea, [James Greenlea], (2nd Lt, Co A, 49th NCST), III: 129; V: 79.
Flemming, R.R., (Cpl, Co H, 27th NCST), II: 462.
Flemming, S.F., (Cpl, Co H, 63rd NCST, 5th Cav), III: 586, 601.
Flemming, W.B., (Lt, Co C, 2nd Vols/12th NCST), I: 651.
Flemming, W.W., (Lt, Adjt, 6th NCST), III: 144, 423, 424; V: 514.
Fletcher, C., (Pvt, Co I, 2nd Vols/12th NCST), V: 508.
Fletcher, Dr. G.W., (Ass't Surg, 25th NCST), II: 291; IV: 635.
Fletcher, Charles M., (Capt, Co D, 6th Battalion/60th NCST), III: 474, 484.
Fletcher, Richard J., (Col, 11th Ala.), V: 584, 585.
Flinn, Josephus, (Cpl, Detached Co, 68th NCST), III: 723.
Flinn, Miles W., (Pvt, Co I, 34th NCST), V: 556.
Flint Hill, Va., I: 563; III: 241.
Flora College, N.C., IV: 607, 613.
Florence, Ala., III: 438, 494, 501.
Florence, S.C., III: 191; V: 68.
Florida, I: 70; II: 701, 737, 738; III: 732; IV: 610, 618; V: 354, 382.
Florida State Seminary, I: 79.
Flow, J.C., (Sgt, Co I, 37th NCST), V: 546.
Flow, J.M.W., (2nd Lt, Co A, 82nd NCST), IV: 131.
Flower, Dr. Josiah C., (Ass't Surg, 47th NCST), IV: 639.
Flowers, George W., (Lt Col, 38th NCST), II: 675, 676, 677, 678, 681, 690, 694, 695; V: 290, 295, 548.
Flowers, J.W., (Pvt, Co A, 10th NCST, 1st Art & Engs, Ramseur-Manly's Battery, Light Art), I: 554; V: 567.
Flowers, James, (Pvt, Co B, Wise's Legion), V: 66.
Flowers, Thomas, (Pvt, Co B, 2nd NCST), I: 175; V: 486.
Flowers, Thomas C., (Pvt, Co G, 38th NCST), V: 557.
Floyd, A.E., (Orderly Sgt, Co D, 8th Vols/18th NCST), II: 63; V: 539.
Floyd, Francis F., (2nd Lt, Co E, 51st NCST), III: 219; IV: 723.
Floyd, James J., (2nd Sgt, Co C, 52nd NCST), III: 223.
Floyd, John Buchanan, (Brig Gen), II: 270; IV: 149.
Floyd, Levi, (Pvt, Co H, 48th NCST), V: 527.

Floyd, W.S., (2nd Lt, Co H, 13th Vols/23rd NCST), II: 187.
Flusser, _____, (Capt, USN; Miami, Perry), I: 446, 447; II: 617, III: 339, 552, 553; V: 175, 181, 320, 321.
Flynn, William S., (Capt, Anderson's Battalion Junior Reserves; Co I, 71st NCST, 2nd Junior Reserves) IV: 26, 29.
Flynt, R.B., (Pvt, Co I, 33rd NCST), V: 545.
Foard, Fred C., (Lt., ADC to Barringer), I: 431; III: 610, 641, 643, 646, 647, 651, 652, 653; IV: 582.
Foard, J.B., (Pvt, Co H, 63rd NCST, 5th Cav), III: 587, 601, 654.
Foard, N.P., [Ford], (Capt, Co F, 9th NCST, 1st Cav), I: 434, 449, 452, 486; III: 605.
Foard, Wyatt, (Pvt, Co B, 59th NCST, 4th Cav), V: 659.
Fogleman, E.M., (Pvt, Co F, 53rd NCST), V: 502.
Fogleman, H.C., (Pvt, Co F, 53rd NCST), V: 502.
Folger, Romulus S., (1st Lt, Adjt, 28th NCST), II: 465, 483; IV: 473; V: 537.
Folk, George N., (Capt, Co D, 9th NCST, 1st Cav; Lt Col, 7th Battalion NCST, Cav; Col, 65th NCST, 6th Cav), I: 418, 483, 484, 485; III: 673, 675, 679, 680, 682-683, 706; IV: 85, 291, 301, 721, 761.
Folk, J.S., (Capt, Co G, 65th NCST, 6th Cav), III: 675, 684.
Foote, Dr. George A., (Surg, 11th Vols/21st NCST), IV: 635.
Foote, J.S., (2nd Lt, Co B, 30th NCST), II: 496.
Foote, James H., (Maj, AAG), I: 51, 52, 53, 137; II: 579.
Foote, Thomas J., (Sgt Maj, Adjt, 2nd Vols/12th NCST), I: 606, 609, 620.
Forbes, A., (Musician, 16th Battalion/75th NCST, 7th Cav), V: 660.
Forbes, A., (Pvt, Co H, 27th NCST), II: 462; V: 524.
Forbes, Arthur, (Sgt, Co F, 30th NCST), V: 492.
Forbes, James, (Pvt, Co F, 30th NCST), V: 492.
Forbes, Samuel H., (1st Lt, Co D, Adam's Battery, Starr's 13th Battalion, Light Art), IV: 353.
Forbis, J.B., (Pvt, Co A, 53rd NCST), V: 501.
Forbis, Richard C., (Pvt, Co, B, 5th Vols/15th NCST), V: 521.
Forcum, John B., (Capt, Co H, 4th NCST), I: 231, 233, 261, 268; V: 484.
Ford, A.J., (Sgt, Co B, 1st NCST), V: 485.
Ford, A.T., (Pvt, Co H, 49th NCST), V: 565.
Ford, Frederick C., (Lt, ADC to Barringer), IV: 582.
Ford, G.B., (Capt, Co K, 50th NCST), III: 203.
Ford, Gaston, (Pvt, Co H, 47th NCST), V: 535.
Ford, J.B., (1st Lt, Co K, 50th NCST), III: 203.
Ford, J.H., (Pvt, Co H, 49th NCST), V: 565.
Ford, James M., (2nd Lt, Co D, 6th Battalion/60th NCST), III: 484.
Ford, John, (Lt, Co G, 6th Vols/16th NCST), IV: 178, 179.
Ford, L.D.H., (Pvt, Co I, 6th NCST), V: 513.
Ford, L..H., (Pvt, Co B, 28th NCST), V: 540.
Ford, P.B., (2nd Lt, Co K, 50th NCST), III: 203.
Ford Road, (nr Five Forks, Va.), III: 396.

Ford's Depot, Va., (South Side Railroad), III: 648.
Forest, ______, (Maj, Engineering Officer, CSN), IV: 418, 419.
Forney, J.J., (3rd Lt, Co B, 54th NCST), III: 268; IV: 702, 707.
Forney's Farm, [Forney's House], (nr Gettysburg, Pa.), I: 612, 633, 634, 636, 637; II: 235; III: 5.
Forrest, J.D., (2nd Sgt, Co I, 52nd NCST), V: 536.
Forrest, James, (Pvt, Co A, Teamster, 2nd Battalion NCST), V: 495.
Forrest, James, (Color-bearer, 44th NCST), III: 31.
Forrest, James, (Pvt, Co D, 48th NCST), III: 120.
Forrest, Nathan Bedford, (Lt Gen), I: 430; III: 501, 553; IV: 498; V: xviii, 170.
Forrester, J.T., [John T.], (2nd Lt, Co F, 37th NCST), IV: 701, 707.
Forrester, John H., (Lt, Co A, 9th NCST, 1st Cav), I: 485.
Forrester, Martin C., (Pvt, Co C, 34th NCST), V: 555.
Forsyth, James R., (Cpl, Co D, 30th NCST), IV: 602.
Forsyth County, N.C., III: 35, 38, 406, 409, 428; IV: 225, 258, 633, 760.
Forsythe, John, (Pvt, Co E, 46th NCST), V: 524.
Fort John W., (Pvt, Co D, 2nd NCST), I: 176; V: 486.
Fort Loudon, (French & Indian War), II: 256.
Fort Necessity, V: 213.
Fort Republic, Va., III: 280.
Forte, John A., (1st Lt, Co A, 31st NCST), II: 512.
Forte, John L., (2nd Lt, Co A, 31st NCST), II: 512.
Forts, Confederate:
    Fort Alexander, (nr Petersburg, Va.), IV: 453.
Fort Anderson, (Cape Fear River; Was Fort St. Philip), II: 650, 751, 754, 756, 761, 762; IV: 268, 304, 305, 311, 327, 331, 357, 418, 419, 423, 428; V: 299, 367, 368.
Fort Bartow, (Roanoke Island), I: 389, 390; II: 1, 2, 508, 509, 510, 511; V: 58, 60, 61, 62, 63, 64.
Fort Blanchard, (Roanoke Island), II: 508, 511; V: 58, 61.
Fort Branch, (Roanoke River at Rainbow Banks), I: xiii, 447, 495, 496, 497, 498, 524, 525, 527, 529, 531, 533; II: 3; III: 720, 726. 727; IV: 16, 17, 27, 353, 354, 439.
Fort Campbell, (Oak Island), II: 650, 751, 761; III: 726; IV: 304, 306, 311, 331, 332, 419, 487.
Fort Caswell, (Cape Fear River), I: 509, 528; II: 111, 113, 629, 650, 750, 751, 752, 753, 755, 756; III: 726; IV: 265, 268, 303, 304, 306, 307, 308, 311, 317, 318, 326, 331, 332, 343, 361, 413, 415, 418, 419, 420, 421, 487, 541, 645; V: 23, 24, 225, 26, 27, 28, 299, 336, 339, 361, 388, 396, 397, 402, 403, 404, 447.
Fort Clark, (Hatteras Island), II: 1; V: 37, 38, 39, 40, 42, 43, 44, 47, 48, 50, 301, 302.
Fort Clifton, (Appomattox River nr Petersburg, Va.), I: 496, 497, 526, 529, 531; III: 355, 357; IV: 357.
Fort Croatan, (nr Otter Creek below New Bern, aka Croatan breastworks), II: 309, 327; III: 680; IV: 84, 90.
Fort Darling, (nr Drewry's Bluff, Va.), III: 40.

Fort Davis, (Cape Fear River), III: 726.
Fort Donelson, (Tenn.), III: 35; V: 244.
Fort Euliss, (nr Hatcher's Run, Va.), II: 454; 509.
Fort Fisher, (at mouth of Cape Fear River), I: xiii, 132, 165, 409, 410, 496, 497, 514, 528, 529, 530, 531; II: 9, 10, 17, 497, 518, 631-650, 747-759, 802; III: 176, 207, 213, 215, 513, 693-695, 726; IV: 4, 6, 38, 39, 41, 45-50, 108, 221, 222, 265, 268, 269, 297, 304, 305, 306-311, 312, 316, 331, 342, 343, 344, 357, 358, 359, 361, 383, 391-392, 398, 402, 410, 416, 419, 421, 422, 423-424, 425, 427, 497, 538, 539-542, 541, 544, 590, 591, 652; V: xv, 6, 23, 28, 217-246, 336, 337, 398, 399, 343, 344, 351, 352, 367, 374, 381, 396, 397, 406, 407, 414, 422, 423, 424, 425, 426, 427, 437, 438, 440, 441, 442, 451, 632.
Fort Forest, (opposite Roanoke Island on mainland), II: 508; V: 58.
Fort Gatling, (nr Fort Fisher), II: 9, 802.
Fort Gilmer, (nr Richmond, Va.), II: 392.
Fort Gregg, (nr Petersburg, Va.), I: 264; II: 59, 61, 62, 670; III: 398; IV: 204, 207, 208, 212, 216, 264, 453, 470, 479.
Fort Gregg, (S.C.), III: 207.
Fort Hamby, (N.C.), IV: 376, 377; V: 285-295.
Fort Hamilton, (Martin County), IV: 348.
Fort Hatteras, (Hatteras Island), I: 501; II: 1, 308, 747; V: 35-56, 299, 301, 302.
Fort Hedrick, (Bald Head Island), II: 761;IV: 421.
Fort Henry, (Tenn.),III: 35.
Fort Hill, (Rodman's Point on Pamlico River), II: 340, 748, 754; III: 233, 234; IV: 253, 519.
Fort Holmes, (opposite Fort Caswell), II: 755, 756, 759, 761; IV: 421.
Fort Huger, (Roanoke Island, aka Battery Huger), I: 389; V: 58, 61.
Fort Huger, (nr Suffolk, Va.), II: 508, 511; V: 58, 61.
Fort Jackson, V: 243, 245, 246.
Fort Johnson, [Johnston] (nr Smithville), II: 497, 749, 752; III: 4; IV: 361, 645; V: 24, 27, 299.
Fort Jones, (nr Plymouth; was Fort Comfort, renamed after the capture of Plymouth; See also: Fort Comfort), III: 346.
Fort Lane, (Neuse River nr New Bern), I: 362, 537; II: 427, 747.
Fort Lee, (Cape Fear River), III: 726.
Fort Macon, (Bouge Island; was both CSA & USA), I: 215, 362, 489, 490, 491, 500, 503, 503, 504, 507, 508, 509, 510, 511, 512, 605; II: 3, 307, 427, 629, 750, 751, 796; III: 35, 314; IV: 413, 607, 629; V: 299, 374, 375, 577, 629.
Fort MacRae, [McRae], (nr Petersburg, Va.), III: 249, 627; IV: 508.
Fort Magruder, (nr Williamsburg, Va.), I: 552.
Fort Mahone, (nr Petersburg, Va.), I: 120; II: 265; III: 16, 17, 56, 58; V: 249, 252.
Fort McAllister, (nr Savannah, Ga.), II: 513; III: 183; IV: 327, 734.

Fort Meares, (Cape Fear River), III: 726.
Fort Mills, (S.C.), II: 416.
Fort Morgan, (Movile Bay, Ala.), V: 420.
Fort Moultrie, (Charleston, S.C.), I: 395; II: 158; IV: 716.
Fort Ocracoke, (Ocracoke Island), V: 35, 36, 40, 41, 43.
Fort Pemberton, (James Island, S.C.), III: 510.
Fort Pender, (nr Smithville), II: 752, 753, 755; IV: 420.
Fort Pitt, (Tenn.), II: 486, 487.
Fort Powell, (Ala.), IV: 684.
Fort Powhantan, Old, (below City Point, Va.), I: 538; II: 429; IV: 502.
Fort Pulaski, (Savannah River, Ga.), IV: 717, 719; V: 623.
Fort Sanderson, (Both CSA & USA; aka Fort Wessels; See also: Fort Wessels), V: 176, 178, 180, 182.
Fort St. Philip, (See: Fort Anderson).
Fort, Spanish, (Mobile Bay, Ala.), I: 768; II: 492, 705, 721.
Fort Sumter, [Sumpter], (Charleston Harbor, S.C.), I: 293, 294, 742; II: 161, 412, 767; III: 386, 674; IV: 243, 421, 491, 498, 716; V: viii, 27, 162, 163, 166, 435, 465, 615, 620, 639, 645.
Fort Sullivan, (Savannah, Ga.), IV: 471.
Fort Thompson, (Neuse River nr New Bern), I: 363; II: 309, 310, 314, 317, 318, 542, 543, 593, 751.
Fort Wagner, (Morris Island, S.C.), I: 392; II: 514; III: 206, 511; V: 161-167.
Fort Walthal, (nr Petersburg, Va.), IV: 489.
Forts, (Federal):
Fort Anderson, (nr New Bern), III: 704; IV: 557.
Fort Comfort, (nr Plymouth; aka Conaby Redoubt), III: 339, 341, 346; V: 176, 186, 187.
Fort Delaware Prison, (Pea Ridge Island in Delaware Bay), II: 184, 420; IV: 257, 321, 327, 497, 683, 713, 725-732, 761; V: 375, 597, 619, 620.
Fort Delaware, Prison life at, IV: 683, 725; V: 375.
Fort Gray, (nr Warren's Neck), III: 337, 338, 348; V: 176, 319.
Fort Hal, (nr Plymouth), III: 343, 344, 345.
Fort Harrison, (nr Richmond, Va.), I: 408, 409; II: 518, 801; III: 213, 214, 218, 219, 220, 358, 374, 505, 512, 690, 691; IV: 495-497, 536; V: 518.
Fort Haskell, [Heiskel], (nr Petersburg, Va.), I: 329; III: 424.
Fort LaFayette, (N.Y.), IV: 734; V: 442, 444, 445.
Fort Massachusetts, (nr Washington, D.C.), II: 247.
Fort McHenry Prison, (nr Baltimore, Md.), II: 254; IV: 257, 612, 726.
Fort Norfolk Prison, IV: 612.
Fort Stedman, [Steadman], (nr Petersburg, Va., aka Fort Hell), I: 155, 156, 290, 329, 334, 601, 650, 651; II: 60, 124, 143, 263, 264, 265, 299, 300, 481, 576, 605, 608, 612, 625; III: 56, 57, 144, 158, 282, 370, 312, 371, 390-394, 423, 424; IV: 205-207, 478, 486, 535, 576, 579.
Fort Stevens, (New Bern), V: 330.
Fort Stevens, [Stephens], (Washington, D.C. defenses),

I: 206, 259; II: 141, 481; III: 13, 749; IV: 526.
Fort Warren, (nr Plymouth), V: 178, 192.
Fort Warren, (Prison, Boston Harbor, Mass.), II: 747; III: 525; IV: 251, 733-743; V: 312, 408, 680.
Fort Wessels, (nr Plymouth, aka 85th Redoubt), I: 321, 526; II: 146; III: 338, 339; IV: 574; V: 176, 178, 180, 182.
Fort Williams, (Plymouth), I: 400, 401, 527; II: 617, 618; III: 339, 341, 342; V: 176, 178, 179, 184, 185, 186, 187, 189, 190.
Fort Worth, (nr Plymouth), V: 176, 188, 189.
Fortress Monroe, (Va.), I: 80, 81, 86, 92, 100, 389, 737; II: 752, 759; III: 134, 336, 386; IV: 77, 87, 572; V: 51, 53, 375, 418, 441, 478.
Fortenburg, Robert A., (Pvt, Co F, 34th NCST), V: 555.
Fortune, B.F., (2nd Lt, Co 3, West's Battalion NCST, Cav), IV: 111.
Fortune, Richard L., (Sgt, Co E, 25th NCST), V: 561.
Fortune, William P., (Capt, Co 3, West's Battalion NCST, Cav), IV: 111.
Forty-five Mile Station, Ga., (Georgia Central Railroad), III: 181.
Foscue's, N.C., II: 82.
Foster, E.S., (2nd Lt, Co A, 70th NCST, 1st Junior Reserves; Ordnance Officer, Nethercutt's Brigade), IV: 5, 12, 18, 591.
Foster, F.L., (Pvt, Co E, 37th NCST), V: 545.
Foster, George, (Pvt, Co D, 6th Vols/16th NCST), IV: 198.
Foster, H, (Pvt, Co F, 3rd Vols/13th NCST), V: 550.
Foster, H.C., (2nd Sgt, Co F, 3rd Vols/13th NCST), V: 550.
Foster, J., (Pvt, Co F, 6th Battalion/60th NCST), III: 482.
Foster, J.M., (Pvt, Co F, 52nd NCST), V: 536.
Foster, James, (Capt, USN, James Adger), V: 408.
Foster, James I., (Capt, Co I, 32nd NCST), I: 736.
Foster, John Gray, (Maj Gen, USA), I: 493, 514, 515, 516, 540, 588; II: 84, 85, 309, 311, 318, 327, 337, 338, 339, 340, 405, 543, 616, 751, 757, 774; III: 4, 86, 87, 173, 179, 183, 186, 187, 320, 459, 507, 508, 553, 740; IV: 103, 251, 263, 264, 325, 326, 430, 484, 557; V: 20, 67, 83, 84, 85, 86, 88, 90.
Foster, Dr. LaFayette, Jr., IV: 595.
Foster, M., (Pvt, Co F, 6th Battalion/60th NCST), III: 482.
Foster, Nathaniel A., (Capt, Co F, 57th NCST), III: 224, 239, 241; IV: 701, 707.
Foster, T.M., (Sgt, Co B, 28th NCST), V: 541.
Foster, William H., (3rd Sgt, Co F, 52nd NCST), III: 224.
Foster's Mills, N.C., III: 210, 680; IV: 15, 16.
Foster's Raid, N.C., III: 320, 459; IV: 325.
Foulkes, Dr. James F., (Capt, Surg, 52nd NCST), III: 223, 225, 227; IV: 640.
Fount, W.C., (Pvt, Co K, 35th NCST), V: 563.
"Four Days of Battle at Petersburg -June 15, 16, 17, and 18, 1864," (by General Beauregard), IV: 534.
Four Mile House, S.C., III: 70.
Foushee, E.T., (3rd Sgt, Co E, 44th NCST), V: 533.
Foushee, James, (Pvt, Co G, 48th NCST), V: 526.

Foushee, Joseph, (Pvt, Co I, 4th Vols/14th NCST), V: 491.
Foust, G.M., (Cpl, Co G, 44th NCST), V: 534.
Foust, J., (Pvt, Co M, 12th Vols/22nd NCST), V: 554.
Fouts, I.G., (Pvt, Co I, 5th NCST), V: 505.
Fowle, Daniel G., (Brig Gen, Adjt Gen. N.C.; Lt Col, 31st NCST; post war Governor of North Carolina), I: 18, 37, 40, 48, 50, 56; II: 507; IV: 249, 483; V: 6.
Fowler, H.D., (Capt, Co I, 1st NCST), I: 137; IV: 721.
Fowler, H.J., (Capt, Co I, 1st NCST), I: 137.
Fowler, J.W., (Pvt, Co F, 35th NCST), V: 563.
Fowler, John, (Pvt, Co H, 6th NCST), V: 513.
Fowler, Dr. Josiah C., (Ass't Surg, 47th NCST), III: 83.
Fowler, M.C., (2nd Lt, Co B, Walker's Battalion, Thomas' Legion; 80th NCST), IV: 118.
Fowler, T.H., (Musician, 6th NCST), V: 511.
Fowler, W., (Pvt, Co G, 1st Vols/11th NCST), V: 530.
Fowler, W.F., (Pvt, Co A, 12th Vols/22nd NCST), V: 553.
Fowler, W.R., (Pvt, Co C, 47th NCST), V: 534.
Fox, A.M., (Pvt, Co G, 26th NCST), V: 532.
Fox, Andrew M., (Pvt, Co G, 34th NCST), V: 556.
Fox, J.A., (Lt, Co F, 58th NCST), III: 433.
Fox, John B., (Lt, Co G, 61st NCST), III: 504.
Fox, N., (Pvt, Co H, 56th NCST), III: 348.
Fox, R.P., (Pvt, Co I, 30th NCST), V: 493.
Fox, Dr. T.S., (Ass't Surg, 66th NCST), IV: 462.
Fox, W., (Pvt, Co G, 37th NCST), V: 546.
Fox, William F., (Col, USA; author of Regimental Losses in the Civil War), II: 360.
Fox's Farm, Va., I: 421.
Fox's Gap, Md., I: 625; II: 115.
Fox's Spring, Va., II: 90, 94, 95.
Foxhall, E.D., (Capt, Co I, 5th Vols/15th NCST), I: 735; V: 519.
Foxhall, Francis D., (2nd Lt, Co B, 33rd NCST), II: 538.
Foy, Christopher D., (Capt, Co H, 67th NCST), III: 686, 704.
Foy, Kit, (Resident of New Bern), II: 322.
Foy, Frank, (2nd Lt, Co F, 66th NCST), III: 686.
Foy, W.G., (Lt, Adjt, 11th Vols/21st NCST), II: 142, 144; IV: 236.
Frada, A.J., (Pvt, Co C, 28th NCST), V: 540.
Frailey, J.M., (Cmdr, USN), V: 242.
Fraley, A.S., (2nd Lt, Co A, 4th NCST), I: 231, 269.
Fraley, J.E., (Lt, Co E, 2nd NCST), I: 161.
Fraley, Dr. J.R., (Ass't Surg, 7th NCST), IV: 632, 472.
Fraley, W.C., [Wilburn C.], (Ordnance Sgt, Co K, 4th NCST), I: 234.
France, F.D.W., (Conscript, Co G, 6th Vols/16th NCST), IV: 186.
Francis, Acains, (AQMS, 6th Vols/16th NCST), V: 551.
Francis, James P., (Pvt, Co H, 34th NCST), V: 556.
Francis, John W., (Maj, 25th NCST), II: 292, 294, 295.
Francis, M., (Pvt, Co C, 11th Vols/21st NCST), V: 514.
Francis, T.A., (Pvt, Co G, 49th NCST), V: 564.

Francis, Uriah, (Pvt, Co C, 11th Vols/21st NCST), V: 514.
Francis, W.R., (Pvt, Co C, 11th Vols/21st NCST), V: 514.
Frank, John A., (Pvt, Co A, 11th Vols/21st NCST), V: 514.
Frankfort, Ky., II: 487, 708, 710, 728, 730.
Franklin, T.P. Siler, (Col, 6th Regt Home Guard), IV: 650.
Franklin, William Buel, (Maj Gen, USA), I: 301, 309; II: 218; IV: 169.
Franklin, N.C., (Macon County), III: 683, 760; IV: 128, 381; V: 271, 653, 654, 655.
Franklin, Tenn., (and Battle of, 1864), II: 492; III: 439, 494-495, 501; IV: 320, 498.
Franklin, Va., I: 494, 495, 522, 578, 587; II: 87, 785, 793; III: 133, 228, 229, 232, 321, 335, 337, 458; IV: 73, 74, 366; V: 17, 83, 84.
Franklin County, N.C., II: 215; III: 288, 686; IV: 483, 518, 595; V: 280, 631.
Franklin Military Institute, (nr Mt. Olive), IV: 420.
Frapps, Miles, (Lt, Co F, 64th NCST), III: 660.
Fraser, John C., (Capt, Fraser's Battery, Ga., Light Art), I: 556.
Frasier, J.C.R., (Musician, 53rd NCST), V: 501.
Frasier, J.L., (Musician, 53rd NCST), V: 501.
Frazer, I.T., (Musician, 3rd Vols/13th NCST), V: 549.
Frazer, James N., (Musician, 3rd Vols/13th NCST), V: 549.
Frazer, John W., (Brig Gen), III: 434, 448, 519, 520, 521, 522, 523, 524, 525, 526, 528, 636, 663, 676, 736, 740; IV: 439.
Frazer, R.J., (Musician, 3rd Vols/13th NCST), V: 549.
Frazer, W.F., (Musician, 3rd Vols/13th NCST), V: 549.
Frazier, E.R., (Pvt, Co I, 13th Vols/23rd NCST), V: 510.
Frazier, F.C., (1st Lt, Co A, 10th Battalion, 2nd Hvy Art), IV: 325, 326, 327, 329.
Frazier, Isaac A., (Musician, Co B, 3rd Vols/13th NCST), V: 549.
Frazier, L.H., (Pvt, Co G, 30th NCST), V: 492.
Frazier, Trenholm & Co., (Shipping Company, Charleston, S.C. & Liverpool, England), V: 387, 400, 460.
Frazier's Farm, Va., (and Battle of, 1862), I: 182, 218, 369, 420, 617, 737, 757; II: 27, 168, 173, 212, 273, 292, 428, 471, 548, 549, 583, 655, 682; III: 39, 40; IV: 158, 200, 501, 551; V: 645.
Frederick, C.C., (4th Cpl, Co A, 38th NCST), V: 557.
Frederick, James R., (Pvt, Co D, 3rd NCST), V: 487.
Frederick, Md., (aka Frederick City), I: 140, 154, 184, 206, 224, 244, 245, 259, 306, 324, 372, 421, 624, 694, 739, 759; II: 32, 70, 96, 218, 219, 234, 245, 274, 431, 432, 531, 552, 585, 656; III: 13, 67, 419, 749; IV: 164, 257, 570, 725; V: 72, 113, 597.
Frederick County, Va., II: 238.
Frederick Junction, Md., I: 573; III: 278.
Fredericksburg, Va., I: 142, 143, 147, 168, 189, 190, 193, 199, 250, 277, 300, 303, 309, 310, 321, 349, 373, 379, 422, 429, 555, 565, 577, 580, 588, 592, 628, 629, 641, 664, 701, 717, 741, 742, 753, 762, 764, 772; II: 34, 35, 36, 71, 87, 116, 167, 170, 225, 227, 228, 233, 275, 296, 341, 438, 446, 476, 477, 582, 586, 609, 610, 657, 658,

660, 679, 687, 753; III: 40, 54, 69, 71, 88, 117, 235, 244, 295, 303, 316, 410, 559, 595; IV: 150, 169, 172, 176, 253, 262, 263, 447, 505, 558; V: 83.
Fredericksburg, Va., (Battles of, 1862), I: 116, 142, 143, 147, 168, 169, 189, 190, 193, 199, 250, 277, 309, 334, 357, 373-375, 422, 554, 609, 629, 643, 664-666, 696, 701, 706, 707, 713, 714, 741, 762; II: 32, 36, 42, 72, 135, 158, 159, 170, 226, 292, 438, 439, 475, 500, 504, 556, 557, 585, 598, 609, 657, 686, 691, 700; III: 5, 69, 70, 79, 81, 117, 129, 256, 268-269, 406-409, 427, 428; IV: 33, 169-171, 174, 188, 202, 236, 325, 397, 441, 448, 466, 504, 525, 552, 571-572, 604; V: 114, 467, 606, 627, 629.
Fredericksburg Road, (nr Spottsylvania, Va., aka Fredericksburg Turnpike), I: 384; III: 77; IV: 475.
Fredericksburg & Central Railroad, III: 24, 586; IV: 195, 196, 197.
Free Mason, II: 285.
Freedle, William E., (Pvt, Co K, 4th Vols/14th NCST), V: 491.
Freeland, W.G., (Capt, Co C, 6th NCST), I: 295.
Freeland, John F., (Capt, Co G, 1st Vols/11th NCST), I: 119, 585.
Freeman, A.H., (1st Lt, Co D, 8th Ga.), IV: 707.
Freeman, B.F., (Cpl, Co K, 44th NCST), V: 534.
Freeman, C.D., (Capt, Co A, Freeman's 26th Battalion NCST), IV: 753; V: 626.
Freeman, Eli, (Capt, Co C, 4th Vols/14th NCST), I: 706, 723, 727, 731.
Freeman, G.W., (Capt, Co B, 35th NCST), II: 623, 627.
Freeman, H.C., (Pvt, Co A, 33rd NCST), V: 543.
Freeman, J.H., (2nd Lt, Co A, 46th NCST), III: 80; V: 520.
Freeman, John T., (Pvt, Co A, 25th NCST), V: 561.
Freeman, M.W., (Pvt, Co A, 28th NCST), V: 540.
Freeman, Nicholas, (Musician, 53rd NCST), V: 501.
Freeman, Robert A., (Pvt, Co A, 25th NCST), V: 561.
Freeman, Spencer M., (Pvt, Co A, 25th NCST), V: 561.
Freeman, W.A., (3rd Sgt, Co B, 3rd Vols/13th NCST), V: 549.
Freeman, W.H., (2nd Lt, Co A, 31st NCST), II: 512.
Freeman, W.N., (Capt, Co C, 25th NCST), II: 291, 292, 301.
Freeman, William W., (2nd Lt, Co I, 10th NCST, 1st Art & Engs, Sutherland's Battery, Light Art), I: 582; IV: 222.
Freeman's Ford, (Nottoway River, Va.), I: 570; III: 623.
Freestone Point, (James River nr Dumfries, Va.), I: 300.
Freeze, Isaac, (Pvt, Co B, 10th Vols/20th NCST), V: 508.
Freitchie, Barbara, I: 694; II: 70.
Freidhiem, A., [Friedheim], (3rd Cpl, Co K, 4th NCST), I: 275; V: 489.
Fremont, John Charles, (Maj Gen, USA), I: 623; II: 147, 149, 153; IV: 230, 233.
Fremont, S.L., (Col, Enginnering Officer), IV: 413, 414, 416, 422.
French, C.A., (Lt, USN, Capt, Southfield), V: 320.
French, James M., (Maj, 63rd Va.), III: 435.
French, Junius B., (Adjt, 13th Vols/23rd NCST), I: 113, 118; II: 189, 236; V: 663.
French, Samuel Gibbs, (Maj Gen), II: 167, 328, 334, 339, 400, 492,

497, 615, 629, 769; III: 4, 167; IV: 263; V: 7, 90.
French, W. Foster, (Maj, 10th Battalion Home Guard; Maj. 7th Battalion Junior Reserves; Lt Col, 72nd NCST, 3rd Junior Reserves), IV: 3, 38, 40, 43, 47, 50, 51, 61, 301, 587, 588, 594, 650.
French, William Henry, (Maj Gen, USA), I: 186, 198; II: 230, 231; III: 242.
French's Farm, Va., III: 115, 124.
French Broad River, N.C., (aka Broad River), III: 474, 527, 670; IV: 112, 123, 380, 381.
Frensley, John L., (Capt, AQM, 32nd NCST; QM, Daniel's Brigade), IV: 513, 518; V: 494.
Fretwell, Dr. John R., (Torpedo Service, CSA), IV: 15, 16, 17.
Friday, J.C., (Pvt, Co H, 52nd NCST), V: 536.
Friday, W.J., (Pvt, Co H, 52nd NCST), V: 536.
Friddle, T.A., (Pvt, Co E, 2nd Vols/12th NCST), V: 507.
Frink, J.O., (1st Lt, Ensign, Co H, 8th Vols/18th NCST), IV: 722.
Fripp, Dr. Clarence A., (Ass't Surg, 14th Vols/24th NCST), IV: 635; V: 559.
Frisby, Soloman, (Pvt, Co F, 6th Battalion/60th NCST), III: 482.
Frobel, ______, (Maj, Frobel's Battalion, Art, ANV), I: 574.
Froelick's Sword Factory, (Kenansville), IV: 265.
From Manassas to Appomattox, I: 611, 615; V: 261.
Froneberger, ______, (Pvt, 72nd NCST, 3rd Junior Reserves), IV: 61.
Front Royal, Va., (and Battle of, 1862), I: 149, 168, 197, 381, 541, 577, 718; II: 116, 233; III: 41, 241, 270, 571; IV: 177, 254.
Front Royal Road, (nr Winchester, Va.), II: 253.
Frost, G.W., (Master, USN), V: 244.
Fry, Birkett Davenport, (Brig Gen), II: 346, 363; III: 300; IV: 251.
Fry, D.A., (Pvt, Co K, 28th NCST), V: 543.
Fry, G.W., (Pvt, Co H, 63rd NCST, 5th Cav), III: 587.
Fry, Hugh Walker, (Maj, 46th Va., Fry's Battalion), V: 59.
Fry, N. Davis, (Pvt, Co C, 25th NCST), V: 561.
Fry, W.A., (1st Lt, Co B, 6th Battalion Junior Reserves; Co E, 70th NCST, 1st Junior Reserves), IV: 13.
Fry House, (McClellan's H.Q., Sharpsburg, Md.), V: 79.
Frying Pan Church, Va., III: 582.
Frying Pan Shoal, N.C., V: 358, 409.
Fulbright, G., (Pvt, Co K, 6th NCST), V: 514.
Fulbright, George, (Cpl, Co E, 34th NCST), V: 555.
Fulcher, Silas, (Cpl, Color-bearer, Co F, 2nd NCST), I: 162.
Fulford, J.T., (2nd Lt, Co G, 30th NCST), II: 497; V: 484.
Fulford, W.Y., (2nd Lt, Co D, 6th Battalion Junior Reserves; Co H, 70th NCST, 1st Junior Reserves), IV: 13.
Fulford, Irvin, (Jr 2nd Lt, Co K, 10th NCST, 1st Art & Engs, Sparrow-Blount's Hvy Art), I: 496, 501, 529.
Fulghum, ______, [Richard Thomas], (Sgt Maj, 9th NCST, 1st Cav), I: 425.
Fulghum, Garry, (1st Lt, Co B, 2nd NCST), I: 158, 159, 175; V: 484.
Fulghum, George W., (Pvt, Co I, 2nd NCST), I: 176; V: 486.
Fulghum, Raiford, (Pvt, Co B, 2nd NCST), I: 175; V: 486.

Fulker Shoals, N.C., II: 509; V: 58.
Fullenwider, H.W., (2nd Lt, Co K, 13th Vols/23rd NCST), II: 188.
Fuller, A.E., (Pvt, Co G, 13th Vols/23rd NCST), V: 510.
Fuller, A.M., (2nd Lt, Co F, 77th NCST, 7th Senior Reserves), IV: 100.
Fuller, E.A., (Sgt, Co G, 13th Vols/23rd NCST), V: 510.
Fuller, J.H., (Lt, Co E, 9th NCST, 1st Cav), I: 486.
Fuller, Thomas C., (1st Lt, Co B, Starr's Battery, Starr's 13th Battalion, Light Art), I: 120, 493, 515, 517, 520; IV: 342, 346, 347, 348, 484.
Fuller, W.L., (Pvt, Co B, 1st Battalion NCST), V: 504.
Fulmore, A.C., (Lt, Co F, 51st NCST), III: 219.
Fulp, E., (Pvt, Co K, 11th Vols/21st NCST), V: 515.
Fulp, M.H., (2nd Lt, Co K, 48th NCST), V: 520.
Fulton, Fewell, (Sgt, Co G, 1 1th Vols/21st NCST), V: 515.
Fulton, H.P., (Pvt, Co G, 11th Vols/21st NCST), V: 515.
Fulton, Saunders F., (Col, 11th Vols/21st NCST), II: 132, 134, 144, 155; IV: 229, 235; V: 11, 680.
Funderburk, S.S., (Pvt, Co E, 48th NCST), V: 526.
Funkstown, Md., I: 544, 557; II: 219; III: 92.
Funston, ______, (Cav), I: 454.
Fuqua, J.H., (Capt, 2nd in command at Salisbury Prison), IV: 753.
Furches, L.A., (Pvt, Co A, 57th NCST), V: 517.
Furchess, W.F., (Sgt, Co E, 16th Battalion/75th NCST, 7th Cav), V: 660.
Furgerson, E.R., (2nd Lt, Co A, 62nd NCST), III: 515.
Furgerson, L., (Pvt, Co G, 46th NCST), V: 525.
Furgeson, S.S., (Pvt, Co F, 37th NCST), V: 546.
Furgus, W.C., (Maj, 42nd Ala.), IV: 707.
Furman, Henry S., (AQMS, 55th NCST), III: 288.
Furman, Robert M., (2nd Lt, Co C, 5th Battalion Junior Reserves; Co H, 71st NCST, 2nd Junior Reserves), IV: 29, 32.
Furr, A., (Pvt, Co K, 28th NCST), V: 543.
Furr, Sol, (Lt, Co B, 7th NCST), I: 375.
Fuss, Allen, (Fayetteville and Harper's Ferry Arsenals), IV: 298.
Fuss, George, (Fayetteville and Harper's Ferry Arsenals), IV: 298.
Fuss, Jeremiah, (Fayetteville and Harper's Ferry Arsenals), IV: 298.
Futrell, T.A., (2nd Sgt, Co G, 46th NCST), V: 525.
Fuzzell's Mills, Va., [Frizzell's], [Fussell's], I: 385, 434; II: 57, 480, 574, 669; III: 332, 618, 619; IV: 469; V: xii.

(G)

Gabriel, Albutress, (Pvt, Co K, 13th Vols/23rd NCST), II: 229.
Gadd, Robert, (1st Lt, Co E, 59th NCST, 4th Cav), III: 457.
Gaddy, J.N., (Pvt, Co D, 37th NCST), V: 545.
Gaddy, J.T., (Sgt, Co K, 26th NCST), V: 532.
Gaddy, Joseph, (Pvt, Co C, 4th Vols/14th NCST), I: 728.
Gaddy, Joseph T., (Pvt, Co D, 4th Vols/14th NCST), V: 490.
Gaddy, R.A., (Pvt, Co I, 53rd NCST), V: 502.
Gaddy, R.B., (Capt, ACS, 59th NCST, 4th Cav), III: 457.
Gage, ______, (Major, Commissary, Clingman's Brigade), II: 511; IV: 482.
Gallard, ______, [Gaillard], (Lt Col, Charleston Battalion), III: 207; V: 152, 167.
Gaillard, A.S., (Lt, S.C.), V: 641.
Gailer, P.B., (2nd Lt, Co I, 69th NCST, 8th Cav), III: 731.
Gaines, Ambrose, (Capt, Co D, 39th NCST), II: 705.
Gaines, James L., (1st Lt, Co G, 9th NCST, 1st Cav, Woodfin's 14th Battalion; Col, 19th NCST, 2nd Cav), I: 439, 474, 486; II: 107; III: 639, 640, 644, 645; IV: 109, 110, 582; V: 567, 657.
Gaines, John C., (Capt, Co F, 44th NCST), III: 23.
Gaines, Margaret, (Mother of Col James L. Gaines), III: 644.
Gaines, Miss Mary, (Resident of Asheville), I: 130.
Gaines, Matthew, (Father of Col James L. Gaines), III: 644.
Gaines' Cross Roads, Va., I: 422; III: 571; IV: 183.
Gaines' Mill, Va., (and Battle of, 1862; aka, 1st Cold Harbor), I: 182, 205, 218, 304, 334, 367, 404, 567, 614, 659, 757; II: 5, 25, 114, 168, 210, 499, 547, 549, 583, 655, 682, 798; III: 12, 29, 96, 115, 246; IV: 157, 234, 551; V: 197, 627.
Gaines' Mill, Va., (2nd Battle of, 1864; aka, 2nd Cold Harbor), I: 205; III: 12; IV: 198.
Gainesville, Fla., V: 384.
Gainsville, Va., II: 87; III: 582.
Gaither, Burgess S., (Congress, CSA), V: 57, 62.
Gaither, J.R., (Capt, Co B, 8th Battalion Junior Reserves; Co E, 72nd NCST, 3rd Junior Reserves), IV: 41, 48, 51.
Gaither, L.G., (1st Lt, Claiborne-Dearing's 7th C.S. Cav; 16th Battalion/75th NCST, 7th Cav), IV: 92.
Gaither, W.G., (Pvt, Co H, 4th NCST), V: 489.
Gaither Dr. William W., (Surg, 28th NCST), II: 371, 382, 395, 410, 412-414, 466; IV: 473, 636.
Gale, ______, (Capt, CSN, Lady Davis), V: 407, 408.

Gales, Seaton, (Maj, AAG, Ramseur-Cox's Brigade), IV: 462, 463; V: 651.
Gallagher, C.K., (Capt, Co E, 4th NCST), I: 232, 271; V: 43, 53.
Gallahar, D.H., (2nd Lt, Co K, 69th NCST, Thomas' Legion), III: 731, 743.
Gallant, J.A., (4th Sgt, Co B, 3rd Vols/13th NCST), V: 549.
Gallant, W.L., (Pvt, Co B, 3rd Vols/13th NCST), V: 549.
Gallaway, A.B., (AQMS, 12th Vols/22nd NCST), V: 553.
Gallaway, A.H., (Maj, QM, Scales Brigade), V: 547.
Galliharn, Alpheus, (3rd Cpl, Co B, 52nd NCST), III: 223.
Gallop, Issac G., (Pvt, Co A, 56th NCST), III: 356.
Gallopp, William, (Pvt, Co A, 56th NCST), III: 347, V: 565.
Galloway, ______, (Capt, Co 10, 79th NCST, 8th Cav), IV: 115.
Galloway, A.H., (Capt, Co F, 45th NCST; Maj, QM, Scales' Brigade), II: 119; IV: 553.
Galloway, A.J., (Lt, Co A, 9th Battalion NCST, 1st Hvy Art), IV: 304.
Galloway, I.F., (2nd Lt, Co H, 62nd NCST), III: 516.
Galloway, J.A., (Lt, Co K, 61st NCST), III: 504.
Galloway, J.E., (3rd Lt, Co K, 62nd NCST), IV: 707.
Galloway, John M., [Gallaway], (Maj, 63rd NCST, 5th Cav), III: 529, 531, 535, 537, 538, 540, 541, 542, 552, 655; IV: 401; V: 651, 671.
Galloway, John W., (1st Lt, Co C, Cumming's Battery, Starr's 13th Battalion NCST, Light Art; Capt., Galloway's Coast Guard), IV: 361, 401; V: 678, 679.
Galloway, R.H., (Musician, 10th Vols/20th NCST), V: 508.
Galloway, Swift, (Capt, Co H, 3rd NCST, temp. Cmdr Salisbury Prison), IV: 752.
Galloway, Thomas S., Jr., (ADC to Pettigrew; Col, 12th Vols/22nd NCST), II: 161, 171, 176, 177, 178; IV: 556; V: 547, 650.
Galt, ______, (Lt, ADC to J.G. Walker), IV: 503.
Galton, H., (Pvt, Co F, 3rd Vols/13thth NCST), V: 550.
Galveston, Tx., III: 302, 307; V: 339, 354, 412.
Gamble, ______, (Owner of Hotel, Florence, S.C.) V: 68.
Gamble, A.J., (Pvt, Co H, 49th NCST), V: 565.
Gamble, B.F., (Cpl, Co D, 33rd NCST), II: 539.
Gamble, Andrew J., (2nd Sgt, Co D, 4th Vols/14th NCST), V: 490.
Gamble, John, (1st Lt, Co F, 12th Vols/22nd NCST), II: 165, 166.
Gamble, John F., (1st Lt, Co D, 4th Vols/14th NCST), IV: 722.
Gammons, G.R., (Pvt, Co D, 43rd NCST), V: 498.
Gant, A.C., (4th Sgt, Co C, 55th NCST), V: 527.
Gant, Evan, (Pvt, Co E, 32nd NCST), V: 496.
Gant, J.M., (Pvt, Co M, 11th Vols/21st NCST), V: 515.
Gant, John, (Pvt, Co F, 57th NCST), V: 517.
Gantt, John C., (Pvt, Co F, 34th NCST), V: 555.
Garbacon Shoals, N.C., V: 17.
Gardin, George H., (Capt, Co B, 12th Vols/22nd NCST), II: 165, 171, 178.
Gardiner, O.P., (Capt, Co I, 38th NCST), II: 676, 678.

Gardman, ______, (Lt, Scales' Brigade), II: 692.
Gardner, ______, (CSN), V: 327.
Gardner, D.W., (Pvt, Co C, 43rd NCST), V: 498.
Gardner, E.T., (Pvt, Co B, 56th NCST), III: 366.
Gardner, H.B., (Sgt, Co A, 16th Battalion/75th NCST, 7th Cav), V: 660.
Gardner, J.M., (Capt, Co C, Littlejohn's 23rd Battalion NCST, Senior Reserves), IV: 399.
Gardner, J.M., (Midshipman, NCN; Lt, CSN, Tallahassee), V: 309, 438.
Gardner, R.W., (Pvt, Co F, 56th NCST), V: 566.
Gardner, Thomas F., (Lt Col, 29th NCST), II: 486, 493.
Gardner, W.H., (Pvt, Co G, 32nd NCST), V: 496.
Gardner, W.T., (Capt, Co E, 50th NCST), III: 202, 203.
Gardner, William Montgomery, (Brig Gen), IV: 375.
Gardner, William R., (2nd Lt, Co K, 31st NCST), II: 512.
Gardener's Bridge, N.C., III: 680.
Garison, J.T., (Capt, Co A, 6th Battalion/60th NCST), II: 481.
Garland, A.B., (Maj, ACS, Garland's Brigade), IV: 521.
Garland, James S., (1st Lt, Co I, 29th NCST), II: 486.
Garland, Samuel, Jr., (Brig Gen), I: 224, 286, 610, 618, 619, 621, 626, 628, 657, 658, 659, 660, 662, 663, 695; II: 114, 115, 207, 209, 211, 220, 221, 223, 238; IV: 521.
Garner, B., (Pvt, Co E, 56th NCST), III: 356.
Garner, J.H., (Pvt, Co C, 32nd NCST), V: 496.
Garner, J.W., (Pvt, Co C, 32nd NCST), V: 496.
Garner, Moses, (3rd Sgt, Co A, 44th NCST), V: 533.
Garner, W.A., (Pvt, Co C, 32nd NCST), V: 496.
Garner, William, (Pvt, Co E, 27th NCST), V: 523.
Garner, N.C., III: 200.
Garnett, ______, (Col, Junior Reserves), III: 633, 634.
Garnett, ______, (Capt, Staff, Robert's Brigade), III: 470.
Garnett, Richard Brooke, (Brig Gen), I: 752; II: 363, 682; IV: 138, 139; V: 106, 148, 150, 151, 156, 157.
Garnett, Theodore S., (Capt, AAG, Robert's Brigade, Cav), II: 108, 109. IV: 580.
Garrason, T.B., (Pilot, Owl), V: 357.
Garrett, ______, (President, Baltimore & Ohio Railroad), III: 750.
Garrett, A., (Pvt, Co G, 3rd Vols/13th NCST), V: 550.
Garrett, Charles T., (1st Lt, Co A, Lusk's 5th Battalion Cav; 1st Lt, Co A & I, 65th NCST, 6th Cav), IV: 287, 290, 292, 702, 707.
Garrett, Dr. Francis M., (Surg, 30th NCST), II: 499; IV: 636.
Garrett, Green, (Capt, N.C. Militia), III: 518.
Garrett, I.W., (Capt, N.C. Quartermaster Department), I: 6, 24, 25, 28.
Garrett, Thomas M., (Col, 5th NCST), I: 281, 284, 286, 288, 289, 639; II: 117, 499; V: xii, 9, 649.
Garrett, W.E., (1st Cpl, Co G, 3rd Vols/13th NCST), V: 550.
Garrett, W.N., (Lt Col, 64th NCST), III: 659, 662, 663; IV: 702, 707.
Garrett, William, (Pvt, Co A, 56th NCST), III: 347.
Garris, E.J., (2nd Lt, Co C, 13th Vols/23rd NCST), II: 184.

Garris, John T., (Pvt, Co G, 55th NCST), V: 528.
Garrison, Alonzo, (Jr 2nd Lt, Co C, 6th Battalion NCST Armory Guard), IV: 296.
Garrison, Ephraim, (3rd Sgt, Co H, 32nd NCST), III: 225.
Garrison, Tobias, (Lt, 3rd NCST), I: 213.
Garrott, Isham W., (Brig Gen), V: 649.
Gartell, ______, (Col, 7th Ga.), I: 347.
Garvin, ______, (Lt, Art, USA), III: 632.
Garysburg, N.C., I: 179, 234, 320, 562, 607, 706, 733; II: 188, 192, 262, 297, 400, 413, 613, 614, 615, 616, 671, 773, 774, 793; III: 125, 131, 162, 232, 331, 337, 456, 529, 530, 550, 551, 553; IV: 73, 244, 266, 339; V: 85, 671.
Gash, ______, (Capt, Co E, 65th NCST, 6th Cav), III: 675, 684.
Gash, H.Y., (2nd Lt, Co D & E, 65th NCST, 6th Cav), IV: 722.
Gash, James M., (2nd Lt, Co K, 62nd NCST), III: 516.
Gaskill, William, (Sgt, Co H, 33rd NCST), II: 540, 578.
Gaskins, David G., (2nd Lt, Co B, McCleese's 3rd Battalion NCST, Light Art), IV: 262.
Gaskins, Edward, (Cpl, Co H, 33rd NCST), II: 540.
Gaskins, Thomas H., (2nd Lt, Co K, 31st NCST), II: 508.
Gaston, Judge ______, (Resident of New Bern), III: 456.
Gaston, J.P., (Adjt, 64th NCST), IV: 702, 707.
Gaston, Perry C., (Adjt, Walker's Battalion, Thomas' Legion, 80th NCST), IV: 117, 128.
Gaston, N.C., II: 263; IV: 11, 15, 358, 359, 430.
Gaston County, N.C., I: 62; II: 182, 234; III: 125; IV: 132, 611.
Gaston House, (New Bern), II: 398.
Gaston Road, I: 320.
Gately, Isaac, (4th Sgt, Co E, 52nd NCST), III: 224.
Gately, T., (Pvt, Co H, 56th NCST), III: 348.
Gates, A.L., (Pvt, Co A, 28th NCST), V: 540.
Gates, E., (Pvt, Co D, 56th NCST), V: 566.
Gates, George W., (2nd Lt, Co G, 6th Battalion NCST, Fayetteville Armory Guard), IV: 297.
Gates, Robert Kell, (Pvt, Co D, 56th NCST), III: 391.
Gates County, N.C., III: 715, 717; V: 84, 210.
Gatesville, N.C., II: 280, 794.
Gatlin, George, (Pvt, Co E, 59th NCST, 4th Cav), V: 659.
Gatlin, John, (Capt, AQM, MacRae's Brigade), V: 529.
Gatlin, John D., (2nd Lt, Co G, 31st NCST), II: 512.
Gatlin, Richard C., (Brig Gen, N.C. Adjt Gen), I: xi, 18, 35, 36, 43, 44, 47, 48, 50, 51, 112; II: 308, 328, 461, 593, 677; III: 314; IV: 44, 414, 646, 651; V: 6, 57, 629, 649.
Gatlin, Richard H., (Capt, Co B, 33rd NCST), II: 538.
Gatlin, Thomas H., (Capt, Co B, 33rd NCST), II: 538.
Gatling, John, Jr., (Capt, AQM, 52nd NCST), II: 414; III: 223, 225, 229, 234.
Gatling, Riddick, (Capt, Co H, 33rd NCST), II: 539, 540, 556, 578; V: 538.
Gauley River, Va., II: 270.
Gay, Alexander, (Pvt, Co A, 43rd NCST), V: 497.

Gay, G.W., (Cpl, Co I, 30th NCST), V: 493.
Gay, James, (Sgt, Co F, 4th NCST), V: 488.
Gay, James F., (Pvt, Co E, 38th NCST), V: 557.
Gay, James K., (Pvt, Co D, 34th NCST), V: 555.
Gay, James W., (Sgt, Co A, 5th Vols/15th NCST), V: 520.
Gay, Lawrence, (Pvt, Co E, 43rd NCST), V: 498.
Gay, S.M., (4th Cpl, Co G, 3rd Vols/13th NCST), V: 550.
Gay, W.T., (1st Lt, Co K, 5th Vols/15th NCST), I: 736.
Gaylord, C.R., V: 678.
Gearner, William, (Pvt, Co E, 27th NCST), II: 462.
Geary, _____, (Cpl, Co C, 7th NCST), I: 368.
Gee, Dr. Charles J., (Surg, 1st NCST then ACS, 35th NCST), I: 136; II: 597; IV: 631.
Gee, George, (Pvt, Co B, Starr's Battery, Starr's 13th Battalion NCST, Light Art), IV: 350.
Gee, John H., (Maj, Fla., Cmdr Salisbury Prison), IV: 754, 755, 757, 760, 764, 765, 769.
Gee, Sterling H., (Capt, AAG & IG, Mat Ransom's Brigade), I: 137; II: 611, 626; III: 146, 348, 397; IV: 572, 578.
Gee House, (nr Petersburg, Va.), V: 617.
Geiger, James H., (Ordnance Sgt, 49th NCST), III: 125.
General Lee, V: 126.
Generals, Confederate, from North Carolina, I: 11; V: 3, 663.
Generals Commissioned by the State, V: 5.
Genet, Citizen, (French), I: 131.
Gentle, R.D., (Pvt, Co H, 11th Vols/21st NCST), V: 514.
Gentry, C., (Pvt, Co G, 58th NCST), III: 453.
Gentry, J.H., (Pvt, Co E, 35th NCST), V: 562.
Gentry, L.C., (Lt, 10th Vols/20th NCST), IV: 707.
Gentry, L.C., (Jr 2nd Lt, Co A, 26th NCST), II: 371, 396, 397.
Gentry, T.R., (Pvt, Co E, 35th NCST), V: 193.
Gentry, Thomas B., (Capt, Co G, 11th Vols/21st NCST), II: 145.
Gentry, W., (Capt, Co L, 58th NCST), III: 434, 447.
George, E.P., (Capt, ACS, 49th NCST), III: 125, 128.
George, Forney, (Lt Col, 8th Vols/18th NCST), II: 16, 20, 34, 39, 41, 74; IV: 473; V: 650.
George, Joseph, (Pvt, Co A, 2nd Battalion NCST), V: 495.
George, LaFayette, (1st Lt, Co H, 69th NCST, Thomas' Legion), III: 731, 754.
George, William, (Pvt, Co G, 1st NCST), V: 572.
Georgetown, Tx., II: 704.
Georgetown Pike, Md., III: 419.
Georgia, I: 70; II: 119, 493, 634, 638, 700, 701, 720, 756; III: 184, 191, 192, 199, 486, 494, 496, 500, 501, 617, 678, 745, 746, 758; IV: 2, 6, 35, 73, 88, 121, 122, 124, 125, 127, 128, 320, 328, 333-335, 382, 400, 404, 452, 482, 504, 517, 537, 618; V: viii, 4, 270, 380.
Georgia Central Railroad, II: 757; IV: 327, 333.
Georgia Troops, II: 163.
Germania Ford, (Rapidan River, Va.), I: 200, 594, 640; II: 381, 664, 693, III: 584, 585.
Gerringer, J.S., (Pvt, Co M, 11th Vols/21st NCST), V: 515.
Gervis, George M., (Pvt, Co B, 2nd Battalion NCST), V: 495.

Getty, George Washington, (Maj Gen, USA), II: 47, 440.

Gettysburg, Pa., (Battle of and Campaign, 1863), I: v, vi, 51, 52, 61, 70, 148, 149, 158, 163, 171, 195, 196, 213, 253, 254, 275, 276, 287, 311-318, 332, 334, 353-359, 379-381, 424, 425, 448, 462, 476, 541-544, 555, 556, 579, 584, 585, 586, 589, 590, 599, 612, 614, 630, 631, 632-640, 644, 672, 697, 698, 699, 717, 718, 719, 720, 742, 764, 765, 777; II: 41, 42, 44, 45, 62, 74, 95, 97, 99, 111, 119, 129, 135, 136, 137, 139, 171, 172, 176, 183, 184, 185, 186, 187, 188, 189, 216, 232-240, 245, 254, 331, 335, 336, 341,343, 344, 345-375, 376, 377, 378, 380, 381, 342, 362, 389, 398, 399, 401, 408, 409, 410, 411, 413, 414, 415, 416, 417, 418, 419, 420, 421, 422, 439, 477, 502, 522, 523, 524, 525, 527-529, 532, 562-567, 568, 586, 587, 613, 660, 662, 674, 691, 693, 700, 712, 715, 753, 776; III: 2, 5, 6, 24, 26, 37, 40-42, 52, 71, 83, 84, 88, 89-92, 93, 103-109, 110, 118, 159, 235-240, 256, 258, 261, 262, 263, 264, 270, 271, 288, 296-303, 382, 389, 411-416, 427, 428, 458, 460, 462, 463, 464, 472, 534-536, 569, 578, 584, 588, 604, 628; IV: 12, 35, 62, 176-184, 192, 237-241, 252, 256, 257, 258, 313, 357, 405, 467, 471, 505, 514, 518, 519, 522, 525, 553, 554, 558, 568, 583, 611, 612, 617, 667, 689, 703, 725; V: ix, xi, xiii, xiv, 7, 88, 100-135, 137-159, 243, 258, 263, 267, 467, 595-616, 627, 628, 640.

Gettysburg Memorial Association, (aka, Gettysburg Federal Memorial Association), II: 360; III: 41.

Gettysburg Park Commission, V: 110.

Gettysburg & Hagerstown Turnpike, IV: 239.

Gettysburg Then and Now, II: 346, 354, 361, 362, 367.

Ghormeley, D.C., (Capt, Co F, Walker's Battalion, Thomas' Legion, 80 NCST), IV: 118, 128.

Gibbon, John, (Maj Gen, USA), II: 47; III: 410; IV: 216; V: 156.

Gibbon, Nicholas, (Capt, ACS, 28th NCST), II: 465; IV: 473; V: 646.

Gibbon, Dr. Robert, (Surg, 28th NCST; Surg., Branch-Lane's Brigade; Surg, Charlotte General Hospital), II: 466; IV: 216, 472, 473, 626, 627, 636, 644.

Gibbons, ______, [A.I.], (Pvt, Co G, 49th NCST), III: 155.

Gibbons, A.S., (Pvt, Co G, 6th NCST), V: 513.

Gibbons, Jack, (Father of A.I., Pvt, Co G, 49th), III: 155.

Gibbs, Alexander, (Pvt, Detached Co, 68th NCST), III: 723.

Gibbs, David, (Pvt, Detached Co, 68th NCST), III: 723.

Gibbs, George C., (Col, 42nd NCST), II: 789, 796; IV: 746, 748, 751.

Gibbs, H.C., (Pvt, Co F, 11th Vols/21st NCST), V: 514.

Gibbs, J.H., (Pvt, Co G, 11th Vols/21st NCST), V: 515.

Gibbs, James W., (1st Lt, Co F, 33rd NCST), II: 539, 573, 578.

Gibbs, Joseph B., (Cpl, Co F, 33rd NCST), II: 540, 578.

Gibbs, Nathaniel, (Pvt, Detached Co, 68th NCST), III: 723.

Gibbs, R.C., (Pvt, Co F, 33rd NCST), V: 544.

Gibbs, Samuel S., (Cpl, Co F, 33rd NCST), II: 540.

Gibbson, A.J., (Pvt, Co G, 49th NCST), V: 564.
Gibson, A.P., (Musician, Mickey's Band, 26th NCST), II: 398.
Gibson, Adolphus, (Capt, ACS, 33rd NCST), II: 537.
Gibson, Charles S., (Lt, Co F, 63rd NCST, 5th Cav), III: 588, 597.
Gibson, D.M., (Pvt, Co F, 63rd NCST, 5th Cav), III: 563.
Gibson, E.D., (Pvt, Co C, 4th Vols/14th NCST), I: 732.
Gibson, George, (1st Lt, Co A, 33rd NCST), II: 538.
Gibson, J.C., (Pvt, Co A, 10th Vols/20th NCST), V: 508.
Gibson, John A., (1st Lt, Co C; ACS, 33rd NCST), II: 539; IV: 474.
Gibson, Leonidas R., (Capt, Co D, 52nd NCST), III: 224, 246.
Gibson, R.B., (2nd Lt, Co B, 27th NCST), II: 458.
Gibson, R.F., (5th Sgt, Co E, 52nd NCST), III: 224.
Gibson, Randall Lee, (Brig Gen), I: 359; II: 492.
Gibson, Samuel B., (Lt, Co K, 9th NCST, 1st Cav), I: 486, 782.
Gibson, William H., (Sgt Maj; 2nd Lt, Co C, 33rd NCST), II: 537, 539, 578.
Giddens, Henry B., (Musician, 10th Vols/20th NCST), II: 113; V: 508.
Giddens, Lewis D., (Musician, 10th Vols/20th NCST), II: 113.
Gieger, James H., (Ordnance Sgt, 49th NCST), III: 125.
Gift, ______, (CSN), V: 327.
Gilberson's, Va., II: 90.
Gilbert, Hyram, (Pvt, Co A, 64th NCST), III: 667, 688.
Gilbert, J.H., (1st Lt, Co E, 57th NCST), IV: 707, 723.
Gilbert, L.W., (Capt, Co H, 58th NCST), III: 433.
Gilbert, Oliver T., (ACS, 3rd Battalion NCST, Light Art), IV: 261.
Gilbert, P.V., (Pvt, Co K, 46th NCST), V: 525.
Gilbert, R.J., (Lt, Co I, 2nd NCST), I: 163.
Gilbert, S.H., (2ns Lt, Co E, 57th NCST), V: 511.
Gilbert, William, (Pvt, Co A, 56th NCST), III: 347.
Gilchrist, John A., (Lt, Co C, 9th Battalion NCST, 1st Hvy Art), IV: 303, 312.
Gilchrist, Robert C., (Maj, 31st NCST), IV: 161.
Giles, John B., (Pvt, Co E, 6th Vols/16th NCST), V: 552.
Gilham, William, (Col, Va.), IV: 142, 143.
Gill, ______, (Engineering Officer, CSN), V: 327, 329.
Gill, G.H., (Maj, 7th Vols/17th NCST), V: 59.
Gill, George, (Pvt, Co G, 49th NCST), III: 155.
Gill, H.L., (2nd Lt, Co D, 42nd NCST), II: 790, 806.
Gill, Ingram A., (Pvt, Co G, 38th NCST), V: 557.
Gill, James A., (Pvt, Co G, 13th Vols/23rd NCST), II: 199.
Gill, Sylvanus P., (Lt, Co F, 47th NCST), III: 84; IV: 700, 707.
Gill, W.J., (2nd Lt, Co D, 30th NCST), II: 496.
Gill, W.P., [W.F.], (2nd Lt, Co G, 13th Vols/23rd NCST), II: 186, 190, 206, 215, 216.
Gillem, Alvan Cullen, [Gilliam], (Maj Gen, USA), V: 285.
Gillespie, Carter W., (Capt, Co D, 5th Battalion, Cav; Capt, Co D, 65th NCST, 6th Cav), III: 674, 675, 677; IV: 271.
Gillespie, E.R., (Pvt, Co K, 47th NCST), V: 535.

Gillespie, J.M., (Lt, Co K, 9th NCST, 1st Cav), I: 486.
Gillespie, J.N., (Pvt, Co A, 3rd Vols/13th NCST), V: 549.
Gillespie, Matthew, (Pvt, Co E, 25th NCST), V: 561.
Gillespie, Thomas D., (2nd Lt, Co B, 1st Vols, "Bethel"), I: 77, 234.
Gillespie, Thomas P., (Musician, 4th NCST), I: 234; V: 488.
Gillet's, N.C., II: 82.
Gilliam, Dr. Francis, [Gillam], (Ass't Surg, N.C.) IV: 631.
Gilliam, George, (Capt, Co C, 52nd NCST), III: 223, 234; IV: 701, 707.
Gilliam, Henry A., (Maj, 7th Vols/17th NCST), II: 1; V: 35, 38, 39, 680.
Gilliam, J.D., (1st Sgt, Co H, 26th NCST), V: 532.
Gilliam, James, (Jr 2nd Lt, Co A, 77th NCST, 7th Senior Reserves), IV: 99, 101.
Gilliam, Julian, (Capt, Co C, 52nd NCST), III: 223, 234.
Gilliam, Thomas H., (2nd Lt, Co I, 7th Vols/17th NCST), II: 2.
Gilliam, William, (Capt, Co 3, Woodfin's 14th Battalion; Co 9, 79th NCST, 8th Cav), IV: 111, 115, 142.
Gilliland, Jesse R., (Capt, Co C, 6th Battalion/60th NCST), II: 741; III: 484, 493.
Gilliland, R.H., (Pvt, Co F, 2nd Vols/12th NCST), V: 265, 268.
Gillis, William I., (Pvt, Co D, 56th NCST), III: 361.
Gillon, M.M., (1st Lt, Co D, 34th NCST), V: 548.
Gilmer, J.C., (Maj, 21st Battalion Home Guard), IV: 650.
Gilmer, John A., (Col, 27th NCST), I: 63, 64, 65; II: 427, 428, 438, 439, 441, 442, 542; III: 378; IV: 504, 573, 574, 753, 754; V: 650, 663.
Gilmer, John E., (Capt, Co M, 11th Vols/21st NCST), II: 145.
Gilmer, Jeremy F., (Maj Gen, Chief Engineer, CSA), I: xii; IV: 410, 415, 416, 427; V: xv, 3, 4, 663.
Gilmore, A., (Cpl, Co G, 48th NCST), V: 526.
Gilmore, J., (Pvt, Co D, 26th NCST), V: 531.
Gilmore, Quincy Adams, [Gillmore], (Brig Gen, USA), III: 191; V: 162, 384.
Gilreath, George, (Capt, Co B, 55th NCST), III: 296, 299.
Gilreath, J.R., (Pvt, Co F, 52nd NCST), V: 536.
Gilreath, James P., (1st Cpl, Co F, 52nd NCST), III: 224.
Gist, States Rights, (Brig Gen), III: 495.
Givens, George A., (Pvt, Co F, 48th NCST), V: 526.
Gladcross' Mill, (nr Petersburg, Va.), II: 781.
Gladden, H.M., (Pvt, Co F, 56th NCST), III: 348.
Glasgow, William N., (5th Sgt, Co B, 52nd NCST), III: 223.
Glasgow, Scotland, V: 335, 359, 409, 410, 470.
Glass, David P., (Lt, Co K, 35th NCST), I: 120; V: 193.
Glass, Ephraim, (Pvt, Co K, 6th Battalion/60th NCST), III: 482.
Glass, George M., (2nd Lt, Co A, 4th Battalion Junior Reserves; Co A, 72nd NCST, 3rd Junior Reserves), IV: 38.
Glass, J.S., (1st Lt, Co F, 77th NCST, 7th Senior Reserves), IV: 100.
Glass, John, (Pvt, Co G, 54th NCST), V: 516.
Glass' Mill, Ga., (nr Chickamauga, Tenn.), III: 487.

Glassgow, L.A., (Pvt, Co I, 2nd Vols/12th NCST), V: 508.
Glendale, Va., (See: Frazier's Farm).
Glenn, Dr. ______, (Surg, 4th Regt Home Guard), V: 630.
Glenn, B.F., (1st Lt, Co A, 82nd NCST), IV: 131.
Glenn, Chalmers, (Capt, Co I, 3rd Vols/13th NCST), I: 653, 655, 695.
Glenn, J.D., (Pvt, Co D, 3rd Vols/13th NCST), V: 550.
Glenn, Mat, (Negro servant of Chalmers Glenn), I: 695.
Glenn, Robert A., (2nd Lt, Co I, 12th Vols/22nd NCST), II: 166, 172; IV: 723.
Glenn, W.T., (2nd Lt, Co C, 6th Battalion Junior Reserves; Co F, 70th NCST, 1st Junior Reserves), IV: 13.
Glidewell, J.P., (Pvt, Co H, 53rd NCST), V: 502.
Glissen, William, (Pvt, Co C, 38th NCST), V: 557.
Glisson, O.S., (Capt, USN), V: 243.
Globe, N.C., II: 331.
Gloucester Court House, Va., I: 733.
Gloucester Point, Va., I: 80, 82; IV: 150.
Gobble, H., (Pvt, Co A, 54th NCST), V: 516.
Goble, Jacob, (Pvt, Co A, 56th NCST), V: 565.
Goddin, N.A.H., (Capt, Co G, 5th NCST), I: 281, 282.
Godon, S.W., (Commodore, USN), V: 242.
Godwin, ______, (CSN), V: 327.
Godwin, Archibald Campbell, (Brig Gen), I: xii, 309, 326; II: 130; III: 279, 405-406, 408, 410, 416, 417, 418, 419, 420, 421; IV: 170, 525, 526, 658, 659, 660, 662, 677, 700, 748, 751 757; V: 9, 10.
Godwin, Condery, (Capt, Co A, 31st NCST), II: 507.
Godwin, J.J., (Pvt, Co D, 30th NCST), V: 492.
Goelet, E.B., (Lt, Co D, 10th Battalion NCST, 2nd Hvy Art), IV: 330, 332.
Goens, Henry, (Pvt, Co E, 6th Vols/16th NCST), V: 552.
Goff, Nathan, Jr., (Col, 37th U.S., Colored), V: 238.
Goins, A.J., (Cpl, Co B, 52nd NCST), V: 535.
Goins, E., (Pvt, Co H, 30th NCST), V: 493.
Gold, P.G., (Cpl, Co H, 28th NCST), V: 542.
Goldsboro, N.C., I: 55, 138, 164, 179, 216, 221, 227, 320, 321, 365, 391, 396, 412, 492, 493, 494, 495, 497, 498, 500, 510, 514, 517, 518, 520, 521, 523, 524, 525, 527, 532, 533, 535, 539, 588, 737, 742, 778; II: 11, 12, 83, 277, 279, 308, 328, 339, 439, 518, 582, 612, 650, 677, 748, 749, 751, 752, 763, 774, 803; III: 1, 4, 66, 71, 87, 114, 129, 130, 170, 194, 197, 199, 200, 206, 216, 217, 227, 229, 232, 274, 319, 322, 329, 333, 335, 350, 459, 505, 506, 508, 531, 553, 554, 681, 692, 693, 696, 698, 699, 708, 709, 711, 722, 725, 726, 727; IV: 3, 10, 11, 20, 21, 25, 30, 31, 32, 37, 38, 39, 42, 45, 50, 51, 52, 53, 55, 56, 57, 108, 110, 221, 252, 263, 265, 325, 326, 336, 344, 348, 350, 351, 358, 392, 393, 398, 402, 430, 484, 498, 505, 543, 549, 558, 592, 613, 652, 653, 760; V: 83, 85, 86, 90, 269, 270, 456, 630, 639, 643.
Goldsborough, ______, (Maj, Md.), V: 623.
Goldsmith, Edward, (Drill Master, 38th NCST), II: 681.
Goldston, C.C., (2nd Lt, Co E, 44th NCST), III: 23.

Goldston, Charles Carroll, (Lt, Co H, 46th NCST), I: 120; III: 82.
Goldston, Robert W., (Jr 2nd Lt, ACS, Co H, 26th NCST), II: 304, 306, 307, 396, 397.
Gonzales, ______, [A.J.], (Col, S.C.), III: 180.
Gooch, Paul, (Pvt, Co E, 46th NCST), V: 524.
Gooch, Samuel L., (Lt, Co K, 61st NCST), III: 504.
Gooch Mountain, N.C., II: 705.
Goodall's Tavern, Va., (Action at, 1864), I: 453, 464-467, 484; III: 596, 597.
Goode, ______, [C.T.], (Col, 10th C.S. Cav), III: 677.
Goode, Dr. Reginald H., (Ass't Surg, 49th NCST), III: 125, 137; IV: 640.
Goode, W. Thomas, (1st Sgt, Co D, 6th Vols/16th NCST), V: 552.
Goode's Bridge, (Appomattox River, Va.), II: 456, 482, 577, 695; III: 252, 399; V: 250.
Gooding, William B., (Capt, Co K, 12th Vols/22nd NCST), II: 166, 172.
Goodloe, Louis D., (Lt, Ordnance Officer, M.W. Ransom's Brigade), IV: 572.
Goodman, ______, (Capt, QM Salisbury Prison), IV: 763.
Goodman, G.C., (Pvt, Co A, 10th Vols/20th NCST), V: 508.
Goodman, George C., (Pvt, Co A, 10th Vols/20th NCST; Detailed, 2nd Corps Provost Guard), II: 118; V: 570.
Goodman, J.F., (Pvt, Co F, 57th NCST), V: 517.
Goodman, J.M., (Pvt, Co A, 10th Vols/20th NCST), V: 508.
Goodman, J.M., (Pvt, Co A, 10th Vols/20th NCST), V: 508.
Goodman, John T., (Musician, 4th NCST), I: 234.
Goodson, John C., (2nd Cpl, Co H, 52nd NCST), III: 225.
Goodson, John F., (2nd Lt, Co K, 13th Vols/23rd NCST), II: 187.
Goodwin, Joseph M., (Pvt, Co D, 5th Vols/15th NCST), V: 521.
Goodwin, Thomas H., (2nd Lt, Co C, 31st NCST), II: 512.
Goolesberry, W.E., [Goolsby, William E.], (2nd Lt, Co L, 11th Vols/21st NCST), IV: 701, 707.
Goose Creek, Va., (nr Middleburg, Va.), II: 96; III: 566.
Goose Creek Salt Works, Tenn., II: 487.
Gordon, ______, [W.W.], (Col, 11th Tenn.), II: 489.
Gordon, A., (Pvt, Co K, 44th NCST), V: 534.
Gordon, A., (Maj, Staff Officer, N.C. Adjt. Gen. Department; AQM, Martin-Kirkland's Brigade; Chief of Staff to Martin), I: v, 49, 50; II: 181; III: 760, IV: 7, 373, 408, 527; V: 1, 654, 665.
Gordon, A.A., (2nd Sgt, Co E, 12th Vols/22nd NCST), V: 553.
Gordon, A.J., (Pvt, Co D, 56th NCST), V: 566.
Gordon, Dr. Alexander, (Ass't Surg, 8th Vols/18th NCST), IV: 473.
Gordon, F.P., (Pvt, Co B, 2nd Vols/12th NCST), V: 506.
Gordon, George I., (Adjt, 5th Vols/15th NCST), I: 734.
Gordon, George T., (Lt Col, 34th NCST), II: 581.
Gordon, J., (Lt, Co H, 2nd Battalion NCST), IV: 245.
Gordon, J.H., (Pvt, Co B, 2nd Vols/12th NCST), V: 506.
Gordon, J.W., (Cpl, Co G, 8th Vols/18th NCST), II: 64; V: 540.
Gordon, James B., (Brig Gen), I: 417, 420, 425, 426, 427, 429, 430, 449, 450, 451, 452, 454,

455, 456, 457, 458, 459, 465, 467, 481, 483, 484, 485; II: 99, 100, 101, 778; III: 465, 534, 535, 536, 537, 538, 569, 570, 574, 575, 576, 578, 581, 582, 585, 592, 594, 595, 596, 597, 600, 602, 603, 604; IV: 581; V: xii, 9. (Cav)
Gordon, John Brown, (Maj Gen), I: 155, 265, 266, 288, 290, 328, 330, 331, 356, 357, 621, 640, 641, 686, 722, 723, 747; II: 50, 54, 60, 120, 125, 141, 243, 246, 260, 262, 263, 264, 300, 481, 536, 670; III: 56, 144, 281, 282, 312, 399, 400, 401, 422, 426; IV: 212, 457, 459, 478, 509, 524; V: 253, 254, 255, 256, 261, 263, 573.
Gordon, L.D., (Pvt, Co F, 2nd Battalion NCST), V: 495.
Gordon, R.M., (Pvt, Co E, 32nd NCST), V: 496.
Gordon, W.C., (2nd Lt, 6th NCST), IV: 722.
Gordon, W.H., (Pvt, Co C, 3rd Vols/13th NCST), V: 550.
Gordon, W.M., (Maj, Superintendent, Hillsboro Military Academy), V: 638.
Gordonsville, Va., I: 142, 189, 297, 323, 324, 365, 366, 370, 381, 382, 449, 451, 465, 557, 567, 594, 608, 620, 623, 666, 739, 742; II: 21, 28, 66, 68, 130, 150, 191, 274, 440, 469, 472, 545, 549, 584, 654, 655, 682; III: 72, 117, 303, 611, 745; IV: 138, 149, 158, 227, 233, 235, 465.
Gore, B.F., (2nd Lt, Co B, 7th Battalion Junior Reserves; Co D, 72nd NCST, 3rd Junior Reserves), IV: 40.
Gore, C.C., (Capt, Co C, 8th Vols/18th NCST), II: 20.
Gore, D.H., (Capt, Co H, 8th Vols/18th NCST), II: 16.
Gore, W.K., (Capt, Co C, 8th Vols/18th NCST), II: 20.
Gorgas, John C., (Capt, Co B, 2nd NCST), I: 158, 159; IV: 723.
Gorgas, Josiah, (Brig Gen Chief of Ordnance Bureau), I: 22; IV: 299, 300.
Gorman, ______, (Capt, 4th Vols/14th NCST), I: 718.
Gorman, James A., (Sgt, Co D, 10th NCST, 1st Art & Engs, Reilly-Ramsay's Battery, Light Art), V: 568.
Gorman, W.R., (Musician, 4th NCST), I: 234.
Gorrell, Henry C., (Capt, Co E, 2nd NCST), I: 161.
Gorrell, R.B., [Albert Burrow], (2nd Lt, Co D, 57th NCST), IV: 707.
Gorrill, R., (Lt, Co G, 2nd Battalion NCST), IV: 245.
Goslin, Junius W., (1st Lt, Co K, 52nd NCST), III: 225.
Goslin, Lafayette H., (2nd Lt, Co I, 33rd NCST), II: 540, 579.
Gosport Navy Yard, (Norfolk, Va.), I: 80; IV: 414.
Goss, Lewis C., (Pvt, Co I, 4th Vols/14th NCST), V: 491.
Gossett, M.C., (Pvt, Co K, 6th Battalion/60th NCST), III: 482.
Governur's Island, [Governor's], (Prison at New York), I: 531; II: 747, 761.
Gowan, B.A., (2nd Lt, Co G, 51st NCST), IV: 723.
Grabb, L.E., (Pvt, Co F, 28th NCST), V: 542.
Grace Church, Va., II: 117.
Gracie, Archibald, Jr., (Brig Gen), II: 7; III: 357, 359, 381, 382, 520; IV: 254, 362.
Graddy, E.G., (Pvt, Co D, 37th NCST), V: 545.
Grady, David T., (Pvt, Co K, 38th NCST), V: 558.
Grady, H.C., (Capt, Co D, 37th NCST), II: 668.

Grady, Henry W., (Resident of Asheville and Atlanta, Son of W.S. Grady), I: 131; IV: 482.
Grady, J.A., (Lt, Co C, 10th Battalion NCST, 2nd Hvy Art), IV: 330.
Grady, L.J., (Pvt, Co A, 43rd NCST), V: 497.
Grady, Lewis J., (Pvt, Co A, 43rd NCST), III: 20.
Grady, P.H., (2nd Lt, Co D, 1st NCST), I: 137.
Grady, R.M.S., (Pvt, Co A, 43rd NCST), III: 20; V: 497.
Grady, W.G., (Lt, Co I, 9th NCST, 1st Cav), I: 486.
Grady, William S., (Maj, 25th NCST), II: 292, 299; III: 372, 374; IV: 482; V: 12.
Gragg, Jackson, (Pvt, Co F, 26th NCST), V: 601.
Graham, _____, (Lt, USA; Burned the bridge at Whitehall), I: 521.
Graham, _____, (Maj, Gatlin's staff), I: 18.
Graham, _____, (Col, Hagood's Brigade), II: 640, 650; V: 167.
Graham, A., (Pvt, Co K, 6th NCST), V: 514.
Graham, A.W., (Judge), V: xv.
Graham, Alexander C., (1st Cpl, Co K, 38th NCST), V: 558.
Graham, B.G., (Lt, Co B, 27th NCST; Ordnance Officer Cooke's Brigade), IV: 504.
Graham, "Bob," (Pvt, Co D, 3rd Vols/13th NCST), I: 684.
Graham, Dr. Daniel McL., [D.L.M. Graham], (Ass't Surg, 37th NCST), I: 119, 122; IV: 474, 637; V: 538.
Graham, Edmund, (Negro servant to Capt W.A. Graham), II: 95.
Graham, F.M., (1st Lt, Co C, 57th NCST), III: 419.
Graham, Hamilton G., (2nd Lt, Co I, 12th Vols/22nd NCST), II: 162, 165, 166.
Graham, J.M., (Pvt, Co B, 33rd NCST), V: 544.
Graham, James A., (Capt, Adjt, 27th NCST; Capt, Co G, 27th NCST; IG Cooke's Brigade), I: 62; II: 425-463; IV: 501, 504, 507, 508, 510, 511, 512; V: 519, 593, 679.
Graham, Jesse, (Fayetteville and Harper's Ferry Arsenals), IV: 298.
Graham, John W., (Maj, 56th NCST), I: 772; III: 139, 314, 318, 322, 328, 331, 333, 337, 341, 342, 343, 348, 362, 363, 365, 378, 389, 390, 391, 392, 393; V: 175, 176, 188, 190, 191, 195, 651.
Graham, Dr. Joseph, (Capt, Co C, 10th NCST, 1st Art & Engs, Brem-Graham-Williams' Battery, Light Art; Surg, 67th NCST), I: 537, 538, 540, 541, 542, 543, 544, 545 546, 547; III: 703; IV: 642.
Graham, Joseph C., (Pvt, Co C, 49th NCST), V: 564.
Graham, N.A., (Lt, Adjt, 3rd NCST), I: 213; V: 484.
Graham, Neil, (Pvt, Co K, 38th NCST), V: 558.
Graham, Robert D., (Capt, Co D, 56th NCST), I: 772; III: 313, 314, 322, 324, 326, 328, 331, 334, 344, 345, 348, 352, 353, 354, 357, 358, 362, 366, 371, 372, 374, 375, 376, 377, 378, 379, 380, 382, 385, 388, 389, 391, 393, 396, 399, 400, 401, 402; V: 15, 188, 189, 191, 559, 618, 669.
Graham, Stark, [Stark P.], (Sgt, Co H, 4th NCST), I: 233.
Graham, W.A., (Maj, AAG N.C.), I: 50, 51, 56, 57; V: 651, 666, 680.
Graham, William A., (Senator, CSA), I: 55, 56, 57, 65; III: 387; V: 478.

Graham, William A., Jr., (Capt, Co K, 9th Vols/19th NCST, 2nd Cav), II: 79, 80, 82, 83, 84, 85, 86, 88, 89, 90, 91, 92, 93, 94, 96, 97, 98, 99, 321, 324, 325.
Graham, N.C., I: 33; IV: 101.
Graham County, N.C., III: 731, 758; IV: 122.
Grahamville, S.C., I: 581; II: 293, 294, 757, 758; III: 179.
Grainger, Jesse W., (Capt, Co B, 5th Battalion Junior Reserves; Co G, 71st NCST, 2nd Junior Reserves), IV: 25, 28, 595.
Grainger County, Tenn., III: 730.
Granburg, Hiram Bronson, [Granberry], (Brig Gen), III: 495.
Grandy, C.W., (AQM, 8th NCST), I: 387.
Grandy, Caleb L., (2nd Lt, Co A, 56th NCST), III: 313.
Grandy, Charles R., (Maj, Norfolk Light Art, Va.), II: 5; IV: 532.
Grandy, Cyrus W., (Capt, Co G, 68th NCST), III: 714.
Granger, Henry F., (Capt, Co K, 33rd NCST), II: 541.
Granger, Henry F., (Pvt, Co C, 27th NCST), II: 462.
Grant, B.L., (Pvt, Co E, 3rd NCST), V: 487.
Grant, Hiram, (Pvt, Co C, 27th NCST), V: 523.
Grant, Jesse, (Pvt, Co C, 27th NCST), II: 462; V: 523.
Grant, John, (1st Lt, Co F, Walker's Battalion, Thomas' Legion, 80th NCST), IV: 118.
Grant, John S., (Capt, Engineering Officer), IV: 424.
Grant, W.R., (Pvt, Co B, 25th NCST), V: 193.
Grant County, Wi., V: 611, 615.
Grantham, David J., (Pvt, Co I, 5th Vols/15th NCST), V: 522.
Graveley, Hill, Va., [Gravel], I: 385; II: 56, 480, 574; IV: 469.
Gravelly Run, Va., I: 436; II: 104.
Granville County, N.C., II: 182, 221, 239, 254, 256; III: 292, 295, 310; IV: 398, 483, 503, 535, 604, 605, 675; V: 265.
Grapevine Bridge, Va., I: 139, 182, 302, 615, 617.
Graves, B.Y., (Lt Col, 11th Vols/21st NCST), II: 144.
Graves, C.L., (2nd Lt, Co H, 12th Vols/22nd NCST), II: 172.
Graves, G.F., (Pvt, Co F, 3rd Vols/13th NCST), V: 550.
Graves, George A., (Capt, Co G, 12th Vols/22nd NCST), II: 172; IV: 701.
Garves, George W., (Pvt, Co B, 8th NCST), V: 193.
Graves, J.H., (Pvt, Co A, 33rd NCST), V: 543.
Graves, John A., (Capt, Co A, 3rd Vols/13th NCST), I: 653; V: 11, 132, 153.
Graves, John A., (Lt Col, 47th NCST), III: 83, 105, 107, 109; V: 11, 132, 153.
Graves, John W., (Capt, Co G, 12th Vols/22nd NCST), II: 163, 165, 166.
Graves, Thomas L., (Sgt, Co A, 61st NCST), III: 512; V: 16.
Graves, W.W., (AQMS, 56th NCST), V: 565.
Graves, William G., (Capt, Co H, 56th NCST), III: 316, 327, 331, 355, 376, 377, 378, 392, 398; V: 191.
Graves, William W., (Capt, Co E, 25th NCST), II: 292.
Graves, William W., (QM Sgt, 56th NCST), III: 319.
Graveyard Hill, (nr Helena, Ark.), IV: 36.
Gray, Caliborn, (1st Lt, Co L, 12th Vols/22nd NCST), II: 165, 166; IV: 171.

Gray, Colin, (Pvt, Co D, 43rd NCST), V: 498.
Gray, D.O., (2nd Cpl, Co E, 52nd NCST), III: 224.
Gray, David Z., (Pvt, Co D, 34th NCST), V: 555.
Gray, E.G., [Eli G.], (2nd Lt, Co G, 54th NCST), IV: 701, 707.
Gray, H.A., (Lt, Co F, 48th NCST), III: 117.
Gray, J.R., (Cpl, Co D, 27th NCST), II: 462; V: 523.
Gray, J.W., (Pvt, Co K, 33rd NCST), V: 545.
Gray, L.S., (1st Lt, Co C, 6th Battalion Junior Reserves; Co F, 70th NCST, 1st Junior Reserves), IV: 13.
Gray, Mat, (Brig Gen), IV: 213.
Gray, P., (Capt, 62nd Ga., Cav), IV: 75, 77, 82.
Gray, Peter, (Pvt, Co I, 6th Battalion/60th NCST), III: 482.
Gray, R., (Pvt, Co I, 6th Battalion/60th NCST), III: 482.
Gray, Robert H., (Lt Col, 12th Vols/22nd NCST), II: 162, 163, 165, 166, 168, 169, 170; IV: 157, 171; V: 11.
Gray, S.W., (Capt, Co D, 57th NCST), III: 427.
Gray, T.R., (1st Lt, Co C, Millard's 9th/20th Battalion Junior Reserves), IV: 386.
Gray, Terrell, (Pvt, Co B, 1st NCST), V: 485.
Gray, William T., (Sgt, Co D, 43rd NCST), V: 498.
Gray's Farm, Va., II: 447.
Gray's Landing, (Roanoke River), V: 181.
Graybeard, Peter, (2nd Lt, Co A, Indian Co, 69th NCST, Thomas' Legion), III: 730.
Grayson, _____, [R.O.], (Sgt Maj, 5th Vols/15th NCST), I: 734.
Graysville, Ga., II: 716.
Grear, Calvin E., (Sgt Maj, 3rd Vols/13th NCST), I: 675.
Great Grandfather Mountain, N.C., (aka, Grandfather Mountain), II: 359.
Great Western Turnpike, (Md.), I: 224.
Greaver, James, [J.D.W.], (Sgt, Co A, 65th NCST, 6th Cav), III: 680.
Greble, John T., (Lt, 2nd U.S. Art), I: 87, 88, 98.
Green, _____, [Benjamin H.], (Maj, Ewell's Staff, Engineering Officer), V: 381.
Green, _____, [Greer, James C.], (2nd Lt, Co I, 26th NCST), II: 397.
Green, Dr. _____, (Civilian living nr Rappahannock River, Va.), II: 90.
Green, A.W., (1st Lt, Adjt, 2nd Battalion NCST; AA & IG, Grimes' Brigade), IV: 252; V: 494.
Green, Augustin, [Augustus F.], (Pvt, Co D, 58th NCST), III: 443.
Green, Dr. Benjamin T., (Lt, Co E; Surg, 5th Vols/15th NCST; Surg, 55th NCST), I: 734, 735; IV: 634, 640; V: 520.
Green, Dr. Charles, H., (Ass't Surg, Walker's Battalion, Thomas' Legion; 80th NCST), IV: 117, 142, 643.
Green, Charles, (Pvt, Co G, 6th Vols/16th NCST), IV: 142.
Green, D.E., (1st Lt, Co F, 5th Vols/15th NCST), I: 735.
Green, D.J., (Pvt, Co I, 43rd NCST), V: 499.
Green, D.O., (Pvt, Co H, 28th NCST), V: 542.
Green, Dan, (Pvt, Co C, 8th Vols/18th NCST), II: 63; V: 539.

Green, Daniel W., (Pvt, Co F, 6th Vols/16th NCST), V: 552.
Green, F.M., (Lt, USN), V: 243.
Green, H.G., (Cpl, Co I, 53rd NCST), V: 502.
Green, Harrison, (Pvt, Co K, 45th NCST), III: 39.
Green, Henry C., (Pvt, Co G, 6th Vols/16th NCST), IV: 142, 143.
Green, Rev. J.B., (Resident, Alexander Co.), V: 288, 289, 290.
Green, J.F., (Ass't Eng, CSN, Tallahassee), V: 438.
Green, J.M., (Sgt, Co H, 28th NCST), V: 542.
Green, J.L., (Pvt, Co H, 28th NCST; Detailed, Invalid Battalion), V: 542, 571.
Green, J.M.J., (Pvt, Co H, 28th NCST), V: 542.
Green, J.M.S., (Pvt, Co H, 28th NCST), V: 542.
Green, Jacob P., (Cpl, Co I, 48th NCST), V: 527.
Green, James E., (2nd Lt, Co I, 53rd NCST), III: 263.
Green, John H., (Sgt Maj, 50th NCST), III: 202.
Green, Joseph, (Pvt, Co C, 10th NCST, 1st Art & Engs, Brem-Graham-Williams' Battery, Light Art), V: 568.
Green, Joseph, (Capt, Co C, 30th NCST), II: 495.
Green, Josiah, (Pvt, Co B, 47th NCST), V: 534.
Green, L.M., (Pvt, Co G, 56th NCST), III: 348.
Green, R.H., (Pvt, Co H, 28th NCST), V: 542.
Green, Samuel, (Pvt, Co I, 56th NCST), III: 348.
Green, Dr. Simon T., (Surg, 46th NCST), III: 65; IV: 639.
Green, T.F., (2nd Lt, Co H, 28th NCST), V: 538.
Green, Thomas, (Pvt, Co I, 25th NCST), V: 562.
Green, W.C., (2nd Lt; Son of J.B. Green of Alexander County), V: 288, 289, 290.
Green, W.P., (Cpl, Co E, 6th Battalion/60th NCST), III: 482.
Green, Walter, (Pvt, Courier, Co B, 27th NCST), II: 461; V: 523.
Green, Wharton J., (Lt Col, 2nd Battalion NCST; ADC to Daniel), I: vii, 463; IV: 243, 244-260 personal account, 513, 519, 700, 707; V: 59.
Green, William, (Purser, Blockade Runner), V: 411.
Green, William Forney, (Col, 1st Regt 3rd Class, Home Guard), I: 733, 736; IV: 650, 653; V: 631, 632.
Green, Dr. William J., (Ass't Surg, 44th NCST), III: 22; IV: 639.
Green's Mill Pond, N.C., III: 215.
Green's Road, (nr Namozine Church), III: 650.
Green Castle, Pa., [Greencastle], I: 148, 194, 541, 579, 698; II: 399, 416, 462; IV: 181, 255.
Green Plains, (nr Drewry's Bluff, Va., aka, Harper's Farm), IV: 404.
Green River Cove, N.C., III: 668.
Green Turtle Cay, V: 382, 411, 430.
Green and Cousin's Crossroads, Va., III: 650.
Greenage, Va., II: 440.
Greenbrier, Va., IV: 149.
Greenbrier Bridge, [Green Brier], IV: 148.
Greenbrier River, Va., I: 753; IV: 141.
Greene, Dr. B.T., (Surg, 55th NCST), III: 288.
Greene, James M., (Pvt, Co F, 3rd NCST), V: 487.
Greene, Matthew M., (1st Lt, Co G, 61st Va.), IV: 403.

Greene, R.S., (Sgt, Co F, Starr's 13th Battalion NCST, Light Art), V: 569.
Greene County, N.C., I: 533; III: 504, 545, 709, 711, 727.
Greene County, Tenn., III: 757.
Greenlee, Dr. E.G., [E.L.], (Ass't Surg, 1st Battalion; Surg, 54th NCST), III: 267; IV: 640, 643.
Greenlee, J.L., (Lt, Co K, 12th Vols/22nd NCST), II: 166.
Greenlee, J.M., (1st Sgt, Co A, Millard's 9th/20th Battalion Junior Reserves), IV: 395.
Greensboro, N.C., I: 59, 60, 61, 62, 63, 64, 386, 409, 446, 499, 531; II: 163, 393, 409, 764, 786, 807; III: 36, 79, 200, 368, 388, 399, 444, 445, 496, 502, 542, 550, 681, 692, 696, 700; IV: 7, 32, 41, 60, 67, 98, 99, 101, 102, 222, 269, 299, 323, 334, 336, 352, 359, 362, 375, 394, 396, 495, 539, 542, 615, 653, 652, 694, 770; V: 7, 276, 468, 478, 629, 630, 632, 633, 639, 654, 665.
Greenville, N.C., I: 391, 511, 540, 577, 588; II: 126, 513, 620, 773, 777, 785; III: 24, 88, 130, 135, 172, 173, 232, 233, 290, 349, 506, 507, 707, 709, 710, 714; IV: 74, 77, 84, 221, 338, 349, 415, 418.
Greenville, Tenn., III: 475, 499, 517, 519, 520, 521, 660, 664, 676, 737, 740, 741; IV: 115, 116.
Greenwich, (Private residence of English Consul in Va.), I: 454, 592.
Greenwich, Va., III: 578, 579.
Greer, E.J., (1st Lt, Co C, 30th NCST), II: 496.
Greer, J.C., (Lt, Co I, 26th NCST), II: 397.
Greer, L.M., (Pvt, Co G, 56th NCST), III: 348.
Greeson, William, (Pvt, Co A, 53rd NCST), V: 501.
Gregg, B., (Pvt, Co C, 10th NCST, 1st Art & Engs, Brem-Graham-Williams' Battery, Light Art), V: 568.
Gregg, David McMurtrie, (Maj Gen, USA), I: 423; II: 390.
Gregg, Hiram, (Pvt, 65th NCST, 6th Cav), III: 680.
Gregg, John, (Brig Gen), I: 729.
Gregg, John Irvin, (Brig Gen, USA), II: 93; III: 563, 564, 565, 566, 598, 630, 631; V: 207.
Gregg, Maxcy, (Brig Gen), I: 309, 666; II: 35, 93, 552, 553, 554, 557, 679, 684; III: 100; IV: 171.
Gregory, A.H., (Lt, Co G, 8th NCST), V: 194.
Gregory, Casper, (Color-bearer, 2nd Vols/12th NCST), I: 639.
Gregory, Dr. Charles G., (Ass't Surg, 30th NCST), I: 119; II: 495; IV: 636.
Gregory, Dr. F.R., (Capt, Co B; Ass't Surg, 70th NCST, 1st Junior Reserves), IV: 12, 13, 14, 17, 642.
Gregory, Frederick W., (Signal Officer, Susan Beirne), V: 380, 405-411.
Gregory, George Henry, (2nd Lt, Co E, 1st Vols, "Bethel"), I: 78, 120, 127; IV: 355.
Gregory, John, (Pvt, Co B, 55th NCST), V: 527.
Gregory, John T., (Lt, Co G; Adjt, 2nd Vols/12th NCST), I: 620, 639, 642.
Gregory, Nathaniel A., (1st Lt, Co I, 13th Vols/23rd NCST; Capt, Co D, 6th Battalion Junior Reserves; Co H, 70th NCST, 1st Junior Reserves; Maj, 71st NCST, 2nd Junior Reserves), II: 187,

231; IV: 11, 12, 13, 28, 587, 594; V: 640.
Gregory, W.H., (2nd Lt, Co B, 70th NCST 1st Junior Reserves), IV: 12.
Gregory, W.H.H., (Adjt, 42nd NCST; Lt, 70th NCST, 1st Junior Reserves), II: 789, 805; IV: 13.
Gresham, Dr. Charles, (Ass't Surg, 53rd NCST), III: 261; IV: 640.
Gresham, John W., (Pvt, Co A, 38th NCST), V: 557.
Gresham, Willis T., (5th Sgt, Co A, 38th NCST), V: 556.
Grey, A.H., [Gray, Augustus H.], (1st Lt, Co B, 57th NCST), IV: 707.
Grier, C.E., (Adjt, 3rd Vols/13th NCST), V: 547.
Grier, Hiram L., (Lt, Co B, 55th NCST), III: 296.
Grier, J.L., (Lt, Co F, 9th NCST, 1st Cav), I: 486.
Grier, John, (Pvt, Co A, 56th NCST), V: 565.
Grier, John C., (2nd Lt, Co I, 1st Vols/11th NCST), I: 120; II: 372.
Grier, John C., (Capt, Co F, 49th NCST), III: 141, 147, 148, 153.
Grier, P.B., [Paul B.], (1st Lt, Co E, 1st Vols/11th NCST), I: 120.
Grier, S.A., (Capt, Co D, 63rd NCST, 5th Cav), I: 119; III: 540, 613, 618, 639, 651, 652.
Grier, W.L., (Capt, Co H, 1st Vols/11th NCST), I: 585, 593.
Griffin, Benjamin W., (Pvt, Co K, 5th Vols/15th NCST), V: 522.
Griffin, George, (Pvt, Co I, 56th NCST), III: 352, 356.
Griffin, George W., (Pvt, Co I, 33rd NCST), II: 544.
Griffin, H.G., (Pvt, Co H, 2nd Vols/12th NCST), V: 507.
Griffin, Dr. Hamilton, (Surg, 6th Battalion/60th NCST), III: 484; IV: 641.
Griffin, Harvey D., (Lt, Co B, 47th NCST), III: 84.
Griffin, J.A., (Pvt, Co E, 48th NCST), V: 526.
Griffin, J.E., (2nd Lt, Co D, 37th NCST), V: 538.
Griffin, James B., (Col, Hampton's Legion), IV: 150.
Griffin, Joel R., (Col, 62nd Ga. Cav), IV: 72, 73, 74.
Griffin, John J., (Pvt, Co E, 48th NCST), V: 526.
Griffin, John S., (Pvt, Co I, 53rd NCST), V: 502.
Griffin, Joseph, (Pvt, Co H, 32nd NCST; Detailed, 2nd Corps Provost Guard), V: 570.
Griffin, Loranie W., (4th Sgt, Co D, 6th Vols/16th NCST), V: 552.
Griffin, M.S., (Pvt, Co I, 30th NCST), V: 493.
Griffin, P.C., (Pvt, Co D, 37th NCST), V: 545.
Griffin, T.H., (2nd Lt, Co K, 5th Vols/15th NCST), I: 736.
Griffin, T.W., (Capt, Co C, 76th NCST, 6th Senior Reserves), IV: 97.
Griffin, W.T., (Pvt, Co H, 32nd NCST), V: 497.
Griffin, W.T., (Pvt, Co D, 37th NCST), V: 545.
Griffinsburg, Va., III: 575.
Griffith, J.H., (Pvt, Co B, 43rd NCST), V: 497.
Griffith, Andrew J., (Capt, Co G, 4th Vols/14th NCST), I: 731.
Grigg, Alfred R., (2nd Lt, Co F, 56th NCST), III: 315; V: 670.
Grigg, Benjamin F., (Capt, Co F, 56th NCST), I: 119; III: 315, 357, 392; V: 670.
Grigg, J.R., (Lt, Co F, 56th NCST), III: 357.

Grimes, Bryan, (Maj Gen), I: xi, xii, 170, 174, 207, 209, 230, 235, 237, 238, 239, 240, 241, 242, 243, 244, 246, 250, 251, 252, 254, 256, 257, 258, 259, 262, 263, 264, 265, 266, 269, 273, 275, 277, 279, 280, 550; II: 62, 238, 504, 505, 523, 531, 533; III: 11, 12, 17, 57, 59, 256, 260, 264; IV: 74, 247, 253, 442, 448, 457, 458, 460, 515, 516, 518, 519; V: xi, xiii, 247-256, 260, 265, 483, 648.
Grimes, D.L., (Pvt, Co C, 3rd NCST), V: 487.
Grimes, George W., (Lt, Co G, 7th Vols/17th NCST), II: 3, 12; IV: 547; V: 44, 46, 47, 680.
Grimes, H.J., (1st Lt, Co B, 10th Va., Cav, N.C. company), V: 627.
Grimes, John, (Resident of Red Banks Roanoke River, Va.), I: 512.
Grimes, Polk, (Negro servant to Bryan Grimes), I: 273.
Grimes, Ruben, (Pvt, Co H, 48th NCST), V: 527.
Grimes, T.F., (2nd Lt, Co B, 10th Va., Cav, N.C. Company), V: 627.
Grimes, W.L., (Pvt, Co H, 48th NCST), V: 526.
Grimes, William, (Brother of Bryan Grimes), IV: 74.
Grimes Road, N.C., III: 172.
Grimmer, Rufus R., (Pvt, Co E, 27th NCST), II: 462; V: 523.
Grimsley, George, (Lt, Co I, 61st NCST), III: 504.
Grimsley, James M., (Lt, Co K, 37th NCST), II: 667, 669; V: 16.
Grimsley, Lowery, (Lt, Co I, 61st NCST), III: 504.
Grimsley, Thomas, (Pvt, Co A, 26th NCST), V: 531.
Grinstead, L.L., (Pvt, Co D, 3rd Vols/13th NCST), V: 550.
Grisby, John Warren, (Col, Ky, 6th Cav), II: 739.
Grissett, Edwin W., (1st Lt, Co C, 78th NCST, 8th Senior Reserves), IV: 107.
Grissom, Dr. Eugene, (Capt, Co D, 30th NCST; Surg, N.C.), II: 495, 498; IV: 629.
Grissom, R.D., (Pvt, Co E, 9th NCST, 1st Cav), V: 657.
Grissom, R.S., (Pilot, Little Hattie), V: 357.
Grissom, Robert, (Pilot, The Lady Davis), V: 407.
Grissom, Thomas, (Pilot, Lilian; Index), V: 357, 369, 373, 409.
Grissom, W.M., (Pvt, Co E, 12th Vols/22nd NCST), V: 553.
Grist, John, (Planter nr Washington), I: 512.
Griswold, Bishop ______, (Chaplain, 33th NCST), II: 579.
Griswold, George, (2nd Lt, Co E, 50th NCST), III: 203.
Griswold, John, (Capt, Co E, 50th NCST), III: 161, 202.
Griswold, John B., (2nd Lt, Co D, 4th NCST; Capt, Griswold's Unattached Co., Senior Reserves), I: 232; IV: 402.
Grizzard, James M., (Capt, Co A, 15th N.C. Militia), IV: 645.
Groce, J.H., (Sgt, Co D, 35th NCST), V: 562.
Groner, J.L., (Pvt, Co A, 10th Vols/20th NCST), V: 508.
Gross, B.F., (Pvt, 21st Ga.), V: 194.
Gross, J.C., (Lt, Co I, 56th NCST), III: 393.
Gross, L.M., (2nd Lt, Co B, Millard's 9th/20th Battalion Junior Reserves), IV: 386.
Gross, Phillip H., (2nd Lt, Co I, 56th NCST), III: 316, 317, 393; V: 559.
Ground Squirrel Bridge, Va., III: 596.
Ground Squirrel Church, Va., I: 465; III: 536, 596, 598, 600.

Grove Street, (Asheville), IV: 386.
Grover, A.C., (Pvt, Co A, 2nd Battalion NCST), V: 494.
Groveton, Va., II: 31; III: 582; IV: 227.
Grubbs, J.F., (Pvt, Co D, 57th NCST), V: 517.
Gualt, A., (Pvt, Co I, 1st Vols/11th NCST), V: 531.
Guard for Home Defence, (See also: Home Guard), IV: 649.
Guard, Old Men's, I: 55.
Gudger, J.C.L., (1st Lt, Adjt, 25th NCST), II: 291, 301.
Gudger, R.V., (Pvt, Co E, 1st Vols, "Bethel"; 1st Sgt, Co C, Brem-Graham-Williams' Battery, Light Art), I: 128; V: 567.
Gudger, James M., (Capt, Co F, 4th Vols/14th NCST), I: 708.
Gudger, John W., (2nd Lt, Co C, 29th NCST), II: 485.
Gudger, William M., (2nd Lt, Co F, 4th Vols/14th NCST), I: 730; V: 484.
Guerrant, H.L., (Capt, Co K, 3rd Vols/13th NCST), I: 701; V: 151.
Guerrant, J.W.S., (4th Sgt, Co K, 3rd Vols/13th NCST), V: 551.
Guess, W.G., [William G.], (Capt, Co C, 6th NCST), IV: 702, 707.
Guest, John, (Cmdr, USN), V: 242.
Guffey, C.A., (2nd Lt, Co G, 4th NCST), V: 484.
Guffey, S.M., (Hospital Steward, Co A, 4th NCST), V: 488.
Guffey, William, (Pvt, Co K, 49th NCST), V: 15
Guffin, George, III: 356.
Guffy, C.A., (2nd Lt, Co G, 4th NCST), I: 233, 272.
Guffy, E.P., (Pvt, Co A, 49th NCST), V: 564.
Guffy, Dr. J.W., (Hospital Stewart, 4th NCST), I: 230, 268.
Guild, Lafayette, (Surgeon-General, CSA), II: 360.
Guilford, F.B., (Pvt, Co I, 4th NCST; Brigade Butcher), V: 489.
Guilford, J.W., (Pvt, Co D, 5th NCST), I: 291; V: 505.
Guilford, Joseph M., (Pvt, Co D, 5th NCST; Detailed, 2nd Corps Provost Guard), V: 570.
Guilford County, N.C., I: 43; III: 35, 38, 260, 262, 264, 545, 550; IV: 73, 103, 415; V: 629, 631, 633.
Guilford Court House, Battle of, (Revolution), II: 359, 599, 735.
Guinea Station, Va., (The place where Stonewall Jackson died), I: 373, 375, 577, 664, 660, 696, 762; II: 227, 679; III: 71.
Guion, B.B., (Capt, Co A, 10th NCST, 1st Art & Engs, Ramseur-Manly's Battery, Light Art), I: 551, 553, 560.
Guion, Henry T., (Lt Col, 10th NCST, 1st Art & Engs), I: 496, 498, 501, 509, 515, 525, 526, 529, 535, 536.
Guion, John, (Sgt Maj, 31st NCST), II: 511.
Gulf of Mexico, (aka, The Gulf), II: 707.
Gulf, The (Moore County), IV: 299.
Gulick, W.B., (Paymaster, N.C. Pay Department), I: 51.
Gulick, James W., (Lt, Co H, 2nd NCST), I: 162.
Gulledge, Elijah, (Pvt, Co I, 43rd NCST), V: 499.
Gulledge, H.M., (Pvt, Co K, 26th NCST), V: 532.
Gulley, John D., (Capt, Co C, 14th Vols/24th NCST), II: 271, 274.
Gulley Station, N.C., I: 58.
Gully, Jacob, (Pvt, Co C, 14th Vols/24th NCST), V: 560.

Gum Spring, Va., III: 582.
Gum Swamp, N.C., (and 1st Battle of, 1863), I: 742; II: 277, 439; III: 117, 131, 323, 329, 333; IV: 221, 346-347, 505.
Gum Swamp, N.C., (2nd Battle of, 1865), III: 324, 327, 332.
Gunter, D.G., (2nd Lt, Co A, 6th NCST), V: 511.
Gunter, H.A., (Adjt, 48th NCST), III: 124.
Gunter, J.H., (Musician, Co D, 35th NCST), V: 562.
Gunter, William, (Pvt, Co D, 61st NCST), III: 507.
Gupton, H.G., (2nd Lt, Co G, 5th Vols/15th NCST), I: 735.
Gurganus, A.J., (2nd Lt, Co E, 3rd NCST), IV: 722.
Gurganus, W.H., (Pvt, Co E, 55th NCST), V: 528.
Gurley, Joseph D., (Artificer, 6th Battalion NCST, Fayetteville Armory Guard), IV: 296.
Guthrie, Archibald, (Pilot, Giraffe), V: 357.
Guthrie, John F., (Lt, Co C, 61st NCST), III: 504, 505.
Guthrie, Julius, (Capt, CSN, Advance), I: 59; V: 471.
Guthrie, T.W., (Cpl, Co H, 33rd NCST), II: 540.
Guy, Alexander, (Pvt, Co A, 43rd NCST), III: 20.
Guy, Amos M., (2nd Lt, Co A, 8th Battalion Junior Reserves; Co F, 72nd NCST, 3rd Junior Reserves), IV: 41, 48.
Guy, C.T., (Lt, Co I, 51st NCST), III: 220.
Guy, W.S., (Lt Col, 3rd Vols/13th NCST), I: 653.
Guyther, John M., (2nd Lt, Co H, 1st NCST), I: 137; IV: 722.
Gwaltney, Rev. L.P., (Civilian), V: 290, 291.
Gwaltney, Rev. W.R., (Chaplain, 1st NCST), I: 136, 150; IV: 604; V: 293, 294.
Gwathmey, ______, (Lt Col, Engineering Officer), IV: 418, 419.
Gwynn, Bruce, (Son of Walter Gwynn), IV: 425.
Gwynn, Walter, (Col, Engineering Officer; N.C. Brig Gen), IV: 415, 416, 425; V: 6.

(H)

Habbitt, John, (2nd Lt, Co H, Walker's Battalion, Thomas' Legion; 80th NCST), IV: 119.
Habeas Corpus, Suspension of, IV: 749-751.
Habnicht, ______, (Chief, CSN, Sirene), V: 448, 449.
Hackett, J.W., (Lt, ACS, 1st NCST), I: 136.
Hackett, James Gordon, (Nephew of Brig Gen James B. Gordon), III: 604.
Hackett, John W., (1st Lt, Co D, 41st NCST, 3rd Cav), II: 770.
Hackett, L.W., (Sgt, Co E, 2nd NCST), I: 176; V: 486.
Hackett, R.N., (Nephew of Brig Gen James B. Gordon), III: 604.
Hackney, B., (Pvt, Co B, 56th NCST), III: 347.
Hackney, D.J., (Musician, Mickey's Band, 26th NCST), II: 398.
Hackney, Jesse E., (Pvt, Co D, 5th Vols/15th NCST), V: 521.
Hackwood, Va., (Battle of, See: also: Winchester), II: 252.
Hackwood Farm, (nr Winchester, Va.), II: 252.
Haddock's Mill, (nr Greenville), IV: 338.
Hadley, Dr. J.M., (Ass't Surg, 4th NCST), I: 230, 268, 279; IV: 484, 632.
Hadley, T.J., (Lt, Co A, 55th NCST), III: 295.
Hadspeth, Wesley, (Capt, Co B, 13th Vols/23rd NCST), II: 183, 224, 231.
Hafner, George, W., (Teamster, Co K, 49th NCST; Detailed, QM Corps), V: 571.
Hagerstown, Md., I: 148, 194, 254, 261, 287, 317, 324, 381, 541, 544, 556, 557, 573, 579, 624, 625, 639, 718; II: 45, 74, 119, 139, 219, 375, 377, 413, 478, 487, 568, 587, 662, 693; III: 5, 7, 41, 88, 109, 239, 271, 416, 462, 463, 472, 570; IV: 177, 182, 255, 405, 468; V: 71, 72, 77.
Hagerstown Road, (aka Hagerstown Pike at Sharpsburg, Md.), I: 142, 225, 307, 308, 311; II: 435; III: 271; V: 77.
Haggard, ______, (Capt, 2nd NCST, USA), II: 618.
Hagler, Paul, (Pvt, Co I, 48th NCST), V: 527.
Hagood, Johnson, (Brig Gen), II: 7, 764; IV: 537; V: 163, 167, 199.
Hahr, F.J., (Maj, Commandant Conscript Camp; Mallet-Hahr's 19th Battalion NCST), I: 118; IV: 383, 548.
Haigh, Charles, (Sgt Maj, 63rd NCST, 5th Cav), I: 119; III: 529, 551, 577, 655.
Haigh, Charles T., (Capt, Co B, 37th NCST), II: 667, 668.
Haigh, George, (Sgt Maj, 63rd NCST, 5th Cav), III: 529.
Haigh, George B., (AQMS, 72nd NCST, 3rd Junior Reserves), IV: 51.

Haigh, George H., (2nd Lt, Conscript Bureau), I: 120.
Haigh, John C., (Cadet, Hillsboro Military Academy Battalion), V: 643.
Haigh, T.D., (Capt, Clarendon Guard, Unattached Co), IV: 402.
Hair, A.M., (Pvt, Co G, 33rd NCST), V: 544.
Hale, Edward J., Jr., (Maj, AA & IG Lane's Brigade), I: 96, 117, 118, 122, 133; II: 483, 484, 572; III: 318, 322, 326, 327, 331-333; IV: 471, 472, 477; V: xi, xii, 537, 651, 654, 680.
Hale, Joe, (1st Lt, Co 4, Henry's 14th Battalion NCST, Cav), IV: 113.
Hale, Peter M., (Maj, 1st Vols, "Bethel"), I: 132.
Haley, William, (Pvt, Co K, 11th Vols/21st NCST), V: 515.
Half Link, Va., II: 471; IV: 465.
Half Sink Bridge, I: 366.
Halifax, N.C., (aka Halifax Court House), I: 498, 532, 533, 535; II: 593, 616, 677; III: 135, 331, 720; IV: 52, 358, 359, 392; V: 272, 282, 318, 337.
Halifax County, N.C., II: 671, 771; IV: 10, 11, 379, 403, 513, 518, 609; V: 315.
Halifax, Nova Scotia, V: 339, 340, 375, 376, 377, 393, 418, 439, 461, 471.
Halifax Road, (nr Malone's Crossing, Va.), III: 620, 633.
Halifax Street, (Petersburg, Va.), IV: 208.
Half-way Station, (Between Richmond & Petersburg, Va.; aka Half-way House), I: 89, 97; II: 88; III: 329, 351; IV: 492.
Hall, ______, (Col, 26th Ala.), II: 230.
Hall, ______, (Lt Col, 39th NCST), II: 729.
Hall, ______, [Wilber G.], (Sgt, Co B, Starr's Battery, Starr's 13th Battalion NCST, Light Art), IV: 348
Hall, Benjamin F., (1st Sgt, Co A, 43rd NCST), III: 17, 18, 20; V: 497.
Hall, C.F., (2nd Lt, Co G, 53rd NCST), III: 263.
Hall, Charles H., (Pvt, Co I, 10th Vols/20th NCST), II: 120.
Hall, Charles M., (Capt, Co A, Millard's 9th/20th Battalion Junior Reserves), IV: 18, 53, 386, 393.
Hall, Constant, (Pvt, Co D, 10th NCST, 1st Art & Engs, Reilly-Ramsay's Battery, Light Art), V: 568.
Hall, Dewitt C., (Pvt, Co K, 34th NCST), V: 556.
Hall, E.D., (Capt, Co H, 40th NCST, 3rd Art, Hvy), II: 746.
Hall, E.G., (Ass't Engineer, CSN, Tallahassee), V: 438.
Hall, Edward, (Capt, Co C, 47th NCST), III: 84
Hall, Edward D., (Maj, 7th NCST), II: 541, 746; IV: 472.
Hall, Edward D., (Col, 46th NCST), I: 158, 361, 362, 364, 365; II: 440, 441, 442, 602; III: 65, 67, 72, 73, 75,; IV: 501, 504, 505, 506; V: 664.
Hall, Frank, (Lt, Co K, 57th NCST), III: 409.
Hall, Guidon, (Pvt, Co D, 10th NCST, 1st Art & Engs, Reilly-Ramsay's Battery, Light Art), I: 571.
Hall, H.A., (Pvt, Co I, 8th Vols/18th NCST), II: 64.
Hall, H.L., (Pvt, Co I, 51st NCST), III: 217.
Hall, Harrison, (Hospital Steward, Co H, 49th NCST), III: 125; V: 564.

Hall, J.O., (Musician, Mickey's Band, 26th NCST), II: 398.
Hall, J.P., (Pvt, Co K, 11th Vols/21st NCST), V: 531.
Hall, J.T., (Pvt, Co B, 43rd NCST), V: 497.
Hall, Dr. J.W., (Surg, Salisbury Priosn Hospital; Surg, Salisbury General Hospital), IV: 625, 626, 627, 629, 746.
Hall, Dr. James K., (Surg, 12th Vols/22nd NCST), II: 162; IV: 633, 635.
Hall, James W., (Pvt, Co D, 56th NCST), III: 347; V: 188.
Hall, Dr. Joel, (Salisbury Hospital), II: 743.
Hall, John, (Pvt, Co A, 38th NCST), V: 556.
Hall, John, (2nd Lt, Co E, 66th NCST), III: 686.
Hall, John J., (Lt, Co I, 2nd NCST), I: 163.
Hall, Joseph G., (1st Sgt, Co F; 2nd Lt, Co F, 52nd NCST), III: 224, 226; V: 169.
Hall, Linnington , (Pvt, Co D, 10th NCST, 1st Art & Engs), V: 50.
Hall, Moses, (Pvt, Co K, 6th Battalion/60th NCST), III: 482.
Hall, R.H., (Pvt, Co G, 8th Vols/18th NCST), II: 64.
Hall, Robert T., (Capt, Co I, 43rd NCST), III: 2.
Hall, S.S., [Stockton S.], (Pvt, Co D, 10th NCST, 1st Art & Eng, Guidon's Battery), I: 571.
Hall, W.D., (2nd Lt, Co C, 69th NCST, Thomas' Legion), III: 730.
Hall, W.G., (Pvt, Co A, 30th NCST), V: 491.
Hall, Dr. W.H., (Ass't Surg, 2nd N.C. General Hospital, Petersburg, Va.), IV: 624, 630.
Hall, W.H., (Musician, Mickey's Band, 26th NCST), II: 398, 399.
Hall, William S., (Pvt, Co H, 4th Vols/14th NCST), V: 491.
Hallam, _____, (Historian), V: 475.
Halleck, Henry Wager, (Maj Gen, Chief of Staff, USA), I: 63; II: 218, 386; IV: 175.
Haller, A.A., (Pvt, Co D, 16th Battalion/75th NCST, 7th Cav), V: 660.
Hallet, E., (Pvt, Co E, 37th NCST), V: 546.
Hallman, _____, [W.M.], (Pvt, Co A, 33rd NCST), II: 578.
Hallman, E., (Pvt, Co E, 57th NCST), V: 517.
Hallman, L., (Pvt, Co G, 57th NCST), V: 517.
Hallman, Robert, (Pvt, Co G, 57th NCST), V: 517.
Hallowell, _____, (Col, 54th Mass., Colored), V: 621, 622, 623.
Halltown, Va., II: 433; IV: 502; V: 213.
Hallyburton, T.C., (Capt, ACS, 56th NCST), III: 316, 318, 322.
Halpon, _____, (Englishman, Capt, Blockade Runner), V: 413.
Halsey, D.P., (Capt, AAG, Garland's Brigade), IV: 521, 523.
Halso, James G., (Pvt, Co A, 43rd NCST), III: 20; V: 497.
Halstead, F.M., (Capt, Co B, 68th NCST), III: 713.
Halton, R.J., (Pvt, Co E, 28th NCST), V: 542.
Halyburton, A.G., (1st Lt, Co B, 12th Vols/22nd NCST), II: 164.
Halyburton, R., (2nd Lt, Co C, 1st Battalion Junior Reserves; Co D, 70th NCST, 1st Junior Reserves), IV: 13.
Ham, H.B., (2nd Lt, Co D, 62nd NCST; Co A, 1 6th Battalion/ 75th NCST, 7th Cav) IV: 91.

Haman, Henry, (Pvt, Co H, 6th Battalion/60th NCST), III: 500.

Hamarskold, Charles J., (Lt Col, 34th NCST), II: 581.

Hambrick, E., (Pvt, Co E, 2nd Vols/12th NCST), V: 507.

Hambrick, J., (Pvt, Co H, 28th NCST), V: 542.

Hambrick, J.F., (Pvt, Co A, 1st Battalion NCST), V: 503.

Hambrick, J.M., (Pvt, Co E, 2nd Vols/12th NCST), V: 507.

Hambrick, John T., (Col, 3rd Regt Home Guard), I: 653, 654, 659; IV: 650.

Hambright, Alfred F., (Hospital Steward, 6th Vols/16th NCST), V: 551.

Hamby, Mrs. _____, (See: Fort Hamby).

Hamilton, _____, [D.H.], (Col, 1st S.C.), II: 677.

Hamilton, Alexander H., (Jr 2nd Lt, Co C, 68th NCST), III: 728

Hamilton, C.H., (Master, USN; Pioneer, Juniata), V: 244.

Hamilton, D.H., (Maj, 3rd Vols/13th NCST), I: 653; V: 641.

Hamilton, R.L., (1st Lt, Co D & E, 65th NCST, 6th Cav), IV: 700, 701, 707.

Hamilton, Simeon E., (Capt, 2nd Choctaw Cav), IV: 696.

Hamilton, V.C., (2nd Lt, Co K, 62nd NCST), III: 516.

Hamilton, W.G., (Pvt, Co D, 26th NCST), V: 572.

Hamilton, W.H., (Sgt, Co E, 4th Vols/14th NCST), I: 710.

Hamilton, William C., (Pvt, Co E, 25th NCST), V: 561.

Hamilton, Bermuda, V: 377, 419.

Hamilton, N.C., I: 446, 447, 448; II: 87, 88, 278, 582, 616; III: 8, 135, 320, 331, 337, 681, 707, 720, 721, 726; IV: 15, 16, 27, 29, 44, 77, 354, 415, 645; V: 181, 318.

Hamilton, Va., III: 279.

Hamilton's Heights, (nr Fredericksburg, Va.), II: 556.

Hamilton's Crossing, Va., I: 143, 144, 190, 191, 309, 310, 588, 628, 713; II: 35, 115, 116, 117, 135, 158, 226, 476, 559, 679; III: 235, 295; IV: 169, 172, 175, 176, 236, 253; V: 93.

Hamin, R., (Pvt, Co C, 45th NCST), V: 500.

Hamlet, N.C., II: 125.

Hamlett, J.F., (Pvt, Co C, 3rd Vols/13th NCST), V: 550.

Hamlin, A.C., (Lt Col, USA; Historian, 11th Corps), II: 40.

Hamlin, Frank M., (2nd Lt, Co D, 4th Battalion Junior Reserves; Co K; 1st Lt, Adjt, 72nd NCST, 3rd Junior Reserves), IV: 4, 38, 39, 48, 51, 52, 54, 591.

Hamlin, Hannibal, (Vice President, U.S.), II: 40.

Hammell, W.R., [Hansell, William R.], (1st Sgt, Co F, 4th NCST), I: 233.

Hammock, _____, (Capt, Crescent), IV: 715, 716.

Hammond, G.W., (Lt Col, 5th Vols/15th NCST), I: 733, 736; V: 519.

Hammond, Hampton B., (Pvt, Co C, 4th Vols/14th NCST; Detailed, 2nd Corps Provost Guard), V: 490, 570.

Hammond, John, (2nd Lt, Co A, 46th NCST), III: 80.

Hammond, W.M., (Capt, AAG & Chief of Staff, Daniels' Brigade), II: 529; III: 35; IV: 513, 516, 517.

Hampden, Augustus Charles Hobart, (Englishman, Capt, Royal Navy; Blockade Runner; Author; Admiral and Chief of the Turkish Navy; aka Capt Roberts & Hobart Pasha),

V: 411, 413, 414, 416, 417, 425, 426-437.
Hampden-Sydney College, II: 804; V: 341.
Hampton, Alexander, (Pvt, Co G, 11th Vols/21st NCST), V: 515.
Hampton, B.F., (Lt, Co E, 64th NCST), III: 660.
Hampton, E.H., (Maj, 29th NCST), II: 485, 492.
Hampton, E.R., (Hospital Steward, Millard's 9th/20th Battalion, Junior Reserves), IV: 385, 386, 389, 390, 391, 393, 394, 395, 396.
Hampton, Frank, (Lt Col, 2nd S.C.), I: 424.
Hampton, J.A., (Lt Col, 68th Battalion Home Guard), I: 136; IV: 650.
Hampton, M.P., (Lt, Co C, 58th NCST), III: 433.
Hampton, S.D., (2nd Lt, Co G, 50th NCST), III: 203.
Hampton, Thomas Preston, (Lt, ADC and son of Lt. Gen. Wade Hampton), III: 630.
Hampton, W.B., (Capt, Co I, 54th NCST), III: 267.
Hampton, Wade, (Lt Gen), I: 62, 63, 133, 299, 342, 352, 420, 423, 425, 430, 434, 435, 436, 438, 460, 461, 462, 463, 464, 470, 481, 482, 772, 775, 776; II: 103, 105, 123, 701, 780, 782, 787; III: 30, 194, 195, 196, 197, 198, 383, 460, 539, 558, 564, 565, 578, 584, 585, 586, 592, 593, 609, 611, 615, 620, 621, 622-624, 625, 626, 627, 628, 629, 630, 632, 633, 634, 635, 636, 681; IV: 43, 56, 58, 88, 104, 149, 150, 151, 152, 352, 390, 498, 547; V: 207, 208, 209, 627, 628.
Hampton, William W., (Jr 2nd Lt, Co C, 26th NCST), II: 303, 396.
Hampton, Va., I: 81, 82, 83, 85, 86, 87, 89, 97, 98, 107.
Hampton Roads, Va., I: 607; V: 305.
Hampton Roads Affair, (See: Peace Commission).
Hampton's Beef Raid, (aka Hampton's Cattle Raid), I: 436, 482; II: 105; III: 540, 622-627; IV: 88..
Hampton's Legion, I: 342; IV: 149, 150, 152, 155, 425.
Hamrick, Amos, (Pvt, Co B, 34th NCST), V: 555.
Hamrick, David, (Pvt, Co D, 55th NCST), V: 528.
Hamrick, Thomas, (Pvt, Co D, 55th NCST), V: 528.
Hancock, A., (Pvt, Co B, 52nd NCST), V: 535.
Hancock, Doctor N., (1st Sgt, Co B, 34th NCST), V: 555.
Hancock, Ezekiel W., [Handcock], (2nd Lt, Co C, 3rd Vols./13th NCST; Col, 77th NCST, 7th Senior Reserves), I: 653; IV: 100.
Hancock, J.T., (Pvt, Co C, 59th NCST, 4th Cav), V: 659.
Hancock, J.W., (Pvt, Co F, 46th NCST), V: 524.
Hancock, James, (Pvt, Co K, 2nd NCST), I: 164.
Hancock, James B., (2nd Lt, Adjt, 40th NCST, 3rd Art, Hvy), II: 745, 746, 747.
Hancock, John M., (Maj, 2nd Battalion NCST), II: 255, 256, 258; IV: 245, 255, 256, 258, 700, 708.
Hancock, Richard D., (1st Lt, Co K, 2nd NCST), I: 164, 173, 175; V: 484.
Hancock, Wheeler, (Lt Col, 77th NCST, 7th Senior Reserves), IV: 103.
Hancock, William, (Pvt, Co F, 11th Vols/21st NCST), V: 194.
Hancock, Winfield Scott, (Maj Gen, USA), I: 116, 152, 171, 285, 481,

596, 601, 610, 611, 679; II: 6, 51, 57, 96, 390, 411, 480, 569, 575, 621, 665, 669, 799; III: 29, 30, 94, 95, 97, 628, 631; IV: 193, 469, 534; V: 108, 156, 207.
Hand, James, (Pvt, Co D, 63rd NCST, 5th Cav), III: 538.
Hand, P.H., (Sgt, Co C, 59th NCST, 4th Cav), V: 659.
Hand, Robert H., (2nd Lt, Co A, 1st Vols/11th NCST), I: 120, 584; IV: 701, 707.
Hand, S.P., [Samuel P.], (2nd Lt, Co K, 3rd NCST), I: 213.
Hand, William L., (Capt, Co A, 1st Vols/11th NCST), I: 119, 583; IV: 701, 707.
Handy, William, (Pvt, Co B, 56th NCST), III: 347.
Hanes, George, (Pvt, Co E, 42nd NCST), II: 799.
Hanes, Spencer J., (Capt, Co E, 42nd NCST), II: 790, 801, 806.
Hanes, William P., (Pvt, Co C, 48th NCST), V: 526.
Hanging Dog, N.C., IV: 122.
Hanging Rock, Va., III: 277.
Hanks, B.J., (Master, CSN, Colonel Hill), V: 36.
Hanks, Edward P., (1st Lt, Co A, 56th NCST), III: 313.
Hanks, G.M., (Capt, Co B, Indian Co, 69th NCST, Thomas' Legion), III: 730.
Hanks, John, (Lt, MacRae's 18th Battalion NCST, Cav), IV: 379.
Hanks, William H., (Pvt, Co K, 10th NCST, 1st Art & Engs), V: 35.
Hanna, Harvey, (Pvt, Co H, 6th NCST), V: 194.
Hannah, ______, [Rody, Pvt], (Sgt, Co A, 6th NCST), I: 344, 345.
Hannah, ______, (Sgt Maj, 1st Regt Home Guard in the Field), V: 631.
Hannah, J. George, (Cadet, Hillsboro Military Academy Battalion), V: 643.
Hanner, James H., (Lt, Co E, 12th Vols/22nd NCST), II: 166.
Hanner, Oran A., (Jr 2nd Lt, Co E, 26th NCST), II: 371.
Hanner, Orren Alston, (Lt, Co D, 26th NCST), II: 371, 372, 396, 397, 419; IV: 701, 707.
Hanner, R.M., (Pvt, Co C, 45th NCST), V: 500.
Hanner, Robert, (Lt, Co I, 12th Vols/22nd NCST), II: 166.
Hanner, Samuel, (Lt, Co I, 63rd NCST, 5th Cav), III: 600.
Hanover, Pa., II: 97, 98, 99, 100; V: 627.
Hanover Court House, Va., (aka Hanover Junction, Slash Church and Battle of, 1862, See also: Slash Church), I: 115, 172, 205, 258, 322, 334, 350, 366, 430, 557, 567, 570, 588, 608, 609, 643, 677, 701, 745; II: 21, 22, 66, 67, 77, 88, 100, 101, 120, 122, 240, 341, 387, 401, 415, 469, 470, 471, 545, 588, 654, 679, 785; III: 11, 24, 66, 71, 77, 88, 111, 119, 129, 234, 235, 246, 277, 604, 608, 609; IV: 151, 197, 357, 465, 522, 554, 558.
Hanover Road, Va., II: 22.
Hanovertown, Va., I: 558; III: 538, 608.
Hanrahan, James A., (Lt, Co E, 55th NCST), III: 296; IV: 700, 707.
Hanshey, J.W., (Sgt, Co E, 30th NCST), V: 492.
Happer, R.W., (Pvt, Co A, Webb's Battery, Starr's 13th Battalion NCST, Light Art), V: 282.
Happers, L., (Pvt, Co H, 2nd Battalion NCST), V: 495.
Happers, W.W., (Pvt, Co H, 2nd Battalion NCST), V: 495.

Happoldt, John W., (1st Lt, Co D, 33rd NCST), II: 539, 578, 579.
Happy Valley, N.C., II: 411.
Haralson, W.C., (Cpl, Co H, 6th NCST), V: 513.
Harbin, A.A., (Maj, 3rd Battalion Home Guard), IV: 650.
Harbin, W.T.J., (Sgt, Co A, 4th NCST), I: 232.
Hardaway, _____, (Maj, Ala.), I: 277.
Hardee, _____, (Son of Lt Gen W.J. Hardee), III: 198.
Hardee, William Joseph, (Lt Gen, and Hardee's Army), I: 56, 57; II: 488, 490, 634, 702, 739, 756, 757; III: 179, 183, 184, 185, 186, 190, 191, 192, 193, 194, 195, 196, 197, 513, 696; IV: 31, 56, 58, 59, 320, 321, 322, 350, 352, 536, 547, 548, 549, 591; V: 270.
Hardee's Tactics, II: 732, 733.
Hardeeville, S.C., II: 758; III: 180, 185, 186.
Hardeman, _____, [Thomas], (Col, 45th Ga.), II: 21, 545.
Harden, J.J., [Irvin J.], (2nd Lt, Co E, 2nd Vols/12th NCST), I: 652.
Harden, James D., (Adjt, 39th NCST), II: 707, 725, 732.
Harden, Dr. James H., (Ass't Surg, 38th NCST), IV: 638.
Harden, Joseph, (2nd Lt, Co D, Walker's Battalion, Thomas' Legion; 80th NCST), IV: 118.
Harden, Thomas, (Pvt, Co G, 49th NCST), V: 564.
Hardenburg, T., [Hardenbergh, Thomas H.], (Sgt, Co K, 10th NCST, 1st Art & Engs), V: 36.
Hardenburg, Selby, (2nd Lt, Co B, 40th NCST, 3rd Art, Hvy), II: 746.
Hardey, W.C., (Pvt, Co D, 10th Vols/20th NCST), V: 508.
Hardgrove, F.M., (Sgt, Co K, 52nd NCST), V: 536.
Hardie, H., (Chaplain), IV: 603.
Hardiman, Thomas, Jr., [Hardeman], (Col, 45th Ga.), II: 677.
Hardin, _____, (Capt, Co B, 5th Battalion NCST, Cav), IV: 271.
Hardin, D.J., (Capt, Co C, 5th Vols/15th NCST), I: 734.
Hardin, James H., (Pvt, Co B, 27th NCST), II: 461; V: 523.
Hardin, W.K., (2nd Lt, Co C, 5th Vols/15th NCST), I: 734.
Harding, Rev. Dr. E.H., (Chaplain, 45th NCST), III: 35; IV: 615.
Harding, Frederick, (Capt, Co K, 41st NCST, 3rd Cav), II: 772; III: 635.
Harding, Henry, (Maj, 61st NCST), III: 503.
Harding, James, (4th Sgt, Co C, 44th NCST), V: 533.
Harding, Oliver P., (Maj, 203rd Pa.), V: 237, 238.
Hardison, _____, (Sgt, Co A, 2nd Corps Engineers), IV: 431.
Hardison, W.H., (Sgt Maj, 32nd NCST), II: 522; V: 495.
Hardison, W.J., (1st Lt, Co E, 7th Vols/17th NCST), II: 3, 7.
Hardister, Agrippa S., (Sgt Maj, 38th NCST), II: 679.
Hardister, Jonathan, (Pvt, Co D, 10th NCST, 1st Art & Engs, Reilly-Ramsay's Battery, Light Art), I: 569.
Hardister, Lindsay C., (2nd Lt, Co B, 52nd NCST), III: 23, 223, 227, 228.
Hardy, H.B., (1st Lt, Co H, 9th Vols/19th NCST, 2nd Cav), II: 80.
Hardy, Jesse, (Pvt, Co D, 27th NCST), II: 462; V: 523.
Hardy, Dr. John G., (Ass't Surg, 1st Vols "Bethel"; Surg, 6th NCST; Surg, 64th NCST), I: 77, 118; IV: 631, 632, 642.

Hardy, Dr. J. Geddings, (Surg, 64th NCST), I: 118; IV: 642.
Hardy, Joseph R., (3rd Cpl, Co A, 4th Vols/14th NCST), V: 489.
Hardy, W.B., (Lt, Va. Art), IV: 695.
Hardy, Washington Morrison, (Col, 6th Battalion/60th NCST; Cmdr Baker's Brigade; Cmdr Hardy's Brigade), I: 78, 118; II: 757; III: 187, 188, 191, 198, 454, 473, 483, 486, 492; IV: 6, 101, 103, 104, 105, 218, 334, 440.
Hare, J.B., (Jr 2nd Lt, Co B, 38th NCST), II: 678, 690.
Hare's Hill, Va., (See also: Fort Stedman), I: 209, 396, 650; II: 124, 263, 452, 534, 625, 670, 673, 801; III: 15, 16, 122, 144, 157-158, 256, 264, 282, 379, 390-394, 396, 425, 601; IV: 450, 494, 509, 516, 519, 523, 526.
Hare House, (nr Petersburg, Va.), II: 799; IV: 362, 535.
Harget, Henry P., (Pvt, Co I, 48th NCST), V: 527.
Harget, James C., (Pvt, Co F, 48th NCST), V: 526.
Hargett, J.M., (2nd Lt, Co G, 1st NCST), I: 137; IV: 722.
Hargrave, W.F., (Capt, Co D, 1st Battalion Junior Reserves; Co I, 70th NCST, 1st Junior Reserves), IV: 13.
Hargrove, Jesse, (Lt Col, 1st Battalion Home Guard), IV: 650.
Hargrove, Tazewell L., (Lt Col, 44th NCST), II: 335; III: 22, 24, 25, 26; IV: 707, 721.
Hargrove, W.W., (5th Sgt, Co E, 1st Vols/11th NCST), V: 530.
Hargrove, Willis W., (AQMS, 34th NCST), II: 582; V: 554.
Hargrove's House, Va., I: 436; II: 104.
Harill, Abram, (Pvt, Co B, 13th Vols/23rd NCST), V: 509.
Harker's Island, N.C., II: 750.
Harkey, D.E., (Pvt, Co F, 49th NCST), V: 564.
Harkey, J.I., (Cpl, Co F, 49th NCST), V: 564.
Harkey, M.L., (Pvt, Co I, 43rd NCST), V: 499.
Harkins, T.J., (Sgt, Co E, 6th Battalion/60th NCST), III: 482.
Harkins, Thomas, (Jr 2nd Lt, Co 2, West's Battalion NCST, Cav), IV: 111.
Harlan Road, Tenn., (aka Harlan County Road), II: 486; III: 521.
Harlee, William F., (Capt, Co A, 13th Vols/23rd NCST), II: 182.
Harman, C.D., (Pvt, Co E, 37th NCST), V: 545.
Harmer, John H., (Pvt, Co D, 13th Vols/23rd NCST), II: 190.
Harmon, A.W., [Harman], (Col, 12th Va.), I: 424.
Harmon, D.C., (Capt, Co D, 58th NCST), III: 433.
Harmon, John J., (Pvt, Co D, 4th Vols/14th NCST), V: 490.
Harmon, P.B., (Pvt, Co E, 2nd Vols/12th NCST), V: 507.
Harnett County, N.C., II: 769, 770; III: 199, 323; IV: 329, 342, 483.
Harney, ______, [Frank M.], (Lt, Co F, 4th Vols/14th NCST), I: 248, 276, 277, 718, 719.
Harney, E.C., (Lt, Co L, 12th Vols/22nd NCST), II: 166.
Harold, Abram F., (2nd Lt, Co C, 9th Vols/19th NCST, 2nd Cav), II: 89.
Harold, Furney, (Pvt, Co C, 2nd NCST), V: 486.
Harper, ______, (Capt, Brig Gen Mott's Staff, USA), III: 632.
Harper, ______, [R.W.], (Col, 1st Ark., Cav), II: 717.
Harper, C.E., (2nd Lt, Co G , 16th Battalion/75th NCST, 7th Cav), IV: 92.

Harper, Charles E., (Capt, Co E, 12th Vols/22nd NCST), II: 165, 168.
Harper, Cornelius, (2nd Lt, Co D, 27th NCST), II: 462.
Harper, F.S., (Pvt, Co A, 12th Vols/22nd NCST), V: 553.
Harper, G.W.F., (Maj, 58th NCST), III: 431, 432, 433, 437, 438, 441, 444, 447; V: xi, 670.
Harper, J.C., (1st Lt, Co H, 2nd Vols/12th NCST), I: 651; V: 503.
Harper, John W., (Jr 2nd Lt, Co C, 8th Battalion Junior Reserves; Co G, 72nd NCST, 3rd Junior Reserves), IV: 42, 54.
Harper, Joseph R., (Pvt, Co G, 4th Vols/14th NCST), V: 490.
Harper, Luby, (2nd Lt, Co I, 66th NCST), III: 686.
Harper, R.W., (Pvt, Co A, Webb's Battery, Starr's 13th Battalion NCST, Light Art), V: 282.
Harper's Farm, (nr Drewry's Bluff, Va.; aka Green Plains), IV: 404.
Harper's Ferry, Va.,(Town, Arsenal and Battles of), I: 39, 40, 81, 147, 172, 189, 206, 259, 261, 286, 307, 324, 326, 372, 373, 421, 422, 533, 575, 624, 625, 663, 672, 696, 718, 739, 740, 759, 760, 762; II: 30, 70, 135, 155, 156, 432, 534, 553, 656, 685; III: 13, 67, 68, 79, 116, 124, 128, 270, 415, 419, 749; IV: 164, 165, 168, 236, 294, 297, 419, 421, 466, 502, 515, 552, 570-571; V: 71, 72, 74, 77, 79, 80, 82, 114, 589, 590, 591.
Harper's Ferry Road, II: 248, 601.
Harrell, Abram F., (Capt, Co C, 19th NCST, 2nd Cav), II: 105.
Harrell, D.J., (Pvt, Co B, Starr's Battery, Starr's 13th Battalion NCST, Light Art), IV: 346.
Harrell, G.K., (1st Lt, Co F, 30th NCST), II: 496.
Harrell, Henry D., (Pvt, Co D, 68th NCST), III: 715.
Harrell, J.N., (Lt Col, 1st NCST), I: 134, 137, 146, 149, 150.
Harrell, J.N., (2nd Lt, Co C, 52nd NCST), III: 223.
Harrell, M., [Harrel], (Pvt, Co L, 58th NCST), III: 453.
Harrell, Nicholas, (Sgt, Co C, 19th NCST, 2nd Cav), II: 102.
Harrell, R.E., (Pvt, Co D, 55th NCST), V: 528.
Harrell, Rivhard, (Pvt, Co C, 10th NCST, 1st Art & Engs, Brem-Graham-Williams' Battery, Light Art), V: 568.
Harrell, Samuel, (Pvt, Co D, 6th Vols/16th NCST), V: 552.
Harrell, W., (Pvt, Co B, NCST), V: 543.
Harrell, W.H., (Pvt, Co B, 45th NCST), V: 500.
Harrell, Walston, (Pvt, Co F, 30th NCST), V: 492.
Harrell, Warren, (Pvt, Co B, 33rd NCST), V: 543.
Harrell, Wiley, (Pvt, Co E, 43rd NCST), V: 498.
Harrell, Dr. William B., (Surg, Wynn's 15th Battalion NCST, Cav), IV: 644.
Harrell, William H., (Pvt, Co D, 55th NCST), V: 528.
Harrell's Store, N.C., IV: 613.
Harrellsville, N.C., II: 793; III: 134, 715, 716.
Harrelson, B.M., (Cpl, Co D, 10th Vols/20th NCST; Prvost Marshall, 2nd Corps), II: 118; V: 569.
Harrellson, B.M., (Pvt, Co D, 10th Vols/20th NCST), V: 508.
Harriet's Chapel, N.C., (nr Kinston), III: 508.
Harrill, Amos, (Sgt, Co E, 56th NCST), III: 347, 356.
Harrill, D.B., (1st Lt, Co C, 34th NCST), V: 548.

Harrill, H., (Pvt, Co I, 56th NCST), III: 348.
Harrill, J.N., I: 135, 137, 146, 149, 150; III: 223.
Harrill, James A., (Pvt, Co B, 34th NCST), V: 555.
Harrill, John N., (Pvt, Co B, 34th NCST), V: 555.
Harrill, Lawson, [Harrell], (Capt, Co I, 56th NCST), I: 766, 771, 772; III: 316, 323, 338, 342, 343, 345, 356, 362, 372, 376, 380, 385, 390, 391, 392, 393; V: 179, 188, 189.
Harrill, Nathan S., (Pvt, Co B, 34th NCST), V: 555.
Harrington, Abner, (Jr 2nd Lt, Co G, 38th NCST), II: 678, 681.
Harrington, Timothy, (Fayetteville and Harper's Ferry Arsenals), IV: 298.
Harrington, Thomas H., (1st Lt, Co H, 19th NCST, 2nd Cav), II: 89.
Harrington, W.M., (Lt, Co D, 58th NCST), III: 433.
Harris, ______, (Lt Cmdr; Capt, Black Warrior), V: 304, 307.
Harris, ______, [James Edward], (Sgt, Co A, 10th Battalion NCST, 2nd Hvy Art), IV: 326.
Harris, A.H., (Lt, Co C, 47th NCST), III: 84.
Harris, Adolphus, (Pvt, Co M, 6th Vols/16th NCST), V: 553.
Harris, B.F., (Pvt, Co C, 32nd NCST), V: 496.
Harris, Burell B., (Pvt, Co I, 34th NCST), V: 556.
Harris, C.L., (2nd Lt, Co I, 42nd NCST), II: 791, 807.
Harris, Cebern L., (Lt, Co I, 69th Battalion Home Guard), IV: 650.
Harris, D.B., (Col, Corps of Engineers, Beauregard's Staff), III: 362.
Harris, David T., (Lt, Co D, 2nd Battalion NCST), IV: 245.
Harris, Edwin Victor, (Capt, Co E, 49th NCST), III: 133, 143, 148.
Harris, F., (1st Cpl, Co E, 46th NCST), V: 524.
Harris, F.S., (Capt, 7th Tenn.), V: 107.
Harris, G.W., (Pvt, Co K, 14th Vols/24th NCST), V: 560.
Harris, H.J., [Harriss], (Capt, Co A, 10th Battalion NCST, 2nd Hvy Art), IV: 329.
Harris, H.W., (Capt, Co E, 35th NCST), V: 559.
Harris, Henry, (Pvt, Co D, 30th NCST), V: 492.
Harris, I.A., (Capt, Co 2, Woodfin's Battalion; Maj., Henry's 14th Battalion; Maj, 79th NCST, 8th Cav), I: 133, 368; IV: 111, 114.
Harris, J.E., [Harriss], (Sgt, Co A, 10th Battalion NCST, 2nd Hvy Art), IV: 326, 335.
Harris, J.F., (Pvt, Co H, 35th NCST), V: 193.
Harris, J.J., [Harriss], (Capt, Co I, 30th NCST), II: 496.
Harris, J.M., (Capt, Co G, 4th Vols/14th NCST), I: 726.
Harris, J.M., (Cpl, Co C, 32nd NCST), V: 496.
Harris, J.M., (Lt, Co C, 26th NCST), II: 372, 396; IV: 701, 707.
Harris, J.N., (Pvt, Co B, 30th NCST), V: 491.
Harris, J.N., (Pvt, Co B, 2nd Vols/12th NCST), V: 506.
Harris, J.R., (2nd Lt, Co B, 4th NCST), I: 231.
Harris, J.S., (Capt, Co B, 7th NCST), I: 375, 378; V: 665.
Harris, James A., (Cpl, Co I, 7th NCST), I: 368.

Harris, James G., (Maj, 7th NCST), I: 361, 385, 386; III: 78; IV: 472; V: 646, 665.
Harris, James R., (2nd Lt, Co K, 9th Vols/19th NCST, 2nd Cav), II: 89.
Harris, John, (Pvt, Co B, 44th NCST), V: 533.
Harris, John L., (Lt Col, 14th Vols/ 24th NCST), II: 270, 271, 286, 287, 290, 614; III: 376, 377, 378.
Harris, John S., (Pvt, Co C, 44th NCST), V: 533.
Harris, Joseph J., (Capt, Co B, 47th NCST), III: 84.
Harris, Julian Shakespeare, (Pvt, Co F, 63rd NCST, 5th NCST), III: 626.
Harris, Kiah P., (Cpl, Co A, 10th Vols/20th NCST), II: 114.
Harris, M., (Pvt, Co A, 1st Vols/11th NCST), V: 530.
Harris, Nathaniel Harrison, (Brig Gen), I: 725.
Harris, Neal, (Pvt, Co B, 45th NCST), V: 500.
Harris, Nick M., (2nd Lt, Co E, 19th NCST, 2nd Cav), II: 80.
Harris, Orrin J., (3rd Cpl, Co F, 52nd NCST), III: 224.
Harris, R., (Pvt, Co C, 44th NCST), V: 533.
Harris, R.S., (2nd Lt, Co E, 5th Vols/15th NCST), I: 735.
Harris, Richard, (Pvt, Co E, 27th NCST), II: 462; V: 523.
Harris, Richard S., (Capt, AQM, 10th Vols/20thNCST; AQM, Johnston's Brigade), II: 112; V: 503.
Harris, Reuben, (5th Sgt, Co I, 52nd NCST), II: 225.
Harris, T., (Pvt, Co C, 2nd Vols/12th NCST), V: 507.
Harris, T.A., (Lt, USN), V: 243.
Harris, T.C., (Lt Cmdr, USN), V: 242.
Harris, T.J.L., (Cpl, Co C, 32nd NCST), V: 496.
Harris, T.P., (Pvt, Co D, 30th NCST), V: 492.
Harris, Thomas W., (Maj, 63rd NCST, 5th Cav), I: 441; III: 529, 530, 541, 643, 649, 654; V: 12.
Harris, W.D., (Lt, Co F, 47th NCST), III: 84.
Harris, Dr. W.H., (Surg, 58th NCST), III: 432; IV: 641.
Harris, W.S., (1st Lt, Co I, 32nd NCST), I: 736.
Harris, Wade H., (Editor, Concord Sun), III: 547.
Harris, Wiley, (Pvt, Co A, 11th Vols/21st NCST), V: 514.
Harris, William, (Lt, Co A, 9th Battalion NCST, 1st Hvy Art), IV: 304.
Harris, Dr. William W., (Ass't Surg, 61st NCST), III: 503; IV: 641.
Harris, Zenah A., (4th Cpl, Co F, 52nd NCST), III: 224.
Harris House, (nr Spottsylvania, Va.), I: 641; II: 243.
Harrisburg, Pa., I: 61, 632; II: 233, 527, 671; V: 81.
Harrisonburg, Va., III: 749.
Harrison, _____, [George P., Jr.], (Col, 32nd Ga.), I: 394; V: 163, 167.
Harrison, H.M., (4th Cpl, Co K, 3rd Vols/13th NCST), V: 551.
Harrison, J.W., (Sgt, Co D, 4th NCST), I: 232.
Harrison, John A., (Capt, Co D, 47th NCST), III: 84.
Harrison, John K., (Capt, Co I, 37th NCST), II: 653.
Harrison, Thomas, (Brig Gen), III: 678.
Harrison, Dr. Virginius, (Surg, Martin-Kirkland's Brigade), IV: 527, 644.
Harrison, W.H., (Pvt, Co G, 61st Va.), V: 569.

Harrison, W.H., (Sgt, Co C, 37th NCST), V: 545.
Harrison, W.H., (Col, 1st Regt Home Guard), II: 746; IV: 650.
Harrison, William C., (Lt, Co D, 64th NCST), III: 660.
Harrison, William H., (President, U.S.), II: 331.
Harrison, William H., (2nd Lt, Co B, 40th NCST, 3rd Art, Hvy), II: 746.
Harrison, William Henry, (Lt, Co I, 47th NCST), III: 85.
Harrison's Landing, Va., I: 305, 334, 420, 539, 694; II: 214, 274, 430, 655, 682; III: 116, 166, 167-170; IV: 158, 235, 356, 446, 502, 551.
Harrison's Old Field, (nr Savannah, Ga.), II: 634.
Harrison House, (nr Spottsylvania, Va.), III: 61.
Harrisonburg, Pa., IV: 665; V: 113.
Harrisonburg, Va., I: 262.
Harriss, Edwin T., (Pvt, Co G, 4th Vols/14th NCST), V: 490.
Harriss, J.P., (Pvt, Co B, 28th NCST), V: 541.
Harriss, Major D., (Pvt, Co A, 4th Vols/14th NCST), V: 489.
Harriss, R.H., (Pvt, Co F, 33rd NCST), V: 544.
Harrow, William, (Brig Gen, USA), V: 106.
Hart, B.T., (1st Lt, Co I, 5th Vols/15th NCST; AIG, Cooke's Brigade), I: 735; IV: 506.
Hart, E.S., (Cpl, Color-bearer, 13th Vols/23rd NCST), II: 244; IV: 723.
Hart, F.A., (Capt, 78th NCST, 8th Senior Reserves), IV: 107.
Hart, J.C., (Pvt, Co I, 26th NCST), V: 532.
Hart, J.J., (Pvt, Co C, 32nd NCST), V: 496.
Hart, J.T., (3rd Lt, Co I, 48th NCST), V: 520.
Hart, J.W., (Sgt, Co I, 13th Vols/23rd NCST), V: 510.
Hart, John, (Pvt, Co G, 48th NCST), V: 526.
Hart, John F., (Pvt, Co I, 13th Vols/23rd NCST), V: 510.
Hart, W.W., (Cpl, Co I, 13th Vols/23rd NCST), V: 510.
Hart, William C., (Sgt, Co E, 5th Vols/15th NCST), V: 521.
Hart's House, (nr Petersburg, Va.), III: 250.
Hart's Island Prison, (USA), IV: 326.
Hartley, D.M., (2nd Lt, Co C, 42nd NCST), II: 790.
Hartline, A., (Pvt, Co E, 1st Vols/11th NCST), V: 530.
Hartington, The Duke of Devonshire, Lord, (Englishman), V: 412.
Hartman, Daniel, (Pvt, Co D, 10th NCST, 1st Art & Engs, Reilly-Ramsay's Battery, Light Art), V: 568.
Hartman, J.W., (Lt, Co F, 51st NCST), III: 219.
Hartman, Jacob, (Pvt, Co E, 5th NCST), I: 292; V: 505.
Hartman, Lewis A., (Musician, 33rd NCST), II: 537; V: 543.
Hartman, W.H., (Capt, Co A, 31st NCST), II: 507, 512.
Hartranft, John Frederick, (Maj Gen, USA), I: 64; III: 394.
Hartsell, J.M., [J.J.], (Lt, 64th NCST), IV: 707.
Hartsfield, Asa A., (Lt, Co C; AQM, 9th Battalion NCST, 1st Hvy Art), IV: 303, 306.
Hartsfield, Jacob A., (1st Lt, Co I, 1st NCST), I: 137; IV: 721.
Hartsfield, Lemuel H., (Capt, Co E, 41st NCST, 3rd Cav), II: 771; IV: 721.
Hartsog, John, (Capt, Co A, 37th NCST), II: 653.

Hartsuff, William, (AAG, to Johnston), IV: 323; V: 78.
Hartzog, A.C., (1st Lt/Ensign, 34th NCST), V: 548.
Harvard College, III: 643.
Harell, Elbert, (Pvt, Co I, 49th NCST), V: 565.
Harward, Charles, (Pvt, Co A, 10th NCST, 1st Art & Engs, Ramseur-Manly's Battery, Light Art), I: 557.
Harvell, John, (Pvt, Co I, 49th NCST), V: 565.
Harvey, E., (Pvt, Co G, 7th Vols/17th NCST), V: 39.
Harvey, Hanna, (Pvt, Co F, 6th NCST), V: 194.
Harvey, Price, (Pvt, Co M, 11th Vols/22nd NCST), V: 515.
Harvey, William H., [Edward], (Pvt, Co K, 10th NCST, 1st Art & Engs, Hvy Art), V: 50.
Harville, T.C., (2nd Cpl, Co K, 3rd Vols/13th NCST), V: 551.
Haskell, J.T., (1st Sgt, Co I, 52nd NCST), V: 536.
Haskell, John C., (Lt Col, Haskell's Battalion, Art), I: 580.
Haskett, Thomas B., (2nd Lt, Co G, 10th NCST, 1st Art & Engs, Pender-Manney's Hvy Art), I: 496, 521, 526, 527, 536.
Haskins, B.B., (2nd Lt, Co F, 1st Vols/11th NCST), I: 585.
Haskins, Blount, (Pvt, Co A, 10th NCST, 1st Art & Engs, Ramseur-Manly's Battery, Light Art), I: 555.
Hass, J.M., (Pvt, Co K, 46th NCST), V: 525.
Hassell, Theodore, (Lt, Ordnance Officer, Martin-Kirkland's Brigade), IV: 527, 547.
Hassel, William, (1st Lt, Co G, 40th NCST, 3rd Art, Hvy), II: 746.
Hasty, N., (Pvt, Co F, 1st NCST), V: 485.
Hasty, S.H., (Pvt, Co I, 53rd NCST), V: 502.
Haswell, T.N., (Pvt, Co F, 47th NCST), V: 535.
Hatch, W.H., (Col, Ass't Confederate Agent of Exchange), V: 624.
Hatcher, Dr. Alfred A., (Surg, 39th NCST), II: 707, 738; IV: 638.
Hatcher's Run, Va., (and Battle of, 1864, aka Burgess Mills), I: 328, 501, 650, 702; II: 61, 124, 143, 176, 182, 262, 290, 361, 390, 391, 449, 450, 481, 533, 534, 589, 782, 783; III: 78, 79, 80, 81, 96, 121, 122, 250, 251-252, 310, 311, 373, 389-380, 396, 422, 428, 466, 627, 628, 630, 637; IV: 88, 90, 478, 508, 509, 524, 526, 567, 568.
Haterick, P.W., (1st Lt, Co A, 53rd NCST), III: 261.
Hathaway, G., (Lt, Co E, 9th Vols/19th NCST, 2nd Cav), I: 441.
Hathaway, J.R.B., (Pvt, Co M, 1st Vols, "Bethel"), I: 133.
Hathaway, James, (Pvt, Co C, 44th NCST), V: 533.
Hathaway, John, (Pvt, Co D, 44th NCST), V: 533.
Hathaway, Nathaniel, (Pvt, Co A, Webb's Battery, Starr's 13th Battalion NCST, Light Art), V: 282.
Hathaway, R., (Pvt, Co F, 30th NCST), V: 492.
Hathcock, Uriah F., (Cpl, Co K, 28th NCST), V: 543.
Hatsell, J.M., (Capt, Co H, 42nd NCST), II: 791, 807.
Hatteras, Cape, N.C., (and Battle of, 1861), I: 4, 388, 489, 694; II: 629, 745, 768; III: 313, 314; IV: 414; V: 6, 35-56, 299, 305, 306, 321, 443, 446, 680.

Hatteras Inlet, N.C., I: 389; II: 1; V: 321.
Hatteras Lighthouse, N.C., V: 56.
Hatton, Robert, (Brig Gen), I: 350, 352.
Haughton, Miss Currie, (Mrs. W.L. London), IV: 517.
Haughton, Charles T., (Capt, Co H, 47th NCST), III: 85.
Haughton, Thomas B., (Chaplain, 50th NCST), III: 202; IV: 617.
Haughton, Thomas H., (Capt, Co A, MacRae's 18th Battalion NCST, Cav), IV: 379, 380.
Hauser, A.J., (Lt, Co D, 1st NCST), I: 120; IV: 722.
Hauser, A.L., (Musician, Mickey's Band, 26th NCST), II: 398, 537, 540.
Hauser, Dr. Robert A., (Capt, ACS, 33rd NCST), II: 537; IV: 474.
Hauser, Robert H., (1st Lt, Co I, 33rd NCST), II: 540.
Havener, D., (Pvt, Co C, 10th NCST, 1st Art & Emgs, Brem-Graham-Williams' Battery, Light Art), V: 568.
Havana, Cuba, V: 339, 386, 416.
Havner, Michael, (Pvt, Co M, 6th Vols/16th NCST), V: 553.
Havner, Philip, (Pvt, Co M, 6th Vols/16th NCST), V: 553.
Haw Creek, N.C., III: 474.
Haw River, N.C., I: 59, 412, 413; III: 200, 700; IV: 32, 60, 352.
Haw's Shop, Va., [Hawes], (and Battle of, 1864), I: 430; II: 101; III: 599, 608, 609.
Hawes, ______, (Sgt, Co F, 10th Vols/20th NCST), II: 118.
Hawes, John R., (Capt, Co E, 8th Vols/18th NCST), II: 16.
Hawfield, J.W., (Pvt, Co F, 49th NCST), V: 564.
Hawkins, A.G., (1st Lt, Co H, 41st NCST, 3rd Cav), II: 771.
Hawkins, A., (Pvt, Co G, 61st Va.), V: 569.
Hawkins, Charles C., (Pvt, Co G, 6th Vols/16th NCST), IV: 216; V: 552.
Hawkins, Hiram, (Col, 5th Ky.), III: 435.
Hawkins, J.B., (Lt, Co C, 25th NCST), II: 299.
Hawkins, J.F., (Musician, 3rd Vols/13th NCST), V: 549.
Hawkins, J.P., (Musician, 3rd Vols/13th NCST), V: 549.
Hawkins, J.W., (Pvt, Co E, 4th NCST), V: 488.
Hawkins, James B, (Pvt, Co I, 34th NCST), V: 556.
Hawkins, John, (Pvt, Co F, 43rd NCST), V: 498.
Hawkins, Rush Christopher, (Brig Gen, USA; One of the several Federal soldiers guilty of war crimes and atrocities in North Carolina such as the burning and pillaging of several cities and towns), V: 50.
Hawkins, Dr. W.J., (President of Raleigh and Gaston Railroad), I: 534; V: 278, 279.
Hawkinsville, Va., III: 623.
Hawks, Rev. Dr. ______, (Resident of New Bern, Father of F.T. Hawks), IV: 425.
Hawks, Francis T., (1st Lt, Co A, 2nd Corps Engineers; AAG, Branch-Lane's Brigade), IV: 425, 428, 431, 472.
Hawley, Ransom G., (Pvt, Co H, 10th Vols/20th NCST), II: 120.
Hawn, E.L., (Pvt, Co A, 2nd Vols/12th NCST), V: 506.
Haws, ______, (Governor of Kentucky), II: 730.
Haws, E., (Pvt, Co G, 10th Vols/20th NCST), V: 509.
Hawse, Ruben J.T., (Lt, Co A, 51st NCST), III: 218.

Haxall's Landing, (James River, Va.), III: 603.
Hay Market, Va., II: 87; III: 582, 583.
Hayden, ______, (Deserter, Outlaw, Yankee), III: 519.
Hayden, J.P., (Pvt, Co I, 45th NCST), V: 500.
Hayden, Tom, (Pvt, Co G, 6th Vols/16th NCST), IV: 192.
Hayes, ______, (Capt, Stoneman's Cav, USA), I: 65.
Hayes, ______, (Pvt, 24th Mi.), II: 369.
Hayes, Abner B., (Lt, Co F, 26th NCST), II: 397.
Hayes, Caleb M., (4th Sgt, Co C, 52nd NCST), III: 223.
Hayes, George W., (Capt, Co A, 9th Vols/19th NCST, 3rd Cav), II: 79, 324.
Hayes, James W., (2nd Lt, Co H, 33rd NCST), II: 540.
Hayes, John S., (Capt, Co G, 25th NCST), II: 292.
Hayes, John W., (Lt, Co H, 9th NCST, 1st Cav), I: 486.
Hayes, Joesph G., (1st Lt, Co F, 5th NCST), I: 288.
Hayes, Joseph L., (Lt, Co F, 5th NCST), I: 120.
Hayes, Julius J., (Pvt, Co D, 68th NCST), III: 715.
Hayes, Rutherford B., (President, U.S.), III: 745.
Hayes, W.A., (Pvt, Co G, 27th NCST), II: 455, 462.
Haymen, S. Layne, (Lt, Co E, 7th NCST), I: 383.
Haymond's Landing, (Roanoke Island), II: 510; V: 60.
Haymount, (Hill in Fayetteville which was the site of the Fayetteville Arsenal), IV: 293, 294.
Hayne, H., (Pvt, Co I, 8th Vols/18th NCST), II: 64.
Haynes, D.A., (Pvt, Co I, 1st Vols/11th NCST), V: 531.
Haynes, Albert Sidney, (Maj, 1st Vols/11th NCST), I: 114, 119, 585; IV: 707; V: 153.
Haynes, J.M., (Pvt, Co I, 3rd Vols/13th NCST), V: 551.
Haynes, John C., (Pvt, Co F, 34th NCST), V: 555.
Haynes, Joseph E., (Adjt, 62nd NCST), III: 515.
Haynes, L.F., (2nd Lt, Co B, 38th NCST), II: 675, 678.
Haynes, P.H., (Pvt, Co E, 16th Battalion/75th NCST, 7th Cav), V: 660.
Haynes, P.P., (Pvt, Co G, 4th NCST), I: 233.
Haynes, T.F., (Pvt, Co I, 28th NCST), V: 543.
Haynes, W.G., (1st Lt, Co E, 77th NCST, 7th Senior Reserves), IV: 100.
Haynes, W.G., (Pvt, Co E, 16th Battalion/75th NCST, 7th Cav), V: 660.
Haynesville, N.C., III: 684.
Haynesville, Tenn., (See: Johnson City).
Hays, A.B., (2nd Lt, Co F, 26th NCST), II: 372, 396, 397.
Hays, Alexander, (Maj Gen, USA), I: 697; III: 580, 581.
Hays, H.H., (Pvt, Co F, 26th NCST), V: 602.
Hays, Harry Thompson, (Maj Gen), I: 319, 357, 359; II: 115; III: 414, 417; IV: 658, 659 768.
Hays, Haunce, (Cpl, Co E, 33rd NCST), II: 539.
Hays, John S., (Maj, Commissary, Walker's Brigade), IV: 503.
Hays, Joseph L., (Lt, Co F, 5th NCST), I: 285.
Hays, W.A., (Pvt, Co G, Musician, 27th NCST), II: 321, 455, 462.

Hays, William, (Pvt, Co D, 68th NCST), III: 715.
Hays, William, (Brig Gen, USA, prisoner at Salisbury), II: 364; IV: 768.
Hayti, V: xviii.
Haywood, Duncan C., (Lt, Co E, 7th NCST), I: 368, 369; III: 111.
Haywood, Dr. E., Burke, (Surg, Raliegh General Hospital), IV: 623, 625, 626, 627, 629; V: 577, 649.
Haywood, Ed. Graham, (Col, 7th NCST), I: 361, 362, 363, 365,, 366, 367, 368, 369, 371, 377, 386; II: 313, 317, 542; IV: 472.
Haywood, Fab J., (Lt, Adjt, 5th NCST), I: 286, 287; IV: 700, 707.
Haywood, Moses, (2nd Lt, Co H, 44th NCST), III: 23.
Haywood, S.S., (Pvt, Co K, 45th NCST), V: 501.
Haywood, W.A, (Pvt, Co G, 2nd Battalion NCST), V: 495.
Haywood, W.H., (Senator, Father of Lt William H. Haywood), III: 111.
Haywood, William H., (Lt, Co K, 7th NCST), I: 383; III: 111.
Haywood County, N.C., II: 493, 723; III: 516, 517, 524, 525, 662, 729, 730, 731, 733, 758, 759; IV: 113, 381, 481, 619; V: 655.
Hazel Grove, (nr Chancellorsville, Va.), II: 476.
Hazel River, Va., (aka Deep Run, Hazel Run), I: 309, 570; II: 29, 87, 133; III: 407, 408, 578, 584; IV: 161, 169, 170.
Hazell, J.C., (Pvt, Co K, 6th NCST), V: 514.
Hazell, W.H., (Pvt, Co K, 6th NCST), V: 514.
Hazelle, M.C., (Capt, Co D, 4th NCST), I: 232.
Head, John W., (Pvt, Co A, 25th NCST), V: 561.
Headen, William J., (2nd Lt, Co E, 26th NCST), II: 304, 396.
Headley, P.D., (Capt, Co L, 11th Vols/21st NCST; Co. B, 1st Battalion NCST), IV: 225.
Headrick, W.H., (Pvt, Co H, 60th NCST), III: 482.
Hearne, James D., (1st Lt, Co I, 52nd NCST), III: 225.
Heath, J.F., [James F.], (2nd Lt, Co F, 67th NCST, Whitford's), IV: 723.
Heath, J.J.F., (Cpl, Co I, 8th Vols/18th NCST), II: 64; V: 540.
Heath, J.W., (Pvt, Co I, 12th Vols/22nd NCST), V: 554.
Heath's Mills, N.C., III: 679.
Heaton, D., (Col, USA, U.S. Treasury Department), I: 33.
Heavner, Peter, (Teamster, Co E, 34th NCST; Detailed, Medical Purveyor's Department), V: 572.
Hebert, Louis, (Brig Gen), II: 756; IV: 267, 268; V: 239.
Hebert, Paul O., (Past Governor of Louisiana, Brig Gen), IV: 40, 41.
Heddin, B.F., (Pvt, Co G, 48th NCST), V: 526.
Hedgecock, E.T., (Pvt, Co G, 2nd Battalion NCST), V: 495.
Hedgecock, J.C., (Capt, Co A, 11th Vols/21st NCST), II: 132; IV: 230.
Hedgeman River, (Upper Rappahonnock River, Va.), III: 578.
Hedgepeth, A.W., (Pvt, Co G, 27th NCST), II: 462.
Hedger, Rev. B.H., (Yankee), IV: 602.
Hedgeville, Va., [Hedgersville], I: 373; II: 34, 555, 657.
Hedgpeth, A., (Pvt, Co H, 52nd NCST), V: 536.
Hedrick, Alfred M., (3rd Sgt, Co F, 38th NCST), V: 557.

Hedrick, E.M., (Lt, Co H, 58th NCST), III: 433.
Hedrick, John C., (Pvt, Co F, 38th NCST), V: 557.
Hedrick, John J., (Maj, Cape Fear Minute Men, N.C. Militia; Capt, Co C, Starr's 13th Battalion NCST, Light Art; Maj, Engineering Officer; Col, 40th NCST, 3rd Art, Hvy), II: 631, 745, 755, 762; IV: 47, 342, 344, 361, 413, 414, 416, 419, 423; V: 24, 26.
Hedrick, W.H., (Pvt, Co H, Battalion/60th NCST), III: 482.
Hedspeth, Wesley, (Capt, Co E, 13th Vols/23rd NCST), II: 224, 231.
Heebner, Charles, (Drum Major, 10th Vols/20th NCST), II: 113.
Heflin, H.H., (Musician, 46th NCST), V: 524.
Heflin, Jesse F., (Capt, Co E, 46th NCST), III: 81.
Heflin, R.L., [J.R.], (Capt, Co E, 46th NCST), III: 81; V: 519.
Heffner, D., (Pvt, Co C, 28th NCST), V: 541.
Heffner, G., (Pvt, Co C, 28th NCST), V: 541.
Heffner, S., (Pvt, Co C, 28th NCST), V: 541.
Hefner, F.L., (Pvt, Co H, 37th NCST), V: 546.
Hefner, W.R., (Pvt, Co F, 37th NCST), V: 546.
Hege, Amos, (Pvt, Co B, 1st Battalion NCST), V: 504.
Heggie, A., (2nd Cpl, Co H, 3rd Vols/13th NCST), V: 551.
Heggie, S., (4th Cpl, Co H, 3rd Vols/13th NCST), V: 551.
Heggie, W.J., (Pvt, Co H, 3rd Vols/13th NCST), V: 551.
Heidelburg, Pa., [Heidelberg], I: 311; IV: 255.
Heidelburg Road, [Heidlerburg], (nr Gettysburg, Pa.), I: 633; II: 235.
Height, R., (Sgt, Co E, 9th NCST, 1st Cav), V: 657.
Heilig, John, (Pvt, Co I, 12th Vols/22nd NCST), V: 554.
Heilig, P.A., (Pvt, Co K, 4th NCST), I: 277.
Heinistitle, Hamilton, (Pvt, Co A, 38th NCST), V: 556.
Heintzelman, Samuel Peter, (Maj Gen, USA), II: 203; V: 31.
Heitman, A.M., (Capt, Co A, 6th Battalion Junior Reserves; Co C, 70th NCST, 1st Junior Reserves) IV: 10, 13.
Heitman, J.F., (Capt, Co H, 48th NCST), III: 117.
Helan, W.O., (Pvt, Co A, 12th Vols/22nd NCST), V: 553.
Helena, Ark., (and Battle of, 1863), IV: 36.
Hell Gate, N.Y., V: 439.
Hellard, Jesse, (2nd Lt, Co K, 50th NCST), III: 203.
Hellen, Joseph F., (Lt, Co K, 2nd NCST), I: 163.
Hellen, Joseph F., (2nd Lt, Co H, 40th NCST, 3rd Art, Hvy), II: 747.
Hellers, John, (Sgt, Co B, 4th NCST), I: 232.
Helm, Benjamin Hardin, (Brig Gen), III: 490.
Helms, A.C., (Pvt, Co D, 37th NCST), V: 545.
Helms, A.M., (Pvt, Co E, 30th NCST), V: 492.
Helms, C.L., (Pvt, Co D, 37th NCST), V: 545.
Helms, Calvin, (Pvt, Co B, 5th Vols/15th NCST), V: 521.
Helms, M., (Pvt, Co I, 53rd NCST), V: 502.
Helms, Salathiel, (Pvt, Co A, 48th NCST), V: 526.

Helms, W.M., (Pvt, Co B, 43rd NCST), V: 497.
Helsabeck, E.J., (Pvt, Co F, 11th Vols/21st NCST), V: 514.
Helton, M.L., (Lt, Co F, 13th Vols/23rd NCST), II: 185; IV: 701, 707.
Hemphill, J.Y., (2nd Sgt, Co A, Millard's 9th/20th Battalion Junior Reserves), IV: 396.
Hemphill, Lee, (Lt, Co G, 6th Vols/16th NCST), IV: 153.
Hengan, J.E., (Cpl, Co F, 49th NCST), V: 564.
Henderson, ______, (Lt Col, Wise's Staff), V: 59.
Henderson, ______, (Col, Cumming's Ga. Brigade), III: 197, 443.
Henderson, ______, (3rd Ass't Engineer, Sea Bird), V: 309.
Henderson, Dr. C.A., (Ass't Surg, 6th NCST), IV: 632.
Henderson, E., (Pvt, Co C, 8th Vols/18th NCST; Detailed, Invalid Battalion), V: 571.
Henderson, F., (Lt, 37th NCST), IV: 707.
Henderson, Dr. Francis M., (Ass't Surg, 1st. N.C. General Hospital, Petersburg, Va.), IV: 623, 630.
Henderson, J.M., (Pvt, Co I, 3rd Vols/13th NCST), V: 551.
Henderson, J.W., (Pvt, Co H, 49th NCST), V: 565.
Henderson, John, (Capt), III: 760.
Henderson, Leonard A., (Capt, Co F, 8th NCST), I: 405; V: 203, 204.
Henderson, L.J., (2nd Lt, Co G, 3rd NCST), IV: 722.
Henderson, Robert Miller, (Brig Gen, USA), I: 670.
Henderson, Thomas B., (1st Lt, Co H, 41st NCST, 3rd Cav), II: 771; IV: 722.
Henderson, W.J., (Pvt, Co H, 49th NCST), V: 565.
Henderson, N.C., II: 238; III: 324, 536, 591; IV: 612.
Henderson County, N.C., III: 659, 660, 662, 665, 667, 668; IV: 109, 115, 381, 397, 481.
Henderson Military Institute, II: 238.
Hendersonville, N.C., III: 670, 683.
Hendren, A.N., (1st Sgt, Co F, 3rd Vols/13th NCST), V: 550.
Hendrick, H., (Pvt, Co F, 25th NCST), V: 561.
Hendrick, Henry, (Pvt, Co G, 25th NCST), V: 561.
Hendrick, J., [Hendrix, N.], (Pvt, Co K, 48th NCST), V: 526.
Hendrick, W.F., (Pvt, Co A, 2nd Vols/12th NCST), V: 506.
Hendricks, J.F., (Pvt, Co H, 37th NCST), V: 546.
Hendricks, John H., (Pvt, Co H, 34th NCST), V: 556.
Hendrix, Lee, (Pvt, Co B, 1st Battalion NCST), V: 504.
Hendrix, William, (3rd Lt, Co K, 42nd NCST), II: 791.
Henkel, D.S., (Chaplain, 28th NCST), II: 466; IV: 473, 611.
Henkle, C., (Pvt, Co G, 57th NCST), V: 517.
Henley, Green, (Pvt, Co I, 52nd NCST), V: 536.
Henley, J., (Pvt, Co B, 35th NCST), V: 562.
Henley, J.T., (Pvt, Co K, 26th NCST), V: 532.
Henline, J.H., (Pvt, Co B, 54th NCST), V: 516.
Henly, ______, [Henley],(2nd Lt, Co B, Avery's 17th Battalion NCST), IV: 377; V: 287, 294.
Hennesy, R.J., (3rd Sgt, Co B, 1st Vols/11th NCST), V: 530.
Henningsen, ______, (Brig Gen), V: 307.
Henrahan, W.S., (Lt, Co H, 9th NCST, 1st Cav), I: 486.

Henrico Court House, Va., (and Battle of, 1864), II: 8.
Henry, Dr. A.F., (Ass't Surg, 16th Battalion/75th NCST, 7th Cav), IV: 643.
Henry, E.F., (Pvt, Co I, 43rd NCST), V: 499.
Henry, J.M., (Pvt, Co I, 43rd NCST), V: 499.
Henry, James L., (Jr 2nd Lt, Co K, 26th NCST; Lt, Co G; Adjt, 9th NCST, 1st Ca.; Capt, AAG, Ransom's Brigade; Lt Col 14th Battalion, 79th NCST, 8th Cav), I: 486; II: 372, 397; IV: 113, 114, 569.
Henry, John, (Pvt, Co B, 59th NCST, 4th Cav), V: 659.
Henry, R.M., (Capt, Co D, 62nd NCST), III: 515.
Henry, William, (1st Lt, Co 1, West's Battalion, Cav), IV: 111.
Henry County, Va., IV: 219.
Henry House, (Manassas, Va.), I: 298, 299, 306, 341; V: 585.
Henshaw, W.T., (Pvt, Co B, 1st Battalion NCST), V: 504.
Hensley, A., (Pvt, Co H, 11th Vols/21st NCST), V: 513.
Hensley, H.T., (Pvt, Co A, 3rd Vols/13th NCST), V: 549.
Hensley, John A., (Ordnance Sgt, 58th NCST), III: 432.
Hensley, S.R., (Adjt, 6th Vols/16th NCST), V: 547.
Hensley, W.M., (Pvt, Co C, 21st Ga.), V: 194.
Henson, A., (Pvt, Co I, 53rd NCST), V: 502.
Henson, Thomas G., (Capt, Co K, 61st NCST), III: 504.
Henson, William T., (Pvt, Co I, 25th NCST), V: 562.
Herald, Furney, (Pvt, Co C, 2nd NCST), I: 176.
Heriot, R.L., (Cadet, Hillsboro Military Academy Battalion), V: 643.
Heritage, A.D., (Pvt, Co I, 14th Vols/24th NCST), V: 560.
Heritage, Furnifold G., (Lt, Co F, 2nd NCST), I: 161, 162.
Herman, J.L., (Pvt, Co A, 2nd Vols/12th NCST), V: 506.
Hermatage, (nr Wilmington), IV: 268.
Hermon, D.M., (Cpl, Co C, 28th NCST), V: 541.
Hermon, J.S., (Pvt, Co C, 28th NCST), V: 541.
Hermon, P.J., (Sgt, Co C, 28th NCST), V: 541.
Herndon, Benjamin, (Pvt, Co E, 5th NCST), I: 292; V: 505.
Herndon, E., (Pvt, Co I, 6th NCST), V: 513.
Herndon, E.W., [E.N.], (Maj, QM, Branch-Lane's Brigade), IV: 472; V: 537.
Herndon, H., (Sgt Maj, 58th NCST), III: 432.
Herndon, J.M., (Pvt, Co E, 56th NCST), V: 566.
Herndon, M.C., (Pvt, Co C, 6th NCST), V: 512.
Heroine, A North Carolina, V: 19.
Herren, Arch, (N.C. Militia), III: 518.
Herring, ______, (Herring's Company, 11th Battalion NCST), IV: 338.
Herring, Calvin, (Maj, 27th NCST), II: 457, 461.
Herring, Isaiah, (2nd Lt, Co I, 46th NCST), III: 82.
Herring, John D., (2nd Lt, Co I, 46th NCST), III: 82.
Herring, S.B., (Pvt, Co C, Color-bearer, 38th NCST), II: 676.
Herring, Robert, (Signal Officer, Giraffe), V: 406.
Herring, Thomas J., (Capt, Co B, 51st NCST), III: 218.

Herring, William A., (Capt, Co G, 40th NCST, 3rd Art, Hvy), II: 746.
Herring Creek, Va., I: 431; III: 609.
Herrington, Frank, (Fayetteville and Harper's Ferry Arsenals), IV: 298.
Herrington, Herbert, (Fayetteville and Harper's Ferry Arsenals), IV: 298.
Herrington, Hiram, (Fayetteville and Harper's Ferry Arsenals), IV: 298.
Herrington, James A., (2nd Lt, Co I, 4th NCST), I: 233.
Herrington, James C., (Lt, Co I, 4th NCST), V: 664.
Herrington, Orrie, (Fayetteville and Harper's Ferry Arsenals), IV: 298.
Herrold, William, (Pvt, Co D, 11th Vols/21st NCST), V: 514.
Herron, G.T., (Pvt, Co A, 1st Vols/11th NCST), V: 530.
Hertford, N.C., II: 80; IV: 355; V: 283, 284.
Hertford County, N.C., III: 457, 713, 715, 717; IV: 262, 339, 483, 607; V: 271.
Hesse, M.A., (Sgt, Co K, 6th NCST), V: 513.
Hester, Joseph, (2nd Lt, Co D, 78th NCST, 8th Senior Reserves), IV: 107.
Hester, Robert, (Pvt, Co I, 3rd Vols/13th NCST), V: 510.
Hester, W.H., (Sgt, Co K, 11th Vols/21st NCST), V: 515.
Heth, Henry "Harry," (Maj Gen), I: 378, 381, 547, 589, 592, 593; II: 39, 41, 173, 341, 345, 346, 357, 376, 381, 388, 389, 394, 441, 461, 480, 561, 568, 689; III: 96, 97, 121, 236, 237, 248, 297, 299, 302, 311, 376, 627, 629; IV: 182, 184, 185, 468, 510, 559, 560, 562; V: 96, 103, 115, 116, 118, 120, 130, 135, 138, 587.
Hevener, George W., (Pvt, Co G, 57th NCST), V: 517.
Hewett, ______, (Englishman, Capt, Royal Navy; Blockade Runner), V: 413.
Hewett, John, (Fayetteville and Harper's Ferry Arsenals), IV: 298.
Hewett, Otho, (Fayetteville and Harper's Ferry Arsenals), IV: 298.
Hewett, William, (Fayetteville and Harper's Ferry Arsenals), IV: 298.
Heye, L.G., (Pvt, Co E, Beale's 10th Va., Cav, N.C. company), V: 569.
Heyer, Charles, (Musician, 4th NCST), I: 234; V: 488.
Hiawassee River, N.C., III: 757.
Hibriten Mountain, N.C., IV: 375.
Hickerson, Charles N., II: 653; IV: 474.
Hickerson, Dr. James, (Surg, 37th NCST), II: 653; IV: 474, 637.
Hickford, Va., IV: 388.
Hickman, A.H., (Lt, 54th NCST), IV: 707.
Hickory, N.C., II: 627; III: 445.
Hickory Road, (Petersburg to Appomattox River, Va.), V: 250.
Hickory Nut Gap, N.C., III: 670; V: 654.
Hicks, A.B., (Lt), IV: 420.
Hicks, A.D., (Lt, 28th NCST), IV: 420, 701, 707.
Hicks, Albert R., (Capt, Co A, 5th Battalion Junior Reserves; Co A, 71st NCST, 2nd Junior Reserves), IV: 25, 26, 28.
Hicks, Chesley, (2nd Lt, Co D, 77th NCST, 7th Senior Reserves), IV: 100.
Hicks, Daniel T., (Pvt, Co A, 4th Vols/14th NCST), V: 489.

Hicks, Elkanah, (Pvt, Co B, 6th Battalion/60th NCST), III: 482.
Hicks, F.G., (2nd Lt, Co B, 49th NCST), I: 734.
Hicks, F.Y., (2nd Lt, Co B, 49th NCST), IV: 701, 707.
Hicks, Frank, (Pvt, Co M, 11th Vols/21st NCST), V: 515.
Hicks, J.C., (Co G, 2nd Vols/12th NCST), I: 630.
Hicks, James, (Pvt, Co D, 56th NCST), III: 355.
Hicks, John, (Pvt, Co I, 45th NCST), V: 500.
Hicks, John, (Pvt, Co G, 46th NCST), V: 525.
Hicks, John, (Pvt, Co F, 28th NCST), V: 542.
Hicks, Lewis T., [Louis], (Capt, Co E, 10th Vols/20th NCST), II: 115, 125; IV: 701, 708.
Hicks, R.J., (Pvt, Co F, 55th NCST), V: 528.
Hicks, Dr. Robert I., [Robert J.], (Surg, 13th Vols./23rd NCST; Surg, Garland's Brigade; Senior Surg, Johnston's Brigade), II: 190, 198, 267; IV: 521, 635, 708; V: 503.
Hicks, W.D., (Cpl, Co C, 6th NCST), V: 512.
Hicks' Ford, (Meherrin River, Va.), IV: 44.
Hicks' Run, Va., IV: 388, 390.
Hicksford, Va., I: 321; III: 633, 634.
Higerson, Dr. James, (Surg, 37th NCST), II: 653.
Higginbotham, N.W., (Conscript; Detailed, Invalid Battalion), V: 571.
Higginbotham, Dr. Edward G., (Surg, 33rd NCST; Surg., Branch-Lane's Brigade), II: 537; IV: 472, 474, 637, 644.
Higgins, J.M., (Capt, Co B, 49th NCST), I: 734; III: 152.
Higgins, J.M., (2nd Lt, Co B, 12th Vols/22nd NCST), II: 164, 165.
Higgins, Isaac C., (Lt, Co I, 61st NCST), III: 504, 505.
Higgins, Israel, (Pvt, Co G, 6th Vols/16th NCST), IV: 211.
Higgins, Wiley F., (ACS, 67th NCST), III: 703.
Higgs, George A., (Capt, Co G, 41st NCST, 3rd Cav), II: 771.
Higgs, James, [James A.], (Pvt, Co G, 41st NCST, 3rd Cav), I: 482.
High, H., (Pvt, Co D, 47th NCST), V: 535.
High Bridge, (Appomattox River, Va.), I: 330, 780; II: 62, 402; III: 252, 344, 470; IV: 526; V: 251.
High Point, N.C., I: 5, 7, 9, 112, 386; II: 519, 582, 653, 804; III: 454, 514, 690, 700; IV: 32, 98, 394, 593.
"High Water Mark," V: 605.
Hight, A.C., (2nd Lt, Co G, 5th Vols/15th NCST), I: 735.
Highsmith, L.W., (4th Sgt, Co I, 46th NCST), V: 525.
Highsmith, Robert C., (2nd Lt, Co A, 41st NCST, 3rd Cav), II: 770.
Highley, Gilbert P., [Higley], (2nd Lt, Co F, 51st NCST), III: 212, 219; IV: 723.
Hildebrand, D.A., (Cpl, Co D, 6th NCST), V: 512.
Hildesheimer, Joseph, (Capt, 4th Regt Home Guard; AQM, 2nd Regt 3rd Class, Home Guard), IV: 654; V: 630, 631.
Hill, Albert, A., (Capt, Co G, 7th NCST; Maj, Hill's 22nd Battalion Senior Reserves; Lt Col, 48th NCST), I: 380; III: 113, 117, 123; IV: 6, 398; V: 520.
Hill, Atherton B., (Capt, Co G, 41st NCST, 3rd Cav), II: 497, 771; IV: 379.

Hill, Ambrose Powell, (Lt Gen, 3rd Corps), I: 139, 146, 181, 193, 252, 278, 318, 353, 367, 368, 374, 379, 435, 543, 544, 545, 548, 549, 592, 593, 601, 613, 614, 615, 617, 623, 632, 633, 672, 755, 757, 758, 760, 761, 762, 763, 765; II: 24, 25, 31, 34, 37, 38, 41, 45, 51, 59, 61, 73, 156, 168, 173, 174, 209, 234, 350, 375, 379, 381, 382, 383, 387, 388, 441, 447, 448, 471, 474, 477, 481, 484, 546, 550, 553, 554, 555, 557, 559, 560, 561, 562, 563, 577, 583, 656, 659, 660, 662, 680, 681, 686, 687, 688, 690, 693, 694, 782; III: 27, 30, 72, 92, 143, 243, 244, 304, 332, 367, 413, 556, 560, 620, 621, 632, 731; IV: 43, 155, 157, 164, 165, 166, 175, 179, 180, 184, 185, 187, 195, 212, 465, 467, 477, 505, 510, 551, 562, 567; V: viii, 73, 79, 93, 94, 95, 96, 97, 98, 99, 116, 121, 122, 138, 207, 208.

Hill, Charles W., (Col, USA, Cmdr of Johnson's Island Prison), IV: 681, 692, 693.

Hill, Daniel Harvey, (Maj Gen/Lt Gen: Some authorities do not credit Hill with the higher rank.), I: xi, xii, 40, 77, 78, 83, 84, 85, 93, 94, 95, 96, 98, 100, 101, 103, 105, 106, 107, 108, 111, 112, 115, 117, 121, 124, 126, 138, 139, 141, 142, 165, 166, 167, 168, 174, 180, 181, 185, 186, 187, 188, 189, 242, 246, 248, 249, 283, 286, 293, 347, 350, 379, 494, 522, 539, 540, 541, 555, 573, 575, 578, 588, 610, 613, 614, 615, 618, 619, 624, 626, 628, 643, 657, 658, 659, 660, 693, 696, 733, 742; II: 113, 115, 198, 199, 209, 211, 213, 214, 217, 218, 219, 220, 221, 223, 227, 308, 334, 339, 340, 407, 461, 498, 499, 501, 502, 504, 523, 524, 547, 548, 555, 600, 612, 613, 650, 655, 776, 793, 797; III: 4, 19, 40, 87, 128, 167, 170, 233, 255, 324, 328, 329, 330, 350, 354, 355, 554, 555; IV: 19, 54, 58, 76, 221, 252, 253, 346, 350, 357, 361, 376,418, 444, 445, 457, 514, 529, 530, 531, 537, 544, 547, 557, 558; V: 15, 57, 72, 78, 590, 637, 645, 646, 665.

Hill, Prof. Daniel Harvey, Jr., (Son of Maj Gen D.H. Hill, Professor at NCSU), I: 342; II: 573; III: 327.

Hill, G.H., (Maj, 7th Vols/17th NCST), II: 509.

Hill, George, (Pvt, Co A, 67th NCST), III: 710.

Hill, H.D., (Pvt, Co F, 32nd NCST), V: 496.

Hill, Rev. Dr. H.G., (Chaplain, 3rd Vols/13th NCST), IV: 607.

Hill, Hugo A., (1st Lt, Co A, 33rd NCST), II: 538, 578.

Hill, J.C., (Lt, Co A, 52nd NCST), III: 229.

Hill, J.E., (2nd Lt, Co H, 13th Vols/23rd NCST), II: 187.

Hill, J.L., (Pvt, Co E, 28th NCST), V: 542.

Hill, J.P., (Pvt, Co.A, 3rd NCST), V: 487.

Hill, J.R., (Pvt, Co A, 3rd NCST), V: 487.

Hill, J.R., (Pvt, Co E, 2nd Vols/12th NCST), V: 507.

Hill, Rev. Jacob, (Iredell County), IV: 614.

Hill, James A., (2nd Lt, Co E, 53rd NCST), III: 262.

Hill, James, [James H.], (Maj, AAG to Whiting), II: 648; V: 234, 240.

Hill, John, (Pilot, Sirene), V: 357, 404.

Hill, John F., (Capt, Co E, 34th NCST), II: 581.

Hill, Dr. John F., (Surg, Goldsboro General Hospital; Capt, Co , 73rd NCST, 4th Senior Reserves), IV: 66, 625, 626.

Hill, John H., (2nd Lt, Co H, 40th NCST, 3rd Art, Hvy), II: 747, 763, 765.
Hill, Joseph C., (2nd Sgt, Co A, 52nd NCST), III: 223.
Hill, Joshua B., (Orderly Sgt, 41st NCST, 3rd Cav), II: 772, 785, 786, 787; IV: 582.
Hill, Junius L., (Lt Col, 7th NCST), I: 361, 365, 374, 377; IV: 467, 472; V: 11.
Hill, Dr. Lauriston H., (Surg, 53rd NCST), III: 261; IV: 640.
Hill, M.T., (Pvt, Co I, 37th NCST), V: 546.
Hill, Marcus, (Pvt, Co E, 43rd NCST), V: 498.
Hill, Robert A., (Capt, Co E, 53rd NCST), III: 262.
Hill, Robert C., (Col, 48th NCST), III: 114, 115, 117, 123; IV: 501, 504; V: 10.
Hill, S.V., [Samuel B.], (2nd Lt, Co H, 6th NCST), IV: 707.
Hill, Rev. Samuel J., (Chaplain, 42nd NCST), II: 789, 805; IV: 614.
Hill, Samuel P., IV: 700.
Hill, Sion, (Pvt, Co G, 46th NCST), V: 525.
Hill, T.C., (AQMS, 3rd Vols/13th NCST), V: 549.
Hill, Dr. Thomas, (Surg, 40th NCST, 3rd Art, Hvy), II: 745; IV: 638.
Hill, Thomas, (Pvt, Co A, 10th NCST, 1st Art & Engs, Ramseur-Manly's Battery, Light Art), I: 556, 559.
Hill, Dr. Thomas H., (Surgeon-in-Chief, N.C. Reserves; Surg, Raleigh General Hospital #2), IV: 7, 37, 625, 626.
Hill, W.D., (Pvt, Co F, 47th NCST), V: 535.
Hill, W.H., (Sgt, Co E, 47th NCST), V: 535.
Hill, W.J., (Lt Col, 5th NCST), I: 281, 287, 289; IV: 707.
Hill, W.R., (Cpl, Co D, Millard's 9th/20th Battalion Junior Reserves), IV: 393.
Hill, William, (Capt, ACS, 53rd NCST), III: 261.
Hill, William, (Pvt, Co H, 48th NCST), V: 526.
Hill, William P., (Capt, Co H, 13th Vols./23rd NCST; AAG Garland's Brigade), I: 77; II: 186; IV: 521.
Hill's Ferry, (Roanoke River, Va.), III: 321; IV: 417.
Hill's Point, N.C., III: 172, 173; IV: 74.
Hillard, J., (Sgt, Co C, 2nd Vols/12th NCST), V: 506.
Hillard, A., (2nd Cpl, Co E, 44th NCST), V: 533.
Hilliard, J.H., (Capt, Co B, 4th NCST), I: 232.
Hilliard, Louis, (ACS, 2nd NCST), I: 157.
Hilliard, N.B., (1st Lt, Co E, 44th NCST), III: 23.
Hilliard, Dr. William L., (Surg, 9th NCST, 1st Cav), I: 485; IV: 633.
Hillsboro, N.C., I: 55, 57, 59, 60, 62, 65; III: 403; IV: 32; V: 638, 639, 643.
Hillsboro, Va., II: 248, 432, 601.
Hillsboro Military Academy, (aka Tew's Military Academy), I: 159, 162, 168, 338; II: 167, 598; IV: 10; V: 637-644.
Hilton, ______, (Scout for Hampton), I: 133.
Hilton Head Island, S.C., (Depot and Prison, USA), II: 757; III: 183, 186; IV: 327, 715; V: 384, 620.
Hind, Benjamin, (Hospital Steward, 26th NCST), II: 307, 371, 396.
Hindman, Thomas Carmichael, (Maj Gen), II: 717.

Hines, A.A., (1st Lt, Co G, 38th NCST), V: 549.
Hines, Amos J., (Capt, Co G, 8th NCST), I: 404.
Hines, Benjamin, (Hospital Steward, 26th NCST), V: 531.
Hines, E.D., (Sgt, Co I, 63rd NCST, 5th Cav), III: 589.
Hines, George, (Cpl, Co B, 28th NCST), V: 541.
Hines, George S., (Ordnance Sgt, 47th NCST), V: 534.
Hines, Dr. Harvey L., (Ass't Surg, 1st N.C. General Hospital, Petersburg, Va.), IV: 623, 630.
Hines, Henry, (2nd Lt, Co E, 53rd NCST), III: 262.
Hines, J.B., (Pvt, Co B, 28th NCST), V: 541.
Hines, J.C., (2nd Lt, Co G, 63rd NCST, 5th Cav), III: 589; IV: 723.
Hines, J.J., (Chaplain, 11th Vols/21st NCST), IV: 609.
Hines, Dr. J.M., (Capt, Co K, 45th NCST), III: 36.
Hines, J.S., (Maj, 1st NCST), I: 134, 136, 140.
Hines, J.W., (Pvt, Co C, 5th NCST), I: 291.
Hines, John S., (Capt, AQM, 9th Vols/19th NCST, 2nd Cav; Capt, Cav, MacRae's 18th Battalion NCST, Cav), II: 79; IV: 379, 381.
Hines, M.M., (2nd Lt, Co B, 13th Vols/23rd NCST), I: 120; II: 183.
Hines, Peter E., (Surg, 1st Vols, "Bethel"; Medical Director Department of Petersburg; Medical Director of N.C. General Hospitals), I: 77, 117; IV: 623, 625, 627, 628, 629, 631; V: 577, 649.
Hines, Samuel H., (Capt, Co I, 45th NCST), IV: 721.
Hines, Samuel W., (Pvt, Co G, 38th NCST), V: 557.
Hines, W.R., (2nd Lt, Co D, 5th Battalion Junior Reserves; Co E, 71st NCST, 2nd Junior Reserves), IV: 28.
Hines' Mill, N.C., III: 507.
Hinkle, John L., (Pvt, Co C, 10th NCST, 1st Art & Emgs, Brem-Graham-Williams' Battery, Light Art), V: 568.
Hinnant, E., (Pvt, Co I, 16th Battalion/75th NCST, 7th Cav), V: 660.
Hinrick, _____, (Resident, Elizabeth City), V: 309.
Hinsdale, Mrs. _____, I: 30.
Hinsdale, John W., (AAG, N.C. Reserves; Col, 72nd NCST, 3rd Junior Reserves), III: 1, 19; IV: 7, 35, 36, 37, 38, 42, 50, 51, 52, 53, 59, 61, 65, 351, 499, 588, 594; V: 650, 677.
Hinson, John W., (2nd Lt, AQM, 43rd NCST), III: 1, 3, 19.
Hinson, Joseph C., (Pvt, Co 34th NCST), V: 534.
Hinson's Mills, Va., (Rappahannock River, Va.), III: 559.
Hinton, _____, (Negro, servant to J.H.W. Hinton), III: 721.
Hinton, A., (Sgt, Co C, 47th NCST), V: 534.
Hinton, H.E., (Capt, 10th Battalion Va., Cav), IV: 403.
Hinton, Henry C., (Pvt, Co E. 38th NCST), V: 557.
Hinton, J.M., (Capt, Co E, 4th Vols/14th NCST), V: 484.
Hinton, James H.W., (Col, 68th NCST), I: 342, 387, 527; III: 681, 713, 718, 721, 722; IV: 11, 17, 757, 768.
Hinton, John, (Pvt, Co B, 6th Battalion/60th NCST), III: 500.
Hinton, Joseph W., (Capt, Adjt, 68th NCST), I: 527; III: 681, 713, 714, 722; IV: 17.

Hinton, Sydney A., (Lt, Co H, 47th NCST), III: 85.
Hinton, W.H., (Pvt, Co G, 13th Vols/23rd NCST), V: 510.
Hinton, William J., (Pvt, Co G, 13th Vols/23rd NCST; Detailed, 2nd Corps Provost Guards), V: 570.
Hipp, John M., (Pvt, Co G, 34th NCST), V: 556.
Hipps, J.A., (Sgt, Co B, 6th Battalion/60th NCST), III: 482.
Historians and Contributors, List of, V: xix-xxvi.
History of the Civil War in East Tennessee, IV: 120.
History of the Gettysburg Memorial Association with an Account of the Battle, III: 41.
Hiwassee River, N.C., IV: 125.
Hix, John, (Pvt, Co G, 26th NCST), V: 532.
Hix's Mill, N.C., V: 289.
Hobart Pasha, (See: A.C.H. Hampden).
Hobbs, Edward S., (Lt, Co G, 7th Vols/17th NCST), II: 7.
Hobbs, James C., (Pvt, Co B, 13th Vols/23rd NCST), V: 509.
Hobbs, William, (Pvt, Co H, 45th NCST), V: 500.
Hobbs' Mill, N.C., IV: 221.
Hobdy's Point, (north side York River, Va.), I: 737.
Hobgood, A., (Sgt, Co I, 13th Vols/23rd NCST), V: 510.
Hobert, ______, (Capt, 7th Wi.), V: 613, 614.
Hobson, ______, (Lt, 6th Battalion/60th NCST), III: 498.
Hobson, Caleb B., (Lt Col, 51st NCST), III: 206, 210, 214, 218; V: 11.
Hobson, Henry, (Sgt, Co H, 63rd NCST, 5th Cav), III: 534, 654.
Hobson, J.W., (Pvt, Co A, 1st Battalion NCST), V: 504.
Hobson, James M., (Capt, Co E, 2nd NCST), I: 161; II: 265; IV: 722.
Hobson, John M., (Lt, Co E, 2nd NCST), I: 161.
Hobson, Richmond P., (Lt, son of James Hobson), I: 161; II: 265.
Hobson, Santiago, (Cousin of W.H. Hobson), III: 586.
Hobson, T.C., (Pvt, Co A, 1st Battalion NCST), V: 504.
Hobson, W.H., (Pvt, Co H, 63rd NCST, 5th Cav), III: 586, 587.
Hockaday, James, (Capt, Co E, 78th NCST, 8th Senior Reserves), IV: 107.
Hockaday, W.L., (Lt, Co B, 10th Battalion NCST, 2nd Hvy Art), IV: 329.
Hocutt, E.R., (Pvt, Co C, 24th NCST), V: 193.
Hodge, Abram, (Pvt, Co D, 10th NCST, 1st Art & Engs, Reilly-Ramsay's Battery, Light Art), I: 574.
Hodge, John W., (Pvt, Co G, 2nd Battalion NCST), V: 495.
Hodges, B.F., (Pvt, Co F, 45th NCST), V: 500.
Hodges, G.C., (Pvt, Co C, 32nd NCST), V: 496.
Hodges, J.D., (Pvt, Co H, 63rd NCST, 5th Cav), III: 587, 588, 589, 654.
Hodges, J.E., [James E.], (Capt, Co B, 32nd NCST), IV: 721.
Hodges, J.F., [James F.], (Capt, Co A, 45th NCST), IV: 700, 708.
Hodges, J.W., (Pvt, Co C, 11th Vols/21st NCST), V: 194.
Hodges, Noel B., (2nd Lt, Co B, 40th NCST, 3rd Art, Hvy), II: 746.
Hodges, William R., (Capt, Co I, 58th NCST), III: 434.
Hodgins, R.W., (Co D, 4th NCST), I: 232.

Hoey, John E., (Adjt, 29th NCST), II: 486, 489.
Hoey, Samuel A., (Capt, Co H, 34th NCST), II: 581.
Hofflin, Marcus, (2nd Lt, Co K; Capt, Co K; Capt, ACS, 4th NCST), I: 230, 231, 234, 269.
Hoffman, _____, (Col, 56th Pa.), III: 279.
Hoffman, Burrell, (Pvt, Co F, 38th NCST), V: 557.
Hoffman, David, (Pvt, Co F, 38th NCST), V: 557.
Hoffman, John, (Pvt, Co E, 59th NCST, 4th Cav), V: 659.
Hoffman, Joseph, (Pvt, Co C, 10th NCST, 1st Art & Engs, Brem-Graham-Williams' Battery, Light Art), V: 568.
Hoffman, L.M., (2nd Lt, Co B, 2nd Battalion Junior Reserves; Co C, 71st NCST, 2nd Junior Reserves), IV: 28.
Hofler, Job, (1st Sgt, Co C, 52nd NCST), III: 223.
Hofler, Peterson, (3rd Cpl, Co C, 52nd NCST), III: 224.
Hofler, William O., (2nd Cpl, Co C, 52nd NCST), III: 223.
Hoge, _____, (Lt, CSN), V: 327, 331.
Hoge, David, (Pvt, Co B, 34th NCST), V: 555.
Hoge, M.R.G., (Son of Rev. Moses D. Hoge), V: 343.
Hoge, Rev. Moses D., (of Richmond, Va.; Passenger on the Advance), V: 337, 341-344 personal account, 362.
Hogg, T.D., (Maj, Chief Commissary, N.C.), I: 17, 37, 48, 51, 56.
Hoggard, H.E., (Capt, Co A, 12th Battalion NCST, Cav), IV: 339.
Hoke, Dr. George M., (Ass't Surg, 1st Battalion NCST), IV: 643.
Hoke, J.B., (Pvt, Co A, 2nd Vols/12th NCST), V: 506.
Hoke, John F., (Col, 13th Vols/23rd NCST, Brig Gen Adjt Gen N.C.; Col, 73rd NCST, 4th Senior Reserves; Col, 2nd Brigade Senior Reserves), I: 4, 5, 18, 124, 125, 126, 127, 561;, II: 188, 190, 198, 201, 202; IV: 6, 66, 67, 440; V: 5, 66, 650.
Hoke, P.C., (Pvt, Co A, 2nd Vols/12th NCST), V: 506.
Hoke, Robert F., (Maj Gen), I: vii, xi, xii, xiv, 8, 48, 78, 111, 113, 114, 115, 116, 117, 118, 127, 309, 310, 357, 398, 496, 526, 558; II: 5, 10, 11, 12, 36, 130, 135, 139, 140, 144, 282, 311, 315, 320, 321, 323, 325, 515, 516, 517, 518, 519, 520, 537, 544, 545, 547, 548, 552, 558, 578, 579, 616, 618, 619, 647, 751, 764, 778, 797, 798, 802; III: 7, 8, 9, 10, 96, 132, 135, 177, 178, 195, 196, 197, 200, 215, 273, 274, 275, 334, 335, 337, 339, 343, 345, 346, 348, 349, 350, 351, 357, 407, 410, 427, 513, 694, 704, 705, 708, 722, 727, 910; IV: 18, 19, 20, 22, 30, 31, 33-34, 54, 58, 59, 84, 85, 166, 199, 222, 237, 241, 242, 268, 361, 379, 393, 427, 428, 429, 473, 474, 488, 496, 525, 526, 528, 531, 534, 535, 537, 541, 542, 543, 544, 545, 546, 573, 574, 575, 593; V: xii, 4, 175, 177, 178, 182, 183, 184, 190, 192, 193, 197, 199, 204, 241, 318, 321, 325, 573, 606, 649.
Hoke, W.A., (Uncle of Joseph W. Alexander, CSN), V: 680.
Hoke, William J., (Col, 38th NCST; Col, Hoke's Brigade Detailed Men), I: 75, 78, 91, 98, 118, 122, 125, 127; II: 676, 677, 679, 681, 687, 690, 691, 692, 693, 694; IV: 129, 133, 155, 176, 180, 400, 440, 551; V: 7.

Hoke's Farewell Address, IV: 32.
Holbroke, William A., (Jr 2nd Lt, Co B, 39th NCST), II: 705.
Holbrooke, Josiah, [Holbrook], (Capt, Co B, 13th Vols./23rd NCST), II: 183.
Holcombe, W.P., (Lt, ADC Robert's Cav Brigade), II: 108, 109; IV: 580.
Holcombe's Legion, III: 231.
Holden, E. Brock, (1st Lt, Co B, 59th NCST, 4th Cav), III: 457, 469.
Holden, J.A., (2nd Lt, Co F, 19th NCST, 2nd Cav), II: 89, 96.
Holden, James P., (Pvt, Co E, 25th NCST), V: 561.
Holden, Joseph W., (Jr 2nd Lt, Co D, 31st NCST), II: 507.
Holden, Richard, (Cpl, Co E, 5th Vols/15th NCST), V: 521.
Holden, Sam, (Pvt, Co E, 48th NCST), V: 526.
Holden, W.W., (Newspaper editor, political agitator, Reconstruction Governor of N.C. In that position he was rightfully seen by many as having sold out the state and her citizens for his own gain. He is widely viewed as a traitor.), I: 65; II: 240, 756; III: 75, 375, 380, 383, 389.
Holden-Kirk War, IV: 371.
Holder, Abram, (Pvt, Co A, 5th NCST), I: 291; V: 504.
Holder, H., (Pvt, Co I, 26th NCST), V: 532.
Holder, J.A., (Sgt, Co A, 28th NCST), V: 540.
Holder, L., (Pvt, Co A, 12th Vols/22 NCST), V: 553.
Holding, Calvin, (Pvt, Co A, 10th NCST, 1st Art & Engs, Ramseur-Manly's Battery, Light Art), I: 559.
Holdsclaw, William, (Pvt, Co I, 49th NCST), V: 565.
"Hole in the Wall Light," V: 450.
Holeman, James, (Pvt, Co A, 46th NCST), V: 524.
Holeman, James A., (Capt, Co A, 14th Vols/24th NCST), II: 271.
Holiday, ______, (Col at Morris Island Prison), III: 590.
Holland, ______, (Col, 107th Illinois), II: 734.
Holland, Daniel, (Pvt, Co B, Bladen Stars, 36th NCST, 2nd Art & Engs, Light Art), II: 632; V: 352.
Holland, E.E., (Capt, Co G, 77th NCST, 7th Senior Reserves), IV: 100.
Holland, Elisha, (Pvt, Co C, 43rd NCST), V: 498.
Holland, Gold G., (Capt, Co H, 28th NCST), II: 475, 480, 483; V: 538.
Holland, Henry, (Pvt, Co A, 6th NCST), V: 512.
Holland, J.F., (Musician, Co A, 30th NCST), V: 491.
Holland, J.H., (Pvt, Co A, 45th NCST), V: 499.
Holland, J.Q., (Capt, Co B, 2nd Battalion Junior Reserves; Co C, 71st NCST, 2nd Junior Reserves), IV: 25, 28.
Holland, James R., (Sgt, Co H; AQMS, 49th NCST), III: 125; V: 564.
Holland, Jesse, (2nd Lt, Co C, 66th NCST), III: 686.
Holland, R., (Pvt, Co H, 1st Vols/11th NCST), V: 530.
Holland, T.J., (Sgt, Co H, 28th NCST), V: 542.
Holland, W.H., (Pvt, Co E, 56th NCST), III: 347.
Holland, W.P., (2nd Lt, Co D, 62nd Ga.; 16th Battalion/75th NCST, 7th Cav), IV: 91.
Holland, William, (Pvt, Co D, 10th NCST, 1st Art & Engs, Reilly-Ramsay's Battery, Light Art), V: 568.

Holland, William A., (Maj, 40th NCST, 3rd Art, Hvy), II: 745, 746, 756, 762, 764; V: 651.
Hollar, A.D., (Pvt, Co C, 28th NCST), V: 541.
Hollar, David, (Pvt, Co F, 38th NCST), V: 557.
Holler, Gilbert, (Pvt, Co F, 13th Vols/23rd NCST), V: 510.
Holler, J.E., (Pvt, Co F, 13th Vols/23rd NCST), V: 510.
Holliday, H.W., (Sgt, Co H, 1st NCST), V: 485.
Holliday, J.G., (Capt, Co A, Wynn's 15th Battalion NCST, Cav), IV: 365, 368.
Holliday, R.H., (1st Lt, Co F, 6th Battalion NCST, Fayetteville Armory Guard), IV: 297.
Holliday, T.S., (2nd Lt, Co G, 1st NCST), I: 137.
Holliday, Walter, [Holladay], (1st Lt, Ordnance Officer, Garland-Johnston's Brigade), IV: 521.
Hollingsworth, J.B., (Pvt, Co G, 56th NCST), III: 348; V: 566.
Hollingsworth, J.B., (Pvt, Co A, 63rd NCST, 5th Cav), III: 577.
Hollingsworth, John, (Pvt, Co E, 25th NCST), V: 561.
Holloman, Joseph, (2nd Lt, Co E, 68th NCST), III: 714.
Holloman, Kindred, (Pvt, Co D, 68th NCST), III: 715.
Holloman, W.D., (Capt, AQM, 59th NCST, 4th Cav), III: 457.
Holloway, G.W., (Pvt, Co F, 26th NCST), V: 602.
Holloway, J.M., (Pvt, Co F, 26th NCST), V: 602.
Holloway, John B., (2nd Lt, Co F, 26th NCST), II: 304, 358, 372, 396, 397; V: 601.
Holloway, Kinet, (Musician, 6th NCST), V: 511.
Holly Shelter, (nr Wilmington), III: 70.
Hollywood Cemetery, (Richmond, Va.), II: 801.
Holman's Ford, (Yadkin River), V: 286, 287, 289, 291, 292.
Holmes, G., (ACS, 46th NCST), III: 65.
Holmes, Gabriel, (Capt, 1st Battalion NCST Junior Reserves; Co I, 70th NCST, 1st Junior Reserves; Son of Lt Gen T.H. Holmes), IV: 13.
Holmes, H.B., (Pvt, Co D, 43rd NCST), V: 498.
Holmes, J.A., [James A.], (Sgt, Co C, 4th NCST), I: 233.
Holmes, James C., (Capt, Co A, 30th NCST), II: 495.
Holmes, John, (Orderly Sgt, Co D, 4th NCST), I: 232; V: 488.
Holmes, John F., (Pvt, Co C, 4th NCST), V: 488.
Holmes, L.A., (2nd Lt, Co B, 5th Vols/15th NCST), I: 734.
Holmes, M.C., (Pvt, Co E, 5th Vols/15th NCST), I: 745.
Holmes, Melville, (Pvt, Co G, 13th Vols/23rd NCST), II: 247.
Holmes, Owen, (Capt, Co I, 46th NCST), III: 65, 82; V: 519.
Holmes, R.J., (Pvt, Co C, 4th NCST), V: 488.
Holmes, Robert Q., (Pvt, Co C, 4th NCST; Detailed, 2nd Corps Provost Guard), V: 570.
Holmes, Theophilus H., (Lt Gen), I: xi, 12, 112, 179, 216, 217, 342, 507; II: 83, 164, 328, 334, 427, 428, 461, 587, 596, 677; III: 4, 163, 165, 166, 179; IV: 5, 7, 9, 11, 12, 13, 14, 35, 36, 37, 42, 44, 50, 52, 65, 66, 97, 99, 100, 101, 105, 107, 129, 131, 133, 397, 398, 400, 501, 511, 587, 646; V: 7, 668.

Holmes, Theophilus H., Jr., (1st Lt, ADC to Holmes, Son of T.H. Holmes), IV: 37.
Holmes, W.R., (Cpl, Co B, 56th NCST), III: 366.
Holsenback, John W., (Pvt, Co D, 56th NCST), III: 347.
Holshouser, ______, [Otho], (Sgt, Co K, 4th NCST), I: 278.
Holshouser, M.A., (Pvt, Co C, 57th NCST), V: 517.
Holshouser, Rufus, (Pvt, Co D, 10th NCST, 1st Art & Engs, Reilly-Ramsay's Battery, Light Art), I: 574.
Holsomback, William, (Pvt, Co E, 5th Vols/15th NCST), V: 521.
Holston River, Tenn., III: 518, 742, 743.
Holt, B.A., (Pvt, Co K, 28th NCST), V: 543.
Holt, D.A., (Pvt, Co E, 5th NCST), I: 292; V: 505.
Holt, E.J., (1st Lt, Co A, 16th Battalion/75th NCST, 7th Cav), IV: 90, 91, 94, 95, 96, 580; V: 659.
Holt, Edwin, (Chairman of the Board, N.C. Railroad), I: 338.
Holt, G.W., (Pvt, Co E, 3rd Vols/13th NCST), V: 550.
Holt, G.W., (Pvt, Co E, 12th Vols/22nd NCST), V: 553.
Holt, H., (Pvt, Co E, 3rd Vols/13th NCST), V: 550.
Holt, H.S., (Pvt, Co E, 3rd Vols/13th NCST), V: 550.
Holt, Isaac, (Pvt, Co F, 45th NCST), V: 500.
Holt, J., (Pvt, Co K, 54th NCST), V: 516.
Holt, Jesse M., (1st Lt, Co F, 53rd NCST), III: 262.
Holt, L. Banks, (1st Lt, Co I, 8th NCST), IV: 497.
Holt, Dr. P.A., (Ass't Surg, 2nd Vols/12th NCST; Surg., 6th NCST), IV: 632, 633.
Holt, Dr. W.A., (Surg, Pender-Scales' Brigade; Surg., Goldsboro General Hospital), IV: 551, 626, 627, 629, 644.
Holt, W.H., (Lt, Co D, 35th NCST), II: 610.
Holt, W.N., (Lt, Co H, 55th NCST), III: 288, 296.
Holt's Factory, (Haw River), I: 413.
Holton, H., (Pvt, Co E, 1st Vols/11th NCST), V: 530.
Holton, Samuel R., (1st Lt, Co H, 56th NCST), III: 316, 348, 378; V: 189.
Holy Shelter Road, (nr Wilmington), IV: 358.
Home Guard, Ga., IV: 322.
Home Guard, N.C., (There were at least 78 Battalions and 9 Regiments of Home Guard organized into at least 2 Brigades and those whose identities have not been totally forgotten are listed below. See also: Collett Leventhorpe and J.W. McElroy), I: v, xiii, 52, 53, 54, 165; IV: 224, 372, 376, 408, 440, 645, 647, 649, 650, 654; V: 1, 2, 6, 7, 599, 602, 629-636.
Home Guard Battalions:
1st Home Guard, Goldsboro;
2nd Home Guard, Franklinton;
3rd Home Guard, Mocksville;
4th Home Guard, Pittsboro;
7th Home Guard, Kenansville;
10th Home Guard, Lumberton;
14th Home Guard, Lexington;
18th Home Guard, Wadesboro;
21st Home Guard, Mt. Airy;
22nd Home Guard, Wentworth;
23rd Home Guard, Williamsboro;
24th Home Guard, Lillington;
26th Home Guard, Rockingham;
27th Home Guard, Clinton;
29th Home Guard, Mosely Hall;
37th Home Guard, Salisbury;
48th Home Guard, Asheboro;

59th Home Guard, Carthage;
63rd Home Guard, Charlotte;
64th Home Guard, Winston;
68th Home Guard, Wilkesboro;
69th Home Guard, Chimney Rock;
72nd Home Guard, Burnsville;
80th Home Guard, Wilson;
Home Guard Regiments:
Burr's 7th Regiment, IV: 440.
Cole's 1st Regiment, V: 629-636.
Draughan's 3rd Regiment, IV: 650.
Cole's 4th Regiment, V: 629-636.
Hambrick's 3rd Regiment, IV: 650.
Home Guard Brigades:
J.W. McElroy's, IV: 650.
Collett Leventhorpe's, IV: 650.
Home Guard, Pa., V: 115, 116.
Home Guard, Va., III: 614; IV: 44, 244.
Homer, J.Q., (Pvt, Co A, 56th NCST), V: 565.
Homing Creek, N.C., III: 477.
Honbager, John, (Pvt, Co D, 10th NCST, 1st Art & Engs, Reilly-Ramsay's Battery, Light Art), V: 568.
Honey Hill, S.C., II: 757; IV: 333.
Honeycutt, Frank, (Pvt, Co B, 26th NCST), II: 352, 353, 374.
Honeycutt, J.B., [Hunnicutt], (Pvt, Co C, 5th NCST), I: 291; V: 505.
Honeycutt, R.D., (Cpl, Co E, 47th NCST), V: 535.
Honeycutt, S., (Pvt, Co C, 28th NCST), V: 541.
Hood, A.I., (Father of W.S. Hood), II: 608.
Hood, Ezekiel, (2nd Lt, Co K, 10th NCST, 1st Art & Engs, Sparrow-Shaw's Hvy Art), I: 525.
Hood, J., (Pvt, Co K, 54th NCST), V: 516.
Hood, J.H., (Pvt, Co H, 35th NCST), V: 563.
Hood, J.T.C., (Orderly Sgt, Co F, 26th NCST), V: 532, 599-601, 602.
Hood, John Bell, (Gen, demoted to Lt Gen and Hood's Army), I: 186, 308, 570, 573, 574, 626, 768; II: 88, 218, 514, 602, 720; III: 268, 339, 407, 439, 454, 493, 500; IV: 152, 192, 372, 498, 543 V: 270, 679.
Hood, W.L., (Cpl, Co K, 30th NCST), V: 493.
Hood, William S., (Pvt, Co H, 35th NCST, Orderly to Mat & Robert Ransom), II: 604, 605, 607, 608, 625; IV: 576; V: 78.
Hook, J.A., (Pvt, Co K, 35th NCST), V: 563.
Hooker, Henry H., (2nd Lt, Co D, 40th NCST, 3rd Art, Hvy), II: 747.
Hooker, Joseph, (Maj Gen, USA; aka "Fighting Joe," and Hooker's Army), I: 169, 186, 250, 251, 310, 376, 379, 424, 628, 629, 696, 697, 707, 714, 715, 716, 764; II: 36, 40, 171, 203, 228, 229, 230, 232, 233, 234, 501, 602, 658, 659, 688; III: 410, 533, 557, 560, 561, 567; IV: 163, 169, 172, 173, 176, 411, 522, 552, 553, 558; V: xvi, 80, 96, 114.
Hooker, Samuel D., (Pvt, Detached Co, 68th NCST), III: 723.
Hookerton, N.C., I: 588; III: 234.
Hooks, Boaz F., (Maj, 3rd Battalion Senior Reserves; Maj, 78th NCST, 8th Senior Reserves IV: 3, 108, 399.
Hooks, William, (2nd Lt, Co E, 62nd Ga.; 16th Battalion/75th NCST, 7th Cav), IV: 91.
Hoole, James L., (Lt Cmdr, NCN; Capt, Forest), V: 304, 306, 307.

Hoop Pole, N.C., I: 489.
Hooper, A.D., (Capt, Co G, 62nd NCST), III: 516; IV: 701, 707.
Hooper, A.J., (Pvt, Co A, 3rd Vols/13th NCST), V: 549.
Hooper, H.R., (QM, N.C. Reserves), IV: 7.
Hooper, J.N., (2nd Lt, Co B, 2nd Battalion Junior Reserves; Co C, 71st NCST, 2nd Junior Reserves), IV: 28.
Hooper, James P., (Pvt, Co M, 6th Vols/16th NCST), V: 553.
Hooper, James P., (Pvt, Co B, 59th NCST, 4th Cav), V: 659.
Hooper, Joseph A., (Capt, Co E, 12th Vols/22nd NCST), II: 166.
Hooper, R.L., [Rufus L.], (Capt, Co F, 54th NCST), IV: 702, 707.
Hoover, D.B., (Pvt, Co A, 2nd Vols/12th NCST), I: 630.
Hoover, J.M., (2nd Lt, Co K, 46th NCST), III: 82.
Hoover, Sumpter A., (Pvt, Co C, 4th NCST; Detailed, 2nd Corps Provost Guard), V: 488, 570.
Hoover, W.G., (Pvt, Co C, 10th NCST, 1st Art & Engs, Brem-Graham-Williams' Battery, Light Art), V: 568.
Hoover, W.W., (Pvt, Co C, 48th NCST), V: 526.
Hope Slater, (Negro jail in Baltimore used to house Confederate prisoners), IV: 665.
Hopewell, Va., (and Hopewell Road), III: 562, 563.
Hopkins, ______, (Pvt, 69th NCST, Thomas' Legion), III: 662.
Hopkins, George W., (Lt, Co M, 58th NCST), III: 434, 437, 447.
Hopkins, H., (Pvt, Co D, 43rd NCST), V: 498.
Hopkins, James A., (Capt, Co E, 45th NCST), III: 42.
Hopkins, Martin, (Pvt, Co E, 45th NCST), V: 500.
Hopkins, N.H., (Jr 2nd Lt, Co H, 38th NCST), II: 676.
Hopkins, P., (Pvt, Co D, 52nd NCST), V: 536.
Hopkins, P.J., (Pvt, Co I, 3rd Vols/13th NCST), V: 551.
Hopkins, W.H., (Pvt, Co H, 2nd Battalion NCST), V: 495.
Hopper, J.A., (Pvt, Co H, 28th NCST), V: 542.
Hopper, J.N., (2nd Lt, Co C, 71st NCST, 2nd Junior Reserves), IV: 28.
Hopper, R.M.S., (2nd Lt, Co A, 34th NCST), V: 548.
Horah, George, (1st Lt, Co B, 46th NCST), III: 76, 80.
Horan, ______, [G.P.], (1st Lt, Co G, 49th NCST), III: 148.
Horde, William F., (Cpl, Co B, 33rd NCST), II: 538.
Hornaday, E.H., [E.M.], (Ordnance Sgt, 26th NCST), II: 307, 371, 396; V: 531.
Horn, A., (Sgt, Co C, 53rd NCST), V: 501.
Horn, Abel, (Pvt, Co E, 3rd Vols/13th NCST), V: 550.
Horn, L.H., (Pvt, Co I, 8th Vols/18th NCST), II: 64.
Horn, Noah, (Pvt, Co H, 48th NCST), V: 526.
Horn, S.E., (Musician, 6th NCST), V: 511.
Horn, S.R., (2nd Lt, Co C, 53rd NCST), III: 262.
Horn, W.H., (Musician, 55th NCST), V: 527.
Horne, H.R., (Jr 1st Lt, Co D, Webb's Battery, Bogg's 12th Va. Battalion, Hvy Art; Co A, Webb's Battery, Starr's 13th Battalion NCST, Light Art), I: 120; IV: 355, 356, 357, 358; V: 282.
Horne, H.W., (Capt, Co C, 3rd NCST), I: 119; IV: 721.

Horne, J.R., (Pvt, Co A, 10th NCST, 1st Art & Engs, Ramseur-Manly's Battery, Light Art), I: 556.
Horne, Jesse, (Pvt, Co A, 43rd NCST), III: 20; V: 497.
Horne, Lion, (Sgt, Co K, 14th Vols/24th NCST), V: 560.
Horne, N.A., (Cpl, Co H, 56th NCST), III: 356.
Horne, R.H., (2nd Lt, Co A, Webb's Battery, Starr's 13th Battalion NCST, Light Art), IV: 355.
Horne, W.W., (Pvt, Co E, 2nd Vols/12th NCST), V: 507.
Horner, ______, (Capt, CSN, Flora), V: 409.
Horner, J.H., (Capt, Co E, Vols/23rd NCST), II: 184.
Horner, Thomas, (Pvt, Co K, 6th NCST), V: 514.
Horran, G.D., (2nd Lt, Co B, 49th NCST), I: 734.
"Horse-Jockey Battalion," (Name given to a band of Yankee horse theives), V: 655.
Horse Shoe, The, (aka: Bloody Angle, The Mule Shoe, Lee's Salient, at Spotsylvania, Va.), I: 202, 203, 289, 548, 642, 702, 724, 725, 726, 745; II: 49, 51, 52, 75, 243, 244, 383, 530, 571, 666; III: 46, 47-52, 60, 258.
Hores Shoe Bend, (Etowah River, S.C.), II: 742.
Horton, Miss ______, (Became Mrs. A.L. Stough), IV: 613.
Horton, A.V., (2nd Lt, Co H, 31st NCST), II: 512.
Horton, Augustus H., (Capt, Co C, 26th NCST), II: 303, 307, 396.
Horton, J.G., (Pvt, Co I, 56th NCST), V: 566.
Horton, J.P., (Capt, Co C, 58th NCST), III: 433.
Horton, J.W., (2nd Lt, Co D, 5th Vols/15th NCST), I: 735; V: 519.
Horton, Jonathan, (Capt, Co B, 37th NCST), II: 653.
Horton, N., (2nd Lt, Co B, 37th NCST), IV: 700, 707.
Horton, Phineas, (2nd Lt, ACS, 26th NCST), II: 303, 371, 396.
Horton, Rufus D., (Capt, Co C, 26th NCST), II: 371, 396, 397, 398.
Hoskins, Calhoun, (Lt, Co K, 61st NCST), III: 504.
Hospitals, Confederate:
  Atlanta, Ga., II: 743.
  Augusta, Ga., II: 743.
  Carolina City Hospital, (nr New Bern), II: 413.
  Charlotte General Hospital, IV: 626.
  Charlotte Wayside Hospital, IV: 624, 627; V: 473.
  Chimborazo, (nr Richmond, Va.), III: 607.
  Columbia, S.C., II: 743.
  Craven General Hospital, (N.C. hospital at Richmond), IV: 624, 629.
  Danville, Va., III: 653.
  Fayetteville General Hospital, IV: 626, 627, 629.
  Fincastle, Tenn., IV: 275.
  Goldsboro General Hospital, IV: 625, 627.
  Goldsboro Wayside Hospital, IV: 624, 625, 626; V: 473.
  Greensboro General Hospital, IV: 428, 431.
  Greensboro Wayside Hospital, V: 473.
  Greenville, Tenn., III: 521.
  Howard Grove Hospital, (nr Richmond, Va.), IV: 629.
  Jacksonville, Va., (nr Richmond, Va.), III: 111.
  Kittrell Springs Wayside Hospital, IV: 606.
  Macon, Ga., II: 743.
  Marine Hospital, (nr Wilmington), IV: 221.

North Carolina, 1st General Hospital, (Petersburg, Va.), IV: 623, 630.
North Carolina, 2nd General Hospital, (Petersburg, Va.), IV: 624, 629, 634.
Petersburg, Va., III: 314.
Pettigrew Hospital, (aka Raleigh Fair Grounds Hospital; This facility became the Confederate Soldiers' Home), IV: 626, 627; V: 577, 578.
Raleigh General Hospital #1, IV: 623, 626, 627, 629; V: 649.
Raleigh General Hospital #2, (Peace College), IV: 625, 627.
Raleigh Wayside Hospital, IV: 624; V: 473.
Richmond, Va., I: 51, 672.
Salisbury General Hospital, II: 743; IV: 626, 627.
Salisbury Prison Hospital, IV: 625.
Salisbury Wayside Hospital IV: 624, 625, 627; V: 473.
Tarboro Wayside Hospital, IV: 624, 625, 627.
Wake Forest Wayside Hospital, IV: 627.
Weldon Wayside Hospital, IV: 624, 625; V: 473.
Wilmington General Hospital #1, IV: 391, 625, 627, 629.
Wilmington General Hospital #2, IV: 625, 627, 630, 636.
Wilmington Wayside Hospital, V: 473.
Wilson General Hospital, IV: 625, 627, 629; V: 194.
Winder Hospital, (nr Richmond, Va.), II: 389, 418; III: 54; IV: 201, 600.
Hospitals, Federal:
Baltimore, Md., IV: 689.
David's Island, New York, N.Y., II: 419; IV: 404, 703.
Frederick City, Md., IV: 689.
St. Elizabeth Hospital for the Insane, (nr Washington, D.C.), IV: 318.
Hospitals Established, IV: 623, 627; V: 443.
Hot Springs, N.C., (Madison County), II: 297; III: 662, 664, 671, 756; IV: 287.
Hot Springs, Va., IV: 147, 148, 149.
Hotchkiss, _____, [James T.], (Sgt, Co K, 56th NCST), III: 391.
Hotchkiss, Jed, (Maj, Jackson's Topographer), I: 100, 622, 626, 632; IV: 411.
Hotten, John Camden, (Englishman, Publisher), V: 414.
Houck, George W., (Pvt, Co D, 6th NCST), I: 337.
Houck, J.B., (2nd Lt, Co A, 26th NCST), II: 371, 396, 397.
Houffstichler, David R., (Pvt, Co H, 34th NCST), V: 556.
Houghton, Lord _____, I: 725.
Houk, A.W., (Sgt, Co D, 6th NCST), V: 512.
Houk, Calvin, (N.C. Militia), IV: 372.
Houk, William, (Pvt, Co D, 6th NCST), V: 512.
Houk, William A., (Lt Col, 34th NCST), II: 581.
Houp, J.A., (Pvt, Co C, 4th NCST), V: 488.
House, Mr., _____, (Civilian), II: 124.
House, A., (Pvt, Co G, 57th NCST), V: 517.
Houser, A.J., (2nd Lt, Co D, 1st NCST), I: 136.
Houser, A.P., (1st Lt, Co D, 1st NCST), I: 137.
Houser, C.E., (Pvt, Co B, 1st Battalion NCST), V: 504.
Houser, Emanuel, (Blacksmith, Co K, 49th NCST; Detailed, QM Corps), V: 571.

Houser, William, (Pvt, Co B, 1st Battalion NCST), V: 504.
Houston, ______, (Lt, Va.), IV: 671.
Houston, A.H., [A.W], (Adjt, 5th Vols/15th NCST), I: 734; V: 519.
Houston, H.V., (Lt, Co C, 51st NCST), III: 219.
Houston, J.F., (Cpl, Co C, 28th NCST), V: 541.
Houston, J.M., (Pvt, Co C, 28th NCST), V: 541.
Houston, John, (Pvt, Co E, 6th NCST), V: 512.
Houston, John, [John W.], (Pvt, Co D, B & A, 65th NCST, 6th Cav), III: 680.
Houston, R.B.B., (2nd Lt, Co G, 52nd NCST), III: 228.
Houston, Sam, (Gen., Tx.), III: 683.
Houston, Dr. Thomas A., (Ass't Surg, 65th NCST, 6th Cav), III: 663; IV: 642.
Houston, W.H., (Capt, Co C, 82nd NCST), IV: 131.
Houston, W.G.P., (3rd Cpl, Co G, 52nd NCST), III: 224.
Houston, W.J., (Capt, Co I, 9th NCST, 1st Cav), I: 418, 424, 483, 486.
Hovis, Moses S., (Pvt, Co G, 34th NCST), V: 556.
Howard, Rev. ______, (Chaplain), IV: 601, 602.
Howard, Alvis B., (2nd Lt, Co C, 33rd NCST), II: 539.
Howard, B.W., (Pvt, Co K, 57th NCST), V: 518.
Howard, Benjamin A., (Sgt, Co D, 2nd NCST), I: 176; V: 486.
Howard, Charlie, (Pvt, Co A, 10th NCST, 1st Art & Engs, Ramseur-Manly's Battery, Light Art), I: 557.
Howard, E.W., (Pvt, Co I, 6th NCST), V: 513.
Howard, Dr. E. Lloyd, (Surg, 27th NCST), II: 461; IV: 636.
Howard, F., (Pvt, Co A, 8th Vols/18th NCST), II: 63; V: 539.
Howard, F.W., (Pvt, Co C, 28th NCST), V: 541.
Howard, Frank, (Pvt, Barrington's Co, Whitford's 11th Battalion NCST, Hvy Art; Co B, 67th NCST), V: 18.
Howard, G.W., (Pvt, Co G, 28th NCST), V: 542.
Howard, Henry, (Pvt, Co A, 8th Vols/18th NCST), II: 63; V: 539.
Howard, Henry, (Pilot, Fannie), V: 357.
Howard, J., (Pvt, Co C, 56th NCST), III: 347.
Howard, J.R., (Sgt, Co D, 27th NCST), II: 462; V: 523.
Howard, John, (Maj, 2nd NCST), I: 158; V: 11.
Howard, John E., (Musician, 6th Vols/16th NCST), V: 551.
Howard, John W., (2nd Lt, Co A, 41st NCST, 3rd Cav), II: 770.
Howard, Joseph, (Pvt, Co K, 55th NCST), V: 528.
Howard, Joseph W., (1st Lt, Co K, 44th NCST), III: 23.
Howard, Lewis W., (2nd Lt, Co A, 41st NCST, 3rd Cav), II: 770.
Howard, Oliver Otis, (Maj Gen, USA), I: 629, 638; II: 501; V: 114, 118.
Howard, R.G., (Pvt, Co G, 44th NCST), V: 534.
Howard, Richard, (Lt, Co B, 64th NCST), III: 660; IV: 701, 707.
Howard, Samuel, (Pvt, Co H, 63rd NCST, 5th Cav), III: 586.
Howard, W.C., (Lt, Co F, 48th NCST), III: 119.
Howard, W.J., (2nd Sgt, Co G, 1st Vols/11th NCST), V: 530.
Howard, William, (Sgt, Co A, 8th Vols/18th NCST), II: 63.

Howard, William, (2nd Lt, Co D, 1st NCST), I: 137; II: 63.
Howard, William, (Lt, Co B, 2nd NCST), I: 158.
Howard, William H., (Capt, Co A, 57th NCST), III: 405.
Howard's Dam, Va., (nr Battery No. 45), IV: 479.
Howard's Gap Road, N.C., III: 670.
Howard's Grove, Va., I: 79; II: 21, 68.
Howell, A.J., (Pvt, Co H, 43rd NCST), V: 499.
Howell, D.L., (Cpl, Co D, 4th NCST), I: 232.
Howell, Drewry D., (Pvt, Co D, 4th Vols/14th NCST), V: 490.
Howell, E.G., (Pvt, Co E, 6th Battalion/60th NCST), III: 482.
Howell, George W., (Capt, Co I, 25th NCST), II: 292.
Howell, J.A., (Capt, Co C, 42nd NCST), II: 790, 806.
Howell, J.C., (Cmdr, USN), V: 243.
Howell, J.J., (1st Cpl, Co A, 46th NCST), V: 524.
Howell, James H., (Pvt, Co D, 10th NCST, 1st Art & Engs, Reilly-Ramsay's Battery, Light Art), V: 568.
Howell, James K., (Chaplain, 1st NCST), I: 136; IV: 604.
Howell, John T., (2nd Sgt, Co H, 34th NCST), V: 556.
Howell, P.F., (1st Sgt, Co G, 61st Va.), V: 569.
Howell, Paul, (Pvt, Co F, 26th NCST), V: 602.
Howell, R.P., (Capt, AQM, 62nd Ga., Cav), IV: 92.
Howell, William, (Pvt, Co H, 34th NCST), V: 556.
Howerton, Samuel W., (Chaplain, 5th Vols/15th NCST), I: 734; III: 405; IV: 608.
Howerton, Dr. William H., (Capt, Co H, 57th NCST), I: 62; III: 406.
Howie, J.H., (Pvt, Co K, 30th NCST), V: 493.
Howie, S.E., (Pvt, Co H, 35th NCST), V: 563.
Howie, Sanford G., (Capt, Co F, 35th NCST), II: 603, 625, 627; V: 77.
Howington, J., (Cpl, Co E, 37th NCST), V: 545.
Howland, Levi, (67th NCST), III: 706.
Howlett's House, (nr Petersburg, Va. and Battle of 1864), III: 355, 357; IV: 530-531.
Howser, A.J., (2nd Lt, Co K, 1st NCST), IV: 722.
Hoyle, D.P., (Pvt, Co C, 10th NCST, 1st Art & Engs, Brem-Graham-Williams' Battery, Light Art), V: 568.
Hoyle, James, (Pvt, Co G, 6th Vols/16th NCST), IV: 209, 210.
Hoyle, Joel J., (Lt, Co F, 55th NCST), III: 296, 310.
Hoyle, Lemuel J., (Capt, Co I, 1st Vols/11th NCST), I: 119, 585.
Hubbard, ______, "Squire," V: 292.
Hubbard, H.C., (Sgt, Co I, 5th NCST), I: 292; V: 505.
Hubbard, J.A., (Pvt, Co N, 11th Vols/21st NCST), V: 515.
Huckabee, A.A., (Pvt, Co F, 8th Vols/18th NCST), II: 64.
Hudgin, L., (Pvt, Co D, 3rd Vols/13th NCST), V: 550.
Hudgins, L.A., (Pvt, Co G, 21st Ga.), V: 194.
Hudnell, ______, (Lt, Randolph's Howitzers, Va.), I: 106, 127.
Hudson, A., (Pvt, Co I, 46th NCST), V: 525.
Hudson, Abram, (Pvt, Co F, 26th NCST), V: 601.
Hudson, Ambrose, (Pvt, Co F, 26th NCST), V: 602.
Hudson, Coleman J., (Pvt, Co H, 10th Vols/20th NCST; Detailed, 2nd Corps Provost Guard), V: 570.

Hudson, Daniel, (Cpl, Co G, 6th NCST), V: 513.
Hudson, Daniel L., (Capt, Co G, 37th NCST), II: 660, 668, 670.
Hudson, Hinton J., (2nd Lt, Co C, 38th NCST), II: 675, 678.
Hudson, J., (Pvt, Co I, 6th NCST), V: 513.
Hudson, James, (Pvt, Co B, 1st Vols, "Bethel"), V: 577, 578.
Hudson, Joel, (Pvt, Co B, 56th NCST), III: 366.
Hudson, Joseph, (Pvt, Co A, 2nd Battalion NCST), V: 495.
Hudson, Josiah, (Pvt, Co H, 10th Vols/20th NCST), II: 119.
Hudson, N., (Pvt, Co F, 6th Battalion/60th NCST), III: 482.
Hudson, Noah, (Pvt, Co D, 6th Battalion/60th NCST), III: 482.
Hudson, S., (Pvt, Co I, 46th NCST), V: 525.
Hudson, W.H., (Pvt, Co F, 13th Vols/23rd NCST), V: 510.
Hudson, W.J., (Lt, Co E, 2nd Battalion NCST), IV: 245.
Hudspeth, A.M., (Pvt, Co F, 26th NCST), V: 602.
Hudspeth, G.W., (Pvt, Co F, 26th NCST), V: 602.
Hudspeth, John T., (Pvt, Co I, 1st Vols/11th NCST), V: 531.
Hudspeth, R.N., (Lt, Co F, 26th NCST), II: 396, 397; V: 602.
Hudspeth, Robert, (Sgt, Co F, 26th NCST), II: 359; V: 600, 601.
Huff, David, (Pvt, Co H, 43rd NCST), V: 499.
Huff, James T., (Maj, 6th Battalion/60th NCST), III: 474, 478, 482, 496.
Huff, John A., (Pvt, Co E, 5th Mich. Cav, Allegedly shot J.E.B. Stuart), III: 598, 599.
Huff, Leonard C., (1st Lt, Co H, 6th Battalion/60th NCST), III: 474, 491.
Huff, W.H., (Pvt, Co D, 10th NCST, 1st Art & Engs, Reilly-Ramsay's Battery, Light Art), I: 569.
Huffhines, Samuel, (Pvt, Co A, 53rd NCST), V: 501.
Huffman, ______, (Capt, Hoke-Godwin-Lewis' Brigade), IV: 526.
Huffman, A.F., (Pvt, Co E, 2nd Vols/12th NCST), V: 507.
Huffman, Cyrus, (Pvt, Co D, 6th NCST), V: 512.
Huffman, D., (Pvt, Co E, 1st NCST), V: 485.
Huffman, J., (Pvt, Co A, 11th Vols/21st NCST; Detailed, Invalid Battalion), V: 571.
Huffman, J.S., (Pvt, Co E, 3rd Vols/13th NCST), V: 550.
Huffman, W.A., (Pvt, Co F, 13th Vols/23rd NCST), V: 510.
Huffman, W.L., (Pvt, Co A. 2nd Vols/12th NCST), V: 572.
Huffman, William, (Pvt, Co E, 6th Vols/16th NCST), V: 552.
Huffman, William S., (Pvt, Co F, 38th NCST), II: 690.
Hufman, Noah, (3rd Cpl, Co K, 46th NCST), V: 525.
Hufstedler, John, (Lt Col, 25th Ark.), II: 716, 717.
Huffstleter, E.M., (Pvt, Co B, 28th NCST), V: 541.
Huger, Benjamin, (Maj Gen), I: 350, 613, 617; II: 204, 214, 294, 331, 508; IV: 246, 300, 501; V: 57, 58.
Huggins, George W., (Lt, Co I, 8th Vols/18th NCST), II: 28.
Huggins, James B., (2nd Lt, Co C, Cumming's Battery, Starr's 13th Battalion NCST, Light Art), IV: 361.
Huggins, James J., (2nd Lt, Co E & I, 10th Vols/20th NCST), IV: 701, 708.
Huggins, W.H., (Pvt, Co E, 10th Vols/20th NCST), V: 509.

Hughes, Francis, (Pvt, Co K, 6th NCST), V: 513.
Hughes, J.C., (Pvt, Co A, 56th NCST), V: 565.
Hughes, Dr. James B., (Surg, 2nd NCST), I: 157; IV: 631.
Hughes, James S., (Cpl, Co K, 33rd NCST), II: 541.
Hughes, Job C., (Cpl, Color-bearer, 56th NCST), III: 346, 347, 355.
Hughes, John, (AQM, 7th NCST), IV: 472.
Hughes, John, (Maj, 58th NCST; AQM, Hoke-Godwin-Lewis' Brigade), II: 553-554; III: 453; IV: 526.
Hughes, John H., [John W.], (1st Lt, Co E, 31st NCST), II: 507, 512.
Hughes, Jordon, (Lt, Co H, 51st NCST), III: 220.
Hughes, Nicholas Colin, (Capt, AAG to Pettigrew), I: 157, 158, 163; II: 358; IV: 556, 568; V: 131.
Hughes, Noah H., (Capt, Co A, 56th NCST), III: 313, 338, 346, 366; V: 179, 191.
Hughes, Paschal C., (Maj, 39th NCST), II: 705, 706, 724.
Hughes, Theodore J., (Capt, Purser of the Advance), II: 83, 84; V: 453, 455, 456.
Hughes, Thomas, (Pvt, Co K, 6th NCST), V: 514.
Hughes, Dr. W.R., (Ass't Surg, 31st NCST), II: 511; IV: 637.
Huling, ______, (Col, Maine), III: 48, 49.
Hull, E.R., (Pvt, Co C, 11th Vols/21st NCST), V: 530.
Humber, William H., (Pvt, Co H, 27th NCST), II: 462; V: 524.
Humby, Joseph, (Pvt, Co A, 34th NCST), V: 554.
Humes, William Y.C., (Brig Gen), III: 679.
Humfries, J.L., (Pvt, Co H, 1st Vols/11th NCST), V: 530.
Humphrey, Andrew Atkinson, (Maj Gen, USA), I: 601; II: 230.
Humphrey, Benjamin Grubb, (Brig Gen), I: 722.
Humphrey, Henry W., (Capt, Co A, 35th NCST), II: 613, 627.
Humphrey, John F., (2nd Lt, C. B, 5th Battalion Junior Reserves; Co G, 71st NCST, 2nd Junior Reserves), IV: 28.
Humphrey, L.W., (1st Lt, Co B, 41st NCST, 3rd Cav), II: 770.
Humphreys, S.C., (AC Sgt, 35th NCST), V: 562.
Humphries, John, (Pvt, Co C, 5th Vols/15th NCST), V: 521.
Humphries, Lawson, (Pvt, Co C, 5th Vols/15th NCST), V: 521.
Humphries, Lewis, (Pvt, Co I, 34th NCST), V: 556.
Humphries, Perry G., (Pvt, Co C. 5th Vols/15th NCST), V: 521.
Humphries, Sumner, (Pvt, Co C, 5th Vols/15th NCST), V: 521.
Hundley, T.A., (Pvt, Co G, 43rd NCST), V: 498.
Hungarytown, Va., III: 614.
Hunnicutt, E.M., [Huneycutt], (1st Lt, Co H, 42nd NCST), II: 791, 807.
Hunsucker, J.P., (Pvt, Co E, 32nd NCST), V: 496.
Hunsucker, Marcus, (Pvt, Co F, 38th NCST), V: 557.
Hunt, B.F., (1st Lt, Co I, 38th NCST), II: 678.
Hunt, C.A., (Capt, Co K, 4th NCST), I: 272.
Hunt, Henry Jackson, (Maj Gen, USA, Chief of Artillery, Meade's Staff), V: 102, 103, 141.
Hunt, J.M.B., (Capt, Co B, 2nd Vols/12th NCST), I: 639.
Hunt, J.W., (Pvt, Co B, 2nd Vols/12th NCST), V: 506.
Hunt, James M., (Capt, Co D, 33rd NCST), II: 539, 578.

Hunt, L.H., (Capt, Co C, 3rd Vols/13th NCST; AAG, Scales' Brigade), IV: 553.
Hunt, M.T., [M.F.], (1st Lt, Co E, 5th NCST), I: 291; V: 503.
Hunt, R.W., (2nd Lt, Co B, 49th NCST), I: 734.
Hunt, S.H., (Lt, USN, Pioneer, Fort Jackson), V: 245.
Hunt, Seward H., (Capt, Co C, 3rd Vols/13th NCST), I: 665.
Hunt, Weldon S., (Sgt, Co B, 33rd NCST), II: 538.
Hunter, C.A., (Cpl, Co H, 30th NCST), V: 492.
Hunter, David, (Maj Gen, USA; One of the most notorious criminals of the war. Guilty of countless war crimes and atrocities, had he lived during any other age he would have faced a war crimes tribunal and been sentenced to death for his crimes against humanity. I: 153, 172, 205, 259, 323, 324, 462, 645, 727; II: 122, 141, 245, 503, 531; III: 358, 277, 419, 746, 748, 749; IV: 515, 683.
Hunter, E.L., (Lt, Co F, 36th NCST, 2nd Art & Engs), V: 239.
Hunter, G.W., (Capt., Co. B, 13th Vols./23rd NCST), II: 183.
Hunter, Dr. H.H., (Surg, 9th NCST, 1st Cav), I: 485; IV: 633.
Hunter, J.M., (Pvt, Co H, 35th NCST), V: 563.
Hunter, M.B., (Pvt, Co A, 1st Vols/11th NCST), V: 530.
Hunter, R.B., (Pvt, Co C, 10th NCST, 1st Art & Engs, Brem-Graham-Williams' Battery, Light Art), V: 568.
Hunter, R.M.T., (Senator, CSA), III: 386.
Hunter, S.C., (2nd Lt, Co A, 82nd NCST), IV: 131.
Hunter, S.W., (Sgt, Co B, 43rd NCST), V: 497.
Hunter, Samuel B., (Capt, Co F, 36th NCST, 2nd Art & Engs, Pamlico Battery), II: 630, 635, 651.
Hunter, Silas C., (1st Lt, Co H, 35th NCST), II: 598.
Hunter, Thomas, (Lt, Co D, 64th NCST), III: 660.
Hunter, Thomas T., (Lt Cmdr, NCN; Capt, Curlew), V: 304, 307.
Hunter, W.G., (1st Lt, Co D, 5th Battalion, Junior Reserves; Co E, 71st NCST, 2nd Junior Reserves; Adjt, 71st NCST, 2nd Junior Reserves), IV: 28.
Hunter, William W.N., (1st Sgt, Co G, 40th NCST, 3rd Art, Hvy), II: 765.
Hunter's Raid, I: 153; III: 745.
Hunter's, Pa., I: 425.
Huntersville, Va., IV: 140, 141, 149, 406.
Huntington, F.F., (Lt, 16th N.Y., Hvy Art), V: 238.
Huntley, Stephen, (2nd Lt, Co K, 43rd NCST), III: 3.
Hunton, Eppa, (Brig Gen), III: 400; V: 204.
Huntsville, Tenn., IV: 271, 273.
Hupp's Hill, Va., II: 259.
Hurley, Alexander F., (3rd Sgt, Co A, 52nd NCST; 1st Lt, Co A, 52nd NCST), III: 223; V: 529.
Hurley, E., (Lt, Co L, 58th NCST), III: 434.
Hurley, L., (Capt, Co L, 58th NCST), III: 434.
Hurst, L.H., (Sgt, Co B, 56th NCST), III: 347, 366.
Hurst, Robert, (Pvt, Co G, 14th Vols/24th NCST), V: 560.
Hurst, William M., (1st Cpl, Co A, 38th NCST), V: 557.
Hurtt, D.W., (Maj, 2nd NCST), I: 163, 169, 171.
Huse, Samuel, (Lt, USN), V: 243.

Huske, Benjamin Robinson, (Maj, 48th NCST), I: 78, 90, 118, 126, 127, 129; III: 113, 114, 115, 123, 124; V: 12, 651.

Huske, James W., (2nd Lt, Co B, 52nd NCST), I: 120; III: 228, 246, 250.

Huske, Wright, (Capt, Co H, 1st Vols, "Bethel"), I: 75, 78, 91, 126, 127; IV: 294.

Huss, Pinkney J., (Pvt, Co E, 34th NCST), V: 555.

Hussey, Marcellus L., (Cpl, Co I, 5th Vols/15th NCST), V: 522.

Hussey, T.C., (Hospital Steward, 46th NCST), III: 65; V: 524.

Huston, J.K., (QMS, 72nd NCST, 3rd Junior Reserves), IV: 51.

Hutcheson, William J., (Pvt, Co E, 38th NCST), II: 690.

Hutcherson, David, (Lt, Co C, 9th NCST, 1st Cav), I: 485.

Hutchings, Dr. John W., (Surg, 4th Vols/14th NCST; Surg., 59th NCST, 4th Cav; Surg, 68th NCST), III: 457, 713; IV: 457, 634, 641, 642.

Hutchings, S. (Pvt, Co C, 6th NCST), V: 512.

Hutchins, J., (Pvt, Co I, 28th NCST), V: 543.

Hutchins, R.H., (Pvt, Co F, 28th NCST), V: 542.

Hutchins, W.F., (Pvt, Co C, 4th NCST), V: 488.

Hutchinson, B.C., (Pvt, Co C, 4th Vols/14th NCST), I: 731.

Hutchison, Pleasant, (Pvt, Co H, 12th Vols/22nd NCST; Detailed, HQ QM Corps), V: 572.

Hutchison, Scott B., (Pvt, Co G, 34th NCST), V: 556.

Hutson, John, (Pvt, Co I, 34th NCST), V: 556.

Hutson, William, (Pvt, Co F, 6th Battalion/60th NCST), III: 480.

Hyatt, J.B., (2nd Lt, Co E, 6th Battalion/60th NCST), III: 474, 475, 476, 478, 482.

Hyatt, Rice, [N.T.], (Pvt, Co F, 69th NCST, Thomas' Legion), III: 662.

Hyatt, Thaddeus C., (Lt, Co F, 25th NCST), II: 297.

Hybart, T.L., (Capt, Co A, 7th Battalion Junior Reserves; Co H, 72nd NCST, 3rd Junior Reserves), IV: 40, 41.

Hyde, Thomas, (Pvt, Co D, 10th NCST, 1st Art & Engs, Reilly-Ramsay's Battery, Light Art), V: 568.

Hyde County, N.C., I: 362; II: 541, 561; III: 723, 724; IV: 348, 620.

Hyman, G.F., (Sgt Maj, 3rd Vols/13th NCST), V: 549.

Hyman, John D., (Capt, ACS, 4th NCST), I: 230, 268.

Hyman, Joseph H., (Col, 3rd Vols/13th NCST), I: 654, 673, 674, 676, 680, 683, 684, 686; II: 178, 697; IV: 442, 554; V: 547.

Hyman, Samuel A., (1st Lt, Co F, 31st NCST), II: 507, 512.

Hyman, S. Layne, (Lt, Co E, 7th NCST), I: 383.

Hyman, Theodore B., (2nd Lt, Co G, 41st NCST, 3rd Cav), II: 771.

Hyman, Theophilus C., (Capt, Co B, 33rd NCST), II: 538, 578.

Hyman, W.A, (1st Sgt, Co D, 44th NCST), V: 533.

Hymes, ______, [Hyams, Isaac S.], (Lt, Drill Master, 39th NCST), II: 727.

(I)

Ianson, Dr. ______, [Richard W.], (Ass't Surg, 9th Vols/19th NCST, 2nd Cav), II: 88.
Icard, W.P., (Pvt, Co K, 35th NCST), V: 653.
Icard Station, N.C., II: 293; III: 445.
Idol, A.M., (Pvt, Co B, 1st Battalion NCST), V: 504.
Idol, J.N., (4th Sgt, Co B, 1st Battalion NCST), V: 504.
Ihrie, R.R., (Lt Col, 4th Battalion Home Guard), I: 733, 736; IV: 650.
Illinois, II: 702; V: 53.
Ijames, J.D., (4th Sgt, Co F, 3rd Vols/13th NCST), V: 550.
Imboden, John M., (Brig Gen), II: 257, 258; III: 270, 271, 746; IV: 181.
Index of Illustrations, V: 719-731.
Index of Parole Lists, V: 683-717.
Indian Creek, Tenn., IV: 115.
Indian Grove Gap, N.C., IV: 380.
Indina Territory, IV: 1.
Indina Woods, N.C., III: 135.
Indians in Battle, III: 736.
Indiana, II: 702; IV: 275; V: 411.
Ingalls, Rufus, (Maj Gen, USA), III: 560.
Ingle, A., (Pvt, Co A, 53rd NCST), V: 501.
Ingle, Albert, (Sgt, Co A, 53rd NCST), V: 501.
Ingle, R.W., (Pvt, Co M, 11th Vols/21st NCST), V: 515.
Inglis, James, (Sgt Maj, 58th NCST), III: 432, 437.
Inglish, S.M., [English, Samuel W.], (Capt, Co K, 65th NCST, 6th Cav), IV: 708.
Ingold, A.M., (Pvt, Co G, 46th NCST), V: 525.
Ingold, William, (Pvt, Co F, 53rd NCST; Detailed, 2nd Coprs Provost Guard), V: 570.
Ingraham, S.M., [Ingram], (1st Lt, Co E, 38th NCST), II: 675, 678.
Ingram, Benjamin G., (Pvt, Co A, 4th Vols/14th NCST), V: 489.
Ingram, Eli, (2nd Lt, Co H, 69th NCST, Thomas' Legion), III: 731.
Ingram, James R., (1st Cpl, Co K, 52nd NCST), III: 225.
Ingram, Joel, (Sgt, Co F, 4th Vols/14th NCST), I: 724.
Ingram, S.M., (1st Lt, Co E, 38th NCST), II: 678.
Ingram, Thomas, (Pvt, Co K, 11th Vols/21st NCST), V: 515.
Ingram, William A., (Pvt, Co H, 38th NCST), V: 558.
Ingram, William L., (2nd Lt, Co K, 26th NCST), II: 372, 374, 397.
Inman, A.A., [Aaron A.], (3rd Lt, Co D, 8th Vols/18th NCST), IV: 701.
Inman, J.P., (Cpl, Co D, 8th Vols/18th NCST), II: 64; V: 539.
Inspector-General, A.N.V., II: 446, 449.

Investigating Committee, IV: 247.
Ion, (One of Brig Gen M.W. Ransom's horses), III: 398.
Irby, Hogan, (Pvt, Co F, 48th NCST), V: 526.
Irdell County, N.C., I: 269; II: 792, 799, 806; IV: 379, 616; V: 292, 295.
Iredell, C.J., (Capt, Co E, 9th NCST, 1st Cav), I: 441, 486, 782.
Iredell, Cameron T., (Capt, Co C, 47th NCST; Ordnance Officer, Pettigrew's Brigade), III: 84, 103, 106; IV: 556.
Iredell, James Johnston, (Maj, 53rd NCST; Maj, 2nd Battalion NCST), II: 592, 593, 675; III: 258, 260; IV: 258, 259, 515; V: 12, 651.
Irelan, J.E., (Pvt, Co E, 10th Vols/20th NCST), V: 509.
Ireland, David, (Seaman, Gordon), V: 35.
Ireland, J.F., (Capt, Co D, 10th Vols/20th NCST), II: 112.
Ireland, V: 385.
Irvine, Ky., (and Battle of 1863), IV: 279, 280, 281-283, 285.
Irying, J.H., (Pvt, Co G, Color-bearer, 38th NCST), II: 676.
Isaac & Samuel, (Financial House, London, England), V: 454.
Isbell, James M., (Capt, Co A, 12th Vols/22nd NCST), II: 165.
Isle of Wight County, Va., I: 689; II: 515.
Isley, E., (Pvt, Co E, 27th NCST), II: 462; V: 502.
Isley, E., (Pvt, Co F, 53rd NCST), V: 502.
Isley, Lewis N., (Pvt, Co B, 27th NCST), II: 461; V: 523.
Isley, Martin V., (Sgt, Co H, 5th Vols/15th NCST), V: 522.
Isley, S.M., (Pvt, Co F, 53rd NCST), V: 502.
Isley, William, (Pvt, Co K, 47th NCST), V: 535.
Israel, F.J., (Pvt, Co D, 6th Battalion/60th NCST), III: 482.
Israel, J.M., (ACS, 6th Vols/16th NCST), I: 751; IV: 138.
Israel, J.N., (ACS, 6th Vols/16th NCST), IV: 138.
Israel, Pleas, (2nd Lt, Co A, 6th Battalion/60th NCST), III: 473.
Isaacs, G., (Pvt, Co A, 28th NCST), V: 540.
Iverson, Alfred, (Brig Gen), I: xii, 287, 612, 628, 634, 637, 643; II: 112, 114, 119, 225, 233, 235, 239; IV: 281, 522.
Iverson's Pit, (Gettysburg, Pa.), I: 637.
Ivester, A.P., (5th Sgt, Co F, 55th NCST), V: 528.
Ivey, A., (Pvt, Co G, 61st Va.), V: 569.
Ivey, Thomas J., (Jr 1st Lt, Co I, 10th NCST, 1st Art & Engs, Sutherland's Battery, Light Art), I: 582; IV: 222.
Ivey, William H., (2nd Lt, Co H, 19th NCST, 2nd Cav), IV: 722.
Ivor Station, Va., I: 522; II: 515, 776, 793; III: 211, 329; IV: 74, 357, 488, 489.
Ivy River, N.C., IV: 114.

(J)

Jack Mountain, Pa., III: 463, 569, 570, 588.
Jack's Shop, Madison County, Va., (and Battle of, 1863), I: 381, 426, 449, 452, 453, 448; II: 45, 99, 478, 568; III: 464, 472, 572-574, 579, 589, 590.
Jackey, Prof. Charles E., (Chief Musician, 55th NCST), III: 288, 295.
Jacksboro, Tenn., III: 434, 736; IV: 271, 290-291.
Jackson, ______, (Col, 48th N.Y.), V: 163.
Jackson, ______, (Midshipman, Ellis), V: 309, 310, 311.
Jackson, ______, [J.F.B.], (Col, 39th Ga.), II: 727.
Jackson, A.J., (2nd Lt, Co H, 30th NCST), II: 497; IV: 600.
Jackson, A.R., (Pvt, Co E, 12th Vols/22nd NCST), V: 553.
Jackson, Alfred E., (Brig Gen), III: 520, 739, 742-743; IV: 172.
Jackson, Andrew, (President, U.S.), II: 416.
Jackson, C.H., (Pvt, Co A, 11th Vols/21st NCST), V: 514.
Jackson, Conrad Feger, (Brig Gen, USA), IV: 236.
Jackson, Eli, (2nd Lt, Co I, 6th Battalion/60th NCST), III: 475.
Jackson, G.W., (Cpl, Co H, 33rd NCST), II: 540.
Jackson, George, (Col, Jackson's Battalion: 7th, 8th, 9th Junior Reserves), IV: 29, 39, 42, 43, 108, 265, 268, 383, 399, 440, 589.
Jackson, H.R., (Brig Gen), IV: 140, 400.
Jackson, J., (Pvt, Co E, 45th NCST), V: 500.
Jackson, J.J., (Capt, Co G, 5th Vols/15th NCST), I: 735.
Jackson, J.R., (Pvt, Co E, 12th Vols/22nd NCST), V: 553.
Jackson, J.R., (Pvt, Co H, 8th Vols/18th NCST), II: 64.
Jackson, J.W., (Pvt, Co E, 12th Vols/22nd NCST), V: 553.
Jackson, Jack, (Negro, servant to Stonewall Jackson), II: 551.
Jackson, John A., (Pvt, Co H, 26th NCST), II: 375; V: 532.
Jackson, John A., (2nd Lt, Adjt, 44th NCST), III: 22, 23.
Jackson, John Q., (Lt, Co E, 61st NCST), III: 504, 505.
Jackson, Olin, (Pvt, Co B, 56th NCST), III: 366.
Jackson, Samuel, (Pvt, Co K, 48th NCST), V: 527.
Jackson, Thomas Jonathan "Stonewall," (Lt Gen, 2nd Corps), I: 83, 115, 138, 143, 144, 145, 146, 149, 153, 165, 169, 170, 172, 181, 185, 190, 192, 193, 218, 223, 250, 252, 275, 286, 299, 303, 305, 306, 310, 335, 339, 341, 347, 353, 370, 373, 377, 378, 421, 554, 567, 569, 572, 612, 613, 614, 615, 617, 619, 621, 622, 623, 624,

625, 628, 629, 631, 659, 665, 666, 667, 668, 672, 696, 697, 707, 709, 710, 713, 715, 716, 717, 718, 757, 762, 763; II: 21, 26, 28, 29, 30, 31, 32, 34, 36, 37, 38, 59, 66, 67, 68, 70, 71, 72, 73, 118, 126, 131, 134, 135, 147, 148, 150, 153, 154, 156, 158, 169, 171, 177, 208, 209, 210, 214, 216, 218, 219, 222, 228, 230, 232, 233, 250, 300, 383, 406, 433, 469, 472, 473, 476, 479, 500, 504, 531, 550, 551, 553, 555, 556, 557, 558, 559, 560, 562, 563, 584, 586, 601, 602, 603, 604, 607, 654, 656, 657, 658, 659, 660, 682, 683, 684, 688, 701, 768, 792; III: 69, 115, 116, 269, 278, 410, 427, 550, 556, 568, 643, 731, 748; IV: 155, 157, 158, 160, 162, 165, 167, 168, 169, 170, 172, 173, 175, 179, 227, 228, 231, 233, 234, 235, 297, 356, 411, 441, 444, 465, 466, 467, 503, 522, 552, 571; 703, 718, 728, 731; V: viii, xvi, xviii, 72, 77, 78, 81, 93, 94, 95, 96, 97, 98, 99, 129.

Jackson, W.C., (Musician, 46th NCST), V: 524.

Jackson, W.S., (2nd Lt, Co G, 5th Vols/15th NCST), I: 735.

Jackson, Wes., (Pvt, Co C, 35th NCST), V: 562.

Jackson, N.C., II: 277, 614; III: 330, 458, 717; IV: 27, 359; V: 272.

Jackson County, N.C., I: 767, 768; II: 439, 705; III: 518, 730, 731, 733, 759; IV: 113, 381, 481; V: 173, 655.

Jackson, Miss. II: 734; III: 484, 485, 486, 499.

Jackson River, Va., II: 270.

Jackson River Depot, Va., II: 270.

Jackson's Mill, N.C., II: 762; IV: 54.

Jacksonville, Fla., V: 384.

Jacksonville, N.C., II: 775.

Jacobs, Benjamin J., (Capt, Co C, 78th NCST, 8th Senior Reserves), IV: 107.

Jacobs, Darby, (Pvt, Co G, 5th Vols/15th NCST), V: 522.

Jacobs, J.W., (1st Lt, Co A, 5th Vols/15th NCST), I: 734.

Jacobs, Jesse C., (Capt, Co L, 1st Vols, "Bethel"), I: 110.

Jacobs, John, (Chief Musician, 32nd NCST), V: 495.

Jacobs, John M., (1st Lt, Co E, 56th NCST), III: 315, 347.

Jacobs, Joseph, (Pvt, Co D, 56th NCST), V: 566.

Jacob's Ford, (Rapidan River, Va.), III: 585, 586, 590.

Jacocks, J.A., (Pvt, Co A, Webb's Battery, Starr's 13th Battalion NCST, Light Art), V: 282.

James II, (King of England), V: 473.

James, H.H., [Henry H.], (Sgt, Co H, 4th NCST), I: 233.

James, J.E., (Pvt, Co A, 6th Battalion/60th NCST), III: 481.

James, James W., (Pvt, 56th NCST), III: 380.

James, John, (Pvt, Co A, 11th Vols/21st NCST), V: 514.

James, Matthew, (Pvt, Co H, 27th NCST), II: 462.

James, Phillip A., (4th Sgt, Co D, 52nd NCST), III: 224.

James, R., (Pvt, Co H, 27th NCST), II: 462; V: 523.

James, R.J., (Bugler, Co B, 12th Vols/22nd NCST), V: 553.

James, R.P., (Adjt, 10th Vols/20th NCST), II: 112.

James, Robert, (Lt, Co C, 51st NCST), III: 218.

James, Robert, (Lt, Co C, 51st NCST), III: 218.

James, Redden, (Sgt, Co F, 6th Battalion/60th NCST), III: 489.

James, T.J., (Pvt, Co G, 43rd NCST), V: 498.
James, Theodore C., (Adjt, 3rd NCST), I: 213.
James, W.C., (Pvt, Co D, 28th NCST), V: 541.
James, W.M., (3rd Sgt, Co B, 12th Vols/22nd NCST), V: 553.
James, William A., (Teamster, Co D, 42nd NCST; Detailed, QM Corps), V: 571.
James, William H., (Capt, Chief Engineer, Wilmington), IV: 417, 419.
James City, Va., II: 81; III: 578.
James Island, S.C., I: 391, 392, 742; II: 513; III: 206, 510, 511; IV: 484; V: 163.
James River, Va., I: 80, 82, 305, 321, 323, 384, 396, 408, 430, 434, 435, 463, 470, 482, 538, 539, 552, 559, 580, 597, 600, 602, 616, 617, 618, 654, 655, 662, 678, 702, 737, 738, 739, 742, 746, 747, 754, 757; II: 4, 56 57, 58, 75, 76, 88, 101, 104, 133, 140, 212, 274, 285, 391, 429, 430, 518, 548, 574, 621, 768, 779, 783, 797, 799, 801; III: 4, 39, 77, 96, 114, 116, 130, 139, 162, 163, 166, 168, 169, 184, 213, 247, 249, 255, 275, 276, 307, 308, 317, 329, 350, 351, 354, 355, 358, 359, 374, 399, 540, 553, 602, 603, 604, 609, 611, 615, 618, 619, 622, 627, 688, 691; IV: 86, 158, 208, 209, 261, 357, 362, 411, 446, 478, 493, 494, 497, 502, 529, 534, 536, 538; V: 326.
James River Squadron, IV: 733.
Jameson, W., (Ensign, USN; Pioneer, Iosco) V: 245.
Jamestown, N.C., I: 386.
Jamestown Island, II: 776.
Jamesville, N.C., I: 446; III: 337; IV: 16, 82; V: 177.
Jamesville Road, (nr Plymouth), III: 338; V: 177.
Jamison, John, (Pvt, Co F, 63rd NCST, 5th Cav), III: 618.
Jamison, Miles S., (Pvt, Co D, 34th NCST), V: 555.
Jarman, J.R., (Cpl, Co K, 26th NCST), V: 532.
Jarman, L., (Pvt, Co A, 35th NCST), V: 562.
Jarman, W., (Pvt, Co A, 35th NCST), V: 562.
Jarrett, O.M., (Pvt, Co K, 46th NCST), V: 525.
Jarrett, George, (Pvt, Co F, 58th NCST), III: 453.
Jarrett, J.A., (Capt, Co C, 26th NCST), II: 358, 371, 396, 397.
Jarrett, J.M., (1st Lt, Co C, 5th Vols/15th NCST), I: 734.
Jarrett, J.W., (2nd Lt, Co C, 5th Vols/15th NCST), I: 734.
Jarrett, W.D., (Pvt, Co H, 45th NCST), V: 500.
Jarrett, William A., (Pvt, Co B, 35th NCST), V: 562.
Jarratt's Station, Va., [Jarett's] I: 386; II: 58, 450, 481, 576, 669; III: 122, 135, 311, 350.
Jarrette, Hosea, (Pvt, Co E, 32nd NCST), V: 496.
Jarvis, D.W., (Lt, Co B, 61st NCST), III: 504.
Jarvis, J.A., (Lt, Co F, 64th NCST), III: 660.
Jarvis, John A., (Capt, Co D, 29th NCST), II: 485, 493.
Jarvis, S.A., [Simeon A.], (2nd Lt, Co H, 54th NCST), IV: 700, 708.
Jarvis, T.J., (Capt, Co B, 8th NCST, later Gov. of N.C.), I: 403; IV: 490, 537.
Jasper, ______, (Sgt, Lane's Brigade), II: 2, 158; IV: 471.
Jay, Joseph McD., (Pvt, Co G, 6th Vols/16th NCST), IV: 216; V: 552.

Jay, William H.M., (Pvt, Co G, 6th Vols/16th NCST), IV: 216; V: 552.
Jean, W.P., (Pvt, Co G, 28th NCST), V: 542.
Jefferson, Va., IV: 161.
Jefferson County, Tenn., III: 730.
Jefferson County, Va., V: 213.
Jefferson Medical College of Philadelphia, II: 413.
Jefferson Street, (Plymouth), V: 189.
Jeffords, R.J., (Lt Col, 5th S.C., Cav), II: 3; IV: 266, 528.
Jeffreys, J.G., (Pvt, Co B, 3rd Vols/13th NCST), V: 549.
Jeffreys, Lea, (Pvt, Co A, 3rd Vols/13th NCST), V: 549.
Jeffreys, W.A., (Sgt, Co I, 41st NCST, 3rd Cav), II: 786.
Jeffries, C.E., (Pvt, Co E, 46th NCST), V: 524.
Jenk's Bridge, Ga., IV: 327, 328.
Jenkins, ______, (Col, 146th N.Y.), I: 150, 200.
Jenkins, ______, [Bennett P.], (2nd Lt, Co B, 33rd NCST), II: 578.
Jenkins, ______, (Capt, Co E, 2nd Regt Home Guard), IV: 653.
Jenkins, Dr. ______, (Surg, 46th NCST), III: 65; IV: 639, 657.
Jenkins, Aaron, (Pvt, Co C, 10th NCST, 1st Art & Engs, Brem-Graham-Williams' Battery, Light Art), V: 567.
Jenkins, B.P., (2nd Lt, Claiborne-Dearing"s 7th C.S., Cav; Co I, 16th Battalion/75th NCST, 7th Cav), IV: 91, 701, 708.
Jenkins, Carley, (Pvt, Co I, 6th NCST), V: 513.
Jenkins, E.J., (Pvt, Co A, 33rd NCST), V: 543.
Jenkins, Edward, (Pvt, Co C, 10th NCST, 1st Art & Engs, Brem-Graham-Williams' Battery, Light Art), V: 567.
Jenkins, Frederick H., (Capt, Co B, 33rd NCST), II: 538.
Jenkins, H., (Pvt, Co K, 37th NCST), V: 546.
Jenkins, H.J., (1st Lt, Co A, Wynn's 15th Battalion, Cav), IV: 365, 722; V: 677.
Jenkins, Henry, (1st Lt, Co I, 34th NCST), V: 548.
Jenkins, J.A., (Pvt, Co B, 28th NCST), V: 541.
Jenkins, J.F., (Pvt, Co E, 1st Vols, "Bethel"), I: 128.
Jenkins, J.H., (Pvt, Co B, 33rd NCST), V: 543.
Jenkins, J.P., (1st Lt, Co F, 1st NCST), I: 137.
Jenkins, James H., (Sgt, Co B, 33rd NCST), II: 538.
Jenkins, Joseph, (Maj, 1st Regt 3rd Class, Home Guard), IV: 653.
Jenkins, Joseph P., (Lt, Co H, 32nd NCST), I: 620.
Jenkins, M., II: 775.
Jenkins, Micah, (Brig Gen), I: 494, 522, 548; II: 88, 775, 776.
Jenkins, Newsom E., (Sgt Maj, 4th Vols/14th NCST), V: 489.
Jenkins, Samuel, (Pvt, Co C, 10th NCST, 1st Art & Engs, Brem-Graham-Williams' Battery, Light Art), V: 567.
Jenkins, T.M., (2nd Lt, Co I, 6th NCST), IV: 701, 708.
Jenkins, Thomas, (Pvt, Co D, 6th Vols/16th NCST), V: 552.
Jenkins, Thomas G., (Lt, Co C, 46th NCST), III: 76, 81; V: 520.
Jenkins, W.A., (Lt. Col, 46th NCST), III: 64, 65, 81; V: 651.
Jenkins, W.A., (Pvt, Co I, 6th NCST), V: 513.
Jenkins, W.A., (Sgt, Co H, 11th Vols/21st NCST), V: 515.

Jenkins, W.B., (2nd Lt, Co B, 50th NCST), III: 203.

Jenkins, Wilson T., (Capt, Co A, 4th Vols/14th NCST), I: 168, 274, 708; V: 484.

Jennett, Robert, (Sgt, Co F, 33rd NCST), II: 539, 578.

Jennings, James A., [James R.], (Capt, Co G, 1st Vols/11th NCST), I: 77, 119, 585.

Jennings, L.R., (Sgt, Co D, 33rd NCST), V: 544.

Jennings, Nathaniel B., (2nd Lt, Co G, 1st Vols/11th NCST), I: 585.

Jennings, W.L., (Lt, Co A, 63rd NCST, 5th Cav), III: 577.

Jericho Ford, Va., II: 55, 480, 573, 668; III: 246; IV: 196-198, 469.

Jericho Mills, Va., I: 384.

Jerman, E.W., (Pvt, Co K, 43rd NCST), V: 499.

Jerome, E.A., (Capt, Co I, 53rd NCST), III: 263.

Jerome, R.J., (2nd Lt, Co B, 5th Vols/15th NCST), I: 734.

Jerome, R.P., (Maj, 5th Vols/15th NCST), I: 733, 734.

Jerusalem Plank Road, (nr Petersburg, Va.), I: 482; II: 450; III: 140, 360, 362, 363, 364, 371, 373; IV: 362.

Jesse Scouts, (Dressing in Confederate uniforms these scouts of Sheridan's cavalry penetrated Lee's lines and attempted to disrupt the A.N.V. in any manner that they could. If captured in uniform they could, and were in some cases, executed as spies. A good number of Federal officers saw this practice as underhanded and in violation of the spirit of the Rules and Articles of War - which it was. Evidently even the men responsible for sending these spies/scouts on their missions felt the same way as they attempted to deny the practice after the war. The evidence and records of their operations remains too strong for those feeble denials to be taken seriously.), I: 782.

Jessup, Isaac, (2nd Lt, Co B, Starr's Battery, Starr's 13th Battalion NCST, Light Art), I: 120; IV: 350.

Jetersville, Va., [Gettersville], I: 480, 778, 780; II: 62, 109, 482; III: 283; IV: 90, 454.

Jewel, ______, (Pvt, Co B, 10th NCST, 1st Art & Engs, Guion's Hvy Art), I: 509.

Jewett, R.B., (Sgt Maj, 9th Battalion NCST, 1st Hvy Art), IV: 306.

Jimtown, N.C., III: 497.

Jinks, H., (Cpl, Co H, 47th NCST), V: 535.

Johns, Dr. Anthony B., (Capt, Co H, 3rd Vols/13th NCST; Ass't Surg, 45th NCST; Capt, 72nd NCST, 3rd Junior Reserves), IV: 50, 639.

Johns, William R., (Capt, Conscript Bureau), IV: 50, 51.

John's River, N.C., IV: 375.

Johnson, ______, (Master, NCN), V: 309.

Johnson, ______, (Pvt, Ambulance driver, 11th Vols/21st NCST), II: 143.

Johnson, ______, (Lt, Breathed's Battery Horse Art), II: 90 91.

Johnson, ______, (Capt, Engineer, Lee's Staff), II: 441.

Johnson, A.H., (Pvt, Co H, 11th Vols/21st NCST), V: 515.

Johnson, A.J., (Cpl, Co E, 45th NCST), V: 500.

Johnson, A.M., (2nd Lt, Co H, 11th Vols/21st NCST), V: 511.

Johnson, A.R., (Capt, Co G, 26th NCST), II: 390, 395, 396, 397; V: 529.
Johnson, Andrew, (President, U.S.), I: 63, 65; III: 519, 734, 741; IV: 22, 32.
Johnson, B.C., (Pvt, Co B, 56th NCST), III: 366.
Johnson, Bushrod Rush, (Maj Gen), II: 176, 285, 287, 391, 490, 713, 718, 720, 730; III: 357; IV: 491.
Johnson, Balden, (Fayetteville and Harper's Ferry Arsenals). IV: 298.
Johnson, Bradley T., (Brig Gen), I: 646; II: 123, 251; IV: 375, 758, 760, 762, 763; V: 213-216 personal account.
Johnson, C.R., (Sgt, Co E, 43rd NCST), V: 498.
Johnson, Carson, (1st Lt, Co D, 6th Battalion Junior Reserves; Co H, 70th NCST, 1st Junior Reserves), IV: 13.
Johnson, Dr. Charles E., (Col, Surgeon General, North Carolina), IV: 623, 624, 628.
Johnson, Cornelius, (1st Lt, Co E, 30th NCST), II: 496; IV: 600.
Johnson, D., (Pvt, Co C, 10th NCST, 1st Art & Engs, Brem-Graham-Williams' Battery, Light Art), V: 568.
Johnson, David, (Capt, Co F, 2nd NCST), I: 176; II: 618; V: 486.
Johnson, David, (Pvt, Detached Co, 68th NCST), III: 723.
Johnson, Dugald, (Pvt, Co H, 46th NCST), V: 525.
Johnson, E., (Pvt, Co H, 46th NCST), V: 525.
Johnson, E.H., (Pvt, Co B, 1st NCST), V: 485.
Johnson, E.M., (Pvt, Co E, 30th NCST), V: 492.
Johnson, Edward, (Maj Gen), I: 147, 148, 150, 171, 193, 198, 204, 288, 290, 315, 316, 548; II: 50, 120, 243, 384, 480, 571; III: 6; V: 596; IV: 469; V: 596.
Johnson, Dr. Elisha G., (Maj, 69th NCST, Thomas' Legion), III: 730, 732.
Johnson, Frank S., (Lt, Adjt, 72nd NCST, 3rd Junior Reserves), IV: 51.
Johnson, George W., (Lt Col, 7th Vols/17th NCST), II: 1.
Johnson, Griffin, (Pvt, Co K, 6th Vols/16th NCST), V: 552.
Johnson, H.C., (Pvt, Co G, 26th NCST), V: 532.
Johnson, H.L., (Pvt, Co D, 26th NCST), V: 531.
Johnson, Hiram, (Sgt, Co G, 26th NCST), II: 374.
Johnson, I.J., (1st Lt, Co E, 30th NCST), II: 496; V: 484.
Johnson, Isaac M., (Pvt, Co G, 34th NCST), V: 556.
Johnson, J.H., (Pvt, Co A, 56th NCST), III: 347.
Johnson, J.H., (2nd Lt, Co K, 44th NCST), III: 24, 37.
Johnson, J.J., (Pvt, Co H, Colorbearer, 38th NCST), II: 676.
Johnson, J.N., (1st Sgt, Co C, 44th NCST), V: 533.
Johnson, J.W., (1st Lt, Drill Master, M.W. Ransom's Brigade), V: 559.
Johnson, J.W., (Pvt, Co D, 1st NCST), V: 485.
Johnson, Jacob, (Pvt, Co E, 59th NCST, 4th Cav), V: 659.
Johnson, James, (Pvt, Co A, 4th NCST; Detailed, 2nd Corps Provost Guard), V: 570.
Johnson, James, (Pvt, Co E, 26th NCST), V: 532.
Johnson, Dr. James, (Surg,2nd Vols/12th NCST), I: 606; IV: 633.
Johnson, James D., (Pvt, Co H, 5th NCST), I: 292; V: 505.

Johnson, James F., (Capt, Co C, 9th NCST, 1st Cav), I: 782.
Johnson, James H., (Sgt, Co F, 5th Vols/15th NCST), V: 521.
Johnson, James M., (Sgt, Co I, 5th Vols/15th NCST), V: 521.
Johnson, James Theodore, (Col, 35th NCST), II: 579.
Johnson, Jesse, (Pvt, Co G, 48th NCST), V: 526.
Johnson, John, (Pvt, Co A, 8th Vols/18th NCST), II: 63; V: 539.
Johnson, John, (Pvt, Co F, 7th NCST), V: 538.
Johnson, John C., (Cpl, Co B, 10th Vols/20th NCST; Detailed, 2nd Corps Provost Guard), V: 569.
Johnson, John H., (Chief Musician, 61st NCST), III: 503.
Johnson, John R., (Pvt, Co K, 2nd Vols/12th NCST), I: 630.
Johnson, John T., (Pvt, Co G, 34th NCST), V: 556.
Johnson, Joseph P., (Musician, 6th Vols/16th NCST), V: 551.
Johnson, Joshua, (Pvt, Co H, 6th NCST), V: 194.
Johnson, Jourdan, (Pvt, Co G, 48th NCST), V: 526.
Johnson, L.A., (Capt, Co A, 59th NCST, 4th Cav), III: 457, 464, 468.
Johnson, Lee, (2nd Lt, Co B, 13th Vols/23rd NCST), II: 183.
Johnson, Lem., (Pvt, Co I, 57th NCST), V: 518.
Johnson, Lucius J., (Maj, 7th Vols/17th NCST), II: 2, 5; IV: 538, 544, 545, 546; V: 11, 651, 680.
Johnson, M.C., (Pvt, Co G, 54th NCST), V: 516.
Johnson, McC., (Pvt, Co C, 11th Vols/21st NCST), V: 514.
Johnson, M.O., (Pvt, Co E, 30th NCST), V: 492.
Johnson, Miles, (Lt, Co F, 9th NCST, 1st Cav), I: 486.
Johnson, Nathan J., (Lt Col, 115th N.Y.), V: 238.
Johnson, P.J., (Capt, Co K, 35th NCST), V: 559, 663.
Johnson, R.B., (Capt, AQM, 62nd NCST), III: 515.
Johnson, R.F., (Pvt, Co E, 43rd NCST), V: 498.
Johnson, R.S., (Pvt, Co H, 13th Vols/23rd NCST), V: 510.
Johnson, R.W., (Senator, Ark., Father of Lt. F.S. Johnson), IV: 51.
Johnson, Robert, (Chief Clerk, Fayetteville Arsenal), IV: 299.
Johnson, Robert, (Cpl, Co D, 5th NCST), V: 505.
Johnson, S.M., (1st Lt, Claiborne-Dearing's 7th C.S. Cav; Co E, 16th Battalion/75th NCST, 7th Cav), IV: 92.
Johnson, Stewart L., [Johnston], (Capt, Co H, 7th Vols/17th NCST), II: 2; V: 15, 44, 46, 47, 49, 50, 680.
Johnson, Thomas A., (Sgt, Co G, 34th NCST), V: 556.
Johnson, Thomas D., (AQM, Walker's Battalion, Thomas' Legion, 80th NCST), IV: 117.
Johnson, Thomas L., (Capt, Co A, 1st NCST), I: 150; IV: 721.
Johnson, W., (Pvt, Co H, 59th NCST, 4th Cav), V: 659.
Johnson, W., (2nd Lt, Co E, 78th NCST, 8th Senior Reserves), IV: 107.
Johnson, W., (Pvt, Co F, 16th Battalion/75th NCST, 7th Cav), V: 660.
Johnson, W., (Pvt, Co C, 3rd NCST), V: 487.
Johnson, W.A., (Pvt, Co K, 2nd NCST), I: 164.

Johnson, W.H., [Johnston, William H.], (Capt, Co K, 13th Vols/23rd NCST), IV: 708.

Johnson, W.L., (Pvt, Co I, 10th Vols/20th NCST), V: 509.

Johnson, W.P., [Johnston, William P.], (Pvt, Co C, 9th NCST, 1st Cav), IV: 723.

Johnson, W.P., (Cpl, Co G, 26th NCST), V: 532.

Johnson, W.R., (Pvt, Co B, 1st NCST), V: 485.

Johnson, Waverly, [Johnston], (Lt, ADC to Matt Ransom; 2nd Lt, Co E, 6th Battalion Junior Reserves; Co G, 70th NCST, 1st Junior Reserves), II: 619; IV: 13, 490, 572.

Johnson, Wiley, (Pvt, Co A, 5th NCST; Detailed, 2nd Corps Provost Guards), V: 570.

Johnson, William, (Pvt, Co C, 49th NCST), V: 564.

Johnson, William, (Pvt, Co A , 65th NCST, 6th Cav), III: 680.

Johnson, William J., (Pvt, Co A, 5th Vols/15th NCST), V: 520.

Johnson, William R., (of Poplar Lawn), III: 350, 393.

Johnson, Yancey M.C., (Capt, Co L, 12th Vols/22nd NCST), II: 166, 172, 178; V: 548.

Johnson City, Tenn., III: 433, 447, 448, 517, 518.

Johnson's Island Prison, [Johnston's], (Sandusky, Ohio; Lake Erie), I: 466, 481, 584, 590, 599; II: 254, 290, 415, 416, 471, 671, 761; III: 37, 159, 273, 467, 663, 664; IV: 192, 257, 287, 292, 321, 405, 689-696; V: xvi, 88.

Johnson's Island Prison, Life at, IV: 657-687.

Johnson's Island Prison, List of Prisoners, IV: 703-712.

Johnson's Island Prisoners' Letter to Governor Vance, IV: 697-702.

Johnston, ______, (Lt Col, Hampton's Legion), I: 342.

Johnston, ______, (ADC to J.A. Walker), I: 650.

Johnston, Albert Sidney, (Gen), I: 41, 79; III: 382; IV: 415, 498; V: xvi, 395.

Johnston, B.A., (Lt, Co C, 37th NCST), II: 668.

Johnston, Bradley, (Brig Gen), II: 123, 251, 252.

Johnston, Branch, (2nd Lt, Co 2, West's Battalion NCST, Cav), IV: 111.

Johnston, Cary, (Pvt, Co C, 4th Vols/14th NCST), I: 732.

Johnston, D., (Pvt, Co B, 10th Vols/20th NCST), V: 508.

Johnston, Francis M., (Pvt, Co A, 4th Vols/14th NCST), V: 489.

Johnston, Francis W., (Capt, Co E, 25th NCST), II: 292.

Johnston, Rev. Dr. Frontis H., (Chaplain, 48th NCST), IV: 616.

Johnston, G.W., (Lt Col, 7th Vols/17th NCST), V: 35, 38, 39, 40, 42, 47, 50.

Johnston, Gabriel, (Ordnance Sgt, 28th NCST), II: 466.

Johnston, George B., (AAG, Branch's Brigade), II: 466, 467, 471; IV: 472.

Johnston, J.H., (Sgt, Co H, 6th NCST), V: 513.

Johnston, J.J., (Musician, 5th NCST), I: 291; V: 504.

Johnston, J.P., (Pvt, Co G, 28th NCST), V: 542.

Johnston, James Forney, (Ass't ACS, 13th Vols./23rd NCST; ADC, Garland-Iverson-Johnston's Brigade; Capt, Co A, 2nd Vols/12th NCST), II: 189, 242; IV: 521, 523; V: 679.

Johnston, James F., (Capt, Co C, 9th NCST, 1st Cav), I: 441, 485.

Johnston, James T., (Lt Col, 35th NCST), II: 610, 613, 623, 625, 627.
Johnston, Jesse, (Pvt, Co A, 5th NCST), I: 291; V: 504.
Johnston, John H., (Sgt Maj, 44th NCST; 1st Lt, Co K, 44th NCST III: 22; V: 529.
Johnston, Joseph E., (Gen, and Johnston's Peninsula Army, Johnston's Army of the Potomac, Johnston's Army of the West), I: 35, 55, 56, 58, 60, 61, 63, 64, 95, 297, 301, 302, 303, 339, 340, 341, 342, 343, 347, 348, 349, 350, 386, 413, 417, 420, 499, 531, 532, 534, 553, 565, 566, 611, 655, 656, 658, 690, 693, 710, 755, 768, 772, 777, 781; II: 13, 21, 23, 25, 66, 67, 193, 194, 196, 199, 201, 203, 204, 207, 392, 393, 462, 519, 598, 712, 714, 720, 721, 734, 735, 739, 741, 742, 743, 764, 803, 804; III: 79, 192, 193, 194, 195, 196, 199, 200, 201, 217, 306, 317, 381, 394, 396, 400, 437, 439, 442, 443, 444, 445, 454, 484, 485, 492, 493, 496, 497, 499, 500, 502, 513, 514, 542, 699, 700, 709, 710, 727; IV: 4, 5, 20, 21, 30, 31, 32, 43, 55, 56, 57, 58, 59, 61, 62, 67, 69, 98, 105, 108, 114, 123, 128, 141, 151, 222, 226, 269, 302, 312, 322, 323, 335, 350, 351, 352, 359, 360, 362, 369, 383, 394, 419, 425, 429, 430, 431, 438, 439, 442, 481, 483, 495, 498, 499, 500, 547, 548, 549, 592, 593, 620, 694, 731; V: xviii, 29, 32, 255, 270, 271, 273, 274, 276, 277, 279, 280, 354, 468, 471, 472, 478, 643, 649, 654.
Johnston, Philip J., (Capt, Co K, 35th NCST), II: 610, 626, 628.
Johnston, Robert, (Cpl, Co D, 5th NCST), I: 291.
Johnston, Robert D., (Brig Gen), I: xii, 48, 61, 629, 630, 644, 646, 651; II: 117, 119, 120, 121, 187, 189, 201, 205, 206, 223, 230, 236, 238, 239, 241, 242, 244, 246, 252, 260, 261, 263, 264, 266; III: 48, 422, 436; IV: 522, 523; V: 213, 214, 215, 216, 649.
Johnston, Samuel R., (AQMS, 43rd NCST), V: 497.
Johnston, T.L., (Capt, Co A, 1st NCST), I: 136, 150.
Johnston, Thomas D., (Capt, AQM, Walker's Battalion, Thomas' Legion; 80th NCST), IV: 117, 128, 386.
Johnston, W.B., (Capt, Co C, 77th NCST, 7th Senior Reserves), IV: 99.
Johnston, W.E., (Lt, Co F, 2nd Vols/12th NCST), I: 630.
Johnston, William, (Capt, Co H, 57th NCST), III: 411.
Johnston, William, (Col, N.C. Subsistence Department), I: 37, 48; II: 206; V: 519, 649.
Johnston, William A., (Lt Col, 4th Vols/14th NCST), I: 711, 716, 728; IV: 461; V: 484.
Johnston, William H., (Capt, Co K, 13th Vols/23rd NCST), II: 187, 205, 236; IV: 702, 708.
Johnston's Army, (See: Army of Tennessee).
Johnston County, N.C., II: 274, 650; III: 194, 199, 262, 289, 514, 727; IV: 329, 351, 592, 610, 619; V: 280.
Joiner, J.R., (Pvt, Co D, 44th NCST), V: 533.
Joiner, Sydney, (Pvt, Co G, 47th NCST), V: 535.
Joines, Calloway, (Lt, Co I, 61st NCST), III: 504.
Joines, John W., (Lt, Co I, 61st NCST), III: 504.
Joines, Major F., (2nd Lt, Co D, 33rd NCST, Branch's), II: 539, 578; IV: 700, 708.

Joines, W.H., (Lt, Co I, 61st NCST), III: 504.
Jolly, C.D., (Pvt, Co E, 2nd Vols/12th NCST), V: 507.
Jolly, M.N., (Sgt, Co H, 28th NCST), V: 542.
Jonas Ridge, N.C., IV: 372.
Jonathan, N.C., IV: 620.
Jones, _____, (Col, Ft. Caswell), IV: 306, 332.
Jones, _____, (Capt, Va. Cav), I: 89.
Jones, A., (Pvt, Co F, 6th NCST), V: 512, 572.
Jones, A.C., (Pvt, Co F, 32nd NCST), V: 496.
Jones, A.R., (Pvt, Co A, 2nd Battalion NCST), V: 495.
Jones, Andrew J., (Pvt, Co D, 10th NCST, 1st Art & Engs, Reilly-Ramsay's Battery, Light Art), V: 568.
Jones, Arthur N., (Lt, Co C, 10th Vols/20th NCST), II: 114.
Jones, Asa W., (Capt, Co G, 67th NCST), III: 704.
Jones, B., (Pvt, Co E, 47th NCST), V: 535.
Jones, Benjamin, (Pvt, Co A, 3rd NCST), V: 487.
Jones, Bill, (Chief, Lilian; post war Capt, Luloa Murchison), V: 372.
Jones, C.C., (Sgt, Co H, 6th Battalion/60th NCST), III: 482.
Jones, C.C., (Pvt, Co L, 12th Vols/22nd NCST), V: 554.
Jones, C.E., (Pvt, Co H, 26th NCST), V: 532.
Jones, C.L., (Ass't Paymaster, CSN, Tallahassee), V: 438.
Jones, Charles J., (Capt, Co F, 8th NCST), I: 387.
Jones, Rev. Charles P., (Capt, Co D, Adam's Battery, Starr's 13th Battalion NCST, Light Art), IV: 353.
Jones, Charles R., (Lt, Adjt, 55th NCST), III: 288, 296.
Jones, Clinton A., (Pvt, Co G, 25th NCST; AQMS, 25th NCST), II: 291; V: 521.
Jones, Cyrus P., (Lt, Co B, 4th Vols/14th NCST), I: 731.
Jones, D., (Pvt, Co I, 3rd Vols/13th NCST), V: 551.
Jones, D.C., (Pvt, Co K, 3rd Vols/13th NCST), V: 551.
Jones, Daniel McL., (2nd Lt, Co I, 31st NCST), II: 512.
Jones, E.A., (Pvt, Co E, 2nd Vols/12th NCST), V: 507.
Jones, E.P., [Elliotte P.], (Col, 109th Va.Milita), III: 747; IV: 717.
Jones, George T., (2nd Lt, Co E, 50th NCST), III: 203.
Jones, George W., (1st Lt, Co D, 27th NCST), II: 457, 462; V: 519.
Jones, H.M., (Pvt, Co A, 3rd Vols/13th NCST), V: 549.
Jones, Halcott P., (1st Lt, Co E, Dixon's Battery, Starr's 13th Battalion NCST, Light Art), III: 349, IV: 354.
Jones, Hamilton C., Jr., (Col, 57th NCST), I: 271, 281, 354; III: 405, 406, 409, 412, 416, 418, 421, 422, 423, 424, 426, 427, 428; IV: 658, 700, 702, 708; V: 650.
Jones, Hawkins, (Pvt, Co K, 55th NCST), V: 528.
Jones, Henry, (Pvt, Co H, 63rd NCST, 5th Cav), III: 587.
Jones, Isaac A., (1st Lt, Adjt, 5th NCST), I: 281, 284, 286.
Jones, Issac M., (Pvt, Co C, 4th NCST), V: 488.
Jones, J., (Capt, AAG, Cox's Brigade), IV: 463; V: 483.
Jones, J.A., (Pvt, Co H, 45th NCST), V: 500.
Jones, J.A., (1st Sgt, Co K, 3rd Vols/13th NCST), V: 551.
Jones, J.B., (Pvt, Co A, 1st Battalion NCST), V: 503.

Jones, J.D., (Pvt, Co I, 56th NCST), V: 566.

Jones, J.H., (Pvt, Co B, 37th NCST), V: 545.

Jones, J.J., (Pvt, Co E, 26th NCST), V: 532.

Jones, J.K., (Sgt, Co E, 30th NCST), V: 492.

Jones, J.M., (1st Sgt, Co B, 3rd Vols/13th NCST), V: 549.

Jones, J.R., (Pvt, Co D, 11th Vols/21st NCST), V: 514.

Jones, J.R., (AQMS, 35th NCST), V: 562.

Jones, Dr. J.W., (Surg, Tarboro Wayside Hospital), IV: 625, 627, 630.

Jones, James, (Pvt, Co G, 26th NCST), V: 532.

Jones, James, (Pvt, Co E, 27th NCST), V: 523.

Jones, James G.M., (2nd Lt, Co D, 26th NCST), II: 371, 396, 397, 420.

Jones, James H., (Capt, Co H, 11th Vols/21st NCST) II: 145.

Jones, James M., (Capt, ACS, 5th NCST), I: 281.

Jones, Jay Bird, (Alleged Col, USA, Buffalo), III: 136, 506; IV: 575; V: 10, 183.

Jones, Joel, (Lt, Co C, 2nd NCST), I: 159.

Jones, John, (Pvt, Co I, 43rd NCST), V: 499.

Jones, John, (Pvt, Co I, 14th Vols/24th NCST), V: 560.

Jones, John, (2nd Lt, Co F, 62nd NCST), III: 516.

Jones, John G., (Col, 35th NCST), I: 281; II: 597, 600, 606, 612, 613, 622, 623; III: 346, 361; IV: 575; V: 10, 183, 187.

Jones, John M., (1st Lt, Co B, Badham's 3rd Battalion NCST, Light Art), IV: 262, 264, 268.

Jones, John Marshall, (Brig Gen), III: 43.

Jones, John Thomas, (Lt Col, 26th NCST), I: 118, 590, 591; II: 304, 330, 335, 338, 349, 351, 354, 358, 362, 365, 371, 372, 380, 382, 383, 395, 397, 401, 403, 410-411; III: 92; IV: 562; V: ix, 11, 111, 131, 133, 135, 152, 650.

Jones, Joseph, (Capt, Co K, 4th Vols/14th NCST), I: 713.

Jones, Joseph P., (Lt Col, 5th NCST), I: 281.

Jones, Josiah M., (2nd Lt, Co K, 6th Battalion/60th NCST), III: 475.

Jones, L.A., (Pvt, Co K, 41st NCST, 3rd Cav), II: 786.

Jones, L.A., (Pvt, Co F, 32nd NCST), V: 496.

Jones, L.W., [Lewis W.], (Pvt, Co G, 21st Ga.), V: 194.

Jones, Lewellyn, (2nd Sgt, Co A, 55th NCST), V: 527.

Jones, Love, (Pvt, Co I, 6th Vols/16th NCST), V: 552.

Jones, J. Pembroke, (1st Lt, CSN, Capt, Raleigh), V: 232, 298, 447.

Jones, J. Richter, (Col, 58th Pa.), III: 328, 555.

Jones, J. Wiley, (1st Lt, Co I, 47th NCST), III: 85, 108, 112; V: 529.

Jones, Lemuel, (Pvt, Co F, 4th Vols/14th NCST), V: 490.

Jones, LeRoy, (Capt, 76th NCST, 6th Senior Reserves), IV: 97.

Jones, M., (Pvt, Co K, 2nd Vols/12th NCST), V: 508.

Jones, M.L., (Sgt, Co F, 32nd NCST), V: 496.

Jones, M.M., (2nd Lt, Co H, 6th Battalion/60th NCST), III: 474.

Jones, Martial B., (Pvt, Co A, 38th NCST), V: 556.

Jones, Matthew, (Pvt, Orderly, Co E, 27th NCST), II: 462; V: 523.

Jones, N.G., (Pvt, Co I, 43rd NCST), V: 499.
Jones, N.M., (Sgt Maj, 70th NCST, 1st Junior Reserves), IV: 14.
Jones, O.C., (Pvt, Co A, 1st Battalion NCST), V: 503.
Jones, Pride, (Lt Col, 27th NCST), II: 425, 426.
Jones, R.J., (Pvt, Co D, 3rd Vols/13th NCST), V: 550.
Jones, Retus, (Pvt, Co A, 5th NCST), I: 291.
Jones, Robert H., (2nd Lt, Co G, 2nd NCST), I: 162, 175; V: 484.
Jones, Mrs. Robert H., II: 579.
Jones, Robert M., (Musician, 33rd NCST), II: 538.
Jones, Robert T., (2nd Lt, Co B, 59th NCST, 4th Cav), III: 457.
Jones, Rufus, (Pvt, Co A, 5th NCST), V: 504.
Jones, S., (Pvt, Co A, 47th NCST), V: 534.
Jones, S.C., (Lt, Co I, 9th NCST, 1st Cav), I: 486.
Jones, S.G., (Pvt, Co F, 3rd Vols/13th NCST), V: 550.
Jones, Samuel, (Cpl, Detached Co, 68th NCST), III: 723.
Jones, Samuel F., (2nd Cpl, Co G, 4th Vols/14th NCST), V: 490.
Jones, Stephen W., (Capt, Co C, 46th NCST), III: 76, 81.
Jones, T.B., (2nd Sgt, Co K, 44th NCST), V: 534.
Jones, T.G., (Sgt, Co B, 3rd NCST), V: 487.
Jones, T.L., (Lt Col, 2nd Vols/12th NCST), I: 607, 608, 609, 629, 630, 634.
Jones, Thaddeus, (Lt, Co C, 2nd NCST), I: 159.
Jones, Thomas D., (Capt, Co A, 12th Vols/22nd NCST), II: 163, 164, 165, 167, 176.
Jones, Thomas O., (Lt, Co C, 61st NCST), III: 504.
Jones, Thomas P., (Maj, 64th NCST), III: 659, 660, 662; IV: 702, 708.
Jones, Dr. W., (Ass't Surg, 9th NCST, 1st Cav), I: 485; IV: 633.
Jones, W.A., (Sgt, Co I, 1st NCST), V: 485.
Jones, W.D., (Pvt, Co G, 43rd NCST), V: 498.
Jones, W.F., (Capt, Co A, 12th Vols/22nd NCST), II: 161, 163, 165, 167.
Jones, W.G., (Pvt, Co F, 3rd Vols/13th NCST), V: 550.
Jones, W.M., (Lt, Co H, 6th Battalion/60th NCST), III: 482.
Jones, W.T., (1st Lt, Co C, 35th NCST), IV: 723.
Jones, W.W., (2nd Lt, Co D, 69th NCST, Thomas' Legion), III: 730, 754.
Jones, Walter, (Pvt, Co I, 26th NCST), II: 410.
Jones, William A., (Pvt, Co B, 34th NCST), V: 555.
Jones, William B., (Pvt, Co H, 4th Vols/14th NCST), V: 560.
Jones, William B., (2nd Lt, Co G, 4th NCST), I: 233, 272.
Jones, William B., (Chaplain, 61st NCST), IV: 619.
Jones, William E., "Grumble," (Brig Gen), I: 423; III: 742, 746.
Jones, William H., (Maj, 48th NCST), III: 114, 124.
Jones, William L., (Pvt, Co A, 49th NCST), V: 564.
Jones, Willie D., (Capt, Co H, 31st NCST), II: 508.
Jones' Farm, (nr Petersburg, Va. and Battle of, 1864; aka Jones' House), I: 385, 436, 567; II: 58, 61, 76, 104, 385, 481, 575, 576, 669; III: 112, 367, 489; IV: 93, 469, 478, 479.

Jones County, N.C., II: 82, 497, 774; III: 504, 686, 704; IV: 302.
Jonesboro, Ga., (and Battle of, 1864), III: 432, 493.
Jonesboro, Tenn., III: 737, 738, 739, 740, 757; IV: 119.
Jonesville, Va., III: 523, 524.
Jordan Springs, Va., I: 147, 194.
Jordan, Dr. ______, [Jourdan], (Ass't Surg, 13th Vols/23rd NCST), II: 190, 222; IV: 635.
Jordan, A.R., (2nd Lt, Co G, 26th NCST), II: 372.
Jordan, A. Smith, (AQM, 9th Vols/19th NCST, 2nd Cav), II: 88.
Jordan, Edward, (Sgt Maj, 9th Vols/19th NCST, 2nd Cav), II: 89, 92.
Jordan, Edward M., (Lt, Co C; Adjt, 9th Vols/19th NCST, 2nd Cav), I: 441; II: 89, 92; V: 567, 657.
Jordan, Henry B., (1st Lt, Co D, 31st NCST), II: 507.
Jordan, Henry T., (Adjt, 55th NCST), III: 288; IV: 700, 708.
Jordan, Dr. J.P., (Ass't Surg, NCST, 2nd Junior Reserves), IV: 28, 642.
Jordan, James, B., (1st Lt, Adjt, 26th NCST), II: 303, 306, 358, 371, 372, 381, 395, 396, 397, 415; IV: 701, 708.
Jordan, Dr. James C., (Ass't Surg, 70th NCST, 1st Junior Reserves), IV: 14, 642.
Jordan, John M., (Pvt, Co B, 4th Vols/14th NCST), I: 731.
Jordan, John V., (Col, 31st NCST), I: 40; II: 507, 509, 511, 748; IV: 249, 483; V: 59, 60, 63, 64, 65, 88, 89.
Jordan, M.H., (Pvt, Co H, 35th NCST), V: 563.
Jordan, T.N., (Capt, Co F, 5th NCST), I: 287, 288.
Jordan's Farm, (nr Prtersburg, Va.; aka Jordan's House), II: 515; III: 359.
Jowl's Mills, Va., III: 277.
Joyce, A.R., (Pvt, Co I, 28th NCST), V: 543.
Joyce, H., (Pvt, Co K, 12th Vols/22nd NCST), V: 554.
Joyce, J.K.P., (Pvt, Co D, 45th NCST), V: 500.
Joyce, J.M., (Pvt, Co H, 12th Vols/22nd NCST), V: 554.
Joyce, O., (3rd Cpl, Co H, 3rd Vols/13th NCST), V: 551.
Joyce, T.P., (Pvt, Co A, 46th NCST), V: 524.
Joyce, Thomas, (Pvt, Co H, NCST), V: 502.
Joyner, B., (Pvt, Co H, 2nd Vols/12th NCST), V: 507.
Joyner, G.W., (2nd Lt, Co A, 12th Battalion NCST, Cav), IV: 339.
Joyner, Gilbert, (Pvt, Co A, 10th NCST, 1st Art & Engs, Ramseur-Manly's Battery, Light Art), I: 554, 559.
Joyner, Dr. Henry, (Surg, 30th NCST), II: 495, 499; IV: 636.
Joyner, J.L., (Musician, Co D, 30th NCST), V: 492.
Joyner, J.S., [Julius S.], (Capt, Co F, 47th NCST), IV: 701, 708.
Joyner, Jason P., (Capt, Co E, 27th NCST), V: 640.
Joyner, Julius S., (Capt, Co F, 47th NCST), III: 84.
Joyner, L.H., (Pvt, Co B, 47th NCST), V: 534.
Joyner, Robert W., (Capt, Co E, 27th NCST), II: 457, 462.
Joyner, W.B., (Pvt, Co C, 43rd NCST), V: 498.
Joyner, W.B., (Pvt, Co I, 30th NCST), V: 493.
Joyner's Ford, (Blackwater River, Va.), III: 228, 229.

Joyner's Store, Va., III: 321.
Judkins, ______, (Commodore, Englishman), V: 418.
Judson, ______, (Capt, 5th Mi. Cav), III: 598.
Julian, Frank, (Pvt, Co I, 5th NCST), I: 292.
Julian, R.M., (Lt, Co D, 2nd Battalion NCST), IV: 245.
Julich, J.F., (Chief Bugler, 3rd Battalion NCST, Light Art), IV: 261.
Juna-lus-kee, (Cherokee Chief), III: 729.
Junior Reserves, (See also: 70th, 71st and 72nd NCST), I: xiii, 16, 18, 52, 433, 437; II: 11, 635; III: 496, 634, 680, 699, 718; IV: 2, 3, 4, 5, 6, 7, 8, 10, 14, 15, 17, 18, 19, 20, 23, 29, 35, 36, 37, 42, 44, 45, 49, 50, 52, 54, 59, 62, 65, 89, 358, 372, 382, 389, 407, 408, 440, 499, 585, 586, 587, 588, 589, 591, 592, 595, 757; V: 4, 221, 466, 640, 643.
Junior Reserves, Archer's, (Va.), V: 247.
Jaunita, Benjamin W., (Capt, ACS, 47th NCST), III: 84; V: 529.
Justice, G.F., (Lt, 62nd NCST), IV: 701, 708.
Justice, J.A., (Pvt, Co G, 6th Vols/16th NCST), IV: 216.
Justice, J.H., (Pvt, Co K, 12th Vols/22nd NCST), V: 554.
Justice, J.W., (2nd Sgt, Co K, 3rd Vols/13th NCST), V: 551.
Justice, J.W., (Lt, Co A, 12th Vols/22nd NCST), II: 165.
Justice, John, (Lt, Hoke-Godwin-Lewis' Brigade), IV: 526.
Justice, John E., (Pvt, Co G, 6th Vols/16th NCST), V: 552.
Justice, S., (Pvt, Co G, 37th NCST), V: 546.
Justice, T.B., (Resident of Appomattox, Va.), IV: 212.
Juthrie, Julius, (Lt, CSN), I: 59.
Juvenile Heroism, IV: 590.

(K)

Kallum, Charles K., (Pvt, Co D, 11th Vols/21st NCST), V: 194.
Kamschatka, V: 348.
Kanawha River, Va., V: viii.
Kanawha Valley, Va., I: 80; III: 748; IV: 149.
Kane, Charles G., (Sgt, Co F; Sgt Maj, 14th Vols/24th NCST), V: 560.
Kane, Marshall, (Passemger, Advance), V: 362.
Kanipe, H., (Pvt, Co K, 49th NCST), V: 565.
Kanoy, Samuel, (Sgt, Co K, 45th NCST), V: 501.
Kansas, II: 132.
Katz, Aaron, (Sgt Maj, 53rd NCST), III: 261.
Kautz, ______, (Midshipman, USN, Hannah Balch), V: 300.
Kautz, August Valentine, (Maj Gen, USA, See also: Kautz's & Wilson's Raid), I: 432, 467, 470; III: 465, 613, 614, 615, 617.
Kautz & Wilson's Raid, I: 432, 467-470, 467; III: 538.
Kayler, A.L., (Capt, Co E, 6th Vols/16th NCST), V: 547.
Keanansville, N.C., I: 742; II: 277, 297, 610, 623; III: 130.
Kearner, Peter, (Pvt, Co E, 34th NCST), V: 555.
Kearnes, J.N., (1st Lt, Co H, 38th NCST), II: 676, 678.
Kearney, Henry C., (1st Lt, Co E, 5th Vols/15th NCST), I: 733, 734, 735, 747, 748; V: 519.
Kearney, Philip, (Maj Gen, USA), I: 758; II: 134, 203, 205, 599; IV: 164.
Kearns, Alsim J., (Pvt, Co H, 38th NCST), V: 558.
Keebler, ______, [Kibler, John M.], (1st Lt, Co A, 5th Battalion NCST, Cav), IV: 285.
Keen, J.H., (2nd Lt, Co H, 1st NCST), I: 137.
Keen, Dr. Thomas, (Surg, 11th Vols/21st NCST), IV: 635.
Keener, John C., (Maj, 58th NCST), III: 431.
Keener, John S., (Sgt, Co A, 6th Vols/16th NCST), I: 758.
Keener, Peter, (Pvt, Co H, 1st Vols/11tth NCST), V: 530.
Keesler, S.G., (Pvt, Co B, 1st Battalion NCST), V: 504.
Keiser, M., (Pvt, Co B, 28th NCST), V: 541.
Keith, Alexander, Jr., (CSA Agent, Halifax, N.S.), V: 375, 376.
Keith, G.E., (Pvt, Co E, 8th Vols/18th NCST), V: 539.
Keith, James A., (Lt Col, 64th NCST), III: 659, 660, 661, 665.
Keith, John, (Pvt, Co H, 4th Vols/14th NCST), V: 491.
Keith, L.L., (Capt, Co G, 61st NCST), III: 504, 505.
Keith, Thomas W., (Lt, Co I, 64th NCST), III: 660.
Keith, Dr. W.W., (Surg, 6th Vols/16th NCST), IV: 634; V: 547.

Keith, William M., (Capt, Co G, 64th NCST), III: 660.
Keitt, L.M., (Col), V: 167, 200.
Keizer, J.H., (Pvt, Co A, 52nd NCST), V: 535.
Kell, J.F., (Pvt, Co H, 8th Vols/18th NCST; Detailed, Invalid Battalion), V: 571.
Kell, James T., (Lt Col, 30th NCST), II: 495, 496, 497, 499, 504.
Keller, P.J., (Pvt, Co A, 12th Vols/22nd NCST), V: 553.
Keller, S., (Pvt, Co I, 26th NCST), V: 532.
Kelley, T., (Pvt, Co C, 5th NCST; Detailed, Invalid Battalion), V: 571.
Kelly, ______, (Capt, Hebert's Staff), II: 756.
Kelly, A.A., (Pvt, Co C, 37th NCST), V: 545.
Kelly, David P., (Cpl, Co A, 33rd NCST), II: 538.
Kelly, Duncan, (Capt, Co K, 76th NCST, 6th Senior Reserves), IV: 97.
Kelly, G.W., (Pvt, Co D, 26th NCST), II: 374.
Kelly, George, (Pvt, Co D, 26th NCST), V: 531.
Kelly, H.B., (Pvt, Co D, 49th NCST), V: 564.
Kelly, J.C., (AQMS, 28th NCST), II: 465.
Kelly, J.R., (Capt, Co H, 51st NCST), III: 219.
Kelly, James A.O., (Capt, Co F, 50th NCST), III: 161, 202.
Kelly, James E., (Pvt, Co K, 10th Vols/20th NCST), II: 123.
Kelly, James E., (2nd Lt, Co K, 40th NCST, 3rd Art, Hvy), II: 747.
Kelly, John Herbert, (Col, 8th Ark.), III: 435, 436, 451, 452.
Kelly, John M., (Maj, 35th NCST), II: 600, 610; V: 12, 651.
Kelly, John N., (Lt, Co B, 36th NCST, 2nd Art & Engs; Adjt, Fort Fisher), II: 646; V: 233, 239.
Kelly, M.L., (1st Lt, Co D, 62nd NCST), III: 515; V: 708.
Kelly, Samuel A., (Capt, Co G, 4th NCST), I: 231, 233, 261, 269, 279.
Kelly, Thomas, [Thomas J.], (2nd Lt, Co B, 3rd NCST), I: 213.
Kelly, W.J., (Capt, Co F, 78th NCST, 8th Senior Reserves), IV: 107.
Kelly, William, (Pvt, Co E, Color-bearer, 24th Mi.), II: 356.
Kelly, William G., (Capt, Co G, 4th NCST), I: 231, 269.
Kelly's Farm, (Blackwater River, Va.), IV: 357.
Kelly's Field, [Kelley's], (nr Chickamauga, Tenn.), III: 489, 490; V: 171, 173.
Kelly's Ford, (Rappahannock River, Va. and Battles of), I: 162, 164, 171, 255, 319, 382, 422, 423; II: 91, 502, 503; III: 531, 557, 558; IV: 462, 657.
Kellysville, Va., I: 422.
Kelp, J.E., (Pvt, Co A, 54th NCST), V: 516.
Kemp, J.C., (Capt, Co K, 6th Vols/16th NCST), I: 751.
Kemper, James Laivson, (Maj Gen), II: 363; V: 102, 106, 148, 151, 156, 157, 158; V: 584.
Kemper, Joseph B., (Sgt, Co D, 5th Mi.), II: 519, 520.
Kenan, James G., (Capt, Co A, 43rd NCST), III: 2, 3, 19; IV: 694, 701, 708.
Kenan, Thomas S., (Col, 43rd NCST), I: 124, 607; II: 677, 679; III: 1, 2, 6, 19, 163, 171;

IV: 689-696, 697, 698, 700, 702, 708; V: xvi, 611-616, 650, 667.
Kenan, William R., (Sgt, Maj, Acting Adjt, 43rd NCST; Jr 2nd Lt, Adjt, 43rd NCST), III: 1, 2, 12, 18, 20; V: 497.
Kenansville, N.C., III: 19, 322; IV: 91, 265, 267, 331, 420, 599, 609, 694.
Kendall, James S., (Maj, 26th NCST), II: 304, 330, 335, 395, 397, 409.
Kendall, Henry, (Pvt, Co H, 4th Vols/14th NCST), I: 726.
Kendrick, B.F., (Pvt, Co B, 56th NCST), III: 366.
Kendrick, J.M., (2nd Lt, Co H, 13th Vols/23rd NCST), II: 187; IV: 700, 708.
Kennedy, Mrs. ______, (Head Nurse, 1st N.C. General Hospital, Petersburg, Va.), IV: 624.
Kennedy, A.M.D., (1st Lt, Co H, 4th NCST), I: 233, 272.
Kennedy, Rev. Dr. F. Milton, (Chaplain, 28th NCST), II: 466; IV: 473, 611.
Kennedy, J., (Pvt, Co G, 28th NCST), V: 542.
Kennedy, J.B., (Pvt, Co I, 44th NCST), V: 534.
Kennedy, J.W., (Pvt, Co B, 3rd NCST), V: 487.
Kennedy, John Thomas, (1st Lt, ACS, 35th NCST; Capt, Co E, 62nd Ga., Cav; Maj, 62nd Ga. Cav; Lt Col; Col, 16th Battalion/75th NCST, 7th Cav), I: 16; II: 280, 593; IV: 71, 72, 73, 74, 75, 77, 78, 79, 83, 84, 86, 87, 88, 89, 92, 93, 370.
Kennedy, W.B., (Sgt, Co C, 59th NCST, 4th Cav), V: 659.
Kennedy, William, (3rd Cpl, Co E, 52nd NCST), III: 224.
Kennedy, William M., (Pvt, Co A, 1st Vols/11th NCST), V: 530.
Kennedy, William M., (Sgt, Co K, 33rd NCST), II: 541, 579.
Kenney, J.M., (Pvt, Co F, 2nd Battalion NCST), V: 495.
Kenerly, Rev., ______, (Resident of Pitt County), IV: 74.
Kennerly, P.A., (Capt, Co K, 8th NCST), I: 388, 405.
Kennesaw, Ga., (Kennesaw Mountain, and Battle of 1864), I: 768; II: 743; III: 493; V: 648.
Kennon' Landing, Va., (aka Wilson's Wharf), III: 604-607; V: 671.
Kenter, John E., [John F.], (Cpl, Co K, 4th NCST), I: 234.
Kenter, T.J., (Pvt, Co D, 57th NCST), V: 517.
Kentucky, I: 3, 46; II: 487, 701, 702, 707, 709, 710, 729, 730, 731; III: 434, 521, 523, 662, 673, 676, 677-678, 734, 737, 738; IV: 1, 35, 121, 124, 127, 271, 274, 275, 287, 288, 290, 301, 619, 674, 675, 682, 683, 686, 704, 735, 746.
Kentucky Campaign, 1862, II: 708, 710; III: 475; IV: 438.
Kentucky Military Institute, I: 111.
Kentucky River, Ky., II: 730; IV: 276, 280, 285, 286.
Kenyon, John H., (Capt, Co F, 28th NCST), II: 466.
Keogh, Richard, (Capt, Co H, 68th NCST), III: 714.
Kepley, George, (Pvt, Co D, 10th NCST, 1st Art & Engs, Reilly-Ramsay's Battery, Light Art), I: 574.
Kerby, W.W., (Pvt, Co F, 26th NCST), V: 603.
Kerley, R.B., (2nd Lt, Co B, 54th NCST), I: 121.
Kerner, W., (Pvt, Co F, 44th NCST), V: 534.

Kerney, T.H., (1st Lt, Co D, 66th NCST), III: 686.
Kernstown, Va., (and Battles of, Jackson's and Early's Valley Campaigns), I: 206, 261; II: 250, 253, 532; III: 14, 256, 751-752.
Kerr, Mr. ______, (Owner of hotel in Charlotte), IV: 694.
Kerr, B. Knox, (Sgt, Co B, 4th NCST), I: 232.
Kerr, Francis, (Pvt, Co C, 10th NCST, 1st Art & Engs, Brem-Graham-Williams' Battery, Light Art), V: 568.
Kerr, J.B., (Pvt, Co C, 10th NCST, 1st Art & Engs, Brem-Graham-Williams' Battery, Light Art), V: 568.
Kerr, J.T., (Musician, 3rd Vols/13th NCST), V: 549.
Kerr, John, (Pvt, Co H, 63rd NCST, 5th Cav), III: 587.
Kerr, John D., (Capt, Co B, 7th Battalion Junior Reserves; Co D, 72nd NCST, 3rd Junior Reserves), IV: 40, 51, 595.
Kerr, R. Davis, (Pvt, Co F, 63rd NCST, 5th Cav), III: 600.
Kerr, W.A., (Capt, Co C, 4th NCST), I: 231, 232, 270.
Kerr, W.A., (1st Lt, CSN; Capt, Yadkin), IV: 404; V: 298, 327.
Kerr, W.H., (Lt, CSN), IV: 404.
Kerr, W.J., (Sgt, Co F, 6th NCST), V: 512.
Kerr, W.J., (Lt, Co E, 1st Vols/11th NCST), I: 584; V: 663.
Kerr, William J., (Capt, Co D, 7th NCST), I: 369, 377; IV: 467.
Kerrigan, ______, (Capt, Torpedo Service, Engineer Corps, CSA), IV: 424.
Kershaw, Joseph Brevard, (Maj Gen), I: 343, 555, 558; II: 392; V: 199.
Kestler, C., (Pvt, Co C, 48th NCST), V: 526.
Kestler, Jeremiah M., (Capt, Co C, 33rd NCST), II: 538.
Kestler, Robert, (Pvt, Co I, 4th Vols/14th NCST), V: 491.
Ketchey, J.J., (Pvt, Co G, 8th NCST), V: 194.
Ketner, F., (Pvt, Co I, 33rd NCST), V: 545.
Key, A.J., (Pvt, Co A, 28th NCST), V: 540.
Key, David M., (Col, Tenn., Cav), III: 745.
Keyes, Erasmus Darwin, (Maj Gen, USA), III: 330.
Keyser, E.S., (Master, USN), V: 244.
Keyser, Joe, (Fayetteville and Harper's Ferry Arsenals), IV: 298.
Keyser, Louis, (Fayetteville and Harper's Ferry Arsenals), IV: 298.
Keyser, W.H., (Pvt, Co G, 11th Vols/21st NCST), V: 515.
Keziah, P.W., (Pvt, Co F, 35th NCST), V: 563.
Kibler, G.B., (Capt, Co B, 54th NCST), I: 119; IV: 708.
Kidder, G.W., (Lt, Co A, 9th Battalion NCST, 1st Hvy Art), IV: 304.
Kiel, J.H., (3rd Sgt, Co G, 3rd Vols/13th NCST), V: 550.
Kifenic, M.A., (Pvt, Co D, 5th NCST), I: 291.
Kiger, J.A., (Pvt, Co B, 1st Battalion NCST), V: 504.
Killet, John, (Pvt, Co E, 10th Vols/20th NCST), II: 120.
Killett, L.D., (1st Lt, Co C, 43rd NCST), III: 3.
Killian, C.E., (Pvt, Co C, 28th NCST), V: 541.
Killian, S.E., (Pvt, Co K, 46th NCST), V: 525.

Killian, W.F., (Pvt, Co F, 13th Vols/23rd NCST), V: 510.
Kilpatrick, Frank M., (Cpl, Co E, 27th NCST), II: 462; V: 523.
Kilpatrick, H.Y., [Kirkpatrick, Hugh Y.], (Sgt, Co K, 30th NCST), IV: 600.
Kilpatrick, Hugh Judson, (Maj Gen, USA and Kilpatrick's command), I: 56, 92, 427, 438, 451, 459, 461, 463, 464; II: 238, 376; III: 573, 574, 583; IV: 104, 240, 725; V: 270.
Kilpatrick, J.T., (Pvt, Co B, 3rd Vols/13th NCST), V: 572.
Kilpatrick, J.W., (Capt, Co N, 6th Vols/16th NCST; Capt, Co I, 56th NCST), I: 766, 772; III: 316, 317; IV: 137.
Kilpatrick, Miles D., (2nd Lt, Co H, 39th NCST), II: 706.
Kilpatrick, Simon B., (Cpl, Co A, 27th NCST), II: 461.
Kilpatrick, William M., [William W.], (1st Lt, Co C & D, 65th NCST, 6th Cav), III: 680.
Kilpatrick-Dahlgren Raid, (See: Ulric Dahlgren for explanation of raid), I: 428, 459, 464.
Kimbrough, John A., (Musician, 33rd NCST), II: 538.
Kimsey, Joseph A., (Capt, Co I, 69th NCST, Thomas' Legion), III: 731.
Kincaid, George W., (2nd Lt, Co D, 1st Vols/11th NCST), I: 584.
Kincaid, J.P., (2nd Lt, Co A, 59th NCST, 4th Cav), III: 457.
Kincaid, James, M., (1st Lt, Co G, 52nd NCST), III: 224.
Kincaid, John, (Pvt, Co F, 26th NCST), V: 603.
Kincaid, J. Rufus, (2nd Lt, Co F, 41st NCST, 3rd Cav), II: 771.
Kincaid, Robert, (Pvt, Co B, 1st Vols/11th NCST), V: 530.
Kincaid, William J., (Capt, Co D, 1st Vols/11th NCST), I: 119, 584; IV: 702, 708.
King, ______, (ACS, 10th NCST, 1st Art & Engs, Hvy Art, Fort Macon), I: 504, 506.
King, A.D., (2nd Lt, Co D, 38th NCST), II: 675.
King, Alexander M., (2nd Lt, Co H, 53rd NCST), III: 263.
King, Burrill, (Pvt, Co G, 5th Vols/15th NCST), V: 522.
King, C.A., (Capt, Hardee's Staff), IV: 549.
King, Charles H., (QM Sgt, 61st NCST), III: 503.
King, D.W., (Pvt, Co D, 56th NCST), III: 347.
King, Daniel, (Orderly Sgt, Co E, 14th Vols/24th NCST), II: 284.
King, E.H., (Sgt, Co E, 3rd NCST), V: 487.
King, Ezekiel, (Pvt, Co G, 34th NCST), V: 556.
King, H.W., (Pvt, Co A, 13th Vols/23rd NCST), V: 509.
King, Henry, (1st Lt, Co C, 43rd NCST), III: 3.
King, Henry, (Pvt, Co G, 5th Vols/15th NCST), V: 522.
King, J.E., (Pvt, Co F, 10th Vols/20th NCST), V: 509.
King, J.E., [John E.], (2nd Lt, Co E, 3rd NCST), IV: 722.
King, Dr. J.K., (Surg, 4th NCST), I: 230, 268; IV: 632.
King, J.N., (Capt, Prake's Staff, USA), II: 318.
King, J.W., (Pvt, Co A, 13th Vols/23rd NCST), V: 509.
King, Jacob, (Pvt, Co E, 25th NCST), V: 561.
King, James, (Col, Revolutionary War, Great grandfather of Col Stringfield), IV: 123.
King, James, (Pvt, Co D, 38th NCST), V: 557.

King, James A., (2nd Lt, Co B, 56th NCST), III: 314, 378.
King, John Haskell, (Maj Gen, USA), III: 490.
King, L.M., (Musician, 6th NCST), V: 511.
King, M.C., (Sgt, Co K, 6th NCST), V: 513.
King, M.D., (AC Sgt, 6th Battalion/60th NCST), III: 496.
King, Nathan J., (2nd Sgt, Co D, 38th NCST), V: 557.
King, R.W., (1st Lt, Co F, 9th Vols/19th NCST, 2nd Cav), II: 80.
King, Richard M., (2nd Sgt, Co A, 4th Vols/14th NCST), V: 489.
King, S.D., (Pvt, Co A, 30th NCST), V: 491.
King, S.J., (Pvt, Co A, 30th NCST), V: 491.
King, Thomas, (2nd Lt, Co D, 44th NCST), III: 23.
King, W.H., (Sgt, Co K, 8th Vols/18th NCST), II: 64; V: 540.
King, W.P., (Pvt, Co I, 1st NCST), V: 485.
King, W.R., (Pvt, Co I, 47th NCST), V: 535.
King, W.W., (1st Lt, Co A, 4th Battalion Junior Reserves; Adjt, 72nd NCST, 3rd Junior Reserves), IV: 38, 51, 57.
King's Mountain, N.C., (Revolutionary Battle), III: 735.
King's School House, (nr Seven Pines, Va.), II: 599.
King & Queen County, Va., I: 737.
Kingsbury, Charles P., (Capt, antebellum Cmdr., Fayetteville Arsenal, Chief of Staff to McClellan, USA), IV: 300.
Kingston, Ga., II: 704, 742; IV: 273, 290, 613.
Kinlaw, J.C., (Pvt, Co K, 8th Vols/18th NCST), II: 50, 64; V: 540.
Kinney, ______, (Lt, Wise's Legion), II: 510; V: 61, 63, 66.
Kinney, D.F., (Lt, Co F, 7th NCST), I: 380.
Kinney's Farm, Va., II: 470, 471; IV: 465, 471.
Kinney's Landing, Va., III: 553.
Kinsey, James, (2nd Lt, Co A, 40th NCST, 3rd Art, Hvy), II: 746, 747.
Kinsey, Joseph, IV: 701.
Kinsey, Joseph E., (Lt, Co E, 61st NCST), III: 504.
Kinsey, William F., (2nd Lt, Co G, 56th NCST), III: 316.
Kinston, N.C., (and Battles of, 1862 & 1864), I: 9, 10, 12, 320, 321, 365, 391, 395, 396, 397, 402, 411, 420, 493, 494, 495, 514, 515, 516, 517, 520, 522, 526, 527, 531, 532, 538, 540, 581, 587, 588, 742; II: 3, 20, 66, 81, 83, 221, 277, 279, 284, 294, 323, 326, 327, 328, 330, 412, 427, 428, 439, 468, 513, 523, 524, 544, 594, 596, 598, 599, 612, 650, 654, 747, 748, 749, 751, 752, 754, 762, 763, 767, 774, 776, 778, 803; III: 4, 5, 8, 9, 40, 71, 83, 85, 86, 129, 130, 132, 135, 170, 171, 172, 173, 174, 176, 205, 215, 216, 219, 226, 227, 230, 234, 243, 273, 274, 275, 289, 290, 322, 323, 324, 327, 329, 333, 335, 350, 419, 459, 472, 505, 506, 507, 508, 553, 554, 555, 679, 680, 681, 685, 696, 698, 704, 705, 706, 707, 708, 709, 722, 726; IV: 4, 18, 20, 30, 38, 39, 41, 42, 53, 54, 55, 59, 82, 84, 221, 222, 252, 263, 312, 325, 338, 339, 344, 345, 346, 348, 350, 353, 354, 362, 383, 393, 395, 396, 402, 415, 418, 439, 465, 484, 486, 488, 498, 499, 505, 527, 528, 543, 546, 555, 569, 573, 591, 592, 593, 652; V: 2, 7, 19, 20, 85, 86, 269, 270, 326, 332, 333, 631.
Kinyoun, Dr. J.H., (Surg, 66th NCST), III: 685; IV: 642.

Kinzey, Izark D., (Pvt, Co G, 56th NCST), III: 348.
Kirby, ______, (Col, Stoneman's Cav, USA), IV: 116.
Kirby, Edmund, (Lt Col, 58th NCST), III: 432, 435, 450, 452; V: 11.
Kirby, Dr. George L., (Ass't Surg, 2nd NCST; Surg, 2nd NCST; Surg, Anderson-Ramseur-Cox's Brigade), I: 157; IV: 463, 631, 644.
Kirby, W.W., (Pvt, Co F, 26th NCST), V: 603.
Kirby, Wiley, L., (Sgt, Co D, 5th Vols/15th NCST), V: 521.
Kirk, George W., (One time Col, USA turned outlaw), III: 758; IV: 4, 111, 128, 371, 372, 374, 375, 380, 382, 401.
Kirk, J.C., (Pvt, Co H, 35th NCST), V: 563.
Kirk, W.A., (Pvt, Co K, 28th NCST), V: 543.
Kirk's Command, (A deserter himself Kirk assembled in the mountains of western North Carolina and east Tennessee a band of deserters, draft dodgers and common outlaws. This band of criminals attacked all they came in contact with. Civilians, Militia, Home Guard units and finally the regular army forces that were sent against them. Surprisingly, although a deserter, Kirk still claimed his former rank and was welcomed by the Federal forces that committed like depredations in that region. After the war he lead Holden's 1st N.C. Regiment during the Holden-Kirk War.), I: 21; II: 331; III: 664, 666, 718, 719, 757, 758, 759, 761; IV: 113, 114, 372, 380, 386, 588, 655.
Kirkland, Alexander M., (1st Lt, Co E, Cameron's Battery, Starr's 13th Battalion NCST, Light Art), IV: 353.
Kirkland, John, (Capt, AQM, 5th NCST), I: 281.
Kirkland, John H., (2nd Lt, Co B, Wlaker's Battalion, Thomas' Legion; 80th NCST), IV: 118.
Kirkland, S., (Pvt, Co G, 28th NCST, Detailed, Invalid Battalion), V: 571.
Kirkland, Samuel S., (Capt, Co A, 6th NCST; AAG, Scales' Brigade), I: 295, 340; IV: 553.
Kirkland, William W., (Brig Gen), I: xi, xii, 582, 592, 593, 596, 597; II: 1, 8, 9, 12, 129, 131, 137, 144, 378, 381, 385, 801, 803; III: 26, 29, 93, 95, 111, 118, 241, 244, 246; IV: 45, 47, 228, 230, 535, 536, 537, 539, 540, 544, 545, 546, 548, 549, 562, 563, 564, 568.
Kirkman, George, (1st Lt, Co B, 77th NCST, 7th Senior Reserves), IV: 99.
Kirksey, E.J., (Capt, Co E, 6th Vols/16th NCST), I: 751; IV: 137, 143, 148.
Kirksey, J.F., (Pvt, Co B, 10th Vols/20th NCST), V: 508.
Kirmick, M.A., (Pvt, Co D, 5th NCST), V: 505.
Kiser, J.C., (Pvt, Co F, 37th NCST), V: 546.
Kiser, Noah, (Pvt, Co M, 6th Vols/16th NCST), V: 553.
Kissop, J.W., (Pvt, Co I, 37th NCST), V: 546.
Kistler, G.H., (Pvt, Co I, 37th NCST), V: 546.
Kistler, G.L., (Sgt, Co I, 7th NCST), V: 538.
Kistler, Jerry M., (Orderly Sgt, 10th Vols/20th NCST), II: 113.

Kitchin, W.H., (Capt, Co I, 2nd Vols/12th NCST), I: 642; IV: 721.
Kittrell, G.W., (2nd Lt, Co G, 13th Vols/23rd NCST), II: 186.
Kittrell Springs, N.C., (aka Kittrell), I: 4; II: 255, 256; IV: 606.
Kitzmiller, Archibald, (Fayetteville and Harper's Ferry Arsenals), IV: 298.
Kivett, Warren B., (Lt, Co M, 12th Vols/22nd NCST), II: 166.
Kizer, John, (Pvt, Co E, 34th NCST), V: 555.
Kizer, Zimri, (Pvt, Co E, 34th NCST), V: 555.
Klu-Klux Campaign, (aka Holden-Kirk War), IV: 380.
Klutts, A.L., (Pvt, Co A, 57th NCST), V: 517.
Klutts, D., (Pvt, Co C, 8th Vols/18th NCST), II: 63; V: 539.
Klutts, J.C., (Pvt, Co G, 8th NCST), V: 194.
Klutts, W.B., [William B.], (2nd Lt, Co F, 57th NCST), IV: 708.
Klutts, Hon. Theodore F., (Post war N.C. Congressman), V: 657.
Klutta, Jacob, (Pvt, Co K, 57th NCST), V: 518.
Knapp, T. Judson, (1st Lt, Co F, 1st Vols/11th NCST), I: 585.
Kneer, Charles, (Maj, 76th Pa.), V: 238.
Knight, _____, (Fireman, NCN), V: 311.
Knight, Arthur B., (2nd Lt, Co F, 31st NCST), II: 512.
Knight, Charles W., (Lt Col, Co F, 31st NCST), II: 507; III: 207; V: 63, 65, 66, 69, 197.
Knight, E.E., (2nd Lt, Co I, 5th Vols/15th NCST), I: 735.
Knight, Elisha C., (2nd Lt, Co B, 44th NCST), III: 22.
Knight, Harper, (Pvt, Co A, 12th Vols/22nd NCST), V: 553.
Knight, James, (Engineer on the Wilmington & Weldon Railroad), I: 523.
Knight, James S., (1st Lt, Co B, 13th Vols/23rd NCST), II: 184.
Knight, Jim, [James S.], (Pvt, Co A, 3rd NCST), I: 185.
Knight, S.J., (Pvt, Co A, 12th Vols/22nd NCST), V: 553.
Knights of the Golden Circle, V: 115.
Knittle, H., (2nd Lt, Co K, Ball's Legion), IV: 708.
Knott, J., (Pvt, Co B, 2nd Vols/12th NCST), V: 506.
Knott, J.D., (1st Lt, Co I, 13th Vols/23rd NCST), II: 187, 205.
Knott, J.H., (Pvt, Co K, 3rd Vols/13th NCST), I: 692.
Knott, John, (Pvt, Co K, 3rd Vols/13th NCST), V: 551.
Knotts, Harrison B., (Pvt, Co C, 2nd Vols/12th NCST), V: 521.
Knowles, D.J., (2nd Lt, Co K, 66th NCST), III: 686.
Knox, Benjamin Allen, (1st Sgt, Co B, 4th NCST; Detailed, 2nd Corps Provost Guard), I: 232, 272; V: 569.
Knox, George E., (Capt, Co H, 76th NCST, 6th Senior Reserves), IV: 97.
Knox, John G., (Capt, Co A, 7th NCST), I: 367, 372, 375, 383; IV: 474, 475, 721.
Knox, John M., (2nd Lt, Co H, 1st Vols/11th NCST), I: 585.
Knox, S.W., (Pvt, Co C, 37th NCST), V: 545.
Knoxville, Tenn., (and Battle of, 1863), II: 487, 488, 706, 707, 710, 727; III: 436, 475, 660, 663, 664, 666, 677, 678, 679, 729, 732, 733, 737, 738, 740, 741,

742, 743, 760; IV: 111, 117, 123, 124, 125, 128, 272, 273, 274, 290, 291, 380; V: 654.
Koffman, W., (Pvt, Co D, Thomas's Legion; Detailed, Invalid Battalion), V: 571.
Koonce, F.D., (Capt, Co K, 61st NCST), III: 504.
Koonce, H.C., (Lt, Co K, 61st NCST), III: 504.
Koonce, John, (Pvt, Co A, 34th NCST), V: 554.
Koonce, S.E., (Lt, Co G, 2nd NCST), I: 162.
Koonce, S.E., (Lt, Co K, 61st NCST), III: 504.
Koontz, J.H., (Capt, Co A, 42nd NCST), II: 789, 805; IV: 539, 540, 541.
Koontz, W.A., (Pvt, Co A, 54th NCST), V: 516.
Kornegay, Hargett, (Pvt, Co A, 43rd NCST), III: 20; V: 497.
Kornegay, S.H., (Cpl, Color-bearer, Co D, 27th NCST), II: 462; V: 523.
Kornegay, W.F., (Lt, Co H, 9th NCST, 1st Cav), I: 486.
Krider, C.C., (Lt, Co C, 49th NCST), III: 141, 145, 148.
Kriminger, William J., (2nd Lt, Co C, 33rd NCST), II: 539.
Kurfees, Z.C., (Pvt, Co F, 3rd Vols/13th NCST), V: 550.
Kurile Islands, V: 348.
Kurkholder, D.S., (2nd Lt, Co F, Walker's Battalion, Thomas' Legion; 80th NCST), IV: 118.
Kuykendall, E.J., (Lt, Co G, 9th NCST, 1st Cav), I: 486.
Kyle, Jesse K., (Capt, Co B, 52nd NCST), I: 119; III: 223, 246; IV: 721.
Kyle, W.E., (1st Lt, Co B, 52nd NCST), I: 120, 122; III: 223, 236; V: 210, 211, 529.

(L)

Lackey, W.F., (Pvt, Co H, 56th NCST), III: 356; V: 566.
Lacky, James W., (Pvt, Co G, 38th NCST), V: 557.
Lacky, John W., (Pvt, Co G, 38th NCST), V: 557.
Lacky, Moses T., (Pvt, Co G, 38th NCST), V: 557.
Lacky, Robert C., (Musician, Co G, 38th NCST), V: 557.
Lacky, Thomas H., (Pvt, Co G, 38th NCST), V: 557.
Lacy, Rev. B. Tucker, (Jackson's Chaplian), I: 718.
Lacy, Rev. Dr. Drury, Jr., (1st Lt, Adjt, 43rd NCST; AAG, Hoke-Godwin-Lewis' Brigade), III: 1; IV: 526, 616; V: 511.
Lacy, Rev. Dr. W.S., (Chaplain, 47th NCST), III: 83; IV: 601, 614, 616.
Ladd, Dr. Charles H., (Surg, 56th NCST), III: 318, 322; IV: 640.
LaFayette,______, (French Gen), I: 131.
Lafayette, Ga., II: 712; III: 448, 449.
Lafayette Road, (aka Lafayette Pike, nr Chickamauga, Tenn), II: 716; III: 489; V: 170.
Lafevers, D.H., (Sgt, Co B, 54th NCST), V: 516.
Laffoon, Nathan D., (2nd Lt, Co B, 2nd Battalion), IV: 702, 708.
LaGrange, N.C., III: 226, 289.
Laidley, T.T.S., (Maj, antebellum Cmdr., Fayetteville Arsenal), IV: 300.
Lail, A., (Pvt, Co C, 28th NCST), V: 541.
Lail, P.H., (Pvt, Co H, 28th NCST), V: 542.
Lake Erie, IV: 667, 670, 675, 689, 703.
Lake Scuppernong, N.C., (Tyrell County), II: 377.
Lakey, Ellis, (Pvt, Co H, 63rd NCST, 5th Cav), III: 587.
Lamb, Edwin, (Pvt, Co A, 55th NCST), V: 527.
Lamb, G., (Ensign, USN; Pioneer, Peguot), V: 245.
Lamb, George V., (Capt, Co I, 12th Vols/22nd NCST), II: 166, 172, 178; V: 548.
Lamb, Harris, (Pvt, Co D, 2nd NCST), I: 176; V: 486.
Lamb, Ithamer, (Pvt, Co C, 30th NCST), V: 491.
Lamb, J.M., (Pvt, Co B, 45th NCST), V: 500.
Lamb, J.T., (Pvt, Co G, 5th NCST), I: 292; V: 505.
Lamb, John C., (Lt Col, 7th Vols/17th NCST), II: 1, 2, 3, 5, 338; III: 320, 530, 531, 552; IV: 46, 47, 77, 530, 538; V: 11, 35, 38, 40, 42, 680.
Lamb, Leary B., (Pvt, Co D, 2nd NCST), I: 176; V: 486.
Lamb, N.E., (1st Cpl, Co I, 12th Vols/22nd NCST), V: 554.
Lamb, Robert W., (Capt, AQM, 36th NCST, 2nd Art & Engs), II: 630.

Lamb, W.H.H., (Pvt, Co B, 52nd NCST), V: 535.
Lamb, William, (Col, 36th NCST, 2nd Art & Engs, Cmdr of Fort Fisher), I: 528, 530; II: 629, 630, 631, 641, 642, 643, 644, 645, 646, 647, 648, 649, 651, 761; IV: 46, 49, 304, 305, 307, 308, 309, 311, 344, 416, 419, 422, 423, 542, 590; V: xv, 217-246, 337, 351-352, 374, 407, 409, 413, 425, 426, 445.
Lamb, Wilson G., (2nd Lt, Adjt, 7th Vols/17th NCST), II: 2, 3, 7, 8, 10; IV: 345, 543, 545.
Lambe, Branson, (2nd Lt, Co F, 53rd NCST), III: 262.
Lambert, L., (Pvt, Co H, 4th NCST), V: 489.
Lambert, W.J., (2nd Lt, Co E, 26th NCST), II: 371, 372, 373, 396, 397.
Lambeth, B.F., (Pvt, Co M, 48th NCST), V: 527.
Lambeth, Dudley, (Pvt, Co B, 4th Vols/14th NCST), I: 731.
Lambeth, Joseph H., (Maj, 4th Vols/14th NCST), I: 726, 728.
Lambeth, L.D., (Pvt, Co K, 48th NCST), V: 527.
Lammond, Neal, (Pvt, Co C, 4th Vols/14th NCST), V: 490.
Lamont, Dygald, (1st Lt, Co C, Cumming's Battery, Starr's 13th Battalion NCST, Light Art), IV: 361.
Lamson, R.H., (Lt Cmdr, USN, Pioneer, Gettysburg), V: 243, 245.
Lancaster, A.L., (Capt., Co B, 4th Battalion Junior Reserves; Co B, 72nd NCST, 3rd Junior Reserves), IV: 38, 48, 51.
Lancaster, Benjamin H., (Pvt, Co F, 4th NCST; Detailed, 2nd Corps Provost Guards), V: 488, 570.
Lancaster, Byrd, (1st Lt, Co F, 40th NCST, 3rd Art, Hvy), II: 746, 747.
Lancaster, Daniel, (Pvt, Co I, 35th NCST), V: 563.
Lancaster, J.M., (2nd Lt, Co I, 44th NCST), III: 23.
Lancaster, R.B., (Sgt, Co F, 4th NCST), I: 233.
Lancaster, Stephen, (2nd Lt, Co G, 40th NCST, 3rd Art, Hvy), II: 747.
Lancaster, William, (Cpl, Co K, 11th Vols/21st NCST), V: 515.
Lancaster, Ky., II: 487, 708; IV: 286.
Lancaster, Wi., V: 611, 612, 615.
Land We Love, The, IV: 455.
Lander, S.L., (2nd Lt, Claiborne-Dearing's 7th C.S. Cav; 16th Battalion/75th NCST, 7th Cav), IV: 92.
Landers, J.F., (5th Sgt, Co D, 52nd NCST), III: 224.
Landsford, III: 439.
Landis, Augustus, (Capt, Co D, 2nd Vols/12th NCST), I: 620; V: 677.
Lane, ______, (Col, Art, Son of Gen Joe Lane), IV: 208.
Lane, ______, (Col, 49th Ga.), II: 677.
Lane, Abram J., (AQMS, 26th NCST), II: 307, 371, 396.
Lane, Barney, (Capt, Co E, 14th Vols/24th NCST), II: 269, 271, 273, 277, 283, 284, 286.
Lane, Benjamin D., (1st Lt, Co G, 56th NCST), III: 315.
Lane, C.C., [Christopher C.], (2nd Lt, Co A, 3rd NCST), IV: 722.
Lane, Daniel, (1st Sgt, Co F, 2nd NCST), I: 161, 176.
Lane, H.B., (ACS, 31st NCST), II: 511.
Lane, Henry E., (Capt, Co G, 56th NCST), III: 315.
Lane, Henry W., (1st Lt, Co A, 56th NCST), III: 313.
Lane, J.H., (Sgt, Co F, 45th NCST), V: 500.

Lane, J.W., [John W.], (Capt, Co I, 6th Vols/16th NCST), IV: 721.
Lane, James, (Sgt, Co D, 33rd NCST), II: 539.
Lane, James H., (Brig Gen), I: xi, xii, 77, 79, 85, 89, 99, 111, 112, 115, 116, 117, 118, 122, 123, 126, 127, 133, 365, 372, 373, 374, 375, 377, 380, 381, 471, 665; II: 21, 22, 24, 33, 34, 35, 36, 37, 38, 39, 47, 48, 51, 52, 54, 55, 56, 62, 63, 65, 66, 72, 75, 174, 175, 388, 465, 466, 467, 468, 470, 471, 472, 474, 475, 477, 479, 480, 481, 484, 545, 547, 548, 552, 555, 556, 557, 559, 561, 562, 564, 565, 566, 567, 568, 569, 570, 571, 572, 573, 574, 576, 577, 578, 579, 674; III: 90, 91, 332, 358; IV: 194, 199, 209, 435, 442, 465, 466, 468, 469, 470, 471, 472, 473, 475, 476, 477, 478; V: xii, 93-96 personal account, 154, 155, 158, 208, 537, 645-646.
Lane, James L., (Capt, Co D, 40th NCST, 3rd Art, Hvy), V: 240.
Lane, James S., (Capt, Co D, 40th NCST, 3rd Art, Hvy), II: 746, 756.
Lane, Jesse W., (Musician, 10th Vols/20th NCST), II: 113.
Lane, Joel, (Col, Upon whose property Raleigh was built), II: 408.
Lane, John B., (Musician, 10th Vols/20th NCST), II: 113.
Lane, John Randolph, (Col, 26th NCST), II: 304, 305, 308, 333, 335, 336, 337, 338, 342, 351, 352, 353, 358, 387, 389, 390, 393, 395, 396, 397, 399, 401, 403, 408-410, 412, 417, 422; V: 601.
Lane, Joseph, (Brig Gen), II: 408; IV: 209.
Lane, Joseph J., (Ordnance Sgt, 61st NCST), III: 503.
Lane, J. Rooker, (ADC, Branch-Lane Brigade), IV: 467, 472.
Lane, L., (Pvt, Co B, 46th NCST), V: 524.
Lane, L., (Pvt, Co G, 12th Vols/22nd NCST), V: 554.
Lane, Oscar, (ADC, Branch-Lane's Brigade), IV: 472.
Lane, Preston, (Pvt, Co F, 5th NCST), I: 292; V: 505.
Lane, Dr. Thomas B., (Ass't Surg, 28th NCST; Surg, 8th Vols./18th NCST), II: 63, 466; IV: 473, 635, 636; V: 537.
Lane, Thomas J., (Pvt, Co I, 3rd NCST), V: 487.
Lane, W.K., (Capt, Claiborne-Dearing's 7th C.S. Cav; Co F, 16th Battalion/75th NCST, 7th Cav), IV: 72, 91, 93.
Lane, William, (2nd Lt, Co C, 50th NCST), III: 198, 203.
Lane, William G., (Jr 2nd Lt, Co G, 26th NCST), II: 372, 397; IV: 700.
Lane, William P., (Capt, Co C, Millard's 9th/20th Battalion Junior Reserves), IV: 386, 393.
Laney, William De, (Pvt, Co F, 48th NCST), V: 526.
Lang, David, (Col, Fla.), V: 109.
Lang, Robert J., (Cpl, Co E, 27th NCST), II: 462; V: 523.
Langbridge, W.A., (Pvt, Co K, 35th NCST), V: 563.
Langdon, Richard F., (Capt, Co E, 1st NCST), I: 137, 213.
Langdon, Dr. Samuel W., (Surg, 5th Vols/15th NCST), I: 734; IV: 634; V: 520.
Langhon, Arch, (Lt, Co F, 10th Vols/20th NCST), II: 118.
Langley, David P., (Lt, Co G, 8th NCST), I: 401.
Langley, J., (Pvt, Co D, 47th NCST), V: 535.
Langley, L.D., (Lt, Co G, 8th NCST), V: 193.

Lamgley, M.E., (2nd Lt, Co B, 41st NCST, 3rd Cav), II: 770.
Langley, M.F., (1st Lt, Co B, 41st NCST, 3rd Cav), II: 770.
Langsing, William, (Pvt, Co I, 38th NCST), V: 558.
Langston, G.M., (Pvt, Co I, 16th Battalion/75th NCST, 7th Cav), V: 660.
Langthorne, A.R., (Lt, USN), V: 243.
Lanier, H.H., (Lt, Co H, 61st NCST), III: 504.
Lanier, John, (Capt, Co H, 61st NCST), III: 504.
Lanier, William B., (Capt, Co H, 61st NCST), III: 504.
Lankford, Robert W., (Pvt, Co K, 25th NCST), V: 562.
Lankford, William C., (Lt Col, 47th NCST), III: 83, 84.
Lankston, J., (Pvt, Co D, 26th NCST), V: 531.
Lanman, Joseph, (Commodore, USN), V: 242.
Lanneau, J.F., (Capt, Chief Engineer, Hampton's Corps), IV: 425.
Lanning, Robert, (Pvt, Co F, 27th NCST), II: 462; V: 523.
Larkins, G.D., (Pvt, Co F, 32nd NCST), V: 496.
Larkins, R.L., (Pvt, Co C, 30th NCST), V: 491.
Lash, W.A., (Pvt, Co D, 63rd NCST, 5th Cav), III: 536.
Lasley, C.M., (Sgt, Co D, 11th Vols/21st NCST), V: 514.
Lassiter, Dr. ______, (Resident of Petersburg, Va.), III: 393.
Lassiter, Caleb, (Pvt, Co D, 32nd NCST), V: 496.
Lassiter, Hardy J., (Capt, Co D, 35th NCST), II: 596, 600.
Lassiter, James F., (3rd Sgt, Co E, 4th Vols/14th NCST), V: 490.
Lassiter, Jesse W., (Pvt, Co H, 30th NCST; Detailed, Ordnance Reserve Department), V: 572.
Lassiter, Luke, (Pvt, Co A, 10th NCST, 1st Art & Engs, Ramseur-Manly's Battery, Light Art), I: 558.
Lassiter, P.D., (Hospital Steward, 35th NCST), V: 562.
Lassiter, Thomas L., (1st Lt, Co H, 47th NCST), III: 85.
Lassiter, William H., (Pvt, Co I, 14th Vols/24th NCST), V: 560.
Lassiter, Z.W., (Pvt, Co D, 68th NCST), III: 715.
Latham, Alexander C., (Capt, Co B, 10th NCST, 1st Art & Engs, Guion's Hvy Art; Capt, Co F, Latham-Potts-Flanner's Battery, Starr's 13th Battalion NCST, Light Art), I: 501; IV: 341, 354.
Latham, C.H., (1st Lt, Co D, Adam's Battery, Starr's 13th Battalion NCST, Light Art), IV: 353.
Latham, D.G., [Daniel P.], (Capt, Co E, 4th NCST), I: 231, 232, 271.
Latham, J.G., (Sgt, Co A, Webb's Battery, Starr's 13th Battalion NCST, Light Art), V: 282.
Latham, J.R., (Pvt, Co E, 48th NCST), V: 526.
Latham, Julian A., (1st Lt, Co G, 1st NCST), I: 137; IV: 722.
Latham, L.C., (Maj, 1st NCST), I: 134, 135, 137, 146, 149, 150; V: 484, 651.
Latham, S.J., (1st Lt, Co F, 31st NCST), II: 507; V: 66.
Latham's, Charles, (Residence and site of a redoubt nr Plymouth), III: 339, 341; V: 176, 186.
Latimer House, II: 492.
Latta, David S., (Pvt, Co I, 8th Vols/18th NCST), II: 64; V: 540.

Latta, Henry C., (2nd Lt, Co E, 46th NCST), III: 81.
Latta, J.R., (Adjt, 51st NCST), III: 205, 217.
Latta, James G., (2nd Lt, Co A, 66th NCST), III: 685.
Latta, Joseph W., (Capt, Co A, 66th NCST), III: 685.
Lattimore, Daniel, (2nd Lt, Co B, 49th NCST), I: 734; III: 138.
Lattimore, J.L., (Pvt, Co B, 49th NCST), V: 564.
Lattimore, James H., (Pvt, Co F, 34th NCST), V: 555.
Lattimore, Jesse R., (Pvt, Co F, 3th NCST), V: 555.
Lattimore, T.D., (2nd Lt, Co F, 34th NCST), II: 581, 582, 583, 584, 590; V: 548.
Laughinghouse, _____, [Caswell], (Pvt, Co E, 27th NCST), II: 444.
Laughinghouse, Joseph J., (Capt, Co C, 5th Battalion Junior Reserves; Co H, 71st NCST, 2nd Junior Reserves), IV: 28, 595.
Laughinghouse, Samuel, (1st Lt, Co B, 5th Battalion Junior Reserves; Co G, 71st NCST, 2nd Junior Reserves), IV: 28.
Laughlin, James J., (2nd Lt, Co B, 30th NCST), II: 496; IV: 701, 708.
Laughon, Arch, (Lt, Co F, 10th Vols/20th NCST), II: 118.
Laughter, Lewis, (Pvt, Co E, 64th NCST), III: 668.
Laurel Hill, Va., I: 752.
Laurel Mountain, (Madison County), IV: 113, 114.
Laurenburg, N.C., IV: 613.
Laurence, Alexander, (Chief Engineer, CSN, Ella and Annie), V: 445.
Laurens, H., (Sgt, Co F, 3rd NCST), V: 487.
Lauter, F.M., (2nd Lt, Co D, Walker's Battalion, Thomas' Legion; 80th NCST), IV: 118.
Law, Evander Melvor, (Brig Gen), I: 305, 309, 568; II: 718; III: 407, 408.
Law's Gap, N.C., V: 289.
Lawder, P.J., (Pvt, Co D, 11th Vols/21st NCST), V: 514.
Lawhon, C., (Sgt, Co D, 48th NCST), III: 119.
Lawhon, W.H.H., (Capt, Co D, 48th NCST), III: 113, 115, 118, 119, 120, 121, 122, 123; V: 520, 593.
Lawhorn, A.F., (1st Lt, Co F, 10th Vols/20th NCST), V: 503, 509.
Lawhorn, A.F., (2nd Lt, Co A, 30th NCST), II: 496, 498.
Lawhorn, Y.J., (Lt, Co B, 10th Battalion NCST, 2nd Hvy Art), IV: 329.
Lawing, J., (Pvt, Co I, 37th NCST), V: 546.
Lawing, John S., (Pvt, Co G, 34th NCST), V: 556.
Lawing, Dr. John W., (Surg, 69th NCST, Thomas' Legion), III: 730, 733; IV: 642.
Lawley, Francis C., (Englishman, Editor, London Telegraph), V: 411-421.
Lawrence, _____, [Robert J.], (Col, 14th Miss.), I: 699.
Lawrence, A.W., (Capt, Ordnance Officer, 12th Vols/22nd NCST; Ordnance Officer, N.C. Reserves), I: 48; II: 166; IV: 37.
Lawrence, George, (Englishamn), V: 412.
Lawrence, H.C., [Lowrance, Henry Clay], (1st Lt, Co D, 6th Battalion/60th NCST), IV: 708.
Lawrence, Dr. J.J., (Pvt, Co A, 1st Vols, "Bethel"), V: 578.
Lawrence, J.J., (Capt, Claiborne-Dearing's 7th C.S. Cav; 16th Battalion/75th NCST, 7th Cav), IV: 72.

Lawrence, J.W., (Cpl, Co H, 30th NCST), V: 492.
Lawrence, John M., (2nd Lt, ACS, 12th Vols/22nd NCST; 1st Lt, Co B, 8th Battalion Junior Reserves; Co E, 72nd NCST, 3rd Junior Reserves), II: 166, 172; IV: 41, 48, 701, 708.
Lawrence, Joseph J., (Capt, Co F, 40th NCST, 3rd Art, Hvy), II: 746.
Lawrence, Lee, (Pvt, Co A, 1st Battalion NCST), V: 504.
Lawrence, Lewis C., (2nd Lt, ACS, 68th NCST), I: 137; III: 713.
Lawrence, Lewis H., (2nd Lt, Co B, 33rd NCST), II: 538, 578.
Lawrence, N.M., [Nathan M.], (2nd Lt, Co C, 8th NCST), IV: 701, 708.
Lawrence, Peter, (Pvt, Co H, 27th NCST), II: 462.
Lawrence, Rhet, R.L., (Capt, Co K, 44th NCST), III: 23.
Lawrenceburg, Ky., II: 708.
Lawrenceville, Va., I: 434.
Laws, Cyrus, (Pvt, Co D, 56th NCST), III: 347.
Lawson, B.F., (Pvt, Co B, 6th Battalion/60th NCST), III: 482.
Lawson, J.J., (Sgt, Co E, 35th NCST), V: 562.
Lawson, Dr. John W., (Surg, 2nd Vols/12th NCST), I: 651; IV: 633; V: 503.
Lawson, R.H., (Lt Cmdr, USN, Gettysburg), V: 243, 245.
Lawson, Thomas T., (Capt, Co H, 3rd Vols/13th NCST), I: 691, 701.
Lawson, Mrs. Thomas T., I: 701.
Lawsonville, N.C., I: 653.
Lawton, Alexander Robert, (Brig Gen), II: 36, 683.
Lawyer's Road, (nr Cooke's Bridge), III: 622.
Lay's Ferry, Ga., II: 741.
Laycock, J. Erwin, (Cpl, Co D, 56th NCST), III: 355.
Lazel, Lawson, (Pvt, Co F, 38th NCST), V: 557.
Lazenby, J.M., (Pvt, Co A, 33rd NCST), V: 543.
Lazenby, Robert S., (Pvt, Co A, 4th NCST), V: 488.
Lea, J.A., [James A.], (Capt, Co K, 6th NCST), IV: 702, 708.
Lea, James W., (2nd Lt, Co I, 5th NCST), I: 291; V: 503.
Lea, John W., (Col, 5th NCST), I: 281, 284, 287, 288, 289, 290, 291, 296, 351, 651; II: 264, 265; IV: 441, 524; V: 264, 503.
Lea, Thomas L., (Capt, Co E, 6th Battalion Junior Reserves; Co G, 70th NCST, 1st Junior Reserves), IV: 10, 13.
Leach, Miss ______, (Became Mrs. C.C. Dodson), IV: 615.
Leach, D.W., (Pvt, Co I, 5th NCST), I: 292; V: 506.
Leach, Frank, (Lt, Co K, 9th NCST, 1st Cav), I: 486.
Leach, George T., (1st Lt, Co C, 53rd NCST), III: 262; V: 494.
Leach, J.A., (Pvt, Co G, 46th NCST), V: 525.
Leach, J.P., (Pvt, Co C, 53rd NCST), V: 501.
Leach, James M., (Lt Col, 11th Vols/21st NCST), II: 144.
Leach, Dr. John P., (2nd Lt, Co C; Ass't Surg, 13th Vols/23rd NCST), II: 184; IV: 630.
Leach, John, (Capt, Co C, 53rd NCST), III: 261.
Leach, Dr. R.V., (Surg, 2nd Battalion NCST), IV: 643; V: 494.
Lead Works, (nr Petersburg, Va.), IV: 495.
Leadbetter, Danville, [Ledbetter], (Brig Gen, Chief Engineer, AoT), II: 706.

Leak, John W., (Lt Col, 13th Vols/23rd NCST), II: 189, 202-203.
Leak, P.J., (Pvt, Co I, 3rd Vols/13th NCST), V: 551.
Leak, Walter, Sr., (Pvt, Revolution, Grandfather of John W.), II: 202.
Leak, William P., (Pvt, Co C, 4th Vols/14th NCST), V: 490.
Leary, James A., (1st Lt, Co F, 68th NCST), III: 714.
Leatherman, D., (Pvt, Co E, 57th NCST), V: 517.
Leathers, S.N., (Musician, 6th NCST), V: 511.
Leatherwood, Albert N., (2nd Lt, Co E, 39th NCST), II: 705; IV: 722.
Leatherwood, W.H., (1st Lt, Co A, 62nd NCST), III: 515, 525; IV: 702, 708.
Leavel, George, (ADC to Lt Col Ray, 6th Battalion/60th NCST), III: 488.
Leazar, A., (1st Lt, Co G, 42nd NCST; Hoke's Staff), II: 791, 806; IV: 538.
Ledbetter, Miss _____, (Became Mrs. F.M. Kennedy), IV: 611.
Ledbetter, Chealey E., (Pvt, Co G, 38th NCST), V: 557.
Ledbetter, J.A., (Pvt, Co E, 28th NCST), V: 542.
Ledbetter, J.G., (Pvt, Co K, 6th Battalion/60th NCST), III: 482.
Lechrist, Daniel. (Pvt, Co I, 4th Vols/14th NCST), V: 491.
Ledford, Hiram, (1st Lt, Co H, Walker's Battalion, Thomas' Legion; 80th NCST), IV: 119.
Ledford, James, (Pvt, Co K, 49th NCST), V: 565.
Ledford, John, (Pvt, Co C, 10th NCST, 1st Art & Engs, Brem-Graham-Williams' Battery, Light Art), V: 568.
Lee, _____, (Capt, USN, Smith Briggs), II: 515.
Lee, Charles C., (Col, 1st Vols, "Bethel"; Col, 37th NCST), I: 77, 78, 79, 84, 85, 89, 99, 111, 113, 118, 122, 126, 127, 365; II: 22, 23, 310, 327, 471, 542, 548, 653, 654, 655; IV: 474; V: 10, 645, 646.
Lee, Fitzhugh, (Maj Gen), I: 420, 427, 428, 434, 438, 439, 440, 457, 458, 576, 602, 686; II: 101, 108, 123, 391, 783; III: 394, 399, 401, 460, 553, 563, 565, 576, 582, 583, 604, 605, 642, 653, 650; V: 126, 253, 254, 628.
Lee, Frank, (Pvt, Co K, 26th NCST), V: 532.
Lee, George, (Capt, ACS, Grimes' Staff), V: 483.
Lee, George Washington Custis, (Maj Gen), II: 392; III: 339; IV: 404, 427.
Lee, H.D., (Capt, Co D; Maj, 6th Vols/16th NCST), I: 751; IV: 137, 174, 254.
Lee, H.S., (Sgt, Co B, 10th NCST, 1st Art & Engs, Guion's Hvy Art), I: 510, 536.
Lee, J.A., (Pvt, Co A, 5th NCST), I: 291; V: 505.
Lee, J.B., (Ordnance Sgt, Grimes Staff), V: 483.
Lee, J.B., (2nd Lt, Co G, 59th NCST, 4th Cav), III: 457.
Lee, J.H., (Sgt, Co B, 26th NCST), V: 531.
Lee, J.N., (Lt, Co E, 2nd Battalion NCST), IV: 245.
Lee, John, (Maj, W.H.F. Lee's Staff), II: 104.
Lee, John, (Pvt, Co H, 56th NCST), III: 357.
Lee, John W., (1st Cpl, Co G, 4th Vols/14th NCST; Detailed, 2nd Corps Provost Guard), V: 490; V: 569.

Lee, Joshua, (2nd Lt, Co I, 53rd NCST), III: 263; V: 494.
Lee, M.C., (Capt, Co D, 8th Vols/18th NCST), II: 20, 22.
Lee, Monroe, (Pvt, Co C, 5th NCST), I: 291; V: 505.
Lee, Mordecai, (Lt, Co G, 55th NCST), III: 296.
Lee, P., (Pvt, Co G, 61st Va.), V: 569.
Lee, Richard H., (Capt, 16th N.Y. Battery), V: 238.
Lee, Robert, (Pvt, Co I, 49th NCST), V: 565.
Lee, Robert, [Robert J.], (Sgt, Co C, 62nd NCST), III: 667.
Lee, S.S., (Capt, CSN), IV: 743.
Lee, Stephen D. (Lt Gen), I: 352, 565, 566, 626, 733, 751; IV: 137, 138, 139, 140, 146, 150, 151, 254.
Lee, T.G., (Capt, Co D, 4th NCST), I: 232, 233, 271; V: 484.
Lee, T.T., (Lt, Co E, 24th NCST), V: 193.
Lee, William H., (Color-bearer, 1st NCST), I: 151, 152.
Lee, William Henry Fitzhugh "Rooney," (Maj Gen), I: 423, 424, 432, 433, 435, 436, 438, 439, 440, 441, 468, 469, 470, 473, 474, 475, 476, 477, 481, 775, 777; II: 91, 93, 104, 107, 780; III: 460, 562, 592, 595, 608, 609, 610, 612, 613, 614, 615, 619, 622, 623, 624, 625, 627, 629, 630, 634, 640, 642, 647, 650, 652; IV: 88, 90, 142, 144.
Lee, Young J., (2nd Lt, Co D, 50th NCST), III: 203.
Lee's Farewell Address, III: 402; IV: 214-215.
Lee's Farm, (nr Yorktown, Va.), I: 733, 737.
Lee's Mill, N.C., III: 338.
Lee's Mill, Va., I: 737.
Lee's Mill Road, (nr Plymouth), III: 338; V: 176, 182.
Lee County, Va., III: 524.
Lee & Gordon's Mills, Ga., II: 716; III: 449, 487.
Lee & Gordon's Mill Road, Ga., II: 716.
Leecraft, ______, (Leecraft's Co, 11th Battalion NCST), IV: 338.
Leecraft, LaFayette, (Lt, Co G, 10th NCST, 1st Art & Engs, Pender-Graham's Hvy Art), I: 525, 536.
Leesburg, Va., I: 154, 206, 224, 259, 325, 573, 739; II: 32, 96, 217, 247, 431, 552, 585, 685; III: 13, 66, 750; IV: 164, 511.
Leetown, Va., III: 279, 752.
Leffon, N., (Pvt, Co A, 2nd Vols/12th NCST), V: 506.
Leffon, T., (Pvt, Co A, 2nd Vols/12th NCST), V: 506.
Leffon, Y.T., (Pvt, Co A, 2nd Vols/12th NCST), V: 506.
Leftwich, James B., (Pvt, Co G, 4th Vols/14th NCST), V: 490.
Leggett, ______, (Capt, Boatman), II: 795.
Leggett, ______, (Sgt, Co A, 2nd Engineers, CSA), IV: 431.
Leggett, Dr. E.A., (Ass't Surg, 45th NCST), IV: 639.
Leggett, John E., (Capt, Co C, 40th NCST, 3rd Art, Hvy), II: 746, 756.
Leghman, Oliver J., (Musician, 33rd NCST), II: 537.
Lehman, F.T., (2nd Lt, Co H, 33rd NCST), II: 540.
Leham, O.J., (Musician, 33rd NCST), V: 543.
Leham, Peyton T., (Sgt, Co I, 33rd NCST), II: 540.
Leigh, Dr. H.G., (Surg, Raleigh General Hospital #2), IV: 626, 627.
Leigh, J.W., (Pvt, Co C, 6th NCST), V: 512.

Leigh, John H., (2nd Lt, Co E, 43rd NCST), III: 3.
Leigh, Thomas, (Pvt, Co H, 43rd NCST), V: 499.
Leinback, Peter T., (Pvt, Co I, 33rd NCST), II: 544.
Leinster, R.O., [Linster, Robert Osborne], (Ordnance Sgt, Co C, 4th NCST), I: 279; V: 593.
Leister, Thomas R., (Pvt, Co H, 25th NCST), V: 561.
Leitersburg, Md., III: 570.
Leith, James J., (Capt, Co B, 7th Vols/17th NCST), II: 2, 3; V: 680.
Leitts, M.H., (Pvt, Co E, 28th NCST), V: 542.
Lemley, Jacob, (Pvt, Co D, 10th NCST, 1st Art & Engs, Ramseur-Manly's Battery, Light Art), I: 563.
Lemley, W.A., (Musician, Mickey's Band, 26th NCST), II: 398.
Lemmons, A., (Pvt, Co E, 28th NCST), V: 542.
Lemmons, M., (Pvt, Co E, 28th NCST), V: 542.
Lemons, George, (Pvt, Co B, 27th NCST), II: 461; V: 523.
Lengle, F.S., (Pvt, Co I, 53rd NCST), V: 502.
Lennon, ______, [John Cale], (1st Lt, Co H, 51st NCST), III: 219.
Lenoir, Thomas I., (Capt, Co F, 25th NCST), II: 292.
Lenoir, W.W., (Capt, Co A, 37th NCST), III: 433.
Lenoir, N.C., II: 411, 417, 628; III: 683; IV: 375, 376; V: 600.
Lenoir County, N.C., I: 534; II: 747, 771; III: 131, 226, 504, 545, 686, 727; IV: 354, 595.
Lenoir Station, Tenn., (East Tennessee & Georgia Railroad), II: 488, 710, 731, 273.
Lenow Bridge, IV: 368.
Lentz, Luther, (Pvt, Co G, 5th NCST), I: 292; V: 505.
Lentz, R.R., (Sgt, Co C, 37th NCST), V: 545.
Lentz, Robert, (Pvt, Co D, 10th NCST, 1st Art & Engs, Reilly-Ramsay's Battery, Light Art), I: 569.
Lentz, Tobias, (Pvt, Co H, 5th NCST), I: 292.
Leon, L., (Pvt, Co B, 53rd NCST), III: 258, 264.
Leonard, A., (Pvt, Co H, 48th NCST), V: 527.
Leonard, A.B., (Pvt, Co E, 44th NCST), V: 533.
Leonard, Burgess, (Pvt, Co A, 11th Vols/21st NCST), V: 514.
Leonard, H.C., (Maj, 7th Regt Home Guard), IV: 650.
Leonard, J.B., (Cpl, Co E, Millard's 9th/20th Battalion Junior Reserves), IV: 389.
Leonard, James M., (Pvt, Co G, 5th Vols/15th NCST), V: 522.
Leonard, Joseph J., (2nd Lt, Co K, 44th NCST), III: 24.
Leonard, Robert R., (Pvt, Co G, 5th Vols/15th NCST), V: 522.
Leonard, Robert R., (1st Sgt, Co C, 48th NCST), V: 526.
Leonard, W.H., (Sgt, Co G, 5th Vols/15th NCST), V: 522.
Leonhart, J.M., (Pvt, Co I, 1st Vols/11th NCST), V: 531.
Leper, F.W., (Cpl, Co B, 28th NCST), V: 541.
Leroy, C.H., (Ass't Engineer, CSN, Tallahassee), V: 438.
Lesesne, Dr., Charle, (Ass't Surg, 8th Vols./18th NCST), II: 17; IV: 473, 635.
Lesesne, R.M., (2nd Lt, Co B, 8th Vols/18th NCST), II: 63; V: 537.
Leslie, ______, (Gen, USA; Leslie's Division, 9th Corps), II: 622.
Leslie, Charles M.P., (Englishman, Col), V: 412.

Leslie, Frank, (Englishman), V: 410.
Leslie, J.J., (Musician, Co G, 8th Vols/18th NCST), II: 64; V: 540.
Lesley, Isaac, (Pvt, Co C, 49th NCST), V: 564.
Letcher, John, (Governor of Virginia), III: 749; IV: 139, 244.
Letz, J.C., (Lt, Co , 50th NCST), IV: 708.
Leventhorpe, Collett, (Col, 34th NCST; Col, 1st Vols/11th NCST; N.C. Brig Gen, Leventhorpe's Home Guard Brigade; Brig Gen), I: xii, xiii, 52, 583, 586, 589, 590; II: 581, 582, 677; III: 321; IV: 18, 43, 44, 76, 182, 440, 555, 589, 646, 651, 652, 653; V: 7, 83, 84, 85, 88, 89, 120, 630, 631, 632.
Levi, J.T., (Capt, Co L, Louisiana Tigers, Art Co, Walker's Battalion, Thomas' Legion; 80th NCST), IV: 119.
Levister, Richard, (Pvt, Co I, 55th NCST), V: 528.
Lewellen, Thomas, (Pvt, Co F, 45th NCST), V: 500.
Lewey, John, (Pvt, Co A, 53rd NCST), V: 501.
Lewis, Rev. ______, (Col), IV: 671, 673, 674, 679, 686.
Lewis, A.F., [Asa F.], (2nd Lt, Co B, 38th NCST), IV: 708.
Lewis, A.L., (Pvt, Co I, 30th NCST), V: 493.
Lewis, Alexander, (2nd Lt, Co H, 8th Vols/18th NCST), II: 64; V: 537.
Lewis, Augustus M., (Maj, N.C. Quartermaster Department, N.C. Pay Department), I: 23, 45; V: 651.
Lewis, B.M., (Pvt, Co E, 45th NCST), V: 500.
Lewis, Calvin B., (3rd Sgt, Co B, 52nd NCST), III: 223.
Lewis, D.W., (2nd Lt, Co D, 59th NCST, 4th Cav), III: 457, 464.
Lewis, Exum, (Sgt Maj, 5th Vols/15th NCST), I: 734;
Lewis, Exum, (2nd Lt, Co E, 33rd NCST), II: 539, 578.
Lewis, G., (Pvt, Co A, 47th NCST), V: 534.
Lewis, George C., (Capt, Co K, 2nd NCST), I: 164.
Lewis, George N., (Capt, Co D, 47th NCST), III: 84.
Lewis, Henry G., (Maj, 32nd NCST), II: 522; IV: 701.
Lewis, Isaac, (Pvt, Co K, 11th Vols/21st NCST), V: 515.
Lewis, J.H., (Pvt, Co B, 1st Battalion NCST), V: 504.
Lewis, J.J., (Pvt, Co B, 28th NCST), V: 540.
Lewis, J.S., (Pvt, Co F, 30th NCST), V: 492.
Lewis, J.T., (Pvt, Co B, 1st Battalion NCST), V: 504.
Lewis, James J., (Pvt, Co E, Drum-Corps, 4th Vols/14th NCST), I: 711; V: 490.
Lewis, Dr. Joel Battle, (Pvt, Co I, 5th Vols/15th NCST; Ass't Surg & Surg, 43rd NCST), III: 1; IV: 638.
Lewis, John, (Pvt, Co D, 4th NCST), V: 488.
Lewis, John C., (Pvt, Co F, 26th NCST), V: 601.
Lewis, Kindred, (Color Sgt, 2nd NCST), I: 170.
Lewis, Lovett, (Capt, Co D, 4th NCST), I: 232.
Lewis, McCloud, (Fayetteville and Harper's Ferry Arsenals), IV: 298.
Lewis, Nelson, (Pvt, Co E, 49th NCST), V: 564.
Lewis, Dr. O.M., (Ass't Surg, 58th NCST), III: 432; IV: 641.
Lewis, R.G., (Lt, Ass't N.C. Paymaster), I: 45.

Lewis, Robert, (Pvt, Co A, 45th NCST), V: 499.
Lewis, Thomas C., (Capt, Co I, 8th Vols/18th NCST), IV: 719, 721; V: 98.
Lewis, Thomas L., (See: Thomas C.).
Lewis, W.D., (Pvt, Co D, 43rd NCST), V: 498.
Lewis, W.P., (1st Lt, Co C, 10th NCST, 1st Art & Engs, Brem-Graham-Williams' Battery, Light Art), I: 537, 538.
Lewis, Watson, Jr., (of Hertford County), III: 715.
Lewis, William Gaston, (Brig Gen), I: xii, 77, 113, 115, 117, 118, 122, 133; II: 130, 144, 315, 316, 320, 321, 537, 544; III: 1, 4, 6, 7, 8, 18, 274, 277, 284, 285, 341, 342, 346, 355, 400, 422, 426; IV: 474, 526; V: 190, 649, 663, 666.
Lewis House, (nr Manassas, Va.), I: 342, 343, 344, 347, 348; V: 581.
Lewis' Store, (Hertford County), III: 715.
Lexington, Ky., IV: 275, 276.
Lexington, N.C., IV: 653, 770.
Lexington, Va., I: 153, 215; III: 278, 748, 749.
Lexington & Winchester Pike, Ky., IV: 275.
Libby Prison, (Richmond, Va.), III: 600.
Liberty, Va., I: 205; II: 245; III: 12, 277, 419.
Liberty Mills, Va., I: 382, 383, 448, 450; II: 45, 46, 122, 478, 479, 568, 569, 663, 664; IV: 188, 474.
Liddle, ______, [Philip F.], (Col, 11th Miss.), V: 583.
Lierner, ______, (Capt, Engineering Officer), IV: 418.
Lieutenant Run, Va., II: 481; IV: 478.
Life and Campaigns of Lieut.-Gen. Thomas J. Jackson, II: 437.
Light, M.M., (Pvt, Co A, 37th NCST), V: 545.
Lightfoot, ______, [James N.], (Lt Col, 6th Ala.), I: 151.
Lightfoot, Charles E., (Lt Col, 6th NCST; Col, 12th Vols/22nd NCST), I: 295, 338, 339, 344, 346; II: 167; IV: 356; V: 32, 581, 582, 584, 641.
Ligon, Hiram S., (Capt, Co G, 11th Vols/21st NCST), IV: 230.
Liles, Charles M., (Pvt, Co C, 4th Vols/14th NCST), V: 490.
Liles, Edward R., (Maj, 18th Battalion Home Guard; Lt Col, 31st NCST), IV: 650; V: 63, 64, 65, 66, 69, 650.
Liles, Edward R., (Lt Col, 31st NCST), II: 507, 511, 513.
Liles, Joseph E., (Pvt, Co B, 31st NCST), V: 69.
Liles, Junius A., (2nd Lt, Co B, 31st NCST), II: 512, 513.
Liles, W.A., (Capt, Co C, 4th Vols/14th NCST), I: 731.
Lillington, N.W., (Lt, Co H, 55th NCST), III: 296, 306, 307.
Lilly, H.D., (Pvt, Co G, 3rd Vols/13th NCST), V: 550.
Lilly, John W., (2nd Lt, Co G, 52nd NCST), III: 224.
Lilly, Peter B., (2nd Lt, Co H, 43rd NCST), III: 3.
Lilly, S.M., (1st Sgt, Co K, 43rd NCST), V: 499.
Lilly, Samuel S., (Capt, Co I, 52nd NCST), III: 225; V: 529.
Lilly, Thomas, (Capt, Co K, 26th NCST), II: 372, 393, 397, 403, 419.
Lilly, Dr. William H., (Ass't Surg, 52nd NCST), III: 226; IV: 640; V: 529.
Limestone, Tenn., III: 518, 739.
Limestone Bridge, Tenn., (and Battle of, 1863), IV: 121.

Lincoln, Rev. ______, (Gen, Revolutionary War), I: 754.
Lincoln, Abraham, (President, U.S.), I: 39, 56, 71, 73, 81, 102, 115, 294, 337, 500; II: 15, 86, 152, 218, 247, 293, 305; III: 200, 354, 383, 386, 388, 395, 412, 559, 567, 735, 750; IV: 125, 500, 597, 665, 686; V: 73, 74, 81-82, 114, 132, 259, 280, 283, 340, 465, 478.
Lincoln County, N.C., III: 125, 153, 154, 315, 406, 409, 427, 545, 730; IV: 28, 330, 614.
Lincoln County, Va., II: 182, 202, 234.
Lincolton, N.C., I: 61, 111, 500; III: 411, 422; IV: 28, 375, 743.
Lindsay, Andrew D., (Ordnance Sgt, 27th NCST), II: 461; V: 522.
Lindsay, Gavin H., Jr., (2nd Lt, Co K, 54th NCST), IV: 723.
Lindsay, George, [Lindsey], (Sgt, Color-bearer, 6th Battalion/60th NCST), III: 491, 497.
Lindsay, Henry P., (2nd Lt, Co F, 41st NCST, 3rd Cav), II: 771.
Lindsay, J.B., [Lindsey], (2nd Lt, Co B, 31st NCST), IV: 723; V: 64.
Lindsay, J.W., (Pvt, Co F, 56th NCST), III: 348.
Lindsay, John W., (Jr 2nd Lt, Co A, 6th Battalion/60th NCST), III: 483.
Lindsay, R.W., (2nd Lt, Co A, 6th Battalion Junior Reserves; Co C, 70th NCST, 1st Junior Reserves), IV: 13.
Lindsay, W.S., (Pvt, Co D, 45th NCST), V: 500.
Lindsay's Turnout, (nr Charlottesville, Va.), I: 546, 547.
Lindsey, ______, (Author), IV: 120.
Lindsey, B.D., (Pvt, Co A, 8th Vols/18th NCST), II: 63.
Lindsey, Charles B., (Capt, Co B, 31st NCST), II: 507, 512; V: 64.
Lindsey, E.B., [Lindsay, Edwin B.], (1st Lt, Co K, 63rd NCST, 5th Cav), I: 441; III: 541, 600, 643.
Lindsey, J.B., (AQMS, 31st NCST), II: 511.
Lindsey, S.S., (1st Lt, Co I, 62nd Ga. Cav; Co C, 16th Battalion/75th NCST, 7th Cav), IV: 91.
Lindsey, Dr. W.D., (Surg, 48th NCST), IV: 639.
Lineback, Edward, (Bugler, Co A, 11th Vols/21st NCST), V: 514.
Lineback, J.A., (Musician, Mickey's Band, 26th NCST), II: 398.
Lineback, Peter T., II: 544.
Linebarger, ______, [James W.], (Lt, Co H, 49th NCST), III: 137, 148.
Linebarger, J.L., (Pvt, Co H, 37th NCST), V: 546.
Linebarger, Frederick, (3rd Sgt, Co G, 52nd NCST), III: 224.
Linebarger, N.M., (Pvt, Co C, 28th NCST), V: 540.
Linebarger, T. James, (Capt, Co C, 28th NCST), II: 482; V: 537.
Lineberger, J.C., (Pvt, Co G, 8th NCST), V: 194.
Lineberry, Alexander, (Pvt, Co G, 26th NCST), V: 532.
Lineberry, Edwin C., (2nd Lt, Co F, Millard's 9th/20th Battalion Junior Reserves), IV: 387, 393, 395.
Lindberry, R.D., [Linebery], (Pvt, Co B, Starr's Battery, Starr's 13th Battalion NCST, Light Art), IV: 346.
Lineberry, W.S., (Capt, Co C, 6th Battalion Junior Reserves; Co F, 70th NCST, 1st Junior Reserves), IV: 10, 13.
Linens, William, (Pvt, Co K, 47th NCST), V: 535.
Liner, A. Joseph, (1st Lt, Co C, Millard's 9th/20th Battalion Junior Reserves), IV: 386, 391, 393, 395, 396.

Lines, Charles L., (Pvt, Co B, 4th Vols/14th NCST), V: 490.
Lingle, A.D., (Lt, Co H, 58th NCST), III: 433.
Linney, James Polk, (Brother of R.Z. Polk), V: 290, 291, 292, 293, 294, 295.
Linney, Romulus Z., (Pvt, Co A, 7th NCST), IV: 377; V: 285, 290, 295.
Linney, W.C., (Store Owner, Cove Gap), V: 289, 294.
Linster, Robert O., (Orderly Sgt, Co C, 4th NCST), V: 488.
Lippard, C.W., (Lt, Co D, 9th NCST, 1st Cav), I: 485.
Lippitt, A.D., (Lt, Co G, 61st NCST), III: 504.
Lippitt, J.W., (Capt, Co G, 51st NCST), III: 219.
Lippitt, T.B., (Lt, Co G, 51st NCST), III: 219.
Lipscomb, Samuel M., (Musician, Co B, 27th NCST), II: 461; V: 523.
Lipscomb, T.J., (Col, 2nd S.C., Cav), V: 241.
Lipscombe, William A., (Cpl, Co I, 5th Vols/15th NCST), V: 522.
Lisk, J.T., (Pvt, Co E, 28th NCST), V: 542.
Lisk, W.T., (Musician, Co E, 28th NCST), V: 542.
List of General and Field Officers Killed, V: 9.
List of Historians and Contributors, V: xix.
Litaker, Alfred, (Pvt, Co B, 10th Vols/20th NCST), II: 114.
Litaker, James F., (2nd Lt, Co F, 57th NCST), III: 427; IV: 708.
Litchfield, George, (1st Sgt, Co E, 4th NCST), I: 233.
Litchfield, S.J., (1st Lt, Co E, 4th NCST), I: 233, 271, 272.
Litchford, James J., (AQM, 12th Vols/22nd NCST), II: 162.
Littell, John S., (Col, 76th Pa.), V: 238.
Little, Albert, (Sgt, Co E, 32nd NCST), V: 496.
Little, Benjamin F., (Lt Col, 52nd NCST), III: 224, 239; V: 153.
Little, C.C., (Pvt, Co G, 10th Vols/20th NCST), II: 114; V: 509.
Little, Gray, (Resident of Pitt County), IV: 77.
Little, J.C., (Capt, Ordnance Officer, Fort Fisher), II: 648.
Little, J.C., (Pvt, Co F, 30th NCST), V: 492.
Little, J.H., (Sgt, Co H, 27th NCST), II: 462; V: 523.
Little, J.P., (Cpl, Co C, 33rd NCST), II: 579.
Little, John F., (5th Sgt, Co G, 52nd NCST), III: 224.
Little, John G., (Pvt, Co E, 32nd NCST), V: 496.
Little, John M., (2nd Lt, Co A, 13th Vols/23rd NCST), II: 183.
Little, Joshua B., (Capt, Co F, 38th NCST), II: 675.
Little, J. Pinkney, (Ensign/1st Lt, 28th NCST), II: 465.
Little, L., (Pvt, Co C, 2nd Vols/12th NCST), V: 507.
Little, P., (Pvt, Co D, 37th NCST), V: 545.
Little, R.B., (Pvt, Co K, 13th Vols/23rd NCST), V: 510.
Little, T.Y., (Pvt, Co E, 1st Vols, "Bethel"), I: 128.
Little, William, (4th Cpl, Co G, 52nd NCST), III: 224.
Little, Dr. William, (Ass't Surg, N.C.), IV: 630.
Little, William Calvin, (Pvt, Co C, 4th Vols/14th NCST), I: 727, 732.
Little Church, (nr Chancellorsville, Va.), II: 118.
Little Creek, N.C., (aka Little River), II: 337, 338.

Little Fort Valley, Va., I: 327.
"Little Litaker," (Bugler, 9th NCST, 1st Cav), I: 427.
Little River, Va., III: 24.
Little River Turnpike, Va., (nr Manassas, Va.), II: 31, 32; III: 582.
Little Rock, Ark., IV: 36.
"Little Sorrel," (Stonewall Jackson's favorite hores), V: 93.
Little Tennessee River, N.C., IV: 123, 125.
Little Washington, Va., I: 422.
Littlejohn, J.B., (Pvt, Co F, 26th NCST), V: 601.
Littlejohn, J.T., (Maj, Littlejohn's 23rd Battalion Senior Reserves), IV: 6, 398, 399.
Littlejohn, W.H., (Lt, Co A, 51st NCST), III: 209, 218.
Littletown, Pa., I: 425.
Liverman, Jesse, (Pvt, Cook, 7th Vols/17th NCST), V: 39.
Liverpool, England, V: 43, 335, 340, 346, 349, 364, 387, 400, 405, 415, 417, 418, 441, 453, 471.
Lives of Distinguished North Carolinians, IV: 448.
Livingood, H.W., (Pvt, Co D, 57th NCST), V: 517.
Livingood, Lewis, (Pvt, Co K, 11th Vols/21st NCST), V: 515.
Livingston, L, (Pvt, Co B, 1st Vols/11th NCST), V: 530.
Lloyd, ______, (Capt, Lloyd's Battery; Battery disbanded the men going to Manly's and Reilly's Batteries), I: 554, 577.
Lloyd, G.E., (Pvt, Co D, 30th NCST), V: 492.
Lloyd, J.L., (Sgt, Co G, 28th NCST), V: 542.
Lloyd, Whitmel P., (Lt Col, 2nd Regt. Home Guard), I: 77, 113, 118; IV: 653.
Lockett, D.S., (2nd Lt, Co A, 3rd Vols/13th NCST), V: 547.
Lockey, J.M., (Sgt, Co L, 11th Vols/21st NCST), V: 515.
Lockhart, ______, [John S.], (2nd Lt, Co B, 6th NCST), I: 345.
Lockhart, ______, (Chief Engineer, CSN, Susan Beirne), V: 382, 410.
Lockhart, J.T., (Pvt, Co H, 43rd NCST), V: 499.
Lockhart, John P., (Maj, 19th NCST, 2nd Cav), I: 441, 442; II: 80, 89, 107; III: 642.
Lockhart, Joseph G., (Capt, Co E, 56th NCST), III: 315, 338, 342; V: 179, 185, 189, 191.
Lockman, L.A., (Pvt, Co K, 13th Vols/23rd NCST), V: 510.
Lockman, W.L., (Sgt, Co K, 13th Vols/23rd NCST), V: 510.
Lockwood, Henry Hayes, (Brig Gen, USA), III: 753.
Lockwood, Robert, (Capt, CSN, Sirene), V: 442, 445.
Lockwood, Thomas, (Cmdr, CSN; Capt, Gordon, Colonel Lamb), V: 339, 340, 401, 403.
Lockwood's Folly, N.C., IV: 332, 600; V: 358, 396.
Locust Grove, Va., I: 150, 199; II: 120.
Locust Old Field, N.C., (now Canton), III: 757.
Loften, Lafayette, (1st Cpl, Co H, 52nd NCST), III: 225.
Loftin, S.H., (2nd Lt, Co E, 41st NCST, 3rd Cav), II: 771.
Loftin, William, (Ambulance Driver, Co E, 66th NCST; Detailed, QM Corps), V: 571.
Loftin, W.W., (Lt, Co C, 2nd NCST), I: 159.
Loftis, Thomas, (Pvt, Co K, 3rd Vols/13th NCST), I: 656.
Lofton, T.J., (Col, 6th Ga.), V: 241.
Logan, B.F., (1st Lt, Co E, 2nd Vols/12th NCST), I: 651; V: 503.
Logan, H.G., (1st Lt, Co C, 2nd Battalion Junior Reserves; Co

D, 71st NCST, 2nd Junior Reserves), IV: 28.
Logan, Dr. John E., (Ass't Surg, 4th Vols/14th NCST; Surg, Grimes' Division), III: 399; IV: 634; V: 484.
Logan, John F., (Pvt, Co G, 6th Vols/16th NCST), IV: 146.
Logan, R.F., (2nd Lt, Co G, 50th NCST), IV: 203.
Loggins, Thomas, (Pvt, Co H, 11th Vols/21st NCST), V: 515.
Loinback, B.F., (Pvt, Co K, 11th Vols/21st NCST), V: 194.
Lollar, H. Louis, (Pvt, Co C, 4th NCST), V: 488.
Loman, William, (Pvt, Co B, 1st Battalion NCST), V: 504.
Lomax, Lunsford Lindsay, (Brig Gen), I: 454; II: 119.
London, A.T., (Adjt, 70th NCST, 1st Junior Reserves; AAG, Nethercutt's Brigade), IV: 5, 14, 591, 594.
London, Andrew J., (Pvt, Co F, 34th NCST), V: 555.
London, Henry, (Pvt, Co C, 34th NCST), V: 555.
London, Henry A., (Pvt, Co I, 32nd NCST; Courier for Maj Gen Grimes), I: 265; II: 536; IV: 258, 458, 519; V: xii, 497.
London, William L., (Capt, Co K, 32nd NCST; AAG, Daniel-Grimes' Brigade), I: 736; II: 528; III: 46; IV: 260, 513, 516, 517; V: 494.
London, England, V: 417, 453, 454.
London, Tenn., III: 448.
"Lone Star," (War correspondent), V: 184, 186.
Long, A.B., (1st Sgt, Co G, 6th Vols/16th NCST), IV: 153, 163.
Long, Armistead Lindsay, (Brig Gen), V: 138.
Long, B.F., (Chaplain, 4th NCST), IV: 605.
Long, Baxter, (Pvt, Co G, 6th Vols/16th NCST), IV: 185.
Long, Edward, (2nd Lt, Co C, 40th NCST, 3rd Art, Hvy), II: 747.
Long, Frederick, (2nd Lt, Co I, 28th NCST), II: 474.
Long, G.W., (Cpl, Co E, 5th NCST), I: 291; V: 505.
Long, H.C., (Cpl, Co H, 8th Vols/18th NCST), II: 64; V: 540.
Long, H.C., (Capt, Co F, 58th NCST), III: 433.
Long, Hamilton C., (2nd Lt, Co K, 4th NCST), I: 234, 270; V: 664.
Long, Henry H., (Pvt, Co E, 34th NCST), V: 555.
Long, I.P., (1st Lt, Co I, 62nd NCST), III: 516.
Long, J., (Pvt, Co D, 10th Vols/20th NCST), V: 508.
Long, Dr. J.F., (Surg, 53rd NCST), III: 261; IV: 640.
Long, J.J., (Pvt, Co D, 49th NCST), V: 564.
Long, James, (Pvt, Co C, 45th NCST), V: 500.
Long, James M., (Ordnance Sgt, 45th NCST), V: 499.
Long, John O., (Lt Col, 12th Vols/22nd NCST), II: 161.
Long, Joseph, (Pvt, Co K, 11th Vols/21st NCST), V: 194.
Long, Madison M., (Pvt, Co K, 32nd NCST; Detailed, 2nd Corps Provost Guard), V: 497, 570.
Long, Nicholas M., (Capt, AQM, 35th NCST), II: 597.
Long, Richard, (Pvt, Co E, 35th NCST), V: 562.
Long, Richard D., (Cpl, Co K, 5th Vols/15th NCST), V: 522.
Long, Thomas B., (2nd Lt, Co E, 44th NCST), III: 21, 23.
Long, W.J., (Capt, Co C, 31st NCST), II: 512.
Long, William J., (Cpl, Co B, 5th Vols/15th NCST), V: 521.
Long, William M., (Pvt, Co G, 25th NCST), V: 561.

Long, William M., (Pvt, Co E, 35th NCST), V: 562.
Long, William S., (2nd Lt/Ensign, Co A, 1st Vols, "Bethel"), I: 77; III: 22.
Long Bridge, (Chickahominy River, Va.), III: 609.
Long Island, N.Y., V: 439.
Long Island Sound, N.Y., V: 441.
Long Tom, (canon), II: 60, 487, 492.
Longstreet, James, (Lt Gen), I: 138, 181, 196, 350, 379, 494, 522, 542, 547, 548, 555, 558, 595, 611, 613, 614, 615, 617, 619, 621, 622, 624, 626, 628, 631, 632, 633, 661, 676; II: 31, 34, 41, 42, 87, 134, 154, 197, 209, 228, 382, 383, 391, 436, 437, 439, 553, 563, 565, 566, 570, 592, 661, 683, 693, 701, 775, 801; III: 119, 245, 291, 295, 371, 385, 395, 414, 560, 679; IV: 35, 123, 170, 179, 192, 208, 212, 291, 357, 457, 466, 503, 504, 536, 537, 541, 563, 571; V: 72, 112, 122, 123, 124, 127, 129, 138, 172, 208, 261, 263.
Lookout Lighthouse, N.C., (Cape Lookout), I: 490, 502, 503.
Lookout Mountain, Tenn., II: 716; III: 491, 735.
Lookout Valley, Tenn., II: 718.
Loper, J.H., (Cpl, Co I, 16th Battalion/75th NCST, 7th Cav), V: 660.
Lorance, H. Clay, (1st Lt, Co D, 6th Battalion/60th NCST), III: 484, 497.
Lorance, S.N., (Pvt, Co I, 49th NCST), V: 565.
Lord, J.C., (Ensign, USN; Pioneer, Yantic), V: 245.
Lord, William C., (Capt, Co A, 57th NCST), III: 410.
Loring, William Wing, (Maj Gen), I: 112; IV: 142, 144.
Lossing, Benson J., II: 368; III: 513.
"Lost Dispatch,The," (General Lee's Order No. 191, the movement order for the Army of Northern Virginia which resulted in the Battle of Sharpsburg. A copy of this Order, supposedly belonging to General D.H. Hill, was found by Federal soldiers and turned over to General McClellan. The controversy surrounding this incident wrongfully did considerable harm to General Hill's reputation.), II: 218, 219, 554, 555 V: 72, 590, 591.
Lost Mountain, Ga., II: 743.
Louch, A.J., (Master, USN; Pioneer, Mackinaw), V: 245.
Loudermilk, G.N., (2nd Lt, Co B, Walker's Battalion, Thomas' Legion; Capt, Co H, 80th NCST), IV: 118.
Loudon, Tenn., II: 727, 731; III: 678; IV: 273, 291.
Loudon Bridge, Tenn., IV: 273.
Loudon County, Va., II: 95, 248, 432.
Loudon Heights, Md., II: 296, 432, 553, 601, 685; III: 116; IV: 502, 570; V: 74.
Louisburg, N.C., IV: 12; V: 280.
Louisia Court House, Va., I: 578; II: 191.
Louisiana, I: 70, 359; II: 701; IV: 35, 513.
Louisville, Ky., I: 37, 46; II: 708; III: 484; IV: 675.
Louisville, Ky., Federal Prison, IV: 41.
Love, Apollos, (Pvt, Co B, 59th NCST, 4th Cav), V: 659.
Love, C., (Pvt, Co G, 56th NCST), III: 356.
Love, C.G., (Capt, Co C, 5th Vols/15th NCST), I: 734.
Love, C.S., (2nd Lt, Co A, 7th Battalion Junior Reserves; Co H, 72nd NCST, 3rd Junior Reserves), IV: 40.

Love, D., (Negro, servant to Col David Coleman), II: 736.
Love, James R., (Lt Col, 69th NCST, Thomas' Legion), III: 730, 731, 732, 739, 741, 751, 753, 754, 757, 759, 760, 761; IV: 119, 122, 128; V: 654, 655.
Love, John B., (Father of Col J.R. Love, resident of Webster, N.C.), III: 760; V: 655.
Love, Dr. John C., (Ass't Surg, 69th NCST, Thomas' Legion), III: 730, 733; IV: 642.
Love, John S., (Capt, Co I, 64th NCST), III: 660. IV: 708.
Love, Matthew Hale, (Lt Col, 25th NCST), II: 292; V: 559.
Love, Matthew Hale, (Capt, Co A, Indian Co, 69th NCST, Thomas' Legion), III: 730, 732, 760.
Love, R.A., (Pvt, Co D, 49th NCST), V: 564.
Love, R.G.A., (Capt, Co L; Lt Col, 6th Vols/16th NCST; Col, 69th NCST; Col, 62nd NCST), I: 751; III: 515, 517, 521, 524, 525; IV: 137, 138, 151.
Love, Rufus, (Sgt, Co E, 49th NCST), II: 539.
Love, Thaddeus D., (Maj, 14th Vols/24th NCST), II: 269, 271, 279, 280, 288, 290.
Love, Thomas, (Pvt, Sharpshooters, 69th NCST, Thomas' Legion), III: 750.
Love, Dr. William, (Ass't Surg, 29th NCST), IV: 636.
Love, William B., (Capt, Co D, 69th NCST, Thomas' Legion), III: 730.
Lovejoy, Charles C., (2nd Lt, Co B, 12th Battalion NCST, Cav; 1st Lt, Co I, 59th NCST, 4th Cav), III: 85, 485; IV: 339.
Lovejoy, George S., (Lt Col, 4th Vols/14th NCST), V: 11.
Lovelace, G.L., (Pvt, Co I, 56th NCST), V: 566.
Lovelace, J.L., (Pvt, Co H, 28th NCST), V: 542.
Lovell, E.F., [Lovill], (Capt, Co A, 28th NCST), II: 475, 482, 483; V: 154, 537.
Lovell, H.P., [Lovill, Henry P.], (1st Lt, Co A, 54th NCST), IV: 701, 708.
"Lover's Leap," N.C., IV: 112.
Lovett, K., [Lovet], (Pvt, Co D, 8th Vols/18th NCST), II: 64; V: 539.
Lovett, N., (Pvt, Co D, 10th Vols/20th NCST), V: 508.
Lovins, William H., (Capt, Co H, 12th Vols/22nd NCST), II: 166.
Lovitt, William, (Pvt, Co I, 27th NCST), II: 462; V: 524.
Low, J.W., (Pvt, Co H, 48th NCST), V: 527.
Lowder, Eben, (1st Cpl, Co H, 4th Vols/14th NCST), V: 490.
Lowber, H., (Pvt, Co A, 6th Battalion/60th NCST), III: 500.
Lowder, George, (Pvt, Co I, 3rd Vols/13th NCST), I: 665.
Lowdermilk, Reuben, (2nd Cpl, Co B, 52nd NCST), III: 223.
Lowdermilk, Z.H., (2nd Lt, Co H, 3rd NCST), IV: 722.
Lowe, Miss _____, (Became Mrs. E.W. Thompson), IV: 614.
Lowe, _____, [Benjamin F.], (1st Lt, Co K, 3rd Ark.), II: 431.
Lowe, J.A., (1st Lt, Co G, 26th NCST), II: 350, 358, 372, 397.
Lowe, J.T., (Sgt Maj, 28th NCST), II: 465.
Lowe, Jesse F., (Pvt, Co D, 59th NCST, 4th Cav), V: 659.
Lowe, John B., (Pvt, Co C, 5th Vols/15th NCST), V: 521.
Lowe, Milton, A., (1st Lt, Co H, 28th NCST), II: 465, 548.
Lowe, Samuel D., (Col, 28th NCST), II: 465, 466, 468, 482; IV: 473.

Lowe, T.C., (AQMS, 28th NCST), II: 465; V: 540.
Lowe, Thomas L., (Lt Col, 28th NCST), II: 465, 466, 468; IV: 473; V: 11.
Lowery, Rev. _____, (Chaplain), IV: 602.
Lowery, Atlas Dargan, (4th Vols/14th NCST), I: 729.
Lowery, S.J., (1st Lt, Co C, 10th NCST, 1st Art & Engs, Brem-Graham-Williams' Battery, Light Art), I: 537.
Lowman, William, (Pvt, Co A, 13th Vols/23rd NCST), II: 190.
Lowrance, B.A., (Cpl, Co A, 2nd Vols/12th NCST), V: 506.
Lowrance, H.C., (Lt, Co D, 6th Battalion/60th NCST), I: 120.
Lowrance, J.S., (Pvt, Co C, 57th NCST), V: 517.
Lowrance, James C., (Pvt, Co D, 34th NCST), V: 555.
Lowrance, John A., (2nd Lt, Co K, 56th NCST), III: 318.
Lowrance, Lansing, [L.J.], (Pvt, Co D, 1st Battalion NCST), V: 292.
Lowrance, William, (Pvt, Co D, 54th NCST), V: 516.
Lowrance, William B., (2nd Lt, Adjt, 34th NCST; Capt, Co K, 34th NCST), II: 582; III: 80; V: 548.
Lowrance, William M., (Adjt, 34th NCST), II: 582.
Lowrance, William L.J., (Col, 34th NCST), II: 363, 364, 566, 567, 581, 692; III: 300; IV: 180; V: 139, 144, 156.
Lowery, J.T., (Pvt, Co D, 37th NCST), V: 545.
Lowery, John, (Pvt, Co H, 4th Vols/14th NCST), V: 490.
Lowrie, J.B., (2nd Lt, Co H, 1st Vols/11th NCST), I: 585; V: 664.
Lowrie, Patrick J., (1st Lt, AQM, 1st Vols/11th NCST), I: 583, 585.
Lowrie, R.B., (2nd Lt, Co H, 1st Vols/11th NCST), I: 585; V: 529.
Lowry, D., (Capt, 10th Illinois), II: 734.
Lowry, Henry Berry, (Murderer of P.M. Wishart), III: 80.
Lowry, James Marion, (Lt Col, 29th NCST), II: 485, 493.
Lowry, S.J., (1st Lt, Co C, 10th NCST, 1st Art & Engs, Brem-Graham-Williams' Battery; Light Art), I: 537, 538.
Loy, J.N., (Lt, Co E, 35th NCST), V: 193.
Loyall, B.P., (Cmdr, CSN; Capt, Neuse), V: 298, 325-333 personal account.
Lucas, Francis, (Pvt, Co E, 56th NCST), V: 566.
Lucas, G.F., (2nd Lt, Co B, 2nd Battalion Junior Reserves; Co C, 71st NCST, 2nd Junior Reserves), IV: 28.
Lucas, H.C., (Adjt, 1st Vols/11th NCST), I: 583, 586.
Lucas, J.F., [John F.], (Sgt, Co E, 4th NCST), I: 233.
Lucas, Wilson H., (1st Lt, Co A, 33rd NCST), II: 538, 539, 578.
Luce, W.H., (Lt Col), IV: 693.
Luck, John, (Pilot, Albemarle), V: 319, 320.
Luck, William J., (Surg, 59th NCST, 4th Cav), V: 659.
Luckey, Dr. F.N., (Ass't Surg, 28th NCST; Surg, 25th NCST), II: 301, 466; IV: 473, 579, 635, 636; V: 559.
Luckey, William A., (2nd Lt, Co B, 19th NCST, 2nd Cav), II: 89.
Ludlow Street Jail, (N.Y. City), V: 410, 443.
Ludwig, H.T.J., (Drummer & Historian, Co H, 8th NCST), I: ix, 414, 415; IV: 485, 489; V: 180, 185, 190.

Luke, J.M.C., (Capt, Co D, 7th Vols/17th NCST), II: 2; V: 35, 42.
Luke, G. Gratiott, (Lt Col, 56th NCST), III: 313, 318, 320, 321, 326, 336, 341, 355, 358, 362, 394, 397, 398; V: 189.
Lumber River, N.C., IV: 613.
Lumberton, N.C., IV: 613.
Lunsford, A., (Pvt, Co G, 9th NCST, 1st Cav), V: 657.
Lunsford, J.G., (Sgt, Co B, 6th NCST), V: 512
Lunsford, N.L., (Musician, 6th NCST), V: 511.
Lunsford, R.D., (Capt, Co C, 50th NCST), III: 161, 202.
Luray, Va., I: 223.
Luray Pike, I: 223.
Luray Valley, Va., I: 326, 327.
Luria, A.M., (2nd Lt, Co I, 13th Vols/23rd NCST), II: 187, 205, 216; V: 640.
Lusk, Virgil S., (Capt, Co A, 5th Battalion NCST, Cav; Capt, Co I, 65th NCST, 6th Cav), III: 674, 675; IV: 271-292 personal account, 702, 708.
Luther, M.D., (Pvt, Co I, 25th NCST), V: 562.
Luther, R.M., (Pvt, Co A, 52nd NCST), V: 535.
Luther, S.P., (Jr 2nd Lt, Co K, 6th Battalion/60th NCST), III: 475.
Luther, W.N., (Pvt, Co K, 1st Vols/11th NCST), V: 531.
Luther, W.N., (Lt, Co B, 64th NCST), III: 660.
Luther, W.M., (Pvt, Co C, 56th NCST), V: 565.
Lutterloh, Jarvis B., (Lt, Co E, 56th NCST), I: 120; III: 315, 323; IV: 347.
Lutterloh, T.S., (1st Lt, Co D, 19th NCST, 2nd Cav), II: 80.
Lutz, Frank, (Pvt, Co F, 56th NCST), V: 566.
Lyell, J.J., (Ass't Engineer, CSN, Tallahassee), V: 438.
Lyerly, J.H., (Cpl, Co D, 28th NCST), V: 541.
Lyerly, John L., (Cpl, Co K, 4th NCST), I: 234.
Lyerly, Joseph, (Pvt, Co D, 10th NCST, 1st Art & Engs, Reilly-Ramsay's Battery, Light Art), I: 574.
Lyman, ______, (Brig Gen, USA), IV: 522.
Lyman, Jonas W., (Lt Col, 203rd Pa.), V: 238.
Lyman, Theodore, (ADC to Meade, USA), II: 780.
Lynch, A.K., (Pvt, Co I, 56th NCST), I: 772; III: 317.
Lynch, Ceberns, (Pvt, Co C, 3th NCST), V: 555.
Lynch, Humphrey P., (Cpl, Co C, 34th NCST), V: 555.
Lynch, J.C., (2nd Lt, Co A, 66th NCST), III: 685.
Lynch, L.M., (3rd Lt, Co I, 56th NCST), III: 317.
Lynch, Richard, (Pvt, Co A, 4th Vols/14th NCST), I: 730; V: 489.
Lynch, Thomas, (Pvt, Co K, 6th NCST), V: 513.
Lynch, W.F., (Commodore, CSN), II: 509, 510; IV: 404; V: 55, 60, 298, 303, 304, 305-309, 313.
Lynchburg, Va., I: 153, 172, 205, 211, 212, 266, 303, 324, 334, 549, 550, 645, 727, 766; II: 122, 141, 183, 207, 245, 531, 784, 792; III: 12, 13, 18, 58, 59, 252, 258, 277, 396, 400, 419, 745, 748; IV: 124, 142, 515, 523, 525, 607; V: 252, 259, 654.
Lynchburg Road, (nr Petersburg, Va., aka Lynchburg Stage Road), I: 651; II: 266; III: 400; V: 251, 252, 254, 259, 261.
Lynchburg & Petersburg Canal, I: 684.

Lynn, George, (Pvt, Co H, 47th NCST), V: 535.
Lyon, ______, (Judge), III: 350.
Lyon, C.F., (2nd Lt, Co F, 1st Vols, "Bethel"), I: 137.
Lyon, E.H., (Capt, Co C, 13th NCST, 23rd NCST), II: 183, 185.
Lyon, Elanah E., (Capt, Co A, 44th NCST), II: 184; III: 22.
Lyon, H.P., (Sgt, Co A, 10th NCST, 1st Art & Engs, Ramseur-Manly's Battery, Light Art), I: 554.
Lyon, Harrison P., (1st Lt, Co B, 33rd NCST), II: 538, 578.
Lyon, J.W., (Pvt, Co B, 6th NCST), V: 512.
Lyon, James, (Maj, IG, Hoke-Godwin-Lewis' Brigade), IV: 526.
Lyon, John B., (2nd Lt, Co C, 56th NCST), III: 314.
Lyon, John R., (Pvt, Co G, 4th Vols/14th NCST), V: 490.
Lyon, Robert H., (2nd Lt, Co H, 3rd NCST), I: 196, 202, 203, 213; IV: 722.
Lyon, Z.E., (Pvt, Co E, 13th Vols/23rd NCST), V: 510.
Lytle, George W., (Capt, Co A, 49th NCST), III: 128, 138, 148, 152.
Lytle, Thomas Y., (2nd Lt, Co B, 49th NCST), I: 734.
Lytton E., (Lt, 64th NCST), IV: 708.

(M)

Mable, Joel, (Pvt, Co K, 56th NCST), V: 566.
Mable, John, (Sgt Maj, 56th NCST), III: 319.
Mabry, Baker W., (Capt, Co B, 44th NCST), III: 22.
Mabry, Benjamin, (Pvt, Co H, 4th Vols/14th NCST), V: 491.
Mabry, C.R., (Pvt, Co F, 2nd Vols/12th NCST), V: 507.
Mabry, Charles, (Pvt, Co B, 2nd NCST), V: 486.
Mabry, Charles D., (2nd Lt, Co B, 44th NCST), III: 22.
Mabry, Eben, (Pvt, Co H, 4th Vols/14th NCST), V: 491.
Mabry, J., (Pvt, Co F, 2nd Vols/12th NCST), V: 507.
Mabry, James, (Pvt, Co A, 10th NCST, 1st Art & Engs, Ramseur-Manly's Battery, Light Art), I: 553.
Mabry, Leon S., (Lt, Co C, 46th NCST), III: 81.
Mabson, C.B., (2nd Sgt, Co K, 45th NCST), III: 60.
MacKenzie, Ranald Slidell, (Maj Gen, USA), III: 644.
Machey, Charles, (Songwriter), V: 421.
Mackinnon, Luther, (Chaplain, 36th NCST), IV: 613.
MacKoy, A.L., (Surg, 60th NCST), IV: 641.
Macon, C., (Pvt, Co E, 28th NCST), V: 542.
Macon, Gideon, (Pvt, Co F, 2nd Battalion NCST), V: 495.
Macon, Henry A., (Capt, Co F, 43rd NCST), III: 2, 3; V: 180, 194.
Macon, Dr. Henry I., (Surg, 1st NCST), I: 136; IV: 630, 631.
Macon, Jesse A., (2nd Lt, Co F, 43rd NCST), III: 3.
Macon, John A., (Pvt, Co K, 32nd NCST), V: 497.
Macon, Joseph, [Mason, Joseph P.], (Capt, ACS, 58th NCST), IV: 708.
Macon, Ga., IV: 327, 611.
Macon, County, N.C., II: 706, 724; III: 517, 550, 683, 684, 760; IV: 123, 128, 198, 381; V: 653, 656.
Macon Depot, N.C., I: 534.
MacRae, Duncan K., [McRae], (Col, 5th NCST), I: 186, 281, 286, 626, 627, 663, 695; II: 193, 198, 220, 223, 505; IV: 713-719; V: 460, 461, 649.
MacRea, Dr. James A., (Surg, 5th NCST, resigned), I: 281, 282.
MacRae, James C. [Cameron F.], (Chaplain, 5th Vols/15th NCST), I: 734; IV: 607.
MacRae, James C., (Capt, Branch's Staff; Maj, MacRae's 18th Battalion NCST; Maj, AAG, Baker's Brigade), I: 31, 117, 118, 128, 132; IV: 379, 381, 382; V: 271, 281, 282.
MacRae, James C., (Col, 5th NCST), I: 281, 610.
MacRea, Robert B., (Capt, Co C, 7th NCST), I: 361, 369, 371, 372.

MacRae, Walter G., (Capt, Co C, 7th NCST), IV: 719, 721.
MacRae, William, [McRae], (Brig Gen), I: xii, 471, 547, 592, 595, 597, 627, 733, 734, 743; II: 379, 380, 385, 388, 411, 436, 441, 443, 575; III: 21, 26, 29, 31, 32, 33, 34, 95, 98, 100, 247, 250; IV: 442, 504, 506, 536, 563, 564, 565, 566, 567, 568; V: 209, 210, 211, 529, 594, 597.
Madden, M.J., (Pvt, Co F, 43rd NCST), V: 498.
Maddry, Charles, (Pvt, Co B, 2nd NCST), I: 175.
Madeira, Spain, V: 346.
Madison, N.C., I: 689; II: 493; III: 473, 499, 659, 660, 661, 662, 665, 666.
Madison County, N.C., I: 448; II: 293, 297; III: 42, 72, 272, 572, 578; IV: 113, 114, 271, 371, 373, 381.
Madison Court House, Va., I: 383, 449, 675, 676; II: 45, 119, 240, 275, 297, 378, 438, 445, 478, 568, 609.
Madison Green, Va., II: 445.
Madison Street, (Plymouth), V: 188.
Madison & Orange Turnpike, Va., III: 572, 573.
Madre, William, (Odrnance Sgt, 1st Vols/11th NCST), V: 529.
Maffitt, Mrs. Ann Carnicke, (Mother of Capt John N. Maffitt), V: 385.
Maffitt, Eugene, (First Officer, Susan Beirne), V: 379.
Maffitt, John N., (Capt CSN, Lilian, Albemarle, Owl, Florida), I: xiv; IV: 344, 404; V: 311, 364, 376, 381, 385-400, 410, 419, 420, 421, 423, 424, 425.
Maffitt, Mrs. John N., V: 385-404.
Maffitt, Rev. John Newland, (Father of Capt John N. Maffitt), V: 385.
Maffitt, Dr., William, (Uncle of Capt John N. Maffott), V: 385.
Maffitt's Channel, (Charleston, S.C.), V: 386, 399.
Maginnis, J.J., (Capt, Co B, 49th NCST), V: 559.
Maglenn, James, (Chief Engineer, NCN, Advance), V: 335-340.
Magness, D.B., (Capt, Co I, 38th NCST), II: 676; IV: 701, 709.
Magness, Jud, (Capt, Co B, 49th NCST), III: 152.
Magnolia, N.C., (aka Magnolia Station), I: 588, 742; II: 400, 439, 786; III: 87, 206, 216, 232, 319, 321, 693; IV: 505, 558, 617.
Magruder, John Bankhead "Prince John," (Maj Gen), I: 77, 82, 83, 86, 91, 93, 94, 95, 96, 97, 100, 103, 105, 107, 108, 111, 112, 282, 552, 553, 613, 617, 654, 655, 709; II: 332, 521; IV: 570, 579.
Mahone, William "Little Billy," (Maj Gen), I: 175, 265, 435, 555, 599; II: 51, 52, 75, 572; III: 373, 374; IV: 457, 564, 566, 567; V: 252, 617, 618.
Mahoney, Mickey, (2nd Steward, Lilian), V: 370.
Maiden, I.P., [Wilson W.], (Pvt, Co H, 4th NCST), I: 233.
Maine, I: 748; II: 367; V: 439.
Major, C.A., [McGhee], (1st Lt, Co H, 53rd NCST), IV: 709.
Malacca Sea, V: 416.
Malcolm, F., (Pvt, Co E, 45th NCST), V: 500.
Malcolm, James, (Pvt, Co C, 45th NCST), V: 500.
Mall, T.P., [Mull, Peter P.], (2nd Lt, Co F, 55th NCST), IV: 709.
Mallett, C.P., [Charles P.], (1st Lt, Co C, 3rd NCST), IV: 722.
Mallett, E.J., (Lt Col, 61st NCST), V: 651.

Mallett, Edward, (Lt Col, 61st NCST), III: 504, 505; IV: 483, 498; V: 11.

Mallett, John W., (Adjt, 61st NCST; Capt, Co B, MacRae's 18th Battalion NCST), I: 118; IV: 379, 381.

Mallett, Peter, [Mallet], (Col, N.C. Conscript Bureau; Col, Mallett's Battalion NCST), I: 178, 227, 493, 516; IV: 50, 407; V: 677.

Mallett, Richard, (Adjt, 46th NCST), III: 65, 71.

Mallett, Richardson, (Capt, Adjt, 44th NCST), I: 77, 114, 118, 129, 130.

Mallory, J.R., (Pvt, Co D, 2nd Vols/12th NCST), V: 507.

Mallory, S.C., (Pvt, Co D, 2nd Vols/12th NCST), V: 507.

Mallory, S.R., (Secretary of the Navy, CSA), V: 309.

Mallory, W.C., (Pvt, Co D, 2nd Vols/12th NCST), V: 507.

Malloy, Charles, (Capt, Co F, 8th Vols/18th NCST), II: 16.

Malloy, J.D., (Capt, Co D, 51st NCST), III: 209, 211, 219; IV: 722.

Malloy, Thomas P., (Lt, Co D, 7th NCST), I: 384.

Malone, E., (Pvt, Co K, 6th NCST), V: 513.

Malone, John, (2nd Lt, Co E, Cameron's Battery, Starr's 13th Battalion NCST, Light Art), IV: 354.

Malone's Crossing, (nr Ream's Station, Va., aka Malone's Bridge), I: 775; II: 780; III: 620, 621; V: 208.

Maloney, Patrick, (Pvt, Co G, 2nd Wisconsin), II: 345.

Malpass, J.M., (Pvt, Co B, 1st NCST), V: 485.

Malvern Hill, Va., (and Battle of, 1862), I: 139, 159, 162, 163, 164, 165, 182, 213, 219, 244, 282, 286, 305, 334, 340, 369, 420, 431, 538, 553, 569, 609, 614, 617, 619, 620, 621, 622, 628, 639, 643, 661, 694, 733, 741, 758; II: 27, 30, 185, 186, 188, 190, 212, 214, 215, 219, 223, 274, 292, 295, 295, 296, 304, 331, 332, 333, 406, 411, 419, 420, 428, 472, 498, 548, 549, 560, 584, 539, 596, 598, 599, 600, 609, 655, 682, 799; III: 4, 40, 66, 79, 116, 127, 163, 164, 165, 166, 212, 307, 308, 609; IV: 158, 235, 239, 356, 404, 411, 446, 502, 517, 551, 570, 579, 595, 611; V: 668.

Manassas, Va., (and 1st Battle of, 1861, aka Bull Run), I: 3, 22, 39, 164, 179, 216, 244, 282, 286, 290, 297, 298, 299, 300, 306, 332, 334, 339, 341, 342, 343, 345, 346, 347, 348, 349, 417, 419, 420, 457, 499, 546, 571; II: 28, 30, 69, 87, 130, 167, 190, 191, 192, 193, 194, 216, 274, 349, 584, 592, 600, 655; III: 35, 93, 113, 291, 302, 417, 423, 674, 704; IV: 110, 141, 149, 185, 205, 226-227, 241, 419, 481, 505, 703; V: xiv, 29-33, 581, 585, 664.

Manassas, Va., (2nd Battle of, 1862; aka 2nd Bull Run), I: 116, 140, 184, 305, 306, 370, 421, 572, 623, 625, 663, 697, 758, 759, 762; II: 30, 31, 69, 115, 133, 153, 154, 169, 473, 499, 551, 552, 585, 600, 655, 683, 684, 686, 687, 700; III: 66, 72; IV: 33, 160-163, 185, 235, 237, 447, 466, 551, 570; V: 71, 82, 590, 627.

Manassas Depot, Va., II: 30.

Manassas Gap, Va., I: 570.

Manassas Gap Railroad, Va., I: 297, 298, 343; II: 683, 684; IV: 227.

Manassas Junction, Va., I: 223, 234, 235, 298, 370, 564, 753; II: 30, 68, 69, 96, 151, 190, 191, 193, 584, 655, 656, 683, 686; III: 581; IV: 226, 227, 235, 466.
Manassas Road, (at Hagerstown, Md.), I: 223.
Manchester, England, V: 453, 454, 456.
Manchester, N.C., IV: 611.
Manchester, Pa., V: 117.
Manchester, Va., I: 540, 577, 578; III: 692.
Manchester & County Bank, (Manchester, England), V: 454, 456.
Mangum, Hon. Judge W.P., (and owner of "Walnut Hall" plantation), IV: 687.
Mangum Adolphus W., (Chaplain, 6th NCST), IV: 606, 745; V: 626.
Mangum, B.E., (Pvt, Co E, 48th NCST), V: 526.
Mangum, D.C., (Pvt, Co B, 6th NCST), V: 512.
Mangum, E.P., (Pvt, Co D, 30th NCST), V: 492.
Mangum, F.P., (Pvt, Co D, 30th NCST), V: 492.
Mangum, Joseph, (Pvt, Co H, 24th NCST), V: 193.
Mangum, Rufus, (Pvt, Co B, 6th NCST), V: 512.
Mangum, W.C., (Pvt, Co G, 1st Vols/11th NCST), V: 530.
Mangum, Willie P., Jr., (2nd Lt, Co B, 6th NCST), I: 345, 349; V: 31.
Manigault, Arthur Middleton, (Brig Gen), II: 711.
Manley, B.W., (Pvt, Co I, 26th NCST), V: 532.
Manly, Basil C., (Maj, Chief of Art, Hoke's Division), I: 536, 551, 552, 554, 556, 560; IV: 352, 356; V: 651.
Manly, Langdon Cheves, (Capt, Co D, 31st NCST), II: 507.
Manly, Matthew, (Capt, Co D, 2nd NCST), I: 159, 160; IV: 702, 709; V: 640.
Mann, B.M., (Pvt, Co A, 49th NCST), V: 564.
Mann, D.C., (Pvt, Co D, 5th Vols/15th NCST), V: 521.
Mann, D.L., (Pvt, Co F, 6th Battalion/60th NCST), III: 482.
Mann, J., (2nd Lt, Co H, 42nd NCST), II: 791, 807.
Mann, James E., (Capt, Co D, 57th NCST), III: 405.
Mann, Joseph H., (Sgt, Co D, 35th NCST), V: 562.
Mann, S.D., (2nd Lt, Co C, 42nd NCST), II: 790, 806.
Mann, Thomas L., (Pvt, Co D, 1st NCST), V: 485.
Manney, James L., (Capt, Co G, 10th NCST, 1st Art & Engs, Pender-Manney's Hvy Art), I: 491, 492, 495, 496, 501, 511, 512, 513, 515, 522, 525, 526, 536.
Manning, J.D., (Pvt, Co I, 30th NCST), V: 493.
Manning, J.T., (Pvt, Co G, 5th NCST), I: 292; V: 505.
Manning, John, [John, Jr.], (Adjt, Co M, 5th Vols/15th NCST), I: 734, 736.
Manning, John, (Lt, Co H, 61st NCST), III: 504.
Manning, John A., (Capt, Co K, 6th Battalion Junior Reserves; Co K, 70th NCST, 1st Junior Reserves), IV: 12, 13, 29.
Manning, Thomas C., (Adjt Gen, La.), V: 649.
Manning, Van H., (Col, 3rd Ark.), IV: 431, 501, 502, 503.
Manny, George Earl, (Brig Gen), II: 490.
Mansfield, A.W., (Pvt, Co G, 57th NCST), V: 517.
Mansfield, J.B., (Color Sgt, 26th NCST), II: 351, 374.

Mansfield, James, (Pvt, Co H, 45th NCST), V: 500.
Mansfield, Joseph King Fenno, (Maj Gen, USA), I: 141, 185, 186; II: 602; V: 80.
Mansfield, S., (Pvt, Co H, 45th NCST), V: 500.
Manson, John C., (Capt, Co H, 10th NCST, 1st Art & Engs, Pool's Hvy Art), I: 501, 515, 525, 536.
Manson, Dr. Otis F., (Surg, Craven Hospital, Richmond, Va.), I: 51; IV: 624, 629.
Manstook, G.W., (Pvt, Co H, 6th Battalion/60th NCST), III: 482.
Manton, Herbert, V: 300.
Maple Cypress, N.C., III: 710.
Marable, William S., (Capt, 7th Conn.), V: 238.
Marblehead, Hawaii, V: 393.
Marbry, A.C., (Pvt, Co K, 28th NCST), V: 543.
Margaret & Jessie, V: 410, 440, 442, 443, 445.
Marietta, Ga., II: 743.
Marines, C.S., III: 349; IV: 417; V: 220, 223, 237, 240.
Marines, U.S., III: 180; V: 244.
Marion, N.C., II: 627.
Marion, S.C., II: 125.
Marius, J., (Pvt, Co F, 12th Vols/22nd NCST), V: 553.
Markham, A.D., (Capt, 1st Battalion Junior Reserves; Co I, 70th NCST, 1st Junior Reserves), IV: 13.
Markham Station, Va., I: 578.
Marks, J.G., (Pvt, Co B, 53rd NCST), V: 501.
Marks, Mack, (Pvt, Co A, 10th NCST, 1st Art & Engs, Ramseur-Manly's Battery, Light Art), I: 556.
Marks., S.H., (Pvt, Co B, 3rd Vols/13th NCST), V: 549.
Marks, T.S., (Lt, Co D, 35th NCST), V: 559.
Marlborough, Md., V: 417.
Marler, J.B., (Lt, Co E, 58th NCST), III: 433.
Marler, M.S., (Lt, Co B, 54th NCST), I: 120.
Marley, John R., (Pvt, Co G, Color-bearer, 26th NCST), II: 374, 384.
Marloe, W.A., [Marler, William A.], (2nd Lt, Co F, 28th NCST), IV: 701, 709.
Marrow, George, (Pvt, Co H, 6th Battalion/60th NCST), III: 482.
Marrow, J.L., (Lt, Co C, 9th NCST, 1st Cav), I: 485.
Marsh, A.L., (2nd Lt, Co D, 37th NCST), V: 538.
Marsh, A.T., (2nd Lt, Co I, 53rd NCST), III: 264.
Marsh, Edward S., (Maj, 4th NCST), I: 230, 233, 270.
Marsh, George, W., (Capt, Co A, 61st NCST), III: 65, 81, 503.
Marsh, James A., (1st Lt, AQM, 46th NCST), III: 65, 81.
Marsh, Rev. Dr. Robert H., (Chaplain, 26th NCST), II: 306, 396; IV: 611.
Marsh, W.T., (Capt, Co I, 4th NCST), I: 231, 246, 247, 267, 270.
Marsh, William, (Pvt, Co A, 28th NCST), V: 540.
Marsh Creek, (nr Gettysburg, Pa.), II: 343.
Marshall, ______, (Capt, CSN, Index), V: 409, 410.
Marshall, ______, (Col, Pettigrew's Brigade), III: 300.
Marshall, C.M., (Pvt, Co H, 11th Vols/21st NCST), V: 515.
Marshall, E., (Pvt, Co G, 26th NCST), V: 532.
Marshall, G.W., (Pvt, Co G, 7th NCST), V: 538.
Marshall, J.J., (Cpl, Co I, 33rd NCST), II: 540, 579.

Marshall, James, (Pvt, Co C, 10th NCST, 1st Art & Engs, Brem-Graham-Williams' Battery, Light Art), V: 568.
Marshall, James C., (1st Lt, Co A, 13th Vols/23rd NCST; Adjt, 4th Vols/14th NCST), II: 182.
Marshall, James H., (2nd Lt, Co H, 67th NCST), III: 710.
Marshall, James K., (Col, 52nd NCST; Brig Gen N.C. Reserves), I: 110, 118, 122, 225, 519, 590, 591, 592, 593, 599, 600, 604; II: 363, 365, 399; III: 104, 105, 106, 225, 227, 228, 229, 230, 231, 234, 236, 237, 238; IV: 225, 345, 555, 556; V: 10, 101, 102, 108, 111, 120, 124, 139, 144, 156.
Marshall, M.M., (Chaplain, 7th NCST), IV: 472, 606.
Marshall, P., (Pvt, 21st Ga.), V: 194.
Marshall, Peter, (Sgt, Co K, 1 1th Vols/21st NCST), V: 515.
Marshall, N.C., III: 474, 661, 664, 665, 666, 667; IV: 112, 380, 381.
Marshburn, J.H., [Marshbourne, James H.], (Sgt, Co F, 4th NCST), I: 233.
Marsteller, Charles, (2nd Lt, Co C, 1st NCST), I: 136.
Marston, Dr. W.V., (Ass't Surg, 2nd Vols/12th NCST), I: 606; IV: 633.
Martin, ______, (Capt, Co F, 7th Vols/17th NCST), V: 680.
Martin, ______, (Capt, Susan Berine), V: 410.
Martin, ______, (Lt Col, Jeff Davis Legion), I: 421.
Martin, ______, [Rawley W.], (Col, 53rd Va.), V: 157.
Martin, A., (Pvt, Co G, 45th NCST), V: 500.
Martin, A.H., (Capt, Co G, 53rd NCST), III: 267, 283; IV: 555, 556.
Martin, Alexander, (Pvt, Co A, 11th Vols/21st NCST), V: 514.
Martin, B.M., (Musician, 53rd NCST), V: 501.
Martin, B.Y., [Bartlett Y.], (1st Lt, Co A, 34th NCST), IV: 709
Martin, B.Y., (Lt, 53rd NCST), IV: 701, 709.
Martin, C.J., (Lt, 1st Vols/11th NCST), IV: 708.
Martin, E.A., (Capt, Co C, Wheeler's 12th Battalion; Co H, 16th Battalion/75th NCST, 7th Cav), IV: 72, 91, 93, 339.
Martin, Eugene S., (Lt, Co A, 9th Battalion NCST; Ordnance Officer, Nethercutt's Brigade), IV: 5, 304, 591; V: 396.
Martin, Green, (Lt, Co B, 1st NCST), I: 148.
Martin, J.M., (1st Sgt, Co H, 3rd Vols/13th NCST), V: 551.
Martin, J.T., [John T.], (1st Lt, Co L, 11th Vols/21st NCST), IV: 701, 709.
Martin, James G., (Maj Gen N.C.; N.C. Adjt Gen; Brig Gen CSA; aka "Old One Wing"), I: xi, 3, 4, 5, 8, 9, 10, 12, 13, 15, 16, 17, 18, 20, 21, 22, 24, 25, 26, 28, 29, 30, 35, 37, 38, 41, 42, 43, 44, 46, 48, 50, 129, 220, 511, 513, 514, 526; II: 1, 3, 8, 334, 775, 776, 796, 798; III: 85, 86, 87, 132, 133, 226, 227, 289, 290, 319, 320, 334, 685, 756, 759, 760; IV: 77, 127, 265, 266, 372, 373, 375, 416, 418, 426, 442, 527, 528, 529, 530, 531, 532, 533, 534, 535, 536, 537, 555, 556, 624, 646, 756; V: 5, 6, 14, 653, 654, 655.
Martin, John K., (Capt, Co M, 1st Vols, "Bethel"; Capt, Co H, 12th Vols/22nd NCST), I: 110; II: 165, 166, 172.
Martin, M.C.M., (Pvt, Co A, 38th NCST), V: 557.

Martin, Pinkney, (Pvt, Co D, 6th Vols/16th NCST), V: 552.
Martin, R.B., (Pvt, Co F, 35th NCST), V: 563.
Martin, R.G., (Pvt, Co H, 12th Vols/22nd NCST), V: 554.
Martin, R.L., (Pvt, Co A, 33rd NCST), V: 543.
Martin, Shadrach, (2nd Lt, Co H, 12th Vols/22nd NCST), II: 165, 166.
Martin, T.A., (Maj, 3rd Vols/13th NCST), V: 547.
Martin, W.A., (Pvt, Co E, 2nd Vols/12th NCST), V: 507.
Martin, W.A., (Pvt, Co C, 28th NCST), II: 475; V: 541.
Martin, W.D., (Pvt, Co H, 49th NCST), V: 565.
Martin, W.G., (Adjt, 66th NCST), III: 690.
Martin, W.K., Jr., (2nd Lt, Co K, 71st NCST, 2nd Junior Reserves), IV: 29.
Martin, W.S., (AQMS, 45th NCST), V: 499.
Martin, W.T., (Maj Gen), III: 678.
Martin, William, (Fayetteville and Harper's Ferry Arsenals), IV: 298.
Martin, William F., (Col, 7th Vols/17th NCST, Brother of J.G. Martin), I: 495, 523; II: 1, 2, 83, 84, 85, 86; IV: 77, 80, 366, 527, 538, 556; V: 35, 39, 41, 45, 46, 47, 49, 51, 52, 301, 302, 649.
Martin, William J., (Lt Col, 1st Vols/11th NCST), I: ix, 583, 587, 592, 593, 600; II: 394; IV: 562; V: 529.
Martin, William J., (Capt, Co G, 28th NCST), II: 466.
Martin, William Pinckney, (Capt, Co H, 26th NCST), II: 304, 305, 322, 323, 328, 329, 397, 418.
Martin, Miss., II: 491.
Martin's Cross Roads, N.C., V: 282.
Martin County, N.C., I: 533; II: 7, 87, 337, 406, 769, 772; III: 210, 299, 320, 504; IV: 15, 348, 355, 502, 589, 646; V: 50, 67, 110.
Martindale, John Henry, (Maj Gen, USA, Military Gov. of D.C.), II: 470, 623.
Martinsburg, Va., I: 189, 207, 253, 324, 325, 334, 421, 541, 577, 718, 759; II: 32, 34, 134, 135, 170, 233, 275, 437, 608; III: 5, 55, 68, 241, 559, 749; IV: 164, 167, 176, 183, 229, 230, 231, 255, 262, 405, 503, 525, 568.
Martinsburg Pike, Va., I: 207, 208; IV: 229.
Marye's Heights, (nr Fredericksburg, Va.), I: 310, 554, 739, 741; II: 275, 297, 438, 609, 610; III: 69, 269, 407, 410, 411; IV: 448, 504, 571, 572, 579.
Marye's House, (nr Fredericksburg, Va.), II: 297; IV: 1.
Maryland, I: 81, 178, 184, 207, 244, 253, 291, 334, 499, 541, 624, 628, 632, 663, 674, 698, 739; II: 34, 69, 70, 71, 133, 167, 217, 274, 378, 473, 499, 585, 601, 671, 685, 690, 702, 753; III: 4, 13, 14, 40, 66, 67, 116, 270, 278, 460, 462, 560, 664, 674, 737, 751; IV: 93, 165, 176, 447, 514, 572, 605, 704; V: 82, 113, 213, 590.
Maryland Campaign, (The 1862 series of battles that included South Mountain, Harper's Ferry and culminated with the Battle of Sharpsburg.), I: 166, 167, 222, 372, 421, 553, 623-628, 694, 696; II: 42, 77, 171, 217-224, 296, 297, 431, 437, 523, 598, 600, 601, 623, 656, 793; III: 116; IV: 167, 422, 502, 521.
Maryland Heights, Md., I: 206, 324, 326; II: 432, 553, 685; III: 13; IV: 570.
Maryland Line, III: 608.

Marysville, N.C., III: 756, 760.
Maryville, Tenn., IV: 290.
Mason, A., (Pvt, Co H, 30th NCST), V: 492.
Mason, G., (1st Lt, Co C, 4th Battalion Junior Reserves; Co C, 72nd NCST, 3rd Junior Reserves), IV: 38.
Martin, J.J., (Pvt, Co H, 35th NCST), V: 563.
Mason, J.M., (Confederate representative to the Court of St. James), II: 629; V: xvi, 454.
Mason, John C., (Capt, Co H, 10th NCST, 1st Art & Engs, Pool's Hvy Art), I: 515.
Mason, Littleberry W., (Capt, Co G, 61st Va.), IV: 403.
Mason, Otis F., (Chief Surgeon Richmond Hospital), I: 51.
Mason, Robert, (Pvt, Co H, 59th NCST, 4th Cav), V: 659.
Mason, Thomas W., (Lt, ADC to Robert Ransom), IV: 569, 577.
Mason, William, (3rd Ass't Engineer, USN, Niphon), V: 351.
Mason, William D.A., (4th Cpl, Co I, 52nd NCST), III: 225.
Mason Hill, Va., I: 282; II: 192.
Mason and Dixon's Line, IV: 1.
Masonboro, N.C., II: 631; V: 222, 358, 407.
Masonboro Inlet, N.C., II: 631, 632.
Masonboro Salt Works, (nr Masonboro), IV: 357.
Masonboro Sound, N.C., I: 582; III: 509; IV: 39, 42, 100, 103, 221, 244, 391, 539; V: 217, 343, 352, 367, 384, 408.
Massachusetts, II: 367.
Massanutton Gap., Va., II: 21.
Massanutton Mountain, Va., I: 154, 327; II: 259.
Massaponax Creek, Va., II: 35.
Massenburg, A.C., (2nd Lt, ACS, 5th Vols/15th NCST), I: 734, 735.
Massey, J.S., (Pvt, Co H, 56th NCST), III: 357.
Massey, J.W., (Pvt, Co H, 6th NCST), V: 513.
Massey, Jacob, (Chaplain, 62nd NCST), IV: 619.
Massey, May M., (Pvt, Co D, 30th NCST; Detailed, 2nd Corps Provost Guard), V: 570.
Massey, N.M., (Pvt, Co D, 30th NCST), V: 492.
Massey, William H., (2nd Lt, Co G, 33rd NCST), II: 540, 578.
Massie, ______, [Thomas B.], (Col, 12th Va. Cav), III: 576.
Massie, G.T., (Pvt, Co C, 32nd NCST), V: 496.
Massie, J.P., (Pvt, Co C, 32nd NCST), V: 496.
Massie, R.C., (Pvt, Co A, 3rd Vols/13th NCST), V: 549.
Mast, D.P., (Lt, Co D, 9th NCST, 1st Cav), I: 441, 485, 782.
Mast, W.P., (Lt, Co D, 58th NCST), III: 433.
Masten, J., (Col, 2nd Regt, 3rd Class, Home Guard), IV: 650, 654.
Masten, W.L., [William L.], (1st Lt, 11th Vols/21st NCST; Co D, 1st Battalion NCST), IV: 242.
Mastin, J.F., (Sgt, Co G, 54th NCST), V: 516.
Mastin, W.J., (Cpl, Co F, 37th NCST), V: 546.
Matamoras, Mexico, V: 355, 416.
Matheson, A.H., (Sgt, Co D, Millard's 9th/20th Battalion Junior Reserves), IV: 396.
Matheson, Wesley F., (Ensign, Co G, 38th NCST), II: 679, 690.
Mathias, T.L., (Lt, Co G, 9th NCST, 1st Cav), I: 486.
Mathews, J.H., (Pvt, Co C, 32nd NCST), V: 496.
Mathis, Elkanah, (Pvt, Co F, 26th NCST), V: 603.

Mathis, William A., (Lt, Co A, 61st NCST), III: 503.
Mattaponi Creek, Va., [Mattapony], II: 679; III: 54, 305.
Matthews, J., (Cpl, Co C, 56th NCST), III: 356.
Matthews, J.C., (Pvt, Co K, 47th NCST), V: 535.
Matthews, John E., (1st Lt, Co G, 26th NCST), II: 304, 307, 397.
Matthews, Levis J., (Pvt, Co B, 25th NCST), V: 561.
Matthews, M., (Pvt, Co A, Millard's 9th/20th Battalion Junior Reserves), IV: 391.
Matthews, Marcellus S., (Pvt, Co D, 6th Battalion/60th NCST), III: 500.
Matthews, W.G., (Capt, Co F, 1st Vols, "Bethel"), I: 125.
Matthews, William M., (2nd Lt, Co B, 53rd NCST), III: 261; IV: 700, 709.
Maultsby, Samuel W., (Capt, Co H, 51st NCST), III: 211, 219.
Mauney, Samuel, (Pvt, Co M, 6th Vols/16th NCST), V: 553.
Mauney, W.A., (ACS, 28th NCST), II: 465.
Maury, W.L., (Cmdr, CSN; Capt, North Carolina), V: 298.
Maury, Dabney H., (Brig Gen), II: 492.
Maxwell, David G., (Capt, Co H, 35th NCST), II: 598, 605, 607, 608, 613, 628; IV: 405.
Maxwell, James H., (Pvt, Co A, 25th NCST), V: 561.
Maxwell, R.H., (Lt, Co C, 9th NCST, 1st Cav), I: 485.
May, Anthony, (Pvt, Co E, 5th Vols/15th NCST), V: 521.
May, C.A., (Pvt, Co E, 3rd Vols/13th NCST), V: 550.
May, David, (Pvt, Co H, 56th NCST), III: 356.
May, Edward, (Cpl, Co C, 4th NCST), I: 232.
May, H.H., (Pvt, Co A, 53rd NCST), V: 501.
May, H.M., [Hugh M.], (Cpl, Co B, 31st NCST), V: 67.
May, J.W., (Pvt, Co D, 1st NCST), V: 485.
May, John W., (Capt, Co A, 45th NCST), III: 36, 39, 40.
May, L.M., (Capt, Adjt, 69th NCST, Thomas' Legion), III: 733.
May, Luther C., (Adjt, 69th NCST, Thomas' Legion), III: 730, 740.
May, Nathan, (Pvt, Co I, 55th NCST), V: 528.
May, Robert, (Pvt, Co D, 10th NCST, 1st Art & Engs, Reilly-Ramsay's Battery, Light Art), I: 569, 572.
May, Thomas, (Pvt, Co K, 26th NCST), V: 532.
May, Thomas L., (Cpl, Co B, 33rd NCST), II: 538.
May, Turner, (Pvt, Co A, 67th NCST), III: 710.
May, W.C., (Pvt, Co E, 12th Vols/22nd NCST), V: 553.
May, W.H., (Pvt, Co E, 3rd Vols/13th NCST), V: 550.
May, William, (2nd Lt, Co B, 4th Battalion Junior Reserves; Co B, 72nd NCST, 3rd Junior Reserves), IV: 38.
Maybury, J.W., (Pvt, Co A, 1st NCST), V: 572.
Mayer, B.R., (2nd Lt, Co D, 82nd NCST), IV: 131.
Mayer, W.H., (Ensign, USN; Pioneer, Sassacus), V: 245.
Mayfield, Dr. Benjamin, (Surg, Walker's Battalion, Thomas' Legion, 80th NCST), IV: 117, 128, 643.
Mayfield, J.W., (3rd Lt, Co C, 2nd Vols/12th NCST), I: 652.

Mayhew, Thomas W., (Maj, 33rd NCST), II: 537, 539, 561, 562, 578; IV: 474; V: 12.
Maynard, C.G., (Pvt, Co I, 57th NCST), V: 517.
Maynardsville, Tenn., IV: 274.
Mayo, _____, (Pilot, Pantheon), V: 38, 311.
Mayo, Cyrus, (Capt, Mayo's Co, 11th Battalion NCST, Hvy Art; Co B, 67th NCST), IV: 18, 338; V: 229.
Mayo, James M., (Maj, 59th NCST, 4th Cav), II: 642; III: 456, 462, 467; IV: 700, 709.
Mayo, Dr. M.L., (Ass't Surg, 28th NCST), II: 466; IV: 473, 636.
Mayo, Reuben E., (2nd Lt, Co C, 44th NCST), III: 23; IV: 700, 709.
Mayo, Robert, [Robert M.], (Col, 47th Va.), IV: 83; V: 124, 130.
Maynard, Horace, (Congressman, Tenn., Scalawag), III: 734.
Maynard, J.C., (Pvt, Co E, 47th NCST), V: 535.
Mays, David, (Pvt, Co E, 53rd NCST), V: 501.
Mays, M., (Pvt, Co A, 10th NCST, 1st Art & Engs, Ramseur-Manly's Battery, Light Art), I: 556.
Mays, Moses T., (1st Lt, Claiborne-Dearing's 7th C.S. Cav; 16th Battalion/75th NCST, 7th Cav), IV: 91.
McAden, Dr. John H., (Surg, 3rd Vols/13th NCST; Surg, Garland's Brigade; Surg, Scales' Brigade), I: 663; IV: 405, 553, 554, 633, 644; V: 547, 572.
McAfee, Lee M., (Col, 49th NCST), III: 125, 127, 136, 138, 142, 144, 146, 147, 148, 153, 157, 353, 372; IV: 575; V: 650.
McAlister, _____, (Adjt, 78th NCST, 8th Senior Reserves), IV: 108.
McAlister's Independent Command, (In some sources known as McAlister's Battalion, this command consisted, at times, of eleven companies. It patrolled western North Carolina during the late period of the war. Core command consisted of: 1 company 7th NCST, 2 companies 27th NCST, 2 companies 46th NCST, 2 companies 48th NCST and 2 companies 55th NCST.), III: 78, 79.
McAllister, Alexander C., [McAlister], (Lt Col, 46th NCST), I: 60; III: 65, 78, 81; V: 651, 665.
McAllister, Alexander C., (2nd Lt, Co I, 12th Vols/22nd NCST), II: 165, 166.
McAllister, David S., (Cadet Capt, Co B, Hillsboro Military Academy Battalion), V: 644.
McAllister, H.B., (Pvt, Co F, 49th NCST), V: 564.
McAllister, Harvey C., (1st Lt, Co H, 8th NCST), I: 407.
McAllister, James H., (Lt, Acting ACS, 62nd NCST), III: 515.
McAllister, L.A., (Pvt, Co H, 13th Vols/23rd NCST), V: 510.
Malpin, James, [Malpine, James], (Pvt, Co F, 10th Vols/20th NCST; Detailed, 2nd Corps Provost Guard), V: 570.
McArthur, J.A., (Capt, Co I, 51st NCST), I: 119; III: 210, 211, 220.
McArthur, John F., (2nd Lt, Co K, 38th NCST), V: 549.
McArthur, John S., (1st Lt, Co E, 40th NCST, 3rd Art, Hvy), II: 746, 747.
McAuley, J.T., (1st Lt, Co D, 6th Battalion Junior Reserves; Co H, 70th NCST, 1st Junior Reserves), IV: 13.

McAuley, James R., (Capt, Co I, 7th NCST), I: 361, 369, 378, 385.
McAuley, Robert G., (Lt, Co I, 7th NCST), I: 378.
McAuley, William, (Lt, Co I, 12th Vols/22nd NCST), II: 166.
McBee, Ganium C., (1st Lt, Co D, 69th NCST, Thomas' Legion), III: 730.
McBlair, _____, (Capt, CSN, Atlanta), IV: 733.
McBrayer, E.W., (2nd Lt, Co C, 5th Vols/15th NCST), I: 734; V: 519.
McBrayer, Reuben, [Reuben B.], (Sgt, Co D, 71st NCST, 2nd Junior Reserves), IV: 594.
McBrayer, W.A., (Sgt, Co C, 6th Battalion/60th NCST), III: 482.
McBride, John, (Pvt, Co F, 4th NCST), V: 489.
McBride, T.C., (Pvt, Co A, 54th NCST), V: 516.
McBride, W.A., (Pvt, Co B, 27th NCST), II: 461; V: 523.
McBryde, J.A., (Musician, 46th NCST), V: 524.
McBryde, Malcom H., (Capt, Co E, 40th NCST, 3rd Art, Hvy), II: 746, 765; V: 240.
McBryde, W.H., (Pvt, Co E, 56th NCST), III: 347; V: 240.
McCain, D.H., (Pvt, Co H, 35th NCST), V: 563.
McCain, George C., (Capt, Co I, 52nd NCST), III: 225, 237, 239.
McCain, J.W., (3rd Sgt, Co C, 3rd Vols/13th NCST), V: 550.
McCain, W.A., (Pvt, Co C, 3rd Vols/13th NCST), V: 550.
McCall, Ezekial W., (Pvt, Co D, 34th NCST), V: 555.
McCall, George Archibald, (Maj Gen, USA), I: 615.
McCall, J.C., (Pvt, Co I, 37th NCST), V: 546.
McCall, John C., (4th Sgt, Co H, 52nd NCST), III: 225.
McCall, P., (Pvt, Co A, 2nd Vols/12th NCST), V: 506.
McCalla, R.C., (Maj, Thomas' Legion, 80th NCST), IV: 119.
McCallum, A.S., (Pvt, Co C, 4th Vols/14th NCST) I: 732.
McCallum, J.B., (Lt, Co D, 51st NCST), III: 211, 219.
McCallum, J.B., (Pvt, Co G, 14th Vols/24th NCST), V: 560.
McCanless, James C., (Pvt, Co K, 4th NCST), I: 274.
McCarrick, James W., (Master's Mate, NCN), V: 300, 303, 312.
McCarrick, Patrick, (Master's Mate, NCN; Capt, Winslow), V: 299, 303, 304, 307, 312.
McCarthy, _____, (Capt, Richmond Howitzers), I: 556, 559.
McCarver, H.P., (Pvt, Co H, 49th NCST), V: 565.
McCarver, J.E., (Pvt, Co H, 49th NCST), V: 565.
McCaskell, Edward A, (Pvt, Co C, 4th Vols/14th NCST), V: 490.
McCaskell, James A., (Pvt, Co C, 4th Vols/14th NCST), V: 490.
McCaslin, W.B., (Pvt, Co C, 10th NCST, 1st Art & Engs, Brem-Graham-Williams' Battery, Light Art), V: 568.
McCaulay, J.T., (2nd Lt, Co B, 6th Battalion Junior Reserves; Co E, 70th NCST, 1st Junior Reserves), IV: 13.
McCauley, C.M.T., (Capt, Co C, 10th Battalion NCST, 2nd Hvy Art), IV: 330, 334.
McCauley, David, (Pvt, Co D, 1st Vols, "Bethel"), I: 133.
McCauley, G.W., (Capt, Co G, 28th NCST), II: 483.
McCauley, J.T., (Pvt, Co E, 28th NCST), V: 542.
McCauley, S.S., (Lt, Co C, 10th Battalion NCST, 2nd Hvy Art), IV: 330.

McCenney, J.W., (Pvt, Co E, 5th NCST), I: 292.
McChesney, _____, (Col, USA), I: 89, 100.
McCinney, J.W., (Pvt, Co E, 5th NCST), V: 505.
McClammy, C.W., (Maj, 41st NCST, 3rd Cav), II: 769, 770; V: 651.
McCleese, Nelson, (1st Lt, Co B, Badham's 3rd Battalion, Light Art), IV: 261, 263, 264; V: 88, 91.
McClellan, George B., (Maj Gen, USA, General-in-Chief and McClellan's Army), I: 10, 11, 12, 140, 165, 166, 225, 282, 300, 301, 302, 303, 304, 307, 308, 309, 367, 420, 422, 538, 539, 609, 612, 614, 616, 617, 618, 621, 623, 624, 625, 626, 628, 657, 659, 661, 662, 677, 694, 696, 715, 737, 754, 756, 757, 758, 760; II: 25, 26, 27, 66, 67, 69, 84, 115, 116, 133, 148, 149, 150, 152, 153, 156, 193, 196, 197, 203, 207, 208, 211, 212, 213, 214, 216, 218, 219, 222, 273, 274, 328, 348, 430, 499, 545, 549, 555, 560, 603, 655, 657, 682; III: 39, 66, 127, 166, 168, 169, 170, 329, 383; IV: 166, 168, 234, 235, 261, 262, 300, 256, 446, 447, 452, 502, 570, 571, 685; V: 71, 72, 73, 74, 79, 80, 81, 82, 467, 588, 590, 591.
McClellan, H.B., (Maj, J.E.B. Stuart's Staff), I: 424; III: 534.
McCelland, W.S., (Pvt, Co E, 1st Vols/11th NCST), V: 530.
McClennahan, John B., (Capt, Co G, 63rd NCST, 5th Cav), III: 529, 554.
McClenny, Lewis, (Pvt, Co D, 38th NCST), V: 557.
McClue, W.H., (Lt, Co D, 2nd Battalion NCST), IV: 245.
McClure, J.J., (2nd Lt, Co B, 62nd NCST), III: 515.
McCoin, N.L., (Lt, Co A, 10th Battalion NCST, 2nd Hvy Art), IV: 329.
McCollum, A.B., (Capt, Co C, 7th Battalion Junior Reserves; Co I, 72nd NCST, 3rd Junior Reserves), IV: 40, 52.
McCollum, J.Y., (Pvt, Co I, 3rd Vols/13th NCST), V: 551.
McCombs, Dr. James Parks, (Ass't Surg, 1st Vols/11th NCST), I: 583; IV: 633; V: 529.
McCombs, William, (Brig Gen), II: 453.
McConnell, Charles H., (Sgt, 24th Mi.), II: 353.
McConnell, J.M., (Capt, Co F, 69th NCST, Thomas' Legion), II: 394; III: 731, 743.
McConnellsburg, Pa., I: 148, 195.
McCool House, (nr Spottsylvania, Va.), I: 642; II: 243; III: 61.
McCorkle, James, G., (2nd Lt, Co D, 1st Vols/11th NCST), I: 121, 584.
McCorkle, James M., (Capt, AQM, 52nd NCST), III: 225, 229.
McCorkle, L.M., (Lt Col, 81st NCST, Detailed Men), IV: 129, 400.
McCorkle, M.L., (Capt, Co F, 13th Vols/23rd NCST), II: 185.
McCorkle, R.A., (Pvt, Co C, 10th NCST, 1st Art & Engs, Brem-Graham-Williams' Battery, Light Art), V: 568.
McCorkle, Richard, (4th Cpl, Co H, 52nd NCST), III: 225.
McCorkle, Richard G., (2nd Lt, Co E, 1st Vols/11th NCST), I: 121.
McCorkle, Dr. William, (Ass't Surg, 42nd NCST), II: 789; IV: 638.
McCormick, George, (Pvt, Co A, Millard's 9th/20th Battalion Junior Reserves), IV: 389.
McCormick, H., (Pvt, Co E, 1st NCST), V: 485.

McCormick, James L., (Capt, Co D, 1st Battalion NCST, 1st Hvy Art), II: 651; IV: 305, 306, 307, 308, 309, 310, 311; V: 240.
McCormick, M.M., (Pvt, Co G, 14th Vols/24th NCST), V: 560.
McCotter, R.D., (2nd Lt, Co F, 46th NCST), III: 81; V: 520.
McCowan, John Porter, (Maj Gen), II: 488.
McCoy, A., (2nd Lt, Co B, 82nd NCST, Detailed Men), IV: 131.
McCoy, James, (2nd Lt, Co H, 68th NCST), III: 714.
McCoy, Josiah K., (Sgt, Co I, 3rd Vols/13th NCST), I: 656.
McCoy, Robert, (AQMS, 42nd NCST), II: 789.
McCoy, Tobert, (QM of Salisbury Prison), II: 789; IV: 751.
McCoy, William H., (Pvt, Co I, 1st Vols/11th NCST), V: 531.
McCraw, Chesley, (Musician, 5th Vols/15th NCST), V: 521.
McCraw, John C., (Pvt, Co C, 5th Vols/15th NCST), V: 521.
McCreary, P.G., (3rd Sgt, Co A, 12th Vols/22nd NCST), V: 553.
McCreery, W.W., (Capt, AIG, Pettigrew's Brigade), II: 352, 358, 374, 399; IV: 556, 568; V: 131.
McCullen, William, (Pvt, Co D, 38th NCST), V: 557.
McCulloch, Rufus, (Pvt, Co K, 6th NCST), V: 513.
McCullough, Benjamin, (Brig Gen) I: xii.
McCurdy, ______, (Col, Planter, Alexander County), V: 287-288.
McCurdy, Isaac S., (Sgt, Co K, 7th NCST), I: 378.
McCurry, John D., (Pvt, Co H, 55th NCST), V: 528.
McDade, H.T., (Pvt, Co G, 1st Vols/11th NCST), V: 530.
McDade, John H., (2nd Lt, Co G, 1st Vols/11th NCST), I: 121, 585.
McDade, W.H., (Sgt, Co D, 1st Vols, "Bethel"), I: 128.
McDaniel, A.P., (Capt, Co A, 53rd NCST), III: 261.
McDaniel, E.F., (Adjt, 7th Battalion Junior Reserves; Co H, 72nd NCST, 3rd Junior Reserves), IV: 40.
McDaniel, James, (Pvt, Co C, 53rd NCST; Detailed, 2nd Corps Provost Guard), V: 570.
McDaniel, John, (Pvt, Co C, 6th NCST), V: 194.
McDaniel, M.R., [McDonald, Martin R.], (2nd Lt, Co E, 52nd NCST), IV: 709.
McDaniel, Randall, (1st Lt, Co F, 78th NCST, 8th Senior Reserves), IV: 107.
McDaniel, S., (Pvt, Co H, 4th NCST, Corps Teamster), V: 489.
McDaniel, Samuel, (Pvt, Co F, 45th NCST), V: 500.
McDaniel, W.C., (Lt, Adjt, 54th NCST), I: 118; III: 267; IV: 701, 709.
McDaniels, Joseph J., (Pvt, Co C, 34th NCST), V: 555.
McDiarmid, J., (Lt, USN), V: 243.
McDiarmid, Whitfield S., (Chaplain, 38th NCST), II: 679; IV: 613.
McDonald, Alexander, (Artificer, 6th Battalion NCST, Fayetteville Armory Guard), IV: 296.
McDonald, C., (Cpl, Co H, 26th NCST), V: 532.
McDonald, Charles, (Capt, ACS, 10th Vols/20th NCST), II: 112.
McDonald, D.J., (Pvt, Co A, 63rd NCST, 5th Cav), V: 658.
McDonald, Daniel M., (2nd Lt, Co B, 56th NCST), I: 121; III: 314; IV: 700, 709; V: 669.
McDonald, E.A., (2nd Lt, Co D, 13th Vols/23rd NCST), II: 184, 205.

McDonald, G.W., (Pvt, Co A, 8th Vols/18th NCST), II: 63.
McDonald, H.A., (2nd Lt, Co K, 38th NCST), I: 121; IV: 701, 709.
McDonald, J.A., (Pvt, Co C, 35th NCST), V: 562.
McDonald, J.H., (1st Sgt, Co E, 1st Vols/11th NCST), V: 530.
McDonald, James R., (Maj, 51st NCST), I: 118; III: 206, 210, 212, 219; IV: 721.
McDonald, James, T., (Pvt, Co G, 25th NCST), V: 561.
McDonald, John F., (1st Lt, Co G, 33rd NCST), II: 540, 578.
McDonald, John L., (Sgt, Co I, 34th NCST), V: 556.
McDonald, Joseph M., (Capt, 47th N.Y.), V: 237.
McDonald, Lewis, (2nd Cpl, Co C, 55th NCST), V: 527.
McDonald, M.B., (2nd Lt, Co E, 52nd NCST), III: 224; IV: 702, 709.
McDonald, M.S., (Pvt, Co D, 49th NCST), V: 564.
McDonald, N., (Pvt, Co H, 26th NCST), V: 532.
McDonald, William, (Pvt, Co G, 33rd NCST), II: 544.
McDonald, William J., (Pvt, Co B, 56th NCST), V: 669.
McDonald, Worth, (Pvt, Co F, 63rd NCST, 5th Cav), III: 606.
McDonald's House, (nr Chickamauga, Tenn.), III: 489.
McDonall, John, (Pvt, Co C, 3rd NCST), V: 572.
McDougal, George C., "The Boss," [McDougald], (Capt, Chief Engineer, Gordon), IV: 400-404, 442-445, 446-449.
McDougal, James L., [McCormick], (Capt, McDougal's Unatached Co, MacRae's Brigade), II: 651.
McDougald, A., (Pvt, Co H, 46th NCST), V: 525.
McDougald, Alexander B., (2nd Lt, Co E, 56th NCST), III: 315.
McDougald, Daniel, (Capt, Co F, 5th Vols/15th NCST), I: 735.
McDowell, ______, (Pvt, Co A, 1st Vols, "Bethel"), I: 128.
McDowell, B.G., (Lt Col, 62nd NCST), III: 515, 517, 518, 519, 520, 521, 522, 523, 524, 525, 526, 663, 666, 667, 756.
McDowell, Irvin, (Maj Gen, USA), I: 282, 341, 609, 623; II: 545; IV: 226, 447.
McDowell, James C.S., (Lt Col, 54th NCST), I: 78, 118, 309; III: 267, 269, 409; V: 11.
McDowell, John A., (Col, 1st NCST), I: 134, 138, 139, 146, 149.
McDowell, John L., (Lt Col, 34th NCST), II: 581; IV: 169.
McDowell, Dr. Joseph A., (Col, 6th Battalion/60th NCST), I: 13; III: 473, 474, 475, 499.
McDowell, W.E., (Capt, Co E, 65th NCST, 6th Cav), III: 675, 677, 684.
McDowell, William W., (Maj, 6th Battalion/60th NCST), III: 473, 475, 497, 499.
McDowell, William Wallis, (Maj, 51st NCST), I: 78, 85, 90, 118, 125, 127, 129, 131, 156, 170, 173, 551; V: xii, 677.
McDowell, Va., IV: 139.
McDowell County, N.C., II: 163; III: 125, 447, 760; IV: 218, 391, 397; V: 654.
McDowell's Farm, Va., I: 436; I I: 103, 104, 105; III: 621, 627.
McEachern, Hector, (Lt, Co D, 51st NCST), III: 211, 219.
McEachern, Robert J., (Capt, Co D, 51st NCST), I: 119; III: 212, 219.
McElroy, J.W., (Brig Gen, Home Guard), IV: 651; V: 7.

McElroy, John S., (Lt Col, 6th Vols/16th NCST), I: 751, 753, 755, 763; II: 168, 680; IV: 137, 151, 156, 157, 170, 173, 174, 551, ; V: xii, 677.
McEntire, Tom, (Lt, Co G, 6th Vols/16th NCST), IV: 153, 180, 218.
McEntire, W.T., (1st Lt, Co D, 33rd NCST), V: 538.
McEvoy, James, (2nd Lt, Co H, 40th NCST, 3rd Art, Hvy), II: 747.
McEwen, J.M., (Pvt, Co H, 35th NCST), V: 563.
McFadyen, A., [Angus], (Lt, Co A, 63rd NCST, 5th Cav), IV: 700, 709.
McFadyen, A.C., (2nd Lt, Co C, 7th Battalion Junior Reserves; Co I, 72nd NCST, 3rd Junior Reserves), IV: 40.
McFarland, J.A., (Pvt, Co H, 30th NCST), V: 492.
McFarland, W.H., (Sgt, Co I, 54th NCST), V: 516.
McGarlliard, Jones, (Pvt, Co D, 6th NCST), V: 512.
McGathy, Thadeus C., (Pvt, Co G, 34th NCST), V: 556.
McGee, ______, (Pvt, Co K, 52nd NCST), V: 536.
McGee, A., (Pvt, Co E, 6th NCST), V: 512.
McGee, Henry, (Cpl, Co E, 6th NCST), I: 345.
McGee, J.A., (Sgt, Co E, 6th NCST), V: 512.
McGee, Dr. James W., (Ass't Surg, 51st NCST), III: 205; IV: 640.
McGee, Joseph B., (Maj, 34th NCST), II: 581.
McGee, N.S., (1st Lt, Co H, 77th NCST, 7th Senior Reserves), IV: 100.
McGee, Thaddeus, (Capt, AQM, N.C.), I: 51.
McGee, W., (Pvt, Co E, 6th NCST), V: 512.
McGehee, Charles A., [McGeehee], (1st Lt, Co H, 53rd NCST), III: 263; IV: 700.
McGehee, Edward P., (Ordnance Sgt, Walker's Battalion, Thomas' Legion, 80th NCST), IV: 117.
McGehee, Henry, (1st Lt, Co H, 3rd Vols/13th NCST), I: 653.
McGehee, W.J., (1st Lt, Co B, Walker's Battalion, Thomas' Legion, 80th NCST), IV: 118.
McGhee, J.C., (Capt, Co I, 58th NCST), III: 434.
McGhee, J.L., (Pvt, Co A, 28th NCST), V: 540.
McGhee, L.L., (Pvt, Co H, 37th NCST), V: 546.
McGhee, Thomas T., (Pvt, Co G, 34th NCST), V: 556.
McGhee House, (nr Cold Harbor, Va.), II: 56.
McGill, A.D., (Sgt, Co H, 30th NCST), V: 492.
McGill, John W., (Lt Col, 8th Vols/18th NCST), II: 41, 63, 74, 572; IV: 473.
McGilvary, J.H., [McGilvery], (Jr 2nd Lt, Co H, 26th NCST), II: 372, 397.
McGilvery, ______, [Freeman], (Brig Gen, USA), V: 299.
McGimpsy, W.W., (2nd Sgt, Co B, 1st Vols/11th NCST), V: 530.
McGinn, N.C., (Pvt, Co B, 3rd Vols/13th NCST), V: 549.
McGinn, W.A., (Pvt, Co B, 3rd Vols/13th NCST), V: 549.
McGinnis, Nathan, (Capt, Co F, 34th NCST), V: 548.
McGinnis, R.C., (Sgt, Co B, 43rd NCST), V: 497.
McGinnis, S.P., (Sgt, Co B, 49th NCST), V: 564.
McGinniss, J.J. (1st Lt, Co B, 49th NCST), I: 734.

McGowan, Samuel, [MacGowan], (Brig Gen), I: 380, 666; III: 252; IV: 375; V: 211.
McGowen, Alexander D., (Pvt, Co A, 38th NCST), V: 556.
McGowen, John Q., (3rd Cpl, Co A, 38th NCST), V: 557.
McGregor, ______, (Capt, Horse Art, Barringer's Brigade), I: 431, 468, 469.
McGregor, John W., (Lt, Co F, 4th Vols/14th NCST), I: 724, 726, 729, 731.
McGruder, ______, [Zachariah S.], (Lt Col, 10th Va. Cav), I: 421.
McGuire, Dr. Hunter, (Medical Director, Jackson's 2nd Corps, ANV), II: 558, 560, 620.
McGuy, John, (Sgt Maj, 16th Battalion/75th NCST, 7th Cav), IV: 72.
McHorney, Benjamin, (1st Lt, Co G, 68th NCST), III: 714.
McIlhany, J.H., (Pvt, Co C, 10th NCST, 1st Art & Engs, Brem-Graham-Williams' Battery, Light Art), V: 568.
McIlhenny, John C., (1st Lt, Co E, 10th NCST, 1st Art & Engs, Moore-Miller's Battery, Light Art), I: 581.
McIlwaine's Hill, (nr Petersburg, Va.), II: 60.
McInnis, Malcom, (Jr 2nd Lt, Co D, 6th Battalion NCST, Fayetteville Armory Guard), IV: 296.
McIntire, A.J., (Ensign, 38th NCST), V: 548.
McIntire, Alexander, (Pvt, Co E, 38th NCST), V: 557.
McIntire, D.M., (1st Lt, Adjt, 38th NCST), V: 548.
McIntire, J.Y., (Lt, Co, 6th Vols/16th NCST), IV: 153, 179, 180, 701, 709.
McIntire, R.M., [Robert M.], (Capt, Co C, 59th NCST, 4th Cav), IV: 701, 709.
McIntire, T.T., (Pvt, Co C, 10th Vols/20th NCST), II: 114.
McIntire, Thomas H.W., (1st Lt, Adjt, 1st NCST), I: 136; V: 484.
McIntosh, Archibald A., (1st Lt, Co H, 30th NCST), II: 496.
McIntosh, D.W., (2nd Lt, Co H, 30th NCST), II: 497.
McIntosh, Frank, (1st Lt, Co F, 8th Vols/18th NCST), IV: 722.
McIntosh, James, (Maj Gen, USA), I: 545; II: 553.
McIntyre, Andrew J., (Capt, Co K, 33rd NCST), II: 541.
McIntyre, David M., (AAG, Scales' Brigade), II: 676, 679, 681, 682, 686, 689, 690, 693; V: 151.
McIntyre, J.Y., (Capt, Co G, 6th Vols/16th NCST), IV: 179.
McIntyre, R.M., (Capt, Co C, 59th NCST, 4th Cav), III: 457.
McIntyre, W.T., (2nd Lt, Co D, 33rd NCST), II: 539, 577, 578.
McIver, ______, (S.C. Supreme Court Justice), II: 725.
McIver, A.A., (Capt, Co G, 14th Vols/24th NCST), II: 272.
McIver, D.M., (Pvt, Co H, 30th NCST), V: 492.
McIver, D.N., (Pvt, Co H, 30th NCST), V: 492.
McIver, James D., (Capt, Co H, 26th NCST), II: 304, 372, 373, 397, 418.
McIver, J.M., (Sgt, Co A, 63rd NCST, 5th Cav), V: 658.
McIver, M.M., (Pvt, Co G, 14th Vols/24th NCST), V: 560.
McJones, Alexander, (2nd Lt, Co I, 40th NCST, 3rd Art, Hvy), II: 747.
McKamy, James A., (Capt, Co C; Maj, Walker's Battalion; Lt Col, Thomas' Legion, 80th NCST), III: 751, 754; IV: 117, 118, 121, 122, 127, 128.

McKamy, John W., (2nd Lt, Co C, Walker's Battalion, Thomas' Legion, 80th NCST), IV: 118.
McKay, Dr. A.L., [McKoy], [Mackay], (Surg, 6th Battalion/60th NCST), III: 484, 485, 486; IV: 641.
McKay, J.A., (Pvt, Co H, 1st Vols, "Bethel"; Pvt, Co C, 10th NCST, 1st Art & Engs, Brem-Graham-Williams' Battery, Light Art), I: 123; V: 568.
McKay, John A.D., (Maj, 31st NCST), II: 508, 511.
McKee, B.H., (Pvt, Co D, 56th NCST), III: 380.
McKee, Bedford, (Pvt, Color-bearer, 56th NCST), III: 392.
McKee, David, (Pvt, Co D, 56th NCST), III: 352.
McKee, James, (Lt, Co C, 7th NCST), I: 120.
McKee, James, (Pvt, Co D, 56th NCST), III: 361.
McKee, R.D., (Pvt, Co G, 37th NCST), V: 546.
McKellar, John, (Capt, Co A, 63rd NCST, 5th Cav), III: 530.
McKenzie, Donald, (Capt, AQM, 5th Battalion NCST, Cav), IV: 271.
McKenzie, J., (Pvt, Co E, 28th NCST), V: 542.
McKenzie, Kenneth, (1st Lt, Co B, 78th NCST, 8th Senior Reserves), IV: 107.
McKenzie, M.S., (Sgt, Co B, 4th NCST), I: 232.
McKenzie, William, (QM Sgt, 51st NCST), III: 205.
McKethan, A.A., (2nd Lt, Co B, 51st NCST), III: 205, 214, 216, 217, 218, 220, 221.
McKethan, E.M., (Resident of Fayetteville), I: 131.
McKethan, E.T., (Lt, Co K, 51st NCST, Hoke's Staff), III: 220.
McKethan, Hector, [McKeithan], (Col, 51st NCST), I: 78, 91, 118, 127; III: 205, 206, 207, 210, 212, 214, 217, 220; IV: 483, 493, 497; V: 162, 197, 198.
McKethan, James K., (Lt, Co G, 8th NCST), V: 194.
McKimmon, Charlie, (Pvt, Co A, 10th NCST, 1st Art & Engs, Ramseur-Manly's Battery, Light Art), I: 559.
McKimmon, James, (2nd Lt, Co A, 10th NCST, 1st Art & Engs, Ramseur-Manly's Battery, Light Art) I: 551, 560.
McKinne, David E., (Capt, Co A, 71st NCST, 2nd Junior Reserves; Adjt, Camp of Instruction at Weldon), IV: 25, 26, 28.
McKinney, A.A., [Adolph A.], (Capt, Co D, 6th Vols/16th NCST), IV: 180, 701, 709.
McKinney, H.R., (Capt, Co A, 46th NCST), II: 454; III: 78, 80, 122.
McKinney, Robert M., (Col, 5th Vols/15th NCST), I: 295, 339, 733, 737, 739; V: 10, 645, 646.
McKinney, S., (Pvt, Co C, 10th NCST, 1st Art & Engs, Brem-Graham-Williams' Battery, Light Art), V: 568.
McKinney, W.H., (2nd Lt, Co G, 53rd NCST), III: 263.
McKinnon, John M., (2nd Lt, Co E, 40th NCST, 3rd Art, Hvy), II: 747.
McKinnon, Rev. Dr. Luther, [McKinnon], (Chaplain, 36th NCST, 2nd Art & Engs), II: 630, 646; IV: 613; V: 233.
McKnight, George, (Adjt Gen Loring's Division), IV: 695.
McKorkle, R.B., (Pvt, Co B, 43rd NCST), V: 194.
McKorkle, W.A., (Pvt, Co H, 57th NCST), V: 517.
McKoy, Allmand A., (Lt Col, 27th Battalion Home Guard;

Col, 78th NCST, 8th Senior Reserves), IV: 108, 650.
McKoy, Henry J., (1st Lt, Co K, 33rd NCST), II: 541, 579.
McKoy, M.G., (Pvt, Co F, 8th Vols/18th NCST), II: 64.
McKoy, Thomas Hall, (Commissary, Branch-Lane's Brigade), IV: 472; V: 537.
McLamb, Minson, (2nd Lt, Co I, 46th NCST), III: 82.
McLarty, J.M., (1st Lt, Co B, 5th Vols/15th NCST), I: 734; V: 519.
McLauchlin, Edward, [McLacklan, Edward T.], (Cpl, Co I, 2nd NCST), I: 171.
McLauchlin, John C., [James C.], (Capt, Co K, 26th NCST), II: 304, 330, 337, 338, 353, 372, 393, 397, 403, 418-419.
McLaughlin, John H., (Pvt, Co D, 34th NCST), V: 555.
McLauchlin, N.A., (Pvt, Co B, Starr's Battery, Starr's 13th Battalion NCST, Light Art), IV: 346.
McLaughlin, M. McR., (Maj, 38th NCST), II: 676, 678, 679, 685, 689, 690.
McLaughlen, Napolean Bonaparte, (Brig Gen, USA), I: 155.
McLaurin, A.L., (Pvt, Co I, 12th Vols/22nd NCST), V: 554.
McLaurin, Daniel J., (Pvt, Co K, 38th NCST), V: 558.
McLaurin, Daniel M., (Capt, Co F, 8th Vols/18th NCST), II: 20.
McLaurin, Jack, (Negro servant to W.H. McLaurin), II: 55.
McLaurin, James T., (Capt, Co B, 4th Tx.), II: 26, 48.
McLaurin, William H., (1st Lt, Adjt, 8th Vols/18th NCST), II: 19, 36, 37, 38, 40, 47, 48, 49, 51, 52, 53, 54, 55, 56, 61, 62, 63, 63; IV: 473.
McLaurin, William T., [Daniel M.], (Capt, Co F, 8th Vols/18th NCST), II: 54, 63.
McLaws, Lafayette, (Maj Gen), I: 555; II: 433; III: 184, 185, 187, 188, 190, 193, 194, 198; IV: 335, 547; V: 73, 128.
McLean, D.H, (1st Cpl, Co C, 10th NCST, 1st Art & Engs, Brem-Graham-Williams' Battery, Light Art), V: 567.
McLean, J.D., (2nd Lt, Co B, 3rd Vols/13th NCST), V: 547.
McLean, J.D., (2nd Lt, Co B, Starr's Battery, Starr's 13th Battalion NCST, Light Art), IV: 346, 349, 352.
McLean, Dr. J.L., (Ass't Surg, 33rd NCST), IV: 474.
McLean, J.C., (Pvt, Co A, 53rd NCST), V: 501.
McLean, J.T., (1st Lt, Co F, 5th Vols/15th NCST), I: 735.
McLean, J. Logan, (Pvt, Co B, 3rd Vols/13th NCST), V: 549.
McLean, James Robert, (Maj, 77th NCST, 7th Senior Reserves), IV: 101, 103.
McLean, Jesse R., (Maj, Conscript Camp at Morganton), IV: 382.
McLean, John P., (1st Lt, Co H, 50th NCST), I: 120; III: 203.
McLean, Nathaniel A., (Lt Col, 78th NCST, 8th Senior Reserves), IV: 107, 108.
McLean, Robert A., (Pvt, Co G, 14th Vols/24th NCST), V: 560.
McLean, Dr. W.D., (Ass't Surg, 26th NCST), IV: 636.
McLean, Dr. William S., (Capt, Ass't Surg, 26th NCST), II: 304, 305, 306, 308, 395, 396, 408.
McLean's House, (Wilmer McLean had left his residence near Manassas early in the war and moved to Appomattox in the hope that he would escape any further occurrence of battles in his door yard. Yet fate had other

plans for McLean as it was to his home and his parlor that generals Lee and Grant came on that fateful day in April of 1865. McLean stood witness to the first and the last great battles of the war.), II: 392.
McLellan, C.C., (2nd Lt, Co A, 7th Battalion Junior Reserves; Co H, 72nd NCST, 3rd Junior Reserves), IV: 40.
McLellan, D.G., (Sgt, Co I, 51st NCST), III: 220.
McLenahan, John B., [McClenahan], (Capt, Co G, 63rd NCST, 5th Cav), III: 554.
McLendon, Benjamin, (Pvt, Co E, 52nd NCST), V: 536.
McLendon, John J., (Pvt, Co C, 4th Vols/14th NCST), I: 731; V: 490.
McLeod, C.M., (Capt, Co H, 6th Vols/16th NCST), V: 547.
McLeod, D., (Cpl, Co H, 26th NCST), V: 532.
McLeod, John, (Pvt, Co C, 35th NCST), V: 562.
McLeod, L.H., (2nd Lt, Co H, 30th NCST), II: 497; IV: 600.
McLeod, M., (1st Lt, Co H, 26th NCST), II: 358, 372, 397; IV: 722.
McLeod, M.D.L., (Maj, 9th NCST, 1st Cav), I: 439, 475, 484, 485, 782.
McLester, J.D., (Lt, 4th NCST), IV: 702, 709.
McLoud, A.S., [Cloud], (Lt Col, 6th Vols/16th NCST), IV: 184, 192, 201.
McManus, Edwin H., (Lt, Co E, 26th NCST), II: 396, 397.
McManus, J.C., (Pvt, Co A, 4th NCST), V: 488.
McMasters, Lewis F., (Lt, Co M, 12th Vols/22nd NCST), II: 166.
McMichael, J.W., (Pvt, Co D, 45th NCST), V: 500.
McMillan, Alexander, (Capt, Co C, MacRae's 18th Battalion NCST), IV: 379.
McMillan Andrew N., (Capt, Co A, 26th NCST), II: 303, 305, 323, 396, 397.
McMillan, D.T., (2nd Lt, Co E, 30th NCST), II: 496.
McMillan, Daniel L., (2nd Lt, Co H, 44th NCST), III: 23.
McMillan, J.J., (1st Lt, Co C, 1st NCST), I: 136; IV: 722.
McMillan, John C., (Capt, Co E, 30th NCST), II: 495, 599; IV: 462, 599.
McMillan, Peter, (Pvt, Co A, Webb's Battery, Starr's 13th Battalion NCST, Light Art), V: 282.
McMillan, Ronald, (Grandfather of T.F. Toon), II: 125.
McMillan, W.D., (Sgt Maj, 51st NCST), III: 214.
McMillan's House, (nr Gettysburg, Pa.), I: 379; II: 660.
McMillan's Woods, (nr Gettysburg, Pa.), III: 299.
McMinn County, Tenn., IV: 126.
McMinnville, Tenn., II: 488.
McMullen, L.W., (Cpl, Co A, Webb's Battery, Starr's 13th Battalion NCST, Light Art), V: 282.
McMurray, Christopher C., (2nd Lt, Co F, 6th Battalion, Fayetteville Armory Guard), IV: 297.
McNabb, ______, (Brig Gen, Ark.), II: 490.
McNair, Archibald J., (2nd Lt, Co E, 40th NCST, 3rd Art, Hvy), II: 747; V: 368.
McNair, Duncan, (Capt, Co H, 3rd NCST), I: 189, 213, 226.
McNair, Rev. Dr. Evander, (Chaplain, 14th Vols/24th NCST), II: 271; IV: 610.
McNair, Evander, (Brig Gen), II: 712, 713, 714, 716, 717, 739; V: 171.
McNair, J.A., (Pvt, Co E, 52nd NCST), V: 536.

McNair, Malcolm, (Capt, Co E, 40th NCST, 3rd Art, Hvy), II: 746.
McNair, Robert G., (Pvt, Co G, 14th Vols/24th NCST), V: 560.
McNate, John, (Cpl, Co G, 33rd NCST), II: 540, 579.
McNeal, A., (Sgt, Co K, 8th Vols/18th NCST), II: 64.
McNeal, James M., (2nd Lt, Co D, 41st NCST, 3rd Cav), II: 771.
McNeal, W.M., (2nd Lt, Co D, 41st NCST, 3rd Cav), II: 771.
McNeely, _____, (Adjt, 82nd NCST, Detailed Men), IV: 131.
McNeely, C.K., [Carmi K.], (Capt, Co D, 34th NCST), IV: 700, 709.
McNeely, F.Y., (Capt, Co K, 4th NCST), I: 231, 267.
McNeely, J.J., (Sgt, Co K, 56th NCST), III: 357.
McNeely, John F., (Capt, Co K, 56th NCST), III: 317, 399; V: 559.
McNeely, Thomas, (Pvt, Co D, 6th NCST), V: 512.
McNeely, William G., (AQM, 57th NCST), III: 405, 427.
McNeely, William Richard, (2nd Lt, Co A, 4th NCST), I: 232, 263, 269.
McNeil, Henry J., (1st Lt, Co H, 30th NCST), II: 496.
McNeil, K.M, (1st Lt, Co F, 5th Vols/15th NCST), I: 735.
McNeill, A., (Sgt, Co K, 8th Vols/18th NCST), II: 64; V: 540.
McNeill, A.B., (Pvt, Co D, 3rd NCST), V: 487.
McNeill, D.G., (Pvt, Co D, 3rd NCST), V: 487.
McNeill, Duncan, (Capt, ACS, 8th Vols/18th NCST), II: 17; IV: 473.
McNeill, George, (Father of Col J.R. McNeill), III: 643.
McNeill, H., (Pvt, Co E, 56th NCST), III: 347.
McNeill, James D., (Senator, CSA, Nephew of Col J.H. McNeill), III: 655.
McNeill, James H., (Col, 63rd NCST, 5th Cav), I: 439, 443, 472, 473; III: 228, 529, 530, 533, 541, 551, 563, 604, 607, 620, 639, 640, 641, 642, 643, 644, 654, 655, 656,; V: 10, 533, 650, 671, 674.
McNeill, James M., (Maj, 63rd NCST, 5th Cav), III: 551; V: 671.
McNeill, James M., (2nd Lt, Co D, 41st NCST, 3rd Cav), II: 771.
McNeill, John N., (2nd Lt, Co H, 46th NCST), III: 82.
McNeill, Malcom D., (1st Lt, Co D, Webb's Battery, Bogg's 12th Battalion Va., Hvy Art; Co A, Webb's Battery, Starr's Battalion NCST, Light Art), IV: 355, 358.
McNeill, Minerva Ruffin, (Mother of Col J.H. McNeill), III: 643.
McNeill, N.A., (1st Lt, Co H, 46th NCST), III: 82; V: 520.
McNeill, N. McK., (Maj, 46th NCST), III: 65, 82; V: 519.
McNeill, N.T., (Pvt, Co E, 56th NCST), III: 323.
McNeill, T.A., (Sgt, Co D, 9th Battalion NCST, 1st Hvy Art), IV: 303.
McNeill, W.M., (2nd Lt, Co D, 41st NCST, 3rd Cav), II: 771.
McNider, W.H., (2nd Lt, Co A, 1st NCST), I: 136.
McNutt, _____, [John W.], (Adjt, 2nd Battalion NCST), IV: 245.
McPhail, John A., (2nd Lt, Co D, 46th NCST), III: 81.
McPhail, W.H., (Pvt, Co K, 38th NCST), II: 690.
McPheeters, A.M., (Maj, Private Secretary to Governor Vance), I: 64.
McPherson, _____, [William D.], (Pvt, Co C, 4th Vols/14th NCST), I: 723.

McPherson, D.C., (Pvt, Co G, 26th NCST), V: 532.
McPherson, J.A., (1st Lt, Co E, 6th NCST), I: 345, 354.
McPherson, James R., (Cpl, Co A, 5th NCST, Detailed, 2nd Corps Provost Guard), V: 569.
McPherson, W.H., (Pvt, Co I, 26th NCST), V: 532.
McPherson's Ridge, (nr Gettysburg, Pa.), II: 344, 349, 351; V: 117, 119.
McPherson's Woods, (nr Gettysburg, Pa.), II: 344, 345, 346, 347, 348, 349, 350, 351, 354, 356, 361, 368, 418.
McPhaul, M.I., (Musician, 46th NCST), V: 524.
McQueen, A.N., (Pvt, Co K, 4th NCST, Teamster), V: 489.
McQueen, Donald, (Capt, Co C, 7th Battalion Junior Reserves; Co I, 72nd NCST, 3rd Junior Reserves), IV: 40.
McQueen, W.B., (Pvt, Co K, 4th NCST), V: 489.
McRae, Alexander, (Maj, 9th Battalion NCST, 1st Hvy Art), IV: 303, 304, 305, 306, 313.
McRae, Cameron F., (Chaplain, 5th Vols/15th NCST), I: 734; IV: 607.
McRae, D.G., (Capt, Co E, 38th NCST), II: 675, 678, 690.
McRae, Duncan, (Pvt, Co K, 38th NCST), V: 558.
McRae, Duncan A., (Adjt, 28th NCST), II: 465; IV: 473.
McRae, Duncan K., [MacRae], (Col, 5th NCST), II: 192, 198, 220; IV: 521, 703.
McRae, Henry, (Capt, Co C; Maj, 8th NCST), I: 387, 492, 511; V: 11.
McRae, Dr. James A., (Surg, 5th NCST), I: 281, 282; IV: 632.
McRae, Dr. James F., (Surg, 3rd NCST), IV: 632.
McRae, John, (AQM, Starr's 13th Battalion NCST, Light Art), IV: 348.
McRae, John B., (2nd Lt, Co B, 78th NCST, 8th Senior Reserves), IV: 107.
McRae, John Burgwyn, (Pvt, Co B, Starr's 13th Battalion NCST, Light Art), IV: 607.
McRae, Montford S., (Sgt Maj, 26th NCST), II: 358, 371, 372, 396.
McRae, Neill, (Pvt, Co G, 14th Vols/24th NCST), V: 560.
McRae, R.S., (Pvt, Co H, 35th NCST), V: 563.
McRae, Robert B., (Maj, 7th NCST), I: 361, 369, 371, 372; IV: 472.
McRae, Walter G., (Capt, Co C, 7th NCST), I: 383; IV: 713.
McRae, William, (2nd Lt, Co B, 78th NCST, 8th Senior Reserves), IV: 107.
McRae, William, (Brig Gen), I: 471.
McRary, John C., (Pvt, Co F, 5th Vols/15th NCST), V: 521.
McRee, Dr. James F., (Surg, 3rd NCST), I: 213; IV: 629, 632.
McRee, Robert C., (Sgt Maj, 3rd NCST), I: 203, 213.
McRorie, Miss Martha, (of Salisbury), I: 561.
McRorie, William F., (Capt, Co A, 4th NCST), I: 231, 257, 269.
McSwain, Bermudas, (Pvt, Co D, 38th NCST), V: 557.
McSwain, G., (Pvt, Co K, 54th NCST), V: 516.
McSween, Alexander, (Pvt, Co G, 68th NCST, 5th Cav, Jeff Davis Legion), V: 658.
McTate, John, II: 540, 579.
McWatson, Malcolm, (2nd Lt, Co F, 50th NCST), III: 203.
Meade, Everard B., (ADC, Branch-Lane's Brigade), IV: 472.
Meade, George Gordon, (Maj Gen, USA and Meade's Army), I: 313,

315, 316, 317, 318, 382, 426, 428, 462, 481, 592, 593, 594, 628, 639, 640, 720; II: 45, 46, 96, 97, 99, 234, 240, 241, 343, 344, 369, 370, 375, 378, 381, 440, 444, 479, 569, 623, 662, 663, 664, 780; III: 26, 42, 43, 72, 73, 92, 93, 107, 239, 242, 244, 303, 465, 560, 570, 578, 581, 582, 585, 586, 594, 611, 626, 628; IV: 182, 183, 184, 1887, 562; V: 110, 114, 121, 122, 128, 138, 139, 141.
Meade, R. Kidder, (Capt, Engineering Officer, CSN), IV: 419, 422.
Meadow Bluff, Va., II: 270.
Meadow Bridge, Va., (aka Brook Church, Chickahominy River, Va.), I: 139, 181, 367, 613, 755; II: 471; III: 601, 602, 603; IV: 152, 155, 465.
Meadow Bridge Road, Va., I: 570; IV: 156.
Meadows, B., (Pvt, Co K, 6th NCST), V: 513.
Meadows, E.H., (ACS, 31st NCST), II: 511, 518, 519; V: 161, 167.
Meadows, James, (1st Lt, Co E, 46th NCST), III: 81.
Meadows, L., (Pvt, Co E, 46th NCST), V: 524.
Meadows, Wiley, (Sgt, Co B, 6th NCST), V: 512.
Meagher, Thomas Francis, (Brig Gen, USA), I: 167.
Meaks, C.W., (Pvt, Co F, 45th NCST), V: 500.
Means, Paul B., (Pvt, Co F, Courier, 63rd NCST, 5th Cav), IV: 582.
Means, T.H., (1st Lt, Co B, 5th Vols/15th NCST), I: 734.
Means, Dr. T.H., (Ass't Surg, 63rd NCST), IV: 641.
Means, W.N.S., (2nd Lt, Co E, 1st Vols/11th NCST), I: 584; V: 664.
Meares, Calvin, (Pvt, Co C, 10th Vols/20th NCST), II: 114.
Meares, D.A., (1st Sgt, Co A, 46th NCST), V: 524.
Meares, E.G., [Edward G.], (Capt, Co D, 3rd NCST), I: 213.
Meares, Gaston H., (Col, 3rd NCST), I: 140, 178, 180, 181, 182, 183, 190, 212, 215, 216, 217, 219, 221; IV: 649; V: 9, 649.
Meares, J.A., (Lt, Co H, 51st NCST), III: 214, 219.
Meares, John, (Pvt, Co B, 8th Vols/18th NCST), II: 63; V: 539.
Meares, Oliver P., (Capt, 30th N.C. Militia; Lt Col, 8th Vols/18th NCST), II: 16, 17, 18, 19; III: 503, 508; IV: 473; V: 27, 650.
Meares, Reddin, (Pvt, Co E, 43rd NCST), V: 498.
Meares, Dr. William B., (Lt, Ass't Surg, 10th Vols./20th NCST; ADC to M.W. Ransom), II: 112; IV: 572, 578, 635.
Mears, James B., (Cpl, Co K, 5th Vols/15th NCST), V: 522.
Mears, William J.L., (Pvt, Co D, 2nd NCST), I: 176; V: 486.
Mebane, B.Y., (2nd Lt, Co F, 6th NCST), II: 140.
Mebane, G.A., (Pvt, Co F, 6th NCST), V: 513.
Mebane, John T., (Capt, Co F, 68th NCST), III: 714.
Mebane, T.Y., (Pvt, Co F, 6th NCST), V: 512.
Mebane, W.A., (2nd Lt, Co F, 6th NCST), V: 511.
Mebane, W.A, [William A.], (2nd Lt, Co F, 27th NCST), IV: 702, 709.
Mebane, W.N., (2nd Lt, Topographical Engineer, 3rd Vols/13th NCST; Ordnance Officer, Cooke's Brigade), I: 689, 690; IV: 508; V: 519.
Mechanicsville, Va., (and Battle of, 1862), I: 138, 180, 181, 165, 217,

242, 304, 367, 609, 612, 613, 614, 694, 738, 755, 757, 762, 772; II: 21, 25, 39, 67, 114, 168, 207, 209, 471, 498, 547, 549, 583, 655, 680, 687; III: 39, 76, 77, 79, 277; IV: 156, 198, 262, 355, 397, 446, 551; V: 197.
Mechancisville Bridge, Va., I: 613.
Mechanicsville Pike, Va., I: 180, 217, 658, 737.
Mechanicsville Road, Va., II: 22.
Mechum's Station, Va., I: 567.
Mecklenburg County, N.C., I: 61; II: 628, 792, 799; III: 125, 260, 317, 318, 319, 360, 368, 378, 406, 456, 457, 545; IV: 405, 406, 616.
Mecklenburg County, Va., II: 239, 589, 591.
Medals, Confederate, I: 378.
Medearis, John E., (QM Sgt, 58th NCST), III: 432.
Medical Corps, N.C., IV: 623-644.
Medical Department, IV: 623.
Mediterranian Sea, V: 385.
Medley, Benjamin F., (Pvt, Co C, 4th Vols/14th NCST), V: 490.
Medlin, Willis, (Pvt, Co I, 48th NCST), V: 527.
Meekins, F., (Pvt, Co A, 35th NCST), V: 495.
Meekins, John W., (Pvt, Detached Co, 68th NCST), III: 723.
Mehagen, R., (Pvt, Co G, 3rd Vols/13th NCST), V: 551.
Meherrin Creek, N.C./Va., (aka Meherrin River), III: 633, 634; IV: 44, 368; V: 283.
Meigs, H.P., (Musician, 53rd NCST), V: 501.
Meinung, A., (Musician, Mickey's Band, 26th NCST), II: 398.
Melbourne, Australia, V: 347.
Melcher, M., (Pvt, Co G, 33rd NCST), V: 544.
Melvin, J., (Sgt, Co D, 9th Vols/19th NCST, 2nd Cav), V: 658.
Melvin, John T., (Capt, Co I, 36th NCST, 2nd Art & Engs, Bladen-Richardson-Melvin's Battery, Light Art), II: 630, 634; V: 239.
Melvin, William, (Pvt, Co K, 8th Vols/18th NCST), II: 64; V: 540.
Memorial Association of Winchester, II: 132.
Memphis, Tenn., IV: 605.
Mennis, F.E., (Pvt, Co C, 57th NCST), V: 517.
Mercer, ______, [John T.], (Col, 21st Ga.), II: 148; III: 8, 274, 337, 339; V: 175, 180.
Mercer, Hugh Weedon, (Brig Gen), IV: 254.
Mercer, Oliver, (Lt, Co G, 10th Vols/20th NCST), II: 127.
Mercer, Willie, (Pvt, Co A, 55th NCST), V: 527.Merchant's Hope Church, (nr Petersburg, Va.), II: 431; IV: 502.
Meredith, ______, [Solomon], (Brig Gen, USA), V: 613.
Meridian, Miss., II: 491, 492, 721, 734; III: 499.
Merrick, J.C., (Pvt, Co G, 6th NCST), V: 513.
Merrick, James, (Fayetteville and Harper's Ferry Arsenals), IV: 298.
Merrimon, Augustus S., (Capt, N.C. Subsistence Department), I: 37.
Merrimon, J.H., (Adjt, 65th NCST, 6th Cav), III: 683.
Merritt, B.H., (Pvt, Co G, 30th NCST), V: 492.
Merritt, E.J., (1st Lt, Co K, 32nd NCST), I: 736.
Merritt, Joshua, (Pvt, Co D, 4th NCST), V: 488.
Merritt, Wesley, (Maj Gen, USA), I: 481.
Merritt House, (nr Kinston), II: 83.
Merry, J.F., (Ensign, USN; Pioneer, Osceola), V: 245.
Merry Hill, N.C., II: 793.
Mersey River, England, V: 349.

Merton, Stephen H., (2nd Lt, Co B, 41st NCST, 3rd Cav), II: 770.
Messemer, Moses, (Pvt, Co F, 57th NCST), V: 517.
Messer, Whitley, (Pvt, Co C, 5th NCST), I: 291; V: 505.
Messinger, B., (Pvt, Co A, 46th NCST), V: 524.
Metts, James I., (Capt, Co G, 3rd NCST), I: 177, 194, 214, 215; IV: 701, 708; V: 484.
Meyer, Francis X., (Lt Col, 117th N.Y.), V: 237.
Mexico, V: 354.
Michael, J.M., (Pvt, Co I, 56th NCST), III: 357.
Michael, John, (Capt, Co H, 48th NCST), III: 114, 115.
Michigan, II: 367; V: 294.
Mickey, Samuel T., (Capt, Chief Musician, 26th NCST), II: 398-400.
Mickey, William, (Sgt, Co I, 11th Vols/21st NCST), V: 515.
Mickey's Band, Samuel T., II: 336, 362, 381, 397-400.
Mickle, J.C., (Pvt, Co B, 26th NCST), V: 531.
Mickle, William, [William N.], (2nd Lt, Co K, 37th NCST), II: 661, 674.
Micks, Dr. T.R., (Surg, Fayetteville General Hospital #1), IV: 625, 627, 629.
Middle Mountain, Va., IV: 147.
Middleburg, Va., I: 424; II: 95, 96; III: 456, 461, 462, 472, 532, 559, 560, 561, 562, 563, 564, 565, 586, 637.
Middleburge, Pa., V: 117.
Middleton, George W., (Pvt, Co A, 38th NCST), V: 556.
Middleton, Hugh, (2nd Lt, Co D, 46th NCST), III: 81.
Middleton, R.M., (1st Lt, Co A, 38th NCST), V: 548.
Middletown, Md., [Middleton], I: 261, 327, 421, 647; II: 259, 533; III: 278, 749, 750, 755; IV: 164.
Middletown Academy, (Middletown, Conn.) I: 133.
Midgett, J.S., (Orderly Sgt, 33rd NCST), V: 543.
Midyett, John S., (Ordnance Sgt, 33rd NCST), II: 537, 578.
Midyett's Hammocks, N.C., II: 508; V: 58.
Milburnie, N.C., IV: 430.
Miles, D.H., (Brig Gen, USA), II: 135.
Miles, J., (Pvt, Co H, 56th NCST), III: 348.
Miles, Warren, (Pvt, Co B, 59th NCST, 4th Cav), V: 659.
Milford Station, Va., I: 428; II: 679, III: 10, 585, 592; IV: 150.
Military Conscription, IV: 2, 407.
Military Courts, V: 8.
Military Equipment, I: 34; III: 542; V: 471.
Militia, Archer's, II: 621.
Militia, The, N.C., I: v, xiii, 40, 41, 74, 337; II: 401; IV: 224, 372, 645-647, 652; V: 5, 25, 466, 477.
Militia, N.C., Regiments:
13th N.C. Militia, IV: 645.
____ N.C. Militia, (Bertie County), IV: 646; V: 6.
____ N.C. Militia, (Cape Fear Minute Men), V: 24, 25.
____ N.C. Militia, (Edgecombe County), V: 6.
____ N.C. Militia, (Guilford County), V: 629.
____ N.C. Militia, (H.J.B. Clark's), IV: 647.
15th N.C. Militia, (Halifax County, Lower), IV: 645; V: 6.
____ N.C. Militia, (Halifax County, Upper), IV: 645.
____ N.C. Militia, (Martin County), IV: 646; V: 7.
____ N.C. Militia, (Northampton County), IV: 645; V: 6.
____ N.C. Militia, (Smithville

Guards), V: 24, 25.
____ N.C. Militia, (Warren County), IV: 645; V: 6.
____ N.C. Militia, (Washington County), IV: 646; V: 6.
30th N.C. Militia, (New Hanover County), V: 25, 27.
Militia, Ohio, IV: 678, 680, 683.
Militia, Pennsylvania, IV: 238; V: 130.
Militia, Smith's, (Ga.), III: 179, 180.
Millburn, Va., I: 753.
Mill Creek, N.C., III: 759, 760; V: 654.
Mill Spring, Tenn., III: 677.
Millard, Dr. D.T., (Maj, 9th/20th Battalion NCST), III: 496; IV: 3, 386, 587.
Millboro, Va., IV: 149.
Millen, Ga., II: 757; IV: 327.
Miller, ______, (Resident of Shelby), IV: 202.
Miller, Rev. ______, (Capt, 4th NCST), IV: 605.
Miller, A., (Pvt, Co E, 32nd NCST), V: 496.
Miller, A.H., [A.A.], (Capt, Co K, 57th NCST), IV: 700, 709.
Miller, A.P., (Pvt, Co E, 2nd Vols/12th NCST), V: 507.
Miller, Alfred, (Capt, Co K, 57th NCST), III: 405, 409.
Miller, Alexander, (Capt, Co K, 2nd NCST), I: 164; IV: 700, 709.
Miller, Alexander, (Lt Col, 11th Vols/21st NCST), II: 138, 144; V: 12.
Miller, B.F., (Capt, Co H, 10th NCST, 1st Art & Engs, Pool's Hvy Art), I: 501, 515, 522, 525, 526, 536.
Miller, C.A., (2nd Lt, Co G, 42nd NCST), II: 791.
Miller, Caleb A., (Pvt, Co D., 10th NCST, 1st Art & Engs, Reilly-Ramsay's Battery, Light Art), V: 568.
Miller, D., (Pvt, Co H, 56th NCST), III: 348.
Miller, D.M., (Lt, Co E, 2nd Vols/12th NCST), I: 621.
Miller, David L., (Musician, 6th Vols/16th NCST), V: 552.
Miller, DeWitt C., (Pvt, Co D, 68th NCST), III: 715.
Miller, Eli H., (Lt Col, 34th NCST), II: 581, 585; IV: 159, 164; V: 12.
Miller, Frank M., (Sgt Maj, 6th Battalion/60th NCST), III: 484, 483, 492, 493.
Miller, G.C., (1st Lt, Co K, 34th NCST), V: 548.
Miller, G.P., (Pvt, Co E, 2nd Vols/12th NCST), V: 507.
Miller, George W., (Pvt, Co L, 11th Vols/21st NCST), V: 515.
Miller, Gibson L., (Musician, 33rd NCST), II: 538; V: 543.
Miller, H.C., (Sgt, Co B, 4th NCST), I: 232.
Miller, H.W., (2nd Lt, Co G, 42nd NCST), II: 791.
Miller, Henry, (Pvt, Co D, 10th NCST, 1st Art & Engs, Reilly-Ramsay's Battery, Light Art), I: 574.
Miller, Henry, (Pvt, Co H, 63rd NCST), III: 587.
Miller, Henry M., (Maj, Commissary, Ramseur-Cox's Brigade), I: 540; IV: 462, 463; V: 483.
Miller, J.H., (Capt, Co A, 11th Vols/21st NCST), II: 145; V: 515, 516, 518.
Miller, J.M., (Pvt, Co H, 28th NCST), V: 542.
Miller, J.O., (Capt, Co E, 10th NCST, 1st Art & Engs, Moore-Miller's Battery, Light Art), I: 581; V: 175.
Miller, J.R., (Pvt, Co I, 27th NCST), II: 462; V: 524.
Miller, J.S.R., (Capt, Adjt, 1st NCST), I: 136, 137, 142, 148.

Miller, Jacob H., (1st Lt, Co F, 13th Vols/23rd NCST), II: 185.
Miller, Dr. James A., (Surg, 8th Vols/18th NCST; Surg, Branch-Lane's Brigade), II: 17, 20; IV: 472, 473, 635, 644.
Miller, James A., (1st Lt, Co K, 50th NCST), III: 203.
Miller, James, C., (Sgt, Co A, 34th NCST), V: 554.
Miller, James R., (Pvt, Co D, 56th NCST), III: 347, 370.
Miller, Jesse, (Capt, Co E, 31st NCST), II: 507.
Miller, Jesse W., (Capt, Co A & C, 57th NCST), III: 409.
Miller, John, (Musician, 46th NCST), V: 524.
Miller, John, (Sgt, Scout, 10th NCST, 1st Art & Engs, Pool's Hvy Art), I: 532, 533, 535.
Miller, John A., (Capt, Co I, 58th NCST), III: 433, 447.
Miller, John B., (Musician, 6th Vols/16th NCST), V: 552.
Miller, John E., (Capt, Co H, 53rd NCST), III: 263.
Miller, Dr. John F., (Surg, 34th NCST), II: 582; IV: 637.
Miller, John H., (Capt, Co A, 21st NCST), V: 511.
Miller, John M., (2nd Lt, Co E, 62nd Ga., Cav; Co K, 16th Battalion/75th NCST, 7th Cav; Capt, Co C, 9th NCST, 1st Cav), I: 418, 483, 484, 485; IV: 91.
Miller, Joseph C., (Lt, Co K, 7th NCST), I: 369.
Miller, L.W., (Pvt, Co A, 37th NCST), V: 545.
Miller, Lewis, (Pvt, Co F, 11th Vols/21st NCST), V: 514.
Miller, Nelson A., (Capt, Co B, Avery's 17th Battalion NCST), IV: 373, 375.
Miller, P.J., (Lt, Co G, 8th NCST), V: 194.
Miller, R., (Pvt, Co A, 37th NCST), V: 545.
Miller, S.E., (2nd Lt, Co D, 21st NCST), V: 511.
Miller, Thomas C., (Lt, Co K, 53rd NCST), I: 136; III: 264; IV: 700, 709.
Miller, Virgil P., (Musician, 33rd NCST), II: 538.
Miller, W.L., (Capt, Thomasville Rifles, 4th Vols/14th NCST), I: 124.
Miller, W.T., (Conscript; Detailed, Invalid Battalion), V: 571.
Miller, William J., (Capt, Co K, 53rd NCST), III: 264.
Miller, Willis L., (Pvt, Co F, 63rd NCST, 5th Cav), III: 594.
Millertown, Pa., III: 236.
Millet, H.H., (Musician, 53rd NCST), V: 501.
Millican, Daniel W., (Pvt, Co B, 38th NCST), V: 557.
Millican, L.S., [Mullican, Lewis S.], (Sgt, Co G, 4th NCST), I: 233.
Milligan, ______, (Capt, Signal Corps, ANV), II: 776.
Milliken, Samuel J., (Pvt, Co B, 6th Vols/16th NCST; Detailed, Invalid Battalion), V: 552, 571.
Milling, W.R., (Pvt, Co H, 13th Vols/23rd NCST), V: 510.
Mills, Dr. Columbus, (Surg, 6th Vols/16th NCST), I: 751, 771; IV: 138, 178, 634.
Mills, F.M., (Pvt, Co K, 4th NCST), V: 489.
Mills, George H., (Ordnance Officer, Pender's Brigade; 1st Lt, Co G, 6th Vols/16th NCST), IV: 137-219 personal account.
Mills, H.A., (Pvt, 24th Va.), V: 195.
Mills, J.P., (Musician, Co E, 53rd NCST), V: 502.
Mills, James L., (Pvt, Co I, 3rd NCST), V: 487.

Mills, Joseph C., (Capt, Co G, 6th Vols/16th NCST), IV: 170, 218.
Mills, Joseph C., (1st Lt, Co G, 33rd NCST), II: 540, 573, 578, 579.
Mills, Julius, (Pvt, Co I, 27th NCST), II: 462; NCST), V: 524.
Mills, Otis P., (Capt, Co G, 56th NCST), III: 315; V: 191.
Mills, Rufus, (Sgt, Co B, 4th NCST), I: 232.
Mills, W.C., (Pvt, Co I, 7th NCST), V: 572.
Mills Gap Road, N.C., III: 670.
Millsaps, J.F., (Cpl, Co A, 33rd NCST), V: 543.
Millsaps, J.T., (Pvt, Co A, 33rd NCST), V: 543.
Millsaps, Peter P., (Pvt, Co K, 34th NCST), V: 556.
Millstead, William H., (Cpl, Co A, 7th NCST), I: 378.
Millwood, Va., I: 579; II: 438, 609; III: 560, 750.
Milner, Dudley, (Yorkshireman), V: 418.
Milroy, Robert Huston, (Maj Gen, USA; Another of the several Federal officers, who, had he lived in any other era, would have been tried and convicted as a war criminal. There were few, if any, of the Rules and Articles of War which he did not violate on a regular basis), I: 147, 194, 310, 659, 718; II: 66, 233; III: 41, 270, 411, 559; IV: 254.
Milton, G., (Pvt, Co K, 28th NCST), V: 543.
Mine Run, Va., (and Battle of, 1863), I: 149, 171, 198, 255, 288, 334, 382, 485, 546, 639, 640, 720, 743; II: 45, 46, 74, 99, 120, 172, 227, 241, 445, 479, 569, 664; III: 7, 73, 94, 243-244, 258, 303, 585; IV: 186-188, 190, 506.
Mine Run Campaign, I: 171, 198, 288, 320, 428, 594; II: 120, 569, 587, 664; III: 7.
Minie, ______, (Capt, French Army, Inventor of the "Minie Ball"), I: 109.
Minish, A.W., (Pvt, Co H, 11th Vols/21st NCST), V: 515.
Minnesota, II: 367.
Minnesota Indians, III: 362.
Minor, Henry, (Pvt, Co H, 63rd NCST, 5th Cav), III: 587.
Minor, Richard V., (1st Lt, Co E, 13th Vols/23rd NCST), II: 185.
Minter, B.W., (Capt, Co E, 53rd NCST), III: 262; IV: 702.
Minton, A., (Pvt, Co H, 8th Vols/18th NCST), II: 64; V: 540.
Minton, Thomas, (Pvt, Co C, 26th NCST), II: 389.
Misenheimer, Daniel, (Pvt, Co D, 10th NCST, 1st Art & Engs, Reilly-Ramsay's Battery, Light Art), I: 574.
Misenheimer, G.A., (Pvt, Co K, 4th NCST), V: 489.
Misenheimer, George A., (4th Cpl, Co A, 52nd NCST), III: 223.
Misenheimer, J.M., (Sgt, Co A, 10th Vols/20th NCST), V: 508.
Misenheimer, James, (Pvt, Co H, 8th NCST), I: 401.
Misenheimer, Joseph F., (Cpl, Co C, 33rd NCST), II: 539, 578.
Missionary Ridge, Tenn., (and Battle of, 1863), III: 491, 500; III: 436, 437, 453, 491-492, 743; V: 173.
Mississippi, I: 70; II: 701, 712, 734, 737; III: 440, 499; IV: 35, 612; V: 653.
Mississippi River, II: 710, 712; III: 130, 307, 664; IV: 256; V: viii, 5, 653.
Missouri, II: 702; IV: 1, 35, 259, 704.
Missouri River, II: 701.
Mitchel, A.M., (Pvt, Co L, 11th Vols/21st NCST), V: 515.

Mitchel, B.A., (Sgt, Co L, 11th Vols/21st NCST), V: 515.
Mitchel, John H., (Sgt, Co G, 32nd NCST), V: 496.
Mitchel, William, (Pvt, Co B, 2nd Battalion NCST), V: 495.
Mitchell, _____, (Correspondent, New York Herald), IV: 240.
Mitchell, A.A., (Capt, Co H, 6th NCST; Capt, Co F, 77th NCST, 7th Senior Reserves), I: 296; IV: 100.
Mitchell, B.S., (Lt, Co G, 12th Vols/22nd NCST), II: 166.
Mitchell, Dr. Charles A., (Ass't Surg, 40th NCST, 3rd Art, Hvy), II: 745; IV: 638.
Mitchell, Charles S., (Pvt, Co D, 5th Vols/15th NCST), V: 521.
Mitchell, Henry, (Pvt, Co D, 68th NCST), III: 715.
Mitchell, J., (Pvt, Co C, 3rd Vols/13th NCST), V: 550.
Mitchell, J.H., (2nd Lt, Co E, 13th Vols/23rd NCST), II: 185.
Mitchell, James T., (Pvt, Co D, 2nd NCST), I: 176; V: 486.
Mitchell, James T., (Capt, Co C, 3rd Vols/13th NCST), I: 653.
Mitchell, James T., (Pvt, Co H, 56th NCST), V: 566.
Mitchell, James T., (Capt, Co B, 59th NCST, 4th Cav), III: 457.
Mitchell, John, (5th Sgt, Co E, 46th NCST), V: 524.
Mitchell, John, (Pvt, Co I, 1st NCST), V: 485.
Mitchell, Lueco, (2nd Lt, Co D, 10th NCST, 1st Art & Engs, Reilly-Ramsay's Battery, Light Art), I: 577.
Mitchell, M.H., (3rd Sgt, Co B, 44th NCST), V: 533.
Mitchell, Mason T., (1st Lt, Co H, 12th Vols/22nd NCST), II: 172.
Mitchell, Perry, (Pvt, Co D, 68th NCST), III: 715.
Mitchell, R.J., (Maj, 46th NCST), III: 64, 65, 81.
Mitchell, Robert L., (2nd Lt, Co G, 12th Vols/22nd NCST), II: 172.
Mitchell, Rush J., (1st Lt, Co G, 30th NCST), II: 496.
Mitchell, Sydney W., (Capt, Co H, 47th NCST), III: 85, 108.
Mitchell, Dr. T.J., (Ass't Surg, 58th NCST), III: 432; IV: 641.
Mitchell, W.L., (Lt Col, 12th Vols/22nd NCST), II: 166, 171, 178; V: 547.
Mitchell, W.S., (Capt, Co B, 66th NCST), III: 686.
Mitchell County, N.C., II: 331, 493; III: 431, 432, 447, 719; IV: 271, 371, 373, 374.
Mitchell's Ford, (Bull Run Creek, Va.), I: 149, 199; II: 130; IV: 226.
Mitchell's Sound, N.C., II: 293.
Mitchner, R.S., (Pvt, Co E, 5th Vols/15th NCST), V: 521.
Mitchener's Station, N.C., (aka Mitchner's Depot), III: 515; IV: 21, 31.
Mitchie, Dr. James, (Surg, 59th NCST, 4th Cav), III: 457; IV: 641.
Mittag, W. McK., (2nd Lt, Co H, 34th NCST), V: 548.
Mix, _____, (Col, USA, Mix's Cav), II: 84.
Mizel, _____, (Lt, USA, at Plymouth), III: 552.
Mizel, Alfred, (Capt, Co H, 1st NCST), I: 137, 150; V: 484.
Mizel, J.R., (1st Lt, Co H, 1st NCST), I: 137, 150.
Mizzell, Adolphus, (Pvt, Co B, 9th NCST, 1st Cav), V: 657.
Moad, John, (Pvt, Co C, 10th NCST, 1st Art & Engs, Brem-Graham-Williams' Battery, Light Art), V: 568.
Mobile, Ala., (City, Bay and Wharf), II: 492, 737; III: 486;

IV: 329, 424, 442, 684, 687; V: 386, 412, 420, 424.
Mobley, Dr. John C., (Surg, Starr's 13th Battalion NCST, Light Art), IV: 341, 644.
Mock, C.S., (Pvt, Co B, 1st Battalion NCST), V: 504.
Mock, J.A., (Pvt, Co E, Beale's 10th Va., Cav, a N.C. company), V: 569.
Mocksville, N.C., II: 806; III: 590, 655.
Model Farm, (nr Petersburg), II: 271.
Moffat, ______, (Maj, QM, Salisbury Prison), IV: 758, 759.
Moffitt, A.A., [Alfred A.], (Capt, Co F, 8th Vols/18th NCST), IV: 702, 708.
Moffitt, E.A., (2nd Lt, Co H, 44th NCST), III: 23.
Moffitt, Dr. G.B., (Ass't Surg, 37th NCST), IV: 474.
Moffitt, M.H., (Sgt, Co F, 2nd Battalion NCST), V: 495.
Moffitt, William D., (Capt, Co H, 44th NCST), III: 23.
Moir, R.L., (Capt, Co H, 3rd Vols/13th NCST), I: 698; V: 547.
Moltz, Mayfield, (Pvt, Co C, 10th NCST, 1st Art & Engs, Brem-Graham-Williams' Battery, Light Art), V: 568.
Monday, W.F., (Pvt, Co E, 37th NCST), V: 545.
Monday's, N.C., IV: 381.
Money, H., (Pvt, Co H, 54th NCST), V: 516.
Monie, J.M., [Cpl], (Pvt, Co H, 9th NCST, 1st Cav), V: 593.
Monk, C.B., (Capt, Corps of Engineers), IV: 420.
Monk's Neck, Va., I: 434.
Monk's Neck Bridge, Va., III: 30, 628; V: 207.
Monocacy, Md., (aka Monocacy Junction, Monocacy Bridge, and Battle of, 1864), I: 154, 172, 206, 259, 306, 324, 334, 645; II: 32, 122, 141, 184, 245, 246, 274, 290, 431, 531, 601; III: 13, 55, 67, 278, 419, 750; IV: 525.
Monocacy River, Md., I: 172, 206, 694, 739; II: 32, 601.
Monroe, C.S., (Jr 2nd Lt, Co I, 6th Battalion/60th NCST), III: 475.
Monroe, D.A., (Capt, Co K, 38th NCST), I: 119; II: 678.
Monroe, Malcolm N., (2nd Lt, Co B, 6th Battalion/60th NCST), IV: 296.
Monroe, Neill J., (Lt, Co E, 8th NCST), I: 390.
Monroe, Neill L., (Artificer, 6th Battalion NCST, Fayetteville Armory Guard), IV: 296.
Monroe, Thomas J., (4th Cpl, Co C, 52nd NCST), III: 224.
Monroe, N.C., II: 627; IV: 431.
Monroe, Va., III: 321.
Monroe County, Tenn., III: 730.
Monroe Street, (Plymouth), V: 176, 189.
Montague, A.B., (Pvt, Co A, 44th NCST), V: 533.
Montague, E.B., (Maj, Montague's Battalion, Va.), I: 83, 89, 91, 93, 94, 105.
Montague, P.H., (Capt, Co E, 82nd NCST, Detailed Men), IV: 132.
Montague, T.J., (Pvt, Co D, 54th NCST), V: 516.
Montague, T.J., (Sgt, Co H, 56th NCST), III: 356.
Monteith, R.J., (Pvt, Co A, 1st Vols/11th NCST), V: 530.
Monterey, Va., IV: 139, 140.
Montgomery, A.D., (Pvt, Co A, 3rd Vols/13th NCST; 1st Lt, ADC, Scales' Brigade), IV: 553; V: 547.
Montgomery, Dr. D.A., (Surg, 3rd Vols/13th NCST), IV: 633.
Montgomery, G.W., (Cpl, Co D, 56th NCST), III: 347.

Montgomery, George W., (2nd Lt, Co F, 44th NCST), III: 23, 347.
Montgomery, J., (Pvt, Co A, 53rd NCST), III: 264.
Montgomery, J.T., (Pvt, Co A, 53rd NCST; Detailed, Invalid Battalion NCST), V: 571.
Montgomery, J.W., (Pvt, Co A, 53rd NCST), V: 501.
Montgomery, John C., (1st Lt, Co F, 44th NCST), III: 23.
Montgomery, N.G., (Pvt, Co A, 1st Battalion NCST), V: 504.
Montgomry, R.C., (Pvt, Co F, 2nd Vols/12th NCST), V: 507.
Montgomery, Robert C., (Pvt, Co F, 2nd Vols/12th NCST), V: 265, 266.
Montgomery, Thomas, (Pvt, Co K, 32nd NCST), V: 497.
Montgomery, W., (2nd Lt, Co C, 13th Vols/23rd NCST), II: 184.
Montgomery, Walter A., (2nd Lt, Co F, 2nd Vols/12th NCST), I: 605, 651; V: 257-268 personal account, 503.
Montgomery, William J., (Maj, 28th NCST), II: 465, 466, 467; IV: 473; V: 651.
Montgomery, Dr. William T., (Surg, 48th NCST), IV: 639; V: 520.
Montgomery County, N.C., II: 206, 234, 586; III: 78; IV: 760.
Monterey Springs, Md., II: 238.
Montgomery, Ala., I: 80, 81, 551; II: 190, 403, 597.
Monticello, Ky., III: 662; IV: 271, 273.
Moody, ______, (Capt, Co D, 10th NCST, 1st Art & Engs, Ramseur-Manly's Battery, Light Art), I: 565.
Moody, J.H., (1st Lt, Co E, 69th NCST, Thomas' Legion), III: 730.
Moody, J.J., (Pvt, Co H, 46th NCST), V: 525.
Moody, J.M., (Pvt, Co E, 6th NCST), V: 512.
Moody, John A., (Capt, Co K, 28th NCST), II: 466.
Moody, John M., (Resident of Weldon, His property was the site of Camp Daniel), IV: 10.
Moody, Thomas W., (1st Lt, Co D, Webb's Battery, Bogg's 12th Battalion Va., Hvy Art; Co A, Webb's Battery, Starr's 13th Battalion NCST, Light Art), IV: 355.
Moody, Dr. William S., (2nd Lt, Co E; Ass't Surg, 56th NCST), III: 315; IV: 630.
Moody's Farm, (nr Gettysburg, Pa.), III: 331, 335, 337.
Moon, E.L., (Pvt, Co A, 12th Vols/22nd NCST), V: 553.
Moon, L., (Pvt, Co G, 26th NCST), V: 527.
Mooney, A., (Pvt, Co B, 55th NCST), V: 533.
Mooney, Isaac, (Pvt, Co F, 34th NCST), V: 555.
Mooneyham, Gaston H., (Pvt, Co E, 47th NCST), III: 112.
Moore, ______, (Lt, Artillery, at Hatteras), V: 48.
Moore, Alexander Duncan, (Capt, Co E, 49th NCST; Col, 66th NCST), I: 581; II: 3, 497; III: 152, 685, 686, 688, 692; IV: 270, 302, 527, 530, 532, 538; V: 10.
Moore, Alexander S., (Cpl, Co E, 5th Vols/15th NCST), V: 521.
Moore, Andrew J., (Capt, Co F, 61st NCST), III: 504.
Moore, Augustus M., (Adjt, 3rd Battalion NCST, Light Art), IV: 261, 266, 267.
Moore, Hon. B.F. (Adjt, 6th Vols/16th NCST), I: 17, 20, 45.
Moore, B.F., (Board of Auditors), I: 20, 28, 31, 753.
Moore, B.R., (Lt Col, 41st NCST, 3rd Cav), V: 650.

Moore, Benjamin, (Capt, Co B, 62nd NCST), III: 515.
Moore, Benjamin F., (1st Lt, Co H, 43rd NCST), III: 3; V: 494.
Moore, Carroll, (Father of James D. Moore), II: 331.
Moore, D., (Pvt, Co K, 35th NCST), V: 193.
Moore, D.A., (Jr 2nd Lt, Co K, 38th NCST), II: 676.
Moore, D.O.H.P., (Pvt, Co H, 28th NCST), V: 542.
Moore, Daniel M., (Sgt, Co C, 33rd NCST), II: 539.
Moore, Daniel W., (Ensign, 33rd NCST), II: 537.
Moore, E., (Pvt, Co A, 28th NCST), V: 540.
Moore, E.H., (2nd Lt, Co B, 7th Battalion Junior Reserves; Co D, 72nd NCST, 3rd Junior Reserves), IV: 40.
Moore, Edward, (AQMS, 28th NCST), II: 465.
Moore, Edwin S., (Adjt, 10th Vols/20th NCST), II: 125; III: 112, 122, 124.
Moore, F.M., (2nd Lt, Co H, 30th NCST), II: 497.
Moore, Francis, (Pvt, Co D, 4th Vols/14th NCST), V: 490.
Moore, Fred W., (Capt, Co E, 1st NCST), I: 137; V: 484.
Moore, G.B., (1st Lt, Co G, 53rd NCST), III: 263.
Moore, G.M., Sr., (Pvt, Co H, 28th NCST), V: 542.
Moore, H.C., (Pvt, Co I, 53rd NCST), V: 501.
Moore, H.C., (Lt, Adjt, 38th NCST), II: 693; IV: 700, 709.
Moore, Henry, (Pvt, Co K, 43rd NCST), V: 499.
Moore, Henry, (Pvt, Co E, 8th Vols/18th NCST), II: 64; V: 539.
Moore, Henry H., (Teamster, Co H, 8th NCST, Detailed, QM Corps), V: 571.
Moore, Hugh, (Pvt, Co C, 35th NCST), V: 562.
Moore, Hugh, (Pvt, Co E, 45th NCST), V: 500.
Moore, J.E., (2nd Lt, Co K, 41st NCST, 3rd Cav), II: 772.
Moore, J.F., (Pvt, Co D, 44th NCST), V: 533.
Moore, J.F., (Pvt, Co E, 41st NCST, 3rd Cav; Detailed, Invalid Battalion), V: 571.
Moore, J.F., (Capt, Co G, 61st NCST), III: 504.
Moore, J.M., (Pvt, Co B, 1st NCST), V: 485.
Moore, J.M., (2nd Lt, Co B, 30th NCST), II: 496.
Moore, J.P., (Chaplain, 11th Vols/21st NCST), IV: 609.
Moore, J.S., (Pvt, Co K, 5th Vols/15th NCST), V: 522.
Moore, J.T., (Pvt, Co B, 56th NCST), III: 347.
Moore, James, (Lt, 5th NCST), IV: 709.
Moore, James D., (Pvt, Co F, 26th NCST), II: 330, 331, 369; V: 600-601, 603.
Moore, James V., (2nd Lt, Co K, 19th NCST, 2nd Cav), II: 80.
Moore, Jesse S., (Ordnance Sgt, 6th Vols/16th NCST), V: 551.
Moore, John, (Pvt, Co I, 45th NCST), V: 500.
Moore, John, (Capt, Co I, 48th NCST), III: 117.
Moore, John, (Lt, Co H, 64th NCST), III: 660.
Moore, John, (Capt, Co E, 8th Vols/18th NCST), IV: 701, 708.
Moore, John E., (Sgt Maj, 26th NCST), II: 396.
Moore, John M., (Pvt, Co F, 44th NCST), V: 534.

Moore, John R., (Adjt, 16th Battalion/75th NCST, 7th Cav), IV: 72, 93.
Moore, John T., (Pvt, Co F, 44th NCST), V: 534.
Moore, John W., (Maj, 3rd Battalion NCST, Light Art), I: 19, 705; III: 674, 675; IV: 261, 263, 264, 265, 267, 268; V: 651.
Moore, John W., (See: Julius W.).
Moore, John W., (Capt, ACS, 19th NCST, 2nd Cav), II: 79.
Moore, John W., (Col, 203rd Pa.), V: 238.
Moore, Joseph, (Pvt, Co I, 43rd NCST), V: 499.
Moore, Julian G., (Capt, Co C, Moore's 3rd Battalion NCST, Light Art), IV: 262, 264, 265.
Moore, Julius W., (Capt, Co H, 41st NCST, 3rd Cav), III: 674; IV: 721; V: 256.
Moore, L., [Leander], (1st Lt, Co E, 3rd NCST), I: 213.
Moore, Lewis H., (Cpl, Co G, 33rd NCST), II: 540.
Moore, M.V., (Capt, AQM, 65th NCST), I: ix; III: 673, 674, 675, 677, 681, 683, 683.
Moore, Matthew C., (Capt, Co I, 11th Vols/21st NCST), II: 145.
Moore, N.M., [N.W.], (Capt, Co B, 62nd NCST), IV: 709.
Moore, R.H., (Col, 65th Ga.), III: 435.
Moore, R.N., (Sgt, Co A, 49th NCST), V: 564.
Moore, Robert G., (Pvt, Co E, 5th Vols/15th NCST), V: 521.
Moore, Roger, (Lt Col, 41st NCST, 3rd Cav), I: 442, 443, 480, 778, 779, 780; II: 769, 780; IV: 349.
Moore, S.A., (Pvt, Co A, 3rd Vols/13th NCST), V: 549.
Moore, Dr. S.P., (Surg Gen, CSA), IV: 626, 627.
Moore, S.R., (Capt, Co F, 30th NCST), II: 495, 496, 503; V: 484.
Moore, Samuel, (Pvt, Co F, 43rd NCST), V: 498.
Moore, Simeon, [Simon], (Pvt, Co B, 2nd NCST; Detailed, 2nd Corps Provost Guard), I: 175; V: 486, 570.
Moore, Simon H., (Sgt, Co E, 5th Vols/15th NCST), V: 521.
Moore, Styring S., (Chaplain, 26th NCST), II: 396.
Moore, Rev. Dr. Theophilus W., (1st Lt, Chaplain, 13th Vols/23rd NCST), II: 185, 189; IV: 610.
Moore, Thomas C., (1st Lt, Co I, 10th NCST, 1st Art & Engs, Sutherland's Battery, Light Art), I: 582; IV: 221, 222.
Moore, Thomas J., (Lt, Artillery Officer to D.H. Hill), I: 117, 118.
Moore, Thomas J., (Adjt, 59th NCST, 4th Cav), III: 456.
Moore, Thomas J., (1st Lt, Co C, 33rd NCST), II: 539, 578.
Moore, Thomas L., (Lt, CSN), IV: 404.
Moore, W.A., (1st Lt, Co B, 66th NCST), III: 686.
Moore, W.H., (Chaplain, 12th Vols/22nd NCST), III: 730; IV: 610.
Moore, W.M.B., (Maj, 30th NCST), II: 495, 496; IV: 462.
Moore, W.P., (2nd Lt, Co A, 19th NCST, 2nd Cav), II: 80.
Moore, W.P., (Pvt, Co H, 6th Battalion/60th NCST), III: 482.
Moore, W.P., (Capt, Co E, 51st NCST), III: 219.
Moore, W.P., (Capt, Co F, 63rd NCST, 5th Cav), II: 88; III: 588, 674, 675, 684.
Moore, Walter R., Jr., (Lt, Sharpshooters 5th NCST), I: 290.
Moore, William, (Pvt, Co D, 6th Vols/16th NCST), IV: 198.

Moore, William H., (Chaplain, 12th Vols/22nd NCST), IV: 610.
Moore County, N.C., I: 386; II: 303, 359, 418, 421, 627; III: 78, 125, 319, 512; IV: 299.
Moore's Bridge, Battle of, Revolution, II: 359.
Moore's Mill, Va., II: 782.
Moore's Roster, (aka Roster of North Carolina Troops), I: 7, 13, 14, 16, 23, 114, 133, 295, 339, 414, 705, 734; II: 113, 145, 161, 205, 214, 224, 231, 395, 496, 578, 583, 589, 703, 768, 770; III: 1, 115, 318, 517, 530, 549, 674, 675, 701, 715, 722, 761; IV: 6, 7, 65, 99, 100, 107, 108, 119, 270, 301, 315, 316, 337, 339, 341, 342, 383, 385, 393, 395, 403, 404, 407, 609, 610, 612, 628; V: 313.
Mooreman, Rev. _____, (Tract Society at Richmond), IV: 765.
Mooresville, N.C., V: 665.
Moose, G.W., (Pvt, Co A, 2nd Vols/12th NCST), V: 506.
Moose, W.A., (Musician, 4th NCST), I: 234.
Mooser, W.H., (Pvt, Co K, 46th NCST), V: 525.
Mooter, C.H., (Sgt, Co M, 11th Vols/21st NCST), V: 515.
Moran, Rev. Dr. R.S., (Chaplain, 50th NCST), III: 161, 202; IV: 617.
Moravian Falls, N.C., V: 292.
Morehead, Hon. J.M., (Governor of North Carolina and father of J. Turner Morehead), I: 64; III: 575, 586.
Morehead, J.M., (Lt Col, 55th NCST), I: 160, 161.
Morehead, James T., (Col, 53rd NCST), III: 36, 52, 255, 256, 257, 259, 260, 264, 265; V: 650.
Morehead, John Henry, (Col, 45th NCST), I: 160, 161; III: 35, 36, 37, 163; V: 10, 650.
Morehead, Joseph M., (Lt, Co E, 2nd NCST), I: 161.
Morehead, J. Turner, (Lt, Adjt, 63rd NCST, 5th Cav), III: 465, 529, 534, 536, 551, 575.
Morehead City, N.C., (See also: Carolina City), I: 503; II: 84, 307, 308, 309, 594, 629, 751, 777; III: 132, 133; IV: 74, 265, 266, 487, 528; V: 19.
Morell, George Webb, (Maj Gen, USA), I: 609; II: 213.
Moreno, _____, [Celestino S.], (2nd Lt, Co G, 6th Battalion/60th NCST), III: 494.
Morgan, _____, (Capt, Ky.), V: 620.
Morgan, D.S., (Pvt, Co C, 32nd NCST), V: 496.
Morgan, E.W., (1st Lt, Co C, 69th NCST, Thomas' Legion), III: 730.
Morgan, George W., (Pvt, Co D, 57th NCST), V: 517.
Morgan, George, (Pvt, Co F, 26th NCST), V: 602.
Morgan, George Washington, (Brig Gen, USA), II: 487, 708, 728.
Morgan, Grey, (Pvt, Co F, 30th NCST), V: 492.
Morgan, H.P., (Pvt, Co C, 32nd NCST), V: 496.
Morgan, J.B., (Lt, Co F, 58th NCST), III: 433.
Morgan, J.L., (Pvt, Co E, Color-bearer, 6th Battalion/60th NCST), III: 477, 482.
Morgan, James, (Pvt, Co A, 47th NCST), V: 534.
Morgan, John, (Pvt, Co E, 6th Battalion/60th NCST), III: 482.
Morgan, John, (Pvt, Co A, 47th NCST), V: 534.
Morgan, John A., (Lt, Adjt, 1st NCST), I: 136, 147.
Morgan, John H., (Brig Gen), IV: 115, 275, 276, 682, 683, 715; V: 382.

Morgan, Joseph, (Pvt, Co D, 10th NCST, 1st Art & Engs, Reilly-Ramsay's Battery, Light Art), V: 568.
Morgan, Nathan, (Pvt, Co H, 5th NCST), I: 292; V: 505.
Morgan, R.H., (Pvt, Co C, 32nd NCST), V: 496
Morgan, T.L., (Pvt, Co H, 4th NCST), V: 489.
Morgan, W.Y., (Maj, 25th NCST), II: 292.
Morgan, Washington, (Maj), II: 729.
Morgan, Whitfield, (1st Lt, Co 6, Henry's 14th Battalion; Co D, 79th NCST, 8th Cav), IV: 113, 114.
Morgan, Z., (Pvt, Co K, 56th NCST), III: 357.
Morganton, N.C., II: 293; III: 718, 720; IV: 4, 41, 116, 218, 271, 372, 373, 376, 379, 382, 386, 605, 652, 653; V: 654.
Moring, John H., (Pvt, Co A, 10th NCST, 1st Art & Engs, Ramseur-Manly's Battery, Light Art), I: 557.
Moring, John J., (Cpl, Co H, 47th NCST), V: 535.
Morphis, G.B., (Pvt, Co H, 3rd Vols/13th NCST), V: 551.
Morphis, S.F., (Pvt, Co H, 3rd Vols/13th NCST), V: 551.
Morrell, ______, (Engineer, Atlanta), IV: 742.
Morrill, W.H., (Capt, ACS, 27th NCST), II: 425, 426, 437; IV: 512.
Morris, A.F., (Pvt, Co I, 6th NCST), V: 513.
Morris, B.T., (Capt, Co A & E, 64th NCST), III: 659, 660, 665, 666, 667, 670, 671.
Morris, Calvin J., (QMS, 41st NCST, 3rd Cav), II: 769.
Morris, D.W., (Pvt, Co H, 35th NCST), V: 563.
Morris, E.W., (Pvt, Co C, 6th NCST), V: 512.
Morris, H.R., (1st Lt, Co B, Indian Co, 69th NCST, Thomas' Legion), III: 730.
Morris, Isaac E., (2nd Lt, Co K, 12th Vols/22nd NCST), II: 165,166.
Morris, J.A., Sr., (2nd Lt, Co E, 5th Vols/15th NCST), I: 735; V: 519.
Morris, J.A., (Pvt, Co F, 35th NCST), V: 563.
Morris, J.E., (Pvt, Co K, 10th Vols/20th NCST), V: 509.
Morris, J.W., (Lt, Co E, 64th NCST), III: 660.
Morris, James H., (Capt, Co F, 43rd NCST), I: 119; III: 3, 11.
Morris, John F., (Pvt, Co H, 14th Vols/24th NCST), V: 560.
Morris, Norman G., (Pvt, Co A, 4th Vols/14th NCST), V: 489.
Morris, Richard T., (Cpl, Co H, 34th NCST), V: 556.
Morris, S.E., (Pvt, Co H, 35th NCST), V: 563.
Morris, T.W., (Pvt, Co H, 46th NCST), V: 525.
Morris, Thomas A., (Pvt, Co K, 10th Vols/20th NCST), II: 119.
Morris, W.G.B., (Capt, Co B, 64th NCST), III: 516, 660; IV: 702, 709.
Morris, W.L., (Lt, Co E, 64th NCST), III: 660; IV: 700, 708.
Morris, Washington, (Surg, Henry's 14th Battalion, 79th NCST, 8th Cav), IV: 643.
Morris, William, (Pvt, Co E, 56th NCST), V: 566.
Morris, William G., [Morriss], (Lt Col, 37th NCST), II: 672; IV: 474; V: 154.
Morris Island, S.C., I: 392, 393, 394, 395; II: 514, 757; III: 206, 207, 209, 210, 510, 511, 590;

IV: 485, 486, 505; V: 161, 167, 619, 620, 621, 678.
Morris Island Prison, (After the capture of Morris Island by Federal forces a prison was established to house Confederate troops. Against the Rules and Articles of War and International law gun emplacements were erected at the prison site. Because of this the prisoners held there were under the constant danger of being bombarded. In the most real of terms Federal soldiers used prisoners as human shields.), II: 184, 185, 244; IV: 713-724; V: ix, 619-625.
Morris' Mill, Va., III: 635.
Morrisett, Stephen W., (Capt, Co F, 31st NCST), II: 507, 512.
Morrisey, D.G., (1st Lt, Co A, 38th NCST), II: 675, 678.
Morrisey, Dr. Samuel B., (Surg, 51st NCST), III: 205; IV: 640.
Morrisitt, Willis, (2nd Lt, Co B, 68th NCST), III: 713; IV: 640.
Morrison, ______, [James J.], (Col, 1st Ga. Cav), III: 679.
Morrison, A., (Pvt, Co H, 54th NCST), V: 516.
Morrison, A.A., (Pvt, Co E, 37th NCST), V: 545.
Morrison, Alexander S., (Pvt, Co C, 4th Vols/14th NCST), I: 731; V: 490.
Morrison, Daniel, (Pvt, Co A, Webb's Battery, Starr's 13th Battalion NCST, Light Art), V: 282.
Morrison, E.F., (Sgt, Co A, 4th NCST), I: 232.
Morrison, Elam F., (Ordnance Sgt, Co A, 4th NCST), I: 230; V: 488.
Morrison, George, (Capt, Chief Engineer, Advance), V: 361, 363.
Morrison, J.D., (Lt, Co F, 58th NCST), III: 433, 435.
Morrison, J.M., (Pvt, Co A, 49th NCST), V: 564.
Morrison, John A., (1st Lt, Co G, 50th NCST), III: 203.
Morrison, Joseph G., (Capt, Co F, 57th NCST, Adjt, 57th NCST, ADC to Stonewall Jackson, brother-in-law to Jackson and D.H. Hill, on Hoke's Staff), II: 558; III: 427.
Morrison, L., (Pvt, Co H, 37th NCST), V: 546.
Morrison, Thomas W., (Pvt, Co C, 4th Vols/14th NCST), V: 490.
Morrison, Dr. Washington, (Surg, Henry's 14th Battalion, 79th NCST, 8th Cav), IV: 113.
Morrison, William W., (Capt, N.C. Subsistence Department), I: 37.
Morriss, D.D., (Pvt, Co H, 46th NCST), V: 525.
Morriss, E., (Pvt, Co G, 3rd Vols/13th NCST), V: 551.
Morriss, W.B.D., (Pvt, Co E, 7th NCST), V: 538.
Morriss, William E., (Pvt, Co H, 4th Vols/14th NCST), V: 490.
Morristown, Tenn., III: 664, 665, 756.
Morrisville, N.C., IV: 430.
Morrow, ______, (Outlaw), II: 301.
Morrow, B.F., (Capt, Co K, 30th NCST), II: 496.
Morrow, D.F., (1st Lt, Co G, 28th NCST), II: 483; V: 538.
Morrow, G.W., (Pvt, Co I, 7th NCST), V: 539.
Morrow, Henry A., (Col, 24th Mi.), II: 355, 356.
Morrow, J.L., (Lt, Co C, 9th NCST, 1st Cav), I: 435, 452, 470, 485.
Morrow, W.J., (2nd Sgt, Co G, 44th NCST), V: 534.
Morrow, Dr. William H., (Ass't Surg, 67th NCST), III: 703; IV: 642.

Morse, C.C., (Pilot, CSN, Cornubia, Kate, Advance), V: 357. 406, 407.
Mortar Bed, The, (nr Petersburg, Va.), III: 370.
Mortar Hill, (nr Petersburg, Va.), II: 289; III: 690.
Morton, A.B., (Pvt, Co C, 4th Vols/14th NCST), I: 731.
Morton, Alexander B., (1st Cpl, Co C, 4th Vols/14th NCST), V: 490.
Morton, Dr. Charles S., (Surg, 57th NCST), III: 405, 427; IV: 641.
Morton, George A., (Pvt, Co C, 4th Vols/14th NCST), I: 731; V: 490.
Morton, J., (Musician, Co K, 28th NCST), V: 543.
Morton, J.J., (Pvt, Co I, 56th NCST), III: 357.
Morton, Jacob, (Pvt, Co G, 3rd NCST), V: 487.
Morton, P.F., (Pvt, Co C, 4th Vols/14th NCST), I: 732.
Morton, Peter F., (4th Sgt, Co C, 4th Vols/14th NCST), V: 490.
Morton, W.A., (2nd Lt, Co C, 42nd NCST), II: 790.
Morton's Ford, (Rappahannock River, Va.), I: 381, 382, 639; II: 119, 120, 478, 568, 662; III: 42.
Mosby, John S., (Col, Mosby's Partisan Rangers), II: 150, 152; III: 534, 625, 750.
Mosely, Richard E., (Capt, Co , 12th Va.), IV: 403.
Moseley, ______, (Maj, Moseley's Art Battalion), I: 581, 582.
Moseley, A.G., (Capt, Co A, 38th NCST), II: 675, 678.
Moseley, C.T., (Pvt, Co K, 5th Vols/15th NCST), V: 522.
Moseley, J.H., (Pvt, Co E, 10th Vols/20th NCST), V: 509.
Moseley, Nathan S., (1st Lt, Co F, Sharpshooters, 2nd Vols/12th NCST), I: 97, 630, 639, 642; IV: 722; V: 184.
Moseley, Richard E., (Capt, 61st Va.), IV: 403; V: 569.
Mosley's Creek, N.C., (nr Kinston), III: 553.
Mosely Hall, [Moseley], (now LaGrange), III: 553; IV: 54, 263-265, 383.
Moser, Dan, (Pvt, Co I, 57th NCST), V: 518.
Moser, Israel, (2nd Lt, Co H, 77th NCST, 7th Senior Reserves), IV: 100.
Moser, James K., (Pvt, Co I, 11th Vols/21st NCST), V: 515.
Moses, G.C., (Col, 2nd Regt, Home Guard), IV: 650, 653.
Moss, A.A., (Col, 76th NCST, 6th Senior Reserves), IV: 97.
Moss, H.R., (Pvt, Co C, 2nd Vols/12th NCST), V: 507.
Moss, Kit, (Pilot, CSN, Advance), V: 336.
Moss, Ira J., (Pvt, Co C, 2nd Vols/12th NCST), V: 507.
Moss, J.C., (Lt, Co C, 39th NCST), II: 729.
Moss, J.E., (Pvt, Co C, 2nd Vols/12th NCST), V: 507.
Moss, Patterson, (Pvt, 65th NCST, 6th Cav), III: 680.
Moss, Peter M., (Ordnance Sgt, 5th Vols/15th NCST), I: 734; V: 520.
Moss, W.B., (Pvt, Co B, 6th NCST), V: 512.
Moss Neck, Va., I: 375; II: 72, 476, 477, 558, 559, 562, 586, 658, 660, 687; IV: 171.
Moss Neck Church, Va., IV: 172.
Motley, John, (Pvt, Co D, 45th NCST), V: 500.
Motley, T., (Pvt, Co K, 28th NCST), V: 543.
Mott, Gershom, (Maj Gen, USA), II: 47; III: 631.
Mott, Dr. Walter B., (Ass't Surg, 5th Vols/15th NCST), I: 734; IV: 634.

Mount, S.G.R., (AQM, 39th NCST), II: 707.
Mount, Samuel S.C., (Capt, Co C, 39th NCST), II: 705, 737.
Mount Airy, N.C., V: 285.
Mount Holly, N.C., IV: 611.
Mount Jackson, Va., I: 155, 209; II: 258, 261; III: 15, 278, 279, 280; IV: 603.
Mount Olive, N.C., III: 693; IV: 420.
Mount Pleasant, S.C., I: 395; II: 514.
Mount Pleasant Pike, Tenn., III: 438.
Mount Sidney, Va., I: 262; II: 258.
Mount Vernon, Ky., IV: 286, 287.
Mount Tabor, N.C., II: 125.
Mount Tirza, N.C., IV: 419.
"Mountain Dew," V: 473.
Mountain House, Md., II: 115.
Mountain Run, Va., III: 575.
Mountcastle, W.D., (Pvt, Co B, 24th Va.), V: 195.
Mouse Creek, Tenn., III: 679.
Mowrey, A., (2nd Cpl, Co K, 4th NCST), V: 489.
Mowry, A.J., (Pvt, Co K, 57th NCST), V: 517.
Moxley, C., (Chaplain, 48th NCST), IV: 616.
Mud Tavern, Va., III: 277.
Mulberry Island, Va., I: 689, 690.
Mulder, J., (Pvt, Co G, 61st Va.), V: 569.
Muldoon, Arthur, (Pvt, 36th NCST, 2nd Art & Engs), V: 227.
Mulford, W.H., (Federal, Agent of Exchange), V: 624.
Mull, Lacob, (Pvt, Co A, 13th Vols/23rd NCST), V: 509.
Mull, P.K., (2nd Lt, Co E, 25th NCST), V: 559.
Mull, Peter M., (Capt, Co F, 55th NCST), III: 287, 289, 290, 293, 296, 307.
Mull, Peter P., (Lt, Co F, 55th NCST), III: 296.
Mullen, James M., (Pvt, Co A, Webb's Battery, Starr's 13th Battalion NCST, Light Art), IV: 360; V: 269-284 personal account.
Mullen, S.P., (AC Sgt, 56th NCST), V: 565.
Mullen, Stephen C., (ACS, 56th NCST), III: 319.
Mulligan, James Adelbert, (Brig Gen, USA), III: 751.
Mullin, A., (Pvt, Co I, 1st Vols/11th NCST), V: 531.
Mullins, Henry, (Capt, Co C, 5th NCST), I: 282, 284.
Mullis, John, (Pvt, Co H, 55th NCST), V: 528.
Mullis, William, (2nd Sgt, Co H, 55th NCST), V: 528.
Mumford, William, (Pvt, Co D, 2nd NCST), I: 176; V: 486.
Mumfordville, Ky., II: 709.
Mumma's Farm House, (nr Sharpsburg, Md.), I: 185, 225.
Mummasburg Road, (nr Gettysburg, Pa.), I: 633, 634, 635; II: 235.
Munday, James D., (Pvt, Co G, 52nd NCST), V: 536.
Munday, John, (Pvt, Co A, 12th Vols/22nd NCST), V: 553.
Munday, William M., (2nd Lt, Co K, 13th Vols/23rd NCST), II: 188, 236.
Munden, William J., (1st Lt, Co A, 68th NCST), III: 713.
Munford, Thomas Taylor, (Brig Gen), I: 739; II: 783; IV: 142.
Munn, Daniel, (Capt, Co B, 36th NCST, 2nd Art & Engs, Bladen Stars), I: 528; II: 630, 635, 636, 646; V: 233, 239, 351.
Munroe, Donald D., (Lt, Co H, 2nd NCST), I: 162.

Murchison, D.R., (Capt, AQM, 54th NCST; QM, Lewis' Brigade), III: 267; V: 511.

Murchison, H.C., (Cpl, Co H, 56th NCST), III: 356.

Murchinson, John R., (Lt Col, 8th NCST), I: 405; III: 212; IV: 488, 493, 573; V: 11, 183, 197, 203.

Murchinson, Kenneth, (Capt, Co F, 5th Vols/15th NCST), I: 735.

Murchinson, Kenneth M., (Col, 54th NCST; Col, 24th Battalion Home Guard), III: 267, 269, 271; IV: 650, 658, 662, 709; V: 650.

Murchinson, Murdock D., (Pvt, Co C, 38th NCST), V: 557.

Murdaugh, Robert K., (Pvt, Co G, 38th NCST), V: 557.

Murdaugh, T.F., (2nd Lt, Co G, 38th NCST), V: 549.

Murdaugh, W.H., (Lt, CSN), V: 39, 44, 46, 47, 302.

Murdoch, Dave, (Pvt, Co C, 4th NCST), V: 488.

Murdock, Alexander, (Ordnance Sgt, 2nd NCST), I: 163.

Murdock, Alexander G., (Jr 2nd Lt, Co H, 38th NCST), II: 678; IV: 700, 709.

Murdock, C.D., (Sgt, Co A, 4th NCST), I: 232.

Murdock, Dr. William H., (Ass't Surg, Henry's 14th Battalion, 79th NCST, 8th Cav), IV: 113, 643.

Murfrees' Station, N.C., III: 134.

Murfreesboro, N.C., II: 271, 522, 776; III: 134, 321; IV: 26, 359; V: 270, 272, 283, 627.

Murfreesboro, Tenn., (and Battle of, 1864, See also: Stone's River), II: 488, 490, 491, 702, 710, 711, 724, 731; III: 438, 474, 476-481, 483, 495, 499, 501, 663; IV: 498.

Murph, D.M., (Pvt, Co C, 33rd NCST), V: 544.

Murphy, Charles, (Pvt, Co A, 63rd NCST, 5th Cav), III: 574.

Murphy, D., (Pvt, Co K, 8th Vols/18th NCST), II: 64; V: 540.

Murphy, Dr., David, (Father of Charles Murphy), III: 574.

Murphy, G.B., (Capt, Co G, 5th Vols/15th NCST), I: 735; V: 519.

Murphy, J.H., (Pvt, Co G, 16th Battalion/75th NCST, 7th Cav), V: 660.

Murphy, J.S., (Pvt, Co G, 8th NCST), V: 194.

Murphy, John, (Pvt, Co B, Starr's Battery, Starr's 13th Battalion NCST, Light Art), IV: 351, 352.

Murphy, Rev. Dr. Joseph W., (Chaplain, 32nd NCST; Chaplain, 43rd NCST), II: 524; III: 1; IV: 612, 614.

Murphy, P., (Pvt, Co K, 44th NCST), V: 534.

Murphy, Dr. R.R., [B.B.], (Pvt, Co K; Ass't Surg, 6th Vols/16th NCST), IV: 218, 634; V: 547.

Murphy, Robert, (Pvt, Co B, 1st Battalion NCST), V: 504.

Murphy, Robert J., (Capt, Co A, 36th NCST, 2nd Art & Engs, King's Battery), II: 630, 634; V: 239.

Murphy, W.F., (Capt, Co K, 51st NCST), III: 211, 220; IV: 721.

Murphy, W.T., (Lt, CSN), IV: 404.

Murphy, N.C., II: 301, 706; III: 738, 756, 757; IV: 122, 126, 127, 128.

Murray, A., (Pvt, Co I, 3rd NCST), V: 487.

Murray, E.P.G., (2nd Lt, Co I, 62nd NCST), III: 516; IV: 702, 709.

Murray, G.W., (Lt, Co F, 4th Vols/14th NCST), I: 723, 731.

Murray, Hugh F., [Muray], (2nd Lt, Co A, 5th Battalion Junior Reserves; Co A, 71st NCST, 2nd Junior Reserves), IV: 28, 594.

Murray, John, (Englishman, Publisher), V: 414.
Murray, John W., (Pvt, Co E, 7th NCST), V: 538.
Murray, Timothy A., (Cpl, Co F, 33rd NCST), II: 540, 578.
Murray, W.J., (Pvt, Co D, 2nd Vols/12th NCST), V: 507.
Murray, William G., (Pvt, Co A, 47th NCST), V: 534.
Murray, William R., (Lt, Adjt, 53rd NCST), III: 259, 261.
Murrell, Joe, (Pvt, Co K, 35th NCST), V: 563.
Murrell, Porter R., (Pvt, Co D, 25th NCST), V: 561.
Muse, Btaxton, (Pvt, Co B, 25th NCST), V: 561.
Muse, J.M., (Sgt, Co H, 57th NCST), III: 427.
Muse, W.T., (Cmdr, NCN; Capt, Ellis; Cmdr, Naval Station Wilmington; Commodore, CNS, North Carolina), IV: 404; V: 35, 36, 38, 39, 50, 299, 300, 301, 303, 312.
Mustin, D.R., (Pvt, Co G, 43rd NCST; Detailed, Invalid Battalion), V: 571.
Myers, A.C., (1st Sgt, Co D, 52nd NCST), III: 224.
Myers, Abraham, (Maj, N.C. Quartermaster Department), I: 6, 23, 24, 362; IV: 760, 761.
Myers, Alexander L., (Cpl, Co C, 33rd NCST), II: 539.
Myers, Charles D., (Adjt, 8th Vols/18th NCST), II: 7; IV: 473.
Myers, Ezekiel, (Lt, Co D, 10th NCST, 1st Art & Engs, Reilly-Ramsay's Battery, Light Art), I: 580.
Myers, Joseph D., (Capt, Co K, 67th NCST , a Cav Co attached to the 67th), III: 704.
Myers, W., (Capt, Myers' Unattached Company, Perquimans County), V: 678.
Myers, William R., (Capt, Co G, 34th NCST), II: 581.
Myers, William W., (1st Lt, Co D, 10th NCST, 1st Art & Engs, Reilly-Ramsay's Battery, Light Art), I: 561, 563, 574, 652.
Myrick, John R., (Lt, Co E., 3rd U.S. Art), V: 238.
Myrover, J.H., (2nd Lt, Co B, Starr's Battery, Starr's 13th Battalion NCST, Light Art), I: 120; IV: 341, 346, 348, 349.

(N)

Nag's Head, N.C., II: 509; V: 59.
Nahunta, N.C., III: 725.
Nail, John A., (5th Sgt, Co F, 3rd Vols/13th NCST), V: 550.
Nall, Ira, (Pvt, Co E, 26th NCST), II: 387.
Nance, Buren, (Pvt, Co H, 6th NCST), V: 513.
Nance, E.A., (Pvt, Co E, 7th NCST), V: 538.
Nance, W., (Pvt, Co H, 8th Vols/18th NCST), II: 64; V: 540.
Namozine Church, Va., I: 442, 479, 480; II: 108, 783, 784; III: 470, 648, 649, 650-653; IV: 582.
Namozine Creek, Va., III: 252.
Nansemond County, Va., III: 504.
Nansemond River, Va., II: 88.
Nantahala Mountains, N.C., III: 757, 758; IV: 122, 381.
Nantahala River, N.C., III: 757; IV: 125.
Nants, W.K., (Pvt, Co C, 10th NCST, 1st Art & Engs, Brem-Graham-Williams' Battery, Light Art), V: 568.
Nants, W.R., (Pvt, Co C, 10th NCST, 1st Art & Engs, Brem-Graham-Williams' Battery, Light Art), V: 568.
Nantucket, Mass., V: 386.
Nantz' Shop, Va., I: 431.
Napier, Sir Charles, (Admr, English), V: 425.
Napier, G.W., (Tobacco Trader), IV: 218.
Napier, H.J., (Pvt, Co C, 4th Vols/14th NCST), I: 732.
Nash, ______, [Edwin], (Col, 4th Ga.), V: 247.
Nash, Fred, (Capt, Ordnance Officer, Kiriland's Brigade; AAG, Walker's Brigade), IV: 562, 564.
Nash, George, (Pvt, Co B, 12th Vols/22nd NCST), V: 553.
Nash, Solomon, (Pvt, Co D, 6th NCST), V: 512.
Nash County, N.C., III: 686.
Nashville, Tenn., (and Battle of, 1864), I: 768; II: 490, 492, 514, 710, 721; III: 432, 438, 439, 454, 476, 584, 494, 495, 501, 732; IV: 682.
Nashville Campaign, II: 720.
Nashville Pike, (nr Murfreesboro, Tenn.), III: 477.
Nassau, III: 37; IV: 691; V: 335, 339, 340, 335, 356, 358, 361, 381, 382, 385, 386, 391, 395, 405, 410, 416, 419, 430, 431, 432, 441, 442, 447, 448, 450, 453, 459, 471.
National Cemetery, (nr Gettysburg, Pa.), V: 102, 138, 142, 153.
National Farmers Alliance, II: 422.
National Road, (at South Mountain, Md.), I: 573.
Natural Bridge, Va., II: 122, 245.
Naval Academy, U.S., III: 287, 733.
Naval Battalion, CSN, IV: 403, 404; V: 313.
Naval Detachments, Sailors and Marines, V: 240.

Naval & Military Board, CSA, V: 299.
Navy, C.S., III: 8; IV: 404, 417, 528; V: ix, 219, 223, 240, 313, 315, 316, 325, 345, 356, 400, 437, 441.
Navy, C.S., Vessels in North Carolina, V: 298.
Navy, C.S., Scharf's, V: 355.
Navy, North Carolina, V: 299-313, 679.
Navy, North Carolina Vessels in, V: 299.
Navy, Turkish, V: 425, 426.
Navy, U.S., II: 722; IV: 305, 307, 417; V: 218, 224, 299, 300, 302, 312, 345, 346, 375, 385, 416, 437.
Naylor, B.T., (2nd Lt, Co E, 42nd NCST), II: 791, 806.
Neagle, Dr. John L., (Ass't Surg, N.C.), IV: 631.
Neal, A.F., (2nd Lt, Co I, 3rd Vols/13th NCST), I: 671, 672.
Neal, A.W., (Pvt, Co B, 10th Vols/20th NCST), V: 508.
Neal, D.D., (Pvt, Co D, 55th NCST), V: 528.
Neal, F.M., (Pvt, Co A, 3rd Vols/13th NCST), V: 549.
Neal, J., (Cpl, Co I, 3rd NCST), V: 487.
Neal, J.B., (Lt, AQM, 9th NCST, 1st Cav), I: 485, 486.
Neal, J.C., (2nd Lt, Co B, 6th Battalion Junior Reserves; Co E, 70th NCST, 1st Junior Reserves), IV: 13.
Neal, J.N., (Pvt, Co E, 2nd Vols/12th NCST), V: 507.
Neal, James M., (Capt, Co B, 12th Vols/22nd NCST), II: 162, 163, 164, 165.
Neal, John H., (Pvt, Co F, 2nd Vols/12th NCST; Detailed, 2nd Corps Provost Guard), V: 570.
Neal, O.M., (2nd Lt, Co K, 32nd NCST), I: 736.
Neal, Oliver S., (Pvt, Co F, 33rd NCST), II: 544.
Neal, Thomas B., (Chaplain, 14th Vols/24th NCST), IV: 610.
Neal, W.B., (Lt), IV: 709.
Neal, William D., (Sgt Maj, 40th NCST), II: 745.
Neale, E.S., (Cpl, Co K, 2nd Vols/12th NCST), V: 508.
Neall, S.R., (2nd Lt, Co F, 49th NCST), V: 559.
Neathery, John B., (Lt, N.C. Adjt Gen Department), I: 51; V: 678.
Neave, Edward B., (Musician, 4th NCST), I: 234; V: 488.
Nebraska Territory, II: 412.
Needham, Henry, (2nd Lt, Co D, 69th NCST, Thomas' Legion), III: 730.
Needham, Thomas N., (Pvt, Co C, 10th NCST, 1st Art & Engs, Brem-Graham-Williams' Battery, Light Art), V: 567.
Neely, Thomas W., (1st Lt, Co A, 1st Vols/11th NCST), V: 530.
Neese, J.A., (Pvt, Co A, 53rd NCST), V: 501.
Neff, David, (Capt, Co G, Walker's Battalion, Thomas' Legion, 80th NCST), IV: 118, 123, 127.
Negroes, Impressing, I: 53.
Neill, J.R., (AQM, Co K, 29th NCST), II: 486.
Neill, John C., (Pvt, Co H, 14th Vols/24th NCST), V: 560.
Neill, L.C., (Capt, Co K, 62nd NCST), III: 516; IV: 701, 709.
Nelson, ______, [Richard M.], (Adjt, 35th NCST), II: 597.
Nelson, Lord Adm. ______, I: 729; V: 413.
Nelson, E.R., (2nd Lt, Co F, Walker's Battalion, Thomas' Legion, 80th NCST), IV: 118.
Nelson, George H., (2nd Lt, Co A, 62nd NCST), III: 515.

Nelson, H.E., (2nd Lt, Co D, 2nd Battalion Junior Reserves; Co F, 71st NCST, 2nd Junior Reserves), IV: 28.
Nelson, Isaac, (1st Lt, Co D, 52nd NCST), III: 224.
Nelson, Isaac H., (Lt, 32nd NCST), IV: 700, 709.
Nelson, J.M., (Pvt, Co M, 11th Vols/21st NCST), V: 515.
Nelson, J.O., (Pvt, Co B, 33rd NCST), V: 544.
Nelson, James, (Pvt, Co D, 3rd Vols/13th NCST), V: 550.
Nelson, James, (1st Lt, Co H, 6th Battalion/60th NCST), III: 474.
Nelson, John B., (Capt, ACS, 5th Battalion NCST, Cav), IV: 271.
Nelson, John H., (2nd Sgt, Co D, 52nd NCST), III: 224.
Nelson, John N., (2nd Lt, Co E, 12th Vols/22nd NCST), II: 164, 166.
Nelson, Miles, (Pvt, Co G, 56th NCST), III: 324.
Nelson, P.C., (Pvt, Co F, 32nd NCST), V: 496.
Nelson, Samuel L., (Pvt, Co G, 27th NCST), II: 462; V: 523.
Nelson, Thomas A.R., (Scalawag, Congressman, Tenn.), III: 734.
Nelson, W.B., (2nd Lt, Co A, 29th NCST; Capt, Co B, Walker's Battalion, Thomas' Legion, 80th NCST), II: 485; IV: 118.
Nelson, William, (2nd Lt, Co F, 9th Vols/19th NCST, 2nd Cav), II: 80.
Nelson, William M., (QMS, Walker's Battalion, Thomas' Legion, 80th NCST), IV: 117.
Nelson's Farm, (nr Malvern Hill, Va.), I: 570.
Nesbitt, Dr. A.M., (Surg, 6th NCST), IV: 632.
Nethercutt, Jesse A., (Pvt, Co A, 38th NCST), II: 690, 698.
Nethercutt, John H., (Maj, Nethercutt's Battalion; Col, 66th NCST; Cmdr, Junior Reserves Brigade), I: xiii; II: 11, 513; III: 685, 689, 697, 699; IV: 4, 5, 30, 31, 55, 56, 302, 351, 394, 538, 545, 591; V: 19.
Netherland, John, (Scalawag, Congressman, Tenn.), III: 734.
Neuse River, N.C., I: 391, 402, 493, 494, 495, 515, 516, 517, 518, 519, 520, 524, 526, 587, 588; II: 80, 308, 309, 311, 318, 339, 513, 541, 593, 745, 749, 751, 752, 777, 803; III: 4, 86, 135, 170, 171, 229, 230, 289, 323, 507, 508, 553, 696, 698, 704, 705, 706, 708, 709, 710, 722; IV: 18, 20, 30, 53, 54, 55, 81, 92, 252, 253, 263, 264, 325, 326, 336, 350, 360, 415, 416, 430, 487, 537; V: 17, 18, 57, 86, 87, 88, 90, 303, 325, 326, 327, 330, 331, 631.
Neuse River Bridge, (nr Goldsboro), III: 206, 220, 229, 230; IV: 108, 326, 344-346, 398.
Neuse River Road, (Kinston to New Bern), III: 333.
Neva River, Russia, V: 425.
Never Caught, V: 414, 416.
New Baltimore, Va., I: 457, 458, 459; III: 242, 583; IV: 184, 185.
New Bedford, Mass., V: 346, 348.
New Bern, N.C., (and Battle of, 1862), I: xiii, 3, 4, 7, 11, 12, 14, 15, 116, 138, 164, 179, 216, 362, 363, 371, 391, 490, 493, 499, 502, 503, 509, 515, 516, 524, 537, 538, 540, 588, 737, 742; II: 3, 20, 62, 80, 81, 82, 83, 84, 277, 279, 284, 294, 308, 309-327, 329, 330, 337, 338, 340, 389, 398, 406, 408, 414, 425, 426, 427, 439, 467, 468, 497, 513, 541-544, 549, 580, 593, 594, 595, 597, 598, 599, 600, 629, 653, 747, 748, 749, 750, 751, 752, 774, 777, 778; III: 4,

35, 40, 83, 85, 178, 206, 227, 290, 324, 349, 459, 507, 513, 553, 554, 696, 703, 708, 709; IV: 12, 18, 30, 31, 53, 54, 72, 76, 81, 82, 92, 110, 221, 263, 270, 302, 326, 338, 353, 358, 361, 367, 393, 414, 424, 428, 482, 484, 498, 541, 543, 547, 556, 557, 562, 592, 611, 615, 619, 620, 646, 647; V: 19, 20, 83, 84, 85, 270, 300, 303, 359, 629, 631.

New Bern Campaign, 1863, II: 612, 616, 751, 754, 768; III: 87, 117, 130, 131, 170-171, 173, 174, 176, 233, 234, 328; IV: 252, 514.

New Bern Campaign, 1864, I: 8, 9, 321, 363, 391, 396, 397, 402, 411, 495, 496, 526, 540; II: 4, 11, 80, 129, 140, 519, 523, 524, 619, 650, 653, 762, 797, 803; III: 7, 8, 9, 83, 132-133, 170, 177, 210, 273-274, 275, 328, 333, 333-335, 350, 419, 555, 679, 680, 681, 704, 705, 726; IV: 72, 84, 85, 241, 242, 265, 266, 267, 392, 486-489, 525, 528, 573, 575; V: 325, 327, 328, 330, 332, 333, 663.

New Bethel Crossroads, N.C., I: 687.

New Bridge, (Chickahominy Creek/River, Va.), I: 612, 617.

New Bridge Road, (nr Richmond, Va.), I: 350.

New Brunswick, Conn., IV: 739.

"New Dip," V: 473.

New Hampshire, I: 671.

New Hanover County, N.C., I: 581; II: 16, 66, 769, 770; III: 205, 217, 457, 503, 504, 688 IV: 303, 354, 483, 484, 725.

New Hope Church, Ga., (and Battle of, 1864), II: 702, 720, 742; III: 433, 493.

New Hope Church, (Rutherfordtown), IV: 212.

New Hope Church, Va., I: 557; III: 14, 15, 163, 366, 749.

New Inlet, N.C., II: 17, 18, 631, 632, 634, 748, 751, 752; IV: 45, 46, 303, 304, 305, 307, 419; V: 23, 303, 336, 337, 351, 358, 362, 367, 397, 406, 409, 422, 441, 442, 443.

New Jersey, II: 367.

New Kent Court House, Va., I: 737; IV: 151, 152.

New Market, Va., (and Battle of), I: 174, 208, 262, 264, 326, 373, 457, 649, 762; II: 71, 259, 261; IV: 169.

New Market Bridge, Va., (and Road), I: 85, 87, 89, 98, 101.

New Market Gap, Va., I: 142, 189; IV: 169.

New Market Heights, Va., (nr Malvern Hill), II: 799.

New Market Races, II: 531.

New Market Road, (nr Frazier's Farm, Va.), I: 738.

New Mexico, IV: 1, 511.

New Orleans, La., IV: 305, 329, 743.

New Providence Island, V: 355, 453.

New River, N.C., II: 774; III: 553; V: 18.

New River Bridge, Va., III: 745.

New Salem, Va., II: 30.

New South Quay, Va., III: 321.

New York, (aka Empire State), II: 367, 747; III: 383; V: 81.

New York, N.Y., I: 103, 539; IV: 295, 734; V: 385, 386, 393, 410, 411, 414, 417, 418, 427, 429, 430, 439, 441, 443, 445.

Newby, W.H., (Cpl, Co K, 32nd NCST), V: 497.

Newby, W.H., (Pvt, Co F, 49th NCST), V: 564.

Newell, D.S., (Pvt, Co H, 35th NCST), V: 563.

Newell, J.A., (Pvt, Co K, 57th NCST), V: 517.

Newfound Mountains, N.C., (aka Pisgah Mountains), III: 558.

Newfoundland, V: 416.
Newkirk, _____, [George B.], (Sgt, Co E, 30th NCST), IV: 602.
Newkirk, A.W., (Capt, Co A, 41st NCST, 3rd Cav), II: 497, 770, 774.
Newland, John & Sons, (English textile manufacturer), I: 33.
Newman, L.H., (Lt Cmdr, USN), V: 242.
Newman's Farm, (nr Liberty Mills, Va.), I: 382.
Newport, N.C., (and Battle of, 1864, aka Shepperdsville), I: 363, 496, 526; II: 3; IV: 74, 90, 266, 528.
Newport, Tenn., III: 756; IV: 619.
Newport News, Va., I: 82, 83, 87, 89, 100, 654; IV: 404.
Newsom, Alfred, (Pvt, Co D, 3rd NCST), V: 487.
Newsom, James D., (Lt, Co H, 47th NCST), I: 551; III: 85, 108; IV: 700, 709.
Newsom, James D., (2nd Sgt, Co C, 10th NCST, 1st Art & Engs, Brem-Graham-Williams' Battery, Light Art), I: 551.
Newsom, John, (Pvt, Co B, 1st Battalion NCST), V: 504.
Newxom, John G., (Sgt, Co B, 30th NCST), V: 491.
Newsom, S.D., (2nd Lt, Co K, 21st NCST), V: 511.
Newsom, W.H., (2nd Lt, Co H, 9th Vols/19th NCST, 2nd Cav), II: 80.
Newsom, N.C., (Burned by Yankees), IV: 26.
Newsome, Owen, (Pvt, Co D, 3rd NCST), V: 487.
Newspapers:
Asheville Citizen, I: ix, 5, 6, 7.
Atlanta Constitution, III: 683.
Atlanta Intelligencer, II: 739.
Atlanta Journal, I: 130.
Charleston Courier, I: 104.
Charleston Mercury, I: 129.
Charlotte Observer, I: ix.
Christian Advocate, II: 806.
Concord Sun, III: 547, 548, 642.
Fayetteville Carolinian, V: 363.
Fayetteville Observer, I: ix, 129, 448, 452; III: 343, 347, 348, 510; V: 187, 188.
Franklin Press, III: 550, 554.
Galveston News, III: 307.
Harper's Weekly, II: 217.
Illustrated News, Frank Leslie's, V: 410.
Knoxville Journal Tribune, IV: 120-121.
Knoxville Whig, III: 733.
London Herald, I: 256.
London Telegraph, V: 411.
London Times, V: 411.
New Bern Observer, I: ix, 4.
News and Observer, Raleigh, I: ix.
New York Herald, I: 102; IV: 240, 671.
New York Tribune, I: 102; V: 51.
North Carolina Standard, III: 375, 506.
Petersburg Express, I: 75, 103; IV: 495.
Philadelphia Enquirer, IV: 730.
Raleigh Confederate, V: 180.
Raleigh Morning Post, I: ix.
Raleigh Observer, III: 431.
Raleigh Post, II: 605.
Raleigh Register, V: 578.
Richmond Dispatch, I: 104, 129.
Richmond Enquirer, III: 600; V: 135, 599, 601.
Richmond Examiner, I: 38, 76, 79, 104, 129, 362; II: 250; V: 179, 181, 191, 599, 601.
Richmond Sentinel, II: 422.
Richmond Whig, I: 104.
Robensonian, IV: 613.
Sandusky News, IV: 678.
Siler City Messenger, II: 422.
Statesville American, I: 279.

Waynesville Courier, I: ix.
Wilmington Daily Review, V: 403.
Wilmington Journal, II: 467, 468; III: 511.
Wilmington Messenger and Star, I: ix.
Newton, George W., (Pvt, Co I, 13th Vols/23rd NCST), V: 510.
Newton, R.R., (Pvt, Co C, 10th NCST, 1st Art & Engs, Brem-Graham-Williams' Battery, Light Art), V: 567.
Newton, S.B., (2nd Lt, Co E, 30th NCST), II: 496.
Newton, T.W., (Pilot, Eugenia), V: 357.
Newtown, Va., [Newton], (and Battle of, 1864), I: 261, 327; II: 132; III: 278, 750.
Newton Academy, (nr Asheville), II: 722.
Niblock, George, (Pvt, Co D, 57th NCST), V: 517.
Nichollaison, G.A., (Ass't Surg, Starr's 13th Battalion NCST, Light Art), IV: 644.
Nicholas, Emperor of France, V: 425.
Nicholls, Francis Reddin T., (Brig Gen), I: 195, 359.
Nicholls, P., (Capt, 66th NCST), IV: 709.
Nichols, B.F., (2nd Lt, Claiborne-Dearing's 7th C.S. Cav; 16th Battalion/75th NCST, 7th Cav), IV: 92.
Nichols, B.G., (Sgt, Co K, 30th NCST), V: 493.
Nichols, Jefferson, (Pvt, Co K, 57th NCST), V: 517.
Nichols, John H., (2nd Sgt, Co E, 52nd NCST), III: 224.
Nichols, John S.A., (Capt, Co E, 1st Vols/11th NCST), I: 584; V: 663.
Nichols, Risden T., (1st Lt, Co D, 13th Vols/23rd NCST), II: 184.
Nichols, S.W., (Lt, USN; Pioneer, Shenandoah), V: 244.
Nichols, Samuel, (3rd Cpl, Co A, 10th NCST, 1st Art & Engs, Ramseur-Manly's Battery, Light Art), I: 551.
Nichols, W.A., (Lt, 37th NCST), II: 661.
Nicholson, ______, (Capt, Co A, 74th NCST, 5th Senior Reserves), IV: 69.
Nicholson, ______, I: 368.
Nicholson, A.J., (Lt, Co C, 46th NCST), III: 81.
Nicholson, E.A.T., (AAG, Garland-Iverson-Johnston's Brigade), IV: 523.
Nicholson, Edward T., (Capt, AG, J.A. Walker's Brigade; AIG, Branch-Lane's Brigade), I: 650; II: 673; IV: 472, 523.
Nicholson, Guilford, (Lt, Co A, 9th Vols/19th NCST, 2nd Cav), II: 79, 83.
Nicholson, H.J., (Pvt, Co H, 7th NCST), I: 368.
Nicholson, J.C., (Pvt, Co K, 33rd NCST), V: 545.
Nicholson, J.L., (Pvt, Co G, 61st Va.), V: 569.
Nicholson, J.N., (1st Lt, Co C, 5th Vols/15th NCST), I: 734.
Nicholson, John H., (1st Lt, Co B, 30th NCST), II: 496; IV: 600, 701.
Nicholson, John H., (Lt, Co B, 30th NCST), IV: 701.
Nicholson, Dr. John P., (Hospital Steward), II: 537, 540, 579.
Nicholson, Dr. John P., (AC Sgt, 33rd NCST), II: 537; V: 543.
Nicholson, John R., (1st Lt, Co C, 13th Vols/23rd NCST), II: 184.
Nicholson, Malcolm, (Sgt, Co D, 13th Vols/23rd NCST), II: 200.
Nicholson, Peter, (Chaplain, 49th NCST), III: 125; IV: 616.

Nicholson, W.A.J., (Lt, Co C, 46th NCST), III: 81.
Nicholson, William, (Fayetteville and Harper's Ferry Arsenals), IV: 298.
Nicholson, William T., (Capt, Adjt, 37th NCST), II: 653, 664, 666, 668, 670, 673; IV: 469, 474, 475, 476.
Nicollaison, Dr. G.A., (Ass't Surg, Starr's 13th Battalion NCST, Light Art), IV: 341, 644.
Niemeyer, John, (2nd Ass't Engineer, Sirene), V: 404, 446-449.
Niell, L.C., (Capt, 62nd NCST), IV: 709.
Nine Mile Road, (nr Richmond, Va.), I: 350, 567, 738; III: 77; IV: 155, 200.
Nineveh, Va., IV: 177.
Nixon, Albert M., (2nd Cpl, Co G, 52nd NCST), III: 224.
Nixon, D.J., (Capt, Co A, 41st NCST, 3rd Cav), II: 770.
Nixon, F.M., (Lt, Co A, 28th NCST), II: 483.
Nixon, H.W., (Pvt, Co E, 3rd NCST), V: 487.
Nixon, John R., (1st Sgt, Co E, 27th NCST), II: 462.
Nixon, Lewis A., (Sgt, Co G, 33rd NCST), II: 540.
Nixon, M.C., (Capt, ACS & AQM, MacRae's 18th Battalion NCST), IV: 11, 13.
Nixon, Dr. Thomas M., (Surg, 68th NCST), III: 713; IV: 642.
Nixon, W.P., (Pvt, Co A, 28th NCST), V: 540.
Nixon, William, (Capt, Co F, 27th NCST), II: 426.
Nobbin, T.W., (Pvt, Co G, 56th NCST), III: 348.
Noble, Albert M., (Capt, AQM/ACS, 18th Battalion NCST), IV: 379.
Noble's Farm, N.C., III: 323.
Nobles, S.W., (Lt, Co E, 61st NCST), III: 503, 504.
Noel's Station, Va., III: 246.
Nolan, A., (Cpl, Co F, 56th NCST), III: 348.
Nolan, J., (Pvt, Co F, 8th Vols/18th NCST), V: 539.
Nolan, Patrick, (Pvt, Co A, 10th NCST, 1st Art & Engs, Ramseur-Manly's Battery, Light Art), I: 556.
Noland, _____, (Sheriff of Waynesville), III: 662.
Noland, James, (Pvt, Co F, 8th Vols/18th NCST), II: 64.
Noland, W.W., (1st Lt, Co M, 6th Vols/16th NCST), IV: 709.
Noland Mountain, N.C., (aka Utah Mountain), III: 518.
Noland's Ford, (Potomac River, Va., aka Nolan's Ferry), II: 217, 431.
Noles, _____, [L.L.], (Maj, 25th Ark.), II: 736.
Noles, John, (Pvt, Co H, 35th NCST), V: 193.
Noel's Station, Va., II: 694; III: 246.
Norcum, Dr. W.A.B., (Ass't Surg, 3rd Battalion NCST, Light Art; Ass't Surg, 2nd N.C. General Hospital, Petersburg, Va.), IV: 261, 624, 630, 643.
Norfleet, Marmaduke W., (Lt, Co C, 47th NCST), III: 84; IV: 700, 709.
Norfolk, Va., I: 6, 607, 608, 657, 694, 709; II: 5, 629, 671; III: 2, 19, 130, 133, 134, 170, 178, 335, 714; IV: 210, 244, 246, 248, 344, 420, 441, 538, 556, 573, 616, 646; V: 270, 299, 300, 303, 304, 305, 307, 308, 309, 312, 323, 328, 329, 339.
Norfolk Navy Yard, V: 445.
Norfolk & Petersburg Railroad, II: 776, 793; III: 329, 370, 390; IV: 362.

Norfolk & Western Railroad, II: 776.
Norman, B., (Pvt, Co C, 11th Vols/21st NCST), V: 514.
Norman, J.C., (Capt, Co E, 53rd NCST), III: 262.
Norman, L.J., (Lt, Co H, 2nd Battalion NCST), IV: 245.
Norman, M.H., (Lt, 10th Vols/20th NCST), IV: 702, 709.
Norman, Preston, (Pvt, Co C, 11th Vols/21st NCST), V: 514.
Norman, T.W., (Pvt, Co B, 2nd Battalion NCST), V: 495.
Norman, Thomas J., (Capt, Co G, 7th Vols/17th NCST), II: 2, 9.
Norman, W.M., (Lt, Co A, 2nd NCST), I: 158; IV: 702, 709; V: 46.
Norment, R.M., (Maj, 46th NCST), I: 124, 607; III: 64, 65, 80.
Norment, George M., (Lt Col, 34th NCST), II: 581, 589; V: 548.
Norment, William S., (Capt, Co D, 8th Vols/18th NCST), II: 16; III: 219; IV: 219.
Norris, John R., (Capt, Co G, 58th NCST), III: 433, 434.
Norris, W.W., (Pvt, Co E, 30th NCST), V: 492.
North, Joshua, (Pvt, Co B, 30th NCST), V: 491.
North Atlantic Squadron, (USN), V: 241.
North Carolina, V: 42.
North Carolina Financial Operations in England, V: 453.
North Carolina General and Field Officers Killed, V: 9-12.
North Carolina Generals, I: xi; V: 3-4.
North Carolina Generals Commissioned by the State, V: 5-7.
North Carolina Heroine, V: 19-20.
North Carolina Military Institute, I: 78, 124, 127, 293, 294, 295, 733; III: 128; V: 637, 645-646.
North Carolina Naval Officers, I: xiv.
North Carolina Railroad, I: 294, 390, 338; III: 129, 313.
North Carolina Railroad, Western, I: 294.
North Carolina Regiments, III: 596.
North Carolina Troops, Where Stationed, 21 November, 1861, V: 13-14.
North Carolina Troops, Number of, V: 1-2, 466.
North Carolina Troops, (Federal), III: 173; V: 655.
North Carolina's Records, V: 463-481.
North Carolinians in Other Commands, IV: 403.
North Carolinians on Military Courts, V: 8.
North Mountain, Va., I: 324, 327.
North Mountain Depot, Va., II: 34, 479, 657.
North River, N.C., V: 17.
North West Lock, Va., IV: 573.
Northampton County, N.C., II: 405, 502, 611, 671; III: 318, 319, 458, 717; IV: 10, 261, 339, 403, 572; V: 271, 282.
Northeast Bridge, [North East], (nr Wilmington), III: 505, 506; IV: 358, 543.
Northeast River, N.C., [North East], I: 410, 411, II: 11, 277, 762; III: 215, 695, 696; IV: 222, 268, 428, 429, 498, 542, 543.
Northeast Station, [North East], (Wilmington & Weldon Railroad), IV: 344.
Northington, G.W., (Sgt, Co G, 2nd Vols/12th NCST), V: 507.
Northington, John S., (Capt, AQM, Garland-Iverson-Johnston's Brigade), I: 606, 651; V: 523.
Northrop, William H., (Capt, Pettigrew's Brigade), IV: 418.

Norton, ______, (Maj, 1st Va.), V: 177.
Norton, J.C., [James C.], (Pvt, Co C, 4th NCST), I: 232.
Norton, W.P., (2nd Lt, Co D, 62nd NCST), III: 515; IV: 709.
Norval, James, (Pvt, Co F, 30th NCST), V: 492.
Norwood, J.T., (Cpl, Co G, 52nd NCST), V: 536.
Norwood, James, (Pvt, Co K, 6th NCST), V: 513.
Norwood, John H. (Capt, Co E, 47th NCST), III: 84; V: 154.
Norwood, R.W., (1st Cpl, Co K, 46th NCST), V: 525.
Norwood, Thomas H., (Capt, Co H, 44th NCST), III: 23; V: 529.
Norwood, Thomas J., (2nd Lt, Co G, 1st Vols/11th NCST), I: 585.
Norwood, Thomas L., (1st Lt, Co A, 37th NCST), V: 538.
Norwood, Thomas L., (Lt, Co A, 37th NCST), II: 662.
Norwood, W.E., (Pvt, Co B, 26th NCST), V: 531.
Norwood, W.L., (Sgt Maj, Henry's 14th Battalion, 79th NCST, 8th Cav), IV: 113.
Notlay, N.C., III: 756.
Notley River, N.C., IV: 125.
Nott, James D., (2nd Lt, Co A, 63rd NCST, 5th Cav), I: 121, 441; III: 643.
Nottaway Bridge, (Nottaway River, N.C.), IV: 366, 367, 369.
Nottaway Court House, Va., III: 612.
Nottaway River, N.C., I: 402; III: 321, 623, 633, 636; IV: 26.
Nova Scotia, V: 377.
Nunn, Henry S. (1st Sgt, Co D, 27th NCST), II: 462; V: 523.
Nunn, William H., (Pvt, Co G, 27th NCST), II: 462; V: 523.
Nutt, Henry, V: 300.
Nutt, W.B., (Pvt, Co I, 57th NCST), V: 517.

(O)

O & A Railroad, I: 593.
Oak Grove Church, Va., III: 621.
Oak Hill, (nr Gettysburg, Pa.), I: 171, 634.
Oak Island, N.C., II: 751, 761; IV: 487.
Oakley, H.W., (Sgt, Co E, 35th NCST), V: 193.
Oakley, Davis, (Pvt, Co C, 30th NCST), V: 491.
Oakley, R.H., (Pvt, Co E, 46th NCST), V: 524.
Oakley, S.M., (Pvt, Co H, 14th Vols/24th NCST), V: 560.
Oakman, H.A., (Lt Col, 30th U.S. Colored), V: 238.
Oaks, J.A., (Pvt, Co A, 11th Vols/21st NCST), V: 514.
Oaks, P.A., [James P.], (2nd Lt, Co A, 11th Vols/21st NCST), II: 146.
Oakwood Cemetery, (Raleigh, aka Soldier's Cemetery), II: 408, 422.
Oates, A.T., (Pvt, Co E, 2nd Vols/12th NCST), V: 507.
Oates, David M., (Adjt, 37th NCST), V: 646.
Oates, David W., (Adjt, 37th NCST), IV: 474.
Oates, James A., (5th Sgt, Co H, 46th NCST), V: 525.
Oates, Robert M., (AQM, 37th NCST; Capt, AQM, Wilcox's Division), II: 653; IV: 474; V: 537.
Oates, T.J., (Adjt, 35th NCST), II: 593.
Oates, W.R., (Pvt, Co E, 2nd Vols/12th NCST), V: 507.
Obenchain, William A., (Lt, Engineering Officer), IV: 418, 419.
O'Brien, E., (Pvt, Co B, 33rd NCST), V: 544.
O'Brien, E.M., (3rd Sgt, Co D, 3rd Vols/13th NCST), V: 550.
O'Brien, J.R., (Pvt, Co D, 3rd Vols/13th NCST), V: 550.
O'Brien, M.J., (Lt, ADC to Col. W.H. Hatch), V: 624.
O'Bryant, Albert, (2nd Lt, Co A, 50th NCST), III: 203.
O'Bryenm, D.A., (Pvt, Co E, 35th NCST), V: 563.
Ocala, Fla., V: 383, 384, 411.
Occoquan Bay, Va., I: 753.
Occoquan Creek, Va., [Opequon] I: 287, 300, 422, 577; II: 224, 251; III: 751, 753; IV: 149, 412.
O'Connor, Thomas, (Lt, Kain's Battery), III: 522.
Ocracoke Inlet, N.C., V: 299, 300, 301, 303, 304.
Ocracoke Island, N.C., V: 40, 299.
Odell, John M., (Maj, 12th Vols/22nd NCST), II: 162, 163, 164, 165, 166, 170, 171.
Odell, Laban, (Maj, 12th Vols/22nd NCST), II: 165, 166, 170; V: 12.
Odell, William H., (Pvt, Co B, 4th Vols/14th NCST), I: 731.
Odom, G.W., (Pvt, Co D, 43rd NCST), V: 498.

Odom, James D., (2nd Lt, Co C, Wheeler's 12th Battalion NCST, Cav), IV: 339.
Odom, James G., (2nd Lt, Co C, Wheeler's 12th Battalion NCST, Cav), IV: 91.
Odom, Richard B., (2nd Lt, Co I, 68th NCST), III: 714.
Odum, J.G., (Lt, 2nd Vols/12th NCST) IV: 710.
Ogburn, S.A., (Sgt, Co D, 57th NCST), V: 517.
Ogeechee River, Ga., II: 757, 758; III: 182; IV: 327, 333.
O'Hagan, Dr. Charles J., (Ass't Surg, 9th NCST, 1st Cav; Surg, 35th NCST), I: 485; II: 597, 613, 619, 620; IV: 579, 633, 637; V: 559.
O'Hara, Gen, _____, (British), I: 754.
Ohio, I: 324, 706; II: 367, 702; III: 273, 734; IV: 275, 276, 666, 682, 689.
Ohio River, II: 701, 707, 708; IV: 1; V: viii.
Okalona, Miss., III: 439.
O'Keefe, K.S., (Lt, 15th N.Y. Engineers), V: 238.
Old Capitol Prison, (Washington City), I: 65; II: 232; IV: 237, 662; V: 422.
Old Castle, (Building in the southern part of Kinston), IV: 344.
Old Church, Va., IV: 151.
Old Church Road, Va, II: 469, 776.
Old Cold Harbor, Va., V: 197.
"Old Hike," (Vermont soldier at Fort Delaware Prison), IV: 727, 728, 729.
Old Men's Guard, (See also: Home Guard), I: 55.
Old North State, I: 103, 177.
"Old North State, The," (Song by Gaston), III: 691.
Old Point Comfort, IV: 294, 676.
"Old Rye," V: 473.
Old South Quay, Va., III: 335.
Old Topsail Sound, N.C., I: 392; III: 322.
Old Town, N.C., IV: 268.
Old Town Creek, Va., III: 247.
Oldham, J.W., (Musician, 35th NCST), V: 562.
Oldham, T.A., (2nd Lt, Co D, 5th Vols/15th NCST), I: 735.
Oldham, T.E., (1st Lt, Co D, 5th Vols/15th NCST), I: 735.
Oldham, T.S., (Capt, Co D, 5th Vols/15th NCST), I: 735.
Oldham, Thomas S., (Cpl, Co D, 5th Vols/15th NCST), V: 521.
Oldham, W.E., (2nd Lt, Co D, 5th Vols/15th NCST), I: 735.
Oldham, W.P., (Capt, Co K, 44th NCST), III: 21, 23, 31; IV: 710; V: 210, 211.
Oldham, Y.A., (Capt, Co D, 5th Vols/15th NCST), V: 519.
Oliphant, J.R., (Pvt, Co K, 56th NCST), V: 566.
Oliver, J.A., (Lt, Co , 57th NCST), IV: 710.
Oliver, Joseph B., (2nd Lt, Co E, 10th Vols/20th NCST), IV: 420, 700, 710.
Oliver, Mercer, (Lt, Co G, 10th Vols/20th NCST), II: 127.
Oliver, William H., (Capt, agent of the N.C. Quartermaster Depar-tment), I: 24, 33, 34; V: 461.
O'Neal, Abram, (Pvt, Co C, 5th NCST), I: 291; V: 505.
O'Neal, E.F., (Lt, Beckett's Battalion NCST), IV: 710.
O'Neal, Edward Asbury, (Col, 3rd Ala.), III: 41.
O'Neal, Frank, (Pvt, Detached Co, 68th NCST), III: 723.
O'Neal, Morgan, (Pvt, Detached Co, 68th NCST), III: 723.
O'Neal, Stanley, (Pvt, Detached Co, 68th NCST), III: 723.

Onslow Bay, N.C., V: 217.
Onslow County, N.C., I: 227; II: 82, 497, 627, 770, 774; III: 319, 504, 686.
Oostanaula River, Ga., II: 739.
Orange County, N.C., II: 436; III: 318, 329, 352, 360, 392, 685; IV: 353, 379, 483, 606, 614, 618, 619; V: 191.
Orange County, Va., I: 448.
Orange Court House, Va., I: 140, 142, 149, 171, 189, 197, 199, 223, 235, 254, 370, 381, 382, 454, 544, 545, 557, 570, 592, 594, 639, 672, 673, 674, 675, 701, 720, 743; II: 28, 29, 45, 46, 119, 194, 240, 372, 378, 379, 413, 420, 438, 445, 446, 478, 551, 568, 585, 587, 662, 693; III: 27, 42, 79, 92, 93, 117, 241, 243, 244, 246, 271, 303; IV: 158, 159, 160, 169, 183, 187, 188, 189, 190, 198, 258, 506, 554, 570, 606, 614.
Orange Court House & Chancellorsville Road, I: 667.
Orange Court House & Fredericksburg Road, III: 243, 244.
Orange Plank Road, Va., (Through the Wilderness), I: 376; II: 36, 47, 48, 381; III: 27.
Orange & Alexandria Railroad, I: 282, 382, 623; II: 91, 193, 194, 569, 663; III: 417.
Ord, Edward Otho Cresap, (Maj Gen, USA), I: 419; III: 344, 385, 395; IV: 458.
Ordnance Department, CSA, I: 39, 43; IV: 296.
Ordnance Department, N.C., I: 5, 23, 25, 39, 43.
Ore, G.W., (Pvt, Co B, 27th Ga., Executed for Mutiny), IV: 55-56.
Oregon, IV: 209.
Oregon Inlet, N.C., V: 300.
Organizing of First Regiment, N.C., I: 124.
Orleans, Va., II: 30; III: 69; IV: 161.
Orman, J.E., (Pvt, Co A, 1st Vols/11th NCST), V: 530.
Ormond, R.D., [Ormand], (2nd Lt, Co B, 28th NCST), II: 483.
Ormsby, T.J., (Pvt, Co I, 3rd NCST), V: 487.
Orr, E.M., (Lt, 65th NCST, 6th Cav), IV: 709.
Orr, J.B., (Lt, 64th NCST), IV: 709.
Orr, J.J., (Pvt, Co K, 30th NCST), V: 493.
Orr, James H., (Resident of Charlotte), I: 61.
Orr, N.D., (1st Lt, Co K, 30th NCST), II: 496.
Orrell, W.C., (2nd Lt, Co E, 12th Vols/22nd NCST), II: 178; V: 548.
Osborn, D.D., (2nd Lt, Co A, 1st Battalion NCST), V: 503.
Osborn, J.H., (5th Sgt, Co A, 26th NCST), V: 531.
Osborn, W.M., (Pvt, Co E, 48th NCST), V: 526.
Osborne, E., (Pvt, Co A, 37th NCST), V: 545.
Osborne, E.N., [Osborn, Ezekiel N.], (3rd Lt, Co H, 54th NCST), IV: 700, 710.
Osborne, Charles L., (Capt, Co E, 25th NCST), II: 292.
Osborne, Edwin Augustus, (Col, 4th NCST), I: 230, 231, 238, 244, 245, 247, 249, 253, 255, 257, 258, 269, 275, 276, 279; IV: 460.
Osborne, Gus, (Negro servant to E.A. Osborne), I: 249, 273.
Osborne, R., (Pvt, Co F, 12th Vols/22nd NCST), V: 553.
Osborne, W.B., (Pvt, Co K, 56th NCST), V: 566.
Osborne, William B., (1st Lt, Adjt, 53rd NCST), III: 260.
Ossabaw Sound, Ga., IV: 733, 734.

Otter Creek, (nr New Bern), I: 363; II: 309, 310, 327, 541.
Ottley, C.M., (Sgt, Co C, 32nd NCST), V: 496.
Ottley, J.J., (Pvt, Co C, 32nd NCST), V: 496.
Our Living and Dead, IV: 65, 99.
Ousby, William C., (Capt, Co F, 43rd NCST), III: 2, 3, 245.
Outlaw, A., (Pvt, Co E, 10th Vols/20th NCST), V: 509.
Outlaw, Edward R., (Capt, Co C, 1st Vols/11th NCST), I: 119, 584, 603; V: 529.
Overby, J.M., (Pvt, Co C, 11th Vols/21st NCST), V: 514.
Overby, L.W., (Pvt, Co B, 2nd Vols/12th NCST), V: 506.
Overby, R.C., (Capt, Co C, 2nd Battalion NCST), IV: 245.
Overman, H., (Pvt, Co G, 26th NCST), V: 532.
Overman, W.H., (Capt, Co A, 2nd Battalion Junior Reserves; Co A, 71st NCST, 2nd Junior Reserves), IV: 25, 28, 595.
Overton, A., (Cpl, Co F, 5th NCST), I: 288.
Overton, Washington F., (1st Lt, Co G, 13th Vols/23rd NCST), II: 186, 231.
Owen, D.W., (Sgt, Co A, 6th Battalion/60th NCST), III: 481.
Owen, J.M., (1st Lt, Co H, 62nd NCST), III: 516.
Owen, R.A., (Lt, 62nd NCST), III: 525.
Owen, Robert L., (2nd Lt, Co C, 62nd NCST), III: 515.
Owen, W.L., (Lt, Co B, 1st Battalion NCST), IV: 236.
Owenby, H.W.N., (Pvt, Co A, 25th NCST), V: 572.
Owenby, W.W., (Pvt, Co A, 25th NCST), V: 193.
Owens, B.N., (Lt, 62nd NCST), IV: 710.
Owens, Dick, (Lt, Co 10, 79th NCST, 8th Cav), IV: 115.
Owens, J.J., (Pvt, Co K, 37th NCST), V: 546.
Owens, J. Henry, (2nd Lt, Co I, 53rd NCST), III: 261, 263.
Owens, Noah, (Pvt, Co F, 46th NCST), V: 524.
Owens, Robert L., (2nd Lt, Co C, 62nd NCST), III: 515; IV: 700, 710.
Owens, T.W., (Cpl, Co E, 43rd NCST), V: 498.
Owens, Thomas, [Owen], (2nd Lt, Co I, 46th NCST), III: 82, 352; V: 520.
Owens, W.A., (Lt Col, 53rd NCST), V: 650.
Owens, W.M., (2nd Lt, Co G, 9th Vols/19th NCST, 2nd Cav), II: 89.
Owens, William A., (Col, 53rd NCST), I: 77, 90, 113, 118, 122, 127, 260, 583; III: 258, 259, 260, 264; V: 10, 650.
Owens, William A., (Maj, 34th NCST), II: 581.
Oxford, Isaac, (Capt, Militia, Caldwell County), V: 292, 294.
Oxford, N.C., IV: 398, 594, 605, 611.
Ox Hill, Va., (and Battle of, 1862, aka Chantilly), I: 224, 306, 334, 371, 759; II: 31, 69, 134, 169, 473, 552, 583, 585, 656, 685; IV: 163-164, 466, 552.

(P)

Pace, E.R., (Sgt, Co I, 1st NCST), V: 485.
Pace, Daniel, (Lt, Co B, 64th NCST), III: 660.
Pace, J.F., (Sgt, Co C, 57th NCST), III: 427; V: 517.
Pace, William H., (Pvt, Co I, 1st NCST), V: 485.
Padgett, J.W., (1st Lt, Co G, 30th NCST), II: 496.
Page, _____, (Resident of Abingdon, Va.), III: 523.
Page, B.J., (Pvt, Co H, 56th NCST), III: 348.
Page, Erasmus F., (Pvt, Co F, 2nd NCST), I: 176; V: 486.
Page, J.M., (Sgt, Co L, 8th NCST; Detailed, Invalid Battalion), V: 571.
Page, Jesse H., (Chaplain, 7th Vols/17th NCST), I: 119; IV: 608.
Page, L.A., (Lt, Co H, 58th NCST), III: 433.
Page, Noah, (Pvt, Co F, 26th NCST), V: 603.
Page, P.A., (Sgt Maj, 47th NCST), V: 534.
Page, W.D., (2nd Sgt, Co G, 12th Vols/22nd NCST), V: 554.
Page, W.L., (4th Sgt, Co G, 12th Vols/22nd NCST), V: 554.
Page, William, (Pvt, Co B, 59th NCST, 4th Cav), V: 659.
Page Valley, Va., I: 149, 197.
Paige, John, (Master's Mate, USN, Niphon), V: 351.
Paine, _____, (Lt Col, Va.), II: 95.
Paine, Charles Jackson, (Maj Gen, USA), II: 10; IV: 542; V: 238.
Paint Rock, N.C., III: 662, 739, 757; IV: 380.
Paisley, William, (Capt, Co D, 82nd NCST, Detailed Men), IV: 131.
Palfret, Francis Winthrop, [Palfrey], (Brig Gen, USA), II: 603; V: 77.
Palmer, George S., (Resident of Richmond, Va.), I: 273.
Palmer, Innis Newton, (Maj Gen, USA), I: 540; III: 133, 350, 705.
Palmer, J.C., (ACS, 53rd NCST), III: 261.
Palmer, John B., (Col, 58th NCST), III: 431, 434, 435, 436, 438, 447, 448, 452, 665, 669, 670 756; IV: 115, 371, 380, 386, 439.
Palmer, John H., (Lt, Co I, 12th Vols/22nd NCST), II: 166.
Palmer, John McAuley, (Maj Gen, USA), II: 4, 11, 12, 619; IV: 218.
Palmer, Joseph Benjamin, (Brig Gen), III: 438, 440, 442, 444, 454, 496, 666, 669, 670, 671.
Palmer, Owen A., (2nd Lt, Co E, 41st NCST, 3rd Cav), II: 771.
Palmer, Valentine J., (1st Lt, Co F, 56th NCST), III: 315, 347, 348, 392, 398; V: 189, 191.
Palmer, W.C., (Pvt, Co D, 7th NCST), V: 572.
Palmer, W.H., (Pvt, Co C, 2nd Vols/12th NCST), V: 507.

Palmer, William, (Pvt, Co A, 33rd NCST), II: 544.
Palmer, William H., (Col, A.P. Hill's Staff), II: 479, 569; V: 94.
Palmer's Legion, III: 431, 447; IV: 380.
Palmyra, N.C., III: 321, 331.
Pamlico, N.C., I: 14.
Pamlico County, N.C., I: 160; II: 749; III: 711.
Pamlico Point, N.C., (Neuse River nr New Bern), V: 303.
Pamlico River, N.C., II: 745, 748, 749, 752, 754; III: 233; V: 303, 307, 310.
Pamlico Sound, N.C., I: 388, 389; II: 509; IV: 414, 620; V: 56, 57, 59, 60, 63, 68, 192, 299, 300, 315, 321.
Pamunkey River, Va., I: 322, 461, 579, 612; II: 101, 776; III: 608; IV: 357.
Panama, II: 416.
Pannell's Bridge, (Staunton River, Va.), III: 654.
Papertown, Va., (Skirmish at, 1863), II: 97.
Pardew, F.C., (Sgt, Co D, 33rd NCST), II: 539, 578.
Parham, F.M., (Pvt, Co F, 6th Battalion/60th NCST), III: 482.
Parham, S.J., (Capt, Co K, 4th NCST), III: 267, 723.
Parham, Samuel G., [Samuel Jones], (Capt, Co K, 54th NCST), IV: 702.
Parham, Samuel R., (Pvt, Co I, 13th Vols/23rd NCST), V: 510.
Parham, T.B., (Pvt, Co K, 54th NCST), V: 516.
Parham, W.A., (Pvt, Co G, 30th NCST), V: 492.
Paris, _____, [Parris] (Capt, Paris' Battery), II: 3; IV: 528.
Paris, Rev. Dr. John, (Chaplain, 54th NCST), III: 268, 285; IV: 618.
Paris, Mrs. Rev. John, III: 285.
Paris, Robert, (Pvt, Co A, 6th Battalion/60th NCST), III: 481.
Paris, Ky., II: 730.
Paris, Va., II: 96, 438, 609; III: 533, 567.
Parish, B.D., (Pvt, Co C, 53rd NCST), V: 501.
Parish, Duncan, (Pvt, Co C, 56th NCST), V: 565.
Parish, James T., (Pvt, Co D, 68th NCST), III: 715.
Parish, W.K., (Capt, Co B, 6th NCST), I: 295.
Parish, W.R., [William K.], (Capt, Co B, 6th NCST), IV: 710.
Parke, John Grubb, (Maj Gen, USA), I: 490, 491, 504, 509, 510, 600, 602; II: 84, 85, 308, 317, 318, 327, 543; IV: 251.
Parker, _____, [Parks, Dabney W.], (Capt, Co E, 54th NCST), III: 267.
Parker, _____, (Capt, CSN, Patrick Henry), V: 326.
Parker, A.J., (Pvt, Co M, 12th Vols/22nd NCST), V: 554.
Parker, A.L., (2nd Lt, Co H, 50th NCST), III: 203.
Parker, Allen B., (Capt, Co I, 31st NCST), II: 512.
Parker, Dr. B.H., (Ass't Surg, 32nd NCST), IV: 637.
Parker, Cader, (2nd Lt, Co D, 4th NCST), I: 232, 271.
Parker, David A., (2nd Lt, Co D, 68th NCST), III: 714.
Parker, David W., (Lt, Co C, 52nd NCST), III: 223; IV: 701, 710.
Parker, Durant A., (Capt, AQM, 28th NCST), II: 465; IV: 473.
Parker, E.S., (ACS, 50th NCST), III: 161, 202.
Parker, Francis M., (Col, 30th NCST), I: 78, 91, 113, 118, 122, 133, 246, 248, 253, 273, 723;

II: 495, 497, 498, 500, 501, 502, 505; IV: 461; V: xi, 78, 593.
Parker, George D., (Capt, Adjt, 36th NCST, 2nd Art & Engs), II: 630, 648; V: 234, 239.
Parker, George P., (3rd Sgt, Co I, 52nd NCST), III: 225.
Parker, George T., (Capt, Co H, 5th NCST), I: 291; V: 503.
Parker, George, W., (2nd Lt, Co D, 44th NCST), III: 23.
Parker, H., (Pvt, Co G, 3rd Vols/13th NCST), V: 551.
Parker, H.P., (Pvt, Co H, 52nd NCST), V: 536.
Parker, J., (Pvt, Co C, 56th NCST), III: 347.
Parker, J.A., (Pvt, Co K, 37th NCST), V: 546.
Parker, J.H, (Musician, 16th Battalion/75th NCST, 7th Cav), V: 660.
Parker, J.M., (Pvt, Co A, 30th NCST), V: 491.
Parker, James, (Lt Cmdr, USN; Pioneer, Minnesota), V: 244.
Parker, James, (Pvt, Co E, 6th Battalion/60th NCST), III: 485.
Parker, James B., (Pvt, Co C, 1st Vols/11th NCST), V: 530.
Parker, James H., (2nd Lt, Co E, 62nd Ga.; Co B, 16th Battalion/75th NCST, 7th Cav), IV: 91.
Parker, John A., (1st Lt, Co K, 68th NCST), III: 714.
Parker, John Alvis, (Pvt, Co D, 56th NCST), III: 364; V: 16.
Parker, John G., (1st Lt, Co A, 27th NCST), II: 457, 461; V: 519.
Parker, M. Pleasant, IV: 701.
Parker, Mark, (Pvt, Co D, 10th NCST, 1st Art & Engs, Reilly-Ramsay's Battery, Light Art), V: 568.
Parker, P.M., (2nd Lt, Co G, 62nd NCST), III: 516.
Parker, R.A., (Pvt, Co I, 10th Vols/20th NCST), V: 509.
Parker, Dr. R.H., (Ass't Surg, 32nd NCST), II: 522; V: 494.
Parker, Richard B., (1st Sgt, Co A, 27th NCST), II: 461; V: 522.
Parker, Richard H., (Pvt, Co B, 1st NCST), I: 142; V: 485.
Parker, S.Y., (2nd Lt, Co F, 4th NCST), I: 233.
Parker, Thomas, (Pvt, Co E, 48th NCST), V: 526.
Parker, W.B., (Pvt, Co A, 10th NCST, 1st Art & Engs, Ramseur-Manly's Battery, Light Art), I: 556.
Parker, W.H., (1st Lt, Co A, 5th Vols/15th NCST), I: 734.
Parker, W.H., (Lt, NCN; Capt, Beaufort), V: 303, 304, 306, 307, 308, 309.
Parker, W.L., (Pvt, Co E, 5th NCST), I: 292; V: 505.
Parker, W.S., (Pvt, Co I, 6th NCST), V: 513.
Parker, W. Fietche, (Lt, Claiborne-Dearing's 7th C.S. Cav; 16th Battalion/75th NCST, 7th Cav), IV: 71, 87, 89, 91.
Parker, Wiley C., (Musician, 33rd NCST), II: 538; V: 543.
Parker, Wiley F., (Capt, Co H, 29th NCST; Co 4, Henry's 14th Battalion NCST, Cav), II: 485, 493; IV: 113.
Parker, Wiley T., (Capt, Co H, 29th NCST), II: 493.
Parker, William T., (Capt, Co E, 33rd NCST), II: 539.
Parker, Willis, (Capt, Co I, 69th NCST, Thomas' Legion), III: 731.
Parker's Store, Va., I: 428, 557; III: 244, 585.
Parkersburg Pike, (nr Staunton, Va.), IV: 138.
Parks, ______, (Lt, Engineer Corps), IV: 418.

Parks, Benjamin, (Capt, Co K, 27th NCST), II: 462.
Parks, Charles M., (Pvt, Hospital Steward, Co G, 27th NCST), II: 462; V: 522.
Parks, D.C., (Pvt, AQMS, Co G, 27th NCST), II: 462; V: 523.
Parks, David C., (Lt, Co A, 9th NCST, 1st Cav), I: 485.
Parks, J.A, (1st Lt, Co A, 6th Battalion Junior Reserves; Co C, 70th NCST, 1st Junior Reserves), IV: 13.
Parks, John Alvis, (Pvt, Co D, 56th NCST), III: 364.
Parks, John P., (Lt, Co D, 34th NCST), II: 584.
Parks, Marcus A., (Col, 52nd NCST), I: 136; III: 224, 225, 226, 237, 238; IV: 701, 710; V: 10.
Parks, Miles, (Pvt, Co D, 10th NCST, 1st Art & Engs, Reilly-Ramsay's Battery, Light Art), I: 569.
Parks, Oliver T., (Capt, Co D, 33rd NCST), II: 321, 539, 578.
Parks, Thomas, (Capt, Co B, 1st Vols/11th NCST), I: 119, 584; V: 529.
Parks, W., (Pvt, Co F, 37th NCST), V: 546.
Parks, W.E., (Pvt, Co M, 11th Vols/21st NCST), V: 515.
Parks, W.F., (Pvt, Co F, 37th NCST), V: 546.
Parks, William, (Pvt, Co D, 10th NCST, 1st Art & Engs, Reilly-Ramsay's Battery, Light Art), I: 574.
Parlier, J.J., (Jr 2nd Lt, Co F, 52nd NCST), III: 224.
Parnell, Frank, (Pvt, Co E, 5th NCST), I: 292; V: 505.
Paroles, Copy of, IV: 213-214.
Parole List at Appomattox, V: 483-574, 667, 680.
Parrish, E.A., (Pvt, Co F, 2nd Vols/12th NCST), V: 507.
Parrish, John, (Pvt, Co H, 26th NCST), V: 532.
Parrish, W.K., (Capt, Co B, 6th NCST), I: 295, 345; IV: 710.
Parrish, W.R., (See: W.K.).
Parrott, E.G., (Cmdr, USN), V: 243.
Parrott, W., (Saddler, Co A, 10th NCST, 1st Art & Engs, Ramseur-Manly's Battery, Light Art), I: 551.
Parsley, William M., (Lt Col, 3rd NCST), I: 178, 182, 191, 192, 193, 196, 203, 204, 207, 210, 211, 212, 213, 227; IV: 459; V: 10.
Parson, T.A., (Pvt, Co E, 28th NCST), V: 542.
Parson, W.R., (Pvt, Co D, 11th Vols/21st NCST), V: 514.
Parsons, J.F., (Pvt, Co D, 9th NCST, 1st Cav), V: 657.
Parsons, T.A., (2nd Lt, Co A, 4th Battalion Junior Reseres; Co A, 72nd NCST, 3rd Junior Reserves), IV: 38.
Parsonage, (at Malvern Hill), I: 182, 183, 219.
Partizan Rangers, [Partisan], (and Partisan Ranger Act), III: 447, 529, 539, 549, 550, 551, 725; IV: 302; V: 270.
Paschall, R.H.M., (Sgt, Co B, 2nd Vols/12th NCST), V: 506.
Paschall, R.H.H., (Pvt, Co C, 2nd Vols/12th NCST), V: 506.
Pasquotank County, N.C., III: 319, 713, 717; IV: 483, 546, 605; V: 17, 18, 312.
Passmore, M., (2nd Lt, Co B, 62nd NCST), III: 515; IV: 710.
"Pat," (Irish nurse at Pettigrew Hospital, Raleigh), V: 578.
Pate, Henry, (Pvt, Co I, 5th Vols/15th NCST), V: 522.
Pate, Stephen W., (Pvt, Co K, 27th NCST), II: 463; V: 524.

Pate, Thomas J., (Pvt, Co D, 4th NCST), V: 488.
Patillo, ______, (Capt, Co K, 2nd Regt Home Guard), IV: 653.
Patillo, John R., (Pvt, Co F, 4th Vols/14th NCST), V: 490.
Patrick, Cornelius, (2nd Lt, Co A, 30th NCST), II: 496.
Patrick, F.F., (1st Lt, Co A, 32nd NCST), IV: 722.
Partick, George, [George W.], (Pvt, Co E, 37th NCST), II: 672.
Patrick, H.M., (Pvt, Co H, 41st NCST, 3rd Cav), II: 786.
Patrick, William H., (Lt, Co B, 61st NCST), III: 504.
Patrick County, Va., IV: 218.
Patten, B., (Pvt, Co I, 57th NCST), V: 517.
Patterson, ______, (Senator, Tenn., Son-in-law of President Johnson), III: 741.
Patterson, ______, (Musician, 4th NCST), I: 234.
Patterson, A.F., (Pvt, Co C, 11th Vols/21st NCST), V: 194.
Patterson, A.H., (Ordnance Sgt, 3rd Vols/13th NCST), V: 549.
Patterson, C., (Pvt, Co H, 52nd NCST), V: 536.
Patterson, C.A., (Cpl, Co A, 10th Vols/20th NCST), II: 118.
Patterson, D.A., (Lt, Co E, 35th NCST), V: 193.
Patterson, D.J., (Pvt, Co A, 45th NCST), V: 499.
Patterson, D.M., (Pvt, Co K, 55th NCST), V: 528.
Patterson, Daniel, (Capt, Co H, 36th NCST, 2nd Art & Engs, Clarendon's Battery), II: 630, 635; V: 225, 239.
Patterson, E.J., (Pvt, Co G, 8th NCST), V: 194.
Patterson, E.W., (Pvt, Co A, 47th NCST), V: 534.
Patterson, F., (Pvt, Co H, 56th NCST), III: 357.
Patterson, Dr. Frank, (Surg, 2nd Battalion NCST; Surg, Daniel's Brigade), IV: 245, 250, 256.
Patterson, Rev. Dr. George, (Chaplain, 3rd NCST), I: 148, 194; IV: 605.
Patterson, H.L., (2nd Lt, Co I, 1st NCST), I: 137; V: 484.
Patterson, J.B., (Pvt, Co A, 10th Vols/20th NCST), V: 508.
Patterson, J.D., (1st Lt, Co H, 56th NCST), III: 316.
Patterson, J.H., (Pvt, Co I, 37th NCST), V: 546.
Patterson, James A., (1st Sgt, Co H, 52nd NCST), III: 225.
Patterson, James D., (Pvt, Co G, 38th NCST), V: 557.
Patterson, James M., (Pvt, Co K, 25th NCST), V: 562.
Patterson, John A., (Cpl, Co F, 8th Vols/18th NCST), II: 64; V: 539.
Patterson, Joseph A., (Sgt, Co C, 33rd NCST), II: 539.
Patterson, Malloy, (2nd Lt, Co D, 46th NCST), III: 81.
Patterson, N. McN. (Pvt, Co F, 8th Vols/18th NCST), II: 64; V: 539.
Patterson, Oliver H., (1st Lt, Co E, 38th NCST), II: 677, 678.
Patterson, Dr. R.A., (Surg, 47th NCST), III: 83; IV: 639.
Patterson, R.F., (Pvt, Co D, 8th NCST), V: 193.
Patterson, Robert E., (Musician, 4th NCST), I: 234; V: 488.
Patterson, Samuel, (Maj, 2nd Regt 3rd Class, Home Guard), I: 106, 128; IV: 654.
Patterson, T.P., (Sgt, Co A, 45th NCST), V: 499.
Patterson, W.A., (Lt, Co G, 64th NCST), III: 660.
Patterson, W.F., V: 290.

Patterson, W.H., (Pvt, Co G, 26th NCST), V: 532.
Patterson, W.T., (Pvt, Co H, 56th NCST), III: 357.
Patterson, William A., (2nd Lt, Co C, 33rd NCST), II: 539.
Patterson, W. Pressly, (Cpl, Co H, 4th NCST), V: 489.
Patterson, N.C., IV: 374; V: 285.
Patton, Augustus W., (AQM, 6th Battalion/60th NCST), III: 473, 483, 484.
Patton, B.F., (Capt, Co B, 6th Battalion/60th NCST), I: 119, 133; III: 473, 474, 483, 497.
Patton, C.L., (Maj, President, University Publishing Company), I: viii.
Patton, David, (Pvt, Co H, 29th NCST), II: 490.
Patton, Miss Fannie, (Resident of Asheville), I: 130.
Patton, Hugh F., (1st Lt, ADC, Cooke's Brigade), IV: 503; V: 519.
Patton, James Alfred, (Jr 2nd Lt, Co E, 1st Vols, "Bethel"), I: 78.
Patton, James P., (2nd Sgt, Co H, 6th Vols/16th NCST), V: 552.
Patton, Dr. John D., (Surg, 50th NCST), III: 202; IV: 640.
Patton, Miss Mary, (Resident of Asheville), I: 130.
Patton, Thomas W., (Capt, Co C, 6th Battalion/60th NCST), I: 119; III: 473, 483, 497, 501.
Patton, William, (Pvt, Co A, 49th NCST), V: 564.
Paul, Gabriel Rene, (Brig Gen, USA), I: 635.
Paul, James A., (2nd Lt, Co C, Walker's Battalion, Thomas' Legion, 80th NCST), IV: 118.
Pay Department, N.C., I: 5, 23, 45.
Payne, A.M., (Pvt, Co G, 32nd NCST), V: 496.
Payne, J.H., (Lt, Co A, 10th NCST, 1st Art & Engs, Ramseur-Manly's Battery, Light Art), I: 554, 558.
Payne, Charles M., (2nd Lt, Co K, 56th NCST), III: 317, 326, 390.
Payne, J.W.A., (Pvt, Co E, 32nd NCST), V: 496.
Payne, John, (Pvt, Co A, 12th Vols/22nd NCST), V: 553.
Payne, Joseph, (Pvt, Co G, 2nd Battalion NCST), V: 495.
Payne, R., (Pvt, Co A, 45th NCST), V: 499.
Payne, W.M., (Maj, AQM, Garland's Brigade), IV: 521.
Payne, William Henry Fitzhugh, (Brig Gen), I: 208; II: 87, 93.
Payne, William R., (Pvt, Co F, 26th NCST), V: 603.
Payne's Farm, Va., (Skirmish at), I: 149, 197, 198.
Paysour, E., (Pvt, Co H, 37th NCST), V: 546.
Payton, W., [Paylor, William], (1st Lt, Co I, 45th NCST), IV: 710.
Pea Patch Island, Del., IV: 726.
Pea Ridge, Tenn., IV: 291.
Pea Ridge, Ark., (and Battle of, 1862, aka Elkhorn Tavern), I: 745; IV: 291.
Peace, Abner D., (Capt, Co E, 13th Vols/23rd NCST), I: 644; II: 185, 236, 262; V: 503, 510.
Peace, P.P., (Lt, Co G, 47th NCST), III: 85.
Peace, Failure to Negotiate, III: 394.
Peace Commission, (and Peace Commissioners), II: 15; III: 386-389, 394, 402; V: 478.
Peach Orchard, (nr Gettysburg, Pa.), I: 556; V: 605.
Peach Orchard, (nr Sharpsburg, Md.), V: 78.
Peach Tree Creek, Ga., (and Battle of, 1864), II: 720.

Peacock, David, (Pvt, Co I, 5th Vols/15th NCST), V: 522.
Peacock, George W., (Pvt, Co D, 34th NCST), V: 555.
Peacock, Joseph, (Pvt, Co A, 27th NCST), II: 461.
Peak, John, [Peake], (Capt, Co B, 6th Vols/16th NCST), I: 751; IV: 137.
Peake's Turnout, Va., II: 21.
Pearce, B.F., [Benjamin F.], (1st Lt, Co K, 54th NCST), IV: 702, 710.
Pearce, J.H.C., (Musician, 52nd NCST), III: 226.
Pearce, Ricks, (Lt, Co L, 6th Vols/16th NCST), V: 666.
Pearce, Samuel M., (Pvt, Co D, 68th NCST), III: 715.
Pearce, W.H., (Pvt, Co B, Starr's Battery, Starr's 13th Battalion NCST, Light Art), IV: 346.
Pearl River, Miss., II: 734, 735; III: 484, 499.
Pearsall, D.M., (Jr 2nd Lt, Co A, 38th NCST), II: 675; III: 1.
Pearsall, David M., (Pvt, Co A, 38th NCST), V: 557.
Pearsall, J.H., (Sgt, Co D, 4th NCST), I: 232.
Pearsall, Jere J., (Pvt, Co A, 43rd NCST), III: 20; V: 497.
Pearsall, John W., (3rd Sgt, Co A, 38th NCST), V: 556.
Pearsall, William F., (1st Sgt, Co A, 38th NCST), V: 556.
Pearson, Charles W., (Capt, Co H, 63rd NCST, 5th Cav), III: 587, 588, 601, 641, 643, 648, 653, 654, 655.
Pearson, Giles William, (Father of Capt C.W. Pearson), III: 655.
Pearson, J.A., (Pvt, Co K, 35th NCST), V: 563.
Pearson, Dr. J.N., [J.F.], (Surg, 5th NCST), I: 291; IV: 632; V: 503.
Pearson, Jacob C., (Musician, 55th NCST), V: 527.
Pearson, James T., (Lt, Co B, 46th NCST), III: 80.
Pearson, John M., (Adjt. 7th NCST), IV: 472.
Pearson, John R., (Lt, Co F, 7th NCST), I: 385.
Pearson, John W., (Adjt, 7th NCST), I: 384.
Pearson, R.C., (Resident of Morganton), IV: 372.
Pearson, Richmond M., (Chief Justice N.C. Supreme Sourt), II: 402, 804; III: 655; IV: 517.
Pearson, Robert P., (Pvt, Co E, 6th Vols/16th NCST), V: 552.
Pearson, W.A., (Maj, Adjt, 2nd Regt Home Guard), IV: 653.
Pearson, W.R., (1st Lt, Co C, 77th NCST, 7th Senior Reserves), IV: 99.
Pearson, William, (1st Lt, Co I, 31st NCST), II: 508, 512.
Peatree, H.S., (Pvt, Co B, 10th Vols/20th NCST), V: 508.
Peay, T.C., (Pvt, Co G, 45th NCST), V: 500.
Peck, Adam, (Lt, Co D, 68th NCST), III: 744, 747.
Peck, J.W., (Capt, Co G, 58th NCST), III: 447.
Peck, Job B., (Lt, Co D, 64th NCST), III: 660.
Peck, John James, (Maj Gen, USA), IV: 338; V: 83, 84.
Peck, Leander, (Pvt, Co G, 6th Battalion/60th NCST), III: 482.
Peden, J.W., (2nd Lt, Co B, 1st NCST), I: 136.
Peden, John T., (Capt, Co B, 55th NCST), III: 296, 307; V: 520.
Pedrick, W.T., (Pvt, Co K, 10th NCST, 1st Art & Engs, Pool's Hvy Art), V: 50.
Peebles J.H., (1st Lt, Co E, 42nd NCST), II: 790, 806.

Peebles, Robert B., (Capt, AAG, Matt Ransom's Brigade), II: 611, 612, 626; III: 315, 397; V: 559.
Peebles' Farm, (and Battle of, 1864, Wilmington & Weldon Railroad), IV: 88, 90.
Peek, Alfred, (Lt, Co C, 64th NCST), III: 660.
Peek, J.B., (Lt, Co G, 64th NCST), III: 660.
Peek, John, (Capt, Co C, 64th NCST), III: 660, 662.
Peek, L.W., (Capt, Co D, 64th NCST), III: 660.
Peek, Levi, (Lt, Co C, 64th NCST), III: 660.
Peek, Zachariah, (1st Sgt, Co B, 6th Vols/16th NCST), V: 552.
Peel, J.H., (Capt, Co A, 5th Vols/15th NCST), I: 734.
Peel, J.W., (Lt, Co B, 9th NCST, 1st Cav), I: 446, 448, 485.
Peel, Robert, (Cpl, Co D, 4th NCST), I: 232.
Peel, T.J., (Pvt, Co H, 56th NCST), III: 357.
Peele, A.E., (2nd Lt, Co D, 57th NCST), IV: 701, 710.
Peele, F., (Cpl, Co D, 33rd NCST), V: 544.
Peele, J.W., (Lt, Co B, 9th NCST, 1st Cav), I: 485.
Peele, J.W., (Editor), IV: 448.
Peeler, ______, [Alfred L.], (Bugler, Co D, 10th NCST, 1st Art & Engs, Reilly-Ramsay's Battery, Light Art), I: 571.
Peeler, Alfred L., (Pvt, Co D, 10th NCST, 1st Art & Engs, Reilly-Ramsay's Battery, Light Art), V: 568.
Peeler, Andrew, (Pvt, Co F, 34th NCST), V: 555.
Peeler, Daniel, (Pvt, Co D, 10th NCST, 1st Art & Engs, Reilly-Ramsay's Battery, Light Art), V: 568.
Peeler, Doctor D., (Pvt, Co F, 34th NCST), V: 555.
Peeler, J.A., (Cpl, Co C, 57th NCST), V: 517.
Peeler, J.M., (Pvt, Co C, 57th NCST), V: 517.
Peeler, John, (Pvt, Co C, 10th NCST, 1st Art & Engs, Brem-Graham-Williams' Battery, Light Art), V: 567.
Peeples, H., (Pvt, Co A, 33rd NCST), V: 543.
Peete, Dr. R.S.F., (Surg, 2nd Vols/12th NCST), I: 606; IV: 633.
Pegg, William, (Pvt, Co G, 6th Battalion/60th NCST), III: 482.
Pegram, ______, (Admr, CSN), II: 93; IV: 254, 578.
Pegram, A.M., (Pvt, Co G, 45th NCST), V: 500.
Pegram, John, (Brig Gen), I: 328; II: 129, 143, 256, 260, 261, 262, 450, 501, 533, 649, 650; III: 677; IV: 254, 290, 524.
Pegram, John C., (Adjt, 9th Vols/19th NCST, 2nd Cav; Capt, AG, M.W. Ransom's Brigade), I: 606, 609; II: 83, 88, 92; III: 338, 359; IV: 253, 254, 572, 575, 578; V: 179, 184.
Pegram, Miles P., (AQM, 37th NCST), IV: 474.
Pegram, R.B., (Pvt, Co B, 30th NCST), V: 491.
Pegram, R.B., (Pvt, Co D, 30th NCST; Detailed, 2nd Corps Provost Guard), V: 570.
Pegram House, (Fight at), I: 600; II: 58, 311, 481, 575; III: 97; IV: 470, 478.
Peldon, Joseph N., (Pvt, Co A, 5th Vols/15th NCST), V: 520.
Pelham, John, (Maj, Stuart's Horse Artillery), I: 422, 713.
Pell, ______, IV: 602.

Pell, William E., (1st Cpl, Co A, 10th NCST, 1st Art & Engs, Ramseur-Manly's Battery, Light Art), I: 551.
Pemberton, John A., (Col, N.C. Ordnance Department), I: 39, 40, 78.
Pemberton, John Clifford, (Lt Gen), I: 171, 552, 709, 767; II: 734; III: 485.
Pender, Mrs. ______, (Passenger, Advance), V: 341, 343.
Pender, J., (Pvt, Co E, 45th NCST), V: 500.
Pender, Josiah, (Capt, Co G, 10th NCST, 1st Art & Engs, Pender-Manney's Hvy Art), I: 363, 501.
Pender, S.M., (2nd Lt, Co I, 5th Vols/15th NCST), I: 735; V: 519.
Pender, Thomas J., (2nd Lt, Co D, 33rd NCST), II: 539.
Pender, Walter, (2nd Lt, Co G, 10th NCST, 1st Art & Engs, Pender-Manney's Hvy Art), I: 501, 521, 536.
Pender, W.N., (Pvt, Co E, 58th NCST), III: 453.
Pender, William Dorsey, (Maj Gen), I: xi, 300, 303, 333, 346, 349, 350, 351, 352, 353, 375, 380, 381, 613, 653, 654, 659, 663, 665, 667, 668, 669, 673, 693, 697, 756, 757, 760, 764, 765; II: 29, 35, 41, 42, 45, 168, 170, 171, 172, 231, 240, 555, 556, 562, 568, 583, 586, 661, 679, 680, 682, 683, 684, 685, 686, 687, 689, 690, 691, 693; III: 159, 237, 339; IV: 37, 153, 155, 156, 157, 160, 161, 163, 164, 165, 167, 170, 173, 175, 176, 180, 181, 254, 551, 552, 553, 554, 555; V: xii, xiii, 4, 9, 95, 104, 116, 121, 151.
Pendergrass, John, (Pvt, Co G, 52nd NCST), V: 536.
Pendergrast, R., (Pvt, Co C, 56th NCST), III: 347.
Pendleton, Rev. Dr. William Nelson, (Brig Gen, Chief of Artillery ANV), I: 81, 144, 208, 558, 559, 564; II: 391, 459; III: 166, 167, 168; IV: 262, 496.
Pendley, William, (Lt, Co A, 64th NCST), III: 660.
Peninsular Campaign, I: 709; II: 25, 194.
Penick, Dixon B., (Lt, Co H, 7th NCST), I: 378, 385.
Penland, J.H., (Pvt, Co F, 6th Battalion/60th NCST), III: 482.
Penland, W.S., (Pvt, Co C, 6th Battalion/60th NCST), III: 482.
Pennington, ______, [John], (Pvt, Co A, 30th NCST), IV: 602.
Pennington, Alexander Cummings McWhorter, (Brig Gen, USA), III: 644.
Pennsylvania, I: 291, 324, 334, 421, 423, 424, 462, 481, 498, 541, 643, 672, 698; II: 74, 182, 233,341, 367, 478, 502, 525, 671, 702; III: 41, 42, 270, 411, 559, 560, 561, 664, 730, 733, 737; IV: 176, 181, 238, 514, 558, 559, 598, 601; V: 81, 82.
Pennsylvania Campaign, (See also: Gettysburg Campaign), I: 192; II: 77, 401; III: 5, 131; V: 113-114.
Penny, Dr. George A., [Penney], (Ass't Surg, 2nd Vols/12th NCST), I: 606, 651; IV: 633; V: 503.
Penny, J.A., (Pvt, Co C, 57th NCST), V: 517.
Penny, J.J., (1st Lt, Co D, 50th NCST), III: 203.
Penny, John A.J., (Pvt, Co E, 4th Vols/14th NCST), V: 490.
Penny, Ransom, (Pvt, Co C, 5th NCST), I: 291; V: 505.

Pennypacker, Galusha, (Col, Pennypacker's Brigade, USA), V: 237.
Pensacola, Fla., III: 494.
Pensacola Bay, Fla., II: 737.
Pensacola Naval Yard, IV: 417; V: 385.
Pense, Jacob, (Pvt, Co E, 5th NCST), I: 292; V: 505.
Penyan, W.E., (5th Sgt, Co I, 48th NCST), V: 527.
Peoples, Martin H., (Capt, Co K, 7th NCST), I: 361, 369.
Peoples, R.G., (Pvt, Co C, 10th NCST, 1st Art & Engs, Brem-Graham-Williams' Battery, Light Art), V: 567.
Pepper, J.R., (Ordnance Sgt, 52nd NCST), III: 226.
Pepper, R.K., (Lt Col, 11th Vols/21st NCST), II: 131, 132, 144; IV: 230; V: 11.
Percy, A.B., (2nd Lt, Co F, 56th NCST), III: 315.
Percy, J.D., (Pvt, Co D, 33rd NCST), V: 544.
Perdue, Thomas, (Pvt, Co C, 27th NCST), II: 462; V: 523.
Perkins, A.W., (Pvt, Co F, 26th NCST), V: 603.
Perkins, Elisha A., (Capt, Co F, 41st NCST, 3rd Cav), II: 771, 775.
Perkins, Frank, (Ensign, Co G, 8th NCST), V: 194.
Perkins, Francis J., (Color-bearer, Co A, 8th NCST), I: 401, 402.
Perkins, Henry, (Pvt, Co A, 64th NCST), III: 668.
Perkins, J.W., (Pvt, Co H, 52nd NCST), V: 536.
Perkins, James M., (2nd Lt, Co D, 44th NCST), III: 23.
Perkins, James M., [2nd Lt, Co. G, 61st Va.], (2nd Lt, 12th Va.), IV: 403.
Perkins, Julius, (2nd Lt, Co F, 31st NCST), II: 512.
Perkins, W.L.M., (2nd Lt, Co F, 43rd NCST), III: 3, 12.
Perkinson, James R., (Pvt, Co C, 5th Vols/15th NCST), V: 521.
Perkinson, S.E., (Pvt, Co G, 43rd NCST), V: 498.
Perkinson's Mill, Va., III: 167.
Perquimans County, N.C., V: 282.
Perrel, D.C, (2nd Lt, Co H, 48th NCST), V: 520.
Perry, A.S., (Capt, Co I, 32nd NCST), I: 736.
Perry, Benjamin L., (Adjt, 58th NCST), III: 432.
Perry, Bradford, (Civilian), IV: 83.
Perry, C.E., (Sgt, Co E, 4th NCST), I: 233; V: 488.
Perry, Daniel R., (1st Lt, Co B, 36th NCST, 2nd Art & Engs, Munn's Hvy Art), II: 646.
Perry, Dr. Daniel W., (Ass't Surg, 73rd NCST, 4th Senior Reserves), IV: 66, 643.
Perry, Edward Aylesworth, (Brig Gen), II: 363.
Perry, Fabius H., (1st Lt, Co H, 31st NCST), II: 508.
Perry, George W., (Pvt, Co D, 68th NCST), III: 715.
Perry, H., (Pvt, Co G, 56th NCST), III: 348.
Perry, Hugh H., (Lt, Co B, 47th NCST), III: 84.
Perry, Isaac R., (Pvt, Co G, 38th NCST), V: 557.
Perry, J.S., (Musicianm 16th Battalion/75th NCST, 7th Cav), V: 660.
Perry, J.W., (Lt, Adjt, Wynn's 15th Battalion NCST, Cav), IV: 365, 368.
Perry, J.W., (Lt, Co A, Littlejohn's 23rd Battalion NCST, Senior Reserves), IV: 399.
Perry, J.W., (Pvt, Co I, 1st NCST), V: 485.

Perry, John D., (3rd Lt, Co A, 7th Vols/17th NCST), II: 7.
Perry, John H., (2nd Sgt, Co D, 68th NCST), III: 715.
Perry, John M., (1st Lt, Co F, Latham-Potts-Flanner's Battery, Starr's 13th Battalion NCST, Light Art), IV: 354.
Perry, Joseph, (Pvt, Co D, 68th NCST), III: 715.
Perry, L.D., (Cpl, Co G, 32nd NCST), V: 496.
Perry, L.R., (Pvt, Co F, 16th Battalion/75th NCST, 7th Cav), V: 660.
Perry, S.R., (2nd Lt, Co I, 30th NCST), II: 497.
Perry, Thomas, (Pvt, Co F, 5th NCST), I: 292; V: 505.
Perry, Thomas L., (1st Lt, Adjt, 4th NCST), I: 230, 231, 270.
Perry, W.H., (Cpl, Co A, 47th NCST), V: 534.
Perry, Willie, (Capt, Co E, 5th Vols/15th NCST), I: 735.
Perryville, Ky., (and Battle of, 1862), II: 487, 702, 705, 709; III: 448; IV: 438.
Perryville, Va., I: 172; II: 709, 730.
Person, B.F., (Lt, Co H, 9th NCST, 1st Cav), I: 486.
Person, Jesse H., (Lt, Co E, 9th NCST, 1st Cav), I: 486.
Person, John B., (2nd Lt, Co D, 9th Vols/19th NCST, 2nd Cav), II: 89.
Person, Samuel J., (Lt Col, N.C. Quartermaster General's Department), I: 23.
Person County, N.C., II: 627; III: 288, 292, 361; IV: 609, 610; V: 111, 187.
Pescud, John S., (Adjt, 4th Battalion Junior Reserves), IV: 38, 595.
Petersburg, Va., I: 12, 117, 155, 156, 209, 264, 297, 320, 321, 328, 365, 395, 396, 397, 398, 399, 402, 405, 431, 432, 434, 436, 442, 538, 539, 559, 577, 578, 581, 742, 781; II: 56, 109, 244, 255, 261, 262, 263, 264, 266, 271, 274, 278, 279, 284, 292, 334, 385, 429, 430, 439, 483, 515, 522, 523, 533, 534, 574, 600, 611, 612, 613, 619, 694, 776, 792, 793, 796; III: 39, 40, 58, 86, 112, 114, 116, 129, 130, 135, 162, 166, 167, 169, 210, 227, 249, 250, 252, 275, 290, 321, 329, 330, 396, 403, 422, 465, 609, 705; IV: 74, 86, 87, 92, 93, 138, 357, 388, 389, 488, 502, 555, 556, 558, 569, 572, 573, 687; V: 326, 628.
Petersburg, Siege of, (and Campaign, 1864-1865,) I: 39, 159, 160, 174, 210, 290, 330, 334, 335, 384-386, 406, 430, 496, 526, 549, 559, 560, 580, 582, 584, 597, 598, 599, 600, 601, 602, 650, 677, 678, 681, 682, 701, 702, 728, 729, 747, 748, 765; II: 4, 6, 7, 8, 45, 58, 59, 60, 61, 62, 63, 75, 76, 77, 108, 112, 124, 143, 144, 173, 174, 287, 288, 298, 336, 386, 387, 390, 391, 400, 411, 417, 419, 421, 447, 448, 452, 454, 480, 481, 482, 515, 518, 519, 534, 576, 577, 588, 589, 611, 612, 621, 622, 623, 624, 625, 670, 694, 695, 720, 773, 778, 781, 783, 786, 790, 791, 797, 799, 800, 801, 805; III: 9, 15, 17, 29, 30, 31, 32, 33, 34, 37, 56, 77, 78, 79, 80, 82, 99, 121, 122, 123, 126, 135, 138, 139, 140, 144, 152, 153, 154-159, 211, 212, 213, 214, 218, 247-248, 256, 260, 261, 262, 263, 275, 277, 281, 282, 307, 308, 310, 312, 317, 349, 350, 351, 352, 353,

354, 359, 360, 362, 363, 366, 367, 368, 466, 372, 374, 376, 380, 382, 385, 390, 391, 398, 419, 425, 426, 427, 458, 467, 468, 470, 505, 512-513, 514, 538, 541, 615, 616, 618, 624, 627, 628, 645, 648, 687, 689, 690; IV: 73, 85-86, 89, 93, 94, 202, 203, 205, 206, 208, 209, 210, 242, 254, 302, 354, 359, 361, 362, 424, 427, 430, 450, 452, 453, 455, 459, 461, 469, 470, 471, 476, 478, 486, 488, 489, 493, 494, 495, 508, 509, 516, 524, 526, 528, 529, 534, 535, 554, 563, 565, 575-576, 589, 615, 718; V: 15, 187, 205, 207, 211, 247, 252, 258, 266, 269, 270, 275.
Petersburg Railroad, I: 577, 747; III: 135.
Petersburg Turnpike, Va., III: 77.
Petersburg & Norfolk Railroad, III: 367.
Petersburg & Richmond Railroad, I: 321; III: 227; IV: 529.
Petersburg & Weldon Railroad, I: 321, 384, 385, 386, 407, 431, 432, 433, 435, 436, 437, 467, 471, 496, 527, 588, 597, 598, 599, 678, 681, 702; II: 56, 58, 87, 103, 105, 254, 261, 299, 387, 450, 481, 574, 576, 588, 615, 625; III: 248, 249, 251, 309, 311; IV: 388, 389, 539, 554, 572, 573, 589.
Peterson, Edward, (Musician, Mickey's Band, 26th NCST), II: 398.
Peterson, J., (Sgt, Co E, 10th Vols/20th NCST), II: 114.
Peterson, T.R., [Patterson, Robert English], (Musician, Cpl, Co C, 4th NCST), I: 233.
Pethel, J.V., (Pvt, Co A, 10th Vols/20th NCST), V: 508.
Petree, William, (Pvt, Co H, 35th NCST), V: 563.
Pettigrew, Mrs. _____, (Of Raleigh, Head Nurse, 1st N.C. General Hospital, Petersburg, Va.), IV: 624.
Pettigrew, J.C., (Pvt, Co A, 3rd Vols/13th NCST), V: 549.
Pettigrew, James Johnston, (Brig Gen), I: xi, 158, 352, 380, 381, 425, 588, 589, 590, 591, 592, 597; II: 42, 43, 44, 161, 167, 171, 334, 335, 336, 339, 340, 342, 343, 344, 347, 352, 353, 357, 358, 359, 362, 364, 365, 366, 375, 376, 377, 380, 399, 407, 409, 564, 566, 567, 568, 598, 661, 662, 793; III: 24, 25, 26, 87, 88, 90, 92, 105, 110, 170, 171, 172, 232, 235, 236, 237, 240, 299, 300, 301, 321, 416; IV: 10, 36, 37, 183, 338, 357, 361, 555, 556, 557, 558-559, 560, 561, 562, 568; V: xii, 4, 9, 10, 15-16, 101, 104, 105, 106, 108, 109, 111, 114, 114, 116, 117, 120, 124, 125, 126, 127, 128, 129, 130, 131, 132, 134, 135, 139, 140, 144, 146, 150, 156, 157, 649.
Pettigrew, Miss Mary L., IV: 624.
Pettigrew, Rev. William S., (Brother of J.J. Pettigrew, Senior Reserves at Fort Fisher), IV: 539.
Pettigrew-Pickett Charge, (aka Pettigrew's, Pickett-Pettigrew's and Pickett's Charge; 15 N.C. Regiments and 9 Va. Regiments were involved in the ill-fated charge. Had Longstreet carried out the orders given him, when they were given instead of sulking, the charge may have stood a chance of success. As it was, Longstreet was no more prompt on that battlefield than he was on most. The delay of several hours casued by his inexcusable

foolishness resulted in the massive loss of life and ultimately brought the battle to an end.), I: 196, 315; II: 43, 44, 74, 360, 362, 367, 415, 416, 478, 562, 587, 661; III: 90, 299, 382; IV: 179-180, 468, 518; V: xiii, 101-159, 596, 609.
Pettigrew's Division Losses, II: 367, 368.
Pettit, H.B., (Pvt, Co E, 25th NCST), V: 561.
Pettit, J.M., (Pvt, Co I, 25th NCST), V: 562.
Pettiway, J.W., (Pvt, Co B, 35th NCST), V: 562.
Pettus, Edmund Winston, (Brig Gen), III: 441.
Pettus, H.M., (Pvt, Co A, 1st Vols/11th NCST), V: 530.
Petty, C.Q., [C.R.], (Maj, 49th NCST), III: 143, 144, 147, 153; V: 559.
Petty, Robert E., (Maj, 35th NCST), II: 620, 623, 626, 627, 670; V: 559.
Petway, Oliver Cromwell, (Adjt, Camp Crab Tree; Lt Col, 35th NCST), II: 304, 592, 593, 595, 597, 600; V: 11.
Peyton, ______, (Maj, Grimes' Staff), V: 255.
Peyton, Henry, (Col, IG, ANV), IV: 453; V: 148, 250, 255.
Peyton's Ford, (Rapidan River, Va.), III: 243.
Pfohl, C.B., (2nd Lt, Co B, 4th Battalion Junior Reserves; Co B, 72nd NCST, 3rd Junior Reserves) IV: 38, 48.
Pfohl, E.A., (Pvt, Co L, 11th Vols/21st NCST), V: 515.
Pfohl, W.J., (Maj, 11th Vols/21st NCST), II: 143, 144; IV: 230; V: 12.
Pfohl, W.T., (Pvt, Co L, 11th Vols/21st NCST), V: 515.
Pharr, S.E.W., (Lt, Co H, 57th NCST), IV: 702, 710.
Phelps, ______, (Col, Cmdr, Newport News, Va.), I: 87.
Phelps, T.S., (Lt Cmdr, USN), V: 242.
Phifer, Charles, (Pvt, 10th NCST, 1st Art & Engs, Pool's Hvy Art) I: 498, 533.
Phifer, Charles W., (Brig Gen), V: 649.
Phifer, David, (Pvt, Co A, 33rd NCST), II: 544.
Phifer, Edward, III: 140.
Phifer, George L., (Bugler, Co A, 10th NCST, 1st Art & Engs, Ramseur-Manly's Battery, Light Art), I: 551.
Phifer, George L., (Capt, Co K, 49th NCST), III: 125, 128, 139, 140, 148, 153.
Phifer, J.A., (Cpl, Co K, 43rd NCST), V: 499.
Phifer, J.L., (Ordnance Sgt, 10th Vols/20th NCST), V: 508.
Phifer, J.W., (Sgt, Co B, 4th NCST), I: 232.
Philadelphia, Tenn., III: 679; IV: 291.
Philadelphia, Pa., IV: 665; V: 374, 619, 621.
Philadelphia, Va., I: 311.
Philadelphia Centennial, 1876, I: 132.
Philbeck, J.P., (Pvt, Co I, 56th NCST), III: 348.
Philippi, Va., I: 86.
Philips, Fred, (2nd Lt, Co I, 5th Vols/15th NCST), I: 735.
Philips, Fred, [Phillips], (Capt, Adjt, 30th NCST), I: 273, 275; II: 499, 500, 502; V: 593.
Philips, Fred Jr., [Phillips], (Visitor to the Sharpsburg battlefield), V: 592.
Phillips, ______, (Capt, Co F, 2nd Regt Home Guard), IV: 653.

Phillips, ______, (Capt, Va. Cav; at Battle of Bethel), I: 89.
Phillips, B.B., (Pvt, Co E, 44th NCST), V: 533.
Phillips, C., (Pvt, Co B, 1st Vols/11th NCST), V: 530.
Phillips, C.T., (Pvt, Co B, 1st Battalion NCST), V: 504.
Phillips, D.C., (Pvt, Co A, 10th NCST, 1st Art & Engs, Ramseur-Manly's Battery, Light Art), I: 555.
Phillips, E., (Pvt, Co E, 44th NCST), V: 533.
Phillips, G., (Pvt, Co B, 47th NCST), V: 534.
Phillips, J., (Pvt, Co G, 28th NCST), V: 542.
Phillips, J.A., (Lt, 64th NCST), IV: 710.
Phillips, J.J., (Sgt, Co G, 33rd NCST), II: 540.
Phillips, J.L., (Capt, Co G, 58th NCST), III: 433, 435.
Phillips, James T., (Capt, Co E, 44th NCST), III: 23.
Phillips, Joseph, (Pvt, Co F, 26th NCST), V: 601.
Phillips, L.C., (Pvt, Co A, 46th NCST), V: 524.
Phillips, Matthew, (2nd Lt, Co E, 77th NCST, 7th Senior Reserves), IV: 100.
Phillips, N.G., (Capt, Co I, 69th NCST, Thomas' Legion), III: 731.
Phillips, R., (Pvt, Co F, 30th NCST), V: 492.
Phillips, Hon. Samuel F., (Board of Auditors), I: 20, 45.
Phillips, Thomas, (4th Sgt, Co A, 38th NCST), V: 556.
Phillips, Thomas P., (2nd Lt, Co I, 34th NCST), V: 548.
Phillips, W.B., [William B.], (Pvt, Co F, 21st Ga.), V: 194.
Phillips, W.E., (Pvt, Co F, 26th NCST), V: 532, 601.
Phillips, Wesley A., (Pvt, Co A, 11th Vols/21st NCST), V: 514.
Phillips, William H., (2nd Lt, Co B, Walker's Battalion, Thomas' Legion, 80th NCST), IV: 118.
Phillips' Farm, Va., I: 420.
Philpot, J.W., (Capt, Co E, 35th NCST), II: 627.
Philpot, S.R., (Pvt, Co E, 9th NCST, 1st Cav), V: 657.
Philyaw, Gideon, (Pvt, Co F, 26th NCST), V: 603.
Philyaw, S.P., (Cpl, Co F, 26th NCST), V: 602.
Phinisee, John H., (Capt, Co G, 25th NCST), II: 292.
Phipps, J.L., (Cpl, Co B, 2nd Vols/12th NCST), V: 506.
Pickard, L., (Pvt, Co I, 6th NCST), V: 513.
Pickens, S.V., (Adjt., Co G, Woodfin's Battalion, 9th NCST, 1st Cav; Adjt, Henry's 14th Battalion, 79th NCST, 8th Cav), IV: 109, 113, 115, 116, 363.
Pickering, C.W., (Capt, USN), V: 243.
Pickett, George E., (Maj Gen), I: 353, 354, 397, 526, 555; II: 3, 41, 42, 43, 44, 88, 364, 391, 564, 616, 751, 777, 797; III: 7, 90, 91, 132, 146, 301, 333, 335, 390, 396, 397, 398, 646; IV: 265, 266, 267, 486, 487, 489, 528, 573; V: 105, 108, 109, 124, 128, 129, 130, 134, 141, 142, 147, 158, 326, 328, 332, 333.
Pickett, I.J., [Isaac J.], (1st Lt, Co F, 3rd NCST), I: 213.
Pickett's Factory, (Swift Creek, Va.), III: 112.
Pickett-Pettigrew Charge, (See: Pettigrew-Pickett Charge).
Picot, Julian, (Capt, Co G, 31st NCST), II: 507, 512.
Piedmont Road, (Railroad), I: 446.
Piedmont Station, Va., I: 340, 341; III: 742, 745, 746.

Pierce, ______, (Maj, N.C. Quartermaster Department), I: 28.
Pierce, A., (Pvt, Co C, 3rd Vols/13th NCST), V: 550.
Pierce, A.L., (1st Lt, Co K, 1st NCST), I: 137.
Pierce, Byron Root, (Maj Gen, USA), I: 87, 88, 89, 92, 96, 97, 98, 100, 107.
Pierce, J.C., (Lt, Co D, 2nd NCST), I: 159.
Pierce, J.P., (Pvt, Co C, Cumming's Battery, Starr's 13th Battalion NCST, Light Art), IV: 362; V: 16.
Pierce, James M., (Pvt, Co F, 43rd NCST), V: 498.
Pierce, Jeremiah, (Pvt, Co D, 10th NCST, 1st Art & Engs, Reilly-Ramsay's Battery, Light Art), V: 568.
Pierce, L.M., (Pvt, Co F, 49th NCST), V: 564.
Pierce, William A., (Maj, 39th NCST), II: 508, 706.
Pierson, ______, (Col, 4th Mass.), III: 328.
Pierson, ______, (Col, Cmdr Johnson's Island Federal Prison), IV: 666, 681.
Pierson, J.M., IV: 702.
Pierson, Sylvester, (Pvt, Co A, Millard's 9th/20th Battalion Junior Reserves), IV: 389.
Pigeon River, N.C., III: 517, 524.
Pigeon River, Camp on, III: 524.
Pike, Oliver M., (2nd Lt, Co L, 12th Vols/22nd NCST), II: 166, 172.
Pike, W.M., (Pvt, Co L, 12th Vols/22nd NCST), V: 554.
Pike, William B., (Pvt, Co H, 2nd NCST), I: 176; V: 486.
Pilkinton, J.A., (Pvt, Co D, 61st NCST), III: 507.
Pilot Mountain, N.C., V: 633.
Pine Mountain, Ga., II: 743.
Pine Mountain Road, Tenn., IV: 274.
Pineville, Ky., IV: 271.
Pineville, N.C., IV: 613.
Pinick, J.C., (Cpl, Co H, 6th NCST), V: 513.
Pinion, E.S., (Pvt, Co F, 29th NCST), V: 173.
Pinkney, R.F., (Cmdr, CSN), V: 298, 313.
Pinkston, H.D., (Pvt, Co K, 26th NCST), V: 532.
Pinner, Benjamin, (Pvt, Co H, 25th NCST), V: 561.
Pinnix, J.N., (Pvt, Co E, 1st Vols/11th NCST), V: 530.
Pinnix, Will, (Pvt, Co A, 3rd Vols/13th NCST), I: 660.
Piper, J.G., (Musician, 6th NCST), V: 511.
Pipkin, E., (Pvt, Co G, 48th NCST), V: 526.
Pipkin, Isaac, (Capt, Co G, 31st NCST), II: 507, 512, 515.
Pipkin, S.D., (2nd Lt, Co F, 5th Vols/15th NCST), I: 735.
Pipkin, S.H., (Cpl, Co A, 30th NCST), II: 498.
Pippin, Calvin, (Pvt, Co B, 47th NCST), V: 534.
Pisgah, Va., IV: 602.
Pisgah Mountains, N.C., (aka, Newfound Mountains), III: 758.
Pistole, James M., (Pvt, Co B, 5th Vols/15th NCST), V: 521.
Pitch Landing, N.C., IV: 26.
Pitcher, A.R., (Orderly Sgt, Co F, 2nd Vols/12th NCST), I: 645.
Pitchford, T.J., (Lt, Co I, 2nd Vols/12th NCST), I: 642.
Pitman, J.P., (1st Lt, Co E, 51st NCST), III: 219.
Pitman, J.W., (Lt, Co B, 58th NCST), III: 432.
Pitman, James M., (Pvt, Co D, 10th NCST, 1st Art & Engs, Reilly-Ramsay's Battery, Light Art), I: 575.

Pitman, John A., (Pvt, Co H, 2nd Vols/12th NCST; Detailed, 2nd Corps Provost Guard), V: 570.
Pitman, N., (Pvt, Co H, 2nd Vols/12th NCST), V: 507.
Pitman, R., (Pvt, Co E, 6th NCST), V: 512.
Pitt, _____, (Capt, 65th NCST, 6th Cav), III: 680.
Pitt, J.W., (2nd Lt, Co F, 30th NCST), II: 496.
Pitt, J.W., (Pvt, Co I, 30th NCST), V: 493.
Pitt County, N.C., I: 102, 533; II: 126, 444, 620, 771, 772; III: 704, 726; IV: 15, 17, 77, 483, 515, 595.
Pittard, G.W., (Pvt, Co K, 6th NCST), V: 514.
Pittman, O.P., (Lt, Co B, 63rd NCST, 5th Cav), I: 120.
Pittman, R.E., (Cpl, Co F, 30th NCST), V: 492.
Pittman, Thaddeus E., (Adjt, 27th NCST), II: 461; V: 519.
Pittman, William, (Pvt, Co C, 43rd NCST), V: 498.
Pitts, _____, (Capt, 65th NCST, 6th Cav), IV: 15, 16.
Pitts, B.F., (Pvt, Co C, 11th Vols/21st NCST), V: 514.
Pitts, F.G., (Capt, Co F, 30th NCST; Capt, Claiborne-Dearing's 7th C.S. Cav; Capt, Co I, 16th Battalion/75th NCST, 7th Cav; Maj, 16th Battalion/75th NCST, 7th Cav), II: 495; IV: 71, 72, 76, 85, 91, 93, 94, 370.
Pitts, John W., (Capt, Co A, 4th Battalion Junior Reserves; Co A, 72nd NCST, 3rd Junior Reserves), IV: 38, 51.
Pitts, Mark B., (2nd Lt, Claiborne-Dearing's 7th C.S. Cav; Co I, 16th Battalion/75th NCST, 7th Cav), IV: 91.
Pittsboro, N.C., I: 265; IV: 431, 517, 610.
Pittsburg, Pa., III: 560; IV: 665.
Plank Road, (aka Orange & Fredericksburg Plank Road, in the Wilderness), I: 743, 744; II: 40, 48, 73, 118, 230, 231, 241, 381, 446, 476, 559, 561, 586, 588, 665, 693; III: 75, 244, 303, 585, 592, 595; IV: 190, 191, 192, 475, 507; V: 93, 95, 96.
Pleasant Hill, N.C., II: 390.
Pleasant Valley, Md., I: 421, 739, 740.
Pleasanton, Alfred, (Maj Gen, USA), I: 421, 423, 424; II: 91, 93; III: 557, 558, 560, 561, 562, 564, 565, 566, 567, 574.
Pleasants, W.H., (Lt, Co G, 47th NCST), III: 85.
Pleasants, Henry, (Brig Gen, USA, Constructed the mine that produced The Crater), III: 372.
Pledger, J.C., (Lt, Co B, 9th NCST, 1st Cav), I: 485.
Pledger, James, (Pvt, Detached Co, 68th NCST), III: 723.
Plemmons, Silas J., (Pvt, Co H, 2nd Battalion NCST), V: 495.
Plemmons, William, (Pvt, Co B, 6th Battalion/60th NCST), III: 482.
Plemmons, William B., (Musician, 6th Vols/16th NCST), V: 552.
Pless, P.J., (Pvt, Co G, 5th NCST), I: 292; V: 505.
Pless, Solomom, (Cpl, Co A, 34th NCST), V: 554.
Plum Run, (nr Gettysburg, Pa.), V: 109.
Plumby, John, (Capt, Co A, 25th NCST), II: 292.
Plumlee, James M., (Pvt, Co H, 25th NCST), V: 561.
Plummer, Kemp, (Maj, 13th Vols/23rd NCST), I: 621, 631, 648, 650.
Plummer, W.T.,(AQM, 1st Regt 3rd Class, Home Guard), IV: 654.

Plyer, D.W., (Cpl, Co D, 28th NCST), V: 541.
Plyer, E.A., (Pvt, Co D, 28th NCST), V: 541.
Plyer, H.D., (Pvt, Co D, 28th NCST), V: 541.
Plyler, Calvin, (Chaplain, 48th NCST), IV: 616.
Plyler, Peter W., (Lt, Co E, 48th NCST), III: 117.
Plymouth, N.C., (and Battle of, 1864), I: xiv, 12, 116, 117, 321, 334, 398, 399, 401, 405, 446, 496, 526, 527; II: 2, 3, 139, 140, 145, 146, 277, 279, 281, 284, 298, 338, 616, 769, 774, 793, 797; III: 8, 9, 10, 130, 135, 172, 177, 178, 179, 274-275, 314, 356, 390, 418, 419, 506, 530-531, 551-553, 680, 687, 704, 706, 707, 720; IV: 15, 16, 17, 27, 40, 72, 82, 90, 92, 103, 166, 242, 401, 435, 436, 488, 525, 528, 531, 573-574, 578, 579, 617, 646, 680; V: xvi, 7, 269, 312, 318, 319, 321, 323.
Plymouth, Capture of, 1864, I: 321; IV: 83-84; V: 175-195.
Po River, Va., II: 49.
Po River Road, (nr Spottsylvania, Va.), III: 28.
Poag, W.J., (Pvt, Co B, 3rd Vols/13th NCST), V: 549.
Pocahontas Bridge, (nr Petersburg, Va.), III: 359, 399.
Pocahontas County, Va., IV: 140, 143.
Pocotaligo, S.C., (aka New Pocotaligo), I: 742; II: 18, 439, 758; III: 70, 71, 117, 186, 187; IV: 103, 333, 422, 505.
Pocotaligo, Old, S.C., III: 186, 188.
Poe, C.C., (2nd Lt, Co K, 32nd NCST), I: 736.
Poe, R.P., (Pvt, Co G, 28th NCST), V: 542.
Poe, S.A., (Pvt, Co G, 28th NCST), V: 542.
Poe, Terry, (Pvt, Co D, 61st NCST), III: 507.
Pogue, W.T., (Maj, Pogue's Battalion Va.), I: 541, 542, 543, 544.
Poindexter, C.B., (1st Lt, CSN; Capt, Arctic), V: 298.
Poindexter, R.H., (Pvt, Co G, 28th NCST), V: 542.
Point Lookout Prison, Md., (Federal), II: 290, 752, 761; III: 159, 590; IV: 48, 404, 497, 603, 664, 670, 675, 683; V: 375.
Point Pleasant, V: 213.
Point of Rocks, Va., I: 140, 184, 224, 372, 694, 739; II: 69, 274, 431, 432, 601; III: 67, 609; IV: 570.
Poisson, John J., (Capt, Co G, 8th Vols/18th NCST), II: 63, 64; V: 537.
Pole Green Church, Va., (and Battle of, 1864), I: 384; II: 447, 480; IV: 198, 507.
Polenta, N.C., V: 600.
Political Prisoners, IV: 754.
Polk, Mrs. ______, IV: 218.
Polk, James K., (President, U.S.), II: 422.
Polk, John A., (2nd Lt, Co K, 26th NCST; 1st Lt, Adjt, 26th NCST), II: 360, 373, 380, 395, 397; V: 529.
Polk, Leonidas, (Lt Gen), II: 492, 731, 732, 742, 743; V: 648, 663.
Polk, Leonidas L., (Sgt Maj, 26th NCST; Lt, Co I, 43rd NCST), II: 307, 396, 421-422; III: 3.
Polk, Thomas, (Col; Relative of Sgt Maj L.L. Polk), II: 422.
Polk County, N.C., III: 475, 499, 659, 660, 668; IV: 198, 216, 381, 397.
Pollard, James, (Ordnance Sgt, Grimes's Staff), V: 483.
Pollard, Rufus, (Pvt, Co C, 53rd NCST), V: 501.

Pollard, T.R., (Pvt, Co C, 49th NCST), V: 533.
Pollard, Ala., II: 737, 738.
Pollard's Southern History of the War, I: 41, 49.
Pollock, Alexander J., (1st Lt, Co H, 55th NCST), III: 287.
Pollock, W., (Pvt, Co I, 10th Vols/20th NCST), V: 509.
Pollocksville, N.C., II: 81, 82; IV: 110, 609.
Pomeroy, Chauncey, (Hospital Steward, 2nd Corps Provost Guard), V: 569.
Pond, ______, (Col, 62nd Oh.), V: 162.
Ponds, G.F., (Pvt, Co H, 43rd NCST), V: 499.
Ponton, ______, (Capt, Co G, 2nd Regt Home Guard), IV: 653.
Pool, Burroughs, (Pvt, Co D, 56th NCST), III: 347.
Pool, D.H., (AAG, to Hardee), III: 185.
Pool, Henry B., (Pvt, Co B, 38th NCST), V: 557.
Pool, Henry C., (Sgt Maj, 10th NCST, 1st Art & Engs, Pool's Hvy Art), I: 496, 527, 574.
Pool, I, (Pvt, Co B, 43rd NCST), V: 497.
Pool, J.K., (Pvt, Co I, 32nd NCST), V: 497.
Pool, J.L., (Pvt, Co G, 6th NCST), V: 513.
Pool, James B., [Poole], (1st Lt, Co G, 37th NCST), IV: 700, 710.
Pool, James H., (1st Lt, Co H, 10th NCST, 1st Art & Engs, Pool's Hvy Art), I: 524, 525.
Pool, John L., (2nd Lt, Co F, 40th NCST, 3rd Art, Hvy), II: 747.
Pool, R.C., (Pvt, Co H, 54th NCST), V: 516.
Pool, Simon B., (1st Lt, Co G, 31st NCST), II: 507, 512; III: 714.
Pool, Stephen D., (Col, 10th NCST, 1st Art & Engs), I: ix, 159, 491, 492, 493, 494, 495, 497, 498, 500, 501, 503, 504, 509, 511, 512, 513, 514, 515, 516, 517, 518, 519, 520, 521, 522, 524, 525, 526, 527, 532, 533, 534, 536; II: 513; III: 290; IV: 325, 350; V: 16, 19, 83, 90, 91, 183.
Pool, Dr. William E., (Ass't Surg, 31st NCST), II: 511; IV: 636.
Pool, William T., (Capt, Co E, 4th Vols/14th NCST), I: 707.
Poole, Simon B., (Capt, Co K, 68th NCST), III: 714.
Poolsville, Md., I: 421; II: 247; III: 561, 750.
Poovey, H.H., (Pvt, Co C, 28th NCST), V: 541.
Poovey, J.A., Jr., (Pvt, Co C, 28th NCST), V: 541.
Poovey, J.A., Sr., (Pvt, Co C, 28th NCST), V: 541.
Poovey, L., (Pvt, Co C, 28th NCST), V: 541.
Poovey, T., (Pvt, Co C, 28th NCST), V: 541.
Poovey, W.H.H., (Pvt, Co C, 28th NCST), V: 541.
Pope, ______, [Simmons B.], (3rd Lt, Co B, 7th Vols/17th NCST), II: 7.
Pope, ______, (Capt, Co A, 2nd Regt Home Guard), IV: 653.
Pope, John, (Maj Gen, USA), I: 223, 305, 306, 370, 371, 421, 623, 758; II: 28, 29, 30, 31, 115, 133, 134, 149, 150, 151, 152, 153, 154, 155, 169, 216, 473, 564, 584, 600, 655, 656, 682, 683; IV: 160, 162, 163, 164, 465, 505, 551, 552.
Pope, Joseph A., (Pvt, Co C, 38th NCST), V: 557.
Pope, Leroy W., (5th Sgt, Co A, 52nd NCST), III: 223.
Pope, William H.H., (Pvt, Co C, 38th NCST), V: 557.
Pope, Willis H., (Capt, Co E, 51st NCST), III: 211, 219.

Poplar Cove, Tenn., III: 662.
Poplar Lawn, Va., (nr Petersburg, Va.), III: 350.
Poplar Point, N.C., (Roanoke River), I: 446; III: 331; IV: 17-18, 354, 589.
Poplar Spring Church, Va., (aka 1st Battle of Ream's Station), III: 619; IV: 93.
Poplar Spring Road, I: 435.
Poplin, D., (Pvt, Co K, 28th NCST), V: 543.
Poplin, George C., (Pvt, Co B, 38th NCST), V: 557.
Poplin, Henry M., (Pvt, Co G, 38th NCST), V: 557.
Poplin, J.A., (Pvt, Co I, 52nd NCST), V: 536.
Poplin, John, (Pvt, Co K, 26th NCST), V: 533.
Poquosin River, Va., I: 111.
Porch, George, (Pvt, Co F, 26th NCST), V: 603.
Porch, John, (Pvt, Co F, 26th NCST), V: 603.
Porcher, ______, (CSN), V: 327.
Port Republic, Va., (and Battle of, 1862), I: 262, 277, 623; II: 132, 133, 147, 258, 504; IV: 231, 233.
Port Royal, S.C., II: 18, 244; III: 184, 186; IV: 175, 237, 734.
Port Royal, Va., (and Battle of, 1863), I: 142, 190, 310; II: 116; III: 410; IV: 171, 172, 228, 237.
Port Royal Road, II: 35, 36, 691; IV: 175.
Port Tobacco, V: 417.
Port Walthal Junction, Va., III: 687; IV: 85, 529.
Porter, ______, (Chaplain, 65th NCST, 6th Cav), III: 683.
Porter, B.H., (Lt, USN; Pioneer, Malvern), V: 242, 244.
Porter, David Dixon, (Adm, USN), I: 496, 497, 528, 529; II: 633, 636, 762; IV: 45, 46, 47, 49, 307, 308, 590, 591; V: 220, 221, 222, 236, 241, 333, 396, 397, 398.
Porter, Fitz John, (Maj Gen, USA), I: 115, 304, 366, 608, 609, 614, 615, 616, 621; II: 21, 22, 115, 210, 470, 546, 549, 654; III: 166; IV: 465.
Porter, Horace, (Brig Gen, USA, ADC to Grant), II: 48.
Porter, J.H., (Master, USN), V: 243.
Porter, James, (Jr 2nd Lt, Co A, 26th NCST), II: 303, 323, 396, 397.
Porter, John L., (CSN, Chief of Construction/Designer of the Albemarle), V: 316.
Porter, Joseph E., (Sgt Maj, 5th Vols/15th NCST; 1st Lt, ADC, MacRae's Brigade), I: 734; IV: 564; V: 529.
Porter, Steve, (Pvt, Co F, Walker's Battalion, Thomas' Legion, 80th NCST), IV: 125.
Porter, Otho M., (Pvt, Co D, 10th NCST, 1st Art & Engs, Reilly-Ramsay's Battery, Light Art), V: 568.
Porter, William, (1st Lt, Co C, 26th NCST), II: 371, 396, 397; IV: 710.
Portland, Me., IV: 740, 741.
Portsmouth, Mass., IV: 739.
Portsmouth Island, N.C., I: 390; II: 521; V: 35, 39, 51, 68, 300, 301, 302.
Portsmouth, Va., V: 328, 329.
Posey, A.E., (2nd Lt, Co 1, Woodfin's Battalion; Capt, Co 8, 79th NCST, 8th Cav), IV: 111, 115.
Post, James F., (Jr 2nd Lt, Co I, 10th NCST, 1st Art & Engs, Southerland's Battery, Light Art), IV: 221.
Poston, A., (Pvt, Co D, 55th NCST), V: 528.

Poston, S., (Pvt, Co E, 2nd Vols/12th NCST), V: 507.
Poteat, B.F., (Pvt, Co H, 7th NCST), V: 539.
Poteat, Felix L., (Lt, Co K, 47th NCST), III: 85.
Poteat, J.W., (Pvt, Co A, 52nd NCST), V: 535.
Poteat, John, (Capt, AQM, 33rd NCST), II: 537.
Poteat, John A., (Pvt, Co F, 2nd NCST), I: 176; V: 486.
Poteat, John M., (Adjt, 1st Vols, "Bethel"; Adjt, 33rd NCST), I: 77, 127; IV: 474; V: 646.
Poteat, Peter, (Pvt, Co G, 1st Vols, "Bethel"), I: 106, 128.
Poteet, William, (Pvt, Co D, 6th NCST), V: 512.
Potomac Railroad, IV: 150.
Potomac River, I: 140, 142, 148, 149, 163, 179, 184, 189, 194, 197, 206, 207, 216, 224, 244, 249, 254, 259, 261, 300, 306, 307, 308, 311, 317, 324, 325, 326, 334, 372, 373, 379, 381, 421, 422, 424, 480, 481, 482, 541, 544, 557, 563, 573, 576, 579, 590, 591, 596, 626, 627, 628, 632, 643, 645, 663, 694, 696, 699, 718, 739, 759, 761, 762, 764, 765; II: 32, 33, 41, 42, 45, 69, 70, 71, 74, 77, 95, 116, 122, 131, 135, 139, 164, 167, 169, 217, 224, 233, 240, 245, 247, 274, 275, 276, 296, 335, 342, 370, 373, 375, 413, 420, 431, 432, 433, 437, 473, 474, 477, 478, 502, 525, 552, 553, 555, 558, 562, 568, 585, 601, 608, 656, 657, 660, 662, 685, 686, 693, 753; III: 7, 13, 14, 42, 55, 67, 68, 88, 92, 109, 110, 116, 117, 128, 131, 235, 239, 240, 241, 271, 279, 296, 416, 420, 462, 464, 534, 535, 560, 561, 570, 571, 749, 750; IV: 149, 150, 164, 166, 167, 168, 176, 177, 181, 182, 183, 239, 241, 254, 255, 412, 426, 466, 468, 502, 515, 522, 552, 553, 570, 571; V: viii, 71, 72, 73, 74, 79, 80, 113, 135, 411, 412, 417, 418, 590, 591, 592, 619, 627.
Potomac Run, Va., I: 500.
Potter, _____, (Capt, Co G, 36th NCST, 2nd Art & Engs, Lamb's Battery), II: 630.
Potter, E.E., (Lt Cmdr, USN), V: 242.
Potter, Edward Elmer, (Brig Gen, USA), III: 173, 174, 175, 176, 373.
Potter, Dr. Francis W., (Surg, 50th NCST), III: 202; IV: 640.
Potter, Henry A., [Henry W.], (2nd Lt, Co F, 3rd NCST), I: 213.
Potter, J.W., (Pilot, Beauregard), V: 357.
Potter's Raid, III: 173, 174, 175, 176; IV: 77-78, 92.
Potts, J.K., (Lt, Co C, 48th NCST), III: 117.
Potts, J.W., (Pvt, Co B, 1st Vols, "Bethel"), I: 128.
Potts, James M., (Capt, Co C, 37th NCST), II: 653.
Potts, John R., (Capt, Co F, Latham-Potts-Flanner's Battery, Starr's 13th Battalion NCST, Light Art), II: 469, 470; IV: 354; V: 43.
Potts, L.A., (Capt, Co C, 37th NCST), I: 119.
Potts, R.B., (1st Lt, Co D, 4th NCST), I: 231, 232.
Potts', Va., (action at, aka Potts' Station, on South Side Railroad), I: 442, 478; III: 648.
Pounds, J.M., (2nd Lt, Co M, 12th Vols/22nd NCST), II: 165, 166.
Pounds, Jesse J., [Pouns], (Pvt, Co G, 10th Vols/20th NCST), II: 118, 125.

Powder Springs, Ga., II: 742.
Powell, _____, (Lt, 10th Battalion NCST), III: 198.
Powell, A.C., (Pvt, Co I, 2nd NCST), I: 176.
Powell, Alexander M., (Orderly to W.R. Cox), IV: 457; V: 486.
Powell, Andrew, (Pvt, Co I, 49th NCST), V: 565.
Powell, B.F., (AQM, 2nd Vols/12th NCST), I: 606.
Powell, C.S., (2nd Lt, Co E, 14th Vols/24th NCST; Lt, Adjt, 10th Battalion NCST, 2nd Hvy Art), IV: 329-337 personal account.
Powell, Charles P., (Adjt, 13th Vols/23rd NCST), II: 189, 190, 216.
Powell, Edward, (Pvt, Co D, 6th NCST), V: 512.
Powell, Edward H., (Lt Col, 10th U.S. Colored), V: 238.
Powell, G.C., (Pvt, Co D, 10th Vols/20th NCST), V: 508.
Powell, J., (Capt, Co F, 76th NCST, 6th Senior Reserves), IV: 97.
Powell, J.R., (Pvt, Co F, 1st NCST), V: 485.
Powell, James J., (3rd Sgt, Co A, 10th NCST, 1st Art & Engs, Ramseur-Manly's Battery, Light Art), I: 551, 555.
Powell, John B., (2nd Lt, Co G, 43rd NCST), III: 3; V: 494.
Powell, John R., (2nd Lt, Co C, Moore's 3rd Battalion NCST, Light Art), IV: 262.
Powell, O.H., (Capt, Co E, 36th NCST, 2nd Art & Engs, Columbus Battery), II: 630, 635; V: 239.
Powell, Pinkney, (Pvt, Co F, 26th NCST), V: 603.
Powell, R.H., (Lt, Co B, 9th NCST, 1st Cav), I: 441, 485, 782.
Powell, R. James, (Pvt, Co H, 44th NCST), V: 534.
Powell, Robert, (Pvt, Co G, 25th NCST), V: 561.
Powell, Robert J., (Ordnance Sgt, 44th NCST), III: 22; V: 533.
Powell, Solomon, (Pvt, Co A, 5th Vols/15th NCST), V: 520.
Powell, Tate, (Pvt, Co I, 49th NCST), V: 565.
Powell, Thomas, (Sgt, Co D, 6th NCST), V: 512.
Powell, Thomas, [Thomas F.], (Sgt Maj, Adjt, 13th Vols/23rd NCST), II: 241.
Powell, Thomas C., (Lt, Adjt, 47th NCST), III: 83, 110; IV: 702, 710.
Powell's River, Tenn., IV: 275.
Powell's Valley, Tenn., III: 736; IV: 275, 286.
Power, Rev. W.C., (Chaplain, 4th Vols/14th NCST), I: 714, 720, 721.
Powers, David, (Pvt, Co I, 2nd NCST), I: 176; V: 486.
Powers, E.P., (Sgt Maj & Ass't Clerk, 6th Battalion NCST, Fayetteville Arsenal), I: 119; IV: 299.
Powers, J.R., (Pvt, Co G, 33rd NCST), V: 544.
Powers, L.E., (2nd Lt, Co A, 11th Vols/21st NCST; Acting Ordnance Officer, lewis' Brigade), II: 147, 148, 149, 150, 155, 156, 157, 159; V: 511.
Powers, W.D., (Pvt, Co I, 3rd Vols/13th NCST), I: 679, 680.
Powers, William C., (Chaplain, 4th Vols/14th NCST), IV: 600, 604, 607, 714; V: 484.
Powhite Creek, Va., I: 304; II: 210.
Prather, E.F., (1st Lt, Co D, Millard's 9th/20th Battalion Junior Reserves), IV: 387.
Prather, J.J., (Ensign, 42nd NCST), II: 789.

Prather, L.L., (Adjt, Mallet-Hahr's 19th Battalion NCST), IV: 383.
Prather, W.S., (Pvt, Co F, 63rd NCST, 5th Cav), III: 606.
Pratt, H.B., (Chaplain, 63rd NCST, 5th Cav), IV: 619.
Pratt, John L. (Capt, Co K, 11th Vols/21st NCST), II: 145.
Pratt, Thomas, (Pvt, Co K, 52nd NCST), V: 536.
Prempert, Henry C., (Drum Major, 2nd NCST), I: 163.
President, The, (Train named for Lincoln), II: 152.
Preston, S.W., (Lt, USN, ADC.; Pioneer, Malvern), V: 242, 244.
Pretson, Samuel J., (Lt Col, N.C. Quartermaster Department), I: 23.
Preston, William, (Maj Gen), III: 435, 478, 479; V: 380.
Price, _____, (Capt, Independent Co, 9th NCST, 1st Cav), IV: 371, 373.
Price, Benjamin, (Fayetteville and Harper's Ferry Arsenals), IV: 298.
Price, Charles, (Capt, Co A, 1st Battalion Junior Reserves; Co A, 70th NCST, 1st Junior Reserves), IV: 9, 12, 594.
Price, D., (Pvt, Co E, 10th Vols/20th NCST), V: 509.
Price, Dury D., (Cpl, Co F, 34th NCST), V: 555.
Price, Ebenezer, (Capt, Co B, 33rd NCST), II: 538, 561, 578.
Price, F.A., [Thomas A.], (1st Lt, Co A, 6th NCST), IV: 710.
Price, H.W., (Pvt, Co I, 56th NCST), III: 348.
Price, Henry F., (Capt, Co H, 27th NCST), II: 457, 462; V: 519.
Price, J.A., (Pvt, Co L, 11th Vols/21st NCST), V: 515.
Price, J.G., (Drummer, 56th NCST), III: 317.
Price, James, (2nd Lt, Co H, 40th NCST, 3rd Art, Hvy), II: 747.
Price, John, (Fayetteville and Harper's Ferry Arsenals), IV: 298.
Price, Joseph, (1st Lt, Co H, 40th NCST, 3rd Art, Hvy), II: 746.
Price, M., (Pvt, Co E, 56th NCST), V: 566.
Price, O.D., (Fifer, Co I, 56th NCST), I: 772.
Price, R.H., (Pvt, Co H, 8th Vols/18th NCST), II: 64.
Price, R.W., (2nd Lt, Co B, 42nd NCST), II: 790, 805.
Price, Richard Nye, (Chaplain, 26th NCST), II: 396.
Price, Thomas R., (Lt, Co C, 46th NCST), III: 78, 81.
Price, Wade, (Pvt, Co E, 56th NCST), V: 566.
Price, William J., (Lt Col, 8th NCST), I: 387; V: 65.
Price, William J., (Pvt, Co G, 25th NCST), V: 561.
Price's Creek Station, N.C., V: 405.
Price's Farm, Va., I: 553.
Pride, William G., (Capt, 1st Conn., Hvy Art.), V: 238.
Primrose, Cicero, (2nd Lt, Co F, 10th NCST, 1st Art & Engs, Andrew-Cogdell's Hvy Art), I: 501, 507.
Primrose, John W., (ACS, 9th NCST, 1st Cav), I: 485.
Prince, Hal, (Horse of Maj J.W. Woodfin), IV: 112.
Prince, Henry, (Brig Gen, USA), III: 575.
Prince, W.A., (1st Lt, Co I, 31st NCST), II: 512.
Prince George County, Va., III: 622.
Princess Anne County, Va., III: 717.
Princeton College, III: 643.
Printer, _____, (Capt, 55th Ga.), III: 526.

Prior, John N., (Maj, 73rd NCST, 4th Senior Reserves; Conscription Officer), I: 118; IV: 66.
Prison, Escapes from, IV: 767.
Prison Guard, (Salisbury, N.C.), V: 626.
Pritchard, A.H., (Cpl, Co G, 32nd NCST), V: 496.
Pritchard, Calvin, (1st Lt, Co G, 37th NCST), IV: 702, 710.
Pritchard, J.J., (Pvt, Co C, 32nd NCST), V: 496.
Pritchard, Malinda, (Traitor and Outlaw), II: 330, 331.
Pritchard, Riley, (Brother of the Traitor and Outlaw Malinda), II: 331.
Pritchett, F.H., (Pvt, Co K, 3rd Vols/13th NCST), V: 551.
Pritchett, William, (Pvt, Co F, 6th Battalion/60th NCST), III: 482.
Privett, Burke, (Chief Bugler, 9th NCST, 1st Cav), I: 778, 779, 780.
Privett, J.C., (2nd Lt, Co H, 16th Battalion/75th NCST, 7th Cav), V: 659.
Privett, James A., (Pvt, Co K, 14th Vols/24th NCST), V: 560.
Proctor, Hence, (Pvt, Co K, 45th NCST), III: 56, 57.
Proctor, Richard G., (Pvt, Co K, 13th Vols/23rd NCST; Detailed, 2nd Corps Provost Guard), V: 570.
Proctor, Samuel, (Pvt, Co I, 48th NCST), V: 527.
Proctor's Creek, Va., II: 88.
Proctor's Station, Va., IV: 556.
Proffett, William H., (Sgt Maj, 1st NCST), I: 136.
Profit, A.A., (Pvt, Co D, 8th Vols/18th NCST), V: 539.
Proffit, B.S., (Capt, Co K, 29th NCST), II: 486, 493.
Proffit, Ira, (1st Lt, Co B, 6th Vols/16th NCST), IV: 702, 710.
Proffit, James C., (2nd Lt, Co K, 29th NCST), II: 486.
Proffit, W.A., (Lt, 6th NCST), IV: 710.
Proffitt, William W., (Lt Col, 58th NCST), III: 431.
Prophet, ______, [Proffitt], (Pvt, Co D, 8th Vols/18th NCST), II: 40.
Prophet, A.N., (Pvt, Co D, 8th Vols/18th NCST), II: 64.
Propst, George A., (Capt, Co A, 52nd NCST), III: 223, 229.
Propst, J., (Pvt, Co C, 33rd NCST), V: 544.
Propst, N.E., (Cpl, Co A, 2nd Vols/12th NCST), V: 506.
Propst, Tobias, (Pvt, Co A, 33rd NCST), V: 543.
Propst, W.W., [William M.], (Capt, Co A, 57th NCST), IV: 710.
Prouty, ______, (Lt, USA), I: 510.
Providence Church, Va., II: 88.
Provisional Army of Virginia, I: 82.
Provo, Jesse M., (Pvt, Co H, 38th NCST), V: 558.
Provost Guard, 2nd Corps, V: 569-570.
Pruden, William D., (1st Lt, Co K, 70th NCST, 1st Junior Reserves), IV: 13, 594.
Pruett, William S., (Pvt, Co D, 55th NCST), V: 528.
Pruitt, A., (Pvt, Co G, 53rd NCST), V: 502.
Pruitt, J.A., (Pvt, Co D, 28th NCST), V: 541.
Pruitt, J.C., (Pvt, Co H, 28th NCST), V: 542.
Pruitt, John, (Pvt, Co H, 28th NCST), V: 542.
Pryor, Roger Atkinson, [Prior], (Brig Gen), I: 693; II: 796; III: 87, 231, 321, 322; IV: 357, 529; V: 84, 85.
Pryor, W.S., (Pvt, Co D, 55th NCST), V: 528.

Pucket, T.E., (Pvt, Co H, 35th NCST), V: 563.
Pucket, William C., (Pvt, Co E, 1st Vols/11th NCST), V: 530.
Puckett, J.W., (Pvt, Co B, 24th NCST), V: 193.
Pugh, Dr. Thomas C., (Ass't Surg, N.C.), IV: 631.
Pugh, William A., (Adjt, 12th Battalion, Cav), IV: 339.
Pugh's Landing, N.C., [Pagh's], (Roanoke Island), II: 509; V: 59, 60.
Pulley, W.E., (Pvt, Co A, 10th NCST, 1st Art & Engs, Ramseur-Manly's Battery, Light Art), I: 552.
Pulley, William, (Jr 2nd Lt, Co H, 31st NCST), II: 508.
Purcell, Dr. J.D., (Ass't Surg, 10th Vols/20th NCST), II: 112; IV: 635.
Purchases for the Army in England, V: 457, 458.
Purdie, Thomas J., (Col, 8th Vols/18th NCST), II: 20, 34, 35, 37, 38, 39, 68, 73; IV: 467, 473; V: 10, 99.
Purdie, Thomas L., (Pvt, Co I, 7th NCST), I: 378.
Purnell, T.R., (Engineering Trooper), IV: 425.
Purnell, W., (Pvt, Co B, 3rd NCST), V: 487.
Purnell, W.T., (2nd Lt, Co K, 71st NCST, 2nd Junior Reserves), IV: 29.
Putman, Devany, (Cpl, Co E, 34th NCST), V: 555.
Putman, Samuel L., (Pvt, Co F, 34th NCST), V: 555.
Putnam, ______, (Col, 7th N.H.; Putman's Brigade; at Morris Island Prison), III: 208; V: 163, 165.
Puryear, Hal S., (Lt, ADC, Clingman's Brigade), IV: 482, 494-495.
Puryear, S.L., (1st Sgt, Co I, 13th Vols/23rd NCST), V: 510.
Purvis, J. Edward, (Sgt Maj, 1st NCST), I: 136.
Purvis, J.R., (Pvt, Co B, 33rd NCST), V: 543.
Purvis, Levi H., (Sgt, Co B, 33rd NCST), II: 538.
Puttick, James, (Musician, 4th Vols/14th NCST), I: 711.

(Q)

Quaker Road, (nr Burgess' Mill, Va.), I: 139; III: 629.
Qualltown, N.C., II: 705; III: 757; V: 655.
Quantico, Va., (aka Quantico Station), I: 300; II: 164.
Quantico Creek, Va., II: 164.
Quartermaster Corps, V: 571-572.
Quartermaster Department, CSA, I: 19, 20, 26; III: 411; V: 353.
Quartermaster Department, N.C., I: 5, 23, 25, 27, 30, 33, 34, 35, 36, 45.
Quartermaster-General, CSA, I: 25, 566.
Quartermaster-General, N.C., I: 29.
Quartermaster's Report, I: 27, 33, 34.
Queen Ann, IV: 719.
Queen, B.N., [Queenn], (2nd Lt, Co G, 62nd NCST), III: 516; IV: 700, 710.
Queen, James, (Pvt, Co H, 52nd NCST), V: 536.
Queenstown, England, V: 418.
Queeny, John, (Pvt, Co C, 10th NCST, 1st Art & Engs, Brem-Graham-Williams' Battery, Light Art), V: 568.
Quewhiffle, (District of Cumberland County), IV: 294.
Quince, R.M., (Lt, Co C, Adjt, 7th NCST), I: 385.
Quince, William, (Lt, Co I, 3rd NCST), I: 213, 221.
Quinn, Hugh, (Sgt, Co F, 1st NCST), V: 485.
Quinn, James, (Pvt, Co D, 27th NCST), II: 462; V: 523.
Quinnerly, Steven S., (Capt, Co E, 66th NCST), III: 686.

(R)

Raborn, C., (Pvt, Co H, 57th NCST), V: 517.
Raby, D.M., (1st Lt, Co G, 69th NCST, Thomas' Legion), III: 731.
Raby, J.B., (2nd Lt, Co G, 69th NCST, Thomas' Legion), III: 731, 744.
Raby, J.W., (Pvt, Co I, 26th NCST; Chaplain, 58th NCST), IV: 619.
Raccoon Ford, Va., (Rappahannock River), I: 4, 87, 288, 428, 557, 570, 639, 720; II: 240; III: 271.
Radcliffe, James D., (Maj, Engineering Officer; Col, 8th Vols/ 18th NCST; Col, 61st NCST), I: 365; II: 17, 18, 654; III: 503; IV: 413, 414, 473, 483.
Radcliffe, R.S., [Robert S.], (Capt, Co F, 3rd NCST), I: 213.
Rader, M.M., (Pvt, Co F, 26th NCST), V: 603.
Radford, T., (Pvt, Co K, 2nd Vols/12th NCST), V: 508.
Radford, William, (Commodore, USN), V: 242.
Rae, W.D., (2nd Lt, Co F, 1st Vols/11th NCST), I: 585.
Ragan, J.C., (Pvt, Co D, 35th NCST), V: 562.
Ragin, Charlton C., (Lt, Co K, 37th NCST), II: 659; IV: 467.
Ragged Island, Va., I: 654.
Raglan, E., (Pvt, Co D, 26th NCST), V: 531.
Raiford, J.T., (Pvt, Co B, 33rd NCST), V: 544.
Raiford, W.P., (Pvt, Co C, 28th NCST), V: 541.
Rainbow Banks, N.C., (nr Hamilton, See Also: Fort Branch, aka Rainbow Bend), I: 447; III: 720; IV: 416, 645.
Raine, Dr. John R., (1st Lt, Co G; Ass't Surg; Surg, 45th NCST), III: 35; IV: 639.
Raines, James Edwards, (Brig Gen), II: 486, 488, 489, 731.
Rains, Gabriel J., (Brig Gen), I: xii, 76, 112; IV: 424; V: xv, 3, 4, 663.
Rainey, J.N., (Pvt, Co C, 3rd Vols/13th NCST), V: 550.
Rainey, J.P., (1st Lt, Co C, 3rd Vols/13th NCST), I: 677.
Raleigh, Evacuation of, I: 55.
Raleigh & Gaston Railroad, N.C., I: 533, 534, 535; V: 274, 278.
Raleigh Powder Mill, (Constructed by Waterhouse & Bowes), I: 44.
Ramsay, F.M., (Lt Cmdr, USN), V: 242.
Ramsay, J.J., (Pvt, Co 1, Woodfin's Battalion; Co 1, Henry's 14th Battalion; 79th NCST, 8th Cav), IV: 112.
Ramsay, John A., (1st Lt, Co D, 10th NCST, 1st Art & Engs, Reilly-Ramsay's Battery, Light Art), I: 561, 562, 565, 566, 567, 569, 570, 571, 572, 573, 575, 576, 579.
Ramsay, Junius N., (Capt, Co I, 8th NCST), V: 490, 491.

Ramsdale, G.W., (Pvt, Co K, 32nd NCST), V: 497.
Ramseur, Charles R., (Sgt Maj, 71st NCST, 2nd Junior Reserves), IV: 28.
Ramseur, Oliver A., (2nd Lt, Co I, 1st Vols/11th NCST), I: 121, 585; IV: 702, 710.
Ramseur, Stephen Dodson, (Maj Gen), I: xi, 134, 155, 169, 170, 173, 174, 206, 207, 209, 209, 250, 251, 252, 253, 255, 256, 257, 263, 274, 275, 278, 325, 515, 536, 551, 643, 646, 711, 714, 724; II: 129, 140, 141, 142, 143, 236, 237, 245, 248, 249, 257, 260, 332, 476, 500, 501, 502, 503, 526, 530; III: 14, 46, 51, 125, 126, 127, 147, 148, 153, 159, 281, 420, 754; IV: 356, 448, 449, 457, 463, 516, 523, 569, 603; V: xiii, 9, 10, 13, 96.
Ramsey, ______, [Wilson A.], (Color-Sgt, Co B, 9th Vols/19th NCST, 2nd Cav), II: 101.
Ramsey, Douglas, (Lt, Rickett's Battery, USA), V: 31, 32.
Ramsey, J.N., (1st Lt, Co A, Ellis' 3rd Battalion, Light Art), IV: 261.
Ramsey, Nathan A., (Capt, Co D, 61st NCST), III: 503, 504, 505, 506 510, 511, 513.
Ramsey, O.H., (Lt, Co A, 64th NCST), III: 660.
Ramsey, R.D., (2nd Lt, Co A, 50th NCST), III: 203.
Ramsey, Thomas J., (Pvt, Co I, 38th NCST), II: 690.
Ramsey, W.F., (Pvt, Co A, 10th NCST, 1st Art & Engs, Ramseur-Manly's Battery, Light Art), I: 556.
Ramsey, William S., (Lt, Co D, 61st NCST), III: 504, 505.
Ramsour, Edward G., (Pvt, Co D, 38th NCST), V: 557.
Rand, Oscar R., (Capt, Co D, 26th NCST; Col, 1st Regt Home Guard), II: 303, 305, 306, 314, 318, 319, 320, 329, 396, 414; IV: 653.
Randal, Horace, [Randall], (Brig Gen), IV: 254.
Randal, J.H., (Lt, 52nd NCST), IV: 701, 710.
Randall, James H., (Lt, Co D, 55th NCST), III: 296.
Randall, Silas D., [Randal], (Capt, Co D, 55th NCST), III: 287, 296; IV: 701, 710; V: 669.
Randall, Willis, (Jr 2nd Lt, Co I, 52nd NCST), III: 225; IV: 710.
Randle, F.P., (Sgt, Co I, 6th Battalion/60th NCST), III: 500.
Randleman, Samuel H., (5th Sgt, Co H, 52nd NCST), III: 225.
Randleman, W.D., (Pvt, Co G, 33rd NCST), V: 544.
Randolph, ______, (Capt, Stuart's Staff), II: 501.
Randolph, ______, [L.C., Surg], (Capt, 9th Va., Cav), I: 480, 778, 779.
Randolph, George W., (Sec of War, CSA), I: 82, 83, 85, 89, 90,93, 94, 95, 97, 100, 108, 109, 110, 111, 138, 181; IV: 158, 446.
Randolph, J.B., (Capt, Co A, 5th Vols/15th NCST), I: 734.
Randolph, John, (Capt, Co H, 9th Vols/19th NCST, 2nd Cav, Spruill's), I: 50; II: 80.
Randolph, T. Edward, (Pvt, Co H, 27th NCST), II: 462.
Randolph, W.M., (Pvt, Co A, 3rd NCST), V: 487.
Randolph County, N.C., I: 413; II: 13, 101, 161, 163, 303, 421, 804; III: 78, 261, 316, 545; IV: 22, 32, 62, 102, 132, 258, 325, 329, 352, 394, 549, 607, 615, 617, 651.
Randolph County, Va., IV: 143.

Randolph-Macon College, Va., II: 202.
Raney, John, (Pvt, Co G, 8th NCST), V: 194.
Rankin, _____, [Nathaniel Patterson], (Capt, McRae's Battalion NCST), II: 651.
Rankin, Alonzo, (Sgt Maj, Millard's 9th/20th Battalion Junior Reserves), IV: 386.
Rankin, J.E., (Adjt, Henry's 14th Battalion, 79th NCST, 8th Cav), IV: 115.
Rankin, John T., (Lt, Co D, 9th Battalion NCST), IV: 305, 719.
Rankin, Nathaniel P., (Maj, 26th NCST), II: 304, 305, 306, 328, 395, 396, 416; III: 148, 530, 549, 550, 551, 554, 589, 650, 655.
Rankin, Robert, (Capt, N.C. Quartermaster Department), I: 23.
Ramkin, Robert G., (Capt, Co A, 9th Battalion NCST, 1st Hvy Art), IV: 303, 304, 305, 306, 311-312; V: 24.
Rankin, S.C., (Capt, Co B, 45th NCST), IV: 702, 710.
Rankin, W.R., (Sgt Maj, 28th NCST), II: 465, 653; V: 540.
Rankin, W.S., (Lt Col, 11th Vols/21st NCST), II: 137, 144; IV: 693, 700, 710.
Rankin, W.W., (Pvt, Co B, 28th NCST), V: 541.
Rankin, Wallace A., (1st Lt, Co H, 49th NCST), III: 148.
Ransom, Matthew W., (Brig Gen), I: xi, xii, 134, 135, 138, 398; II: 277, 280, 281, 283, 284, 285, 298, 299, 332, 593, 596, 597, 598, 600, 603, 604, 605, 606, 607, 608, 609, 611, 612, 613, 614, 615, 616, 617, 618, 619, 620, 625, 626; III: 8, 129, 136, 146, 156, 157, 282, 329, 335, 337, 338, 340, 341, 351, 352, 390, 391, 392, 393, 394, 396, 398, 422; IV: 10, 82, 365, 442, 451, 488, 490, 569, 572, 574, 576, 577, 578; V: xii, 12, 74, 175, 177, 182, 183, 184, 186, 187, 192, 266, 276, 277, 587, 559, 649, 667.
Ransom, Robert, Jr., (Maj Gen), I: xi, 10, 205, 388, 417, 419, 420, 463, 464, 484; II: 20, 83, 273, 274, 275, 276, 294, 295, 297, 298, 328, 332, 334, 428, 431, 461, 544, 596, 597, 599, 602, 603, 604, 608, 609, 610, 612, 613, 776, 777; III: 10, 114, 115, 137, 170, 321, 327, 329, 333, 353, 358, 741, 742; IV: 110, 113, 221, 346, 441, 503, 569, 572, 578; V: 77, 78, 277, 667, 674, 679.
Rape, Samuel, (Pvt, Co E, 48th NCST), V: 526.
Rapidan River, Va., I: 149, 199, 235, 250, 255, 287, 288, 310, 318, 320, 321, 370, 381, 382, 428, 429, 487, 570, 592, 593, 594, 628, 639, 640, 701, 720, 721, 743; II: 4, 40, 42; III: 7, 26, 27, 42, 43, 73, 93, 243, 244, 271, 272, 302, 406, 416, 418, 464, 572, 575, 576, 584, 585, 586, 590, 593; IV: 110, 159, 160, 184, 186, 187, 188, 189, 190, 193, 412, 426, 506, 562, 563, 570, 609, 610, 677; V: 266, 628.
Rapidan Station, Va., I: 334; II: 431, 444, 469; III: 66, 73, 341, 242, 243, 271; IV: 502, 506.
Rappahannock Bridge, Va., II: 91, 191; III: 272-273, 417-419; IV: 658.
Rappahannock River, Va., I: 142, 143, 168, 169, 190, 255, 287, 300, 305, 310, 318, 319, 334, 370, 375, 378, 381, 382, 423, 565, 592, 593, 628, 664, 666, 701, 713, 720, 742, 743, 762, 763, 764; II: 29, 36, 45, 71, 72, 87, 117, 119, 133, 134, 135, 167, 170, 193, 194, 226, 227, 228,

378, 444, 472, 476, 479, 503, 504, 551, 558, 569, 586, 587, 660, 663, 679, 689, 691; III: 42, 73, 235, 269, 272, 273, 407, 410, 417, 418, 460, 461, 464, 558, 559, 564, 571, 572, 575, 577, 584; IV: 110, 150, 161, 168, 169, 171, 172, 174, 175, 176, 185, 227, 236, 237, 252, 411, 412, 426, 448, 552, 553, 657, 659, 662, 748.

Rappahannock Station, Va., I: 318, 319, 428; II: 444, 569; III: 272, 558, 584; IV: 227, 658.

Rascoe, A.B.S., (Pvt, Co H, 43rd NCST), V: 499.

Rasberry, H.H., (Lt, Co E, 61st NCST), III: 504.

Raspberry, Willis J., (Capt, Co F, 66th NCST), III: 686.

Ratchford, ______, (Adjt to D.H. Hill), I: 696; V: 646.

Ratchford, J.W., (Maj, AAG) I: 106, 117, 127, 128.

Ratchford, R.M., (1st Lt, Co H, 13th Vols/23rd NCST), II: 186.

Ratchford, Robert M., (Pvt, Co C, 38th NCST), V: 557.

Ratcliff, ______, [David F.], (Sgt, Co D, 63rd NCST, 5th Cav), III: 539, 618.

Ratcliff, Jeremiah, [Radliff], (2nd Lt, Co C, 62nd NCST), III: 515; IV: 700, 710.

Ratliffe, J.C., (2nd Sgt, Co H, 3rd Vols/13th NCST), V: 551.

Rattlesnake Shoal, S.C., V: 399.

Rawley, James W., (1st Sgt, Co G, 4th Vols/14th NCST), V: 490.

Rawley, T.L., (1st Lt, Co K; Acting Adjt, 3rd Vols/13th NCST), I: 701; IV: 551; V: 547.

Rawls, A., (1st Sgt, Co B, 44th NCST), V: 533.

Rawls, F.M., (Pvt, Co C & I, 29th Ga.), V: 194.

Rawls' Mills, N.C., (and Battle of, 1862), II: 278, 336, 337, 338, 339, 407, 410; IV: 15.

Ray, A.P., (Pvt, Co E, 59th NCST, 4th Cav), V: 659.

Ray, Alexander, (Capt, Co D, 53rd NCST), I: 119; III: 262.

Ray, D.A., (Pvt, Co H, 11th Vols/21st NCST), V: 194.

Ray, D.H., (Lt, Co A, 5th NCST), I: 120.

Ray, David J., (1st Lt, Co B, 6th Battalion/60th NCST), IV: 296.

Ray, David M., (2nd Lt, Co B, 29th NCST), II: 485.

Ray, David S., (1st Lt, Co D, 56th NCST), III: 314, 328.

Ray, E.M., (Pvt, Co E, 47th NCST), V: 535.

Ray, Erastus H., (Lt, Co E, 47th NCST), III: 84.

Ray, G.D., (Lt, Co A, 64th NCST), III: 660.

Ray, J.M., (Lt, Co A, 64th NCST), III: 660.

Ray, James M., (Lt Col, 6th Battalion/60th NCST), III: 474, 475, 477, 479, 482, 483, 485, 486, 488, 490, 491, 497, 500; IV: 116; V: xi.

Ray, Jim, (Capt, Co 6, Henry's 14th Battalion; 79th NCST, 8th Cav), IV: 113, 116.

Ray, John, (Capt, Co K, 2nd Vols/12th NCST), I: 607.

Ray, John H., (Lt, Co A, 9th NCST, 1st Cav), I: 485.

Ray, N.A., (Pvt, Co H, 26th NCST), V: 532.

Ray, Neill W., (Capt, Co D, 6th NCST), I: xi, 293, 296, 304, 308, 332, 323, 333, 336; V: xi, 593, 605-609 personal account.

Ray, R., (Pvt, Co G, 54th NCST), V: 516.

Ray, Thomas, (Lt, Co M, 58th NCST), III: 434.

Ray, Thomas L., (Pvt, Co K, 6th NCST), V: 514.
Ray, William A., (1st Lt, Co B, 29th NCST), II: 485.
Rayle, B.Y., (2nd Lt, Co I, 33rd NCST), II: 540.
Raymer, Nathaniel, (Musician, 4th NCST), I: 234, 279.
Raymond, S. Owens, (Pvt, Co D, 6th Vols/16th NCST), V: 552.
Read, ______, (Lt Col, Chief of Art, Kirkland's Brigade), I: 582.
Read, J.T., (Hospital Steward, 12th Vols/22nd NCST), V: 553.
Read, Theodore, (Col, Ord's Staff, USA), II: 402; III: 344.
Reading, G.W., (Pvt, Co A, 33rd NCST), V: 543.
Ready, J.W., (Capt, 3rd Ark.), II: 434, 437.
Reagan, Hon. J.H., (With Vance at Greensboro), I: 63.
Reagan, Joseph, (Pvt, Co G, 14th Vols/24th NCST), V: 560.
Reams, John, (Color-bearer, Co F, 1st NCST), I: 152.
Reams Creek Campground, N.C., (now Weaverville), II: 705.
Reams Station, Va., (and Battle of, 1864; See also: Poplar Springs Church), I: 385, 432, 435, 436, 454, 467, 470, 471, 590, 599, 678, 702, 747, 775, 776, 778; II: 57, 58, 76, 103, 105, 173, 174, 299, 387, 388, 393, 409, 412, 447, 480, 482, 575, 588, 669, 694, 780, 781; III: 29-31, 77, 78, 80, 82, 85, 97, 111, 112, 121, 248-249, 333, 379, 612, 615, 616, 619, 620-622; IV: 93, 469, 470, 471, 508, 554, 564-565; V: xii, xiii, 207-212, 628, 674.
Reaves, ______, [Reeves, Richard E., Capt, Co A, 28th NCST], (Capt, Co C, 12th Vols/22nd NCST), II: 162.
Reaves, George S., [Reeves, Richard E.], (Pvt, Co G, 10th Vols/20th NCST), II: 114.
Reaves, Samuel, (Capt, Co E, 5th NCST), I: 281.
Reavis, Giles, (Pvt, Co A, 1st Battalion NCST), V: 504.
Reavis, J.G., (Sgt, Co A, 1st Battalion NCST), V: 503.
Rector, Charles W., (Pvt, Co C, 6th Vols/16th NCST), V: 552.
Rector, Lewis, (1st Lt, Co K, 69th NCST, Thomas' Legion), III: 731.
Rector, T.D., (Sgt, Co G, 26th NCST), V: 532.
Rectortown, Va., III: 562.
Red Bank, N.C., I: 492, 511; III: 117; IV: 115.
Red Banks Church, N.C., II: 777.
Red Cross, N.C., IV: 22, 32, 61.
Red Hill, N.C., (nr Washington), IV: 74-76, 90.
Red Infantry, II: 650, 763.
Red Marble Gap, N.C., III: 757.
Red Top, (nr Plymouth), V: 177.
Redd, C.C., (Jr 2nd Lt, Co I, 10th NCSR, 1st Art & Engs, Sutherland's Battery, Light Art), I: 582; IV: 222.
Redd, M.L.F., (Capt, Co E, 3rd NCST), I: 178, 227.
Redd Gap, N.C., (nr Plymouth), III: 338.
Redden, T.C., (Pvt, Co D, 49th NCST), V: 564.
Reddin, Allen, (Pvt, Co D, 25th NCST), V: 561.
Redding, E.L., [E.J.], (2nd Lt, Co E, 4th NCST), I: 231, 232, 272.
Redding, William W., (Cpl, Co D, 56th NCST), III: 347.
Redditt, David F., (Lt, Co B, 61st NCST), III: 504.
Redfearne, W.D., (1st Lt, Co A, 13th Vols/23rd NCST), II: 182.

Redfern, W.I., (Pvt, Co G, 32nd NCST), V: 496.
Redford, Theodrick, (Pvt, Co K, 3rd Vols/13th NCST; Detailed, 2nd Corps Provost Guard), V: 570.
Redford, W.E., (Pvt, Co I, 1st NCST), V: 485.
Redmond, Dennis, (Editor, agricultural paper, Augusta, Ga.), V: 624.
Redman, F., (Pvt, Co C, 3rd Vols/13th NCST), V: 550.
Redman, W.W., Sr., (Pvt, Co E, 54th NCST), V: 516.
Redoubt, 85th, (See: Fort Wessell).
Redwine, G.D., (2nd Lt, Co I, 42nd NCST), II: 791, 807.
Redwine, T.W., (Capt, Co I, 42nd NCST), II: 807.
Reece, G.H., (Pvt, Co I, 28th NCST), V: 543.
Reece, J.M., (Maj, 4th Battalion Junior Reserves), IV: 3, 4, 38, 46, 47, 48, 51, 270, 587.
Reece, W.D., (Pvt, Co A, 1st Battalion NCST), V: 504.
Reece, William P., (Musician, 6th Vols/16th NCST), V: 552.
Reed, C.W., (Lt, CSN, Tacony), IV: 735, 736, 737, 738, 739, 740, 741.
Reed, H., (Pvt, Co A, 9th Vols/19th NCST, 2nd Cav), V: 658.
Reed, J.J., (2nd Lt, Co K, 5th Vols/15th NCST), I: 736.
Reed's Bridge, Ga., II: 716.
Reed's Ford, Tenn., (Chickamauga River), III: 678.
Reedy, ______, (Capt, 3rd Ark.), IV: 503.
Reel's House, (nr Sharpsburg, Md.), V: 79.
Reedy, C.M., (Pvt, Co A, 26th NCST), V: 531.
Reedy, W.B., (Pvt, Co A, 26th NCST), V: 531.
Reems Creek, N.C., III: 434.
Reep, Jonas, (Pvt, Co K, 13th Vols/23rd NCST), V: 510.
Reese, E., (Pvt, Co G, 61st Va.), V: 569.
Reese, Randolph H., (Capt, Co H, 9th Vols/19th NCST, 2nd Cav), II: 89.
Reese, W.B., (Capt, 69th NCST, Thomas' Legion), III: 760.
Reeves, Calvin, (Lt, Co F, 12th Vols/22nd NCST), II: 166.
Reeves, George G., (Lt, Co F, 12th Vols/22nd NCST), II: 166.
Reeves, George Mc., (2nd Lt, Co F, 12th Vols/22nd NCST), II: 165, 166.
Reeves, George R., (1st Lt, Co A, 26th NCST), II: 303, 396.
Reeves, Horton S., [Horton L.], (2nd Lt, Co F, 12th Vols/22nd NCST), II: 165, 166.
Reeves, James H., (Capt, 3rd N.Y.), V: 237.
Reeves, Jesse A., (2nd Lt, Co A, 26th NCST), II: 303, 396.
Reeves, Jesse F., (Capt, Co F, 12th Vols/22nd NCST), II: 162, 163, 166.
Reeves, Malachi W., (1st Lt, Co C, 29th NCST), II: 485.
Reeves, Preston B., [Reaves], (Capt, Co F, 12th Vols/22nd NCST), II: 165, 166.
Reeves, Richard E., (Maj, 28th NCST), II: 465, 466; IV: 473.
Regiments, Confederate, (North Carolina):
"Bethel" (1st Volunteers; See also: 11th NCST), I: ix, 9, 33, 52, 69-133, 603, 736; II: 162; III: 13, 19, 260, 268, 313, 314, 315, 331, 332; IV: 9, 25, 37, 224, 341, 347, 604, 608, 623, 629; V: ix, x, xi, 13, 577-579, 646, 663.
Avery's, (See: 33rd NCST).

Branch's, (See: 33rd NCST).
Burr's, (Home Guard), IV: 44.
Fisher's, (See: 6th NCST).
Jordan's, (See: 31st NCST).
Hinton's, (See: 68th NCST), IV: 768.
Leventhorpe's, (See: 1st Vols./11th NCST).
Marshall's, (See: 52nd NCST).
Walker's, (See: 80th NCST and Thomas' Legion).
Whitford's, (See: 67th NCST).
1st NCST, I: 73, 74, 81, 124, 131, 134-156, 180, 183, 193, 194, 198, 200, 201, 203, 204, 205, 212, 216, 217, 218, 219, 222; II: 596, 597; IV: 372, 435, 441, 449, 459, 578, 604, 631, 725; V: 2, 9, 11, 13, 485, 588, 589, 595-598.
2nd, (Spanish War), II: 423.
2nd NCST, I: 139, 157-176, 215, 244, 245, 246, 251, 254, 260, 500, 502; II: 498, 499, 503, 753; IV: 18, 435, 445, 450, 460, 601, 604, 612, 631; V: 2, 9, 11, 13, 35, 486, 589, 639, 640, 641.
3rd NCST, I: 138, 140, 143, 148, 152, 177-228; II: 20, 426, 437; IV: 18, 51, 435, 441, 449, 450, 459, 605, 632; V: xiv, 2, 9, 13, 74, 487, 589.
4th NCST, I: 164, 167, 170, 172, 229-280, 562, 563; II: 206, 426, 498, 504, 531, 589, 791; IV: 149, 435, 445, 448, 460, 461, 515, 518, 605, 632; V: xiv, 2, 9, 11, 13, 467, 488-489, 589, 664.
5th NCST, I: 3, 118, 244, 281-292, 348, 610, 611, 612, 634, 635, 636, 639; II: 117, 192, 197, 198, 207, 220, 223, 225, 240, 264, 592; III: 406, 652; IV: 436, 441, 521, 524, 606, 632, 703; V: xii, xiv, 2, 9, 11, 264, 504-506, 589.
6th NCST, I: 3, 118, 133, 293-359; II: 135, 140, 167; III: 7, 268, 269, 281, 291, 406, 407, 411, 414, 415, 417, 423; IV: 153, 237, 373, 436, 441, 525, 551, 606, 632, 657, 658, 659, 660, 667, 672, 680; V: 2, 9, 29-33, 175, 194, 511-514, 581-585, 588, 605-609, 641.
7th NCST, I: 3, 271, 361-386, 492, 538, 609; II: 20, 23, 25, 35, 36, 37, 50, 65, 72, 308, 310, 313, 316, 317, 326, 471, 541, 542, 544, 547, 550, 556, 559, 560, 561, 562, 570, 573, 576, 594, 654, 664, 665, 792, 804; III: 78, 268, 274, 300, 314; IV: 435, 465, 467, 472, 474, 606, 632, 713; V: 2, 9, 11, 13, 94, 95, 97, 139, 147, 156, 538-539, 573, 588, 631, 646, 666.
8th NCST, I: 3, 387-415, 511, 512; II: 16, 509, 510, 513, 516, 517, 616, 617; III: 205, 212, 268, 290, 333, 337, 338, 340, 341, 505, 713; IV: 345, 346, 435, 467, 482, 485, 486, 488, 490, 493, 495, 497, 573, 633; V: 2, 9, 11, 13, 55-56, 59, 61, 62, 63, 65, 66, 175, 179, 180, 183, 185, 186, 187, 190, 193, 197, 198, 199, 202, 203, 204, 241, 665.
9th NCST, 1st Cav, (See: Cavalry).
10th NCST, 1st Art & Engs, (See: Artillery).
11th NCST, 1st Vols, I: 4, 9, 51, 118, 119, 132, 133, 583-604; II: 336, 344, 348, 354, 355, 361, 379, 399, 700, 767; III: 24, 87, 93, 103, 104, 105, 106, 229, 242, 260, 300, 321; IV: 43, 182, 263, 326, 436, 555, 557, 562, 605, 606-607, 633; V: 7, 11, 83, 85, 86, 87,

88, 89, 91, 114, 120, 131, 139, 153, 530-531, 640.
12th NCST, 2nd Vols, I: 4, 366, 605-652; II: 22, 83, 119, 121, 207, 220, 225, 230, 236, 240, 241, 246, 249, 265, 267, 545; III: 1, 2, 19, 41; IV: 243, 436, 441, 490, 518, 521, 523, 607, 633; V: 13, 259, 506-508, 589.
13th NCST, 3rd Vols, I: 4, 114, 610, 643, 653-703; II: 170, 178, 207, 220, 221, 225, 455, 582, 680, 687, 695; III: 1, 300, 316; IV: 155, 175, 405, 436, 441, 521, 522, 552, 553, 554, 607, 621, 633; V: 13, 139, 549-551, 589, 641.
14th NCST, 4th Vols, I: 4, 167, 168, 172, 244, 245, 246, 248, 275, 694, 705-732; II: 50, 305, 404, 498, 700; III: 36, 318; IV: 435, 441, 445, 461, 513, 517, 601, 607, 634, 637, 641; V: xiv, 9, 11, 489-491, 589.
15th NCST, 5th Vols, I: 4, 281, 295, 399, 547, 733-749; II: 379, 385, 395, 436, 438, 440, 443, 446, 447, 448, 521, 609; III: 27, 29, 78, 152, 247, 308; IV: 404, 435, 441, 504, 506, 517, 518, 563, 566, 607-608, 634, 638; V: 10, 13, 520-522, 588, 589, 645.
16th NCST, 6th Vols, I: 4, 586, 680, 749, 751-773; II: 168, 174, 582, 680, 700, 702, 704, 707; III: 300, 316, 317, 516, 731; IV: 137-219, 397, 436, 551, 552, 608, 634; V: xii, 10, 13, 139, 551-553, 589, 680.
17th NCST, 7th Vols, I: 4, 12, 119, 495, 511, 512, 523; II: 1, 13, 83, 337, 338, 509, 775, 796, 803; III: 290, 320, 530, 551; IV: 77, 266, 366, 436, 527, 528, 530, 532, 535, 538, 539, 543, 545, 548, 555, 556, 608, 634; V: 11, 13, 15, 35, 41, 42, 55, 59, 241, 301, 302, 640, 680.
18th NCST, 8th Vols, I: 4, 179, 181, 216, 365, 376, 581, 609; II: 15-78, 476, 481, 544, 550, 551, 556, 559, 560, 561, 562, 573, 574, 576, 654, 659, 664, 666, 767; IV: 416, 422, 435, 465, 473, 476, 483, 608, 617, 635; V: 10, 13, 93, 94, 95, 96, 97, 98, 99, 139, 539-540, 588, 653.
19th NCST, 9th Vols, 2nd Cav, (See: Cavalry).
20th NCST, 10th Vols, I: 610, 635, 636, 639; II: 111-159, 207, 220, 225, 767; IV: 425, 436, 441, 521, 522, 523, 608-609, 635; V: xvi, 11, 12, 14, 508-509, 589.
21st NCST, 11th Vols, I: 116, 309, 311, 317, 348, 354; II: 129-159; III: 7, 38, 241, 268, 269, 273, 287, 295, 331, 414, 415, 418; IV: 45, 225, 226, 227, 228, 230, 234, 235, 436, 441, 525, 609, 635; V: 11, 12, 14, 175, 194, 514-515, 588, 641, 666.
22nd, 12th Vols, I: 765; II: 161-180, 455, 582, 598, 679, 695; III: 295, 300; IV: 10, 155, 157, 159, 171, 436, 551, 552, 609-610, 635; V: 10, 11, 12, 14, 139, 553-554, 589, 629, 641.
23rd NCST, 13th Vols, I: vii, 118, 610, 635, 639, 641, 643, 649; II: 117, 118, 181-268, 312; IV: 11, 436, 441, 521, 522, 610, 635; V: 5, 10, 12, 14, 509-510, 589, 640.
24th NCST, 14th Vols, I: 606; II: 269-290, 294, 328, 332, 599, 601, 603, 610, 614, 617; III: 129, 138, 145, 146, 156, 212, 330, 336, 337, 338, 339,

340, 341, 342, 348, 353, 365, 366, 372, 375, 386; IV: 436, 569, 610; V: 14, 175, 179, 180, 182, 183, 184, 185, 186, 187, 189, 193, 560, 588, 627.

25th NCST, I: 5, 581; II: 291-301, 328, 599, 601, 610, 612, 624, 700; III: 129, 136, 141, 143, 145, 146, 156, 157, 322, 324, 327, 328, 337, 338, 340, 343, 348, 357, 364, 372, 373, 374, 386, 390; IV: 126, 404, 436, 481, 569, 635, 636; V: 12, 14, 175, 178, 180, 183, 184, 186, 187, 188, 193, 561-562, 588, 638, 667.

26th NCST, I: 5, 118, 363, 589, 590, 602; II: 44, 81, 272, 294, 296, 303-423, 542, 543, 594, 595, 596, 599, 600; III: 24, 27, 87, 92, 103, 104, 105, 106, 127, 130, 300, 319, 320, 433; IV: 436, 555, 556, 562, 569, 611, 619, 636; V: xiii, xiv, 10, 11, 12, 14, 104, 111, 114, 119, 120, 131, 133, 134, 139, 152, 463, 467, 531-533, 599-603.

27th NCST, I: 5, 118, 187, 354, 413, 465-484, 741; II: 20, 23, 56, 308, 310, 326, 425-463, 542, 593, 594, 609, 610 695; III: 66, 74, 78, 116, 120, 378, 725; IV: 435, 501, 502, 503, 504, 507, 509, 511, 562, 611, 636; V: xiv, 14, 522-524, 588, 640.

28th NCST, I: 5, 112, 115, 365, 375, 376, 609; II: 21, 24, 33, 36, 37, 39, 45, 49, 50, 57, 65, 66, 178, 413, 465-484, 544, 545, 547, 550, 551, 552, 555, 556, 559, 560, 561, 562, 573,575, 576, 654, 659, 664, 666; III: 300, 332; IV: 126, 435,465, 473, 611, 636; V: 10, 11, 14, 94, 97, 139, 154, 540-543, 588, 646.

29th NCST, I: 6, 12; II: 485-494, 700, 708, 711, 712, 727, 731; III: 366, 737; IV: 122, 438, 442, 612, 636; V: 4, 14, 18, 169, 170, 171, 173.

30th NCST, I: 6, 118, 119, 167, 172, 244, 245, 246, 273, 723, 724; II: 495-505; IV: 435, 444, 445, 461, 462, 599, 601, 612, 636; V: xi, 11, 14, 491-493, 589, 667.

31st NCST, I: 6, 40, 163; II: 507-520, 748; III: 205, 207, 209, 505; IV: 249, 263, 435, 482, 483, 636; V: 6, 11, 59, 61, 62, 64, 66, 86, 88, 89, 167, 197, 199, 202, 203, 241, 667.

32nd NCST, I: 6, 116, 620, 739; II: 521-536; III: 4, 5, 41, 49, 162, 256; IV: 252, 260, 436, 513, 514, 515, 516, 517, 518, 612, 614, 637; V: xii, 10, 14, 247, 495-497, 666.

33rd NCST, I: 6, 24, 41, 117, 118, 145, 363, 365, 376, 548, 609; II: 20, 22, 23, 25, 36, 48, 50, 55, 62, 65, 79, 308, 311, 312, 315, 316, 321, 323, 326, 327, 476, 515, 537-580, 594, 595, 654, 659, 664, 666; III: 1, 300; IV: 166, 191, 435, 465, 470, 473-474, 612-613, 637; V: 2, 10, 12, 14, 94, 97, 139, 147, 155, 156, 543-545, 588, 640, 667.

34th NCST, I: 7, 51, 118, 765; II: 168, 174, 581-590, 679, 694; III: 300; IV: 43, 155, 157, 164, 173, 174, 180, 436, 551, 552, 613, 637, 646; V: 7, 10, 12, 14, 140, 554-556, 589.

35th NCST, I: 7, 137, 364; II: 277, 294, 298, 304, 308, 310, 313, 316, 317, 326, 327, 328, 542, 543, 591-628; III: 4, 5, 129, 140, 145, 146, 156, 212, 322, 337, 338, 340, 346,

361, 364, 372, 386, 397, 725; IV: 10, 436, 482, 483, 486, 569, 575, 576, 633, 637, 647; V: 10, 12, 14, 74, 76, 78,175, 179, 180, 183, 184, 186, 187, 190, 193, 562-563, 588.
36th NCST, 2nd Art. & Engs., (See: Artillery).
37th NCST, I: 7, 118, 119, 365, 375, 376, 609; II: 20, 21, 22, 23, 35, 36, 37, 50, 55, 65, 308, 310, 313, 325, 326, 471, 502, 509, 542, 544, 548, 549, 550, 556, 559, 561, 562, 563, 574, 575, 576, 594, 653-674; III: 300, 673; IV: 435, 465, 468, 474, 475, 613, 637; V: xiv, 10, 12, 14, 94, 97, 139, 154, 545-546, 588, 645, 646.
38th NCST, I: 7, 118, 765; II: 47, 168, 582, 675-697; III: 1, 300; IV: 129, 155, 176, 180, 191, 209, 436, 551, 552, 613, 637-638, 646; V: 7, 140, 556-558, 589.
39th NCST, I: 7, 12, 764, 766, 767, 768; II: 487, 492, 699-744; III: 517, 737; IV: 126, 137, 438, 442, 613-614, 638, 646; V: xi, 4, 169, 171, 172, 173.
40th NCST, 3rd Art. & Engs., (See: Artillery).
41st, 3rd Cav, (See: Cavalry).
42nd NCST, I: 7, 8, 9, 119, 271, 365; II: 3, 4, 9, 363, 789-807; III: 320, 321; IV: 266, 357, 436, 527, 528, 530, 532, 537, 538, 539, 544, 545, 614, 638, 748; V: 15, 241.
43rd NCST, I: 10, 117, 118; II: 523, 528, 616, 679; III: 1-20, 41, 162, 163, 170, 256, 274; IV: 9, 29, 252, 260, 436, 513, 514, 518, 612, 614, 638, 689, 691, 694, 697; V: xvi, 175, 180, 190, 194, 497-499, 611.
44th NCST, I: 10, 12, 118, 589, 592; II: 135, 335, 336, 341, 379, 395 412; III: 21-34, 87, 103, 111, 281, 320; IV: 436, 555, 558, 562, 568, 614, 616, 638, 658; V: 10, 114, 533-534.
45th NCST, I: 10; II: 523, 533; III: 1, 4, 24, 35-61, 162, 163, 165, 170, 171, 256, 260; IV: 252, 258, 259, 260, 326, 436, 513, 514, 553, 615, 639; V: 10, 12, 254, 497-501.
46th NCST, I: 10, 60, 365, 741; II: 432, 433, 438, 439, 440, 442, 446, 447, 448, 602, 609, 610, 695; III: 63-82, 122; IV: 435, 501, 502, 504, 505, 506, 509, 615-616, 639; V: 524-525, 588, 665.
47th NCST, I: 10, 12, 101; II: 135, 335,336, 344, 348, 354, 355, 361, 379, 395; III: 83-112, 246, 300, 320; IV: 436, 555, 556, 563, 614, 616, 639, 691; V: 11, 114, 132, 139, 153, 154, 534-535.
48th NCST, I: 10, 118, 741; II: 328, 433, 438, 441, 446, 447, 454, 458, 601, 609; III: 66, 78, 113-124; IV: 25, 435, 501, 502, 504, 616, 639; V: 10, 12, 526-527, 588.
49th NCST, I: 10; II: 294, 328, 455, 490, 500, 573, 599, 601, 612, 616, 619, 624, 639, 793; III: 125-160, 322, 330, 331, 333, 337, 353, 358, 359, 360, 372, 373, 374, 386, 390, 391, 401; IV: 436, 490, 569, 573, 616, 639-640; V: 10, 11, 15, 79, 175, 184, 564-565, 588, 663.
50th NCST, I: 10, 12, 162, 597; II: 3, 284, 636, 796; III: 4, 5, 161-204, 680; IV: 6, 15, 27, 81, 101, 103, 105, 334, 350, 436, 440, 527, 529, 617, 640; V: 241, 668.

51st NCST, (aka Cape Fear Regiment), I: 10, 12, 118, 398, 406; II: 513, 515, 516, 518; III: 205-221, 230, 231, 505; IV: 345, 435, 482, 483, 489, 493, 497, 608, 617, 640; V: 11, 162, 167, 197, 198, 199, 200, 203, 241.
52nd NCST, I: 10, 12, 118, 119, 493, 519, 590, 592, 593, 600; II: 336, 344, 348, 354, 355, 361, 379, 395, 414; III: 21, 24, 87, 103, 104, 105, 106, 223-253, 300; IV: 345, 436, 555, 617-618, 640; V: 10, 12, 83, 114, 120, 139, 153, 535-536.
53rd NCST, I: 10, 260; II: 523, 535, 592; III: 4, 5, 41, 52, 162, 255-265; IV: 252, 258, 260, 436, 513, 618, 640; V: 10, 12, 501-502.
54th NCST, I: 10, 118, 119, 309, 311, 354; II: 170; III: 7, 255, 267-285, 407, 409, 415, 417; IV: 436, 441, 525, 618, 640, 658; V: 11, 12.
55th NCST, I: 10, 353, 492, 511, 512; III: 78, 287-312; IV: 108, 182, 435, 440, 441, 508, 617, 640; V: xi, 11, 12, 101, 110, 527-528.
56th NCST, I: 13, 119; II: 4, 296, 601, 612, 742, 766, 772; III: 129, 131, 136, 139, 145, 146, 156, 174, 313-404; IV: 10, 137, 346, 357, 436, 569, 575, 640; V: 15, 175, 178, 179, 180, 182, 183, 184, 185, 186, 187, 188, 190, 191, 565-566, 668, 669.
57th NCST, I: 13, 271, 309, 311, 317, 354; II: 135; III: 7, 268, 269, 405-429; IV: 170, 436, 441, 525, 526, 611, 658, 751; V: 10, 517-518.
58th NCST, I: 13; II: 700, 701; III: 431-454, 492, 497; IV: 371, 380, 439, 442, 619, 632, 641; V: xi, 11, 12, 169, 172, 670.
59th NCST, 4th Cav, (See: Cavalry).
60th NCST, (See also: 6th Battalion), I: 13, 118, 119; II: 700, 701, 712, 731, 741, 757; III: 431, 436, 444, 454, 473-502, 737; IV: 6, 101, 103, 115, 116, 439, 442, 641; V: xi, 11, 169, 171, 172, 173.
61st NCST, I: 13, 118; II: 513, 516, 517; III: 205, 320, 503-514; IV: 435, 482, 483, 488, 495, 498, 619, 641; V: 11, 16, 197, 199, 202, 203, 241.
62nd NCST, I: 13; II: 700, 701; III: 515-527, 663, 664, 667, 670, 671, 737, 756, 759; IV: 380, 381, 439, 442, 619, 641; V: 654.
63rd NCST, 5th Cav, (See: Cavalry).
64th NCST, I: 13, 119; II: 700, 701; III: 448, 659-671, 759; IV: 380, 381, 404, 439, 442, 620, 642; V: 654.
65th NCST, 6th Cav, (See: Cavalry).
66th NCST, See also: 4th & 8th Battalions), I: 13; II: 3, 4, 9, 796; III: 685-701; IV: 4, 30, 41, 55, 56, 270, 302, 436, 527, 530, 532, 538, 544, 545, 546, 591, 642; V: 10, 11, 241.
67th NCST, I: 14, 18, 51; III: 703-711, 713, 726, 727; IV: 17, 242, 358, 440, 543, 620, 642; V: 2, 6, 17, 18.
68th NCST, I: 14, 18, 51, 527; III: 314, 681, 708, 709, 713-728; IV: 11, 17, 97, 365, 402, 440, 641, 642, 768; V: 2, 6, 18.
69th NCST, (A portion of this regiment was composed of a part of Thomas' Legion. The

entire regiment rarely if ever came to the field as a whole, normally operating as sepa rate battalions. See also: Thomas' Legion), I: 13, 15, 766; II: 487, 700, 701, 759; III: 519, 644, 670, 671, 729-761; IV: 119, 121, 123, 124, 126, 127, 128, 137, 437, 438, 439, 442, 620, 642; V: 653-656.
70th NCST, 1st Junior Reserves, (See also: 1st & 6th Battalions Junior Reserves) I: xiii, 16; II: 598; III: 320, 634, 680, 681, 721; IV: 4, 6, 9-23, 26, 27, 29, 30, 37, 44, 53, 57, 224, 354, 385, 393, 439, 499, 587, 588, 589, 593, 642.
71st NCST, 2nd Junior Reserves, (See also: 2nd & 5th Battalions Junior Reserves), I: xiii, 16; III: 634; IV: 4, 6, 18, 25-34, 44, 53, 224, 358, 392, 393, 439, 499, 587, 588, 589, 591, 593, 642; V: 640.
72nd NCST, 3rd Junior Reserves, (See also: 4th, 7th & 8th Battalions Junior Reserves I: xiii, 16; IV: 4, 6, 7, 18, 30, 35-63, 224, 270, 301, 302, 393, 439, 499, 583, 588, 590, 591, 593, 642.
73rd NCST, 4th Senior Reserves, I: viii, 16; II: 202; IV: 4, 6, 65-67, 97, 99, 107, 224, 351, 398, 440, 643; V: 5, 676.
74th NCST, 5th Senior Reserves, I: vii, 16; IV: 6, 65, 67, 69, 97, 224, 398, 440; V: 5, 676.
75th NCST, 7th Cav, (aka 16th Battalion and Claiborne-Dearing's 7th C.S. Cav; See: Cavalry).
76th NCST, 6th Senior Reserves, I: vii, xiii; IV: 6, 65, 67, 97-98, 224, 398, 440, 643; V: 5, 676.
77th NCST, 7th Senior Reserves, I: vii, xiii; II: 11, 803; IV: 3, 6, 65, 99-105, 107, 224, 334, 397, 398, 440; V: 677.
78th NCST, 8th Senior Reserves, I: vii, xiii; II: 11, 803; IV: 3, 6, 65, 100, 107-108, 224, 383, 398, 440, 643; V: 677.
79th NCST, 8th Cav, (See: Cavalry).
80th NCST, (A portion of this regiment was composed of a portion of Thomas' Legion. The entire regiment rarely if ever came to the field as a whole, normally operating as separate battalions. See also: Walker's Battalion & Thomas' Legion), II: 733; III: 662, 664, 671, 733, 737, 738, 758; IV: 117-128, 437, 438, 439, 442, 643; V: 10, 656.
81st NCST, (1st Regiment of Detailed men), IV: 129, 132, 133, 400, 440, 652.
82nd NCST, (2nd Regiment of Detailed men), IV: 129, 131-132, 400, 440, 652; V: 589, 664, 652.
83rd NCST, (3rd Regiment of Detailed men), IV: 131, 132, 133, 400, 440, 652.
Regiments, Confederate, (Other States):
Alabama, 3rd, III: 41.
Alabama, 4th, (Law's), I: 339, 341, 350, 567; III: 291, 406; V: 109, 582.
Alabama, 5th, I: 662; II: 230; V: 247.
Alabama, 6th, I: 151.

Alabama, 13th, II: 346; III: 300.
Alabama, 15th, II: 130; IV: 232, 234, 525.
Alabama, 26th, II: 230.
Arkansas, 1st, I: 180, 217; II: 167, 717.
Arkansas, 3rd, II: 431, 434, 436, 438; III: 66, 116; IV: 501, 502, 503, 504.
Arkansas, 8th, III: 451.
Arkansas, 25th, I: 767; II: 716, 719, 736.
Florida, 8th, V: 109.
Georgia, 2nd, V: 55, 56.
Georgia, 3rd, I: 388.
Georgia, 4th, I: 138, 141, 143, 180, 184, 190, 224, 225, 226.
Georgia, 6th, IV: 601; V: 241.
Georgia, 7th, (Gartrell's), I: 341.
Georgia, 8th, (Bartow's), I: 341, 342, 349.
Georgia, 12th, II: 130; IV: 525.
Georgia, 14th, IV: 142, 149, 150.
Georgia, 19th, IV: 149, 150; V: 241.
Georgia, 20th, II: 192.
Georgia, 21st, (Mercer's), II: 130, 139, 147, 148; III: 7, 8, 274, 337, 339; IV: 234, 525; V: 175, 194.
Georgia, 23rd, V: 241.
Georgia, 27th, (Zachary's), II: 517, 736; IV: 55, 493, 535; V: 203, 241.
Georgia, 28th, V: 241.
Georgia, 31st, V: 165.
Georgia, 32nd, III: 180, 209; V: 163.
Georgia, 37th, II: 736.
Georgia, 40th, (actually 4th), I: 217, 218.
Georgia, 44th, I: 138, 143, 180, 190, 217, 218.
Georgia, 45th, I: 609; II: 21, 545, 677.
Georgia, 47th, III: 180; IV: 445.
Georgia, 49th, II: 677.
Georgia, 55th, III: 434, 448, 526.
Georgia, 59th, II: 88.
Georgia, 65th, III: 435.
Kentucky, 5th, III: 435, 436, 451.
Louisiana, 10th, II: 272.
Mississippi, 1st, I: 691.
Mississippi, 2nd, (Faulkner-Stone's), I: 339, 341, 347, 348, 350, 352; II: 345, 348; III: 290, 291, 297, 300, 311; IV: 375; V: 582, 583.
Mississippi, 11th, I: 339, 341, 350, 352; III: 290, 291, 297, 300; V: 582, 583.
Mississippi, 16th, II: 130, 147, 148; IV: 234.
Mississippi, 22nd, V: 641.
Mississippi, 26th, III: 290.
Mississippi, 42nd, III: 290, 297, 300.
South Carolina, (Capp's), I: 343.
South Carolina, 1st, II: 677; III: 193, 207.
South Carolina, 2nd, (Kershaw's), I: 343.
South Carolina, 6th, II: 299.
South Carolina, 11th, V: 241.
South Carolina, 21st, II: 641, 643, 645, 646; V: 228, 230, 232, 240, 241.
South Carolina, 22nd, II: 624; 361, 372.
South Carolina, 25th, II: 641, 643, 645, 646; V: 228, 230, 232, 240, 241.
South Carolina, 26th, III: 141, 142, 143.
South Carolina, 27th, V: 241.
Tennessee, 1st, I: 339; III: 300.
Tennessee, 2nd, II: 167.
Tennessee, 7th, III: 300; V: 107.
Tennessee, 11th, II: 486, 489, 490.
Tennessee, 14th, III: 300.
Tennessee, 31st, III: 732.
Texas, 4th, II: 26, 48.
Virginia, 1st, III: 300; V: 177.

Virginia, 3rd, I: 89.
Virginia, 7th, III: 300; V: 194.
Virginia, 8th, III: 300.
Virginia, 9th, I: 693, 694; III: 300.
Virginia, 10th, I: 143, 190, 200.
Virginia, 11th, III: 300.
Virginia, 13th, I: 180; II: 431.
Virginia, 14th, III: 300.
Virginia, 18th, III: 300.
Virginia, 19th, III: 300.
Virginia, 23rd, I: 143, 190, 200.
Virginia, 24th, (Early-Terry's), I: 283, 284, 285, 342, 611; II: 192, 197; III: 163, 300; V: 175, 194.
Virginia, 27th, I: 235.
Virginia, 28th, I: 235; III: 300.
Virginia, 29th, III: 334.
Virginia, 30th, I: 217; II: 431, 432, 438; III: 66, 116, 334; IV: 501, 502, 504.
Virginia, 36th, III: 745, 746, 747.
Virginia, 37th, I: 143, 190, 200.
Virginia, 38th, II: 192; III: 300.
Virginia, 40th, II: 561; III: 300.
Virginia, 45th, II: 341; III: 745, 746.
Virginia, 46th, III: 163.
Virginia, 47th, II: 347, 561; III: 300.
Virginia, 49th, (Extra Billy Smith's), I: 235, 348; V: 62.
Virginia, 50th, II: 72, 73.
Virginia, 51st, III: 745, 746, 752.
Virginia, 53rd, III: 300; V: 157.
Virginia, 54th, III: 452.
Virginia, 55th, II: 347; III: 300, 436.
Virginia, 56th, III: 300.
Virginia, 57th, III: 300; IV: 258.
Virginia, 59th, V: 62.
Virginia, 60th, III: 745, 746, 747.
Virginia, 61st, (Company G, from Halifax and Northampton counties, N.C.), IV: 403; V: 569.
Virginia, 63rd, III: 435, 436, 451.
Regiments, (Federal):
Connecticut, 6th, V: 163, 164, 165, 238.
Connecticut, 7th, V: 163, 238.
Connecticut, 8th, II: 317, 318, 326.
Connecticut, 10th, II: 326; IV: 543.
Connecticut, 11th, II: 326.
Connecticut, 16th, III: 345; V: 175.
Illinois, 107th, II: 743.
Indiana, 13th, V: 238.
Indiana, 19th, II: 346, 347, 349, 354, 355, 361; V: 613.
Indiana, 20th, V: 56.
Indiana, 27th, V: 596.
Kansas, 8th, II: 719.
Kentucky, 1st, III: 678.
Kentucky, 6th, II: 491.
Maine, 1st, (See: Cavalry).
Maine, 3rd, II: 476; IV: 467; V: 96.
Maine, 5th, IV: 660.
Maine, 6th, III: 48, 49.
Maine, 7th, III: 48.
Maine, 9th, V: 163, 164.
Maine, 16th, I: 635.
Maine, 5th, IV: 660.
Massachusetts, 2nd, V: 596.
Massachusetts, 4th, I: 82, 87, 88, 106; III: 328.
Massachusetts, 12th, I: 634, 635.
Massachusetts, 19th, II: 603.
Massachusetts, 21st, II: 311, 312, 313, 314, 316, 317, 326, 543; IV: 249; V: 67.
Massachusetts, 23rd, II: 311, 326.
Massachusetts, 24th, II: 311, 326.
Massachusetts, 25th, II: 311, 326.
Massachusetts, 27th, II: 311, 326.
Massachusetts, 44th, (Colored), III: 180, 181.
Massachusetts, 54th, (Colored), III: 208; V: 163, 164, 621.

Massachusetts, 55th, III: 180, 181.
Massachusetts, 115th, I: 288.
Michigan, 1st, II: 622, 624.
Michigan, 2nd, III: 393.
Michigan, 5th, II: 519, 520.
Michigan, 6th, (See: Cavalry).
Michigan, 17th, II: 667.
Michigan, 24th, II: 346, 347, 348, 349, 353, 354, 355, 356, 361, 368; V: 613.
Michigan, 68th, I: 719.
Minnesota, 2nd, III: 490; V: 172.
New Hampshire, 3rd, V: 163, 238.
New Hampshire, 4th, V: 238.
New Hampshire, 5th, III: 384.
New Hampshire, 7th, V: 163, 238.
New Jersey, 9th, II: 311, 326.
New Jersey, 12th, III: 581.
New Jersey, 13th, V: 77.
New York, 1st, I: 88, 89, 97, 106.
New York, 3rd, I: 87, 88, 93, 95, 97, 98; V: 237.
New York, 5th, (Zouzves), I: 87, 88, 92, 93, 94, 97, 101, 106; IV: 158, 198.
New York, (Brooklyn Zouzves), I: 343, 344, 345; NCST), V: 582, 583, 584.
New York, 7th, I: 82, 87, 88, 93, 106; II: 147, 148.
New York, 8th, III: 345; V: 67.
New York, 14th Militia, II: 345.
New York, 15th, I: 690.
New York, 20th, II: 354.
New York, 25th, II: 470.
New York, 26th, III: 581.
New York, 39th, V: 111.
New York, 47th, V: 237.
New York, 48th, V: 163, 237.
New York, 51st, II: 326; V: 67.
New York, 56th, III: 180.
New York, 64th, II: 500.
New York, 66th, III: 41.
New York, 76th, III: 297.
New York, 80th, II: 346, 347, 361.
New York, 82nd, II: 177.
New York, 83rd, I: 634, 636.
New York, 84th, (aka 14th Brooklyn), III: 298.
New York, 85th, V: 175, 180.
New York, 94th, I: 635.
New York, 95th, II: 345; III: 298.
New York, 97th, I: 634, 636.
New York, 100th, V: 163.
New York, 105th, II: 237.
New York, 112th, V: 237.
New York, 115th, V: 238.
New York, 117th, V: 237.
New York, 120th, III: 578.
New York, 126th, V: 108.
New York, 127th, III: 180.
New York, 142nd, V: 237.
New York, 144th, III: 180.
New York, 146th, I: 150, 200.
New York, 147th, III: 41, 297.
New York, 157th, III: 180; IV: 717.
New York, 169th, II: 649; V: 235, 238.
North Carolina, 2nd, III: 345.
North Carolina, 3rd, V: 655.
North Carolina Volunteers, (Graham's, USA), II: 785.
Ohio, 8th, I: 167; II: 364; V: 105.
Ohio, 25th, III: 180.
Ohio, 62nd, V: 163.
Ohio, 67th, V: 163.
Ohio, 100th, III: 739, 740.
Pennsylvania Corn Exchange Regiment, IV: 466.
Pennsylvania, 11th, I: 634.
Pennsylvania, 46th, I: 630.
Pennsylvania, 51st, II: 311, 326, 668.
Pennsylvania, 56th, III: 41, 297.
Pennsylvania, 58th, III: 328, 555.
Pennsylvania, 76th, V: 163, 164, 238.
Pennsylvania, 83rd, III: 565, 566.
Pennsylvanis, 88th, I: 634, 636.
Pennsylvania, 90th, I: 634, 635.
Pennsylvania, 97th, V: 238.

Pennsylvania, 101st, III: 345; V: 175.
Pennsylvania, 103rd, III: 345; V: 175.
Pennsylvania, 120th, II: 37, 347.
Pennsylvania, 121st, II: 346, 354, 361.
Pennsylvania, 128th, I: 226; II: 559; V: 94, 95.
Pennsylvania, 142nd, II: 346, 347, 354, 361.
Pennsylvania, 143rd, II: 346; III: 41.
Pennsylvania, 149th, II: 346; III: 42.
Pennsylvania, 150th, II: 346.
Pennsylvania, 151st, II: 346, 354, 361.
Pennsylvania, 203rd, V: 238.
Rhode Island, 4th, II: 314, 317, 318, 326.
U.S., 1st, (Colored), V: 238.
U.S., 4th, (Colored), V: 238.
U.S., 5th, (Colored), V: 238.
U.S., 6th, (Colored), V: 238.
U.S., 10th, (Colored), V: 238.
U.S., 14th, (Sykes' Regulars), II: 114, 210.
U.S., 26th, (Colored), III: 180.
U.S., 27th, (Colored), V: 238.
U.S., 30th, (Colored), V: 238.
U.S., 32nd, (Colored), III: 180.
U.S., 35th, (Colored), III: 180.
U.S., 37th, (Colored), V: 238.
U.S., 39th, (Colored), V: 238.
U.S., 102nd, (Colored), III: 180.
Vermont, 1st, I: 82, 87, 88, 106.
Vermont, 6th, II: 691.
Vermont, 8th, I: 263.
Vermont, 13th, V: 149.
Vermont, 16th, V: 149.
Wisconsin, 2nd, II: 345, 346, 347, 348, 361; V: 613.
Wisconsin, 6th, II: 345, 346, 348, 361; III: 298; V: 613.
Wisconsin, 7th, II: 346, 347, 348, 361; V: 611, 613.
Regiments and Brigades, I: xiii.
Regimental Hospital, V: 577.
Regimental Losses in the Civil War, II: 360.
Reich, W.A., (Musician, Mickey's Band, 26th NCST), II: 398.
Reid, _____, (Pvt, Co I, 68th NCST), III: 726.
Reid, A.S., (Capt, AQM, Grimes' Staff), V: 483.
Reid, C.A., (Sgt, Co B, 59th NCST, 4th Cav), V: 659.
Reid, C.A., (Pvt, Co G, 47th NCST), V: 535.
Reid, David, (Pvt, Teamster, Co E, 34th NCST; Detailed, Medical Purveyor's Departmant), V: 555, 572.
Reid, David S., (2nd Lt, Co A, 4th Battalion Junior Reserves; Co A, 72nd NCST, 3rd Junior Reserves), IV: 38.
Reid, George W., (Pvt, Co K, 34th NCST), V: 556.
Reid, H.R., (Musician, 53rd NCST), V: 501.
Reid, J.B., (Maj, Va., Art), V: 175, 178, 184.
Reid, J.B., [John B., Jr.], (Pvt, Co F, 21st Ga.), V: 194.
Reid, J.W., (Musician, 3rd Vols/13th NCST), V: 549.
Reid, James A., (Pvt, Co A, 4th NCST), V: 488.
Reid, James Rufus, (1st Lt, Co C, 4th NCST), I: 231, 269.
Reid, John, (1st Lt, Co I, 39th NCST), II: 707.
Reid, Tim, (Pvt, Co B, 10th Vols/20th NCST), V: 508.
Reid, W.O., (Pvt, Co C, 11th Vols/21st NCST), V: 514.
Reidsville, N.C., I: 687.
Reilly, James, (Maj, Co D, 10th NCST, 1st Art. An Irishman by birth Reilly made the South his home and the military his

career. At the beginning of hostilities he wore the Blue as Ordnance Sergeant of Fort Johnson. Quickly making the decision to cast his lot with his adopted homeland Reilly was commissioned an officer of the 10th NCST and saw action with the Army of Northern Virginia until later in the war when he was transferred back to North Carolina and ultimately to the defense of Fort Fisher. After the woundings of General Whiting and Colonel Lamb the command of Fort Fisher devolved to Reilly. Abandoned by General Bragg and unsupported by General Hoke whose troops were within easy distance, Reilly was left no option but to surrender the fort and what remained of its garrison.), I: 496, 525, 528, 529, 530, 536, 562, 563, 565, 569, 570, 574, 577, 578, 579, 580; II: 635, 641, 646, 647; IV: 49, 307, 391; V: 24, 27, 228, 230, 233, 234, 239.

Reinhardt, Andy, (Pvt, Co B, 57th NCST), V: 517.

Reinhardt, Daniel, (1st Lt, Co K, 13th Vols/23rd NCST), II: 187, 188.

Reinhardt, Hannon W., (Capt, Co C, 41st NCST, 3rd Cav), II: 770.

Reinhardt, J.F., (Pvt, Co K, 1st Vols, "Bethel"), I: 133.

Reinhardt, Wallace M., (1st Lt, Co K, 1st Vols, "Bethel"), I: 78.

Relph, Dorsey, (Pvt, Co C, 56th NCST), V: 565.

Rencher, John G., (1st Lt, Co K, 33rd NCST), II: 541, 579; IV: 129.

Rencher, William C., (Maj, Rencher's 24th Battalion NCST, Detailed Men), IV: 400.

Rendall, W.P., (Lt, Co E, 10th NCST, 1st Art & Engs, Moore-Miller's Battery, Light Art), I: 581.

Rendleman, P.N., (Pvt, Co K, 13th Vols/23rd NCST), V: 510.

Renfree, Stephen, (Pvt, Co C, 43rd NCST), V: 194.

Renfroe, Braswell, (Pvt, Co A, 55th NCST), V: 527.

Renike, John, (Pvt, Co B, 2nd NCST), I: 175; V: 486.

Reno, Edward, [John Edward], (Cpl, Co A, 6th Battalion/60th NCST), III: 496.

Reno, Jesse Lee, (Maj Gen, USA), II: 84, 85, 221, 308, 311, 312, 314, 318, 327, 349, 543; IV: 251, 521; V: 67.

Repition, A. Paul, (Engineering trooper), IV: 425.

Resaca, Ga., (and Battle of, 1864), II: 702, 720, 739, 741; III: 433, 437, 493.

Reserves, Organization of, IV: 1-7.

Respass, Fenner, (Pvt, Detached Co, 68th NCST), III: 724.

Respass, G.W., (Pvt, Co G, 1st NCST), V: 485.

Respass, William O., (Pvt, Detached Co, 68th NCST), III: 724.

Retus, Jones, (Pvt, Co A, 5th NCST), I: 291.

Review and Conclusions, V: vii.

Rex, G.W., (Pvt, Co F, 37th NCST), V: 546.

Reyall, William B., (ACS Sgt, 55th NCST), V: 527.

Reynold's House, (Marye's Heights, nr Fredericksburg, Va.), I: 577.

Reynold's Grove, (See: McPherson's Woods).

Reynolds, Alexander Welch, (Brig Gen, aka "Old Gauley"), II: 710, 724, 739; III: 436.

Reynolds, D., (Pvt, Co G, 33rd NCST), II: 544.

Reynolds, Edwin, (Lt, Co H, 64th NCST), III: 660.
Reynolds, F.S.H., (Capt, Co C, 6th Battalion/60th NCST), III: 473, 482, 483.
Reynolds, Francis A., (Lt Col, 39th NCST), II: 707, 724, 727, 733, 736.
Reynolds, Gauly, (Brig Gen), II: 727.
Reynolds, J.E., (Pvt, Co G, 33rd NCST), V: 544.
Reynolds, J.T., (Capt, Co H, 64th NCST), III: 660.
Reynolds, John Fulton, (Maj Gen, USA), I: 316, 354, 634; II: 345; III: 91, 560; V: 114, 117, 118, 613.
Reynolds, John H., (1st Lt, Co F, 6th Battalion/60th NCST), III: 474, 475, 476, 483, 483, 491, 492.
Reynolds, N.A., (Lt, Co F, 12th Vols/22nd NCST), II: 166.
Reynolds, Pryor, (Capt, AQM, 45th NCST; AQM, Grimes' Brigade), III: 35; V: 494.
Reynolds, S., (Pvt, Co G, 10th Vols/20th NCST), V: 509.
Reynolds, W.P., (Pvt, Co D, 45th NCST), V: 500.
Rhea, ______, (Maj, N.C. Militia), III: 518.
Rhea, Henry K., (Jr 2nd Lt, Co C, 6th Battalion/60th NCST), III: 483.
Rhea, John W., (1st Lt, Co F, 39th NCST), II: 705.
Rhea, Dr. Robert C., (Ass't Surg, 65th NCST, 6th Cav), III: 683.
Rhein, John E., (Capt, Co G, 38th NCST), II: 676, 677.
Rhen, William, (Pvt, Co A, 14th Vols/24th NCST), V: 560.
Rhett, ______, [A.M.], (Col, 1st S.C., Art), III: 193.
Rhett, Robert Barnwell, (AG), I: 348.
Rhind, A.C., (Cmdr, USN), V: 243.
Rhoderick, C.D., (Pvt, Co K, 12th Vols/22nd NCST), V: 554.
Rhodes, D.V., (2nd Lt, Co I, 54th NCST), IV: 710.
Rhodes, David F., (Pvt, Co B, 13th Vols/23rd NCST), V: 509.
Rhodes, E.H., (Capt, Co G, 3rd NCST), I: 179, 227, 228.
Rhodes, Edward A., (2nd Lt, Co C, 1st Vols/11th NCST), I: 584, 590.
Rhodes, F.A., (Lt, Co H, 61st NCST), III: 504.
Rhodes, Ingraham, (Pvt, Co I, 3rd Vols/13th NCST), I: 660.
Rhodes, J.P., (Pvt, Co G, 10th Vols/20th NCST), V: 509.
Rhodes, King J., (Capt, Co E, 56th NCST), I: 119; III: 315.
Rhodes, Noel, (Pvt, Co I, 3rd Vols/13th NCST), I: 660.
Rhodes, R.B., (2nd Lt, Co C, 59th NCST, 4th Cav), III: 457.
Rhodes, Thomas J., (1st Sgt, Co B, 27th NCST), II: 461; V: 523.
Rhodes' Hill , Va., [Rood's Hill], (and Battle of, 1864), I: 155, 264.
Rhyne, A., (Pvt, Co B, 28th NCST), V: 541.
Rhyne, A.H., (Cpl, Co B, 28th NCST), V: 541.
Rhyne, Adam M., (2nd Lt, Co K, 42nd NCST), II: 192, 791, 807; V: 664.
Rhyne, Daniel, (Capt, Co E, 57th NCST), III: 405.
Rhyne, J.B., (Pvt, Co H, 49th NCST), V: 565.
Rhyne, J.W., (Pvt, Co I, 25th NCST), V: 562.
Rice, A.G., (Pvt, Co H, 45th NCST), V: 500.
Rice, B.L., (Lt, 49th NCST), IV: 710.
Rice, Giles H., (Lt Col, 1st U.S., Colored), V: 238.
Rice, Robert L., (Capt, Co A, 44th NCST), III: 22.

Rice, S.C., (Pvt, Co D, 3rd Vols/13th NCST), V: 550.
Rice, Stephen A., (2nd Lt, Co C, 41st NCST, 3rd Cav), II: 770.
Rice's Station, Va., II: 459.
Rice's Turnout, Va., III: 247.
Rich, Daniel, (Pvt, Co F, 2nd Battalion NCST), V: 495.
Rich, H.M., (1st Cpl, Co E, 3 rd Vols/13th NCST), V: 550.
Rich, John R., (Color-Sgt, 29th NCST), II: 489.
Rich, Lewis J., (Pvt, Co A, 43rd NCST), III: 20; V: 497.
Rich, Peter M., (Drum Maj, 25th NCST), II: 291.
Rich, Pinkney, (1st Cpl, Co G, 55th NCST), V: 528.
Rich, W.H., (Pvt, Co F, 26th NCST), V: 603.
Rich, W.R., (Pvt, Co F, 26th NCST), V: 603.
Rich Mountain, Va., IV: 295.
Richard, H.R., (Pvt, Co B, 48th NCST), V: 526.
Richard's Shop, Va., I: 557.
Richards, Major, (Pvt, Co D, 43rd NCST), V: 498.
Richards, Roscoe, (3rd Sgt, Co G, Color-bearer, 27th NCST), II: 443, 448, 462; V: 523.
Richardson, A.H., (Pvt, Co F, 48th NCST), V: 526.
Richardson, B.F., (Capt, Co F, 48th NCST), V: 520.
Richardson, C.J., (Capt, Co C, 1st Battalion Junior Reserves; Co D, 70th NCST, 1st Junior Reserves), IV: 9, 13.
Richardson, Allen, (ACS Sgt, Co F, 2nd Battalion NCST), V: 495.
Richardson, George W., (Pvt, Co F, 12th Vols/22nd NCST), V: 553.
Richardson, Israel Bush, (Brig Gen, USA), I: 186.
Richardson, J.A., (Pvt, Co I, 53rd NCST), V: 502.
Richardson, J.C., (Capt, Co C, 53rd NCST), III: 262.
Richardson, J.R., (Color-bearer, 8th Vols/18th NCST), II: 40.
Richardson, John, (Pvt, Co F, 48th NCST), V: 526.
Richardson, John A., (Lt Col, 36th NCST, 2nd Art & Engs, Bladen Art), II: 630.
Richardson, John A, (Capt, Co E, 62nd Ga., Cav; 16th Battalion, 75th NCST, 7th Cav), IV: 72, 73, 76, 77, 91, 370.
Richardson, John M., (Maj, 11th Vols/21st NCST), II: 144; V: 641.
Richardson, John Q., (Maj, 52nd NCST), III: 225, 238; V: 12.
Richardson, John R., (Sgt, Co A, 13th Vols/23rd NCST), V: 593.
Richardson, John W., (Jr 2nd Lt, Co B, 26th NCST), II: 303, 393, 396, 397.
Richardson, S.N., (Sgt, Co K, 8th Vols/18th NCST), II: 64; V: 540.
Richardson, V.V., (Capt, Co C, 8th Vols/18th NCST), IV: 475; V: 98.
Richardson, W.B., (Chaplain, 32nd NCST), IV: 612.
Richardson, W.E., (Pvt, Co I, 16th Battalion/75th NCST, 7th Cav), V: 660.
Richardson, W.W., (2nd Lt, Co B, 26th NCST), II: 358, 371, 372, 396, 397.
Richardson, William, (Pvt, Co M, 11th Vols/21st NCST), V: 194.
Richie, M., (Sgt, Co D, 28th NCST), V: 541.
Richlands, N.C., IV: 326.
Richmond, ______, [Stephen D.], (Adjt, 49th NCST), III: 125, 127.
Richmond, Calab, (1st Lt, ADC to Ramseur), IV: 462, 463.
Richmond, Ky., II: 708; IV: 276.

Richmond County, N.C., I: vii; II: 16, 66, 182, 202, 263, 750; IV: 354, 355, 618.
Richmond Pike, (Petersburg to Richmond, Va.), III: 135, 138, 139; IV: 489.
Richmond & Danville Railroad, I: 432, 433, 777, 781; III: 58; IV: 93, 454, 539.
Richmond & Fredericksburg Railroad, III: 10, 235.
Richmond, Fredericks & Potomac Railroad, I: 179, 216, 288; II: 440, 657.
Richmond & Petersburg Railroad, III: 247, 359.
Richmond & Yorktown Railroad, IV: 235.
Rickert, J.M., (Pvt, Co C, 4th NCST), V: 488.
Rickerts, Harrison H., (Ordnance Sgt, 34th NCST), V: 554.
Rickets, H.H., [Rickerts], (Sgt Maj, 34th NCST), II: 582.
Ricketts, ______, (Capt, Ricketts' Battery, USA), V: 31, 32, 583, 584.
Ricks, E., (Pvt, Co F, 8th Vols/18th NCST; Detailed, Invalid Battalion), V: 571.
Ricks, J.W., (Pvt, Co K, 45th NCST), V: 501.
Ricks, Robert F., (Cpl, Co I, 5th Vols/15th NCST), V: 522.
Riddick, C.E.C., (Lt, Co B, 5th NCST), I: 288.
Riddick, James, (Capt, Adjt, 34th NCST), II: 582; IV: 551, 553.
Riddick, Richard H., (Col, 34th NCST, AAG, Scales' Brigade), II: 581, 583, 585, 679, 692; IV: 155, 157, 164, 551, 552; V: 10, 552.
Riddick, Simon, (Pvt, Co C, 52nd NCST), V: 536.
Riddick, W.G., (2nd Lt, Co I, 41st NCST, 3rd Cav), II: 772.
Riddle, G.W., (Musician, 46th NCST), V: 524.
Riddle, H.H., (Pvt, Co H, 46th NCST), V: 525.
Riddle, James M., (Hospital Steward, 58th NCST), III: 432.
Riddle, Joseph B.F., (1st Lt, Co H, 13th Vols/23rd NCST), II: 186, V: 503.
Riddle, Thomas H., (Jr 2nd Lt, Co C, 6th Battalion/60th NCST), III: 482, 492.
Riddle's Shop, Va., (Skirmish at, 1864), I: 384, 420; II: 56, 480, 574, 588, 694; III: 609, 618; IV: 200-203, 469.
Ridgely, D.B., (Capt, USN), V: 242.
Ridgeville, S.C., III: 191; IV: 103, 104.
Ridgeway, N.C., I: 417, 498, 534; IV: 110, 359; V: 278.
Ridgeway & Alexander Ferry Road, (Warren County), V: 268.
Rierson, John W., (Maj, 53rd NCST), II: 535; III: 260, 263, 264.
Rierson, Samuel H., (2nd Lt, Co D, 52nd NCST), III: 224; IV: 710.
Riggin, C.D., (Pvt, Co B, 30th NCST), V: 491.
Riggin, C.S., (Pvt, Co B, 30th NCST), V: 491.
Riggins, R.J., (Pvt, Co I, 1st NCST), V: 485.
Riggs, ______, [Azariah J.], (1st Lt, Co F, 10th NCST, 1st Art & Engs, Andrew-Cogdell's Hvy Art), I: 501.
Riggs, B.M., (Pvt, Co G, 3rd NCST), V: 487.
Right, John E., (Ambulance Driver, Co A, 2nd Battalion NCST), V: 495.
Rigsbee, J., (Sgt, Co H, 54th NCST), V: 516.
Riggsbee, Revel, (Pvt, Co D, 5th Vols/15th NCST), V: 521.
Rigsbee, T.S., (Pvt, Co I, 32nd NCST), II: 535.

Riley, B., (Pvt, Co A, 10th NCST, 1st Art & Engs, Ramseur-Manly'sBattery, Light Art), I: 556.
Riley, Elzy, (Pvt, Co D, 56th NCST), III: 355.
Riley, John, (Pvt, Co B, 45th NCST), V: 500.
Riley, Simpson, (Pvt, Co D, 56th NCST), III: 347.
Riley, W.N., (Pvt, Co F, 33rd NCST), V: 544.
Rinaldi, B.F., (Capt, Co A, 8th Vols/18th NCST), II: 63; V: 537.
Ring, Enoch, (Pvt, Co B, 2nd Battalion NCST), V: 495.
Ring, Thomas, (Pvt, Co B, 1st Battalion NCST), V: 504.
Ringo, Judge ______, (Resident of Arkansas), III: 327.
Ringo, Daniel W., (2nd Lt, Sharpshooters, 57th NCST), III: 427.
Ringold, Ga., I: 767; II: 716, 735, 737.
Ringstaff, Henry, (Lt, Co B, 43rd NCST), III: 3; IV: 700, 710.
Rio de Jenerio, Brazil, V: 387.
Rio Grande River, V: 354.
Ripley, Roswell Sabine, (Brig Gen), I: 141, 180, 182, 183, 185, 217, 219, 222, 223, 224, 226.
Ripley, Samuel H., (Sgt, Co C, 5th Vols/15th NCST), V: 521.
Ripon, Va., V: 213.
Rip-Raps, (Part of the outer fortification of Fortress Monroe. The initial construction of which was begun by R.E. Lee while he served as an engineering officer in the U.S. Army.), III: 19.
Rise and Fall of the Confederate Government, IV: 36.
Ritchie, George E., (Lt, Co H, 8th NCST), I: 405.
Ritchie, Irey, [Ivy], (Sgt, Co H, 4th Vols/14th NCST), I: 729.
Ritchie, Jacob, (Pvt, Co I, 5th NCST), V: 505.
Ritter, Dr. Henry P., (Surg, 8th NCST), I: 387; IV: 633.
Ritter, J.S., (2nd Lt, Co I, 9th Vols/19th NCST, 2nd Cav), II: 80.
Ritter, John T., (Jr 2nd Lt, Co B, 6th Battalion NCST), IV: 296.
Rivenbark, Charles W., (Sgt, Co C, 1st NCST), IV: 725, 732; V: 595.
River Bridge, (Salkehatcie River), III: 188; IV: 103.
River Road, (nr Drewry's Bluff, Va.), III: 77.
Riverside, N.C., IV: 112.
Rives, A.L., (Col, Ass't Chief Engineer, CSA), IV: 427.
Rives, Dr. Alexander, (Surg, 61st NCST), III: 503; IV: 641.
Rives, R.W., (Capt, Co H, 1st NCST), I: 137, 139.
Rixeyville, Va., III: 578.
Roach, John R., (Capt, Co I, 44th NCST), III: 23.
Roades, A.J., (Pvt, Co G, 12th Vols/22nd NCST), V: 554.
Roan, W.H., (Lt, Co K, 9th NCST, 1st Cav), I: 486.
Roanoke Bridge, (Roanoke River, Va.), III: 539.
Roanoke Island, N.C., (and Battle of, 1862), I: xiii, 3, 6, 8, 40, 388, 389, 390, 490, 503, 693, 737; II: 1, 81, 221, 308, 398, 508, 509, 510, 511, 593, 629, 768, 773; III: 178, 458, 718; IV: 245, 246, 247-248, 414, 482, 483, 519, 645, 646; V: 6, 7, 42, 57-69, 178, 275, 304, 305, 307, 310, 312, 325, 627.
Roanoke River, N.C., I: xiii, 445, 495, 525, 650; II: 87, 124, 140, 263, 337, 400, 407, 582, 615, 616, 617, 618, 677; III: 8, 135, 321, 331, 337, 338, 339, 340, 343, 345, 346, 530, 531, 552, 680, 681, 706, 707, 718, 726; IV: 10, 15-16, 17, 43, 75, 82, 339, 354, 358, 359, 392, 415, 416, 417, 430, 439, 528,

573, 588, 589, 645, 646, 647, 651; V: 6, 175, 176, 178, 183, 186, 187, 188, 265, 267, 270, 271, 273, 274, 275, 312, 315, 318, 319, 320, 321, 323.

Roanoke Station, Va., III: 615; IV: 97, 608.

Roanoke Valley, N.C., V: 192, 472.

Roark, J.M., (Capt, Co D, 42nd NCST), II: 790.

Robards, Horace L., (2nd Lt, AQM, 38th NCST), II: 676, 677.

Robards, J.H., (Pvt, Co I, 43rd NCST), V: 499.

Robards, J.W., (Pvt, Co D, 2nd Vols/12th NCST), V: 507.

Robards, W.J., (Sgt Maj, 2nd Vols/12th NCST), I: 629, 639.

Robarts, Albert, (Musician, 4th Vols/14th NCST), I: 711.

Robb, ______, [George F.], (1st Lt, Co E, MacRae's 18th Battalion NCST), IV: 379.

Robbins, ______, [Roberson, James R.], (Sgt, Co E, 7th Vols/17th NCST), V: 41.

Robbins, Ephraim, (2nd Lt, Co E, 9th Vols/19th NCST, 2nd Cav), II: 89.

Robbins, J.H., (Chaplain, 9th NCST, 1st Cav; 2nd Vols/12th NCST), IV: 606, 607.

Robbins, J.S., (Lt, Co I, 12th Vols/22nd NCST), II: 166.

Robbins, James M., (1st Lt, Co M, 12th Vols/22nd NCST), II: 166, 172.

Robbins, Richard, (Pvt, Co G, 38th NCST), V: 557.

Robbins, Thomas, (Pvt, Co I, 56th NCST), III: 393.

Robbins, William M., (Maj, 4th Ala.), II: 579; V: ix, 101-112 personal account.

Roberson, ______, (Capt, Co D, 2nd Regt Home Guard), IV: 653.

Roberson, David A., (Capt, Co I, 41st NCST, 3rd Cav), II: 771.

Roberson, George, (Pvt, Co I, 27th NCST), II: 462.

Roberson, H., (Pvt, Co G, 52nd NCST), V: 535.

Roberson, James P., (Lt, Co H, 10th NCST, 1st Art & Engs, Pool's Hvy Art), I: 525.

Roberson, John, (Jr 2nd Lt, Co G, 10th NCST, 1st Art & Engs, Pender-Manney's Hvy Art), I: 501, 525.

Roberson, Joseph, (Jr 1st Lt, Co H, 10th NCST, 1st Art & Engs, Pool's Hvy Art), I: 501.

Roberson, M.A., (Pvt, Co K, 6th Battalion/60th NCST), III: 482.

Roberson, M.M., (2nd Lt, Co H, 5th Vols/15th NCST), I: 73.

Roberson, Monroe, (Pvt, Sharpshooter, Co A, 3rd Vols/13th NCST), I: 674, 675.

Roberson, S.M., (2nd Lt, Co H, 15th NCST), IV: 701.

Roberts, ______, [Edward M.], (Drummer, Pvt, Co K, 4th Vols/14th NCST), I: 728.

Roberts, ______, [Frederick Cox], (Capt, Co B, 63rd NCST, 5th Cav), III: 530.

Roberts, ______, (Englishman, Capt, Blockade Runner; See: A.C.H. Hampden).

Roberts, Charles E., (2nd Lt, Co C, 6th Battalion NCST), IV: 296.

Roberts, Charles M., (Lt, Co B, 9th NCST, 1st Ca.; Maj, Henry's 14th Battalion NCST, Cav), I: 485; II: 293; IV: 113; V: 12.

Roberts, E.B., (Lt, Co I, 7th NCST), I: 383.

Roberts, Frank N., (Capt, Co B, 56th NCST), I: 78, 85, 90, 93, 119; III: 313, 338, 344, 355, 357, 361, 363, 364, 367; V: 179, 188, 189.

Roberts, G., (Pvt, Co H, 56th NCST), III: 357.

Roberts, Gideon M., (Capt, Co C, 2nd NCST), I: 159.
Roberts, Goodson M., (Capt, Co I, 6th Battalion/60th NCST), III: 474, 475, 476, 482, 484, 497.
Roberts, H.H., (Ass't Engineer, CSN, Tallahassee), V: 438.
Roberts, H.L., (Pvt, Co A, 3rd Vols/13th NCST), V: 549.
Roberts, H.L., (2nd Lt, Co F, 38th NCST), II: 675.
Roberts, Isaac, (1st Lt, Co E, 41st NCST, 3rd Cav), II: 771.
Roberts, J.L., (Pvt, Co A, 3rd Vols/13th NCST), V: 549.
Roberts, J.M., (Pvt, Co C, 10th NCST, 1st Art & Engs, Brem-Graham-Williams' Battery, Light Art), V: 568.
Roberts, J.W., [Jones W.], (1st Lt, Co F, 45th NCST), IV: 700, 711.
Roberts, James, (Pvt, Co D, 56th NCST), III: 347, 355; V: 566.
Roberts, James P., (Pvt, Co I, 68th NCST), III: 720.
Roberts, John A., (Capt, Co H, 34th NCST), V: 548.
Roberts, John H., (Col, 4th N.H.), V: 238.
Roberts, John T., (Pvt, Courier, Co A, 27th NCST), II: 461; V: 522.
Roberts, M.P., (Capt, 55th NCST), IV: 700, 710.
Roberts, Philetus W., (Col, 4th Vols/14th NCST), V: 9.
Roberts, Philip A., (Pvt, Co H, 6th Vols/16th NCST), V: 552.
Roberts, Rufus, (Capt, Co G, 49th NCST), III: 128, 153.
Roberts, Stephen W., (1st Lt, Co F, 1st Vols/11th NCST), I: 585.
Roberts, Thomas, (Pvt, Co D, 56th NCST), V: 566.
Roberts, W.H., (3rd Sgt, Co A, 3rd Vols/13th NCST), V: 549.
Roberts, Dr. William C, (Ass't Surg, N.C.), IV: 631.
Roberts, William Paul, (Brig Gen), I: xii, 433; II: 80, 82, 89,96, 99-109 personal account; III: 466, 467, 468, 470, 613, 614, 634, 645; IV: 88, 89, 90, 94, 95, 96, 580, 631; V: 179, 210, 251, 567, 659, 673, 674.
Robertson, Beverly H., (Brig Gen), I: 587; III: 460, 530, 531, 534, 550, 551, 553, 555, 558, 562, 563, 565, 566, 567, 569, 572; IV: 73, 190, 253; V: 85, 86, 87, 88, 90.
Robertson, H.H., (Pvt, Co G, 28th NCST), V: 542.
Robertson, J.P., (Pvt, Co B, 53rd NCST), V: 501.
Robertson, James M., (Capt, Art, USA), III: 596.
Robertson, H. Jasper, (2nd Lt, Co A, 10th NCST, 1st Art & Engs, Ramseur-Manly's Battery, Light Art), I: 551, 555, 560.
Robertson, Jerome Bonaparte, (Brig Gen), II: 718.
Robertson, John, (Pvt, Co E, 44th NCST), V: 533.
Robertson, John C., (Capt, Co F, 40th NCST, 3rd Art, Hvy), II: 746, 747.
Robertson, Leonidas W., (Lt, Co E, 47th NCST), III: 84.
Robertson, M., (Pvt, Co A, 3rd Vols/13th NCST), V: 549.
Robertson, N., (Pvt, Co F, 32nd NCST), V: 496.
Robertson, N.M., (Pvt, Co E, 6th NCST), V: 512.
Robertson, Rufus, (Pvt, Co F, 6th NCST), V: 513.
Robertson, Thomas H., (Pvt, Co D, 45th NCST), V: 500.
Robertson, W.E., (Pvt, Co B, 26th NCST), V: 531.
Robertson, Walter H., (Lt, Ordnance Officer, Pettigrew's Brigade), IV: 556; V: 116, 120, 131.

Robertson, Walter M., (Lt, Ordnance officer, Pettigrew's Brigade), II: 358.
Robertson, William, (QM Sgt, 32nd NCST), V: 495.
Robertson River, Va., III: 572, 574, 575, 576; IV: 506, 507.
Robertson's Run, Va., IV: 184.
Roberson, D., (Pvt, Co H, 16th Battalion/75th NCST, 7th Cav), V: 660.
Roberson, J.P., (Pvt, Co H, 16th Battalion/75th NCST, 7th Cav), V: 660.
Robeson, David G., (Lt, Co A, 9th Battalion NCST, 1st Hvy Art), IV: 304.
Robeson, Evander N., (1st Lt, Co K, 8th Vols/18th NCST), II: 64; V: 537.
Robeson, H.B., (Lt, USN; Pioneer, Colorado), V: 244.
Robeson, John H., (Capt, Co H, 29th NCST), II: 485, 493.
Robeson County, N.C., II: 16, 66, 126, 750; III: 205; IV: 216, 303, 342, 353, 483, 594, 610, 613.
Robinette, Joel B., (Pvt, Co G, 37th NCST), II: 654.
Robinette, John C., (Pvt, Co G, 37th NCST), II: 654.
Robinette, William P., (Pvt, Co G, 37th NCST), II: 654.
Robins, Jonathan, (Pvt, Co C, 30th NCST), V: 491.
Robinson, A., (Cpl, Co C, 30th NCST), V: 491.
Robinson, A.T., (Hospital Steward, 51st NCST), III: 205.
Robinson, Dr. Benjamin, (Capt, Co A, 5th NCST; Surg, 6th Battalion NCST, Fayetteville Armory Guard), I: 284, 287, 288; II: 125; IV: 299.
Robinson, C.F., (AQM, 2nd Battalion NCST), IV: 259.
Robinson, C.H., (ACS, 31st NCST), II: 511.
Robinson, D.C., (Sgt, Co I, 37th NCST), V: 546.
Robinson, George, (Pvt, Co I, 27th NCST), V: 524.
Robinson, Henry W., (Pvt, Co C, 4th Vols/14th NCST), I: 710.
Robinson, Isaac W., (Pvt, Co M, 6th Vols/16th NCST), V: 553.
Robinson, J.L., (AQMS, 6th Vols/16th NCST), I: 751.
Robinson, J.N., [Stephen M.], (2nd Lt, Co H, 5th Vols/15th NCST), IV: 710.
Robinson, Dr. J.S., (Ass't Surg, 72nd NCST, 3rd Junior Reserves), IV: 51, 642.
Robinson, James H., (Capt, Co A, 61st NCST), III: 503, 505.
Robinson, Jethro, (Pvt, Co F, 14th Vols/24th NCST), V: 560.
Robinson, John A., (Capt, Co E, Walker's Battalion, Thomas' Legion, 80th NCST), IV: 118.
Robinson, John Cleveland, (Maj Gen, USA), I: 634.
Robinson, John H. Jr., (Capt, Adjt, 52nd NCST; AAG MacRae's Brigade), I: 118, 123, 133; III: 21, 223, 229, 231, 236, 237, 253; V: 529.
Robinson, John H., (Capt, Co H, 29th NCST), II: 486.
Robinson, John M., (Lt, Co G, 10th NCST, 1st Art & Engs, Pender-Manney' Hvy Art), I: 525.
Robinson, John M., (Capt, Co B, 38th NCST), II: 686, 689, 691; V: 548.
Robinson, John S., (Pvt, Co D, 5th Vols/15th NCST), V: 521.
Robinson, Joseph D., (Pvt, Co C, 5th Vols/15th NCST), V: 521.
Robinson, L., (Pvt, Co E, 57th NCST), V: 517.

Robinson, Dr. L.W., (Ass't Surg, N.C.), IV: 630.
Robinson, Dr. P.G., (Surg, 12th Vols/22nd NCST), II: 171; IV: 635.
Robinson, R.M., (Resident of Charlotte), IV: 189.
Robinson, S.R., (2nd Lt, Co D, 2nd Battalion Junior Reserves; Co F, 71st NCST, 2nd Junior Reserves), IV: 28.
Robinson, Samuel, (Pvt, Co K, 13th Vols/23rd NCST), V: 510.
Robinson, Thomas M., (Capt, AQM, 67th NCST), III: 703, 711.
Robinson, T.C., (Pvt, Co E, 28th NCST), V: 542.
Robinson, T.J., (Superintendent of Laboratory, Fayetteville Arsenal), IV: 299.
Robinson, W.P., (Maj, 66th NCST), III: 696; IV: 544.
Robinson, W.T., (Capt, Co D, 66th NCST), III: 686.
Robinson, William G., (Lt Col, 9th Vols/19th NCST, 2nd Cav), II: 79, 82.
Robinson, Willian O., (Lt, Co B, 8th Vols/18th NCST), II: 62.
Robinsonville, N.C., II: 705.
Roby, ______, (CSN), V: 327.
Rock Creek, (nr Gettysburg, Pa.), I: 148, 315, 316; III: 6; V: 597, 606, 609.
Rockbridge Alum Springs, Va., I: 771; IV: 149.
Rockcastle River, Ky., IV: 288.
Rocketts, (nr Richmond, Va.), I: 563; II: 190.
Rockfish, (District of Cumberland County), IV: 294.
Rockfish, N.C., III: 215, 216.
Rockfish Creek, N.C., II: 762.
Rockfish Gap, Va., I: 303; II: 258.
Rockfish River, Va., III: 748.
Rockford Road, Va., III: 572.
Rockingham, N.C., II: 202, 203; III: 192, 193; IV: 355.
Rockingham County, N.C., I: 653, 687, 692; II: 161; III: 35, 38, 42, 545; IV: 103, 508, 611.
Rocks, The, Va., I: 431.
Rocky Ford, Ga., II: 757; V: 635.
Rocky Ford, N.C., (Catawba River nr Morganton), IV: 375; V: 635.
Rocky Mount, N.C., I: 321, 399, 495, 523, 524; III: 87, 173, 232, 322; IV: 77, 604.
Rocky Mountains, II: 703.
Rockville, Md., I: 259, 325, 424; II: 96, 122, 247; III: 278.
Rockville, N.C., III: 321.
Rockwell, Alfred P., (Col, 6th Conn.), V: 238.
Rockwell, H.C., (Capt, AQM, 51st NCST), III: 205.
Rodes, E.H., (Capt, Co G, 3rd NCST), I: 213.
Rodes, Ingram, (1st Cpl, Co I, 3rd Vols/13th NCST), V: 551.
Rodes, Robert Emmet, (Maj Gen), I: 146, 151, 154, 173, 174, 193, 207, 208, 252, 254, 257, 259, 262, 263, 275, 278, 288, 326, 629, 630, 634, 635, 637, 638, 711, 716; II: 114, 119, 226, 230, 231, 237, 252, 501, 524, 525, 529; III: 41, 46, 49, 55, 260, 279, 749, 751, 753; IV: 253, 449, 457, 515, 516, 523, 603; V: 93, 97.
Rodgers, Council, (Pvt, Co A, 1st Vols, "Bethel"), I: 106, 128.
Rodman, ______, (Col, 4th Rhode Island), II: 314, 317, 318.
Rodman, William B., (Capt, Co C, 40th NCST, 3rd Art, Hvy; Col, Presiding Judge Military Court, G.W. Smith's Corps), II: 746; V: 8, 650.
Rodman's Point, N.C., (aka Rodman's Farm), I: 540; II: 340; III: 172, 173; IV: 76.
Roe, J.W., (Pvt, Co C, 6th NCST), V: 512.

Roebuck, George L., (Pvt, Co B, 33rd NCST), V: 544.
Rossler, J., (Capt, Co F, 3rd Vols/13th NCST), V: 547.
Rogers, ______, (Col, N.C. Militia), III: 518.
Rogers, A.J., (Capt, Co D, 8th NCST), I: 387, 395.
Rogers, Allen R., (2nd Lt, Co I, 41st NCST, 3rd Cav), II: 772.
Rogers, Anselm, (Jr 2nd Lt, Co A, 39th NCST), II: 705.
Rogers, Asbury T., (Maj, 62nd NCST), III: 515, 524; IV: 702, 710.
Rogers, B.F., (2nd Lt, Co D, 5th Battalion Junior Reserves; Co E, 71st NCST, 2nd Junior Reserves), IV: 28.
Rogers, C.M., (2nd Lt, Co D, 30th NCST), II: 496.
Rogers, C.W., (Musician, 46th NCST), V: 524.
Rogers, Calvin J., (Pvt, Co A, 43rd NCST), III: 20; V: 497.
Rogers, D.D., (1st Cpl, Co I, 52nd NCST), III: 225.
Rogers, D.J., (Pvt, Co B, 3rd NCST), V: 487.
Rogers, David, (Capt, Co B, 25th NCST), II: 292.
Rogers, F.L., (1st Lt, Co B, 5th Vols/15th NCST), I: 734.
Rogers, George, (Lt Col, 4th U.S., Colored), V: 238.
Rogers, Henry A., (Maj, 3rd Vols/13th NCST), I: 659.
Rogers, Hiram, (Capt, Co E, 29th NCST), II: 485, 493.
Rogers, Dr. Hugh M., (Surg, 62nd NCST), III: 515; IV: 641.
Rogers, Hugh W., (2nd Lt, Co G, 39th NCST), II: 706.
Rogers, J., (Pvt, Co I, 3rd Vols/13th NCST), V: 551.
Rogers, J.T., (2nd Lt, Co K, 32nd NCST), I: 736.
Rogers, J.T., (Pvt, Co G, 3rd Vols/13th NCST), V: 551.
Rogers, J.V.L., (ACS, 42nd NCST), II: 789.
Rogers, J.W., (Pvt, Co C, 33rd NCST), V: 544.
Rogers, James A., (Capt, Co D; Surg; Maj, 54th NCST), III: 267, 269, 276; IV: 630; V: 12.
Rogers, Joseph M., (Capt, AQM, 35th NCST), II: 597.
Rogers, J. Rowan, (2nd Lt, Co I, 47th NCST), III: 85, 103, 105, 108, 109, 110, 111, 112.
Rogers, John V.B., (Capt, Co A, 9th Vols/19th NCST, 2nd Cav), II: 79, 82, 89.
Rogers, M.L., (2nd Lt, Co D, 30th NCST), II: 496.
Rogers, R., (Pvt, Co B, 47th NCST), V: 534.
Rogers, R.S., (3rd Sgt, Co G, 12th Vols/22nd NCST), V: 554.
Rogers, Sion H., (Col, 47th NCST), III: 83, 86, 320.
Rogers, W.J., (1st Lt, Co A, Ellis' 3rd Battalion NCST, Light Art) IV: 261.
Rogers, W.P., (Pvt, Co C, 48th NCST), V: 526.
Rogers' House, (Emmetsburg Road, nr Gettysburg, Pa.), V: 109.
Rogersville, Tenn., III: 664, 742, 743, 772.
Rogersville & Kingsport Valley, Tenn., III: 742.
Rolando, H., (Cmdr, USN), V: 243.
Rolfe, Dr. ______, [Wolfe, Artemas J.], (Ass't Surg, 9th NCST, 1st Cav), I: 485; IV: 633.
Roll of Honor, I: 52, 378; II: 119; III: 645; V: 15, 17.
Roll of Honor, (in prisons), IV: 764.
Rollins, Augustus W., (Lt Col, 7th N.H.), V: 238.

Rollins, John R., (1st Sgt, Co H, 27th NCST), II: 462; V: 523.
Rollins, M.T., (Cpl, Co H, 47th NCST), V: 535.
Rollins, Wallace, (Capt, Co D, 29th NCST), (Traitor), II: 487, 493.
Rome, Ga., III: 500.
Rome, Italy, V: 417.
Rominger, W.J., (Pvt, Co K, 11th Vols/21st NCST), V: 515.
Roney, John, (2nd Lt, Co H, 5th Vols/15th NCST), I: 735.
Roney, L.H., (3rd Lt, Co I, 57th NCST), III: 427.
Rood, Oliver P., (Pvt, USA), II: 137, 138.
Rook, J.L., (Pvt, Co C, 32nd NCST), V: 496.
Rooker, George W., (4th Cpl, Co A, 4th Vols/14th NCST), V: 489.
Roper, John W., (2nd Lt, Co D, 46th NCST), III: 81.
Rose, F.R., (Regimental Bugler, Co A, 63rd NCST, 5th Cav), III: 577, 655.
Rose, George M., (1st Lt, Adjt, 66th NCST, Nephew of Col McNeill), III: 685, 690, 692, 694, 695, 696, 699, 700, 701; IV: 270, 302, 538.
Rose, L.D., (Pvt, Co C, 2nd Vols/12th NCST), V: 506.
Rose, R., (Pvt, Co F, 33rd NCST), V: 544.
Rose, W.N., Jr., (Cpl, Co E, 14th Vols/24th NCST), II: 269, 273, 277, 279, 283, 286, 287, 290.
Roseboro, James T., [Rosborough], (1st Lt, Co G, 6th NCST), I: 345.
Rosecrans, William Starke, (Maj Gen, USA), I: 752; II: 270, 490, 710, 712, 715, 735, 737; III: 476, 480, 486, 491.
Roseman, F.D., (1st Lt, Co F, 38th NCST), II: 675, 678, 681.
Roseman, Marion, (QM Sgt, 38th NCST), II: 676.
Rosick, George W., (Pvt, Co G, 34th NCST), V: 556.
Rosindale, N.C., V: 401.
Ross, B.B., [Benjamin B.], (Sgt, Co I, 4th NCST), I: 234.
Ross, D.M., (Sgt, Co K, 28th NCST), V: 543.
Ross, Egbert A., (Maj, 1st Vols/11th NCST), I: 77, 90, 94, 118, 124, 127, 133, 583, 587, 589; V: 11, 640, 664.
Ross, G.P., (Pvt, Co K, 28th NCST), V: 543.
Ross, J.H., (Sgt, Co K, 47th NCST), V: 535.
Ross, John, (Capt, Co K, 37th NCST), II: 653.
Ross, John R., (Sgt, Co B, 40th NCST, 3rd Art, Hvy), II: 765.
Ross, L.R., (2nd Lt, Co C, 33rd NCST), II: 539, 578.
Ross, M.J., (Sgt, Co K, 28th NCST), V: 543.
Ross, N.W., (Pvt, Co F, 56th NCST), III: 348.
Ross, R.M., (Ass't Eng, CSN, Tallahassee), V: 438.
Ross, W.A., (2nd Lt, Co K, 37th NCST), II: 670.
Ross, W.J., (Pvt, Co K, 30th NCST), V: 493.
Rosser, Thomas Lafayett, (Maj Gen), I: 427, 436; II: 106, 785; III: 623, 624, 625, 626, 746; IV: 88, 213.
Rothrock, L.H., (1st Lt, Co G, 6th NCST), IV: 700, 710.
Rough Creek Church, Va., V: 265.
Roulhac, Thomas R., (1st Lt, Adjt, 49th NCST), III: 125, 127, 131, 144, 145, 146, 147, 148, 391.
Round Top Mountain, (nr Gettysburg, Pa. There are both Big and Little Round Top Mountains. Listings are to

either), I: 149, 315, 556; II: 363; III: 90, 414; V: 102, 109, 121, 122, 137, 138, 142, 391.

Roundtree, E.A., (Musician, 16th Battalion/75th NCST, 7th Cav), V: 660.

Rountree, Erastus, (Pvt, Co H, 27th NCST), II: 462; V: 524.

Rountree, Richard, (Pvt, Co D, 68th NCST), III: 715.

Rountree, S.J., (2nd Lt, Co B, 5th NCST), IV: 701, 710.

Rouse, George, [George W.], (Pvt, Co D, 3rd NCST), I: 194.

Rouse, Joshua, (Capt, Co E, 76th NCST, 6th Senior Reserves), IV: 97.

Routh, Alexander, (1st Lt, Co K, 46th NCST), III: 76, 82.

Rowan, ______, (Cmdr, CSN), V: 302.

Rowan, ______, (Commodore, USN), V: 311.

Rowan County, N.C., I: 565; II: 792; III: 406, 419, 421, 427;IV: 41, 372, 483, 594, 605, 616; V: 627.

Rowanty Creek, Va., (Starting point of Hampton's Beef Raid), III: 622, 623.

Rowe, A.H., (Pvt, Co K, 46th NCST, Battalion, Light Art), IV: 361, 362; V: 525.

Rowe, David P., (Maj, 2nd Vols/12th NCST), I: 609, 620, 629, 630; II: 230.

Rowe, Henry, (Pvt, Co B, 48th NCST), V: 526.

Rowe, J.D., (1st Sgt, Co K, 46th NCST), V: 525.

Rowe, J.M., (1st Lt, Co C, Cumming's Battery, Starr's 13th Battalion NCST, Light Art), IV: 361, 362.

Rowe, Wiley, (Pvt, Barrington's Co, Whitford's 11th Battalion NCST, Hvy Art; Pvt, Co B, 67th NCST), V: 18.

Rowland, T.C., (Capt, Co D, 2nd Battalion Junior Reserves; Co F, 71st NCST, 2nd Junior Reserves), IV: 25, 28.

Rowland, Thomas W., (Capt, AAG, R. Ransom's Brigade), IV: 569, 577.

Rowland, W.H., (Musician, 55th NCST), V: 527.

Rowser's Ford, (Potomac River, Va.), I: 424.

Roxboro, N.C., II: 222.

Royal, A., (Pvt, Co I, 46th NCST), V: 525.

Royal, Rev. Dr. William B., [Royall], (Chaplain, 55th NCST), III: 288; IV: 618.

Royal Shoals, N.C., V: 36.

Royster, David W., (Pvt, Co K, 4th Vols/14th NCST), V: 491.

Royster, Iowa M., (2nd Lt, Co G, 37th NCST), II: 661, 674.

Royster, R. McD., (Lt, Co K, 55th NCST), III: 296; IV: 700, 711.

Royster, T.D., (Pvt, Co D, 2nd Vols/12th NCST), V: 507.

Royster, Thomas, (Pvt, Co F, 2nd Vols/12th NCST), V: 265.

Royster, W.L., (Pvt, Co A, 44th NCST), V: 533.

Rozell, W.F., (2nd Lt, Co E, 1st Vols/11th NCST), I: 585; V: 664.

Rozell's Ferry, N.C., I: 61.

Ruark, E.R., (2nd Lt, Co C, 30th NCST), II: 496.

Rucker, H. King, (1st Sgt, Co I, 6th Vols/16th NCST), V: 552.

Rucker, Dr. J.L., (Pvt, Co N; Ass't Surg, 6th Vols/16th NCST), I: 634, 771; IV: 634.

Rucker's Legion, (AoT), III: 679.

Rudd, E.W., (Cpl, Co H, 6th NCST), V: 513.

Rude's Hill, Va., II: 258.

Rudhour, J.M., [Rendleman, John M.], (2nd Lt, Co G, 57th NCST), IV: 711.

Rudsil, John, (Pvt, Co D, 28th NCST), V: 542.

Rudsil, S., (Pvt, Co B, 54th NCST), V: 516.
Rudsill, Emanuel, (Color Sgt, 6th Vols/16th NCST), V: 552.
Rudsill, Wiley M., (Pvt, Co M, 6th Vols/16th NCST), V: 553.
Rudler, ______, [Anthony F.], (Col, 37th Ga.), II: 736.
Ruff's Mill, N.C., (aka Blount's Creek Mill), IV: 76-77, 90.
Ruffin, ______, (Chief Justice), III: 643.
Ruffin, J.R., (Pvt, Co B, 33rd NCST), V: 544.
Ruffin, Dr. John K., (Ass't Surg, 5th NCST; Surg, 49th NCST), I: 281, 282; II: 125, 139, 153, 579; III: 125, 139, 153; IV: 579, 632, 639.
Ruffin, Thomas, (Col, 9th NCST, 1st Cav; Presiding Judge, Military Court, E. Kirby Smith's Corps), I: 120, 418, 426, 427, 449, 450, 452, 454, 455, 456, 457, 483, 484, 486; V: 8, 11, 650.
Ruffin, Thomas, (Col, 3rd Vols/13th NCST), I: 643, 654, 655, 656, 663, 695.
Ruffin, Thomas, (1st Lt, Co D, 59th NCST, 4th Cav), I: 120; III: 457, 458, 459, 462, 553, 581; IV: 702, 710.
Ruffin's Mill, (Haw River), I: 412, 413; III: 201.
Ruffin's Run, Va., II: 90.
Rufty, Milas, (Pvt, Co D, 10th NCST, 1st Art & Engs, Reilly-Ramsay's Battery, Light Art), I: 569.
Rufus, Richard W., (Lt, Co H, 61st NCST), III: 504.
Rule, William, (Editor, Knoxville Journal Tribune), IV: 120-121.
Rummage, H.A., (Pvt, Co C, 33rd NCST), V: 544.
Rumple, E.C., (Sgt, Co A, 4th NCST), I: 232.
Rumple, Rev. Dr. J., (Chaplain, Salisbury Prison; 4th NCST), IV: 605, 765.
Rune's Salient (nr Petersburg, Va.), II: 535; V: 248, 249.
Running the Blockade, V: 414, 416, 417.
Runyon, Jacob, (Pvt, Co D, 55th NCST), V: 528.
Rupe, John, (Pvt, Co A, 34th NCST), V: 554.
Rush, Benjamin, (Pvt, Co A, 63rd NCST, 5th Cav), V: 658.
Rush, Benjamin, (Capt, Co B, Starr's Battery, Starr's 13th Battalion NCST, Light Art), I: 113, 121; IV: 342, 345, 346, 349, 350.
Rush, Calvin J., (1st Sgt, Co B, 52nd NCST), III: 223.
Rush, Noah, (Capt, Co H, 38th NCST), II: 676.
Rusher, E.A., (2nd Lt, Co D, 42nd NCST), II: 790, 801.
Russ, Jesse, (Pvt, Co E, 34th NCST), V: 555.
Russ, Dr. Simpson, (Ass't Surg, 8th Vols/18th NCST; Surg, 10th Battalion, 2nd Hvy Art), II: 17, 63; IV: 329, 473, 635, 643; V: 537.
Rush, Z.T., (2nd Lt, Co C, 6th Battalion Junior Reserves; Co F, 70th NCST, 1st Junior Reserves), IV: 13.
Russell, Alexander M., (2nd Lt, Co F, 44th NCST), III: 23, 273.
Russell, Bennett, (5th Sgt, Co H, 4th Vols/14th NCST), V: 490.
Russell, C., (Master's Mate, CSN, Tallahassee), V: 438.
Russell, D.Y., (Pvt, Co I, 8th Vols/18th NCST), II: 64; V: 540.
Russell, David Allen, (Maj Gen, USA), I: 722, 728.
Russell, David M., (Pvt, Co D, 25th NCST), V: 561.

Russell, E., (Capt, Co 5, Henry's 14th Battalion; 79th NCST, 8th Cav), IV: 113.
Russell, E.A., (Sgt, Co H, 2nd Battalion NCST), V: 495.
Russell, E.H., (Lt, Co I, 37th NCST), II: 668.
Russell, E.L., (5th Sgt, Co F, 44th NCST), V: 534.
Russell, Lord Earl, (British Minister of Foreign Affairs), V: 349.
Russell, G.L., (Ordnance Sgt, 12th Vols/22nd NCST), V: 553.
Russell, Henry, (Songwriter), V: 421.
Russell, John C., (2nd Lt, Co E, 46th NCST), III: 81.
Russell, Lee, (Capt, Co L, 12th Vols/22nd NCST), II: 166, 172; IV: 701, 710.
Russell, Robert G., (Sgt Maj, 54th NCST), III: 268.
Russell, T.L., (Cpl, Bradford's Miss. Battery, Light Art), V: 195.
Russell, Walter R., (QM Sgt, 52nd NCST), III: 226.
Russell's Ford, (Robertson River, Va.), III: 578.
Russellville, Tenn., III: 665, 743.
Russia, V: 259, 426.
Russia/Turkey War, V: 425.
Ruth, Andrew J., (Pvt, Co D, 10th NCST, 1st Art & Engs, Reilly-Ramsay's Battery, Light Art), I: 569; V: 568.
Ruth, L.D., (Pvt, Co D, 10th NCST, 1st Art & Engs, Reilly-Ramsay's Battery), I: 569.
Ruther, Glen, (Va.), I: 554.
Rutherford County, N.C., I: 766, 772; III: 161, 189, 315, 316; IV: 109, 110, 163, 198, 202, 216, 373, 397.
Rutherfordtown, N.C., IV: 212, 218-219, 376, 397.
Ruthledge, G.H., (Pvt, 24th Va.), V: 195.
Ruthledge, Henry M., (Col, 25th NCST), II: 286, 291, 293, 294, 295, 297, 300, 301, 332; III: 136, 324, 358, 390, 394, 397; IV: 569; V: 183, 559.
Ryals, H.J., (Maj, 50th NCST), III: 161, 202.
Ryan, ______, (Capt, Sirene), V: 404.
Ryan, ______, [James H., 1st Battalion], (1st Lt, Co C, 9th Battalion NCST, 1st Hvy Art), IV: 303.
Rye Beach, (Mass.), IV: 740.
Ryerson, ______, [Rierson, S.W.], (Pvt, Co G, Color Sgt, 11th Vols/21st NCST), II: 157, 158.
Ryke, Emanuel, (Pvt, Co E, 3rd Vols/13th NCST), V: 550.

(S)

Saddler, T.W., (Pvt, Co B, 43rd NCST), V: 497.
Sadler, James, (Pvt, Detached Co, 68th NCST), III: 723.
Sadler, Julius, (Pvt, Co B, 1st Vols, "Bethel"), I: 133.
Sadler, William, (Pvt, Co H, 45th NCST), V: 500.
Sadler, William H., (Pvt, Co F, 33rd NCST), II: 544.
Safrit, John, (Pvt, Co H, 8th Vols/18th NCST), II: 64.
Saqua LaGrande, Cuba, V: 393.
Sailor's Creek, Va., (and Battle of, 1865), I: 210, 211, 213, 265, 651; II: 265; III: 17, 283, 400, 426, 455; IV: 362, 454, 455, 456; V: 251.
Sain, A., (Pvt, Co F, 3rd Vols/13th NCST), V: 550.
Sain, G.W., (2nd Lt, Co E, Millard's 9th/20th Battalion Junior Reserves), IV: 387.
Saint Augustine, Fla., V: 446.
Saint George, William, (Pilot, Don), V: 357.
Saint Georges, Bermuda, V: 335, 336, 364, 371, 377, 380, 396, 397, 406, 410, 440, 441.
Saint Johns, New Brunswick, V: 362, 375.
Saint Petersburg, Russia, V: 425.
Saint Thomas, Bermuda, V: 410.
Saint George's Channel, England, V: 349.
Saint John's River, Fla, V: 383.
Saint Mary's, (School for girls at Raleigh), I: 57; IV: 59.
Saint Paul's Church, (Hanover Court House), II: 470.
Saint Paul's Church, (Richmond, Va.), III: 398.
Saintsing, J.A., (Pvt, Co B, 30th NCST), V: 491.
Salem, N.C., (aka New Salem), II: 398, 786; III: 288, 307.
Salem, Va., I: 206; II: 95, 245, 438, 440; III: 12, 559; IV: 161.
Salem Church, Va., (and Battle of, 1863), I: 555.
Salem Turnpike, Va., III: 277.
Sales, John, (Jr 2nd Lt, Co E, 6th Battalion/60th NCST), III: 474, 497.
Salisbury, N.C., I: 9, 13, 62, 65, 386, 561, 562; II: 393, 743, 789, 792, 806; III: 405, 410, 418, 428, 502, 681, 720, 727, 760; IV: 4, 6, 12, 28, 66, 67, 97, 129, 132, 325, 372, 387, 400, 595, 616, 651, 694, 745, 746, 751, 770; V: 5, 643, 654.
Salisbury Arsenal, IV: 131.
Salisbury Cotton Factory, (First camp of Co. D, 10th NCST, 1st Art & Engs, later became the Salisbury Prison), I: 561.
Salisbury Machine Shop, I: 22.
Salisbury Prison, (For Confederate deserters, Confederate soldiers awaiting court marshal and Federal P.O.W's), II: 202, 792; III: 406, 720; IV: 2, 66, 69, 98, 100, 387, 398, 430, 606, 651, 745-772; V: 5, 626.

Salkehatchie River, S.C., III: 188, 189; IV: 103, 333, 335.
Salmon, R., (Pvt, Co F, 14th Vols/24th NCST), V: 560.
Salt Bonds, V: x.
Salter, William, (Pvt, Co A, 67th NCST), III: 710.
Saltville, Va., III: 744; V: x.
Saluda River, S.C., III: 439.
Sample, E.A., (Pvt, Co C, 37th NCST), V: 545.
Sampson County, Va., II: 111, 113, 412; III: 738, 740, 741, 744-745; IV: 592.
Sampson County, N.C., III: 205, 503, 545; IV: 483, 484.
Sams, Joe, [Joseph L.], (Pvt, Co D, 29th NCST), II: 492.
Samuel, A., (Pvt, Co G, 11th Vols/21st NCST), V: 515.
Sanderlin, Rev. Dr. George W., (Capt, Co E, 33rd NCST), II: 37, 539, 540, 578.
Sanderlin, Jesse, (Pvt, Co A, 38th NCST), V: 557.
Sanderlin, Willis B., (Maj, 68th NCST), III: 713.
Sanders, David, (Pvt, Co G, 49th NCST), V: 564.
Sanders, E.S., (Lt, Co E, 14th Vols/24th NCST), V: 193.
Sanders, H.B., (Pvt, Co C, 4th Vols/14th NCST), I: 732.
Sanders, Henry, [Saunders, Henry B.], (Pvt, Co C, 4th Vols/14th NCST), I: 710.
Sanders, J.H.D., (Pvt, Co C, 4th Vols/14th NCST), I: 732.
Sanders, John Calhoun, (Brig Gen), III: 143.
Sanders, John W., (1st Lt, Co H, 10th NCST, 1st Art & Engs, Pool's Hvy Art), I: 499, 512, 515, 525, 530, 531, 536.
Sanders, Joseph, "Joe," (Capt, Co A; Maj; Lt Col, 33rd NCST), II: 37.
Sanders, M.W., (Lt, USN, Signal Officer), V: 241.
Sanders, Reed, (Resident of Kentucky arrested by the Lincoln administration without charges or trial, held as a political prisoner at Fort Warren Prison), IV: 735, 737, 738, 739, 740.
Sanders, Rufus, (Cpl, Co C, 47th NCST), III: 112.
Sanders, W.H., (Pvt, Co C, 4th Vols/14th NCST), I: 732.
Sanders, William, (Pvt, Co A, 5th NCST), I: 291; V: 504.
Sanderson's Farm, (nr Plymouth), III: 338, 339.
Sands, B.F., (Capt, USN), V: 243.
Sandusky, Ohio, IV: 665, 666, 667, 668, 689, 704.
Sandwich Islands, (and Sandwich Islanders), V: 347.
Sandy Cross, N.C., III: 335.
Sandy Hook, N.C., III: 561; V: 438, 440.
Sandy Mush, N.C., II: 493.
Sandy Ridge, N.C., III: 323, 333; IV: 302.
Sanford, C.C., (2nd Lt, Co F, 42nd NCST), II: 791, 806.
Sandford, Douglass, (Pvt, Co B, Starr's Battery, Starr's 13th Battalion NCST, Light Art), IV: 349.
Sanford, Frank, (Chaplain, 52nd NCST), IV: 618.
Sanford, G.T., (2nd Lt, Co I, 13th Vols/23rd NCST), II: 187.
Sanford, J.Y., [Standefor, James Y.], (3rd Lt, Co D, 57th NCST), IV: 711.
Sanford, Robert, (Pvt, Co K, 55th NCST), V: 528.
Sanford, William H., (ACS, 7th NCST), IV: 472.
Sanford, N.C., II: 627.
San Francisco, Calif., IV: 415; V: 349.

Sangster's Cross Roads, Va., (nr Manassas, Va.), II: 192.

Sapp, Alfred, (Pvt, Co I, 11th Vols/21st NCST), V: 515.

Sapp, Benjamin, (Pvt, Co K, 48th NCST), V: 527.

Sapp, Jesse, (Pvt, Co K, 45th NCST), III: 39.

Sappony Church, Va., I: 434, 470; III: 615.

Sapps, N.W., (2nd Lt, Co B, 1st Battalion NCST), V: 503.

Sargeant, Philip, (Pvt, Co F, 26th NCST), V: 603.

Sartin, M.R., (1st Sgt, Co G, 12th Vols/22nd NCST), V: 554.

Sartin, R.T., (Pvt, Co B, 2nd Battalion NCST), V: 495.

Sartin, S., (Pvt, Co G, 12th Vols/22nd NCST), V: 554.

Sartin, T.J.E., (Pvt, Co K, 3rd Vols/13th NCST), V: 551.

Sassacus, V: 243, 245, 246.

Sasser, C.J., (Pvt, Co G, 8th Vols/18th NCST), II: 64; V: 540.

Sasser, Edward, (Pvt, Co C, 68th NCST), III: 726.

Sasser, Philemon H., (1st Sgt, Co A, 10th NCST, 1st Art & Engs, Ramseur-Manly's Battery, Light Art), I: 551.

Sasser, Philemon H., (2nd Lt, Co A, 33rd NCST), II: 538, 579.

Sasser, S.A., (Pvt, Co F, 4th NCST), V: 489.

Sasser, Thomas H., (Pvt, Co C, 5th NCST), I: 291; V: 505.

Satchwell, Dr. S.S., (Surg, 25th NCST; Surg, Wilson General Hospital), II: 291, 292, 296, 299, 301; IV: 625, 627, 629, 635; V: 111.

Satterfield, E. Fletcher, (Capt, Co H, 55th NCST), I: 353; III: 292, 296, 299; V: 111.

Satterthwaite, Louis E., (Capt, Co G, 9th Vols/19th NCST, 2nd Cav), II: 80.

Satterthwaite, Thomas H., (1st Lt, Co I, 40th NCST, 3rd Art, Hvy), II: 746

Satterthwaite, Thomas H., (Lt, Co B, 61st NCST), III: 503.

Satterthwaite, William, (1st Lt, Co G, 9th Vols/19th NCST, 2nd Cav), II: 80.

Sauls, E.M., (Pvt, Co K, 27th NCST), II: 463; V: 524.

Sauls, H.J., (Lt, Co H, 9th NCST, 1st Cav), I: 486, 782.

Sauls, James, V., (1st Lt, Co A, 12th Battalion, Cav; Capt, Co K, 59th NCST, 4th Cav), III: 458; IV: 339.

Saulston, N.C., III: 725.

Saunders, A.F., (2nd Lt, Co C, 13th Vols/23rd NCST), II: 184.

Saunders, Alexander, [Sanders], (Pvt, Co A, 26th NCST), II: 358.

Saunders, Alfred, (2nd Lt, Co I, 7th NCST), V: 537.

Saunders, Miss Ann, II: 579.

Saunders, Frank, (Pvt, Co D, 68th NCST), III: 715.

Saunders, Henry, (Pvt, Co M, 6th Vols/16th NCST), V: 552.

Saunders, J., (Pvt, Co H, 1st Vols/11th NCST), V: 530.

Saunders, J.J., (Pvt, Co C, 3rd Vols/13th NCST), V: 550.

Saunders, John, (Pvt, Co G, 2nd NCST), I: 176; V: 486.

Saunders, Joseph H., (Lt Col, 33rd NCST), I: 118; II: 537, 538, 561, 563, 566, 567; IV: 473, 474, 702, 711, 743; V: 155, 650.

Saunders, Lancaster K., (Surg, 7th Vols/17th NCST), IV: 643.

Saunders, Palmer, (CSN), V: 327, 330, 331.

Saunders, R.R., (2nd Lt, Co B, 4 5th NCST), IV: 702, 711.

Saunders Richard B., (2nd Lt, AQM, 1st Vols, "Bethel"), I: 77, 113.

Saunders, Simeon P., (Pvt, Co D, 68th NCST), III: 715.
Saunders, T.L., (Pvt, Co B, 28th NCST), V: 541.
Saunders, Thomas S., (Pvt, Co H, 6th Vols/16th NCST), V: 552.
Saunders, W., (Pvt, Co K, 37th NCST), V: 546.
Saunders, W.M., (Pvt, Co K, 37th NCST), V: 546.
Saunders, William H., (Pvt, Co C, 4th Vols/14th NCST), V: 490.
Saunders, William J., (Chief of Art, Whiting's Staff), I: 551, 529; V: 651.
Saunders, William L., (Maj, 10th NCST, 1st Art & Engs, Semme's Staff), I: 551, 554, 562, 564.
Saunders, William L., (Col, 46th NCST), I: 464; II: 439: III: 64, 65, 70, 75, 76, 79, 80; V: 519, 650, 652.
Saunders' Raid, IV: 272.
Savage, Edward, (Lt Col, 3rd NCST), I: 178, 179, 181, 190, 191, 213, 217, 218, 227.
Savage, Henry, (Capt, Co G, 8th Vols/18th NCST; Collector of Customs at Wilmington), II: 16, 20; V: 368.
Savage, J., (Pvt, Co B, 44th NCST), V: 533.
Savage, J.W., (Pvt, Co E, 33rd NCST), V: 544.
Savage, John, (Pilot, Ella), V: 357.
Savage, John T., (2nd Lt, Co G, 41st NCST, 3rd Cav), II: 771.
Savage, Orren B., (Ass't Surg, 5th NCST), IV: 632.
Savage, W., (Pvt, Co C, 2nd Vols/12th NCST), I: 630.
Savage Station, Va., I: 139, 334, 553, 617, 738; II: 212; IV: 152.
Savannah, Ga., I: 6, 391, 742; II: 18, 513, 634, 757, 758; III: 179, 181-186, 191, 192, 206, 454, 502, 509, 510; IV: 58, 101, 103, 320, 322, 327, 328, 333, 334, 335, 424, 437, 440, 471, 536, 548, 562, 615, 619, 733, 735; V: 300, 312, 386, 454.
Savannah River, Ga., II: 757, 758; III: 183; IV: 322, 335, 733, 734; V: 623.
Savells, M.D., (Pvt, Co I, 56th NCST), V: 566.
Saville, J.C., (Cpl, Co K, 30th NCST), V: 493.
Saville, J.M., [Savile], (2nd Lt, Co H, 1st Vols/11th NCST), I: 121, 585.
Savilles, Thomas P., (Capt, Co A, 56th NCST), III: 313, 366.
Sawyer, ______, (Sherman's Staff, USA), I: 730.
Sawyer, G.A., (Pvt, Co H, 6th NCST), V: 513.
Sawyer, Harvey Andrew, (Capt, Co G, 2nd NCST), I: 162.
Sawyer, Hiram, (Lt, Co G, 2nd NCST), I: 162.
Sawyer, J.S., (Pvt, Co C, 56th NCST), III: 347.
Sawyer, James P., (Pvt, Co A, 25th NCST), V: 560.
Sawyer, Joel A., (Jr 2nd Lt, Co F, 39th NCST), II: 706.
Sawyer, John, (Pvt, Co A, 56th NCST), V: 565.
Sawyer, L., (Pvt, Co A, 56th NCST), III: 347.
Sawyer, Robert W., (Pvt, Color-bearer, Co K, 8th NCST), I: 408.
Sawyer, William G., (Sgt, Co B, 7th NCST), I: 378.
Sayars, J., (Lt, Co H, 2nd Battalion NCST), IV: 245.
Scales, ______, (Maj, QM, Pender's Division), I: 729; IV: 182.
Scales, Alfred M., (Brig Gen), I: xi, 380, 610, 634, 653, 654, 657, 659, 660, 662, 665, 670, 673, 676, 678, 680, 681, 693, 729, 765; II: 41, 42, 43, 44, 117, 170,

171, 174, 175, 460, 661, 680, 687, 690, 692, 693; IV: 155, 175, 177, 180, 184, 201, 552, 553, 554; V: xii, 104, 144, 649.
Scales, E.D., (Pvt, Co H, 3rd Vols/13th NCST; Capt., ACS, Scales' Brigade) IV: 553.
Scales, Frank, [Edward F.], (Pvt, Co F, 3rd Vols/13th NCST), I: 695.
Scales, Hamilton, (Capt, Co H, 12th Vols/22nd NCST), II: 162, 163, 165, 166.
Scales, James Turner, (Maj, 2nd NCST), I: 161, 174, 175; IV: 460; V: 484.
Scales, Dr. Jefferson, (Resident of Staten Island, N.Y.), I: 695.
Scales, John, (2nd Lt, Co H, 3rd Vols/13th NCST), I: 653.
Scales, John L., (Capt, Co D, 45th NCST), III: 36.
Scales, N.E., (Maj, QM, Pender-Scale's Brigade; QM, Wilcox's Division), I: 729; IV: 182, 551; V: 537, 651.
Scales, Dr. Nathaniel M., (Surg, 1st NCST), I: 136; IV: 631.
Scarborough, Ambrose F., (Capt, Co C, 13th Vols/23rd NCST), II: 183, 203.
Scarborough, J.C., (Sgt, Co I, 1st NCST), V: 485.
Scarborough, John C., (Pvt, Co K, 4th Vols/14th NCST), V: 593.
Scarborough, M.F., (2nd Lt, Co I, 1st NCST), I: 137.
Scarborough, W.D., (1st Lt, Co I, 1st NCST), I: 137.
Scarlett, Thomas C., (Pvt, Co D, 56th NCST), III: 370.
Schaller, Frank, (Col, 22nd Miss.), V: 641.
Scharf, ______, (CSN), V: 327, 438.
Schayman, Phillip, (Fayetteville and Harper's Ferry Arsenals), IV: 298.
Schemmermeyer, ______, (Lt, Co D, 10th NCST, 1st Art & Engs, Reilly-Ramsay's Battery, Light Art), I: 565.
Schenck, ______, V: 50.
Schenck, David, (Capt, N.C. Subsistence Department), I: 37.
Schenck, Henry F., (Maj, 56th NCST), III: 315, 318, 323, 324, 331.
Schenck, James Findlay, (Commodore, USN), V: 242.
Schenck, Samuel G., (Adjt, 67th NCST), III: 703.
Schilling, John, (Fayetteville and Harper's Ferry Arsenal), IV: 298.
Schimmelfennig, Alexander, (Brig Gen, USA), I: 145.
Schimmerhorn, ______, (Capt, Wise's Legion), II: 510; V: 61, 66.
Schisano, Leon, (French Vice Consel) V: 304, 312.
Schoesser, Ignaz, (Cpl, Co D, 10th NCST, 1st Art & Engs, Reilly-Ramsay's Battery, Light Art), I: 569, 570, 575.
Schofield, Dr. ______, (Resident of Petersburg, Va.), II: 124.
Schofield, John McAllister, (Maj Gen, USA and Schofield's Army), I: 64, 65, 532, 555; II: 11, 650; III: 513, 681, 696, 726, 727; IV: 57, 222, 498, 592; V: 270.
Schoknett, ______, (Col, Cav, USA), II: 285.
Schoup, J.L., (Pvt, Co B, 4th Vols/14th NCST), I: 731.
Scism, James F., (Pvt, Co H, 34th NCST), V: 556.
Scoggins, J.H., (Pvt, Co C, 2nd Vols/12th NCST), V: 506.
Scoggins, J.L., (Pvt, Co E, 56th NCST), V: 566.
Scoggins, J.O., (Pvt, Co H, 56th NCST), III: 356.

Scotland Neck, N.C., IV: 25; V: 318.
Scott, Allen, (1st Cpl, Co L, 12th Vols/22nd NCST), V: 554.
Scott, David, Jr., (Capt, Co D, 53rd NCST), I: 119; III: 262.
Scott, Edward M., (Capt, Co D, 1st NCST), I: 136.
Scott, Edward M., (Capt, Co G, 12th Vols/22nd NCST), II: 162, 166.
Scott, F.J., (Pvt, Co E, 26th NCST), V: 532.
Scott, G.W., (Pvt, Co A, 11th Vols/22nd NCST), V: 514.
Scott, H.M., (Pvt, Co I, 11th Vols/21st NCST), V: 515.
Scott, J.G., (2nd Lt, Co D, 1st NCST), I: 137.
Scott, J.L., (Pvt, Co C, 45th NCST), V: 500.
Scott, J.W., (2nd Lt, Co A, 53rd NCST), III: 261.
Scott, John, (Cpl, Co E, 5th NCST; Detailed, 2nd Corps Provost Guard), I: 292; V: 505, 569.
Scott, John S., (Col, 1st La.), III: 676; IV: 274, 275, 280, 301.
Scott, O.R., (2nd Lt, Co C, 1st NCST), I: 136, 150.
Scott, T.G., (Pvt, Co I, 28th NCST), V: 543.
Scott, W.L., (Lt Col, 11th Vols/21st NCST), II: 144; V: 650.
Scott, W.R., (Lt, Co F, 9th NCST, 1st Cav), I: 486.
Scott, William, (Pvt, Co E, 14th Vols/24th NCST), II: 272.
Scott, Winfield, (Lt Gen, General-in-Chief, USA), I: 80, 81, 86, 106, 109; III: 129, 727; IV: 410.
Scott County, Tenn., IV: 271.
Scribner's & Sons, Charles, V: 414.
Scuffleton, N.C., IV: 80.
Scuppernong, N.C., IV: 556.
Sea of Okhotsk, V: 348.
Seably, Moore J., (Jr 2nd Lt, Co A, 31st NCST), II: 507.
Seaboard, N.C., IV: 359; V: 272.
Seaboard Railroad, (aka Seacoast Railroad), III: 232, 695; IV: 26, 358.
Seaboard & Roanoke Railroad Bridge, I: 446; IV: 366, 367; V: 271, 272.
Seabolt, T.E., (Cpl, Co D, 6th NCST), V: 512.
Seaford, Wiley S., (Pvt, Co G, 8th NCST), V: 194.
Seagle, George W., (Capt, Co B, 13th Vols/23rd NCST), II: 183.
Seagle, T.J., (1st Lt, Co B, 13th Vols/23rd NCST), II: 183.
Seamon, H.R., (Pvt, Co H, 13th Vols/23rd NCST), V: 510.
Searcey, ______, (Col, Tenn.), III: 442.
Searcy, A.W., (Pvt, Co C, 6th Battalion/60th NCST), III: 482.
Searcy, R.P., (Jr 2nd Lt, Co L, Louisiana Tigers, Walker's Battalion, Thomas' Legion, 80th NCST), IV: 119.
Sears, B.J., (Pvt, Co C, 36th NCST), V: 565.
Sears, P., (Pvt, Co H, 47th NCST), V: 535.
Seawell, Dr. F.H., (Surg, 10th NCST, 1st Art & Engs, Ramseur-Manly's Battery, Light Art), I: 553, 556.
Seckler, G.A.J., [Sechler], (Capt, Co K, 57th NCST), IV: 711.
Seceded, North Carolina, II: 16, 190.
Second Street, (Plymouth), III: 339, 341, 346; V: 176, 184, 185, 188, 189.
Secrest, H., (Pvt, Co B, 43rd NCST), V: 497.
Secrest, Matt, (Pvt, Co K, 45th NCST), III: 58.
Secret Service of the Confederate States in Europe, V: 414.

Seddon, James Alexander, (Sec of War, CSA), I: 547; II: 777; III: 555, 638; IV: 749, 751; V: 437.
Sedgwick, John, (Maj Gen, USA), I: 310, 366, 376; II: 21, 135, 602; III: 417; IV: 195; V: 263.
Sedley Road, (nr Manassas, Va.), I: 341.
Seigle, Thomas L., (2nd Lt, Co C, 10th NCST, 1st Art & Engs, Brem-Graham-Williams' Battery, Light Art), I: 547, 549; V: 567.
Seitz, J.Q., (Pvt, Co K, 46th NCST), V: 525.
Selby, Samuel, (1st Lt, Anderson's Battalion Junior Reserves; Co I, 71st NCST, 2nd Junior Reserves), IV: 29.
Selden, William, (Lt, Engineering Officer), II: 510; V: 61, 62, 66.
Seldon, ______, (Signal Officer, Don), V: 425.
Self, W.G., (Pvt, Co F, 55th NCST), V: 528.
Selfridge, T.O., (Lt Cmdr, USN; Pioneer, Huron), V: 242, 244, 245.
Sellars, R., (Pilot, Venus), V: 357.
Sellers, ______, (Maj, AG to Hood), I: 571.
Sellers, W.G., (Pvt, Co K, 10th Vols/20th NCST), V: 509.
Sellers, William W., (Lt Col, 30th NCST), II: 496, 497, 503; IV: 461; V: 11, 650.
Selma, N.C., (aka Smithfield Station), I: 55; II: 125; III: 199, 439, 699.
Selvy, J., (Pvt, Co H, 37th NCST), V: 546.
Seminary, (aka Theological College at Gettysburg, Pa.), II: 42, 344, 354, 356, 528, 692; III: 6, 298, 299; V: 612, 613.
Seminary Ridge, Pa., (nr Gettysburg, Pa.), I: 312, 315, 316, 317, 379, 380; II: 345, 362, 363, 364, 660; III: 6, 237, 299; V: 102, 104, 119, 120, 123, 124, 125, 126, 127, 128, 137, 139, 606, 608, 609, 611, 613.
Semmes, Paul Jones, (Brig Gen), I: 552, 556.
Semmes, Raphhael, (Rear Adm, CSN), IV: 319; V: 416.
Semple, Edward A., (Lt, Adjt, 57th NCST), III: 405, 410, 427.
Seneca Falls, Va., II: 96.
Senior Reserves, I: vii, xiii, 16, 18, 19, 52, 55, 433; II: 11; IV: 2, 3, 5, 6, 37, 47, 65, 97, 100, 101, 102, 105, 224, 334, 397, 407, 408, 440, 539, 585, 586, 587, 651, 652, 756, 757; V: ix, 1, 5, 466, 629.
Senior Reserves in Virginia, I: 433, 437.
Sensabaugh, Dr. Leonidas F., (Surg, 65th NCST, 6th Cav), III: 683; IV: 642.
Senter, George W., (Pvt, Co G, 25th NCST), V: 561.
Senter, W.H., (1st Lt, Co E, 78th NCST, 8th Senior Reserves), IV: 107.
Sergeant, O., (Sgt Maj, 34th NCST), II: 582.
Sergeant, Robert A., [Sergent], (Pvt, Co D, 3rd Vols/13th NCST), I: 684.
Serralt, W.O., (Pvt, Co D, 4th Vols/14th NCST), V: 572.
Serves, T.O., (Pvt, Co F, 63rd NCST, 5th Cav), III: 618.
Sessoms, John W., (AQM, 68th NCST), III: 713.
Sessoms, Dr. Joseph W., (Ass't Surg, 59th NCST, 4th Cav), IV: 457, 641.
Setser, Joseph, (Pvt, Co F, 26th NCST), V: 602.
Setser, T.W., (Pvt, Co F, 26th NCST), V: 603.

Setser, W.E., (Pvt, Co F, 26th NCST), V: 602.
Settle, David, (3rd Lt, Co H, 3rd Vols/13th NCST), I: 653.
Settle, H. Clay, (Pvt, Co A, 10th NCST, 1st Art & Engs, Ramseur-Manly's Battery, Light Art), I: 556.
Settle, Thomas, (Capt, Co I, 3rd Vols/13th NCST), I: 653, 654, 689.
Settle, N.C., IV: 395.
Settlemire, D.N., (Pvt, Co A, 2nd Vols/12th NCST), V: 506.
Setzer, Alfred, (Pvt, Co F, 38th NCST), V: 557.
Setzer, Marcus, (Pvt, Co A, 2nd Vols/12th NCST; Detailed, 2nd Corps Provost Guard), V: 506, 570.
Setzer, N., (Pvt, Co A, 2nd Vols/12th NCST), V: 506.
Setzer, Pink, (Pvt, Co I, 49th NCST), V: 565.
Setzer, W., (Pvt, Co K, 46th NCST), V: 525.
"Seven Days' Battles," (1862), I: 138, 165, 242, 612-623, 632, 711, 758, 772; II: 66, 67, 68, 83, 149, 201, 207-217, 428, 546; III: 4, 66, 127, 159, 162-166, 255; IV: 37, 155-158, 233, 235, 356, 411, 445, 465, 501, 521, 551, 551, 556, 569; V: 71, 116, 641, 667.
Seven Pines, Va., (and Battle of, 1862, aka Fair Oaks), I: 138, 165, 180, 217, 236, 237, 273, 276, 278, 286, 302, 303, 334, 347, 350, 352, 553, 567, 609, 657, 693, 711, 738, 754, 755, 758, 766, 772, 773; II: 25, 66, 67, 111, 114, 167, 168, 176, 183, 185, 187, 188, 189, 203-207, 212, 213, 219, 223, 238, 254, 262, 274, 294, 334, 336, 428, 498, 546, 598, 599; III: 66, 111, 116, 316, 317, 329; IV: 37, 137, 152-155, 156, 200, 355, 356, 551, 555, 570; V: xiv, 407, 467, 627, 664.
Severs, Henry C., (Pvt, Co K, 4th NCST), I: 279.
Severt, E., (Pvt, Co A, 37th NCST), V: 545.
Sevier County, Tenn., III: 518, 738; IV: 126.
Sevierville, Tenn., III: 738, 739, 756, 759.
Seward, William Henry, (Sec of State, U.S.), III: 386.
Sewell's Point, Va., I: 81; II: 205, 216; III: 19.
Sexton, D.M., (1st Lt, Co F, 5th Vols/15th NCST), I: 735.
Sexton, Hiram, (Pvt, Co H, 2nd Battalion NCST), V: 495.
Seymour, Truman, (Maj Gen, USA), II: 120; V: 163.
Seymour, William H., (2nd Lt, Co A, 56th NCST), III: 313.
Shackelford, Calvin, (Lt, Co K, 6th Battalion/60th NCST), III: 492.
Shackelford, Daniel, (Lt, Co G, 61st NCST), III: 504.
Shackelford, J.H., (2nd Lt, Co C, 4th Battalion Junior Reserves; Co C, 72nd NCST, 3rd Junior Reserves), IV: 38.
Shackelford, James M., (Brig Gen, USA), III: 521.
Shackelford Banks, N.C., I: 490, 502, 504, 509.
Shadburne, ______, (Sgt, Scout for Hampton), III: 624, 625, 626.
Shady Grove, Va., III: 593.
Shafer, P.A., (Sgt, Co A, 4th NCST), I: 232.
Shaffner, Dr. J.F., (Surg, 4th NCST; Surg, 33rd NCST), I: 230, 268, 279; II: 537, 579, 580; IV: 474, 632, 637; V: 484.

Shaking Creek, N.C., (nr Wilmington), IV: 358.
Shaler, _____, [Alexander], (Brig Gen, USA, Cmdr at Johnson's Island Prison), IV: 672, 676, 677, 678, 683.
Shallow Ford, (Yadkin River), IV: 375.
Shankle, H., (Pvt, Co F, 44th NCST), V: 534.
Shankle, Jacob, (Pvt, Co I, 52nd NCST), V: 536.
Shannon, _____, (Englishman, Capt, Blockade Runner), V: 418.
Shannon, Dr. Jesse C., (Ass't Surg, 68th NCST), III: 713; IV: 642.
Sharp, _____, [Sharpe, George A.], (Brig Gen, USA, Deputy Provost Marshal, Army of the Potomac), I: 146, 193.
Sharp, Alfred, (1st Lt, Co A, 77th NCST, 7th Senior Reserves), IV: 99, 101.
Sharp, E., Tenkie, [Tonkie], (Pvt, Co B, 27th NCST), II: 461; V: 523.
Sharp, Eli, (Pvt, Co G, 27th NCST), II: 462; V: 523.
Sharp, Henry C., (Pvt, Co D, 68th NCST), III: 715.
Sharp, Dr. Starkey, (Surg, Wynn's 15th Battalion NCST, Cav), IV: 365, 644.
Sharp, Thomas H., [Sharpe], (Lt Col, 7th Vols/17th NCST), II: 2, 5, 9; IV: 538, 539, 545; V: 41, 42, 44, 680.
Sharp, William, (Lt, CSN), V: 301, 302, 305.
Sharp, William, (Capt, Co D, 59th NCST, 4th Cav), III: 457, 462, 700.
Sharpe, G.W., (Maj, 38th NCST; Lt Col, 5th Regt Home Guard), II: 676, 677; IV: 650.
Sharpe, J.B., (Pvt, Co A, 9th NCST, 1st Cav), V: 489.
Sharpe, R.M., (Capt, Co G, 38th NCST), II: 685; V: 293, 549.
Sharpe, R.P., (Pvt, Co E, 3rd Vols/13th NCST), V: 550.
Sharpe, S.A., (Col, 5th Regt Home Guard), IV: 650.
Sharpe, Van B., (2nd Lt, Co E, 43rd NCST; 1st Lt, Claiborne-Dearing's 7th C.S. Cav; Co I, 16th Battalion/75th NCST, 7th Cav), III: 3; IV: 17, 91.
Sharpe, Wallace, (N.C. Militia, Iredell County), V: 292, 293, 294.
Sharpe, Wash, (Col), V: 289.
Sharpsburg, Md., (and Battle of, 1862, aka Antietam), I: 115, 116, 141, 148, 158, 159, 163, 164, 166, 167, 168, 184, 187, 188, 190, 194, 213, 222, 225, 226, 228, 246, 247, 249, 286, 307, 308, 311, 334, 372, 390, 421, 425, 482, 541, 553, 573, 574, 575, 623, 625, 626, 627, 696, 711, 740, 760, 762; II: 32, 65, 71, 116, 135, 156, 157, 158, 169, 183, 184, 221, 222, 224, 225, 238, 254, 275, 296, 433-437, 438, 474, 499, 545, 553, 554, 555, 585, 593, 598, 601, 605, 623, 625, 656, 686, 687, 700; III: 67, 68, 79, 116, 119, 124, 128, 235, 464, 749; IV: 137, 165-166, 177, 236, 262, 374, 447, 465, 466, 503, 521, 552, 552, 570-571, 576, 577, 579, 718; V: viii, xii, xiv, 71-81, 587, 588, 590, 627, 639, 640, 641.
Sharpsburg Battlefield Commission Report, V: 587-593.
Sharpsburg-Hagerstown Pike, I: 184, 185, 189, 225.
Sharpton, B.F., (Lt, 7th NCST), IV: 711.
Sharpshooters Corps, IV: 225, 474.
Shaver, P.A., (Cpl, Co A, 4th NCST), V: 488.

Shaw, Angus, (1st Lt, Co K, 38th NCST), I: 120; II: 676, 678, 681.
Shaw, C.W., (Lt, Co D, 48th NCST), III: 122.
Shaw, Rev. Colin, (Chaplain, 8th Vols/18th NCST; 51st NCST), II: 17, 20; III: 206; IV: 473, 608, 617.
Shaw, Dr. Daniel M., (Ass't Surg, 26th NCST), II: 306, 307, 395; IV: 636.
Shaw, E.B., (Pvt, Co K, 10th NCST, 1st Art & Engs), V: 50.
Shaw, Eilias F., (Lt Col, 63rd NCST, 5th Cav), I: 439; II: 2; III: 529, 535, 541, 554, 643, 654; V: 11, 41, 671.
Shaw, Henry, (Pvt, Co I, 4th Vols/14th NCST), V: 491.
Shaw, Henry M., (Col, 8th NCST), I: 387, 396, 397, 398, 493, 515; II: 509, 510, 511, 513; III: 274, 333; IV: 250, 251, 345, 346, 482, 486, 487; V: 9, 59, 61, 62, 63, 65.
Shaw, J.H., (Musician, Co B, 3rd NCST), V: 487.
Shaw, J.M., (Pvt, Co K, 6th NCST), V: 514.
Shaw, John, (2nd Lt, Co F, 78th NCST, 8th Senior Reserves), IV: 107.
Shaw, R., (Capt, 4th NCST), IV: 711.
Shaw, R.J., (Lt, Co E, 9th NCST, 1st Cav), I: 486.
Shaw, Robert G., (Col, 54th Mass., Colored), III: 208; V: 163, 164, 165, 621.
Shaw, W., [Norman L.], (Lt, Co D; Capt, Co D; Adjt, 7th Vols/17th NCST), V: 43
Shaw, W.D., (Pvt, Co K, 1st NCST), V: 485.
Shaw, W.E., (Pvt, Co C, 10th NCST, 1st Art & Engs, Brem-Graham-Williams' Battery, Light Art), V: 568.
Shaw, W.H., (Musician, 52nd NCST), III: 226.
Shaw, W.N., (Pvt, Co F, 6th NCST), V: 513.
Shaw, W.P., (2nd Lt, Co D, 59th NCST, 4th Cav), III: 455, 456, 457, 468, 469, 470.
Shaw, William, (Capt, Co K, 10th NCST, 1st Art & Engs, Sparrow-Blount's Hvy Art), I: 501, 525; V: 43, 46, 240.
Sheads, ______, (Owner of the property at Gettysburg on which stands the famed Stone Wall), I: 634, 635.
Shearer, J.M., [James M.], (Capt, Co A, 29th NCST), IV: 701, 711.
Shearer, James W., (Jr 2nd Lt, Co E, 39th NCST), II: 705.
Shearin, Martin, (Lt, Co I, 2nd Vols/12th NCST), I: 651.
Shearin, Thomas W., (Cpl, Co B, 30th NCST), V: 491.
Sheek, M.C., (Cpl, Co A, 1st Battalion NCST), V: 503.
Sheet's Ferry, N.C., IV: 81.
Sheffey, A.M., (Lt, Co I, 64th NCST), III: 660.
Shelby, N.C., IV: 202.
Shelbyville, Tenn., II: 490, 491, 731, 732.
Shell, G.W., (HQ, QM Corps), V: 572.
Shell, Noah, (Lt, Co D, 9th NCST, 1st Cav), I: 485.
Shell, O.P., (ACS, 46th NCST), III: 65, 70.
Shell Point, N.C., (Harker's Island), II: 750.
Shelly, W.W., (2nd Cpl, Co C, 10th NCST, 1st Art & Engs, Brem-Graham-Williams' Battery, Light Art), V: 567.
Shelton, ______, (Lt, Battery D, N.Y. Light Art), I: 150, 200.
Shelton, F.L.R., (Pvt, Co E, 45th NCST), V: 500.

Shelton, Joseph, B., (Capt, Co G, 52nd NCST), III: 224, 228.
Shelton, J. Wesley, (Ensign/1st Lt, Color-bearer, 39th NCST), I: 767; II: 704.
Shelton, W.A., [Sheldon], (Lt, USN), V: 243.
Shelton Laurel Mountain, N.C., III: 660, 661, 666; IV: 381.
Shenandoah River, Va., I: 154, 168, 172, 206, 259, 260, 298, 310, 327, 372, 578, 579, 645; II: 116, 132, 147, 248, 275, 433, 473, 532, 553, 585, 601; III: 14, 116, 241, 278, 422, 571, 746; IV: 138, 168, 177, 233, 466; V: viii, 267.
Shenandoah Valley, Va., (aka The Valley and Valley of Virginia), I: 154, 155, 168, 172, 173, 174, 205, 206, 209, 253, 275, 290, 303, 311, 318, 323, 326, 327, 331, 366, 373, 379, 462, 463, 608, 622, 645, 650, 659, 694, 696, 727, 730, 762; II: 21, 67, 77, 116, 122, 124, 130, 132, 135, 141, 143, 148, 149, 208, 240, 245, 247, 250, 251, 255, 258, 259, 297, 469, 503, 532, 533, 654, 657, 682, 685, 700, 708; III: 14, 37, 55, 69, 258, 261, 269, 281, 411, 419, 420, 421, 422, 466, 550, 559, 744, 745, 746, 748, 750, 751, 754, 755, 756, 758; IV: 167, 168, 169, 176, 177, 183, 227, 231, 234, 236, 262, 356, 437, 439, 449, 452, 515, 523, 524, 551, 603; V: 214, 468, 629.
Shepard, J., (Sgt, Co C, 54th NCST), V: 516.
Shepherd, ______, (Col, Archer's Brigade), V: 150.
Shepherd, Benjamin, [Sheppard], (1st Lt, Co C, 5th Battalion Junior Reserves; Co H, 71st NCST, 2nd Junior Reserves), IV: 29.
Shepherd, Henry E., (1st Lt, Co K, 43rd NCST), III: 3; IV: 702, 711; V: 611, 612.
Shepherd, J.G., (4th Sgt, Co D, 44th NCST), V: 533.
Shepherd, J.M., (Musician, Co G, 35th NCST), V: 563.
Shepherd, Jacob, (Pvt, Co B, 1st NCST), V: 485.
Shepherd, James W., (1st Lt, Co K, 56th NCST), III: 317; V: 663.
Shepherd, Lafayett, (Pvt, Co A, 53rd NCST; Detailed, 2nd Corps Provost Guard), V: 570.
Shepherd, M.L., [Shuford, M.H.], (1st Lt, Co B, 23rd NCST), IV: 711.
Shepherd, Silas, (Pvt, Co D, 10th NCST, 1st Art & Engs, Reilly-Ramsay's Battery, Light Art), V: 568.
Shepherd, William Blount, [Sheppard], (Capt, ADC to Pender, Pettigrew & Martin), II: 170; IV: 527, 551, 552, 556; V: 129, 146.
Shepherdstown, Va., I: 148, 189, 194, 206, 228, 249, 250, 259, 311, 324, 372, 379, 424, 541, 718, 761, 762, 764; II: 32, 42, 71, 74, 169, 176, 224, 275, 276, 342, 433, 437, 474, 477, 555, 562, 585, 608, 656, 686, 687; III: 13, 67, 88, 116, 235, 278, 751; IV: 166-168, 177, 466, 502, 552, 570, 571; V: 79.
Shepherdstown Road, II: 71.
Sheppard, M., (Pvt, Co E, 3rd Vols/13th NCST), V: 550.
Sheppard, W.S., (1st Lt, Co F, 1st NCST), I: 137.
Sheppardson, W.L., (Ass't Surg, CSN, Tallahassee), V: 438.
Sheppardsville, N.C., (now New Port), II: 796, 797; III: 555; IV: 528.

Sheridan, Philip, (Maj Gen, USA, Sheridan's Cav and Sheridan's Army), I: 63, 117, 155, 173, 207, 208, 209, 263, 290, 324, 326, 327, 328, 331, 429, 430, 438, 439, 442, 443, 462, 465, 471, 479, 481, 550, 602, 646, 647, 649, 718, 730, 777, 779, 780, 781; II: 5, 100, 250, 251, 252, 253, 257, 259, 260, 261, 392, 768, 773, 798; III: 15, 55, 56, 58, 59, 145, 280, 281, 396, 397, 399, 401, 420, 421, 422, 425, 437, 469, 470, 494, 536, 595, 596, 598, 599, 600, 601, 602, 603, 611, 638, 640, 642, 644, 746, 751, 752, 753, 754, 755; IV: 90, 94, 95, 205, 213, 216, 452, 457, 509, 523, 576, 577, 687; V: 213, 214, 215, 261, 654.
Sheridan's Raid, III: 595-604.
Sherman, Perry, (Pvt, Co A, 1st Battalion NCST), V: 504.
Sherman, William T., (Maj Gen, USA and Sherman's Army. The most criminal figure to have ever worn the uniform of an American soldier. Responsible for more atrocities than all the military men in this country's history combined.), I: 55, 56, 57, 58, 59, 61, 62, 63, 64, 346, 413, 438, 532, 718, 730; II: 10, 11, 12, 13, 518, 519, 634, 720, 757, 786, 802, 803, 804; III: 79, 181, 183, 184, 186, 191, 192, 194, 195, 199, 200, 201, 216, 217, 388, 394, 396, 437, 439, 442, 492, 493, 494, 496, 497, 501, 513, 611, 614, 617, 694, 696, 698, 699, 700, 708, 726, 727, 746; IV: 20, 21, 22, 30, 31, 32, 35, 54, 56, 57, 59, 61, 62, 103, 104, 105, 114, 120, 123, 132, 293, 299, 312, 320, 321, 323, 327, 328, 333, 335, 336, 350, 351, 353, 359, 360, 394, 400, 430, 440, 452, 483, 495, 498, 499, 500, 547, 548, 549, 583, 591, 592, 593, 683, 684, 747, 759, 770; V: xvi, 18, 270, 271, 275, 276, 277, 278, 279, 280, 282, 436, 632, 633, 654.
Sherrell, W.F., (Lt, Co , 2nd Vols/12th NCST), I: 652.
Sherrill, ______, (Col, USA), V: 156.
Sherrill, ______, (33rd NCST), II: 578.
Sherrill, George W., (Musician, Co C, 8th Vols/18th NCST), II: 63; V: 539.
Sherrill, H., (Pvt, Co A, 12th Vols/22nd NCST), V: 553.
Sherrill, J.A.L., (Pvt, Co A, 2nd Vols/12th NCST), V: 506.
Sherrill, J.G., (5th Sgt, Co A, 12th Vols/22nd NCST), V: 553.
Sherrill, J.L., (Pvt, Co A, 12th Vols/22nd NCST), V: 553.
Sherrill, Jacob, (Capt, 49th NCST), II: 626; III: 148.
Sherrill, James H., (Capt, Co I, 49th NCST), V: 559.
Sherrill, John A.L., (Courier, Garland-Iverson-Johnston's Brigade), IV: 523; V: 506.
Sherrill, Joseph B., (Pvt, Co C, 4th NCST), V: 488.
Sherrill, R.N., (Pvt, Co K, 46th NCST), V: 525.
Sherrill, W., (Pvt, Co A, 49th NCST), V: 564.
Sherrill, W.W., (2nd Lt, Co E, 57th NCST), IV: 702.
Sherrod, Henry H., (Jr 2nd Lt, Co E, 5th Vols/15th NCST), I: 735; V: 519.
Sherrod, John, (Lt, Co H, 9th NCST, 1st Cav), I: 486.
Sherrod, William W., (Ambulance Driver, Co G, 7th Vols/17th NCST; Detailed, QM Corps), V: 571.

Sherrod House, (nr Butler's Bridge & Camp Baker), III: 722; IV: 17.
Sherron, Will H., (Pvt, Co A, 10th NCST, 1st Art & Engs, Ramseur-Manly's Battery, Light Art), I: 556.
Sherron, W.J., (Pvt, Co E, 13th Vols/23rd NCST), V: 510.
Shetley, John, (Pvt, Co B, 6th Battalion/60th NCST), III: 482.
Shetley, William, (Pvt, Co B, 6th Battalion/60th NCST), III: 482.
Shevenell, Leonard, (Pvt, Co G, 25th NCST), V: 561.
Shields, A.C., (Pvt, Co K, 56th NCST), III: 357.
Shields, C.S.D., (Pvt, Co B, 28th NCST), V: 541.
Shields, J.F., (Pvt, Co H, 16th Battalion/75th NCST, 7th Cav), V: 660.
Shields, J.W., (Pvt, Co B, 28th NCST), V: 541.
Shields, James, (Brig Gen, USA), I: 659; II: 66, 133, 147, 149, 153, 250; IV: 233.
Shields, Dr. R.H., (Ass't Surg, 9th Vols/19th NCST, 2nd Cav), II: 79; IV: 635.
Shiloh, Miss., (and Battle of, 1862), I: 753; II: 702, 707; III: 381; IV: 415, 498; V: xvi, 395.
Shines, T.S., (Pvt, Co A, 10th Vols/20th NCST), V: 508.
Shinn, J.W., (1st Lt, Co B, 4th NCST), I: 232, 270, 279.
Shinn, Thomas J., (1st Lt, Co D, 5th Battalion Junior Reserves; Co E, 71st NCST, 2nd Junior Reserves), IV: 28.
Ship, John, (Pvt, Co I, 6th NCST), V: 513.
Shipman, Jackson, (1st Lt, Co D, 39th NCST), II: 705.
Shipman, Thomas J., (Capt, Co D, 6th Battalion/60th NCST), III: 474, 482, 497; IV: 701, 711.
Ship Point, Va., I: 111, 112.
Shipp, Ephraim, (Pvt, Co D, 38th NCST), V: 557.
Shipp, J.M., (2nd Lt, Co L, Louisiana Tigers, Walker's Battalion, Thomas' Legion, 80th NCST), IV: 119.
Shipp, William M., (Capt, Co I, 6th Vols/16th NCST), I: 751; IV: 137.
Shippenburg, Pa., V: 115.
Shiverey's, Md., V: 74.
Shives, A.C., (Pvt, Co F, 3rd Vols/13th NCST), V: 550.
Shoaf, J.W., (Pvt, Co H, 33rd NCST), V: 544.
Shober, Charles E., (Capt, Co B, 49th NCST; Lt Col, 2nd Battalion NCST; Col, 77th NCST, 7th Senior Reserves), III: 36, 38; IV: 99, 100, 103, 107, 252, 255; V: 650.
Shoe, R., (Pvt, Co K, 28th NCST), V: 543.
Shoemaker, N.L., (Pvt, Co F, 32nd NCST), V: 496.
Shoffner, F., (Pvt, Co C, 45th NCST), V: 500.
Shofner, Martin, [Shoffner], (Maj, 34th NCST), II: 581.
Shook, Daniel, (4th Cpl, Co F, 38th NCST), V: 557.
Shook, H.C., (Pvt, Randolph's Howitzers, Va.), I: 106.
Shook, J.P., (Pvt, Co F, 26th NCST), V: 601.
Shook, Franklin, (Pvt, Co F, 38th NCST), V: 557.
Shooting Creek, (Clay County), IV: 381.
Shope, Dock V., (Orderly Sgt, 6th Battalion/60th NCST), III: 497.
Shore, H.L., (Pvt, Co B, 10th NCST, 1st Art & Engs, Pool's Hvy Art), V: 572.

Shore, John H., (1st Lt, Co G, 77th NCST, 7th Senior Reserves), IV: 100.
Short, Benjamin, (Pvt, Co K, 1st NCST), V: 485.
Short, G.W., (3rd Sgt, Co E, 48th NCST), V: 526.
Short, J.B., (Cpl, Co K, 26th NCST), V: 532.
Short, J.E., (Pvt, Co E, 48th NCST), V: 526.
Short, J.W., (Pvt, Co E, 48th NCST), V: 526.
Short, S.A., (Pvt, Co I, 43rd NCST), V: 499.
Short, W.P., (Pvt, Co K, 26th NCST), V: 533.
Short, W.T., (Pvt, Co H, 30th NCST), V: 493.
Shotwell, Alexander H., (Lt, Co C, 34th NCST), II: 584.
Shoup, Julius L., (1st Sgt, Co B, 4th Vols/14th NCST), V: 490.
Shouse, David, (2nd Lt, Co G, 77th NCST, 7th Senior Reserves), IV: 100.
Shouse, E.A., (Pvt, Co B, 1st Battalion NCST), V: 504.
Shown's Crossroads, Tenn., III: 683.
Shreem, J., (Pvt, Co B, 28th NCST), V: 541.
Shropshire, D.H., (Pvt, Co A, 45th NCST), V: 499.
Shropshire, William, (Pvt, Co A, 45th NCST), V: 499.
Shuford, A.H., (Capt, AQM & ACS, 2nd Battalion NCST), IV: 245.
Shuford, D.H., (Pvt, Co E, 32nd NCST), V: 496.
Shuford, F.A., (Cpl, Co C, 4th NCST), I: 232.
Shuford, George, (Musician, 4th NCST), V: 664.
Shuford, M.H., (1st Lt, Co B, 13th Vols/23rd NCST), II: 183; IV: 702.
Shuford, P.C., (Capt, Co E, 32nd NCST), V: 494.
Shuford, P.M., (Pvt, Co F, 55th NCST), V: 528.
Shuford, S.A., (2nd Lt, Co B, 13th Vols/23rd NCST), II: 183.
Shuford, Sidney, (2nd Lt, Co K, 46th NCST), III: 82.
Shuford, W.L., (Sgt, Co A, 4th NCST), I: 232.
Shufford, Solomon, (Pvt, Co F, 13th Vols/23rd NCST), V: 510.
Shugart, J.A., (Pvt, Co A, 1st Battalion NCST), V: 504.
Shuler, John M., (Pvt, Co A, 33rd NCST), II: 544.
Shultz, C.A., (Sgt, Co E, 11 Vols/21st NCST; 2nd Lt, Co B, 1st Battalion NCST), IV: 242.
Siberia, V: 348.
Sibley, G.D., (1st Lt, Co A, 59th NCST, 4th Cav), III: 457.
Sicard, M., (Lt Cmdr, USN; Pioneer, Seneca), V: 242, 245.
Siceloff, A.E., (2nd Lt, Co A, 42nd NCST), II: 789, 805.
Sickles, Daniel Edger, (Maj Gen, USA), I: 353; II: 40, 476, 560; IV: 467; V: 96, 128.
Sidbury, Amos, (2nd Lt, Co E, 3rd NCST), I: 213.
Siddell, H.A., (Musician, Mickey's Band, 26th NCST), II: 398.
Sides, J.M., (1st Lt, Co E, 6th Vols/16th NCST), V: 547.
Sides, John, (Pvt, Co K, 57th NCST), V: 518.
Sides, W.M., (Pvt, Co G, 8th NCST), V: 194.
Sidney, J.B., (2nd Lt, Co B, 31st NCST), II: 512.
Siegel, Franz, (Maj Gen, USA), I: 169, 324; II: 69.
Sifford, D.M., (Pvt, Co B, 28th NCST), V: 541.
Sigman, C.C., (Sgt, Co F, 13th Vols/23rd NCST), V: 510.

Sigman, Devault, (Pvt, Co F, 38th NCST), V: 557.
Sigman, H.S., (Pvt, Co B, 32nd NCST), V: 495.
Sigman, J.C., (Pvt, Co G, 32nd NCST), V: 496.
Sigman, J.E., (Pvt, Co E, 32nd NCST), V: 496.
Sigman, L., (Pvt, Co K, 46th NCST), V: 525.
Sigman, M., (Pvt, Co D, 6th NCST), V: 512.
Sigmon, C.S., (Pvt, Co A, 2nd Vols/12th NCST), V: 506.
Sigmon, J.G., (Pvt, Co C, 2nd Vols/12th NCST), V: 507.
Sigmon, M.L., (Pvt, Co A, 2nd Vols/12th NCST), V: 506.
Sigmon, W.R., (Pvt, Co A, 2nd Vols/12th NCST), V: 506.
Signal Corps, CSA, II: 433; V: 405-411.
Sikes, B.F., (Pvt, Co E, 56th NCST), III: 356.
Sikes, E., (Pvt, Co I, 6th NCST), V: 513.
Sikes, Jacob C., (Pvt, Co B, 5th Vols/15th NCST), V: 521.
Sikes, N., (Pvt, Co K, 8th Vols/18th NCST), II: 64.
Sikes, Theodore M., (Capt, Co H, 3rd NCST), I: 179, 228.
Sikes, W.H., (Pvt, Co D, 28th NCST), V: 542.
Sikes, Wilie J., (Capt, Co B, 8th Vols/18th NCST), II: 20.
Siler, A.R., (Pvt, Co G, 26th NCST), V: 532.
Siler, Columbus F., (Capt, Co M, 12th Vols/22nd NCST), II: 166, 172, 174, 175, 176, 178; V: 548.
Siler, H.W., (Cpl, Co G, 26th NCST), V: 532.
Siler, J.W., (Capt, Co E, 65th NCST, 6th Cav), III: 675, 684.
Siler, Jesse W., (Lt, C. K, 9th NCST, 1st Cav), I: 483, 486.
Siler, Rufus S., (Jr 2nd Lt, Co I, 39th NCST), II: 707.
Siler, Thaddeus P., (Capt, Co K, 9th NCST, 1st Cav; Maj, 65th NCST, 6th Cav; Col, 6th Home Guard), I: 418, 486; III: 673, 683; IV: 650.
Sills, D.N., (Jr 2nd Lt, Co B, 66th NCST), III: 686.
Sills, John, (Pvt, Co E, 2nd NCST), I: 176; V: 486.
Silver, D.R., (Capt, Co K, 58th NCST), III: 434.
Silver, L.D., (Lt, Co K, 58th NCST), III: 434.
Silver, S.M., (Lt Col, 58th NCST), III: 432, 434, 438, 447, 454; V: 670.
Silver Spring, Md., I: 154, 325; IV: 449.
Silverthorn, J.W., (Pvt, Co E, 4th NCST), V: 488.
Silvery, J.M., (Pvt, Co G, 12th Vols/22nd NCST), V: 554.
Simmes, William N., (Pvt, Co D, 56th NCST), III: 355.
Simmons, ______, (Deserter, Outlaw, Yankee), V: 285, 286, 287.
Simmons, A., (Pvt, Co G, 10th Vols/20th NCST), V: 509.
Simmons, David W., (2nd Lt, Co B, 41st NCST, 3rd Cav), II: 770.
Simmons, F.A., (2nd Sgt, Co A, 43rd NCST), V: 497.
Simmons, Frank A., (Sgt, Co A, 43rd NCST), III: 20.
Simmons, J.F., (Maj, QM, R. Ransom's Brigade), IV: 569, 577.
Simmons, J.W., (2nd Lt, Co G, 9th Vols/19th NCST, 2nd Cav), II: 89.
Simmons, Junius C., (1st Lt, Co G, 61st Va.), IV: 403.
Simmons, James O., (Capt, Co I, 34th NCST), II: 581.

Simmons, Williiam, (Pvt, Co G, 10th Vols/20th NCST), II: 120.
Simms, C.C., (Lt, NCN; Capt, Appomattox), V: 304, 307.
Simms, John C., (Pvt, Co E, 5th Vols/15th NCST), V: 521.
Simms, P.N., (2nd Lt, Co F, 4th NCST), I: 231.
Simons, John W., (Pvt, Co D, 68th NCST), III: 715.
Sims, W.B., (2nd Lt, Co I, 13th Vols/23rd NCST), II: 187.
Simonton, ______, (Col, at Ft. Fisher), II: 650.
Simonton, A.K., (Maj, 4th NCST), I: 230, 231, 267; V: 11.
Simonton, R.F., (ACS, 4th NCST), I: 230.
Simpson, Dr. E.B., (Surg, 72nd NCST, 3rd Junior Reserves), IV: 51, 642.
Simpson, J.L, (Pvt, Co G, 6th NCST), V: 513.
Simpson, J.R., (Pvt, Co B, 26th NCST), V: 531.
Simpson, P.D., (Pvt, Co I, 3rd Vols/13th NCST), V: 551.
Sinclair, J.D., (Pvt, Co H, 30th NCST), V: 492.
Singletary, R.W., (Lt Col, 27th NCST), II: 426, 427, 428, 436, 438; III: 23, V: 651.
Sinclair, Arthur, (Cmdr, NCN; Capt, Winslow), V: 302, 312.
Sinclair, Rev. James, (Chaplain, 5th NCST, elected Col 35th NCST), II: 310, 313, 314, 315, 316, 317, 542, 592, 593, 594, 595, 596.
Sinclair, Peter J., (Lt Col, 5th NCST, resigned), I: 281, 282, 284, 286, 287.
Singletary, George B., (Col, 44th NCST), I: 589, 592, 594; II: 425, 426, 427; III: 21, 24; IV: 558; V: 10.
Singletary, Thomas C., (Col, 44th NCST), II: 335, 426, 427; III: 21, 24; IV: 555, 558, 562; V: 650.
Singleterry, S., [Singletary], (Cpl, Co B, 8th Vols./18th NCST), II: 63; V: 539.
Singleton, Dr. B.B., [Singletary], (Ass't Surg, 45th NCST), IV: 639; V: 572.
Singleton, J.B., (Pvt, Co B, 1st Vols/11th NCST), V: 530.
Singleton, James M., (Capt, Walker's Battalion, Thomas' Legion, Co C, 80th NCST), III: 738, 754; IV: 118.
Singleton, Dr. Spiers, (Surg, 36th NCST, 2nd Art & Engs), II: 630; IV: 637; V: 240.
Sink, Andrew, (Pvt, Co B, 4th Vols/14th NCST), I: 731.
Sink, J.F., (2nd Lt, Co A, 42nd NCST), II: 790, 805.
Sinster, R.O., (Co C, 4th NCST), I: 232.
Sisk, F., (Pvt, Co H, 12th Vols/ 22nd NCST), V: 554.
Sisk, J.F., (Pvt, Co H, 12th Vols/22nd NCST), V: 554.
Sisk, R.H., (Lt, Co F, 58th NCST), III: 433.
Sitt, William E., (Capt, Co B, 43rd NCST), III: 2.
Sivels, William, (Pvt, Co B, 32nd NCST), V: 495.
Six Mile House, Va., III: 616.
Skeen, Jesse, (Pvt, Co C, 49th NCST), V: 564.
Skeens, J.Y., (Pvt, Co F, 54th NCST), V: 516.
Sketches of the North Carolina Cavalry Brigade, III: 547, 608, 633, 634, 635, 636, 637, 647, 652.
Skinner, Thomas G., (Lt, Co D, Webb's Battery, Bogg's 12th Battalion Va., Hvy Art; Co A, Webb's Battery, Starr's 13th

Battalion NCST, Light Art), I: 120; IV: 355, 357; V: 282.
Skinner, Thomas L., (Maj, 1st NCST), I: 134, 136, 138, 139; V: 11.
Skinner, William, (Pvt, Co E, 54th NCST), V: 516.
Skirven, George, (Capt, Mallett's Battalion NCST), I: 119.
Slade, H., (Sgt, Co E, 37th NCST), V: 545.
Slade, T.B., (Orderly Sgt, 41st NCST, 3rd Cav), II: 786.
Slade, Thomas T., (Capt, Co H, 12th Vols/22nd NCST), II: 172.
Slade, William, (1st Lt, Co K, 41st NCST, 3rd Cav), II: 772, 777.
Slamm, J.A., (Ensign, USN; Pioneer, Pawtuxet), V: 245.
Slash Church, Va., (aka Hanover Court House), II: 22, 24, 66, 77, 545, 546, 549; IV: 465, 471.
Slate, W.W., (Sgt, Co E, 6th Battalion/60th NCST), III: 482.
Slate, William, (Pvt, Co D, 53rd NCST), V: 501.
Slaughter, John A., (2nd Lt, Co G, 31st NCST), II: 507.
Slaughter, John B., (1st Sgt, Co D, 68th NCST), III: 715.
Slaughter, Nathaniel M.E., (Capt, Co F, 39th NCST), II: 705.
Slaughter, T.D., (Pvt, Co G, 36th NCST), V: 492.
Slaughter, W.H., (Pvt, Co A, 2nd Battalion NCST), V: 494.
Slemp, _____, (Col), III: 23.
Slidell, John, (Confederate diplomat to Europe. One of the two Confederate representatives illegally seized aboard the mail packet Trent while sailing to England. Known as the Trent Affair that event nearly brought England into the war.) II: 629; V: xvii.
Sloan, D.F.A., (Cpl, Color-bearer, 56th NCST), III: 378.
Sloan, G.W., (Pvt, Co D, 35th NCST), V: 562.
Sloan, G.W., (Pvt, Co B, 3rd Vols/13th NCST), V: 549.
Sloan, George, (Capt, Co I, 51st NCST), III: 212, 220.
Sloan, George, (Capt, Co I, 51st NCST), I: 78, 119; III: 220.
Sloan, J.A., (Capt, Co B, 27th NCST), V: 519.
Sloan, J.F., (Pvt, Co K, 56th NCST), V: 566.
Sloan, J.G., (Pvt, Co G, 6th Vols/16th NCST), IV: 198.
Sloan, James, (Capt, state agent, N.C. Quartermaster Department), I: 24.
Sloan, John A., (Capt, Co B, 27th NCST), II: 425, 426, 427, 453, 457, 461.
Sloan, William R., (2nd Lt, Co B, 13th Vols/23rd NCST), II: 183.
Sloat, L.D., (Pvt, Co M, 12th Vols/22nd NCST), V: 554.
Slocum, Henry Warnes, (Maj Gen, USA), I: 615; II: 12.
Slocum, T.W., (Lt, AAG, N.C.), I: 51.
Slocum's Creek, N.C., II: 308.
Sloop, D.A., (Musician, 6th NCST), V: 511.
Sloop, Phillip A., (Sgt, Co D, 34th NCST), V: 555.
Slough, Nelson, (Lt Col, 10th Vols/20th NCST), II: 112, 117, 118, 126, 127.
Sluder, James E., (Pvt, Co F, 6th Vols/16th NCST), V: 552.
Small, E.J., (Capt, Co F, 1st Vols/11th NCST), I: 110, 119; V: 88, 188.
Small, Edward A., (Capt, Co F, 1st Vols/11th NCST), I: 585; IV: 700, 711.
Small, R.M., (Pvt, Co H, 45th NCST), V: 500.

Small, R.S., (1st Lt, Co G, 46th NCST), III: 81.
Small, Robert A., (Lt, Co G, 46th NCST), III: 77.
Smart, D.P., (Pvt, Co I, 56th NCST), III: 357.
Smart, James, (Pvt, Co C, 4th Vols/14th NCST), I: 725, 731.
Smart, Thomas R., (2nd Lt, Co D, 69th NCST, Thomas' Legion), III: 730.
Smart, W.R., (Pvt, Co I, 56th NCST), V: 566.
Smartt, J.P., (Cheatham's Division), V: 173.
Smathers, John H., (Capt, Co C, 69th NCST, Thomas' Legion), III: 730.
Smedes, Rev. Dr. Bennett, (Chaplain, 5th NCST), IV: 606.
Smedes, Edward, (2nd Lt, Co E, 5th NCST), I: 289.
Smedes, Ives, (1st Lt, Adjt, 7th NCST), I: 377, 472.
Smiley, Robert, (Sgt, Co A; ACS Sgt., 25th NCST), V: 561.
Smith, ______, (Col, 20th Ga.), II: 192.
Smith, ______, (Governor of Louisiana), I: 358, 359.
Smith, ______, (Pvt, Co 2, Woodfin's Battalion; 79th NCST, 8th Cav), IV: 112.
Smith, ______, (Signal Officer, Advance), V: 341, 343.
Smith, ______, [John C.], (Pvt, Co G, 5th Vols/15th NCST), IV: 745.
Smith, ______, (2nd Lt, Co C, 5th Battalion Junior Reserves; Co H, 71st NCST, 2nd Junior Reserves), IV: 29.
Smith, ______, (Lt, ADC to Law), I: 309.
Smith, ______, (Lt Col, 128th Pa.), II: 559; V: 94.
Smith, Dr. ______, [Robert H.], (Surg, 9th Vols/19th NCST, 2nd Cav), II: 79; IV: 635.
Smith, A.E., (Sgt, Co F, 8th Vols/18th NCST), II: 64.
Smith, A.M., (2nd Lt, Co K, 38th NCST), II: 676, 678, 686.
Smith, Alexander E., (Sgt, Co F, 8th Vols/18th NCST), II: 64; V: 539.
Smith, Amos, (Pvt, Co B, 57th NCST), V: 517.
Smith, Andrew S., (Cpl, Co G, 6th Vols/16th NCST), V: 552.
Smith, Andrew, (Pvt, Co B, 13th Vols/23rd NCST), V: 509.
Smith, Rev. Dr. Aristides S., (Chaplain, 1st Vols/11th NCST), I: 583; IV: 606; V: 99.
Smith, Arthur S., (Pvt, Co K, 8th Vols/18th NCST), V: 99.
Smith, B., (Capt, Co D, 10th Vols/20th NCST), II: 112.
Smith, B.F., (Capt, AQM, Armistead-Connally's Brigade, Junior Reserves), IV: 18.
Smith, B.G., (Capt, AQM, Junior Reserves Brigade), IV: 591.
Smith, B.J., (1st Lt, Co G, 4th NCST), I: 233, 272; V: 572.
Smith, B.R., Jr., (Capt, Co G, 6th NCST), IV: 702.
Smith, Benjamin Franklin, (Brig Gen, USA), II: 6.
Smith, Benjamin G., (Capt, Co G, 41st NCST, 3rd Cav), II: 771.
Smith, Benjamin Ruth, (Capt, Co G, 6th NCST), I: 345.
Smith, Buckner H., (2nd Lt, Co A, 5th Battalion Junior Reserves; Co A, 71st NCST, 2nd Junior Reserves), IV: 28.
Smith, C.C., (Lt, Co H, 12th Vols/22nd NCST), II: 166.
Smith, C.C., (1st Lt, Co A, 70th NCST, 1st Junior Reserves), IV: 12.

Smith, C.G., (Pilot, Calypso), V: 357.
Smith, C.R., (Pvt, Co E, 48th NCST), V: 526.
Smith, Calhoun M., (1st Cpl, Co I, 4th Vols/14th NCST), V: 491.
Smith, Charles Henry, (Maj Gen, USA), III: 644; IV: 534.
Smith, Charles S., (2nd Lt, Co B, 5th Battalion Junior Reserves; Co G, 71st NCST, 2nd Junior Reserves), IV: 28.
Smith, Decatur S., (Pvt, Co I, 34th NCST), V: 556.
Smith, Downing H., (Capt, Co I, 44th NCST), III: 23.
Smith, E., (2nd Lt, Co B, 3rd Vols/13th NCST) IV: 702, 711.
Smith, E.E., (Brother-in-law of Lt Lineberry), IV: 395.
Smith, E.M., (Capt, USN), V: 242.
Smith, Edward, (2nd Lt, Co C, 54th NCST), III: 273; V: 511.
Smith, Edward, (Capt, Co D, 2nd Battalion NCST), IV: 245.
Smith, Edwin, (Lt, Co B, 2nd Battalion NCST), IV: 245.
Smith, Edmund Kirby, (Gen), I: 299, 339, 343, 346; II: 728; III: 307, 381, 475, 729; IV: 117.
Smith, Enos, (Pvt, Co E, 52nd NCST), V: 536.
Smith, Erastus, (2nd Lt, Co C, 68th NCST), III: 725, 728.
Smith, F., (Pvt, Co I, 37th NCST), V: 546.
Smith, F.R., (Lt, USN; Pioneer, Rhode Island), V: 245.
Smith, Frank, (Lt, USN), V: 243.
Smith, Frederick, (2nd Lt, Co C, 77th NCST, 7th Senior Reserves), IV: 100.
Smith, G.C., (Pvt, Co K, 28th NCST), V: 543.
Smith, G.F., (Capt, Co A, 54th NCST), IV: 711.
Smith, Dr. G.G., (Surg, 70th NCST, 1st Junior Reserves), IV: 14, 642.
Smith, G.R., (1st Lt, Co C, 1st Battalion Junior Reserves; Co D, 70th NCST, 1st Junior Reserves), IV: 13.
Smith, G.W., (Pvt, Co C, 10th NCST, 1st Art & Engs, Brem-Graham-Williams' Battery, Light Art), V: 568.
Smith, Gustavus, "Gus," (AQMS, 10th Vols/20th NCST), V: 508.
Smith, Gustavus Woodson, (Lt Gen), I: 303, 350, 494, 521, 522; II: 339, 757, 774; III: 4, 179, 180, 229; IV: 344; V: 85, 86, 90, 94.
Smith, H.H., (Pvt, Co C, 35th NCST), V: 562.
Smith, H.H., (2nd Lt, Co A, 5th NCST), I: 121.
Smith, Herny, (Pvt, Co B, 2nd Battalion NCST), V: 495.
Smith, Henry C., (Capt, Co C, 10th Vols/20th NCST), II: 114.
Smith, Ira W., (Cpl, Co G, 7th NCST), I: 378.
Smith, H.W., (Pvt, Co I, 26th NCST), V: 532.
Smith, J., (Pvt, Co H, 54th NCST), V: 516.
Smith, J.A., (Pvt, Co C, 53rd NCST), V: 501.
Smith, J.B., (Pvt, Co F, 1st Vols, "Bethel"; AQM, Starr's 13th Battalion NCST, Light Art), I: 128; IV: 348.
Smith, J.F., (2nd Sgt, Co H, 1st Vols/11th NCST), V: 530.
Smith, J.J., (Pvt, Co C, 32nd NCST), V: 496.
Smith, J.P., (Pvt, Co I, 16th Battalion/75th NCST, 7th Cav), V: 660.
Smith, J.W., (1st Lt, Co E, 6th Battalion Junior Reserves; Co G, 70th NCST, 1st Junior Reserves), IV: 13.

Smith, Jack, (Pvt, Co B, 4th Vols/14th NCST), I: 726.
Smith, Jackson, (Pvt, Co G, 52nd NCST), V: 536.
Smith, Dr. James, (Surg, 55th NCST), III: 288; IV: 640.
Smith, James A., (3rd Sgt, Co C, 4th Vols/14th NCST), V: 490.
Smith, James L., (Pvt, Co C, 4th Vols/14th NCST), V: 490.
Smith, Jefferson A., (Pvt, Co B, 4th NCST), V: 488.
Smith, Jesse T., (Lt, Co B, 51st NCST), III: 218.
Smith, John B., (Signal Officer, Advance), V: 361.
Smith, John E., (Pvt, Co A, 43rd NCST), III: 20; V: 497.
Smith, John F., (Col, 112th N.Y.), V: 237.
Smith, John L., (Capt, Co A, 9th NCST, 1st Cav), I: 441, 485, 782.
Smith, John N., (Lt, Drill Master & ACS, 41st NCST, 3rd Cav), II: 769.
Smith, John W., (1st Lt, Co H, 31st NCST), II: 512.
Smith, Joseph A., (Pvt, Co G, 27th NCST), II: 462; V: 523.
Smith, Joseph Hale, (Lt, Henry's 14th Battalion; 79th NCST, 8th Cav), IV: 113, 114.
Smith, Joshua, (Pvt, Co A, 2nd Battalion NCST), V: 494.
Smith, Josiah W., (2nd Lt, Co C, 68th NCST), III: 725.
Smith, Josiah W., (1st Lt, Co I, 66th NCST), III: 686.
Smith, L.B., (Pvt, Co E, 26th NCST), V: 532.
Smith, Dr. L.H., (Ass't Surg, 2nd NCST; Adjt, 5th Battalion NCST, Cav), I: 157; IV: 271.
Smith, Miss Kate, (Resident of Asheville), I: 130.
Smith, Kirby, V: 584.
Smith, Leroy, (Pvt, Co G, 56th NCST), III: 348.
Smith, Lovelace, (Pvt, Co G, 11th Vols/21st NCST), V: 515.
Smith, Milton, (Capt, Co B, 2nd Battalion NCST), IV: 245.
Smith, Martin Luther, (Maj Gen, Chief Engineer, ANV), IV: 197, 427, 533, 534.
Smith, Maurice Thomas, (Lt Col, 55th NCST), III: 287, 288, 289, 292, 294, 295, 298, 302; V: 11, 110, 651.
Smith, Melancthon, (Capt, USN), V: 321.
Smith, Moses, (Pvt, Co H, 6th Vols/16th NCST), V: 552.
Smith, N.G., (Lt, Co B, 2nd Battalion NCST), IV: 245.
Smith, N.S., (Lt, Adjt, 3rd Vols/13th NCST), I: 695, 6 98, 699; IV: 711.
Smith, Nat S., (1st Lt, Co H, 3rd Vols/13th NCST), IV: 700.
Smith, Norfleet, (1st Lt, Co G, 41st NCST, 3rd Cav), II: 771.
Smith, Owen, (1st Lt, Co C, 8th Vols/18th NCST), II: 63; V: 537.
Smith, P.T., (Pvt, Co G, 8th Vols/18th NCST), II: 64; V: 540.
Smith, Perry, (AQMS, Co C, 10th NCST, 1st Art & Engs Brem-Graham-Williams' Battery, Light Art), I: 546.
Smith, Peter, (1st Lt, Co G, 12th Vols/22nd NCST), II: 165, 166, 172.
Smith, Peter, E., (One of the builders of the Albemarle), V: 318.
Smith, R.A., (Sharpshooter, 10th Vols/20th NCST), II: 125.
Smith, R.B., (Pvt, Co G, 37th NCST), V: 546.
Smith, R.B., (2nd Lt, Co F, 5th Vols/15th NCST), I: 735.

Smith, R.P., (Pvt, Co G, 56th NCST), III: 356.
Smith, R.W., (Pvt, Co E, 55th NCST), V: 528.
Smith, Robert, (Pvt, Co G, 56th NCST), V: 566.
Smith, Robert, (Pvt, Co H, 34th NCST), V: 556.
Smith, Robert H., (2nd Lt, Co I, 39th NCST), II: 707.
Smith, Rufus, (5th Sgt, Co E, 4th Vols/14th NCST), V: 490.
Smith, S., (Sgt, Co A, 56th NCST), III: 347.
Smith, S.E., (1st Lt, Co C, Millard's 9th/20th Battalion Junior Reserves), IV: 386.
Smith, Saunders, (Pvt, Detached Co, 68th NCST), III: 723.
Smith, Sidney, (Pvt, Co G, 11th Vols/21st NCST), V: 515.
Smith, Simon A., (Pvt, Co K, 4th Vols/14th NCST), V: 491.
Smith, Thomas, (AQMS, 4th Vols/14th NCST), V: 489.
Smith, Thomas A., (Col, 36th Va.), III: 745,751, 753.
Smith, Thomas McGehee, (Maj, 45th NCST; IG, Daniel's Brigade), III: 36, 38, 54; IV: 513; V: 12.
Smith, W.A., (Pvt, Co B, 28th NCST), V: 541.
Smith, W.B., (Sgt, Co I, 7th NCST), V: 539.
Smith, W.B., (Pvt, Co E, 28th NCST), V: 542.
Smith, W.H., (Pvt, Co C, 5th NCST), V: 505.
Smith, W.H., (Capt, N.C. Militia), IV: 646.
Smith, W.H., (Sgt, Co K, 5th NCST), I: 291.
Smith, W.H., (Sgt, Co K, 26th NCST), II: 374.
Smith, W.J., (Pvt, Co C, 53rd NCST), V: 501.
Smith, W.J., (Musician, 46th NCST), V: 524.
Smith, W.P, (Pvt, Co E, 48th NCST), V: 526.
Smith, W.R., (Pvt, Co H, 13th Vols/23rd NCST), V: 510.
Smith, W.R., (Resident of Edward's Ferry. Owner of the field in which the Albemarle was built), V: 315.
Smith, W.S., (Sgt, Co K, 30th NCST), V: 493.
Smith, W.T., (Sgt Maj, 43rd NCST), III: 2.
Smith, William, "Extra Billy," (Governor of Virginia), I: 64, 148, 342, 343, 346, 347, 348.
Smith, William, (Pvt, Co D, 11th Vols/21st NCST), V: 514.
Smith, William, (Pvt, Co B, 5th NCST), I: 291; V: 505.
Smith, William, (Pvt, Co C, 5th NCST), I: 291.
Smith, William A., (Pvt, Co G, 14th Vols/24th NCST), V: 560.
Smith, William A., (3rd Cpl, Co I, 52nd NCST), III: 225.
Smith, William F., (Lt, Co A, 61st NCST), III: 503.
Smith, William F., (Pvt, Co G, 34th NCST), V: 556.
Smith, William Farrar, "Baldy," (Maj Gen, USA), II: 621.
Smith, William L., (Pvt, Co H, 13th Vols/23rd NCST; Detailed, 2nd Corps Provost Guard), V: 570.
Smith, William R., (Pvt, Co B, 59th NCST, 4th Cav), V: 659.
Smith, Winfield, (Pvt, Co F, 63rd NCST, 5th Cav), III: 563.
Smith County, Va., IV: 375.
Smith House, Jesse, (West College and Haywood Streets, Asheville), IV: 110.
Smith's Ferry Road, N.C., III: 193.
Smith's House, (nr Averaboro), III: 193.

Smith's Island, N.C., (See also: Bald Head Island), II: 632, 745, 748, 750, 754; IV: 265, 307, 421, 422.
Smith's Mill, N.C., IV: 265.
Smith's Shop, Va., II: 173.
Smithers, J.P., (Pvt, Co E, 45th NCST), V: 500.
Smithey, H., (Pvt, Co F, 52nd NCST), V: 536.
Smithfield, N.C., I: 412; II: 12, 518, 763, 764, 803; III: 193, 194, 195, 199, 217, 440, 442, 444, 454, 496, 502, 698, 699, 709, 727; IV: 20, 30, 55, 57, 59, 312, 335, 336, 350, 352, 394, 429, 430, 439, 498, 499, 547, 549, 592, 593.
Smithfield. Va., (and Battle of), I: 154, 207, 552, 654; II: 515; III: 14.
Smithfield Depot, II: 12.
Smithville, N.C., (now Southport), II: 111, 113, 639, 749, 752, 756, 761; III: 4, 205, 505, 726; IV: 40, 41, 43, 105, 268, 304, 305, 306, 311, 317, 318, 332, 361; V: 24, 25, 26, 225, 357, 358, 363, 373, 376, 377, 387, 395, 403,404, 406.
Smoketown Road, (nr Sharpsburg, Md.), I: 307, 308.
Smokey Mountains, III: 737, 739, 756, 758, 759; IV: 121, 122, 123, 124, 380, 381.
Smoot, D.G., (2nd Lt, Co G, 4th NCST), I: 233, 272.
Smyer, M.N., (2nd Lt, Co K, 46th NCST), III: 78, 82.
Smyer, R.A., (2nd Cpl, Co K, 46th NCST), V: 525.
Smyrna, N.Y., II: 492.
Smyth, Thomas Alfred, (Maj Gen, USA), V: 107, 153, 154, 156, 157.
Snead, E.D., (Capt, Co C, 5th NCST; Co C, Freeman's 26th Battalion NCST; Capt, Sneed's Unattached Co), I: 281, 282; IV: 401, 753; V: 626.
Sneed, Richard G., (1st Lt, Co A, 44th NCST), III: 21, 22.
Sneed, William M., (Lt, 2nd Vols/12th NCST), I: 638.
Snead's House, (nr Bentonville), III: 195.
Sneel, S.K.W., (Pvt, Co B, 10th Vols/20th NCST), V: 508.
Snelling, William N., (2nd Lt, Co D, 26th NCST), II: 395, 396, 397, 421; V: 152, 529.
Snicker's Gap, Va., (and Battle of, 1864), I: 154, 190, 206, 259-261, 664, 696; II: 34, 71, 170, 247, 474, 555, 657; III: 14, 259, 279, 565, 569; IV: 168, 460.
Snicker's Ferry, (Shenandoah River, Va.), III: 750.
Snicker's Ford, (Shenandoah River, Va.), I: 206, 259, 260, 578; III: 14, 256, 259, 260, 263.
Snicker's Neck, Va., I: 143, 144, 191.
Snider, George V., (2nd Lt, Co A, 9th Vols/19th NCST, 2nd Cav), II: 80.
Snipes, M.L., (2nd Lt, Co D, 6th NCST), V: 511.
Snipes, William H., (Pvt, Co H, 14th Vols/24th NCST), V: 560.
Snodgrass Hill, (nr Chickamauga, Tenn.), II: 703, 715, 716, 737; III: 435, 451-453; V: 172, 173.
Snow, A.L., (Pvt, Co C, 11th Vols/21st NCST), V: 514.
Snow, Byrd, (Capt, Co C, 11th Vols/21st NCST), II: 143, 145.
Snow, George H., (2nd Lt, Co H, 33rd NCST), II: 540, 579.
Snow, John A., (1st Lt, Co G, 2nd Vols/12th NCST), I: 650.
Snow, M.W., (Pvt, Co I, 8th Vols/18th NCST), V: 572.
Snow, Shugan, (Capt, Co I, 2nd Vols/12th NCST), I: 608, 627.
Snow, Thomas, [Samuel Thomas], (1st Lt, Co I, 5th NCST), I: 285.

Snow Ball Fight, (aka Great Snow Battle), I: 666; II: 227, 379, 664; III: 74.

Snow Hill, N.C., I: 517.

Snowden, Thomas H., (Pvt, Co A, Webb's Battery, Starr's 13th Battalion NCST, Light Art), V: 282.

Snuggs, G.D., (Pvt, Co K, 4th NCST), I: 274, 279; V: 489, 665.

Sockwell, D.R., (Lt, 63rd NCST, 5th Cav), I: 441; III: 643.

Soco Creek, N.C., III: 759.

Soco Gap, N.C., (in Balsam Mountains), III: 518, 758-759.

Soliders of North Carolina Praised by Jefferson Davis, II: 58.

Soles, Rev. J., (Chaplain, 36th NCST), II: 125.

Soley, Prof. J.R., (USN), V: 414, 416.

Somers, Peter H., (Pvt, Co E, 27th NCST), V: 523.

Somerset, Ky., IV: 128.

Somerton, Va., III: 335.

Sommers, James A., [James E.], (1st Sgt, Co C, 4th NCST), I: 232.

Sommerville, J.B., (Lt, Co B, 37th NCST), II: 669.

Sommerville, Tenn., II: 176.

Somerville Ford, Va., (Rapidan River), III: 271; IV: 160.

Sonoma, N.C., III: 730.

Sonwell, W.W., [Sonell], (Lt, 57th NCST), IV: 711.

Soots, John, (2nd Lt, Co B, 77th NCST, 7th Senior Reserves), IV: 99.

Sorrell, Elijah, (Pvt, Co C, 25th NCST), V: 560.

Sorrell, Lewis, (Pvt, Co H, 6th Vols/16th NCST), V: 552.

Sorrels, A.R., (Pvt, Co I, 56th NCST), I: 772.

Sorrels, H.R., (Pvt, Co I, 56th NCST), III: 317.

Sorey, J.W., (Chief Bugler, 41st NCST, 3rd Cav), II: 769.

Sossoman, J.P., (Cpl, Color-bearer, Co K, 56th NCST) III: 346, 348, 378.

Sou-ate-Owle, (Capt, Co A, Indian Co, Walker's Battalion, Thomas' Legion, 80th NCST), IV: 126.

Sou-ate-Owle Camp No. 1268 U.C.V., (Cherokee), IV: 126.

South, Dr. ______, IV: 719.

South Anna Bridge, III: 71.

South Carolina, I: 70, 537, 581; II: 4, 293, 701; III: 184, 186, 191, 192, 318, 440, 496, 708, 738, 745, 758; IV: 2, 6, 20, 124, 125, 132, 204, 213, 328, 335-336, 382, 404, 431, 440, 537, 618.

South Carolina Military Academy, V: 637, 638.

South Carolina Troops, II: 163.

South Lowell, III: 360.

South Mills, N.C., II: 280; III: 133, 335; IV: 365, 646.

South Mountain, Md., (and Battle of, 1862), I: 140, 141, 166, 172, 184, 225, 244, 571, 573, 579, 624, 625, 632, 633, 663, 695, 696, 739; II: 115, 190, 218, 219, 224, 238, 247, 348, 499; III: 472; IV: 164, 521; V: 591, 664.

South Mountain Campaign, I: 140. South Quay, Va., I: 494, 522; III: 134, 321; IV: 357, 366, 368.

South River, N.C., V: 17.

South Side Railroad, Va., I: 328, 432, 442, 467, 468, 469, 478, 601; II: 102, 455, 782, 783; III: 251, 396, 398, 470, 611, 614, 628, 629, 648; IV: 509.

South Washington, N.C., I: 742.

South Watauga, (See: Carter's Depot).

South West Creek, N.C., (and Battle of, 1865), I: xiii; III: 215-216, 507, 513, 696-698, 708, 722;

IV: 4, 18-19, 30, 31, 53-55, 311, 312, 325, 387, 393, 543-547, 592.
Southampton County, Va., III: 228.
Southard, R., (Pvt, Co H, 45th NCST), V: 500.
Southerland, Boney, (2nd Lt, Co C, 78th NCST, 8th Senior Reserves), IV: 107.
Southerland, Bryan, (Capt, Co B, 41st NCST, 3rd Cav), II: 770.
Southerland, Edward, (Capt, Co A, 51st NCST), III: 209, 218.
Southerland, John R., (Pvt, Co A, 38th NCST), V: 557.
Southerland, Samuel M., (Lt, Co C, 46th NCST), III: 81.
Southerland, Thomas J., [Sutherland], (Capt, Co I, 10th NCST, 1st Art & Engs, Sutherland's Battery, Light Art), I: 496, 528, 582; IV: 222.
Southerland, W.J., (Lt, Co A, 51st NCST), III: 211, 218.
Southerland's Farm, Va., II: 695.
Southerland's Station, Va., (aka Southerland Depot; on South Side Railroad), I: 748; II: 175, 534, 589, 783; III: 32, 15, 99, 251, 648.
Southern Express Company, V: 624.
Southern Historical Society, IV: 403.
Southern Historical Society Papers, I: 622, 729; V: 413.
Southern Railway System, I: 445.
Southwest Department, Confederate, IV: 749, 751.
Spaight, Ashley W., (Brig Gen), V: 649.
Spainhour, James H., (Chaplain, 1st NCST), I: 136; IV: 604.
Spainhour, R.A., (Pvt, ACS, 1st NCST), I: 136; V: 485.
Spake, Philip, (Pvt, Co D, 56th NCST), V: 566.
Spangler's Woods, (nr Gettysburg, Pa.), III: 299.
Spann, J.J., (Maj, 65th NCST, 6th Cav), III: 674, 681, 683; V: 651.
Sparks, Dr. Benjamin W., (Ass't Surg, 41st NCST, 3rd Cav), II: 769; IV: 638.
Sparks, Cotton, (Lt, Co I, 61st NCST), III: 504, 505.
Sparks, M.T., (Pvt, Co H, 3rd Vols/13th NCST), V: 551.
Sparks, William A., (Pvt, Co B, 34th NCST), V: 555.
Sparrow, Thomas, (Capt, Co G, 7th Vols/1th NCST; Maj, 10th NCST, 1st Art & Engs), I: 489, 496, 501, 502, 525, 527, 536; V: 35-56 personal account, 680.
Spaugh, D.A., (Pvt, Co E, Beale's 10th Va., Cav), V: 569.
Spaugh, T.H., (Pvt, Co K, 11th Vols/21st NCST), V: 515.
Spaulding, Lilburn A., (Pvt, Co K, Color-bearer, 24th Mi.), II: 356.
Speace, A.J., (Pvt, Co D, 57th NCST), V: 517.
Spear, S.P., (Col, 28th NCST), II: 57.
Spears, A.J., (Pvt, Co I, 37th NCST), V: 546.
Spears, M.O., (Pvt, Co A, 10th Vols/20th NCST), V: 508.
Spears, S., (Capt, Co D, 5th Battalion Junior Reserves; Co E, 71st NCST, 2nd Junior Reserves), IV: 25, 28.
Spears, Samuel Perkins, [Spear], (Brig Gen, USA), II: 277, 614, 615, 616; III: 25, 26; IV: 572.
Speck, John F., (Capt, Co G, 57th NCST), I: 119; III: 405, 409.
Speed, ______, (Capt, Co B, 2nd Regt Home Guard), IV: 653.
Speed, D.S., (Capt, Co B, 1st Battalion Junior Reserves; 70th NCST, 1st Junior Reserves), IV: 9, 12.

Speed, Edward A., (2nd Lt, Co B, 6th NCST), IV: 667, 702, 711.
Speed, Miss Mollie, IV: 667.
Speed, Dr. R.K., (Surg, 7th Vols/17th NCST), II: 2.
Speed, Thomas, (1st Sgt, Co I, 55th NCST), V: 528.
Speer, William H.A., (Lt Col, 28th NCST), II: 465, 466, 482, 483; III: 333; IV: 469, 473; V: 10.
Spell, Gaston, (Pvt, Co A, 30th NCST), V: 491.
Spell, W., (Pvt, Co I, 46th NCST), V: 525.
Speller, Charles W., (Jr 2nd Lt, Co F, 59th NCST, 4th Cav), III: 457.
Speller, J.J., (Commandant Conscript Camp Guard), I: 110, 120.
Spence, Joseph N., (Pvt, Color-bearer, Co A, 8th NCST), I: 408.
Spencer, ______, (Capt, Unattached Co), IV: 402.
Spencer, A.F., (Capt, Co D, 2nd Vols/12th NCST), I: 649.
Spencer, J.A., (Lt, Co F, 46th NCST), III: 81.
Spencer, Joseph, (Pvt, Detached Co, 68th NCST), III: 723.
Spencer, P.J., (Pvt, Co C, 28th NCST), V: 541.
Spencer, S., (Pvt, Co C, 28th NCST), V: 541.
Spencer, William G., (2nd Lt, Co L, 12th Vols/22nd NCST), II: 165, 166.
Spencer, William N., (Capt, Detached Co, 68th NCST), III: 723.
Sperryville, Va., I: 570, 623.
Sperryville Turnpike, (Sperryville to Culpepper, Va.), III: 465, 575.
Spicer, H.L., (Sgt, Co K, 5th Vols/15th NCST), V: 522.
Spicer, John W., (1st Lt, Co B, 41st NCST, 3rd Cav), II: 770.
Spicer, W.F., (Cmdr, USN), V: 243.
Spikes, Addison, (Pvt, Co A, 10th NCST, 1st Art & Engs, Ramseur-Manly's Battery, Light Art), I: 555, 559.
Spinola, Francis B., (Brig Gen, USA), I: 588; II: 340; IV: 557.
Spivey, Caleb M., (Cpl, Co D, 10th Vols/20th NCST), II: 114.
Spivey, Cornelius, (2nd Lt, Co E, 56th NCST), III: 315, 366.
Spivey, David W., (Capt, Co K, 14th Vols/24th NCST), II: 270, 272.
Spivey, F.M., (2nd Lt, Co H, 9th Vols/19th NCST, 2nd Cav), II: 89.
Splann, James T., (Pvt, Co D, 6th Vols/16th NCST), V: 552.
Sponcellor, Jacob, (Fayetteville and Harper's Ferry Arsenals), IV: 298.
Spotswood House, (New Bern), II: 86.
Spotts, J.H., (Cmdr, USN), V: 243.
Spottsylvania, Va., (aka Spottsylavnia Court House, Battle and Campaign of 1864), I: 115, 116, 151, 152, 159, 160, 164, 171, 172, 180, 202, 213, 255, 256, 257, 258, 276, 277, 278, 288, 289, 383-384, 404, 430, 460, 465, 548, 558, 594, 596, 612, 639, 641, 677, 701, 702, 723, 724, 725, 726, 744, 745; II: 5, 49, 50, 51, 52, 57, 59, 75, 112, 120, 126, 173, 182, 184, 185, 189, 241, 242, 243, 262, 381, 383, 384, 387, 411, 420, 447, 480, 502, 522, 523, 529, 531, 571, 572, 573, 588, 592, 665, 666, 668, 694, 720; III: 11, 28-29, 36, 37, 38, 43, 45, 76, 77, 79, 82, 95, 111, 119, 246, 256, 258, 259, 260, 261, 277, 305-306, 385, 592, 594, 595, 688; IV: 173, 191, 193-196, 247, 258,

411, 425, 449, 468, 469, 471, 475, 476, 507, 515, 522, 554, 563, 610, 678; V: 78, 104, 258, 619.
Spring Bank, (Neuse River nr Goldsboro), I: 523, 524; IV: 326.
Spring Green, N.C., III: 506, 680, 722.
Spring Green Church, N.C., III: 721.
Springfield, Va., II: 193; III: 361.
Springs, A.A., (Pvt, Co B, 53rd NCST), V: 501.
Springs, Dr. J.M., (Ass't Surg, 53rd NCST), IV: 640.
Springs, John M., (Capt, AQM, 53rd NCST), III: 260, 261.
Springs, Joseph, (Pilot, Alice), V: 357.
Springs, Thomas, (Pvt, Co C, 3rd NCST), V: 487.
Sprinkle, J., (Pvt, Co E, 1st Vols/11th NCST), V: 530.
Sprinkle, Thomas, (Pvt, Co H, 4th NCST), I: 276.
Sprinkle, William R., (Pvt, Co B, 38th NCST), V: 557.
Spruill, S.B., (Col, 9th Vols/19th NCST, 2nd Cav), II: 79, 81, 83, 106; V: 308.
Spruill's Regiment (See: 9th Vols/19th NCST, 2nd Cav).
Sprunt, James, (Purser, Lilian), V: ix, xv, xvi, 351, 358, 359, 363-385 personal account, 395, 406, 410, 411, 442, 446, 457.
Sprunt, James A., [James M.] (Chaplain, 10th Vols/20th NCST), II: 112; IV: 608.
Sprunt, Mary K., V: 369.
Spurgeon, Rev. C.H., I: 725.
Spurlin, G.W., (Pvt, Co I, 56th NCST), III: 357.
Squiggins, W.J., (Capt, Co D, 24th NCST), V: 193.
Squires, J.B., (Pvt, Co K, 30th NCST), V: 493.
Squires, James, (Pvt, Co K, 6th NCST), V: 514.
Squires, M.D., (Cpl, Co F, 49th NCST), V: 564.
Squirrel Level Road, (nr Petersburg, Va.), III: 249; IV: 88.
Stafford, ______, (Midshipman, Ellis), V: 302.
Stafford, D.L., (Pvt, Co F, 2nd NCST), V: 572.
Stafford, F.M., (Pvt, Co G, 6th Vols/16th NCST), IV: 198.
Stafford, J.C., (Capt, Co K, 48th NCST), III: 117.
Stafford, J.L., (Lt, Co H, 7th NCST), I: 384.
Stafford, J.M., (Pvt, Co D, 16th Battalion/75th NCST, 7th Cav), V: 660.
Stafford, John, (Pvt, Co K, 35th NCST), V: 563.
Stafford, John, (Pvt, Co B, 37th NCST), V: 545.
Stafford, Joseph B., (AQM, 43rd NCST), III: 1.
Stafford Heights, Va., (opp. Fredericksburg, aka Stafford Hills), I: 741; II: 226; IV: 176.
Stage Road, (towards Coggin's Point), III: 622.
Stahl, Julius, [Stahel], (Maj Gen, USA), III: 558.
Staley, D.J., (Pvt, Co I, 3rd NCST), V: 487.
Staley, E., (Pvt, Co H, 30th NCST; Detailed, Invalid Battalion), V: 571.
Stallings, A.J., (Sgt, Co K, 4th Vols/14th NCST), V: 560.
Stallings, Caswell, (Pvt, Co C, 4th Vols/14th NCST), V: 490.
Stallings, E., (Pvt, Co F, 30th NCST), V: 492.
Stallings, H.H., (Pvt, Co A, 12th Vols/22nd NCST), V: 553.
Stallings, Hosea, (Pvt, Co F, 26th NCST), V: 602.

Stallings, J.N., (4th Sgt, Co A, 12th Vols/22nd NCST), V: 553.
Stallings, James, (Pvt, Co G, 43rd NCST; Detailed, 2nd Corps Provost Guard), V: 570.
Stallings, R.G., (Sgt, Co I, 6th NCST), V: 513.
Stallings, Rufus, (Pvt, Co F, 30th NCST), V: 492.
Stallings, Theophilus, (AQMS, 30th NCST), V: 491.
Stallings, Walter S., (Col, 2nd NCST), I: 159, 160, 172, 173, 260; IV: 460; V: 10.
Stallings, William, (Pvt, Co F, 26th NCST), V: 602, 603.
Stamer, A.R., (2nd Lt, Co A, 1st NCST), I: 136.
Stamer, William C., (Pvt, Co G, 25th NCST), V: 561.
Stamper, John, (Pvt, Co A, 26th NCST), II: 374.
Stamper, M.D., (1st Lt, Co G, 5th Vols/15th NCST), I: 735.
Stamy, J., (Pvt, Co D, 1st NCST), V: 485.
Stanback, G.L., (Pvt, Co C, 4th Vols/14th NCST), I: 732.
Stancell, S.T., (Capt, Co A, 5th Vols/15th NCST), I: 734.
Stancill, G.W., (1st Lt, Co G, 3rd Vols/13th NCST), V: 547.
Stancill, J.F., [Stansill], (Maj, 4th NCST), I: 230, 231, 232, 261, 268, 279; IV: 461.
Stancill, William H., [Stalcil], (Pvt, Co H, 27th NCST), II: 462; V: 524.
Standardsville Road, (nr Liberty Mills), I: 382; II: 478, 568.
Stanford, S.M., (Capt, Co C, 51st NCST), III: 218.
Stanley, Edward, (Without authority in law and in violation of the Constitution, native of North Carolina, resident of California, Stanley was appointed by Lincoln to be the Governor of North Carolina. His stay as imposter head of state was short for even he could not abide the abuses of the Lincoln administration and its military.), I: 14; II: 86.
Stanley, J.B., (Capt, Co B, 10th Vols/20th NCST), II: 111.
Stanley, Peter, (Pvt, Co C, 30th NCST), IV: 600.
Stanley, R.M., (Ensign, 37th NCST), II: 668.
Stanley, S., (Pvt, Co C, 54th NCST), V: 516.
Stanley, William F., (2nd Lt, Co G, 40th NCST, 3rd Art, Hvy), II: 747.
Stanly, A.G., (Pvt, Co I, 3rd Vols/13th NCST), V: 551.
Stanly County, N.C., II: 792; IV: 132, 760.
Stannard, George Jerrison, (Maj Gen, USA), II: 364; V: 109, 142, 149, 156.
Stannard Mills, Va., III: 277.
Stanton, Edwin M., (Sec of State, U.S.), I: 57, 63; III: 336, 560, 750, 754; IV: 1, 685, 770, 771.
Stanton, Ned, [Edward], (Pvt, Co E, 8th Vols/18th NCST), II: 18.
Stantonsburg, N.C., I: 498, 535, 536; III: 711.
Starbuck, J.W., (Pvt, Co K, 52nd NCST), V: 536.
Stark, Samuel, (Pvt, Co C, 10th NCST, 1st Art & Engs, Brem-Graham-Williams' Battery, Light Art), V: 568.
Starke, Lucien D., (Capt, ACS, 7th Vols/17th NCST; Commissary, Martin-Kirkland's Brigade), II: 1, 2, 5; IV: 527, 528, 530, 531, 538, 556.
Starke, Rufus, (2nd Lt, Co K, 44th NCST), III: 24.

Starke, W.N., (AAG, Hill's 3rd Corps), IV: 476.
Starke, William Edwin, (Brig Gen), II: 683.
"Star Spangled Banner, " V: 50.
Starling, J., (Pvt, Co C, 8th Vols/18th NCST; Detailed, Invalid Battalion), V: 571.
Starling, J.M., (2nd Lt, Co F, 28th NCST), II: 483.
Starnes, Hugh, (Pvt, Co A, 48th NCST), V: 526.
Starnes, Martin, (Pvt, Co A, 52nd NCST), V: 535.
Starnes, Thomas, (Pvt, Co H, 30th NCST), V: 492.
Starnes, William, (Pvt, Co B, 26th NCST), V: 531.
Starns, S.R., [Starnes], (Pvt, Co H, 5th NCST), I: 292; V: 505.
Starr, A., (Pvt, Co C, 28th NCST), V: 541.
Starr, Joseph B., (Capt, Co F, 1st Vols, "Bethel"; Capt, Co B, Starr's Battery; Lt Col, Starr's 13th Battalion NCST, Light Art), I: 75, 78, 90, 112, 113, 118, 126, 127, 133, 519, 520; II: 513; IV: 294, 341, 342, 344, 349.
Starr's Farm, (Totopotomy Creek, Va.), II: 574.
State Library, N.C., I: 53, 102.
State Troops, I: 1-5; II: 16, 79, 162, 181, 192; V: 2, 5, 6, 8.
States in the War, V: 464.
States of the Confederacy, V: 464.
Statesville, N.C., I: 55, 65; III: 445; IV: 241, 405, 605; V: 292, 295.
Station, Ivor, II: 515.
Staton, George H., (Pvt, Co I, 5th Vols/15th NCST), V: 522.
Staton, J.B., (Pvt, Co E, 9th Vols/19th NCST, 2nd Cav), V: 658.
Staton, Neill B., (Pvt, Co B, 26th NCST), II: 375. 376.
Staton, Robert M., (Ensign, 37th NCST), II: 653.
Staton, Simon B., (Sgt, Co I, 5th Vols/15th NCST), V: 522.
Statt, Wiley, (Pvt, Co B, 2nd NCST), I: 175.
Staunton, J.R., (Pvt, Co G, 30th NCST), V: 492.
Staunton, Va., I: 153, 206, 303, 311, 326, 327, 567, 645, 766; II: 245; III: 13, 270, 745-748, 749, 754, 756; IV: 138, 143, 147, 149, 167, 180, 515.
Staunton River, Va., I: 290, 432, 433, 434; II: 392; III: 611, 615, 617, 618.
Staunton River Bridge, III: 611, 614, 615, 617.
Staynes, A.S., IV: 702.
Steadman, John, (Pvt, Co G, Ambulance driver, 6th Vols/16th NCST), IV: 203, 204.
Steadman, Joseph, (Pvt, Co G, 6th Vols/16th NCST), IV: 216; V: 552.
Steadman, Joshua, (Pvt, Co G, 6th Vols/16th NCST), IV: 216; V: 552.
Steagall, George W., (Pvt, Co A, 27th NCST), II: 461.
Stearns, O.P., (Col, 39th U.S., Colored), V: 238.
Stearnes, Jesse J., (Pvt, Co H, 55th NCST), V: 528.
Stedman, Charles M., (Maj, 44th NCST), I: 118, 123, 776; II: 395; III: 21, 22, 23, 24, 28, 34; IV: 326, 568; V: 207, 212, 529, 651, 664.
Stedman, Robert Winship, (Pvt, Co F, 1st Vols, "Bethel"; Co B, 61st NCST; 2nd Lt, Co A, 44th NCST), I: 128; III: 22, 28, 32, 511.
Steed, Alexander L., (2nd Lt, Co G, 43rd NCST), III: 3.
Steedman, C., (Capt, USN), V: 242.
Steel, J.C., (Musician, 4th NCST), I: 234.

Steel, J.H., (Pvt, Co A, 30th NCST), V: 491.
Steel Breast Plates, (An affectation purchased and carried into the field by a relative few during the early war. These devices, much like those worn by knights or Spanish explorers, provided absolutely no protection from the rifles of the day. Due to their wieght, discomfort and lack of protection they were abandoned by their owners.), III: 170.
Steele, ______, (Englishman, Capt, Blockade Runner), V: 413, 417.
Steele, D.W., (Sgt, Co B, 4th NCST), I: 232.
Steele, J.J.C., (Capt, Co B, 26th NCST), II: 303, 305, 336, 396.
Steele, James C., (Musician, 4th NCST), V: 488.
Steele, Joseph, (Pvt, Co B, 5th Vols/15th NCST), V: 521.
Steele, Manly S., (Lt, Co C, 9th NCST, 1st Cav), I: 441, 485, 782.
Steele, Sinclair Preston, (2nd Lt, Co A, 8th Battalion Junior Reserves; Co F, 72nd NCST, 3rd Junior Reserves), IV: 41, 48.
Steen, Ransom H., (1st Lt, Co G, 46th NCST), III: 81.
Stegal, Rabon, (2nd Lt, Co A, 31st NCST), II: 507.
Stegall, A., (Pvt, Co D, 37th NCST), V: 545.
Stegall, F.R., (Pvt, Co C, 3rd Vols/13th NCST), V: 550.
Stegall, George W., (Pvt, Co A, 27th NCST), V: 522.
Step, John, (Jr 2nd Lt, Co 3, Woodfin's Battalion; Lt, Co 9, 79th NCST, 8th Cav), IV: 111, 115.
Stephens, ______, (Sgt, 6th Battalion NCST), IV: 298.
Stephens, A.H., III: 386.
Stephens, Alexander Hamilton, (Vice President, CSA), III: 383, 386, 387; IV: 718.
Stephens, Benjamin, (Pvt, Co B, 59th NCST, 4th Cav), V: 659.
Stephens, Donnie, [Noah Downie], (Pvt, Co K, 10th Vols/20th NCST), II: 114.
Stephens, Enoch, (2nd Lt, Co B, 68th NCST), III: 713.
Stephens, J.R., (Pvt, Co H, 3rd Vols/13th NCST), V: 551.
Stephens, Dr. Lewis, (Ass't Surg, 39th NCST), II: 707.
Stephens, Thomas, (Pvt, Co D, 3rd Vols/13th NCST), V: 550.
Stephens, W., (Pvt, Co D, 3rd Vols/13th NCST), V: 550.
Stephens, Dr. W.G., (Surg, 3rd Vols/13th NCST), IV: 633.
Stephens, W.H., (Pvt, Co H, 3rd Vols/13th NCST), V: 551.
Stephens, William D., (Pvt, Co D, 38th NCST), V: 557.
Stephens' Iron Works, Thad, Pa., IV: 181.
Stephensburg, Va., IV: 160.
Stephenson, Amos, (Pvt, Co A, 5th Vols/15th NCST), V: 520.
Stephenson, D., (Cpl, Co C, 53rd NCST), V: 501.
Stephenson, J.A., (Capt, Co D, Millard's 9th/20th Battalion Junior Reserves), IV: 387.
Stephenson, James W., (Jr 2nd Lt, Co G, 38th NCST), II: 675, 685.
Stephenson, John, (Pvt, Co C, 53rd NCST), V: 501.
Stephenson, Joseph, [Stevenson], (2nd Lt, Co B, 10th NCST, 1st Art & Engs, Guion's Hvy Art), I: 501, 536.
Stephenson, Martin L., (2nd Lt, Co F, Latham-Potts-Flanner's Battery, Starr's 13th Battalion NCST, Light Art), IV: 354.

Stephenson, Robert T., (Pvt, Co A, 5th Vols/15th NCST), V: 520.
Stephenson, Thomas W., (1st Lt, Co C, 4th NCST), I: 232, 249, 271.
Stephenson, Wesley A., (2nd Lt, Co G, 38th NCST), II: 678, 685.
Stephenson's Depot, Va., [Stevenson's, Steven's], (and Battle of, 1864), I: 147, 207, 325, 645; II: 248; V: 214.
Stepp, Tisdale, (Pvt, Co F, 4th Vols/14th NCST), I: 723.
Steppes, George, [George W.], (Cpl, Co C, 10th Vols/20th NCST), II: 121.
Sterling, Campbell & Albright, (Publishing House, Goldsboro), V: 456.
Sterling, J.W., (Musician, 3rd Vols/13th NCST), V: 549.
Sterling, James R., (1st Lt, Co H, 40th NCST, 3rd Art, Hvy), II: 746, 747.
Sterling, Richard, (Adjt, 4th Regt Home Guard), V: 630.
Sterrett, ______, (Capt, CSN), IV: 741.
Sterrett, Samuel, (CSN, Son of above), IV: 741.
Stett, Bunyon, (Pvt, Co B, 2nd NCST), I: 175.
Steuart, George H. "Maryland," (Brig Gen), I: 147, 193, 199, 202, 204.
Stevens, ______, (Col, Foster's 2nd Brigade, USA), II: 337.
Stevens, C.T., (2nd Lt, Co A, 30th NCST), II: 496.
Stevens, Cornelius, (1st Lt, Co D, 44th NCST), III: 23.
Stevens, David, (Sgt Maj, 61st NCST), III: 503.
Stevens, Isaac Ingalls, [Stephens], (Maj Gen, USA), IV: 164.
Stevens, Dr. J.M., (Capt, Ass't Surg, 6th Battalion/60th NCST), III: 474, 475, 484; IV: 641.
Stevens, Dr. Lewis, (Ass't Surg, 39th NCST), IV: 638.
Stevens, Marcus C., (Lt, Co G, 55th NCST), III: 296, 302, 311.
Stevens, Merritt, (Pvt, Co F, 6th Battalion/60th NCST), III: 479.
Stevens, Thomas, (Ordnance/Commissary/AQMS, Fayetteville Arsenal), IV: 296.
Stevens, W.V., (2nd Lt, Co F, 4th NCST), I: 233, 271.
Stevens, William, (Pvt, Co D, 35th NCST), V: 562.
Stevens, Witt, (Col), IV: 427.
Stevensburg, Va., I: 428, 639; III: 575, 576, 584; IV: 177.
Stevenson, ______, (Col, Foster's command, USA, at Rawle's Mill), II: 338.
Stevenson, Bervin, (Sgt, Co B, 33rd NCST), II: 538.
Stevenson, Carter Littlepage, (Maj Gen, Chief Engineer ANV), I: 494; II: 486, 487, 706; III: 332, 434, 444.
Stevenson, James M., (Lt, 30th N.C. Militia; Maj, 36th NCST, 2nd Art & Engs), II: 630, 634, 646, 756; IV: 361; V: 27, 233, 239.
Stevenson, T.W., (Lt, Co C, 4th NCST), I: 262.
Stevenson, Thomas, (Musician, 10th Vols/20th NCST), II: 113; V: 508.
Stevenson, Thomas Greeley, (Brig Gen, USA), III: 208.
Stevenson, William M., (Capt, Co B, 61st NCST), III: 503, 504.
Stevenson's Depot, Va., I: 261.
Steward, ______, (Color-bearer, Co C, 35th NCST), II: 606.
Steward, J.R., (Cpl, Co K, 5th Vols/15th NCST), V: 522.
Stewart, A.L., (Pvt, Co A, 33rd NCST), V: 543.
Stewart, A.T., (Maj, 58th NCST), III: 432, 433, 447; V: 12, 670.

Stewart, A.W., (Pvt, Co K, 45th NCST), V: 501.
Stewart, Alexander Peter, (Lt Gen), II: 717, 720, 731, 732, 733, 734; V: 172.
Stewart, Alfred, (Pvt, Co E, 45th NCST), V: 500.
Stewart, Alfred, (Pvt, Co H, 53rd NCST; Detailed, 2nd Corps Provost Guard), V: 570.
Stewart, Alfred S., (Jr 2nd Lt, Co F, 26th NCST), II: 304.
Stewart, Calvin, [Colin], (Capt, Co D, 46th NCST), III: 64, 81.
Stewart, D., (Sgt, Co D, 33rd NCST), V: 544.
Stewart, D.L., (Cpl, Co G, 57th NCST), V: 517.
Stewart, Daniel, (1st Lt, Co D, 46th NCST), III: 81.
Stewart, J.A., (2nd Lt, Co F, 41st NCST, 3rd Cav), II: 771.
Stewart, J.M., (Capt, Co D, 76th NCST, 6th Senior Reserves), IV: 97.
Stewart, J.W., (Pvt, Co G, 43rd NCST), V: 498.
Stewart, John J., (Lt, Co B, 46th NCST), III: 80.
Stewart, M., (Pvt, Co H, 56th NCST), III: 357.
Stewart, T.J., (1st Lt, Co G, 40th NCST), IV: 711.
Stewart, Thomas J., (Sgt, Co A, 1st Vols, "Bethel"), I: 128.
Stewart, W.S., (Pvt, Co B, 53rd NCST), V: 501.
Stikeleather, John A., (Sgt, Color-bearer, Co A, 4th NCST), I: 232, 239, 243, 263, 279; V: 488.
Stilley, Dr. Burton, (2nd Lt, Co K, 41st NCST, 3rd Cav), II: 772, 785, 786.
Stilley, Robert F., (Barrington's Co, Whitford's 11th Battalion NCST, Hvy Art; Co B, 67th NCST), V: 18.
Stilt, Edward W., (Capt, Co I, 37th NCST), I: 119; V: 664.
Stilts, Robert H., [Stitt], (Lt, Co A, 48th NCST), III: 115.
Stinson, David D., (Pvt, Co B, 5th Vols/15th NCST), V: 521.
Stinson, E. Burette, (Musician, 4th NCST; Sgt Maj, 4th NCST), I: 234, 271, 279; V: 488, 664.
Stinson, George M., (Pvt, Co B, 5th Vols/15th NCST), V: 521.
Stinson, J.B., (Pvt, Co A, 4th NCST, Brigade Courier), V: 488.
Stinson, James A., (Courier, Anderson-Ramseur-Cox's Brigade), I: 271; IV: 463.
Stinson, Robert W., (Lt, Co G, 46th NCST), III: 82.
Stinson, W.W., (Pvt, Co H, 7th NCST), V: 538.
Stith, Dr. L.H., [L.A.], (Ass't Surg, 2nd NCST), I: 158; IV: 631.
Stith, T.B., (2nd Lt, Co F, 4th NCST), I: 233, 271.
Stitt, J.M., (1st Lt, Co A, 48th NCST), V: 520.
Stitt, William E., (1st Lt, Co B, 43rd NCST; Capt, Grimes' Staff), III: 2, 3, 12; IV: 516; V: 483, 664.
Stockard, J.R., (Capt, Co H, 5th Vols/15th NCST), I: 735.
Stockton, ______, (68th NCST), III: 718.
Stockton, Frank D., (Lt, Adjt, 7th NCST; Adjt of Salisbury Prison), I: 365; IV: 472, 753.
Stockton, J.B., (2nd Lt, Co H, 4th NCST), I: 233, 254, 272.
Stockton, John, I: 254, 272.
Stoddard, Albert H., (Lt, ADC to Kirkland), IV: 536, 544, 546, 562, 564.
Stokeley, Charles, (Pvt, Co B, 6th Battalion/60th NCST), III: 482.
Stokely, H.C., (Pvt, Co A, 8th NCST), V: 193.

Stokely, W.R., (Jr 2nd Lt, Co H, 6th Battalion/60th NCST), III: 474.
Stokes, D.E., (2nd Lt, Co D, 1st NCST), I: 137.
Stokes, D.E., (2nd Lt, Co K, 1st NCST), I: 137.
Stokes, J.J., (1st Lt, Co G, 12th Vols/22nd NCST), II: 165.
Stokes, James T., (Lt, Co G, 12th Vols/22nd NCST), II: 166.
Stokes, Mumford Sidney, [Montford], (Col, 1st NCST), I: 126, 134, 135, 136, 139; V: 9.
Stokes County, N.C., II: 145, 155, 163; III: 261, 264; IV: 218, 258; V: 633.
Stone, ______, [John M.], (Col, 2nd Miss.), III: 311; IV: 375.
Stone, A.W., (Capt, Co K, 28th NCST), II: 483; V: 538.
Stone, Charles Pomeroy, (Brig Gen, Stone's Brigade, USA), II: 346, 347.
Stone, E., (Pvt, Co E, 6th NCST), V: 512.
Stone, F.J., (Resident of Stoneville), I: 661.
Stone, G.W., (Sgt, Co I, 9th Vols/19th NCST, 2nd Cav), V: 658.
Stone, J.N., (Pvt, Co I, 6th NCST), V: 513.
Stone, L., (Pvt, Co I, 33rd NCST), V: 545.
Stone, R.D., (Pvt, Co I, 6th NCST), V: 513.
Stone, R.J., (Sgt, Co I, 13th Vols/23rd NCST), V: 510.
Stone, T.A., (Co D, 2nd Vols/12th NCST), I: 630.
Stone, W.E., (Pvt, Co C, 3rd Vols/13th NCST), V: 550.
Stone, W.J., (Capt, Co H, 5th Vols/15th NCST), I: 735.
Stone, Willie, (Pvt, Co H, 3rd Vols/13th NCST), I: 661.
Stone, William E., (Cpl, Co I, 33rd NCST), II: 540.
Stone Bridge, (See: Burnside's Bridge).
Stone Castle, III: 582.
Stone House, (nr Manassas, Va.), I: 572.
Stone House Mountain, Va., III: 575.
Stone's Mill, Va., II: 87.
Stone's River, Tenn., (See also: Murfreesboro), II: 488, 491, 710; III: 476, 477, 478, 480.
Stoneman, David, III: 760.
Stoneman, George, (Maj Gen, USA and Stoneman's Cavalry), I: 61, 62, 65, 386; II: 87, 773; III: 669, 670, 671, 760; IV: 41, 67, 128, 132, 374, 460, 770; V: 285, 287, 632, 639, 654.
Stoneman's Raid, I: 22, 588; I II: 669; IV: 132, 373, 375, 558, 653, 770; V: 635.
Stonestreet, J.H., (Pvt, Co F, 3rd Vols/13th NCST), V: 550.
Stoney Ridge, Ga., (and Battle of, 1864), III: 492.
Stoney Creek, Va., [Stony], I: 435, 436, 439, 471; II: 58, 255, 263, 782; III: 29, 135, 350, 615, 636; IV: 88, 388, 390, 563; V: 628.
Stoney Creek Depot, Va., III: 616.
Storm, D., (Sgt, Co B, 8th Vols/18th NCST), II: 63.
Storr's Farm, (Totoptamoy Creek, Va.), II: 56, 480, 574.
Story, Edward F., (Lt, Co C, 61st NCST), III: 504.
Story, W.C., (Ensign, 27th NCST) II: 443.
Stott, Bunyon, (Pvt, Co B, 2nd NCST), V: 486.
Stott, John, (Pvt, Co A, 47th NCST), V: 534.
Stott, W.E., (2nd Sgt, Co A, 47th NCST), V: 534.

Stott, Wiley, (Pvt, Co B, 2nd NCST), V: 486.
Stough, A.L., (Chaplain, 37th NCST), II: 653; IV: 474, 613.
Stough, R.J., (Cpl, Co K, 56th NCST), III: 378.
Stoup, Solomon, (2nd Lt, Co C, 33rd NCST), II: 539, 578.
Stout, H.M., (Pvt, Co H, 46th NCST), V: 525.
Stovall, Marcellus A., (Brig Gen), III: 488.
Stovall, Wilkins, (Lt, Co K, 55th NCST), III: 296; IV: 711.
Stowe, Abram, (Pvt, Co M, 6th Vols/16th NCST), V: 553.
Stowe, C.T., (ACS Sgt, 37th NCST), V: 545.
Stowe, George C., (Capt, Co I, 33rd NCST; Lt Col, 74th NCST, 5th Senior Reserves), II: 540; IV: 69.
Stowe, Herbert DeLambert, (ACS, 37th NCST), II: 653; IV: 474.
Stowe, James L., (Pvt, Co M, 6th Vols/16th NCST), V: 553.
Stowe, Jasper, (Lt Col, 82nd NCST, 2nd Detailed Men), IV: 131.
Stowe, Leroy W., (Capt, 6th Vols/16th NCST; Lt Col, 73rd NCST, 4th Senior Reserves), IV: 66.
Stowe, R.B., (Pvt, Co B, 28th NCST), V: 541.
Stowe, Samuel N., (Maj, 28th NCST), II: 465, 467, 483; IV: 413, 473.
Stowe, Willaim A., (Col, 6th Vols/16th NCST), I: 753, 763; IV: 151, 174, 196, 197, 201, 210, 212, 213, 215; V: 547.
Strachan, Dr. J.B., (Surg, 32nd NCST), IV: 637; V: 494.
Stradley, Rev. J.A., (Chaplain, 2nd NCST), IV: 601, 604.
Stradley, Joseph, (Capt, Co H, 29th NCST), II: 493.
Strahl, Otho French, (Brig Gen), III: 495.
Straight, Dr. James L., (Surg, 6th Battalion/60th NCST), III: 486, 641.
Straits, N.C., I: 503; IV: 620.
Strange, Benton A., (Capt, Co A, 39th NCST), II: 704.
Strange, Burgess S., (Pvt, Co I, 4th Vols/14th NCST), V: 491.
Strange, French, (Adjt, 5th NCST), I: 118, 136.
Strange, James William, (Capt, Co F, 6th Battalion, Fayetteville Armory Guard; Capt, Co D, 9th Vols/19th NCST, 2nd Cav), II: 80, 82, 89, 93; III: 655; IV: 297; V: 273, 274.
Strasburg, Va., [Strasburg], (and Battle of, 1864), I: 206, 262, 297, 326, 339; II: 143, 260, 261; III: 14, 279, 749, 750, 754; V: 231, 526, 603.
Strawberry Plains, Tenn., III: 520, 664, 730, 737, 738; IV: 123, 273.
Strawbridge, ______, (Col, 76th Pa.), V: 163.
Strayhorn, Sidney G., (Pvt, Co G, 27th NCST), II: 462; V: 523.
Strayhorn's, N.C., (now University Station), I: 63.
Street, William J., (2nd Lt, Co K, 2nd NCST), I: 164, 175; V: 484.
Street's Ferry, N.C., (Neuse River), III: 173, 175, 176; IV: 81-82.
Streeter, E.H., (1st Lt, Co B, 31st NCST), II: 512.
Strickland, B.R., (Pvt, Co A, 10th NCST, 1st Art & Engs, Ramseur-Manly's Battery, Light Art), I: 555.
Strickland, George S., (Pvt, Co E, 5th Vols/15th NCST), V: 521.
Strickland, H.O., (Pvt, Co I, 30th NCST), V: 493.
Strickland, J.L., (Pvt, Co A, 47th NCST), V: 534.

Strickland, J.S., (Pvt, Co B, 3rd NCST), V: 487.
Strickland, James, (Pvt, Co D, 43rd NCST), V: 498.
Strickland, Jere, (Pvt, Co A, 43rd NCST), III: 20; V: 497.
Strickland, L., (Pvt, Co I, 16th Battalion/75th NCST, 7th Cav), V: 660.
Strickland, N.C., (Pvt, Co C, 3rd Vols/13th NCST), V: 550.
Strickland, Nicholas, (Pvt, Co E, 5th Vols/15th NCST), V: 521.
Strickland, Philip, (Cpl, Co C, 7th NCST), I: 378.
Strickland, S.H., (Pvt, Co D, 43rd NCST), V: 498.
Strickland, Samuel, (Pvt, Co C, 5th NCST), I: 291; V: 505.
Strickland, Thomas, (Pvt, Co K, 1st NCST), V: 485.
Strickland, W.R., (Pvt, Co C, 5th NCST), I: 291; V: 505.
Strickland, William S., (Pvt, Co E, 5th Vols/15th NCST), V: 521.
Strider, John, (Pvt, Co K, 56th NCST), III: 348.
Stringfield, W.W., (Maj, 69th NCST, Thomas' Legion), III: 518, 729, 730, 732, 736, 739, 741, 743, 744, 746, 747, 748, 750, 752, 754, 756, 757, 758, 759, 760, 761; IV: 119, 123, 124, 127, 128; V: 653-656.
Stringfellow, Charles S., (Maj, AAG N.C. Reserves), III: 524; IV: 7, 38, 52.
Stringham, Silas Horton, (Admr, USN), II: 1; V: 46, 51, 52, 301, 302.
Stripe, Levin J., (Musician, 33rd NCST), II: 538.
Stronach, A.B., V: 679.
Stronach, George T., (Ordnance Sgt, 4th Vols/14th NCST), V: 489.
Stroanch, W.C., (Sgt, Co H, 47th NCST), V: 535.
Strong, George Crockett, (Maj Gen, USA), V: 163, 165.
Strong, George V., (Maj, 27th NCST), II: 425, 426.
Stroop, Ephraim, (Pvt, Co K, 48th NCST), V: 527.
Stroup, Miles A., (Pvt, Co F, 34th NCST), V: 555.
Strowd, Samuel, (Pvt, Co D, 27th NCST), II: 462; V: 523.
Strudwick,Dr. William, (Surg, Fort Macon), IV: 629.
Strupe, C., (Pvt, Co D, 11th Vols/21xt NCST), V: 514.
Stuart, Alfred T., (Lt, Co F, 26th NCST), II: 396.
Stuart, J.E.B., (Maj Gen), I: 61, 146, 193, 251, 252, 381, 419, 420, 421, 422, 423, 424, 425, 426, 427, 428, 429, 449, 450, 451, 452, 453, 454, 455, 457, 458, 459, 462, 467, 481, 629, 630, 632, 633, 764; II: 38, 39, 40, 73, 87, 91, 93, 96, 97, 100, 219, 233, 275, 370, 477, 501, 568, 603, 659, 689, 701; III: 40, 272, 276, 339, 460, 462, 466, 531, 533, 534, 536, 537, 556, 558, 559, 560, 562, 563, 564, 565, 566, 567, 568, 569, 570, 571, 572, 573, 574, 575, 576, 578, 579, 580, 581, 582, 583, 585, 586, 593, 594, 596, 598, 599, 629; IV: 170, 173, 182, 186, 187, 188, 254, 571; V: xvii, 96, 113, 589.
Stuart, Ruben, (Orderly Sgt, Co B, 10th Battalion NCST, 2nd Hvy Art), IV: 333.
Stuart, William D., (Lt Col, 3rd Va.), I: 82, 89, 91, 93, 94, 95.
Stuart, William R., (Pvt, Co H, 14th Vols/24th NCST), V: 560.
Stuart's Maryland Raid, II: 87.
Stuart's Wharf, (nr Smithville), V: 403.
Stubbs, Jesse R., (Brig Gen), I: xiii.
Stubenville, Ky., III: 677.
Strudevant, ______, II: 515.

Sturdivant, Caswell H., (Capt, Co K, 43rd NCST), III: 2, 3.
Sturdivant, William A., (Pvt, Co E, 4th Vols/14th NCST), V: 490.
Styers, B.B., (Pvt, Co I, 3rd Vols/13th NCST), I: 659.
Styron, D.C., (2nd Lt, Co I, 4th NCST), I: 233, 270; V: 664.
Sublett's Ford, Va., I: 573.
Subsistence Department, N.C., I: 37.
Sudderth, C.F., (Pvt, Co F, 26th NCST), V: 532.
Sudderth, Charles M., (1st Lt, Co F, 26th NCST), II: 358, 371, 372, 396, 397; V: 602.
Sudderth, J.G., (Jr 2nd Lt, Co I, 26th NCST), II: 372, 397.
Sudderth, James W., (Lt, Co A, 12th Vols/22nd NCST), II: 165.
Sudderth, John M., (Pvt, Co F, 26th NCST), V: 603.
Sudderth, John R., (Capt, AQM, 33rd NCST), II: 537; IV: 474.
Sudderth, T.F., (Pvt, Co F, 26th NCST), V: 603.
Sudley's Ford, (Bull Run Creek), I: 223; II: 30, 31; IV: 162, 163.
Sudley Road, (nr Manassas, Va.), V: 582, 583, 584, 585.
Suffolk, Va., I: 158, 398, 578, 587, 628, 654, 737; III: 4, 130, 167, 291, 293-294, 458; IV: 74, 92, 441, 488, 573; V: 83, 84.
Suffolk, Capture of, (1864), III: 133, 134.
Suffolk, Siege of, (1863), I: 495, 522, 523, 578; II: 88, 228, 280, 281, 522, 616, 775, 785; III: 4, 211, 335, 336, 458; IV: 92, 357, 488.
Sugar Loaf, N.C., I: 409, 410, 582; II: 518, 638, 639, 640, 641, 802; III: 215, 693, 694; IV: 39, 40, 43, 45, 47, 49, 50, 222, 268, 426, 427, 497, 539, 541, 542, 693; V: 217, 222, 225, 227.
Sugar Loaf Landing, N.C., II: 18.
Sugg, John, (Pvt, Co C, 47th NCST), V: 534.
Sugg, Josiah T., (Hospital Steward, 5th Vols/15th NCST), I: 734; V: 520.
Suggs, John H., (Musician, Co C, 27th NCST), II: 462; V: 523.
Suggs, R.S., (2nd Lt, Co I, 5th Vols/15th NCST), I: 735.
Suits, G.W., (Pvt, Co I, 3rd Vols/13th NCST), V: 551.
Sulavin, John B., (Pvt, Co A, 2nd Battalion NCST), V: 495.
Sullivan, A.M., (Lt, Co C, 51st NCST), III: 219.
Sullivan, H.F., (Pvt, Co K, 45th NCST), V: 501.
Sullivan, Henry, (Pvt, Co A, 38th NCST), V: 557.
Sullivan, Thomas, [Sutherland, Thomas H.], (Pvt, Co A, 65th NCST, 6th Cav), III: 680.
Sullivan, William H., (Pvt, Co I, 4th Vols/14th NCST), V: 491.
Sullivan's Island, S.C., I: 392, 395; II: 514, 515; III: 209, 510, 511; IV: 66, 485, 486; V: 620, 622.
Sully, Ed, (Lt, McGregor's Battery), I: 460.
Sulphur Springs, N.C., II: 486.
Summerel, Burt T., (Musician, 55th NCST), V: 527.
Summers, ______, [John F.], (1st Lt, Co E, 49th NCST), III: 148.
Summers, A., (Maj, 4th Regt Home Guard; Maj, 1st Regt Third Class Home Guard), V: 630, 631.
Summers, A.L., (Cpl, Co H, 4th NCST), I: 233.
Summers, James A., (Capt, Co A, 33rd NCST), II: 538, 578, 579.
Summers, Julius A., (1st Lt, Co H, 4th NCST), I: 233, 272.

Summers, N.C., (Pvt, Co C, 4th NCST; AQMS, 4th NCST; Detailed, Medical Purveyor's Dept), V: 488, 572.
Summers, P., (Pvt, Co K, 3rd Vols/13th NCST), V: 551.
Summers, Peter H., (Pvt, Co E, 27th NCST), II: 462.
Summers, Thomas, (Pvt, Co C, 4th NCST), V: 488.
Summerow, H.M., (Cpl, Co H, 52nd NCST), V: 536.
Summerow, P.W., (Pvt, Co I, 26th NCST), V: 532.
Summerson, William A., (1st Lt, Co H, 52nd NCST), III: 225.
Summey, Albert T., (Resident of Asheville), IV: 112.
Summey, D.F., (AQM, 6th Vols/16th NCST), I: 751; IV: 138.
Summey, Dr. Daniel F., (Surg, N.C.), IV: 629.
Summit, Va., II: 679.
Sumner, ______, [William T., Cpl], (Sgt, Color-bearer, Co F, 27th NCST), II: 442.
Sumner, A., (Maj, 4th Regt Home Guard), IV: 650.
Sumner, Benjamin H., (ACS, 38th NCST), II: 676, 678, 681.
Sumner, Ed E., (1st Lt, Co D, 1st NCST), I: 78, 114, 120, 136.
Sumner, Edwin Vose, (Maj Gen, USA), I: 186, 617; II: 602.
Sumner, N.N., (2nd Lt, Co A, Millard's 9th/20th Battalion Junior Reserves), IV: 386.
Sumner, R.R., (Farrier, Co H, 7th NCST), IV: 711.
Sumpter County, S.C., III: 684.
Sumter, S.C., IV: 614.
Sumterville, S.C., III: 191.
Surgeon-General, CSA, II: 360.
Surratt, ______, (Capt, 73rd NCST, 4th Senior Reserves), IV: 66.
Surrender, Johnston's, IV: 32, 62.
Surrender, Last, V: 653.
Surrender, Lee's, III: 284; V: 247, 257.
Surry County, N.C., III: 259, 264; IV: 218, 258, 387, 760; V: 285, 633.
Surry of the Eagle's Nest, I: 668.
Susquehanna River, Pa., I: 311.
Suther, G.W., (Pvt, Co C, 33rd NCST), V: 544.
Sutherland's Depot, Va., (aka Station or Tavern), I: 155, 209, 748; II: 391, 455; IV: 509.
Suttle, D.D., (2nd Lt, Co I, 38th NCST), IV: 701, 711.
Suttle, G.W., (1st Lt, Co B, Millard's 9th/20th Battalion Junior Reserves), IV: 386.
Sutton, Benjamin, (Pvt, Co C, 38th NCST), II: 690; V: 557.
Sutton, Daniel M., (Cpl, Co K, 8th Vols/18th NCST), II: 64; V: 540.
Sutton, J.M., (Capt, Co A, 53rd NCST), III: 261, 264.
Sutton, John, (Pvt, Co D, 6th Vols/16th NCST), V: 552.
Sutton, John M., (Capt, Co C, Moore's 3rd Battalion NCST; Capt, Co C, 10th NCST, 1st Art & Engs), I: 119; III: 264; IV: 262; V: 42, 240.
Sutton, Joseph, (Pvt, Co A, 6th Vols/16th NCST), I: 767.
Sutton, Lewis, (Pvt, Co C, 38th NCST), V: 557.
Sutton, Louis B., (Capt, Co F, 59th NCST), I: 119, 133; III: 457; IV: 702, 711.
Sutton, Richard, (Pvt, Co C, 27th NCST), II: 462; V: 523.
Sutton, Stark Armistead, (1st Lt, Adjt, 44th NCST; ADC to Pettigrew), I: 110, 118; III: 22; IV: 556.
Sutton, Thomas N., (Pvt, Co I, 8th Vols/18th NCST), II: 65, 66, 69, 70, 77, 551.

Sutton, William, (Capt, Co A, 40th NCST, 3rd Art, Hvy), II: 745, 748.
Sutton, William M., (Capt, Co F, 68th NCST), III: 714.
Sutton, Dr. William T., (Ass't Surg, 11th Vols/21st NCST; Surg, 44th NCST; Surg, Howard Grove Hospital, Richmond; Surg, Early's Corps), III: 22; IV: 629, 635, 638; V: 511.
Swain County, N.C., III: 730, 753, 757, 759; IV: 122, 126.
Swain, D.L., (Governor, N.C.), I: 55, 56, 57; II: 722; III: 375, 456; IV: 748.
Swain, J.B., (Pvt, Co G, 6th Battalion/60th NCST), III: 482.
Swain, John L., (Capt, Co E, 7th Vols/17th NCST), II: 2.
Swain, J.R., (2nd Lt, Co C, 30th NCST), II: 496.
Swain, J.S., (Lt, Co G, 2nd Battalion NCST), IV: 245.
Swain, M., (Pvt, Co H, 54th NCST), V: 516.
Swain, William, (Capt, Co G, 36th NCST, 2nd Art & Engs, Lamb-Potter-Swain's Battery), II: 634; V: 239.
Swallow, ______, (Col, USA), V: 153.
Swan, Dr. ______, (Surg, Advance), V: 341.
Swan Point, N.C., (Pamlico River), II: 749.
Swann, W.M., (Capt, Co H, 30th NCST), II: 496.
Swannanoa, N.C., IV: 386.
Swannanoa Gap, N.C., IV: 375; V: 654.
Swannanoa River, N.C., III: 474, 497, 760.
Swearengain, E.S., (3rd Sgt, Co I, 52nd NCST), V: 536.
Swearinger, W.F., (Pvt, Co K, 28th NCST), V: 543.
Sweetman, ______, (Capt, 2nd Engineers), IV: 418, 430.
Sweezy, H.A.L., (1st Lt, Co I, 56th NCST), I: 766, 772; III: 316, 317, 321, 378.
Sweezy, J.H., (1st Lt, Co I, 56th NCST), I: 766; III: 316.
Swepson, Mr. ______, (Resident of Haw River), I: 59.
Swift, J.W., (Pvt, Co C, 11th Vols/21st NCST), V: 514.
Swift Creek, N.C., I: 209; IV: 81.
Swift Creek, Va., II: 264, 533, 797; III: 15, 135, 139, 162, 351, 359; IV: 489, 529.
Swift Creek, Camp at, I: 14.
Swift Run Gap, Va., II: 131.
Swindell, Alvin, (Pvt, Detached Co, 68th NCST), III: 723.
Swindell, E.S., (Capt, Detached Co, 68th NCST), III: 723; IV: 402.
Swindell, John, (Pvt, Detached Co, 68th NCST), III: 723.
Swindell, Joseph, (2nd Lt, Co F, 33rd NCST), II: 539, 578.
Swindell, William M.B., (Capt, Co H, 33rd NCST), II: 540, 551.
Swing, John H., (Pvt, Co I, 4th Vols/14th NCST), V: 491.
Swink, D.B., (Lt, Co H, 28th NCST), II: 484.
Swink, George B., (Color-bearer, 57th NCST), III: 421.
Swinson, [Swinton], ______, (Historian), II: 173, 174, 368, 782, 783; III: 533.
Swinson, J.E., (Lt, Co B, 51st NCST), III: 218.
Swinson, Robert J., (2nd Lt, Co H, 66th NCST), III: 686.
Sycamore Church, Va., III: 622, 623, 625.
Sycamore Street, (Petersburg, Va.), I: 678; III: 366.
Sykes, Francis B., (2nd Lt, Co G, 68th NCST), III: 714.

Sykes, George, (Maj Gen, USA), I: 615; II: 210; III: 575.
Sykes, J.J., (Pvt, Co G, 28th NCST), V: 542.
Sykes, John P., (Capt, Co K, 66th NCST), III: 686.
Sykes, T.N., (Pvt, Co D, 54th NCST), V: 516.
Sykesville, Pa., I: 425.
Symons, James V., (Lt Col, 76th NCST, 6th Senior Reserves), IV: 97.

(T)

Tabb Street Presbyterian Church, (Petersburg, Va.), IV: 603.
Tabor, W.K., (Lt, Co E, 64th NCST), III: 660.
Taft, Godfrey E., (2nd Lt, Co E, 55th NCST), III: 296; V: 520.
Taft's Store, N.C., III: 507.
Tah-le-quah, (Capital of the Cherokee Nation), IV: 126.
Tait, George, (Maj, 8th Vols/18th NCST; Lt Col, 40th NCST, 3rd Art, Hvy; Col, 79th NCST, 8th Cav; Col, 69th NCST), II: 16, 17, 20, 745, 746, 759; IV: 115.
Tait, J.C., (1st Lt, Co F, 41st NCST, 3rd Cav), II: 771.
Tait, Robert, (Capt, ACS, 8th Vols/18th NCST), II: 16, 20; IV: 473.
Talbert, ______, (Resident of Alexander Co.), V: 293.
Talbert, T.F., (Pvt, Co E, 43rd NCST), V: 498.
Talcott, T.M.R., (Col, 1st Engineers, CSA), IV: 427.
Taliaferro, William Booth, (Maj Gen), II: 29, 472, 655, 684; III: 194, 197, 209, 210; V: 162, 163, 165, 167.
Taliaferro's Mill, Va., II: 21, 469, 470.
Tall Tower, (nr Petersburg, Va.), I: 328.
Talley, Martin VanBuren, (Capt, Co E, 6th Battalion NCST), IV: 297.
Talley, V., (Fayetteville and Harper's Ferry Arsenals), IV: 298.
Talley's Mill, (nr Spottsylvania, Va.), III: 305.
Tally, Rev. ______, (Chaplain, 39th NCST), IV: 614.
Tally, F.W., (Sgt, Co D, 28th NCST), V: 541.
Tally, S.J., (2nd Lt, Co E, 44th NCST), III: 23.
Tally, W.M., (Pvt, Co E, 44th NCST), V: 533.
Talton, T.R., (Sgt, Co I, 35th NCST), V: 563.
Tamplin, Thomas H., (Capt, Co A, 68th NCST), III: 713.
Tankersley, Felix, (1st Lt, Co F, 37th NCST), II: 670.
Taney, J.B., (Ensign, USN; Pioneer, Tacony), V: 245.
Tanner, Dr. ______, [Isaac S.], (Surg, 11th Vols/21st NCST), II: 149.
Tanner, C.P., (3rd Lt, Co I, 56th NCST), III: 317, 357, 396.
Tanner, Thomas, (Pvt, Co A, 1st Battalion NCST), V: 504.
Tansell, ______, (Col, IG, District of Cape Fear), II: 759.
Tansill, Robert, (Col, 2nd Va, Hvy Art), II: 679; IV: 49.
Tapley, Mark, IV: 715.
Tapping, Samuel, (2nd Lt, Co C, 44th NCST), III: 23.
"Tar Heel," (Name used by Maj J.W. Graham in an article in the Fayetteville Observer to describe the men of North Carolina.), V: 188.

Tar Heels, III: 376-377.
Tar River, N.C., I: 321, 498, 511, 533, 535, 539; II: 773; III: 40, 88, 172, 349; IV: 74, 75, 77, 82, 83, 415, 430; V: 270, 271, 280.
Tarber, W.K., (Lt, 64th NCST), IV: 711.
Tarboro, N.C., I: 102, 273, 323, 399, 492, 495, 497, 498, 511, 523, 524, 527, 532, 533, 535, 554, 577, 578, 673; II: 278, 279, 338, 339, 513, 748, 793, 797; III: 24, 117, 173, 177, 178, 179, 199, 210, 319, 320, 337, 339, 506, 681, 687, 709, 720; IV: 15, 16, 17, 27, 44, 77, 79, 80, 90, 92, 312, 353, 358, 415, 620; V: 177, 271.
Tarboro Railroad, III: 507.
Tralton, J.B., (Pvt, Co K, 43rd NCST), V: 499.
Tarpky, J.H., (Sgt, Co K, 47th NCST), V: 535.
Tart, John, (Pvt, Co B, 56th NCST), III: 356.
Tart, L.L., (Pvt, Co B, 56th NCST), III: 366.
Tate, Dr. Hugh W., (Ass't Surg, 54th NCST), IV: 640.
Tate, J.C., (1st Lt, Co F, 41st NCST, 3rd Cav), II: 771.
Tate, J.M., (1st Lt, Co C, 62nd NCST; Capt, AQM, Wilcox's Division), I: 584; III: 515, 525; IV: 700, 711; V: 537.
Tate, John N., (AQM, 1st Vols/11th NCST), I: 583, 584.
Tate, Joseph W., (2nd Lt, Co F, 33rd NCST), II: 539, 578.
Tate, Junius C., (Capt, Co E, 5th Battalion NCST, Cav; Co G, 65th NCST, 6th Cav), III: 675, 684; IV: 271.
Tate, Robert A., (1st Lt, Co B, 12th Vols/22nd NCST), II: 165, 171.
Tate, Samuel McDowell, (Lt Col, 6th NCST), I: 296, 313, 317, 354, 358; III: 281, 423; IV: 271, 661; V: 593, 635.
Tate, Samuel P., (1st Lt, Co B, 12th Vols/22nd NCST), II: 165, 171, 178; V: 548.
Tate, W.G., (Pvt, Co K, 3rd Vols/13th NCST), V: 551.
Tate, Dr. W.H., (Ass't Surg, 54th NCST), III: 268.
Tate, W.J., (Sgt, Co H, 16th Battalion/75th NCST, 7th Cav), V: 660.
Tatem, ______, (Capt, 1st S.C.), V: 162.
Tatham, Lee B., (Capt, Co D, 25th NCST), II: 292.
Tatham, P.A., (Capt, Co F, 9th Vols/19th NCST, 2nd Cav), IV: 711.
Tatum, ______, (Capt, 1st S.C.), III: 207.
Tatum, M.N., [M.M.], (Sgt, Co A, 8th Vols/18th NCST), II: 63; V: 539.
Tatum, P.A., (Capt, Co F, 9th Vols/19th NCST, 2nd Cav), II: 80, 89, 93; IV: 702, 711.
Tatum, W.C., (1st Lt, Co E, Walker's Battalion, Thomas' Legion, 80th NCST), IV: 118.
"Tax in Kind," V: x.
Tay River, (nr Spottsylvania, Va.), IV: 193.
Tayloe, Langley, (Capt, Co E, 68th NCST), III: 714.
Taylor, ______, (Negro servant to Lt W.P. Taylor, shot by a Yankee), III: 719.
Taylor, ______, (Capt, Wynn's 15th Battalion NCST, Cav), IV: 365.
Taylor, ______, (Pvt, Co F, 4th NCST), I: 258.
Taylor, ______, (Midshipman, NCN; Capt, Fanny), V: 305, 307.
Taylor, A., (Pvt, Co K, 33rd NCST), V: 545.
Taylor, A.A., (Musician, 3rd Vols/13th NCST), V: 549.
Taylor, A.A., (Pvt, Co C, 32nd NCST), V: 496.

Taylor, A.J., (Capt, Co E, 7th NCST), I: 361.
Taylor, Absalom, (Cpl, Co K, 33rd NCST), II: 541.
Taylor, A. John, (Pvt, Co F, 26th NCST), V: 601.
Taylor, Alford P., (Pvt, Co G, 4th Vols/14th NCST), V: 490.
Taylor, B.H., (Pvt, Co B, 33rd NCST), V: 544.
Taylor, Benjamin, (Pvt, Co F, 26th NCST), V: 603.
Taylor, Cam H., (2nd Lt, Co B, Indian Co, 69th NCST, Thomas' Legion; 1st Lt, Co I, Indina Co, Walker's Battalion, Thomas' Legion, 80th NCST), III: 730; IV: 119, 126.
Taylor, Frank M., (Capt, Co B, 56th NCST), I: 119; V: 267.
Taylor, George William, (Brig Gen, USA), I: 370; II: 473.
Taylor, H., (1st Cpl, Co D, 44th NCST), V: 533.
Taylor, H.H., "Tip," (Capt, AAG, Thomas' Legion), III: 740.
Taylor, Henry S., (Sgt, Co K, 33rd NCST), II: 541.
Taylor, Hillary, (Capt, Co D, 68th NCST), III: 714, 716.
Taylor, Horatio, (Pvt, Co D, 68th NCST), III: 715.
Taylor, J.A., (Musician, Co G, 35th NCST), V: 563.
Taylor, J.H., (Lt, Adjt, 51st NCST), III: 220.
Taylor, J.M., (Capt, Co G; Maj, 5th NCST), I: 287, 289, 291; V: 503, 506.
Taylor, J.W., (Capt, Co K, 32nd NCST), I: 736.
Taylor, J.W., (Musician, 16th Battalion/75th NCST, 7th Cav), V: 660.
Taylor, Jacob W., (Capt, Co B, 9th Battalion NCST, 1st Hvy Art), II: 651; IV: 303, 305, 312.
Taylor, James, (Capt, Co B, Indian Co, 69th NCST, Thomas' Legion), III: 730.
Taylor, James M., (1st Lt, Co F, 62nd NCST), III: 516.
Taylor, John Douglas, (Lt Col, 36th NCST, 2nd Art & Engs), II: 630, 650, 651; III: 709; IV: 304, 306, 311, 312; V: 650.
Taylor, John J., (Color-Sgt, Co E, 53rd NCST), III: 259.
Taylor, John L., (Pvt, Co I, 45th NCST), V: 500.
Taylor, John T., (Capt, Co B, 2nd Vols/12th NCST), I: 620.
Taylor, John W., (Capt, Co C, 9th Battalion NCST, 1st Hvy Art), IV: 306.
Taylor, Joseph W., (2nd Lt, Claiborne-Dearing's 7th C.S. Cav; 16th Battalion/75th NCST, 7th Cav), IV: 91.
Taylor, K.B., (Pvt, Co E, 24th NCST), V: 193.
Taylor, K.R., (Sgt Maj, 3rd NCST), V: 487.
Taylor, Leander F., (Pvt, Co I, 6th Vols/16th NCST), V: 552.
Taylor, Lewis G., (Pvt, Co F, 2nd NCST), I: 176; V: 486.
Taylor, Lewellyn, (Pvt, Co D, 56th NCST), III: 347.
Taylor, M.F., (Capt, Co B, 2nd Vols/12th NCST), I: 620, 639; V: 267.
Taylor, Marble Nash, (A pretender to the head of state of North Carolina. Taylor was allegedly "elected" to the position of Governor by citizens of thirty eastern counties. Although he nor they had any legal authority to hold elections for any office, most especially for the governorship of the state, Taylor attempted to claim his position under the protection of

Burnside and his invasion forces. The so-called governor and his administration were eventually rejected in Washington and the strange episode in the attempted usurpation of political authority ended a quick and natural death.), II: 631.
Taylor, Mark P., (Cpl, Co K, 33rd NCST), II: 541.
Taylor, Matthew P., (Maj, 6th Battalion NCST, Fayetteville Armory Guard), IV: 293, 294, 297, 298, 299.
Taylor, Rev. N.G., (Scalawag from Tenn., Father of Governor Robert Taylor), III: 734.
Taylor, P.C., (Pvt, Co E, 43rd NCST), V: 498.
Taylor, Richard, "Dick," (Lt Gen), II: 492, 551, 721.
Taylor, Richard P., (Capt, Co G, 30th NCST), II: 495.
Taylor, Robert "Bob," (Governor of Tennessee), III: 734.
Taylor, S., (Pvt, Co G, 56th NCST), III: 348.
Taylor, S.B., (Lt Col, 35th NCST), II: 613, 623, 626, 627; V: 190, 193.
Taylor, Silvester, (Lt, Co I, 2nd NCST), I: 163.
Taylor, Spottswood B., (Capt, Co H, 53rd NCST), III: 263, 265.
Taylor, T.J., (Pvt, Co G, 11th Vols/21st NCST), V: 515.
Taylor, T.W., (1st Lt, Co B, 70th NCST, 1st Junior Reserves), IV: 12.
Taylor, Thomas, (Pvt, Co D, 56th NCST), V: 566.
Taylor, Thomas, (Lt, Co K, 47th NCST), III: 85.
Taylor, Thomas E., (Englishman, Capt, Blockade Runner), V: 414, 416, 417.
Taylor, Thomas J., (Pvt, Co D, 56th NCST), III: 347.
Taylor, Thomas T., Taylor, (Pvt, Co D, 68th NCST), III: 715.
Taylor, Travis J., (Pvt, Co D, 68th NCST), III: 715.
Taylor, Walter H., (AG, ANV), I: 399, 541; II: 399, 517; III: 594; IV: 367; V: 130.
Taylor, W.R., (Capt, USN), V: 242.
Taylor, William, IV: 700.
Taylor, William, (Pvt, Co C, 68th NCST), III: 726.
Taylor, William B., (Capt, Co A, 1st Vols/11th NCST), I: 119, 123, 133, 584; V: 529.
Taylor, William P., (2nd Lt, Co D, 68th NCST), III: 714, 719.
Taylor, William S., (1st Lt, Co K, 33rd NCST), II: 541.
Taylor, William T., (Capt, Co B, 56th NCST), I: 119; III: 314, 318, 393.
Taylor's Ferry, N.C., III: 135.
Taylor's Ford, (Watauga River, Tenn.), III: 740.
Taylorsville, Tenn., I: 288, 640; II: 120, 240, 241, 470; III: 25, 71, 234; IV: 374, 375; V: 285.
Teachey, Daniel, (2nd Lt, Co E, 30th NCST), II: 496; IV: 600.
Teachey's Depot, N.C., II: 762.
Teague, A.A., (Musician, 46th NCST), V: 524.
Teague, E., (Pvt, Co C, 33rd NCST), V: 544.
Teague, J.A., (Pvt, Co I, 26th NCST), V: 532.
Teague, John A., (2nd Lt, Co E, 29th NCST), II: 485, 488, 493; V: 18.
Teague, M.M., (Capt, Co F, 46th NCST), III: 81.
Teague, Samuel E., (Lt, Co C, 26th NCST), II: 397.
Teague, Vandevere, (Capt, Co H, 55th NCST), III: 287.

Teal, T.H., (Pvt, Co I, 53rd NCST), V: 502.
Teal, W.E., (Pvt, Co D, 3rd NCST), V: 487.
Teal, W.J., (Pvt, Co D, 14th Vols/24th NCST), V: 560.
Tecumseh, (Creek Indian Chief), III: 740.
Telegraph Bridge, (Chickahominy River, Va.), II: 547.
Telegraph Road, (nr Fredericksburg, Va.), I: 742; II: 438; III: 129.
Telfain House, Ga., III: 185.
Telford's Depot, Tenn., III: 739.
Temple, Judge O.P., (Tenn.), IV: 124.
Temple, R.F., (ACS Sgt, 47th NCST), V: 534.
Temple, William G., (Lt Cmdr, USN), V: 243.
Templeton, John Y., (Lt, Co G, 7th NCST), I: 377, 378, 385.
Templeton, Sim, (Yorkshireman, Jockey), V: 418.
Ten Mile House, N.C., II: 82, 83, 87.
Tennent, James A., (Lt, Ass't Engineer, Topographical Corps), IV: 425.
Tennent, Rev. John C., (Chaplain, 32nd NCST), IV: 612; V: 494.
Tennessee, (and East Tennessee), I: 7, 21, 41, 72, 557, 766, 767; II: 15, 367, 415, 486, 491, 700, 701, 707, 710, 712, 731, 735; III: 491, 501, 517, 519, 521, 659, 661, 664, 665, 673, 674, 676-677, 713, 719, 729, 733, 734, 735, 737, 738, 739, 742, 744, 746, 755, 757; IV: 1, 35, 111, 114, 119, 120, 121, 122, 123, 124, 125, 126, 127, 218, 272, 275, 276, 290, 301, 371, 372, 374, 375, 380, 387, 404, 439, 572, 618, 619, 651; V: 7, 285.
Tennessee Abandoned, III: 738.
Tennessee River, II: 710; III: 438, 494, 500, 678, 757, 758; IV: 122, 123, 126, 290, 291.
Tennessee Valley, East, II: 706.
Tenth Legion, Va., II: 258.
Terceira Island, V: 415.
Terrell, ______, (Capt, AAG, Laws' Brigade), III: 291, 292, 293.
Terrell, J.H., (2nd Lt, Co I, 1st NCST), I: 137.
Terrell, J.M., (Lt, Co C, 10th Battalion NCST, 2nd Hvy Art), IV: 330, 332.
Terrell, James W., (AQM, 69th NCST, Thomas' Legion), III: 730, 732.
Terrell, Jefferson, (Pvt, Co B, 59th NCST, 4th Cav), V: 659.
Terrell, John, (Pvt, Co C, 49th NCST), V: 564.
Terrell, Jospeh, (Pvt, Co B, 59th NCST, 4th Cav), V: 659.
Terrell, T.T., (Capt, Co G, 5th Vols/15th NCST), I: 735.
Terrell, William S., (Capt, 39th NCST), II: 728.
Terrell, William S., (1st Lt, Co A, Indina Co, 69th NCST, Thomas' Legion), III: 730.
Terry, Rev. ______, (Passenger, Advance), V: 341, 343.
Terry, Alfred Howe, (Maj Gen, USA), I: 531; II: 643, 647; III: 694; IV: 308, 353, 541, 542, 543, 547, 590, 591; V: 237, 241, 270, 396.
Terry, B.M., (Pvt, Co F, 33rd NCST), V: 544.
Terry, Ephraim B., (4th Cpl, Co K, 52nd NCST), III: 225.
Terry, J.C., (Pvt, Co D, 2nd Vols/12th NCST), V: 507.
Terry, J.D., (Pvt, Co H, 3rd Vols/13th NCST), V: 551.
Terry, S.W., (Lt, USN, ADC), V: 242.
Terry, Stephen O., (Cpl, Co K, 9th Vols/19th NCST, 2nd Cav), II: 96.

Terry, T.L., (Pvt, Co B, 46th NCST), V: 524.
Terry, William Richard, (Brig Gen), I: 283; II: 616; III: 337; V: 175, 191.
Tesh, George W., (Pvt, Co H, 5th Vols/15th NCST), V: 522.
Tessenear, Jack, (Pvt, Co I, 56th NCST), III: 356.
Tessenear, Joe, (Pvt, Co I, 56th NCST), III: 356.
Tester, Joseph, (Pvt, Co D, 59th NCST, 4th Cav), V: 659.
Tew, Charles Courtenay, (Col, 2nd NCST), I: 126, 157, 158, 160, 167, 168, 215, 245, 246, 248, 500; II: 499, 500, 753; V: 9, 35, 78, 629, 637-641.
Tew, J.J., (Lt, Co K, 51st NCST), III: 220.
Tew, Newberne, (Pvt, Co I, 10th Vols/20th NCST), II: 119.
Tew's Military School, (See: Hillsboro Military Academy).
Texarkana, Ark., I: 549.
Texas, I: 70, 178; II: 331, 493, 724; III: 683, 733; IV: 618; V: 454.
Thacker, Isaac, (Pvt, Co H, 45th NCST), V: 500.
Thaggard, W.C., (Pvt, Co H, 46th NCST), V: 525.
Thames River, England, V: 438.
Tharington, Willis, (Pvt, Co E, 5th Vols/15th NCST), V: 521.
Thatcher, Henry K., (Commodore, USN), V: 242.
Thaxton, Henry S., (2nd Lt, Co B, 59th NCST, 4th Cav), III: 457.
Thayer, N.M., (Pvt, Co B, 37th NCST), V: 545.
Thereof, ______, (Officer, Shenandoah), V: 345.
Therrill, William, (Pvt, Co A, 48th NCST), V: 526.
Thigpen, ______, (Chaplain, 6th Ga.), IV: 601.
Thigpen, Andrew M., (1st Lt, Co C, 44th NCST), III: 23.
Thigpen, James R., (Capt, Co E, 43rd NCST), III: 2, 3.
Thigpen, Kenneth, (Jr 2nd Lt, Co A, 1st Vols, "Bethel"), I: 113, 129.
Thigpen, L., (Pvt, Co H, 59th NCST, 4th Cav), V: 659.
"Thin Gray Line of Tar Heels, The" V: 213.
Third Street, (Plymouth), V: 176, 185, 186.
Thom, Joel J., (Sgt, Co B, 27th NCST), II: 461; V: 523.
Thomas, ______, [James], (Pvt, Co C, 49th NCST), III: 148.
Thomas, ______, (Capt, CSN, Chief Officer, The Lady Davis), V: 408.
Thomas, Abel, (Pvt, Co A, 7th Vols/17th NCST), II: 13.
Thomas, Andrew J., (Jr 1st Lt, Co K, 10th NCST, 1st Art & Engs, Sparrow-Blount's Battery Hvy Art), I: 501; V: 43, 46.
Thomas, Dr. B.S., (Ass't Surg, 4th NCST), I: 230; IV: 632.
Thomas, Bryan, (Pvt, Co A, 38th NCST), V: 557.
Thomas, Dr. C.A., (Surg, 56th NCST), III: 318, 321; IV: 640.
Thomas, Calvin, (Pvt, Co K, 26th NCST), V: 533.
Thomas, Charles H., (Capt, AQM, 5th Vols/15th NCST), I: 734; V: 520.
Thomas, Columbus A., (Capt, Co E, 9th Vols/19th NCST, 2nd Cav), II: 80.
Thomas, Daniel, (Pvt, Color-bearer, 26th NCST), II: 366, 374.
Thomas, Edward Lloyd, (Brig Gen), I: 380; II: 35, 36, 478, 555, 565, 683, 684; IV: 196, 197.
Thomas, F.E., (2nd Lt, Co A, 6th Battalion Junior Reserves; Co C, 70th NCST, 1st Junior Reserves), IV: 13.

Thomas, G.W., (Pvt, Co K, 5th Vols/15th NCST), V: 522.
Thomas, George Henry, (Maj Gen, USA), I: 768; II: 715; IV: 125; V: 172.
Thomas, H., (Pvt, Co B, 53rd NCST), V: 501.
Thomas, Isaac H., (Sgt, Co H, 4th NCST), V: 489.
Thomas, H.T., (Pvt, Co H, 30th NCST), V: 493.
Thomas, J.F., (Pvt, Co H, 3rd Vols/13th NCST), V: 551.
Thomas, J.F., (Pvt, Co B, 28th NCST), V: 541.
Thomas, J.H., (Cpl, Co H, 43rd NCST), V: 499.
Thomas, J.J., (Lt, AQM, 47th NCST), III: 84.
Thomas, J.M., (Pvt, Co L, 12th Vols/22nd NCST), V: 554.
Thomas, J.P., (Col, S.C.), V: 638.
Thomas, James, (Pvt, Co K, 6th NCST), V: 514.
Thomas, James H., (Pvt, Co D, 27th NCST), II: 462; V: 523.
Thomas, John W., (Pvt, Co H, 43rd NCST), V: 499.
Thomas, L., (Pvt, Co G, 45th NCST), V: 500.
Thomas, L.A., (Pvt, Co F, 26th NCST), II: 374.
Thomas, Marion, [Toms, Marion C.], (Capt, Co A, 6th Battalion/60th NCST), III: 497.
Thomas, Moses, (Pvt, Co D, 42nd NCST), II: 799.
Thomas, N., (Pvt, Co E, 26th NCST), V: 532.
Thomas, R.W., (Capt, Co K, 55th NCST), III: 296, 302, 307.
Thomas, S.A., (Pvt, Co E, 26th NCST), V: 532, 603.
Thomas, S.J., [Jesse], (Pvt, Co C, 4th NCST), I: 232.
Thomas, S.M., (1st Lt, Co D, 46th NCST), III: 81.
Thomas, Stanhope, (AQMS, 48th NCST), V: 526.
Thomas, W.B., (Pvt, Co B, 28th NCST), V: 541.
Thomas, W.B., (Cpl, Co K, 30th NCST), V: 493.
Thomas, W.H., (Pvt, Co E, 56th NCST), III: 347.
Thomas, W.H., (Pvt, Co E, 35th NCST), V: 563.
Thomas, W.Y., (Pvt, Co H, 3rd Vols/13th NCST), V: 551.
Thomas, William, (Pvt, Co A, 38th NCST), V: 557.
Thomas, Dr. William George, (Quarantine Physician, Wilmington), V: 368.
Thomas, William H., (Col, 69th NCST, Thomas' Legion), III: 729, 730, 732, 735, 738, 739, 745, 761; IV: 121, 122, 124, 128; V: 655.
Thomas, William J., (2nd Lt, Co E, 56th NCST), III: 315.
Thomas, Wilson, (Pvt, Co K, 26th NCST), V: 533.
Thomas' Legion, (aka Thomas' Legion of Indians and Highlanders; See also: 69th and 80th Regiments), I: 13, 15, 766; III: 729-761; IV: 117-128, 380, 437, 439; V: 655.
Thomason, B., (Pvt, Co H, 37th NCST), V: 546.
Thomason, C.R., (Pvt, Co E, 46th NCST), V: 524.
Thomason, James, (Pvt, 24th Va.), V: 195.
Thomasson, W.A., (Pvt, Co D, 43rd NCST), V: 498.
Thompson, ______, [Thomas P.], (Capt, Co G, 5th NCST), I: 282.
Thompson, A.A., (Pvt, Co F, 6th NCST), V: 513.
Thompson, Messrs., (Shipbuilders of Glasgow), V: 419.
Thompson, A.J., (Pvt, Co D, 8th Vols/18th NCST), II: 64.

Thompson, A.M., (Lt, Co H, 51st NCST), III: 220.
Thompson, D., (Pvt, Co G, 43rd NCST), V: 498.
Thompson, D., (Pvt, Co H, 56th NCST), III: 348.
Thompson, D.S., (1st Lt, Co H, 5th Vols/15th NCST), I: 735; V: 519.
Thompson, David A., (1st Sgt, Co D, 38th NCST), II: 690.
Thompson, David J., (Pvt, Co G, 55th NCST), V: 528.
Thompson, E., (Pvt, Co G, 46th NCST), V: 525.
Thompson, E.T., (1st Lt, Co A, 28th NCST), IV: 702, 711.
Thompson, Eugene W., (Chaplain, 43rd NCST), III: 1; IV: 614; V: 494.
Thompson, Frederick, (Capt, Co E, 8th Vols/18th NCST), II: 20.
Thompson, G.A., (Pvt, Co A, 63rd NCST, 5th Cav), III: 577.
Thompson, George A., (Pvt, Co F, 6th NCST), V: 513.
Thompson, George, (Pvt, Co D, 34th NCST), V: 555.
Thompson, George S., (Capt, AQM, 28th NCST; QM, Branch-Lane's Brigade), II: 465; IV: 472, 473.
Thompson, George W., (Resident of Wake County), I: 711.
Thompson, George W., (1st Lt, Co K, 68th NCST), III: 714.
Thompson, George W., (2nd Lt, Co A, 31st NCST), II: 512.
Thompson, Giles W., (Lt, Co E, 51st NCST), III: 209, 219.
Thompson, J., (Pvt, Co F, 33rd NCST), V: 544.
Thompson, J.A., (Pvt, Co F, 33rd NCST), V: 544.
Thompson, J.C., (Pvt, Co F, 26th NCST), V: 534, 603.
Thompson, J.W., (Pvt, Co A, 57th NCST), V: 517.
Thompson, Dr. Jacob, (Ass't Surg, 11th Vols/21st NCST), IV: 635.
Thompson, Jacob, (Inspector-General, Miss.), V: 649.
Thompson, Hon. Jacob, (Ass't Surg, 11th Vols/21st NCST), V: 649.
Thompson, James A., (1st Lt, Co F, 29th NCST), II: 485.
Thompson, James N., (5th Cpl, Co A, 10th NCST, 1st Art & Engs, Ramseur-Manly's Battery, Light Art), I: 551, 553.
Thompson, John, (Capt, 7th Conn.), V: 238.
Thompson, John F., (Pvt, Co G, 27th NCST), II: 462; V: 523.
Thompson, Joseph, (Pilot), V: 369.
Thompson, L.J., (Lt, Co F, 8th NCST), I: 401.
Thompson, Monroe, (Pvt, Co D, 61st NCST), III: 507.
Thompson, Marcellus, (Lt, ACS, 4th Vols/14th NCST), I: 711, 712.
Thompson, N., (Pvt, Co H, 46th NCST), V: 525.
Thompson, R.L., (Sgt, Co E, 47th NCST), V: 535.
Thompson, R.R., (Pvt, Co I, 12th Vols/22nd NCST), V: 554.
Thompson, S.A., (Sgt, Co H, 56th NCST), III: 356.
Thompson, S.T., (Lt, Co I, 28th NCST), II: 484; V: 538.
Thompson, Stephen, (Pvt, Co E, 52nd NCST), V: 536.
Thompson, T.F., (2nd Lt, Co F, 4th NCST), I: 233.
Thompson, T.H., (Pvt, Co G, 28th NCST), V: 542.
Thompson, T.J., (Pvt, Co B, 35th NCST), V: 562.
Thompson, Thomas B., (4th Sgt, Co G, 52nd NCST), III: 224.
Thompson, Thomas E., (2nd Lt, Co F, 4th NCST), I: 231, 271.
Thompson, Thomas M., (Pilot, Atlanta), V: 357.

Thompson, Dr. V.O., (2nd Lt, Co C; Ass't Surg, 46th NCST; Surg, Jenkins' Brigade), III: 65; IV: 639; V: 520.
Thompson, W.A., (2nd Lt, Co B, 13th Vols/23rd NCST), II: 183.
Thompson, W.A., (Sheriff, Wayne County; Capt, Co D, 62nd Ga., Cav; Co A, 16th Battalion/75th NCST, 7th C.S. Cav), IV: 72, 73, 77, 78, 91, 92.
Thompson, W.J., (Musician, 3rd Vols/13th NCST), V: 549.
Thompson, W.L., (Pvt, Co F, 26th NCST), V: 601.
Thompson, W.P., (Cpl, Co G, 44th NCST), V: 534.
Thompson, William, (Pvt, Co G, 27th NCST), II: 462; V: 523.
Thompson, William, (Pvt, Co H, 56th NCST), III: 348.
Thompson, William B., (Maj, 10th NCST, 1st Art & Engs), I: 500, 525, 536.
Thompson, William D., (1st Sgt, Co G, 52nd NCST), III: 224.
Thompson, William G., (2nd Lt, Co F, 3rd Vols/13th NCST), V: 547.
Thompson, William H., (Capt, Co C, 1st NCST), I: 136, 150, 151; V: 484.
Thompson, Willie, (Pvt, Co K, 27th NCST), II: 463; V: 524.
Thompson's Ford, (Rappahonock River, Va.), II: 90.
Thomson, B.T., (Pvt, Co C, 49th NCST), V: 564.
Thomson, T.L., (Pvt, Co C, 49th NCST), V: 564.
Thon, John T., (Pvt, Co C, 10th NCST; 1st Art & Engs, Berm-Graham-Williams' Battery, Light Art), V: 568.
Thornburg, J.L., (Pvt, Co B, 28th NCST), V: 541.
Thornburg, M.A., [Thorneburg, M.M.], (2nd Lt, Co C, 28th NCST), II: 483; V: 538.
Thornburg, W.L., (Capt, Co H, 38th NCST), II: 678, 680, 692.
Thorne, Edward A., (Lt, Ordnance Officer, Ransom's Brigade), IV: 570, 578; V: 5, 12.
Thornton, B.W., (2nd Lt, Co B, 56th NCST), I: 121; III: 344, 347; V: 189, 669.
Thornton, L.G., (Sgt Maj, 8th NCST), I: 387.
Thornton, R.W., (1st Lt, Co B, 56th NCST), I: 120; IV: 314, 701, 711; V: 669.
Thornton, S.C., (2nd Lt, Co I, 62nd Ga., Cav; 16th Battalion/75th NCST, 7th Cav), IV: 91.
Thornton, S.J., (Lt, Co G, 8th NCST), V: 194.
Thornton's Legion, (Ala.), III: 434.
Thoroughfare Gap, (Roanoke River nr Plymouth), V: 319.
Thoroughfare Gap, Va., I: 306; II: 30, 31, 133, 134, 334; III: 562; IV: 161; V: 676.
Thorp, R.S., (Pvt, Co C, 53rd NCST), V: 501.
Thorpe, A., (1st Lt, Co B, 70th NCST, 1st Junior Reserves), IV: 12.
Thorpe, John, (Pvt, Co A, 1st Vols, "Bethel"), I: 119, 127.
Thorpe, John H., [Thorp], (Capt, Co A, 47th NCST), I: 100, 101, 119, 127; II: 395; III: 83, 84, 100, 101; V: 529.
Thorpe, L., (Pvt, Co H, 4th NCST), V: 489.
Thorpe, Peterson, (Hospital Steward, 55th NCST), III: 288; V: 527.
Thorpe, S.C., (2nd Lt, Co C, 30th NCST), II: 496.
Thrailkill, W.J., (Musician, Co D, 35th NCST), V: 562.
Thrash, A.B., (Capt, Co I, 25th NCST), II: 292.
Thrash, P.H., (Capt, Co F, 6th Vols/16th NCST), I: 751; IV: 137.

Thrash, Patrick, (Capt, ACS, 62nd NCST), III: 515.
Threadgill, John H., (1st Lt, Co I, 43rd NCST), III: 3.
Threadgill, S.H., (Cpl, Co I, 43rd NCST), III: 18.
Threadgill, W.C., (Cpl, Co C, 4th Vols/14th NCST), I: 732.
Three Creeks, Va., III: 634.
Thruston, James, (CSMC), IV: 735, 737, 741, 739.
Thruston, Dr. Stephen D., (Capt, Smithville Guards, N.C. Militia; Col, 3rd NCST), I: 178, 184, 185, 187, 190, 191, 192, 198, 203, 207, 225, 226, 227, 459; IV: 459; V: 24, 25.
Tice, J., (Pvt, Co K, 43rd NCST), V: 499.
Tice, Solomon, (2nd Lt, Co G, 77th NCST, 7th Senior Reserves), IV: 100.
Tickle, W.R., (Pvt, Co M, 11th Vols/21st NCST), V: 515.
Tiddy, James, (1st Lt, Co E, 34th NCST), IV: 701, 711.
Tidwell, W.B., (Capt, Co A, 9th Vols/19th NCST, 2nd Cav), II: 89.
Tillery, Richard C., (1st Lt, Co F, 40th NCST, 3rd Art, Hvy), II: 746.
Tillett, Isaac N., (Lt, 1st Vols/11th NCST; Capt., Co G, 59th NCST, 4th Cav), I: 119; III: 457; IV: 702, 711.
Tilley, E.N., (Pvt, Co B, 6th NCST), V: 512.
Tillinghast, John Huske, (Chaplain, 26th NCST; Chaplain, 44th NCST), II: 396; III: 22, 702, 711; IV: 614.
Tilliison, Thomas, (Pvt, Co G, 11th Vols/21st NCST), V: 515.
Tilloston, W.R., (Pvt, Co I, 13th Vols/23rd NCST), V: 510.
Tilman, ______, (Pvt, Co E, Color-bearer, 44th NCST), III: 33, 34.
Tilman, George, (Pvt, Co E, 35th NCST), V: 563.
Tilson, J.E., (Lt, Co K, 64th NCST), III: 660.
Tilson, William E., (Capt, Co K, 64th NCST), III: 660.
Timberlake, ______, [John C., Lt Col], (Maj, 53rd Va.), V: 157.
Timberlake, G.W., (Resident of the Winchester area), II: 116.
Tinnen, O.B., (Pvt, Co G, 28th NCST), V: 542.
Tinnin, William J., (1st Sgt; ACS Sgt., 56th NCST), III: 370.
Tipton, Thomas G., (Pvt, Co B, 58th NCST), III: 450.
Tisdale, N.D., (Pvt, Co H, 2nd Vols/12th NCST), V: 507.
Tisdale, Thomas, (2nd Lt, Co I, 30th NCST), II: 497.
Titusville, Fla., IV: 615.
Tobey, F.A., [Toby], (Capt, Co A, 58th NCST), III: 432, 450, 452, 453.
Todd, Charles B., (Sgt Maj, 34th NCST), II: 582; V: 554.
Todd, David, (Pvt, Co H, 63rd NCST, 5th Cav), III: 587.
Todd, David L., (Pvt, Co G, 34th NCST), V: 556.
Todd, Daivd S., (Pvt, Co G, 34th NCST), V: 556.
Todd, Elliott, (Sgt, Co B, 2nd NCST), I: 175; V: 486.
Todd, J.B., (Lt, Co D, 9th NCST, 1st Cav), I: 485.
Todd, J.C., (Capt, Co G, 34th NCST), V: 548.
Todd, James E., (Capt, Co H, 31st NCST), II: 512.
Todd, John W., (Pvt, Co G, 34th NCST), V: 556.
Todd, Joseph W., (Lt, Co D, 9th NCST, 1st Cav), I: 485; III: 635.
Todd, L., (Pvt, Co D, 10th Vols/20th NCST), V: 508.
Todd, L.A., (2nd Lt, Co F, 28th NCST), V: 538.

Todd, Lawson N., (Pvt, Co G, 34th NCST), V: 556.
Todd, Moses, (Pvt, Co D, 68th NCST), III: 715.
Todd, R.J., (Pvt, Co I, 37th NCST), V: 546.
Todd, Simon, (Pvt, Co D, 68th NCST), III: 715.
Todd, William H., (Lt, Co C, 1st Vols/11th NCST), I: 584.
Todd's Point, (nr Smithfield, Va.), I: 552.
Todd's Tavern, Va., (and Battle of, 1864), I: 430, 558; II: 101; III: 538.
Toder, A.A., (Pvt, Co K, 35th NCST), V: 563.
Tolar, Alfred H.H., (Capt, Co K, 8th Vols/18th NCST), V: 98-100.
Tolar, Calvin R., (Pvt, Co E, 14th Vols/24th NCST), V: 560.
Tolbert, Frank, (Pvt, Co F, 44th NCST), V: 534.
Toler, Thomas, (Pvt, Co E, 14th Vols/24th NCST), II: 287.
Tolson, James H., (Capt, Co A, 67th NCST), III: 704, 709, 710.
Tombs, The, (Federal Prison, New York City), V: 410.
Tomlin, H.W., (Pvt, Co A, 33rd NCST), V: 543.
Tomlinson, E., (2nd Lt, Co C, 53rd NCST), III: 262.
Tomlinson, John H., (2nd Lt, Co C, 53rd NCST), III: 262.
Tommer, W.G., (AQM, 10th Battalion NCST, 2nd Hvy Art), IV: 329.
Toms, Marion C., (Capt, Co A, 6th Battalion/60th NCST), I: 119; III: 475, 481.
Tonnoffski, George, (Courier, Kirkland's Brigade), IV: 546.
Toodles' Harriet, (Federals built a redoubt in Mrs. Toodles' yard nr Plymouth), III: 339, 345; V: 177.
Toon, Anthony F., (Father of T.F. Toon), II: 125.
Toon, Mary McMillan, (Mother of T.F. Toon), II: 125.
Toon, Thomas Fentress, (temp. Brig Gen), I: xii, 644; II: 111-127 personal account; IV: 436, 523; V: 652.
Toon, William H., (Lt Col, 10th Vols/20th NCST), II: 112, 117, 125.
Topsail Island, N.C., III: 206.
Topsail Sound, N.C., III: 71, 176; IV: 484.
Torbert, Alfred Thomas Archimedes, (Maj Gen, USA), II: 258.
Torpedoes, (The name given the weapons that would now be known as land and/or naval mines), V: 220.
Torrance, J.N., (Capt, Co H, 49th NCST), III: 145, 148, 153; V: 559.
Total Number of Confederate Troops, V: 3.
Totapotamoy Creek, Va., I: 303, 322, 334, 597; II: 56, 75, 480, 574; IV: 507.
Towey, J.H., (Pvt, Co E, 2nd Vols/12th NCST), V: 507.
Towles, G.F., (IG to Terry, USA), I: 531.
Towles, James, (Pvt, Co K, 4th Vols/14th NCST), V: 491.
Town Creek, N.C., IV: 311, 428.
Townes, W.H., (Lt, Co D, 55th NCST), III: 292, 296, 310.
Towns, ______, [Randolph], (Lt Col, 62nd Ga., Cav), IV: 73.
Townsell, M.L., (Pvt, Co F, 26th NCST), V: 601.
Townsend, A.E., (Pvt, Co C, 28th NCST), V: 541.
Townsend, James T., (Capt, Co H, 44th NCST), III: 23.
Townsend, Frederick, (Brig Gen, USA), I: 87, 88, 93, 94, 95, 96, 97, 98.

Toxaway, N.C., IV: 381.
Tract Society at Richmond, IV: 765.
Tracy, Dr. J.W., [Tracey], (Ass't Surg, 37th NCST; Surg, 4th Vols/14th NCST; Surg, Raleigh Fairgrounds Hospital), IV: 474, 626, 627, 634, 637.
Trader, Henry G., (AQMS, 8th NCST; AQM, 3rd Battalion NCST, Light Art), I: 387; IV: 261.
Trafalgar, I: 729.
Tramel, H.B., (Pvt, Co B, 32nd NCST), V: 495.
Trammell, Thomas, (Pvt, Co K, 49th NCST), V: 565.
Transon, Charles, (Musician, Mickey's Band, 26th NCST), II: 398.
Transon, Julius A., (Musician, Mickey's Band, 26th NCST), II: 398.
Tranter's Creek, N.C., I: 514; I II: 21, 24, 233; IV: 82.
Transylvania County, N.C., III: 668; IV: 115, 271, 381, 397, 481.
Traveler, (Originally given the name Jeff Davis this magnificent animal became the best know of all American war horses. Described as a "Confedreate Gray," Traveler was General Robert E. Lee's favorite mount. This horse was as recognizable in both armies as was the general himself. So powerful is the memory and mystic of the great steed that he has taken on almost a human persona in the minds of many. So beloved was he by the general, that when Washington college constructed a new house for Lee the stable was connected to the house with a covered walk and Lee commented that it was fitting that he and Traveler should sleep under the same roof -so to speek. In life and death the general and Traveler remain connected. While the mortal remains of Lee rest in the chapel of the now Washington and Lee University those of the mighty Traveler are but a scant few yards away in the chapel yard.), II: 384, 447; IV: 456; V: 93.
Traywick, Dr. B.S., (Sgt Maj; Ass't Surg, 10th Battalion NCST, 2nd Hvy Art), IV: 329, 330.
Tredegar Iron Works, (Richmond, Va.), V: 317.
Tredwell, Adam, (Paymaster, NCN, Ass't Paymaster CSN), V: 313.
Treece, J.C., (Pvt, Co F, 5th NCST), I: 292.
Treloar, J.W., (2nd Lt, Co D, 6th Battalion Junior Reserves; Co H, 70th NCST, 1st Junior Reserves), IV: 13.
Trenchard, S.D., (Cmdr, USN), V: 243.
Trent River, N.C., I: 402, 526; II: 81, 309, 311, 322, 541, 774; III: 132, 135, 170, 324, 349, 705; IV: 84, 487, 573; V: 325, 332.
Trent Road, (nr Wise's Fork), IV: 54.
Trenton, N.C., (aka Trenton Court House), I: 365; II: 81, 323, 325, 329; III: 132, 135, 289; IV: 54, 84, 221; V: 19.
Trescott, Dr. George E., (Surg, 37th NCST; Surg, Branch-Lane's Brigade), IV: 472, 474, 644; V: 538.
Trevilian Station, Va., (and Battle of, 1864), I: 303, 430, 462.
Trexier, Allen, (Cpl, Co D, 10th NCST, 1st Art & Engs, Reilly-Ramsay's Battery, Light Art), I: 567.
Trickey, Willia H., (Capt, 3rd N.H.), V: 238.

Trigg, R.C., (Col, 54th Va.), III: 436, 452.
Trimble, Issac Ridgeway, (Maj Gen), I: 143, 190, 380; II: 39, 42, 43, 129, 132, 133, 167, 171, 363, 364, 562, 563, 564, 566, 567, 587, 661, 692; IV: 180, 230, 232, 233, 234, 468, 471; V: 101, 108, 109, 111, 124, 127, 128, 140, 144, 146, 151, 156.
Trinity College, N.C., IV: 22, 32, 41, 62, 394, 595, 746; V: 651.
Trinity Spire, N.Y., IV: 121.
Triplet, L.H., (Pvt, Co B, 37th NCST), V: 545.
Triplett, Dr. _____, IV: 603.
Triplett, J.H., (2nd Lt, Co B, 1st Vols/11th NCST), I: 121.
Tripp, Charles, (Sgt, Co I, 4th NCST), I: 234.
Tripp, Dr. Clarence A., (Ass't Surg, 61st NCST), IV: 641.
Tripp, Edward, (2nd Lt, Co I, 4th NCST), I: 233, 272.
Tripp, William H., (Capt, Co B, 40th NCST, 3rd Art, Hvy), II: 745, 748, 756.
Trippville, Va., II: 66.
Tristan Island, Brazil, V: 346, 347.
Tritt, W., (Lt, 64th NCST), IV: 711.
Trostle Place, (nr Gettysburg), V: 109.
Trott, B.W., (2nd Lt, Co H, 41st NCST, 3rd Cav), II: 771.
Trotter, A.G., (Pvt, Co B, 53rd NCST), V: 501.
Trotter, J.J., (2nd Lt, Co A, 2nd Battalion Junior Reserves; Co B, 71st NCST, 2nd Junior Reserves), IV: 28.
Trotter, Thomas B., (2nd Lt, Co C, 1st Vols, "Bethel"), I: 77.
Trotter, Turner P., (2nd Lt, Co A, 2nd Battalion Junior Reserves; Co B, 71st NCST, 2nd Junior Reserves), IV: 28.
Troublefield, Peter B., (Capt, Co C, 38th NCST), II: 675.
Trout, Gaither, (Pvt, Co I, 50th NCST), III: 189.
Troutman, David, (Cpl, Co A, 33rd NCST), II: 538.
Troutman, J.J., (Sgt, Co C, 4th NCST), I: 232.
Troy, R.P., (Capt, Co G, 46th NCST), III: 65, 78, 81; V: 519.
Troy, T.S., (2nd Lt, Co G, 46th NCST), III: 65, 66, 71, 76, 81.
Troy, N.C., IV: 431.
Truce, J.C., (Pvt, Co F, 5th NCST), V: 505.
Truelove, J.G., (1st Lt, Co F, 28th NCST), II: 483.
Trull, William R., (Capt, Co C, 69th NCST, Thomas' Legion), III: 730.
Truxham, W.S., (Lt Cmdr, USN), V: 243.
Tryon, _____, (Colonial Governor of North Carolina), IV: 60.
Tuckaseegee River, N.C., III: 757; IV: 121.
Tucke, E.P., (Sgt Maj; 2nd Lt, Co E, 9th Vols/19th NCST, 2nd Cav), II: 79, 89.
Tucker, _____, (Commodore, CSN), III: 400.
Tucker, _____, (Capt, Cmdr Hillsboro Military Academy Battalion), V: 643.
Tucker, _____, (Col, Conscription Officer at Salisbury Prison), IV: 767.
Tucker, C., (Pvt, Co C, 33rd NCST), V: 544.
Tucker, C.E., (Pvt, Co K, 43rd NCST), V: 499.
Tucker, Darling, (Pvt, Co A, 52nd NCST), V: 535.
Tucker, E., (1st Cpl, Co F, 46th NCST), V: 524.
Tucker, Hardin E., (Pvt, Co I, 38th NCST), V: 558.
Tucker, Henry, (Pvt, Co F, 46th NCST), V: 524.

Tucker, J.B., (Lt, Co B, 2nd Battalion NCST), IV: 245.
Tucker, J.H., (Pvt, Co H, 2nd Vols/12th NCST), V: 507.
Tucker, J.J., (Capt, Co E, 2nd Battalion NCST), IV: 245, 711.
Tucker, J.L., (Pvt, Co E, 55th NCST), V: 528.
Tucker, J.R., (Commodore, Naval Battalion, CSA), IV: 404.
Tucker, James, (Pvt, Co G, 56th NCST), III: 356.
Tucker, James B., (1st Lt, Co A, 2nd Battalion NCST), V: 494.
Tucker, John B., (2nd Lt, Co A, 44th NCST), III: 22.
Tucker, N.C., (2nd Lt, Co F, 9th Vols/19th NCTS, 2nd Cav), II: 89.
Tucker, Rufus S., (Maj, AAG N.C.), I: 50, 51, 492, 513; II: 771, 773, 775; III: 290; V: 651.
Tucker, T.P., (Pvt, Co K, 46th NCST), V: 525.
Tucker's Farm, Va., III: 620.
Tulifinny Iron Works, S.C., [Tallifanny], IV: 101.
Tullafuiney Bridge, [Tullafuiney], II: 578.
Tullafuiney River, S.C., [Tullifuiny], [Tullifinny], II: 757; III: 187; IV: 103.
Tullahoma, Tenn., II: 710; III: 480, 483, 484, 499.
Tumbro, Alexander D., (Capt, Co D, 4th NCST), I: 231, 232.
Tumbro, J.R., (Musician, Co D, 4th NCST), I: 232.
Tuning's House, (Wilderness, Va.), IV: 475.
Tunnage, J.J., (Sgt, Co G, 8th NCST), V: 193.
Tunstall, George D., (Lt, Co G, 47th NCST), III: 85.
Tunstall, Thomas J., (Capt, AQM, 41st NCST, 3rd Cav), II: 769.
Tupelo, Miss., III: 439.
Turbyfield, J.L., (Musician, Co C, 28th NCST), V: 541.
Turchin, John Basil, [Ivan Vasilevitch Turchininoff], (Brig Gen, USA; Deserter and embezzler of regimental funds from the Imperial Russian Army. Convicted by court martial in the U.S. as a murderer and war crimminal while serving in a volunteer unit. As a portion of his punishment he was cashiered from military service. Reinstated to command, given a regular army commission and promoted to general by Lincoln who evidently did not consider the murder of unarmed prisoners of war to be a crime.) IV: 254.
Turkey Bend, Va., (aka Turkey Hill), III: 119.
Turkey Creek, N.C., II: 493; III: 474.
Turkey Creek, Va., (nr Cold Harbor), I: 384, 420.
Turkey Ridge, Va., (and Battle of, 1864) I: 745; II: 56, 75, 574, 588; IV: 531.
Turnage, Henry C., (Musician, 55th NCST), V: 527.
Turnage, Joseph, (Musician, Co A, 3rd NCST), V: 487.
Turnage, M., (Pvt, Co F, 16th Battalion/75th NCST, 7th Cav), V: 660.
Turnage, Robert, (Pvt, Co K, 33rd NCST), II: 544.
Turnbull, John R., (Capt, Co F, 2nd Vols/12th NCST), I: 627, 642, 650.
Turner, ______, (Maj, at Salisbury Prison), IV: 762.
Turner, ______, (Capt, 73rd NCST, 4th Senior Reserves), IV: 66.
Turner, Alexander, (Pvt, Co D, 10th NCST, 1st Art & Engs, Reilly-Ramsay's Battery, Light Art), V: 568.

Turner, Alexander, (2nd Lt, Co B, 70th NCST, 1st Junior Reserves), IV: 12.
Turner, Andrew J., (2nd Lt, Co A, 68th NCST), III: 713.
Turner, B.B., (Capt, Ordnance Officer, Lee's Cav Brigade), II: 94.
Turner, C.S., (3rd Lt, Co A, 33rd NCST, Branch's), IV: 701, 711.
Turner, Columbus L., (2nd Lt, Co A, 33rd NCST), II: 538, 578, 579; IV: 701.
Turner, D.N., (Pvt, Co E, 30th NCST), V: 492.
Turner, George, (Pvt, Co A, 10th Vols/20th NCST), II: 118.
Turner, Dr. H., (Ass't Surg, 2nd Regt Home Guard), IV: 653.
Turner, H.C., (2nd Lt, Co K, 28th NCST), V: 538.
Turner, H.G., (Capt, Co H, 13th Vols/23rd NCST), II: 186, 226, 236; IV: 701, 711.
Turner, H. Clay, (Sgt Maj, 52nd NCST), III: 225, 226.
Turner, J.B., (2nd Lt, Co H, 42nd NCST), II: 791, 807.
Turner, J.F., (Pvt, Co I, 57th NCST), V: 518.
Turner, J.N., (Capt, Co D, 9th Vols/19th NCST, 2nd Cav), II: 89, 103, 104; V: 666.
Turner, J.W., (2nd Cpl, Co C, 4th Vols/14th NCST), I: 731.
Turner, James N., (Capt, Co B, 9th Vols/19th NCST, 2nd Cav), I: 441; II: 80, 89, 103.
Turner, J. Calder, (Capt, Co A, 6th NCST), IV: 700, 711.
Turner, J. McLeod, (Lt Col, 7th NCST), I: 271, 361, 367, 371, 375, 379, 380, 386; IV: 472; V: 665.
Turner, John C., (2nd Lt, Co C, 4th NCST), I: 232; V: 484.
Turner, John L., (Lt, Co F, 9th NCST, 1st Cav), I: 477, 486.
Turner, John W., (Capt, Co I, 76th NCST, 6th Senior Reserves), IV: 97.
Turner, John W., (2nd Sgt, Co C, 4th Vols/14th NCST), V: 490.
Turner, John Wesley, (Maj Gen, USA), III: 371.
Turner, Josiah, (Capt, Co K, 9th Vols/19th NCST, 2nd Cav), II: 80, 82; IV: 523.
Turner, N.G., (Capt, Co A, 9th NCST, 1st Cav), I: 436, 485.
Turner, T.L., (Pvt, Co K, 49th NCST), V: 565.
Turner, Thomas, (Pvt, Co I, 46th NCST), V: 525.
Turner, Vines E., (Capt, Adjt & AQM, 13th Vols/23rd NCST; AQM, Early's Division), II: 186, 189, 199, 201, 209, 211, 215, 220, 221, 234, 255, 265, 267, 268; V: 503.
Turner, W.G., (2nd Lt, Co E, 6th NCST), IV: 702.
Turner, W.S., (2nd Lt, Co E, 1st Vols/11th NCST), I: 585.
Turner, Walter S., [William J.], (Pvt, Co G, 3rd Vols/13th NCST), V: 667.
Turner, William, (2nd Lt, Co D, 56th NCST.), III: 315, 328, 398.
Turner, William, (Cpl, Co D, 56th NCST), III: 347.
Turner's Gap, Md., I: 625; II: 219, 221; V: 72.
Turnington, W.A., (Pvt, Co G, 32nd NCST), V: 496.
Turpin, J., (Capt, Co C, 62nd NCST), III: 515; IV: 700, 711.
Turrentine, S.W., (Pvt, Co B, 6th NCST), V: 512.
Tuscarora, N.C., II: 81, 82.
Tuscarora Indinas, IV: 60.
Tuten, R.R., (Lt, Co A, 4th NCST), I: 234, 270.
Tuten, Noah B., (2nd Lt, Co I, 4th NCST), I: 231, 233, 270; V: 664.

Tuten, T.A.E., (2nd Lt, Co I, 40th NCST, 3rd Art, Hvy), II: 747.
Tuton, John, (Pvt, Co A, 3rd NCST), V: 487.
Tutor, T., (Pvt, Co G, 61st Va.), V: 569.
Tutor, William O., (2nd Lt, Co I, 31st NCST), II: 512.
Tutterrow, G.W., (Pvt, Co F, 3rd Vols/13th NCST), V: 550.
Tuttle, C.A., (Pvt, Co E, 26th NCST), V: 603.
Tuttle, C.M., (Pvt, Co G, 11th Vols/21st NCST), V: 515.
Tuttle, D.P., (3rd Sgt, Co D, 52nd NCST), III: 224.
Tuttle, J.W., (2nd Cpl, Co D, 52nd NCST), III: 224.
Tuttle, Marcus G., (1st Lt, Co C, 8th Battalion Junior Reserves; Co G, 72nd NCST, 2nd Junior Reserves), IV: 42, 48.
Tuttle, Romulus Morrison, (Capt, Co F, 26th NCST), II: 336, 358, 371, 373, 396, 397, 403, 416, 417; V: 131, 599-603.
Tuttle, William A., (2nd Lt, Co A, 12th Vols/22nd NCST), II: 171, 178; V: 547.
Tweed, James H., (Pvt, Co F, 6th Battalion/60th NCST), III: 482.
Twisdale, A.G., (Pvt, Co G, 43rd NCST), V: 498.
Twitty, Birchet T., (Hospital Steward, 34th NCST), V: 554.
Twitty, Francis L., (Maj, 34th NCST), II: 581.
Twitty, R.C., (Lt, Adjt, 9th NCST, 1st Cav), I: 478, 479, 486.
Twitty, T.B., (AQM & Hospital Steward, 34th NCST), II: 582.
Twitty, W.L., (Capt, Co C, Avery's 17th Battalion NCST, Cav), IV: 373, 376.
Two Brothers, The, IV: 405-406.
Two Years at Fort Delaware, V: 595, 597.
Tyack, Joseph L., (Pvt, Co I, 13th Vols/23rd NCST), V: 510.
Tyer, John E., (Sgt, Co E, 27th NCST), II: 462; V: 523.
Tyler, Dr. John Tazwell, (Surg, 8th Vols/18th NCST), I: 103; IV: 473.
Tyler, Robert Ogden, (Maj Gen, USA), II: 5; III: 561.
Tyler, Tx., II: 608.
Tyman, J.W., (Chief Engineer, CSN, Tallahassee), V: 438.
Tyrell County, N.C., II: 161, 377, 508; IV: 261, 262; V: 57, 58, 60.
Tyson, Allen, (Pvt, Co F, 16th Battalion/75th NCST, 7th Cav), V: 660.
Tyson, Edwin, (Lt, Co G, 48th NCST), III: 117.
Tyson, H.C., (Pvt, Co H, 26th NCST), V: 532.
Tyson, James H., (1st Lt, Co D, 78th NCST, 8th Senior Reserves), IV: 107.
Tyson, Lemuel, (Pvt, Co E, 55th NCST), V: 528.
Tyson, S.H., (Pvt, Co F, 16th Battalion/75th NCST, 7th Cav), V: 660.
Tyson, W.A., (Cpl, Co H, 59th NCST, 4th Cav), V: 659.
Tyson, W.H., (Capt, Co K, 32nd NCST), I: 736.

(U)

Underdown, J.W., (Pvt, Co F, 26th NCST), V: 603.
Underdown, William, (Pvt, Co F, 26th NCST), V: 602.
Underwood, D.A., (Maj, 42nd NCST), II: 789, 790.
Underwood, Dr. George C., (Lt, Ass't Surg, 26th NCST), II: 303, 304, 320, 321, 324, 326, 357, 360, 361, 366, 370, 372, 379, 385, 388, 390, 395, 397, 423; IV: 636.
Underwood, H.M., (Pvt, Co D, 10th Battalion NCST, 2nd Hvy Art) IV: 335.
Underwood, J.A., (Cpl, Co H, 30th NCST), V: 492.
Underwood, J.B., (Capt, Co K, 51st NCST), III: 220, 503.
Underwood, J.P., (Pvt, Co C, 10th NCST, 1st Art & Engs, Berm-Graham-Williams' Battery, Light Art), V: 568.
Underwood, J.R., (Pvt, Co C, 10th NCST, 1st Art & Engs, Berm-Graham-Williams' Battery, Light Art), V: 568.
Underwood, J.W., (Pvt, Co C, 10th NCST, 1st Art & Engs, Berm-Graham-Williams' Battery, Light Art), V: 568.
Underwood, John, (Pvt, Co D, 28th NCST), V: 542.
Underwood, Joseph B., (Capt, Co A, 61st NCST), III: 503.
Underwood, Robert, (Pvt, Co C, 10th NCST, 1st Art & Engs, Berm-Graham-Williams' Battery, Light Art), V: 568.
Uneka Mountains, N.C., IV: 380.
Unicoi, Tenn, III: 757.
Union, Va., II: 96; III: 563.
Union County, N.C., II: 303, 415; III: 428; IV: 329, 330.
Union County, Tenn., III: 731.
Union Depot, Tenn., (aka Zollicoffer, now Bluff City, See: Bluff City).
Union Mills, Va., II: 192.
United Confederate Veterans, II: 727; III: 549, 732, 750; IV: 315.
United Confederate Veterans, John T. Jones Camp, II: 410.
United Confederate Veterans, 2nd N.C. Brigade, IV: 517.
United Daughters of the Confederacy, Col C.C. Blacknell Chapter, II: 256.
United States Antietam Board, V: 587.
United States Ford, (Rappahannock River, Va.), I: 101, 146, 193; II: 37, 664; IV: 174; V: 677.
University of Heidelburg, Germany, III: 295.
University of North Carolina, I: 553, 560, 587; II: 202, 239, 335, 403, 405, 410, 596, 598, 611, 671, 674, 722; III: 456; IV: 10, 51, 60, 120, 481, 515, 517, 577, 608; V: 643, 647-652.
University of Pennsylvania, II: 412.

University of Virginia, I: 79; II: 806; III: 636.
University Publishing Company, V: xv.
Upchurch, Albert E., (Capt, Co A, 55th NCST), III: 295.
Upchurch, Isham S., (Pvt, Co G, 6th Vols/16th NCST), IV: 216.
Upchurch, Richard, (Pvt, Co F, 26th NCST), V: 603.
Upper Ford, (Potomac River, Va.), III: 67.
Upper Trent Road, N.C., III: 323.
Upperville, Va., I: 424, 578; II: 96, 116, 438, 609; III: 69, 456, 461, 472, 533, 559, 560, 561, 563, 564, 565, 566, 567, 587, 637; V: 674.
Upshur, J.H., (Lt Cmdr, USN), V: 243.
Upshur, Dr. W.H., (Surg, 9th Vols/19th NCST, 2nd Cav), II: 88; IV: 635.
Upton, Emory, (Maj Gen, USA), III: 273.
Urbana, Va., I: 421, 422.
Usry, Henry, (Pvt, Co B, 56th NCST), III: 366.
Ussery, J., (Pvt, Co E, 28th NCST), V: 542.
Utah, III: 259.
Utley, Mrs. Kate Roulhac, (Daughter of Col McNeill), III: 655.
Utley, Leinster, (1st Lt, Co C, 31st NCST), II: 705.
Utley, T. Jefferson, (1st Lt, Co I, 41st NCST, 3rd Cav), II: 771.

(V)

Vail, Thomas L., (Lt, Co H, 9th NCST, 1st Cav), I: 486.
Valentine, George W., (Pvt, Co D, 68th NCST), III: 715, 717.
Valle Crucis, N.C., IV: 374.
Valley Campaign, 1862, (Stonewall Jackson's), I: 153, 206, 645; II: 66, 133, 248, 531, 533, 792; III: 259, 270; IV: 124, 441.
Valley Campaign, 1864, (Early's), I: 117, 153, 162, 164, 209, 264, 274, 326, 327, 645, 727; II: 141, 245, 248-261, 503, 531, 533; III: 15, 37, 56, 259, 281, 418, 420, 732, 744; IV: 124, 437, 516.
Valley Lee, Md., IV: 605.
Valley Mountain, Va., I: 752, 753, 771; IV: 141, 142, 143, 147, 155.
Valley Pike, (Shennandoah Valley, Va.), I: 147, 303, 327, 328, 645, 647, 648, 664; II: 71; III: 746, 751, 753; IV: 228, 231; V: 213.
Valley River, N.C., III: 757; IV: 125.
Valley River, N.C., (now Andrews), IV: 126.
Valley River, Va., IV: 142.
"Valley of Death," (nr Gettysburg, Pa.), V: 605.
Van Amringe, Stacy, (Lt, Co G, 61st NCST), III: 504.
Vanbenthusen, A.C., (Capt, CSN), V: 240.
VanBokkelen, John S.F., (Capt, Adjt, 3rd NCST), I: 189, 212, 226.
Vance, David, (Col, Revolutionary), II: 723.
Vance, Robert, (Sgt, 197th Ill.), II: 723.
Vance, Robert B., (Brig Gen), I: ix, xi; II: 485, 486, 487, 488, 489, 490, 491, 493, 711, 731, 743, 746, 748, 762; III: 663, 664; IV: 371, 379, 380, 438, 612; V: xii.
Vance, W.A., (Lt, Co A, 58th NCST), III: 432, 453.
Vance, Zebulon Baird, (Brig Gen; Governor of North Carolina), I: 17, 18, 25, 28, 29, 30, 31, 32, 33, 34, 35, 36, 38, 41, 42, 44, 47, 48, 50, 54, 55, 56, 57, 58, 60, 61, 62, 63, 64, 65, 144, 363, 413, 435, 470, 471, 708, 721, 775; II: 46, 58, 81, 121, 240, 272, 273, 274, 305, 306, 307, 310, 311, 314, 320, 321, 322, 323, 324, 325, 326, 327, 328, 329, 330, 331, 332, 334, 357, 388, 395, 398, 400, 401, 402, 403, 405, 404, 406, 407, 412, 414, 481, 505, 542, 543, 575, 600, 722, 723, 756, 774, 781; III: 75, 127, 167, 179, 244, 319, 375, 383, 388, 389, 621, 661, 692, 703, 718; IV: 2, 21, 22, 31, 59, 242, 318, 326, 331, 352, 373, 375, 403, 404, 407, 443, 455, 456, 469, 498, 523, 566, 569, 624, 625, 626, 651, 652, 657, 697, 698, 702, 758; V: ix, 4, 5, 7, 192, 212, 353, 358, 359, 360-361, 437, 438, 453, 454, 458, 460, 461, 463-481, 481, 629, 630, 632, 633, 635, 650.

Vance County, N.C., II: 256.
Vance's, Z.B., Legion, III: 433.
Vanderslice, John M., (Pvt, Co D, 8th Pa.), II: 346, 354, 360, 362, 363, 364, 367.
Van Dervear, Ferdinand, (Brig Gen, USA), III: 436.
Van Dike, Joshua, (Pvt, Co F, 34th NCST), V: 555.
Van Dorn, Earl, (Maj Gen), II: 192.
Vandyke, L.S., (Pvt, Co H, 13th Vols/23rd NCST), V: 510.
Van Eaton, B.R., (Pvt, Co E, Beale's 10th Va, Cav), V: 569.
Van Eaton, R.T., (Pvt, Co H, 57th NCST), V: 517.
Van Eaton, Richard, (Pvt, Co A, 57th NCST), III: 427.
VanEberstein, William, [VonEberstein], (Sgt, Ordnance Officer, Ft Ocracoke), V: 35.
Vaner, J.G., (Pvt, Co G, 46th NCST), V: 525.
VanHook, John C., (Lt Col, 50th NCST), III: 161, 177, 202, 680; IV: 15, 350.
Vanhorne, Joseph, (Pvt, Co H, 1st NCST), I: 142.
Vanlandingham, M., (Pvt, Co C, 46th NCST), V: 524.
Vanlandingham, R.P., (Sgt, Co C, 2nd Vols/12th NCST), V: 506.
VanLeer, Rush, (Engineer, Frazer's Brigade), III: 523.
Vann, D., (Pvt, Co B, 56th NCST), III: 366.
Vann, W.A., (Chaplain, 3rd Vols/13th NCST), IV: 607.
Vann, William, (2nd Lt, Co A, 12th Battalion NCST, Cav; 1st Lt, Co K, 59th NCST, 4th Cav), III: 458; IV: 339, 458.
Vannoy, A.M., (Pvt, Co B, 1st NCST), V: 485.
Vannoy, E.R., (2nd Sgt, Co F, 52nd NCST), III: 224.
Vannoy, J.A., (Musician, 53rd NCST), V: 501.
Vannoy, W.W., (1st Lt, Co B, 1st NCST), I: 136.
Vanpelt, Charles, (Pvt, Co A, 52nd NCST), V: 535.
Vanpelt, William, (Pvt, Co A, 52nd NCST), V: 535.
Vass, A., (Pvt, Co F, 6th NCST), V: 513.
Vassar, ______, (Lt, Macon Light Artillery), II: 615.
Vaughan, Alonzo, (Hospital Steward, 54th NCST), V: 516.
Vaughn, B.C., (Pvt, Co E, 35th NCST), V: 563.
Vaughn, D., (Pvt, Co E, 13th Vols/23rd NCST), V: 510.
Vaughn, R.Y., (Pvt, Co H, 6th NCST), V: 513.
Vaughn, John C., (Brig Gen), III: 524, 745, 748; IV: 121.
Vaughn, Maurice H., (Chaplain, 3rd NCST), IV: 605.
Vaughn, Monroe, (Cpl, Co B, 6th NCST), V: 512.
Vaughan, R.T., (Pvt, Co K, 12th Vols/22nd NCST), V: 554.
Vaughn, William, (Fifer, Drum Corps, 4th Vols/14th NCST), I: 711.
Vaughn, William T., (Cpl, Co D, 43rd NCST), V: 498.
Vaughn Road, (nr Reams Station, Va.), II: 389, 417; III: 251, 627.
Vaughn's House, (See: Yellow Tavern, Va.).
Vause, Robert B., (2nd Lt, Co A, 40th NCST, 3rd Art, Hvy), II: 746, 748, 762.
Veach, James L., (Cpl, Co B, 38th NCST), V: 557.
Veach, W.D., (Pvt, Co B, 4th Vols/14th NCST), I: 731.
Veazey, E., (Pvt, Co E, 13th Vols/23rd NCST), V: 510.

Veazey, W.C., (Pvt, Co B, 6th NCST), V: 512.
Venable, Charles S., (Col, ADC, Lee's Staff), II: 146, 479, 569, 571, 572, 668; III: 579; IV: 468; V: 138.
Venable, Thomas B., (Maj, N.C. Quartermaster Department, Lt Col, 14th Vols/24th NCST), I: 23, 105; II: 269, 272.
Venters, Brinson, (Capt, Co A, 35th NCST), II: 627.
Venters, Silas W., (2nd Lt, Co I, 66th NCST), III: 686.
Verbal, D., (Lt, Co , 57th NCST), IV: 711.
Verdiersville, Va., III: 27, 592.
Vermont, II: 367.
Versailles, Ky., II: 487, 490.
Vessels, (CSN, USN, Civilian, Foreign):
  Abigail, (Whaling Bark, Yankee), V: 348.
  Adelaide, (Norfolk & Baltimore Bay Steamer, Yankee), V: 52, 53.
  Adriatic, (Ship, Yankee, Captured), V: 439.
  Advance, (North Carolina owned Steamer, Blockade Runner; aka Ad-vance and Frolic; See also: Lord Clyde and Frolic), I: 17, 30, 31, 32, 42, 46, 53, 54; II: 632; III: 319; IV: 45, 319, 326, 331, 458, 471, 472; V: ix, xvi, 5, 243, 312, 335-340, 341-344, 357, 358-363, 379, 406, 438, 458, 460, 471, 472.
  Agnes Fry, (Steamer, Blockade Runer), V: 357.
  A.J. Bird, (Schooner, Yankee; Captured), V: 440.
  Alabama, (Steamer, Commerce Raider, CSN), V: 345, 346, 415, 437, 472.
  Alabama, (Steamer, USN), V: 243.
  Albermarle, (Ironclad Ram, CSN), I: xiv, 321, 496, 525, 527; II: 2, 140, 146, 616, 618, 619; III: 8, 177, 178, 331, 338, 339, 340, 342, 343, 346, 706; IV: 15, 27, 40, 317, 404, 416, 528, 573, 574; V: 175, 176, 180, 181, 182, 188, 190, 192, 298, 312, 315-323, 364, 396.
  Albermarle, (Gunboat, USN), III: 680.
  Albert, (Royal British Yatch), V: 425.
  Alice, (Steamer, Blockade Runner), V: 357.
  A. Lincoln, (Bark, Yankee; Captured), V: 441.
  Alma, (Bark, Yankee), V: 346.
  Amelia, (Ironclad Steamer, Blockade Runner, CSN; The fifth in a series of names given this ship when she entered British service after the war. Previously she had been named: Atlanta, Tallahassee, Olustea and Chemeleon; See also: Atlanta and Talahassee), V: 441.
  Annie, (Steamer, Blockade Runner), II: 632, 633.
  Antonica, (Steamer, Blockade Runner), V: 357, 358.
  Appomattox, (Steamer, Gunboat, NCN), V: 304, 307, 308, 309.
  Arabian, (Steamer, Blockade Runner), V: 442.
  Arctic, (Floating Battery, CNS), V: 298.
  A. Richards, (Brig, Yankee; Captured), V: 439.
  Aries, (Yankee), V: 243.
  Arrow, (Steamer, Yankee), V: 17.
  Aster, (Tug, USN), II: 633.
  Atlanta, (Ironclad Steamer, Blockade Runner, CSN; aka Amelia, Chameleon, Olustee, and Tallahassee; See also:

Amelia, and Talahassee), III: 605; IV: 733, 735, 742; V: 357, 437.
Atlantic, (Schooner, Yankee; Captured), V: 438.
Aureole, (Ship, Yankee; Captured), V: 440.
Banshee, (Steamer, Blockade Runner), II: 632; V: 357, 414, 437, 440.
Barracowta, (Bark, English), V: 349.
Bay State, (Bark, Yankee; Captured), V: 439.
Beaufort, (Steamer, Gunboat, NCN), IV: 248; V: 300, 303, 304, 305, 306, 307, 308, 309, 680.
Beauregard, (Transport, CSN), IV: 248.
Beauregard, (Steamer, Blockade Runner), V: 357, 358.
Billow, (Brig., Yankee; Captured), V: 439.
Black Warrior, (Schooner, NCN), V: 304, 307, 310.
Bombshell, (Tender to the Albemarle, CSN), V: 194, 321.
Britannia, (Steamer, Blockade Runner; Captured), V: 243, 357.
Brooklyn, (Screw Sloop, USN), V: 242, 244, 245.
Calypso, (Steamer, Blockade Runner), V: 357.
Canonicus, (Ironclad, USN), V: 242, 245.
Carrie Estelle, (Brig, Yankee; Captured), V: 438.
Carroll, (Schooner, Yankee; Captured), V: 439.
Catskill, (Monitor, USN), V: 162.
Ceres, (Gunboat, USN), V: 175, 180, 321.
Chameleon, (Ironclad Steamer, Blockade Runner, CSN; aka Amelia, Atlanta, Olustee and Tallahassee; See: Amelia, Atlanta and Tallahassee).
Charleston, (Steamer, Blockade Runner), V: 357.
Cherokee, (USN), V: 243.
Chicamauga, (Steamer, Cruiser, CSN; See also: Edith), II: 639; IV: 427; V: 225, 376, 397, 437, 438, 441, 442.
China, (Cunard Steamer, English), V: 340, 418.
Chippewa, (Gunboat, USN), I: 509; II: 751; V: 162, 242, 245.
City of Petersburg, (Steamer, Blockade Runner), V: 357.
Colonel Hill, (Steamer, CSN), V: 36, 51, 64.
Colonel Lamb, (Steamer, Blockade Runner), V: 339, 340, 357, 401.
Colorado, (Screw Frigate, USN), II: 637; V: 242, 244, 245.
Columbia, (Steamer, USN), II: 632.
Commodore Hull, (Gunboat, USN), V: 321.
Condor, (Steamer, Blockade Runner), V: 357.
Congress, (Frigate, USN), I: 607; V: 332.
Constitution, (aka "Old Iron Sides," Man-of-War, USN), V: 385.
Coquette, (Steamer, Blockade Runner), V: 357.
Cora, (CSN), V: 181.
Cornubia, (Steamer, Blockade Runner; aka The Lady Davis), II: 632; V: 357, 406, 407, 408.
Cotton Plant, (Tender to the Albemarle, CSN), V: 321.
Crescent, (Steamer, Transport, CSN), IV: 714, 715.

Crusader, (Pre-war, Steamer, USN), V: 386.
Cuba, (War Ship, Cuban), V: 363.
Cumberland, (Frigate, USN), I: 607; V: 45, 301.
Curlew, (Steamer, Gunboat, NCN), II: 510; V: 60, 303, 304, 306, 308, 310.
Daniel Webster, (Side-Wheel Steamer, Transport, USN), I: 539; II: 429, 430.
Dawn, (Gunboat, USN), III: 605.
Dee, (Steamer, Blockaade Runner), V: 357, 358.
DeMollay, (Steamer, Transport, USN), II: 761.
Diadem, (Schooner, Yankee; Captured), V: 439.
Dolphin, (Pre-war, Brig, USN), V: 386.
Dolphin, (Steamer, Blockade Runner), V: 357.
Don, (Steamer, Blockade Runner), II: 632; V: 357, 425, 426-434, 459.
Douro, (Steamer, Blockade Runner), V: 357.
Dream, (Steamer, Blockade Runner), V: 358.
Driver, (War Ship, English), V: 425.
Dupont, (Schooner, Yankee; Captured), V: 439.
Eagle, (Steamer, Blockade Runner), V: 357.
Edith, (Twin Screw Steamer, Gunboat; Became the Cruiser Chichamauga, CSN; See also Chichamauga), V: 441.
Edwards, (Whaler, Yankee), V: 346, 347.
E.F. Lewis, (Schooner, Yankee; Captured), V: 440.
Eliza Barse, (Brig, Blockade Runner), V: 377, 378.
Elizabeth, (Steamer, Blockade Runner), V: 401.
Ella, (Steamer, Blockade Runner), V: 357, 358.
Ella and Annie, (Steamer, Blockade Runner), V: 357, 443, 444, 445.
Ellis, (Steamer, Gunboat, NCN), V: 36, 37, 38, 44, 300, 301, 302, 303, 304, 306, 307, 308, 309, 311, 312.
Ellis, (Schooner, Yankee; Captured), V: 439.
E.M. Downing, (Steamer, CNS), V: 35.
Emily, (Steamer, USN), V: 17.
Emma, (Steamer, Blockade Runner; Captured), V: 243, 357.
Emma L. Hull, (Bark, Yankee; Captured), V: 441.
Empress Theresa, (Bark, Yankee; Captured), V: 440.
Eolus, (USN), V: 243.
Escort, (Transport, USN), III: 173.
Etta Caroline, (Schooner, Yankee; Captured), V: 439.
Eugenia, (Steamer, Blockade Runner), V: 357.
Fannie, (Steamer, Blockade Runner), V: 355, 357.
Fanny, (Steamer, Gunboat, NCN), V: 51, 53, 302, 303, 304, 307, 308, 309.
Firedog, IV: 333.
Flora, (Steamer, Blockade Runner), V: 357, 409.
Flora McDonald, (Steamer, Engineer Corps, CSA), IV: 429.
Floral Wreath, (Schooner, Yankee; Captured), V: 439.
Florida, (Cruiser, CSN; See also: Oreto), V: 399, 400, 415, 420, 437.

Florie, (Steamer, Blockade Runner), V: 419, 420, 425.
Forest, [Forrest], (Steamer, Gunboat, NCN), II: 510, 610; V: 60, 304, 306, 307, 308, 309, 310.
Fort Jackson, (USN), V: 243, 245, 246.
Frolic, (Name given the Blockade Runner Advance after its capture. Converted to a Steamer, Gunboat, USN), V: 339, 363.
Fort Donelson, (USN), V: 244.
Fulton, (Transport, USN), V: 442, 443.
Galena, (Gunboat, USN), III: 39.
Gallatin, (USN), V: 386.
General Lyon, (Steamer, Transport, USN), II: 761.
General Whiting, (Steamer, Blockade Runner), V: 450.
Georgia, (Cruiser, CSN), V: 366.
Georgiana McCall, (Steamer, Blockade Runner), V: 358.
Gertrude, (Steamer, Blockade Runner), V: 357.
Gettysburg, (Steamer, USN), V: 236, 245, 246, 371, 372.
Gibraltar, (See: Sumter).
Giraffe, (Steamer, Blockade Runner; See also: R.E. Lee), V: 357, 406.
Glenavon, (Schooner, Yankee; Captured), V: 439.
Goodspeed, (Schooner, Yankee; Captured), V: 440, 441.
Gordon, (Steamer, Blockade Runner), V: 35, 401.
Governor Buckingham, (Boat, USN), V: 243.
Granite City, (Steamer, Blockade Runner), V: 357.
Great Eastern, (Laid the Transatlantic Cable), V: 413.
Hanna Balch, (Brig, USN; Captured), V: 300.
Hansa, (Steamer, Blockade Runner), V: 357, 459.
Harriet Lane, (Steamer, Gunboat, USN), V: 45, 301, 302.
Havelock, (Steamer, Blockade Runner), V: 357.
H.C. Brooks, (Brig), V: 43.
Hebe, (Blockade Runner, English), II: 632, 633; V: 351, 352, 357, 358.
Henry Nutt, (Schooner, Yankee; Captured), V: 300.
Herbert Manton, (Schooner, USN), V: 300.
Hero, (Staemer, Blockade Runner), V: 357.
Howard, (Schooner, Yankee; Captured), V: 439.
Howquah, (USN), V: 243.
Huron, (Steamer, Gunboat, USN), V: 242, 245.
Index, (Steamer, Blockade Runner), V: 371, 409, 410.
Iosco, (Double-ender Gunboat, USN), V: 242, 245.
Iroquois, (USN), V: 345.
Isaac Wells, (Steamer, Transport), II: 639.
Itasca (Brig, USN), V: 299.
James Adger, (Steamer, Gunboat, USN), II: 632, 633; V: 351, 352, 408, 419.
James Funk, (Pilot Boat, Yankee; Captured), V: 438, 439.
James Petteway, (Engineer Corps, CSA, Steamer, Transport/Supply Ship), II: 760; IV: 403, 418.
J.E. Coffee, (Side Wheeler Gunboat, NCN; See also: Winslow), V: 299.
Josiah Achorne, (Schooner, Yankee; Captured), V: 439.

Junaluska, (Steamer, Gunboat, NCN), V: 303.
Juniata, (Screw Sloop, USN), V: 242, 244, 245.
Junietta, (Corvette, USN), V: 450.
Kansas, (Steamer, Gunboat, USN), V: 242, 245.
Kate, (British, Steamer, Blockade Runner), II: 632, 748, 750, 752; V: 357, 401, 402, 403.
Kate II, (Steamer, Blockade Runner, English), II: 753.
Kearsage, (USN), V: 346.
Keystone State, (Steamer, USN), V: 243, 369, 372, 373, 374, 410, 443.
Lady Davis, (See: Cornubia).
Lamont, (Schooner, Yankee; Captured), V: 439.
Leopard, (Steamer, Blockade Runner), I: 32; V: 453.
Leopard, (Schooner, Yankee; Captured), V: 439.
Let Her Be, (Steamer, Blockade Runner), V: 357.
Let Her Rip, (Steamer, Blockade Runner), V: 357.
Lilian, (Steamer, Blockade Runner), V: 243, 351, 357, 363, 364, 369, 371, 372, 374, 375, 376, 395, 411, 420, 422, 423, 425, 387, 419, 421, 424, 440.
Little Ada, (USN), V: 243.
Little Hattie, (Steamer, Blockade Runner), V: 357.
Little Nattie, (Blockade Runner), II: 632.
Lord Clyde, (See also: Advance), I: 17, 30, 32.
Logan, (Steamboat, CSN), I: 82.
Louisiana, (Butler's failed pow der boat, USN), II: 635; V: 243.
Luola Murchinson, (Steamer, Post-war), V: 372.
Lynx, (Steamer, Blockade Runner), V: 357.
Macedonian, (Pre-war, Frigate, USN), V: 385.
Mackinaw, (Double-ender, Gunboat, USN), V: 242, 245.
Magnolia, (Schooner, Yankee; Captured), V: 439.
Mahopoc, (Ironclad, USN), V: 242.
Malvern, (Flagship, 1st attack on Fort Fisher, USN), V: 242, 244, 245.
Mark L. Potter, (Bark, Yankee; Captured), V: 441.
Mary Celest, (Steamer, Blockade Runner), V: 357, 358.
Maumee, (Screw Gunboat, USN), V: 242.
Mayflower, (Transport, USN), III: 605.
Mercy C. Howes, (Schooner, Yankee; Captured), V: 439.
Merrimack, [Merrimac], (See: Virginia).
Miami, (Side-wheeler Steamer, Gunboat, USN), II: 617; III: 339; V: 175, 180, 181, 320, 321, 323, 396.
Maintanomah, (Gunboat, USN), IV: 343.
Maratanza, (Double-ender, Gunboat, USN), V: 242, 245.
Margaret and Jessie, (Steamer, Blockade Runner), V: 355, 357, 410, 440, 442, 443, 445.
Mary K. Sprunt, (Steamer, Blockade Runner), V: 369.
Mattabesett, (Gunboat, USN), V: 321.
Milo, (Whaler, Yankee), V: 348.
Minnesota, (Frigate, Flagship of the North Atlantic Blockading Squadron, USN), II: 632, 637; V: 45, 52, 224, 244, 245, 301, 302, 351.

Minquas, (Steamer, USN), III: 710; V: 18.
Moccasin, (USN), V: 243.
Modern Greece, (Steamer, Blockade Runner), IV: 343; V: 351, 352, 358.
Mohican, (Screw Sloop, USN), V: 242, 244, 245.
Monadnock, (Ironclad, USN), V: 242.
Monitor, (First Federal ironclad. The name applied to all Federal ironclad vessels of any type.), I: 608.
Montawk, (Monitor, USN), V: 162.
Montgomery, (Gunboat, USN), V: 243, 245, 246, 440.
Monticello, (Steamer, Man-of-War, USN), I: 81; II: 750; V: 37, 38, 243, 254, 246, 301, 374.
Moselle, (Post-war Vessel), V: 375.
Mystic, (Steamer, USN), III: 710; V: 18.
Nansemond, (USN), V: 243.
Nantucket, (Monitor, USN), V: 162.
Nashville, (Steamer, Blockade Runner), I: 510, 511.
Nathaniel Chase, (Schooner, USN), V: 300.
Nereus, (USN), V: 243, 245, 246.
Neuse, (North Carolina built ironclad ram constructed near Kinston), V: 86, 298.
Neva, (Schooner, Yankee; Captured), V: 439.
New Ironsides, (Ironclad, USN), IV: 306; V: 162, 224, 242.
Nighthawk, (Steamer, Blockade Runner), II: 632; V: 414.
Niphon, [Nyphon], (Gunboat, USN), V: 351, 445.
North America, (Schooner, Yankee; Captured), V: 439.
North Carolina, (Ironclad), IV: 404; V: 298.
Northampton, (Steamer), V: 325.
North Heath, (Steamer, Blockade Runner), V: 357, 364.
Nyack, (Screw Gunboat, USN), V: 242, 243.
Old Dominion, (Steamer, Blockade Runner), V: 357.
Olustea, (Ironclad Steamer, Blockade Runner, CSN; aka Amelia, Atlanta Chameleon and Tallahassee; See: Amelia, Atlanta, and Tallahasee).
Oreto, (Gunboat, CSN, See also: Florida), V: 387, 420, 424.
Osceola, (Double-ender, Gunboat, USN), V: 243, 245, 246.
Ottowa, (Gunboat, USN), V: 162.
Owl, (Steamer, Blockade Runner), V: 357, 381, 387, 396, 399, 400, 410.
Pantheon, (Schooner, CSN), V: 36, 38, 39.
Patapsco, (Monitor, USN), V: 162.
Patrick, Henry, (Steamer, CSN), V: 326.
Paul Jones, (Gunboat, USN), V: 162.
Pawnee, (Steam Gunboat, USN), I: 80; V: 56, 301, 501.
Pawtuxet, (Double-ender, Gunbost, USN), V: 243, 245, 246.
P.C. Alexander, (Schooner, Yankee; Captured), V: 439.
Pearl, (Schooner, Yankee; Captured), V: 439.
Penobscot, (Steamer, USN), II: 632.
Pensacola, (Steamer, Sloop-of-War), II: 164.
Perry, (Steamer, Gunboat, USN), III: 552.

Pequot, (Screw Gunboat, USN), III: 605; V: 242, 245.
Pet, (Steamer, Blockade Runner), V: 357.
Peterhoff, (Steamer, Gunboat, USN), II: 755; IV: 317.
Petrel, (Gunboat, USN), V: 410.
Pontoosuc, (Double-ender, Gunboat, USN), V: 243, 245, 246.
Powhatan, (Side-wheeler Steamer, USN), V: 242, 244, 245.
Proney, (Corvette, French), V: 303, 304, 312.
Pungo, (Steamer, Blockade Runner), II: 753.
Quaker State, (USN), V: 243.
Raleigh, (Steamer, Gunboat, NCN), V: 298, 300, 303, 304, 308, 309, 312, 680.
R.E. Lee, (Steamer, Blockade Runner; See also: Giraffe), V: 355.
Republic, (USN), V: 244.
Restless, (Schooner, Yankee; Captured), V: 439.
Rhode Island, (USN), V: 243, 245, 246, 420.
Rouen, (Steamer, Blockade Runner), V: 410.
Rowan, (Brig, Yankee; Captured), V: 439.
R.R. Cuyler, (USN), V: 243.
Rubart E. Packer, (Schooner, Yankee; Captured), V: 439.
Saint Louis, (Pre-war Vessel, USN), V: 385.
Samuel Chase, (Schooner, CSN), V: 39.
Santee, (USN), V: 345.
Santiago de Cuba, (Federal ship involved in the illegal siezure of Confederate Ambassadors Slidell and Mason in what has come to be known as "The Trent Affair."), V: 243, 245, 246, 338, 339.
Sarah A. Boyce, (Ship, Yankee; Captured), V: 438.
Sarah B. Harris, (Schooner, Yankee; Captured), V: 439.
Sarah Louise, (Schooner, Yankee; Captured), V: 439.
Sassacus, (Double-ender Gunboat, USN), V: 243, 245, 246, 321, 322, 440.
Saugus, (Ironclad, USN), V: 242, 245.
Scotia, (Steamer, Blockade Runner), II: 752; V: 357.
Seabird, (Schooner, NCN), V: 17, 304, 307, 308, 309, 311, 312.
Seawitch, (Schooner, USN), V: 299.
Seneca, (Gunboat, USN), V: 162, 242, 245.
Shenandoah, (Cruiser, CSN), I: xiv; IV: 404; V: ix, xvi, 345-350, 437.
Shenandoah, (Screw Sloop, USN), V: 242, 244, 245.
Shooting Star, (Ship, Yankee; Captured), V: 441.
Sirene, (Steamer, Blockade Runner), V: 401, 402, 403, 404, 442-450.
Smith Briggs, (Steamer, Butler's flagship, USN), II: 515.
Southfield, (Gunboat, USN), II: 617; III: 178, 339, 552; V: 175, 180, 181, 320, 323, 396.
Speedwell, (Bark, Yankee; Captured), V: 441.
Spokane, (Schooner, Yankee; Captured), V: 439.
Spunkie, (Steamer, Blockade Runner), IV: 358.
S.R. Spaulding, (Steamer, USN), IV: 248, 251; V: 68.
St. Louis, (Ship), V: 385.
Stag, (Steamer, Blockade Runner), V: 397.

State of Georgia, (Steamer, USN), V: 337.
Stonewall Jackson, (Steamer, Blockade Runner), V: 357.
Storm King, (Steamer, Blockade Runner, English), V: 364.
Suliote, (Bark, Yankee; Captured), V: 439.
Sumter, [Sumpter], (Cruiser, CSN; See also: Gibraltar), I: 20; II: 632, 759; IV: 319; V: 415, 436.
Susan Beirne, (Steamer, Blockade Runner), V: 377, 379, 380, 381, 410.
Susquehannah, (Side-wheel Steamer, USN), V: 45, 46, 242, 244, 245, 301.
Swash, V: 37.
Tacony, (CSN), IV: 735; V: 245, 246.
Tacony, (Double-ender Gunboat, USN), V: 243, 245, 246.
Tallahassee, (Ironclad Steamer, Blockade Runner, CSN; aka: Amelia, Atlanta, Chameleon and Olustea,; See also: Amelia and Atlanta), IV: 427; V: 376, 437, 438, 439, 440, 441.
T.D. Wagner, (Brig, Yankee; Captured), V: 440.
Tennessee, (Cruiser, CSN), I: 54.
Thistle, (Steamer, Blockade Runner), V: 357.
Ticonderoga, (Screw Sloop, USN), V: 242, 244, 245.
Transit,(Schooner, USN), V: 300.
Tristram Shandy, (USN), V: 243, 245, 246.
Tuscarora, (Screw Sloop, USN), V: 242, 244, 245.
Unadilla, (Steamer, Gunboat, USN), V: 242.
Uncle Ben, (Steamer, Gunboat, NCN, CSN), V: 303.
Underwriter (Steamer, Gunboat, USN), I: 495, 526; III: 133; IV: 487; V: 325, 331-333.
Vanderbilt, (USN), V: 243, 245, 246, 419.
Vapor, (Schooner, Yankee; Captured), V: 440.
Venus, (Steamer, Blockade Runner), II: 632; V: 357, 358.
Victoria, (Royal British Yatch), V: 425.
Victory, (Steamer, Blockade Runner), V: 357.
Virginia, (Formerly the U.S. Merrimac which was burned and abandoned by Federal forces in Virginia. Raised and rebuilt as the first ironclad war ship.), I: 607, 608; III: 169; IV: 733; V: 305, 316, 317.
Wabash, (Screw Frigate, USN), V: 45, 224, 242, 244, 245, 301.
Wachusett, (USN), V: 345.
Weehawken, (Monitor, USN), V: 162.
White, (Tug), IV: 248.
Whitehead, (Gunboat, USN), V: 175, 180, 181, 321.
Wilderness, (USN), V: 243.
William Bell, (Pilot Boat, Yankee; Captured), V: 438.
William McGilvery, (Schooner, USN), V: 299.
William Thompson, (Whaler, Yankee), V: 348.
Winslow, (Side-wheel Steamer, Gunboat, NCN; See also: J.E. Coffee; At the fall of Hatteras Island this ship was repeat edly fired upon while under a flag of truce at the orders of federal general Benjamin F. Butler), V: 39, 51, 299, 300, 301, 302, 303, 304, 312.
Wissahickon, (Gunboat, USN), V: 162.

Wyalusing, (Gunboat, USN), V: 321.
Wyoming, (War Ship, USN), V: 345.
Yadkin, (Steamer, Gunboat), V: 298.
Yantic, (Steamer, Gunboat, USN), V: 242, 245.
Vessels from Nassau, V: 355.
Vessels Saved, II: 632.
Vestal, C.M., (1st Sgt, Co L, 12th Vols/22nd NCST), V: 554.
Vestal, H.T., (Pvt, Co H, 54th NCST), V: 516.
Vestal, M.E., (Pvt, Co G, 26th NCST), V: 532.
Vick, E.M., (Pvt, Co C, 32nd NCST), V: 496.
Vick, J.J.B., (1st Lt, Co E, 9th Vols/19th NCST, 2nd Cav), II: 80.
Vick, J.W., (Capt, Co E, 7th NCST), I: 380.
Vick, S.S., (Capt, Co E, 2nd Vols/12th NCST), I: 652.
Vick, W.P., (2nd Lt, Co A, 5th Vols/15th NCST), I: 734.
Vickers, _____, [George F.], (Sgt., Co E, 59th NCST, 4th Cav), III: 466.
Vickers, Hiram, (Sgt, Co C, 6th NCST), V: 512.
Vickers, J.H., (Sgt, Co H, 56th NCST), III: 466.
Vickers, W.D., (Pvt, Co E, 56th NCST), V: 566.
Vickers, W.M., (Pvt, Co E, 56th NCST), III: 324.
Vickery, William, (Pvt, Co F, 48th NCST), V: 526.
Vicksburg, Miss., I: 171, 767; II: 232, 369, 491, 710, 712, 734, 735; III: 389, 485, 499, 664, 737; IV: 35, 256, 498, 583; V: viii, 212, 461.
Victoria, Queen of England, V: 425.
Victoria Cross, I: 161.
Vidiersville, Va., II: 240, 664; III: 93, 243, 244.
Vigal, Dr. John A., (Ass't Surg, 33rd NCST), II: 537, 578, 580; IV: 474, 637; V: 538.
Vincent Creek, (Morris Island, S.C.), III: 207.
Vincent, Strong, (Brig Gen, USA), III: 565, 566.
Vienna, Va., I: 419, 480.
Villapique, John Bordenaue, (Brig Gen), IV: 254.
Vinagum, D.V., (Pvt, Co F, 3rd Vols/13th NCST), V: 550.
Vines, Charles, (2nd Lt, Co F, 30th NCST, 1st Lt, Co E, 43rd NCST), II: 496; III: 3.
Vines, John A., (Capt, Co E, 43rd NCST), III: 2.
Vines, William T., (Pvt, Co C, 30th NCST; Detailed, 2nd Corps Provost Guard), V: 570.
Vinson, James W., II: 303, 396.
Vinson, John, (Pvt, Co G, 26th NCST), II: 374, 401.
Virginia Central Railroad, I: 366, 384, 567, 609; II: 148; III: 235; IV: 138.
Virginia Collegiate Institute, IV: 426.
Virginia Creek, N.C., III: 176.
Virginia Military Institute, I: 79; II: 161, 304, 342, 403, 404, 406, 593; III: 690; V: 94, 637.
Vizetelly, Frank, (Crewman, Lilian), V: 421.
Vogdes, _____, (Maj, USA), IV: 747.
Voliver, Asa, (Pvt, Detached Co, 68th NCST), III: 723.
Volunteers, Numbering of Regiments Changed, I: 4, 5.
Volusia County, Fla., II: 415.
Von Eberstien, William H., (Ordnance Sgt, 7th Vols/17th NCST),V: 35.

Von Moltre, ______, (German author), II: 563.
Voris, Alvin Coe, (Col, 67th Oh.), V: 163.
Voyles, Enoch, (Jr 2nd Lt, Co G, 39th NCST), II: 706.

(W)

W & A Railroad, II: 739, 741.
Wachovia National Bank, II: 398.
Waddell, Alfred M., (Lt Col, 41st NCST, 3rd Cav), II: 769; V: 650.
Waddell, Duncan C., (1st Lt, Co G, 1st Vols/11th NCST), I: 585; II: 388.
Waddell, G.W., (Pvt, Co G, 27th NCST), II: 462; V: 523.
Waddell, James I., (Capt, CSN, Shenandoah), I: xiv; IV: 404; V: 346, 347, 348, 349, 350.
Waddell, John, (Pvt, Co I, 43rd NCST), V: 499.
Waddell, John E., (Pvt, Co B, 6th Battalion/60th NCST), III: 482.
Waddell, John T., (Pvt, Co I, 43rd NCST), V: 499.
Waddill, J.M., (2nd Lt, Co B, 46th NCST), III: 63, 65, 66, 78, 79, 80, 81, 82.
Waddill, John B., (2nd Cpl, Co C, 4th Vols/14th NCST), I: 732; V: 490.
Wade, ______, (Deserter, Outlaw; Alleged Maj, Mi), V: 285, 286, 287, 289, 290, 292, 293, 294, 295.
Wade, Benjamin O., (Capt, Warren Guard, 1st Vols, "Bethel"; Col, 2nd Vols/12th NCST), I: 124, 607, 608, 609, 620, 621, 629, 630, 643; II: 22, 545; IV: 243.
Wade, G.L., (Pvt, Co C, 10th NCST, 1st Art & Engs, Brem-Graham-Williams' Battery, Light Art), V: 568.
Wade, W.A., (Pvt, Co D, 54th NCST), V: 516.
Wade, W.H., (Musician, Co F, 5th Vols/15th NCST), V: 521.
Wadford, Allen, (Pvt, Co D, 30th NCST), V: 492.
Wadesboro, N.C., IV: 611.
Wadsworth, James Samuel, (Maj Gen, USA), II: 344, 345.
Wagg, Samuel P., (Capt, Co A, 26th NCST), II: 358, 360, 371, 372, 373, 396, 397, 415.
Wagner, Andrew, (Capt, Co F, 24th Mi.), II: 356.
Wagoner, C.J., (Pvt, Co C, 57th NCST), V: 517.
Wagoner, J.W., (Pvt, Co I, 28th NCST), V: 543.
Wagoner, Jacob, (Sgt, Co K, 47th NCST), V: 535.
Waggoner, D.H., (Sgt, Co A, 6th Battalion/60th NCST), III: 481.
Wagstaff, J.W., (Pvt, Co B, 1st NCST), V: 485.
Waightstill, Dr. Collett, (Ass't Surg, N.C.), IV: 630.
Wainwright, John, (Lt, 97th Pa.), V: 238.
Wainwright, T.A., (Pvt, Co G, 43rd NCST), V: 498.
Wait, G.N., (Pvt, Co G, 28th NCST), V: 542.
Waites, ______, (Lt, Blake Artillery), V: 167.
Wait's Shop, Va., III: 94.
Wake County, N.C., II: 303, 408, 412, 414, 419, 771; III: 112, 124,

260, 458; IV: 317, 329, 483, 517, 594, 608, 616; V: 6, 280, 631.
Wake Forest, N.C., I: 581; V: 651.
Wake Forest College, II: 125, 162, 412, 623; IV: 425.
Walcott, ______, (Capt, Co B, 21st Mass.), II: 313.
Walden, John W., (Capt, Co E, 48th NCST), III: 113.
Waldo, Joseph T., (1st Lt, Co F, 31st NCST), II: 512.
Waldrop, ______, [Waldrep], (Pvt, Co D, 29th NCST), II: 488.
Walker, Mrs. ______, (Resident of Valley River), IV: 127.
Walker, ______, (Brig Gen, Hancock's Staff, USA), V: 211.
Walker, ______, (Passenger, Advance), V: 343.
Walker, ______, (Pre-war Ordnance Sgt, USA, Fort Caswell), V: 27.
Walker, ______, [George F], (Capt, Co A, 51st NCST), III: 218.
Walker, Arthur M., (2nd Lt, Co A, 7th NCST), I: 378;
Walker, Arthur M., (Capt, Co C, 48th NCST), III: 113, 115.
Walker, B.J., (Pvt, Co G, 45th NCST), V: 500.
Walker, Dr. Benjamin M., (Surg, 41st NCST, 3rd Cav), II: 769; IV: 638.
Walker, C.H., (Pvt, Co B, 30th NCST), V: 491.
Walker, Dr. Charles F., (Sgt Maj, Walker's Battalion, Thomas' Legion, 80th NCST), IV: 117, 128.
Walker, D.C.F., (2nd Lt, Co B, Walker's Battalion, Thomas' Legion, 80th NCST), IV: 118.
Walker, D.D., (2nd Lt, Co F, 62nd NCST), III: 516.
Walker, David L., (Capt, Co H, 39th NCST), II: 706.
Walker, H., (Pvt, Co B, 44th NCST), V: 533.
Walker, Dr. H.J., (3rd Lt, Co B, 3rd Vols/13th NCST), IV: 405-406, 701.
Walker, Henry, (Pvt, Co K, 6th NCST), V: 514.
Walker, Dr. J.C., (Surg, Wilmington General Hospital No. 2), IV: 625, 627.
Walker, J.J., (1st Lt, Co E, 46th NCST), III: 81.
Walker, J.M., (Pvt, Co H, 6th NCST), V: 513.
Walker, J.P., (Pvt, Co K, 53rd NCST), V: 502.
Walker, J.T., (Pvt, Co C. 2nd Vols/12th NCST), V: 507.
Walker, J.W., (2nd Lt, Co G, 66th NCST), III: 686.
Walker, James, (Pvt, Co E, 35th NCST), V: 563.
Walker, James A., (Maj Gen), II: 262, 264, 265; V: 259, 260.
Walker, John G., (Maj Gen), I: 180, 187, 217, 563, 650; II: 167, 428, 431, 432, 438, 461, 601, 602, 778; III: 66, 68, 115, 116, 422, 423; IV: 501, 502, 503, 572; V: 74, 253.
Walker, John H., (3rd Sgt, Co F, 4th Vols/14th NCST), V: 490.
Walker, John W., (ACS, 25th NCST), II: 291.
Walker, John W., (Pvt, Co K, 34th NCST), V: 556.
Walker, Joseph M., (1st Lt, Co I, 56th NCST), III: 316, 317, 393, 398.
Walker, Dr. Joshua C., (Surg, 3rd NCST), I: 213; IV: 128, 630, 632.
Walker, L. Jasper, (Color-bearer, Co B, 3rd Vols/13th NCST), IV: 405-406.
Walker, Leroy Pope, (Sec of War, CSA), I: 80, 82; II: 406.
Walker, Norman, (Maj, Agent & QM, St. Georges, Bermuda), V: 364.

Walker, R.L., (Sgt, Co K, 6th NCST), V: 513.
Walker, Robert E., (1st Lt, Co G, 10th NCST, 1st Art & Engs, Pender-Manney's Hvy Art), I: 501, 525.
Walker, Samuel, (1st Lt, Co E, 53rd NCST), III: 262.
Walker, Virgil H., (Jr 2nd Lt, Co K, 52nd NCST), III: 225.
Walker, W.M., (Pvt, Co K, 3rd Vols/13th NCST), V: 551.
Walker, W.R., (Pvt, Co K, 53rd NCST), V: 502.
Walker, William, (Pvt, Co K, 6th NCST), V: 514.
Walker, William, (Seaman, Black Warrior), V: 311.
Walker, William, (Resident of Cherokee County), III: 662.
Walker, William C., (Lt Col, 29th NCST; Lt Col, Walker's Battalion, Thomas' Legion; Col, 80th NCST), II: 485, 486, 493; III: 662; IV: 117, 118, 119, 121, 122, 123, 125, 126; V: 10.
Walker, William Henry Talbot, (Maj Gen), II: 491, 716.
Walker, William Jordan, (Capt, Co K, 41st NCST, 3rd Cav), II: 772, 775.
Walker William S., (Brig Gen, "Live Oak"), II: 461; III: 349, 356; IV: 505.
Walkup, Samuel H., (Col, 48th NCST), II: 441; III: 113, 114, 123; V: 520, 650.
Wall, A.D., (Pvt, Co K, 45th NCST), V: 501.
Wall Aaron N., (Pvt, Co D, 6th Vols/16th NCST), V: 552.
Wall, B., (Pvt, Co I, 3rd Vols/13th NCST), V: 551.
Wall, H. Clay, (Sgt, Co A, 13th Vols/23rd NCST), I: vii, ix; II: 195, 199, 267, 268.
Wall, J.M., (2nd Lt, Co A, 59th NCST, 4th Cav), III: 457.
Wall, J.B., (Pvt, Co E, 8th Vols/18th NCST), II: 64; V: 539.
Wall, James M., (Capt, Co A, 13th Vols/23rd NCST), II: 182, 224.
Wall, L.B., (Pvt, Co E, 8th Vols/18th NCST), II: 64; V: 539.
Wall, R.H., (Pvt, Co I, 56th NCST), III: 348; V: 566.
Wall, W.C., (Capt, Co F, 13th Vols/23rd NCST), II: 184, 185, 224, 246; V: 503.
Wall's Ferry, S.C., IV: 104, 105.
Wallace, J.S., (Pvt, Co H, 13th Vols/23rd NCST), V: 510.
Wallace, W.C., (Capt, Co D, Wlaker's Battalion, Thomas' Legion, 80th NCST), IV: 118, 123.
Wallace, John O. (2nd Lt, Co D, 5th Battalion Junior Reserves; Co E, 71st NCST, 2nd Junior Reserves), IV: 28.
Wallace, John R., (Sgt Maj, 38th NCST), V: 556.
Wallace, Lewis, "Lew," (Maj Gen, USA, author of Ben Hur), I: 172, 259, 290, 324, 645; II: 122, 245, 246; III: 13, 55, 419, 749, 750.
Wallace, William Henry, (Brig Gen), II: 625.
Wallace, William W., (Drum Maj, 56th NCST), III: 319.
Waller, ______, (Col, 9th NCST, 1st Cav), I: 474, 778.
Waller, Fred, (Pvt, Co B, 46th NCST), V: 524.
Walser, H.C., (Pvt, Co A, 11th Vols/21st NCST), II: 146.
Walsh, Edward D., (Capt, Co F, 10th NCST, 1st Art & Engs, Andrew-Cogdell's Hvy Art), I: 501, 525, 529; V: 240.
Walsh, T.C., (ACS Sgt, 5th Vols/15th NCST), I: 734.

Walston, Caleb B., (Capt, Co C, 68th NCST), III: 714.
Walston, Caleb P., (1st Sgt, Co A, 56th NCST), III: 313.
Walston, John, (Sgt, Co F, 30th NCST), V: 492.
Walston, John D., [Wallston], (Cpl, Color-bearer, Co E, 27th NCST), II: 462; V: 523.
Walston, Ralph, (Pvt, Co F, 30th NCST), V: 492.
Walston, W.R., (Pvt, Co F, 43rd NCST), V: 498.
Walston, William, (Pvt, Co E, 43rd NCST), V: 498.
Walston, William P., (1st Lt, Co C, 68th NCST), III: 714.
Walters, ______, [Walter, Alfred B.], (Capt, Co F, 51st NCST), III: 219.
Walters, Abram G., (Capt, Co F, 34th NCST), II: 581, 583.
Walters, B.C., (Pvt, Co E, 35th NCST), V: 563.
Walters, L.M., (Pvt, Co K, 53rd NCST), V: 502.
Walters, W.B., (2nd Lt, Co B, 50th NCST), III: 203, 512.
Walthall, Edward Cary, (Maj Gen), II: 711.
Walton, Benjamin, (1st Lt, Co D, 31st NCST), II: 512.
Walton, James B., (Col, Hood's Staff), I: 571.
Walton, James T., (Capt, Co K, 33rd NCST), II: 541, 578, 579.
Walton, Samuel J., (2nd Lt, Co D, 6th Battalion NCST), IV: 296.
Walton, Thomas B., (2nd Lt, Co I, 68th NCST), III: 714.
Walton, T. George, (Capt, Co F, 41st NCST, 3rd Cav), II: 771.
Walton, T. George, (Col, 8th Home Guard), IV: 376, 650, 653, 654; V: 635, 636.
War Records, The State's, V: 463.
War of the Rebellion, (aka Records of the Rebellion, War of the Rebellion: Official Records of the Union and Confederate Armies), I: 107, 295, 335, 341, 347, 350, 351, 356, 359, 414; II: 44, 86, 93, 137, 177, 178, 224, 360, 369, 447, 492, 519, 524, 527, 529, 703, 716, 719; III: 9, 79, 204, 302, 334, 383, 385, 387, 401, 452, 454, 497, 520-653, 663, 670, 678, 679, 681, 708, 718, 737, 754; IV: 4, 6, 7, 19, 21, 65, 71, 94, 100, 101, 108, 114, 119, 121, 127, 221, 222, 242, 247, 268, 270, 300, 302, 315, 338, 339, 348, 349, 350, 352, 353, 383, 387, 397, 401, 408, 441, 472, 507, 524, 526, 570, 571, 579, 581, 646, 647, 652, 653; V: vii, 2, 7, 8, 81, 82, 299.
War of the Rebellion, (aka Records of the Rebellion, War of the Rebellion; Official Records of the Union and Confederate Navies), V: 302, 303, 305-311, 345.
Ward, ______, (Capt, USA), I: 65.
Ward, A.C., (1st Lt, Co A, 41st NCST, 3rd Cav), II: 770.
Ward, Benjamin F., (2nd Lt, Co G, Walker's Battalion, Thomas' Legion, 80th NCST), IV: 118.
Ward, E.H., (Capt, Co D, 5th Vols/15th NCST), I: 735.
Ward, E.W., (Capt, Co B, 41st NCST), II: 770, 774.
Ward, George D., (1st Lt, Co B, 12th Battalion, Cav; Capt, Co I, 59th NCST, 4th Cav), III: 458; IV: 339.
Ward, George W., (1st Lt, Co B, 3rd NCST), I: 213.
Ward, George W., (Capt, Co K, 41st NCST, 3rd Cav), II: 772.
Ward, J.A., (Pvt, Co A, 54th NCST), V: 516.

Ward, J.D., (Pvt, Co B, 45th NCST), V: 500.
Ward, J.H., (Pvt, Co H, 11th Vols/21st NCST), V: 515.
Ward, J.J., (Pvt, Co K, 10th Vols/20th NCST), V: 509.
Ward, J.L., (Capt, Co G, 6th Battalion/60th NCST), III: 475, 482.
Ward, J.R., (Pvt, Co G, 28th NCST), V: 542.
Ward, John W., (Lt, Co H, 63rd NCST, 5th Cav), III: 586.
Ward, McD., (Pvt, Co F, 10th Vols/20th NCST), II: 118.
Ward, M.M., (Lt, Co C, 2nd Vols/12th NCST), I: 647.
Ward, R.H., (Capt, Co I, 3rd Vols/13th NCST), I: 653, 655, 658, 665, 668, 670, 674, 675, 676.
Ward, Mrs. R.H., (Wife of above), I: 676.
Ward, Richard, (Pvt, Co A, 27th NCST), II: 461; V: 522.
Ward, Samuel Alston, (Cpl, Co C, 2nd Vols/12th NCST), I: 630, 647.
Ward, Thomas, (Pvt, Co I, 35th NCST), V: 563.
Ward, Thomas F., (Pvt, Co G, 27th NCST), II: 462; V: 523.
Ward, W., (Pvt, Co D, 30th NCST), V: 492.
Ward, W.H., (Lt, CSN, Tallahassee), V: 438, 440.
Ward, W.P., (Capt, Co I, 27th NCST), II: 426.
Ward, William E., (Sgt Maj, 27th NCST), II: 461; V: 522.
Ward's Farm, (nr Norfolk, Va.), I: 607.
Wardell, T.R., (Sgt Maj, Fort Fisher), IV: 342.
Ware Bottom Church, Va., (and Battle of, 1864; aka Clay's Farm), II: 298; III: 315, 316, 355, 356, 359; IV: 362.
Warford, J.E., (Pvt, Co K, 32nd NCST), V: 497.
Waring, R.P., (Capt, Co B, 43rd NCST; AG, J.F. Hoke's 2nd Brigade Junior Reserves; Adjt, 73rd NCST, 4th Senior Reserves), IV: 6, 66.
Waring, Robert P., (Lt Col, Jeff Davis Legion), I: 423; III: 2.
Wark, ______, (Capt, Pilot), V: 382, 383.
Warley, A.F., (Capt, CSN, Albemarle), V: 323.
Warlick, David, (Sgt, Co B, 57th NCST), V: 517.
Warlick, J.L., (2nd Lt, Co B, 1st Vols/11th NCST), I: 121, 584.
Warlick, L., (Pvt, Co E, 32nd NCST), V: 496.
Warlick, L., (1st Lt, Co D, 6th NCST), IV: 702.
Warlick, Pinkney, (1st Lt, Co K, 35th NCST), II: 628.
Warlick, Portland A., (2nd Lt, Co B, 1st Vols/11th NCST), I: 121, 584.
Warlick, R.M., (2nd Lt, Co K, 49th NCST), I: 121.
Warm Springs, N.C., III: 473, 474; IV: 112, 381.
Warm Springs, Va., (now Bath Court House), IV: 147, 149.
Warner, G.H., (Chief Musician, 3rd Vols/13th NCST), V: 549.
Warren, (One of Gen Grimes' horses), I: 265; V: 251.
Warren, Burrill, (4th Cpl, Co I, 46th NCST), V: 525.
Warren, Edward, (Col, Surgeon General, N.C.), I: 50, 51, 56; IV: 624, 628.
Warren, Gouverneur Kemble, (Maj Gen, USA), I: 318, 382, 437, 471, 481, 599; II: 105, 390, 694; III: 29, 246, 248, 580, 631, 633; IV: 16, 43, 184, 388, 390, 564; V: 207.

Warren, H.M., (Capt, Co F, 4th NCST), I: 233, 270, 279.
Warren, J.H., (Sgt, Co F, 52nd NCST), V: 536.
Warren, James, (Pvt, Co K, 3rd Vols/13th NCST), V: 551.
Warren, James C., (2nd Lt, Co H, 68th NCST), III: 714.
Warren, James P., (4th Sgt, Co F, 52nd NCST), III: 224.
Warren, John C., (1st Lt, Co C, 52nd NCST), III: 234.
Warren, John T., (Pvt, Co E, 2nd NCST; Detailed, 2nd Corps Provost Guard), I: 176; V: 486, 570.
Warren, Dr. L.L., (Surg, 7th Vols/17th NCST), I: 119.
Warren, Dr. Llewellen P., [Llewellyn], (1st Lt, Co M, 1st Vols,"Bethel"; Surg, 26th NCST), I: 110, 119; II: 371, 395; IV: 636; V: 529.
Warren, Micajah, (Pvt, Co I, 3rd Vols/13th NCST), I: 660.
Warren, P.M., (Capt, Unattached Co, Chowan County), V: 678.
Warren, R., (Pvt, Co K, 12th Vols/22nd NCST), V: 554.
Warren, R.F., (Musician, 52nd NCST), III: 226.
Warren, W., (Pvt, Co C, 6th NCST), V: 512.
Warren, Dr. W.C., (Surg, 2nd N.C. General Hospital, Petersburg, Va.), IV: 624, 629.
Warren, W.C.P., (Pvt, Co H, 49th NCST), V: 565.
Warren, W.M., (3rd Sgt, Co A, 47th NCST), V: 534.
Warren, Y.B., (Pvt, Co I, 57th NCST), V: 518.
Warren County, N.C., I: 417; II: 162, 176, 599; IV: 483; V: 265, 266, 268.
Warren Junction, N.C., V: 276, 277.
Warren Plains, N.C., II: 263.
Warren's Neck, N.C., (nr Plymouth), III: 337, 339, 348; V: 176, 177, 178, 182, 319.
Warrenton, N.C., I: 3, 134; II: 472, 479; III: 318; IV: 482, 605, 606; V: 268, 270, 276, 277, 453.
Warrenton, Va., I: 223, 373, 422, 427, 454, 457, 553, 554, 592, 762; II: 45, 87, 95, 99, 267, 355, 440, 657; III: 66, 242, 578, 580, 581, 582, 583; IV: 184.
Warrenton Junction, Va., IV: 661, 662.
Warrenton Pike, Va., I: 306, 341, 427, 572; III: 571.
Warrenton Road, (nr Culpepper, Va.), II: 479, 663.
Warrenton Springs, Va., (aka Warrenton White Sulphur Springs, Warrenton Sulphur Springs), I: 305, 318, 334, 370, 570, 592; II: 29, 68, 472, 551; III: 578; IV: 161.
Warrick, ______, (Resident of Clover Lick, Va.), IV: 141.
Warsaw, N.C., I: 742; III: 130, 206, 271, 319.
Wartrace, Tenn., III: 484.
Warwick Island, Va., I: 552.
Warwick River, Va., I: 709.
Washburn, Francis, (Lt Col, 4th Mass.), I: 87, 88, 89, 93, 96; II: 402.
Washburne, T.J., (Pvt, Co E, 2nd Vols/12th NCST), V: 507.
Washington, Mrs. Byrd, (Resident of Winchseter, Va.), II: 256.
Washington, George, (Resident of Kinston), III: 322.
Washington, George, (Gen; President), I: 131; II: 196, 254, 256; IV: 150, 670, 671; V: 213.
Washington, George L., (ADC to R.F. Hoke), IV: 429.
Washington, James A., (Col, 50th NCST), I: 162, 163; III: 161, 202; IV: 81; V: 650.

Washington, John A., (Col, ADC to Lee, Last owner of Mt. Vernon), IV: 144, 146.
Washington, John C., (Col, Resident of Kinston area), IV: 18, 30, 53.
Washington, N.C., (aka Little Washington), I: 321, 402, 492, 496, 512, 513, 521, 526, 527, 539, 540, 577, 578, 588; II: 3, 80, 279, 284, 337, 339, 340, 524, 523, 619, 677, 748, 749, 751, 754, 773, 775, 793, 797; III: 5, 9, 40, 88, 117, 130, 135, 172-173, 177, 179, 233, 255, 275, 289, 290, 320, 349, 459, 472, 530, 553, 680, 687, 703, 705, 706, 707, 749; IV: 15, 16, 44, 72, 74, 75, 76, 83-84, 92, 221, 253, 349, 514, 519, 557, 646; V: 36, 192, 269, 303.
Washington, Va., I: 578; III: 269.
Washington Academy, (Washington), I: 512, 513.
Washington City, (aka Washington D.C.), I: 154, 172, 206, 259, 282, 290, 299, 318, 325, 331, 334, 382, 424, 462, 544, 592, 624, 632, 645, 709, 724, 727, 758; II: 15, 66, 70, 71, 88, 96, 122, 130, 134, 141, 155, 164, 214, 232, 241, 244, 246, 247, 259, 386, 503, 531, 532, 569, 656, 670, 753; III: 13, 35, 37, 41, 55, 91, 92, 169, 200, 256, 258, 259, 263, 278-279, 389, 399, 419, 560, 610, 749, 750; IV: 7, 32, 61, 66, 69, 108, 141, 237, 261, 299, 318, 321, 449, 515, 562, 612, 662, 663, 664, 665, 718, 735; V: 81, 82, 213, 373, 386, 412, 417, 443, 464, 587, 591, 627.
Washington College, Lexington, Va.(Later known as Washington and Lee College), I: 78.
Washington County, N.C., II: 508, 769, 772; IV: 605, 646; V: 57.
Washington County, Tenn., III: 517, 518, 738, 757.
Washington Road, (nr New Bern), III: 334.
Washington Road, (nr Plymouth), V: 177, 178, 189.
Washington Street Road, (nr Petersburg, Va.), I: 549.
Washington's Hill, (nr Kinston), IV: 325.
Washington and Jamesville Road, (nr Plymouth), III: 338; V: 176.
Watauga, Tenn., III: 735; IV: 371, 373, 374.
Watauga County, N.C., III: 443, 445, 447, 683; IV: 401; V: 169, 285, 287.
Watauga River, Tenn., III: 676, 739, 740; IV: 374.
Water Street, (Plymouth), III: 340, 341, 342, 344; V: 176, 187, 188, 189.
Waters, John O., (Color-Sgt, 38th NCST), II: 676, 681.
Waters, N.R., (Pvt, Co E, 48th NCST; Detailed, Invalid Battalion), V: 571.
Waters, Samuel B., [Watters], (Lt, Adjt, 8th Vols/18th NCST), II: 20; IV: 473.
Watford, J.J., (Capt, Co F, 59th NCST, 4th Cav), I: 119.
Watford, Joseph, (Pvt, Wynn's 15th Battalion NCST, Cav), IV: 368.
Watkins, A.A., (Pvt, Co B, 2nd Vols/12th NCST), V: 506.
Watkins, Dr. B.S., (Ass't Surg, 25th NCST), IV: 635; V: 559.
Watkins, George W., (Pvt, Co D, 10th NCST, 1st Art & Engs, Reilly-Ramsay's Battery, Light Art), V: 568.
Watkins, J.B., (Pvt, Co D, 1st Vols/11th NCST), V: 530.
Watkins, J.F., (Pvt, Co E, 10th Vols/20th NCST), V: 509.
Watkins, J.M., (Pvt, Co C, 4ht Vols/14th NCST), I: 732.

Watkins, P.B., (Musician, Co I, 3rd NCST), V: 487.
Watkins, Richard, (Pvt, Co E, 43rd NCST), V: 498.
Watkins, T.J., (Pvt, Co C, 4th Vols/14th NCST), I: 732.
Watkins, W.C., (Pvt, Co A, 13th Vols/23rd NCST), II: 224.
Watkins, William H., (Pvt, Co C, 4th Vols/14th NCST), V: 490.
Watlington, _____, [William P.], (Capt, Co F, 54th NCST), III: 267.
Watlington, E.R., (Pvt, Co I, 3rd Vols/13th NCST), V: 551.
Watmough, P.G., (Lt Cmdr, USN), V: 242.
Watson, A.C., (1st Lt, Co B, 4th NCST), I: 231, 269.
Watson, Dr. Alfred A., (Chaplain, 2nd NCST), I: 157, 158; IV: 604.
Watson, Andrew, (Pvt, Co A, 5th NCST), I: 291; V: 504.
Watson, B., [G.H.], (3rd Lt, Co C, 10th Vols/20th NCST), II: 120.
Watson, C.A., (2nd Lt, Co I, 4th NCST), I: 233.
Watson, Cyrus B., (2nd Sgt, Co K, 45th NCST), III: 35-61 personal account; IV: 258-259; V: 682.
Watson, E.L., (Capt, Co C, 51st NCST), III: 218.
Watson, E.W., (Pvt, Co F, 48th NCST), V: 526.
Watson, Eli, (Pvt, Co I, 43rd NCST), V: 499.
Watson, G.W., (2nd Lt, Co C, 50th NCST), III: 203.
Watson, H.B., (Col; Cmdr of Camp Mangum), III: 318.
Watson, Israel B., (Lt, Co I, 2nd NCST), I: 163; IV: 700.
Watson, J.J., (2nd Lt, Co H, 6th Battalion Junior Reserves; Co H, 70th NCST, 1st Junior Reserves), IV: 13
Watson, James H., (Lt, Co K, 47th NCST), III: 85, 109; IV: 701.
Watson, James F., (Chaplain, 6th Vols/16th NCST), IV: 608; V: 547.
Watson, John F., (Pvt, Co G, 25th NCST), V: 561.
Watson, Jones M., (2nd Lt, Co G, 1st Vols/11th NCST), I: 121.
Watson, R.H., (Co F, 4th NCST), I: 233.
Watson, Robert F., (Sgt, Musician, Co F, 33rd NCST), II: 538, 539, 578.
Watson, Samuel C., (2nd Lt, Co F, 33rd NCST), II: 539.
Watson, T.B., (Pvt, Co F, 2nd Vols/12th NCST), V: 265, 266, 268.
Watson, T.B., (Pvt, Co G, 43rd NCST), V: 498.
Watson, T.C., (Capt, Co B, 4th NCST), I: 232.
Watson, Thomas, (Pvt, Detached Co, 68th NCST), III: 723.
Watson, Thomas S., (1st Lt, Co A, 43rd NCST), III: 19.
Watson, William G., (Capt, Co A, 8th Battalion Junior Reserves; Co F, 72nd NCST, 3rd Junior Reserves), IV: 41, 43, 51.
Watt, W.T., (Pvt, Co B, 3rd Vols/13th NCST), V: 549.
Watts, _____, (Orderly Sgt, Naval Battalion), IV: 404.
Watts, C.L., (Sgt, Co D, 1st Vols, "Bethel"), I: 128.
Watts, John, (Pvt, Co F, 52nd NCST), V: 536.
Watts, S.W., (Civilian), I: 446.
Watts, Thomas, (Pvt, Co C, 26th NCST), V: 531.
Watts, W., (Pvt, Co E, 6th NCST), V: 512.
Watts, W., (Pvt, Co D, 9th NCST, 1st Cav), V: 657.
Watts, W.H., (Capt, Co E, 77th NCST, 7th Senior Reserves), IV: 100.

Waugh, James B., (Capt, Co A, 2nd NCST), I: 158.
Waugh, S.A., (Pvt, Co B, 1st Battalion NCST), V: 504.
Waugh, W.D., (Chaplain, 64th NCST), IV: 620.
Waxhaw, N.C., II: 415.
Wayne County, N.C., I: 163, 534; II: 113, 591, 593, 597; III: 161, 199, 686, 704, 711, 725, 727; IV: 73, 77, 330, 617.
Waynesboro, Ga., II: 756.
Waynesboro, Va., II: 258, 261; IV: 138.
Waynesburg, Pa., I: 541.
Waynesville, N.C., I: 154, 262, 303, 541, 698; III: 515, 518, 730, 733, 738, 756, 757, 760, 761; IV: 121, 123, 127, 128, 442; V: 5, 653, 654, 655.
Waynesville White Sulphur Springs Hotel, V: 653.
Wayt, John Henry, I: 77.
Weant, Natt J., (Musician, 4th NCST), I: 234; V: 488.
Wear, Robert H., (Pvt, Co H, 34th NCST), V: 556.
Wear, William (Pvt, Co H, 34th NCST), V: 556.
Wearing of the Gray, I: 668.
Weatherman, H.H., (2nd Lt, Co C, 2nd Battalion Junior Reserves; Co D, 71st NCST, 2nd Junior Reserves), IV: 28.
Weathersby Road, (nr New Bern), II: 311, 314, 321, 322, 324, 542, 543.
Weatherspoon, S., (2nd Lt, Co G, 7th NCST), IV: 701.
Weaver, ______, (Sgt, Co D, 33rd NCST), II: 562.
Weaver, A.W., (Lt Cmdr, USN), V: 242.
Weaver, B.F., (Capt, Co F, 1st Battalion Junior Reserves; Co I, 70th NCST, 1st Junior Reserves), IV: 13.
Weaver, D.W., (Lt, Co G, 8th NCST), V: 194.
Weaver, G.W., (2nd Lt, Co D, 33rd NCST), II: 539, 652, 578; IV: 467.
Weaver, Hal H., (2nd Lt, Co H, 4th NCST), I: 231, 247, 272.
Weaver, James Thomas, (Lt Col, 6th Battalion/60th NCST), II: 741; III: 473, 475, 481, 483, 488, 490, 496, 500, 501; V: 11.
Weaver, P.D., (Sgt, Co I, 4th Vols/14th NCST), I: 248.
Weaver, Preston J., (4th Sgt, Co I, 4th Vols/14th NCST), V: 491.
Weaverville, Va., III: 579.
Weaverville and Greenwich Road, Va., III: 579.
Webb, ______, (Brig Gen, USA), V: 148, 151, 156, 157.
Webb, Mrs. ______, (Resident of Louisville, Ky.), IV: 675.
Webb, A.C., (1st Lt, Co C, Millard's 9th/20th Battalion Junior Reserves), IV: 386.
Webb, A.D., (Pvt, Co F, 8th Vols/18th NCST), II: 64.
Webb, A.S., (2nd Lt, Co E, 13th Vols/23rd NCST), II: 185.
Webb, Alexander Stewart, (Maj Gen, USA), II: 546.
Webb, Alexander S., (2nd Lt, Co K, 44th NCST), III: 22, 24.
Webb, Franklin, (Pvt, Co D, 2nd NCST), I: 176; V: 486.
Webb, Rev. G.M., (Resident of Rutherford County), IV: 202.
Webb, H., (Pvt, Co E, 52nd NCST), V: 536.
Webb, H.W., (Pvt, Co K, 37th NCST), V: 546.
Webb, J.G., (Pvt, Co F, 56th NCST), III: 348.
Webb, J.R., (Pvt, Co K, 35th NCST), V: 563.
Webb, James E., (Capt, Ordnance officer, Robert's Cav Brigade), II: 108, 109; IV: 580.

Webb, John, (Pvt, Co F, 30th NCST), V: 492.
Webb, John, (Resident of Granville County), IV: 675.
Webb, John C., (1st Lt, Co E, Cameron-Dickson's Battery, Starr's 13th Battalion NCST, Light Art), IV: 354, 403.
Webb, John M., (2nd Lt, Co A, Ellis' 3rd Battalion, Light Art), IV: 261.
Webb, Joseph C., (Lt Col, 27th NCST), II: 426, 438, 443, 444,447, 456, 457, 461; III: 378.
Webb, Kate, (Sister of Col R.F. Webb, Resident of Baltimore), IV: 663, 664.
Webb, Lewis H., (Capt, Co D, 13th Vols/23rd NCST; Co. D, Bogg's 12th Va., Hvy Art; Co A, Webb's Battery, Starr's 13th Battalion NCST, Light Art), II: 184; IV: 341, 355, 356; V: 269, 271, 273, 274-283.
Webb, Louise, (Resident of Baltimore, Sister of Col R.F. Webb, 6th NCST), IV: 663, 664.
Webb, Newell, (Musician, Co F, 30th NCST), V: 492.
Webb, Richard G., [Richard S.], (Chaplain, 44th NCST), III: 22; IV: 614, 615, 616.
Webb, Robert F., (Col, 6th NCST), I: 295, 339, 345; IV: 657-687, 702, 711; V: 581.
Webb, Mrs. Robert F., (Wife of Col R.F.), IV: 667, 675.
Webb, W.A., (Capt, CSN, Atlanta), IV: 733, 734, 743.
Webb, W.C., (Sgt, Co E, 52nd NCST), V: 536.
Webb, W.D., (1st Sgt, Co K, 26th NCST), V: 532.
Webb, W.P., (ACS, 55th NCST), III: 288.
Webb, W.R., (1st Lt, Co H, 5th Vols/15th NCST), I: 735.
Webb, Walter J., (Pvt, Co A, Webb's Battery, Starr's 13th Battalion NCST, Light Art), V: 282.
Webb, William C., (Jr 2nd Lt, Co I, 38th NCST), II: 676, 678.
Webb, William E., (Pvt, Co A, 4th Vols/14th NCST), V: 489.
Webb's Ford, N.C., IV: 202.
Webber, J.S., [Weber], (Sgt, Co E, 2nd Vols/12th NCST), I: 630.
Weber, Maxwell, (Brig Gen, USA), II: 122; V: 50, 51.
Weber, P.A., (Maj, 6th Mi. Cav), II: 376.
Webster, ______, (Capt, USN), IV: 740.
Webster, A.W., (Pvt, Co E, 26th NCST), V: 532.
Webster, Daniel, (Politician, U.S.), I: 349.
Webster, J.B., (Pvt, Co L, 11th Vols/21st NCST), V: 515.
Webster, J.F., (Cpl, Co C, 48th NCST), V: 526.
Webster, John, (Pvt, Co D, 4th Vols/14th NCST), V: 490.
Webster, John J., (2nd Lt, Co F, 53rd NCST), III: 263.
Webster, R.B., (Pvt, Co D, 35th NCST), V: 562.
Webster, T.A., (Sgt Maj, 35th NCST), V: 562.
Webster, W.S., (Capt, Co E, 26th NCST), II: 304, 305, 396.
Webster, N.C., III: 733, 738, 757, 760; IV: 113, 121; V: 655.
Wedden, C.S., (AQMS, 70th NCST, 1st Junior Reserves), IV: 14.
Weddington, S.A., (Cpl, Co A, 10th Vols/20th NCST), V: 508.
Weden, Dan, (Pvt, Co E, 3rd Vols/13th NCST), I: 670.
Wedington, W.M., (Pvt, Co F, 10th Vols/20th NCST; Detailed, Invalid Battalion), V: 571.
Weede, Charles T., (Pvt, Co H, 14th Vols/24th NCST), V: 560.

Weeks, John A., (Pvt, Co D, 38th NCST), V: 557.
Weeks, Dr., S.B., (UNC), V: 647.
Weir, Andrew, (Pvt, Co B, Starr's Battery, Starr's 13th Battalion NCST, Light Art), IV: 346.
Weir, Samuel P., (2nd Lt, Co F, 46th NCST), II: 439; III: 70, 81; IV: 505.
Weir, William M., (Capt, Co D, 4th Vols/14th NCST), I: 707.
Weir's Cave, Va., I: 262, IV: 233.
Weisiger, Davis Adams, (Brig Gen), II: 51, 572; IV: 403.
Weitzel, Godfrey, (Maj Gen, USA), II: 637; IV: 46, 48, 590; V: 220.
Welborn, Calvin H., [Wilborne], (1st Lt, Co L, 12th Vols/22nd NCST), II: 166, 178; V: 548.
Welborn, J.H., (Adjt, 12th Vols/22nd NCST), II: 171.
Welborn, L., (Lt, Co B, 4th Vols/14th NCST), I: 731.
Welborn, R.W., [Wellborn], (1st Lt, Co B, 6th Battalion Junior Reserves; Co E, 70th NCST, 1st Junior Reserves), IV: 13.
Welch, A.H., (Ambulance Driver, Pvt, Co G, 2nd Battalion NCST), V: 495.
Welch, A.H., (Sgt, Co F, 69th NCST, Thomas' Legion), III: 747.
Welch, A.L., (Pvt, Co B, 1st Battalion NCST), V: 504.
Welch, A. Lon, (Sgt, Co A, Walker's Battalion, Thomas' Legion, 80th NCST), IV: 126.
Welch, J.J., (1st Sgt, Co B, 1st Battalion NCST), V: 504.
Welch, James, (Capt, Co I, Indina Co, Walker's Battalion, Thomas' Legion, 80th NCST), IV: 119.
Welch, John A., (2nd Lt, Claiborne-Dearing's 7th C.S. Cav; Co E, 16th Battalion/75th NCST, 7th Cav), IV: 92.
Welch, Julius M., (Capt, Co E, 69th NCST, Thomas' Legion), III: 730, 733, 743, 747.
Welch, Lucius M., (ACS, 69th NCST, Thomas' Legion), III: 730, 733.
Welch, Moses, (Sgt, Co G, 2nd Battalion NCST), V: 495.
Welch, R.S., (Pvt, Co E, 35th NCST), V: 563.
Welch, William T., (1st Lt, Co F, 69th NCST, Thomas' Legion), III: 731, 741, 754.
Welch Coal, (aka Cardiff Coal), V: 341, 419, 472.
Welch's Creek, (nr Plymouth), V: 180.
Weldon, J.C., (Pvt, Co F, 43rd NCST), V: 498.
Weldon, N.C., I: 6, 164, 297, 320, 365, 399, 402, 445, 446, 493, 515, 524, 561, 562, 577, 578, 588, 733; II: 255, 270, 277, 278, 281, 282, 613, 614, 615, 616, 671, 677, 753, 776, 777, III: 86, 117, 130, 131, 133, 134, 135, 162, 199, 275, 329, 330-331, 335, 337, 350, 368, 550, 687, 717, 718; IV: 4, 10, 11, 15, 17, 25, 26, 27, 29, 39, 43, 44, 297, 312, 357, 358, 359, 365, 366, 369, 383, 390, 396, 572, 573, 606; V: 68, 269, 270, 271, 272, 273, 274, 275, 315.
Weldon Bridge, N.C., II: 390, 615, 677, 773; III: 330; V: 20.
Weldon Road, (Railroad), II: 299, 447, 574, 694, 699; III: 29, 77, 97, 317, 376, 377, 540, 610, 611, 616, 619, 620, 621, 633; IV: 93; V: 207.
Welford's Ford, (Rappahannock River, Va.), II: 90.
Welford's Furnace, (nr Chancellorssville, Va.), V: 93.
Welles, L.M., [Wells], (Sgt, Co E, 2nd Vols/12th NCST), I: 630.

Wellington, ______, (British Gen), II: 564.
Wells, ______, (Chaplain, Branch's Brigade), II: 398.
Wells, A.N., (Chaplain, 26th NCST), IV: 611.
Wells, C.W., (Lt, Co I, 64th NCST), III: 660.
Wells, D.M., (Pvt, Co K, 6th Battalion/60th NCST), III: 482.
Wells, D.O., (Lt, Co I, 9th NCST, 1st Cav), I: 486.
Wells, F.S., (Lt, USN), V: 243.
Wells, J.D., (2nd Lt, Co G, 52nd NCST), III: 224.
Wells, J.K., (Pvt, Co E, 2nd Vols/12th NCST), V: 507.
Wells, John, (Pvt, Co D, 47th NCST), V: 535.
Wells, John C., (Pvt, Co B, 2nd NCST), I: 175.
Wells, John D., (2nd Lt, Co F, 4th NCST), V: 484.
Wells, John G., (Pvt, Co B, 2nd NCST), V: 486.
Wells, John K., (Capt, Co C, 2nd Battalion Junior Reserves; Co D, 71st NCST, 2nd Junior Reserves), IV: 25, 28.
Wells, M.L., (1st Lt, Co D, 6th Vols/16th NCST), V: 547.
Wells, O.C., (Capt, Junior Reserves), IV: 595.
Wells, P.B., (Pvt, Co E, 2nd Vols/12th NCST), V: 507.
Wells, Robert, (Sgt, Co 6, Henry's 14th Battalion; Co D, 79th NCST, 8th Cav), IV: 114.
Wells, S.W., (Sgt, Co I, 8th Vols/18th NCST), II: 64.
Wells, W.N., (Master, USN; Pioneer, Montgomery), V: 245.
Wells, William, (Maj Gen), II: 784.
Wells, William S., (Pvt, Co C, 10th NCST, 1st Art & Engs, Brem-Graham-Williams' Battery, Light Art), V: 568.
Wells', Farm, (nr Petersburg, Va.), I: 384; II: 574
Welsh, Henry N., (Pvt, Co B, 11th Vols/21st NCST; 1st Battalion NCST), IV: 241.
Welsh, John, (Pvt, Co B, 26th NCST), V: 531.
Wemyss, William P., (Capt, Co D, 6th Battalion NCST, Fayetteville Armory Guard), I: 119; IV: 296.
Werley, G.W., (Pvt, Co E, 1st Vols, "Bethel"), I: 128.
Werth, ______, [W.H.], (Capt, 3rd Va.), I: 93.
Wessels, Henry Wilson, (Brig Gen, USA), II: 139, 282, 617, 618; III: 178, 342, 343, 344, 345; IV: 76, 574; V: 175, 190, 321.
Wesson, James D., (1st Sgt, Co H, 34th NCST), V: 556.
West, Elic, (1st Lt, Co E, 6th Battalion/60th NCST), III: 474.
West Erwin, (2nd Lt, Co F, 6th Battalion/60th NCST), III: 475, 476.
West, Fleming, (Pvt, Co I, 13th Vols/23rd NCST), V: 510.
West, Frank, (Pvt, Co C, 10th NCST, 1st Art & Engs, Brem-Graham-Williams' Battery, Light Art), V: 568.
West, George, (Pvt, Co F, 12th Vols/22nd NCST), V: 553.
West, George, (ADC to D.H. Hill), IV: 376.
West, Hardaman, (Pvt, Co I, 13th Vols/23rd NCST), V: 510.
West, Hezekiah, (Chaplain, 69th NCST, Thomas' Legion), III: 730; IV: 620.
West, James, (2nd Lt, Co F, 69th NCST, Thomas' Legion), III: 731.
West, Nick W., (Artificer, Co A, 10th NCST, 1st Art & Engs, Ramseur-Manly's Battery, Light Art), I: 551, 557.

West, Speight B., (Capt, temp Cmdr of 5th NCST), I: 287.
West, W. Riley, (Capt, Co K, 6th Battalion/60th NCST), III: 474, 478, 482, 484.
West, William Riley, (1st Lt, Co G, 9th NCST, 1st Cav; Capt, Co 1, Woodfin's 14th Battalion NCST, Cav), IV: 109, 111.
West India Regiment, (Royal British Army), V: 431.
West Indies, V: xviii, 355, 377, 446.
West Point, Va., I: 82, 566; II: 194, 471.
West Point Military Academy, (aka United States Military Academy), I: 249, 362, 483, 606, 697, 711; II: 161, 339, 341, 405, 542, 598, 599, 724, 732, 796; III: 36, 126, 318, 320, 322, 339, 516, 530, 551, 685, 729; IV: 12, 13, 37, 254, 409, 414, 415, 418, 424, 443, 445, 513, 646; V: 74, 78, 264, 637.
West Virginia, (Without sanction in law and specifically in violation of provisions of the Constitution thirty some odd counties located in western Virginia were wrongfully designated a state. The creation of the so-called state of West Virginia was but one of the criminal acts committed by Lincoln for which neither he nor his minions have been called to account.), I: 318, 324; IV: 138.
"West Woods," (nr Sharpsburg, Md), II: 603; III: 129; V: 76.
Westall, W.L., (Sgt, Co H, 6th Vols/16th NCST), IV: 198.
Western North Carolina Railroad, III: 718, 719, 757; IV: 116, 371, 372, 759; V: 653.
Western Plank Road, N.C., IV: 353.
Westminster, Md., II: 97.
Westmoreland, A.H., (2nd Lt, Co D, 53rd NCST), III: 262.
Westmoreland, W.N., (2nd Lt, Co D, 53rd NCST), III: 262.
Weston, James A., (Maj, 33rd NCST), II: 537, 539, 557, 562, 564, 570, 571, 573, 574, 577, 578, 579, 580; IV: 474; V: 538, 667.
Weston, Samuel R., (Pvt, Co F, 33rd NCST), II: 544.
Weston, W.S., (Pvt, Co B, 12th Vols/22nd NCST), V: 553.
Westover, Va., II: 115; III: 169.
Westray, George W., (Lt, Co A, 47th NCST), I: 120; III: 84, 99, 100.
Westray, Thomas, (Lt, Co A, 47th NCST), III: 84, 103; V: 529.
Wetherington, Roderick, (Lt, Co F, 2nd NCST), I: 161.
Wexler, Rev. E.C., (Chaplain, 29th NCST), II: 730; IV: 612.
Whaley, M., [Whaler], (2nd Lt, Co A, 33rd NCST), II: 538.
Wharnecliffe, Countess of, V: 418.
Wharton, ______, [Ward, Nathan Owen], (2nd Lt, Co C, 9th Vols /19th NCST, 2nd Cav), I: 441.
Wharton, Gabriel, (Brig Gen), I: 384; III: 751, 752.
Wharton, J.E., (Capt, Co K, 63rd NCST, 5th Cav), III: 530, 550.
Wharton, John A., (Maj Gen), II: 488; III: 678.
Wharton, R.W., (Maj, 1st Battalion NCST; Lt Col, 67th NCST), III: 703, 704, 707, 710, 711; IV: 225-242 personal account.
Wharton, W.D., [Wharten], (2nd Lt, Co K, 63rd NCST, 5th Cav), III: 643.
Wharton, William W., (Capt, Co G, 45th NCST), V: 494.
Wheat Field, The, (nr Gettysburg, Pa.), II: 349, 350; V: 605.
Whedbee, William H., (Pvt, Co A, Webb's Battery, Starr's 13th Battalion NCST, Light Art), V: 282, 283.

Wheeler, C.C., (Pvt, Co I, 63rd NCST, 5th Cav), V: 674.
Wheeler, G.W., (ACS, 2nd Regt 3rd Class, Home Guard), IV: 654.
Wheeler, H., (Pvt, Co E, 56th NCST), III: 347.
Wheeler, H.C., (Lt, Co G, 2nd Battalion NCST), IV: 245.
Wheeler, J.B., (Pvt, Co G, 45th NCST), V: 500.
Wheeler, J.H., Jr., (Adjt, 6th Vols/16th NCST), I: 751.
Wheeler, J.H., (Pvt, Co E, 8th Vols/18th NCST), II: 668.
Wheeler, J.K., (2nd Lt, 6th Battalion Junior Reserves; Co K, 70th NCST, 1st Junior Reserves), IV: 13.
Wheeler, James, (2nd Lt, Co E, 46th NCST), III: 81.
Wheeler, Joseph, (Maj Gen and Wheeler's Cavalry), I: 60; II: 710; III: 185, 194, 197, 727; IV: 498.
Wheeler, Noah, (Pvt, Co C, 43rd NCST), V: 498.
Wheeler, Oliver C., (Lt, Co E, 12th Vols/22nd NCST), II: 166, 172.
Wheeler, Samuel J., (Maj, Wheeler's 12th Battalion NCST, Cav), II: 398, 399; III: 458; IV: 339.
Wheeler, W.H., (Capt, Co G, 2nd Battalion NCST), IV: 245, 252, 259.
Wheeler, Woodbury, (Lt, Adjt, 6th Vols/16th NCST; Lt, Latham's Battery; Capt, Co D, 10th Battalion NCST, 2nd Hvy Art), II: 311, 320; IV: 137, 139, 154, 186, 201, 315, 317, 318, 320, 323, 330.
Wheeler's Raid, I: 60.
Wheeless, A.B., (Pvt, Co I, 43rd NCST), V: 499.
Wheeliss, J.W., (Sgt, Co K, 32nd NCST), V: 497.
Whegget, Joseph, (Co E, 4th NCST), I: 233.
Whichard, D.F., [D.D.], (Cpl, Co E, 2nd Vols/12th NCST), V: 507.
Whisenhundt, J.C., (Pvt, Co K, 35th NCST), V: 193.
Whisenhundt, William, (Pvt, Co F, 13th Vols/23rd NCST), V: 510.
Whisnant, Adam, (Pvt, Co F, 34th NCST), V: 555.
Whisnant, D.D., (Cpl, Co E, 2nd Vols/12th NCST), V: 507.
Whisnant, Eli, (2nd Lt, Co A, 49th NCST), V: 559.
Whisnant, J., (Pvt, Co C, 55th NCST), V: 527.
Whisnant, Philip S., (Capt, Co A, 82nd NCST, 2nd Detailed Men), IV: 131.
Whitaker, ______, (Lt, 18th Pa.), III: 584, 585.
Whitaker, Cary W., (Capt, Co D, 43rd NCST), I: 78, 119; III: 2, 16.
Whitaker, David, (2nd Lt, Co A, Indian Co, 69th NCST, Thomas' Legion), III: 730.
Whitaker, David C., (1st Lt, Co K, 71st NCST, 2nd Junior Reserves), IV: 29.
Whitaker, David M., (Lt, Co C, 47th NCST), III: 84.
Whitaker, J.B., (Capt, Co D, 4th NCST), I: 231; II: 425.
Whitaker, J.R., (Pvt, Co D, 43rd NCST), V: 498.
Whitaker, James, H., (Capt, Co E, 2nd Vols/12th NCST), I: 607.
Whitaker, James R., (2nd Lt, Co G, 1st Vols/11th NCST). I: 585.
Whitaker, John H., (Maj, 9th NCST, 1st Cav), I: 418, 420, 424, 445, 483, 485; V: 11, 651.
Whitaker, John S., (1st Lt, Co D, 43rd NCST), I: 120, 123; III: 3; V: 494.
Whitaker, M.T., (Capt, Co I, 1st Vols, "Bethel"), I: 78, 114, 127.

Whitaker, Noah, (Pvt, Co G, 32nd NCST), V: 496.
Whitaker, Samuel, (Pvt, Co A, 33rd NCST), II: 544.
Whitaker, Spier, Jr., (1st Lt, Adjt, 33rd NCST), I: 118, 123; II: 537, 574, 578, 579; IV: 474; V: 97-98, 538.
Whitaker, Stephen, (Capt, Co E, Walker's Battalion; Maj, Walker's Battalion, Thomas' Legion, 80th NCST), IV: 117, 118, 127, 128; V: 653, 656.
Whitaker, T.L., (Lt, Co D, 24th NCST), I: 120.
Whitaker, W.H., (Pvt, Co D, 43rd NCST), V: 498.
Whitaker, W.S., (Pvt, Co H, 56th NCST), III: 357.
Whitaker, William, (Pvt, Co F, 5th NCST; Detailed, 2nd Corps Provost Guard), V: 570.
White, ______, (Pvt, Wynn's 15th Battalion NCST, Cav), IV: 367.
White, ______, [Alexander P.], (Capt, Co B, 56th NCST), III: 314.
White, ______, (Lt Col, 4th Vols/14th NCST), I: 719.
White, ______, (Capt, Co I, 2nd Regt Home Guard), IV: 653.
White, ______, (Maj, Ordnance Department), III: 550.
White, A.M., (Sgt, Co C, 4th NCST), I: 232.
White, Abb M., (Sgt, Co C, 4th NCST), V: 488.
White, Alexander P., (Capt, Co C, 56th NCST), III: 314, 393; V: 191.
White, Dr. Alonzo, (Ass't Surg, 58th NCST), III: 432; IV: 641.
White, Alphonso, (Pvt, Co A, Webb's Battery, Starr's 13th Battalion, Light Art), V: 282.
White, Augustus A., (Sgt, Co D, 43rd NCST), V: 498.
White, A. Sidney, (ACS Sgt, 6th Vols/16th NCST), V: 552.
White, B.F., (Capt, Co F, 6th NCST), I: 344, 345; IV: 700; V: 581, 582, 583, 584, 585
White, Bryan, [Bryant, J.], (Pvt, Co D, 10th Vols/20th NCST), II: 122.
White, C.R., (Pvt, Co E, 55th NCST), V: 528..
White, Charles A., (Capt, Co E, 67th NCST), III: 704.
White, Rev. David, (Chaplain, 107th Ill.), II: 743.
White, Edward, (Capt, AAG, Clingman's Brigade), IV: 482, 492, 493; V: 198, 205.
White, Edward F., (Capt, Co I, 67th NCST), III: 704.
White, Dr. Franklin J., (Surg, 47th NCST), III: 83; IV: 639.
White, G.W., (Capt, Co K, 5th Vols/15th NCST), I: 736.
White, George, (Capt, ADC to Pettigrew), IV: 556.
White, George Rufus, (1st Lt, Co A, 8th Battalion Junior Reserves; Co F, 72nd NCST, 3rd Junior Reserves), IV: 41, 48.
White, H.F., (2nd Lt, Co M, 6th Vols/16th NCST), V: 547.
White, J.B., (ACS Sgt, Co H, 49th NCST), V: 564.
White, J.H., (Pvt, Co C, 37th NCST), V: 545.
White, J.W., (Capt, AQM, 27th NCST), V: 520.
White, John, (N.C. Special Commissioner to England), I: 17, 30, 31, 32; V: 359, 453-461, 471.
White, John H., (Sgt, Co G, 43rd NCST), V: 498.
White, J. Harvey, (Capt, Co A, 53rd NCST), III: 261.
White, Joseph C., (1st Lt, Co C, 4th NCST), I: 231, 232, 269.

White, Joseph M., (Capt, Co E, 67th NCST), III: 710.
White, Julius, (Maj Gen, USA), II: 32, 685; IV: 164.
White, L.M., (1st Lt, Co A, 30th NCST), II: 496, 578.
White, Leonidas S., (4th Sgt, Co M, 6th Vols/16th NCST), V: 553.
White, Dr. Lorenzo, (Ass't Surg, 6th Battalion/60th NCST), IV: 641.
White, Moses J., (Col, Cmdr of Fort Macon), I: 489, 490, 491, 502, 503, 504, 505, 506, 507, 508, 509, 510.
White, O.P., (1st Lt, Co I, 46th NCST), III: 82.
White, P.R., (4th Cpl, Co F, 55th NCST), V: 528.
White, Robert, (Jr 2nd Lt, Co D, 6th Battalion/60th NCST), III: 476.
White, Robert A., (1st Lt, Co B, 28th NCST), V: 538.
White, S.J., (3rd Cpl, Co F, 55th NCST), V: 528.
White, Samuel C., (Pvt, Co K, 4th Vols/14th NCST), V: 491.
White, Solomon H., (Capt, Co G, 32nd NCST; Capt, Co E, Ellis' 3rd Battalion NCST, Light Art), I: 120; IV: 264.
White, T.A., (Pvt, Co K, 43rd NCST), V: 499.
White, T.J., (Pvt, Co E, 32nd NCST), V: 496.
White, VanVuren, (2nd Lt, Co F, 68th NCST), III: 714.
White, W., (Pvt, Co A, 28th NCST), V: 540.
White, W., (Pvt, Co A, 2nd Vols/12th NCST), V: 506.
White, W.J., (Lt, AQM, 9th NCST, 1st Cav), I: 485, 486.
White, W.P.A., (Pvt, Co A, 9th Vols/19th NCST, 2nd Cav), V: 658.
White, William, (Pvt, Co K, 1st Vols, "Bethel"), I: 106, 128.
White, William, (Lt, Co F, 6th Battalion/60th NCST), III: 482, 488.
White, Dr. William Edward, (Ass't Surg, 7th NCST), I: 361; IV: 472, 632.
White, William F., (1st Sgt, Co F, 34th NCST), V: 555.
White, W. Hargrave, (Financial Agent in England), V: 456.
White, W. Lee, (2nd Lt, Co I, 33rd NCST), II: 479, 540.
White, William T., (Jr 2nd Lt, Co K, 6th Battalion/60th NCST), III: 484, 492.
White, Wilson A., (Capt, Co I, 26th NCST), II: 397.
White, Wilson, S., (Capt, Co I, 26th NCST), II: 304, 305, 306.
White Church, N.C., II: 82.
White Hall, N.C., (and Battle of, 1862; now Seven Springs), I: 585, 587; II: 513, 751; III: 86, 472, 553-554; IV: 263, 326, 416; V: 83-93.
White House, Va., (Plantation of the Lee family formerly owned by President George Washington), II: 440; III: 330; IV: 152.
White Oak Road, (nr Five Forks, Va.), I: 439, 442, 477, 478; II: 109, 391, 782, 783; III: 145, 396, 397, 467, 469, 472, 628, 629, 645, 646, 647; IV: 94.
White Oak River, N.C., IV: 265, 424.
White Oak River Bridge, N.C., IV: 528.
White Oak Swamp, Va., (and Battles of), I: 139, 305, 334, 434, 470, 568, 569, 612, 616, 617, 668, 694, 738; II: 104, 105, 108, 207, 272; III: 77, 80, 116, 247, 307, 609, 619; IV: 200, 501, 570.

White Plains, N.Y., V: 385.
White Post, Va., IV: 177.
White Sulpher Springs, Va., "II: 122, 270; IV: 403.
White's Farm, (nr Richmond, Va.), III: 619.
White's Ford, (nr Leesburg, Va.), I: 325, 645; II: 247.
White's Tavern, Va., I: 434; II: 786; III: 619.
Whitehall, Va., [White Hall], I: 430, 587; II: 101; III: 263, 554, 594, 595, 636, 645; V: 83, 86, 91.
Whitehead, A.J.M., (Capt, Co I, 7th Vols/17th NCST), II: 2.
Whitehead, B., (Pvt, Co D, 43rd NCST), V: 498.
Whitehead, D.F., (ACS, 44th NCST), III: 22.
Whitehead, H.G., (Capt, Co E, 55th NCST), IV: 700.
Whitehead, Howell G., (Capt, Co E, 55th NCST), III: 296.
Whitehead, I.J., (Pvt, Co E, 10th Vols/20th NCST), V: 509.
Whitehead, James S., (Maj, 51st NCST), V: 12.
Whitehead, James T., (Maj, 55th NCST), III: 287, 288.
Whitehead, Dr. M., (Surg, Salisbury Wayside Hospital), IV: 625, 627.
Whitehead, William, (Pvt, Co A, 1st Battalion NCST), V: 504.
Whitehurst, H.C., (Capt, Co I, 40th NCST, 3rd Art, Hvy), II: 746, 748, 756.
Whitehurst, James J., [Whitehead, Augustus J.M.], (Lt, Co I, 7th Vols/17th NCST), V: 40, 42, 46.
Whitehurst, N.J., (Capt, Co G, 1st Vols, "Bethel"), I: 137.
Whitehurst, Samuel S., (2nd Lt, Co G, 9th Vols/19th NCST, 2nd Cav), II: 80.
Whitener, P.S., (Pvt, Co K, 35th NCST), V: 193, 261.
Whiters, Marcus S., (Pvt, Co M, 6th Vols/16th NCST), V: 553.
Whiteside, W.E., (Pvt, Co B, 28th NCST), V: 541.
Whitesides, Noah H.P., (Sgt, Co C, 34th NCST), V: 555.
Whitfield, A.W., (Pvt, Co B, 40th NCST, 3rd Art, Hvy), II: 765.
Whitfield, Bryan F., (Lt, Co H, 9th NCST, 1st Cav), I: 486.
Whitfield, George F., (Col, 27th NCST), II: 425, 426, 438, 442, 443.
Whitfield, N.B., (Lt, Co H, 2nd NCST), I: 161, 162.
Whitfield, Nathan B., (Lt Col, 29th Battalion Home Guard), I: 159; IV: 650.
Whitford, David P., (Capt, Co F, 67th NCST), III: 704.
Whitford, Edward, (Maj, 67th NCST), III: 703, 705, 706.
Whitford, John N., (Lt Col, Whitford's 11th Battalion; Col, 67th NCST), I: 14; II: 322, 340; III: 703, 706, 707, 708, 710; IV: 17, 81, 338, 358, 359, 543; V: 17, 271, 272.
Whiting, ______, (Lt, USA), III: 680.
Whiting, George M., (Capt, Co C, 47th NCST), III: 84; IV: 701.
Whiting, Jasper, (Maj, Johnston's Staff), I: 350.
Whiting, W.H.C., (Maj Gen), I: xi, xii, 299, 304, 497, 528, 530, 569, 581; II: 27, 214, 634, 635, 636, 638, 641, 642, 643, 646, 647, 648, 651, 747, 755, 760, 761, 774, 776, 797; III: 137, 138, 159, 291, 354; IV: 39, 43, 46, 47, 49, 152, 263, 265, 268, 296, 297, 305, 307, 311, 316, 416, 418, 421, 423, 424, 425, 431, 484, 487, 527, 529, 530, 537, 542, 590; V: xiii, 9, 223, 225, 227, 228, 229, 233, 234, 235, 239, 240, 352, 406, 407, 437, 450.

Whitley, Augustus, (Sgt, Co E, 55th NCST), III: 299.
Whitley, Benjamin, (Pvt, Co A, 47th NCST), V: 534.
Whitley, H.H., (Pvt, Co B, 1st NCST), V: 485.
Whitley, J.A., (Sgt, Co E, 55th NCST), V: 110, 669.
Whitley, Jesse K., (Sgt, Co C, 5th NCST), I: 291; V: 505.
Whitley, John, (Pvt, Co E, 43rd NCST), V: 498.
Whitley, John W., (2nd Lt, Co C, 40th NCST, 3rd Art, Hvy), II: 747.
Whitley, M., (1st Lt, Co E, 62nd Ga., Cav; 16th Battalion/75th NCST, 7th Cav), IV: 91.
Whitley, M., (Pvt, Co K, 28th NCST), V: 543.
Whitley, M. Lafayette, (2nd Lt, Co A, 27th NCST), II: 461.
Whitley, N.L., (2nd Lt, Co A, 27th NCST), II: 457; V: 519.
Whitley, S.A., (2nd Lt, Co H, 27th NCST), II: 458.
Whitley, S.B., (Sgt, Co E, 4th NCST), I: 233.
Whitley, Thomas W., (Pvt, Co K, 28th NCST), V: 543.
Whitley, Wiley, (Pvt, Co B, 33rd NCST), II: 544.
Whitley, Tenn., IV: 271.
Whitlock, Jackson, (Pvt, Co C, 6th Battalion/60th NCST), III: 482.
Whitlock, Logan T., (1st Lt, Co C, 11th Vols/21st NCST), II: 145, 146.
Whitlock, N.J., (Capt, AQM, Grimes' Staff), V: 483.
Whitmel, Dickerson, (Pvt, Co B, 6th Vols/16th NCST), V: 552.
Whitmire, G.W., (2nd Lt, Co H, 62nd NCST), III: 516; IV: 516, 711.
Whitmore, James, (Pvt, Co D, 43rd NCST), V: 498.
Whitmore, John, (2nd Lt, Co B, Starr's Battery, Starr's 13th Battalion NCST, Light Art), I: 120; IV: 342, 346, 347.
Whitner, J.P., (Pvt, Co K, 35th NCST), V: 563.
Whitner, L.R., (Sgt, Co A, 2nd Vols/12th NCST), V: 261, 506.
Whitney, John, (Pvt, Detached Co, 68th NCST), III: 723.
Whitson, James M., (Col, 8th NCST), I: 387, 397, 405.
Whitted, John M., (2nd Lt, Co G, 8th Vols/18th NCST), II: 64; V: 537.
Whitted, Dr. W.D., (Ass't Surg, 6th Vols/16th NCST), IV: 138, 634; V: 520.
Whitted, Walter A., (Capt, Co G, 55th NCST), III: 296, 302, 307, 310, 312.
Whittenberry, J.M., IV: 701.
Whittier, John Greenleaf, II: 70.
Whittington, B.G., (1st Lt, Co K, 29th NCST), II: 486.
Whittington, M.S., (Cpl, Co A, 53rd NCST), V: 501.
Whitty, Joseph, (Capt, Co K, 31st NCST), II: 508, 512.
Whitworth, ______, (Capt, 26th NCST), II: 340.
Whitworth, William R., (Pvt, Co B, 13th Vols/23rd NCST), V: 509.
Wiatt, Francis L., (Maj, 48th NCST), III: 113, 124.
Wicker, C.D., (Pvt, Co H, 30th NCST), V: 493.
Wicker, E., (Pvt, Co H, 46th NCST), V: 525.
Wicker, Jesse J., (Capt, Co H, 30th NCST), II: 496, 497.
Wicker, John A., (Pvt, Co H, 46th NCST), V: 525.
Wier, S.P., [Weir], (2nd Lt, Co F, 46th NCST), II: 439.
Wiggins, A.M.G., (1st Lt, Co E, 62nd Ga., Cav; Co K, 16th

Battalion/75th NCST, 7th Cav) IV: 91.
Wiggins, Al, (Lt, Co G, 41st NCST, 3rd Cav), II: 785.
Wiggins, Bartimeus, (Fifer, Co D, 68th NCST), III: 715.
Wiggins, Octavius A., (1st Lt, Co E, 37th NCST), II: 653, 667, 668, 669, 670, 671, 672, 673, 674; V: 16.
Wiggins, R.H., (Pvt, Co F, 2nd Vols/12th NCST), V: 507.
Wiggins, Thomas H., (2nd Lt, Co K, 37th NCST), V: 538.
Wiggins, W.A., (2nd Lt, Co E, Walker's Battalion, Thomas' Legion, 80th NCST), IV: 118.
Wiggs, T.N., (Pvt, Co I, 16th Battalion/75th NCST, 7th Cav), V: 660.
Wiggs, W.H., (Cpl, Co I, 16th Battalion/75th NCST, 7th Cav), V: 660.
Wightman, Garvin, (Pvt, Co B, Starr's Battery, Starr's 13th Battalion NCST, Light Art), IV: 349.
Wightman, George W., (ACS, 5th NCST), I: 118.
Wilbor, Alfred W., (Orderly Sgt, 1st NCST), V: 485.
Wilborn, W.D., (Pvt, Co K, 45th NCST), V: 501.
Wilborne, Calvin H., (Lt, Co L, 12th Vols/22nd NCST), II: 178.
Wilburne, J.E., (Pvt, Co F, 4th NCST), V: 489.
Wilcox, Cadmus Marcellus (Maj Gen), I: xii, 381, 547, 679, 680, 681; II: 45, 47, 48, 61, 62, 172, 484, 568, 665, 668, 693; III: 332; IV: 194, 197, 200, 201, 207, 476, 477, 478, 554.
Wilcox, Daniel, (2nd Cpl, Co F, 52nd NCST), III: 224.
Wilcox, Edwin W., (Sgt, Co D, 10th NCST, 1st Art & Engs,Rielly-Ramsay's Battery, Light Art), V: 568.
Wilcox, G.W., (2nd Lt, Co D, Millard's 9th/20th Battalion Junior Reserves), IV: 387.
Wilcox, George, [Willcox], (Capt, Co H, 26th NCST), II: 352, 371, 374, 397, 420, 421; V: 519.
Wilcox, George, (Capt, Co H, 46th NCST), III: 82.
Wilcox, H.H. (Lt, Liddell's Brigade), II: 421.
Wilcox, Orlando B., (Brig Gen, USA), III: 30, 373; V: 583.
Wilcox, Robert P., [Willcox], (Pvt, Co H, 26th NCST), II: 421.
Wilcox, W.M., [Willcox], (Lt, Linddell's Brigade), II: 421.
Wilcox's House, (nr White Oak Swamp, Va.), III: 619.
Wilcox's Landing, Va., I: 431; III: 609.
Wild, Edward Augustus, (Brig Gen, USA), III: 605, 606.
Wild Cat Creek, Va., II: 679.
Wilder, J.D., [J. Dickson], (Capt, AQM, 12th Vols/22nd NCST), II: 171.
Wilder, James J., (Pvt, Co E, 5th Vols/15th NCST), V: 521.
Wilder, Jesse, (2nd Lt, Co C, 59th NCST, 4th Cav), III: 457.
Wilder, John Thomas, (Brig Gen, USA), III: 679.
Wilderness, The, Va., (and Battle of, 1864), I: 149, 150, 200, 288, 334, 383, 404, 430, 547, 548, 557, 558, 580, 594, 595, 596, 612, 629, 640, 675, 676, 701, 743, 744, 747; II: 5, 47, 48, 49, 72, 74, 120, 173, 176, 228, 348, 381, 382, 385, 409, 410, 417, 420, 445-447, 479, 502, 519, 569, 570, 588, 665, 694; III: 27-28, 37, 43, 44, 75, 76, 77, 79, 80, 81, 94, 110-111, 118, 244-245, 246, 256, 258, 303-305, 332, 368, 371, 593-594, 688; IV: 187, 190-193, 201, 259, 313, 371,

425, 468, 475, 507, 510, 514, 522, 554, 563, 583, 610, 615; V: 104, 258, 263.
Wilderness Campaign, I: 429, 546, 640, 642; II: 100, 399; III: 358, 466.
Wilderness Road, (Mine Run to Wilderness, Va.), IV: 188.
Wilderness Tavern, II: 241.
Wiles, Elbert J., (Pvt, Co A, 34th NCST), V: 554.
Wiley, ______, (Capt, Advance), V: 335, 336, 337, 339, 341, 343, 361, 379, 380, 471.
Wiley, C., (Pvt, Co F, 12th Vols/22nd NCST), V: 553.
Wiley, E.R., (Cpl, Co M, 11th Vols/21st NCST), V: 515.
Wiley, Eli, (Cpl, Co M, 11th Vols/21st NCST), II: 138.
Wiley, J.C., (Pvt, Co B, 3rd Vols/13th NCST), V: 549.
Wiley, W.J., (Lt, Co F, 63rd NCST, 5th Cav), III: 555, 557, 563, 570, 575, 618, 654; V: 664.
Wiley, William G., (Pvt, Co C, 5th Vols/15th NCST), V: 521.
Wilfong, Charles, (2nd Lt, Co B, 8th Battalion Junior Reserves; Co E, 72nd NCST, 3rd Junior Reserves), IV: 41.
Wilfong, G.M., (Pvt, Co A, 2nd Vols/12th NCST), V: 506.
Wilfong, W.M., [Y.M.], (Capt, Co A, 2nd Vols/12th NCST), I: 609, 642.
Wilford Station, Va., I: 300.
Wilkes County, N.C., I: 483; II: 303, 389; III: 569, 604; IV: 218, 376, 379, 387, 651; V: 285, 286, 287, 288.
Wilkerson, Harris, (Pvt, Co D, 56th NCST), III: 347.
Wilkerson, John, (Pvt, Co A, 14th Vols/24th NCST), V: 560.
Wilkerson, W.H., (Pvt, Co H, 1st Vols/11th NCST), V: 530.
Wilkerson's Bridge, Va., III: 622.
Wilkesboro, N.C., IV: 697; V: 285, 286, 289.
Wilkey, D.F., (Pvt, Co E, 26th NCST), V: 532.
Wilkins, ______, (Pvt, Co D, 30th NCST), IV: 602.
Wilkins, Jack, (ACS, 6th Vols/16th NCST, aka Uncle Jack), IV: 153.
Wilkins, James M. [Wilkinson], (Lt, Co H, 14th Vols/24th NCST), V: 193.
Wilkins, L.P., (2nd Lt, Co K, 50th NCST), III: 203.
Wilkins, Samuel, (Capt, Co K, 50th NCST), III: 161, 203.
Wilkins, W.J., (Pvt, Co H, 12th Vols/22nd NCST), V: 554.
Wilkins, W.T., (Pvt, Co G, 6th Vols/16th NCST), IV: 140, 218.
Wilkins, William T., (2nd Lt, Co C, 34th NCST), V: 548.
Wilkinson, J.F., (Pvt, Co A, 2nd Vols/12th NCST), V: 506.
Wilkinson, J.G., (Cpl, Co L, 11th Vols/21st NCST), V: 194.
Wilkinson, John, (Capt, CSN; Chickamauga, Chameleon), V: 355, 397, 411, 440, 441.
Wilkinson, John W., (2nd Lt, Anderson's Battalion Junior Reserves; Co I, 71st NCST, 2nd Junior Reserves), IV: 29.
Wilkinson, Thomas D., (Lt, Co B, 61st NCST), III: 504.
Willard, Alverious, (Pvt, Co K, 11th Vols/21st NCST), V: 515.
Willard, John A., (Musician, 33rd NCST), II: 538.
Willard, William H., (Textile Manufacturer), I: 32.
Willcox, Herman Husband, (Pvt, Co H, 26th NCST), II: 421.
William and Mary College, I: 691; II: 198.
Williams, ______, (Ensign, USN; Pioneer, Kansas), V: 245.

Williams, ______, (Civilian), I: 446.
Williams, Mrs. ______, (In her garden John Hunt Morgan was killed), IV: 115.
Williams, A.H.A., (Lt, Co F, 55th NCST), III: 296.
Williams Arthur B., (Capt, Co C, 10th NCST, 1st Art & Engs, Brem-Graham-Willliams' Battery, Light Art), I: 537, 538, 540, 544, 545, 547, 548, 549, 550; II: 321, 324, 446; III: 382, 399, V: 567.
Williams, B.B., (Sgt, Co G, 4th NCST), I: 233.
Williams, Dr. B.B., (Ass't Surg, 34th NCST), II: 582; IV: 637; V: 548.
Williams, Benjamin B., (1st Lt, Co E, 68th NCST), III: 714.
Williams, Billy, (Negro servant to 1st Lt Marshall Williams), III: 281.
Williams, Buckner D., (1st Lt, AQM, 30th NCST; Maj, QM, Ramseur-Cox's Brigade), II: 495, 496, 502; IV: 462, 463.
Williams, C.H., (Sgt, Co D, 2nd Vols/12th NCST), V: 507.
Williams, C.L., (Sgt, Co I, 6th NCST), V: 513.
Williams, Charles, (Pvt, Co A, 1st Vols, "Bethel"), I: 106, 196, 128.
Williams, Charles M., (3rd Cpl, Co D, 52nd NCST), III: 224; V: 536.
Williams, D., (2nd Lt, Co B, 41st NCST, 3rd Cav), II: 770.
Williams, D.W., (Pvt, Co F, 16th Battalion/75th NCST, 7th Cav), V: 660.
Williams, David "Pap," (Capt, Co K, 3rd NCST), I: 179, 182, 213, 228.
Williams, Dr. Donald, (Ass't Surg, 5th Vols/15th NCST), I: 734; IV: 634.
Williams, E.H., (1st Lt, Co I, 31st NCST), II: 512, 518.
Williams, E.J., (Lt, Co I, 31st NCST), I: 120.
Williams, Edward H., (Pvt, Co F, 7th NCST), I: 378.
Williams, G., (Pvt, Co I, 10th Vols/20th NCST), V: 509.
Williams, G.S., (Pvt, Co I, 6th NCST), V: 513.
Williams, Gay M., (Lt, Co F, 4th Vols/14th NCST), I: 728.
Williams, Gary F., (Capt, Co A, 30th NCST), II: 495; IV: 602.
Williams, George, (Cpl, Co A, 1st Vols, "Bethel"), I: 100, 101, 127.
Williams, Gideon H., (Pvt, Co K, 25th NCST), V: 562.
Williams, H.P., (Pvt, Co H, 4th NCST), I: 233.
Williams, Dr. H.W., (Ass't Surg, 5th NCST), I: 291; IV: 632; V: 503.
Williams, Henry, (Pvt, Co A, 56th NCST), III: 347.
Williams, Henry, (Lt, Co H, 61st NCST), III: 504.
Williams, Henry Clay, (Sgt, Co B, 5th NCST), I: 291; V: 505.
Williams, I.W., (Pvt, Co H, 57th NCST), V: 517.
Williams, Isaac, (Pvt, Co H, 5th NCST), I: 292; V: 505.
Williams, J.B., (1st Lt, Co B, 7th Battalion/72nd NCST, 3rd Junior Reserves), IV: 40.
Williams, J.C., (2nd Lt, Co C, 31st NCST), II: 512.
Williams, J.D., (2nd Lt, Co A, 1st NCST), I: 136.
Williams, J.D., (Pvt, Co C, 10th NCST, 1st Art & Engs, Brem-Graham-Williams' Battery, Light Art), V: 568.
Williams, J.E., (3rd Lt, Co A, 9th Vols/19th NCST, 2nd Cav), IV: 701.

Williams, J.F., (Pvt, Co I, 6th NCST), V: 513.
Williams, J.H., (Pvt, Co I, 6th NCST), V: 513.
Williams, J.M., (Lt, USN), V: 243.
Williams, Dr. J.M., (Surg, 73rd NCST, 4th Senior Reserves; Surg, 76th NCST, 6th Senior Reserves), IV: 66, 97, 643.
Williams, J.M., (1st Lt, Co C, 54th NCST; AA & IG Lewis' Brigade), V: 511.
Williams, J.P., (Capt, Co G, 55th NCST), III: 287, 290.
Williams, J.R., (Pvt, Co B, 33rd NCST), V: 544.
Williams, J.R., (Pvt, Co H, 6th NCST), V: 513.
Williams, J.R., (Sgt, Co D, 4th NCST), I: 232.
Williams, J.R., (Pvt, Co G, 3rd Vols/13th NCST), V: 551.
Williams, J.T., (Pvt, 21st Ga.), V: 194.
Williams, J.W., (2nd Lt, Co C, 28th NCST), II: 484; NCST), V: 538.
Williams, Jacob, (Pvt, Co H, 2nd NCST; Detailed, 2nd Corps Provost Guard), I: 176; V: 486, 570.
Williams, Jacob E., (2nd Lt, Co A, 9th Vols/19th NCST, 2nd Cav), II: 89.
Williams, James, (Pvt, Co K, 25th NCST), V: 562.
Williams, James, Jr., (2nd Lt, Co C, 66th NCST), III: 686.
Williams, James F., (2nd Lt, Co D, 9th Vols/19th NCST, 2nd Cav), II: 80.
Williams, James T., (Capt, Co D, 44th NCST), V: 529.
Williams, James W., (2nd Lt, Co G, 1st Vols/11th NCST), I: 121, 585.
Williams, James W., (Capt, Co E, 8th NCST), I: 387.
Williams, Jesse P., (Capt, Co I, 66th NCST), III: 686.
Williams, Jesse P., (Col, Engineer Corps), IV: 420.
Williams, John, (Ambulance Driver, Pvt, Co G, 2nd Battalion NCST), V: 495.
Williams, John, (1st Lt, Co A, 40th NCST, 3rd Art, Hvy), II: 746.
Williams, John A., (ACS, 14th Vols/24th NCST), II: 269, 271.
Williams, John Q., (Pvt, Co C, 43rd NCST), V: 498.
Williams, John R., (2nd Lt, Co F, 56th NCST), III: 315; V: 191.
Williams, John Stuart, (Brig Gen), III: 739, 740, 741, 524; V: 95.
Williams, John T., (Pvt, Co H, 34th NCST), V: 556.
Williams, John T., (Pvt, Co C, 2nd Vols/12th NCST), IV: 702.
Williams, John W., (2nd Lt, Co H, 33rd NCST), II: 540.
Williams, J. Marshall, (Capt, IG Lewis' Brigade), I: 120, 123; III: 267, 268, 273, 280, 281, 284, 285.
Williams, Joseph, (Grandfather of Lt Sol. W.W. Stringfield), III: 732.
Williams, Joseph, (Pvt, Co A, 48th NCST), V: 526.
Williams, Lerus, (Pvt, Co C, 56th NCST), III: 347; V: 565.
Williams, Lewis S., (Capt, Produce Loan Agent), I: 77, 113, 124, 125.
Williams, M.M., (1st Lt, Co H, 59th NCST, 4th Cav), III: 458.
Williams, Mrs. Maggie, (Wife of Col Solomon Williams, daughter of Capt Pegram, CSN), II: 93.
Williams, Oliver, (Lt, Co C, 10th Vols/20th NCST), II: 118, 119, 120, 125, 127.
Williams, Orrin, (Capt, Co G, 2nd NCST), I: 158, 159, 162.

Williams, R.L., (Capt, Co K, 2nd Vols/12th NCST), I: 631, 642.
Williams, R.S., (Capt, Co I, 3rd Vols/13th NCST), I: 653, 662, 655-687 personal account; V: 547.
Williams, R.S., (Pvt, Co E, 28th NCST), V: 542.
Williams, Robert, (Pvt, Co H, 2nd NCST), I: 176; V: 486.
Williams, Robert, (Purser, Index), V: 371, 379, 410.
Williams, Robert A., (1st Lt, Co D, 3rd Vols/13th NCST), V: 547.
Williams, S., (Pvt, Co I, 6th NCST), V: 513.
Williams, S., (Pvt, Co H, 47th NCST), V: 535.
Williams, Samuel V., (1st Lt, Co C, 44th NCST), III: 23.
Williams, Seth, (Pvt, Co C, 4th Vols/14th NCST), V: 490.
Williams, Solomon, (Col, 2nd Vols/12th NCST, Col, 9th Vols/19th NCST, 2nd Cav, Spruill's), I: 424, 606, 608, 609; II: 83, 87, 88, 90, 91, 92, 93, 94; III: 2, 9, 19, 532; IV: 244, 253, 254; V: 10.
Williams, Solomon B., (Pvt, Co A, 25th NCST), V: 561.
Williams, Stephen, (Lt, Co C, 2nd NCST), I: 159.
Williams, Dr., Thomas E., (Surg, 9th Vols/19th NCST, 2nd Cav), II: 100.
Williams, T.W., (Cpl, Co H, 33rd NCST), II: 540, 578.
Williams, Thomas H., (2nd Lt, Co E, 43rd NCST), III: 2, 3.
Williams, W., (Pvt, Co E, 3rd Vols/13th NCST), V: 550.
Williams, W.A., (Pvt, Co G, 5th NCST), I: 292; V: 505.
Williams, W.A., (2nd Sgt, Co D, 44th NCST), V: 533.
Williams, W.A., (4th Sgt, Co C, 10th NCST, Brem-Graham-Williams' Battery, Light Art), NCST), V: 567.
Williams, W.B.W., (Pvt, Co A, 10th NCST, 1st Art & Engs, Ramseur-Manly's Battery, Light Art), I: 555.
Williams, W.D., (1st Lt, Co G, 29th NCST), II: 485.
Williams, W.F., (Pvt, Co B, 6th NCST), V: 512.
Williams, W.G., (2nd Lt, Co D, 31st NCST; Adjt, 66th NCST), II: 512; III: 685, 690.
Williams, W.H., (Capt, Co I, 55th NCST), III: 296.
Williams, W.H., (3rd Sgt, Co D, 44th NCST), V: 533.
Williams, W.H., (Pvt, Co E, 1st NCST), V: 485.
Williams, W.H., (Capt, Co I, 55th NCST), IV: 701.
Williams, W.J., (1st Lt, Co G, 66th NCST), III: 686.
Williams, W.L., (Pvt, Co K, 14th Vols/24th NCST), V: 560.
Williams, W.M., (Pvt, Co G, 46th NCST), V: 525.
Williams, W.P., (Pvt, Co I, 48th NCST), V: 527.
Williams, W.R., (Lt, Co B, 9th NCST, 1st Cav), I: 485.
Williams, W.T., (Capt, Co I, 2nd Vols/12th NCST), I: 607.
Williams, William, (Pvt, Co E, 5th NCST), I: 292; V: 505.
Williams, Wiliiam, (Pvt, Detached Co, 68th NCST), III: 723.
Williams, William B., (2nd Lt, ACS, 43rd NCST), III: 1, 3.
Williams, William R., (2nd Lt, Co K, 1st NCST; Capt, Co F, 43rd NCST; 1st Battalion Junior Reserves, 70th NCST, 1st Junior Reserves; Co K, 71st NCST, 2nd Junior Reserves), I: 137; II: 137, 485; III: 2; IV: 11, 12, 20, 27, 29.
Williams, Wilson H., (Capt, Co I, 55th NCST), III: 287, 289, 290, 296; IV: 701.

Williams, William T., (Capt, Co H, 32nd NCST; Lt Col, 1st Battalion NCST), II: 521, 522; III: 281; IV: 245.
Williams, William T., (Lt Col, 1st Battalion NCST; 32nd NCST), II: 521.
Williams, Willis, (Pvt, Detached Co, 68th NCST), III: 723.
Williams, Z.T., (Lt, Co F, 2nd Battalion NCST), IV: 245.
Williams, Zimri, (Pvt, Co H, 3rd NCST), V: 487.
Williamsburg, Va., (and Battle of, 1862), I: 165, 235, 282, 283, 300, 301, 552, 553, 554, 610, 612, 655, 690, 691, 693, 710, 711, 737, 754; II: 167, 197-200, 206, 223, 238, 254, 294, 613; III: 317; IV: 151, 152, 445; V: xiv, 645.
Williamsburg Road, (Richmond to Williamsburg, Va.), I: 617; II: 114, 203, 294, 331, 599; III: 77; IV: 151, 570.
Williamson, ______, (CSN), V: 327.
Williamson, ______, (Col, Ark.), II: 739.
Williamson, Alonzo, (Pvt, Co K, 10th Vols/20th NCST), II: 114.
Williamson, B.P., (Lt, Co C, 2nd Battalion NCST), IV: 245.
Williamson, B.R., (Lt, Co C, 2nd Battalion NCST), IV: 245.
Williamson, Benjamin, (Pvt, Co A, 1st Battalion NCST), V: 504.
Williamson, C.D., (Cpl, Co D, 5th Vols/15th NCST), V: 521.
Williamson, Edward, (2nd Lt, Co H, 66th NCST), III: 686.
Williamson, George, (Maj, 8th NCST), I: 387; IV: 249.
Williamson, George, (Lt, Co G, 47th NCST), III: 85.
Williamson, Henry, (Pvt, Co A, 30th NCST), V: 491.
Williamson, Hiram, (Pvt, Co D, 5th Vols/15th NCST), V: 521.
Williamson, J.A., (Pvt, Co B, 1st Battalion NCST), V: 504.
Williamson, J.N., (1st Lt, Co A, 3rd Vols/13th NCST), V: 547.
Williamson, J.W., (Capt, Co D, 1st NCST), I: 136.
Williamson, James A., (2nd Lt, Co C, 41st NCST, 3rd Cav), II: 770.
Williamson, M.T., (2nd Lt, Co E, 4th NCST), I: 233, 271.
Williamson, P., (Pvt, Co H, 16th Battalion/75th NCST, 7th Cav), V: 660.
Williamson, R.A., (2nd Lt, Co D, 78th NCST, 8th Senior Reserves), IV: 107.
Willianson, T.G., (Lt, Co F, 7th NCST), I: 378.
Williamson, W.R., (Pvt, Co K, 10th Vols/20th NCST), II: 114.
Williamsport, Md., I: 149, 197, 372, 422, 425, 557, 695, 718; II: 32, 70, 233, 238, 240, 376, 378, 553, 585, 656, 685; III: 5, 240, 270, 462, 463, 464, 569, 570, 571, 751; IV: 164, 183, 239, 241, 255; V: 628.
Williamsport Ford, (Potomac River, Va.), II: 376.
Williamston, N.C., I: 446, 447, 495, 523; II: 279, 337, 338; III: 179, 210, 319, 337, 680, 721, 722, 726; IV: 15, 16, 17, 75, 77, 82, 617, 646; V: 7.
Williford, B.B., (1st Lt, Co I, 30th NCST), II: 496.
Williford, W.C., [Willie H.], (1st Lt, Co F, 36th NCST, 2nd Art & Engs, Hvy), II: 642; V: 229.
Williford, W.J., (2nd Lt, Co K, 42nd NCST), II: 791, 807.
Williford, William, (Musician, 33rd NCST), II: 538.
Willington, Billy, (Chief Engineer, Sirene), V: 445.
Willis, D.H., (Sgt, Co D, 3rd NCST), V: 487.

Willis, Henry, (Pvt, Co B, 59th NCST, 4th Cav), V: 659.
Willis, J.C., (Pvt, Co F, 37th NCST), V: 546.
Willis, James R., (1st Sgt, Co F, 55th NCST), V: 528.
Willis, M.V., (Pvt, Co B, 28th NCST), V: 541.
Willis R.L., (Sgt, Co D, 5th NCST), I: 291; V: 505.
Willis, William, B., (Pvt, Co , 7th Vols/17th NCST), V: 41, 43, 46, 47.
Willis, William Henry, (Col, 4th Ga.), I: 722.
Willis Church, Va., I: 420.
Willis Heights, (nr Fredericksburg, Va.), II: 609, 610.
Willoughby, Henry J., (Pvt, Co H, 43rd NCST), V: 499.
Willoughby, Joseph, (Drummer, Co D, 68th NCST), III: 715.
Willoughby Run, (nr Gettysburg, Pa.), II: 235, 344, 347, 348, 349, 351, 354; III: 236, 299; V: 118, 613.
Wills, George W., (2nd Lt, Co D, 43rd NCST), I: 121; III: 3.
Wills' Farm, (nr Petersburg, Va.), I: 384.
Willson, William M., (Hospital Steward, 1st Vols/11th NCST), V: 530.
Wilmer, Rev. Mr. ______, (Post war Bishop of Louisiana), II: 377.
Wilmington, N.C., I: 4, 7, 10, 11, 12, 12, 17, 30, 32, 43, 52, 54, 216, 391, 392, 395, 409, 410, 411, 412, 509, 514, 528, 530, 531, 579, 581, 582, 583, 586, 587, 742, 776; II: 3, 9, 10, 11, 16, 18, 20, 113, 123, 277, 293, 330, 439, 467, 468, 479, 497, 513, 514, 518, 612, 631, 634, 635, 638, 646, 650, 651, 747, 749, 750, 752, 753, 754, 756, 759, 762, 763, 768, 769, 797, 802, 803; III: 4, 21, 70, 71, 130, 132, 170, 176, 191, 205, 206, 214, 215, 216, 318, 319, 321, 322, 328, 332, 456, 503, 505, 508, 512, 513, 615, 687, 691, 692, 693, 694, 695, 726; IV: 4, 6, 29, 39, 40, 42, 43, 45, 46, 50, 53, 55, 67, 92, 97, 100, 103, 108, 221, 222, 224, 246, 247, 248, 263, 265, 267-269, 270, 295, 296, 297, 303, 304, 311, 313, 316, 317, 318, 319, 320, 326, 329, 330, 331, 333, 342, 343, 359, 358, 359, 365, 367, 383, 386, 388, 390, 393, 397, 399, 401, 402, 413, 414, 417, 418, 419, 420, 421, 422, 423, 424, 425, 426, 428, 429, 438, 439, 440, 484, 487, 497, 505, 527, 528, 529, 530, 538, 539, 540, 541, 542, 547, 572, 573, 588, 589, 592, 594, 604, 605, 608, 625, 645, 652, 691, 716, 760; V: x, 23, 24, 25, 26, 27, 217, 221, 222, 223, 240, 270, 299, 303, 326, 335, 336, 337, 338, 339, 342, 343, 354, 355, 356, 359, 360, 363, 364, 367, 368, 376, 379, 384, 386, 387, 393, 395, 396, 399, 400, 401, 403, 405, 406, 407, 408, 409, 410, 411, 412, 413, 419, 421, 422, 423, 424, 425, 426, 430, 431, 433, 437, 438, 439, 440, 441, 442, 443, 446, 447, 450, 451, 454, 458, 459, 471, 573, 624, 640, 643.
Wilmington Custom House, V: 360.
Wilmington, Retreat from, II: 10, 11; III: 696.
Wilmington Road, (nr New Bern), III: 334.
Wilmington, Columbia & Augusta Railroad, V: 446.
Wilmington & Manchester Railroad, III: 726.
Wilmington & Weldon Railroad, (aka Weldon Road), I: 523, 533; II: 10, 277, 299, 447, 467, 513, 574, 677, 694, 699, 768, 772; III: 29, 77, 97, 129, 206, 213, 229, 231, 317, 376, 377, 508, 540, 610, 611, 616, 619, 620, 621, 633, 726; IV: 43, 88, 93, 108, 265, 312, 325, 326, 344, 346, 348, 558, 563; V: 207, 269.

Wilmington, Weldon & Petersburg Railroad, II: 780.
Wilson, Albert, (Pvt, Co F, 6th NCST), V: 513.
Wilson, B. Franklin, (1st Lt, Co K, 42nd NCST), I: 120; II: 791, 792, 807.
Wilson, Benjamin J., (Pvt, Co E, 25th NCST), V: 561.
Wilson, C.H., (Pvt, Co I, 54th NCST; Detailed, 2nd Corps Provost Guard), V: 570.
Wilson, Charles R., (2nd Lt, Co D, 56th NCST), III: 315, 339, 347, 356, 398; V: 180.
Wilson, E.A., (Chaplain, 67th NCST), IV: 620.
Wilson, F.C., (Pvt, Co F, 10th Vols/20th NCST), II: 118.
Wilson, F.R., (Pvt, Co F, 6th Battalion/60th NCST), III: 482.
Wilson, G.W., (Chaplain, 29th NCST), IV: 604, 612.
Wilson, J., (Pvt, Co F, 6th Battalion/60th NCST), III: 482.
Wilson, J.H., (1st Cpl, Co B, 1st Battalion NCST), V: 504.
Wilson, J.J., (Pvt, Co F, 10th Vols/20th NCST), II: 118.
Wilson, J.J., (Pvt, Co H, 49th NCST), V: 565.
Wilson, J.L., (Pvt, Co K, 46th NCST), V: 525.
Wilson, J.M., (Maj, QM, Ramseur's Brigade), IV: 462.
Wilson, J.T., (Maj, 38th NCST), II: 678, 679, 694; V: 548.
Wilson, J.W., (Maj, QM, Ramseur's Brigade), IV: 462.
Wilson, James, (Pvt, Co G, 6th Battalion/60th NCST), III: 482.
Wilson, James, (1st Lt, Co 3, West's 14th Battalion NCST, Cav; 79th NCST, 8th Cav), IV: 111.
Wilson, James, (Sailor, CSN), V: 329.
Wilson, James A., (1st Lt, Co K, 56th NCST), III: 317.
Wilson, James Harrison, (Maj Gen, USA; See also: Kautz-Wilson Raid), I: 431, 467, 470; III: 611, 612, 614, 615, 616-617, 618.
Wilson, James L., (Pvt, Co I, 7th NCST), V: 538.
Wilson, James W., (Capt, Co F, 6th NCST), I: 296.
Wilson, James W., (Capt, AQM, 49th NCST), III: 125; V: 651.
Wilson, John, (Sgt, Hospital Steward, 1st Vols/11th NCST), I: 587.
Wilson, Dr. John, (Surg, 1st Vols/11th NCST), I: 583, 587.
Wilson, Dr. John, Jr., (Surg, 1st Vols/11th NCST; Chief Surg at Salisbury Prison), IV: 579, 633, 763, 764, 765.
Wilson, John F., (2nd Lt, Co C, 38th NCST), II: 675, 678, 679.
Wilson, Joseph H., (3rd Lt, Co K, 42nd NCST), I: 121, 133; II: 791, 807.
Wilson, Joseph J., (1st Lt, Co H, 13th Vols/23rd NCST), II: 186.
Wilson, Joseph W., (Sgt, Co C, 34th NCST), V: 555.
Wilson, L.L., (Pvt, Co B, 28th NCST), V: 541.
Wilson, Leander, (Pvt, Co D, 6th NCST), V: 512.
Wilson, M.A., (Pvt, Co H, 35th NCST), V: 563.
Wilson, Ozias S., (Pvt, Co F, 6th Vols/16th NCST), V: 552.
Wilson, R.E., (Capt, Co B, 11th Vols/21st NCST; Co A, 1st Battalion NCST), II: 145; IV: 225, 236, 242.
Wilson, R.M., (2nd Lt, Co E, 62nd NCST), III: 516; IV: 701.
Wilson, Robert, (Pvt, Co A, 53rd NCST), V: 501.
Wilson, S.M., (Cpl, Co I, 6th Battalion/60th NCST), III: 482.

Wilson, S.N., (Capt, Co A, 34th NCST), II: 581.
Wilson, S.W., (Pvt, Co B, 53rd NCST), V: 501.
Wilson, Stephen P., (1st Lt, Co G, 59th NCST, 4th Cav), III: 457.
Wilson, T.W., (1st Lt, Co F, 13th Vols/23rd NCST), II: 185.
Wilson, Thomas H., (Pvt, Co K, 6th Battalion/60th NCST), III: 482.
Wilson, W.C., [Willson], (2nd Lt, Co F, 42nd NCST), II: 791, 795.
Wilson, W.S., (Sgt, Co H, 53rd NCST), V: 502.
Wilson, W.W., (Pvt, Co E, 16th Battalion/75th NCST, 7th Cav), V: 660.
Wilson, William, (Pvt, Co H, 49th NCST), V: 565.
Wilson, William, (Capt, Co B, 26th NCST), II: 303, 315, 318, 330, 358, 371, 372, 396, 397, 399, 403, 415, 418.
Wilson, William A., (Sgt, Co K, 35th NCST), V: 563.
Wilson, William J., (Capt, Co I, 62nd NCST), III: 516; IV: 701, 711.
Wilson, Dr. William R., (Ass't Surg, 14th Vols/24th NCST; Surg, Ransom's Brigade), II: 269, 271; IV: 635, 644.
Wilson, William S., (Lt, Co E, 55th NCST), III: 296.
Wilson, N.C., I: 495, 524, 533; III: 709, 726, 727; IV: 388, 594, 613, 620; V: 194.
Wilson County, N.C., I: 498, 533, 535; III: 458, 503, 504, 704.
Wilson's Farm, Va., (aka Wilson's House), I: 436; II: 105; III: 472, 627, 628, 630; V: 674.
Wilson's Raid, (aka Kautz-Wilson Raid), I: 467-470; III: 538, 611-618.
Wilson's Wharf, Va., (aka Kennon's Landing), III: 604-607.
Wimbish, J., (Lt Col, 23rd Battalion Home Guard), IV: 650.
Winborne, Calvin H., (2nd Lt, Co L, 12th Vols/22nd NCST), II: 172.
Winborne, Jesse, (Bugler, Co I, 41st NCST, 3rd Cav), II: 772, 775.
Winborne, John Q., (Lt, Co D, 47th NCST), III: 84.
Winbourne, R.W., [Wilburne], (2nd Lt, Co I, 12th Vols/22nd NCST), II: 166, 172.
Winchester, John R., (Lt, Adjt, 48th NCST), III: 124; V: 520.
Winchester, T., (1st Sgt, Co I, 3rd Vols/13th NCST), V: 551.
Winchester, W.G., (Pvt, Co A, 48th NCST), V: 526.
Winchester, W.H., (1st Lt, Co I, 3rd Vols/13th NCST), I: 655, 671, 672.
Winchester, Ky., IV: 278, 279, 280, 281.
Winchester, Va., (and Battles of), I: 147, 154, 163, 168, 172, 173, 194, 207, 208, 261, 287, 297, 298, 308, 310, 318, 325, 326, 327, 334, 339, 340, 373, 541, 554, 577, 623, 628, 644, 645, 647, 648, 649, 672, 718, 728, 762; II: 95, 96, 116, 123, 131, 132, 135, 141, 188, 233, 238, 239, 248, 250, 251, 252, 253, 254, 255, 256, 258, 261, 275, 437, 475, 524, 532, 555, 556, 608; III: 14, 37, 41, 55, 68, 69, 88, 241, 256, 257, 259, 260, 262, 263, 270, 278, 279, 280, 303, 406, 411, 420, 427, 559, 561, 741, 749, 751, 753-754; IV: 122, 128, 167, 176, 225, 228-231, 254, 459, 460, 461, 503, 515, 517, 519, 523, 525, 571, 602; V: 213-216.
Winchester, Va., Confederate Cemetery at, V: 467.
Winchester Road, (nr Stephenson Depot, Va.), II: 248.

Winchester-Harper's Ferry Road, Va., II: 553.
Winder, Charles S., (Brig Gen), I: 140; II: 550; IV: 416, 428, 446.
Winder, John C., (Capt, Co A, 2nd Engineers; Maj, Johnston's Staff, Son of C.S. Winder), IV: 413, 416, 419, 425, 428, 429, 430.
Winder, John Henry, (Brig Gen, Provost Marshal General), IV: 751, 759.
Winding Stairs, N.C., IV: 372.
Windley, Robert, (2nd Lt, Co I, 40th NCST), II: 747.
Windley, William, (1st Lt, Detached Co, 68th NCST), III: 723.
Windsor, N.C., III: 135, 321.
Windsor, S.C., II: 416.
Windsor Road, (nr Suffolk, Va.), II: 775.
Windsor Station, Va., III: 232.
Winecoff, Frank, (2nd Lt, Co D, 5th Battalion Junior Reserves; Co E, 71st NCST, 2nd Junior Reserves), IV: 28.
Winecoff, Mack, (Pvt, Co H, 7th NCST), I: 382.
Wingate, R.M., (Pvt, Co E, 32nd NCST), V: 496.
Wingfield, Dr. R.T., (Surg, 5th NCST), I: 282; IV: 632, 634.
Winkler, James, (Pvt, Co D, 6th NCST), V: 512.
Winkler, Jospeh, (Pvt, Co F, 26th NCST), V: 603.
Winnamac, Indiana, II: 369.
Winninfham, A.J., (Pvt, Co I, 12th Vols/22nd NCST), V: 554.
Winningham, E.H., (1st Lt, Co I, 12th Vols/22nd NCST), II: 165, 166.
Winslow, ______, (Capt, Battery D, N.Y. Light Art), I: 151.
Winslow, Warren, (Secretary of the Naval & Military Board, CSA), V: 299, 302.
Winstead, Dr. J.B., (Ass't Surg, 47th NCST), III: 83; IV: 639.
Winstead, J.F., (Cpl, Co E, 35th NCST), V: 562.
Winstead, K.H., (1st Lt, Co E, 9th Vols/19th NCST, 2nd Cav), II: 89.
Winstead, W.E., (1st Sgt, Co F, 4th NCST), I: 233.
Winston, B.H., (Lt, Co I, 55th NCST), III: 296; IV: 701.
Winston, Duncan C., (1st Lt, Co C, 1st Vols/11th NCST), I: 584.
Winston, Hon. F.D., (Co L, 1st Vols, "Bethel"), I: 133.
Winston, John A., (Col, Randolph Howitzers, Va.), I: 82.
Winston, John R., (Col, 45th NCST), III: 36, 37, 55; IV: 691, 711; V: 254, 255, 494.
Winston, Norfleet, (Cpl, Co E, 5th Vols/15th NCST), V: 521.
Winston, P.H., (Board of Auditors), I: 20, 45.
Winston, T.F., (Pvt, Co H, 3rd Vols/13th NCST), V: 551.
Winston, N.C., II: 398, 806; IV: 259.
Winter's Gap, Tenn., (Cumberland Mountains), IV: 273.
Winters, John, (Pvt, Co K, 1st NCST), V: 485.
Winthrop, Francis Bayard, (of Connecticut, Father of Theodore), I: 97.
Winthrop, Theodore, (Maj, Washburn's Battalion, USA), I: 90, 91, 96, 99.
Winton, N.C., (Burned by Yankees), II: 613, 615; III: 134; IV: 26; V: 270, 283, 627.
Wise, ______, (Lt, CSN), V: 39.
Wise, H.A., (Pvt, Co G, 4th NCST), V: 489.
Wise, Henry Alexander, (Maj Gen), II: 6, 270, 508, 509, 510, 612; III: 163; IV: 87, 149, 244, 246, 247, 530; V: 57, 58, 59, 66.

Wise, J.J., (Lt, Co A, 58th NCST), III: 432.
Wise, J.N., (Pvt, Co E, 6th NCST), V: 512.
Wise, M.M., (Capt, Co B, Wynn's 15th Battalion NCST, Cav), IV: 365.
Wise, William B., (Capt, Co C, 7th Vols/17th NCST), II: 2.
Wise, Z., (Pvt, Co I, 1st Vols/11th NCST), V: 531.
Wise's Fork, N.C., (and Battle of, 1865; aka Cobb's Mill), I: 411; II: 11, 81, 277, 612, 762, 803; III: 290, 323, 324,
Wise's Fork, N.C., 554, 697, 722, 726; IV: 54, 312, 346, 543.
Wise's Legion, II: 510, 799; IV: 244, 246; V: 61, 63, 65, 66, 627.
Wiseman, A.N., (2nd Lt, Co K, 4th NCST), I: 234, 272; V: 664.
Wiseman, Dr. Alfred W., (Ass't Surg, 7th NCST), IV: 472, 632.
Wiseman, Dr. Joseph W., (Ass't Surg, 42nd NCST), II: 789, 805; IV: 638.
Wiseman, Martin D., (Capt, Co A, 58th NCST), III: 432, 447.
Wiseman, W.H., (Lt, Co A, 58th NCST), III: 432, 435.
Wishart, Frank M., (Capt, Co B, 46th NCST), III: 76, 80.
Wishart, Wellington, (1st Lt, Co A, 46th NCST), III: 80.
Wiswall, Howard, (Capt, Co K, 7th Vols/17th NCST), II: 2.
Witherington, ______, [Stephen], (2nd Lt, Co I, 49th NCST), III: 145.
Witherington, I.K., (1st Lt, Co E, 66th NCST), III: 686.
Withers, E.B., (Lt Col, 3rd Vols/13th NCST), V: 547.
Withers, Jones Mitchell, (Maj Gen), I: 607; II: 489.
Witherspoon, Hiram, (Capt, Co G, 7th NCST), I: 361.
Witherspoon, J.G., (Capt, Co K, 30th NCST), II: 496.
Witherspoon, I.K., (1st Lt, Co E, 66th NCST), III: 686.
Witherspoon, Stephen, III: 145.
Witherspoon, W.H., (Cpl, Co B, 1st NCST), V: 485.
Withers, E. Benton, (Lt Col, 3rd Vols/13th NCST), I: 673, 674, 679, 680, 693, 702.
Wofford, H.J., (Pvt, Co A, 54th NCST), V: 516.
Wofford, J.E., (Pvt, Co A, 54th NCST), V: 516.
Wofford, William Tatum, (Brig Gen), I: 555.
Wolf, A., (Pvt, Co F, 12th Vols/22nd NCST), V: 553.
Wolf, C.H., (Musician, 53rd NCST), V: 501.
Wolf, J.W., (Pvt, Co F, 49th NCST), V: 564.
Wolf, Martin M., [Wolfe], (Capt, Co E, 12th Vols/22nd NCST), II: 166.
Wolf, W.C., (Pvt, Co F, 56th NCST), III: 357.
Wolf, William C., (Sgt, Co B, 5th Vols/15th NCST), V: 521.
Wolf, William T., (Pvt, Co B, 5th Vols/15th NCST), V: 521.
Wolf River, III: 662.
Wolf Run Shoal, Va., I: 753; IV: 150.
Wolford, ______, (Brig Gen, USA), III: 677; IV: 292.
Wolftown, Va., III: 572.
Wolseley, Field Marshal The Right Honorable Viscount, (Englishman), V: 411, 417.
Womack, D.G., (Pvt, Co A, 3rd Vols/13th NCST), V: 549.
Womack, Elisha, (Pvt, Co K, 13th Vols/23rd NCST), V: 510.
Womack, Jefferson, (Pvt, Co D, 61st NCST), III: 507.
Womack, Jones, (Pvt, Co I, 56th NCST), V: 566.

Womack, W.T., (1st Sgt, Co D, 1st Vols/11th NCST), V: 530.
Woman's Rights Party, IV: 665.
Womble, I., (Pvt, Co D, 10th Vols/20th NCST), V: 508.
Womble, John T., (Lt, Co H, 47th NCST), III: 85.
Womble, Thomas, (Pvt, Co A, 13th Vols/23rd NCST), V: 509.
Wood, ______, (Col of expedition against the Underwriter), I: 495, 526.
Wood, ______, (Superintendent Old Capitol Prison, Washington, D.C.), IV: 662, 663.
Wood, ______, (Capt, Co H, 2nd Regt Home Guard), IV: 653.
Wood, ______, (Capt, AAG, Garland's Brigade), IV: 521.
Wood, ______, (Pvt, Wynn's 15th Battalion NCST, Cav), IV: 368.
Wood, Benjamin, (Ensign, USN; Pioneer, Tristrain Shandy), V: 243, 245.
Wood, Rev. Dr. Frank H., (Chaplain, 12th Vols/22nd NCST), IV: 609.
Wood, Francis D., (Pvt, Co G, 6th Vols/16th NCST), IV: 215, 216; V: 552.
Wood, Furney, (Pvt, Co B, 56th NCST), III: 367.
Wood, G.H., (Ensign, USN; Pioneer, Chippewa), V: 245.
Wood, Henry, (Pvt, Co H, 63rd NCST, 5th Cav), III: 587.
Wood, Henry S., (Lt, Co C, 2nd Battalion NCST), IV: 245.
Wood, J.B., (Master, USN; Pioneer, Maratanza), V: 245.
Wood, J.W., (Pvt, Co E, 54th NCST), V: 516.
Wood, James, (Capt, Co I, 34th NCST), V: 548.
Wood, James H., [Jamse A.], (Col, 4th NCST), I: 230, 231, 244, 256, 257, 258, 260, 267, 275, 495; IV: 460; V: 9.
Wood, Jasper N., (Sgt, Co H, 5th Vols/15th NCST), V: 522.
Wood, John Taylor, (Commodore, CSN; Capt, Tallahassee), III: 133; V: 326, 328, 329, 330, 331, 332, 333, 438, 439, 440.
Wood, Spier W., (Capt, Co A, 5th Vols/15th NCST), I: 734.
Wood, T.J., (1st Sgt, Co I, 12th Vols/22nd NCST), V: 554.
Wood, Dr. Thomas F., (Ass't Surg, 3rd NCST), I: 213; IV: 632; V: 484.
Wood, Uzzell T., (Pvt, Co E, 30th NCST), V: 492.
Wood, W.R., (Capt, Co G, 9th NCST, 1st Cav), I: 418, 484, 485, 486.
Wood, Rev. William A., (Chaplain, 4th NCST; 1st Vols/11th NCST), I: 230, 270, 279; IV: 605, 607.
Wood, William T., (Pvt, Co E, 4th Vols/14th NCST), V: 490.
Wood's Brick Yard, (nr New Bern), II: 398.
Woodall, Ira T., (Capt, Co I, 14th Vols/24th NCST), II: 270, 272.
Woodall, Marvin J., (Lt, Co D, 26th NCST), II: 396, 397, 421.
Woodard, J.W., (Sgt, Co I, 16th Battalion/75th NCST, 7th Cav), V: 660.
Woodard, James S., (Capt, Co C, 43rd NCST), III: 2.
Woodard, Jesse F., (1st Lt, Co D, 10th NCST, 1st Art & Engs, Reilly-Ramsay's Battery, Light Art), I: 561, 562, 563, 567, 580; V: 568.
Woodard, John B., (Pvt, Co F, 4th NCST), V: 488.
Woodburn, D.P., (Cpl, Co H, 38th NCST), II: 690.
Woodburn, J.D., (Sgt, Co K, 26th NCST), V: 532.
Woodburn, T.M., (2nd Lt, Co B, 77th NCST, 7th Senior Reserves), IV: 99.

Woodcock, Henry M., (Musician, Co E, 8th Vols/18th NCST), II: 64; V: 539.
Woodfin, Miss Anna, (Daughter of N. Woodfin), I: 130, 131.
Woodfin, John W., (Capt, Co G, Woodfin's 14th Battalion, 9th NCST; 1st Cav; Maj., Woodfin's 14th Battalion NCST; Maj, 9th Vols/19th NCST, 2nd Cav), I: 483, 484, 486; II: 79, 81, 87; III: 664; IV: 109, 110, 111, 112; V: 12.
Woodfin, Nicholas, (Col, State Senator, Prominent public figure of Buncombe county and western N.C.) I: 130, 131; II: 722; IV: 110.
Woodfin, Miss Sallie, (Daughter of N. Woodfin), I: 131.
Woodfin Mountain, N.C. (now Lookout Mountain), IV: 110.
Woodhouse, M.S., (Pvt, Co A, 1st Battalion NCST), V: 504.
Woodley, ______, (Pvt, Co H, 7th Vols/17th NCST), V: 35.
Woodruff, J.E., (Pvt, Co C, 32nd NCST), V: 496.
Woodruff, R.W., (1st Lt, Co A, 11th Vols/21st NCST; Co A, 1st Battalion NCST), IV: 242; V: 503, 504.
Woodruff, W.E., (2nd Lt, Co A, 5th Vols/15th NCST), I: 734.
Woods, John F., (4th Cpl, Co E, 52nd NCST), III: 224.
Woods, S.K., (Pvt, Co G, 27th NCST), II: 462; V: 523.
Woods, W.D., (Pvt, Co G, 27th NCST), II: 462; V: 523.
Woods, William G., (Prisoner, Johnson's Isand), IV: 700.
Woodside, John C., (Pvt, Co D, 34th NCST), V: 555.
Woodstock, Va., IV: 231.
Woodville, N.C., I: 577; IV: 546.
Woodward, B.W., (Lt, Co A, 64th NCST), III: 660.
Woodward, C.W.W., (2nd Lt, Co I, 30th NCST), II: 497.
Woodward, James F., (1st Lt, Co D, 6th Battalion NCST), IV: 296.
Woodard, Jesse F., (Lt, Co D, 10th NCST, 1st Art & Engs, Reilly-Ramsay's Battery, Light Art), I: 576, 580.
Woodward, N.W., (Lt, Co A, 64th NCST), III: 660.
Woodward, William J., (Military Storekeeper, Fayetteville Arsenal), IV: 299.
Woody, C.C., (Pvt, Co D, 54th NCST), V: 516.
Woody, James, (Pvt, Co B, 6th Battalion/60th NCST), III: 482.
Woody, James D., (Pvt, Co K, 14th Vols/24th NCST), V: 560.
Woody, John, (of Madison County, Murdered by Yankee deserters/outlaws), III: 662.
Wool, John Ellis, (Maj Gen, USA), V: 82.
Wooster, J.L., (1st Lt, Co E, 1st NCST), I: 137.
Wooten, ______, (Guide, Battle of South West Creek), IV: 545, 546.
Wooten, Council, (Color-bearer, 66th NCST), III: 698.
Wooten, Edward W., (2nd Lt, Co K, 40th NCST, 3rd Art, Hvy), II: 747.
Wooten, H.C., (Sgt, Co A, 53rd NCST), V: 501.
Wooten, J.T., (Musician, 53rd NCST), V: 501.
Wooten, John W., (2nd Lt, Co G, 33rd NCST), II: 540, 578; V: 538.
Wooten, Robert, (Capt, Co G, 33rd NCST), II: 540, 578.
Wooten, Shade, (Capt, Co C, 27th NCST), II: 448, 457.
Wooten, Thomas, (Pvt, Co A, 3rd NCST), V: 487.

Wooten, Thomas J., (Maj, 8th Vols/18th NCST), II: 42, 59, 60, 63, 74, 175, 481, 576, 669; IV: 470, 471, 473, 476, 477, 478, 479.

Wooten, W.F., (Capt, Co D, 27th NCST), II: 425, 426.

Wooten, W.O., [Wootten], (Sgt, Co F, 4th NCST), I: 233, 270; V: 488.

Wootten, Leven, (Pvt, Co I, 43rd NCST), V: 499.

Workman, G.B., (Pvt, Co G, 28th NCST), V: 542.

Workman, L.H., IV: 702.

Workman, S.H., (1st Lt, Co G, 44th NCST), III: 23.

Works on Blockade Running, V: 414, 416.

Worley, A.P., (Pvt, Co H, 2nd Battalion NCST), V: 495.

Worley, B.T., (Pvt, Co H, 2nd Battalion NCST), V: 495.

Worley, Curtis, (Pvt, Co D, 27th NCST), II: 462; V: 523.

Worley, G.W., (2nd Lt, Co K, 1st Vols/11th NCST), I: 121.

Worley, S.F., (Sgt, Co I, 35th NCST), V: 563.

Wortburgh, Tenn., IV: 273.

Worth, ______, [Shubal G.], (Lt, Adjt, 9th Vols/19th NCST, 2nd Cav), II: 101.

Worth, J.W., (AQMS, 71st NCST, 2nd Junior Reserves), IV: 28.

Worth, John, (Pvt, Randolph's Howitzers, Va.), I: 106.

Worth, John M., (Col, 76th NCST, 6th Senior Reserves), V: 677.

Worth, Jonathan, (Post War Governor of North Carolina), III: 714; V: 455.

Worth, Shubal G., (Lt Col, 48th Battalion Home Guard), IV: 650.

Worth, Shubal G., (Capt, Co I, 12th Vols/22nd NCST), II: 162, 163, 165, 166.

Wortham, George, (Adjt, Cape Fear Minute Men, N.C. Militia; Capt, Co B, 2nd Vols/12th NCST; Col, 50th NCST), I: 124, 607; III: 161, 198, 202; IV: 105, 527; V: 26.

Wounding of Jackson, V: 96-100.

Wran, John, (Pvt, Co K, 3rd Vols/13th NCST), V: 551.

Wray, Aaron, (AQMS, Woodfin-Henry's 14th Battalion), IV: 113.

Wray, Thomas H., (1st Lt, Co C, 31st NCST), II: 507, 512.

Wren, P.A., (Pvt, Co C, 45th NCST), V: 500.

Wren, William, (Pvt, Co G, 49th NCST), V: 564.

Wrenshall, Charles C., (6th Sgt, 10th NCST, 1st Art & Engs, Ramseur-Manly's Battery, Light Art), I: 551, 552.

Wright, ______, (Lt, Ordnance Officer, Wright's Brigade), IV: 503, 504.

Wright, ______, (Col, Cav, Ga.), III: 197.

Wright, ______, (Col), V: 303.

Wright, A.B., (Pvt, Co E, 2nd Vols/12th NCST), V: 507.

Wright, A.D., (1st Lt, Co B, 42nd NCST), II: 790, 805.

Wright, A.R., (Col, 2nd Ga.), V: 55, 56.

Wright, Aaron, (AQMS, Henry's 14th Battalion NCST), IV: 113.

Wright, Adam Empie, (Asst Surg, Wilmington Hospital), IV: 630.

Wright, Ambrose Ransom, (Brig Gen), II: 57; IV: 195.

Wright, Clement G., (Maj, 4th Battalion NCST; Lt Col, 66th NCST), III: 685, 689, 696; IV: 270, 538; V: 11, 651.

Wright, D.D., (Pvt, Co E, 33rd NCST), V: 544.

Wright, David, (Pvt, Co M, 12th Vols/22nd NCST), V: 554.

Wright, E.J., (Pvt, Co D, 11th Vols/21st NCST), V: 514.
Wright, Elias, (Col, Wright's Brigade, USA), V: 238.
Wright, F.H., (Pvt, Co E, 33rd NCST), V: 544.
Wright, Horatio Gouverneur, (Maj Gen, USA), I: 63, 200, 327, 602; II: 10.
Wright, J.G., (1st Lt, Co E, 1st NCST), I: 137.
Wright, J.M., (2nd Lt, Co A, 59th NCST, 4th Cav), III: 457.
Wright, J.R., (Pvt, Co C, 45th NCST), V: 500.
Wright, J.W., IV: 700.
Wright, James A., (Capt, Co E, 1st NCST), I: 137, 139.
Wright, John C., (2nd Lt, Co I, 46th NCST), III: 82.
Wright, John C., (Pvt, Co E, 1st Vols, "Bethel"), I: 128.
Wright, John T., (2nd Lt, Co F, 78th NCST, 8th Senior Reserves), IV: 107.
Wright, K., (Pvt, Co D, 10th Vols/20th NCST), V: 508.
Wright, M.M., (Pvt, Co M, 11th Vols/21st NCST), V: 194.
Wright, Newton, (Pvt, Co F, 34th NCST), V: 555.
Wright, Noah, (Pvt, Co F, 34th NCST), V: 555.
Wright, S.G., (Pvt, Co D, 33rd NCST), V: 544.
Wright, S.J., IV: 701.
Wright, Samuel C., (1st Lt, Co E, 6th Battalion/60th NCST), III: 474, 475, 482.
Wright, Samuel F., (2nd Lt, Co A, 13th Vols/23rd NCST), II: 183.
Wright, T.W., (2nd Lt, Co F, 46th NCST), III: 66.
Wright, Thomas H., (Sgt Maj, 46th NCST), V: 524.
Wright, W.G., (Cpl, Co I, 4th NCST), V: 489.
Wright, William B., (Pvt, Co G, 4th Vols/14th NCST), V: 490.
Wright, William W., (Capt, Co H, 28th NCST), II: 466.
Wright, Willoughby, (Pvt, Co G, 59th NCST, 4th Cav), V: 659.
Wright, Wilson, (Pvt, Co G, 59th NCST, 4th Cav), V: 659.
Wrightsville, N.C., IV: 221, 426; V: 336, 358.
Wrightsville Sound, N.C., IV: 42, 425.
Wyatt, ______, (Civilian), II: 124.
Wyatt, Andrew, (Sgt, Co B, 26th NCST), II: 400, 401.
Wyatt, Eli, (Pvt, Co D, 10th NCST, 1st Art & Engs, Reilly-Ramsay's Battery, Light Art), I: 572.
Wyatt, Henry Lawson, (Pvt, Co A, 1st Vols, "Bethel;" Considered for years the first Confederate soldier to give his life for his country Henry Wyatt is now seen by some as merely the first North Carolinian to do so. Some allude to a Virginian that may have been killed before Wyatt. Nonetheless Henry Lawson Wyatt is memorialized with a fine statue on the capitol grounds in Raleigh.), I: v, 100, 101, 102, 106, 127, 128; II: 17; V: 577.
Wyatt, Isham, (Father of Henry L.), I: 102.
Wyatt, John Henry, (ACS, 1st Vols, "Bethel"), I: 77.
Wyatt, Lucinda, (Mother of Henry L.), I: 102.
Wyatt's, Va., III: 627.
Wyatt's Bridge, (Nottoway River), III: 633.
Wyndham, Percy, (Col, USA, Cav, mercenary), IV: 231.
Wynn, Cope, (Pvt, Co H, 63rd NCST, 5th Cav), III: 587.

Wynn, John, (2nd Lt, Co K, 1st NCST), I: 137.
Wynns, James M., (Capt, Co C, 9th Vols/19th NCST, 2nd Cav), II: 80, 89, 99; IV: 365, 368, 369.
Wynns, J.M., (Lt Col, 15th Battalion NCST), V: 651.
Wyrick, George, (Pvt, Co M, 11th Vols/21st NCST), V: 194.
Wyrick, M.W., (1st Sgt, Co E, 12th Vols/22nd NCST), V: 553.
Wyson, J.P., (Pvt, 24th Va.), V: 195.

(Y)

Yadkin County, N.C., III: 287, 732; IV: 218, 225, 387, 760.
Yadkin Bridge, (nr Salisbury), I: 386; III: 727.
Yadkin River, N.C., IV: 375, 759; V: 286, 289, 291, 292, 293, 294, 630.
Yadkin Valley, N.C., V: 286.
Yale University, I: 339.
Yancy, C., (Pvt, Co A, 2nd Vols/12th NCST), V: 506.
Yancy, J.E.R., (Pvt, Co B, 2nd Vols/12th NCST), V: 506.
Yancey, George H., (Lt, Co E, 9th NCST, 1st Cav), I: 486.
Yancey, George W., (2nd Lt, Co C, 4th Battalion Junior Reserves; Co C, 72nd NCST, 3rd Junior Reserves), IV: 38, 48.
Yancey, John, (Pvt, Co C, 10th NCST, 1st Art & Engs, Brem-Graham-Williams' Battery, Light Art), V: 568.
Yancey, Dr. John, (Surg, 29th NCST), IV: 636.
Yancey County, N.C., III: 431, 432, 447, 757; IV: 371, 380, 612; V: 32.
Yandle, A.F., (2nd Lt, Co I, 37th NCST), II: 669; V: 538.
Yarborough, David, (2nd Lt, Co K, 44th NCST), III: 23.
Yarborough, J.J., (Sgt, Co E, 35th NCST), V: 193.
Yarborough, Richard F., (Lt, Co G, 47th NCST), III: 85.
Yarborough, William H., (Col, 5th Vols/15th NCST), I: 733, 736; V: 519.
Yarborough, Zachariah, (1st Sgt, Co E, 48th NCST), V: 526.
Yarrington, J.B., (Lt, 12th Vols/22th NCST), IV: 711.
Yates, Edwin A., (Chaplain, 1st Vols, "Bethel"), I: 77; IV: 604.
Yate, John W., (Pvt, Co A, 52nd NCST), V: 535.
Yazoo City, Miss., II: 491, 734.
Yeates, Jesse Johnston, (Maj, 31st NCST), II: 507.
Yell, ______, (Col, N.C. Regt's in Mexican War), I: 216.
Yellow Creek, Tenn., II: 486; III: 521.
Yellow Fever, I: 15.
Yellow House, (nr Hatcher's Run, Va.), III: 121.
Yellow River, Fla., II: 737.
Yellow Tavern, Va., (and Battle of, 1864; aka Vaughn's House), I: 429; II: 409, 786; III: 248, 466, 596, 598, 599, 600, 602; IV: 151, 503.
Yellowley, Edward C., (Capt, Co G, 8th NCST; Lt Col, 68th NCST), I: 388; III: 678, 708, 713, 719, 721, 726; V: 55, 56, 651.
Yelton, J.W., (Pvt, Co H, 8th Vols/18th NCST), II: 64; V: 540.
Yelverton, Wyatt E., (Lt, Co D, 2nd NCST), I: 159, 160.
Yelvington, R.H., (Ensign, Co C, 50th NCST), III: 203.
Yerby's Yard, (The lawn of a residence at Fredericksburg, Va.), II: 476.

Yodel, S.A., (Lt, Co I, 28th NCST), II: 483.
Yoder, George M., (2nd Lt, Co F, 38th NCST), II: 677.
Yon, M.C., (Cpl, Co D, 48th NCST), III: 119.
Yona-gus-kee, (Cherokee Chief), III: 727, 759.
Yopp, ______, [Franklin V.B.], (3rd Lt, Co G, 51st NCST), III: 219.
York, Isacc J., (Sgt, Co A, 33rd NCST), V: 543.
York, J.B., (1st Lt, Co D, 45th NCST), V: 494.
York, J.L., (Pvt, Co M, 12th Vols/22nd NCST), V: 554.
York, John, (Pvt, Co G, 6th NCST), V: 513.
York, Joseph, (Pvt, Co M, 12th Vols/22nd NCST), V: 554.
York, L.C., (Pvt, Co A, 28th NCST), V: 540.
York, R.W., (Maj, 6th NCST), I: 296; IV: 661.
York, W.C., (2nd Lt, Co D, Millard's 9th/20th Battalion Junior Reserves), IV: 387.
York, Pa., I: 311, 632; II: 135; III: 411, 412; IV: 665.
York, Pa., Old Fair Grounds, I: 311.
York Collegiate Institute, (Alexander Co.), V: 289.
York River, Va., I: 80, 81, 82, 300, 655, 737; III: 131, 317; IV: 152, 261, 357.
York River Railroad, Va., I: 613, 691, 738; II: 115; III: 139; IV: 153, 262.
York Road, (nr Gettysburg, Pa.), I: 356.
Yorktown, Va., (and Battle of, 1862), I: 73, 75, 76, 80, 81, 83, 89, 99, 100, 101, 111, 112, 114, 128, 129, 132, 133, 235, 282, 286, 300, 301, 334, 349, 552, 565, 654, 690, 709, 736, 737, 742, 753, 766, 772; II: 167, 194, 196, 197, 254; III: 317; IV: 150-152, 342; V: 664.
Yorktown Centennial, 1881, I: 132.
Yorktown Depot, II: 193.
Young, ______, (Lt Col, Cobb Legion), I: 420, 427.
Young, ______, (Maj, Sheridan's Scouts), I: 481, 779, 780, 781, 782.
Young, ______, (Cpl, 1st Mi.), II: 622.
Young, A.J., (Pvt, Co E, 24th NCST), V: 193.
Young, A.P., (Pvt, Co D, 57th NCST), V: 517.
Young, B.F., (2nd Lt, Co A, Millard's 9th/20th Battalion Junior Reserves), IV: 386.
Young, Daniel A., (Sgt Maj, 10th Battalion NCST, 2nd Hvy Art), IV: 330, 334.
Young, David M., (2nd Lt, Co I, 29th NCST), II: 486.
Young, G.W., (Lt Cmdr, USN), V: 243.
Young, H.H., (Pvt, Co G, 2nd NCST), I: 176; V: 486.
Young, Isaac J., (Capt, Co G, 13th Vols/23rd NCST), II: 185, 186, 189, 209, 210, 211, 215, 216.
Young, J.W.C., (Ordnance Sgt, 55th NCST), III: 288; V: 527.
Young, James M., (Capt, Co K, 1st Vols/11th NCST), I: 120, 128, 585, 603; V: 529.
Young, John, (ADC, 38th NCST), II: 681.
Young, John Augustus, (Lt Col, 4th NCST), I: 230, 235, 241, 266, 280; V: 676.
Young, John D., (Capt, Co C, 34th NCST; Capt, Sharpshooters, Scales' Brigade), II: 174; V: 548.
Young, John Graham, (Ass't Ordnance Sgt, Co A, 4th NCST; Sgt Maj, 4th NCST), I: 230, 271, 279; V: 488.

Young, John P., (Capt, Co B, 7th NCST), I: 369, 377; IV: 467; V: 646.
Young, Joseph, J., (Capt, AQM, 26th NCST), II: 303, 306, 322, 326, 357, 358, 370, 371, 395, 407, 408, 414, 420; V: 600.
Young, Julius M., (ACS, 25th NCST), II: 291.
Young, Larry, [Leary], (Pvt, Co I, 4th Vols/14th NCST; Detailed, 2nd Corps Provost Guard), V: 491, 570.
Young, Lenoir R., (Capt, Co F, Walker's Battalion, Thomas' Legion, 80th NCST), III: 754; IV: 118.
Young, Louis G., (Lt, ADC to Pettigrew; Capt, AAG to William MacRae), II: 408, 566, 567; III: 21, 110; IV: 555, 556, 558, 559, 561, 562, 563, 565, 566, 567, 568; V: ix, 95, 113-132, personal account, 209.
Young, M.A., (Pvt, Co K, 1st Vols/11th NCST), V: 531.
Young, Pierce Manning Butler, (Maj Gen), I: 436, 775; III: 537, 538, 558, 608; IV: 182, 582.
Young, Dr. Peter W., (Surg, 38th NCST), II: 676; IV: 637; V: 548.
Young, R.H., (Cpl, Co A, 3rd NCST), V: 487.
Young, Dr. R.W., (Ass't Surg, 2nd Vols/12th NCST), I: 606; IV: 633.
Young, Robert S., (Maj, 7th NCST), I: 361, 367; IV: 472.
Young, S.A., (Lt, Co A, 10th Battalion, 2nd Hvy Art), IV: 329.
Young, S.P., (Pvt, Co K, 6th Battalion/60th NCST), III: 482.
Young, Dr. Samuel, (Ass't Surg, 2nd Battalion NCST), IV: 245, 329, 643.
Young, Samuel M., (2nd Lt, Co H, 1st Vols/11th NCST), I: 586.
Young, Thomas J., (Capt, Co H, 25th NCST), II: 292; V: 559.
Young, W.R., (Lt, Sharpshooters, 13th Vols/23rd NCST), I: 680; IV: 701, 712.
Young, W.R., (2nd Lt, Co I, 32nd NCST), I: 736.
Young, William, (Pvt, Co D, 5th NCST), I: 291; V: 505.
Young, William H., (Adjt, 55th NCST), III: 288; IV: 701, 712.
Young, William Hugh, (Brig Gen), II: 492.
Young, Wilton L., (1st Lt, Co L, 5th Vols/15th NCST; Maj, 10th Battalion, 2nd Hvy Art), I: 736; IV: 317, 329, 334, 418, 419.
Youngblood, Thomas R., (Capt, Co C, 50th NCST), III: 202, 203.
Yount, A., (Pvt, Co E, 6th NCST), V: 512.
Yount, A.E., (Pvt, Co C., 28th NCST), V: 541.
Yount, D. McD., (Capt, Co F, 38th NCST), II: 675, 678.
Yount, D.P., (Pvt, Co E, 2nd Vols/12th NCST), V: 507.
Yount, F., (Pvt, Co C, 28th NCST), V: 541.
Yount, J., (Pvt, Co C, 10th NCST, 1st Art & Engs, Brem-Graham-Williams' Battery, Light Art), V: 568.
Yount, J.A., (1st Lt, Co F, 38th NCST), II: 678; V: 549.
Younts, Charles W., (Cpl, Co A, 10th Vols/20th NCST), II: 119; V: 508.
Yountz, William C., (Pvt, Co I, 4th Vols/14th NCST), V: 491.

(Z)

Zachary, ______, [Charles T.], (Col, 27th Ga.), IV: 20, 535, 536; V: 203.
Zanzibar, Prince of, V: 349.
Zeke's Island, N.C., II: 17, 18, 20, 631, 633, 748.
Zent, Samuel M., (Lt Col, 13th Ind.), V: 238.
Zephyr Puff, (Brand of Smoking Tobacco), V: 266.
Ziegler, John, (Pvt, Co H, 16th Battalion/75th NCST, 7th Cav), V: 660.
Ziegler's Grove, (nr Gettysburg, Pa.), V: 126.
Ziglar, Joshua D., (Lt, Co H, 12th Vols/22nd NCST), II: 166.
Zigler, Samuel B., (Lt, Co H, 12th Vols/22nd NCST), II: 166.
Zigler's Grove, (nr Gettysburg, Pa.), II: 363.
Zimmerman, H., (Pvt, Co K, 35th NCST), V: 563.
Zimmerman, Israel, (Pvt, Co F, 26th NCST), V: 603.
Zoller, S., (Pvt, Co H, 2nd NCST; Detailed, Invalid Battalion), V: 571.
Zollicoffer, Felix Kirk, (Brig Gen), I: xii; III: 736; IV: 125, 284.
Zollicoffer, Tenn., (See: Bluff City).
Zouaves, Louisiana, (1st Battalion, La.), I: 82.
Zouaves, Texas, II: 281.
"Zouzves," The, (Hawkin's N.Y.), V: 584.

BIBLIOGRAPHY

Boatner, Mark Mayo, III. The Civil War Dictionary. Revised Edition. New York: David McKay Company, Inc., 1987.

Clark, Walter, ed. Histories Of The Several Regiments And Battalions From North Carolina In The Great War 1861-1865, Written by Members of the Respective Commands. 5 vols. Raleigh, North Carolina: The State, E.M. Uzzell Printer and Binder, 1901; Wendell, North Carolina: Broadfoot's Bookmark, Avera Press, 1982.

Evans, Clement A., ed. Confederate Military History; A Library of Confederate States History, in Seventeen Volumes, Written by Distinguished Men of the South, and Edited by General Clement A. Evans of Georgia. Extended Edition. 19 vols. Edited by Robert S. Bridges and others. Atlanta, Georgia: Confederate Publishing Company, 1899; Wilmington, North Carolina: Broadfoot Publishing Company, 1987.

Hewett, Janet B., ed. The Roster of Confederate Soldiers 1861-1865. 16 vols. Wilmington, North Carolina: Broadfoot Publishing Company, 1995.

Jones, Rev. J. William, and others, eds. Southern Historical Society Papers, 1876-1959. 55 vols. Richmond, Virginia: Southern Historical Society, 1876-1959; Wilmington, North Carolina: Broadfoot Publishing Company and Morningside Bookshop, 1990-1992.

Jordan, Weymouth T., Jr., and others. North Carolina Troops 1861-1865 A Roster. 14 vols. Raleigh, North Carolina: Division of Archives and History, 1966-1998.

Long, E.B., and Barbara Long. The Civil War Day By Day: An Almanac 1861-1865. New York, 1919; New York: Doubleday and Company, Da Capo Press, 1987.

Scott, R.N., and Others, eds. War Of The Rebellion: Official Records Of The Union And Confederate Armies. 130 vols. Washington, D.C., 1880-1901; Harrisburg, Pennsylvania: The National Historical Society, by Edwards Brothers, 1871-1985.

Wise, Jennings C. The Long Arm Of Lee: The History Of The Artillery Of The Army Of Northern Virginia. New York: Oxford University Press, 1959.